'This extremely appealing collection pulls off that hardest of tricks: it is simultaneously authoritative and exciting, its findings new as well as true. The Hellenistic age was an age of marvels and this impeccably edited work is itself a Hellenistic marvel. Scholars, students and interested non-professionals will devour it with pleasure and go away nourished, as I did.'

Professor Simon Hornblower, University College London

'Blackwell and Erskine have done a splendid job with the Hellenistic *Companion* and I'm extremely pleased to have a copy, both as a guide for my own contributions and for future reference. It is, I think, the best comprehensive book on the Hellenistic world available and a "must have" for everyone working in this field.'

Professor Waldemar Heckel, University of Calgary

'*The Companion to the Hellenistic World* is very impressive indeed both in its breadth and its depth, and sets an exhilaratingly high standard for the new series.'

Professor Justina Gregory, Smith College

BLACKWELL COMPANIONS TO THE ANCIENT WORLD

This series provides sophisticated and authoritative overviews of periods of ancient history, genres of classical literature, and the most important themes in ancient culture. Each volume comprises between twenty-five and forty concise essays written by individual scholars within their area of specialization. The essays are written in a clear, provocative, and lively manner, designed for an international audience of scholars, students, and general readers.

A COMPANION TO THE HELLENISTIC WORLD

Edited by

Andrew Erskine

Blackwell
Publishing

© 2003, 2005 by Blackwell Publishing Ltd

BLACKWELL PUBLISHING
350 Main Street, Malden, MA 02148-5020, USA
9600 Garsington Road, Oxford OX4 2DQ, UK
550 Swanton Street, Carlton, Victoria 3053, Australia

First published 2003 by Blackwell Publishing Ltd
First published in paperback 2005 by Blackwell Publishing Ltd

1   2005

Library of Congress Cataloging-in-Publication Data

A companion to the Hellenistic world / edited by Andrew Erskine.
    p. cm. — (Blackwell companions to ancient history)
ISBN 0-631-22537-4 (alk. paper) — ISBN 1-4051-3278-7 (pbk. : alk. paper)
    1. Mediterranean Region—History—To 476. 2. Greece—History—Macedonian Hegemony, 323–281
B. C. 3. Greece—History—281–146 B. C. 4. Hellenism.
I. Erskine, Andrew. II. Series.

DE86.C65 2003
938'.07–dc21

                                                                2002015293

ISBN-13: 978-0-631-22537-9 (alk. paper) — ISBN-13: 978-1-4051-3278-7 (pbk. : alk. paper)

A catalogue record for this title is available from the British Library.

Set in 10 on 12 pt Galliard
by SPI Publisher Srervices, Pondicherry, India.

For further information on
Blackwell Publishing, visit our website:
www.blackwellpublishing.com

Contents

Figures

Contributors

Sheila L. Ager is Associate Professor of Classical Studies at the University of Waterloo in Canada. Her research deals chiefly with political history in the Hellenistic period, in particular the relations between the city-states and the great powers of the age, as well as those between the city-states themselves. She is the author of *Interstate Arbitrations in the Greek World, 337–90* BC (Berkeley, 1997).

Susan E. Alcock is Arthur F. Thurnau Professor and Associate Professor of Classical Archaeology at the University of Michigan, and the recent recipient of a MacArthur Fellowship.

Michel Austin is Honorary Senior Lecturer in Ancient History at the University of St Andrews in Scotland. His research has been concerned with Greek social and economic history and with the Hellenistic period. He is the author of *The Hellenistic World from Alexander to the Roman Conquest* (Cambridge, 1981); a revised and enlarged edition is in preparation.

Patrick Baker has been Professor of Ancient Greek History in the Department of History at Laval University, Québec, Canada since 1998. His research interest focuses on the military institutions in the Greek cities of the Hellenistic world. He is the author of one opuscula: *Cos et Calymna 205–200 a.C.: esprit civique et défense nationale* (Québec, 1991) and several articles on related topics. He is currently working on a book entitled *Armies and Defence Organization in the Greek Cities of Western Asia Minor*.

Richard A. Billows is Professor of Greek and Roman History at Columbia University in the City of New York. Though he has published articles on various periods and aspects of Greek and Roman history and material culture, his primary publications to date have been concerned with Hellenistic politico-social institutions. He is the author of *Antigonos the One-Eyed and the Creation of the Hellenistic State* (Berkeley, 1990) and of *Kings and Colonists: Aspects of Macedonian Imperialism* (Leiden, 1995).

David Braund is Professor of Black Sea and Mediterranean History in the Department of Classics and Ancient History at the University of Exeter. From 2002–2005 he is a Leverhulme Major Research

Fellow, working on a book on the north coast of the ancient Black Sea. His earlier books include *Georgia in Antiquity* (Oxford, 1994).

Angelos Chaniotis is Professor of Ancient History at the University of Heidelberg. His research interests include the history of institutions, society and religion in the Hellenistic and Imperial periods. He is co-editor of the *Supplementum Epigraphicum Graecum* and the author of *Historie und Historiker in den griechischen Inschriften* (Stuttgart, 1988) and *Die Vertraege zwischen kretischen Staedten in der hellenistischen Zeit* (Stuttgart, 1996).

Emma Dench is Senior Lecturer in Ancient History at Birkbeck College, University of London. Her current research interests are issues of identity and empire in the Hellenistic and Roman worlds. She is the author of *From Barbarians to New Men: Greek, Roman, and Modern Perceptions of Peoples from the Central Apennines* (Oxford, 1995).

Peter Derow teaches in Oxford, where he is Hody Fellow and Tutor in Ancient History of Wadham College and University Lecturer (C.U.F.) in ancient history. He has worked mostly on Hellenistic history and epigraphy and Roman republican history, and he has long had a particular interest in Polybius and dealings between Rome and the Greeks. His publications include articles and reviews in these areas, and he is the author (with Roger S. Bagnall) of *Greek Historical Documents: the Hellenistic Period* (1981; a new edition is in preparation for Blackwell).

Claude Eilers is Associate Professor of Classics at McMaster University, Ontario, Canada. He recently held a Humboldt fellowship at the University of Cologne in Germany. He is the author

of *Roman Patrons of Greek Cities* (Oxford, 2002).

Andrew Erskine is Reader in Classics at the University of Edinburg. A specialist in Hellenistic history, he is the author of *Troy between Greece and Rome: Local Tradition and Imperial Power* (Oxford, 2001), *The Hellenistic Stoa: Political Thought and Action* (London, 1990), and numerous articles on the ancient world.

Rebecca Flemming is lecturer in ancient history at King's College London. Her research has focused on women and medicine in the ancient world, both separately and together. She is the author of *Medicine and the Making of Roman Women: Gender, Nature, and Authority from Celsus to Galen* (Oxford, 2000).

Vincent Gabrielsen is Professor of Ancient History at the Department of History, University of Copenhagen. His research has focused on Classical Greek and Hellenistic history, in particular the social and economic aspects of naval warfare. His publications include *Financing the Athenian Fleet: Public Taxation and Social Relations* (Baltimore and London, 1994) and *The Naval Aristocracy of Hellenistic Rhodes* (Aarhus, 1997).

Jennifer E. Gates is a doctoral student in the Interdepartmental Program in Classical Art and Archaeology (IPCAA) at the University of Michigan.

Privatdozent Dr Klaus Geus teaches Ancient History and Greek at the University of Bamberg, Germany. His research has focused on the social and scientific history of the Hellenistic and Roman period. He is the author of *Prosopographie der literarisch bezeugten Karthager* (Leuven, 1994) and *Eratosthenes of Kyrene: Studien zur hellenistischen Kultur-*

und Wissenschaftsgeschichte (München, 2002).

Erich S. Gruen is Gladys Rehard Wood Professor of History and Classics at the University of California, Berkeley. He has worked on the Roman Republic, relations between the Hellenistic world and Rome, and cultural connections among Greeks, Romans, and Jews from the Hellenistic period through the early Roman Empire. His most recent books are *Heritage and Hellenism: the Reinvention of Jewish Tradition* (Berkeley, 1998) and *Diaspora: Jews amidst Greeks and Romans* (Harvard, 2002).

Richard Hunter is Regius Professor of Greek at the University of Cambridge and a Fellow of Trinity College. His principal research interest is post-classical Greek literature, particularly Hellenistic poetry, comedy, and the novel. He has edited Apollonius of Rhodes and Theocritus, and his many books include *Theocritus and the Archaeology of Greek Poetry* (Cambridge, 1996). His most recent books are (with Marco Fantuzzi) *Muse e modelli: la poesia ellenistica da Alessandro Magno ad Augusto* (Bari, 2002) and *Theocritus: Encomium of Ptolemy Philadelphus* (2002).

Elizabeth Kosmetatou is Fellow of the Flemish Fund for Scientific Research at the Catholic University of Leuven. Her research has focused on Hellenistic history, epigraphy, archaeology, and literature, especially the construction of the ancient political spectacle. She is the author of numerous articles on Attalid political and ideological self-definition.

John Ma is Fellow and Tutor in Ancient History, Corpus Christi College, Oxford. His interests are the historical geography of Asia Minor, Greek epigraphy and the Hellenistic polis. He has written a monograph on Antiochos III and the cities of Western Asia Minor, and is currently working on honorific statues in the Hellenistic period.

Brian McGing is a Fellow of Trinity College Dublin. His research interests concentrate mainly on Hellenistic Asia Minor, Judaea and Greco-Roman Egypt. He has been heavily involved in Trinity College's government-funded Mediterranean and Near Eastern Studies research project, an investigation of cultural encounter in the lands of the eastern Mediterranean. His publications include *The Foreign Policy of Mithridates VI Eupator King of Pontus* (Leiden, 1986) and *Greek Papyri from Dublin* (Bonn, 1995).

Stephen Mitchell is Leverhulme Professor of Hellenistic Culture at the University of Exeter. His research has focused on the archaeology, epigraphy and history of Asia Minor from the Hellenistic to the Late Roman periods. He is the author of *Anatolia: Land, Men, and Gods in Asia Minor* (Oxford, 2 vols, 1993), *Cremna in Pisidia: an Ancient City in Peace and in War* (Wales and London, 1995) and *Pisidian Antioch: the Site and its Monuments* (Wales and London, 1998).

Phillip Mitsis is Alexander S. Onassis Professor of Hellenic Culture and Civilization at New York University. He has taught at Cornell, the University of Pittsburgh, and Princeton. He has written on topics in ancient and early modern philosophy, Greek tragedy and modern Greek poetry.

David S. Potter is Professor of Greek and Latin at the University of Michigan. He is the author of *Literary Texts and the Roman Historian* (London, 1999), *Prophecy and History in the Crisis of the Roman Empire* (Oxford, 1990), *Prophets and Emperors: Humans and Divine Au-*

thority from Augustus to Theodosius
(Cambridge, Mass., 1994) and *Losing
Power: a History of the Roman World* AD
180–395 (forthcoming), co-editor of
*Life, Death and Entertainment in the
Roman Empire* (Ann Arbor, 1999), and
editor of the forthcoming Blackwell
Companion to the Roman Empire.

Gary Reger is Professor of History at
Trinity College in Hartford, Connecti-
cut. His research interests include the
economy and epigraphy of the Hellenistic period, especially in Asia Minor. He is
the author of *Regionalism and Change in
the Economy of Independent Delos* (Berkeley, 1994), and is currently working on a
book on Mylasa in Karia.

Jane E. Rempel is a doctoral student in
the Interdepartmental Program in Classical Art and Archaeology (IPCAA) at
the University of Michigan.

Jane Rowlandson is a lecturer in Ancient History at King's College London.
She is the author of *Landowners and
Tenants in Roman Egypt* (Oxford,
1996), has edited a sourcebook, *Women
and Society in Greek and Roman Egypt*
(Cambridge, 1998), and has published
articles on the social history of Ptolemaic
and Roman Egypt.

Tanja S. Scheer was Gerda-Henkel research scholar (1994–96) in Rome. She
is Privatdozentin of Ancient History in
the Historic Department of the Ludwig-
Maximilians-Universität in Munich and
since 2002 Heisenberg research fellow
at the Albert-Ludwigs-Universität in
Freiburg. Her research interests are in
Greek and Roman cultural history, history of ancient religion and gender history. She has published *Mythische
Vorväter. Zur Bedeutung griechischer
Heroenmythen in kleinasiatischen Städten*
(1993) and *Die Gottheit und ihr Bild.
Untersuchungen zur Funktion grie-*

*chischer Kultbilder in Religion und Poli-
tik* (2000).

Joseph Scholten is Visiting Associate
Professor of Classics at the University of
Maryland. He specializes in Hellenistic
political history, with a particular concentration on the construction of regional
identities and institutions. He is author
of *The Politics of Plunder: Aitolians and
their Koinon in the Early Hellenistic Era,
ca. 279–17 BC* (Berkeley and Los Angeles,
2000).

Andrew Stewart is Professor of Ancient
Mediterranean Art and Archaeology at
the University of California at Berkeley.
He is the author of *Attika: Studies in
Athenian Sculpture of the Hellenistic Age*
(London, 1979), *Greek Sculpture: an Exploration* (New Haven, 1990), *Faces of
Power: Alexander's Image and Hellenistic
Politics* (Berkeley, 1993), and *Art, Desire,
and the Body in Ancient Greece* (Cambridge, 1997). He is completing a book
on Pergamene dedications on the Akropolis of Athens, and excavates the Persian, Hellenistic and Roman levels at the
seaport of Dor in Israel.

Dorothy J. Thompson, a Fellow of the
British Academy, teaches ancient history
at Cambridge, where she is a Fellow of
Girton College and Isaac Newton Trust
Lecturer in the Faculty of Classics. Her
research is mainly on Egypt in the period
following its conquest by Alexander of
Macedon; she has written books and
many shorter studies on Ptolemaic
Egypt. Her most recent book *Memphis
under the Ptolemies* (Princeton, 1988)
was awarded the James H. Breasted
Prize by the American Historical Association.

Riet van Bremen teaches Ancient History at University College London. She
is the author of *The Limits of Participation: Women and Civic Life in the Greek*

East in the Hellenistic and Roman Periods (Amsterdam, 1996). She is currently preparing an edition of the dossier of imperial letters to the Epicureans in Athens and is writing a study of the sanctuaries at Panamara and Lagina in Caria.

Preface

This *Companion to the Hellenistic World* was conceived during a sabbatical in Rome in Jubilee year 2000. The initial invitations were mailed from an internet café close to the Pantheon; the first contributor was gained over a meal in Trastevere and not a little grappa. The resulting volume presents a wide-ranging picture of the Hellenistic world and gives a sense of the vitality of recent scholarship. Hellenistic history shades into Roman history, and the *Companion* seeks to integrate the two rather than merely nod acknowledgement to Rome with a final chapter. It is Frank Walbank who has done so much to explore this interplay and it is to him that this collection is dedicated.

My task as editor has been made easier by the enthusiasm and efficiency of all the contributors and by the constant encouragement of Al Bertrand at Blackwell. The typescript was guided through its final stages by Angela Cohen and Louise Spencely. I am particularly grateful to Joan Wright for translating chapter 13 from its original German. Wolfgang Blümel, Andy Meadows and Christine Morris all kindly gave me assistance with illustrations. And Michelle I would like to thank for things too numerous to mention.

Andrew Erskine
Galway, 5 November 2002

Acknowledgements

Quotations from vols. 4–6 of W. R. Paton's translation of Polybius are reprinted by permission of the publishers and the Trustees of the Loeb Classical Library, Loeb Classical Library vols. 159–61, Cambridge, Mass.: Harvard University Press, 1925, 1926, 1927. The Loeb Classical Library is a ® registered trademark of the President and Fellows of Harvard University.

Ancient Authors:
Abbreviations and Glossary

The spellings of Greek names in the list below are the conventional latinized ones and are for the most part those used in the main text, but where a transliterated spelling has been preferred in the main text that is indicated in brackets. Dates, often only approximate, are taken from *OCD*[3].

Ach. Tat.	Achilles Tatius, Alexandrian novelist, 2nd c. AD
Aen. Tact.	Aeneas Tacticus, 4th c. BC, *Siegecraft*
Aesch.	Aeschylus, Athenian tragedian, first half 5th c. BC
PV	*Prometheus Vinctus*
Supp.	*Supplices*
Ampelius	Ampelius, 3rd–4th c. AD, *Liber memorialis*
Anth. Pal.	*Anthologia Palatina* (*Palatine Anthology*)
App.	Appian, Greek historian, 2nd c. AD
BC	*Bella civilia* (*Civil Wars*)
Hann.	*Hannibalic War*
Ill.	*Illyrian Wars*
Mith.	*Mithridatic Wars*
Syr.	*Syrian Wars*
Arist.	Aristotle, Greek philosopher, 384–322 BC
Cael.	*De caelo*
Eth. Nic.	*Nicomachean Ethics*
Mete.	*Meteorologica*
Pol.	*Politics*
frag. Rose	V. Rose (ed.). *Aristotelis qui ferebantur librorum fragmenta*. Leipzig, 1886
[Arist.] *Ath. Pol.*	*Athenaion politeia* (*Constitution of the Athenians*)
Oec.	*Oeconomica*
Aristid.	Aelius Aristides, 2nd c. AD
Panath.	*Panathenaic oration* (*Or.* 1)
Rom. Or.	*To Rome* (*Or.* 26)

Arr.	Arrian, Greek historian, *c.* AD 86–160
Anab.	*Anabasis*
Ind.	*Indica*
Tact.	*Tactica*
Artem.	Artemidorus Daldianus, 2nd c. AD, *On Dreams*
Athen.	Athenaeus, c. AD 200, *The Deipnosophists*, learned conversation at dinner
Avien. *Or.*	Avienus, Latin poet, 4th c. AD, *Ora maritima*
Caes.	C. Iulius Caesar (100–44 BC)
BC	*Bellum Civile*
[Caes.] *Alex.*	*Bellum Alexandrinum*
Celsus *Med.*	A. Cornelius Celsus, 1st c. AD, *De medicina*
Cic.	M. Tullius Cicero, Roman politician and writer, 106–43 BC
Att.	*Epistulae ad Atticum* (*Letters to Atticus*)
Deiot.	*Pro rege Deiotaro*
Div.	*De divinatione* (*On Divination*)
Fam.	*Epistulae ad familiares* (*Letters to Friends*)
Flac.	*Pro Flacco*
Leg.	*De legibus* (*On Laws*)
Off.	*De officiis* (*On Duties*)
Pis.	*In Pisonem*
Rep.	*De republica* (*On the Republic*)
Sen.	*De senectute* (*On Old Age*)
II *Verr.*	*In Verrem* (*Verrines*), Actio secunda
Clem. Al. *Protr.*	Clement of Alexandria, bishop, late 2nd–early 3rd c. AD, *Protrepticus*
Cleomed.	Cleomedes, probably 4th c. AD, author of astronomical treatise
Columella	Columella, 1st c. AD, *De re rustica*, an agricultural manual
Curt.	Q. Curtius Rufus, 1st or 2nd c. AD, *History of Alexander*
Dem.	Demosthenes, Athenian orator, 384–322 BC
Ol.	*Olynthiacs*
D.H. *Ant. Rom.*	Dionysius of Halicarnassus (Dionysios of Halikarnassos), 1st c. BC, *Roman Antiquities*
Dio	Cassius Dio, Greek historian of Rome, *c.* AD 164– after 229
Dio Chrys.	Dio Chrysostom, Greek orator and philosopher, mid-1st c.–early 2nd c. AD
Diod.	Diodorus Siculus (Diodoros of Sicily), author of a world history, 1st c. BC
D.L.	Diogenes Laertius, probably early 3rd c. AD, *Lives of the Philosophers*
Eur. *Andr.*	Euripides, Athenian tragedian, *c.* 480s–407/6 BC, *Andromache*
Euseb. *Chron.*	Eusebius of Caesarea, bishop and scholar, *c.* AD 260–339, *Chronica*
Eutrop.	Eutropius, historian, 4th c. AD, *Breviarum ab urbe condita*
Frontin. *Str.*	Sex. Iulius Frontinus, 1st c. AD, *Strategemata*

Gal.	Galen, Greek medical writer, 2nd c. AD, cited according to edition of Kühn or *CMG* series
AA	*De anatomicis administrationibus* (*On Anatomical Procedures*)
Comp. Med. Gen.	*De compositione medicamentorum per genera*
Comp. Med. Loc.	*De compositione medicamentorum secundum locos*
PHP	*De placitis Hippocratis et Platonis* (*On the Doctrines of Hippocrates and Plato*)
Sem.	*De semine* (*On the Seed*)
Trem. Palp.	*De tremore, palpitatione, convulsione et rigore*
Ven. Sect. Er. Rom.	*De venae sectione adversus Erasistrateos Romae degentes*
[Gal.] *Intro.*	*Introductio*
Hdt.	Herodotus of Halicarnassus (Herodotos of Halikarnassos), historian, 5th c. BC
Hes. *Theog.*	Hesiod, Greek poet, *Theogony*, probably *c.* 700 BC
Hom.	Homer
Il.	*Iliad*
Od.	*Odyssey*
Isoc. *Phil.*	Isocrates (Isokrates), Athenian orator, 436–338 BC, *Philippus*
Jos.	Josephus (Josephos), Jewish historian, 1st c. AD
AJ	*Antiquitates Judaicae*
Ap.	*Contra Apionem*
BJ	*Bellum Judaicum* (*The Jewish War*)
Just.	Justin, *Epitome*, of the *Historiae Philippicae* of Pompeius Trogus
Lib.	Libanius, rhetorician, 4th c. AD
Livy	Livy, probably 59 BC–AD 17; history of Rome cited as 'Livy'
Epit.	*Epitome*
Per.	*Periochae*
Lucan	Lucan, Latin poet, AD 39–65, *De bello civili*
Lucian *Macr.*	Lucian, 2nd c. AD, *Macrobii*
Lucr.	Lucretius, Epicurean Latin poet, 1st c. BC, *De rerum natura* (*On the Nature of Things*)
Lycoph.	Lycophron (Lykophron), Hellenistic poet, *Alexandra*
Lyd. *Mens.*	John Lydus, 6th c. AD, *De mensibus*
Macc.	*Maccabees*
Macrob. *Sat.*	Macrobius, late empire, *Saturnalia*
Mart. *Spect.*	Martial, Latin poet, 1st c. AD, *Spectacula*
Men.	Menander, Athenian playwright, late 4th–early 3rd c. BC
Dysk.	*Dyskolos*
Sik.	*Sikyonios* (ed. R. Kassel 1965)
Ovid *Met.*	Ovid, Latin poet, 43 BC–AD 17, *Metamorphoses*
Paus.	Pausanias, Greek traveller, 2nd c. AD, *Description of Greece*
Philo	Philo, Jewish writer, early 1st c. AD
Conf.Ling.	*De confusione linguarum*
In Flacc.	*In Flaccum*

Leg.	*Legatio ad Gaium* (*Embassy to Gaius*)
Mos.	*The Life of Moses*
Spec.Leg.	*De specialibus legibus*
Phot. *Bib.*	Photius (Photios), 9th c. AD, *Bibliotheca*
Pind. *Pyth.*	Pindar, Boiotian poet, late 6th–mid 5th c. BC, *Pythian Odes*
Plato	Plato, Athenian philosopher, *c.* 429–347 BC
Rep.	*Republic*
[Plato] *Ep.*	*Epistulae*
Pliny	Pliny the Elder, AD 23/4–79
HN	*Naturalis historia* (*Natural History*)
Plut.	Plutarch, Greek biographer and philosopher, mid-1st c. to 2nd c. BC
Aem.	*Aemilius Paulus*
Alc.	*Alcibiades*
Alex.	*Alexander*
Ant.	*Antony*
Arat.	*Aratus*
Caes.	*Caesar*
Cleom.	*Cleomenes*
Crass.	*Crassus*
Demetr.	*Demetrius*
Eum.	*Eumenes*
Flam.	*Flamininus*
Luc.	*Lucullus*
Lys.	*Lysander*
Mar.	*Marius*
Mor.	*Moralia*
Phil.	*Philopoemen*
Pomp.	*Pompey*
Pyrrh.	*Pyrrhus*
Sol.	*Solon*
Sull.	*Sulla*
Polyaen.	Polyaenus, 2nd c. AD, *Strategemata*
Polyb.	Polybius (Polybios), Greek historian, *c.* 200–*c.* 118 BC
Ps.-Callisthenes	The Alexander Romance attributed to Kallisthenes, ed. W. Kroll (1926), trans. R. Stoneman (1991)
RG	*Res gestae Divi Augusti*
Rufus *Onom.*	Rufus, physician, late 1st c. AD, *Peri Onomasia* (*On Nomenclature*)
Scribon. *Comp.*	Scribonius Largus, physician, 1st c. AD, *Compositiones*
S.H.A. *Tyr. Trig.*	Scriptores Historiae Augustae, *Tyranni Triginta*
Sor. *Gyn.*	Soranus, physician, late 1st–early 2nd c. AD, *Gynaecology*
Strabo	Strabo, *c.* 64 BC–after AD 20, *Geography*
Suda	*Suda*, a lexicon compiled in 10th c. AD (ed. A. Adler, Stuttgart 1928–38)
Suet.	Suetonius, Latin biographer, *c.* AD 70–*c.* 130
Aug.	*Divus Augustus*
Dom.	*Domitian*

Iul.	*Divus Iulius*
Tib.	*Tiberius*
Tac. *Ann.*	Tacitus, Latin historian, *c.* AD 56–after *c.* 118, *Annals*
Theocr. *Id.*	Theocritus, Greek poet, 3rd c. BC, *Idylls*
Theophr.	Theophrastus (Theophrastos), Greek philosopher, late 370s–early 280s BC
Char.	*Characters*
Hist. pl.	*Historia plantarum*
Thuc.	Thucydides, Athenian historian, 5th c. BC
Trogus *Prol.*	Pompeius Trogus, Augustan historian, *Prologi*
Val. Max.	Valerius Maximus, Latin writer, 1st c. AD
Vell. Pat.	Velleius Paterculus, early imperial, *Historiae Romanae*
Vitr. *De arch.*	Vitruvius, late 1st c. BC, *De architectura*
Xen.	Xenophon, Athenian writer, *c.* 430–mid 4th c. BC
Anab.	*Anabasis*
Cyr.	*Cyropaedia*
Hell.	*Hellenica*
Mem.	*Memorabilia*
Zonar.	Johannes Zonaras, Byzantine historian, 12th c. AD

Reference Works: Abbreviations

For fuller information on papyrological publications, see Oates et al. 2001.

AHB	*Ancient History Bulletin*
AJA	*American Journal of Archaeology*
AJAH	*American Journal of Ancient History*
AJP	*American Journal of Philology*
AncSoc	*Ancient Society*
ANRW	*Aufstieg und Niedergang der römischen Welt*. Berlin 1972–
ANSMN	*Museum Notes* (American Numismatic Society)
APF	*Archiv für Papyrusforschung*
ASNP	*Annali della Scuola Normale Superiore di Pisa, Classe di Lettere e Filosofia*
ATL	Meritt, B., Wade-Gery, H. and McGregor, M. *The Athenian Tribute Lists*. 1939–53
Austin	Austin, M. M. *The Hellenistic world from Alexander to the Roman conquest: a selection of ancient sources in translation*. Cambridge 1981
BCH	*Bulletin de Correspondance Hellénique*
BD	Bagnall, R. and Derow, P. *The Hellenistic Period: Historical Sources in Translation*. Oxford 2004 (earlier edition, Chico, California 1981)
BE	*Bulletin épigraphique*, published in *REG*
BGU	*Aegyptische Urkunden aus den Staatlichen Museen zu Berlin, Griechische Urkunden*. Berlin 1895–
BICS	*Bulletin of the Institute of Classical Studies*
BMC	*Catalogue of the Greek Coins in the British Museum*
BSA	*Annual of the British School at Athens*
Burstein	Burstein, S. M. *The Hellenistic Age from the battle of Ipsos to the death of Kleopatra VII*. Translated Documents of Greece and Rome 3. Cambridge 1985

CAH²	*Cambridge Ancient History.* 2nd edn. Cambridge 1961–
Chrest.Wilck	Mitteis, L. and Wilcken, U. *Grundzüge und Chrestomathie der papyruskunde.* Vol. 1: *Historischer Teil.* Leipzig 1912
CIJ	Frey, J. B. *Corpus Inscriptionum Iudaicarum.* Rome 1936–52
CIL	*Corpus Inscriptionum Latinarum.* 1863–
CJ	*Classical Journal*
CMG	*Corpus Medicorum Graecorum.* 1909–
CP	*Classical Philology*
CPCActs	*Acts of the Copenhagen Polis Center*
CPJ	Tcherikover, V. and Fuks, A. *Corpus Papyrorum Judaicarum.* Cambridge, Mass. 1957–64
CQ	*Classical Quarterly*
CRAI	*Comptes rendus de l'Académie des Inscriptions et Belles-Lettres*
Davies *EGF*	Davies, M. *Epicorum Graecorum Fragmenta.* Göttingen 1988
DdA	*Dialoghi di Archeologia*
DHA	*Dialogues d'Histoire Ancienne*
EA	*Epigraphica Anatolica*
FGrH	Jacoby, F. *Die Fragmente der griechischen Historiker.* 1923–
GGM	Müller, C. *Geographici Graeci Minores.* Paris 1855–61
GRBS	*Greek, Roman and Byzantine Studies*
HSCP	*Harvard Studies in Classical Philology*
HTR	*Harvard Theological Review*
I.Cret.	Guarducci, M. *Inscriptiones Creticae.* Rome 1935–50
I.Didyma	Rehm, A. *Didyma* II: *Die Inschriften.* Berlin 1958
I.Ephesos	Wankel, H., Merkelbach, R. et al. *Die Inscriften von Ephesos.* 1979–81 (*IK* 11–17)
I.Erythrai	Engelmann, H. and Merkelbach, R. *Die Inschriften von Erythrai und Klazomenai.* 1972–73 (*IK* 1)
I.Iasos	Blümel, W. *Die Inschriften von Iasos.* 1985 (*IK* 28)
I.Ilion	Frisch, P. *Die Inschriften von Ilion.* 1975 (*IK* 3)
I.Lamp.	Frisch, P. *Die Inschriften von Lampsakos.* 1978 (*IK* 6)
I.Laodikeia	Corsten, T. *Die Inschriften von Laodikeia am Lykos.* Vol. 1. 1997 (*IK* 49)
I.Louvre	Bernand, E. *Inscriptions grecques d'Égypte et de Nubie au Musée du Louvre.* Paris 1992
I.Magn.	Kern, O. *Die Inschriften von Magnesia am Maeander.* Berlin 1900
I.Mylasa	Blümel, W. *Die Inschriften von Mylasa.* 1987–88 (*IK* 34–5)
I.Perg.	Fränkel, M. *Die Inschriften von Pergamon.* Berlin 1890 (Vol. 1), 1895 (Vol. 2)
I.Perinthos	Sayar, M. H. *Perinthos-Herakleia: Marmara Ereglisi und Umgebung; Geschichte, Testimonien, griechische und lateinische Inschriften.* Vienna 1998
I.Priene	Hiller von Gaertingen, F. *Die Inschriften von Priene.* Berlin 1906

I.Sestos   Krauss, J. *Die Inschriften von Sestos und des thrakischen Chersones.* 1980
                  (*IK* 19)

I.Stratonikeia   Şahin, M. Ç. *Die Inschriften von Stratonikeia.* 1981–90 (*IK* 21–2)

IG   *Inscriptiones Graecae.* 1873–

IGRR   Cagnat, R. *Inscriptiones Graecae ad res Romanas pertinentes.* Paris 1906–27

IK   *Inschriften griechischer Städte aus Kleinasien.* Bonn 1972–

ILLRP   Degrassi, A. *Inscriptiones Latinae Liberae Rei Republicae.* Florence 1963
                  (Vol. 2), 1965 (Vol. 1^2)

ILS   Dessau, H. *Inscriptiones Latinae Selectae.* Berlin 1892–1916

IOSPE   Latyschev, B. *Inscriptiones antiquae orae septentrionalis Ponti Euxini
                  Graecae et Latinae.* St Petersburg 1885–1901

Iscr.Cos.   Segre, M. *Iscrizioni di Cos.* Rome 1993

ISE   Moretti, L. *Iscrizioni storiche ellenistiche.* Florence 1967–76

JEA   *Journal of Egyptian Archaeology*

JHS   *Journal of Hellenic Studies*

JRA   *Journal of Roman Archaeology*

JRS   *Journal of Roman Studies*

JSav   *Journal des Savants*

LDAB   Leuven Database of Ancient Books, http://ldab.arts.kuleuven.ac.be

LSAM   Sokolowski, F. *Lois sacrées de l'Asie Mineure.* Paris 1955

MDAI   *Mitteilungen des deutschen archäologischen Instituts.* (A) Athens,
                  (C) Cairo, (I) Istanbul, (R) Rome

Milet   *Milet, Ergebnisse der Ausgrabung seit dem Jahren 1899.* Berlin 1906–

ML   Meiggs, R. and Lewis, D. *A Selection of Greek Historical Inscriptions to the
                  End of the Fifth Century* BC. Rev. edn. Oxford 1988

MRR   Broughton, T. R. S. *The Magistrates of the Roman Republic.* New York
                  1951–2. Suppl. in 1986

OCD[3]   Hornblower, S. and Spawforth, A. *The Oxford Classical Dictionary.* 3rd edn.
                  Oxford 1996

OGIS   Dittenberger, W. *Orientis Graeci Inscriptiones Selectae.* Leipzig 1903–5

P.Adler   *The Adler Papyri.* Oxford 1939

Pap. Lugd.-Bat.   *Papyrologica Lugduno-Batava.* Leiden

PCPS   *Proceedings of the Cambridge Philological Society*

P.Eleph.   Rubensohn, O. *Elephantine Papyri.* Berlin 1907

P.Grenf. I   Grenfell, B. *An Alexandrian Erotic Fragment and other Greek Papyri chiefly
                  Ptolemaic.* Oxford 1896

P.Hal.   *Dikaiomata: Auszüge aus Alexandrinischen Gesetzen und Verordnungen
                  in einem Papyrus des philologischen Seminars der Universität Halle.* Berlin
                  1913

P.Haun.   *Papyri Graecae Haunienses*

P.Hib   *The Hibeh Papyri.* London. Vol. 1, ed. Grenfell, B. P. and Hunt, A. S,
                  1906; Vol. 2, ed. Turner, E. G. and Lenger, M.-Th., 1955

P.Köln	*Kölner Papyri.* Opladen 1976–
P.Lond.	*Greek Papyri in the British Museum.* London 1893–
P.Mich.Zenon	Edgar, C. C. *Papyri in the University of Michigan Collection.* Vol. 1: *Zenon papyri.* Ann Arbor 1931
P.Oxy	*The Oxyrhynchus Papyri.* London 1898–
PSI	*Papiri Greci e Latini, Pubblicazzioni della Società italiana per la ricerca dei papiri greci e latini in Egitto.* Florence 1912–
P.Rev.	*Revenue Laws of Ptolemy Philadelphus.* Ed. B. Grenfell, Oxford, 1931; and again by J. Bingen, Göttingen, 1952 (in *SB*)
P.Tebt.	Grenfell, B. P. et al. *The Tebtunis Papyri.* London 1902–76
P.Tor.Choach.	Pestman, P. W. *Il Processo di Hermeias e altri documenti dell'archivio dei choachiti, papiri greci e demotici conservati a Torino e in altre collezioni d'Italia.* Turin 1992
P.Yale	Oates, J., Samuel, A. and Welles, C. B. *Yale Papyri in the Beinecke Rare Books and Manuscript Library.* New Haven 1967
RC	Welles, C. B. *Royal Correspondence in the Hellenistic Period.* New Haven 1934
RDAC	*Report of the Department of Antiquities of Cyprus*
RDGE	Sherk, R. K. *Roman Documents from the Greek East:* Senatus Consulta *and* Epistulae *to the Age of Augustus.* Baltimore 1969
RE	Pauly, A., Wissowa, G., and Kroll, W., *Realencyclopädie des classischen Altertumswissenschaft.* 1893–
REA	*Revue des études anciennes*
REG	*Revue des études grecques*
REL	*Revue des études latines*
Rh.Mus.	*Rheinisches Museum für Philologie*
Robert *OMS*	Robert, L. *Opera Minora Selecta.* 7 vols. Amsterdam 1969–90
SB	Preisigke, F. et al. *Sammelbuch griechischer Urkunden aus Ägypten.* 1915–
SCI	*Scripta Classica Israelica*
SEG	*Supplementum Epigraphicum Graecum.* 1923–
Sel.Pap.	Hunt, A. S, Edgar, C. C. and Page, D. L. *Select Papyri,* 4 vols, Loeb Classical Library, Cambridge, Mass. 1950
Sherk	Sherk, R. K. *Rome and the Greek East to the Death of Augustus,* Translated Documents of Greece and Rome 4, Cambridge 1984
*SIG*³	Dittenberger, W. *Sylloge Inscriptionum Graecarum.* 3rd edn. Leipzig 1915–24
Supp. Hell.	Lloyd-Jones, H. and Parsons, P. *Supplementum Hellenisticum.* Berlin 1983
SV	*Die Staatsverträge des Altertums.* Munich. Vol. 2: *von 700 bis 338 v. Chr.,* ed. H. Bengtson, 1962; Vol. 3: *von 338 bis 200 v. Chr.,* ed. H. H. Schmitt, 1969
TAM	*Tituli Asiae Minoris.* 1901–
TAPA	*Transactions and Proceedings of the American Philological Association*

Tod   Tod, M. N. *Greek Historical Inscriptions.* Oxford 1946–48

UPZ   Wilcken, U. *Urkunden der Ptolemäerzeit (ältere Funde).* Berlin and Leipzig. Vol. 1: *Papyri aus Unterägypten,* 1922–27; Vol. 2: *Papyri aus Oberägypten.* 1957

ZPE   *Zeitschrift für Papyrologie und Epigraphik*

CHAPTER ONE

Approaching the Hellenistic World

Andrew Erskine

1 Alexander's Legacy

After his victory at Actium in 31 BC Augustus pursued his defeated rivals, Antony and Kleopatra, to Alexandria in Egypt. After capturing the city, he soon had the opportunity to view its sights. One of the few places he is known to have visited during his residence there is the tomb of Alexander the Great. Rome's future emperor is said to have reverently placed a golden crown on the embalmed body laid out in front of him and then scattered flowers on it. When asked if he would also like to see the tombs of Ptolemies, the Greco-Macedonian dynasty that had ruled over Egypt since the death of Alexander, he abruptly dismissed the suggestion, saying that 'he wanted to see a king, not some corpses'. So, at least, reports Suetonius in the early second century AD (Suet. *Aug.* 18, cf. Dio 51.16, Erskine 2002a).

This story in many ways captures the Hellenistic Age. It was the transforming power of Alexander that brought Alexandria into existence, a major Greek city which had grown up in the foreign land of Egypt, something which would have been unthinkable to a Greek of the fifth century BC. Here, as the dead Alexander lies before the new ruler of the world, the beginning and the end of the Hellenistic period meet, Alexander the Macedonian king who changed the East by his conquest of the Persian empire, Augustus the Roman who overthrew the last of the successor kingdoms with his occupation of Ptolemaic Egypt. The Ptolemies themselves are of no interest; they are simply written out of history, and with them go the centuries that intervened between Alexander and the coming of Rome. The Roman emperors wanted to look back to the almost mythical figure of Alexander; they saw themselves as heirs not to the kingdoms that developed out of Alexander's empire but as the heirs of Alexander himself.

Of course Augustus may never have uttered the disparaging comment attributed to him by Suetonius; such anecdotes tend to evolve with each telling. Nonetheless, the dismissive outlook evident in the story reflects a general and continuing neglect of the Greek world after Alexander. From antiquity onwards this has been seen as a period of decline, both political and cultural. The great figures of the Greek past were to be found in earlier times, not in the years following Alexander. This way of thinking about the past was not limited to Romans; Greeks of the early empire would often by-pass their Hellenistic ancestors and look for inspiration to the Classical period. A complex attitude can already be detected during the reign of Augustus; Latin poets may have admired and emulated their Alexandrian predecessors but a critic such as Dionysios of Halikarnassos could see Alexander as marking a turning-point in literary culture and one for the worse (cf. Gelzer 1979). This has had important consequences for the study of the Hellenistic world. Whereas Classical literature was valued and preserved, its post-Alexander counterpart has survived only very poorly.

This neglect was to continue until the nineteenth century when Johann-Gustav Droysen virtually invented the Hellenistic period in a series of studies devoted to Alexander and his successors. For him Alexander's conquests led to a fusion of Greek and Oriental culture that eventually gave Christianity the opportunity to flourish. Since the publication of Droysen's work the discovery of new inscriptions and papyri has provided historians with an ever-increasing wealth of evidence to exploit, allowing a far more subtle and nuanced picture to emerge.

Nonetheless, in spite of the work of some great scholars the Hellenistic world has never received the same degree of attention as its Classical predecessor. The dominance of Classics as an academic discipline among the elite of more modern times has kept the ancient world alive but it has also tended to exclude those areas that have less to contribute to Classics as traditionally understood. It is therefore the periods that produce the literary canon that are most studied: Classical Greece (Herodotos, Thucydides, tragedy), Republican Rome (Cicero, Sallust), the Roman Empire (Horace, Vergil, Tacitus). To appreciate the Hellenistic world one must abandon the value system that sees the centuries after Alexander as some kind of epilogue to the achievement of Classical Greece. Increasing interest in Hellenistic literature, philosophy and art in their own right suggests that this is changing, perhaps in part as a result of the recent decline of traditional Classics, but also because academics, however categorized, are asking different questions about both present and past.

On the simplest level the Hellenistic period is defined and bounded by political events. Alexander's conquest of the sprawling Persian empire marks the beginning, but his premature death in 323 BC was followed by the fragmentation of his possessions as leading figures in the Macedonian military struggled for control. Out of these conflicts emerged three main dynasties: the Antigonids in the Macedonian homeland; the Seleukids in Asia; and the Ptolemies in Egypt, supplemented in the later third century by the Attalids in Asia Minor. The period traditionally ends with the fall of the Ptolemaic kingdom to Rome after Actium, the culmination of two centuries of Roman success in the East. All historical periods are in some sense the arbitrary constructs of historians. If political events are the criteria, then establishing the end of the Hellenistic period is problematic. Alexander may have created a dramatic and decisive beginning but the end is not so neat; the extension of Roman power occurred gradually, affecting different areas at different times. The disappearance of the last of the successor kingdoms is a convenient terminal point rather than one of profound significance. The present volume takes the narrative of events through to the death of Augustus, in order to allow some consideration of Augustus' role in the creation of a Roman East.

As Droysen saw, however, the Hellenistic period is as much a cultural phenomenon as a political one. It may have its origins in a political event – the demise of the Persian empire – but that event was to have enormous repercussions beyond politics, repercussions that would not recognize Actium as a boundary. When the Greco-Macedonian elite took power throughout much of the east, they not only replaced the old order, they also brought their own way of life. Greek cities were founded and developed – centres of Greek culture and language in an alien environment, cities such as Alexandria in Egypt, Antioch on the Orontes, Seleukeia on the Tigris, or in the far east the Greek settlements in Baktria, now in modern Afghanistan. A sign of the cultural change that had taken place was the location of the world's largest collection of Greek books; this library was to be found not in Athens nor in one of the old Greek cities but in Egypt. Change, of course, is always easier to notice than continuity and it is important not to overlook the latter. To understand the Hellenistic world it is essential to grasp both.

Greek communities and culture settled among non-Greek populations. It is the resulting cultural interaction that offers one of the more fascinating areas of study. Its extent and nature have been the subject of considerable debate: in which direction did influence go? Or did Greeks and non-Greeks remain largely separate? What did it mean anyway to be Greek? What was the relationship between immigrant and native, between town and country? To what extent did non-Greeks, such as Iranians or Egyptians, participate in the royal administration and up to what level? The answers and approaches to such questions may change from region to region. The area conquered by Alexander was vast and varied; its very diversity acts as a warning against too uniform a response, a point increasingly stressed in modern scholarship. Greek culture may have been new to Baktria but there had long been coexistence and interaction in Asia Minor between Greeks and Karians, Greeks and Lykians, and so on. And the Greeks of Asia Minor were in any case very different from those of say Athens or Sparta. Other areas may rarely have seen a Greek.

The present volume begins with a section of narrative before adopting a thematic approach. Some chapters are concerned with subjects that have long interested students of Hellenistic history, others are less familiar. Topics may vary – dynasties, religion, the *polis* (city-state), local tradition, geography – but underlying themes recur – regionalism and diversity, cultural interaction, ethnicity, change and continuity. Old certainties have disappeared; it used, for instance, to be commonplace to lament the death of the *polis*, crushed by the rise of the kings, but now there is an increasing tendency to stress the vitality of civic life.

It is the legacy of Alexander, both political and cultural, that gives the Hellenistic period its sense of unity and coherence. This may lead to an over-emphasis on the Greek at the expense of what is more regional. Alternative perspectives are possible. The Seleukids when considered as part of the history of Iran may look rather different from the dynasty presented as part of Greco-Macedonian history. From the perspective of a student of Greek history Alexander can be viewed as the founder of the Hellenistic world, but a historian of the Persian or Achaimenid empire might reasonably hold him to be 'the last of the Achaimenids' (Briant 1996: 896). Thus our ideas of change and continuity are themselves dependent on emphasis and perspective.

2   Reviewing the Evidence

The Classical period offers the historian a series of dominating texts – Herodotos, Thucydides, Xenophon – which shape the way we think about the period and establish a framework for further investigation. The Hellenistic world, on the other hand, has none of this, a circumstance that is at once both frustrating and liberating. There are no contemporary narrative histories until Polybios' account of the rise of Rome appears in the mid-second century BC and even here, disappointingly, much of his text is now lost. Nor can too much enlightenment be sought among later historians whose coverage of the Hellenistic period is sketchy at best.

There has always been a tendency for scholars investigating the ancient world to prioritize histories but the study of ancient history has changed over time. Its goal is not simply (if it ever was) to produce a political narrative; issues, such as economic activity, gender, ethnicity and cultural change, are at the forefront of current historical investigations; yet the emphasis on the importance of historical texts remains. There is often a sense, not shared by historians of more modern periods, that history is merely a commentary on these ancient texts.

The historian of the Hellenistic period might regret the lack of such texts and the resulting haziness in narrative and chronology, but there is much by way of compensation. In particular there is no shortage of alternative source material: large quantities of papyri unearthed in Egypt, the inscriptions that were so much part of Greek civic life, coins minted by cities and kings, continuing archaeological discoveries, both through excavation and survey. This body of evidence is growing all the time. A satisfactory narrative may be elusive but the variety and richness of the source material available gives the historian the chance to confront other questions and issues. Thus, for example, although individual wars, such as the Second Syrian War or the Chremonidean War, may be badly documented, much can said about the phenomenon of warfare itself.

The challenge lies in combining all this evidence, material that often pulls in different directions. Papyri tell of administration and life in rural Egypt, inscriptions reveal something of the values and society of Greek cities, literary texts focus on personalities and kings. What survives is a partial and in some ways rather fragmented picture, oriented towards the Greek elite. The non-Greek inhabitants of this world are not, however, completely without a voice, although it still tends to be the elite who speak, sometimes in Greek, sometimes in native languages. Texts appear on various materials and in various scripts; there is Egyptian in hieroglyphs and demotic, Akkadian on cuneiform tablets from Babylonia, Hebrew from Judaea. These can offer a different perspective, although they are not so plentiful as we might want nor are they so familiar to classically-trained historians. The rest of this chapter will offer a survey of the written evidence available, beginning with the Greco-Roman literary tradition, before turning to inscriptions and papyri, and finally to non-Greek voices from the Hellenistic world. The handling of the evidence of archaeology and art is treated elsewhere in this volume (Alcock et al.; Stewart).

3   Literature

The lack of contemporary histories means that students of the Hellenistic world must often turn to later writers, who may have lived centuries after the events they are describing. Even here the focus is much greater on some periods than others; Alexander's reign and the wars with Rome attract the most attention.

The only Hellenistic history to survive in any quantity is the study of Rome's rise to power written by Polybios in the second century BC. Polybios was a member of a distinguished family from Megalopolis in the Peloponnese; he had been a high-ranking official in the Achaian League, one of the more powerful confederacies in Greece, but after the Roman victory over the Macedonian king Perseus in 168 his political career came to an abrupt end. The following year he was among a thousand Achaians deported to Italy where he was compelled to remain until 150. He used this enforced leisure in Rome to begin his history, an ambitious work of high quality in forty books which took the whole Mediterranean as its subject. After two introductory books the history proper commences with the 140th Olympiad (220–216 BC), the date at which he believed the history of Italy and Libya merged with that of Greece and Asia (1.3). He sought to explain to his fellow Greeks 'how and by what sort of government in less than 53 years the Romans came to conquer and rule almost the whole inhabited world' (1.1.5). These 53 years ended with the fall of the Macedonian kingdom in 168/7, but he later decided to extend his history so that it covered not only Rome's acquisition of power (bks 3–29) but also the years that followed, up to 145/44 (bks 30–39). As a contemporary observer he offers a rare insight into Roman expansion and the Greek reaction to it, but his work is not exclusively concentrated on Rome; there is, for instance, an important account of the history of the Achaian League, much about the early years of Antiochos III, a vivid picture of disturbances in Alexandria. Only the first five books are intact, the remainder surviving in 'fragments', albeit some quite substantial. These are largely the work of Byzantine excerptors, although numerous citations can also be found in Strabo, Athenaeus and Plutarch. Some idea of what is missing can be obtained from the Latin historian Livy, who used Polybios extensively as his source for events in the east in books 31–45 of his history of Rome, although his work too is incomplete, ending in 167 BC.

Other historians from the Hellenistic period are for the most part only known through the work of their successors. Lost are the early writers on Alexander, such as Aristoboulos of Kassandreia (*FGrH* 139), Kallisthenes of Olynthos (*FGrH* 124), Kleitarchos (*FGrH* 137) and Ptolemy I of Egypt (*FGrH* 138); so too are the major third-century figures, Douris of Samos, Hieronymos of Kardia, Phylarchos, and Timaios of Tauromenion. Douris' writings included a history of Macedonia from 370 through to the time of the battle of Koroupedion in 281, a history of Samos of which he was tyrant, and a rather sensational biography of fellow tyrant Agathokles of Sicily (*FGrH* 76). Hieronymos' history, spanning the years from the death of Alexander in 323 to the death of Pyrrhos in 272, is probably the most serious loss from this period. He was closely involved in the struggles of the successors, in the service first of his compatriot Eumenes and afterwards of the early Antigonids, and was consequently well-informed if slightly partial. Much used by later writers such as Diodoros and Plutarch, his work appears to have been of an especially high standard (*FGrH* 154). Phylarchos covered the central section of the third century, moving from the death of Pyrrhos to the death of the Spartan king Kleomenes in 220/19. His sympathetic portrait of the revolutionary Kleomenes, which features prominently in Plutarch's *Lives of Agis and Kleomenes*, provoked the Achaian Polybios to subject Phylarchos to a savage critique (*FGrH* 81; Polyb. 2.56–63). The Sicilian historian Timaios was another victim of Polybian polemic; he is criticized for spending too much time with books, not seeing cities and places for himself, and lacking political and military experience, charges that reveal much about Polybios' own conception of history. Timaios was, nonetheless, a very influential historian who wrote extensively on the western Greeks during some fifty years spent as an exile in Athens (*FGrH* 566; Polyb. 12). The most important lost work from the later Hellenistic period is probably the continuation of Polybios written by the Stoic polymath Poseidonios from Apameia in Syria. One of the leading intellectuals of the first century BC and close to members of the Roman elite, he wrote a history in 52 books covering the years from 146 to the 80s BC.

These lost writers form the basis of the accounts that survive; sometimes they are cited by name, at other times material is unattributed, leaving modern historians to speculate on a likely source. Named citations are rather misleadingly referred to as 'fragments', a term that suggests that they are verbatim quotations that have somehow become displaced from their original text. Occasionally this may indeed be the case, for instance if the text has been preserved on papyrus, or is among the extracts from historians collected for the Byzantine emperor, Constantine VII Porphyrogenitus. More often these citations are abridgements or re-wordings of what was written and may even have been reproduced from memory. Some abridgements can be substantial, notably the so-called *Bibliotheca*, or 'Library', of Photios, a ninth century AD scholar who wrote numerous summaries of books he had read. These included works now completely lost, such as *On the Red Sea* by Agatharchides of Knidos (*FGrH* 86) or the history of his home-town written by Memnon of Herakleia Pontike (*FGrH* 434). The modern historian needs to be wary of placing too much faith in the evidence of such 'fragments'; far from offering an authentic glimpse at a lost text, the process of selection, re-wording, and abridgement may have done much to distort the original work (cf. Brunt 1980).

Alexander's career is well documented in later writers; Arrian and Q. Curtius Rufus both wrote histories of his reign, Diodoros of Sicily devoted book 17 of his world-history to the Macedonian king, and Plutarch included a life of Alexander among his *Parallel Lives*. The most authoritative treatment was written in the second century AD by Arrian, a distinguished Greek author from Nikomedia in Bithynia, whose friendship with the emperor Hadrian brought him a consulship. His self-consciously stylish history was based primarily on the writings of Ptolemy I, who served as an officer with Alexander before establishing himself as king of Egypt, and of Aristoboulos, who also accompanied Alexander on campaign. Arrian concluded with the death of Alexander, but he also wrote ten lost books entitled *The Affairs after Alexander*, which covered the four years after the king's death; in addition to a summary by Photios some quite lengthy fragments of this survive on papyrus and in medieval manuscripts (*FGrH* 156; Dreyer 1999b). Curtius' account in ten books, composed in the first or second century AD and extending as far as the immediate aftermath of Alexander's death, may be admirable as a moralizing work of rhetoric, but as history it is less satisfactory.

It is to the Augustan age that we owe the only extant narratives of the hundred years or so which followed Alexander's death, one in Greek by Diodoros, the other in Latin by Pompeius Trogus, although Trogus is known only through a later and not always reliable abridgement composed by a certain Justin. Both are universal histories, that is to say they take the history of the world as their subject, or rather the Greco-Roman world. Their composition at this time and the emphasis they place on the Hellenistic period may indicate a sense of closure, a realization that Rome now controlled the East and that the era of the great kingdoms was over. Diodoros' history, written in forty books between approximately 60 and 30 BC, began in the mythological past and extended until 60 BC. It thus included Pompey's victory over Mithradates and the subsequent reorganization of the East which resulted in the end of the Seleukid kingdom. The implications of this would not have escaped Diodoros who records Pompey's verdict on his own achievement: he 'brought the limits of Roman rule to the limits of the earth' (Diod. 40.4). Pompeius Trogus, a Gaul who wrote a history in 44 books some years after Diodoros, showed a similar awareness, but for him it is with Augustus that the whole world becomes Roman (Just. 44.8). At this point universal history turns into Roman history.

In books 18–20 Diodoros provides a valuable narrative of the turbulent years after the death of Alexander, years during which the king's successors (known as the Diadochoi) battled with each other for power and territory. For his material Diodoros is usually believed to have drawn heavily on Hieronymos of Kardia, a belief which has helped to give his account greater authority. Book 20, which ends in 302 with the prelude to the battle of Ipsos, is, however, the last book to survive complete, the remaining twenty known mainly through Photios and Byzantine excerpts. It is left, therefore, to Pompeius Trogus, as processed by Justin, to tell the narrative of the third century. Whether Justin was selecting the parts he liked, abridging Trogus, or doing both, is not clear; it is possible that Justin's text is as little as one tenth the length of Trogus' original text. Nevertheless, whatever Justin was doing, he has bequeathed a very unsatisfactory and often sketchy narrative to generations of frustrated historians, yet one that offers tantalizing sights of otherwise unknown events.

Once the Romans become involved in the East, our knowledge of the narrative becomes better, but its Romano-centric character means that the record can be silent when Rome has no one to fight there. In addition to Polybios and Livy, there is Appian, an Alexandrian Greek who in the second century AD wrote a history of Rome's conquest of the world. Rather than organizing his history on strictly chronological principles, he structured it around the peoples conquered by the Romans, an approach which served to emphasize the geographic and ethnographic extent of the Roman empire. Valuable where more reliable sources are lost, Appian is especially useful for events in the first century BC, in particular for Rome's wars with Mithradates.

The narrative and nature of the Hellenistic world can be further illuminated by others whose writings are not directly historical. Three stand out: Plutarch, Pausanias and Strabo. Plutarch, an extraordinarily prolific and wide-ranging writer from

Chaironeia in Boiotia, was active in the late first and early second century AD. In addition to numerous essays collected together now under the title, the *Moralia*, his output included a series of biographies, the *Parallel Lives*, in which illustrious Greeks are paired with Roman counterparts; his prime concern here is with the moral character of his subjects. He treats a number of leading Hellenistic figures, though significantly none of the major monarchs; there are no lives of such as Seleukos I, Ptolemy I, or Antiochos III. Instead we read of those who evince the spirit of Classical Greece, men who try to stand up for the *polis* against the great powers, the Athenian Phokion, the Achaians Aratos and Philopoimen, the revolutionary kings of Sparta, Agis and Kleomenes. Several *Lives* do feature those who operate outside the *polis* but they tend to be the unorthodox and atypical: Eumenes of Kardia, Greek secretary of Alexander turned warlord, Demetrios Poliorketes, the womanizing, heavy-drinking son of Antigonos the One-eyed, Pyrrhos, king of Epeiros and Alexander *manqué*. His Roman *Lives* include some who were commanders in wars in the East, notably, T. Quinctius Flamininus, L. Aemilius Paullus, Sulla and Pompey. Together all these lives with their characterization and anecdote add personality to our image of the Hellenistic age.

A very different type of text is the *Geography* of Strabo of Amaseia, a native of Pontos writing during the reign of Augustus. This seventeen-book opus takes as its subject not people or events but places, and thus encapsulates the known world at the conclusion of the Hellenistic period. It is as if Augustus has brought history to an end and all that is left is to describe the world Rome rules. As Strabo moves around the Mediterranean, he tells of the cities that populate it, their present and their past; Korakesion prompts a digression on Cilician piracy, Pergamon comes with a history of the Attalids, his own residence in Alexandria allows him to offer an eye-witness portrait of the late Hellenistic city, and everywhere local traditions are evoked, whether through stories or monuments. Local traditions feature prominently too in Pausanias' *Description of Greece*, a guidebook to ancient Greece written in the second century AD. Detailed descriptions of sites and monuments are supplemented by stories, historical and mythological, some widely-known, others local. Both Strabo and Pausanias are valuable for giving a sense of the variety and complexity of the Greek world; these are places inhabited and distinct rather than absorbed into a streamlined narrative.

It is not only historical texts that will be discussed and cited in the chapters that follow. Poetry, scientific writings and philosophy can reveal much about Hellenistic society, its ways of thinking, its values and its ideology. Poetry has survived rather better than history. There are the *Idylls* of Theocritus, the *Argonautica* of Apollonios of Rhodes, the hymns of Callimachus, the mimes of Herodas, the enigmatic *Alexandra* of Lykophron, and the *Phaenomena* of Aratos of Soloi. Some scientific writing survives, perhaps as it was less vulnerable to the vagaries of style: the astronomical works of Aristarchos and Hipparchos, and the mathematical writings of Euclid, Archimedes, and Apollonios of Perge. Philosophical texts fare much worse. Apart from Theophrastos' *Characters* and some philosophical letters and maxims of Epicurus little now remains of the voluminous output of the Hellenistic schools.

4 Inscriptions

In many cultures texts are written for public display; they may be epitaphs, dedications, or advertisements; they may be inscribed on stone or bronze, pasted on hoardings, or lit up in neon. Greek fondness for inscription is evident in the tens of thousands of inscribed texts that survive from the cities of the Hellenistic East, especially the cities of Asia Minor, but it is not the quantity that is distinctive so much as the character of the texts themselves. Many of these are civic decrees, treaties and letters from kings, in other words documents that were not primarily intended for public display. The original text, written on a more manageable material such as papyrus, would most likely have been kept in a city archive. Far from being short and simple, these texts were frequently detailed and dense; for instance, a treaty between Rhodes and the Cretan city of Hierapytna runs to over a hundred lines (*SIG*³ 581; Austin 95), while almost two hundred lines remain of the incomplete decree honouring Protogenes of Olbia on the Black Sea for services to his native city (*SIG*³ 495; Austin 97). Accumulatively documents such as these, edited and published by specialist scholars known as epigraphists, provide an invaluable resource for the study of the Hellenistic world (for an example, Figure 19.1).

Such texts have an immediacy that a historical narrative, often composed much later, does not have. It is not merely that they are contemporary but that in reading the text of an inscription we are faced with the participants and their concerns in a very direct way. Obscure cities come to life, both in their local preoccupations and occasionally, more alarmingly, as they are drawn into the conflicts of the powerful. The city of Teos on the coast of Asia Minor furnishes us with a good number of such documents. Here we find inscribed the regulations for a school which has been established with money donated by Polythros, a prominent local citizen; the teachers will include a kithara-player to teach the children music and the school interestingly provides for the education of both boys and girls (*SIG*³ 578; Austin 120). When pirates occupy the harbour, the wealthy of Teos whose names are all inscribed contribute to a fund to rid the city of the intruders and reclaim their captured fellow-citizens (*SEG* 44.949). Antiochos III's take-over of the city prompts extensive cult honours as it adjusts to the disappearance of Attalid power in the region (Herrmann 1965a: 33–40; Ma 1999: nos. 17–18).

Only a selection of a city's public documents will ever have been inscribed and it is worth considering why some become civic monuments. If we look at the Teian texts discussed above, it is evident that their content is varied – education, piracy and royal cult – but in each case, directly or indirectly, someone is remembered and honoured by the act of inscription, Polythros, the contributors, the king. This is not to suggest that all inscription is honorific but in a culture in which the rich are expected to perform services for their city honour is highly prized and may consequently help to shape our image of a city. It may even be the city itself which is honoured. An important verse inscription, recently discovered in Halikarnassos, begins by asking 'What is it that brings honour to Halikarnassos?'; the response, a fascinating insight into civic pride and local tradition, outlines the city's mythical past before turning to celebrate its poets and historians (Isager 1998; Lloyd-Jones 1999).

The decision to inscribe is often contained within the document itself and may be justified by reference to future observers; the permanence of a treaty can be represented by engraving it on stone, thus the following clause negotiated between Rhodes and Hierapytna:

> And so that what was resolved about the alliance and the treaty might be engraved on stone stelai and visible for all time, let the people (of Rhodes) set up a stele at Rhodes in the sanctuary of Athena, and let the *poletai* (officials responsible for letting state contracts) put out to tender a contract for making the stele out of Lartian stone and for engraving and erecting in the sanctuary what was decided by the cities about the alliance, as directed by the commissioner for works, at a cost of not more than 100 drachmas. Let the treasurers pay for this expense out of the fund for matters to do with decrees. Let the Hierapytnians also engrave the alliance and erect it among themselves in whatever sanctuary they think fit. (*SIG*³ 581.95–101; Austin 95)

Inscribed stones were both symbols of civic life and part of the physical make-up of the city. This is vividly demonstrated by the agora of Magnesia-on-the-Maeander. Inscribed on the south and west walls of the city's central public space was an impressive collection of over sixty decrees and royal letters from around the Greek world. Magnesia had launched a major diplomatic campaign to ensure recognition of its newly-established panhellenic festival of Artemis Leukophryene and these documents, collected from the cities and kings visited by their ambassadors, were the outcome. Here the aspirations of the city have become a physical presence within the city (*I.Magn.* 16–87; Rigsby 1996: 179–279). The bulk of Hellenistic inscriptions come from Greek cities and their sanctuaries, a striking testament to the vitality of civic life in this period and a useful rejoinder to those who see Alexander as marking the end of the *polis*.

5 Papyri

In 1900 the excavation of a cemetery at Tebtynis in the Fayum area of Egypt produced somewhat unexpected results. Workmen, hoping to find humans buried with their most valued possessions, found instead dozens of mummified crocodiles, carefully preserved and interred by pious Egyptians. One of the men, uninhibited by a sense of religious awe in the face of these sacred animals, gave vent to his frustration by smashing up a crocodile with his spade. The rips in the mummy casing exposed handwriting; waste papyri, in a form of papier mâché known as cartonnage, had been moulded round the body of the animal (Bowman 1986: 173). This ancient practice, developed for the mummification of both humans and sacred animals, has been a vital source of papyrus texts for the Ptolemaic and the Augustan periods.

Papyrus was a writing material made from the *Cyperus papyrus*, a plant that grew in the marshes and lakes of Egypt and especially in the Nile Delta. Outside Egypt it was rare, giving the region a virtual monopoly over papyrus production. Although used for writing throughout the ancient world, it has survived best in Egypt, where it has been found as cartonnage, in rubbish dumps, and in the ruins of buildings. An important reason for its survival in Egypt is the climate; the dry ground of the desert is ideal for its preservation. There may, however, be other factors at work; although papyri have been found elsewhere, for example at Qumran near the Dead Sea, at Dura-Europos on the Euphrates, and carbonized at Herculaneum in Italy, its availability in Egypt may have meant that it was more readily used there than elsewhere (Bagnall 1995: 26–9). Expense and distance from Egypt may have encouraged the use of alternative materials, for instance the fragments of pottery known as ostraka or wooden writing tablets such as those found at a rather later period at the Vindolanda fort on Hadrian's Wall (Bowman 1994).

Like inscriptions papyri have a sense of immediacy, but whereas inscriptions offer the public, monolithic face of the city, monumentalized in stone, papyri take us closer to the individual. The subject matter of the Egyptian papyri is varied: petitions, private letters, deeds of sale, wills, marriage contracts, tax records, assorted documents from the state administration. Such documents will often survive without context, but sometimes whole collections, linked together by an individual or a place, have been discovered. Here it is possible to study the inter-relationships between the documents as names, families, problems and themes recur, allowing the creation of a context and a fuller picture of the world that produced the documents. Two of the more important collections, or archives as they tend to be known, are the mid-third-century Zenon archive and the second-century texts from the sanctuary of Sarapis in Memphis. Zenon was the manager of a large estate at Philadelphia in the Fayum, a property of Apollonios, chief minister of Ptolemy II. This collection of some two thousand documents gives a remarkable insight into the running of an estate, ranging from agricultural matters (where Zenon's approach is fairly experimental), problems with tenants, both Greek and Egyptian, to dealings with Apollonios and the state administration (Pestman 1981; Clarysse and Vandorpe 1995). The much smaller archive of Ptolemaios, a man who spent about twenty years of his life in seclusion in the Sarapeion at Memphis, has provided the focus for an important study of the interaction between Greek and Egyptian culture at the city which had for centuries been considered its capital and which remained its religious centre even after the court had moved to Alexandria (D. J. Thompson 1988: 212–65). Other archives allow similar studies (Lewis 1986).

Papyri offer a valuable point of access to the world of native Egyptians. Not only are Egyptians a common presence in the Greek papyri that survive but there are also a substantial number of documents written in a script of Egyptian known as demotic. Especially in the early years of Ptolemaic rule Egyptians would often use demotic as the appropriate language for contracts and other transactions among themselves, though that gradually gave way to the language of the Greek rulers (D. J. Thompson 1994b). Papyri thus can make a significant contribution to modern debates about culture and ethnicity in Egypt, revealing a complex society in which the ethnic character of the individual, as expressed for instance in name and language, may change according to context (Bagnall 1995: 20; D. J. Thompson 2001; Rowlandson, this volume).

Abundant as the papyrological evidence is, there is also a need for the historian to exercise a certain degree of caution. Alexandria and the Nile Delta were the most populated regions of Egypt but the dampness of the soil has not favoured the survival of papyri. Papyri tend to come from marginal areas where dry conditions and lack of later settlement have aided preservation – or from areas such as the Fayum where the desert has reclaimed the land. Nor is this material evenly spread out over time. This presents a problem for the historian: how safe is it to generalize from such evidence? Can one extrapolate from one well-documented village to others? Can such local Egyptian evidence illuminate the Hellenistic world beyond Egypt? It is important to be aware of such methodological problems but not to be paralyzed by them. The careful and sensitive use of comparative material can do much to illuminate beyond the immediate context (Bagnall 1995).

6 Other Voices

Alexander's conquest of the Persian empire brought a large number of different cultures and peoples under Greco-Macedonian rule. The native voice, however, is not so readily heard as its Greek counterpart. This is partly a problem of evidence; there is less of it and, being in less well-known languages, it is not as accessible as writings in the more familiar Greek and Latin. It may also, however, be a problem of perspective; the ancient historian frequently comes to the Hellenistic world with a classical training and sees Greek rule as the unifying factor. This can lead to an over-emphasis on Greekness and Greek culture. While much of the non-Greek population may remain silent, some still speak to us, notably the Babylonians, the Egyptians and the Jews.

Texts in Aramaic, a semitic language written in alphabetic script, are quite widely dispersed, largely because of its role as one of the main languages of the now-defunct Persian administration. For instance, when the Mauryan king Asoka sought to spread the word of Buddha to the inhabitants of his Indian kingdom, the languages he chose for his north-western territories were Aramaic and Greek, as is attested in a bilingual inscription on a pillar from Kandahar in modern Afghanistan. This is not the only bilingual text of Asoka in the region; Aramaic was also used in combination with Prakrit, a language of India (Thapar 1997; MacDowell and Taddei 1978: 192–8). At the other end of the former Persian empire Aramaic is to be found among the languages used in Jewish writings, and features in the Dead Sea Scrolls of the Qumran community, discovered in caves there in the 1940s and 1950s (Beyer 1984). Its continuing importance in administration is demonstrated by its use in various bilingual Greek/Aramaic documents from Seleukid Babylonia (S. Sherwin-White 1987: 23–5).

Jewish religion placed considerable emphasis on the written word; hence a large amount of Jewish religious writing survives, notably the scriptures that go to make up the Old Testament, mostly in Hebrew but with a little Aramaic. The demands of the large Greek-speaking Jewish diaspora generated Greek translations of these scriptures that together came to be known as the Septuagint, reputed to have been begun by a team of seventy-two scholars working in Alexandria at the request of Ptolemy II. This pressure for Greek texts is evident also in the first two books of Maccabees, both important sources for the history of the Jewish people in the second century. They give two separate and varying accounts of the circumstances and consequences of the revolt of Judas Maccabaeus, the first written in Hebrew but translated into Greek, the second composed in Greek, probably abridged from a more substantial work by a certain Jason of Cyrene. Many of these Greek-speaking Jews would have lived in Egypt, primarily but not only in Alexandria. The city of Herakleopolis along the Nile valley, for example, has recently turned up an important collection of Jewish papyri in

Greek; the texts include petitions to the archon of the *politeuma* of the Jews, valuable evidence for Jewish social organization in Egypt (Cowey and Maresch 2001).

In Egypt there was a large, native population, some of whose concerns, as was noted in the previous section, have been unearthed on papyri in both demotic Egyptian and in Greek. Papyrus preserves not only the more everyday aspects of their life but also literature written in demotic. Narrative fiction, such as the adventures of Setna Khaemwase, or moral guidance, as in the *Instructions of Ankhsheshonqy*, stand in a long Egyptian literary tradition that goes back well before the Ptolemies (Tait 1994; texts in Lichtheim 1980). But it was the priests and temples that were the chief medium for the transmission of Egyptian tradition; here that tradition was articulated through the archaizing scripts of hieratic and hieroglyphic, scripts that emphasized the priests' role as the keepers of arcane knowledge. Nonetheless, the priests had a dual role; they connected the Egyptian people with their past but at the same time they were at the interface between the people and their Greek rulers. Their decrees honouring the Ptolemaic kings would be inscribed in hieroglyph, demotic and Greek, as for example the Kanopos decree and the famous Rosetta stone that played such a crucial role in the modern decipherment of hieroglyphic script (*OGIS* 56, 90; trans. Austin 222, 227). One priest, Manetho, even wrote a history of the Pharaohs in Greek, thus presenting the Egyptian past to the Greek present. This, unfortunately, survives only through later writers.

Babylonia, too, had long, literate cultural traditions which continued through Persian and into Seleukid rule. Again there is archaizing, evident in the use of Akkadian, a language no longer spoken; it was written in cuneiform script, usually formed by impressing the end of a reed into clay tablets. This language was the preserve of scholars, centred on temples, and finding expression in documents such as chronicles, astronomical diaries, legal texts, administrative documents and horoscopes. Such archaizing, far from being a sign of a moribund culture, is a sign of the strength and resilience of Babylonian tradition under a series of foreign rulers. The chronicles on the wars of the successors and on the early Seleukids, incomplete though they are, give a valuable Babylonian perspective on the events of the time (Grayson 1975a: nos. 10–13). As in Egypt, the temples may act as the custodians of indigenous tradition but their officials can also address a Greek-speaking audience, although by virtue of using Greek they are altering their voice. Thus Berossos, a Babylonian priest, produced the *Babyloniaka*, a history of Babylon in three books, which now exists only in fragments; it is evident, even so, that it is shaped by the principles of Greek historiography (*FGrH* 680; Burstein 1978; Kuhrt 1987).

However much our evidence may show an accommodation between the native population and Greco-Macedonian intruders, there is one form of literature that suggests an underlying resentment. From a number of parts of this Hellenistic world there were prophetic writings, exercises in wishful thinking, that often foretold the overthrow and expulsion of foreign rulers, whether individuals or peoples. From Babylon there is the Dynastic prophecy written in Akkadian; it is critical of Alexander and seems to date from the period of the successors (S. Sherwin-White 1987: 10–14). The apocalyptic *Book of Daniel*, written in Hebrew and Aramaic around the time of the Maccabaean revolt, culminates by dramatically prophesying the end of contemporary empires and the emergence of the kingdom of God. Out of Egypt come the *Demotic Chronicle* and the *Oracle of the Potter*, the latter, a Greek translation from the Egyptian, foretells the abandonment of Greek Alexandria and revival of the traditional capital of Memphis (A. B. Lloyd 1982; Koenen 1968; Burstein 106).

Just as the non-Greek population and their priests could express themselves in the language of the rulers, so the Greek kings could adopt a native voice. An inscribed foundation cylinder from a temple in Babylonian Borsippa allows Antiochos I to speak in Akkadian and importantly in the manner of a native king (Kuhrt and Sherwin-White 1991). In Egypt royal decrees were sometimes translated into demotic and may today survive only in demotic (cf. Burstein 97). The visual equivalent of this is the way in which portraits of Ptolemy I and his successors show these kings as Pharaohs (figure 7.2), a striking expression of the complex and multifaceted character of Alexander's legacy.

FURTHER READING

There are a number of surveys of the Hellenistic World, each with its own approach, notably Préaux 1978 (in French), Green 1990, Walbank 1992, Shipley 2000; Will 1979–82 offers a thorough political history; Rostovtzeff's *The Social and Economic History of the Hellenistic World* (1941) is a classic. For an overview of recent scholarship, see Cartledge 1997. Translations of source material, in particular inscriptions and papyri, are usefully collected in Austin 1981, Bagnall and Derow 2004, Sherk 1984, and Burstein 1985. *OCD*[3] is an invaluable reference work for anyone interested in the ancient world.

Translations of the writers discussed in this chapter can usually be found in the Loeb Classical Library (Harvard UP) or Penguin Classics. The importance of Polybios is matched by Walbank's monumental commentary (1957–79); for a more concise assessment, see Walbank 1972; see also Derow 1979, Eckstein 1995 and Erskine 2000. For other authors note: Appian (Brodersen 1989), Arrian (Bosworth 1988), Curtius (Baynham 1998), Diodoros (Sacks 1990), Justin (Yardley and Develin 1994, which provides translation), Livy (Luce 1977), Pausanias (Habicht 1985, Arafat 1996, Alcock et al. 2001), Plutarch (C. Jones 1971, Russell 1972), Strabo (K. Clarke 1999, J. Engels 1999, Dueck 2000). S. Swain 1996 offers a valuable survey of Greek writers of the early centuries AD with particular emphasis on their attitude to Rome. More literary texts are discussed in Hunter, this volume. Alexandrian science, literature and scholarship are treated exhaustively in Fraser 1972.

The 'fragments' of lost writers are collected (without translation) and discussed in F. Jacoby, *Die Fragmente der griechischen Historiker* (*FGrH*; relevant Jacoby references are given in the text above). For fragments of Poseidonios, see Edelstein and Kidd 1989 with Kidd 1988 (commentary) and 1999 (translation). What is left of lost Alexander historians is translated in Pearson 1960. Burstein 1989 translates and discusses Agatharchides. Important studies of individual writers include Hornblower 1981 on Hieronymos, Momigliano 1977: 37–66 on Timaios and Pédech 1989 on Douris and Phylarchos.

Millar 1983 and Pleket 1996 provide accessible introductions to the often confusing world of inscriptions; so too does the 1961 essay by Louis Robert, the French epigraphist who dominated the discipline for much of the twentieth century. Important collections include the *Inscriptiones Graecae* (*IG*), Dittenberger's *OGIS* and *SIG*[3], Moretti's *ISE* and Welles's study of royal letters (*RC*, with translations). New publications are reviewed annually in *SEG* and *Bulletin Épigraphique* (*BE*), the latter incorporated in *Revue des Études grecque* since 1888. For recent epigraphy of Asia Minor, see the invaluable account of Ma 2000a.

The best guides to papyrology are Turner 1980, with an emphasis on literary papyri, and Bagnall 1995, directed at the historian. The best representative sample of Greek papyri (arranged by type of document and date, including a translation but almost no editorial help) is still the Loeb *Select Papyri*, vols. I and II, eds A. S. Hunt and C. C. Edgar (Cambridge, Mass. 1932–34). Rowlandson 1998 is a model collection of papyri in translation with useful introduction. The bewildering array of papyrological abbreviations are decoded in the *Checklist* of Oates et al. 2001. Although the *Checklist* now includes Demotic papyri, for various reasons it has not been usual in Egyptology to cite texts in this way, but rather by inventory number with the full reference to their place of publication. Depauw 1997 is an important guide both to what is available in Demotic and where it has been published.[1]

Babylonia and its literature are discussed in Oelsner 1986 and Kuhrt and Sherwin-White 1987; some texts are available in translation: Grayson 1975a (chronicles), Grayson 1975b (prophecies, with S. Sherwin-White 1987) and Sachs and Hunger 1988, 1989 (astronomical diaries). Jewish literature is surveyed in Schürer 1979, and more recently in Alexander 2001, cf. also Gruen, this volume. For the Dead Sea Scrolls, see the encyclopedia of Schiffman and Vanderkam 2000. A basic reference work for the archaeology and culture of the Near East, including Babylonia, Palestine and Egypt, is Meyers 1997.

1   This paragraph written with Jane Rowlandson.

PART I

Narratives

CHAPTER TWO

After Alexander: the Emergence of the Hellenistic World, 323–281

David Braund

Alexander the Great has become such an enormous figure that he tends easily to overshadow everyone and everything around him. His coruscating campaign through Asia Minor and Iran to Afghanistan and the Indian sub-continent forcibly carried Hellenic culture beyond the wildest imaginings of earlier Greek imperialists. At the climax of his success, at Babylon in 323 BC, he died, romantically young, ensuring the power of his legend in centuries to come, tinged and enhanced with human frailties. However, just as Alexander's spectacular father, Philip II, suffers in his great shadow, so the aftermath of the imperialist adventure may seem at first sight to have been very much an anti-climax.

Alexander had left his world with no particular direction. Death had not been expected; in any case his supercharged romance had little time for responsibility. The world he left behind had been changed fundamentally, but what sort of 'new world order' was to follow? In 323 BC no-one knew, except, as legend had it, Alexander himself, who predicted war with his dying breath (Diod. 18.1.4; Arr. *Anab.* 7. 26.3; Curt. 10.5.5; Just. 12.15.6–8). There were relations of Alexander for whom claims to power might be made, but none was even nearly ready to fill his shoes: his only recognized son was still in Roxane's womb. There were also his generals, at various ages and stages in their careers and with large numbers of men under arms or available for war. Women too would play key roles: such is the habit of monarchies. What kind of succession could there be? The throne of Macedon itself had tended to change hands in bloody fashion, so that war and murder were to be expected. Now the prize was far more extensive and diverse. Alexander's campaign had cut so great a swathe through the empire of Achaimenid Persia that he had effectively replaced the Persian king while also remaining king of Macedon and master of Greece. And yet much of the Achaimenid Empire had not really been conquered at all: Cappadocia was held by an Ariarathes. Caucasia had been passed by, though part of the Achaimenid sphere (Braund 1994; Knauss 2001). Eastern limits were negotiable and to be disputed (Schober 1984; Bosworth 1996; Holt 1999). It was most unclear that a single man

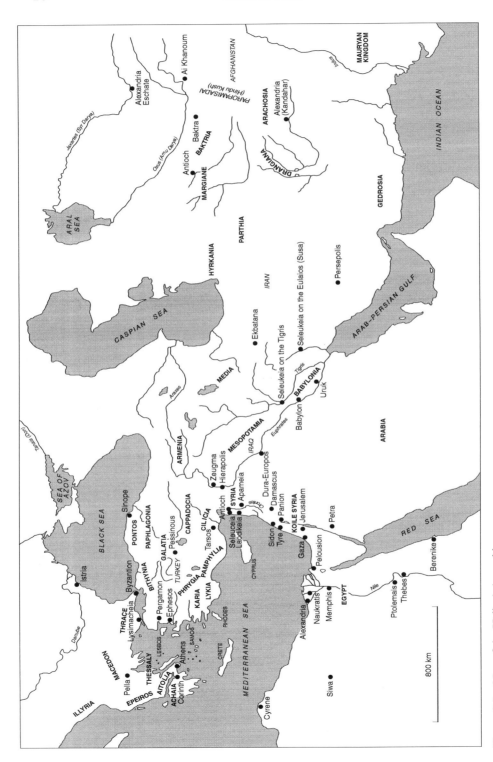

Figure 2.1 Map of the Hellenistic world

would be able to emerge from the flurry of competitors to seize for himself the whole prize in all its scale and diversity. It was still less clear that any such success could be stabilized in the longer term: Alexander himself had not managed that before his death.

For more than forty years, from 323 to 281, these issues were fought out across a huge expanse of territory, entailing Greece, Asia Minor, the Mediterranean Sea, Egypt, Central Asia, Iran and India. The extended conflict was marked by recurrent alliances and 'Peaces' between some or most of the leading players, reminding us that diplomacy was as important as actual fighting. These arrangements, however much couched in the language of established harmony, were made to be put to use or broken. Accordingly, for the modern student of the period the sense of anti-climax after 323 may be made to seem still more depressing by the fragmented complexities of numerous individuals, a dizzying scatter of places and a whirlwind of events which seem all too often to come to nothing. The absence of a single ancient narrative – a Thucydides, say – to select what matters, to give a dominant interpretation and to guide us through the tangle does nothing to raise faltering spirits. Instead our principal source is Diodoros, Books 18–20, much of which seems to come from Hieronymos of Kardia, who was a participant in some of the events described and who knew leading figures (Hornblower 1981).

However, while Alexander's long shadow is not to be denied (and is worth consideration in its own right: Stewart 1993a), the years 323–281 have a lot to offer even so, conveyed to us by a range of ancient voices and material evidence, neither simply Greek (Erskine, this volume). These years show first the consequences of the great imperialist adventure in a world which, from a Greek perspective at least, had now expanded massively, however much some Greeks had penetrated eastwards before Alexander's campaign. From the morass of competition, really major figures do emerge, most notably Antigonos Monophthalmos ('the One-Eyed') until his death in 301, Seleukos I until his death in 281 and the judicious Ptolemy, who died in 283. The expanded world was carved up between the more successful competitors again and again, leaving challenging political shapes on the map, together with the abiding notion of potential unification. Moreover, it is in these years that monarchy re-emerges as the dominant form in Greek history, after a marked hiatus, with its roots both in Macedonian and in local practices. The Hellenistic world which Alexander had instigated was to be a world with great cities – including his own foundations – but it was above all to be a world of kings. Perhaps most exciting and yet most elusive is the rich cultural mix that developed (and not without controversy) in the aftermath of Alexander. It is most visible, as ever, among the ruling elite. Meanwhile, as for the more humble, the overwhelming majority, we are nonplussed through the haziness and the diversity of local stories played out in the very many microcosms of this extensive world, just visible in the archaeological record (Alcock 1994; cf. Shipley 2000). In short, everything was possible in 323, except a peaceful succession.

1   Babylon and Triparadeisos: from Perdikkas to Antipater

Perdikkas was the first to achieve pre-eminence in the aftermath of Alexander's death. He had been the closest of his friends in 323, and he was on the spot, in Babylon, to manage matters (on the progress of events, Errington 1970). It was said that Alexander had given him his signet-ring, symbolic of his wishes, which Perdikkas claimed to champion. The Macedonian army, in assembly to consider the future, offered Perdikkas the kingship, but he demurred. Our key source here, Quintus Curtius Rufus of the first half of the first century AD, may well have inserted an echo of the posturings of early Roman emperors, especially Tiberius in AD 14 (Curt. 10.6; Badian 1962; Bosworth 1971: 128). His whole stance as the guardian of Alexander's interests required hesitation, for Alexander's widow was pregnant and might produce a son and heir. As Alexander's champion Perdikkas could hardly seize the throne from the king's son: much better to be regent, if there were to be a son. And so he waited. Meanwhile, the claims of Herakles, the son of Iranian Barsine and said to be Alexander's, were rejected fiercely: Alexander had not acknowledged his paternity. The importance of Alexander's blood, where it could be proved, is confirmed by the emergence of his half-brother Philip Arrhidaios, who was acclaimed by the army as Perdikkas hesitated. Philip Arrhidaios, we are told, was mentally disabled: some blamed Olympias, in the fog of propaganda surrounding the succession-crisis (on which Bosworth 1971). But, however much disabled, Philip Arrhidaios was Alexander's half-brother even so; and he was on the spot at Babylon, available for use by others (Diod. 18.2; Plut. *Alex.* 77; cf. Athen. 13.557d). However, kingship had not been the only option touted. Ptolemy had suggested that Alexander's friends might rule as a council; that would have undermined Perdikkas' predominance. A certain Meleagros, characterized as the worst of demagogues (a simplification at best: Heckel 1992: 165–70), had urged the army to seize a heritage that was really its own, causing a riot, until changing his position to support for Arrhidaios.

While the army had the strength, the friends of Alexander were well placed to manipulate and ultimately control it. Meleagros was a nuisance to them and was murdered; a solution could be achieved. Perdikkas avoided the kingship but took 'the care of the whole kingdom', on behalf of Alexander's new-born son and no doubt Arrhidaios too. The technicalities of his uncertain titulature need not detain us (Bosworth 1971: 131–2; Billows 1990: 54–7; Heckel 1992: 366–70). More important, two key figures were absent from these crucial events at Babylon: Antipater and Krateros. Antipater had been holding Macedon and thus Greece for Alexander ever since the latter had left for Asia in 334; he was still there, though Alexander had set about his removal (encouraging rumours that he had killed Alexander, no less: Bosworth 1971). For Krateros had been sent to replace him, though he was proceeding with no great urgency. While Perdikkas secured his pre-eminence in Babylon, Krateros was still in Cilicia, vaguely *en route* to Macedon, his awkward task now still more unattractive.

Neither Antipater nor Krateros could be forgotten even at Babylon. They were invited, in their absence, to share power in Macedon and Greece. Key satrapies of Alexander's empire were parcelled out to the others who mattered. Ptolemy got Egypt, Lysimachos Thrace, Leonnatos Hellespontine Phrygia, and Antigonos Monophthalmos Greater Phrygia. Cappadocia and Paphlagonia were to be conquered by Leonnatos and Antigonos and then handed to Eumenes of Kardia. Perdikkas himself was careful to have the army-assembly reject, on grounds of practicality, the grand schemes envisaged by Alexander, especially in the west. Roxane's baby son, however, was enthusiastically acclaimed; this was Alexander IV.

However, the settlement was illusory in large part. There were major loose ends. In Greece, Athens and the Aitolians in particular saw in Alexander's death the opportunity for revolt (Habicht 1997). This was the so-called Lamian War: Antipater was besieged in Lamia in Thessaly, until Leonnatos' intervention from Phrygia broke the opposition at the cost of his own life. Meanwhile Antipater, doubtless disgruntled through his absence from Babylon, had entered negotiations not only with Leonnatos but also with Ptolemy (who had tried to undermine Perdikkas at Babylon) and with Alexander's powerful mother, Olympias. Meanwhile, in summer 322 Krateros finally reached Macedon, but he accepted Antipater's seniority and command. Athens was seized, after losing the Battle of Krannon: a Macedonian garrison was installed at Munychia, dominating the port at Piraeus (Green 1990: 36–8, captures the mood). Antipater gave his daughter Phila in marriage to Krateros, cementing their relationship, while another daughter, Nikaia, was sent to Perdikkas, evidently in the hope of a rapprochement, though Perdikkas himself was apparently inciting Greek opposition to Antipater (Diod. 18.48.2). Indeed, Perdikkas declared his hand by rejecting Nikaia and instead marrying Kleopatra, who was no less than the sister of Alexander and had been sent to Asia by Olympias. Meanwhile, Antigonos Monophthalmos fled to Antipater and Krateros: he had left the task of conquering Cappadocia to Perdikkas and could expect retribution. It has been plausibly suggested that he was less than happy with the outcome at Babylon (Billows 1990: 56–7).

Ptolemy remained aligned with Antipater's coalition, at a careful distance. By his good fortune, Alexander had expressed the wish that his body be deposited at Siwa: its possession could only be talismanic. Accordingly, in 321 Ptolemy attacked the Perdikkan force escorting it in Syria and brought it forcibly to Egypt, where he deposited it at Memphis. Early in 320 Perdikkas invaded Egypt to recover the body, but fared badly until he was killed by his own officers, led by Peithon, satrap of Media, notably abetted by the young Seleukos (Erskine 2002a). Meanwhile, there had been fighting in the north, where Eumenes defended the Hellespont with mixed success against Antipater and Krateros. While Krateros was killed, Antipater branded Eumenes a Greek rebel who was to be executed (Errington 1970: 67).

Within a few years of Alexander's death, his forces had gone to war with each other and his two favoured friends – Perdikkas and Krateros – were dead. A new arrangement was needed, reached at Triparadeisos in northern Syria in 320. The key question was how to replace Perdikkas, within a broader new scheme. Antipater was the obvious choice, but preferred to avoid the role: Perdikkas' fate was doubtless a warning, while the army was restless for lack of pay and incited to action, we are told, by Eurydike, the wife of Philip Arrhidaios. Antipater may also have felt his age: he was already in his seventies. With Ptolemy ensconced in Egypt, Antigonos Monophthalmos, already satrap of Greater Phrygia, was given control of Asia and the task of dealing with Eumenes. Antipater's main ambition seems to have been to retain his dominance in Macedon, but he was careful to have his son Kassandros as Antigonos' second-in-command, while his daughter Phila, now a widow after the death of Krateros, married Antigonos' son, Demetrios. Triparadeisos doubtless left Antipater feeling in control: Kassandros could be expected to keep watch over the principal threat to his supremacy, Antigonos. Triparadeisos had also brought Seleukos, hitherto a cavalry-commander, to a new prominence: he was given Babylonia. Alexander's shaky empire had not quite fragmented, for Antipater could plausibly imagine himself at its head. But the process of fragmentation was very far advanced for all that and Antipater's death would soon be a further step. Throughout, Macedonians dominated the struggle; only the Greek Eumenes was a significant exception. By contrast, Iranians played no part in the forefront of these power-politics; even the Iranian wives assigned by Alexander had in part been set aside. However, that tendency can be exaggerated (S. Sherwin-White 1987: 6–7; certainly Seleukos kept his, Apame). We should not neglect the presence of non-Greeks in important administrative and military roles not far beneath the great Macedonians: occasional inscriptions in particular offer salutary examples of such figures in Asia and Egypt (Briant 1985; Billows 1990: 310–11; Sherwin-White and Kuhrt 1993: 121–5).

2   Antigonos the King

Antipater returned from Triparadeisos to Macedon with 'the kings', as they could be grandly termed, that is the disabled Philip Arrhidaios (alias Philip III) and Roxane's son, Alexander IV, scarcely more than a toddler. Their possession confirmed his pre-eminence, but his age was against him and the new arrangements: his death in 319 decapitated the structure agreed at Triparadeisos. To take his place he himself, on his death-bed, had appointed Polyperchon, who no doubt seemed a safe pair of hands, but who was to show himself unequal to the enormous task, whether or not the sources give an unfairly hostile picture of him, as seems likely (Hornblower 1981: 224–5). In a bid to bolster his new authority, presumably, Polyperchon took the dangerous step of recalling Olympias from exile in Epeiros: on an optimistic view, an association with Alexander's mother as well as 'the kings' gave Polyperchon all the cards (Billows 1990: 84). But Antipater had (curiously perhaps) passed over his own energetic son, Kassandros, who went in search of allies against Polyperchon. Kassandros had already figured in the arrangements around Triparadeisos in a way in which Polyperchon had not: Antigonos, Ptolemy and Lysimachos gave him their support. After all why should they accept Polyperchon in Antipater's position? He was no Antipater.

For his part, Polyperchon attracted Eumenes, whose condemnation to death was overlooked. Antigonos had not long ago reached his own agreement with Eumenes, which had allowed Eumenes to escape the fastness of Nora in the northern Tauros, where Antigonos had been besieging him in 319/18. Antigonos too had overlooked Eumenes' condemnation. Legalistic niceties were malleable, as the moment required, and in any case were open to dispute. Warfare was renewed: while Polyperchon fought in Greece, Eumenes resumed hostilities with Antigonos in Asia, claiming the support of the dead Alexander, who, he said, had appeared to him in a dream. Alexander's name was still a potent force (Diod. 18.60–2; Billows 1990: 85). In Macedon in 317 Eurydike, Philip Arrhidaios' wife, declared for Kassandros, fracturing the foundation of Polyperchon's position as guardian of 'the kings'. Olympias reacted violently: the two women met at the head of their respective armies on the borders of Epeiros and Macedonia. But Eurydike's forces would not fight: Olympias was Alexander's mother. In victory and with Polyperchon's support she swiftly executed Philip Arrhidaios and forced Eurydike to suicide, as Alexander himself might well have done (Athen. 13.560f from Douris of Samos; cf. Bosworth 1971).

She soon paid the price: Kassandros executed her in turn early in 315, having forced his way into Macedonia and starved her out of her retreat in Pydna. Polyperchon sought refuge in the Peloponnese, where he maintained hostilities. However, Kassandros enjoyed the greater popularity among the Greek cities: at Athens, in particular, Demetrios of Phaleron was presiding on his behalf from about 317 and over the next ten years would be honoured with no less than 300 statues, we are told, which at least indicates Athenians' desire to curry favour (Parker 1996: 258). Now, with Philip Arrhidaios, Eurydike and Olympias all done to death, the child-'king' Alexander IV gained a singular importance. Kassandros now had him. He kept the boy under guard with Roxane at Amphipolis, while in 315 he married a sister of Alexander the Great, Thessalonike. The direction of his ambitions was clear enough.

In Asia, meanwhile, Eumenes had also died, executed by Antigonos at the very beginning of 315. Having appropriated the royal treasury at Susa, Eumenes had inflicted significant losses upon Antigonos' forces at the Battle of Paraitakene in 316 and all but won the Battle of Gabiene at the turn of the same year, save that Antigonos had gained the crucial prize of Eumenes' baggage-train, women and all. That was enough for the elite Macedonian infantry, who exchanged Eumenes for their baggage: by that means Antigonos emerged victorious, as his ally Kassandros had prospered also in Europe.

However, Antigonos seems to have been too eager to enforce his authority. Seleukos in particular refused to accept it: we are told that he insisted that he owed his satrapy not to Antigonos but to the services he had performed for Alexander, having been awarded it at Triparadeisos. Wisely, he then fled to Ptolemy in Egypt, who received him with generosity and enthusiasm: Seleukos is said to have told Ptolemy that Antigonos wanted 'the whole kingdom of the Macedonians'; that is, to take the place vacated by Alexander (Diod. 19.55–6). Ptolemy and Seleukos therefore recruited Kassandros and Lysimachos to test Antigonos' ambitions by claiming some of his territories and shares of the booty he had taken from Eumenes. In response, Antigonos prepared for war, sending help to his erstwhile enemy Polyperchon in the Peloponnese to prosecute his rumbling war against Kassandros. However, the ensuing conflict is most notable for its high-energy diplomacy: past friends had become enemies, but might hope to become friends again in pursuit of their own interests. The search for support also entailed the many cities. It is in this context that we find the glimmer of an ideal amongst the power-hungry machinations of ambitious individualists: the so-called 'proclamation of Tyre'. For in 314, besieging Ptolemy's forces in Tyre, Antigonos called a military assembly at which he denounced Kassandros for killing Olympias, holding Alexander IV and Roxane, forcing (allegedly) Thessalonike to marry him and, by these acts, showing his ambitions to rule the Macedonians. Further he added that Kassandros had acted against Macedonian interests by restoring the hated Olynthians to their city, re-established in his own name (Kassandreia), and by re-building Thebes, which Alexander had razed. Antigonos decreed that Kassandros must either undo these wrongs and acknowledge him as his superior and the guardian of Alexander IV, or become an enemy. And finally, he decreed that all the Greeks (that is, the Greek cities) should be free, ungarrisoned and live under their own laws. All this was a bid for support: Antigonos hoped that the Greek cities would embrace the prospect of freedom and resist Kassandros in particular. However, the discourse of freedom for Greeks had been heard often enough since the fifth century to warn all but the most gullible. In 386 the King's Peace had used such talk of freedom to make Greece subject to Persia and its Spartan allies. And the invocation of freedom for Greeks remained a commonplace of public posturing well after Antigonos too, used even by the Romans. The very notion tends to tautology: he who gives such freedom thereby suggests his power to take it away at will and thereby underlines his implied mastery. Yet, hollow or not, Ptolemy thought it as well to counter Antigonos' self-presentation as champion of Greek freedom: he too promised freedom to the Greeks.

Throughout, our predominantly Greek sources lay particular emphasis on Greek perspectives, including such appeals for Greek backing. The fact that all the major players in these power-politics were Macedonian (or at least Greek) strengthens that tendency still further. Reasonably so, perhaps. But we should not lose sight of the fact that these would-be rulers needed to maximize their support in a shifting and dangerous world: that meant serious attention to the aspirations of non-Greek elites and non-Greek troops. Eumenes had worked to build support among the Cappadocians (Plut. *Eum.* 4; S. Sherwin-White 1987: 15); better attested, thanks to Babylonian evidence, are Seleukos' constructive dealings with the non-Greeks of Babylon. Seleukos had taken care to build strong personal relationships with the elite of Babylon and had earned their favour by so doing. In sharp contrast, Antigonos was to prefer extreme violence against them and their property, making his own position there harder to maintain (Diod. 19.91; Sherwin-White and Kuhrt 1993: 8–10). Non-Greeks too had parts to play, which no Macedonian could afford to ignore.

In winter 312/11 the Battle of Gaza brought Antigonos down to earth (on the date, Billows 1990: 134 n. 67): Ptolemy and Seleukos inflicted a defeat upon his son, Demetrios. Diplomacy now suited most: in summer 311 a peace was concluded once more. Kassandros was declared general of Europe until Alexander IV reached maturity. Lysimachos was to retain Thrace; Ptolemy would keep Egypt, as well as the cities he had brought under his sway in Cyrenaica to the west and Arabia to the east. Antigonos himself would have the whole of Asia, while the Greeks should be autonomous. There is a notable absence from these arrangements: no mention is made of Seleukos. Perhaps Ptolemy had thought it best to abandon him, or at least to agree to his omission; conceivably, Seleukos had already directed his energies to Central Asia and made it easier for others to overlook him (Diod. 19.105 with Simpson 1954; Austin 1981: 57; Will 1984: 50; Billows 1990: 134).

We are fortunate in having Antigonos' gloss on the agreement in the form in which he presented it in a letter to the city of Skepsis in the Troad and doubtless to other cities besides. Skepsis inscribed his letter and, to show its joy, developed its festival in his honour into a cult, with precinct, altar and cult-statue. In his letter Antigonos lays emphasis on the freedom of the Greeks, as might be expected, but even in so doing his injunction upon them to swear support for the agreement, evidently in conjunction with other cities, immediately indicates the severe limitations upon that freedom (*OGIS* 5, trans. Austin 31). It is easy enough to see why the people of Skepsis thought it best to flaunt their joy and their gratitude (*OGIS* 6, trans. Austin 32). It is easy also to see why Antigonos persisted in his noisy support for Greek freedom: that sounded much better than any reference to defeat at Gaza or to the substantial compromise that the peace of 311 meant for him by contrast with his bullish proclamation at Tyre (Will 1984: 51–2, splendidly cynical).

At the same time, the peace of 311 indicates the growing problem of Alexander IV for Kassandros, and by extension also for Antigonos and the others. Alexander IV was entering his teenage years; already we are told there were murmurings that he should be given power. In theory at least the realm of Alexander the Great might even now be passed *en bloc* to a son and heir. Kassandros took the obvious and brutal step: he had him murdered, together with Roxane. Now there were only Alexander's sisters, Kleopatra and Thessalonike (Kassandros' wife), and (arguably) the young Herakles, Barsine's son, whose claim had been rejected at Babylon but who had lived on at Pergamon, evidently nurtured by Antigonos, just in case.

Kassandros' rivals were tellingly silent about the murder of 'the king', Alexander the Great's son. Roxane mattered much less in that, although Alexander's widow, she was an outsider, an Iranian, and a woman to boot. Kassandros will have blamed others for the killings, but implausibly, for Roxane and her boy were in his custody. However, while we may assume disquiet elsewhere (Billows 1990: 141 on the army; cf. Austin 1986), Kassandros' rivals seem to have made nothing of it (Diod. 19.105 with Gruen 1985: 253–4). Even Antigonos, who had made so much of Kassandros' mistreatment of Alexander IV and Roxane outside Tyre, seems not to have levelled the obvious criticism at him now. All had reason to be pleased that the inconvenience of Alexander the Great's son and heir had been removed. But that did not preclude them, had they wished, from now stressing their loyalty to 'the king' and denouncing Kassandros even so: hypocrisy was not a problem and protestations of loyalty were easier with 'the king' safely dead. Perhaps there was criticism, not preserved in our fractured sources; perhaps the killings had been agreed in advance and the agreement kept for once.

Indeed, one wonders how far the news was bruited abroad; there is a sense of secrecy and even denial surrounding the death of Alexander the Great's heir. It is startling to find that the regnal year of Alexander IV continues to be used for dating purposes well after his death: in Egypt we find two demotic documents dated in that way as late as 305/4 BC (*P. Dem. Louvre* 2427, 2440, with Gruen 1985: 258, esp. n. 30). His death raised an enormous question for which there was not yet an answer. All the events and posturings of the previous decade and more had taken place in the context of the notional rule of 'the king', or while Philip Arrhidaios was alive 'the kings'. This was not an issue of legal nicety or any kind of constitutional rule-book, but a whole world-view, which gave meaning to the claims and actions of the leading players. The proclamation at Tyre and the agreement of 311 are enough to show that all pre-eminence was still imagined as deriving from Alexander the Great's son. Accordingly, the murder of Alexander IV set a large question mark beside the positions of the leading men: for whom were they acting? Of course at the level of power-politics the answer was the same as it had been since the tumultuous debates at Babylon in 323: those in power were acting for themselves. However, it was not immediately clear that such an answer, though realistic, was entirely sufficient. There was something to be gained by not making much of the death of Alexander IV: the status quo could hold while new stances were worked out and adopted.

It was only after four years, in 306, that Antigonos Monophthalmos finally took the step of calling himself 'king', and also bestowing the title on his own son and heir, Demetrios. The intervening years after 310 were spent in tension and low-level conflicts. In 309 the hopeful Herakles had finally been done away with. Polyperchon had tried to use him against Kassandros: they came to terms, which brought Polyperchon the return of his property in Macedonia and a place in Kassandros' hierarchy as general of the Peloponnese at the price of Herakles' murder. Henceforth Polyperchon lived on in this relative obscurity, outliving both Kassandros and Antigonos, from whom he had received Herakles and no doubt encouragement to use him (Billows 1990: 140–3).

In these years also Ptolemy had gone on the offensive, pursuing ambitions not only in the Eastern Mediterranean but into the Aegean too. He promoted himself, once again, as the champion of Greek freedom, especially (as before) against Antigonos, whom he held to have broken the conditions of the peace of 311 in that regard. Moreover, he sought to marry Kleopatra, sister of Alexander the Great and almost the last living link to his legend: Antigonos had held her at Sardis since 321. Meanwhile, he was making overtures to Polemaios, Antigonos' disaffected nephew who had carved out a strong position for himself in central Greece: initial co-operation on Kos was soon ended by Ptolemy's decision to kill this awkward new ally, who seemed not to know his place. To exploit his death Ptolemy set about establishing himself in Corinth and Sikyon, with much talk of Greek freedom: a lukewarm Peloponnesian response caused him to limit his schemes, place garrisons in his two cities, and return to Egypt after coming to an arrangement with Kassandros (cf. Billows 1990: 145 n. 18 envisaging a restored League of Corinth). Meanwhile, dealings with Kleopatra had also begun well and finished badly for Ptolemy. Wooed by all the leading players on account of her lineage, Kleopatra plumped for Ptolemy in 309/8 but was caught on her way to him and murdered by some of her women, evidently at Antigonos' surreptitious behest (Diod. 20.37; on her grand marital history, Billows 1990: 143 n. 15). Ptolemy returned alone, but he had shown the scope of his ambitions, which encompassed far more than Egypt and its environs.

In Asia proper, Seleukos had been engrossed well to the east of Babylonia, in the so-called Upper Satrapies of Central Asia, while Antigonos' son Demetrios seized and ravaged Babylonia in his absence. After returning to defeat Antigonos, as it seems (we rely on Polyaen. 4.9), Seleukos made a pact with him in 308, which allowed him to spend the next five years building his realms in the east, especially against the Indian ruler Chandragupta (alias Sandrokottos: see Holt 1999, esp. 28). That allowed Antigonos to turn his full attention on the west: he sent his favourite son, the energetic Demetrios, to take Athens away from his namesake, Demetrios of Phaleron, the philosopher and friend of Kassandros.

With a mixture of military acuity and adroit proclamation of the liberation of Athens and restoration of the ancestral constitution, Antigonos' son swiftly took the city, while Demetrios of Phaleron retired to Thebes. Kassandros had been occupied in a fruitless campaign in Epeiros. The Athenians responded to the Antigonid regime with a string of extravagant honours, associating Antigonos and his son with the gods: for what it is worth, the biographer Plutarch considered this to be the cause of Demetrios' later obnoxious behaviour (*Demetr.* 8–10; Austin 34; Parker 1996: 258–9, adducing *SEG* 30.69). Athens was now a democracy once more, but very much under Antigonid control. Demetrios next took Megara and in winter 307/6 set about organizing Greek cities against Kassandros, before setting off to engage Ptolemy in Cyprus; its position had already made it a major bone of contention. In 306, with bravura tactics once more, Demetrios crushed the Ptolemaic forces on Cyprus, winning a key naval victory off Salamis on the east of the island; Athenian ships played a distinguished part. Cyprus now belonged to Antigonos and would remain in Antigonid hands for more than a decade to come (Billows 1990: 151–5).

This was the moment at which Antigonos became king in 306. Our sources relate the theatrical arrival of an envoy from Demetrios, discreetly reporting the great victory to Antigonos, who was busy building his new capital, Antigoneia-on-the-Orontes, in northern Syria near the site of the later city of Antioch (on its location, Diod. 20.47 with Sherwin-White and Kuhrt 1993: 11). The envoy (Aristodemos, a well-established servant), after a stately progress to Antigonos' presence, finally gave his report. His first words were stunning: 'Hail, King Antigonos!' Immediately a diadem was produced and bestowed upon Antigonos by his entourage; King Antigonos then sent another diadem to Demetrios with a letter addressing him too as king.

The theatricality was appropriate to the dramatic event: for the first time since 323 there was now a king who could rule for himself and over an extensive realm, after some seventeen years of bloody conflict and shifting diplomacy (Plut. *Demetr.* 17–18; Gruen 1985, esp. 255). Less clear is the extent to which the play was actually staged by Antigonos or written up thereafter for public consumption: our fullest account, Plutarch in his *Life* of Demetrios, is well-known for his penchant for drama in his *Lives* and in this *Life* in particular (DeLacy 1952 remains the classic study). However that may be, it is clear enough that Antigonos' assumption of the royal title followed hard upon the (unusually clear-cut and substantial) victory in Cyprus; given that the essence of kingship was military victory, the logic was impeccable. Demetrios' kingship was thus not only convenient for the succession to ageing Antigonos, but also was seen to be deserved. That Antigonos appears at this critical moment also as a builder of cities further confirms his proper claim to royalty: to build cities was itself appropriate to a king (Shipley 2000: 59–86 and the works cited there). However, the particular power of the dramatic story of his acquisition of the title resides in the initiative coming not from Antigonos but from others, most immediately his entourage, but also the army on Cyprus which had sent Aristodemos to make his statement. To be king was a personal matter: the title moved with the king, unrestricted by any territorial associations. Antigonos, and by his grace Demetrios, were kings, but it remained to be seen what they would rule. In their wilder dreams they no doubt envisaged Alexander the Great's realm.

The importance of these events is not to be diminished. And yet some perspective is required: it is all to easy to be beguiled by grandeur. None of Antigonos' rivals rushed to assume a royal title for themselves: documentary evidence shows that both Ptolemy and Seleukos waited until the first half of 304. As to Lysimachos, 304 is likely enough, but we simply do not know. Kassandros seems to have waited longer still, perhaps until 302 (Gruen 1985). Their delay demands explanation. On the other hand, the royal title had been bandied about even before 306. The debates of 323 apart, we are told that Seleukos had sported it when dealing with non-Greeks (Plut. *Demetr.* 18) and also claimed to have been hailed as king by the oracle of Apollo near Miletos before setting out to Babylonia in 312 (Diod. 19.90.4). Moreover, Athenian honours for Antigonos and Demetrios in 307 had included the bestowal of the royal title upon them: little enough for the divine (Plut. *Demetr.* 10; cf. above). There were no rules for the assumption of kingship. The sheer power of those who followed

Alexander could only attract the title, for royalty was central to the discourse of power, while the death of Alexander IV in particular encouraged the use of the title. While subjects eager to express their loyalty might well proffer kingship, it was for the leaders to decide whether and when to accept it. In 306 Antigonos considered the moment right, buoyed by victory, and no doubt incited the offer. The others could afford to await reactions, and hope perhaps to turn Antigonos' striking gambit to their own diplomatic advantage; their powers were not immediately affected. Once they had seen Antigonos' innovation accepted, they followed his example and chose their moments as best they could to do so. In making their respective moves, there is no reason to suppose that Kassandros, Seleukos, Ptolemy and Lysimachos each had any less ambition than Antigonos or one another (*pace* Will 1984: 57–8). Each may well have had dreams of becoming the new Alexander. After all Antigonos was already 76 years of age and would soon create a vacancy which the bold Demetrios might not be able to fill for long.

3   From the Siege of Rhodes to the Battle of Ipsos

Be that as it may, King Antigonos was still seeking to expand his realm: while Antigonos failed to press home his advantage over Ptolemy (Billows 1990: 162–5), Rhodes was the next objective for Demetrios. The Rhodians had declined Demetrios' invitation to join in the campaign against Cyprus, preferring to continue to hedge their bets, and winning Antigonid enmity in the process (Diod. 20.46.6). Rhodian sea-power and Rhodes' strategic location between the Aegean and the eastern Mediterranean were enough to attract hostile action (cf. Berthold 1984). Demetrios was sent to take the island and set about a siege which was to earn him the familiar name 'Poliorketes' ('Besieger'). After a year or more, from 305 into 304, and despite the deployment of a panoply of innovative technology, the exasperated Antigonos called off his Besieger and both sides turned to diplomacy (Diod. 20.99; Ager 1996: 59–61): Ptolemy, in particular, had kept the island supplied, so that talks proved to be the better option. No doubt Ptolemy thought Rhodes some consolation for the loss of Cyprus: it was perhaps easier now for Ptolemy too to be king. However, it was not all success: the Antigonids did gain a measure of control over Rhodes. While the island was to be ungarrisoned, use its own laws and not pay tribute, the Rhodians were to become the allies of Antigonos (with specific exception for any campaign against Ptolemy). Moreover, Demetrios was to choose 100 hostages to ensure that the Rhodians kept their word: these were kept together at Ephesos (Diod. 20.107.4 for their release). Understandably after a year's siege even a mixed outcome was very welcome to the Rhodians, who celebrated with enthusiasm. Kassandros and Lysimachos were honoured with statues for their parts in supporting the island, while the crucial role played by Ptolemy brought him a cult, sanctioned by the oracle of Ammon. Moreover, the island was re-built and beautified, not least with the famous Colossus (Green 1990: 33; Shipley 2000: 44).

Demetrios sailed on to Greece, where he spent winter 304/3 in Athens, which had been hard pressed by Kassandros. There, we are told, he set up house in the Parthenon and, even discounting the more lurid stories, partied hard. These tales of impiety and debauchery are expressions of a profound political and religious debate at Athens over the nature of the city's relationship with the king whom it had made a god. Demetrios ensured that his man, Stratokles, held sway against serious challenge from Demochares, who championed a more democratic democracy, liberated from Antigonid control (Parker 1996: 260–4; Austin 35; Chaniotis, this volume). Demochares was also a historian, though we know little of his work (Billows 1990: 337–9). After that busy winter, Demetrios swiftly removed Ptolemy's garrisons from Sikyon and Corinth (where he installed his own) in spring 303 and campaigned on into the Peloponnese, where he married Deidameia, sister of Pyrrhos of Epeiros and important enough to have been once betrothed to Alexander IV. Pyrrhos was no friend of Kassandros: this promised to be a useful marriage. To consolidate the Antigonid position in central and southern Greece Demetrios proceeded, in 302, to reproduce a version of Philip II's League of Corinth, with himself and his father as its leaders, much as Ptolemy may have envisaged in 308. The Antigonids could thereby pose as the champions of Greek liberty through unity, but their own concern to dominate revealed the posture for the political gambit that it surely was. We may recall Antigonos' letter to Skepsis, which raised the same issues, as well as the proclamation outside Tyre and Demetrios' activities in Athens, Sikyon and Corinth: the Antigonids showed a commitment at least to the posture, suggesting its utility (*SV* III.446; Austin 42).

At this juncture, Antigonos and his son finally bit off more than they could chew. Kassandros sought terms, having lost his influence in central and southern Greece and envisaging an Antigonid assault upon Macedonia itself. He was rebuffed and thus given no choice but to fight: Antigonos had told him, it seems, that he should hand over all his possessions, including Macedonia. If Antigonos were to remove Kassandros, Lysimachos could not hope to keep Thrace, now at last more or less under his control. Lysimachos and Kassandros had already been co-operating successfully to mutual benefit and perhaps even with a measure of friendly affection. They united immediately against Antigonos and Demetrios and soon brought in Ptolemy, who had had his own troubles with them, especially in the loss of Cyprus. Seleukos, who had finally reached an accommodation with Chandragupta, could expect nothing good from Antigonid domination and was also quick to offer support.

Kassandros and Lysimachos took the initiative. Kassandros turned south into Greece against Demetrios, who was having himself initiated into the Eleusinian Mysteries in Athens: inconclusive conflicts followed in Thessaly. Meanwhile, Lysimachos and a part of Kassandros' army under his general Prepelaos had crossed into Asia and quickly made a series of gains there: several cities and even some of Antigonos' commanders in western Asia Minor threw in their lots with the invaders. However, Antigonos came up from Syria in force and, as winter 302 came on, pressed Lysimachos back into north-west Asia Minor, where Lysimachos had usefully married Amestris, once wife of Krateros and a niece of Darius himself: she was in control of the key city of Herakleia Pontike (Diod. 20.107–10; Ameling and Jonnes 1994). Demetrios, having made a truce with Kassandros on Antigonos' orders, himself crossed to Asia, won back key cities and penned in Lysimachos' forces. Attempts at relieving Lysimachos across the Black Sea proved disastrous (Diod. 20.112). In the meantime Ptolemy had forged into Syria and besieged Sidon, but withdrew again to Egypt when exaggerated accounts of Lysimachos' difficulties reached him. By contrast Seleukos had entered Cappadocia with a great army, which included some 480 war-elephants from India; he joined with Lysimachos' army as it made its way south.

In 301 the decisive battle was fought at Ipsos in Phrygia. If Antigonos and Demetrios had achieved a clear victory, there would have been little left to oppose them but Ptolemy, still in Egypt. But it was Kassandros, Lysimachos and Seleukos who had the victory. King Antigonos, now an octogenarian, was killed in battle, while our sources attribute much of the blame for the crushing defeat to Demetrios, who is said to have charged off in hot pursuit with his cavalry at the height of the battle and to have been too slow to return to the fray, with dire consequences for his father and the rest of the army. We should not ourselves charge to follow this tradition in detail, for it is in the hands of the dramatizing and moralizing Plutarch (*Demetr.* 29–30).

4   After Ipsos: the Emergence of Dynasties

Demetrios himself escaped the defeat and rode on to Ephesos, where he took ship and set about recovering his position by sea, without the guidance of Antigonos. Demetrios had shown his naval competence before, notably against Ptolemy off Cyprus, and the island was still his. In the Aegean, perhaps as early as 315/14, Antigonos had formed the islands of the central Aegean into a league which seems to have amounted to a federal state, centred upon a council on Delos: it had been a useful tool of Antigonid power and Demetrios could expect support for his naval campaigns there too (Austin 1981: 359; Billows 1990: 220–5). Corinth was also available. But not Athens, where Demetrios had used up his store of goodwill and now after Ipsos seemed to have little to offer. The city, controlled by Lachares, turned instead to Kassandros (Habicht 1997).

The victors at Ipsos also had to contend with the new situation after Antigonos. Seleukos soon quarrelled with Ptolemy over Phoenicia, which was to remain a bone of contention between their dynasties for centuries after. Ptolemy made an ally of Lysimachos, who held much of Asia Minor; Seleukos turned to Demetrios, but they soon fell out. In 298/7 Kassandros' death caused still more instability: his young sons fought a civil war, which included matricide against Kassandros' widow, Thessalonike, the surviving sister of Alexander the Great. Demetrios seized his chance in 294, taking Athens by siege, campaigning in the Peloponnese and at last seizing Macedon for himself, killing one of Kassandros' sons and forcing the other into exile with Lysimachos, who had troubles enough of his own, held captive briefly by the Getai of the lower Danube (Delev 2000). Demetrios' wife was Kassandros' sister, Phila: his claim to rule Macedon was more than military. Meanwhile, Pyrrhos of Epeiros had been extending his kingdom into Macedonian territory, fortified by good relations with both Ptolemy and Agathokles of Syracuse (Meister 1984); he also had ambitions in central Greece where he caused trouble for Demetrios in Aitolia and Boiotia. However, Demetrios was nothing if not energetic: he restored order and even seized Kerkyra (Corfu) and Agathokles' daughter, who had brought it to Pyrrhos as her dowry. Demetrios and Pyrrhos managed to reach a peace of sorts in 289, but only after protracted conflict in Greece.

Ptolemy, whose hand may be seen in some of Pyrrhos' activities, had taken back Cyprus in 295 and a few years later also the league of the islanders (Bagnall 1976: 136–58; Austin 218). In 288/7 he took from Demetrios Sidon and Tyre too, while Lysimachos and Pyrrhos were pressing him in Macedon itself. In 287 Athens revolted against him, supported by Pyrrhos. Demetrios made a desperate bid for Asia, where his forces dwindled away; in 286 he was captured by Seleukos in the Tauros and met his end. Again, Plutarch seeks to moralize (*Demetr.* 46ff.). Ptolemy soon died too, albeit more comfortably, in 283, having handed power to his son and heir Ptolemy II Philadelphos in 285. Lysimachos was the great beneficiary in all this, gradually making Macedon his own, together with Thrace and much of Asia Minor, a formidable kingdom, but one beset by palace intrigue – apparently formidable even by Hellenistic standards (Shipley 2000: 48–51 is nicely nuanced on this, while Ogden 1999 encompasses Hellenistic dynastic standards in general). Pyrrhos had been forced back, despite an alliance with Demetrios' son, Antigonos Gonatas, who had been left behind in Greece; as yet not quite a leading player, he had much of the Peloponnese, a foothold in Thessaly and more besides.

Seleukos seized the moment, perhaps incited by Lysimachos' problems at home and in his uneasy kingdom, but with ambition enough besides. Having invaded western Asia Minor, he defeated and killed Lysimachos at the Battle of Koroupedion near Sardis in 281. However, after crossing into Europe, evidently *en route* to claim Macedon, Seleukos was murdered by Ptolemy Keraunos, a son of Ptolemy, who had sought Seleukos' patronage, having lost his hopes of the throne of Egypt when Ptolemy had rejected his mother Eurydike in favour of Berenike, mother of Philadelphos. True to his sobriquet (Keraunos, or 'Thunderbolt') the murderer was quick to conceal his crime and had his victim's army proclaim him king.

The years 323–281 had been full of war and diplomatic complexities after the shattering loss of Alexander. Yet, amid all the conflict and fragmentation that ensued, Macedonian control of Alexander's heritage had been maintained for the most part and gradually stabilized, even at its eastern limits. By 281 a new world order had developed and the foundation had been set for the king-orientated practices of a Hellenistic world which would find in these years the roots and exemplars of its traditions. Two of the great dynasties were broadly in place: most firmly the Ptolemies, but also the Seleukids, for Seleukos had already appointed his successor, Antiochos I, before setting out to Koroupedion. The Antigonids were in a more parlous state, but Antigonos Monophthalmos and Demetrios Poliorketes would certainly be remembered, while Antigonos Gonatas, Monophthalmos' grandson, had already started to make his own way.

FURTHER READING

Broad studies of the Hellenistic world devote early chapters to this period: Shipley 2000 is up-to-date and thoughtful, while Austin 1981 is the most advanced collection of documents and texts, with commentary. Green 1990 offers a fine general treatment, which wears its considerable learning lightly. The opening chapters of volume 7.1 of the second edition of the *Cambridge Ancient History* (1984) are also rich in ideas, information and bibliography. The key discussion of the literary tradition and much besides is Hornblower 1981, with Shipley 2000 for the full range of sources, including archaeology, on which see also Alcock 1994. On the abiding importance of Alexander after 323, see Stewart 1993a; on the earlier history of key

Hellenistic figures under Alexander, Heckel 1992. The large issue of the continued importance of non-Greeks is suggestively treated by Briant 1985.

The dominant individual of these years, Antigonos Monophthalmos, has been studied very fully: Wehrli 1968, Billows 1990, with much also on Demetrios Poliorketes. On Antigonos' assumption of kingship, Gruen 1985 is excellent. Each dynast(y) has received good modern work. On Kassandros and all things Macedonian, the magisterial Hammond and Walbank 1988 is standard. On Lysimachos, Delev 2000 is a valuable starting-point; also Lund 1992. On Seleukos, Sherwin-White and Kuhrt 1993 is outstanding (and has caused debate: Ma 1999: 7 and the literature he cites), supplemented with the biographical treatment of Mehl 1986 and Grainger 1990a, together with e.g. Braund 1994 and Holt 1999 on the Caucasus and Baktria/ India respectively. On Ptolemy and his dynasty, see now Hölbl 2001, Huss 2001, with Bagnall 1976 on Ptolemaic administration outside Egypt. Of the various cities, Athens has been well-served: Habicht 1997, with Parker 1996 on religious matters. On Rhodes, Berthold 1984. On Herakleia Pontike, Ameling and Jonnes 1994 offer a learned, source-led starting-point.

CHRONOLOGICAL NOTE

The dating of the events in the years of the successors through to 311 is complex and controversial. The present chapter follows the low chronology advocated by R. M. Errington in *JHS* 90 (1970) 49–77 and *Hermes* 105 (1977) 478–504. Recently, however, A. B. Bosworth and P. Wheatly have revived the high chronology, A. B. Bosworth, *Chiron* 22 (1992) 55–81, P. Wheatley, *Phoneix* 52 (1998) 257–81, all underpinning A. B. Bosworth, *The Legacy of Alexander: Politics, Propaganda and Warfare under the Successors* (2002). Thus, for example, the low chronology would date it to the previous year, though the sequence of events remains the same.

CHAPTER THREE

An Uneasy Balance:
from the Death of Seleukos
to the Battle of Raphia

Sheila L. Ager

'There is nothing about Lykourgos that is not a matter of dispute,' says Plutarch in his introduction to the *Life* of the Spartan legislator, 'not his family, or his travels, or his death, or his reforms, or even when he lived.'

Plutarch was speaking of the obscurity of a pre-Classical period, but the same might be said for other times in Greek history, and of these, by far the most impenetrable is the third century BC. Like Plutarch, we are faced with the task of reconstructing not only *why* or *how* things happened, but simply *what* happened. Our only surviving continuous narrative for much of the period is Justin, whose predilection for tales of court intrigue and treachery, aberrant sexuality and murder make him one of the soapiest of the ancient writers. It is true that the third century does offer some compensation for the lack of literary sources in the wealth of surviving papyri and inscriptions. The challenge, however, lies in interpreting this material without a context. The temptation to flights of reconstructive fancy is great, and we may be in danger of seeking too much of a coherent pattern in a century where chaos theory might be a better methodology.

1   Chaos: the Years from 281 to 276

The term 'chaos' might be extreme for some regions of the Hellenistic world in 281. After all, in Egypt Ptolemy II had safely followed his father on the throne in 283, with minimal succession trauma. All the same, even Ptolemy felt the need to rid himself of superfluous siblings – two brothers were executed or assassinated, and it is worth noting that Ptolemy Keraunos had already left Egypt 'in fear' because their father had named his younger half-brother as heir (Paus. 1.7.1; App. *Syr.* 62). The monarchies were all new ones, with no firmly established pattern of succession, and elsewhere the situation was not so tranquil even as in Egypt. With the deaths of Lysimachos and Seleukos, royal control in the regions of Macedon and Asia Minor was severely shaken. Lysimachos had left no viable heir, though his eldest son by Arsinoe lived to trouble his contemporaries, and to trouble generations of modern scholars even more. Seleukos, on the other hand, left a highly competent heir: his son by the Iranian Apame, Antiochos I. In 281 Antiochos had already been co-regent for over a decade. Even so, he was going to face serious challenges posed both by his father's victory and by his death.

Justin touches briefly on Ptolemy Keraunos' political and military successes in establishing his rule in Macedon in the face of inherited enmities – he defeated Demetrios' son Antigonos Gonatas in a naval battle, and made peace with Seleukos' son Antiochos in the winter of 281/0 – but the historian saves his pen for the story that really caught his interest: the interaction of Keraunos with his half-sister Arsinoe, the widow of Lysimachos. It was imperative that Keraunos neutralize the claims of Arsinoe's sons to the throne of their father's kingdom. A marriage with his half-sister was the perfect solution; for Arsinoe herself, this may have been an opportunity unhoped for, one that would enable her to be a queen again (Carney 1994). The only hindrance to the success of this plan was Arsinoe's eldest child, Ptolemy, who, while young, was far from naive. He warned his mother against the marriage; that he had no intention of quashing his own ambitions is evident from the fact that he shortly embarked on a military campaign against his new stepfather. This ill-mannered behaviour may have prompted Keraunos to the action so luridly described by Justin: the murder of Arsinoe's younger boys in their mother's arms (Just. 24.3; Heinen 1972: 75–83).

Keraunos might have succeeded in his bid for power in Macedon had it not been for a singular event that had long term repercussions: the invasion of the Celts. About February of 279, a Celtic band invaded Macedon, and repaid Keraunos for all his crimes (as Justin saw it) by killing him in battle and sticking his head on a pike. An invasion later in the year that penetrated all the way to Delphi had an even greater impact on the Greek mind, and though the Celts were driven out of Greece, they subsequently irrupted into Asia Minor, and 'filled it like a swarm' (Just. 25.2.8). There they became a constant danger, always simmering beneath the surface, and frequently boiling over, making their own contribution to the destabilizing forces at work in the third century (*OGIS* 765, trans. Burstein 17; *I.Erythrai* 24, 28; Mitchell, this volume).

To one individual, however, the Celts proved a blessing in disguise. Antigonos Gonatas was still wearily searching for a territorial kingdom in which to situate himself. After an abortive effort in Asia Minor (an effort which culminated peacefully in a marriage alliance that made Gonatas Antiochos I's brother-in-law twice over), Gonatas returned to the European side of the Hellespont. There he encountered and defeated a force of Celts near Lysimacheia (Memnon *FGrH* 434 F10; Trogus *Prol.* 24; Just. 25.1–2; Hammond and Walbank 1988: 581). Macedon, in the meantime, had been in a desperate condition. The sources name several would-be rulers after Keraunos' death, including Ptolemy the son of Lysimachos, but in reality Macedon remained in a pitiable state of anarchy for years. Gonatas, fresh from his victory at Lysimacheia, was the most viable candidate the wounded country had seen in some time. The kingdom without a king and the king without a kingdom had found each other, and by 276 Antigonos Gonatas was ruler of Macedon.

The state of documentation in the Seleukid kingdom is so tattered that it has provided scholars with the opportunity (depending on one's point of view) either to reconstruct carefully a real but vanished episode, or to fabricate entirely an ephemeral non-event: the so-called 'War of the Syrian Succession', a war between Antiochos I and Ptolemy II (*c.* 280/79). Given that the very existence of this war is in doubt, it seems best not to include it in the 'canon' of Syrian Wars that begins with the First Syrian War of 274–271. The term 'Syrian War' has long been recognized as a misnomer, since much of the fighting during the Syrian Wars took place elsewhere than in this cul-de-sac at the eastern end of the Mediterranean. But wherever the fighting took place, the Syrian border between the Ptolemaic and the Seleukid empires was an eternal hot spot, a point of friction that in the third century was never alleviated.

Chief among the contemporary sources for the putative succession war is an inscription from Ilion (*OGIS* 219, trans. Austin 139), which refers to the troubles Antiochos faced from rebels in Seleukis (north Syria), and to the attacks of external enemies from outside the kingdom. This inscription is usually dated to the years immediately after Antiochos' accession, and it is assumed that those enemies include Ptolemy II. Vigorous arguments about the date – whether the inscription refers to Antiochos I or to Antiochos III – mean that the hypothesis of a Syrian war at the time of Antiochos I's accession remains an unresolved question (Mastrocinque 1987/8; Piejko 1991; C. Jones 1993; cf. Ma 1999: 254–9). Nevertheless, it is certain that Antiochos did face a number of challenges, particularly in Asia Minor, where the difficulties of establishing Seleukid influence in the remains of Lysimachos' kingdom were exacerbated by the presence of the unruly Celts. But as with Gonatas, a military victory over the Celts promised glory and (perhaps more important) legitimation for a Macedonian ruler. Antiochos defeated them in the famous 'elephant battle', perhaps *c.* 270 (or a little later), as a result of which he was given the cognomen 'Saviour' (App. *Syr.* 65; Wörrle 1975).

The mid-270s, with Gonatas established in Macedon and Antiochos having successfully weathered whatever succession crisis he faced, have conventionally been held to be the beginning of the 'stable' years. Whether this was so or not remains to be seen.

2 Ptolemy Against the World: the First Syrian and Chremonidean Wars

While his counterparts Gonatas and Antiochos were battling to secure their kingdoms, Ptolemy II was gaining a reputation (in the modern world at any rate) for being an unwarlike, and downright un-Macedonian monarch. The eminent old-school historian W. W. Tarn had this to say about him:

> Alone of the kings of his time he was no warrior.... The prince who presided over Egypt's age of gold was but a sickly creature, a devotee of pleasure in all its forms, ever seeking new pastimes and new sensations..., one who exhausted every form of luxury, and who, prostrated by gout, envied the simple joys of the beggars below his window, even while he dabbled in search after the elixir that should make him immortal. (1913: 216)

An outmoded prejudice, of course, inspired by admiration for Ptolemy's enemy, the Stoic Gonatas. Ptolemy fought his own share of battles, though not always in person;

no one today would see it as a cause for criticism that he had other dimensions to his character. The common pattern of tensions in the third century saw Ptolemy at odds with his neighbours Antiochos I and II over the 'Syrian' question on the one hand, and with Gonatas in Greece and the Aegean on the other. Whether the Antigonids and Seleukids, friendly since 278, combined to stand against Ptolemy in any effective or consistent way is one of the open questions of third century history. The diplomatic isolation of Egypt may have been among the factors that prompted Ptolemy II to send an embassy to Rome in 273 (Hauben 1983). The Romans responded amicably, though their ambassadors declined the lavish gifts Ptolemy tried to present to them; no doubt Ptolemy's descendant Auletes could have wished that the Romans of his day would display a similar lack of avarice.

Whether or not Ptolemy made major gains against Antiochos I in a war around 280/79, Ptolemaic holdings were certainly extensive by this time. In the Aegean Egypt had assumed the leadership of the Nesiotic ('Island') League, and had established a presence along the Karian and Ionian coasts (*SIG*[3] 390, trans. Austin 218, *c.* 280–278, date disputed by Hazzard 2000: 47–58; *SIG*[3] 322, trans. Burstein 25; *SEG* 1.363, trans. Austin 135). Ptolemaic foreign policy is often interpreted as 'defensive imperialism' (Will 1979: 153–208), the premise being that the Ptolemies were primarily interested in securing the strategic and economic well-being of Egypt itself. Their holdings beyond its borders – Syria, Cyprus, Cyrene, various places along the coast of Asia Minor and in the Aegean – would have been intended as a perimeter ring that would not only provide a forward defence, but that would also bring Egypt the vital natural resources that she herself could not supply, such as timber and metals. This view has much to be said for it, but it is open to challenge on some points. In this context let it simply be said that for a state that was interested primarily in security rather than aggrandisement, the Ptolemaic regime was extraordinarily active outside its own borders. The Aegean, where the sea both united and divided, and made the islands both liminal and central to the rivalries of the kingdoms, became a frequent battleground. And one of the most crucial of those borders was the frontier between Ptolemaic and Seleukid Syria, which for most of the third century ran along the Eleutheros river and through the Bekaa valley (Grainger 1991: 67).

Like the putative War of the Syrian Succession, the First Syrian War (274?–271?) is known to us only through fragmentary and scattered references. Pausanias refers to collusion between Antiochos I and his son-in-law, Magas, Ptolemy's half-brother and ruler of Cyrene (1.7.1–3). The collusion was not very well co-ordinated, and amounted to little, except that Magas did succeed in establishing a degree of independence for himself in Cyrene. A Babylonian astronomical diary informs us that in 274/3 Antiochos abandoned for the moment his Asia Minor pursuits, advancing to Syria to confront the Egyptian enemy (Sachs and Hunger 1988: no. 273; Sherwin-White and Kuhrt 1993: 46–7; Austin 141). We learn from an Egyptian hieroglyphic document, the 'Pithom stele', that in early 273 Ptolemy was at Pithom on the eastern borders of Egypt to defend Egypt against invasion, and that he may have conducted an (unsuccessful?) campaign in Palestine (Lorton 1971). The war was perhaps over by 271/0, and may have had a finale that Ptolemy had cause to celebrate, if the stupefyingly extravagant pageant of Ptolemy II described by the Rhodian writer Kallixeinos is to be dated to that year (Athen. 5.196–203).

Figure 3.1 Dynastic advertising: gold *mnaieion* of Ptolemy II, showing himself and his sister Arsinoe II on the reverse (left), and their parents, Ptolemy I and Berenike I on the obverse (right). Courtesy of the British Museum

At Ptolemy's side when he was at Pithom in January of 273 was his new(ish) bride: his older sister Arsinoe. After her disastrous marriage to her half-brother Keraunos, she had fled to Samothrace, and then to Egypt. She was evidently willing to give both queenship and brother-marriage another try, and at some point before 274 she married her full brother Ptolemy II. The incestuous marriage (whence both Arsinoe and Ptolemy are known by the epithet 'Philadelphos') provoked revulsion among Greeks, though it may have been more acceptable to the Egyptian population. The court poet Theocritus, in one of his more sycophantic moments, tried to clean up the marriage for Greek consumption by likening it to the marriage of Zeus and Hera (*Id.* 17), but the more commonly held view was no doubt expressed in the indelicate remark of Sotades (Athen. 14.621a). Theocritus' position was clearly the more rewarding one to hold – the tactless Sotades was sealed in a lead jar and dropped into the sea to drown.

In the past Arsinoe has been seen as far more ambitious, competent and politically ruthless than her (allegedly) indolent and sensual brother. This view has been rejected (Burstein 1982; Hazzard 2000: 81–100), but the epigraphic and numismatic evidence does suggest that Arsinoe II – for whatever reason – held a unique position. An Egyptian inscription refers to her as 'the king of Upper and Lower Egypt' (Quaegebeur 1998: no. 42), and Ptolemy issued a remarkable coinage emphasizing the marital partnership by presenting his profile side-by-side with that of his sister-wife (Mørkholm 1991: no. 297; figure 3.1). Among the Ptolemaic foundations or refoundations along the coasts of Asia Minor, Greece, and the islands are no less than twelve 'Arsinoes' (G. Cohen 1995). And one of the most hotly debated pieces of Arsinoe-evidence is the famous inscription from Athens, *SIG*[3] 434/5, a document which brings us to the next Ptolemaic conflict: the Chremonidean War (trans. Austin 49).

The inscription records a decree, moved by one Chremonides and passed in Athens in the archonship of Peithidemos (268/7 or 265/4; Heinen 1972; Gabbert 1987; Habicht 1997; Dreyer 1999a). The Athenians resolve to fight against 'those who are trying to destroy the laws and the ancestral constitutions of the cities, those who have wronged the cities and broken treaties'. The reference, while unspecified, is clearly to

Antigonos Gonatas. Since assuming control of Macedon, Gonatas had worked to consolidate his control both there and at the key points later to be called the 'fetters of Greece': Demetrias in Thessaly, Chalkis on the island of Euboia, and Corinth on the Isthmus. The Athenian port of Piraeus was also in his hands, and we do not need to look much further for Athenian motivation in declaring war on Gonatas, though Gonatas' aggressions in Euboia will also have been alarming (Knoepfler 1993; Habicht 1992; 1997: 143).

The years since 276 had been challenging ones for the Antigonid ruler. He had been forced to deal with the intrusions of the bellicose ruler of Epeiros, Pyrrhos, back from his Italian adventure in 275/4. Pyrrhos had mounted an invasion of Macedon that had actually forced Gonatas back on his coastal holdings. Diverted from there by an opening in the Peloponnese, Pyrrhos met his death fighting both Spartans and Macedonians at Argos in 272, after being stunned by a roof tile dropped on his head by an Argive woman (Just. 25.4–5; Plut. *Pyrrh.* 26–34; Polyaen. 8.68). Gonatas no doubt heaved a sigh of relief to have the plaguey, but peculiarly feckless Pyrrhos out of the way, and took the opportunity to extend his influence in the Peloponnese (Just. 26.1, 1–3). Sparta would not have been happy, and so, in spite of the brief co-operation with Gonatas in 272, the Spartans and their king Areus were equal partners with Athens in the Chremonides decree. Indeed, Areus' name figures so conspicuously in the decree, and in the rarefied literary evidence for the ensuing war, that we might be tempted to call this the 'Arean War'.

Prominent also in the anti-Macedonian coalition recorded in the inscription was the name of Ptolemy, who was evidently eager to support the 'common freedom of the Greeks', in accordance with the policy 'of his ancestors and his sister'. The reference to a woman in this context is extraordinary and has led to much debate on the role of Arsinoe in the Chremonidean War; it is even more striking when we consider that she had probably been dead for some time (efforts have been made to date her death to 268, but in all likelihood she was dead by July 270; Cadell 1998). The view was long held that Arsinoe instigated the war in order to have Ptolemy, her son by Lysimachos, enthroned in Macedon. But there is no need to seek Ptolemaic motivation in pressure from a domineering sister-wife – still less in an altruistic and disinterested support of Greek freedom. Ptolemaic policy had long been friendly to Athens' efforts to resist the Antigonids (Habicht 1992), and Philadelphos may have been alarmed at the ramifications of Macedonian recovery, particularly if Gonatas was developing the naval arm of the Macedonian military (Will 1979: 220–1).

Pausanias, one of our very few literary references, says that 'nothing remarkable' came of the Ptolemaic support for Athens (1.7.3). Archaeological, epigraphic, and numismatic evidence from Attica acts as a corrective on Pausanias' remark, showing that Ptolemy's commander Patroklos was doing perhaps the best he could with what resources he had (McCredie 1966; Heinen 1972: 152–4; Habicht 1997: 145). In the end, however, it really did come down to nothing remarkable. Areus was killed fighting on the Isthmus of Corinth, and Athens was finally forced to capitulate, in the spring of 262 or 261. Not only did Gonatas still hold the Piraeus, he now installed a garrison in the city of Athens itself, and imposed a pro-Macedonian governor for the next several years. And perhaps it was as a finale to the Ptolemaic–Antigonid hostilities in the Chremonidean War that Antigonos triumphed in a naval victory over Ptolemy's fleet in a sea battle off the island of Kos.

If the Battle of Kos was indeed fought at the close of the Chremonidean War, it would mean that Ptolemy was right to be concerned about Antigonid naval activity. Antigonos' fleet may also have been assaulting Ptolemaic interests along the Karian and Ionian coast (*RC* 14, Austin 270). By the close of the 260s, Ptolemy's naval pre-eminence was, at the very least, no longer unchallenged. As for Gonatas, he had secured his rule in Macedon, and ensured that individual states like Athens or Sparta could not effectively challenge him in Greece again.

In Asia, Antiochos I died in 261, having throughout his reign been engaged in the 'many wars' that Memnon speaks of (*FGrH* 434 F9). Towards the end of his reign a new enemy appeared where once there had been a friend. Eumenes, the nephew of Philetairos of Pergamon, took over upon his uncle's death in 263, and very shortly demonstrated that he intended Pergamon to be independent, defeating Antiochos in battle near Sardis *c.* 262 (Strabo 13.4.2). Antiochos was no more than about sixty years of age when he died and left his kingdom to his homonymous son, but no doubt much of his life energy had gone into the strenuous efforts to maintain his immense kingdom with its many unstable frontiers.

3 Mid-Century Crisis: the Second and Third Syrian Wars and the Kings' Household Dilemmas

By the time two generations had passed, all the rulers of the Successor kingdoms were related to one another. Ptolemy III was a second cousin to Antiochos II, and a first cousin, once removed, to Antigonos Gonatas; Gonatas and Antiochos, for their part, were uncle and nephew. But blood relationships amongst royalty rarely do much to uphold conventional family values. If the third century witnessed little strife between the closely related Antigonids and Seleukids, it was only because their spheres of interest rarely clashed. Dynastic rivalries and succession crises are a continuing thread in the story of the relationship between Ptolemies and Seleukids. The tale of the Third Syrian War illustrates just how bloody royal blood relationships could get, and it demonstrates also that the vaunting ambitions of the period of the Diadochoi never really disappeared. Of particular interest during the Second and Third Syrian Wars is the question of whether Antigonos Gonatas intervened in these conflicts, forcing the Ptolemies to fight on more fronts than they wanted. The sea battles of Kos and Andros, events which float in the literature without anchors, are often set in the context of these wars (Kos is generally dated either to *c.* 261 or to *c.* 255, Andros to 246/5). The notion that Gonatas worked the Aegean front for his Seleukid relatives during these wars will suit those who find conspiracy theories attractive, but there is no proof of any kind.

We have little indication of fighting in Syria itself during the Second 'Syrian' War (260?–253). An ostrakon bearing a demotic Egyptian text that calls for an inventory of the land of Egypt may have bearing on the economic measures necessary for the conduct of the war, and may refer to a victorious Ptolemaic campaign in Syria (Bresciani 1978; Hölbl 2001: 44; Burstein 97). Much of what evidence there is, however, points to conflict in Asia Minor. The naval state of Rhodes may have taken the side of Antiochos II – a notable circumstance, as the interests of Rhodes and the Ptolemies usually ran in the same track (*SIG*³ 725, trans. Burstein 46; Frontin. *Str.* 3.9, 10; Polyaen. 5.18; Seibert 1976). The *polis* of Miletos was a more passive victim of royal rivalries. Sometime around 259 Miletos fell under the sway of a tyrant, an Aitolian emigré by the name of Timarchos. Subsequently the Milesians were the first to give Antiochos II the sobriquet *Theos* ('the God') when he wrested the city from Timarchos' control and killed the tyrant, thereby bringing the Milesians into the Seleukid camp. Before his death, Timarchos may also have disrupted Ptolemaic control of Samos (App. *Syr.* 65; Frontin. *Str.* 3.2, 11).

Timarchos is also connected to the most mysterious and controversial figure of the third century BC: the elusive and ever-challenging 'Ptolemy the Son'. The prologue to the vanished book 26 of Trogus tells us that 'in Asia the son of King Ptolemy, with Timarchos as his ally, revolted against his father'. There seems to be no question that this rebellious offspring is the same as the 'Ptolemy, son of Ptolemy' who appears in numerous papyri as the co-regent of Ptolemy II Philadelphos between 267 and 259. His disappearance from the co-regency in 259 must be connected to his rebellion, though whether as cause or effect is indeterminable. But who exactly *was* 'Ptolemy the Son'? Was he Ptolemy III Euergetes, who ultimately succeeded to the throne in 246 (a next to impossible choice)? Was he a bastard son of Philadelphos, who had enough mistresses that one of his descendants made a catalogue of them (a popular choice)? Was he a son of Philadelphos and Arsinoe II, in spite of all the sources say about that incestuous marriage being childless? Was he an unattested son of Phila-delphos and his first wife, and hence the full brother of Euergetes? Was he an adoptive son of Philadelphos, none other than the son of Arsinoe by her first husband Lysimachos? The last – that 'Ptolemy the Son' is to be identified with the son of Arsinoe and Lysimachos, adopted by his uncle-stepfather – is a choice that had fallen out of favour, but has recently been reformulated (Huss 1998). Huss's argument resurrects an old rationale for the Chremonidean War: Philadelphos, who had no desire to undergo the same experience as his half-brother Keraunos, was seeking a throne for his mettlesome adoptive son that would settle him far away from Egypt. A papyrus that is most important for Ptolemaic history in the third century (*P.Haun.* 6) may contribute the information that the Son (having reconciled with his adoptive family after the revolt of 259), fought in the Battle of Andros, and went on to make conquests for the Ptolemaic side on the coast of Thrace. He would have died some time after 239, having led a most stimulating life and reached at least sixty-plus years of age. Huss's position is eloquently argued, but no doubt we have not heard the last of Ptolemy the Son (Tunny 2000; Gygax 2000). The discovery of a new inscription or papyrus could bring about a complete reshuffling of all the pieces.

The finale to the Second Syrian War sowed the seeds of the Third Syrian War. The peace settlement in 253 was sealed with a marriage alliance: Antiochos II was to repudiate his wife Laodike, the mother of his sons Seleukos and Antiochos, and marry Philadelphos' daughter Berenike. Philadelphos will surely have insisted that Antio-chos get his heir from the Ptolemaic princess, passing over his sons by Laodike (Beyer-Rotthoff 1993:18–19); Berenike's father is said to have been so desirous that his daughter prove fertile that he regularly sent her Nile water to drink. The marriage settlement calls into question the general (if tentative) consensus that the outcome of the Second Syrian War, because of his losses in the Aegean, was unfavour-able to Ptolemy II. The marriage in fact proved to be unfavourable to the Seleukids, imposing on their dynasty the burden of 'amphimetric strife' (Ogden 1999: 128–9). Amphimetric strife – the conflict between royal children of the same father and different mothers – had already destroyed the house of Lysimachos. Philadelphos, married to a survivor of that conflict, knew very well what might ensue.

As it turned out, Philadelphos was dead (January 246) by the time the crisis arose in the Seleukid house, a crisis precipitated by the death of Antiochos a few months later. Rumour (Seleukid) had it that Antiochos had reconciled with his wife Laodike and had named her son Seleukos as his heir. Other rumours (Ptolemaic) claimed that Laodike had poisoned Antiochos and declared her son his father's successor. Berenike instantly declared her own infant son as the king, barricaded herself in her position at Antioch, and sent out a call for help. The classic amphimetric strife was underway, and was to have far-reaching consequences.

Berenike's brother, Ptolemy III Euergetes, responded to her call and set out with his forces to come to her rescue in Antioch, intent on ensuring the accession of his own nephew to the Seleukid throne. Before he arrived, the rules of the game had changed drastically: Berenike and her son were murdered (Just. 27.1; App. *Syr.* 65). Emotional ramifications aside, this was strategically a most awkward turn of events for Euergetes. With Berenike and the child still living, he could play the role of defender of the rightful heir; with their deaths, he became a foreign invader. It would therefore have been expedient to keep the news of the murders from spreading as long as possible. A curious anecdote in Polyaenus suggests that the murders were indeed covered up for a time (8.50). But a far more remarkable piece of evidence is a papyrus from Gourob, which appears to be a sort of war 'bulletin' issued by Ptolemy himself (*FGrH* 160, trans. Austin 220; Piejko 1990). Like most war bulletins, it presents only the good news: Ptolemy arrives in Seleukeia, the port city at the mouth of the Orontes, to the cheering of the crowds, and has the same astonishingly warm reception in Antioch itself, the very heart of Seleukis. After all the rejoicing and backslapping, he then, 'as the day was getting on towards evening, went in to the sister'. The unadorned statement provokes suspicion that she was already dead (after all, why wasn't she at the celebrations?), and that Ptolemy conspired to conceal his sister's death as long as he could.

It was to his immediate advantage. The ancient sources are unanimous in saying that from Antioch, Euergetes went on to an astonishing and unparalleled assault on the Seleukid realm. From Syria he advanced to Mesopotamia and, according to one exuberant writer, secured the country all the way from the Tauros mountains to India without a single military engagement (Polyaen. 8.50; Just. 27.1; App. *Syr.* 65). In fact, if it were not that the king was recalled by the news of an insurrection in Egypt, says Justin, he would have taken over the entire Seleukid kingdom (cf. *P.Haun.* 6.15; Peremans 1978; 1981; McGing 1997). Just how far Ptolemy actually went (probably only as far as Babylon), or how lasting his 'conquests' were (already by 245 his enemy Seleukos II was recognized formally as king there), are debatable points. How far his propaganda claimed he went is another matter. A lost inscription from Adoulis on the Red Sea lists Ptolemy's version of events:

> Great King Ptolemy (III) ..., having inherited from his father the kingdom of Egypt and Libya and Syria and Phoenicia and Cyprus and Lykia and Karia and the Kyklades islands, led a campaign into Asia with infantry and cavalry and fleet and Troglodytic and Ethiopian elephants.... Having become master of all the land this side of the Euphrates and of Cilicia and Pamphylia and Ionia and the Hellespont and Thrace and of all the

forces and Indian elephants in these lands, and having made subject all the princes in the
(various) regions, he crossed the Euphrates river, and after subjecting to himself Mesopotamia and Babylonia and Susiana and Persis and Media and all the rest of the land up to
Baktria . . . . (*OGIS* 54, trans. as BD 26; also Austin 221)

This expedition of Euergetes at the beginning of the Third Syrian War is perhaps
better understood as a kind of 'triumphal progress' than a military campaign, possible
because there was as yet no organized resistance to him. Ptolemaic seizure of
the entire Seleukid empire was not sustainable, and Ptolemy had sufficient demands
on him back in the Mediterranean. Aside from the native rebellion in Egypt, there
was also the old enemy Antigonos Gonatas to consider. Antigonid efforts to interfere in Cyrene after Philadelphos' half-brother Magas died (*c.* 250, bizarrely choking
to death because he was so grossly fat), by sending out a half-brother of Gonatas
(known as 'Demetrios the Handsome') to marry Magas' daughter Berenike, had
backfired. Berenike was not taken with Macedon's marital candidate (perhaps because
her decorative fiancé was having an affair with her mother Apame), and had
Demetrios assassinated. She thereupon married her cousin Euergetes, and brought
Cyrene once more under Ptolemaic rule (Just. 26.3.2–8). But if things went
poorly for Antigonid schemes in Cyrene, Gonatas was still able to fetch a blow to
Ptolemaic interests in the Aegean in late 246 or early 245. This is the now widely
accepted date for another Antigonid naval victory over Ptolemaic forces, the Battle
of Andros.

The Battles of Kos and Andros have been seen as forcing a decisive
rollback in Ptolemaic power in the Aegean (for sources and a discussion of the
possible dates of these battles: Buraselis 1982: 119–51; Reger 1985; Hammond
and Walbank 1988: 587–600). Certainly after about 260 the Antigonid presence is
more apparent in the Aegean, and the evidence for Ptolemaic leadership in the
Nesiotic League disappears. But nothing in the sources tells us that either Kos or
Andros was a crushing defeat for the Ptolemies. If Euergetes did suffer a naval defeat
in the Aegean in the early years of the Third Syrian War, he also made *gains* along the
coast of Thrace and in the Hellespontine region (*OGIS* 54; *P.Haun.* 6, 7; Bagnall
1976: 162), not to mention in Ionia, where Samos seems to have once again become
Ptolemaic (*SEG* 1.366, trans. Austin 113).

The chief significance of the Third Syrian War lies not so much in the monumental,
and ephemeral, territorial gains advertised in the Adoulis inscription, but rather in the
thorough shaking it gave to the Seleukid dynasty. Seleukeia, one of the four cities of
Seleukis, and Antioch's outlet to the Mediterranean, remained Ptolemaic until 219
and would have served as a constant reminder of the outrage of Euergetes' progress
through the heart of the empire, a political, strategic, and economic choke-hold on
the Seleukids (Jähne 1974; Beyer-Rotthoff 1993: 51–2). While the claims of Ptolemy's propaganda about the war are surely inflated, it is still true that Seleukos II had
found it almost impossible to counter the Egyptian offensive effectively. By 241 he
was forced to offer his younger brother Antiochos the rule in Asia Minor in return for
his support against Ptolemy, a move that prompted Ptolemy to conclude a peace
treaty (Just. 27.2.9). But Seleukos was now about to face enormous grief from the
fourteen year old Antiochos, who 'had a lust for power beyond his years' (Just.
27.2.7; Yardley trans.).

4   Internal Affairs: the Years from 241 to 221

In 240/39 Antigonos Gonatas died at the age of eighty. Aside from the Battle of Andros, he had been little involved with the international scene in recent years. Affairs in Greece – the revolt of his nephew Alexander, the seizure of Corinth in 243 by the Achaian general Aratos – had absorbed most of his energies. For the next two decades, with few pauses, the Achaians were to be hostile to Macedonian interests in Greece, and Ptolemaic Egypt lost no opportunity to create trouble for the Antigonids there. Already in 250 Philadelphos had granted Aratos 150 talents to 'fight the good fight', and in 243 the Achaians named Euergetes their *hegemon* by land and sea (Plut. *Arat.* 11–13; 24). No doubt this was an honorific position – subventions were enough at this stage to protect Ptolemaic interests in the Aegean. Gonatas did little to harm those interests in the last few years of his reign, and his son and heir Demetrios II (239–229) was too busy fighting the 'Demetrian War' against both Achaians and Aitolians to take much note of affairs in the wider world of the kingdoms (Scholten, this volume).

The Seleukids too were preoccupied with internal calamity after the end of the Third Syrian War. At one end of the empire, Seleukos II had to cope with the peeling away of his eastern satrapies. The sources unfortunately do not give us an unambiguous picture of the events that eventually saw Baktria and Parthia established as independent kingdoms, and there is much debate about the dates involved, but the movement seems to have begun by about the middle of the third century (Just. 41.1–5; Strabo 11.9.2–3; Arrian *FGrH* 156 F31–2; App. *Syr.* 65). Rebellion by Seleukid governors, rebellion that the king did not have the time or manpower to suppress, forms part of the picture. Another ingredient was the infiltration of the nomadic Parni, who eventually established themselves and their rule in Parthia. The apostasy of the eastern empire did not occur overnight (Sherwin-White and Kuhrt 1993: 84–90, 107–11), but the sources are unanimous in connecting at least the beginning of the defections to the circumstances of the Third Syrian War (or perhaps even earlier). We must therefore add troubles in the east to the difficulties Seleukos II had to face (Will 1979: 281–90; Musti 1984: 210–20).

More immediately before the eyes of contemporary Mediterranean observers were the problems that Seleukos was having with his little brother. Rumoured to be rapacious in his 'lust for power', Antiochos received the nickname *Hierax*, the 'Hawk'. Almost immediately upon the conclusion of peace with Ptolemy, Seleukos found himself at war with his sibling, who had the support of their mother Laodike. Hierax defeated Seleukos near Ankyra in 240 or 239 and forced him out of Asia Minor (Just. 27.2, 10–12; Athen. 13.593e; Plut. *Mor.* 184a, 489a–b). But things did not thereupon go swimmingly for Antiochos – a new opponent presented himself in the person of Attalos, who had succeeded to the rule of Pergamon in 241. Attalos was not one to let his own good deeds go unpraised: numerous monuments and inscriptions attest to his victories over Antiochos Hierax and over Hierax's sometime mercenaries, the Galatian descendants of the Celts (*OGIS* 272–280; Austin 197; Burstein 85). By 228 he had closed Asia Minor to Hierax. But Attalos' attitude towards the Hawk was not an ideological one. He was not supporting the 'rightful' king, Seleukos II, against a usurper – he was intent, rather, on the aggrandizement of Pergamon and the creation of his own monarchy.

After his defeat in Asia, Hierax appeared in Alexandria, prompting us to wonder whether he had not received some Ptolemaic support all along, perhaps in the favourite form of financial subsidies to pay his Galatian mercenaries (Just. 27.3.9–10). It is true that Euergetes kept him confined in some way – his departure from Alexandria is described as an escape – but then that was also the fate of another Ptolemaic subvention recipient, Kleomenes, a few years later. Hierax fled to Thrace and was murdered (ironically, by Celts) in 227, shortly before his brother Seleukos was killed in a fall from his horse (226/5; Just. 27.3.12). Seleukos was succeeded by his son Seleukos III, but the latter did not survive his accession for long. He was assassinated in 223 (by a Celt) as he was marching into Asia Minor to confront Attalos (Polyb. 4.48, 8; App. *Syr.* 66). For the troubled Seleukid kingdom, this death marked a sea change. It brought Seleukos III's younger brother Antiochos to the throne, the Antiochos who was to do so much to reconstitute the empire of Seleukos I.

Whether or not Euergetes chose to offer financial support to Hierax (or to Attalos for that matter), there is no doubt that he continued his practice of subventions to anti-Macedonian forces in the Balkans (perhaps on occasion even dispatching troops: *P.Haun.* 6.18; Scholten 2000: 176). The subsidies to the Achaian League initially negotiated by Aratos continued for some years, but the Ptolemies were equal opportunity employers. When Kleomenes III, the most energetic king to rule Sparta since Areus, approached Egypt to talk about subsidies, Euergetes was open to discussion. He was no doubt all the more open as the forces of containment working on Macedon seemed to be weakening. After the death of Demetrios II in 229, the throne was given (in trust for Demetrios' young son Philip) to Demetrios' cousin Antigonos III Doson. In 227 Doson mounted a naval expedition to Karia in southwestern Asia Minor (Trogus *Prol.* 28; Polyb. 20.5, 7–11; Crampa 1969). His motivation in doing so remains mysterious – perhaps a reassertion of Macedonian naval interests in the Aegean, perhaps a desire to fish in the troubled waters of an Asia Minor weary from Seleukid–Attalid conflict – but in any case his success in Karia will have been deeply troubling to Euergetes, who had interests in the same region and no desire to see Macedonian naval power anywhere near the Ptolemaic sphere.

Also troubling to Euergetes was the behaviour of his old friends the Achaians. Not only had they failed to prevent this display of Antigonid maritime ambition, they were now wavering in their loyalty to anti-Macedonian sentiment. Alarm at the indefatigable energies of the Spartan Kleomenes had prompted an Achaian approach to Macedon in 227/6; news of these negotiations was certain to sound Ptolemaic alarm bells (Polyb. 2.48–50). Kleomenes began to look like the better risk, and Euergetes, probably in the winter of 226/5, withdrew his financial support from the Achaian League and began to forward it instead to Kleomenes (Polyb. 4.51). Kleomenes responded gratefully and without subtlety to the subventions with a issue of coins bearing the Ptolemaic eagle (Mørkholm 1991: 149).

But the Ptolemies, if generous, could be erratic supporters (as the Achaians had already discovered). Egypt's motivation was not altruistic, in spite of the claims of the Chremonides decree; it was driven by a calculated self-interest, exemplified by Euergetes' demand in 224 that Kleomenes render up his mother and his children to be detained in Alexandria as hostages for his good behaviour (Plut. *Cleom.* 22). When Doson and the Achaians – as was surely now inevitable – concluded an alliance in 224, and when other Greeks subsequently joined in a coalition against Kleomenes,

Euergetes saw no sense in continuing to bet on a lost cause. Ten days before the battle at Sellasia in July 222, he sent a message telling Kleomenes that he was withdrawing his support and recommending that the Spartan king make the best peace he could. Kleomenes fought the battle anyway – committed to the restoration of the antique Sparta and everything it stood for, he had little choice – and went down to defeat.

Ptolemy III Euergetes, Antigonos III Doson, and Seleukos III were all of different generations, but their deaths were closely contemporary. Seleukos III was murdered in 223, and Euergetes was dead by February 221; Doson died in midsummer of the same year. In all three kingdoms, youthful – and unseasoned – kings now came to the throne.

5   Succession (Melo)Drama: the Young Kings and their Villainous Advisors

Polybios asserts that this moment – the accession of Philip V in Macedon, Ptolemy IV Philopator in Egypt, and Antiochos III in Asia – was a watershed in world history (4.2). The 'balance' that had existed in the previous decades was about to shift dramatically, and furthermore, the Romans were about to step onto the Hellenistic stage. Of the new monarchs, two, in Polybios' view, had more talent than their predecessors had shown in some time, while one was not only depraved, but useless. Drawing on Polybios' judgement, Justin puts it succinctly:

> These boy-kings had no men of riper years to guide them, but in their enthusiasm to follow in the steps of their forefathers, they all revealed great natural abilities. The sole exception was Ptolemy; villainous in seizing his realm, he was also inefficient in administering it. (29.1.8–9; Yardley trans.)

It is difficult to liberate ourselves from this view and the notion that Ptolemy IV was a weak and vicious libertine who single-handedly sank the power that Ptolemaic Egypt had been during the third century. And yet Ptolemy IV did manage to retain (more or less) the external possessions he had inherited from his father; the native uprisings that occurred in Egypt during his reign had not only been attested before, but may in some measure be attributable to the oppressive economic measures instituted not by himself, but by his grandfather (Huss 1976; Turner 1984; Hölbl 2001: 63, 153).

There is a suspicious structural similarity in Polybios' accounts of the early years of the three kings. All three are initially subjected to the conflicting pressures of a wicked and a wise advisor, a model for which the historiographic *locus classicus* is Herodotos' account of the young king Xerxes. Antiochos and Philip successfully rid themselves of their villainous Rasputins, but Ptolemy IV never did (Polybios' answer, of course, to the problem of Ptolemaic decline). During the Social War of 220–217, when Philip and his new Achaian allies finally embarked on open warfare with the Aitolian League (for decades a crotchety neighbour of both the Achaians and Macedon), one Apelles, 'who had the most influence with the king', concocted a conspiracy to discredit the Achaian Aratos and to damage Philip's prospects in the war. Before the war was over, Philip had seen the light and disposed of Apelles' group through execution and enforced suicide (Polyb. 4.76, 82–7; 5.1–28). As for Antiochos III, he had inherited a kingdom with a basic structural weakness, and a history of secession and internecine strife. Upon his accession more of the upper satrapies fell away in revolt: Molon in Media and his brother Alexander in Persia rebelled against Seleukid authority (222; Polyb. 5.40–56). Vicious in himself, Antiochos' chief advisor Hermeias also appears to have given the young king bad advice, persuading him to embark on a campaign against Ptolemaic holdings in Syria rather than against Molon (221). The Syrian campaign failed utterly, while Molon's affairs prospered. In the end Antiochos was forced to deal with Molon himself; the rebellion was successfully put down, and Molon committed suicide (220). By now, Antiochos was suspicious of Hermeias, and had him quietly done away with.

Ptolemy IV was unfortunate enough to have a similarly evil *daimon* in the person of Sosibios, and doubly unfortunate in that he was in himself too inept to cope without his advisor. Polybios gives us an object lesson in Sosibios' nefarious dealings with the Spartan Kleomenes, in exile in Alexandria after the disaster at Sellasia. Using the same techniques as Hermeias (the ever-useful if slightly tired device of the forged letter), Sosibios destroys Kleomenes, allowing Polybios to record an epitaph of a man 'by nature most commanding and kingly' (Polyb. 5.39.6, who had had few kind words for Kleomenes so long as he was an enemy of Achaia). The weakness, however, of Polybios' portrait of Sosibios – and this perhaps is why the real Ptolemy IV did not divest himself of the real Sosibios – is that unlike Apelles or Hermeias, Sosibios, far from harming the king's cause, saved it during the Fourth Syrian War.

In 219, Antiochos was ready to make an attempt on Syria again. He may well have been provoked by his misgivings about the relationship between Ptolemaic Egypt and his cousin Achaios, who had been operating with great success against Attalos in Asia Minor in recent years. Already under suspicion, in 220 Achaios put on the diadem and proclaimed himself king in Asia Minor (Polyb. 5.57.5). We have no ironclad proof that Ptolemy was supporting him in his venture, though it would admittedly be a Ptolemaic sort of thing to do. The chief Seleukid achievement in the Fourth Syrian War (219–217) was Antiochos' recovery of the port city of Seleukeia. Although he scored military successes in the Ptolemaic province, he was stalled by the machinations of Ptolemy's ministers Sosibios and Agathokles, who persuaded him to agree to a four-month truce in which to negotiate. The negotiations gave Egypt enough time to train an army that included, for the first time, 20,000 native Egyptians armed as hoplites (Polyb. 5.63–7). When the two armies met on the battlefield near Raphia (June 22, 217), the Ptolemaic forces defeated Antiochos' troops, and the Seleukid king was forced to give up his Syrian ambitions – for the present.

Polybios remarks that it was an enormous mistake in the long run to enlist the Egyptian troops (he thus manages to belie neatly the real success of Ptolemy IV and Sosibios at Raphia). Until now, the Macedonian rulers of Egypt had eschewed the use of native troops, contemptuous of their unwarlike character in much the same way as the British of the colonial era were (the Egyptian peasant 'would make an admirable soldier', writes a British field marshal in the 1910 *Encyclopedia Britannica*, 'if only he wished to kill some one!'). But emboldened now by their success at Raphia, and filled with nationalist fervour, the Egyptians rebelled against their foreign masters – 'immediately', Polybios says (5.107.1), though he seems to be telescoping events which took place much later in Philopator's reign (McGing 1997). It was this upsurge in the native Egyptian movement for independence, combined with Ptolemy

IV's character being 'rather too much inclined for peace' (5.87.3), that Polybios saw as disastrous for the future of the Ptolemaic empire.

Philopator's peaceful inclinations were on display in Greece as well, where his ambassadors attempted to mediate a settlement to the Social War between Philip and the Aitolians (Polyb. 5.100). What contribution the Ptolemaic envoys made to the Peace of Naupaktos is difficult to determine. Polybios claims that what really prompted Philip to make peace in the late summer of 217 was the news of the recent victory of Hannibal at Lake Trasimene and the world of opportunity opened up by the Roman defeat there (5.101–2). Whether Polybios' essay at mind-reading is right or wrong, it is true that the Roman world was soon to intrude itself more and more into the consciousness of the eastern Mediterranean, till now so dominated by Ptolemies, Seleukids, and Antigonids.

6   Conclusion: a 'Balance of Power'?

The phrase 'balance of power' repeatedly appears in discussions of the third century BC, generally with a disclaimer. The assertion that the Ptolemaic, Seleukid, or Antigonid kings consciously aimed at merely limited power out of an ideological sense that a triangulated balance of strong kingdoms would produce a world that was healthiest and happiest for everyone is a precarious one (though Hölbl has recently claimed to see in the settlement at the end of the Fourth Syrian War 'the consummate statecraft of the Ptolemies and their long-term policy of a balance of power' [2001: 131]). F. W. Walbank, in a discussion of Antigonid sea power, states the qualified view well: 'the three major monarchies in practice operated a balance of power which, however, was never accepted in principle' (Walbank 1982: 234). Walbank's view is that the Antigonids in the naval realm were *not* being purely defensive, but rather were actively pursuing aggressive expansionism – they just weren't very good at it. And that may well be the whole story of Hellenistic 'balance of power' in a nutshell.

Because the Ptolemies never controlled the entire Aegean or all of Asia Minor (and because of the claims of Polybios) we have the sense that Ptolemaic imperialism was purely 'defensive', and that it was all the result of tidy planning. But this is a view based to a large extent on hindsight. Just because Euergetes' wild adventure in the heart of the Seleukid empire in 246/5 had little lasting effect does not mean that he never thought it might. The fragility of the balance is particularly well illustrated by that episode. The claim that Ptolemaic foreign policy was defensive in its nature, and that the Ptolemies accepted the principle of limited power, inevitably tends to soften our estimation of their imperialism. Yet *any* imperial power can claim – and even sincerely believe – that its expansionism is based on the needs of security and defence. 'It may have been wrong to take this empire,' says Perikles in fifth-century Athens, 'but it would be dangerous to give it up' (Thuc. 2.63.2).

Viewed from the perspective of the Greek cities of Asia Minor, the third century, far from being a time of stability and equilibrium, was a time of great turmoil and often anguish. This chapter has focused almost exclusively on matters of war. The Hellenistic kings were all the descendants of a warrior culture, and their power and their kingship were measured by their arms. This period demonstrates to perfection that the Hellenistic world was always a fluid and dynamic one, and that the eastern Mediterranean was never in these years the settled, stable place it came to be under the Roman empire. The balance of the third century, if there was one, was of a Herakleitan rather than a Pythagorean character, based not on harmony, but on tension and strife.

FURTHER READING

It has been remarked many times in the course of this chapter that the third century is one of the most challenging in all of ancient history in terms of primary source materials. Any day we may find another Gourob Papyrus or another Adoulis inscription, another Chremonides decree or another *P.Haun.* 6. If and when we do, all our assumptions will have to be revisited, from the finest details to the broadest conclusions. Important re-examinations of some of the most significant documents may be found in Bülow-Jacobsen 1979, Piejko 1990, 1991 and C. Jones 1993.

Will 1979–1982 remains the best broad survey of the political/military history of the Hellenistic world, though it now stands in need of updating; it is especially useful for the collation and discussion of primary sources. In English, the second edition of the *Cambridge Ancient History* (Vol. 7.1, 1984, covering the Hellenistic period from 323 to 217) offers a number of important essays. More recent syntheses (Green 1990 or Shipley 2000) are valuable, although their added emphasis on social and cultural history inevitably curtails the discussions of political narrative. Specialized studies of the individual Hellenistic kingdoms include Hammond and Walbank's *History of Macedonia* iii (1988), dealing with the years between 336 and 167; Sherwin-White and Kuhrt's *From Samarkhand to Sardis* (1993), a somewhat idiosyncratic, but commendable study of the Seleukid kingdom; and Hölbl's *History of the Ptolemaic Empire* (2001) and Huss's *Ägypten in hellenistischer Zeit* (2001).

Much of the debate and discussion of the tangled web of third century history is to be found in specialized monographs and articles. They are too many to list here in their entirety, but following are a few examples. Most are not unnaturally concerned with reconstruction of the military struggles of the period. For perspectives on the Syrian conflicts: Lorton 1971, Jähne 1974, Huss 1977, 1978, Bresciani 1978, Clarysse 1980, Peremans 1981, Hauben 1983, 1990, Mastrocinque 1987/8, and McGing 1997; discussions of Ptolemaic foreign policy under Ptolemies III and IV may be found in Huss 1976 and Beyer-Rotthoff 1993. On the events and chronology of the Chremonidean War: McCredie 1966, Heinen 1972, Gabbert 1987, 1997, Habicht 1992, 1997, Knoepfler 1993, and Dreyer 1999a. Aegean affairs are the focus of Merker 1970, Buraselis 1982, Reger 1985, 1994c, and much of Bagnall 1976. For a new evaluation of Ptolemaic activity in the Aegean, and of the Ptolemaic monarchy in general, Hazzard 2000 should be consulted. Hazzard also discusses the perpetually intriguing Arsinoe II, as do Burstein 1982, Carney 1994, and Quaegebeur 1998; her enterprising son is the focus of a major study by Huss 1998; see also Tunny 2000.

CHAPTER FOUR

The Arrival of Rome: from the Illyrian Wars to the Fall of Macedon

Peter Derow

This story might begin in many places. For Polybios it all started with the First Illyrian War (229–28). On his account this was Rome's 'first crossing with military force into Illyria and these parts of Europe, as well as the first diplomatic involvement with places in Greece' (2.12.7). The second part of this statement is incorrect, or at least misleading, but about the first there is no question. This was indeed the first appearance of Roman arms and warships across the Adriatic, and this war and its aftermath created a situation that can rightly be said to have been the beginning of the process known as the Roman conquest of Greece. Over the next sixty years there followed a series of actions and reactions by Romans and by Greeks. At every stage a new situation was created as people responded to changing circumstances. But there was a kind of continuity, too, and after those two generations the fell sway of Rome had increased and been affirmed, to the point that there was nothing left but 'to give heed to the Romans and obey them in their orders' (Polyb. 3.4.3, writing of the time after the eradication of the Macedonian monarchy in 167). Players on both sides contributed to this outcome.

1 The Adriatic

There had been Illyrians and there had been piracy in this sea long before the 230s. What there had not been was a strong Illyrian state such as emerged in this decade under the leadership of Agron, king of the Ardiaioi, continued after Agron's death at the end of the decade by Queen Teuta, his wife. Piracy became more insistent, and, more important, Agron began to extend his political dominion southwards and to more Greek places. The Achaian and Aitolian Leagues were unable to stop him from gaining a foothold at Phoinike in Epeiros. To the north, the Greeks of Pharos were already under his control, but the Greeks of Issa still held out. For Polybios it was complaints about Illyrian piracy, lodged before the Senate by Italians, that prompted the Romans to send an embassy in 230 to Teuta. For Appian, whose account is to be given at least as much weight, it was a plea from the Greeks of Issa that elicited the Roman *démarche*. For both, it was the murder of a Roman ambassador that led to the Roman declaration of war. But there was more to it than this, for neither provides a satisfactory explanation of this level of Roman concern with Adriatic affairs.

The answer lies on the western shores of the Adriatic and in a development of much longer standing than the rise of the Ardiaioi. After the battle of Sentinum in 295 Roman dominion in Italy was extended across the peninsula to the Adriatic. This was quickly confirmed by the foundation of colonies on the coast in the 280s: Sena Gallica, Hadria and Castrum Novum. They were the beginning of a process that continued with the foundations of Ariminum (268), Firmum Picenum (264), and, finally, Brundisium (244). These were citizen and Latin colonies, and it was above all the sea that connected them to the wider world. It is against this backdrop of fifty years of Roman presence along the Adriatic coast that the events of the 230s must be seen and understood: by then Adriatic affairs were altogether relevant to Rome's dominion in Italy. And the importance of the northern Adriatic for Rome in the 230s

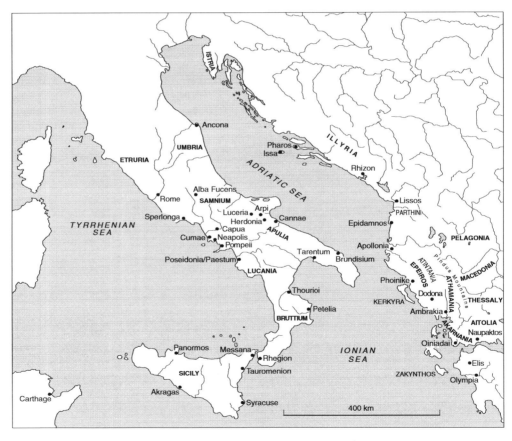

Figure 4.1 Map of Italy and the West

was more than a little enhanced by the quest for territory and control in the Po Valley in which the Romans were then engaged.

It made sense for Italians sailing in the Adriatic to appeal to Rome against the depredations of Illyrian pirates (Polyb. 2.8.2; one must wonder to what extent these were from the coastal colonies of Italy). It made sense for the Greeks of Issa to turn their attention in the same direction (App. *Ill.* 7). The Adriatic was visibly in part a Roman sea, and already a few years before this some Akarnanians had appealed to Rome (Just. 28.1–2; on the historicity, but relative inconsequentiality, of this, Dany 1999: 98–119). The Senate took cognizance. Roman ambassadors were sent to the Illyrian monarch in the company of the envoys from Issa. They were set upon by pirates, and one Roman, Coruncanius, and the Issaian Kleemporos were killed (whether before or after an interview with Queen Teuta is unclear; Appian's version, that there was no interview, seems preferable: Derow 1973a; cf. Errington 1989a: 86–8). The result was war. Both consuls of 229 were sent across the Adriatic, with fleet and two consular armies (the usual expeditionary force at the time).

The war was short. Both consuls triumphed, thereby establishing the world to the east of Italy as one where triumphs might be gained. Even more consequential for the history of Greece was the immediate aftermath of the war. In the course of it, a number of Greek cities and some inland tribes surrendered themselves to the Romans. Whether some or all of them became allies of Rome in some formal sense, or whether they entered into a vaguer kind of 'friendship and alliance' with the victors is disputed (for alliance, especially in the case of Pharos, see Derow 1991; BD 31, but also Eckstein 1999; further on formal relations of Rome and Greek states: Hammond and Walbank 1988: 601–10). Roman envoys were sent to the unsuccessful opponents of the Illyrians, the Achaian and Aitolian Leagues (in 228 by the consul who wintered in Greece), and also to Athens and to Corinth (in 227 by the Senate). They portrayed Rome's intervention as a service to Greeks, and report has it that the Romans (or perhaps just the Roman envoys?) were admitted to the Isthmian Games at Corinth and into citizenship and the Eleusinian Mysteries at Athens. The Romans had arrived. The ships and the soldiers left, but Roman interest in the area remained.

During the next few years Roman pre-eminence in the Adriatic and on the shores of Illyria and north-western Greece was challenged by Demetrios of Pharos. Agron's erstwhile lieutenant, he had fallen afoul of Queen Teuta, signalled his availability to the Romans before they arrived and handed over to them Pharos and Kerkyra which he controlled. From the Romans he received no great reward for this (App. *Ill.* 8; Polybios' assertion, 2.11, that they granted him much is surely a construction designed to demonstrate ingratitude on Demetrios' part) and soon set about improving his situation. He allied himself with Antigonos Doson, with whom he fought at Sellasia (222), and made common cause with Istrian pirates in the north. By the end of the decade he had detached people and places from their Roman connection and was attacking cities Polybios describes as 'subject to the Romans' (3.16: whether officially allies or friends, this is how they were perceived, a perception explicitly shared by Philip V of Macedon: Polyb. 7.9.13).

For some years the Romans did nothing about this. Indifference is not the explanation. As early as 226 they were deeply concerned about the Gauls in and around the Po Valley and the hostile reaction of the Gauls to Roman settlement in that area (Polyb. 2.13); this was not resolved until Marcellus' great victory at Clastidium in

222. In 221 both consuls were sent against the Istrians, Demetrios' partners (Eutrop. 3.7; cf. Dell 1970), and the consuls of 220 led an expedition 'as far as the Alps' (Zonar. 8.20: which Alps, and whether this had to do with the sequelae of the Gallic conflict or with the Istrians, we do not know). Demetrios would be next, and so he was, in 219, when both consuls were again sent to Illyria. The inevitability of this must help to explain Demetrios' otherwise bizarrely provocative conduct in 220: he was preparing for the inevitable Roman attack. He had to do so on his own: Doson had died, and the young Philip V who succeeded him was becoming embroiled in the Social War. This second Illyrian War was even shorter than the first. Both consuls triumphed. Illyria and the Adriatic had been disrupted and Roman authority challenged. The Romans set things back to rights at the earliest opportunity, when free of the more pressing task as was always their way. Demetrios fled to the young king Philip and took refuge at his court.

2   Macedon

It is unlikely that the Romans had much interest in Macedon before this (despite Polyb. 3.16 and Holleaux 1928), but they were not unaware of Demetrios' presence at Philip's court. In 217 an embassy was sent to Philip requesting the surrender of Demetrios (Livy 22.33.3). This was the first contact between the two states. Demetrios was not surrendered, and the Romans were of course not in a position to do anything about it: they were at war with Carthage and Hannibal was in Italy. For Philip, on the other hand, Rome's preoccupation provided opportunity, and his own preoccupation with the Social War came to an end with the Peace of Naupaktos in September 217.

The idea that the opportunity perceived by Philip included thoughts of universal dominion derives only from Polybios' exorbitant ascription to the king of Alexander-like aims (5.101–2; Philip was of course not related to Alexander, and Polybios' romantic account of Philip's reception of the news of Trasimene raises all manner of difficulties, not least chronological: see Derow 1976: 276 n. 36) and Livy's even more exorbitant rendition of the alliance struck in 215 between Philip and Hannibal (23.33). Polybios gives us the document (7.9). Detailed provisions for military co-operation are absent. What we do have is the provision that the Romans were no longer 'to be masters (*kyrioi*) of Kerkyra, Apollonia, Epidamnos, Pharos, Dimale, the Parthinoi or Atintania' (7.9.13): Philip's aim was to remove Roman authority from the eastern shore of the Adriatic. He built ships in the winter of 217/6, but the Adriatic expedition of summer 216 was aborted. Then came the alliance with Hannibal and, in 214, a seaborne attack on Orikos near Apollonia. But the Romans had learned of the link between Hannibal and Philip and, accordingly, of Philip's Adriatic designs. A fleet was sent to Orikos. Philip was forced to burn his ships and to retreat home overland. So had begun the so-called 'First Macedonian War'. The conflict was not notable for battles between Roman and Macedonian forces, for it included none of these, and it was not in any sense resolved by the Peace of Phoinike that brought it to a halt in 205. Its significance was otherwise.

After abandoning any naval pretensions in the west, Philip operated by land, and he was successful, gaining control of the Adriatic port of Lissos in 213. This created a problem for the Romans. To commit a small fleet to the region was one thing, to commit a land army was something else again. An ally in Greece was needed, and one was found in the Aitolian League. To judge from Livy's account (25.23) it seems that the Romans had been angling for the support of the Aitolians for a time before the alliance was struck in 211. To judge from the Polybian record (9.37), it was the Aitolians who dragged the Romans into a Greek conflict. This likely reflects a difference of emphasis rather than of fact. The Aitolians were happy to take advantage of Philip's Roman concerns in order to re-open the questions of the Social War that the Peace of Naupaktos had not really resolved and to extend their own authority at the expense of Macedon; the Romans needed a land-based ally in their conflict with Philip. Each had their own reasons for making common cause with the other against Philip, and this is nowhere clearer than in the alliance itself, of which part is preserved on stone (*SV* III.536; trans. BD 33, Sherk 2; cf. Livy 26.24). What survives seems to begin with the statement that the Aitolians are to make war on Philip and his allies (the list of the latter may be filled in from Polyb. 9.38.5 and 11.5.4: Epeirotes, Achaians, Akarnanians, Boiotians, Thessalians, Euboians, Phokians, Lokrians). It continues:

> If the Romans take by force any of these peoples, let it be permitted, as far as concerns the *demos* (people) of the Romans, for the *demos* of the Aitolians to have these cities and lands; whatever (the) Romans take besides the city and land, let (the) Romans have. If Romans and Aitolians together take any of these cities, let it be permitted, as far as concerns the *demos* (of the Romans) for the Aitolians to have these cities and lands; whatever they take besides the city, let it belong to both together. If any of these cities go over to, or surrender to, the Romans or the Aitolians, [let it be permitted, as far as concerns the] *demos* of the Romans, for the Aitolians to takes these people and the cities and the lands [into their] state . . .

Philip, and especially his allies, will be the object of a Roman–Aitolian war. The Aitolians will gain territory and booty. The Romans will gain from Philip's occupation with the war and indeed from booty as well: the profit from enslavement in particular must have been substantial. The new allies began their co-operation in Akarnania, taking cities and enslaving populations. That set the pattern for the conflict over the next few years, and Philip could only attempt heroically to defend his allies. It was the Social War all over again, only much more vicious. The difference was not lost on Greeks of the time. An Akarnanian envoy at Sparta in 210, endeavouring to dissuade the Spartans from joining the Romans and Aitolians, asks the Aitolian envoy 'But who makes common cause with you at present or what kind of alliance do you invite them (i.e. the Spartans) to enter? Is it not an alliance with barbarians?' (Polyb. 9.37.5–6) The contrast with previous Spartan resistance to the barbarians (in the form of the Persians) is explicitly drawn. After referring to more recent Aitolian history, the Akarnanian continues:

> How, when one knows of this, can one help viewing with suspicion the advance of the Romans and with detestation the unprincipled conduct of the Aetolians in venturing to make such treaties? Already they have robbed the Akarnanians of Oiniadai and Nasos, and it is but the other day that it together with the Romans seized on the unhappy city of Antikyra, selling its inhabitants into slavery. So the Romans are carrying off the women and children to suffer, of course, what those must suffer who fall into the hands of aliens

(*allophyloi*), while the Aitolians divide the houses of the unfortunate people among themselves by lot. A fine alliance this for anyone to determine to join and specially for you Lakedaimonians, who, when you conquered the barbarians, decreed that the Thebans were to pay a tithe to the gods for having decided under compulsion, but alone among the Greeks, to remain neutral during the Persian invasion. (Polyb. 9.39.1–5, trans. Paton)

The Spartans were deaf to these pleas. They joined the new alliance, as did the Messenians around the same time. For both, the present Peloponnesian picture was, we may judge, the more important: the Achaian League was for them the greater threat. Another adherent was Attalos I of Pergamon. He already had connections with the Aitolian League, and he very soon became Rome's most influential ally in the East (a position assumed after his death in 197 by his son Eumenes). The war went on, and revulsion at the nature of its conduct grew apace. Nothing like this, with populations being enslaved, had been seen in Greece for a long time (cf. Tarn and Griffith 1952: 80–2), nor had such 'barbarians' and 'aliens'.

The Social War had been widely seen in the Greek world as a dangerously inter-necine affair. A number of states, including Rhodes, Chios, Byzantion and Ptolemaic Egypt tried to mediate a settlement of it (Polyb. 5.100). It had ended with the Aitolian Agelaos of Naupaktos warning of 'the clouds in the west' and the danger they posed for Greeks (Polyb. 5.104). This recrudescence of the Social War elicited more attempts at mediation from yet more people. The language of mediation is infused with hostility to the Romans. It is informed also by a kind of panhellenism and a related fear about the future. In an address to the Aitolians in 207 a Rhodian speaker refers to numerous attempts by Ptolemy, Rhodes, Chios and Byzantion to bring an end to the war. He begs them 'as if the whole of the islanders and all the Greeks who inhabit Asia Minor were present here and were entreating you to stop the war and decide for peace – for the matter concerns them as much as ourselves – to come to your senses and relent and agree to our request' (Polyb. 11.4.6). He continues:

You say that you are fighting with Philip for the sake of the Greeks, that they may be delivered and may refuse to obey his commands; but as a fact you are fighting for the enslavement and ruin of Greece. This is the story your treaty with the Romans tells, a treaty formerly existing merely in writing, but now seen to be carried out in actual fact. Previously the words of the treaty involved you in disgrace, but now when it is put in action this becomes evident to the eyes of all. Philip, then, is but the nominal pretext of the war; he is in no kind of danger; but as he has for allies most of the Peloponnesians, the Boiotians, the Phokians, the Lokrians, the Thessalians, and Epeirotes, you made the treaty against them all, the terms being that their persons and personal property should belong to the Romans and their cities and lands to the Aitolians. Did you capture a city yourselves you would not allow yourselves to outrage freeman or to burn their towns, which you regard as a cruel proceeding and barbarous; but you have made a treaty by which you have given up to the barbarians the rest of the Greeks to be exposed to atrocious outrage and violence. This was not formerly understood, but now the case of the people of Oreos and that of the unhappy Aiginetans have exposed you to all, Fortune having of set purpose as it were mounted your infatuation on the stage. Such was the beginning of this war, such are already its consequences, and what must we expect its end to be, if all falls out entirely as you wish? Surely the beginning of terrible disaster to all the Greeks. (6) For it is only too evident, I think, that the Romans if they get the war in Italy off their hands – and this will be very shortly, as Hannibal is now confined in quite a small district of Bruttium – will next throw themselves with their whole strength on Grecian lands on the pretext that they are helping the Aitolians against Philip, but really with the intention of conquering the whole country. Should the Romans when they have sub-jected us, determine to treat us kindly, the credit and thanks will be theirs; but if they treat us ill it is they who will acquire the spoil of those they destroy and sovereignty over the survivors, and you will then call the gods to witness then neither any god will be still willing, nor any man still able to help you. (11.5–6.4, trans. Paton; cf. already 10.25 for similar fear about the future)

Evidence for this resurgent panhellenism is found not only in speeches reported by Polybios (on which, see above all, Walbank 1965, esp. 248–9). At precisely the same time as these sentiments were being uttered in Greece, something remarkable was occurring at Magnesia-on-the-Maeander (for the epigraphical dossier from which alone we know about this, Rigsby 1996: 179–279).

Some years before all this (in 221/20) the Magnesians, in response to an appear-ance of their patron deity, Artemis Leukophryene, had sought recognition for a panhellenic festival in her honour and recognition of their city as sacred and inviol-able. The attempt failed for lack of support. They renewed it in 208/7. Envoys were dispatched all over the Greek world, and this time they met with resounding success. Favourable responses came from kings (Ptolemy IV, Attalos I, Antiochus III and his son, and, implied in one text, Philip V), from Leagues (Boiotian, Aitolian, Akarna-nian, Epeirote, Phokian and Achaian), and from dozens of Greek cities throughout the Mediterranean world (all of them, according to the Magnesian decree).

How much this concatenation of panhellenic (and anti-barbarian: anti-Roman, that is) concern and sentiment affected the progress of the war in Greece must remain a matter of conjecture. But there was clearly something in the air. In 206, after concluding peace with Philip (see below) the Aitolians sponsored a wide-ranging appeal from the Dorians of Kytinion for assistance in rebuilding their city, damaged by earthquake in the early 220s and by years of warfare. Their appeal, known only from an inscription from Xanthos in Lykia, was elaborately couched in terms of shared hellenic ancestry (*SEG* 38.1476; cf. Hammond and Walbank 1988: 339; Erskine 2001: 164–5).

In 207 and 206 the Romans contributed little support to their allies. Their great success at the River Metaurus in 207 meant that Hannibal was effectively stranded in the south of Italy, and they focused their attention on him. Attalos withdrew from the conflict to deal with incursions by King Prusias of Bithynia. In 206 Philip, no longer obliged to devote all his effort to the defence of his allies, forced the Aitolians to negotiate a peace. The Romans, recent inactivity notwithstanding, appear to have been willing to carry on the war. In 205 a sizeable force was sent to Epidamnos. Philip came as far as the territory of Apollonia, but the Romans, having failed to draw the Aitolians back into the war, did not go out to meet him. Epeirote mediators had no trouble in persuading Philip to the negotiating table, and the Roman general, Sempronius, did not demur. Peace was agreed at Phoinike in Epeiros in 205. Atinta-nia, attached to Rome since the first Illyrian war, was ceded to Philip, but there were no other territorial adjustments of any significance; the peace effectively re-established the situation before the conflict (Livy 29.12).

But if it made no concrete difference, the Peace of Phoinike redefined the political constellation of Greece in the most striking way. On the one side was Philip, to whom were added in the treaty Prusias, king of Bithynia, the Achaians, Boiotians, Thessalians, Akarnanians and Epeirotes. On the other side were now the Romans, to whom were added the Ilians, King Attalos, Pleuratos, Nabis, tyrant of Sparta, and the Eleians, Messenians and Athenians. Two things were clear. One, that there were now two sides in Greece: Philip and his allies on the one hand, the Romans and their allies on the other. Two, that the settlement was temporary. About this Livy is explicit: peace was voted at Rome 'since, now that the war had shifted to Africa, they wished *for the present* to be relieved of all other wars' (29.12.16; Derow 1979: 6–8).

Roman interests in general were not restricted in the same way. In 205/4 it was decided, in response to omens and the advice of the Sibylline books, to import the cult of the Magna Mater to Rome. A team of illustrious envoys was sent to Pessinous in northwestern Asia Minor to fetch the image of the deity. They were assisted in this by Attalos, and 'five quinqueremes were assigned to the deputation so that in a manner worthy of the dignity of the Roman people it might approach lands where it was desirable that the Roman name should win for itself the highest respect' (Livy 29.11; Erskine 2001: 205–18).

3   The Roman Conquest

For Rome the next few years saw the final stages of the war with Hannibal, which ended with the victory of Scipio Africanus at Zama in North Africa in 202 and the peace imposed upon Carthage in 201, including a huge indemnity of 10,000 talents. This was to be paid over the next 50 years in yearly instalments of 200 talents and is better seen as an insistence by Rome upon the subordination of Carthage than as a serious quest for imperial profit. With the end of that conflict the Romans were indeed relieved of all other serious conflicts (and this in a way they had not been for a very long time). Philip in the meanwhile turned his attention mostly towards the Aegean, where he found himself increasingly at odds with Rhodes and King Attalos. There was some contact between Macedon and Rome during this time. In 203 'allied cities from Greece' are reported to have appealed to Rome against Macedonian depredations (Livy 30.26). The Romans took cognizance of this in a minor way. Also reported is a Macedonian contingent fighting alongside Hannibal at Zama, but the fact that these troops do not appear in Polybios' account of the battle, on which that of Livy is otherwise clearly based, must indicate fabrication (Livy 30.33, Polyb. 15.11). Philip had no reason to provoke Rome, and there is no other reason to think that he did so.

Certainly another conflict between Rome and Macedon began in 200, the so-called second Macedonian war. Polybios' view, that there was only one war between Philip and the Romans, which began with Philip's alliance with Hannibal and ended with the battle of Kynoskephalai in 197, is worth taking very seriously (Polyb. 3.32; cf. Derow 1979: 10–11; Polybios' view finds an echo in Livy (31.1) and later, more strikingly, in Florus (1.23), whose 'first Macedonian war' embraces what are now conventionally known as the first and second). It would seem that for Polybios, as for Livy's Romans (see section 2 above on 29.12.16), the Peace of Phoinike was not seen as concluding the issue between Rome and Philip in any more than a very temporary way. Still, the conflict renewed in 200 was something quite different than what had gone before: it is the circumstances and nature of this renewal that invite attention.

In 201, when the Hannibalic war was finally ended, there arrived at Rome embassies from Attalos and the Rhodians and from the Aitolians (on the date of the Aitolian embassy, see Derow 1979: 7–8). The latter complained of Philip's treatment of them and appealed to the Romans to renew the old conflict. Attalos and the Rhodians, who had been fighting Philip in the Aegean, sought Roman support in their conflict with Philip and against his expansionist campaigns. The Aitolian appeal was rejected. This cannot be taken to indicate any lack of willingness on the part of Rome to engage with Philip: it was at just this time that they did decide to engage. It must indicate something else, and evidently it indicates that the Romans had decided not to engage with Philip in the way that they had done before. They were not unaware of what had been said in Greece about them and their alliance with the Aitolians (on which see section 2 above), and they were about to define themselves to the Greeks in a wholly new way. The reports of Attalos and the Rhodians were taken on board, and an embassy was despatched. For what it shows about this redefinition and about the extent of Roman interest to the east, it is a most extraordinary embassy. The Roman envoys went to Athens, where they met with Attalos and the Rhodians in early spring 200, and where Attalos made clear to the people of Athens the hostility of the Romans (as well as his own and that of the Rhodians) towards Philip (Polyb. 16.25–6). Polybios goes on:

> At the time that the Roman legates were present in Athens Nikanor, Philip's general, overran Attika up to the Academy, upon which the Romans, after sending a herald to him in the first place, met him and asked him to inform Philip that the Romans 'called upon' that king to make war on no Greek states and also to give such compensation to Attalos for the injuries he had inflicted on him as a fair tribunal should pronounce to be just. If he acted so, they added, he might consider himself at peace with Rome, but if he refused to accede the consequences would be the reverse. Nikanor on hearing this departed. The Romans had conveyed the contents of this communication to the Epeirotes at Phoinike in sailing along that coast and to Amynander, going up to Athamania for that purpose. They had also apprised the Aitolians at Naupaktos and the Achaians at Aigion. After having made this statement to Philip through Nikanor they sailed away to meet Antiochos and Ptolemy for the purpose of arranging a settlement. (trans. Paton)

Philip is presented with an ultimatum which takes the form of a Roman order. It is an ultimatum to which he could not possibly accede, at least not without acknowledging Roman dominion in place of his own. This is the first time that the syndrome of orders and obedience, which will characterize and indeed define Rome's *imperium* for some time to come, appears on the hellenic stage (on this syndrome, Derow 1979: 5–6). Whatever were the niceties of Roman fetial procedure at the outset of this war (on the basis of which the people voted for war against Philip 'on account of arms borne against and injuries done to allies of the Roman people', Livy 31.6), this ultimatum had nothing to do with them. It was a clear declaration of intent by Rome to occupy the central position in Greek affairs. And it was, of course, wonderful propaganda: a declaration that the Romans were no longer the 'barbarians' they had been not long before but instead the protectors of Greeks. Philip becomes the villain. As well as to Philip (to whom the ultimatum was delivered in person at Abydos later in 201: Polyb. 16.34; by that time Roman forces were landing in Greece), the message was conveyed to other Greeks, all of whom are allied or connected with Philip. This group includes, pointedly, the Aitolian League: this is indeed the new Rome. And the new Rome has a very wide purview indeed. The Roman embassy was to travel also to Antiochos III and Ptolemy V, who were engaged in the Fifth Syrian War, to bring about a settlement between them. That the request for this intervention came from Ptolemy, whose father had helped the Romans during the Hannibalic war with a subvention of grain (Polyb. 9.11a) and who appears to have solicited Rome's help (Polyb. 15.25), is most likely. Certainly it was Antiochos who was winning the war against Ptolemy: the Roman *démarche* can only have been to the latter's benefit. This was the first contact between Rome and the Seleukid king.

In Greece, the Roman war was initially entrusted to P. Sulpicius Galba, consul of 200. He had been consul in 211 and as proconsul had conducted most of the earlier war: the old Rome had not been entirely eclipsed. Little progress was made, and the Aitolians were received back on side. (On what (if any) formal terms the Aitolians renewed their Roman connection will remain a serious question.) He was succeeded by P. Villius Tappulus, consul of 199, who spent little time in Greece (and most of that dealing with a mutiny of Roman soldiers), before being succeeded by T. Quinctius Flamininus, consul of 198, who arrived in Greece early in his consular year. It was Flamininus (on whose background, Badian 1971), who completed the redefinition of Rome for the Greeks. His diplomatic achievements were many, the most significant amongst them being to secure the alliance of the Achaian League, prominent now under the leadership of Philopoimen. This was accomplished in 198 by the able diplomacy of his brother Lucius (who promised Corinth to the Achaians: see below), aided in no small way by the presence at Corinth of a Roman fleet trained on the northern Peloponnese. Even so, the Achaian decision to abandon Philip for Rome was a close run thing. The League was riven on the question of Rome, and it remained so for the rest of its life.

The adherence of the Achaians enabled Flamininus to put himself at the head of a group of allies. Polybios' account of a meeting between Flamininus and these allies (including Amynander of Athamania and representatives of King Attalos, the Achaians, Rhodians, Aitolians and Athenians) and Philip (accompanied by a Boiotian and an exiled Achaian opponent of the alliance with Rome) in the winter of 198/97 shows that the interests of Rome's allies were to be represented; it shows also how all essential decisions were to remain with Flamininus and Rome (Polyb. 18.1–12). On this occasion ambassadors from Philip and from Flamininus and the allies went to Rome, notionally with an eye to negotiating an end to the war. Philip's envoys were surprised by a question about the king's continued occupation of the 'fetters of Greece' (Chalkis, Demetrias and the Acrocorinth; how they could not have been expecting this is another serious question). With this comes the first secure mention of the idea of the 'freedom of the Greeks' in this context. The idea went back a long way (cf. Gruen 1984: 132–57). The chief contemporary exponent of liberation was Antiochos III (most notably during his sojourn in southwestern Asia Minor in 204–202, where he also sponsored an extensive, and successful, campaign by the Teians for recognition of their city as sacred and inviolable: known only from inscriptions, Rigsby 1996: 280–325). At Rome the negotiations foundered, as no doubt they were intended to do. Flamininus' allies, both Roman and (perhaps unwitting) Greek, secured the continuation of the war and of Flamininus' command. The war came to an end in 197 when Roman and Macedonian armies chanced upon one another at Kynoskephalai in Thessaly. A battle was fought on ground much better suited to the flexible Roman legion than to the Macedonian phalanx. Philip was defeated and obliged to sue for peace.

There was uncertainty in Greece about the nature of the settlement that would come. In Boiotia a hint might have been seen in Flamininus' connivance in the murder of the pro-Macedonian boiotarch Brachylles: the Roman was anxious to gain the adherence of the Boiotians 'because he was looking ahead to Antiochos' (Polyb. 18.43). For public consumption the ten Roman commissioners, dispatched to assist Flamininus in the settlement of Greece, brought with them a decree of the Senate about the peace with Philip. The main points were:

> All the rest of the Greeks in Asia and Europe were to be free and subject to their own laws; Philip was to surrender to the Romans before the Isthmian Games [summer 196] those Greeks subject to his rule and the cities in which he had garrisons; he was to leave free, withdrawing his garrisons from them, the towns of Euromos, Pedasa, Bargylia and Iasos, as well as Abydos, Thasos, Myrina and Perinthos; Flamininus was to write to Prusias in the terms of the Senate's decree about restoring the freedom of Kios.... [Philip was to pay the Romans] a thousand talents, half at once and the other half by instalments extending over ten years. (Polyb. 18.44, trans. Paton)

The most striking thing here is, of course, the extension of the Roman order to cover Asia Minor, where Antiochos was at the time affirming and seeking to increase his dominion (on this dominion and its nature, Ma 1999). In Greece there was widespread approbation. The Aitolians, however, angry at Flamininus' refusal to give them credit for their part in the victory over Philip or proper reward for their participation in the war, observed that the fetters of Greece were being taken over by the Romans and that what was happening was a change of masters for the Greeks and not liberation (Polyb. 18.45.6). There were those who believed them. There was also uncertainty on the Roman side about the fetters, and Flamininus needed his best diplomatic skills in dealing with the ten Roman commissioners:

> [He pointed out to them] that if they wished to gain unmixed renown amongst the Greeks and in general convince all that the Romans had originally crossed over not in their own interest but in that the liberty of Greece, they must withdraw from every place and set free all the cities now garrisoned by Philip. The hesitation felt in the conference was due to the fact that, while a decision had been reached in Rome about all other questions, and the commissioners had definite instructions from the Senate on all other matters, the question of Chalkis, Corinth and Demetrias had been left to their discretion on account of Antiochos, in order that with an eye to circumstances they should take any course on which they determined.... Flamininus persuaded his colleagues to set Corinth free at once, handing it over to the Achaians, as had originally been agreed, while he remained in occupation of the Acrocorinth, Demetrias and Chalkis. (Polyb. 18.45.9–12, trans. Paton)

The question was, evidently, one of how best to deal with Antiochos. For some (led, one imagines, by the senior commissioner, P. Sulpicius Galba) it was to maintain military strongholds in Greece. For Flamininus it was to gain the goodwill of as many Greeks as possible by doing the opposite. Flamininus carried the day. At the Isthmian Games in the summer of 196, the Roman herald proclaimed that the Greeks of Greece who had been under Philip's control (they were named) would be free, free from garrison and tribute, and governed by their own laws. (The list included the Corinthians, the Euboians and the Magnesians of northern Greece, in whose territories lay the three fetters, Acrocorinth, Chalkis and Demetrias, which, in the event, the Romans held garrisoned for another two years, thereby adding further fuel to the Aitolians claims, which Flamininus was still trying to defuse in 194: *RDGE* 33; trans. BD 36, Sherk 4.) The crowd received the announcement with thunderous enthusiasm.

After the games the Roman commissioners turned to deal with envoys from Antiochos. The message was clear and its tone even clearer:

> They ordered him, as regards the cities of Asia, to keep his hands off those which were autonomous and make war on none of them and to withdraw from those previously subject to Ptolemy and Philip which he had recently taken. At the same time they enjoined him not to cross to Europe with an army, for none of the Greeks were any longer being attacked by anyone or the subjects of anyone, and they announced in general terms that some of their body would come to see Antiochos. (Polyb. 18.47, trans. Paton)

The meeting happened at Lysimacheia on the European side of the Hellespont (once a Seleukid possession and now recently reoccupied) later in the summer of 196. The Roman demands were repeated. Antiochos had answers to them. About the autonomous cities of Asia, Antiochos' reply was that 'it was not proper for them to receive their liberty by order of the Romans, but by his own gracious favour' (Polyb. 18.51), which reflects and reveals very nicely an essential difference between the natures of Hellenistic monarchy and Roman *imperium*. The Romans went a step further in their challenge to Antiochos' dominion and invited representatives from Smyrna and Lampsakos to submit their disputes with Antiochos to them. Antiochos suggested the Rhodians as arbitrators, and with that the meeting ended, but not the question of Smyrna and Lampsakos. The Lampsakenes had themselves already been in contact with Rome by way of an embassy in the winter of 197/6 (for all this *SIG*³ 591; trans. BD 35, Sherk 5). Referring to their kinship with Rome, through association with Athena Ilias (on the importance of Troy in dealings between Greeks and Rome, see Erskine 2001), they had sought from the Senate to be included in the peace that was being made with Philip. Significantly, the Senate had granted this and promised to protect them. Also significantly, the Lampsakene envoys, on their way to Rome, had approached (and gained promises of protection from) Roman officers in Greece, including Lucius Flamininus, in charge of the fleet, and a quaestor: the Lampsakenes approached high-ranking Romans as they would have approached high-ranking courtiers of a hellenistic king. The Lampsakenes may be forgiven for dealing in the only way they knew. What the Roman officials thought they were doing is another question; the tendency of Roman officials to behave in such a plenipotentiary way would only increase.

Flamininus and the Roman army remained in Greece. A reason for doing so was found in the occupation of Argos by Nabis of Sparta (erstwhile ally of the Romans), against whom Flamininus led his allies in a war of liberation. The business was soon accomplished, and by 194 Flamininus was travelling about Greece arranging things. An indication of Roman intentions may be found in his organization of Thessaly, where power was put in the hands of the wealthy (Livy 34.51, not the only indication of such Roman preference). In 194 he finally vacated the fetters and led the victorious forces back to Rome for a magnificent triumph. Even before Flamininus' return Scipio Africanus had been elected to the consulship as war with Antiochos was envisaged at Rome (Livy 34.53).

Contact between Antiochos and Rome was renewed in the winter of 194/93 when the king sent an embassy seeking friendship and alliance, and thereby normalization of relations (Livy 34.57–9). The response was uncompromising: either Antiochos stayed out of Europe or the Romans would extend their connections with cities in Asia Minor. Antiochos' envoys had the power to agree to nothing of the kind. The matter was postponed and the Senate dispatched an embassy to Antiochos.

On the same occasion, one of Antiochos' envoys laid before the Senate the request of Teos for recognition of its city and territory as inviolable (this had been sought from Greek states a dozen years before: Rigsby 1996: 280–325). The Roman reply of 193 is preserved on stone. The Teian request is granted, but in a particularly and revealingly Roman way, both in the special relationship to the gods that is claimed and, above all, in the conditional reference to the future at the end:

> ...And that we continue always to value most highly reverence towards the gods one might best reckon from the favour with which we have for these reasons met from the supernatural. We are convinced, moreover, that the special honour we show to the divine has become thoroughly clear to all from many other things as well. Wherefore, for these reasons and on account of our good-will towards you and on account of the esteemed ambassador, it is our decision that your city and land are to be sacred, as is even now the case, and inviolable and free from tribute at the hands of the *demos* of the Romans, and we shall try to increase both the honours to the god and our kindnesses to you, so long as you maintain your good-will towards us even after this. (*RDGE* 34; trans. BD 39, Sherk 8)

As well as meeting with Antiochos, the Roman envoys toured widely. They returned to Rome in the spring of 192 and reported that there was 'no sufficiently ripe cause for war' against anyone except Nabis of Sparta (Livy 35.22), who had occupied coastal towns in Lakonia in contravention of the Roman settlement. A force was dispatched against Nabis. The absence of a sufficiently ripe cause for war against Antiochos did not prevent the Romans from preparing for war against him. Both consuls of 192 had been held in readiness for that. An army and fleet were made ready for one of the consuls to be elected for 191, and in the summer of 192 a force under the praetor Baebius (whose province had been changed from Spain) was sent to mainland Greece (see Livy 35 for Roman dispositions during 192).

In the autumn of 192 two things happened almost simultaneously. Well into October Antiochos sailed with a small force to Demetrias. The Aitolians, whose manoeuvres against Rome and (increasingly) in favour of Antiochos had continued (Badian 1959), had prepared the way, and a mission led by Flamininus to shore up support for Rome in Greece had failed in general, and in particular at Demetrias, where the people believed they were to be handed over to Philip in return for his support of Rome against Antiochos. In early November Rome declared war against Antiochos. (This happened at the beginning of the Roman consular year 191, but the Roman calendar was then seriously out of joint with the solar year: Derow 1973b, 1976, with the small caveat noted at Walbank 1979a: vi.) The Roman declaration had nothing to do with Antiochos' crossing: no connection is made between the two in Livy, and the chronology tells decisively against. Two quite separate questions are, accordingly, raised. One: why Antiochos crossed into Greece when and as he did; two: why Rome declared war against him.

The answer to the question about Rome is, in general, quite clear. Even before the end of the war against Philip the Romans had had Antiochos in their sights. The dealings between the two have been characterized as a kind of 'cold war' (Badian 1959). It was more a matter of the Romans making a series of demands, with Antiochos trying to find ways of responding to them: this was not unlike the situation with Philip a few years before, when the Romans ordered him to make war on no Greeks, and the outcome could scarcely have been different. In detail, a question does remain. In the spring of 192 the Romans had found 'no sufficiently ripe reason for war' against Antiochos. When did they find one, and what was it? The answer to this may be found in the offer, made by Antiochos after the war had begun, to withdraw from the cities of Lampsakos, Smyrna, and Alexandria Troas, 'from which the war took its beginnings' (Polyb. 21.13). Exactly what lies behind this is beyond recovery, but the implication is clear. And we know that the Senate had undertaken to protect Lampsakos at the time of the Lampsakene embassy of 197/6 (see above). Nothing similar is known for sure about the other two cities, but it is known that the inhabitants of Smyrna in 195 dedicated a sanctuary to the deified City of Rome (Tac. *Ann.* 4.56), perhaps in search of goodwill and benefit, perhaps as a gesture of thanks for something. Most striking of all might be the form of the Roman declaration of war against Antiochos (Livy 36.1). It contains no reference to wrongs done by Antiochos, whether to the Romans or to their allies, and in this respect it is unique amongst surviving Roman declarations of war. The people were asked simply whether they wished to declare war against Antiochos and those who followed him. This was a war for conquest outright, perhaps indeed the only one of its kind during this period.

Antiochos' conduct late in 192 may be seen in general as a response to the determined pressure of Rome in the preceding years, expressed in a series of orders. In particular there were dealings (of which we have not the details) to do with Lampsakos, Smyrna and Alexandria Troas, and a Roman force had entered mainland Greece in the summer. When the Aitolians invited Antiochos to Demetrias, the point had come where he had to respond. That he had not been planning this is indicated by the evident insufficiency of the force with which he crossed. This must indicate also that he hoped to find widespread antipathy towards Rome in Greece and correspondingly widespread support for himself. One of the most interesting things in the whole affair is that it seems at least part of his hope was by no means unfounded. Polybios reports that when the Achaians declared war on Antiochos four months before the Roman crossing into Greece in early spring 191 – around the time of Antiochos' crossing, that is – nearly all the other Greeks were alienated from the Romans (39.6). Even allowing for some exaggeration on Polybios' part (but there is no evidence to suggest such), this is a strong statement. Apparently the enthusiasm so loudly voiced at the Isthmian Games in 196 had over the next four years largely evaporated in Greece. It is difficult, if not impossible, to trace this development in detail, but one must conclude in general that the freedom the Greeks believed they were getting was different from the freedom the Romans believed they were bestowing. That disaffection from Rome did not translate into support for Antiochos and his Aitolian allies is less of a surprise. In the case of Epeiros the reason is known. They would be the first to receive the Roman onslaught, and, as such they would not join unless substantial military protection were provided for them, and Antiochos, who had crossed with a small force, was in no position to do this (Polyb. 20.3). In some other places, for example in Boiotia and Thessaly (see above), one may imagine that those whom the Romans had helped into power were glad of their situation and accordingly desirous of maintaining the authority of their benefactors.

The war itself was not a long affair. The Romans were quick off the mark. Their fleet was in the Aegean in time to intercept Antiochos' transports early in 191. Antiochos himself was defeated in battle at Thermopylai by the army that arrived, also early in the year, under M'. Acilius Glabrio, consul of 191. He retreated to Asia Minor whither he was followed and then defeated again at Magnesia-by-Sipylos by the Romans under L. Cornelius Scipio (Africanus' brother, consul of 190, who took the cognomen Asiaticus) in January 189. The Aitolians were reduced in 189 by M. Fulvius Nobilior, consul. They were obliged by treaty to swear to uphold the majesty and *imperium* of the Roman people and to pay an indemnity of 500 talents, sufficient to bankrupt them. Antiochos was obliged to cede all his territory to the west of the Tauros mountains and to pay an indemnity of 15,000 talents, 3000 at once with the rest to be paid in annual instalments: this was the most profitable war the Romans had ever fought, and the indemnity from Antiochos may reasonably be judged to have altered forever the nature of Rome's public economy. By the settlement known as the Peace of Apameia the Romans organized the Greek East as they saw fit. It had not been a war fought alongside allies, but those who had supported Rome were rewarded, most notably Eumenes of Pergamon and the Rhodians in Asia Minor. But all the rewards were precarious, wholly dependent upon continuing support of Rome's dominion.

In the space of twelve years (200–188) the Romans had reduced the two greatest survivors of Alexander the Great's empire, the Macedonian and Seleukid kingdoms. In doing so they established in their place, throughout the Greek world, the dominion of Rome. For Polybios this was not established until 167 and the end of the Macedonian monarchy. He had his own reasons for choosing this date (cf. Walbank 1994), and there is a formal sense in which the dominion of Rome could not replace that of Macedon whilst the kingdom of Macedon still existed. But in practical terms, as the sequel shows, the point had effectively been reached where, as Polybios put it (3.4), there was nothing left but 'to give heed to the Romans and obey them in their orders'. Roman supremacy is revealingly recognized by Eumenes. In granting a request made to him by the inhabitants of Tyriaion in rural southeastern Phrygia he wrote, not long after 188: 'any (favour) bestowed on you by me at this moment would be durable, since I have full authority by virtue of having received it from the Romans who gained power both by war and by treaty' (Jonnes and Ricl 1997). That Rome's authority was to be uniquely supreme was also the Roman view.

4   The Beginning of Roman Rule

The post-Apameia era began as it was to continue for some time, with numerous embassies from the Greek world to Rome, as individuals and groups sought Roman support for their own purposes. Rome was, and was perceived as, the sole arbiter of affairs. They were the 'cops of the world' (Ochs 1966). Many were there in the spring of 187. More than ever before were there in the spring of 183, as the situation became ever clearer. Amongst the most enthusiastic were Eumenes, who came to denounce Philip for taking possession of some Thracian cities, and a group of Spartans, who came to protest about Achaian treatment of Sparta (which had been brought into the Achaian League in 192). In both cases the Senate took cognizance of the complaints. In the case of Macedon, this was the beginning of a period of pressure by Rome upon Philip which resulted, according to Polybios, in the decision of that king to formulate plans of military resistance to Rome. This was, perhaps, not surprising. Rome's war against Philip had been ended when conflict with Antiochos was already envisaged and with that conflict in mind; as it drew nearer, concessions had been made to Philip to keep him on side. But the Romans were ever slow to forgive. At the same time, Eumenes had established himself as the most reliable king in the east. If the Roman decision to lend support in the case of the discontented group at Sparta is more surprising, it is also the more revealing. The Achaians had recently been the most reliable state in Greece, but in accepting the appeal from some Spartans, the Senate effectively condoned a breach in the constitution of the League: dealings with foreign states were the province of the League, and not of individual cities within it, let alone of groups of individuals within the cities. The effect, inevitably, was to foster dissension, and the possibility of fragmentation, within the Peloponnese and within the League. Whether the Romans intended to do this is another question. Probably not. The power of Rome to decide things had been won by war and by treaty, as Eumenes put it. Roman policy consisted in the exercise of that power; there was little need to manipulate people. By seeking the support or approval of Rome, people manipulated and weakened themselves and thereby affirmed that power. The Roman response to the Spartans' *démarche* is perhaps the sort of thing Polybios had in mind when he said, writing of a later time and context but with reference to the period before 168, that 'measures of this kind are very frequent among the Romans, by which they avail themselves with profound policy of the mistakes of others to augment and strengthen their own empire, under the guise of granting favours and benefiting those who commit the errors' (31.10.7, trans. Shuckburgh; cf. Derow 1979: 14 n. 39). This more (or less) cynical view also has its place in the interpretation of the years after Apameia.

There were still in Achaia in the 180s those who believed (or hoped) that it was still possible to deal with the Romans on a basis of *isologia*, on the basis, that is, that genuine dialogue was possible, that the laws and institutions of the Achaians could carry weight against the force of Roman orders, that expressions of Roman power could be attenuated by reasoned argument. They were deceived in their belief (or hope). Whilst the question of Sparta was still unsettled, Messene revolted from the Achaian League. The Achaians sought Roman support. Rome's temporizing response 'made it entirely clear to everyone that so far from shirking and not caring about the less important items of foreign affairs, they were displeased if all matters were not referred to them and if everything was not done in accordance with their decision' (Polyb. 23.17). In the end, the Achaians dealt successfully with both Sparta and Messene. An embassy was sent to Rome to report this. One of the Achaian envoys, Kallikrates of Leontion, told the Senate that in all the democratic states of Greece there were two groups, one which advocated adherence to Roman orders at the expense of local institutions and one which did not. The latter were more popular with the population at large; if the Romans wanted their orders obeyed, they must support those who promised obedience. Polybios reckoned that it was 'now for the first time that the Senate adopted the aim of weakening those members of the several states who worked for the best, and of strengthening those who, rightly or wrongly, appealed to its authority' (24.10). But this had been the Roman way for some time: Kallikrates was not responsible for a change in Roman policy, although he was responsible for denouncing Polybios as insufficiently pro-Roman after the war against Perseus and thereby securing the latter's deportation to Rome. Kallikrates himself, armed with Rome's approbation, returned to be elected to the chief magistracy of the Achaian League.

It might have gone on that way for some time, with the combination of Roman orders and Rome's adherents gradually eroding Greek independence, but the situation was significantly altered in 179 with the death of Philip V and the accession of his son Perseus. Philip's other son, Demetrios, had fallen prey to the blandishments of Romans who wished to see him succeed to the Macedonian throne in preference to Perseus and victim at home to what was effectively a charge of treason; his father was obliged to order his execution. Perseus began his reign by renewing Macedon's alliance with Rome and by seeking favour in Greece at large. In the latter, which amounted to a resuscitation of the good name and repute of Macedon, he was remarkably successful. Alliances and connections were formed or renewed, with Prusias, with Seleukos, with Delphi and with Rhodes. Early in his reign, his half-sister married Prusias II, and he himself married Laodike, daughter of Seleukos IV; at Delphi, 'liberated' from Aitolian control by the Romans in 191 and since then the preserve of pro-Romans, he regained two Macedonian votes in the Delphic Amphiktyony; in return for a gift of timber, the Rhodians escorted Perseus' Seleukid bride to Macedon. Rome noticed. In 178 an appeal from the Lykians against Rhodes met with favour at Rome. By the settlement of 188 the Lykians had been given over to the Rhodians; now the Romans, apprised of the Rhodian escort and rapprochement with Perseus, decided that that had not been the case. Perseus himself did nothing hostile towards Rome. He did not need to: his growing influence and popularity amongst Greeks (he very nearly succeeded in normalizing relations with the Achaians, but Kallikrates persuaded them that that would be against the wishes of Rome and thereby carried the day) meant that he was an alternative focus for Greek political attention. The nature of Rome's dominion was such as not to allow any alternative focuses.

In Greece and areas adjacent the growth of Perseus' popularity and influence was matched by diminution in that of Eumenes, who had based his authority upon Roman supremacy. In 172 Eumenes went to Rome and denounced Perseus (whilst noting his success at winning support amongst the Greeks at the expense of Rome) at length. For the Romans that was enough, particularly in a time of unrest, which the 170s in Greece certainly were (problems of debt and the threat of civil war arising therefrom were especially rife in Aitolia, Thessaly and the north). Preparations for the war began, and an embassy went to Greece, led by Q. Marcius Philippus. Philippus tricked Perseus into accepting the possibility that peace with Rome was still possible (he prided himself upon this trickery on his return to Rome; most approved) and did what he could to disarm support for Perseus (notably in Boiotia, where he secured the dissolution of the Boiotian League). The possibility of peace was illusory. The consul entrusted with the war against Perseus reached Greece in 171 even earlier in the year than had been managed in 191. The Roman accusations against Perseus were inscribed at Delphi, presumably at the same time (*SIG*[3] 643; trans. Sherk 19; BD 44). These latter were effectively a repetition of the list of allegations that Eumenes had brought to Rome in 172. Amongst them was the accusation that Perseus was fomenting social revolutions (*neoterismoi*) in the states of Greece. Rome was defending an order of things. The freedom of the Greeks was no longer an issue, even in the propaganda. Nor were alliances. This was a Roman war, and the Romans chose to fight it without military allies: offers of assistance were declined.

Early in the war Perseus defeated the Romans in a cavalry engagement. Though of no special military moment, it evoked a groundswell of support across Greece for the king (Polyb. 27.9–10: Polybios does his best to persuade that this did not betoken real affection for Perseus, or hostility to Rome, on the part of the rank and file; one may wonder if he intended his defence of the Greeks as much for a contemporary audience as for a more distant posterity). The early years of the war were marked more by the indiscipline and rapacity of the Romans, troops and generals alike, than by military success. Order was restored in 168 when L. Aemilius Paullus (consul in 182 and now again) took command, and the inevitable triumph of Italian manpower came at the battle of Pydna in June 168. The Illyrian King Genthios, who had allied himself to Perseus, was defeated in the same year after a very short campaign.

The military challenge to Rome's control was at an end. Unencumbered by obligations, the Romans proceeded to the settlement of Greece. Something is known of the arrangement of affairs in Achaia, Aitolia and Epeiros:

> During the year before the battle the Achaeans and Aetolians had been treated with circumspection and a measure of indulgence. During the year following it Roman ambassadors visited the Achaeans again. This time they informed them that one thousand individuals (among them Polybius), whose loyalty had become suspect, were to be deported to Italy. This list was drawn up by Callicrates and those of his party. This was harsh, but gentle when compared to the handling of Aetolia, where 550 leading men were murdered while Roman soldiers surrounded the council-chamber and others driven into exile (Livy 45.28.7). A fate even more special was reserved for Epirus, particularly for the Molossians, who had taken the side of Perseus during the war and from among whom had originated the plot to kidnap the consul Hostilius in 170. After the laxity of the earlier years of the war the Roman army had had discipline imposed upon it. The patience of the soldiers was rewarded when Aemilius Paullus led them home in 167. In accordance with a decree of the Senate seventy towns of Epirus (mostly Molossian) were given to them to plunder. One hundred and fifty thousand people were said to have been sold into slavery as a result of Paullus' march to the sea (Polyb. 30.15).... In these and the other states of mainland Greece the ascendancy of the pro-Romans was assured by deportations, bloodbaths and fear. For the moment, however, the states remained intact. (Derow 1989: 317)

The warring kingdoms were dismembered. Macedon was divided into four rigorously separate states and Illyria into three. In both cases these states were to pay to Rome as tribute half what had been paid as taxes to their kings. This was, on the one hand, the available alternative to an indemnity; it was also an enduring sign of subject status. So was Roman dominion in Greece insisted upon and re-established.

Differently striking, and certainly portentous, was the Roman treatment of Rhodes and Eumenes. Rhodes had not supported Perseus in the war, or opposed Rome, but it was home to a significant pro-Macedonian faction. In 169 Q. Marcius Philippus tricked the Rhodians into thinking that Rome would welcome an attempt to mediate an end to the Macedonian war. The mediation came in June 168 and was, of course, far from welcome. Delos was declared a free port, a very damaging blow indeed to the Rhodian economy which was so dependent upon harbour taxes. It might have been worse: there were those at Rome who wanted war against Rhodes. This was successfully opposed by, amongst others, Cato the Elder, who had a very clear notion of why the Rhodians had acted as they did and of what it was all about (his words preserved by Aulus Gellius 6.4.16):

> And I really think that the Rhodians did not wish us to end the war as we did, with a victory over king Perseus. But it was not the Rhodians alone who had that feeling, but I believe that many peoples and many nations agreed with them. And I am inclined to think that some of them did not wish us success, not in order that we might be disgraced, but because they feared that if there were no one of whom we stood in dread, we should do whatsoever we chose. I think, then, that it was with an eye to their own freedom that they held that opinion, in order not to be under our sole dominion and enslaved to us.

Eumenes, who had done more than anyone to help Rome into the war against Perseus, was rejected outright by the Romans as soon as it was over. When he arrived in Italy on his way to Rome to offer his congratulations, he was ordered to depart the country forthwith. It was said that he had sought to make common cause with Perseus against Rome. This seems scarcely credible. But, if it was not that, what was his crime? Perhaps there did not have to be one. With Macedon gone, Eumenes' Pergamon was the most influential (and popular) Greek player left on the Greek stage: exactly what Eumenes had wanted, exactly what the Romans did not. Returning to Greece after his dismissal from Italy, Eumenes was met by a delegation from the Ionian League, who presented him with a very honorific decree indeed which praised him as 'common benefactor of the Greeks' and bestowed great and public honours upon him (known from Eumenes' letter accepting the honours, *OGIS* 763; trans. BD 47): this was surely seen as unwelcome competition, whether or not it was intended as such (on the idea of Romans as common benefactors, Erskine 1994). Roman policy towards Pergamon in the years following continued in the same vein and did much to humble and destabilize that kingdom. Polybios remarks that 'the harsher the conduct of the Romans to Eumenes the more attached to him did the Greeks become' (31.6.6). A sure sign of things to come. Pergamon was bullied into trepid docility (see *RC* 61; BD 50; Sherk 29), but others would not be, not in Greece in 146, not in Asia in 88.

FURTHER READING

The first port of call for an extended narrative of this period is *Cambridge Ancient History* VIII (2nd edition, 1989; with references and extensive bibliography). The chapters by Holleaux in the first edition of volumes VII (1928) and VIII (1930) remain unsurpassed for elegance (the original French versions, even more elegant, may be found in Holleaux 1952 and 1957), even if the necessity to disagree frequently imposes itself. As indeed it does with Holleaux 1921, with which modern study of Roman expansion in the Greek world may be reckoned to have begun and which should still constitute essential reading. Two monumental monographs on the subject appeared in the 1980s, Gruen 1984 and Ferrary 1988. Both are essential reading (and contain full bibliographies). The former is deservedly the most influential book on the subject to have appeared since Holleaux 1921 and the one with which there is perhaps most disagreement in the preceding pages; the world around the historian changes. Prior to those, and reacted to by those but still rightly influential, are Badian 1958a and W. Harris 1979, who did so much to define basic questions still under discussion: as it has been put, with some risk of oversimplification, 'Badian's Romans like clients / they're not very big on alliance / for Harris they're mean / and psychotically keen / on glory, on war, and on triumphs'. But at the base of it all lie above all the incomparable Polybios of Megalopolis, Livy of Patavium, and the evidence of inscriptions; the full incorporation of the last into the story has still some way to go. Most of the lines of narrative and interpretation, not separable things, in the preceding pages have been put forward or adumbrated in Derow 1970, 1973a, 1979, 1984, 1989, 1990, 1991. In addition to the items cited in these pages, a few further suggestions for reading can be made: Briscoe 1973, 1981, Freeman 1893, de Ste Croix 1981, Walbank 1944 and Dao 2002, the last a very recent and resonant reminder of the interest of this period of history, and of the importance of studying it, for the world of today. There are a number of less recent works in both categories; they exemplify precision and elegance of thought and expression and illustrate the importance of passion for the writing of history. All the more modern books referred to contain hugely useful bibliographies amongst much else.

CHAPTER FIVE

Subjection and Resistance: to the Death of Mithradates

Brian McGing

1 Introduction

On 29 August 168 BC Isias wrote a letter to her husband Hephaistion urging him to leave the temple of Sarapis in the old Egyptian capital of Memphis, where he was delaying, and come home:

> When I received your letter..., in which you announce that you are in seclusion in the Sarapeion at Memphis, for the news that you are well, I straightway thanked the gods. But about your not coming home, when all the others who had been secluded there have come, I am ill-pleased: having steered myself and your child through such bad times and been driven to every extremity owing to the price of corn I thought that now at least, with you at home, I should enjoy some respite... (*UPZ* I 59 = *Sel.Pap.* I 97)

Hephaistion was very probably a soldier in the army of the Ptolemies who had been involved in the recent war against Antiochos IV of Syria (169–8 BC), and had stopped off in Memphis on his way home. We cannot be sure exactly what he was doing in the Sarapeion: it would be nice to think he was celebrating his release from the army, but it is more likely he was trying to improve his finances (D. J. Thompson 1988: 230–1). It is not often that we get a reflection of great events in the lives of ordinary people, but one of the most famous displays of Roman arrogance and power lay behind Hephaistion's decommissioning from the army. Just a few weeks before Isias sent her letter, the Roman legate C. Popillius Laenas had confronted Antiochos at Eleusis, a suburb of Alexandria, and demanded that he cease his assault on Egypt (which was on the verge of final success) and withdraw to Syria. When Antiochos asked for time to consult his advisors, Popillius drew a circle around him in the sand and said he must answer before leaving the circle (Polyb. 29.27). Antiochos wisely backed down, and in due course Hephaistion found himself free to go home.

No doubt Isias knew little or nothing of Popillius and the dramatic events taking place during the difficult summer when her husband was off at the war. The Greek politician and historian, Polybios, on the other hand, was right at the centre of what was happening in those exciting times and provides our most important historical source. He understood it was Rome's victory over Perseus, king of Macedon, at the battle of Pydna, on 22 June 168, that forced Antiochos to yield to Popillius' 'diplomacy'. In fact victory in this Third Macedonian War (172–168) marked, for Polybios, a watershed. Roman rule was now established in the Mediterranean, not in the sense of a territorial empire, but to the extent that for all the peoples of the region the parameters of what was politically possible were now seriously circumscribed: obey Rome's orders or face destruction in war (Derow 1979). This may have been clear to Polybios in retrospect, but not everyone necessarily accepted it at the time. In the century covered by this chapter, from the defeat of Perseus to the death of Mithradates Eupator in 63 BC, Hellenistic armies fought five major wars against Rome in the Greek east: the Macedonian pretender Andriskos, the Achaian League, the Attalid pretender Aristonikos and the famous king of Pontos, Mithradates VI Eupator, all asserted their independence in war, but without success. Ironically each bid for freedom drew Rome a little further into the Greek world: in 168 Rome held no territory whatever in the eastern Mediterranean; in 63 she had a string of provinces and protectorates in the region. If Pydna marked the end of one process – the establishment of Roman dominance – the struggle against Mithradates marked another – the commitment of Rome to empire (Kallet-Marx 1995: 341).

The big political story of the period for the Greek world, then, was undoubtedly its relationship with the new Mediterranean superpower; but it was not the only story. Even in geopolitical terms, there was one other major player in the region – Parthia – and for the Seleukids at least, it was their main problem: they succumbed not so much to Roman interference, irritating and debilitating as that was, but to the irresistible force of Parthian expansion. And in the matter of organizing their own internal affairs and their own relationships with each other, the monarchies and cities of the Greek east went about their business in the accustomed fashion. Arbitrations, alliances, treaties, marriages, benefactions, were the very stuff of Hellenistic inter-state relationships; and they continued as before. Although Rome had now effectively forced herself into membership of the club of Hellenistic states, this did not fundamentally affect the continuation of normal Hellenistic practices: the Greeks simply accepted the Senate, indeed invited it, as one of the participants in the diplomatic processes of the Greek east (Gruen 1984: Vol. I). And the new member did not have to be involved in everything: even wars, if they were sufficiently distant or unimportant, could sometimes be conducted without reference to Rome. In spite of these continuities, however, there was, not surprisingly, a new unease among the Greeks. The Romans might be content to play the power game largely by Greek rules, but military superiority meant that they could change the rules whenever they liked. Realization of this threat caused some individual Greek politicians to spend a great deal of time looking over their shoulder, nervously gauging likely Roman reaction to events. And with good reason. If at times Roman policy in the Greek east seemed distinctly lackadaisical and unconcerned, it is also the case that very little happened without at least attracting an investigative commission from the Senate. An examination of the 160s and 150s will bring out some of the main trends of the period.

2 The Aftermath of Pydna

The Roman settlement of affairs after their victory at the battle of Pydna must have shaken the Greeks. Naturally, those who opposed Rome suffered the worst. Most dramatic was the suppression of the Macedonian monarchy: the line of kings stretching back into archaic times was now brought to an end and the kingdom split into four independent republics, tributary to Rome, but 'free' (Livy 45.29–30; Gruen 1984: 423–9). Macedon's ally, Illyria, shared the same fate. In Epeiros, which had sided with Perseus, 150,000 people were said to have been sold into slavery (Polyb. 30.15). Perhaps even more shocking was the treatment of those states, including friends and allies, who took no part in the fighting, but about whose loyalty Rome was not satisfied. On the mainland leading Aitolians were murdered in their council-chamber, and a thousand Achaians were deported to Italy (Derow, this volume).

Elsewhere Rhodes, a staunch ally and friend of Rome, suffered badly for its ill-timed attempt at mediation (Gruen 1984: 569–72; Habicht 1989: 336–8; Ager 1996: no. 121). Karia and Lykia, granted to them twenty years earlier as a reward for their help in the war against Antiochos III, were now taken away; so too were the valuable towns of Kaunos and Stratonikeia – they provided an annual income of 120 talents – although their acquisition by Rhodes was nothing to do with Rome; and, worst of all, Delos was made a free port, attracting business that reduced Rhodes' own harbour income from one million drachmas to 150,000 (Polyb. 30.31). Desperate to regain the favour of Rome the Rhodians tenaciously sought a treaty, finally succeeding in 164/3. It is difficult to imagine that such severe punishment can have resulted solely from an offer of mediation by loyal allies. Both Prusias II of Bithynia and Ptolemy VI of Egypt also offered to arbitrate, without annoying Rome in the least, although Prusias subsequently felt it advisable to behave with a degree of servility that disgusted Polybios (30.18). A growing sense of invincibility might have seen the Senate happy to cut smug allies down to size, but there is also room for suspicion that Rhodes was not quite so unambiguously loyal as they later made out.

The Senate also harboured grave suspicions about the loyalty during the war of another good friend of theirs, Eumenes II of Pergamon (Polyb. 29.5; 30.1). In spite of the military assistance he afforded Rome, he was now humiliated and his authority in Asia Minor undermined (Gruen 1984: 573–8): his Galatian subjects had rebelled in 168, and, possibly, received encouragement from Rome; when Eumenes travelled to Rome to ask the Senate for help, he was refused a hearing and turned back at Brundisium; and when he finally defeated the Galatians the Senate declared them free. In 164 the Roman commissioner C. Sulpicius invited accusations against Eumenes and spent ten days in Sardis listening to them (Polyb. 31.6). But, as Polybios observed, the more Rome mistreated Eumenes, the better the Greeks liked him.

Virtually the only Greek state to be rewarded by Rome after the war was Athens (Habicht 1997: 213–19). At the beginning of the second century in their need for protection against Macedon the Athenians had turned to Rome, and thereafter wisely pursued a solidly pro-Roman policy. In 167 the Senate awarded them Delos, Lemnos and the land of Haliartos (Polyb. 30.20). Polybios was highly critical of the Athenian acquisition of Haliartos – they should have striven harder to protect its freedom, rather than grab it for themselves – and was obviously pleased to observe that in getting Delos and Lemnos they 'were taking the wolf by the ears' (a reference to later disputes). Of course they were no longer a major military power. Perhaps this weakness, combined with a reputation as a great intellectual centre, enabled them to pursue their own, and benefit from other states', diplomatic policies that did not have to reflect Roman prejudices (Habicht 1997: 220–7). While Rome had defeated Antiochos III in 190 and continued to interfere troublesomely in Seleukid affairs thereafter, this did not prevent Athens enjoying excellent relations with Seleukos IV, and particularly with Antiochos IV, whose lavish sponsorship of work to complete the huge Peisistratid temple of Olympian Zeus in Athens had still not seen it finished when he died in 164. If the Senate chose to humiliate Pergamon after the defeat of Perseus, Athens continued to maintain, and reap the benefits of, its close friendship with the Attalid kingdom (the most spectacular visual evidence of this friendship was provided by the stoas of Eumenes II and of his brother Attalos II). The Ptolemies had acted as Athens' main protector in the third century, and although Rome took over this role in the second century, the Athenians remained the closest of friends with the Ptolemies and their courtiers (Habicht 1992: 68–90).

If Ptolemies and Seleukids could continue to pursue independent diplomatic policies, they could also conduct internal wars in their own kingdoms. In the early 160s Ptolemy VI had to put down a dangerous native revolt in the north of Egypt led by Dionysios Petosarapis and another one in the Thebaid (Diod. 31.15a; 17b; McGing 1997: 289–95). Antiochos IV, when faced with what seemed to be a Jewish insurrection during his invasion of Egypt, reacted with a ferocious, but unwise, persecution of the Jews – the famous 'abomination of desolation' (Daniel 11:31). If the Jews had not actually been in revolt when Antiochos thought they were, they certainly took up arms when he attempted to destroy their religion (Gruen, this volume). Antiochos quickly backed off when he realized his mistake, but he had set in motion the Maccabaean revolt, which was to plague the Seleukid government in the coming generations. Antiochos also had to face revolt in his eastern territories. Having been rebuffed in his attempt to conquer Egypt, he turned his attention to the problem. In 166 he held a magnificent parade at Daphne in the outskirts of Antioch (Polyb. 30.25–6; Diod. 31.16.2). Although not entirely military in character, it contained an impressive display of military might. Polybios thought the intention was to outdo Aemilius Paullus, who the year before had celebrated his victory at Pydna in similar fashion. No doubt Antiochos' intentions were various. Although he had yielded to Rome, he had also won a great victory over the Egyptians. A demonstration of power, then, to his own people and to Rome, a celebration of victory and perhaps an announcement of his new campaign in the east, launched the following year. We know very little of what happened on this campaign or even of what Antiochos intended, as the sources are poor and he died in 164, too soon to identify his precise objectives, but Seleukid control in the east was crumbling and Antiochos was clearly trying to shore it up (Mørkholm 1966: 166–80; Habicht 1989: 350–3). While this was all far too distant to elicit Roman intervention, it is interesting to observe that the Senate still kept a watchful and worried eye on Antiochos. Gaius Sulpicius and Manius Sergius were despatched to check that he was not conniving with Pergamon to attack Rome (Polyb. 31.1.6–8). And the parade at Daphne had not gone unnoticed: Tiberius Gracchus had led a delegation to investigate, but succumbed to Antiochos' charm and found nothing to cause concern (Polyb. 30.27).

That the Senate was concerned, and was ready to meddle in Seleukid affairs, is evident from their treatment of the royal succession. The seeds of Seleukid dynastic weakness had been sown in the aftermath of Rome's victory over Antiochos III in 189. Antiochos' younger son, the future Antiochos IV, had been held as a hostage in Rome, while his elder brother, Seleukos IV, became king in 187. On Seleukos' assassination in 175, Antiochos IV won the throne against the obvious legal claims of Seleukos' eldest son, Demetrios, who then replaced Antiochos IV as hostage in Rome. Thus was established a most damaging split in the Seleukid royal house, with two branches of the family contending for the throne (Sherwin-White and Kührt 1993: 221). It was a split which, with only a minimum of effort, Rome was able and pleased to exploit. When Antiochos IV died Demetrios made a strong plea that he be allowed to take up the throne, but the Senate backed Antiochos V, the young son of Antiochos IV, because, in the opinion of Polybios (31.2.7, trans. Paton), 'they were suspicious of a king in the prime of life like Demetrios and thought that the youth and incapacity of the boy who had succeeded to the throne would serve their purpose better'. With an ineffective boy-king on the throne the Senate sent off a commission with instructions 'in the first place to burn the decked warships, next to hamstring the elephants and by every means to cripple the royal power'. At about the same time another mode of interference in Seleukid affairs presented itself to the Senate – support of the rebellious Jews. In 164 there was initial diplomatic contact (II *Macc.* 11.34–8), and in 161 Judas Maccabaeus apparently succeeded in winning a treaty of alliance with Rome and a letter from the Senate threatening Demetrios, who in 162 had finally managed to escape from Rome and win the Seleukid throne (I *Macc.* 8; Jos. *AJ* 12.414–19; Gruen 1984: 42–6). As there was no Roman response at all to the subsequent defeat and death of Judas at Seleukid hands, it seems unlikely that the Senate intended anything very practical with the treaty; but it was perhaps no harm to make hostile diplomatic noises against Demetrios and let him know that they might choose to offer real assistance to the Jews if it suited them. Attempts to weaken the Ptolemaic dynasty also, by playing off Ptolemy VI Philometor against his younger brother Ptolemy VIII Physkon, are identified by Polybios in the year 163/2 (Polyb. 31.10; Gruen 1984: 692–702). This sort of cynical manipulation he now regarded as a feature of Roman policy:

> Decisions of this kind are now very frequent with the Romans; they rely on the mistakes of others to increase and secure their own empire in a statesmanlike way, by doing favours and appearing to confer benefactions on the offenders. That is why, seeing the greatness of the Egyptian kingdom and fearing that should it ever find a leader he might become excessively arrogant, they appointed as ambassadors Titus Torquatus and Gnaeus Merula to establish Ptolemy in Cyprus and carry out at once the king's design and their own. (cf. Derow, this volume, section 4)

Polybios' viewpoint is Rome's: he does not tell us whether the Ptolemies or Seleukids felt nervous about how their actions might be interpreted at Rome. There is reason to think, however, that at least some of the Greek states were extremely nervous. Even in the relatively harmless area of dynastic marriage, in 161/0 Ariarathes V, the new king of Cappadocia, found his proffered bride, Laodike, too hot to handle: she was the sister of the Seleukid king Demetrios, currently enjoying the extreme disfavour of the Senate, and widow of Rome's defeated enemy, Perseus of Macedon. Diodoros (31.28) states that in turning her down he yielded to Roman pressure, or at least acted in deference to Rome. The case is undoubtedly an exception – the royal houses of the Greek east usually pursued a vigorous and fully independent marriage policy (see the list in Seibert 1967: 129–34) – but it shows just how beholden to Rome a Hellenistic king might feel. The most famous piece of evidence in this connection is the letter of about 156 from Attalos II of Pergamon to Attis, priest of Kybele, concerning joint action they were planning against the Galatians (*RC* 61, Austin 208). The matter was discussed among Attalos' advisers and although they initially thought otherwise, gradually the view prevailed that it would be extremely dangerous to proceed without consulting the Romans. If they acted unilaterally and were successful, 'the result would be jealousy, displeasure and hostile suspicion'. Failure would be disastrous, 'for they would not stir a finger, but would look on with satisfaction, as we had undertaken such a great project without consulting them'. So Attalos decided to keep the Romans closely informed. This is exactly the same policy as enunciated by the pro-Roman Achaian politician, Kallikrates, in 154/3: the Achaians should not go to war with anyone or send help to anyone without taking the advice of Rome (Polyb. 33.16.7–8). Similarly Ophelas, the *epimeletes* (governor) of the island of Delos in the year 147/6, is praised in an honorific inscription for his unquestioning acceptance of Rome's will (Tréheux and Charneaux 1998: 241–2): not only did he maintain the friendship and goodwill of the Romans, he even increased it, by following closely their written instructions, by welcoming Roman ambassadors to the island and by observing the decisions of the Senate communicated by the ambassadors. These were states and politicians in relatively close contact with Rome, but even some further afield felt it necessary to be a 'friend' of Rome. An inscription dating from 155 BC (or 179) records a treaty between king Pharnakes I of Pontos and the Crimean city of Chersonesos, in which both parties undertake to 'maintain their friendship with the Romans and do nothing contrary to them' (*IOSPE* I² 402, trans. Sherk 30). Pharnakes had fought a war against his neighbours in Asia Minor during the 180s, so his activities were not without interest to the Senate, but that Rome should be a central element in a treaty between two such distant states is testament to her growing influence, and to the recognition of this among the Greeks.

No doubt many states when faced with tricky political decisions acted in the same nervous fashion. But there are also signs of greater boldness. Demetrios, who, as we saw, had been kept hostage in Rome while the Seleukid throne that was rightfully his went to Antiochos V, eventually lost patience with the Senate's repeated refusal to let him go. In 162 he escaped from Rome, seized the throne and executed Antiochos (Polyb. 31.11–15; I *Macc.* 7.1–4: App. *Syr.* 47). This was a beginning to his reign bound to displease Rome. The Senate almost immediately bestowed its favour on a pretender, Timarchos, satrap of Media (Diod. 31.27a), made a treaty with the Jewish rebels and put pressure on Ariarathes V of Cappadocia not to marry Demetrios' sister. Demetrios did try to mend diplomatic fences with the Senate, but he never really succeeded: in 150 he was defeated and killed by a pretender to the throne, named Alexander Balas, who was backed primarily by a coalition of Pergamon, Cappadocia and Egypt, but who had also received the verbal support of the Senate (Gruen 1984: 585–6; 666–8). Rome's commitment to Demetrios' enemies was purely verbal and senatorial intervention in his affairs may not have amounted to a sustained campaign to topple him, but the Fathers were consistently ill-disposed to him throughout his reign. Perhaps accepting this as a fact of life from the beginning, he set about looking after his own interests regardless of Rome (Habicht 1989: 356–62). He defeated and killed Timarchos and Judas Maccabaeus, and then started meddling in Cappadocian affairs, engineering in 159/8 the removal of Ariarathes V and instalment of the latter's brother, Orophernes, on the throne (App. *Syr.* 47; Diod. 31.32).

Although in response to embassies from all concerned the Senate suggested that Cappadocia should be split between Ariarathes and Orophernes, Attalos II of Pergamon used military force to re-establish Ariarathes on the throne in 156 (Gruen 1984: 584–5). This he seems to have done without either permission or response from Rome. Similarly, some seven years later in 149, there is nothing to suggest that he looked for senatorial approval before invading Bithynia and helping Nikomedes II to take the throne from Prusias II (App. *Mith.* 4–7). It is all in curious contrast with the rather timid policy he outlined to the priest Attis (above). But the kings of Asia Minor in this period do seem to have engaged in a degree of independent action against each other without always eliciting a very vigorous reaction from Rome. In 156, for instance, Prusias II of Bithynia invaded Pergamon, thus starting a war that lasted until 154 (Habicht 1956: 101–10; Gruen 1984: 586–9). Prusias repeatedly ignored the rather tame efforts of the embassies despatched by the Senate to bring about a cessation of hostilities, and even maltreated the Roman ambassadors (Polyb. 33.7). When his friendship and alliance with Rome were cancelled, however, he must have realized that he was not going to have an entirely free hand; but it was only the formation of a coalition by Attalos, involving Mithradates IV of Pontos and Ariarathes V of Cappadocia, coupled with yet another Roman embassy, that finally brought his defiance to an end. Prusias had to pay an indemnity, but the treaty ending the war really only restored the *status quo*. Such senatorial lethargy may have encouraged Ariarathes and Attalos at about this time to attack the city of Priene, which appealed for assistance first to Rhodes and then Rome (Polyb. 33.6; Ager 1996: no. 143). Roman diplomacy perhaps helped to restrain the aggressors in the end, but Ariarathes and Attalos had displayed no hesitation in attacking in the first place. And while Pergamon and Bithynia were conducting their war, Rhodes and Crete were also engaged in a war (155–153) that attracted little urgent interest in Rome (Gruen 1984: 578–9). Both sides first appealed to the Achaian League for help, presumably on the assumption that they would get more effective attention there than from the Senate: in due course they did turn to Rome, and again, it may have been a Roman embassy that hastened an end to the war, but it seems to be the case that up till this point the combatants had set about the business of war against each other with no obvious concerns for Roman reaction (Ager 1996: no. 144).

3 The Revolt of Andriskos and the Achaian War

This sort of inter-state wrangling was possible for one very good reason: it offered no real threat to Rome's ultimate authority. But if Greek states harboured any doubts about the limits of their independence, two wars in the 140s will have set them right on the matter. The first reinforced the lesson of Pydna: direct military challenge to Roman authority would meet the full force of Rome's military might. In 150–148 a pretender to the Macedonian throne, named Andriskos, offered just such a challenge, although it took the Senate some time to realize what was happening (Gruen 1984: 431–3; Kallet-Marx 1995: 31–6). Andriskos claimed to be a son of Perseus, and in a remarkably short time, with Thracian backing, managed to win control of Macedon and threaten Thessaly. Polybios was perplexed at the turn of events (36.10; 17): Andriskos had appeared from nowhere, 'dropped out of the sky', as he famously put it, and he could not understand why the Macedonians supported him. The rapidity of his success may have been surprising, but there can be little doubt about the main reasons for Andriskos' appeal: the Macedonians missed their monarchy and their independence. Although there is only little explicit statement of hostility to Rome (Zonar. 9.28), it is hard to imagine that this was not one of the driving forces behind the Macedonian revolt. Their last two kings had been defeated by Roman armies and the Senate had abolished their monarchy and deprived them of their political freedom. Even if they were not ruled directly by Rome, they knew who their main enemy was. Not surprisingly they did not like their subjection to Roman authority, and when an opportunity to redress the situation presented itself, they embraced it. In 150 Rome sent a single legate, P. Scipio Nasica, to solve the problem diplomatically: he saw that the matter was a great deal more serious than the Senate had realized, and the following year the praetor P. Iuventius Thalna was despatched with a legion, only to suffer a shocking defeat and death. Finally in 148 the Senate responded adequately: a Pergamene fleet and two legions under the command of Q. Caecilius Metellus brought Andriskos' challenge to an end. Although it is usually assumed that in the wake of the Andriskos affair Macedon now became a Roman province, under direct Roman rule, it may be that the Senate simply decided on a regular military commitment to the defence of Macedon's frontier with Thrace (Kallet-Marx 1995: 11–41).

There were aspects of the other war of this period more difficult for the Greeks to interpret. After a long history of loyal support whenever they were called on for help, in 146 the Achaian League fought a suicidal war against Rome, ending in defeat, the destruction of Corinth and the dissolution of the league (Polyb. 38.9–18; Paus. 7.14–16). What happened? Did they themselves simply devise a disastrous new policy towards Rome, disturbed by social pressures perhaps (Fuks 1970) and driven by a new breed of anti-Roman politician? Or did Rome deliberately provoke them by deciding to dismember the Achaian League (Larsen 1968: 492; W. Harris 1979: 240–4)? Or did a series of tragic miscalculations carry both Rome and the Achaians into a war neither side had really intended (Gruen 1976)? The sources will hardly allow a definitive answer, but the Achaian relationship with Rome was an uncomfortable one, made all the more uncomfortable by the league's own internal problems and the arbitrary exercise of senatorial power. In the 160s and 150s the Achaians repeatedly sought the return from Italy of their countrymen deported after Pydna. Although they finally succeeded in 150 (Polyb. 35.6), they were refused before, in Polybios' opinion (30.32.8), to keep them obedient to the strongly pro-Roman Kallikrates. The frequency of their requests indicates that the Achaians, understandably, regarded it as a pressing matter. In addition to this source of bitterness some of Rome's diplomatic intervention must have tested Achaian patience. In 164, for instance, an old argument between Sparta and Megalopolis flared up again and Roman arbitration was sought (Ager 1996: no. 135). The Senate sent C. Sulpicius Gallus and M'. Sergius (Polyb. 31.1.6–7). In Pausanias' hostile account – our only source – Gallus behaved badly, refused to adjudicate and handed the matter over to Kallikrates (7.11.1–3). If this might be taken to mean that Rome simply reasserted the league's authority to manage its own affairs, Pausanias' continuation of the story would be difficult to reconcile with such an interpretation: the Senate not only supported the wish of the citizens of Pleuron to secede from the league, he says, but also encouraged Gallus to detach as many additional states as possible. Clearly nothing came of this, but we are in a period only shortly after Pydna, when we can see Rome throwing her weight about elsewhere; and even if Pausanias' narrative is deemed unreliable in detail, perhaps it correctly reflects a far from tolerant Senate, quite prepared to threaten the Achaian League. A decade later (156–5), when Athens and Oropos were in dispute, things seem to have been more calmly managed (Ager 1996: no. 141): the Senate was prepared to delegate the details of the arbitration to Sikyon and to see Achaian authority upheld, even if they did tinker with the details by reducing the fine imposed on Athens from 500 to 100 talents.

By 150/149, when once again the relationship of Sparta to the league emerged as the central issue of Achaian politics, there was no particular sign of impending trouble. The league's wish to hold on to a reluctant Sparta was an old problem and there was no reason to think that it would not be sorted out, at least temporarily, with the usual mixture of hostilities and arbitration. But the Achaians were unlucky with the timing of their problem: the revolt of Andriskos in Macedonia not only brought a Roman army to Greece, it also preoccupied the Senate for the best part of two years, and the resulting Roman inattention to events in the Peloponnese may have misled the Achaians into thinking that they could sort out matters exactly as they pleased (Derow 1989: 321–2). Certainly the Achaian leaders began military operations against Sparta, ignoring Metellus' advice to wait for the arrival of a Roman embassy. When an embassy did finally arrive, in the summer of 147, its leader, L. Aurelius Orestes, brought a brutal message from the Senate: Sparta, Corinth, Argos, Herakleia and Orchomenos were to be detached from the league (Paus. 7.14–15). The Achaians must have been stunned, as they had no reason to think that they had fallen so foul of Rome. The usual explanation of the Senate's action is that they lost patience with the league's stubbornness and quarrelsome internal relations, and issued an ultimatum which they knew would lead to war. But Polybios' report (38.9.6) about Sextus Julius Caesar explaining to the Achaians that this was all just meant to frighten them into a less presumptuous, more pliable mode of behaviour, not to dissolve the league or force them into war, might just be true (Gruen 1976): as we saw above, if we can believe Pausanias, exactly the same sort of threat had been made in 164. On this occasion, war resulted because, in Polybios' opinion (38.10–13), Kritolaos deliberately led the Achaians into it. When war was declared on Sparta, it was really against Rome (Polyb. 38.13.6). And yet the possibility remains that this was still a game of bluff and that even right at the end the Achaians were shocked to find themselves at war with Rome: Polybios himself argues that Diaios and Kritolaos were labouring under the misconception that Rome was afraid of war with the Achaians on account of their campaigns in Spain and Africa and would put up with anything (38.10.10). At any rate when the league army moved against Herakleia they encountered Metellus and his army, and disaster came swiftly. Three defeats in rapid succession saw off the Achaian challenge and left Corinth exposed: it was sacked and then burnt to the ground (Paus. 7.16–17).

4   Continuity and Change after the Achaian War

Traditionally 146 has often been seen as representing the end of independent Greek history. Events certainly conspire to make it look a time of great significance. Macedon defeated yet again and the central Greeks humbled, Corinth destroyed. By happy, or unhappy, coincidence, Carthage too was, of course, razed to the ground in 146. Polybios' decision to end his history at this point leaves a loud silence in our coverage of the subsequent period: he adds considerable authority to the notion of the year 146 as a turning point. And with the standard modern interpretation of events in Greece being that after the defeat of Andriskos Macedon was turned into a Roman province, to which much of Greece was attached after the defeat of the Achaian League, the case looks secure: 146 represents a vital moment in the decline of Greece and the rise of Rome. This was always a view, however, that regarded Greek history as primarily that of the Greek mainland. There is no doubt that the Achaian war marked another increment in the growth of Roman power, but many of the states of the Greek east were not directly affected by it, and it can be argued that in the period after 146 continuity outweighed change.

Just as after Pydna, so after the defeat of the Achaian League, there was bound to be a reckoning for the losers. It was administered by the victorious Roman general, L. Mummius, and a senatorial commission sent to assist him. The details are preserved in a problematic and much discussed passage of Pausanias (7.16.9–10). He gets one thing very clearly wrong: he says Roman governors were now regularly assigned to Achaia, but we know this was not the case until 27 BC. As well as destroying the defences of cities that opposed Rome, Mummius, we are told, suppressed democracies, imposed a tribute on Greece, forbade the rich from holding property outside their own state, disbanded the leagues and ordered the Boiotians and Achaians to pay indemnities to the states they attacked. Pausanias adds that not many years later Rome took pity on the Greeks, restored the leagues and the right to hold property abroad and remitted some of the fines Mummius had imposed. Quite how much of this, if any, Pausanias has got right, is difficult to say (Kallet-Marx 1995: 57–96). It is not at all clear that Greece became tributary at this time, although it is hard to imagine that the Achaians did not have to pay a war indemnity – and to Rome, not just to other Greek states. That there were some constitutional measures imposed is confirmed by Polybios who was instructed by the senatorial commission to go round the cities and explain anything they did not understand 'until they got used to the constitution and the laws' (39.5.2). An inscription from the city of Dyme also mentions 'the constitution given to the Achaians by the Romans' (*RDGE* 43, trans. Sherk 50). Whether this refers to a new constitution for the Achaian League, or for the individual cities that had formerly made up the league, is not clear; but from a practical point of view it does not really matter. For whether or not the league was in some form allowed to revive – and there are later references to it, although nothing secure until the early first century – to all intents and purposes it disappears from the stage of political history as a leading actor. This is hardly surprising. When the Macedonians were defeated in 167 Rome suppressed their monarchy, the driving force behind the military challenge to Rome. Similarly in 146 the Achaians made their challenge, lost and paid the price: it was inconceivable that the Senate would leave a politically effective Achaian League in place.

This much was to be expected, and its importance should not be underestimated, but the idea that something fundamental changed rests primarily on modern notions of Roman imperial 'annexation': Macedon is annexed and turned into a 'province' in 148, and Greece made subject to the authority of its governor in 146. In other words the whole status of the Greeks changes, and they now become, in a way they were not before, part of 'the Roman empire'. This standard interpretation has been challenged recently with some force (Kallet-Marx 1995: 11–56). After 146 Macedonia was almost certainly assigned regularly to a Roman commander as a *provincia*, but as a *provincia* in the sense of a commission; and the commission, so the argument would run, was the defence of Macedonia's Balkan frontier, not the administration of an annexed territory. This will not have necessitated any change in the status either of Macedonia, or of Greece. The Roman commander on the spot was naturally a focus of attention in the region and there are records of his involvement in the disputes and affairs of Greece. But this no more demonstrates that Greece was now formally subject to Roman jurisdiction than any of the other examples of proconsular intervention in Greek affairs before 146 demonstrated it. Informally, of course, it was another matter. If the genesis of the Achaian War was difficult for the Greeks to understand, its message, yet another reaffirmation of the post-Pydna world, was not: they were subject to the *imperium* of Rome, which meant, ultimately, that they had to do what they were told. On the other hand this authority was more of a distant threat than a constant pressure, and they were not told to do very much. For most of the Greek world business went on as usual.

Some even benefited from the outcome (Kallet-Marx 1995: 90–3). Profuse votes of thanks to Mummius may have been more strategic than sincere, but reluctant members of the Achaian League, such as Sparta, Elis, Argos and Herakleia, must have been delighted finally to be freed from its control. Strabo (10.5.4) tells us that the destruction of its trading rival, Corinth, was of great advantage to Delos. The Athenians, who before the war had been making aggressive moves on Oropos, probably did not win possession of it subsequently, but may have been rewarded with some disputed islands instead. In general Athens' close and friendly relations with Rome, and with the monarchies of the Greek east, flourished in the second half of the century (Habicht 1997: 269–87). Greek states also continued to fall out with each other and look to third parties, sometimes Rome, sometimes not, for arbitration. The land dispute of two Thessalian communities, Italos and Thebes (145–137 BC), was submitted to Makon of Larisa (Ager 1996: no. 153), while a panel of judges from Asia Minor initially arbitrated between Narthakion and Melitaia (*c.* 143. Ager 1996: no. 154). When Rhodes and Stratonikeia fell out, the disputants thought about going to Rome, but decided instead to submit the case to the Karian city of Bargylia (*c.* 130. Ager 1996: no. 160). If a problem did make its way to the Senate the fathers usually established ground rules and handed on the details to someone else. When Sparta, for instance, encouraged perhaps by the outcome of the Achaian war, took her old dispute with Messenia to Rome, the Senate asked Miletos to give judgement on the basis of who possessed the disputed land when Mummius came to Greece: 600 judges found in favour of Messenia (*c.* 138. Ager 1996: no. 159). For persistent aggression against each other it would be hard to beat the record of the Cretans in the second half of the second century (Chaniotis 1996: 49–56). Gortyn and Knossos were the leading troublemakers, but their allies – Hierapytna and Olos (Gortyn), Lato and Itanos (Knossos) – were not slow to take up arms in support, or indeed in their own separate interests. The Senate did intervene from time to time (with mixed success), particularly in the outbreak of hostilities between Hierapytna and Itanos in 115–114 (Chaniotis 1996: 333–7; Ager 1996: no. 158), but the evidence, mostly epigraphic, gives the distinct impression of the states involved fighting, making and breaking treaties, generally going about their business, with only scant regard for Rome.

Cretan affairs were perhaps too local to threaten the *imperium* of Rome and worry the Senate unduly, but it is slightly more surprising to see in the same period the affairs of the Jews, Seleukids and Ptolemies inextricably linked in a series of intrigues, alliances and wars that elicited little reaction in Rome. The expansionist policies of the Hasmonaean princes (Rajak 1994: 287–96), particularly John Hyrkanos and Alexander Jannaeus, were pursued within the bounds of the Seleukid empire, and, therefore, presumably, not of major concern to the Senate. It is possible that when besieging Jerusalem in 135/4 (Jos. *AJ* 13.236–46) Antiochos VII Sidetes received a diplomatic shot across his bows – if the *senatus consultum* reported by Josephos (*AJ* 13.257–64) belongs at this time – but in view of the careful watch Rome kept on eastern Mediterranean events in the first half of the century, it is interesting to observe what seems to be a diminishing concern in the second half. In the final two decades of the century such apparent indifference may have had more to do with the crises in Numidia and on Rome's northern frontier than with a real lack of interest, but it is also the case that by this stage, indeed well before, the two greatest Hellenistic royal houses, the Seleukids and Ptolemies, were in an advanced state of decline. Both were plagued by extreme dynastic dissension, at times exacerbated, as we have seen, by Roman meddling. In the case of the Seleukids the Jewish drive for independence added a further debilitating factor. These distractions fatally weakened the defence of their empire against Parthian encroachment, and with the defeat and death of Antiochos VII Sidetes in 129 the Seleukids were all but finished: the once mighty empire now comprised Cilicia and northern Syria (Habicht 1989: 362–73: Shipley 2000: 320–5). The Ptolemies faced no such foreign threat, but their internal problems were, if anything, even more acute. On an embassy to the east in 140/39 (or possibly 144/43), Scipio Aemilianus noted what Polybios had earlier observed, that Egypt had the potential to become a great power if ever it found worthy rulers (Diod. 33.28b.1–3). This it singularly failed to do, and its political history from this time is a sad and complicated story of decline – civil war, revolt, dynastic intrigue, local rivalry, administrative breakdown (D. J. Thompson 1994a: Shipley 2000: 207–13). Perhaps symbolic of Egyptian weakness is the attitude of deference to a Roman senator required of local officials organizing his visit to the Fayum in 112 BC:

> Lucius Memmius, a Roman senator, who occupies a position of great dignity and honour, is making the journey from Alexandria to the Arsinoite nome to see the sights. Let him be received with special magnificence and take care that at the proper spots the guest-chambers be prepared and the landing-places to them be got ready with great care, and that the gifts of hospitality mentioned below be presented to him at the landing-

places . . . In general take the utmost pains in everything that the visitor may be satisfied . . . (*Sel. Pap.* II. 416; BD 69)

It would be a mistake to read too much into the hospitable reception of an important person, but in the course of the second century institutional recognition and acceptance of Roman domination is increasingly evident. The cult of the goddess *Roma* developed and spread round the Greek east in this period (Mellor 1975: 27–110). How elaborate and central to the life of a city it could be is well illustrated by an inscription from Miletos of about 130 BC, which describes the working of the cult there (*LSAM* 49, trans. Sherk 41). A regular timetable for sacrifice to 'the People of the Romans and to Roma' is specified, often in conjunction with a special occasion, such as the entry into office of the new gymnasiarchs; and Roman Games are established. 'The people of Rome' crop up on inscriptions from all over the Greek world; and increasingly they are referred to as 'the common benefactors' (Erskine 1994). A practice develops, particularly in the second half of the century, of Greek states, even very minor ones, seeking a formal treaty of alliance with Rome (Kallet-Marx 1995: 184–97). Such diplomatic niceties – the terms treat both signatories as equal partners – had little practical effect, but were probably reassuring expressions of loyalty for the Greeks to be able to make and the Senate to accept. Rather more than a diplomatic nicety was the strange decision we witness for the first time in 155 BC of certain Hellenistic kings to bequeath their kingdom to Rome. In that year Ptolemy VIII Physkon published his will as follows:

> May it be allowed me, with the favour of the gods, to take vengeance fittingly upon those who contrived the unholy plot against me and sought to deprive me not only of my kingship but also of my life. If anything human should befall me before I leave successors to my kingship, I leave the kingdom that belongs to me (i.e. Cyrene) to the Romans, with whom I have from the beginning truly maintained friendship and alliance; . . . (*SEG* 9.7; Austin 230)

Even if this was only a strategy to protect himself against further assassination attempts, and he never thought that Cyrene would really fall to Rome, it was still a striking, and, one would think, far from obvious notion. How would the idea even occur to a Ptolemy? It is no doubt witness to the way in which Hellenistic monarchs regarded their kingdoms as personal possessions, but it is also distinctly defeatist in conception. There is no fight left in Physkon, indeed the Romans are not even the enemy: they are viable heirs to the kingdom of the Ptolemies. He seems to accept as inevitable the dominance of Rome. The will was never activated, as Physkon lived long and fathered heirs, but when Attalos III of Pergamon died in 133 having bequeathed his kingdom to Rome, the result was very different indeed: the Senate accepted the bequest (*RDGE* 11, trans. Austin 214), and established for the first time a Roman presence in Asia.

We are not told what the still youthful but heirless Attalos intended with his will, and there is much debate, but the idea that he was taking defensive measures against dynastic challenge, just like Ptolemy VIII Physkon, is an attractive one (Gruen 1984: 592–6). Aristonikos, supposedly an illegitimate son of Eumenes II, made his bid for the throne only shortly after Attalos' death: perhaps it was clear beforehand that he was already planning to contest the throne, and that Attalos, who had no expectation of dying in the near future, was trying to discourage him with the terms of the will. There is disagreement on how keen the Senate was to take up the inheritance (e.g. W. Harris 1979: 147–9; A. Sherwin-White 1984: 80–4), but once Attalos had involved them in the future of Pergamon, it was no longer a local matter to be decided locally: Aristonikos' defiance constituted a military challenge to the *imperium* of Rome, and a vigorous, probably armed, Roman intervention became inevitable. Aristonikos enjoyed some success at the beginning – Phokaia and Leukai went over to his side (Strabo 14.1.38; Just. 37.1.1), and he was able to capture Myndos, Samos and Kolophon (Florus 1.35.4) – so there must have been elements in the state who saw their best interests served by a continuation of the monarchy (Macedonian colonists of the interior perhaps – Collins 1980: 83–7). Strabo tells us that he also sought the support of the poor and of slaves, probably when he found he was losing, or could not find, more influential support elsewhere; but it is now generally thought unlikely that he presented himself as a great social revolutionary (Gruen 1984: 597). Opposition came especially from the Greek cities of the coast, many of which, like Pergamon (*OGIS* 338, trans. Austin 211), had perhaps been declared 'free' in Attalos' will; and in due course the kings of Cappadocia, Bithynia, Paphlagonia and Pontos entered the fray when the Senate asked for their help. The fathers may, as so often, have been slow to catch up with events – neither consul was assigned Asia as a province in 132, and when one of the consuls of 131, P. Licinius Crassus, was sent out with an army he was defeated and killed – but they eventually brought overwhelming force to bear: in 130 and 129 Marcus Perperna and Manius Aquillius defeated Aristonikos and ended the war.

After the war Manius Aquillius and a senatorial commission of ten settled the affairs of the region (Magie 1950: 154–8; Kallet-Marx 1995: 109–22). Loyal kings were rewarded with parcels of Attalid territory – Mithradates V of Pontos was given Phrygia and the Cappadocians got Lykaonia – but the rest, allowing for the freedom of certain cities, became part of the new Roman province of Asia. There might be disagreement about the exact date of provincialization, but there can be no doubt that Aquillius set in motion a process that soon saw Attalos' kingdom become part of the territory of the Roman empire, territory to be governed directly, exploited economically and protected militarily. It is theoretically possible that if Aristonikos had not appeared, Rome might have dealt with Attalos' bequest differently, but in bringing order to the disruption caused by Aristonikos' bid for power the Senate confirmed their decision to take a physical stake in Asia. Another Hellenistic kingdom had disappeared to be replaced by Rome. On a vastly larger scale the following half century would see the same process repeated.

5 The Mithradatic Wars

While Rome was sorting out its new territory of Pergamon, in the royal house of Pontos there was growing up the young prince whose military challenge to Rome would do so much to ensure the demise of a politically independent Hellenistic world. Mithradates VI Eupator Dionysos succeeded to the throne when his father was assassinated in 120. He belonged to a powerful and noble Persian family, probably directly related to the great Darius himself, which in the fifth and fourth centuries had held sway as dynasts over the regions of Mysia and Mariandynia on the Propontis and further east along the south shore of the Black Sea (Bosworth and Wheatley 1998). Towards the end of the fourth century one of their number, the Mithradates later known as Ktistes ('founder'), was forced to retire to the mountains of Paphlagonia from where he began to build what was to emerge in the course of the third century as the kingdom of Pontos. We know little of its early history (McGing 1986: 15–42; Hind 1994a: 129–33). Although there is no reason to think that the royal family denied or played down their Iranian origins and Achaimenid connections, they also presented a Greek face to the world: Greek coins, Greek diplomatic practices, marriage alliances with the Seleukids all placed the kingdom firmly in the world of Hellenistic monarchies. Eupator's grandfather Pharnakes (*c.* 196–170/155) was the first to bring Pontos to the attention of Rome (section 2 above), and both Mithradates IV and V treated their 'friendship' with Rome seriously, the latter's loyalty in the war against Aristonikos being rewarded, as we have seen, with the territory of Phrygia.

When Eupator had established himself securely on the throne (by about 116), his first major initiative was across the Black Sea in the Crimea where the citizens of Chersonesos, their city sacked by hostile Scythian neighbours, invited him to champion their cause (Strabo 7.4.3). A remarkable inscription (*SIG*³ 709, trans. BD 56) records the resulting campaigns of his general, Diophantos, who subjected the whole area, including the Bosporan kingdom (Strabo 7.4.4), to Pontic rule. The chronology of the rest of Mithradates' expansion in the Euxine cannot be fixed, but the literary, epigraphic and numismatic evidence shows that in due course he came to control, either directly or indirectly, almost its entire circuit (de Callataÿ 1997: 245–64). Aggressive ambitions in Asia Minor, however, were more dangerous (Hind 1994a: 140–4; McGing 1986: 66–88). As Pharnakes' war against his neighbours had demonstrated, hostile coalitions could be formed and there was always the threat of Rome. Probably early in his reign Mithradates murdered his sister Laodike's husband Ariarathes VI of Cappadocia, thus enabling her to rule as regent for her own young son Ariarathes VII, but after that we hear little of Asia Minor until, taking advantage of Rome's northern difficulties in the last decade of the century, Mithradates and his Bithynian neighbour, Nikomedes III, carved up Paphlagonia between them. They ignored a Roman order to withdraw; Nikomedes installed his own son as king and Mithradates annexed part of Galatia. This happy alliance between the two kings did not last long. In about 103/102 we find Nikomedes invading Cappadocia and marrying Laodike, only for Mithradates to expel them both, restore his nephew Ariarathes VII briefly, but then murder him and declare his own young son as king (Ariarathes IX).

Up to this point, about 100 BC, Rome had largely ignored these dynastic intrigues. The famous embassy to the east of Gaius Marius in 99/8 (Plut. *Mar.* 31), however, may show a change of senatorial attitude. 'Be stronger than the Romans,' he told Mithradates, 'or obey their commands in silence'. The king took the latter option when in about 96 the Senate ordered him out of Cappadocia, Nikomedes having stirred the pot by producing a pretender to the Cappadocian throne and appealing to Rome. Cappadocia was declared 'free' (Paphlagonia too), but the Cappadocians in fact wanted a king and chose Ariobarzanes. Although chronological uncertainties make it very difficult to follow the precise course of events in this whole period (de Callataÿ 1997: 186–214), it is clear that Ariobarzanes had difficulty taking possession of, or holding onto, his throne in the face of a Cappadocian intervention by Mithradates' new ally and son-in-law, Tigranes king of Armenia. Rome's response – the restoration (or installation) of Ariobarzanes by an army under the command of L. Cornelius Sulla – was sensational. When threatened directly, by Andriskos, for instance, or Aristonikos, the Senate had always been quite prepared to fight, but they had previously shown no inclination to use force of arms in dealing with the local affairs of the Anatolian kings. The message to Mithradates must have been crystal clear. If he had not already decided on war with Rome, he surely did now. He waited until Italy was convulsed by the Social War, and then annexed Bithynia and Cappadocia. The inept Roman diplomacy that followed cast Rome in the role of aggressor and Mithradates of aggrieved victim.

This was perhaps part of the reason for the remarkable degree of success he achieved initially. In outline the story of the war is simply told (A. Sherwin-White 1984: 121–48). Mithradates' armies swept across Asia Minor, easily defeating the first line of Roman and allied opposition. They met resistance from certain cities, usually swiftly overcome, except in the case of Rhodes, and subsequently Patara in Lykia, both of which Mithradates besieged but failed to capture (App. *Mith.* 24–7). Others, like Kos, Magnesia, Ephesos and Mytilene, offered an enthusiastic welcome to the invading forces (App. *Mith.* 21). With most of Asia Minor in his possession Mithradates then moved into Greece, where astonishingly, given their previous loyalty to Rome, the Athenians went over to his side. The real test, however, was still to come. Mithradates' success to this point was largely a product of perfect timing – Rome was far too busy with the Social War to do anything about him – but sooner or later he was going to have to face the full force of a Roman response. It arrived in the summer of 87, when Sulla landed in Greece with five legions. Support for Mithradates melted away and Sulla drove the Pontic forces into Athens. They held out stoutly over the winter of 87/86, but on the 1 March 86, the city fell. In two subsequent battles Sulla was also victorious, and Mithradates withdrew to Asia. Here he again met with defeat at the hands of the Roman general, Fimbria, and after lengthy negotiations, made peace with Sulla in 85. He had to pay a war indemnity, return prisoners, relinquish all his conquests and merely confine himself to his own kingdom – a settlement that even Sulla's own troops recognized as lenient (Plut. *Sull.* 24).

In the end victory was a relatively straightforward matter – the Roman army was quite simply a mightier fighting force than anything the Pontic side could muster – but more interesting is the degree of support Mithradates won in the first two years of the war. For his own Anatolian subjects, and indeed for other inhabitants of the region, the respectability of his Achaimenid family connections gave him great authority; and he had undoubtedly made himself very attractive to the Greeks (McGing 1986: 89–108). He championed the cause of the Black Sea colonies against their barbarian neighbours; he also built up a reputation in the Aegean and mainland Greek world as a leading philhellenic benefactor; his court was full of Greeks and, in most respects, was structured along standard Hellenistic lines; he created an image of himself as a new Alexander come to rescue the Greeks; and, perhaps above all, he was successful. When faced with the dreadful dilemma of whom to support in a war between Rome and the rich, powerful and civilized kingdom of Pontos, those who chose the latter probably did so, at least in part, for the simple reason that they thought they were backing the winner. There was also the pragmatic consideration for the Asiatic Greeks that Mithradates was the man on the spot: with a victorious Pontic army at the city gates and no hope of Rome's protection, it called for a very stout heart to deny the king of Pontos. And how many wanted Rome's protection? It seems clear that Rome had managed to make herself very unpopular since the creation of the province of Asia, in particular because of the activities of her tax-farmers (Diod. 37.5–6; Kallet-Marx 1995: 138–48). The famous massacre of Romans and Italians ordered by Mithradates in 88 (App. *Mith.* 22–3), an order carried out with no little enthusiasm by some of the Greek states, is usually seen as evidence of accumulated hatred for Rome. While this idea may have been overplayed by scholars to a certain extent (Kallet-Marx 1995: 153–8), it would be difficult to disagree with Appian's conclusion that the cause of the atrocity was more hatred of the Romans than fear of the king.

It would also be difficult to exaggerate just how damaging and disruptive the war had been for the states of the Greek east. It did not matter which side they took, nearly all lost out at some stage. Those who resisted Mithradates were punished by him, but then rewarded by Sulla – Stratonikeia, for instance (App. *Mith.* 21: *RDGE* 18, trans. Sherk 63) – while a pro-Mithradatic stance met with heavy penalties after the war – reprisals, a massive fine and the billeting of Roman troops during the winter of 85/84 (App. *Mith.* 61–2; Plut. *Sull.* 25). Over ten years later the 20,000 talent indemnity that Sulla imposed on the Greek cities of Asia had been paid twice over, but so high were the rates of interest at which the Greeks were forced to borrow that the total debt was now 120,000 talents (Plut. *Luc.* 20.4). Asia truly 'had her fill of misery' (App. *Mith.* 63). The Athenians fared no better, but for a city which had identified so closely with the Pontic cause – Mithradates functioned as one of the mint magistrates in 87/86 BC and may well have been elected Eponymous Archon the previous year – they can hardly have expected otherwise (Habicht 1997: 303–21). Their chief punishment was the cruel siege and murderously destructive sacking of the city. Sulla also seems to have forced new laws on them, or made some sort of constitutional intervention (App. *Mith.* 39). Although in the wake of the war Rome acquired no new territory, Appian does tell us that the majority of people in Asia Minor, Greece and Macedonia were now for the first time made tributary (*Mith.* 118). This represents a huge increase in Rome's stake in the east. Her authority in the region had been shaken to its foundations, but although Sulla made no infrastructural changes to ensure it did not happen again, the range and whole process of war produced in the aftermath a much more intrusive Roman presence.

Mithradates retired to Pontos with his prestige severely damaged, but his ambition fully intact. He had to deal with revolt in his Colchian and Bosporan domains (App. *Mith.* 64), but also continued to intrigue adventurously against Cappadocia. It may have been in response to this activity that Sulla's legate L. Licinius Murena made a series of raids on Pontic territory, known as the Second Mithradatic War (Glew 1981). The crisis lasted from 83 to 81. Mithradates finally reacted to Murena's bullying and inflicted a sharp defeat on him, but neither Rome nor Pontos wanted war just yet: Sulla called off Murena and relations were patched up. The final confrontation, the Third Mithradatic War, arose in connection with Bithynia. When

Nikomedes IV died in 74 he left his kingdom to Rome, a bequest the Senate immediately accepted (Eutrop. 6.6.1). Whatever the exact excuse he used, Mithradates was not going to put up with this, and in the spring of 73 his forces swept through Paphlagonia and invaded the new Roman province (A. Sherwin-White 1994: 238–70). Plutarch (*Luc.* 7) reports that the Bithynians welcomed the invaders and that disaffection with Rome broke out in Asia, but unlike at the beginning of the first war, this time Rome was prepared: two Roman proconsuls and an army were waiting. Although the Roman fleet was easily defeated at Chalkedon, the entire Pontic advance foundered at the first major obstacle it encountered. Mithradates put virtually his whole effort into capturing the city of Kyzikos on the Propontis, but was outwitted by the able L. Licinius Lucullus and forced to withdraw in disorder (App. *Mith.* 72–6). This was by no means the last throw of the dice for Mithradates, but it was the last serious challenge he posed. In some five years of campaigning Lucullus pursued him through Bithynia and Pontos, and on into Armenia, where the king took refuge with his son-in-law, Tigranes. When Lucullus' victorious offensive ran out of political support at Rome and stalled, Mithradates slipped back to Pontos at the end of 68 and defeated the occupying Roman forces. It was only a temporary reprieve, however. In 66 Gnaeus Pompeius was appointed to the command and swiftly routed Mithradates who fled to his Bosporan kingdom. Here in 63, amid stories that he was planning to invade Italy by land, like a Hannibal from the east, he finally succumbed to the treachery of his son, Pharnakes, and committed suicide.

The war had not touched Greece this time and the Greek cities of Asia had largely escaped too, but the campaigns of Lucullus and Pompey brought Roman arms into Pontos, to the Caucasus, to Armenia and south into Palestine. This time there was to be no retreat, no return to the status quo. Asia Minor and the eastern Mediterranean was a world now owned by Rome, and Pompey set about institutionalizing this ownership with the formation of new provinces in Bithynia-Pontus and Syria, and the establishment of compliant 'client' kings to rule in Rome's interests (Eilers, this volume). It would be wrong to blame Mithradates for all of this: there were other factors drawing Rome inexorably eastwards. The Senate had, for instance, long been exercised by the problem of piracy. A special piracy command in Cilicia had been given to M. Antonius in 102, and an important inscription preserves the text of a law of about 100 BC, which, among other things, established Cilicia as a *provincia* to deal with the pirates (Hassal et al. 1974; Sherk 55). In 74 Cretan piracy was targeted by the Senate, and the culmination of this process was Pompey's massive, and brilliantly successful, command in 67 (Gabrielsen, this volume). Campaigns against the Scordisci and Thracians in the last decade of the second century and further offensives in the Balkans and western Black Sea area during the 70s, show a continuing and growing Roman commitment in that region (Kallet-Marx 1995: 223–7; 296–9). But although Rome had interests that would probably have seen her in due course take over the eastern Mediterranean anyway, Mithradates was the catalyst for the process. He challenged Rome for possession of Greece and Asia Minor, and to the victor went the spoils. But to keep the spoils entailed a degree of involvement and commitment that Rome had not previously exhibited. Mithradates shook the Senate out of such complacency. In the new order that was created from the chaos of the Mithradatic wars, the Greek east, in a political sense, disappeared and in its place the eastern Roman empire emerged.

FURTHER READING

The second edition of the Cambridge Ancient History contains extensive coverage of particular subjects within the period of this chapter, most importantly Derow (Roman policy from Pydna to the fall of Corinth) and Habicht (the Seleukids and dynasties of Asia Minor) in *CAH*² 8 and Hind (Mithradates VI), Rajak (later Hasmonaeans), A. N. Sherwin-White (campaigns of Pompey) and Thompson (later Ptolemies) in *CAH*² 9. For all events in Asia Minor Magie 1950 is still an excellent account. The Seleukid empire is interestingly treated by S. Sherwin-White and A. Kuhrt (1993), but there is nothing comparable for Ptolemaic Egypt, where the best help is to be found in the various works of Dorothy Thompson and Willy Clarysse. Inevitably, virtually any interpretation of Greek history in the second century BC will depend to a certain extent on interpretations of Roman imperialism, a controversial subject with huge bibliography. In English, two of the most influential studies in recent decades have been W. Harris 1979, who argued for pugnacious and persistent Roman aggression, and Gruen 1984. One of Gruen's great strengths was to view Roman imperialism in its Greek context, a line of investigation continued most profitably for the period after 148 BC in Kallet-Marx 1995. The Greek context is also the subject of J.-L. Ferrary's important 1988 study of Roman policy in the Greek world from the Second Macedonian War to the Mithradatic wars. For Greek resistance to Rome, Thornton 2001. For sources, see chapter 1 above, but note also the new Budé text and translation, with extensive introduction and notes, of Appian's *Mithridateios* (Paris 2001).

CHAPTER SIX

A Roman East:
Pompey's Settlement to the
Death of Augustus

Claude Eilers

1 Pompey's Reorganization

Pompey is said to have boasted that before his campaigns Asia had been Rome's most distant province, and that now it was in the middle of Rome's dominions (Pliny *HN* 7.99). His boast was not without justification: his conquests had redrawn the map of the eastern Mediterranean and his reorganization of the region fundamentally altered the geopolitical landscape. Some territories now came under Rome's direct control as provinces; others were given to local dynasts who had proven themselves loyal to Rome or useful to Pompey, men who could be trusted to govern in Rome's interests.

Much of Mithradates' kingdom of Pontos was added to the existing province of Bithynia. This new province, which included much of the south coast of the Black Sea, lasted well into the Empire. Pompey's organizational intervention here went beyond the creation of a new province. Where Roman provincial administration had been successful in the east, it was based on the foundation of the Greek civic system. Pontos, however, had been a centralized monarchy, and therefore had not developed such a system. Pompey therefore divided the provincial territory into cities, each with a large dependent territory. Strabo sums up the process for Zela, one of the new cities: 'Pompey added many districts to it and called it a city' (Strabo 12.3.37). Civic constitutions were created that included Roman features that favoured the wealthy classes (Magie 1950: 1232–4).

Where this process was impossible or impractical, Pompey assigned territories to local dynasts. For example, much of the Pontic hinterland, as well as Armenia Minor, was given to the Galatian tetrarch, Deiotaros, along with the title 'king'. Pompey showed similar generosity towards Ariobarzanes I, king of Cappadocia. He had been a loyal ally of Rome for decades, and Pompey confirmed and expanded his kingdom, though he soon resigned in favour of his son, Ariobarzanes II.

There had been territory under Roman control in southern Asia Minor for many years, an area that was sometimes named (somewhat misleadingly up to this point)

'Cilicia'. To this territory Pompey added Cilicia Pedias and Cilicia Tracheia, making a new substantial entity, which became one of Rome's most important eastern provinces and continued to grow in the coming years. In 58 Cyprus, which had belonged to Ptolemaic Egypt, was added, and two years after that part of Phrygia, which had been part of the province of Asia. The new province was important enough that its governors were ex-consuls, one of which was the famous orator Cicero, whose correspondence from these years gives us valuable insight into the ways in which Roman provinces were governed (Treggiari 1978). Cilicia now occupied much of central Asia Minor, including the strategic highway that ran from Laodikeia, through Lykaonia to Tarsos and the Cilician gates.

The most dramatic change in Pompey's reorganization took place in Syria, where the Seleukid dynasty, which had been near death for decades, was not revived. What remained of the once great empire now became the Roman province Syria. In theory, its governors were to hold office for one year and then return to Rome. In practice it was not so: most held office for two or three years and used the extended terms to pursue their own ambitions. In the coming decades, for example, it was used by Gabinius as a base from which to meddle in Egyptian affairs, and by Crassus to launch his ill-fated invasion of Parthia (A. Sherwin-White 1984: 271–89).

In the aftermath of this long period of war, many cities were in a sorry state. For the most part, the region now began to recover, profiting from the relative neglect of the Romans. There were, of course, occasional problems, and Roman governors could be as unscrupulous as before. For example, the first governor of Asia after Pompey's return to Rome, L. Valerius Flaccus, demanded money from several cities to build a fleet to meet the now-diminishing threat of piracy. The ships were never built, and he apparently pocketed the money. Money was also extorted elsewhere on other pretexts, the details of which became public in his trial a few years later (Cic. *Flac.* 27–33). Cicero's speech in his defence, the *pro Flacco*, provides a glimpse of the problems that a dishonest governor could present to provincials. As difficult as such circumstances were to the specific parties involved, the sums involved were small compared to the crushing burdens imposed by Sulla or by Rome's competing factions in the decades to come. Roman governors had virtually unlimited freedom of action in their province: only after they returned to Rome was it possible to revoke their decisions or seek compensation by bringing action against them in Rome (Lintott 1993: 43–69). Most cities, however, were not keen to pursue such legal remedies. In the worst cases, little could be done, and they presumably regarded their losses as an unavoidable cost of being under Roman rule. Normally, however, Greek cities could iron out difficulties by getting Roman patrons to intervene on their behalf (Eilers 2002).

When things went wrong, however, the effects could be catastrophic. An instructive example of this is the case of Salamis in Cyprus. It had become part of the province of Cilicia in 58. Shortly after this, when Salamis needed money, it managed to borrow it from M. Iunius Brutus, who had accompanied his uncle Cato when he annexed the province for Rome (both were formal patrons of the city). Although the loan was forbidden under the *lex Gabinia*, Brutus managed to get the Senate to pass two decrees that allowed him to circumvent the law's provisions, and a large sum was lent to Salamis in the name of his agents there at the extortionate interest rate of 4 per cent per month. Unsurprisingly, the city's finances soon became seriously compromised, and by the end of the decade Brutus' agents were using Roman cavalry (authorized by

Cicero's predecessor as governor) to intimidate Salamis' council into paying the debt. At one point the councillors were besieged in their senate house and five of them starved to death (Cic. *Att.* 6.1.6).

There were problems elsewhere, too. In several Cilician cities the economic crisis was serious enough that they were eight years in arrears in the payment of their taxes. Special levies were necessary: in Laodikeia, a poll tax and a tax on doors were necessary (Cic. *Fam.* 3.8.5). Cicero was inclined to blame these problems on the cupidity of his predecessor, whom he compared at one point to a wild animal (Cic. *Att.* 5.16.2). The fact that eight years' taxes were in arrears, however, suggests that the problem was larger than one extortionate official.

Through these years Athens remained a loyal ally of Rome. It was legally autonomous, and free to conduct its own internal affairs. The Romans, for the most part, respected its autonomy. For a short period in the mid-50s the authority of the governor of Macedonia was expanded to include Athens and other cities in Achaia. This measure, however, was inspired more by the internal politics of Rome than by any sincere desire to encroach on the autonomy of these cities, and the measure was short-lived (Habicht 1997: 339–41).

Over the preceding centuries Athens had benefited from the generosity of sympathetic monarchs, who were keen to prove their philhellenism by funding civic projects there. Many of these dynasties no longer existed, but their role was now fulfilled by prominent Romans. One of these was the financier, T. Pomponius Atticus, a friend and confidant of Cicero, who made a donation of grain Athens (Cic. *Att.* 6.6.2). Others made gifts of money, including such notables as Pompey and Julius Caesar, both of whom are known to have donated fifty talents (Plut. *Pomp.* 27.3; Cic. *Att.* 6.1.25). At the sanctuary at Eleusis, a monumental gateway built by Ap. Claudius Pulcher is still to be seen (*CIL* 3.547 = *ILLRP* 2 1.401). In this regard, Athens seems to have been unique; similar gifts are rarely attested in other Greek cities.

In 54, the Roman senator M. Licinius Crassus arrived in Syria with a large army, which he would lead across the Euphrates to attack Parthia. The war was unjustifiable. Parthia was at peace with Rome and had abided to the agreement that it had made with Pompey. The motives arose from personal ambition: Crassus desired conquests to make his military reputation equal to Pompey and Caesar, and Parthia offered the best opportunity. That, of course, was not completely out of character for the Romans. Little was accomplished in his first year in Syria: some preliminary raids were made against Mesopotamia, and temple treasuries in Jerusalem and Hierapolis were seized. Nothing in this prepared the Greek east for the shock that came in 53, when the invasion ended in disaster at Carrhae: most of Crassus' army was lost and he himself was killed. According to Plutarch (*Crass.* 33), his head was used as a prop in a production of the *Bacchae*: a graphic, though gruesome, illustration both of the wide diffusion of Hellenistic culture throughout the near east, and of how deeply the Parthians were offended by Crassus' treachery.

The episode was highly destabilizing to the region. Parthia, which had been non-aggressive and preoccupied with its own problems, was now an open enemy. Luckily for Rome, internal discord prevented an immediate counter-attack. The new situation, however, led Roman allies to equivocate. The most obvious example of this was Antiochos of Kommagene, whose kingdom lay on the Euphrates bank and included strategic approaches to Syria and Cappadocia. He was in a very delicate position, trying to survive between two hostile superpowers, and for the moment, safety dictated co-operation with Parthia (Sullivan 1990: 194–7).

Parthia's military response came in 51 BC, when Pakoros, son of the king Orodes, led a large Parthian army into Syria. The only Roman troops in the region were the remnants of two of Crassus' legions under the command of Cassius, a subordinate of Crassus, and two under-strength legions in Cilicia under Cicero. Cassius devised a simple, though inglorious, strategy to minimize Rome's losses. He withdrew within the walls of Antioch and refused to give battle. The Parthians lacked the resources and patience for a long siege, and so after a few weeks they retired. In the summer of the next year the Parthians again invaded. Again the Romans (now under Calpurnius Bibulus) held Antioch and waited, and again the Parthians withdrew. For now, the region was safe from Parthia (A. Sherwin-White 1984: 290–7).

2 The Civil War

By the end of the 50s parts of the Greek east had recovered from the economic and political crises of the Mithradatic wars. These crises, however, would soon return, as Rome was plunged into a period of civil strife that would last almost two decades. The crisis fell especially heavily on the Greek east, which not only became an important theatre of war, but also an important recruiting ground for troops, and the treasury that both sides used to fund their efforts.

Soon after Caesar invaded Italy in 49 BC, his opponents withdrew to the provinces, including Greece and Asia Minor. Here, they began to collect the resources needed to confront Caesar. Lentulus Crus, the anti-Caesarian consul, for example, was able to raise two legions in Asia (Caes. *BC* 3.4). Deiotaros of Galatia, Ariobarzanes of Cappadocia, and other kings who owed their kingdoms to Pompey's earlier decisions all furnished the troops asked of them. Maritime cities supplied ships. Money was extracted from all, even Rome's tax-farmers, and new taxes were introduced to raise money: a head-tax on slaves and children, and taxes on pillars and doors are mentioned, as well as 'loans' of the next year's taxes. Soldiers and rowers were conscripted, and, when winter came, Roman troops were billeted (Caes. *BC* 3.3–5, 31–2).

The showdown, when it came, occurred in southern Thessaly at Pharsalos, with a decisive victory for Caesar. Pompey fled. He is said to have considered flight to Parthia, but in the end escaped to Egypt, over which he claimed a special guardianship. The decision, as it turned out, was the wrong one. The Ptolemaic court decided that receiving him would mean entering a war against Caesar on the losing side. He was separated from his escort on the pretext of being taken to the king and assassinated (App. *BC* 2.83–4; Plut. *Pomp.* 77–8).

Following Pharsalos, Caesar was in control of the east, and to him came embassies from its cities and kingdoms. The occasion gave Caesar an opportunity to exercise the clemency in which he took pride. Not only did he make no onerous demands of money or resources on them, but he lowered their taxes and reduced the role that the hated tax-farmers played in the collection of taxes (Magie 1950: 405–7). The ancient privileges of some cities were confirmed; other cities even won new ones. In Pergamon, for example, 'sacred territories' were returned to the gods (*IGRR* 4.304). Caesar's goodwill was a great relief to the cities of Asia: they knew from experience the harm that a vengeful conqueror could inflict. Unsurprisingly, they showered Caesar with honours, some of which have survived epigraphically. As one would expect, their praise is high. An inscription from Pergamon, for example, lauds him as the 'saviour and benefactor of all Greeks', while another from Ephesos calls him a 'god made manifest and common saviour of human life' (Raubitschek 1954; Sherk 79).

Some individuals who had supported Pompey were, however, punished. A large fine was imposed on Deiotaros, for example, but that is hardly surprising since he had been one of the last to abandon Pompey. More significant is the fact that he retained his kingdom. He could hardly expect better. From Asia, Caesar left for Egypt in pursuit of Pompey, leaving Asia Minor in the care of a trusted supporter.

Caesar arrived in Alexandria a few days after Pompey's death and found himself drawn into the middle of a quarrel between Ptolemy XIII and his elder sister, Kleopatra VII. Caesar tried to arbitrate, but the small size of his military escort undermined his ability to dictate terms, and he was forced to hold up in Alexandria for the winter, with Kleopatra as his mistress, until reinforcements were brought by Mithradates of Pergamon (an influential supporter of Caesar related to several Asia Minor dynasts) and Hyrkanos, the Jewish high-priest in Jerusalem ([Caes.] *Alex.*; Jos. *AJ* 14.133–9). When he left in mid-47, Kleopatra was ruling jointly with an even younger brother, Ptolemy XIV, and had borne Caesar a son, Caesarion.

Caesar, having settled the dynastic struggle in Egypt, moved northwards, first through Palestine, where he rewarded the help that Hyrkanos had given him in Alexandria (Jos. *AJ* 14.190–212). He was anxious to return to Rome, but first he had to deal with a serious problem in Asia Minor. Pharnakes, son of Rome's old nemesis, Mithradates, had used Roman civil strife as an opportunity to recover his father's territories by invading Asia from his kingdom in the Crimea. He had moved virtually unopposed into Lesser Armenia and Cappadocia. Caesar's man in Asia Minor, Domitius Calvinus, scrambled to put together a suitable army, hastened into Pontos, forced a battle, but was soundly defeated, leaving Pharnakes as master of Pontos. Caesar now came to the rescue, catching up with his adversary near Zela. Two decades earlier Pharnakes' father had defeated one of Lucullus' legates there, and now the son apparently thought that the coincidence was a favourable omen. His father's victory, however, was not repeated. Within a few hours Caesar's legions had routed him. Caesar's arrival and victory were so quick that they inspired his famous boast, *veni vedi vici*, 'I came, I saw, I conquered' ([Caes.] *Alex.* 69–77; Suet. *Iul.* 37.2; Plut. *Caes.* 50.2). His departure was as swift as his arrival. Caesar had other pressing matters, and began his long journey homewards, escorted and entertained along the way by Deiotaros, who was subsequently tried in Rome for plotting against Caesar *en route* (Cic. *Deiot.*; Sullivan 1990: 165–9).

Rome's civil war dragged on for some time in other parts of the empire. Caesar, however, was sufficiently in control in the east that the outlines of a provincial policy are visible. Earlier in his career he had passed a strict law governing official behaviour in the provinces, and his interest in the health of the provinces continued. Most importantly for Asia was the transfer of responsibilities of tax-collection from Roman *publicani* to the cities' own officials. Asia was put in the capable hands of Servilius Isauricus (cos. 48), who took steps to aid the recovery of his province (Magie 1950: 416–17).

3 Triumvirate

A return to stability did not come. In March 44 Caesar was assassinated in Rome, and the Mediterranean world was plunged again into another period of conflict, this one longer and more destructive. The Greek east suffered especially. In 43 BC the two leaders of the conspiracy against Caesar, Brutus and Cassius, abandoned Rome and took up commands in the east. They had neither money, nor troops, and it was clear that they needed both for their looming struggle against Caesar's supporters. The money was to come from their new provinces. Taxes that were destined for Italy were seized, and diverted to their own purposes (Vell. Pat. 2.62.3; App. *BC* 4.5). Brutus demanded of the cities of Asia Minor a sum equivalent to ten years' taxes. Cities that resisted were attacked. Rhodes, for example, was compelled to surrender all gold and silver in the city, whether it was public, private, or sacred. In Lykia Brutus made an example of Xanthos, which was stormed and almost completely destroyed. For the allied kings the situation was no safer. For hesitating when asked to send aid to Cassius, Ariobarzanes III, the young king of Cappadocia, was put to death and the royal treasury seized (App. *BC* 4.63; Dio 47.33.1).

Brutus and Cassius amassed their troops in Asia in the summer of 42, and marched their combined armies into Macedonia to face the Caesarian forces led by Mark Antony, a protégé of Caesar, and Octavian, Caesar's adopted son. Caesar's assassins were defeated near Phillippi, and this at first brought some relief to Asia. The east now fell under the control of Antony, and he made some gestures towards a return to Caesar's policies. A letter of his to Hyrkanos has survived in which he remarks that Asia must be allowed to recover, as if from a great illness (Jos. *AJ* 14.312). Whether these intentions were sincere is unclear: he too needed money and land for his soldiers, and he soon announced in Ephesos that the cities of Asia must provide it for him (App. *BC* 5.5.21). The cities were naturally desperate: their money, jewellery and silverware had already been surrendered to Brutus and Cassius. In the end, Antony's demands were reduced: only nine years' tribute was required to be paid over the next two years (App. *BC* 5.6.21–7).

Ptolemaic Egypt would be an important ally, and its queen, Kleopatra, was summoned to meet Antony in Tarsos. Hearing that he had been greeted as a 'new Dionysos' in Ephesos, Kleopatra decided to take on the role of the 'new Aphrodite' and cruised up the Kydnos River in a gilded barge. The rumour spread that Aphrodite was revelling with Dionysos for the good of Asia (Plut. *Ant.* 26). Clearly she made a good impression, for she soon became Antony's most important political ally in the east; he saw to it that her personal enemies, including her sister, were eliminated. What is more, the relationship soon took a romantic turn. Antony spent the winter in Egypt, and in the following year she gave birth to twins.

While Antony was wintering in Egypt, however, several new crises arose. Before the Battle of Philippi, Cassius had sent Q. Labienus to Parthia to seek support, and he had become stranded there. Now he joined Pakoros, the son of the Parthian king, in leading an army across the frontier into Roman Syria. Many of the Roman troops stationed in Syria had served under Brutus and Cassius and therefore welcomed Labienus – thus preventing a repetition of the passive strategy that had been successful in the invasions of 51 and 50. From Syria the Parthians swept through Cilicia and into Asia. To make matters worse, a political crisis in Italy prevented Antony from coming to their defence. For now, it had to be abandoned to Labienus and the Parthians, who met little opposition except in Karia, where several cities resisted and suffered terribly. Nine years later, the suffering of Mylasa could still evoke Roman sympathy. In 31 BC, Octavian wrote to them of their 'overwhelmed city, many citizens made captives, some murdered, some burnt with the city, with the brutality of the enemy sparing neither shrines nor temples' (*SIG*³ 768, trans. in Sherk 91). A Roman counter-attack was inevitable and came the following year, led by Ventidius Bassus, a subordinate of Antony. He was able to re-establish Roman control very quickly: the Parthian forces were driven out of Asia and Labienus was himself killed.

Once Antony was again in firm control of the east, he had a free hand to organize its affairs. His policy departed from Pompey's, who assigned territories to dependent kings only when the existing civic structures were deemed too primitive for Roman administration. By contrast, Antony preferred client-kings over provinces. This approach had several advantages. It meant, for example, that his revenues were more predictable, since dynasts paid fixed tribute rather than taxes that varied with the economic output of a province. The policy also freed him from the headaches associated with conducting minor campaigns against the rebellious tribes in places like Isauria or the Amanos. As Strabo noted, kings were always on the spot and armed (14.5.5–9). This allowed Antony to concentrate on Parthia and Rome.

Antony's dispositions took shape over the next few years. Competence and loyalty were rewarded with additional territories, but there were also reversals and reassignments. By 36, however, his settlement was largely in place. Deiotaros had died in 39, and his territories were divided up. By 36, however, most of them had been reunited under the control of his former minister, Amyntas, who now carried the royal title (Sullivan 1990: 171–4). Most of Pontos was now under the rule of Polemon, son of Zenon, of Laodikeia. As far as we know, he had no royal blood in his veins. Rather, he and his father had led the resistance of their city against the Parthians during the invasion. Their loyalty was rewarded first with a small kingdom in Cilicia, and then with a larger one in Pontos. Cappadocia came into the hands of Archelaos, grandson of a general of Mithradates. He had been hereditary ruler-priest of Pontic Komana, a small principality in eastern Pontos (Sullivan 1990: 183–5). Antony's policy was a sensible one, and the quality of the monarchs whom Antony appointed is evidenced by the fact that most survived the defeat of Antony at Actium, and thrived under Augustus.

Antony's most important ally was Kleopatra, and her possessions were also expanded to include Cyprus, eastern Cilicia, Crete and Cyrene (Jos. *AJ* 14.392–7, 406; *BJ* 1.288–92, 297; Dio 49.32.5). She celebrated the donation by establishing a new regnal era. Henceforth, the years of her reign were counted from this date (Sherk 88; Sullivan 1990: 270–2). These distributions were consistent with Antony's policy of strengthening the dependent kings in the region. But the alliance was personal also. Sometime in the winter of 37/36, Antony acknowledged that the twins born to Kleopatra three years earlier were his own. Some form of marriage occurred at this point, which alienated many Romans, especially since Antony had not yet divorced his Roman wife, Octavia, sister of Octavian (Plut. *Demetr. Ant. Compar.* 41; Livy *Per.* 131). Antony, it was charged (with some justification) was becoming less a Roman magistrate, and more a Hellenistic monarch. But there were also some practical strategic advantages. Formalizing his alliance with Kleopatra enhanced his status in the east and signalled his intention to stay in the east for the long term.

This policy of downloading problematic regions to client-kings allowed Antony to pursue his own ambitions, which included mounting an expedition against Parthia in the summer of 36. His immediate aim was to invade Media from Armenia and capture its chief city. This would avoid repeating Crassus' mistake of attacking Parthia through territory that was tactically disadvantageous. Despite the strategic superiority of Antony's plan, his invasion failed miserably. In order to hasten his arrival in Media, Antony advanced ahead of his siege equipment, which was insufficiently defended. The Parthians attacked the column and destroyed it, rendering his objective unattainable and inspiring the king of Armenia to switch his alliance to Parthia at the worst possible moment. After some hesitation, Antony was forced to retreat, but through territory that was now hostile. The march homewards was gruelling, and by the time the legions were safe in Roman territory, Antony had lost a third of his forces (Plut. *Ant.* 34–50). The setback was significant, both to his military resources and to his reputation as a general. He tried to undo some of the damage by undertaking a new campaign, this time against the king of Armenia for his treachery. He successfully occupied Armenia in 34 BC, and led its king in a grand procession in Alexandria (Magie 1950: 427–40; Debevoise 1938: 123–38). This, however, gave his Roman rivals an opportunity to attack him. The procession was sufficiently like a Roman triumph that he could be charged with yet another anti-Roman act – transferring a sacred Roman ritual away from Rome.

Antony's campaigns against Parthia were expensive, both in terms of manpower and money, and they now revealed the dangerous degree to which he had come to depend on Kleopatra. Naturally, this support came at a price, and Antony announced further grants to Kleopatra and her children, including giving them sovereignty over Armenia, Syria, Phoenicia and Cilicia. Antony even minted coins that had his portrait on one side and Kleopatra's on the other (Sullivan 1990: 273–5).

The rivalry between Octavian and Antony had always been strong, and their relations had deteriorated seriously over the preceding years. This would now resolve itself through arms, and both sides began to mobilize for the coming struggle. Serious divisions arose, however, among Antony's Roman supporters, mostly over Kleopatra. Domitius Ahenobarbus, perhaps the most illustrious of Antony's supporters and the consul of 32, was publicly rude to her (Vell. Pat. 2.84). Others urged Antony to send her back to Alexandria (Plut. *Ant.* 56.2). Some supporters even defected to Octavian. The critical moment came when Octavian illegally seized and made public the contents of Antony's will, which revealed that he wanted to be buried in Alexandria. In the light of Antony's earlier behaviour towards Kleopatra, this was easily presented as treason. Roman public opinion now clearly swung behind Octavian, and more supporters abandoned Antony.

War was inevitable. Antony was forced to mobilize the east's resources, already seriously depleted by earlier strife. No property was safe. One of his subordinates even cut down the sacred grove of Asklepios in Kos to provide timber to build warships (Dio 51.8.3; Val. Max. 1.1.9). The east again was forced to supply labour, animals and troops. Plutarch reports that the citizens of Chaironeia, including his great-grandfather, were compelled to carry grain down to the sea under the whips of

Antony's agents. They were in the process of bringing a new load when news came of Antony's defeat at Actium on 2 September 31 BC (Plut. *Ant.* 68.4).

Antony's defeat clearly signalled his end, though he escaped with Kleopatra to Alexandria, where they tried to organize further resistance. Their attempts, however, were futile, as Antony's supporters, seeing that victory was impossible, defected to Octavian in a steady stream. Alexandria fell in the summer of 31. Antony died, probably by his own hand; Kleopatra was captured and lived another nine days before taking her own life.

4 The Augustan Principate

Octavian's triumph at Actium settled the question of who would dominate the Mediterranean world, and freed the east from the disastrous strife that had beset it for so long. With peace came prosperity and the long, slow process by which the Greek east was finally reconciled to Roman rule in a unified empire.

It was not an easy task. Much of the Greek world was in a sorry state. In mainland Greece, Strabo, who wrote later in Augustus' reign, reports that the countryside became depopulated and the local economies impoverished (8.7.5–8.3; 9.2.16–18). This description is probably exaggerated (Alcock 1993), but economic pressures existed nonetheless. Many parts of the Greek east had never fully recovered from the Mithradatic wars and had suffered many hardships in Rome's civil strife. An anecdote from Josephos (*AJ* 16.18ff.) illustrates the problem. In 14 BC Herod came to Asia Minor to meet Agrippa. In Chios he discovered that the city's stoa, which had been destroyed during the Mithradatic occupation almost seventy years earlier, was still in ruins. Out of generosity he paid for its renovation. The situation in Delos was similar. It had been sacked by one of Mithradates' generals during the Mithradatic war and again by pirates in 69. Some parts of the city were abandoned, and Delos never fully recovered (cf. *Anth. Pal.* 9.408, 421). These cases may not have been typical. But they well illustrate that what the Greek east most needed was a period of peace and reconstruction.

Following the battle of Actium, Octavian remained in the region and was able to assess the state of much of the Greek east and address some of its problems. The wealth of Egypt put him in a position to be generous. He distributed grain to some cities and remitted the debts of others (Dio Chrys. 31.66; Plut. *Ant.* 68). He made some significant changes. Egypt was turned into a province governed by equestrian governors, a major innovation. Cyprus and Crete again became provinces. In 27 BC Augustus (as now he was named) revamped Rome's provincial system. The older, wealthier and more peaceful provinces became 'public' provinces, governed by proconsuls selected by seniority and the lot. Other, 'imperial', provinces were governed by legates appointed by Augustus. The east saw both kinds of province. Syria, with its legions and the potentially problematic Parthian frontier, was under a legate, while most provinces – Asia, Achaea, Macedonia – had proconsuls, at least to begin with (Dio 53.13–15).

As had been the case under Antony, large areas remained under the control of allied kings. Archelaos of Cappadocia, Amyntas of Galatia, Polemon of Pontos and Herod of Judaea all owed their positions to Antony, and had remained loyal to him until his defeat was inevitable. They managed, however, to transfer their loyalty to Octavian and not only saved their kingdoms, but in time became the bulwarks of Augustus' eastern network, imposing peace on warlike local tribes and providing a buffer between Rome and Parthia.

Galatia was especially important in the system, given that it included the main land route from Asia to Syria. In 25 BC, its king, Amyntas, was killed while attempting to pacify the Homanadenses, one of several bellicose tribes of the Tauros. The area was too important to leave in the inexperienced hands of Amyntas' son, Pylaimenes, and so Augustus annexed Galatia and governed it through legates (Dio 53.26; Mitchell 1993: 73–6). The pacification of these tribes took several decades more of concentrated effort, including the foundation of veteran colonies, the building of a military road, and several major campaigns (Dio 55.28; Levick 1967: 24–41). The changes that accompanied provincialization were significant. Before Roman rule, central Asia Minor was not highly urbanized. There were, of course, trading-centres, forts and villages, but these were nothing like the typical Greek city in status or structure. Now the region benefited from a conscious policy of urbanization, with the foundation of cities that to this day remain important, such as Ankyra, modern Ankara (Mitchell 1993: 87–91; Levick 1967: 193–4).

The annexation of Galatia demonstrated that the major provincial realignment of 27 would not be the final word, and other changes are attested (cf. Dio 54.4.1). Augustus' burden was significant, especially the duty to oversee almost all the trouble spots on Rome's frontier. Some of the responsibilities were passed to Agrippa, his closest political ally and soon to be his son-in law. In 23 Agrippa was sent to the east with sweeping authority to oversee this part of the empire. Little is known of his actions in the region, but when he returned in 21 BC, Augustus himself journeyed east for two years, only to be replaced again by Agrippa.

These moves were intended at least in part to keep pressure on Rome's Parthian rival. Their victories over Crassus and Antony, and their invasion of Syria and Asia, were still fresh in people's minds. The situation was also unstable in Armenia, which after Antony's departure on the eve of Actium had fallen into the hands of pro-Parthian elements. Augustus' strategy was to keep Parthia off-balance by keeping the threat of military action alive and encouraging a rival to the Parthian throne, who was living in exile in Syria (Dio 51.18.2–3). In the mid-20s Tiridates somehow managed to kidnap the young son of Phraates IV of Parthia, and took him to Rome. At about the same time, pro-Roman elements in Armenia rose up and demanded a new ruler, Tigranes III, who was also living in exile in Roman territories. Augustus returned the young Parthian prince to his father, which proved to be the gesture needed to make a diplomatic breakthrough possible (Dio 53.33.2; Debevoise 1938: 136–7). The standards and prisoners captured from Crassus and Antony were returned, and no objection was made when Augustus sent the young Tiberius, son of his wife Livia, to install the pro-Roman Tigranes III on the Armenian throne (Dio 54.8.1; *RG* 29; A. Sherwin-White 1984: 323–41). The success was celebrated in Rome and the empire as a bloodless victory and became a central theme of Augustan propaganda (*RG* 29).

Agrippa spent a second period supervising the east from 18–13 BC, but now concern about the region was fading as the Parthian threat continued to diminish. Thus, no one was sent to replace him as overseer of the eastern provinces. Indeed, by 10 BC, relations were sufficiently restored that Phraates IV sent his four sons to live in

Rome. This was done in order to prevent them being used by his enemies as challengers to his own position (Strabo 16.1.28; *RG* 32.2; Braund 1984: 12–13). In 6 BC, however, events required the creation of a new eastern command. Tigranes III of Armenia had recently died. Rome had a preferred replacement, but Tigranes' son (Tigranes IV) successfully opposed him and turned to Parthia for support (Dio 55.9.4; Tac. *Ann.* 2.4). Tiberius, who was now Augustus' son-in-law, was given sweeping authority as a preparation for an eastern command. Internal politics in Rome intervened, however, and Tiberius (for reasons that have been debated ever since), retired from public life to Rhodes, where he would remain for almost a decade (Levick 1976: 31–49). For now, the Armenian problem was left to fester.

The situation in the east soon became even more unsettled. First, in 4 BC, Herod died. He had been an important figure in the near east for a generation. Although he was originally an appointee of Antony, he became a trusted part of Augustus' eastern network of allied kingdoms. The history of his reign, however, was marked by civil unrest and dynastic turmoil that led to the trial and execution of several of the sons groomed to succeed him. When he died in 4 BC, his will instructed that his kingdom be divided among three surviving sons, none of whom were well suited to rule. Augustus upheld Herod's wishes and awarded the lion's share of the kingdom to Herod's son Archelaos. While the Herodian princes were in Rome arguing their cases, however, rebellion broke out at home, and Rome's Syrian legions had to intervene (Jos. *BJ* 1.211–2.166; *AJ* 14–17; Schürer 1973: 287–329).

The instability in the region was even further exacerbated when Phraates IV of Parthia was murdered in 3/2 BC by his wife and son, who then took the throne as Phraates V (or Phraatakes). He took a strongly anti-Roman line, especially in Armenia, where he supported the anti-Roman Tigranes IV. Tiberius' retirement had prevented a timely intervention in Armenia. It now provided an opportunity, however, for Augustus' grandson Gaius to acquire military experience, to gain exposure in the provinces, and to be showcased as a future *princeps*. Gaius' send-off and progress eastwards were as much about show as reality. Grand ceremonies in Rome marked his departure and Rome's poets celebrated his coming success. So, too, did the cities of the Greek east. In Athens, for example, he was celebrated as the 'New Ares' (*IG2*² 3.3250, trans. Braund 1985: no. 55), and a Greek poet prophesied an easy victory: 'Go forth to the Euphrates, son of Zeus, for already the Parthians are deserting to you on eastern feet' (*Anth. Pal.* 9.297).

In 1 BC Gaius set out for the east, accompanied by Augustus' most trusted friends. For now, there was no need to hurry. In AD 1 he led an expedition in Nabataean Arabia against nomadic raiders (Romer 1979; Bowersock 1983: 56). He then made his way to the Parthian frontier, where he met in conference with the young Parthian king, Phraatakes (Vell. Pat. 2.101). A new understanding was reached, and Gaius then advanced into Armenia, with Parthian acquiescence, to install the Roman candidate on the Armenian throne. Anti-Roman elements were less accommodating, however, and revolted, throwing the country into turmoil and compelling Gaius to intervene with the legions accompanying him. During the siege of a rebel stronghold, however, Gaius was wounded; eighteen months later, he died (A. Sherwin-White 1984: 325–7).

The dynastic turmoil of the preceding decade was now more or less resolved in favour of Tiberius. He was now adopted by Augustus, effectively designating him as successor. This turmoil, however, had not been confined to the imperial house, or to Rome. Cities and kings in the east had a strong interest in the succession, and jockeyed for position among the possible successors. Some tried to abandon their connections with Tiberius while Gaius prevailed, including Tiberius' old friend Archelaos, king of Cappadocia, whom he defended in a trial in Rome in the 20s (Levick 1971). He tried to demonstrate his loyalty to Gaius by publicly insulting Tiberius, thereby earning Tiberius' lifelong enmity and causing his eventual downfall (Dio 57.17.3–5). Others in the east seem also to have been drawn into the struggle (Bowersock 1984).

The competition to honour the emperor and his family is one of the most striking developments of this period. Indeed, in at least one case the competition was formal. In 9 BC the provincial assembly of Asia announced the winner in a long-standing contest to find the most appropriate honour for Augustus 'whom, for the benefit of mankind, providence has filled with excellence, as if it had sent him as a saviour for us and our descendants' (*OGIS* 458, trans. in Sherk 101). The prize was a gold crown, and it was won by Paulus Fabius Maximus, the governor, who proposed that the province should adopt a new calendar that began the year on Augustus' birthday (23 Sept.), with the first month named 'Caesar' in his honour.

The most extreme example of such honours is, of course, the introduction of the public cult of the emperor in the east. Ruler cult had long been practised in the Greek east, first for Hellenistic kings, and later (on occasion) for Roman officials in the Republic (Chaniotis, this volume). Almost immediately after Antony's defeat, representatives from two cities asked permission to establish a cult for the new ruler. Octavian proceeded cautiously, not wanting to offend the sensibilities of the Roman elite and thus repeat the mistake of his adoptive father. Non-Romans were allowed to worship him in two cities in conjunction with the cult of the goddess Roma, which had a long history in Asia Minor, while Romans worshipped Roma and the deified Julius in Ephesos and Nikaia (Dio 51.20.6–7; Mellor 1975).

From these modest beginnings, the phenomenon of ruler worship exploded. It spread throughout the cities of the Greek east, and by the end of Augustus' reign most cities of any importance had introduced some aspect of the imperial cult alongside their traditional religious observances. Temples and altars were built, rituals introduced, priesthoods and festivals established. Even minor figures within the imperial house were sometimes included. The development and spread of the imperial cult, however, should not be interpreted merely as extreme obsequiousness. The new cults succeeded because they did not replace traditional systems, but supplemented them, and provided a context in which Roman power could be contextualized for a Greek constituency (S. Price 1984).

The new system also resulted in new opportunities for civic elites. Maintenance of the cult of Rome and Augustus fell to the provincial assembly, where the elites of provincial cities found a new venue for their ambition. Such competition, however, acted to align their interests with Rome and the emperor (Magie 1950: 447–52). The imperial cult also illustrates the degree to which the emperor dominated the provincial conception of the empire and their place in it. The corollary of this was the gradual disappearance under Augustus of senatorial patrons of cities (Eilers 2002; Nicols 1990). When provincials looked to the centre of the Roman world, they saw the Emperor there (Millar 1984a). The last decade of Augustus' life was a time of personal disappointment for him, and setbacks for the Empire. The death of Gaius in Syria in AD 4 destroyed his plans for the succession. But there were growing problems elsewhere. Decisive action became necessary in Judaea, where Archelaos proved to be unsuitable for rule and an obstacle to stability in the region. In AD 6, he was removed, apparently for his heavy-handedness in dealing with dissent, and Judaea became a Roman province (Jos. *BJ* 2.111; Dio 55.27.6). The process included a census, which implied the coming imposition of Roman taxation, an event that found its way (erroneously) into the story of Christ's birth (Luke 2:1–3 with Millar 1993: 46). The census was accompanied by resistance and unrest, and the new province, supervised by equestrian officials, proved difficult to govern.

The problems in the east soon faded into the background, as a major rebellion in Pannonia in AD 6 required a transfer of resources and manpower towards the empire's northern frontier. This was done partly by resorting to the unusual expedient of appointing governors for the public provinces for two years instead of one (Dio 55.28.2), and partly by transferring the only legionary contingents in Asia Minor to the northern front (Vell. Pat. 2.112.4, with Mitchell 1976). No sooner had this rebellion been finally settled in AD 9 than a new rebellion broke out in Germany. Unsurprisingly, the east receded from view. Indeed, in the coming century, no emperor would visit Asia.

FURTHER READING

No single ancient source gives us an account of the experience of the whole of the east for the whole of our period. There are periods during the civil wars where the east takes centre stage, and so become approachable through Appian's *Civil Wars*, Dio's *History*, or Plutarch's *Life of Antony* (which is best read with Pelling 1987 and 1996). Normally, however, one must piece together scattered literary and documentary sources. Much of the leg-work has been done by others. Magie 1950 provides a comprehensive, though now somewhat dated, treatment of Roman Asia Minor. A. N. Sherwin-White (1984) describes the political manoeuvring over the Ancient Near East up to the death of Gaius. For the evolution of central Anatolia, see especially Mitchell 1993, which begins with our period and goes far beyond it. The details concerning the dependent kings of the period are handily collected by Sullivan 1990, but only up to the battle of Actium; for a somewhat wider perspective, see Braund 1984. For the impact of the new Augustan principate on the provinces generally, see Millar 1984a; and on the imperial cult, S. Price 1984. Important documents in the original languages can be found in *SIG*³, *OGIS*, *RDGE*, and the most important documents pertaining to Augustus are conveniently collected by Ehrenberg and Jones 1976; translations of many of these documents are available in Sherk 1984 and Braund 1985.

PART II

Protagonists

CHAPTER SEVEN

The Ptolemies and Egypt

Dorothy J. Thompson

1   Setting the Scene

When Alexander died in 323 BC, Ptolemy son of Lagos, Macedonian general and historian of Alexander's conquests, made straight for Egypt, a country he first met together with the Conqueror. Here, with a keen eye on the geography and natural wealth of the region, he inaugurated the most long-lasting of the Hellenistic dynasties.

On his invasion in 332 Alexander had gained swift recognition as ruler in succession to the unpopular Persians. His foundation of Alexandria on the coast, with its rich agricultural hinterland and double harbour, formed a new Mediterranean focus for the country. Here he built a temple to the goddess Isis, and at Memphis he sacrificed to Egyptian Apis and the other gods. These acts combined with his visit to the oracle of Ammon, out in the western desert at Siwa, to provide a clear policy statement for his successors (Arr. *Anab.* 3.1–5). Control of the wealth and power of Egypt depended on a rule attuned to the existing sensibilities of a people whose religion and culture were deeply established.

A local Greek, Kleomenes of Naukratis, was left in control by Alexander. Supported by military garrisons and local administrators, Kleomenes proved successful in revenue-raising. How far, on liquidating the man himself, Ptolemy adopted Kleomenes' system remains speculative; he was certainly more conciliatory towards the priests than was the latter. Strengthened no doubt by the successful hijack of the embalmed remains of the Conqueror (Erskine 2002a), at first Ptolemy governed the region on behalf of Alexander's heirs. In 304, however, he followed Antigonos and took the Greek title of king, so regularizing his position as the new monarch of Egypt (see now *P. Köln* VI 247.ii.28–38; Braund, this volume).

The country he ruled consisted of some 23,000 square kilometres of fertile land which extended some 320 kilometres along the narrow valley of the Nile from the first cataract in the south to the Delta and the Mediterranean coast. The broad-stretching, well-watered Delta to the north was difficult to cross; the entry to Egypt from the east ran south from Pelousion to Memphis. From Heliopolis at the Delta's apex, the

Kanopic branch of the Nile ran north to Alexandria from where the coastal route ran
west to Cyrene, a key Ptolemaic possession. From Memphis, there was access overland
to the rich lake province of the Fayum. To the south lay Thebes with its great temples at
Karnak and Luxor, another historic centre of the country. Ptolemy's foundation of a
further full Greek city in the south, Ptolemais Hermeiou, marks a deliberate attempt to
spread Ptolemaic control along the full valley of the Nile. By the 290s there were
Greeks well-established in Thebes which, despite Ptolemais, remained the key centre of
Upper Egypt (Clarysse 1995: 1; Depauw 2000: 32).

Bounded on either side by desert – Libya to the west and Arabia to the east – the
thin strip of the Nile valley was linked to the Red Sea by caravan routes from Dendera,
Koptos and Edfu (Apollonos Polis Megalê) (Alcock et al., this volume, section 3); to

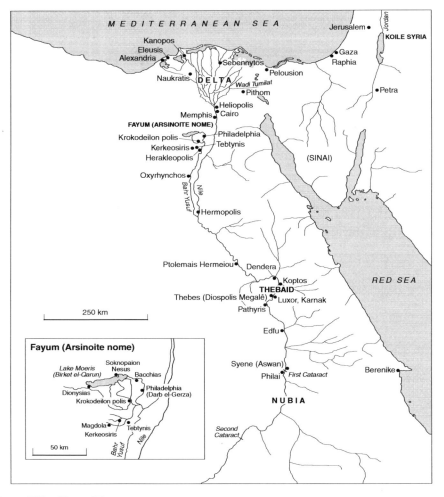

Figure 7.1   Map of Egypt

the north across the Delta, a canal along the Wadi Tumilat joined the river to the head of the Red Sea. From various points along the valley south from Oxyrhynchos caravan trails ran west to the oases. A postal service, most probably a Persian inheritance, provided speedy communication along the valley (*Sel.Pap.* II 397 [*c.* 255 BC]) and new foundations on the Red Sea coast formed staging posts for the transports bringing African elephants for the Ptolemaic army, together with ivory and Nubian gold for the royal treasury (Strabo 17.1.45; Burstein 1996b). Egypt was a rich country and the annual flood of the Nile allowed extensive irrigation agriculture (Bowman and Rogan 1999).

The agricultural wealth of Egypt allowed Ptolemy to develop the country's finances, and the natural frontiers for defence aided his consolidation of an effective and lasting power-base. When his competitor Perdikkas attacked in 321, Ptolemy's forces combined with the crocodiles of the Nile to defeat the invader (Diod. 17.33–6); it was not until the mid second century that a rival dynast, the Seleukid king Antiochos IV of Syria, succeeded in (briefly) conquering Egypt.

With a strong base at home and an Aegean empire, Ptolemy made use of family and friends in his management of his kingdom and its dependencies. His stepson Magas was installed in Cyrene in 301; that city was to prove a fertile source of both troops and scholars for the Ptolemies. His brother Menelaos governed Cyprus from 310 until 306, when it fell to the Antigonids. In setting up a monarchic system in which cities had little part to play, Ptolemy made use both of the newcomers and existing administrative classes. As Diodoros reports in what is a reliable account for these early years, 'he treated the natives with kindness' (18.14.1). Native temples were recognized with donations of land recorded in hieroglyphics, the sacred script of Egypt (D. J. Thompson 1994b: 72). A royal loan of 50 talents helped meet mummification costs for an Apis bull, and the Memphite cult of the deified (mummified) bull as Osorapis lay behind the development of the new Greek cult of Sarapis. Among his native advisors Manetho of Sebennytos, high priest of Heliopolis and historian, seems likely to have played a key role.

Egyptian religion had never been exclusive; presenting themselves to immigrant and local populations in different forms, the gods of Egypt had a long and powerful life. Horus the Behedite of Edfu was Apollo for the Greeks, Ra became Helios, Amun of Thebes was Zeus, and so on. For the Greek immigrants, however, it was their human guise which was preferred to Egyptian animal forms. In promoting the cause of native gods, their festivals and cults and in temple-building, Ptolemy I and his successors found a sure way to establish their rule.

An important feature of the Ptolemaic administration set up by Ptolemy I was that it was a literate system, one that was administered by scribes at all levels in writing. It is only in the reign of Ptolemy II that a change in burial practice occurred with important consequences for our knowledge of this system. The introduction of mummy casing formed from waste papyri known as 'cartonnage', a form of papier mâché, has provided information unparalleled in the ancient world. Given the dry climate of Egypt, papyri used for cartonnage preserve intact not only literary texts but also the papers, both public and private, of those involved in the administration of the country. Once discarded, these recycled texts now give insights to the modern historian that are all the more precious given the absence of more regular historical accounts and the different sorts of issues that they treat.

Such histories as do survive – that of Polybios, in fragments only, of Diodoros, of importance mainly for the early period, or the lurid and headline-grabbing stories of Pompeius Trogus, excerpted by Justin – may for Egypt be filled out not only by inscriptions but, more particularly, by the evidence of papyri. Regularly devoid of a wider context and surviving often in fragments, such texts create their own problems but also offer great possibilities. The view of Ptolemaic Egypt they allow is a patchwork one, a kaleidoscopic picture in which the hand of the historian needs a firm control. To write history from papyri is a formidable challenge (Bagnall 1995).

2   The Ptolemaic System

Under a dynastic rule, political stability depends on a trouble-free form of succession. The Ptolemaic dynasty was a family one which in normal times provided a clear and easy change of rule between the generations. Sometimes, however, and especially in the second and first centuries, sibling rivalry in an extreme form, aggravated by the rivalry of related queens, threatened central control; this was the case with the two sons of both Kleopatra I and III. With brother–sister marriage added to Macedonian royal polygamy (from the reign of Ptolemy II), the family relationships of the Ptolemies at times are barely credible (Whitehorne 1993; Ogden 1999: 67–116). But in the third century at first the succession ran smoothly. Ptolemy II ruled together with his father before taking over completely. His reign ran from 285 and he continued his father's work in shaping the new system. Indeed, given the survival of cartonnage, it is from his reign that details emerge of many institutions which may well have preceded his reign. In his policies, as already for his father, the interrelated issues of defence, revenue-raising and wider administrative control take their place beside cultural issues affecting the mixed and varied population of his kingdom, which are highlighted in this early period.

The supply of soldiers was a problem for all Hellenistic monarchs. The success of Ptolemy I's innovatory policy of settling soldiers on the land was proved in 306, when Ptolemaic soldiers, defeated on Cyprus by Demetrios, preferred to desert back home to Egypt rather than accept good pay from the victor (Diod. 20.47.4). Cavalrymen were endowed with plots of 100 or 80 arouras (27.5 or 22 hectares), infantrymen with smaller plots. For others, billets were provided in the homes of Egyptians, accompanied often by tension and trouble, as in this memorandum (*Sel.Pap.* II 413 [241 BC]):

> We find that several of the houses in Krokodeilon polis which were earlier used for housing troops have had their roofs demolished by their owners; likewise, altars have been built against their doors to prevent their use as billets . . .

Settlement was concentrated in the Fayum, where the combination of expertise of Macedonian drainage and Egyptian irrigation engineers resulted in widespread reclamation and a new garden province for Egypt (D. J. Thompson 1999a). The royal input to this development project is marked in the names of the area. Egypt was traditionally divided into nomes and the Fayum, earlier known as the Marsh, under Ptolemy II was renamed the Arsinoite nome after his sister and wife. More than one village in the region was called Arsinoe; Philadelphia was named for her, and under Ptolemy III Euergetes (the Benefactor) the nome capital Krokodeilon polis became Ptolemais Euergetis. Here, as elsewhere, new royal names were marked upon the landscape of Egypt; the new settlers generally flourished. It is also from this exceptional area that much of the Ptolemaic cartonnage derives, presenting a somewhat biased picture.

Population registers from the period show that settler families were larger, more complex and certainly better endowed than those of Egyptian peasants who were their neighbours (D. J. Thompson 2002). In the second century the system of allotments (*klêroi*) was extended to the Egyptian infantrymen recruited for the Fourth Syrian war. Land grants became smaller as time went on with the development of other forms of recruiting and retaining the loyalty of the army. From the reign of Ptolemy VI, the introduction of *politeumata* provided a new source of identity for different (often army) communities; starting in the same reign and continuing under his brother, a series of new urban foundations with dynastic names (Philometoris, Kleopatra, Euergetis) served as garrison points especially in the south (Kramer 1997; Heinen 1997). As in other policy areas, over time approaches to the problem might differ; the basic concern with defence remained.

The wealth of the crown depended to a large degree on the success of agricultural production. As new areas, like the Fayum, were brought under cultivation, so new crops were introduced. Naked *durum* wheat proved popular and eventually supplanted the traditional husked emmer-wheat; bread took over from porridge as a standard food. Some experiments, like the cabbage from Rhodes that turned bitter (Athen. 9.369f.), were not altogether successful but, as with new breeds of animals (sheep from Euboia, pigs from Sicily), the introduction of vines, olives, and other cash crops will have had a significant impact on the agricultural scene of Egypt (D. J. Thompson 1999b). They also proved an important source of revenue and, whilst rents and taxes on cereal crops were charged and levied in kind, those on orchards and vines came in cash. For an important new feature of the Ptolemaic system was that it was now monetarized, with taxes collected in cash as well as in kind.

In the Fayum, most land was nominally 'royal land', belonging to the king. Some land was ceded to cleruchs and temples ('cleruchic' and 'sacred land'); on this only smaller taxes were charged. On most of the land, however, the crown levied rents and taxes, which regularly amounted to over half annual production. In the southern Nile valley, in contrast, a similar level of charge in the form of a harvest tax (Vandorpe 2000b) was made on the cultivated area of what was there labelled 'private land'. Such land could be bought or sold; it often belonged to temples but was subject still to royal taxation. This prerogative of levying charges on all the land of Egypt and the high level of these illustrate well the overriding power of the monarchy. The resulting revenue enabled Egypt to become engaged in Aegean-wide politics – she even ran a garrison in Attica during the Chremonidean war (268–266) – and to wage a series of wars against her closest rivals, the Seleukids, with whom she struggled for control of Palestine and the Gaza strip, in antiquity known as Hollow Syria (Koile Syria).

Behind the levy of land rents lay the operation of the land survey. From 258, a demotic ostrakon found in the Karnak temple at Thebes records an order made when the pharaoh (Ptolemy II) was away at Daphne, involved in the Second Syrian war:

A survey of Egypt was ordered, specifying field by field their irrigation possibilities, their location, their quality, their arable portions, their relation to the property of the protector gods, their (common) borders with the fields of the benefices themselves and of the royal fields, specifying area by area the size of the parcels and vineyards, noting when the fields of the area are dry – likewise the pastures – and the water channels, the fields that are free and vacant, the high fields, and the fields that are (artificially) irrigated, their basins and the embankments that are ploughed and cultivated, specifying orchard by orchard the trees with their fruits, the gardens, the high fields and the low parcels, their footpaths, the list of leased parcels with their equipment, the decisions concerning the price in connection with them, the emoluments of the priests, the emoluments of the dependents of the reigning king, and, in addition, their taxes, the total of the expenditures for the welfare of Egypt and its sublime freedom, of its cities and of its temples. (Burstein 97; Zauzich 1984)

Drawn up at village level, passed on up the administrative hierarchy through the royal scribe of the nome to the *dioikêtês*, or chief financial minister of the country, annual land surveys prepared once the flood had subsided were supplemented in early spring by surveys of crops in the fields. Each year, in theory at least, the crown could reckon how great the income would be. The bureaucratic structures and scribal work involved come clearly through the texts (Verhoogt 1998).

Land revenues, however, did not suffice to meet the needs of the state, and under the Ptolemies, perhaps for the first time in Egypt, a poll-tax was introduced in the form of the salt-tax. Earlier, records of the country's population were compiled to register the manpower available for corvée labour, both for special tasks and for regular annual work on the irrigation ditches and dikes. Known mainly from the third century, the salt-tax was a low level tax that was charged on men and women alike; women paid a lower rate and over the course of the third century the general rate was lowered more than once (Clarysse and Thompson 1995). The salt-tax was charged and collected in cash; such a pervasive charge played a significant part in progressive monetization. The registers of taxpayers, organized on a household basis as also by tax-category and occupation, provide details of household composition and structure (Bagnall and Frier 1994; D. J. Thompson 1997 and 2002). Tax-collection was a complex business, an interesting mix of public and private which is typical of much of the Ptolemaic system. Taxes were farmed out to the highest bidder, with solid guarantees required before any contract was issued. It was state collectors, however, who played a major role in collection on the ground. Greek financial structures were thus added to the existing system of state control (von Reden 2001). The same amalgam of interests may be found in other aspects of the system. The state gave – in grants, for instance, made to temples – and it collected; others were financially responsible for any potential shortfall.

State involvement was pervasive in most economic aspects of Egypt. In agriculture, a crop schedule detailed the crops that were to be sown (*P.Yale* 36.2–3 [232 BC]; *P.Tebt.* III 703.57–60 [*c.* 242 BC], translated Austin 253 and 256). The cultivation and exploitation of oil crops were centrally controlled at every stage (BD 114 [259 BC]; Bingen 1978a); textile production was closely watched, and some other forms of production were subjected to monopoly control (Préaux 1939: 93–116; Bingen

1978a). All was carefully watched by an army of officials, who in turn were carefully controlled (*P.Tebt.* III 703, trans as Burstein 101, extracts):

> During your tours of inspection, try to encourage each individual .... The sowing of the nome in accordance with the plan for planting is to be one of your prime concerns .... It is your responsibility that the designated provisions are transported to Alexandria .... Go also to the weaving sheds ... and take special care that the looms are in operation .... Conduct an audit also of the revenues, village by village .... Make a list of the royal houses and of the gardens associated with them .... Take particular care that no fraud occur or any other wrongful act .... (Thus) you will create security in the countryside and increase the revenues significantly .... You should behave well and be upright in your duties, not getting involved with bad company, avoid any involvement in corruption, believe that if you are not accused of such things, you will merit promotion, keep this memorandum to hand and write concerning each matter as required.

These short extracts from a long exhortatory memorandum spell out the royal ideology; as is clear from a mound of complaints, the practice was often different. The fact that all was written down enables us to trace some of the conflicting pressures involved at different levels of such a bureaucratic system (D. J. Crawford 1978).

Where did the Ptolemies find the men to run their administration and how did they keep them loyal? Figures are always uncertain but new data from the Fayum suggest that immigrants represented a small percentage of the population, perhaps 10–15 per cent overall, unevenly distributed with a heavy concentration in Alexandria and Lower Egypt (*P.Count* 1 [254–231 BC]; D. J. Thompson 2001: 312). The use, therefore, of existing personnel was essential, and the hieroglyphic evidence of Egyptian sarcophagi and statues allows us to trace some of those involved (D. J. Thompson 1992: 44–5). So do the papyri themselves since in the early generations demotic was still used alongside Greek, and Greek itself is on occasion written with the Egyptian rush (not the Greek pen) allowing us to identify Egyptian scribes at work (Tait 1988). Language too is a give-away; Egyptian scribes did not always write good Greek (Clarysse 1993). Such an open, non-exclusive approach on the part of the new rulers to those already in post may have been inevitable. Nevertheless, this was typical of the Ptolemaic approach to rule. Native law-codes and courts were also left in place; such an approach was no doubt important in winning support.

In some ways, however, an active policy of hellenization can be charted. In Alexandria, the Library and the Museum (Erskine 1995) formed the physical embodiment of a royal policy of patronage in which Greek language and literature were privileged (Hunter, this volume). Throughout the countryside, an active encouragement of Greek schooling can be traced in the numbers of teachers in post and in the salt-tax remission that they shared with coaches, actors and victorious athletes. The survival and spread of Greek literary works is witness to the speed and success of this policy (Clarysse 1983; *LDAB*). At the same time, the willingness of some Egyptians to 'go Greek', take on Greek names and adopt Greek ways (the acquisition, for instance, of household slaves) is a not uncommon reaction to a new controlling power. Moreover, the third-century status of 'tax-Hellene' also brought some financial benefits to its holders (D. J. Thompson 2001: 307).

3   Ptolemies and Temples

Running the administration, the levy of rents and taxes, economic concerns and matters of law and order form the regular stuff of government. In Egypt, two further factors need consideration: the age-old power of the temples and the related role of the Ptolemies themselves, the new rulers of Egypt. The temples were major land-holders with developed economic institutions as well as centres of cult, and no resident ruler could afford to antagonize the gods of Egypt. Traditionally, the pharaoh formed a key link between the gods and his people. Relations with the temples took many different forms. Already as satrap, Ptolemy I had restored some possessions to Delta temples (Hölbl 2001: 3) though, as becomes clear later on, 'restoration' might be a somewhat relative term in respect to control of land. Royal rulings regulated the way that the temples were financed. In 263 the tax (*apomoira*) on vineyards and orchards was designated for the new cult of Arsinoe, the sister-wife of Ptolemy II, who had been introduced as a temple-sharing goddess to all Egyptian temples (Koenen 1993: 66–9; Clarysse and Vandorpe 1998; Chaniotis, this volume). As with other temple income, this was first collected and checked by crown officials and only later passed on to the temple. In the second century a grant or *syntaxis* is known which paid for the costs of cult and was administered by pharaoh's agents within the temple. Meanwhile the temples enjoyed the freedom of running them-selves, but always within the overarching framework of the royal administration.

From Memphis, the former capital of the country, the gravestones of the high priests of Ptah provide a lineage to set besides that of the Ptolemies. Over the three centuries of Ptolemaic rule, there were 13 high priests of Ptah to match the reigns of 13 Ptolemaic dynasts (D. J. Crawford 1980). The life histories of these priests, at least in the first century, testify to their close relations with the court at Alexandria; the exchange of state visits between ruler and high priest underlines the intimate involve-ment of these two authorities (D. J. Thompson 1988: 106–54). The royal coronation – Egyptian style – of the king took place in the temple of Ptah, at least from the reign of Ptolemy V, and possibly even earlier.

At a national level it was for royal coronations and other major events that the priests from all Egypt came together. In 196 the priestly representatives, who had gathered to celebrate the recent coronation of Ptolemy V, produced the encyclical we know as the Rosetta decree, famous for the role it played in the decipherment of hieroglyphs (Parkinson 1999; Greek version, *OGIS* 90). As in the 'Kanopos decree' of 238 (*OGIS* 56), the priests present themselves as enjoying a reciprocal relationship with the crown in terms of mutual benefits (BD 164–5; Austin 222; 227). With a heavy overlay of Egyptianizing imagery, the decree that the priests record has a basic form that is Greek:

> King Ptolemy...has conferred benefits in many ways on the temples and their staffs and on those subject to his rule, as he is a god from a god and goddess just as Horus, the son of Isis and Osiris, the defender of his father Osiris; (and) being in matters concerning the gods benevolently inclined, he has assigned to the temples revenues in money and grain....With good fortune, it has been resolved by the priests of all the temples in the land that [all] honours belonging to King Ptolemy, the eternal, beloved of Ptah, god Epiphanes Eucharistos, and likewise those of his parents, the gods Philopatores and those

of his grandparents, the gods Euergetai [and] those of the gods Philadelphoi and those of the gods Soteres, shall be increased greatly... (Clarysse 2000a)

[and so on.]

Good relations were crucial and, in all important respects, each understood the other. The decree was set up bilingually in three scripts: in hieroglyphs, the ancient script of Egypt, in demotic, its more cursive form, and in Greek, the language of the new rulers. The honours granted the king were those of Egyptian religion, of statues, crowns and statue cult, and the annual celebration of his birthday and the day of his accession.

4 The Ptolemaic Monarchy

Of the major Hellenistic kingdoms, Egypt was the most subject to monarchic rule. With only three full Greek cities (Alexandria, Naukratis in the Delta and Ptolemais in the south), it was through a centralized administration that the Ptolemies ruled. Initiatives came as royal decrees but the king's physical presence, accompanied by his family, was important to his people (Clarysse 2000b: 39–40). In the mid second century, for instance, the king was regularly present in the old Egyptian capital of Memphis for 1 Thoth, the start of the new year, and times of both trouble and triumph were marked by royal progresses up and down the Nile. Religious festivals, the inauguration of a temple, the installation of a sacred bull, were times of celebration in Egyptian cultic life. Royal participation helped to reinforce the monarchy (for Ptolemy I as pharaoh, figure 7.2).

There was a Greek background too to monarchy. Since Xenophon's study of the education of the Persian king Cyrus, the *Cyropaedia*, treatises on kingship had entered literary production. Plutarch records the advice given to Ptolemy I to acquire such studies on kingship; they contained advice that even a king's best friend would hesitate to give him (*Mor.* 189d). The king surely had many friends; the title of 'friend' became an official one for trusted courtiers and, as elsewhere in the Hellenistic world, the system was soon broadened out with 'first friends', 'relatives of the king' and other such ranks defined in a court hierarchy (Mooren 1977; Herman 1997). Those who ran the royal administration were fitted into this honorific structure.

The pharaoh's image was also important. Here too the Ptolemies conformed to a more general pattern discussed elsewhere in this volume (cf. Ma in chapter 11). The use of royal epithets started with Ptolemy I, who was also known as Soter (Saviour). As though echoing this epithet it was, according to the poet Poseidippos, a statue of Zeus Soter that topped the Pharos, the great lighthouse of Alexandria. Later kings (with their queens) adopted similar epithets: Ptolemy II Philadelphos (sister-loving), Ptolemy III Euergetes (benefactor), Ptolemy IV Philopator (father-loving), Ptolemy V Epiphanes (made manifest), and so on. Such epithets certainly carried divine connotations for their holders though not yet full divine status. For Ptolemaic kings and queens, that came in other ways.

In Alexandria the foundation of a cult to Alexander provided through its priest a new way of dating the years ('in the reign of Ptolemy, in the priesthood of Menelaos son of Lagos for the fifth year' is how 284 was marked in one text (*P.Hib.* I 84a.1–2);

Figure 7.2   Ptolemy I: Macedonian Pharaoh. © British Museum, London

as Soter's brother, Menelaos was a worthy holder of the post (Clarysse and Van der Veken 1983: 4)). In 272/271 the cult, as Theoi Adelphoi (brother/sister gods), of the ruling sovereign and his queen (Ptolemy Philadelphos and Queen Arsinoe) was added to that of Alexander as, in time, was that of successive kings and queens. By the reign of Ptolemy IV what had now become a true dynastic cult was granted its own cult quarters in Alexandria: the Sêma or Sôma, where the mummified remains of Alexander and the Ptolemies were on display. In the same reign, a similar cult was initiated in the south at Ptolemais, where Soter, as that city's founder, took the place of Alexander. Regularly employed in the dating formula for all legal contracts and official texts, the dynastic priesthood together with related priestesses for Ptolemaic queens offered a role for the sons and daughters of prominent families in both Alexandria and Ptolemais. Centred in these two cities, this was a Greek dynastic cult.

In the Egyptian temples, royal cult was somewhat different. Already in the Luxor temple, Alexander had been shown on temple walls as pharaoh offering cult to the local god, but it was Arsinoe, sister-wife of Ptolemy II, who was the first of the Ptolemies to be introduced to Egyptian temples, as a temple-sharing goddess worshipped alongside the cult of the main divinity (Hölbl 2001: 85, 101–3). The innovation proved a great success and was followed by successive kings and, particularly, queens (Quaegebeur 1988; 1989). Indeed, the royal names of Arsinoe and Berenike entered the otherwise exclusively Egyptian nomenclature of priestly families.

Ruler cult can play an important role in binding a kingdom together. So it was with the Ptolemies. Images were produced, of different materials and size to suit the pockets of those who bought them; they enjoyed wide circulation. Royal oaths played a part in formal undertakings; sacrifices to the rulers would form the start to any senior official's day. When kings are divine, they enjoy an added strength and authority. As priests and, simultaneously, as gods, the Ptolemies enjoyed an embedded position within Egyptian society.

5   The Troubled Second Century

In a land survey from Edfu south of Thebes, year 16 of Ptolemy IV Philopator (207/206) was a defining year (*P.Haun.inv.* 417); as recorded on the temple walls of the great temple of Horus there, in that year 'ignorant rebels' interrupted the building works. In Thebes, no taxes were paid to the royal bank from September 207 until 192/191. In effect, there was civil war in the region, as the old centre of Thebes and much of the south came under the control of rebel pharaohs, first Haronnophris (205–199) and then Chaonnophris (199–192/191) (Pestman 1995). Their very names carry meaning: 'Horus is Osiris' and 'Osiris still lives'. The powerful gods of Egypt backed these new pharaohs in their control of Upper Egypt. The knot that tied the two lands was loosed; the land of the white crown, the realm of the bee, was lost to Ptolemy, who now held Lower Egypt only, land of the red crown, realm of the sedge.

This was a hard time for Egypt and its people. Trouble at court compounded that in the south. In Alexandria, a palace coup had resulted in the death (in 204) of Ptolemy IV and his more popular queen, Arsinoe III. Ptolemy V was merely a youngster under the control of more sinister figures at the court. With the south in revolt, the young king came under attack from the east and along the Phoenician coast. The battle of Panion on the edge of the Golan Heights in 200 brought an end to Ptolemaic control of the area. It was in this troubled period that the king celebrated, first, his coming of age in Alexandria and then, on 27 November 197, his coronation as pharaoh in Memphis. This royal coronation was the occasion for the priestly convention that resulted in the Rosetta decree (*OGIS* 90).

It was not until 186 that, somewhere further to the south, Chaonnophris was finally defeated by Komanos, general of Ptolemy V. The effects of the rebellion were felt for many generations. One resulting dispute over a house in Thebes, appropriated in the time of the 'trouble' under Ptolemy V, was still before the courts in 125. The case was finally thrown out in 117, some 88 years after the complainant's father had left town to fight (*UPZ* II 160–2 = *P.Tor.Choach.* nos. 11–12). In times of trouble, property was rarely secure; deeds might be lost or burnt, and general insecurities and local conflicts came to the surface (*SB* V 8033 [182 BC]; VIII 9681 [175–169 BC]).

Some thirty years later Antiochos IV of Syria took advantage of further internal unrest, this time among the two sons of Ptolemy V. He invaded Egypt in two successive years (170/168) and was crowned king at Memphis. It was a rough time for Ptolemy VI and Ptolemy VIII, who despite an uneasy coalition found that many important Egyptians joined the Syrian cause (*P.Köln* IV 186). The Syrian king only left the country when Rome intervened. In an encounter at Eleusis outside Alexandria, the Roman envoy handed Antiochos an ultimatum and drew a circle round him on the ground. He should agree to Roman terms, leaving Egypt by a given date, before he stepped out of the circle. The king complied (McGing, this volume, section 1, Diod. 31.1–2; Polyb. 29.27; Ray 1976: 127).

Trouble, however, continued and in their joint rule the two sons of Ptolemy V were far from reconciled. Shortly after, a further revolt was raised by one Dionysios Petosarapis (Diod. 31.15). This time, trouble started at court with a prominent military man. Dionysios is described by Diodoros, our only source for these events, as a 'friend' of the king, as well as an individual with a good military record. His second name – 'gift of Sarapis' – may have been adopted when he went into rebellion. Dionysios sought to exploit the rivalry of the kings and, in doing so, he involved the Alexandrian populace. There was a demonstration in the stadium – a favourite place for such events – and Dionysios sought to establish the younger Ptolemy VIII in place of his older brother, Ptolemy VI. The two kings refused to be used, though some 4000 soldiers still rose to support Dionysios. He fled to the eastern suburb of Eleusis where he was defeated. Plunging naked into the river, he swam across and retreated to the Egyptians whom he incited to revolt. Many indeed came to join him and documents from the period bear testimony to the widespread nature of the ensuing upheaval. Attacks were made on local temples – this was no straightforward Greek/Egyptian conflict – existing enmities played out (McGing 1997).

There was still more trouble in the Thebaid. In the countryside more generally dissident elements took advantage of the situation to forcibly eject homeowners, burn records, or pursue personal vendettas (*Chrest.Wilck* 9.31–6 [165 BC]); *UPZ* I 19.6–9 [163 BC]). From Memphis the loss of burial stelae for Apis bulls and high priests of Ptah in this period is just one sign of these troubled times. In Pathyris no taxes were paid in the years 168–165 (Vandorpe 2000a: 406). For the same three years, the priests failed to chant the titulature of the king following the 'invasion of the Mede', as Antiochos is termed in an Egyptian graffito from Elephantine (Vittmann 1997: 264). No eponymous priests are known in Alexandria from 169 to 165 (Clarysse and Van der Veken 1983: 26); chanting only recommenced at the end of year 5, in late September 165. There can be no clearer statement of the loss of Ptolemaic control.

As is often the case in wartime, those not directly involved suffered the most, as illustrated by Isias in the letter to her husband quoted on p. 71 above. Bad times led to high prices and life was hard for Hephaistion's wife, child and mother. As if to reinforce the plea for her husband's return, Isias appends her own signature to the letter (Cribiore 2001: 91). The explanation for these and later troubles is normally presented in terms of growing native unrest. The Achaian historian Polybios is responsible for this emphasis when he comments on the effects of the battle of Raphia, the engagement in which Ptolemy IV Philopator had finally won the Fourth Syrian War (219–217) and recovered Hollow Syria:

> The king just mentioned, in arming the Egyptians for the war against Antiochos, was
> pursuing a policy which was expedient in present circumstances but out of line for the
> future. For the Egyptians were elated by the success at Raphia and could no longer
> endure to take orders, but looked out for a leader and a figurehead, thinking they were

well able to maintain themselves as an independent power. In this they finally succeeded not long afterwards. (Polyb. 5.107.1–3; Austin 225)

Polybios later describes the ensuing struggles not as a regular war with pitched battles, naval encounters, sieges and events worthy of note but rather as characterized by mutual savagery and general lawlessness (Polyb. 14.12.3–4). How far can his analysis be accepted?

Polybios, deported to Rome after the battle of Pydna in 168 and an admirer of that city's power, perhaps visited Egypt sometime later as part of a Roman embassy (Walbank 1979b); he is likely to have thought long and hard about Egypt which was still an independent power. He sees events in military terms, with a tension existing between those who give and those who receive orders. The latter of course were Egyptians, and though these might be called 'ignorant' or 'impious' rebels (as on the temple walls at Edfu or in the Rosetta decree) or, more often, simply natives (*enchórioi*), it is only in the revolt of Thebes with its native pharaohs that any real ethnic element or secessionist movement can be traced. Even then Upper Egypt was far from united. Whereas in some more recent accounts a nationalist Egyptian agenda has been stressed, it is notable that contemporary descriptions are rather made in terms of 'trouble' or 'upset' (*taraché*) or of non-dealing (*ameixia*). Rebellion, as so often, took many different forms; it is not easy to disentangle the different strands or different groups who were involved within the population (Pestman 1995; McGing 1997).

Despite attempts to deal with the troubles (*UPZ* I 110; 163), from this date, as already seen at Eleusis, a new power enters the picture. In the continuing struggles, it is to Rome that Ptolemies increasingly flee in hope of restoration – Ptolemy VI, VIII and, most disastrously, XII all made that journey. Rome was now an ever-present force. In Alexandria problems continued at court, affecting the rest of the kingdom. On the death of his elder brother in 145, Ptolemy VIII took over the throne and also, as queen, his brother's widow, Kleopatra II, who was also their sister. Not long after, he took as second queen his niece, Kleopatra III, the daughter of his existing wife. This dynamite exploded in a civil war between the two queens (132–130). In middle Egypt, surveys of the Arsinoite and Herakleopolite nomes record land as being from 'before year 39' (132/131) and 'after year 40' (131/130), but still in year 43 (128/127) the eponymous priests are listed not, as usually, 'in Alexandria' but rather in 'the camp of the king' (*BGU* III 993.ii.6–7). Kings in trouble needed their priests to endorse their rule with chanting. Ptolemy VIII eventually came out on top and the two queens were reconciled, but the insecurity of rule and latent splits within the kingdom had once again been revealed: Alexandria and the countryside, different groups within the capital, Greeks and Egyptians, Upper and Lower Egypt. The hostile reaction of some Egyptians to what was still seen as foreign rule – the rule of the 'girdle-bearers' (one of the many forms of paramilitary police) with their 'city by the sea', can be found in the Potter's oracle, an apocalyptic text which foretells destruction to the Greeks and their rule upheld by force; in age-old eastern imagery, the gods of Egypt would return home together with their statues (*P. Rainer G.*19 813 in Koenen 1968: 200–9, cf. Burstein 106).

On the death of Ptolemy VIII in 116, the power of his younger widow over the succession of her two sons, Ptolemy IX Soter and Ptolemy X Alexander, again brought civil war to Egypt. Succession to the throne remained a flash point. So too did the south, particularly Thebes, eventually destroyed by Ptolemy IX after another fierce uprising in 88. The historically valuable cache of some hundreds of priestly statues buried beneath a court in the Karnak temple (de Meulenaere 1995: 83–4) may belong to this sack of the city when, in the words of Pausanias (1.9.5), the king 'did such damage that there was nothing left to remind the Thebans of their former prosperity'. Pausanias reflects the Alexandrian view. Thebes in practice recovered, with the support of its well-established Greco-Egyptian families (*OGIS* 186 (62 BC); 194 (39 BC), translated Burstein 110–11). It was to revolt again in the early years of Roman control.

6   Egypt and Rome

Following the troubles under Ptolemies VIII Euergetes II, IX Soter and X Alexander, Rome was an ever-present player in the period. Ptolemies now visited Rome; Roman senators in turn came to Egypt. It was to the north-west and no longer Seleukid Asia that the focus had turned. Yet Egypt was the last of the Hellenistic kingdoms to fall to Rome, and her ability to avoid an earlier takeover must to some degree reflect Ptolemaic success as much as Roman unwillingness to get embroiled in actual control of this rich province.

It was indeed the wealth of Egypt which was noted by visiting Romans. When Scipio Aemilianus visited the country with a Roman embassy in 140/139, the visitors were horrified by the lavishness of Ptolemaic hospitality but impressed by the natural resources of Egypt, particularly the flood of the Nile; all it lacked was rulers worthy of their kingdom (Diod. 33.28b.1–3; Athen. 12.549 d–e).

Two features of the later period of Ptolemaic rule reflect growing weakness at the centre. Egypt and her key territories of Cyrene and Cyprus no longer formed an entity. In 163, for instance, Ptolemy VI Philometor controlled Egypt and Cyprus while his brother Ptolemy VIII Euergetes II ruled Cyrene; in 107 there was a three-way split, with Ptolemy X Alexander I in Egypt, Ptolemy IX Soter II in Cyprus and Ptolemy Apion in Cyrene. Such a division of territory and interests was not to Egypt's advantage.

A second feature which marks the period is the practice pioneered in Egypt of leaving a kingdom to Rome. The first example came in 155, when Ptolemy VIII (from Cyrene) made a conditional legacy to Rome of 'his rightful kingdom' should he die a childless death (*SEG* 9.7). Such a bid for Rome's support was perhaps a form of insurance policy against attack from his brother; it was never put into effect. Others, however, followed suit – Attalos III of Pergamon in 133 and Ptolemy Apion, who on his death in 96 willed Cyrene to Rome. Finally, in 87 Ptolemy X Alexander left Egypt to Rome (Badian 1967). Rome only took the legacy up in 58, when eventually she annexed Cyprus (only). Egypt proper remained intact. When Ptolemy XII Auletes died in 51, he failed to leave Rome his kingdom outright; it was simply left under the guardianship of that power.

Rome, however, was not a power to go away, and in the last generations of Ptolemaic Egypt domestic developments and policies became increasingly subordinated to that power. Ejected by his subjects from his throne when Rome took Cyprus over, Ptolemy XII used up all the surplus of his wealthy kingdom and promised much more in his efforts at restoration. Figures in ancient sources are notoriously unreliable but Cicero is claimed to have reported an annual income from Egypt of some 12,000 talents (Strabo 17.1.13). Half of that sum was earlier promised by Auletes to Pompey and Caesar for his recognition as friend and ally of Rome, and when eventually the governor of Syria moved to put him back in power his bribe stood at 10,000 talents.

The last thirty years of Ptolemaic rule were a difficult time for Egypt and Kleopatra VII who, inheriting her father's debts and an encumbered throne, was obliged seriously to devalue the currency and even, after Actium, to plunder the temples (Dio 51.5.4–5). Earlier, under Ptolemy II, it had been high officials who were granted gift-estates and other privileges. In these final years, it was Antony's general Publius Canidius who received preferential treatment:

> We have allowed to Publius Canidius and his heirs annually to export 10,000 artabas of wheat *c.* 400,000 litres and to import 5000 Koan amphoras of wine, free of tax levied by anyone and of any other charge whatsoever. And we have also granted him to be untouched in respect of all the lands that he holds in the countryside. He is to be given exemption for the present and future both from charges for the regular government account and for that of me and my children . . .

is the start of a royal order from 33 which records this (van Minnen 2000). Egypt's agricultural wealth was now in others' hands. So soon was the rest of Kleopatra's kingdom. As victor at Actium, Octavian took Alexandria on 3 August 30. When invited, the new ruler refused to visit the Apis bull (Dio 51.16.5, 17.4–5). Conciliation was not the Roman way. Kleopatra died soon after, a self-inflicted royal death from a cobra's fangs, but Caesar's son Ptolemy XV, her designated heir, was not to succeed her. The Romans had come to stay.

FURTHER READING

The period is well served both by general studies and by collections of (mainly papyrological) sources in translation which provide an introduction to the possibilities and problems of this form of historical evidence, cf. Bagnall 1995. Will 1979–82 is a detailed political study of the whole period, not just of Egypt, cf. Green 1990, Shipley 2000. Bowman 1986, with good illustrations, introduces Egypt also in the Roman period. Turner 1984 and D. J. Thompson 1994a treat the Ptolemies only, as does A. Lloyd 2000, with an emphasis on the Egyptian side which is shared by the best general coverage, Hölbl 2001. Huss 2001 (in German) is the fullest of recent studies, reasonably conventional in coverage; his renumbering of the later Ptolemies is likely to prove problematic. Of the source books, Austin 1981, Bagnall and Derow 2004, Burstein 1985 and Rowlandson 1998 (on women) are all probably the best collections. On papyri, see Erskine, this volume, section 5 with further reading there. For historiographical essays, see Samuel 1989 (Greek in outlook) or Burstein 1996a (wider coverage). Individual cities are studied by Fraser 1972 (Alexandria), D. J. Thompson 1988 (Memphis) and Vleeming 1995 (Thebes). For economic history Préaux 1939 remains fundamental; see also, D. J. Thompson 1997, Clarysse and

Vandorpe 1998, on taxation, Bingen forthcoming, on this and much else, von Reden 2001 on monetization, and Mørkholm 1991, on coinage. For social history, Lewis 1986 is a lively study of papyrological archives. On education and literacy, see Ray 1994, D. J. Thompson 1994b, Cribiore 1996 and 2001, and T. Morgan 1998; on ethnicity, Clarysse 1998 and D. J. Thompson 2001; on culture, Koenen 1993; for Egyptian literature, Lichtheim 1980. Several edited collections include key studies: Maehler and Strocka 1978, Criscuolo and Geraci 1989, Johnson 1992 and Green 1993. The catalogues of recent exhibitions provide an important visual record of the mix of Greek and Egyptian that characterizes Ptolemaic Egypt: Bianchi et al. 1988, *La gloire d'Alexandrie* 1998, Clarysse and Willems 2000 and Walker and Higgs 2001, all with introductory pieces. Finally, Baines and Málek 1980 is an invaluable atlas.

CHAPTER EIGHT

The Seleukids and Asia

Michel Austin

> Not infected by the Christian zeal which later became the liberal itch, the Seleucids did not try to convert anybody – either to the true religion or good plumbing. They left people as dirty and blissful as they had been before the Macedonian conquest. 'A wise and salutary neglect' [...] maintained peace within the Seleucid Empire. (Bickerman 1966: 97)

1 Introduction

The Seleukids reckoned the year when Seleukos recovered control of Babylon from his rival Antigonos as the beginning of their empire (October 312 in the Macedonian calendar, April 311 in the Babylonian). This was the start of the 'Seleukid era', a novel method of reckoning by the continuous years of the dynasty and not by the years of individual kings. From then on the sequence of rulers ran down to 63 when Pompey deposed the last king in the dynasty and created the Roman province of Syria. The name 'Seleukids', though conventional and convenient, is actually used by only one ancient writer (App. *Syr.* 48–50, 65, 67). It is not found anywhere else and is completely missing from the numerous Greek inscriptions that relate to the Seleukid kings or emanate from them. Literary sources refer to them in a variety of ways – among others 'the kings descended from Seleukos', or 'the kings of Asia', or the 'kings of Syria/the Syrians', or 'the Syrian kings'. The last two designations are the most common, though they are not attested before the second century (first in Polybios), in the latter part of which the Seleukid empire was progressively reduced to its Syrian component, sizeable but only a fraction of the whole. One other collective designation frequently found in classical writers is simply 'the Macedonians' (Edson 1958), whose rule over Asia followed that of the Persians in a succession of eastern empires, a scheme first formulated in Herodotos (1.95–6, 130; cf. Polyb. 29.21).

None of these designations was used by the rulers, who consistently describe themselves in their letters, inscriptions, and coins simply as 'King Seleukos', 'King Antiochos' etc., and never as kings of any particular land, country or people. Royalty was thus a matter of recognized personal status, not tied to a specific ethnic or geographical context, and there was no 'official' description of the Seleukid empire.

2   The Seleukid Empire

The Seleukid empire was an artificial construct, created piecemeal by Seleukos I over his long career, and handed over to his successors as an inheritance, to be preserved, recovered if any part was lost, or even enlarged if the opportunity arose. It therefore had no pre-existing shape, and no final shape either. Whether Seleukos had a clear and consistent imperial vision from early in his career cannot be determined. At any rate his ambitions grew with success and seemingly embraced vast designs. Alone of his rivals he named not just cities after himself and members of his family (Seleukeia, Antioch, Laodikeia, Apameia) but entire regions: the name Seleukis to describe North Syria, and perhaps an even wider expanse of territory, is attested early in the reign of his son and successor Antiochos I (*OGIS* 219; Austin 139). Reportedly he and his son wanted to give the Indian Ocean the names Seleukis and Antiochis (Pliny *HN* 2.167–8). No less ambitious in its implications was the introduction of the Seleukid era, possibly by Antiochos I rather than Seleukos himself (Sherwin-White and Kuhrt 1993: 27).

But Seleukos' work was left unfinished. At the end of his life in 281 his empire stretched from Baktria in the east to the Levantine coast and the Hellespont; he had just acquired control of western Asia Minor and established a foothold in Thrace on the European mainland, reportedly on his way to take control of the vacant throne of Macedon. This latter ambition soon had to be dropped by Antiochos I after his accession. Different parts of the empire were controlled to varying degrees: there is an obvious contrast between the regions acquired early and consolidated, and those that Seleukos had not had time to assimilate effectively. Thus he placed his stamp firmly on Babylonia and North Syria with major new foundations – Seleukeia on the Tigris in Babylonia, Antioch, Seleukeia in Pieria, Apameia and Laodikeia by the sea in North Syria. But other areas were problematic. Considerable time and energy were devoted by Antiochos I under Seleukos in an apparent effort to establish control over the 'upper satrapies' to the east of Mesopotamia, but with only mixed results. Western Asia Minor, the domain of at first Antigonos then Lysimachos, was a recent acquisition and remained contested ground between a series of protagonists, a constant source of difficulties despite intensive efforts by successive rulers. After Ipsos in 301 Seleukos had also had to yield temporarily to Ptolemy his claims to Koile Syria, and his ambitions to develop maritime power in the Levant remained unfulfilled. Seleukid weakness at sea was never made good subsequently, and Koile Syria was a recurring source of friction between the two dynasties. The chequered history of the Seleukid empire after the death of its founder is outlined elsewhere in this volume and will not be repeated here.

For all its territorial fluctuations the empire remained in essence similar throughout: a conglomerate of many different peoples and lands who happened to be at any given time under Seleukid rule. There was no way of describing the empire apart from the person of its ruler: when the Romans imposed the Peace of Apameia on Antiochos III in 188, they demanded compliance from 'Antiochos and those under his orders' (*hypotassamenoi*, Polyb. 21.43 cf. 11.34; the phrase is common). The hallmarks of the empire were territorial expansion and diversity of peoples and cultures. It fell into major geographical regions – Babylonia, western Iran and to the east the 'upper satrapies' as far as Baktria; to the west North Syria and western Asia Minor. For administrative purposes the empire was divided into territorial provinces adapted from Persian practice (mostly satrapies), though their number and size fluctuated. But the constituent elements were smaller entities. A decree of Smyrna from the reign of Seleukos II provides a convenient shorthand:

> (King Seleukos) guaranteed to the people (sc. of Smyrna) its autonomy and democracy, and wrote to the kings, the dynasts, the cities and the peoples requesting that the sanctuary of Aphrodite Stratonikis be recognised as inviolate and our city as holy and inviolate. (*OGIS* 229; Austin 182)

This gives a summary of the political entities known to the world of the time (not just in the Seleukid empire): kings – the major monarchies of the day, rulers with the royal title *basileus* like the Seleukids themselves; dynasts – numerous petty rulers not of royal status, whose sphere of power was generally local, such as Olympichos of Labraunda in Karia, active from the reigns of Seleukos II to the early years of Antiochos III and known chiefly from a series of inscriptions from Labraunda (Isager 1990: 84–8); very numerous cities with their own political institutions, Greek and non-Greek, some ancient, others newly founded; and peoples whose organization was not based on the city model, such as the Jews in Palestine. To these might be added 'temple-states', where a sanctuary of a god or goddess controlled land and peoples from which revenues were raised, such as the sanctuary of Zeus of Baetokaike in North Syria, known from an inscription involving a King Antiochos of uncertain date and identity (*RC* 70; Austin 178).

As the Smyrna decree shows, Seleukid kings assumed the continued existence of all such entities and dealt with them on an individual basis, dispensing status, privileges or punishment in return for loyalty displayed or withheld. The empire was thus like a network of bilateral relationships between the ruling king and the communities in their sphere of power. The links probably had to be renewed or at least confirmed at the accession of a new ruler (cf. *OGIS* 223; *RC* 15; Austin 183: embassy from Erythrai to Antiochos I or II): the empire was as it were recreated with each successive king. All this generated a vast amount of communications and correspondence, only partly reflected in the surviving evidence.

There is no reason to suppose that Seleukid rule was in the first instance anything but an imposition on the peoples of the empire. Even communities that outwardly professed loyalty saw them as outsiders. For instance a decree of Ilion in the Troad in honour of (probably) Antiochos I after his accession implies that cities like Ilion and the Seleukid kingdom were distinct entities:

> He (sc. the king) has come to the provinces this side of Mt Tauros (i.e. Asia Minor)... and has at once restored peace to the cities and has advanced his interests and the kingdom to a more powerful and brilliant position. (*OGIS* 219; Austin 139)

There was thus no automatic reason for the subjects to accept Seleukid rule, which lacked any ultimate legitimacy, no matter how much rulers might try to enhance their own status. From inscriptions it is known that Antiochos III created a divine cult of his living queen Laodike in 193, modelled on a cult of himself created some time earlier, and effective throughout the empire (Austin 158; Sherwin-White and Kuhrt 1993: 203–10). But no literary source makes any mention of this in the narrative of events in the 190s when Antiochos was attempting to re-establish Seleukid rule in Asia Minor and Thrace: the story is told in purely political and military terms.

The sincerity of outward expressions of loyalty to the rulers can never be taken at face value, and communities could move in and out of the Seleukid allegiance depending on changing circumstances. Miletos, courted already by Seleukos I not least because of the sanctuary of Apollo at Didyma, from whom the dynasty claimed to be descended, is found in the Ptolemaic orbit in the reign of Ptolemy II (*RC* 14; Austin 270), but reverts to the Seleukid fold under Seleukos II (*RC* 22; Austin 186). In their communications with the city neither king lets it out that Miletos had changed its allegiance more than once. Smyrna, obsequious in its profession of loyalty to Seleukos II (*OGIS* 229; Austin 182), is found in the 190s making a determined stand against Antiochos III and seeking Roman support against him (Livy 33.38). Nor was this confined to parts of the empire that might be thought of as 'peripheral'. Seleukeia in Pieria, one of the four major Seleukid cities in North Syria, where Seleukos I was buried, was under Ptolemaic control from 241 to 219 (Polyb. 5.58–61). To attempt to draw maps of the Seleukid empire with clear-cut 'frontiers' is misleading.

The loyalty or at least acquiescence of subjects thus depended ultimately on self-interest and the changing circumstances of the moment. Seleukid rule had to rely on a judicious blend of pressure and persuasion, as may be seen from the activities of Antiochos III in Asia Minor in 197/6:

> In the same year King Antiochos . . . sought to bring all the cities of Asia back to their former status within the empire. He could see that the remainder would submit to his rule without difficulty . . . but Smyrna and Lampsakos were asserting their freedom and there was a danger that if they were granted what they sought, other cities might follow their example. And so he himself sent an army from Ephesos to besiege Smyrna and ordered the troops stationed at Abydos to proceed to the siege of Lampsakos . . . . In fact he was not relying so much on the fear inspired by force, but through envoys he would send them conciliatory messages and reproach them for their rashness and obstinacy; he sought in this way to raise the hope that they would soon have what they were seeking, but only when it was sufficiently clear to themselves and to all others that it was from the king that they had obtained their freedom and that they had not seized it in favourable circumstances. (Livy 33.38)

It should be added that Antiochos' hopes were not fulfilled: several years later, Smyrna and Lampsakos were still resisting the king (Ma 1999: 94–100, 173–4).

3   The Seleukids as a Military Monarchy

It will be seen that the Seleukid monarchy was in the first instance military in character. It was not a constitutional entity but had at its core a human group, unelected and unac-countable: the 'king, his friends, and his military forces', to use a phrase that appears in texts and documents of the period. Simply put, the monarchy consisted of the king as war leader and his band of followers: their cohesion was cemented by a common interest in maintaining control of an empire from which they derived their wealth and status. The primary function of empire, from the point of view of the rulers, was to draw on the resources, material and human, provided by the subject peoples. Taxation in whatever form was thus the hallmark of monarchical rule, and tax-exemptions always a special privilege carefully mentioned as such (cf. van der Spek 2000).

The military character of the monarchy can be illustrated in many ways (Austin 1986). As the age of the Successors had shown, royal status was derived in the first instance from military achievement. Commenting on Antiochos III's eastern *anabasis* of 212–205 Polybios writes: 'It was this campaign which made him appear worthy of royalty, not only to the peoples of Asia but to those in Europe as well' (11.34). Victory gave the ruler possession of territory and peoples: the empire was 'territory won by the spear' (*doriktetos chora*), a concept the Seleukids appealed to subsequently in justification of their rule (Polyb. 5.67 in 219/18; 28.1.4 in 170/69). The major steps in the growth or contraction of the empire related to military events: notably the battles of Ipsos in 301 (gain of North Syria from Antigonos), Koroupedion in 282 (gain of Asia Minor from Lysimachos), Panion in *c*. 200 (gain of Koile Syria from Ptolemy V), Magnesia in 189 (loss of Asia Minor), or the defeat and death of Antiochos VII in 130–29 (final loss of Mesopotamia and all the eastern provinces). The kings expected to take personal command of major campaigns, maintained a close personal relationship with the soldiers, and are shown in action predominantly in military contexts. It has been debated what was the 'centre' of the Seleukid empire, and what was its 'capital city'. The debate may be somewhat artificial and the answer depends on the period concerned. The 'centre' was in practice wherever the king happened to be, and kings were frequently on the move: the careers of Seleukos I and Antiochos III took them from one end of their empire to the other (Austin 2001: 102).

Polybios' narrative of the early reign of Antiochos III gives a good glimpse of the Seleukid monarchy in action over a period of several years, from 223 till 217 (see esp. 5.41–2, 45, 49–52, 55–6, 58). The material is clearly derived from a well-informed source which remains characteristically anonymous (Polybios himself was not even born at the time). The chief business of the monarchy is assumed to be war: the death of a king and the accession of the next ruler were always a time of danger for the monarchy and opportunity for its opponents, internal or external, and a new king had to prove himself through action (Antiochos III's predecessor and elder brother Seleukos III had been assassinated in Asia Minor in 223 after a short reign). The question at issue in Polybios' account is which of the various military tasks Antiochos III should concentrate on himself or delegate to others – dealing with Molon, the rebellious satrap of Media, or resuming war against Ptolemy. Decisions were made within a very restricted circle – the king himself and the most influential of his followers and advisors – hence personalities determine policy. The attack and recapture of Seleukeia in Pieria from Ptolemy IV in 219 was due to the personal intervention of Apollophanes, the king's doctor, who was himself from Seleukeia: no one had apparently paid any attention to the fact that the city had been in Ptolemaic hands for two decades (5.58–61). In general all concerned assumed that military forces were available for use, but no calculations seem to have been made as to the expected costs and benefits of any given campaign. Specialization of governmental functions at the highest levels was conspicuous by its absence. Still less did the leading figures give any thought to the possible impact of military activity on the peoples of the empire.

From the perspective of the subjects, military pressures were a recurring manifestation of Seleukid rule. After the defeat of Antiochos III at Magnesia in 189 the peoples of Asia Minor looked forward to being relieved of 'tribute, garrisons and other royal injunctions' (Polyb. 21.41.2). Garrisons appear to have been normal in all the major Seleukid centres (Babylon, the four major cities in North Syria etc.) but are also found elsewhere (Ma 1999: 113–21, 139–40, 155). Occasionally the evidence provides an insight into the impact of war in one part of the empire on another area, as known for instance from an astronomical diary from Babylon concerning the war between Antiochos I and Ptolemy II Philadelphos in 274/3 (cited in Sherwin-White and Kuhrt 1993: 46). At times of military activity there was a recurring problem in controlling the actions of the army: not even Antiochos III could secure the discipline of his soldiers towards the local populations (Austin 2001: 92 and n. 8). It goes without saying that many parts of the empire will often have been at peace, but the available evidence makes it impossible to document this.

4 The Kings and Their Subjects

Military pressures, overt or implicit, could not be the only way of maintaining the obedience of subjects. In a world where public opinion mattered the kings were sensitive to their reputation, and royal discourse was adapted to suit local audiences. From numerous Greek inscriptions in Asia Minor one gains the impression that the Seleukids cared for Greek ideals – the protection of the Greeks, the democracy and autonomy of the cities, their political harmony and prosperity (e.g. *OGIS* 222; Austin 143: the League of Ionians; *OGIS* 229; Austin 182: Smyrna; *OGIS* 237; Ma 1999 no. 26B, 331–4: Iasos). Elsewhere the language was modified: the old classical antithesis between Greeks and the 'barbarians of Asia' was inappropriate in an empire that was mostly non-Greek. Hence the rhetoric of defence against barbarians could only be applied selectively, to peoples outside the empire, as the nomads of central Asia (Polyb. 11.34.5), or the Thracians in Europe (Ma 1999: 91), or to a special case like the Celtic tribes that caused havoc in Europe and western Asia Minor (Paus. 10.20.5, cf. Polyb. 21.41.2). But at Babylon Antiochos I used traditional Babylonian terminology to present himself as legitimate king and protector of Babylonian cults and traditions (Austin 189; Kuhrt and Sherwin-White 1991). After the conquest of Koile Syria from Ptolemy V in *c.* 200 Antiochos III granted through his governor various favours and fiscal privileges to the Jews and guaranteed them the use of their national customs (Jos. *AJ* 12.138–46).

The sincerity or otherwise of such pronouncements is perhaps not a relevant issue: the formal language of diplomatic relations followed conventions that were used and understood by all sides. It is usually impossible to assess the degree of loyalty or resistance to Seleukid rule, which will have depended on circumstances and the balance of pressures at any given time. It can be assumed from various indications that the Seleukid kings will have had their local supporters in individual communities, a regular technique of all ancient empires. Greek writers for their part did not mince words: 'the kings were anxious to destroy the democracy in the cities' (Memnon *FGrH* 434 F11); 'at the start of their reign all kings may dangle the name of freedom and call friends and allies those who share in their hopes, but once they are involved in government they deal with those who trusted them no longer as allies but as masters'

(Polyb. 15.24). These writers were of course thinking in the first instance of the relations between the kings and the Greek world: how the Seleukids dealt with their non-Greek subjects was of lesser concern to them.

Modern perceptions of the Seleukids have evolved in time and mirror to some extent the rise and fall of European colonial history. In the early twentieth century one influential approach saw the Seleukids as champions of the west (the Greek world) in an eastern context (Bevan 1902; Bouché-Leclerq 1913–14; Meyer 1925). After World War II the emphasis shifted, and Seleukid history came to be seen increasingly as a continuation of the history of the ancient Near East, and in particular the Persian empire (Kreissig 1978; Briant 1990; Kuhrt and Sherwin-White 1991). It goes without saying that modern writing on the Seleukids cannot all be categorized as belonging solely to one or the other of these two approaches (Bikerman 1938 and Rostovtzeff 1941: I.422–542, II.695–705, 841–70 are two illustrations). And it is realistic to assume that perceptions will continue to evolve: the identity and orientation of the Seleukids elude precise definition.

The view of the Seleukids as champions of Hellenism in the east receives only equivocal support in the ancient evidence. Plutarch's rhetorical *On the Fortune or the Virtue of Alexander*, the starting point of many a modern myth on this period, singles out Alexander as (supposedly) the bringer of Greek civilization to the east and contrasts him with the kings who came after, to their disadvantage (I 328c–329a; II 336f–337a, 338a–c, 341a). In his *Lives* Plutarch fails to rise to the bait of presenting any of the Hellenistic kings, Seleukids or others, as champions of Hellenism: for the most part they were not even fit for biographical treatment. The Roman encounter with Antiochos III added further negative traits to the image of the rulers. The Roman commander Manlius Vulso is made to invoke environmental determinism to denigrate the Ptolemies and Seleukids:

> The Macedonians who hold Alexandria in Egypt, who dwell in Seleukeia and Babylonia and in other colonies scattered throughout the world, have degenerated into Syrians, Parthians, Egyptians. (Livy 38.17, in 189; cf. Livy 36.17 on Antiochos III)

Equally negative is the presentation of the Macedonian monarchies in Justin's *Epitome* of Pompeius Trogus: an underlying theme of his account is that of the decline of the Macedonians after Alexander, through greed and internecine conflicts.

A different and positive slant on Seleukid history is given late in the day by Libanius of Antioch, writing from a partisan local perspective:

> And so the men of that time ... lived in happiness in the midst of barbarians, producing a city (Antioch) which was a true Hellas and keeping their way of life pure in the midst of so much corruption all around them (§68) [...] (Seleukos I) planted so many cities on the earth that they were enough to bear the names of the cities of Macedonia and to be named also for the members of his family [...] (§101) [...] You may go to Phoenicia and see his cities there, and you may come here to Syria and see even more and greater ones of his (§102). He extended this fair work as far as the Euphrates and the Tigris, and, surrounding Babylon with cities, he planted them everywhere, even in Persia; in a word he left bare no place that was suitable for receiving a city, but in his work of spreading Hellenic civilisation he brought the barbarian world quite to an end (Lib. 11, *Antiochicus* of AD 360, trans. G. Downey §103).

This, it should be added, is dubious history: Libanius' fanciful presentation of the Seleukids in this speech (11.69–131) says more about the Antiochenes' view of themselves in the fourth century AD than it does about the historical record of Seleukid times.

The comparison of the Seleukids with the Persian empire suggested by more recent research seems a fruitful approach. The Seleukid empire included many of the lands and peoples that had once been under Persian rule, and shared with its predecessor the same general problems of distance, communications, information and control. Like the Achaimenids before, the Seleukids started by accepting the *status quo* and tried to use it to their advantage. Their approach was 'supra-national' in that the status of subject communities was not determined by race or culture, and outward respect was shown by the rulers for local traditions and cults: piety was a royal attribute, though that did not prevent some kings from plundering temples when in financial straits. Local elites were co-opted wherever possible: their support was essential in raising the tribute that was the foundation of the empire.

Yet all this arose from similarity of circumstances rather than deliberate imitation. When Seleukid kings appealed to precedent to justify policy decisions, it is regularly their own ancestors who are invoked (e.g. I *Macc.* 15.5), sometimes also previous kings from Alexander onwards (e.g. *OGIS* 223; Austin 183: Erythrai), but never the Persian kings. Whereas Alexander's preoccupation with the Persians looms large in his reign, there is a conspicuous absence of any mention of the Persians in texts emanating from the Seleukids (the Ptolemies, by contrast, did make some use of anti-Persian propaganda that was traditional in Egypt, cf. *OGIS* 54, 56). At Babylon Antiochos I, going perhaps beyond the policy of his father Seleukos I (Scharrer 1999), presented himself in the guise of a Babylonian king (Austin 189; Kuhrt and Sherwin-White 1991). But no Seleukid ruler ever contemplated linking himself to the Persian past. Other dynasties in the post-Alexander world did: the dynasty of Pontus, which claimed a connection with the Achaimenid Persians, and the dynasty of Kommagene in the first century BC, whose ruler Antiochos I deliberately mixed Persian, Greek and Macedonian elements in his monuments on Mt Nemrud in a way no Seleukid ruler would probably have dreamed of.

In reality the Macedonian origins of the Seleukids and their emergence in the post-Alexander context meant that though ruling an Asiatic empire they would have to remain part of the larger Greek world of the time, and part of the 'club' of royal dynasties that dominated the age. The history of the near east was now much more closely involved with the Greek world than previously. The Hellenistic kings were seen as Greek rulers both by Greek writers (such as Polybios) and by a variety of eastern sources. The Seleukid era was 'the era of the Greeks' (I *Macc.* 1.10). A similar view is found in Indian sources (Thapar 1997: 256, 273, 304). Babylonian sources note the ambition of Seleukos I at the end of his career to attempt to return to 'Macedon, his native land', and this tallies with the presentation in the Greek sources (Briant 1994a: 463–7). At Babylon Antiochos I, while presenting himself as Babylonian king, also makes a point of emphasizing his Macedonian origin (Austin 189; Kuhrt and Sherwin-White 1991: 76–7, 83). Furthermore, the Macedonian conquest was seen in Jewish sources as a violent event which ushered in a period of turbulence (I *Macc.* 1.1–9). For the author of the Book of Daniel (11.2–29) the world was torn in a long struggle between the 'King of the North' (the Seleukids) and the 'King of the South' (the Ptolemies).

Membership of the wider Greek world had numerous consequences for the Seleukids. Culturally, they belonged to that world. The gods they imported to their empire were of Greek origin: Apollo was the ancestor of the dynasty. Greek was the language of court and communication with the rulers, none of whom is known to have used any other language. The coinage of the Seleukids, as that of the other Hellenistic dynasties, was purely Greek in its style, iconography and legends, and with very few exceptions made no concessions to the eastern context in which they operated (Zahle 1990). There was a Seleukid mint at Babylon, but issues from it carried no reference to Babylon or to Babylonian cults.

The question of manpower is crucial. As a band of immigrants into the eastern world the rulers needed to build up the human basis of their support. Sketchy as is the evidence, it suggests that the backbone of the new Seleukid foundations was drawn from the Greek world (Briant 1982: 227–79). The settlers of Antioch, for example, came from Antigonos' foundation of Antigoneia on the Orontes and included Athenians and Macedonians (Grainger 1990b: 95, 152). Antioch in Persis received a contingent of colonists from Magnesia on the Maeander (*OGIS* 233; Austin 190). Less clear-cut is the recruitment of the Seleukids' military forces. Large-scale conscription was used by them from their subject peoples, as had been the practice of previous eastern empires. The roll-call of the Seleukid army in major campaigns shows extensive recruitment by the kings of peoples from Asia, as can be seen from the battle of Raphia in 217 (Polyb. 5.79), or the battle of Magnesia in 189 (Livy 37.40–1). But important uncertainties remain. There is no agreement whether the core of the Seleukid army, the heavy cavalry and the phalanx, were of predominantly Macedonian/Greek origin, or included large numbers of eastern soldiers trained in a Macedonian style of fighting (Sherwin-White and Kuhrt 1993: 53–7, 214; against, Bar-Kochva 1989: 90–115). There is also a striking dearth of evidence to demonstrate the military use of peoples from the core of the empire, Babylonians and Syrians: it is not clear whether this reflects a deliberate policy on the part of the rulers to exclude them from any military function (Walbank 1988: 110–12).

More decisive is the evidence for the origins of the closest followers of the kings – those who belonged to the select circle of 'friends' who shared the king's life and acted as his advisors, governors and commanders. These are the men prominent, for example, in Polybios' account of the early years of Antiochos III, and they were in practice the governing class of the Seleukid empire. Despite suggestions to the contrary and continued controversy, all the available evidence indicates that they were overwhelmingly from the Greek world (Habicht 1958, though with questionable figures; Sherwin-White and Kuhrt 1993: 121–4; Savalli-Lestrade 1998: 216–34). This is hardly surprising: to share in the king's life on a daily basis fluency in Greek was in practice a prerequisite. It is only at the lower levels of administration and government, and at the local level, that non-Greeks are likely to be found more frequently.

In practice the western part of the Seleukid empire exerted a constant pull on the rulers, from the reign of the founder onwards. After years of activity in Babylonia, Iran and the far east, then in North Syria, Seleukos I turned his attention at the end of his reign to western Asia Minor which he conquered from Lysimachos. He then crossed into Thrace, and both Greek and Babylonian sources report his intention to return to his native Macedon (above). All his successors down to Antiochos III devoted considerable time and effort to affairs in Asia Minor. Seleukid involvement and rivalry with the Ptolemies is also a thread that runs continuously through almost the whole of their history. The rivalry was not limited to conflicts over the possession of Koile Syria, as the conventional listing of 'Syrian Wars' between the two dynasties misleadingly suggests, but extended to the whole of the western part of the Seleukid empire, including the control of the eastern Mediterranean and Aegean, in which the Ptolemies held the advantage.

Membership of the wider Greek world did not necessarily carry with it any cultural 'mission' on the part of the rulers. In one particular field, that of the promotion of Greek intellectual and literary activity, which both Ptolemies and Attalids took seriously as a manifestation of royal power and status (Erskine 1995), the Seleukid record is much slighter than that of their rivals. After a tentative beginning under the first two rulers the momentum seemed to flag, and no Seleukid city achieved the cultural eminence of Alexandria under the Ptolemies (Austin 2001). More generally, it may be doubted whether the rulers had any policy of 'hellenizing' their empire. Their foundation of Greek-style cities, reliance on immigrant colonists and soldiers from the Greek world, and recruitment of a circle of followers of predominantly Greek extraction all served primarily imperial purposes. The intention was not to supersede the cultural and ethnic diversity of their empire which the rulers seem from their actions to have taken for granted.

Any 'hellenization' that did take place, in the Seleukid empire or elsewhere, usually resulted not from royal policy and initiatives but from the wish of individual non-Greeks to adopt features of the Greek life-style which, for a variety of possible reasons, they found attractive or useful (Sherwin-White and Kuhrt 1993: 141–9, 186–7). This is clearly attested among the Jews of Palestine in the second century: the Jewish evidence, for all its hostility to the Seleukid rulers, makes abundantly clear that the moves towards 'self-hellenization' were all initiated within Jewish circles. They did not depend on any preconceived royal policy, though it was assumed that the Seleukid ruler would give them his blessing (I *Macc.* 1.11–15, II *Macc.* 4.7–17). The Jewish sources also make clear that after the conquest by Antiochos III Seleukid power was tacitly accepted by rival Jewish leaders who competed for royal support (II *Macc.* 3.1–13, 4.1–6 etc.). The attempt of Antiochos IV to ban Jewish customs in 167 came late in the day: despite extensive modern debate it remains notoriously obscure in its scope, purpose and motives, and in any case it was soon rescinded (Gruen, this volume).

Babylonia shares with the Jews of Palestine the benefit of local source material of non-Greek origin: both are known chiefly from indigenous evidence rather than classical sources, which are sketchy in comparison. Babylonia holds a special place in the Seleukid empire, as the starting point of Seleukid rule and a wealthy and populous province at the heart of the empire's communications between east and west. Both classical and Babylonian sources give some indication of the efforts of the rulers to secure their rule through conciliation of the local elites and outward respect for Babylonian traditions, which involved the performance of royal ritual and the maintenance of temples (Diod. 19.90–2 for Seleukos I; Kuhrt and Sherwin-White 1991 and Scharrer 1999: 127–8 for Antiochos I; generally Kuhrt and Sherwin-White 1987, chs. 1–3 and Sherwin-White and Kuhrt 1993: 149–61; Kuhrt 1996). Yet at the same time they sought to place their own stamp on the region. The significance of the foundation of Seleukeia on the Tigris by Seleukos is debated (the exact date in the reign of Seleukos I is uncertain), though the available sources give an ambivalent impression. Greek sources suggest it was intended as a counterpoise to Babylon, and feared as such by the Babylonian priesthood (App. *Syr.* 58). A large and powerful city, Seleukeia on the Tigris was no ordinary foundation, but was treated by the Seleukids as one of their 'capitals', while Babylon was not (Invernizzi 1994). Babylonian sources refer to Seleukeia as the 'royal city' and classical sources allege that the Seleukids deliberately favoured Seleukeia at Babylon's expense (Strabo 16.1.5; Pliny *HN* 6.122). Babylon had a garrison and a Greek population (the remains of a Greek theatre have been found), but no attempt was made by the rulers to turn it into a Greek city. Uruk, on its side, shows very little evidence of any Greek presence, though two local dignitaries are known to have assumed a Greek name in addition to their original Babylonian one: Anu-uballit, governor of Uruk under Antiochos II, had received the name Nikarchos from Antiochos I and under Antiochos III another Anu-uballit called Kephalon founded a temple to Anu in honour of the Seleukid king (Sherwin-White and Kuhrt 1993: 150–1, 158–9).

5 Conclusion

It has been debated whether the Seleukid empire should be characterized as 'strong' or 'weak' (Kuhrt and Sherwin-White 1987: 2–3; Sherwin-White and Kuhrt 1993: 7–8; cf. Ma 1999: 174–8 for a complex view). But the two terms are perhaps not in practice mutually exclusive: both may be appropriate, depending on the context and the point of view. It may also be suggested that a distinction always needs to be drawn between absoluteness of royal power in theory, and effective power in practice.

The Seleukid dynasty was certainly remarkable for its longevity. Rival monarchies did spring up in the course of Seleukid history, but on the edges of the empire and not in its central parts – the Attalids of Pergamon in Asia Minor, and the rulers of Baktria in the far east. Attempted usurpations came to grief and had no lasting effect, as shown by the fate of Molon, satrap of Media in 222–220, that of Achaios in Asia Minor in 220–213, or by the bid for power of Diodotos Tryphon in *c.* 145–139/8. After Tryphon there were no more 'usurpers' in Seleukid history: conflicts for power were within the dynasty itself. Territorially the empire endured despite numerous ups and downs. Even after the effective loss of control of the far east and the loss of Asia Minor after the peace of Apameia (188) it was still large, rich and powerful. Its decline has often been dated too early: it was not until the defeat and death of Antiochos VII in battle with the Parthians in 130–129 that the loss of Babylonia and western Iran became permanent. Even in its final period of decay, when an increased number of rivals competed for an ever decreasing empire in North Syria, it was difficult to remove the dynasty: it took the intervention by Tigranes of Armenia to replace Seleukid rule from 83 to 69, and the Romans to terminate the Seleukid dynasty once and for all in 63. One obvious element of strength for the rulers was the fragmentation of the empire, which lacked collective institutions and thus any possibility of concerted action on the part of the subjects. When Antiochos III sought to re-establish Seleukid control over Asia Minor in 197/6, only Smyrna and Lampsakos resisted him, but individually and without any local support: they looked to distant Rome for assistance.

On the other hand the Seleukid empire had all the limitations of monarchical empires. The risks inherent in dynastic struggles could never be eliminated, as shown by the conflict of the two rival brothers Seleukos II and Antiochos Hierax, the rivalry between the descendants of the two brothers Seleukos IV and Antiochos IV, and the proliferation of rival and short-lived rulers in the final decades of the dynasty. The size of the empire created obvious problems for the rulers: 'We would do well to see all ancient kingdoms and empires as no more than changing patchworks of control' (Millar 1984b: 18). The argument that the Seleukids were overstretched is easily made and difficult to refute (cf. e.g. Will 1979: 262–3, 272–5; Heinen 1984: 421–2). It is a tenable view that the western preoccupations of the rulers had a part to play in their loss of control in the far east: the evidence of coinage strongly suggests that Diodotos the satrap of Baktria broke away from the Seleukids and proclaimed himself king in the reign of Antiochos II (*Topoi* 4.2, 1994: 436–42, 474–507, 513–19; Holt 1999; Lerner 1999). It is by no means certain that the eastern '*anabasis*' of Antiochos III from 212–205, designed to restore control, did achieve its objectives: this was the last Seleukid incursion into this part of the empire and henceforward it went its own way without regard to the Seleukid rulers.

Nor is this merely a modern analysis after the event: the contradictory pulls at the heart of Seleukid policy are openly revealed in Polybios' account of the debates at the court of Antiochos III in the years after his accession. Yet the Seleukid kings were always reluctant to give up formally anything that had once belonged to the dynasty. In 196 at Lysimacheia Antiochos III lectured the Romans in all seriousness on his claim to the Thracian Chersonese: Seleukos had defeated Lysimachos in battle and his kingdom thus belonged to the Seleukid dynasty (Polyb. 18.51). After the Peace of Apameia the same Antiochos III is reported to have thanked the Romans for providing him with a more manageable empire (Val. Max. 4,1 ext.9). This shows at least that the king had a sense of humour: he and his predecessors had devoted enormous time and energy to securing control of Asia Minor against their rivals (Ma 1999).

One difficulty in any assessment of the Seleukids is the disappearance of reputable historical writing on them in antiquity, if any ever existed. Only a few rulers stand out more conspicuously in the surviving tradition, notably Seleukos I, Antiochos III and Antiochos IV. Of these only Seleukos I secured a lasting reputation as the founder of an empire and an undefeated conqueror. 'In my view it is beyond dispute that Seleukos was the greatest king of those who succeeded Alexander, of the most royal mind, and ruling over the greatest territory, next to Alexander himself' (Arr. *Anab.* 7.22.5). Antiochos III had the misfortune of facing the Romans and being defeated by them: this obscured the achievements of the earlier part of his reign, as may be seen in Livy's unbalanced account (Books 33–38). Antiochos IV on his side had the misfortune of being pilloried by the Jewish tradition as a persecutor. From a Roman perspective the dynasty as a whole had failed like others to stand up to the challenge of Rome: not surprisingly references to the Seleukids are scanty in Roman literature. It was only in North Syria that Seleukid memories were kept alive and adapted to serve contemporary local purposes, as may be seen in Libanius in the fourth century AD and in an even more garbled form in the sixth century AD in the Chronicle of John Malalas of Antioch (Book VIII). Any estimate of the Seleukids is thus provisional. Modern views have shifted in step with changing perceptions of the 'Hellenistic world'. No consensus has emerged and the debate can be expected to continue.

A NOTE ON SOURCES

The poverty of the available evidence for the Seleukid empire is a permanent draw-back. No proper account of the dynasty's history has survived. The nearest to a continuous narrative of the 'Hellenistic period' is Justin's mediocre and rhetorical *Epitome* of the *Philippic Histories* of Pompeius Trogus. The only available outline of Seleukid history is a sketchy summary in Appian's *Syrian History* 45–70. Neither writer gives the slightest indication of what contemporary sources ultimately lay behind their material. Other literary evidence is very scattered – Diodoros, Livy, Plutarch, Polybios, Strabo and others. Coins, archaeological evidence and above all inscriptions contribute important sidelights. In general the source material is charac-terized by its randomness, its unevenness in time and space (information becomes increasingly sparse the further east one looks), the Greek slant of the evidence (the vast majority of inscriptions come from the Greek world, and above all from western Asia Minor), and the lack of information about the personalities of the rulers them-selves and of their followers. The availability of non-Greek material provides a partial compensation, notably Jewish literature concerning their relations with the Seleukids in the second century, and Babylonian documentary evidence: both provide a differ-ent perspective on the Seleukids and illuminate aspects largely neglected by the Greek evidence (see further Erskine, this volume). But in general any modern reconstruc-tion of Seleukid history is no more than an unreliable patchwork, and arguments from silence are worthless: *caveat lector.*

FURTHER READING

On the present state of Seleukid studies cf. Briant 1990 and the articles in Brodersen 1999. A good starting point for the post-war re-evaluation of the Seleukids is Kuhrt and Sherwin-White 1987 and Sherwin-White and Kuhrt 1993, who argue that Seleukid history should be seen from a near-eastern perspective and as a continuation of the Persian empire, with its centre in Babylonia. The approach underplays the Seleukids' western connections and should be read in conjunction with the articles in *Topoi* 4: 1994. Ma 1999 is a richly documented and searching study which gives a wider perspective on Seleukid history than its title implies. Bikerman 1938 retains much of value despite its age. The prosopographical compilation of Grainger 1997, though useful, is unsystematic and leaves gaps. For the dynastic relations of the Seleukids there are contrasting approaches by Seibert 1967 ch. 3 and Ogden 1999 ch. 5. On the Seleukid personnel of government see Savalli-Lestrade 1998: 3–122, 216–36, 245–87, 399–403. For studies of particular kings see Mehl 1986, Mørkholm 1966 and Schmitt 1964. For some particular aspects cf. Bar-Kochva 1976 and 1989, Bilde et al. 1990, G. Cohen 1978 and 1995, Grainger 1990b, Holt 1999, Lerner 1999, Orth 1977.

CHAPTER NINE

Macedon and the Mainland, 280–221

Joseph B. Scholten

1 On the Eve of the Gauls: a Political Topography of the Southern Balkans

The third-century Balkans offer an opportunity not only to follow the development of political events but also the changing character of Greek political organization. This chapter takes as its focal point the political travails of Macedonia, especially the Antigonid regime and its attempts to control the behaviour of various immediate neighbours. The final failure of the independent city-states of the Greek mainland, particularly Athens and Sparta, as effective points of resistance to Macedonian hegemony emerges as a major theme, as does the increasing success of regional states/governments (*sympoliteiai/koina*) in this same capacity. The Aitolian and Achaian commonwealths dominate the latter discussion.

If we were to transport a party of State Formation theorists to this region in early 280 (just ahead of an only slightly less fractious group of Celts) they probably would share at least one fundamental observation: the farther south they ventured, the more sophisticated and complex the political institutions of the human communities that they encountered. As seekers after the truth about how it is that humans form 'states', they would also note, however, that wherever they wandered across the southern Balkans of the third, and indeed the fourth, century, they came across peoples struggling with (or against) the process of creating regional identities and governmental institutions (Cabanes 1993a).

Farthest north and west they would find Celts and Illyrians in the earliest stages of this process. The fundamental socio-economic building block of these peoples was similar to that of their more southerly neighbours: an extended family of farmers/stockbreeders gathered with close neighbours into villages (Halstead 1987). The latter supplemented their livelihood by trading with and raiding against neighbouring communities; and these families/settlements identified and co-operated with others in both immediate and more remote proximity to form ever larger, albeit ever more fragile, political communities. Two Illyrian coalitions achieved a measure of stability, and so regional importance: the Ardiaioi along the Adriatic coast between Skodra and the river Neretva; and the Dardanians who inhabited, roughly, modern Kosovo (Hammond 1966; Cabanes 1988; 1993a).

Thracian speakers to the east and south had forged more durable regional coalitions. Those inhabiting the Danubian foothills of the Star Planina range (anc. Haemos) that divides modern Bulgaria had come together as the powerful Triballi. Between the Haemos and Rhodope ranges, stretching east from the headwaters of the Hebros river to the Black Sea coast, an 'Odrysian' state had emerged, governed from the urbanized settlement of Seuthopolis (Archibald 1998). Further south and east, in European Turkey, were additional, although less stable, Thracian coalitions (Papazoglou 1978; Hoddinott 1981).

The regional state formation trend would be clearest, for our itinerant theorists, among the southernmost, Greek-speaking peoples of the Balkans. Here, the fundamental socio-economic unit, the extended family and its dependents (Gk: *oikos*/pl. *oikoi*), had long since become the building block of ever larger, and increasingly formalized local and district groups such as the clan (*genos*) and the tribe (*phyle*). And while settlement patterns for most remained rooted in the village (*kome*) and their livelihood tied to agriculture, stockbreeding and its close derivatives, local settlement and status hierarchies also arose early on.

In the lands furthest south, certain of these populations had achieved a degree of nucleation, and often even of urbanization, to establish what our experts would identify as 'central places' controlling and exploiting surrounding 'hinterlands'. The Greeks called this consolidation of a territory (*chora*) around a central site (*astu*) *synoikismos*, that is to say 'the coming together of *oikoi*' and their dependents. This was often achieved by means of a cult or sanctuary at the central site frequented by the residents of the *chora*. The result was that most familiar of Mediterranean state forms: the independent city-state (Snodgrass 1980; 1993).

Greeks, however, dubbed their version a *polis*, and distinguished it from those of neighbouring peoples by its extension of formalized responsibilities and rights, particularly in the area of self-governance, to a relatively broader segment of its population, typically to adult males who possessed a certain level of wealth. Contemporary classical scholarship recognizes this distinction by designating the *polis* not simply as a city-state, but rather as a 'citizen-state' (M. Hansen 1993).

Yet not all, and perhaps not even most, mainland Greek speakers of the early third century BC resided in villages that were part of a *polis*. North of an imaginary line stretching from the Gulf of Corinth to the pass at Thermopylai, any additional level of identity and loyalty beyond family, clan and tribe came more commonly in the form of the *ethnos* ('people' or 'nation'; pl. *ethné*). Although focused, as the *polis* was, around a common cult/sanctuary and, again like the *polis*, bolstered by a unifying body of kinship myth, an *ethnos* was physically much more extensive than a typical *polis*. For that reason it was both potentially much more powerful and in practice much less internally cohesive than a *polis*, except when threatened from outside (Hall 1997).

Nonetheless, the *ethnos* does appear early on as the fundamental unit in even greater entities, such as the *Amphiktyoniai* ('dwellers round about') that form in the late Archaic era to regulate regional sanctuaries of growing panhellenic importance, such as those of Demeter at Anthela, Apollo at Delphi, Poseidon at Kalauria, and Zeus at Olympia or Dodona (Tausend 1992). Some *ethné*, in particular that of the Thessalians, were prominent political actors in this earlier period. Indeed, even

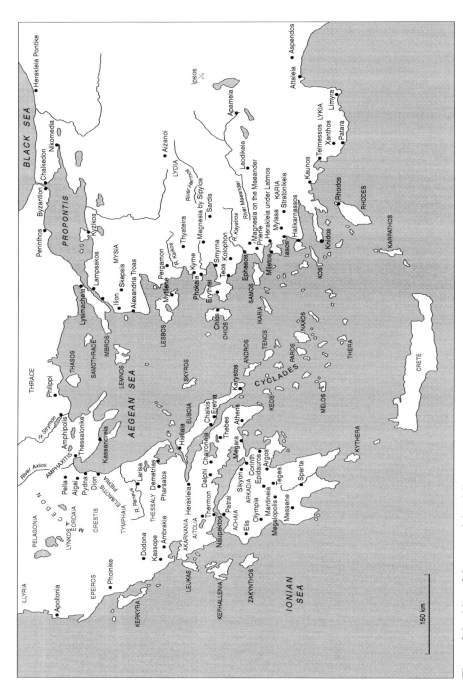

Figure 9.1 Map of Greece and Asia Minor

citizens of the independent *poleis* eventually came to see themselves as members of some *ethnos*. Particularly during the fourth century, many of these *ethné* attempted to bridge the gap between the local and the regional by developing stronger, federal political institutions, based upon a varying mix of direct democracy and proportional representation (Larsen 1968: 173–302; Beck 1997).

Yet a tension always remained between regional and local identity, interests and loyalty, even in areas where local settlements had not coalesced into *poleis* (Cabanes 1985). Whether these regional polities could be transformed into stable regional states capable of routinely marshalling their resources for common purposes, in particular for war, was a question which had animated the history of the southern Balkans for the preceding century (Cabanes 1989; 1993a). It would continue to underpin events and developments in the area between 280 and 221.

2 The Arrival of the 'Others'

The seminal event for this area and era occurred at the outset. In the late 280s and early 270s a series of Celtic war parties arrived on the scene. The movement of these 'Gauls' into the southern Balkans set off shock waves that reverberated into the farthest corners of the Hellenistic world. In summer 280 separate bands approached via each of the three major routes into the southern Balkans from the Danube bend (Paus. 10.19.4–7; cf. Hammond 1982: 619–24; Garaöanin 1982: 75–8).

The population they encountered comprised the most powerful and institutionally stable Hellenic regional state of the day: the *ethnos* of the Macedonians. It had not always been so, of course. Local interests, particularly those of the populations of highland districts in the Pindos foothills – Pelagonia, Lynkos, Eordaia, and farther out, along the upper Haliakmon, Orestis, Tymphaia, and Elimeia – long resisted attempts by clans of the fertile plain between the Haliakmon and Axios, under the leadership of the Argead clan based at Aigai, to forge a more perfect union. The lowlanders' efforts were both helped and hindered by external pressures. One source was in the north and west. Regular incursions by Illyrian neighbours allowed Argead leaders to foster Macedonian identity and their own legitimacy. That is, if the Argead in question survived the campaign. Those that did still had to face trouble from the opposite quarter. Macedonia's Aigaian coastline was dotted with *poleis* whose leaders constantly resisted the Argeads' state-building activities (and fomented further resistance among the Macedonian elite). The *metropoleis* further south that had dispatched these colonies played the same game (Hammond and Griffith 1979; Borza 1990; Errington 1990; Hatzopoulos 1996).

Philip II's ability to transform Pella into the focal point of a monarchic state commanding the allegiance of all the various Macedonians, and to use the region's abundant resources to crush its various antagonists – Illyrian, Thracian and Hellenic – is a tribute, of course, to his own talents (Borza 1990: 198–230). The subsequent military achievements of Alexander and his various marshals likewise reflect the genius of their authors. But all also reflect the latent power of a unified Greek *ethnos*, albeit the most populous among them. And none could have happened without the efforts of earlier Argeads, who built first Aigai and then Pella, and nurtured regional identity and solidarity via common institutions, such as the cult and sanctuary of Zeus at Dion, in the shadow of Mount Olympos (Borza 1990: 167, 172–4). Fortunately for the Celts approaching from the west, their own timing was impeccable. In 280 the Macedonian *ethnos* remained a stable and potentially powerful monarchic state (Billows 1995: 183–220). In preceding years, for example, it had continued to suppress any re-emergence of central authority among the Dardanians, thus, ironic-ally, clearing the way for the Gauls.

Of late, however, the kingship of the Macedonians had been the object of conten-tion between several post-Argead pretenders. The current ruler was a newcomer to the scene: Ptolemy Keraunos, a disinherited son of Ptolemy I of Egypt. Keraunos had only gained the kingship within the previous year, and then through the murder of his erstwhile patron Seleukos I, in the aftermath of the battle of Koroupedion. Eager to establish his legitimacy, Keraunos declined an offer of alliance and assistance from the Dardanians, and refused to bribe the Gallic intruders into a change of course. Confronting them with only a scratch force, he met defeat and death. As Celts paraded his head on the point of a spear, the Macedonian army evaporated, leaving the Gauls to run amok among Macedonia's communities and cantons.

That they were able to do so, and for an extended period, was a further conse-quence of the troubles that had immediately preceded their arrival. When the Gauls severed Keraunos' connection to his cranium, they also metaphorically decapitated the *ethnos* of the Macedonians. Local communities and their institutions, no doubt, continued to function, and district/cantonal ties and government probably did as well. But the Macedonians as an *ethnos* did not. Between the internecine bloodletting of the 280s, and the handiwork of Celtic broadswords, the leadership cadre that had been the key element of the Macedonian state temporarily disintegrated (Borza 1990: 230–52; Errington 1990: 5). Successive pretenders to the throne were unable to rally the *ethnos*. Enough gathered under the leadership of a certain Sosthenes to expel the initial invaders, but Sosthenes' forces were soon brushed aside by yet another Gallic coalition that arrived in the late summer via the third route (the Vardar/Axios corridor) bent on pushing further south (Euseb. *Chron.* 1.235; Diod. 22.4; Just. 24.6.1–2; Hammond and Walbank 1988: 253–4). At least two individuals, Pyrrhos and Antigonos Gonatas, may have possessed the combination of prestige and ability needed to bring order to Macedonia. But, having lost out in the earlier struggles, both were preoccupied and far from the scene. The absence of Pyrrhos was particu-larly unfortunate for the Macedonians. A charismatic military leader, he had already ruled them for at least a brief period, despite the fact that by birth he was a member of the Aiakid clan that led another *ethnos*: the Molossians. In the recent past Pyrrhos' origins had worked against his attempts to assert authority among the Macedonians. In this instance they may well have helped, for Pyrrhos now would have brought the Molossians into the fray on behalf of the Macedonians.

Molossis lay south and west of the Lakes District in the Pindos mountains. The heart of this region was the highland plain of Lake Ioannina that links two central places – Passaron, the region's political seat, with its cult of Zeus Areios, and the pan-hellenic sanctuary of Zeus at Dodona, with its oracle. The peoples and settlements of Molossis had formalized their identity through the adoption of regional governmen-tal institutions that may have been even more complex than those of the Macedonians (Cabanes 1993a). Their Aiakid 'king' led the *ethnos* in war and cult. But alongside him the Molossians collectively elected an annual board of officials to deal with daily and internal affairs, assisted by a council of representatives from Molossis' various districts. And king and people swore a mutual oath to respect the rules of governance established by custom (Plut. *Pyrrh.* 5; Hammond 1967: 487–524).

This Molossian government (*koinon*: Hammond 1967: 528), in turn, had under its control the Ionic coastal districts of Elinia and Kassopia, between the Thyamis river delta and the later site of Nikopolis on the Ambrakian Gulf. Pyrrhos had also gained control of the powerful *polis* east of Kassopia that gave that Gulf its name, transforming the eponymous central place of that one-time Corinthian colony (mod. Arta) into his answer to Pella. At the same time Pyrrhos had managed to pry the peoples of Parauaia and Tymphaia, which lay between Molossis and the upland cantons of western Macedonia, out of the orbit of the *ethnos* to their east (Hammond 1967: 525–54). Furthermore, as 'king' of the Molossians Pyrrhos was also 'general' of an even larger regional entity: the 'alliance of the mainlanders' (*symmachia* of the Epeirotes). Two other tribal groups to the west had co-operated in the creation of this alliance, if only to check the further westward expansion of the Molossian state. The Chaonians' lands began south and just inland of the colonial *polis* Apollonia on the Adriatic, straddling the Aous river valley and the plain of Phoinike in southern Albania. Their neighbours, the Thesproti, controlled the succeeding mountains, along with the portions of the Thyamis and Acheron river valleys inland of Elinia and Kassopia (Hammond 1967: 557–94).

While the precise degree of Pyrrhos' control over this Epeirote alliance remains unclear, when he did manage to rally it to the side of his own Molossian state, the combination could be a match for whatever resources the current ruler of the Macedonians could muster. Presumably the Gallic incursions of 280 would have offered incentive for Epeirote unity, and there seems little reason to doubt that the defeated Macedonians would have rallied around Pyrrhos, recent antagonisms notwithstanding. In the current circumstances, it seems clear whom the Macedonians would have viewed as 'us' and whom as 'them'.

But Pyrrhos was away, and so the Gauls did play. After some additional, leisurely months of pillaging the communities of the Macedonian lowlands, the fourth wave headed south around Mount Olympos and into the second largest plain (after central Macedonia) of the Greek-speaking southlands: that of Thessaly (Diod. 22.9; Paus. 10.19.12; Just. 24.6.2–4).

Bounded on the south by the low Othrys range, the west by the Pindos, and the east by Ossa-Pelion, Thessaly was both watered and united by the river Peneios and its tributaries. This watershed also made the plain ideal for agriculture, which in turn produced a large population. As noted above, the various communities of the plain developed a common identity, and effective regional governance, at a remarkably early date. Local clans and settlements coalesced into four regional polities, the 'tetrads' of Hestiaiotis in the northwest, Pelasgiotis in the northeast, Phthiotis in the southeast, and Thessaliotis in the southwest. The common sanctuary of the *ethnos* was that of Athena Itonia, in Thessaliotis. In addition to leaders for each of these regions ('tetrarchs'), the Thessalians also chose a common leader (*archon*) whose primary duties seem to have been military and cultic (Helly 1995). As time passed, however, the early unity of the Thessalians, which was reflected in their place of honour at the head of the various *ethnē* of the Delphic–Anthelic *Amphiktyonia* that controlled the sanctuary at Delphi, gradually dissipated in the face of internal rivalries. As in the lands further south, certain settlements among the Thessalian tetrads began to dominate their neighbours and adopt the institutions and behaviours of independent citizen-states. At sites such as Larisa, Pherai and Pharsalos, clans such as the Aleuadai asserted control over surrounding territories, often reducing part of the nearby population to a dependent status (the *penestai*: Ducat 1994). As these *poleis* grew in size and complexity, so did the rivalry between them within the *ethnos*. As a consequence, for long stretches the archonship went unfilled. When some individual did achieve the status to assume it, as Jason and Alexander of Pherai did in the 370s and 360s, internal opposition, whether local or regional, soon surfaced to thwart (i.e., eliminate) him. Fearful neighbours were only too happy to encourage such Thessalian fratricide (Larsen 1968: 12–26).

It took an outsider to reunite the Thessalians. Rather than face the prospect of the rise of another Jason to threaten all he had accomplished in Macedonia, Philip II decided to impose order in Thessaly, and then assumed the archonship himself. He thereby not only stabilized his own hold on power in the north, but also added greatly to his ability to control the affairs of the southern Greeks. As *archon* of Thessaly, Philip could command quick access to central and western Greece, and add the considerable manpower of Thessaly to the even greater pool he had in Macedonia. His son continued this custom, and the Thessalian cavalry played a key role in Alexander's conquest of the Achaimenid empire (Westlake 1935; Sordi 1958).

All successful rulers of Macedon after Alexander followed this lead with regard to Thessaly. Demetrios Poliorketes went so far as to place an eponymous stronghold, Demetrias, on the Gulf of Pagasai. It served as his capital, linking his Macedonian holdings to those in the south. Demetrios' successors maintained Demetrias, because of its easy access to Pelasgiotis and Phthiotis, as one of the key links in a chain of bases from which they projected their power throughout the southern mainland, the infamous 'fetters of Greece' (Polyb. 18.11.5; Walbank 1967: 563; Errington 1990: 151, 155, 162).

Their care was clearly born of experience. Any weakening in the stability of the Macedonian state invariably tipped the balance in Thessaly between those who supported (and were supported by) Philip's arrangement, and those who opposed it. The Thessalian cavalry that earlier had fought alongside Alexander turned and fought against his regent, Antipater, during the Lamian War that broke out upon news of Alexander's death. Keraunos' demise seems to have had a similar liberating effect. When the Gauls were finally ejected from Greece, a Thessalian delegation reappears at the head of the list of participants at the next meeting of the Delphic–Anthelic *Amphiktyonia*. When the Macedonian king was their *archon*, the Thessalian delegation yielded this position to his personal delegation (Lefèvre 1998a).

At the time of the Gauls' arrival in their lands, however, the communities of Thessaly seem to have been more concerned with pragmatic matters. Most appear to have presented a matador's defence, waving the invaders on towards the south (Paus. 10.19.12). Some may even have joined the newcomers' excursion (Just. 24.7.2), an early example of the contingency of Celtic otherness in the eyes of the Hellenistic world (cf. Mitchell, this volume).

As this swelling band descended into the plain south of Mt. Othrys inhabited by the small *ethnos* of the Malians and commanded by their central site, Lamia, the invaders finally found their way blocked. An immediate hurdle was the river Spercheios, which emptied into the sea not far to the east (Béquignon 1937). Just beyond it, another mountain barrier loomed: the Oita-Knemis range. Two routes crossed it most directly: one, the Duo Vouna pass west of Mt. Knemis (mod. Kallidromos) and east of Mt. Oita, past the *polis* Herakleia Trachis; the other, the more usual and famous pass of Thermopylai between the Malian Gulf and the north face of Knemis/Kallidromos (Pritchett 1985: 190–216; 1989: 118–22). Both routes, however, were guarded by a combined force of at least 26,000 infantry and 1500 cavalry, drawn from the polities of central and southern Greece (Paus. 10.20.3–5).

Many of the states contributing to this blocking force were familiar players in Greek politics: the small *ethnos* of the east Lokrians, on whose western border Thermopylai lay; that of the Phokians, west and south of the Lokrians; that of the Boiotians, beyond Phokis, and presumably led by its dominant member state, the *polis* of Thebes; the great *polis* of Athens, and its smaller neighbour and rival Megara. Not coincidentally, these polities lay along the normal overland route between Thermo-pylai and the Isthmus of Corinth. All, however, were also members of the council of the old Delphic–Anthelic *Amphiktyonia*. This organization had served as a rallying point for common resistance to threats to central Greece often in the past, and so may also have done so on this occasion.

Equally likely as organizer of this coalition, however, is also its most unlikely member. Pausanias tells us that the largest contingent among the Greek forces along the Thermopylai–Herakleia front was supplied by another *ethnos*: that of the Aitolians. This polity was an outgrowth of an older cultic community centred on the sanctuary of Apollo at Thermon, at the east end of Lake Trichonis (Antonetti 1990a). East and north of the Trichonis basin, including the central course of the Acheloos river, Aitolians also dwelt in the mountainous regions drained by the rivers Evenos, Mornos and Karpenesiotis, and their tributaries. Settlements in this rugged region were numerous, and in its latest, most complex form the Aitolian state referred to its fundamental constituent units as '*poleis*' (Funke 1985; Bommelje et al. 1987). With the possible exception of Kallion in the east, however, none achieved the degree of complexity modern scholars tend to associate with the term *polis*. Most *poleis* of Aitolia proper remained of the rudimentary kind: looser, canton-like collections of scattered villages (cf. Funke 1997).

Outsiders recognized the existence of an Aitolian *ethnos* by the outbreak of the great Peloponnesian Wars of the later fifth century. The subsequent, negative image of Aitolians as semi-feral brigands whose Hellenism was in doubt dates from this period, promoted by Athenian writers upset at the Aitolians' slaughter of an Athen-ian-led incursion up the Mornos valley in 426 (Antonetti 1990b: 43–143). Yet these same writers' claim that the Aitolians and their neighbours clung to an antiquated, more Homeric set of interpersonal conventions and social structures cannot be totally dismissed, as it squares with the limited archaeological data currently at our disposal.

Such conditions would also explain the Aitolian inability to rally for common actions other than self-defence. Across the fourth century the base of the triangle-shaped lands of the Aitolian *ethnos* edged southward, to the north coast of the Gulf of Corinth between the mouth of the Acheloos in the west and Tol(o)phon in the east. During the same years Aitolians developed their common political structures enough that their government, termed the '*koinon* of the Aitolians' (Tod 2.137), was deemed worthy of study by Greek political philosophers (Arist. frag. 473 Rose). Yet these coastal districts, Aiolis, the Naupaktia and the lands of the small *ethnos* of the West

(Ozolian) Lokrians, did not come under Aitolian control through communal action by their *ethnos/koinon*, but rather through the good offices of powerful third parties, such as the Boiotian *koinon* during the Theban hegemony, or the Macedonians under Philip. The direct threat of Macedonian imperialism prompted increasing Aitolian involvement in regional affairs, particularly in the early stages of the Lamian/Hellenic war. But the Aitolians quit that contest half way through, and were feckless allies to various of the Diadochoi, particularly the Antigonids (Scholten 2000: 13–19; cf. Grainger 1999: 54–86).

Only at the outset of the third century did the Aitolians as a polity begin to play a regular, active role in the affairs of mainland Greece. Their most important act was assuming control over the Parnassos massif, probably as a buffer for communities of eastern Aitolia. As the new territories included Delphi, however, the Aitolians' move earned them only further grief. In 289 the Antigonid master of Macedonia, Demetrios I Poliorketes, declared a Sacred War and attacked (Plut. *Demetr.* 40–1: Athen. 6.253b–f; Lefèvre 1998b); eight years later the Spartan king Areus assembled a Peloponnesian coalition and did the same (Just. 24.1.1–7). Aitolian tradition would have dictated withdrawal back into their rough hinterlands in reaction to these two experiences; instead, a new generation of leaders led their fellows into further engagement. In the year following Areus' (unsuccessful) attack, Aitolian forces seized control of the old Spartan stronghold at Herakleia Trachis, commanding both Duo Vouna and Thermopylai (Paus. 10.20.9). When the Celts came calling the year after that, the Aitolian *ethnos* was waiting for them (Scholten 2000: 19–25).

There were some notable absences from the Greek defenders at Thermopylai in 279/78. The Akarnanians, the Aitolians' western neighbours, stayed home. They were no friends of the Aitolians, having fought them for generations over control of the central and lower Acheloos river valley that stretched between Akarnania's two most advanced settlements, Stratos and Oiniadai (Schoch 1997: 1–72; Dany 1999: 1–61). More surprising as absentees were the peoples of the Peloponnesian peninsula in general, and in particular the Spartans, who had anchored an earlier, epic defence of that pass against a barbarian horde. The easiest explanations for this circumstance are proximity and topography. Between Thermopylai and the Peloponnese lay the lands of the Lokrians (east and west), Phokians, Boiotians and Megarians, to say nothing of the allure of Attika. And any raiders who might persevere would then confront two formidable natural obstacles: the Isthmus of Corinth in the east, and the Rhion–Antirrhion strait to the west. It is no coincidence that the only Peloponnesian polity to attempt to send a contingent north were the Patraians (Paus. 7.18.5, 20.3; 10.22.4): theirs is the closest *polis* on the south side of the latter waterway.

The Patraians' actions, however, may also signal another reason for the Peloponnesian abstention: regional political chaos. Patrai was a key community within one of the oldest of the *ethnê* of the Peloponnese: that of the Achaians. Their lands comprised a series of small alluvial plains that open onto the Corinthian Gulf coast from the mountains of the northern Peloponnese. At least a dozen settlement areas – some with a central site of sufficient complexity and hinterlands to behave as a *polis* – arose there along the stretch running west from modern Xylokastro to past Dyme: Pellene, Aigira, Aigai, Bura, Helike, Aigion, Rhypes, Patrai, Pharai, Olenos, Dyme and Tritaia (but cf. Walbank 1957: 230–2). The members of these communities had forged a common regional identity in the Archaic and Classical eras around the cult and sanctuary of Zeus Homarios, near Aigion (Larsen 1968: 80–9). In the earlier fourth century the Achaians had been sufficiently ambitious and cohesive to lay hold of the coastal plain of Aiolis along the north shore of the Gulf – including the Homeric-vintage settlements at Pleuron and Kalydon – as well as the Naupaktia. They had also been advanced and flexible enough in their thinking about their common identity to extend its bounds across the Rhion–Antirrhion strait, offering full membership in the *ethnos* to the populations of these two communities (Bommeljé 1988; Merker 1989).

In the second book of his history the Achaian statesman Polybios presents an account of the growth of his own *koinon* in the Peloponnese, as a parallel to that of Rome in the Mediterranean. Immodest as this decision may seem, it does shine a few points of light into the historiographical gloom that otherwise obscures developments on the mainland and elsewhere prior to events of the 220s. For present purposes it is noteworthy that Polybios indicates that, by the early third century, Macedonian interventions (most likely Antigonid, in the main) had not merely ended the Achaians' extramural experimentation; they had caused the *ethnos* itself to dissolve (Polyb. 2.40.5–6). At the time of the Celtic invasions, the four westernmost communities of Dyme, Patrai, Tritaia and Pharai had only just re-established their ethnic federation, probably taking advantage of the decline in Antigonid fortunes in preceding years (Walbank 1957: 233). The Patraians' dispatching of a force in 279/78 may thus also represent an act of renewed Achaian self-assertion across the Corinthian Gulf. It would require a further generation, however, for the other surviving communities to reforge their lost links to each other (cf. Urban 1979: 1–12).

To the south of Achaia, conditions in the Peloponnese in 279 are more obscure. In Lakonia, the Spartan king, Areus I, had only recently rallied the region in defence of Delphi – but against the Aitolians, and unsuccessfully. Consequently, whatever aspirations he harboured now had to confront two obstacles: a) a manpower shortage among the Lakedaimonians perpetuated by the refusal of their richest citizens to adjust a severe imbalance in individual landed wealth to the needs of Sparta's age-old socio-political regimen or vice versa; b) the revived suspicions of Sparta's Peloponnesian neighbours (Just. 24.1.7; Cartledge and Spawforth 1989: 31–3, 41–3). Not that the Argives to the north and east, the Messenians to the west, or the Megalopolitans to the west and north ever doubted the Spartans' bad intentions. But other communities – the eastern Arkadian *poleis* of Tegea, Mantineia and Orchomenos; the plutocratic oligarchy that controlled Elis; the Achaian *ethnos*; Corinth – were historically more willing to follow a Spartan lead. This difference in opinion about Sparta in fact helped keep the Megalopolitans from uniting with their fellow Arkadians to form a cohesive *ethnos* (Larsen 1968: 180–95). Instead, the anti-Spartan *poleis* were tailor-made friends to Macedonia, and the entire region a paradise for the recruiting agents of the mercenary armies of the Hellenistic age. Except for Corinth. Its wealth and location had made it a key prize in the contests of the Diadochoi; currently, Antigonos Gonatas held the keys to its lofty citadel, and so to the rest of the Peloponnese (Paus. 10.20.5; Hammond and Walbank 1988: 250–1).

In the event, the general absence of Peloponnesians from the anti-Gaulish coalition was not critical. The Aitolian-dominated force held the Herakleia–Thermopylai line so capably that a Gaulish flying column chose to make a difficult countermarch around Mt. Oita and into eastern Aitolia (Pritchett 1996: 173–90), in order to draw off the keystone of the Greek coalition. This move, including the sack of underdefended Kallion, had the desired effect: the Aitolians at Thermopylai headed home to help, their allies scattered, and the rest of the Celtic force headed for Delphi (Paus. 10.20–2).

That was the extent of the Gauls' success. A Phokian-led force stopped the Gauls before Delphi. In gratitude, the Delphic–Anthelic *Amphiktyonia* returned to the Phokians the two votes on the council the latter had lost as a result of their sacrilegious behaviour during the Third Sacred War. Meanwhile, the Patraians, at great cost, kept the Celts from reaching the Peloponnese. As both Gaulish bands attempted to withdraw, they found their return routes lined with Aitolians and other Hellenic ill-wishers; few Celts made it back (Scholten 2000: 31–7).

While the eradication of Brennos' Gallic coalition ended the Celtic threat to the southern mainland, it did not end Celtic mischief in the southern Balkans. In Macedonia, confusion reigned for several more years (Hammond and Walbank 1988: 253–8); in Thracian lands trouble lasted even longer. The various raiding bands that beset the region were anything but stable. Brennos' band, most notably, had reached a parting of the ways ere it even got to Macedonia. The defectors led by a certain Leonnorios and a certain Luturios preferred to take the southeasterly route, into Thrace. Some made it as far as Lysimacheia on the Gallipoli peninsula, others would eventually cross over into Asia Minor (Mitchell, this volume).

3   Antigonos Takes Charge

The presence of these Celts at Lysimacheia gave Antigonos Gonatas, son of Macedon's former king, Demetrios Poliorketes, an excuse to intervene. His forces crushed them, a success that in turn vaulted him, however precariously, into the leadership of the Macedonian *ethnos* (D.L. 2.141; Just. 25.1–2). Given the chaos that preceded his return, Antigonos' ability in the aftermath of the battle of Lysimacheia a) to re-establish order in Macedonia, b) to reassert Macedonian control over the Thessalian *ethnos*, c) to reconstruct Macedonia's hegemony in the southern mainland, and d) to survive as king to a ripe old age before succumbing to nature, must be considered among the more remarkable political achievements of the third-century Greek world. His career, therefore, and those of his successors, Demetrios II (Gonatas' son, regn. 240/39–230/29), and Antigonos III Doson (Gonatas' nephew, regn. 229–222/1), offer a suitable framework for the following narrative of political developments in the southern Balkans down to 221.

The study of the Antigonids is handicapped by evidence that is limited and often biased, concentrating on failure rather than success. As a consequence, the Antigonid regime gives the appearance of lurching from crisis to crisis. Obviously we cannot ignore the evidence we do have. But its nature should also not blind us to the long stretches of peace that the Antigonids brought to their homeland, years that allowed the Macedonian *ethnos* to recover from the Gallic disaster, to return to its previous prosperity, and so to participate in the larger institutional developments that were sweeping across neighbouring lands in the mid-to-late third century.

The first challenge to Gonatas' position was the return in 275 to Epeiros, and then Macedonia, of the (briefly) once and future king, Pyrrhos. The seeming effortlessness of Pyrrhos' march into Upper Macedonia, his defeat there of Gonatas, and his subsequent seizure of the central Macedonian plain, might easily mislead us into ignoring Antigonos' accomplishments in the preceding two years. The equal ease with which Gonatas re-established his dominance once Pyrrhos' attention wandered indicates that Gonatas had already done much to erase any doubts left by his father's mis-reign. A major step was his quick reassertion of Macedonian control over Thessaly, evidenced by Pyrrhos' attention to that region (Diod. 22.11; Just. 25.3.5–8; Plut. *Pyrrh.* 26; Paus. 1.13.2; Walbank 1984a: 230).

By 272 Gonatas was in a position to shadow Pyrrhos when the latter led his forces south to the Peloponnese. And he contributed in no small way to the failure of Pyrrhos' serial attacks there against Sparta and Argos. When the man whom Gonatas himself likened to a talented but undisciplined craps-shooter met his end during an ill-advised nocturnal sneak attack against Argos, Gonatas himself moved aggressively to assure friendly regimes in as many Peloponnesian polities as possible (Plut. *Pyrrh.* 26–34; Paus. 1.13.6–7; Just. 25–6; Fellman 1930; Hammond and Walbank 1988: 259–66).

4 The Last Stand of the *Polis*

Gonatas' bold steps into the political vacuum left by Pyrrhos' death may have helped to spark the second apparent threat to Antigonos' regime: the so-called Chremonidean War of the 260s. While some of the roots of this conflict may be found in broader struggles between the major Hellenistic regimes (Ager, this volume), fundamentally it was simply a renewal, albeit the final one, of the long-running twilight struggle of the *poleis* of southern Greece against Macedonian hegemony (Heinen 1972; Habicht 1997: 142–9).

Fittingly, the list of participants in the anti-Antigonid coalition is headed by the Athenians and the Spartans. Areus, apparently reinvigorated after the repulse of Pyrrhos, was a prime mover, intent as ever on establishing himself among the great kings of his day (Heinen 1972: 117–39; Will 1979: 223; Cartledge and Spawforth 1989: 35–6). The motion by the Athenian statesman Chremonides contains a ringing call to the defence of Greek freedom; the fact that this slogan had long since become a mainstay of anti-Macedonian rhetoric does not necessarily mean that its use here is purely formulaic (Austin 49; Lehmann 1988). Gonatas seems to have moved in the early 260s to expand his influence in Euboia from his base at Chalkis (Knoepfler 1993: 338–9; 1995: 141–4). For an Attic population already outraged by his continuing occupation of the Piraeus (Habicht 1979:102–7), Gonatas' activism on the other side of the Euboian channel must have been alarming indeed.

The extent of the coalition (which also included the *poleis* of eastern Arkadia, the Achaians, Eleians, Phigaleians and unnamed Cretan allies), its backing by the Ptolemaic regime, the apparent length of the struggle, and the likelihood that at one point during its course Pyrrhos' son and successor, Alexander II, emulated his father by driving Gonatas from central Macedonia, together leave the impression that the Chremonidean coalition posed a grave threat to Gonatas' regime. Once again, however, it is important to keep matters in perspective. Alexander's campaign, whose precise date and relationship to the struggle in the south remain unclear, was the only genuine setback Gonatas experienced during these years, and seems to have had even less impact than had Pyrrhos' raid in the previous decade (Just. 26.2). Otherwise, the Macedonian fetters served Gonatas well. His base at Corinth kept

Areus and his Peloponnesian allies from coming to the Athenians' aid, indeed Areus was killed in one of the attempts to break through (Trogus *Prol.* 26; Plut. *Agis* 3; Paus. 3.6.5–6). Gonatas was thus free to strangle Attika from Piraeus and Chalkis. Ptolemaic forces countered by establishing a base at Koroni on the east Attic coast, but that measure, or any other they undertook, was ineffective (Paus. 1.1.1, 1.7.3, 3.6.4–6; Caskey 1982). Whatever was the precise relationship of the enigmatic naval battle of Kos to this struggle on the mainland, the result was the same: Sparta's quest for revival died with Areus at Corinth, and Athens was forced to surrender. Gonatas' dominance over mainland Greek affairs was even greater than before.

It was an epochal moment, particularly for Athenians, as exemplified by the fate of the statesman and writer Philochoros (*FGrH* 328). Unable (or unwilling) to go flee into exile (and Ptolemaic service), as did so many other members of Athens' anti-Macedonian leadership (Étienne and Piérart 1975), Philochoros was captured and executed by Antigonid forces. With him died the long tradition of Atthidography; never again was Athens' history and lore the recipient of such single-minded investigation and glorification (Jacoby 1949). Sparta had lost one king and some of his followers, but little else. A generation later it would produce a new group ready to make yet another run at revival. Athenians lost their independence. Gonatas installed a governor and garrison at Athens, and occupied the various forts of Attika (Habicht 1997: 146). Athenians' will to power was so shattered that Gonatas could loosen his grip after only a few years (Paus. 3.6.6). Moreover, when the Antigonids' opponents liberated Athens in 229 by buying out Attika's remaining Antigonid garrisons, the Athenians responded by adopting a policy of strict neutrality (Habicht 1997: 173–8).

Antigonos Gonatas' victory in the Chremonidean War was not entirely without cost to him. It was probably no accident that one major mainland coalition was conspicuous by its absence from the (admittedly scanty) historical record for Gonatas' struggles both with Pyrrhos and also with the Spartan–Athenian alliance: the Aitolians, and their Boiotian and Phokian friends. Aitolians, of course, probably had little love for Areus after his antics of the late 280s (section 2 above). But their experience with Gonatas' father in the early 280s had been even less pleasant, and could have been disastrous had not Pyrrhos come to their rescue (Lefèvre 1998b). Further, when Gonatas tried to assure a friendly regime in Elis in the aftermath of Pyrrhos' death, Aitolians played no small part in helping their old friends to thwart him (Gómez Espelosín 1991; Scholten 1990). Yet neither do Aitolians (nor their allies) seem to have played an active role in support of Pyrrhos' last campaign. Evidently some Aitolians were hesitant to boost further the fortunes even of an old friend and benefactor (Scholten 2000: 49–51). Inaction was, of course, hardly unprecedented Aitolian communal behaviour (Scholten 2000: 13–25). And in the aftermath of Kallion it would not be surprising had many Aitolian leaders and their followers preferred to stay home and tend to their own troubles rather than sallying forth again to seek new ones.

Other developments during the same years, however, suggest that not all Aitolians were eager to melt back into the hills. Inscriptions at Delphi recording the activities of the Delphic–Anthelic *Amphiktyonia* reveal a new member-*ethnos* in the early 270s: the Aitolians (*CID* 4.12). Whatever had been the relationship between these two communities previously (Arnusch 2000), in the wake of the Gauls the legitimacy of the Aitolians' control over Apollo's oracle was less easily questioned. Lest any visitor forget their sacrifices, and particularly the suffering of Kallion, the Aitolian community (and individual Aitolians) bedecked the sanctuary with memorials to their heroism (Reinach 1911; Jacquemin 1985; Scholten 2000: 37–45).

More significantly, the *ethnos* also seems to have resorted to a tactic it had employed episodically in the past: territorial expansion. The same Amphiktyonic inscriptions that record the Aitolians' acquisition of their first seats at the Delphic–Anthelic table also seem to reveal subsequent increases in the size of the Aitolian delegation. By the conclusion of the Chremonidean War, six or seven Aitolian delegates were voting at council meetings (*CID* 4.38, 4.43). At the same time, some traditional delegations were not doing so: Dolopians, Ainianes, Metropolitan Dorians, East Lokrians (Scholten 2000: 240–9). The obvious inference is that the Aitolians' new votes were those of these smaller *ethnē*.

Less clear is the process by which these switches occurred. Again, one explanation seems obvious: the Aitolians' simply seized the votes, in order to convert the council into an instrument of Aitolian propaganda. Yet, if such was their goal, the Aitolians pursued it at a surprisingly dilatory rate: it is not until the later 240s that Aitolians clearly use the Amphiktyonic council to bolster their own agendas, and not until the 230s that Aitolians have an absolute majority of Amphiktyonic votes. Epigraphic evidence from Thermon suggests an alternative explanation. They document the fitful but steadily growing election of individuals from many of the effected *ethnē* to the executive board of the Aitolian association. The Aitolians may not, therefore, have brazenly occupied these neighbouring lands, but rather absorbed them, through extension to the residents of these territories of full rights in the Aitolian political community. The change in the ethnic identification of the Amphiktyonic votes controlled by these lands was, in this scenario, simply a reflection of the acquisition of an additional political identity, of membership in a Greater Aitolia.

Self-redefinition is a constant feature of human history, and the ancient Greeks were skilled practitioners of the art. For Aitolians, the experience of 279/8, to say nothing of the turmoil surrounding the final struggle of Pyrrhos and Gonatas, provides a reasonable context for a reconsideration of the human boundaries of their political identity, particularly when an expansion of their conceptual horizons could solidify the loyalty of neighbours whose lands could act as a buffer against the outside for the communities of the old *ethnos*. New adherents too could benefit. Membership in Greater Aitolia not only freed neighbouring *ethnē* from the age-old threat of Aitolian raiding, it also offered protection against the perhaps more frightening prospect of a resurgent, Antigonid Macedonia. Dolopians, Dorians of the Metropolis, Lokrians east and west, may all in fact have sought admission to the Aitolians' polity (Scholten 2000: 45–70).

Nor was the Aitolian *ethnos* the only member state of the Delphic–Anthelic *Amphiktyonia* engaged in such vote swapping during these years. Documents dating to the later 270s and 260s show first the Boiotian and then the Phokian delegations growing from two to three, and then back to two votes, in short succession, while the single vote of the East Lokrian *ethnos* disappears, reappears, and then re-disappears. At the end of the chain, the Aitolian delegation rises by one (Lefèvre 1995: 169–80; Scholten 2000: 245–6). It looks as though two age-old rivals within the Amphiktyonic coalition got into a tussle about territory, and not necessarily with the approval of the object of their contention. The Aitolians apparently settled the issue by bringing the communities of Epiknemedian Lokris into Greater Aitolia, along with the pass at Thermopylai which lay within these lands (Scholten 2000: 68–70).

This seeming instability within their own alliance would certainly help to explain the Aitolians' abstention from the Chremonidean War. For Gonatas, at least, keeping the Aitolian community (and its military and strategic resources) on the sideline was perhaps an acceptable outcome. Indeed he may have encouraged it by declining to contest Aitolian influence at Delphi, and the creeping growth of Greater Aitolia (Errington 1990: 170; Knoepfler 1995: 156; but Hammond and Walbank 1988: 289). Whether he connived at the Boiotian–Phokian rivalry is unknowable at present, but certainly he would have been glad at least to keep them out of action, as much as their Aitolian allies.

If Antigonos hoped that this policy might win the Aitolians and their associates to his side, he was probably disappointed. True, the admittedly slim record of Alexander's II's foray into Macedonia offers no sign that the Molossian received any help from his once and future allies. But when Alexander was himself, in turn, driven from his realm by a Macedonian counter-attack (Just. 26.2.11–12), Aitolians undoubtedly offered Alexander comfort and support for his own return to power. Moreover, the period of Gonatas' triumph also witnessed a much belated Amphiktyonic recognition of the Lagid *Ptolemaieia* festival. An attempt to curry favour with Philadelphos in the face of Antigonos' crushing of Ptolemy's erstwhile allies? Another and less ambiguously self-defensive action probably also belongs to these years: an alliance between the Aitolians and their long-time nemesis to the west, the *ethnos* of the Akarnanians (*IG* 9.1^2.1, 3). The terms of the treaty hint at a larger coalition of the polities of western Greece, from Olympia (Elis) in the south to Dodona (Molossis) in the north (Scholten 2000: 77–83; cf. Grainger 1995a: 328).

The Chremonidean War thus left the Greek mainland in something of a cold peace. Gonatas was clearly the dominant player, with the resources of Macedonia and Thessaly at his disposal, while two of the three greatest traditional powers of the south, Athens and Sparta, were broken or neutralized. The network of bases and friendly regimes by which Antigonos had choked off the recent threat was intact, and even enhanced. The third older power, Thebes and the Boiotian *ethnos*, was allied with the greatest potential threat to Gonatas' position, the Aitolian *koinon*, but was increasingly subordinate to its erstwhile protégés. And the wandering of the East Lokrian Amphiktyonic vote (to say nothing of the anomaly of the Akarnanian alliance) indicates that there were tensions within the Aitolian alliance that Gonatas could exploit, if need be.

5   The Emergence of Achaia

By about 255 Gonatas felt secure enough to lift his foot a bit from the neck of the Athenians (Paus. 3.6.6; Habicht 1997: 152). Victory at the naval battle of Kos may have added to his confidence. These same years, however, may also have seen actual fracturing within the Aitolian coalition. Boiotian and Phokian attendance at Amphiktyonic gatherings is sporadic across the 250s, and these same years seem the best location for an Aitolian–Epeirote agreement to partition Akarnania (Scholten 2000: 83–91). If Antigonos had any thoughts of trying to exploit the Aitolians' preoccupations, however, another pair of interrelated events late in the decade quelled them.

The first was the emergence at Sikyon in the northeast Peloponnese of an ambitious and energetic young leader: Aratos, son of an assassinated tyrant of the city. In 251 Aratos brought an end to more than a decade of tumult there by driving out the latest tyrant, recalling Sikyon's many exiles, and then aligning his *polis* with the Achaian *ethnos* to the west (Plut. *Arat.* 2–9). In preceding years the latter had reacquired all of its traditional member-communities; Doric Sikyon, however, had never been among them. Whether the parties to this new breach of old ethnic boundaries were acting under the influence of their Aitolian neighbours across the gulf or were simply harking back to Achaian actions of the early fourth century, the addition of Sikyon immediately raised Greater Achaia to a prominent power in the Peloponnese and, potentially, beyond (Urban 1979: 9–37; Walbank 1984a: 243–6). There was a problem, however: what sort of relationship did the members of this association want with the Antigonids? It seems clear that the communities of the old Achaian *ethnos* had expelled many an Antigonid garrison or Antigonid-friendly regime in the process of reconstructing their political community after 281 (Walbank 1957: 233–4). But Sikyon's recent leadership, Aratos' father included, had had a much warmer relationship with Gonatas.

This potential source of internal tension was to be resolved by a second development. Antigonos governed his holdings in southern Greece through a viceroy, who handled the bases at Chalkis, Piraeus and Corinth. By the later 250s Gonatas' half-brother, Krateros, had been succeeded in this post by his own son, Alexander. At some point, but probably before Aratos' coup, Alexander rebelled against Gonatas (Orsi 1987; Hammond and Walbank 1988: 296–303). For Achaians, Alexander's action was a godsend, and they quickly threw their support to him. Aratos and the Sikyonians then had to change their allegiance (Plut. *Arat.* 18; Trogus *Prol.* 26; Urban 1979: 38–45).

The loss of his bastions at Corinth and Chalkis was a severe blow to Gonatas' carefully constructed control mechanism in the southern mainland, although with garrisons in Attika and friends such as Aristomachos at Argos he still retained enough resources to contain his nephew (*SIG*³ 454, *ISE* 1.23). It is probably no coincidence that in the following years Aratos and the Achaians convinced the Boiotians to break from the Aitolian coalition. A failed Aitolian coup at Sikyon just prior to Aratos' successful one certainly gave this *nouveau* Achaian reason to acquire his adoptive *ethnos*' old animosity towards Aitolians (Polyb. 20.4–5; Plut. *Arat.* 4, 16).

The attempt against Sikyon in fact signals the emergence in these same years of a new generation of Aitolian leaders who were ready and willing to exploit more fully their polity's expanding power and influence. A less belligerent move in the same direction was the Aitolians' decision, probably in the late 250s, to reorganize a local festival they had founded in commemoration of the deliverance of Delphi into a Panhellenic affair intended to equal the greatest such traditional gatherings (*SIG*³ 408; Nachtergael 1977: 209–390; Elwyn 1990; Champion 1995; Scholten 2000: 237–8). It is easy to imagine that this development might have symbolized to uneasy Boiotians the final reversal of the power dynamic in their century-old relationship with the Aitolians, and thus opened them to Achaian approaches. It must also be noted, however, that the Boiotian alliance with his own Achaian allies opened for Alexander an overland connection between his otherwise isolated bases at Chalkis and

Corinth. It therefore seems reasonable to guess that Alexander was somehow involved in the Achaian–Boiotian alliance (Scholten 2000: 85–8).

Yet, while probably a greater threat to Gonatas' position than the Chremonidean uprising, Alexander's revolt brought no direct long-term consequence. Greater Aitolia played the part of ally, whether officially or as mere enemies of enemies, crushing the Boiotians in 245 at Chaironeia (Scholten 2000: 93, 123–7). The Boiotians then returned to the Aitolian fold. More importantly, at about this same time Alexander himself died, leaving his rump kingdom to his widow Nikaia. By 243 Gonatas was able to trick her into surrendering to him the keys to Acrocorinth (as well as Chalkis?), thereby re-establishing the dominant position he had held in the later 260s and 250s (Plut. *Arat.* 17; Polyaen. 6.5; Picard 1979: 274–8).

Tyche, however, had one more reversal to inflict upon the ageing Antigonos. In 243, during his second term as governor-general (*strategos*) of Greater Achaia, the still-young Aratos achieved his most famous exploit: the seizure of Acrocorinth by a daring night assault. In its immediate aftermath, the Corinthians followed their Sikyonian neighbours across the ethnic divide and into Achaian-ness (Polyb. 2.43.4–6; Plut. *Arat.* 18–24; Polyaen. 4.3.6; Urban 1979: 48–53). Greater Achaia thereby raised its importance in Greek politics by yet another order of magnitude. Furthermore, soon afterwards the Achaians secured an alliance with the Spartans, reviving (yet again) under a new, reformist Eurypontid king: Agis IV (Plut. *Arat.* 31, *Agis* 13).

These final indignities tempt us to conclude that, at the time of his death (early 239?: Ehrhardt 1975: 140), Antigonos II Gonatas left to his son, Demetrios II, a regime in decline. Once again, however, some perspective is needed. As far as concerns Aratos, the Achaians and the Spartans, it is important to note that in 241 they were unwilling (or unable?) to confront a relatively small Aitolian raiding party as it crossed the isthmus into the Peloponnese. Aratos eventually eliminated this band, but only after sending Agis and his Spartans home out of fear for their progressive agenda, and as the Aitolians were in the process of sacking the important eastern Achaian settlement at Pellene (Plut. *Arat.* 31–2, *Agis* 14–15; Scholten 2000: 123–7). Furthermore, whatever the nature of his relationship with the Aitolians, Antigonos certainly bequeathed to Demetrios a healthy string of client regimes in key Peloponnesian *poleis* such as Argos and Megalopolis. More importantly, however, and from a broader perspective, any troubles Gonatas left to his son were in the south. There is no hint of upheaval in Thessaly after the late 270s, and with the exception of the two brief Epeirote forays Macedonia itself seems to have enjoyed a period of tranquillity equal to that of the halcyon days of Philip II and Alexander III. For a Macedonian monarch of any era, that was a remarkable accomplishment (Will 1979: 338–43).

6   Demetrios II ('The Aitolian'?)

If the realm which Antigonos II Gonatas bequeathed to his son, Demetrios II, was secure and healthy, that which Demetrios left to his young son Philip V a decade later was anything but. Our historical tradition for third-century Greece is always spotty, at best, but it becomes particularly thin for Demetrios' reign. What does seem clear is that Demetrios spent much of his kingship battling an unusual southern alliance, and ended it – suddenly – while fighting a new wave of invasions from Macedonia's Illyrian neighbours (Ehrhardt 1975: 198–223).

What was unusual about Demetrios' southern opponents was not only their identity – those age-old adversaries, the Aitolians and the Achaians – but the nature of their polities. For the first time, resistance to Macedonian domination over southern Greece was not being led by a coalition of independent *poleis*, but rather by an alliance of regional states, and a close one, at that (Scholten 2000: 139–44). Furthermore, Demetrios may have prompted this coalition of two of the largest Greek *koina* by his own dealings with another such entity: the Epeirote state. Our sources indicate that, after recovering his throne in the late 260s, Alexander II had continued his family tradition of friendship with the Aitolian state. Indeed, as noted above, at some point in the 250s or, perhaps, early 240s Alexander II had joined the Aitolians in partitioning Akarnania. According to Justin the assertiveness implicit in the Aitolians' participation in this pact led to the troubles of the 230s (28.1.1). When Alexander died, probably in the late 240s, his widow Olympias came to fear the growing power and ambitions of Aitolians, individually and collectively. Accordingly, she abandoned the Aiakid–Antigonid rivalry and instead offered her daughter to Demetrios in marriage; Demetrios accepted. It was, most likely, in reaction to this turn of events that Aitolian–Achaian relations began to warm, leading to friendship and then alliance. By spring 238 the Aitolians and Achaians, together with the Boiotian *koinon*, were at war with the Macedonian–Epeirote axis that also included the Thessalian *ethnos* (Plut. *Arat.* 33; Polyb. 2.44; Hammond and Walbank 1988: 317–23; Scholten 2000: 132–9).

At least during its early course, this conflict was no particular disaster for Demetrios. If he, rather than his grandfather, is the Demetrios nicknamed 'Aitolikos' mentioned by Strabo (10.2.4), then Gonatas' son in fact raided the south Aitolian coastal plain of Aiolis, destroying the venerable settlement at Pleuron in the process (Ehrhardt 1978). Moreover, by 235, if not before, Demetrios seems to have struck at the Aitolians' Achilles' heel, boldly marching into Boiotia. Once again, enough Boiotians were conflicted about Aitolian power that the region defected to Demetrios (Scholten 2000: 153–7). Furthermore, at some point one of Demetrios' generals inflicted a serious defeat upon Achaian forces in the Peloponnese (Plut. *Arat.* 34).

If Demetrios is indeed 'Aitolikos', it is also possible that this nickname was no compliment. For while he was pressuring his enemies' weak spots, the Achaian–Aitolian alliance was pushing back, and with greater effect the longer the war continued. Already by 235, Aratos and his Peloponnesian cohorts convinced one of Demetrios' most important Peloponnesian supporters, the tyrant Lydiades of Megalopolis, to defect. Other Arkadian communities and regimes followed Lydiades' lead into Greater Achaia. By the late 230s, Antigonid influence in the Peloponnese had essentially evaporated (Urban 1979: 88–96; Hammond and Walbank 1988: 329–31; Scholten 2000: 157–62).

More seriously, these same years saw similar developments along the western, southern and northern frontiers of Macedonia itself. In Epeiros, fate (aided, in all likelihood, by Aitolian pressure) led to the extinction of the Aiakid dynasty. Those members who did not succumb to nature were exterminated by rebellions in the capital, Ambrakia. That southern region, along with the adjoining land of the Amphilochians, then became part of Greater Aitolia. The more northerly and westerly portions of Epeiros reconstituted themselves as a democratic regional state, the *koinon* of the Epeirotes, with its central site at Phoinike in Chaonia (Cabanes 1976: 97–100, 198–200).

The allegiance of this new state, however, remained very much in play due to developments further up the Adriatic coastline. There, among the Illyrian population, new regional coalitions and leadership were emerging and putting pressure on neighbouring communities. Eventually their activities would lead to the first of the great Roman military interventions in eastern Mediterranean matters, the First Illyrian War of 229. Before then, however, Demetrios was able to transform the westernmost of these Illyrian groups, led by Agron, from a threat into an ally. Most famously, in 231 he arranged for an Illyrian force to sail to the relief of Medeon in Akarnania, which Aitolian forces had under siege. In the following year, Agron's widow independently turned the attention of her followers to the Epeirote *koinon*. In response to an Epeirote appeal, an Aitolian–Achaian relief force stopped the Illyrians, but the Epeirotes nonetheless opted to sign a pact with their attackers (as well as independent Akarnania) to oppose the Achaian–Aitolian coalition. Finally, in spring 229, yet another Illyrian force set out, this time against Epidamnos, Apollonia and Kerkyra. The Aitolian–Achaian alliance once again demonstrated remarkable internal cohesion and organizational skill in responding to this renewed threat, but failed to stop it at a naval battle off the Pachoi islands. In the end, Epeiros remained hostile, but also weakened (Hammond and Walbank 1988: 332–5; Scholten 2000: 145–53).

Demetrios' greater failures, however, occurred simultaneously, along the northern and southern frontiers of the heartland of his realm. To the south, it appears that Aitolians made concerted and at least partially successful efforts to revive old anti-Macedonian feelings in Thessaly. Amphiktyonic documents indicate that by the late 230s the Aitolians were seating at least 11 delegates at the Delphic–Anthelic council. According to the interpretative approach adopted above, these votes reflect the addition of further Amphiktyonic lands to Greater Aitolia, most likely the remaining small *ethnē* of east central Greece, followed by the western portion of Phthiotic Achaia (Scholten 2000: 250–1). A more direct danger to Macedonia, however, arose in the later 230s in the form of a resurgent Dardanian kingdom. Demetrios' preoccupation with this threat may, in fact, have forced him to buy Agron's assistance, and prompted opportunistic action by his opponents to the south. Worse, his campaign against the Dardanians proved to be Demetrios' swan song, and a disastrous one at that. Whether or not Demetrios actually died in the course of being routed by the Dardanians, the fact remains that by early 229 Macedonia's army had been shattered, and its king was dead (Polyb. 2.44). As Demetrios' son, Philip V, was not even ten years old (Tarn 1940), the Macedonian *ethnos* was again effectively leaderless. The situation that Demetrios II left was thus as precarious as that of 280/79, or 360/59 (Hammond and Walbank 1988: 335–6; Errington 1990: 173–5).

To be fair to Demetrios, he had more than his unfair share of bad fortune. His opponents to the south, the Achaian and Aitolian *koina*, had blazed new trails in mainland Greek political thinking and behaviour by the remarkable degree of co-operation and co-ordination that they achieved. It is typical of their performance against Demetrios, and their potential as a counterweight against Macedonia, that at the same time they were sallying forth against an Illyrian fleet, Aitolians and Achaians also moved aggressively to exploit the Macedonian king's death. In the Peloponnese, the tyranny at Argos finally gave way and joined its *polis* into Greater Achaia. Aratos also turned his people's attention eastward, bringing Megara and Aigina into their association, and brokering the buyout of the Antigonid garrisons in Attika. Athenian gratitude, however, did not extend to joining the Achaian association (Plut. *Arat.* 34; Paus. 2.8.6; Urban 1979: 63–70; Habicht 1997: 173–6). Aitolians seem to have scored coups whose potential was even greater. In Boiotia, at the very least pro-Antigonids lost their recent ascendancy. More importantly, significant portions of Thessaly openly rebelled against Macedonian control, and may even have joined the Aitolian association (Scholten 2000: 165–70).

7   The Kleomenian Crisis (229–222)

As in the other major crises noted above, however, so too in this one the Macedonian *ethnos* found an extraordinary leader to turn the tide. Antigonos III 'Doson' was Demetrios II's cousin; having survived the debacle of the assassination of his father, he had achieved sufficient stature in Macedonia to be designated guardian of Philip and commander of Macedonian forces (Ehrhardt 1975: 224–40; le Bohec 1993). His performance fully justified his peers' judgement. After rallying the *ethnos* to drive back the Dardanian threat, Doson then aimed a bold stroke, not at the Thessalian rebels, but rather at their Aitolian sponsors. Most likely moving from Chalkis, Doson led an army through east-central Greece, detaching Opous from Boiotia (as punishment for fecklessness? Scholten 2000: 259–60), 'liberating' Phokis from Aitolian domination, sacking Kytinion in Doris, and trapping an emergency Aitolian levy near Delphi. The revolt in Thessaly collapsed along with Aitolian resistance. By spring 227 Doson was 'king' in his own right, and secure enough to embark on a venture to Karia. He returned after only one campaign season, however, perhaps because events in southern Greece had taken an unexpectedly promising turn (Bousquet 1988; Hammond and Walbank 1988: 337–45; Walbank 1989).

The Spartans had stayed out of Macedon's war with the Achaian–Aitolian alliance, but can hardly have been disinterested in its later course. For while the additions of Megalopolis and Argos to Greater Achaia lessened the danger to Lakonia from the hated Macedonians, they also threatened to transform the Achaian association itself into an even greater nightmare: a Peloponnesian regional state dominated by Sparta's traditional enemies. The prospect of such a turn of events may have played some part in the Spartan alliance with the Achaians in the late 240s, and a contemporaneous attempt by Agis IV to address the stark socio-economic inequities at Sparta that crippled her ability to defend herself (Cartledge and Spawforth 1989: 38–46). Aratos' fear of that programme's regional potential, both political and social, led to him to snub Agis, thus opening the door for the powers that were in Sparta to eliminate Agis and suppress his supporters (Plut. *Agis* 13–16; *Arat.* 31–2). Yet the ability of a massive Aitolian raid (launched on the convenient pretext of aiding Agis' party?) to plunder Lakonia soon afterwards must have brought home to all Sparta's pathetic weakness (Polyb. 4.34.9; 9.34.9; Plut. *Cleom.* 10; 18; Scholten 2000: 264–8). Thus in 229, while Aitolians and Achaians were busy fending off Illyrians and courting the Macedon's allies, the Agiad Kleomenes III led an army out of Lakonia and into eastern Arkadia, perhaps not so much out of delusions of lost grandeur as of fear of encirclement (Polyb. 2.46.2–3, 57.1–2; Plut. *Cleom.* 5, 14; Walbank 1984b: 456; Cartledge and Spawforth 1989: 46–50).

The objects of Kleomenes' first campaign, Tegea, Mantinea, Orchomenos and Kaphyai, were probably carefully chosen. At that time these *poleis* were not part of Greater Achaia, but rather in some sort of alliance with Greater Aitolia (Polyb. 2.46.2). Aitolia had long had interests in the western Peloponnese centred on Elis, but these were eastern Arkadian communities which had only come to the Aitolians to avoid being Achaian, most likely because their long-time adversaries within Arkadia, the Megalopolitans, were exercising growing influence within Greater Achaia (Will 1979: 371–4). Thus, Kleomenes' attack was not random, but aimed at a political fault-line – both within Greater Achaia, and also between the Aitolian and Achaian associations. It succeeded on both scores, perhaps even better than some in Sparta would have wished. Achaians faulted Aitolians for Sparta's acquisition of eastern Arkadia, Aitolian preoccupations in 229 notwithstanding, and the productive (and promising) union between the two *koina* began to deteriorate. Achaians did not help matters by meddling in the following years in Elis and other areas of Aitolian interest in the western Peloponnese (Scholten 2000: 186) But it is just as clear that the members of the Achaian association were equally at odds with each other over what to do about Sparta. Aratos seems to have tried to avoid open war, while others such as Lydiades of Megalopolis favoured a more aggressive approach.

Yet the thinking in Sparta was no more unified. Indeed, the *status quo* group there began to fear the prestige Kleomenes was accruing by his success. Kleomenes, for his part, was preparing to force Spartans to grasp its opportunity. Late in 227, having left Sparta's citizen army on manoeuvres, Kleomenes with the assistance of mercenaries carried out a purge in Sparta that drove away 80 or so of the wealthiest residents of Lakonia (Plut. *Cleom.* 7–11). The connection to Agis IV's early reform programme of what Kleomenes did next, as well as his overall goal, is much debated. What seems clear is that land was confiscated, and then distributed to a Spartiate population whose ranks had swelled to near 5000 by the enrolment of select resident aliens (*metoikoi*) and tributary Lakonians (*perioikoi*). These men were to resume the ancient Spartan way of life, and their sons were enrolled in a revived *agoge*. While this programme was carried out under the guise of returning to the ancestral, 'Lykourgan' constitution, at least one facet suggests a less idealistic agenda: the army of this new Sparta was to fight, not as hoplites, but as Macedonian-style phalangites (Will 1979: 374–5; Walbank 1984: 458–9; Cartledge and Spawforth 1989: 50–3; Erskine 1990: 123–49)

Freed in the same process from oversight by traditional bodies such as the board of ephors or the council of elders (*gerousia*), Kleomenes proceeded in the next two years (226–225) to fracture the Achaian association (Plut. *Arat.* 39; *Cleom.* 12–16; Polyb. 2.51–2). Greater Achaia's disintegration is certainly attributable, on some level, to Aratos' singlemindedly rapid expansion of his *koinon*, a policy which stands in contrast to Greater Aitolia's more fitful but durable growth. He may well deserve less blame (or credit) for what ensued. For Kleomenes, too, had been in too great a hurry. Already in late 227, Megalopolitans began to approach their old Macedonian masters for relief against the even more hated Lakedaimonians. Our sources see Aratos' hand behind this appeal and subsequent ones; it is just as likely, however, to reflect the disintegration of Achaian unity. Certainly, the end point of this tiger-ride cannot have appealed to Aratos, his family's history notwithstanding (Polyb. 2.47–51; Plut. *Arat.* 38.11–12; *Cleom.* 16; Gruen 1972; cf. Urban 1979: 117–58; Walbank 1984: 461–5).

In spring 224, with Argos having gone over to Sparta and Kleomenes besieging Acrocorinth and Sikyon, the Achaian assembly voted to ask Antigonos Doson to come to the rescue. His price: the surrender of Acrocorinth to his control and the transfer of Megara to the Boiotian association. The Achaians agreed; by autumn Argos had switched sides again, Kleomenes had withdrawn to Sparta, and Doson was at Corinth, with even bigger plans (Plut. *Arat.* 41–4; *Cleom.* 17–21; Polyb. 2.52–4). Following in the footsteps of Philip II and his own great-grandfather (and namesake), Antigonos organized yet another 'League of Corinth', although this third version is better known as the 'Hellenic Alliance' (Larsen 1968: 325–6; Walbank 1988: 345–53).

Like its predecessors, Doson's creation was clearly an instrument of Macedonian diplomacy, yet one equally designed to take account of the mainlanders' sensibilities. While its constitutional details are vague, it had the customary *synedrion* of allies, and a leader or *hegemon*: Doson, of course. Unlike previous Macedonian-sponsored alliances of Greek states, however, Doson's *symmachia* was not made up of *poleis*; rather, its constituents were all regional entities: the Achaians, Thessalians, Macedonians, Boiotians, Phokians, Akarnanians and Epeirotes (Walbank 1984b: 468–9). As we have seen, the coalitions of the war of Demetrios II had already anticipated this shift; Doson's alliance simply confirmed that the days of the *polis* as a primary agent in Hellenic military affairs were at an end. It is also important to keep in mind, however, that the powers of this new organization, and particularly of its *hegemon*, were limited. Decisions were taken by the synedrion, but even then were not binding on a member state unless ratified by that state's citizenry. While this provision might seem to be self-defeating, it in fact was quite ingenious. Doson and his successors thereby would be able to gain sanction for police actions without risking driving unenthusiastic allies into opposing arms.

In this first instance, not surprisingly, most allies were on board. When Doson and Kleomenes finally came face to face at Sellasia in 222, the Macedonian's army included contingents from Achaia, Akarnania, Boiotia and far off Epeiros (Polyb. 2.65). The core of his army, however, was Macedonian or mercenary, and its superb training prevailed: Kleomenes' phalangites were slaughtered, he himself fled (ultimately, to Alexandria, and a futile end: Polyb. 2.69.10–11, 5.35–9; Plut. *Cleom.* 29–37; Just. 28.4.9–12), and Doson became the first conqueror ever to enter Sparta. There, following the example of his uncle at Athens decades earlier, he installed a governor. Perhaps because he had ready at hand a body of supporters in Kleomenes' exiled opponents, Doson also left the Spartans a good deal of autonomy. Once again appealing to the 'Lykourgan' past, the ephorate was re-established; but, for the moment, no kings were installed. Nor is it clear whether Sparta joined the Hellenic alliance immediately. In fact, Doson's treatment was lenient, perhaps to maintain the Spartans as a counterweight to other Peloponnesian powers.

Just as likely, however, any mercy in Doson's clean-up after Sellasia was a matter of haste. For no sooner had he begun to settle matters in Sparta than messengers arrived announcing that Macedonia was awash once again with Illyrians. Doson therefore departed for the north, and upon arrival drove off the invaders. But, as in the case of his cousin in 230/29, so too Doson fell ill during the campaign, and presently died (Polyb. 2.70, Plut. *Cleom.* 30; date of death: Walbank 1957: 290 vs. Walbank 1984b: 472).

Doson left the now-adolescent Philip a much stronger realm than had Demetrios. The homeland was secure, and its military as well-trained and formidable as it had been in memory. Thessaly was quiet; both the Aitolian and Achaian associations had been humbled, and their alliance shattered; Sparta's ability to make mischief in the southern mainland had been broken; the other major (and minor) regional states of Greece were united in a Macedonian-led mutual defence organization centred at Corinth, whose acropolis Antigonid troops once again held. Only Athens and Attika remained beyond Doson's grasp, and their population had forsworn further adventures on behalf of ideals and slogans. Unfortunately for the tranquillity of the neighbourhood, the stability of Doson's settlement depended upon the reputation he had achieved across his brief reign. That was one item that he could not pass along to his stepson, Philip V.

8 A Theoretical Retrospective

The preceding narrative, focused on macropolitical events, leaves the impression that the southern Balkans of the third century BC were the scene of continuous bloodletting and destruction. Yet a different focus would bring other, more heartening developments into the foreground. Were we to ask our time-travelling theoreticians to compare the situation at Doson's death to that they had found in 280, they would undoubtedly note a remarkable consensus among at least the Greek communities of this area. Across these same years, the vast majority seem to have come to the conclusion that their interests were best served by membership in a regional political community. The two most notable exceptions, Sparta and Athens, are also notable for the unusually large size of their territory. Part of their disinterest/resistance may stem from the fact that each already *was* a regional state. The case for Athens is all the stronger as one of the fundamental characteristics of the third-century regional states was a common citizenship shared by all citizens of member-communities (*sympoliteia*). The demesmen of Attika had adopted such a regional identity and loyalty already by the end of the sixth century BC, if not earlier.

Elsewhere, however, existing regional identities and entities took on greater salience and substance. Central institutions and offices began to proliferate, and the constitutional prerogatives of the various levels of governance – the details of *sympoliteia* – were worked out. These details varied, of course: the powers and nature of the Aitolian assembly, council and executive differed from those of the Achaian union. But they – and other sympolities – shared a common set of institutions. Even the old Macedonian *ethnos* was part of this general trend. The precise nature of the Macedonian monarchy remains a matter of heated debate among scholars, as does the relationship of that executive to other levels of governance. But recent work has made it clear that, by the later portion of the third century at the latest, Macedonians had elaborated their local and intermediate layers of authority and – like their neighbours to the south – were involved in an ongoing process of refining the rules of their *sympoliteia*. The fact that their chief executive office was held for life and was hereditary, rather than elected annually and not open to consecutive terms by a single individual (as was true for the Achaian and Aitolian *koina*) meant that capable and ambitious occupants could enhance its status and power within the Macedonian *koinon*, and relative to that of the *strategoi* in more republican regional states (Hatzopoulos 1996: 487–96). The Epeirote peoples reacted against that concentration of powers by replacing their monarchic executive – the Aiakid dynasty – in the 230s (Larsen 1968: 279; does the case of Sosthenes, *strategos* in Macedonia during the Gallic incursions, represent a similar movement, albeit one aborted by the arrival of Antigonos Gonatas? Cf. Hammond and Walbank 1988: 254). Yet all alike remained regional states, nonetheless (Cabanes 1993a). This rough uniformity would hardly surprise our observers, who have long since noted the tendency of polities to adopt and adapt the characteristics of their regional peers (Renfrew 1986). The Epeirote evolution also reflects the general third-century trend toward more thoroughly sympolitical regional states.

As inveterate model-makers, our consultants would also inevitably test the question of 'What If?' They would hardly be pathbreakers here: mainland Greece's likely future development if Romans had never arrived is a venerable topic. More hopeful analyses might note the trajectory of the third century, and imagine yet a fourth level of identity and governance emerging in subsequent decades and centuries, perhaps even a United States of Greece. There are signs that political loyalties and boundaries were indeed becoming increasingly complex, malleable and situational in this area and era: the Akarnanian–Aitolian isopoliteia (*IG* 9.1^2.1.3), or the embassy to Xanthos of 206/5, in which the participants present themselves by local, area and regional identities, at once Kytiniotes, Metropolitan Dorians, and Aitolians (Bousquet 1988). Cynics would point to the subsequent reversion of the Aitolian–Akarnanian relationship to its traditional violence as well as that of the Achaian–Aitolian alliance of the 230s, or to the turmoil experienced by the Achaian union when it attempted to absorb the communities of Arkadia.

These conflicts and rivalries, which continued after the arrival of the Romans, at the very least suggest that in the late third century the peoples of the southern Balkans were still some way from that next step, a union of the unions, that could have produced a superstate capable of keeping the area out from under the looming shadow of the 'Clouds arising in the West' (Polyb. 5.104). Yet it is also true that many of the regional identities and institutions that emerged in the third century continued to thrive for centuries after their political eclipse by Rome. Certainly, one can only agree with F. W. Walbank's view that their development reflects 'the continuing ability of the Greeks to respond to a new political challenge with new solutions' (1992: 157).

FURTHER READING

Ancient literary sources (and other documents then known) for nearly every matter discussed here may be found in Will 1979–82, along with sensible interpretations thereof. On the nature of Greek regional states, see Gschnitzer 1955, Giovaninni 1971; Walbank 1976–77; Hatzopoulos 1996: 487–96; Hall 1997. Works on specific regions and *poleis* are proliferating: for Achaia, also Rizakis 1991, 1995, 1998,

Harter-Uibopuu 1998, Ossana 1999, Dixon 2000; for Aitolia, Antonetti 1987, Ager 1989; Bakhuizen 1987, Bommeljé and Doorn 1991 (and volumes 2 and 3 of the series *Studia Aetolica* [Amsterdam, forthcoming]), Dietz et al. 1998, Pantos 1985, Papapostolou 1987–90, 1983–98, Pritchett 1991a; 1992; Themelis 1979, and D. Rousset's forthcoming publication of the inscriptions found by the French excavations at Kallion; for Akarnania, also Habicht 1957, Lang 1994, and forthcoming reports from recent work in and around Stratos (led by P. Funke, H-J. Gerhke, and L. Kolonas); for Arkadia, Jost 1985, Nielsen 1996, Nielsen and Roy 1999; for Boiotia, Feyel 1942, Étienne and Knoepfler 1976, Roesch 1982, Schachter 1981– 86, Buck 1993, Nafissi 1995; for Doris, Rousset 1989, 1990; for eastern Lokris, Fossey 1990; for western Lokris, Lerat 1952; for Phokis, Fossey 1986, McInerney 2000; for Thessaly, Decourt 1990, Decourt et al. 1995; for Makedonia, Errington 1978, Buraselis 1982, plus the summaries of finds from ongoing excavations at Amphipolis, Dion, Pella, Vergina – and a myriad of other sites – in the annual *Archaeological Reports*; on Athens, in addition to the works of Habicht see also Frösén 1997, Dreyer 2000 (challenging); on Delphi and the Amphiktyonia, see also Flacelière 1937, Bousquet 1989, Sánchez 2001; on Sparta, Africa 1961, Oliva 1971, Marasco 1980. Up-to-date biographical studies of players in this chapter's events are in short supply. On Antigonos Gonatas, Gabbert 1997 (a bit slender, perhaps in reaction to the always overimaginative Tarn 1913); for Demetrios II, Ehrhardt 1975; on Doson, le Bohec 1993; on the women of the Makedonian court (neglected here), Carney 2000 (a *tour de force*); for Pyrrhos, Lévêque 1957; for Aratos, Walbank 1933. Finally, on Doson's Hellenic Alliance, Scherberich 2001.

CHAPTER TEN

The Attalids of Pergamon

Elizabeth Kosmetatou

And finally, I constantly . . . kept before your eyes these our contemporaries Eumenes and Attalos, telling you how, inheriting a small and insignificant kingdom, they increased it so much that it is now inferior to none, simply by their concord and agreement and their faculty of mutual respect. (Polybios, 23.11.7–8, trans. Paton)

A remarkable family of low origins, the Attalids created a kingdom that put its mark on the political, social and cultural developments of the Hellenistic period and beyond. In the process they became masters of the art of cultivating an 'international' image, by manipulating contemporary events and making the best of every opportunity to construct and reconstruct their public persona, thereby rationalizing and legitimizing their power (Gruen 2000: 17). Ancient authors such as Strabo and Pausanias considered them to be the most representative Hellenistic dynasty and speak admiringly of their deeds as reflected on their numerous dedications that survived well into the Roman period and retained their function as non-verbal cues on the emotions and attitudes of spectators (Strabo 13.4; Paus. 1.6.1; J. Engels 1999: 277–89). Modern scholars sometimes attribute to them a far greater influence, especially on their contemporary and later artistic developments, a view which has been under serious revision lately. It would, then, be fair to say that the Attalids were successful in creating their own sense of who they were, which after so many centuries continues to influence and even on occasion to deceive.

1 From Rags to Riches: the Origins of the Attalid Dynasty

Even though the Attalids figure as the Greek dynasty *par excellence*, becoming instrumental in diffusing Hellenism both in Asia Minor and among the Romans, their rise to such extraordinary power was an anomaly. Philetairos, the dynasty's founder, was half-Greek at best. Born in about 343 in Tieion, a Paphlagonian backwater on the Black Sea, he was reportedly a eunuch, son of Attalos and Boa, the latter said to be a flute-player and a courtesan (Lucian *Macr.* 12.7; Athen.

13.577b; L. Robert 1963: 320). Scholars generally agree that the name of his father points to a Macedonian origin, but one may wonder at Macedonian presence at Tieion as early as 344 (Hammond and Griffith 1979: 458–63, 484–9). One may even wonder whether the original name of Philetairos' father was not closer to the attested indigenous Attales that was conveniently hellenized in the aftermath of Alexander's campaign, but this supposition must remain conjecture at the current state of the evidence (Masson 1962: 131; Zgusta 1964: 105–8; Billows 1995: 104 n. 67). Even if the family were not originally Greek, however, Greek presence in the area may account for Attalos and Boa's decision to give their children Greek names, a practice that was not unusual in Asia Minor (Hdt. 7.27; Zgusta 1964: no. 1310). Nonetheless, Philetairos' personal ambition, in all likelihood cultivated by the upstart pretensions of his family, and his undeniable political shrewdness, landed him high positions, and historical circumstances offered even greater opportunities. It was well-known that eunuchs were highly valued by the Persian kings for their presumed trustworthiness as servants with no ambitions for self-aggrandizement since they could never have offspring to whom they might bequeath wealth and power. Of course, circumstances proved their masters time and again wrong (Hdt. 8.105; Xen. *Cyr.* 7.60–5). Since eunuchs continued to assume high positions in court, thereby raising the fortunes of their kinsmen (Hdt. 4.43), Philetairos' family may have chosen this cruel path for him in the hope that it would lead to a brilliant career.

Following Alexander's conquest of the Persian empire, parts of the administration continued to serve their new Macedonian masters, who seem to have shared local ideas on the value of eunuch administrators (Badian 1958b; Scholl 1987: 115–17). Philetairos, who was about twenty years old when Alexander died, became an officer of Antigonos Monophthalmos, serving under his general Dokimos, whom he followed in 302 to join the ranks of Antigonos' rival Lysimachos of Thrace. He was eventually stationed at Pergamon, in charge of the Thracian treasure of nine thousand talents. Historical circumstances, as well as personal ambition, led Philetairos to a policy of gradual, steady and careful emancipation. The ancient sources mention the struggles and intrigue in Lysimachos' court which in 283 culminated in the murder of Agathokles, son and heir-apparent of Lysimachos, and victim of queen Arsinoe's false accusations. A number of Lysimachos' officers, including Philetairos, declared themselves inconsolable following the wrongful death of such a brilliant and promising young man, and so afraid of Arsinoe's schemes, that they formed a conspiracy, and defected to Seleukos I of Syria. The Thracian and Syrian armies met at Koroupedion in 281, and Lysimachos lost in a day both his life and kingdom. He had probably never thought it possible that Philetairos could betray him. But betray him he did: as a eunuch, it may not have been possible for him to have children, but nothing could prevent him from having a nephew. Following various manoeuvres, he was able to ingratiate himself with his new master Seleukos I, and his successor Antiochos I, and achieve a certain qualified autonomy for Pergamon. His nephew Eumenes I was thus able to succeed him in power in 263 without incident (E. Hansen 1971: 14–38; Billows 1990: 418–19).

Philetairos was not the first eunuch to assume a degree of independence in the area. Hermias of Atarneus, the philosopher-ruler of parts of Mysia, had set up his own domain in the middle of the fourth century but had been executed by the Persian king on charges of treason (Trampedach 1994: 66–79). Philetairos was more successful and should be credited with establishing the foundations for Attalid policy that his successors were wise enough to follow and build on. Squeezed between the powerful Hellenistic empires, he successfully turned his small artificial territory into a well-organized domain by manipulating all the conflicts in that turbulent period, including the Gallic invasions and the wars of the Diadochoi (*IG* 11.1105; Nachtergael 1977). His delicate perseverance during the conflict between the Seleukids and Ptolemy Keraunos following the collapse of the kingdom of Thrace earned him substantial autonomy: Following the treacherous assassination of Seleukos I by Keraunos, Philetairos made a successful bid for the king's body which he properly cremated and duly sent off to his son and successor Antiochos I (App. *Syr.* 63). It was probably after this that he received the right to issue coinage in his name featuring the posthumous portrait of Seleukos I on the obverse (Newell 1936). He also initiated the brilliant policy of forging non-threatening ties with neighbouring city-states: he assisted Kyzikos in its struggle against the Galatians by sending a gift of grain and advertised his patronage of Apollo Chresterios at Mysian Aigai (*OGIS* 312; 748; Allen 1983: 98–121). At the same time he secured his borders by hiring mercenaries and founding at least one military colony which was known as Philetaireia during the reign of Eumenes I (*I.Perg.* 13; Kosmetatou 2001). His nominal Seleukid master apparently did not consider these actions as suspicious, and relations between Antiochos I and Philetairos must have remained cordial since the Pergamene's great nephew by the name of Attalos married Antiochis, a niece of Antiochos I, by whom he fathered the later king Attalos I.

2 Rise and Fall of a Kingdom

Eumenes I (263–241) continued his predecessor's policy of careful emancipation from the Seleukid empire and prepared the ground for eventual revolt. Conflicts among the Hellenistic kings, the secession of local rulers from the kingdom of Syria, and the ever-present threat of the infamous Galatians, allowed Eumenes to take advantage of the ensuing power gap (*IG* 11.1105). He continued his predecessor's policy of establishing relations with neighbouring city-states, took steps in order to protect his borders by maintaining military colonies, and eventually declared Pergamon's independence. Even though he was victorious over Antiochos I's punitive expedition of *c.* 261, he never assumed the diadem (*I.Perg* 13; Strabo 13.4.1–2; E. Hansen 1971: 21–2). The portrait-coins in the name of Philetairos, that were probably issued soon after his victory over Antiochos I, must have been among Eumenes' first attempts to display his newly acquired independence (Westermark 1961).

The final step towards the creation of a kingdom was taken by his nephew and successor Attalos I (241–197) who was the first Pergamene ruler to score an important victory against the Galatians in *c.* 237, that earned him the diadem and a spear-won kingdom, allowing him to claim conquest through military victory as the foundation of his kingship. This time-honoured principle was especially used in Macedonian royal propaganda and put Attalos on an equal footing with the other Hellenistic kings (Billows 1995: 24–30; for a portrait bust of Attalos, figure 11.1). Even though Attalos was the first Pergamene king, he acknowledged humble Philetairos as the founder of his dynasty by continuing to mint Eumenes I's portrait-coins of Philetairos, linking Philetairos to his own military successes against the Gauls in the context of a series of dedications on Delos, and by continuing to sponsor festivals in the name of Philetairos following his great-great uncle's tradition (e.g. *IG* 11.1105–10; *ID* 346, 366). He also built on Philetairos' policies by establishing the principles followed by all his successors in Pergamene foreign policy: aggressive construction of a public image; the consolidation and expansion of Pergamene territory; and the cultivation of ties and subsequent forging of alliances with cities, leagues and states that were presumably too weak, or located too far away, to pose a threat to the survival of his kingdom. Alliances with the great powers, especially Macedon and Syria, were to be avoided at all costs as suspicious and dangerous.

Initially Attalos I played a lone hand in his bid for an empire by exploiting the internal conflicts within the kingdom of Syria that eventually saw the collapse of Seleukid power in Asia Minor. Already during the reign of Eumenes I the Third Syrian War had broken out, which began as a war for succession between the two wives of Antiochos II and drew in Ptolemy III, brother of queen Berenike. Seleukos II, son of Laodike, prevailed, but his kingdom was dealt a serious blow by the loss of territory to Ptolemaic Egypt. A few years later (*c.* 239) Seleukos II's rule was challenged by his younger brother Antiochos Hierax who was stationed in Asia Minor. Attalos I did not interfere in the so-called 'War of the Brothers' at first. In around 230, however, Hierax and his Galatian allies chose to attack Pergamon, provoking an Attalid reaction. Attalos I conquered the greatest part of the Seleukid possessions in Asia Minor and, at the same time, concluded alliances with the most important cities in the area, including Smyrna, Sardis, Aizanoi and localities in the Troad (Polyb. 4.48.7; Ma 1999: 43–8; Ager, this volume, sections 3–4). He duly advertised his victories over Hierax and his 'barbarians' by sponsoring at least one triumphal monument, the base of which (the so-called 'long base') was discovered at Pergamon and was reconstructed brilliantly by Marszal (1998; figure 10.1).

Attalos I's newly augmented territory did not remain under his control for long. Upon his succession to the Seleukid throne, Antiochos III, continuing his father's policy of regaining what he considered to be rightfully his, appointed his cousin Achaios as governor for Asia Minor west of the Tauros mountains with the express purpose of recovering all the lost land. Achaios was successful in driving Attalos I back into his pre-230 borders and reconquering most of Asia Minor, but the Pergamene king and the allies in the Troad that his dynasty had carefully cultivated in the

2 m

Figure 10.1 Reconstruction of the 'Long Base' at Pergamon by John Marszal. Courtesy of J. Marszal

previous decades managed to stop the Seleukid general's advances further north (Kosmetatou 2001; Erskine 2001: 173–5). Further losses for the Pergamenes were prevented following Achaios' assumption of the diadem and the royal title in 220, an act which forced Antiochos III to conclude an alliance with Attalos I against the usurper (Polyb. 4.48.7–11, 5.107.4; *OGIS* 236; Allen 1983: 58–65; Ma 1999: 54–63).

Although Pergamon seemed to be safe from Seleukid aggression following Attalos I and Antiochos' alliance against Achaios, it was obvious to Attalos that the Seleukid king would not leave the Attalid kingdom to its own devices, especially since he had initiated an elaborate military expedition and propaganda whose main theme centred around the recovery of his 'ancestral holdings' (Herrmann 1965a; Ma 1999: 26–52). Furthermore, the aggression of Philip V and Prusias I of Bithynia posed serious threats to the continuing existence of the Pergamene kingdom. In this context, Attalos turned his interest to Greece by cajoling Macedon's enemies, including Aitolia and Athens. He also moved to create an entangling relationship with Rome, aimed at restraining the ambitions of the Syrian, Macedonian and Bithynian kings, reinforcing Pergamene influence in Greece and Asia Minor, and expanding the relatively small kingdom of Pergamon. Eventually it was to become one of the largest Hellenistic kingdoms in the second century BC, at least theoretically.

In the First Macedonian War Attalos I had been a rather ineffective participant on the Roman side, but the working relationship between Pergamon and Rome was to grow closer. In 205, towards the end of the long struggle against Hannibal, the Romans consulted the Sibylline Books where it was prophesied that Carthaginians would be driven out of Italy if Rome introduced the cult of Magna Mater. Attalos I was instrumental in the transfer of the Great Mother and her sacred stone from Asia Minor to Rome in the following year, an act which opened a new chapter in the affairs of the Hellenistic East (Gruen 1990: 5–33; Erskine 2001: 205–24). Following Philip V's continuing aggression in the Aegean, which undermined Pergamene and Rhodian interests, and backed by the Achaian League, Sparta, and several cities in Greece, Attalos I brought Rome back to the East for the Second Macedonian War, in which he was an active participant this time. He actually died as a result of a stroke that he suffered in 197 while trying to raise the Thebans against Philip V, probably shortly before the battle at Kynoskephalai (Allen 1983: 10 n. 6; Ma 1999: 265).

Attalos' policies were consistently followed by his two sons and successors: Eumenes II (197–158) and Attalos II (160–138). The former inherited a diminished kingdom, an added enemy in the form of Pharnakes of Pontos, and spent most of the 190s continuing his father's work in complaining to Rome about Antiochos III's imperialism. His energy and effectiveness worried Antiochos enough to prompt him to offer the Attalid king a daughter in marriage. This was a crossroads moment for Pergamene policy: Eumenes' brothers, who had always been his closest advisors and allies, recommended that he make a 180-degree turn from his predecessors' consistent policies and accept Antiochos' proposal, but Eumenes' desire to play for higher stakes prevailed (Gruen 1984: 544–5; Ma 1999: 92). The Roman victory over Antiochos at Magnesia and the Apameia settlement that followed changed the political map of Asia Minor. Eumenes II made significant gains as Pergamon and Rhodes divided Seleukid possessions in the region between themselves (Gruen 1984: 640–3; Derow, chapter 4 above). He made serious efforts to control his newly expanded kingdom by introducing, among other measures, a new monetary policy to the largest part of his territory sometime between 188 and 181. The new cistophoric coinage circulated only in parts of the Attalid kingdom, and the Attalids do not appear to have imposed it as the exclusive currency everywhere. The coinage is named after the 'cista mystica', a circular wicker basket accompanied by a snake on the coin's obverse (Kosmetatou 1998).

The following decades were far from peaceful for Eumenes II, as they were marked by continuous wars with Prusias of Bithynia (187–183) and Pharnakes of Pontos (183–179). During the Third Macedonian War (171–168) Pergamon fought again on the side of Rome, but towards its end Eumenes incurred Roman displeasure which was displayed, among other things, in the Senate's declaration of Galatian autonomy (Polyb. 30.19; 30.28; Livy *Per.* 46; Just. 38.6.4). Although Pergamon never suffered the Rhodian fate of losing its political independence and commercial supremacy in the Mediterranean, and Eumenes' masterful manoeuvres managed to stabilize his relationship with Rome, the Pergamene alliance with the Romans remained unequal to the end of the Attalid dynasty. Gruen is probably correct to question the commonly held, and perhaps oversimplified, opinion that during the last decade of his reign Eumenes II held his position at the pleasure of the Roman senate, no longer able to formulate his own policies (Gruen 1984: 573–5; 2000: 17–18). Although Eumenes openly acknowledged Rome's hand in the expansion of his kingdom, he nevertheless conducted his own wars by his own initiative, made his own settlements and concluded his own alliances. He married Stratonike, the daughter of the Cappadocian king Ariarathes IV, a former enemy of the Romans who wished to ingratiate himself with the new superpower, and even openly schemed against his neighbours (Jonnes and Ricl 1997; Ma 1999: 248; Gruen 2000: 19–20). He involved himself in the dynastic conflicts of the Seleukid kingdom by helping Antiochos IV onto the Syrian throne, a policy that his brother Attalos II later favoured as well, when he promoted the interests of the pretender Alexander Balas in 153 (Gruen 1984: 646–68). Attalid intrigue and the quest for larger territory, rather than true love, may have been the motive behind the marriage of Eumenes' youngest brother Athenaios to Kallipa, former mistress of Perseus, the last king of Macedon (Diod. 32.15.5). The Pergamene king had been especially interested in Thrace – his ambitions may have included parts of Macedonia as well – and he had noticed that his brother Athenaios, one of Pergamon's most competent diplomats, had been a particular favourite with the Romans (cf. Gruen 1984: 562). Although our sources are scarce and ambiguous, Eumenes' insatiable appetite for territory and his apparent desire to expand his kingdom westward may have alarmed the Romans and some Greeks, leading them to suspect the Pergamene of wishing to fill the power gap left by the collapse of the Macedonian kingdom.

In the decades following the Peace of Apameia Eumenes II embarked on a lavish building programme, transforming Pergamon into one of the showpieces of the Hellenistic world. He extended the sanctuary of Athena Nikephoros and refounded the Nikephoria festival in 181 which acquired panhellenic status (C. Jones 1974; 2000). He also expanded the famous Library of Pergamon which was probably founded by his father Attalos I and was second only to that of Alexandria (Nagy 1998). It was perhaps in the late 180s that construction of the magnificent and breathtaking Great Altar began; it featured a dramatic Gigantomachy frieze which ran along the outside of the building's base, depicting the struggle of gods against monstrous giants (cf. figure 29.2), and a second, smaller frieze around its internal courtyard narrating the life and deeds of the hero Telephos, the legendary forefather of the Attalid dynasty. Although the Great Altar is considered by most scholars as the crown of Hellenistic art, we know surprisingly little about it. The only surviving ancient author to mention it is Ampelius (8.14). We do not know to whom it was dedicated, when exactly it was built, its purpose or its impact on artistic developments of the period, while its reconstruction remains a matter of fierce debate among art and architectural historians. However, scholars agree that the popular Gigantomachy theme probably symbolized Attalid victories against the Galatians and functioned as a symbol of the struggle of good vs. evil and the forces of civilization vs. the 'barbarians' (Hoepfner 1996; Kästner and Heilmeyer 1997; Ridgway 2000a: 19–102; Stewart 2000).

Although Attalos I and his successors had envisaged the Pergamene and Roman alliance as a relationship of equals, a bilateral partnership based on their shared values of Greek civilization, it became apparent during the reign of Attalos II that this pact had turned into a one-way dependency of the Pergamene kingdom on the goodwill of Rome. Attalos II continued most of his brother's policies, but mainly focused on keeping his kingdom together rather than entertaining ambitions for further expansion. He maintained his alliance with Cappadocia and Syria and in the 140s supported Rome's wars against the Macedonian pretender Andriskos and against Corinth. He also kept up the Pergamene tradition of offering magnificent gifts to important Greek allied cities like Athens, where he built at least one stoa (Hopp 1977: 57–106; Gruen 1984: 584–92; J. Engels 1999: 286–9).

After a long reign of twenty years, Attalos II was succeeded by Eumenes II's son, Attalos III (138–133), but sources for his reign are scarce and confusing. Ancient authors describe him as a brutal, eccentric, unpopular king who was uninterested in governing, loved his mother pathologically and was consumed by the study of botany and pharmacology. Nevertheless, he must have been a competent student in his chosen disciplines, since none other than Galen speaks admiringly of his achievements (Diod. 34.3; Just. 36.4.1–5; Gal. *Comp. Med. Gen.* 13.416). Moreover, the surviving epigraphic evidence, which includes information on his cultic benefactions and at least one military success, show him in a favourable light. Even though official documents usually present us with a 'party-line' of sorts, Attalos III seems to have retained cordial relations with the Romans, and there is no information on internal strife in the kingdom during his reign. At any rate, his premature death in 133 started a chain reaction of events that eventually led to Roman suzerainty in Asia Minor. Possibly faced with a dynastic challenge initiated by Aristonikos, who claimed to be a bastard son of Eumenes II, the childless Attalos bequeathed his kingdom to Rome. His will may have been modelled on that of Ptolemy VIII Physkon, but it definitely came as a natural consequence of political and military developments that had begun many decades before (Hopp 1977: 107–47; Gruen 1984: 592–610; J. Engels 1999: 292–7).

An emergency situation arose immediately after Attalos III's death before Rome could react to news of the will. Proclaiming Eumenes II as his father, Aristonikos organized a rebellion which initially met with some success. He promptly took the diadem, assumed the name of Eumenes III and issued cistophoric coinage from the mints of Thyateira, Apollonis and Stratonikeia (Robinson 1954). Faced with the fierce opposition of city-states and of the kings of Bithynia, Pontos, Cappadocia and Paphlagonia, who naturally aimed at carving up the Pergamene kingdom, and after suffering a heavy naval defeat, he recruited slaves. Although his supporters were fighting against the professional, formidable and disciplined Roman army, they nevertheless scored significant successes, until they were finally defeated in 130. Aristonikos himself was captured and led away to execution in a Roman prison. Judging western Asia Minor as too unstable, the Roman senate assumed responsibility for its security, restored law and order, organized its reconstruction and imposed a settlement among the powers of the region. The Attalid treasury and royal estates had already been bequeathed to Rome, and the eventual annexation of the entire region was a natural consequence of continuous Roman involvement in the area over a long period of time (Gruen 1984: 596–608; Hopp 1977: 135–47; Mileta 1998; McGing, this volume, section 4).

3   The Public and Political Image of the Attalids

Much has been written on the largely successful efforts of the Attalids to cast a shadow over their dubious origins with a blaze of cultural glory, rivalling Classical Athens (Schalles 1985; Gruen 2000). Surviving and/or presumed Attalid monuments have been analysed to destruction, and this chapter will not dwell on the problems associated with the reconstruction of the infamous Attalid sculptural dedications. Emphasis will be given instead to the fundamentals of Attalid image-making by exploring and evaluating a number of themes prevalent in the construction of Pergamene ideology.

A first priority which was consistently assumed as such by all Attalid rulers was the creation of the ideal leader, a type that they endeavoured to fit. As Murray Edelman has observed leadership in this sense can be associated with dramaturgy, and he has stressed that 'regardless of the consequences of officials' actions, which contemporaries cannot know, the ability to create oneself as the ideal type maintains followings' (1988: 40). The Attalids undoubtedly maintained a following through the ages – even though the impact of their propaganda continuously changes with the times – since their reputation remains pristine to this day, and they are continuously credited by art historians as instrumental agents in setting the style and as great innovators (cf. Savalli-Lestrade 2001: 78). It is true that dramaturgy has become more important and relevant in our modern age of mass communication and flood of information, but theatricality and the staging of public life occupied a central position in the Hellenistic world. It allowed the central players – individuals such as kings, or groups, such as the various leagues of cities – to construct an image of themselves which deceived partly because it distorted reality, constructed illusions and controlled the emotions and thoughts of the public (Chaniotis 1997a).

Theatricality was an integral element of Hellenistic public life and played an important role in political attempts to control the emotive responses and affect audiences' attitudes towards the powers that be. It would be a mistake, however, to associate theatricality exclusively with high drama as displayed in the architecture, town planning and art of the period (Pollitt 1986: 230–49). The concept itself is an important theme in Attalid dynastic propaganda, but it bears no relation to grand 'theatrical' performances in public life, along the lines of the spectacular procession of

Ptolemy II Philadelphos (Athen. 5.196a–203e). Attalid actions were never exaggeratedly massive, nor did they offer great thrills to their audiences, because subtlety was their motto and this turned out to be more effective in the long run. In choosing this policy the Pergamene rulers probably took into account the peculiarities of their own rise to power and their family's difference in situation, it being so decidedly beneath the glamorous origins of the Diadochoi.

First, it was necessary to clean up their own origins, and this problem was taken care of, probably by Eumenes I and Attalos I. A fragmentary inscription from Pergamon, dated to the Roman period, informs us that a sufficiently aristocratic pedigree was attached to the Attalids who were thus incorporated into the genealogies of the previous masters of Pergamon (*OGIS* 264). Rather than attempt to hide the fact that Philetairos was a eunuch, with all its demeaning associations of slavery and sexual exploitation, his successors boldly put him forward as a founding father, whose portrait graced Attalid coinage continuously for more than seventy years. A sad story was attached to his fate. He supposedly became a eunuch as a result of a tragic accident. While still an infant, Philetairos was taken by his nurse to a large funeral. Caught in a terrible crowd, he was crushed! In a flash of genius, the family realized that the only career option open for the thus cruelly incapacitated Philetairos was to be trained among other eunuchs as a royal administrator. This unlikely story is narrated by Strabo (13.4) who mainly used pro-Attalid sources in relating the history of the kingdom of Pergamon.

Next, it was essential for the Attalids to construct a state mythology which would rival the religious policies of other Hellenistic kingdoms and would allow the Pergamene rulers to fabricate much-needed fictional dynastic and legendary genealogies. It would also establish a link with Alexander the Great who often figured in Hellenistic royal propaganda. The Attalids could not claim to be the long-lost illegitimate descendants of Philip II, as Ptolemy I had attempted in his early years as king (Curt. 9.8.22; Paus. 1.6.2), but they were somehow lucky in their obscurity. For a short while in the late fourth century Pergamon had been the seat of Herakles, son of Alexander the Great and Barsine, before mother and son were murdered by Polyperchon who thus put an end to their claims over Alexander's empire (Kosmetatou 1995; 2000: 45–6). The Attalids could, therefore, present themselves as the legitimate successors of this Herakles. Their new mythology reinforced this link: the Arkadian hero Telephos was adopted as the dynasty's legendary forefather. He was the son of Auge, an Arkadian princess who was seduced by the hero Herakles and cast away by her father. She gave birth to Telephos in Mysian Teuthrania, over which region the hero reigned. Telephos featured in legends related to the Trojan war: the wandering Achaians landed in Mysia on their way to Troy and plundered the area, until they were stopped by Telephos and his troops who defended the country. The hero was wounded by Achilles in battle and could only find relief by going to Greece, blackmailing the Achaians into providing a cure, and leading them to Troy in return (Stewart 1996b; Gruen 2000). Interestingly, Telephos' sons by the name of Tarchon and Tarsenos (and perhaps Eurypylos as well) sided with the Trojans against the Greeks, an aspect of the story that played an important role later.

In choosing Telephos as legendary forefather, the Attalids established a link with his father Herakles, the legendary patriarch of the Argead dynasty of Macedon, to which Alexander the Great and Philip II belonged. Further mythical origins had to be established, however, which would link the Attalids more closely to Alexander the Great. Following the well-established practice of Greek cities to assign themselves a real or fictitious eponymous *ktistes*, and favoured by the name of their capital which offered a lot of possibilities, the Attalids chose Pergamos, a very marginal hero, as their own legendary founder. Pergamos was one of the sons of Andromache and Neoptolemos, son of Achilles. According to legend, he became king of the Epeirote tribe of the Molossians and eventually ended up in Mysia in response to an invitation of Grynos, grandson of Telephos. Pergamos distinguished himself in war, killed the king of Teuthrania, renamed his capital after himself and ruled. The Attalids did not use his myth in their state mythology very much. The archaeological record suggests that at least one small *heroon*, dedicated to *Pergamos Ktistes*, was built in Pergamon, probably in the third century, and his head with the same legend occurs on some bronze coins of the Roman Imperial period. However, the hero Pergamos played a role in Attalid state propaganda by providing further links to Alexander the Great and by associating the Attalid dynasty with the royal families of Epeiros and therefore with Olympias, the mother of the Macedonian conqueror. Next, Pergamos' name, which he supposedly gave to his capital, conveniently provided a further association between the Attalid capital and Troy, a city that Homer on occasion also calls Pergamon (Kosmetatou 1995; for further discussion of mythology and Pergamene traditions, see Scheer, this volume).

An important element in the creation of the Attalid image was the construction of leaders who possessed qualities that their contemporary rulers lacked. These were, of course, the proverbial Attalid family values. All ancient authors agree on this point: the Attalid family was always united, no feuds ever took place and every member of the family wholeheartedly supported the reigning monarch, who invariably followed on the footsteps of his predecessors and implemented the same, consistent policy that had been formulated since the foundation of the Attalid kingdom (Polyb. 23.11.7–8). This practice was sharply contrasted to the infamous family feuds that repeatedly broke out in other Hellenistic monarchies. Attalos I's image as a family man who married Apollonis, a simple girl from Kyzikos, for love, never cheated on her and became a most virtuous father (Polyb. 18.41) was sharply juxtaposed in the minds of Hellenistic audiences to the Ptolemaic sibling marriage that initially shocked the Greeks and the ensuing murderous habits of these monarchs against members of their own family (Carney 1987). Apollonis, Attalos' wife, was credited with rising to the occasion of her unexpected acquisition of royal status and with teaching her children the importance of family values (Polyb. 22.20). This image of a strong, perpetually united family certainly influenced Polybios in his assessment of the Attalids, as well as modern scholars. In discussing the enigmatic philosopher Daphitas, who was reportedly executed by an otherwise unidentified Attalos for writing jeering verses against the Attalids, Fontenrose cites Attalos I's character, including his relations with his wife and sons, to reject any involvement of this 'wise and just king' in such a horrible and unreasonable act (1960: 85–6)!

While the successful collaboration between Attalos I and Apollonis' four sons is not a matter of dispute among historians, Eumenes II and his brother, the later Attalos II, knew the importance of carefully staging a royal appearance that would bring glory and renown to the dynasty. Eumenes II is said to have appeared in public surrounded by his brothers in the guise of bodyguards, a scene that the Alexandrians would surely never witness during the turbulent reigns of Ptolemy VI and Ptolemy VIII (Plut. *Mor.* 480c). At any rate, this impressive scene left a significant mark on the Greeks to the extent that Polybios used it in his portrayal of Philip V of Macedon as tragic hero. In a manner that echoed Aeschylus' *Persians*, in which the poet chose to glorify the deeds of the Greeks in the Persian wars by having their enemies praise them, Philip V in Polybios' history pays tribute to his enemies, the Attalids, by underlying the unity of their family as instrumental to the preservation and expansion of their rule. Philip bitterly juxtaposes the proverbial Attalid brotherly love to the hatred among his sons that brought down his own kingdom (Polyb. 23.11; Haegemans and Kosmetatou 2002).

Furthermore, promoting their mother as the uniting force of the royal family became an important policy: Eumenes II, Attalos II and Apollonis famously visited the latter's native city of Kyzikos around 185. The two sons made a carefully staged public appearance, framing their mother and holding both her hands during their tour of the city's public buildings. This visit was surely supposed to remind spectators of the most famous sons of Greek history, Kleobis and Biton, whose legend was narrated by Herodotos (Hdt. 1.31; Polyb. 22.20; Walbank 1979a: 211; Chaniotis 1997a: 239), and it may have inspired the later construction of a temple to the dowager queen, presumably after her death, whose columns were adorned with reliefs narrating scenes of filial piety, including the stories of Kleobis and Biton, the Attalid forbears Dionysos and Telephos, and Roman heroes such as Romulus and Remus (*Anth. Pal.* 3.1–19; Kuttner 1995: 168). Even though Eumenes and Attalos acted by instinct in forming their propaganda, they had understood the following important principle that modern political psychologists have better formulated: in the context of ideology, people tend to draw their preferred leader toward their conception of the ideal which usually corresponds to their own positions and even personal characteristics (Granberg 1993: 109–11).

The image that emerges then is that of a virtuous family with habits to which the common man could relate. Attalid queens were primarily wives and mothers, involving themselves in the cult of matron goddesses, sponsoring very limited architectural projects and never involving themselves in politics. Their role in dynastic propaganda was always very limited inasmuch as it supported the image of the reigning ruler. It was a very dull court, without a whiff of a scandal, which brings to mind the bourgeois, austere and virtuous habits of King George III of England, whose excellent relationship with his wife and reported devotion to his children led everyone to consider his as the dullest court in Europe. Last, but not least, the Attalid rulers were never deified during their lifetime, even though they received limited divine honours (*I.Perg.* 246; *OGIS* 332; *IG* 2^2 885; Chaniotis, this volume). One may therefore conclude that they became popular partly because they appealed to the common man, while retaining their royal status (Ferguson 1906).

The Pergamene rulers did indeed acquire a reputation as the consummate benefactors who catered to the needs of the common man. They provided grain to allied cities in times of famine and sponsored basic education by paying teachers' salaries (*OGIS* 748; *SIG*³ 671–2; Diod. 31.36; Polyb. 31.31). They also became famous builders. In his study on architecture Vitruvius (5.9.1) refers to the stoa that Eumenes II built next to the theatre of Athens, the sole purpose of which was to protect the audience from sudden showers. Indeed large public utilitarian buildings, mainly stoas, were sponsored by the Attalids for the benefit of the public which duly appreciated them (Coulton 1976). However, it is noteworthy that these expensive gifts had certain express purposes which they strictly served. Firstly, they marked the Attalid presence in sanctuaries or major Greek cities such as Delphi and Athens; secondly, they reinforced existing alliances between the Attalids and specific cities, as happened in the case of the stoa that was built in Termessos, a gesture that aimed at exploiting the conflicts between Termessos and its neighbouring Selge, a city which had been a thorn in the eye of Attalos II in his continuous efforts to control rebellious Pisidia (Kosmetatou 1997: 32–3). It seems that the sponsoring of an architectural project on the part of Pergamon did not necessarily aim at boosting the local economy, nor did it provide jobs for the locals. A study of the remains of Eumenes II's Athenian stoa has demonstrated that the materials, plans, and perhaps even the artists, were provided by Pergamon (Korres 1983). The same thing probably also happened at Delphi where Attalos I built a stoa close to the temple of Apollo (Scheer, this volume).

Two more elements in Attalid dynastic propaganda contribute to the building up of the portrait of leadership. The first involves the construction of historical accounts relating to the infamous Galatian raids in Greece and Asia Minor; the Attalids are repeatedly the victorious saviours (Mitchell, this volume). The Gauls probably came to Asia Minor in 278 and may have been defeated at some point by Philetairos. His contribution to the war effort, however, went beyond the battlefield: according to the epigraphic record he seized the opportunity to contribute to the reconstruction of cities that were worst hit by the raids (*IG* 11.1105; *OGIS* 748). A dramatic increase in Attalid prestige occurred under Attalos I who pointedly refused to pay tribute to the Gauls and scored a decisive victory over them. Somewhat exaggeratedly, he compared his victory to the Persian defeat at the hands of the Greeks in the early fifth century, and duly celebrated it by setting up a massive monument on the Athenian Acropolis depicting famous mythological battles: a Gigantomachy, an Amazonomachy, the victory of the Athenians over the Persians at Marathon and his own destruction of the Gauls. The base of this very controversial monument, which may have included as many as 120 bronze statues, was recently rediscovered in the Acropolis Museum (Paus. 1.25.2; Wenning 1978; Schalles 1985; Stewart 2004). Subsequent Attalid victories against the Gauls were likewise celebrated in Pergamon, Delos and elsewhere, to the extent that the brief testimony of ancient authors like Pliny and Pausanias has led many modern scholars to associate any sculptural depiction of victories over barbarians or Gauls with the Attalid patronage (Pliny *HN* 34.84.2; Ridgway 1990: 275–312; Marszal 1998; 2000). Upon closer examination of the evidence, however, it becomes clear that the Attalids were rather more successful than other contemporary victors over the Gauls in advertising their achievement. The Aitolians certainly fought against the Gauls in the third century in their attempt to protect Delphi. So too did Antigonos Gonatas, the Seleukid kings and even Ptolemy II (Nachtergael 1977). Some of these even advertised their victories: Callimachus mentions the Ptolemaic victory in his *Hymn to Delos* (v. 185–7), Gallic shields were featured on Ptolemaic coinage, and there is some evidence that monuments were erected. Recently, Barbantani made a case for the association of two fragmentary elegiac poems preserved on papyri with Ptolemaic battles. Significantly, the second poem (SH 958) uses the same association of the Galatians and the Persians at

Marathon (490 BC) that was used as a theme in Attalos I's propaganda (Barbantani 2001).

Royal victories over the Gauls should not be regarded in such a simplistic way, however. Upon closer examination of the events surrounding the majority of these skirmishes, a link can be found between the Gallic threat as a real problem for autonomous city-states and attempts by the powers of the time to counteract it. In this context, the Attalids appeared as the champions of the Greeks who tirelessly sought a way to cope with their problems. In most cases, however, these same Hellenistic kings were the agents responsible for the presence, and raids, of the Gauls in the first place, since the Gauls were used as mercenaries as a matter of course in royal armies (Mitchell, this volume). They were formidable warriors, but unreliable in their loyalty, as they often revolted and subsequently raided various areas causing mayhem. One example will suffice: During his conflict with the Seleukid general Achaios, and while he was wooing allies in the Troad, Attalos had to deal with indiscipline among his Galatian Aigosages mercenary troops that he had brought from Europe, presumably Thrace. He was faced with three difficult choices: First, he could simply let them go, in which case they might have joined Achaios against him. A second, more radical solution dictated their treacherous slaughter by his other, more reliable, troops, thereby assuring himself of notoriety and a reputation as an unreliable employer. He chose the lesser of the three evils, often chosen by other military commanders, and the only one that had a chance of working by promising to return them to their original home, grant them land for a settlement and attend to their requests. The first promise was probably not carried out, because Polybios expressly reports that the Galatian Aigosagoi were settled somewhere along the coast of the Hellespont (5.78.5). His next reference to Attalos' negotiations with Lampsakos, Alexandria Troas and Ilion may suggest that the king came to an understanding with these important cities, who therefore allowed the foundation of this settlement in their neighbourhood. They were soon to regret it. The Galatians did not show any inclination towards farming, a peaceful life and the forging of neighbourly ties, nor did they show any interest in integrating themselves into the region. They chose instead the usual career that the literary sources so often associated with them – that of marauders. The silence of the ancient sources about any hostility on the part of the cities of the Troad towards Attalos I, who brought these troops to the area in the first place, suggests that the local population could understand and appreciate the king's effort to fight off Achaios that kept him continuously occupied for the next year. They may also have been bribed into siding with him, of course. The Pergamene king probably somehow helped the cities of the Troad to respond effectively to the threat, most likely by financing part of their campaign. It may have been around that time that Ilion expressed its gratitude to Attalos by naming one of its tribes after him, an honour that it had previously bestowed only on Alexander the Great. A solution to the continuous Galatian raids in the region was offered by King Prusias of Bithynia who eventually scored a formidable defeat against them and showed considerable cruelty by slaughtering them all (Kosmetatou 2001).

Victories against the Gauls could therefore become grossly exaggerated, taken out of their original context, and reinterpreted as examples of royal military prowess. Still, ancient authors tended to disregard the circumstances surrounding most of these raids and did not acknowledge the responsibility of the glowing victors who brought the Gauls into the area in the first place. One more important aspect of the celebration of Gallic victories by the setting up of public victory monuments was to divert the public's attention from the fact that some of these battles basically took place in the context of a war where Greeks fought against Greeks, and rather focus on the annihilation of the 'barbarian' mercenary troops at the service of their enemy.

Lastly, Attalid propaganda focused on providing a rationale for certain controversial choices in Pergamene policy, in particular what the Greeks perceived as an Attalid alliance with the Romans against fellow Greeks. Towards the end of the third century Attalos I sought the help of independent Greek cities and leagues, as well as the Romans, with a view to guaranteeing his own survival and checking once and for all any Macedonian and Syrian aggression, real or presumed. The strategy followed was simple, time-honoured and effective: a certain, not necessarily deceptive and false, problem was linked to a constructed solution. In this case the problem of Macedonian and Syrian aggression could be tackled by a declaration of war, the course of action favoured by the Attalids; to achieve this they exaggerated the problem and provoked existing fears, thus maximizing the support from their allies. In order to arouse public interest and influence the foreign policy of the Hellenistic world, Attalos I, and his sons after him, appealed to very specific concerns. The Romans had recently emerged victorious following a very difficult struggle with Hannibal and were extremely apprehensive of future aggression coming from the East. The Greek city-states had been traumatized by past experiences with Macedon, and a subsequent rapprochement between Macedon and Syria rattled nerves across the region. All this was suitable material for exploitation; on later occasions, such as the propaganda campaign against Perseus, other anxieties could be stirred.

At any rate, even though many cities offered their support to the Attalid cause, the Macedonian Wars, as well as the eventual defeat and breakdown of the Seleukid and Macedonian kingdoms, did not go down well with the Greeks. A debate arose on the origins of the Romans whom some Greeks declared as kinsmen (Gruen 1992: 6–21). Pergamon had been the chief ally of the Romans, and the main aim of Pergamene foreign policy was the expansion of their kingdom at the expense of Syria and preferably Macedon as well. In this context, the Attalids, anxious to refute anyone who dismissed the Romans as barbarians (Derow, this volume), adopted a strategy that would persuade the Hellenistic world that the Romans were really Greeks, or at least closely associated with the Greek legendary past. These views are echoed in later authors who deal in part with the question of the Greeks in the Roman world. Mythology was again used in order to suggest that the Attalids and the Romans were kinsmen, and that their alliance was therefore natural and justified. As the Roman elite showed a vivid interest in everything Greek at the time and were eager to become part of the sophisticated East, the Attalids also sought to cater to Roman cultural insecurities, thereby securing more benefits from their all-powerful allies.

This policy may be reflected in one of the more enigmatic literary works to survive from the Hellenistic period, the *Alexandra* attributed to Lykophron of Chalkis (Kosmetatou 2000; contrast Erskine 2001: 152–6). This poem has the length of a tragedy and the form of an inflated tragic messenger's speech. The action takes place on the day of the departure of Paris for Greece and for the rape of Helen, during which an unnamed slave of King Priam of Troy reports to his master the incomprehensible prophecies of his daughter Kassandra, after whose obscure name, Alexandra, the poem is named. The prophetess predicts the Trojan War and its aftermath, and amidst a formidable and overwhelming quantity of, mostly rare, myths, whose protagonists are never disclosed directly, she foretells the evils that would befall both the Trojans and, especially, the victorious Greeks as a result. The prophecies culminate in a narration of the Italian adventures of various Homeric heroes on their way home from Troy and of the eventual triumph of the Romans who claimed descent from the Trojans. In particular, a certain passage has been plausibly interpreted as referring to the Roman general T. Quinctius Flamininus, the victor over Philip V at Kynoskephalai in 197 (v. 1446–50). The poet also mentions a certain alliance presumably between Flamininus and a certain descendant of Alexander the Great, through his son Herakles, who also boasts Trojan ties (v. 799–804). Since Pergamene mythology partly focused on the association of Pergamon with the Trojan legend, the Attalids are the only Hellenistic rulers to fit the description of Flamininus' ally. Arguing in favour of this theory is Lykophron's apparent incorporation of a number of myths that clearly belonged to the Attalid 'state mythology', including the adventures of Telephos, and especially his sons who travelled with Aeneas to Italy and became forefathers of local populations. This type of Attalid ideological mythography structured many Roman myths: Dionysios of Halikarnassos mentions that Italy was colonized by various groups of Greeks, including Pelasgians, Arkadians and Peloponnesians from Elis (*Ant. Rom.* 1.17–31). Significantly, the Trojans, the legendary forefathers of the Romans, were presumed to come from Arkadia, just like the Attalid Telephidai (C. Jones 1995: 240). Echoes of Attalid influence on the Roman mythological tradition may also be found, as Hardie has argued, in major iconographies in Virgil's *Aeneid* that may have been initially structured by Attalid ideological mythography (Hardie 1986: 85–156). Kuttner has also recently studied possible Roman republican responses to Hellenistic Pergamon, and this type of research deserves to be further pursued as it opens new avenues for in-depth analyses and an increase in our understanding of early Roman–Greek relations (Kuttner 1995).

4 Conclusion

Like many successful leaders the Attalids were able to manipulate political controversy and manoeuvre in such a way as to impose a certain interpretation of their actions and policies. They were able to present themselves as benevolent, enlightened, true successors to Alexander's legacy, rather than authoritarian rulers. Their wars were just, rather than aggressive; they had the public interest, especially the freedom of the Greeks, at heart; and they belonged to the giant players of the period following an alliance with Rome that was justified on the basis of political developments and the mutual understanding between the two presumed kinsmen – the Roman and Pergamene peoples. One could argue that just as the qualities of leaders are constructed, so too are beliefs about the successes and failures of their policies, precisely because these judgements depend on the interpretation and ideological definitions of the issues. We may therefore perhaps conclude that the Attalids were not successful in their endeavours: they constantly fought wars and never controlled their expanded kingdom in its entirety, but only imposed their rule on parts of it, while their supposed bilateral alliance with Rome became a one-way dependency of the kingdom which eventually reverted to its real masters, brought to Asia Minor, after all, by the ambitious and manipulating Attalids themselves. However, this is not the prevailing assessment of the Attalids in the ancient sources, and this view often influences our assessment of Pergamon in these our modern times as well, when their propaganda still works because it is based on simple, timeless rules, and their monuments still glitter, making this the most photogenic and appealing dynasty of all.

FURTHER READING

The main ancient source on the lives and deeds of the Attalids remains Polybios, although Strabo discusses their reigns as well, mainly using sources that were friendly to the Pergamene kings. Our reconstruction of the history of the kingdom of Pergamon generally relies equally on the primary sources, ancient historiography, the epigraphical evidence and the archaeological record. The secondary literature on Pergamon is enormous. E. V. Hansen's *The Attalids of Pergamon* (1971) remains the most comprehensive, if somewhat outdated, study, long surpassed by epigraphical discoveries and many specialized studies by modern scholars, including important works on Attalid coinage and finances. Hopp's 1977 book on the late Attalids remains a classic, however. Gruen 1984: 529–610 treats Attalid relations with Rome; Allen 1983 focuses more on the administration of the kingdom. In the last decade or so, a particularly welcome revision of traditional theories on the Attalids, especially their cultural policies, has been undertaken by a number of scholars. The most important aspect of these works is the happy collaboration and dialogue between prominent researchers on Pergamon, after a particularly long period which saw the recycling of the same theories on Pergamene sculpture that most resembled a house of cards, and whose formulation sometimes violated the rules of critical thinking. The best starting points for the study of the Attalids and their capital would therefore be: Dreyfus and Schraudolph 1996; Koester 1998, from which one should single out the very important article by W. Radt, director of the Pergamon excavations, that sums up recent field research in the area; and de Grummond and Ridgway 2000. For the debate about the nature of Attalid art and its influence one can consult Wenning 1978; Schalles 1985; Andreae 1988; 1990; 1991a; 1991b; Ridgway 1989; 1990; 2000a; 2000b; Queyrel 1989; Marszal 1991; 1998; 2000; Hoepfner 1996; 1997; Stewart 2000 and this volume; Pollitt 2000; Green 2000; and Stewart 2004. On the Attalid cistophoric coinage, Kleiner and Noe 1977; Mørkholm 1979; Kleiner 1980; Le Rider's important series of articles (1973–92); Bauslaugh 1990; R. Ashton 1994; Kosmetatou 1997; 1998; 1999; Kinns 1999. For discussion of some recent epigraphic material, H. Müller 1989; 2000. Finally for the archaeological research at Pergamon, the Deutsches Archäologisches Institut's ongoing magnificent publication of the series *Altertümer von Pergamon* and many of its satellite specialized studies remain indispensable works that present the available material evidence. For an illuminating recent study, H. Müller and M. Wörrle, Ein Verein in Hinterland Pergamous zur Zeit Eumenes' II. *Chiron* 32 (2002), 191–235.

PART III

Change and Continuity

CHAPTER ELEVEN

Kings

John Ma

1   Introduction: in Search of Unity

Take one particular, relatively well documented case, a particular king in this age of kings: Antiochos III, the Great (Megas), the 'Great King' of the Seleukid realm (regn. 223–186). Here are some moments in his long reign. Antiochos in the ancient Ionian *polis*, Teos: entering the town with royal Friends and troops, giving a speech before the *ekklesia*, proclaiming the city 'holy and inviolate and free from tribute', as confirmed in a follow-up interview and celebrated by the Teians in a long epigraphical dossier (*c.* 203). Antiochos III in Babylon (187): sacrificing and prostrating himself in the great temple of Marduk, the Esagil, appearing before the assembled Babylonians, being presented with 'a golden crown . . . a golden box of Beltiya, and the purple garment of King Nebuchadnezzar'. Quite different the impression from Antiochos III in Elymais, the following year: marching East, plundering a local shrine, slaughtered in a night attack launched on his camp by the local population in revenge for the spoliation. We could yet multiply such images: young Antiochos on his morning constitutional, retiring to relieve himself, taking his time while his Friends knife to death a troublesome but solidly entrenched minister; shortly after, Antiochos marrying his Pontic bride at Zeugma, the city on the Euphrates crossing; dancing in arms and listening to hexameter verse (if not quite at the same time, at least at the same feast); the thirty-year old king deciding in royal council how the usurper, his cousin, will die (ears and nose sliced off, decapitated, the head sewn into a donkey hide and the body impaled atop Mt. Tmolos); the fifty-year-old king marrying an eighteen-year-old beauty from Chalkis, and renaming her 'Euboia', perhaps implying that he is taking the land as well as the girl; camping in the Hindu Kush; sacrificing at Delphi; the military leader campaigning against troops of Ptolemy IV and Ptolemy V, Attalos I, Philip V, against rebels in his kingdom (including his uncle), against Parthians, Baktrians, Pisidians, Thracians, and finally Romans (why them?); personally and rashly leading cavalry charges, as he did in at least three major battles (two of which he duly lost); receiving a mouth wound and losing some teeth in hand to hand combat during one of these charges, in Baktria; in Baktria still, meeting with the

Figure 11.1 Before and after: Hellenistic kingship is good for your hair. This head of Attalos I, ruler of the Pergamon-centred principality, was reworked to accommodate a stone 'wig' of carefully swirling locks, complete with royal diadem. The change occurred when Attalos I took the title of king (some time in the 230s), and expresses the godlike, impressive, 'charismatic' image that was the visible shape of Hellenistic kingship: Smith 1988, 79–81 (the photographs are taken from *Altertümer von Pergamon*, Vol. 7, plates 31–2)

son of an opponent and judging him worthy of the royal title, by demeanour (an act of royal styling, but one which covered and resolved a very real military stalemate); Antiochos himself being judged kingly, on his return from a six-year long armed tour in the Eastern regions of the Seleukid empire. These items (hardly exhausting the variety of Antiochos' life) are derived from the literary and epigraphical material (Schmitt 1964; Sherwin-White and Kuhrt 1993; Ma 1999); if we wanted a visual image, we could turn to a fine sculpted head in the Louvre, which probably represents Antiochos III, with a specific choice among all the possible elements in the vocabulary of royal representation: hard, active, dynamic (Smith 1988). But will the real Antiochos please stand up?

Antiochos III is not unique in the diversity of images available for his exercise of kingship; a similar collage could be given for many other Hellenistic rulers, drawn from other dynasties (for instance the Ptolemies, or the smaller kingdoms of Bithynia, Pontos, Cappadocia). The evidence was always plentiful, and has recently multiplied remarkably, thanks to epigraphical finds (notably in Asia Minor, for the Seleukids and especially the Attalids). Scholars have studied individual dynasties (notably the Antigonids) or individual kings; most importantly, they multiplied the viewpoints on Hellenistic kingship: the Near-Eastern dimension of the Seleukid empire, argued for by A. Kuhrt and S. Sherwin-White (but see Austin, this volume, for a cautious view); the interaction between Ptolemies and Egyptian priests (see Thompson, this volume); the institutions of the royal state (Billows 1995; Savalli-Lestrade 1998); the role of images in projecting royal ideology to different audiences (Smith 1988); ruler cult as a phenomenon of interaction between king and subject, but also as a way for Greek cities to come to terms with a supra-poliadic power (S. Price 1984); kingship as a discursive, performative phenomenon, manifested in speech-act (Bertrand 1990; Ma 1999); the Achaimenid model of kingship, deeply influential (Briant 1996). These are only a few of the recent developments in studies of Hellenistic kings, but they determine the scope of the present, selective, essay on the theme.

The increase in available evidence, the elaboration of new concepts and models and our sharpened awareness for the diverse nature of Hellenistic kingship make writing about the phenomenon much more challenging, if much more interesting (Gruen 1996). As for the rest of the Hellenistic period, we can no longer mingle portentous clichés, tralatician statements and quotations from a rather small body of ancient texts. I might give the following *dictionnaire des idées reçues*, telegraphically condensed in the interests of brevity and caricature. Kingship alien and abhorrent to Greeks (*polis*, Herodotos, Athenian democracy). Alexander (deep and *unique* impact of). Personal monarchy (not kings *of* but . . . *in* Egypt!) But Antigonid exception? Hardly. Plutarch, *Demetrios*. Military monarchy (compulsory quote: Suda s.v. *basileia*). *Nomos empsuchos* (see also 'glorious slavery', *Peri basileias* treatises). Institutionalized charisma (*deinos*, other adjectives transcribed from the Greek into English, truncated quotations, etc.), patrimonial state, power theory (here, according to age of scholar and date of piece, quote homeopathic doses of M. Weber, M. Foucault, C. Geertz, P. Bourdieu). Patronage, euergetism, ruler cult (compulsory tut-tutting quote: Athenian ithyphallic hymn for Demetrios Poliorketes).

None of these elements is necessarily false or misleading, and they underpin useful accounts, even recent ones (e.g. Ma 1999, and this volume). However, they will not determine the present essay: the insistence on diversity in recent work on Hellenistic kingship requires a broadening of horizons to accommodate the plurality of the phenomenon. The topic is an important one: one does not need to subscribe to the ill-documented, recurrent but rhetorically and heuristically useful cliché about the 'end of the *polis*' in the Hellenistic world to recognize the following few points about the period. The kings and their states extended both to the ancient near-east and the Greek world a system of competing imperial states, a situation which had disappeared in the near-east with the emergence of the unitary world empire of the Achaimenids. The kingdoms were the dominant forces in high political history of the period; they developed powerful concrete and ideological forms to express their dominance. These forms are the subject of this chapter: I wish to survey the diversity of interactions, but also argue that diversity was subsumed within an imperial discourse where local multiplicity could be made to speak of unity and dominance. This analysis is derived from P. Briant's analyses of the Achaimenid empire; which is hardly surprising, since the strategies deployed by the Hellenistic kings were inherited from the Achaimenids, an aspect of continuity which Briant himself has emphasized.

2   Local Interlocutors: Interaction and Role Assignment

Kings appeared in a diversity of local roles and under a diversity of local images, interacting with communities, elites and traditions in the various areas they ruled (Herz 1996). This chameleon quality is strikingly illustrated by the images that have survived for the kings in non-Greek regions, where, without speaking the actual languages, Ptolemies and Seleukids were recast in local idioms of kingship, especially religious. In Egypt, the king interacted with the shrines and the priestly elites, notably in Memphis: patronage, visits, sacrifice, building activity, participation in ritual activity intensified with time; the Ptolemaic king, in interacting with the Egyptian priests, appeared as pharaoh (Peremans 1987; D. J. Thompson 1988, 1990; Koenen 1993; cf. figure 7.2). In return for kingly acts of beneficence (perceived or proclaimed: gift, victory, amnesty), the Egyptian priests, meeting in assemblies ('synods'), decided on various gestures of praise for the king, named with pharaonic (or pharaoh-like) titles. The resulting decisions were published in hieroglyphic and demotic (as well as Greek): the famous Rosetta stone bears one such document (the 'Memphis decree' passed in 196 for Ptolemy V). The synod decrees make clear that interaction between Ptolemies and priests generated material manifestations, again in local idioms: building in the temples, and the production of images of the kings in traditional pharaonic guise. Recent archaeological activity in Alexandria, notably around the Pharos, seems to indicate that monumental statuary in Egyptian style was widespread even in that city, a foundation of Alexander (and hence, according to our categories, a 'Greek' city) and the centre of power. Two colossal statues, lately found underwater, of (perhaps) Ptolemy II and Arsinoe II once stood in front of the Pharos: Egyptian by size, hard-stone material and visual style, they seem to imply that an Egyptian visual style was adopted as part of the vocabulary of kingship early on and quite openly (Bagnall 2001: 229–30; the statues were reassembled outside the Petit Palais in Paris in 1998; they now stand outside the modern Bibliotheca Alexandrina).

The other example that has been studied and pondered in detail is the Seleukid interaction with temple and city in Babylonia, where the king presented himself as 'the king of the world, king of Babylon, king of lands', in the traditional titulature (Kuhrt and Sherwin-White 1991; Sherwin-White and Kuhrt 1993). A cuneiform Akkadian document, the 'Borsippa cylinder' (a building inscription, deposed in the foundations of a temple), gives the Babylonian voice of Antiochos I (268 BC). Speaking as the legitimate king, in the local idiom, he issued a kingly narrative of temple-building (complete with the kneading of mud-brick by the ritually pure royal hands), and prayed to Nabu for protection over the dynasty. Another example comes from the reign of Antiochos III, and has already been mentioned: the king accomplished ritual gestures (prayer, sacrifice) in the Esagil, and in turn was greeted by the local population and priests. The robe of Nebuchadnezzar, given or shown to Antiochos III, might stand as a symbol of the roles which Hellenistic kings had to perform within local traditions.

In this respect, it might be fruitful to consider again the Hellenistic kings' interaction with the Greek cities. The whole issue of autonomy and city liberty, the 'Stadt und Herrscher' debate that has obsessed scholars of the Hellenistic period (as indeed it did the Greek sources; e.g. Ma 1999), might be another local tradition, which the kings had to accommodate by playing a specific role to be found within modes of interaction. An obvious qualification might be that kings were not part of the political landscape in the Greek world, whereas kingship had been an integral part of Egyptian and Babylonian social and political organization. But such a statement would be too sweeping. In addition to bearing in mind the diversity of Greek political organization, it is important to point out that many Greek cities had experienced centuries of Achaimenid rule, more or less direct, with strategies of control and interaction that directly inspired those of the Hellenistic kings. Furthermore, the classical age had seen a variety of experiments in integrating the *polis* within massive, hegemonic formations: the Athenian empire (in both its fifth- and fourth-century incarnations) invented forms of autonomy and liberty compatible (more or less by fiat or legal fiction) with tribute paying, and found ways to make the local communities accept external sources of legal authority – the decrees of the Athenian demos (e.g. *ATL* II T78d; *SV* II.320). The long, detailed, and rather unlikely provisions in the charter of the confederation of Greek states, as conceived by Antigonos Monophthalmos and Demetrios Poliorketes in 302 (*SV* III.446), might be interpreted as an early example of kingship accommodating a local discourse and local tradition (freedom, panhellenism, the 'Common Peaces' of the fourth century culminating with the League of Corinth founded by Philip II in 338; federal institutions to mediate between *polis* and bigger state formation). Finally, the culture of the late classical age had seen a number of shifts and developments towards 'big-manism': individualistic military leadership and monarchical-leaning theoretical thinking, which can be seen in Xenophon, Isokrates or even Aristotle (on the shifts, see notably Aymard 1967). The idioms of kingship adopted before Greek audiences were not exclusively about the local traditions of civic freedom, but drawn from a much broader set of concerns and images.

Hellenistic kings accommodated local autonomy in various forms of interaction to achieve legitimacy: legal forms (grants of privileges, the negotiation of statuses), but also the symbolical game of reciprocity (*eunoia, charis*), played out through a shared, ritualized language of euergetism and honours (Bringmann 1993; Bringmann et al. 1995; Gauthier 1985; see the case of Teos, section 1 above: *SEG* 41.1003). But the kings also chose from many other elements of Greek culture: the military-charismatic style of the fourth century; aristocratic display (luxury, gift-giving, horse-racing, dedications in panhellenic shrines); ethical and philosophical justifications; a Macedonian tradition of aristocratic culture shared by peers, solidified into a court system, which itself played an important role in a state formation; finally, god-like greatness, as made clear in the surviving portraits of the kings (Smith 1988; Stewart 1993a) and in court poetry (Hunter 2003, on Theocritus 17 and its construction of royal identity along the lines of Zeus' greatness). On the practical level, there arose a type of citizen-interceder, who mediated between the king and his potential for benefaction, and his fatherland: Kallias of Sphettos, an Athenian notable, served as a Ptolemaic officer, and helped his city on many occasions (Shear 1978, see also *Iscr.Cos.* ED 229, for a whole dynasty of such citizen intermediaries between Kos and the Ptolemies, then Rome). All these elements form the hodge-podge sometimes termed 'Hellenistic kingship: theory and practice' in the Greek world.

The Greek material, detailed and familiar, makes two points clear: firstly, the impact of the interaction between local community and king; secondly, and most importantly for the present essay, the important role of interaction in shaping royal behaviour and the kingdoms themselves. These points can be seen in the Babylonian or Egyptian contexts as well as in the Greek *poleis*. In the latter, interaction with the kings had a considerable impact: institutional and ideological aspects of civic life, actual and abstract, were concerned. In subordinate cities, royal pronouncements had legal force, and had to be accommodated within local law (Gauthier 1993). Dynastic loyalty reshaped civic discourse: that cardinal form of *polis* self-expression, the decree, could be made to mention the king's interests among the various reasons for collective action (Ma 1999: 228–35). Royal statues, honorific or cultural, erected in conspicuous spots, redrew civic space. Ruler cult reshaped civic ritual, at important moments of political and social life. At Teos and Iasos, under Antiochos III, ruler cult was deliberately woven into the fabric of the *polis* (Herrmann 1965a, with *SEG* 41.1003; Nafissi 2001; Chaniotis, this volume). A statue of the king in the council-house of the Teians became the centre for a whole nexus of gestures, shifted to this new venue (sacrifices by entering magistrates, graduating ephebes, victorious athletes); a fountain named after the Seleukid queen, Laodike III, was to be used for sacred purposes (sacrifices, nuptial baths). At Iasos, a cult of Laodike as Aphrodite was overlaid on the *rites de passage* of citizen marriage. The latter cult was inaugurated in response to a benefaction by Laodike, to provide dowries for poor citizen women: a gesture which carried royal intervention, however welcome, deep into the social structures of a *polis*. Interaction with the king inevitably amounted to interference with local discourses, even as the royal interlocutor found ways to engage with the local communities within their idioms. This is strikingly illustrated by the Egyptian material: ruler cult in the Egyptian shrines was an innovation, an invented tradition assembled in response to the Ptolemies' demands and needs (D. J. Thompson 1990). The decrees of the priestly synods, which seem so foreign to the Classicist and hence clear evidence for the Ptolemies adopting non-Greek roles, in fact show clear influence of Greek documents, especially the honorific decree which the *poleis* produced for the kings: the Egyptian documents were probably produced along Greek models, perhaps even phrased or thought in Greek before being rephrased into Egyptian forms, in response to expectations and norms expressed by the Ptolemies (Clarysse 2000c).

The process of interaction, where kings spoke local idioms to the various communities, was dynamic. Local communities changed because of dialogue with the kings; conversely, the kings accepted locally assigned and locally meaningful roles, as illustrated above, which inevitably shaped their behaviour on the ground. Whether the defender of a *polis'* liberty and privileges before a panhellenic audience, or a pious, tradition-minded royal worshipper in a Babylonian king, a Hellenistic ruler accepted commitments before the local communities. Such commitments were taken seriously by both parties, the result of bargaining and negotiation, where the local actors often achieved considerable success, as pointed out for Egypt and Babylonia (D. J. Thompson 1988; Gruen 1996). The collaborative process reflects the kings' need for legitimacy, and for acceptance by the local communities: consent was granted on local terms. The small city of Herakleia under Latmos, in Karia, illustrates this point. When taken over by Antiochos III, it presented a long list of desiderata (a team of twenty-two men went to see the Seleukid high officer, Zeuxis) – exemption from billeting and various taxes (notably on cattle and beehives, local resources of this city between lake and mountain), grants of money and grain – all of which Antiochos agreed to (*SEG* 37.859). Most striking is the case of the harbour tax. The Herakleians had earlier farmed this tax out, presumably among the citizens, the sum from the highest bid being assigned in the civic budget for the oil-anointment of the young men in the *gymnasion*: the harbour tax was burdened with civic obligation, or at least civic purpose (the arrangement itself perhaps reflects a history of specific resources, local needs and financial fine-tuning). When Antiochos took the city, the local harbour tax became an imperial tax, levied to the profit of an outside power;

nonetheless, the Herakleians obtained that Antiochos continue to pay the grant to the gymnasium. The king financed a civic institution, recognizing the need and the obligation that went along with taking over local revenue. Antiochos III could have refused to do so, lived with Herakleian discontent and repressed eventual dissent by force; what matters is precisely that he did not do so.

Royal power as a field of negotiation: the archetype, Alexander himself, needed to engage in this activity; his military victories were followed by constant negotiation, bargaining and accommodation of the local traditions of cities, elites, ethnic groups. The 'Orientalization' of Alexander is merely a reflection of this necessary process (Briant 1996: 862–84). Seen at this level, the Hellenistic kings exist merely as a bundle of local commitments, a series of roles assigned by the subjects, an endless and ubiquitous process of exchange and negotiation to achieve acceptance by different constituencies. The various spheres were not completely segregated (as has been said, too often). Borrowings occurred, between non-Greek and Greek images of kingship, notably in Egypt (Koenen 1993): for instance, the old image of Persians or Asiatics as enemies of Egypt and its king was expressed in Greek. Such permeability needs to be analysed in the context of the wider phenomenon it hints at – the factors for unity in Hellenistic kingship.

3 Unity: Practices and Ideology

The Hellenistic kingdom was a state, a set of centralized and autonomous institutions, exercising control and coercion over a territory. Kingship as roads, garrisons, governors and officials – the phenomenon has been much studied, notably in classic works by E. Bikerman and M. Rostovtzeff (Bikerman 1938; Rostovtzeff 1941). Recently discovered evidence has confirmed the existence of royal roads, measured by milestones (Callieri 1995), and also the generalized practice of control and administration: the Seleukid, but also the Antigonid and the Attalid kingdom were administered through complex state apparatuses similar to the long-known bureaucracy of Ptolemaic Egypt (Musti 1966; Sherwin-White and Kuhrt 1993: 40–71; Hatzopoulos 1996; Malay 1996, 1999: nos. 2, 179, 182; on Egypt, Orrieux 1983.)

The purpose of the structures of control was to carry out the extraction of surplus from the local communities. The kings and their men levied tribute, the emblematic form of imperial taxation, but they also took their cut of local produce: for instance a leg off every boar and deer in the mountain city of Aigai, fees for pasture rights, dues on beehives (*SEG* 33.1034; 37.859); movement of goods was taxed in harbours. In some cases, resources were exploited directly by the king, to be resold by his administrators, notably in the case of timber and grain (Gauthier 1989: 22–33; Briant 1994b, on *RC* 3–4). A remarkable case is the tar of the Nabataean Dead Sea, which Antigonos Monophthalmos was looking forward to collecting and reselling (his Friend, none other than the historian Hieronymos of Karia, was defeated in his attempt to realize his master's vision of imperial extraction and profit: Diod. 19.100.1–3). Finally, the royal state could consume local surplus directly, when the kings and their armies were billeted on local communities, which had to provide for the troops. The forms of exploitation were varied, according to local resources and negotiation with the communities concerned; however, the general principle of a state apparatus whose main function was to control and to take was not negotiable. Apart from the great kingdoms (Ptolemaic, Seleukid, Antigonid, Attalid), a system of royal officials and administrations appears in smaller realms, such as the kingdom of Cappadocia, where the city of Hanisa had to send ambassadors to keep the royal treasury from taking over some intestate property, or the Baktrian kingdom, where the treasury at Ai Khanoum attests a royal bureaucracy of extraction and palatial accumulation (Robert 1963: 457–523; Rapin 1992). Extraction was an essential part of the royal state's operations, and the fiscal nature of a Hellenistic kingdom could be expressed quite crudely, even in the interaction with local communities: a Ptolemaic officer baldly wrote to the citizens of Arsinoe in Cilicia that they should prosper well in order to pay more taxes (*SEG* 39.1426).

It is tempting to focus on the bureaucratic aspects of the royal state: autonomous in function, organized according to rules, rationale and administrative knowledge. Continuity in administrative practice pertained even as individual kingdoms disappeared. Achaimenid administration was followed by Alexander's, then by Ptolemaic or Seleukid government. The Achaimenid colonization in the Lydian plain was followed by Macedonian colonists, and Macedonian colonists replaced, or lived side by side with Achaimenid barons: the name of a Lydian community, 'Hyrkanioi Makedones', was a palimpsestic reflection of the historical change of the late fourth century, but also of continuities. (This community, the descendants of landed soldiers from two successive waves of imperial colonists, drawn from their respective imperial diasporas, turned itself into a Greek *polis*; but that is another story). The satrapal centre of Sardis and the Persian-occupied settlement of Kelainai remained important under the Seleukids; the Achaimenid seat at Meydancιk Kale, in Cilicia, became a Ptolemaic fort, complete with garrison, *gymnasion* and dedications for the king (*SEG* 31.1321). A governor, Olympichos, stayed in office in Karia, while control of the area passed from Seleukids to Antigonids, in the second half of the third century (Crampa 1969). Recent documents have shown that when the Attalids definitely took over Asia Minor from the Seleukids, they retained the Seleukid institutions of 'high-priest' and 'official in charge of sacred incomes', for control of the local shrines (H. Müller 2000). A particularly instructive example of the autonomy of the royal state can be found in an honorific decree from Apollonia under Salbake, a Seleukid foundation in Eastern Karia. The document is worth quoting:

(. . . it seemed good to the council and the people of the Apollonians: – since Philo . . . son of . . .) earlier was continuously well [inclined in general towards the] people and in particular towards each [one of the citizens]; [having been named hip]parch over the [troops which stay with us], he ensures a complete state of discipline; ambassadors having been sent to Ktesikles the . . . and to Menandros the manager of finances (*dioiketes*), concerning the interests of the people, he put himself forward with great [zeal] when the ambassadors left, and travelling with them he made efforts so that all the things which we were asking for should be procured; moreover, when Demetrios the controller of finances (*eklogistes*) summoned the ambassadors concerning the matters which Demetrios the official in charge of the sanctuaries had brought to his attention, and laid claims against the ambassadors concerning the sacred villages of Saleioi in the mountains and Saleioi in the plain, . . . he invited Demetrios to change none of the privileges which the people enjoyed under his . . . , but to let them be as they had been until the present time, and he not only delivered to the ambassadors, who were sent at a later time about the matter of the villages mentioned above, a letter addressed to Demetrios and which agreed with the (people's) decree, but he also went to meet him and spoke to him with great zeal, as the ambassadors bore witness, since they had heard him; in general, he does not cease to be always responsible for some good towards the citizens; – let it seem good to the council and the people of the Apollonians: – to praise Philo . . . on account of his quality and his goodwill towards the people; to give him and to his descendants citizenship and exemption from all the taxes which the city has control of; to invite him to front seating every year, and to crown him with a gold crown in the gymnic contest which is celebrated in honour of king S[eleukos]. (J. and L. Robert 1954: no. 166)

The city praised a garrison commander for helping it in its dealings with various officials, based in Sardis, who seem to have had a good idea of the area and the share of its resources which the royal administration was entitled. The financial officials tried to claim the 'sacred villages' as part of the royal tax base (rather than subordinate communities in the territory of Apollonia under Salbake): in so doing, they pursued their own autonomous goals of revenue raising, even at the detriment of a royal foundation and, in all probability, earlier royal arrangements to sustain this colony.

However, it is just as important to realize that the various operations carried out by the kings and their men were also ideological. Administrative geography was never merely practical, but also expressed power and extension; institutions and logistics made empire visible. A royal order, given by Antiochos III in Iran, was passed on from official to official, until finally displayed in a multitude of local shrines (one example was found, at modern Pamukçu in Mysia, *SEG* 37.1010). This was the world of the verb *suntasso*, to order someone to order; the Pamukçu stele displayed the generative power of the language of empire. The effect of language and of concrete processes of administration was to create 'imagined empire', a space of unity and efficacy filled with the royal presence (whereas the kingdoms could be quite ragged on the ground, with enclaves, difficult lines of communication and the constant proximity of rival kingdoms).

Generally, royal state ideology subsumed the local into the unitary, by assuming the existence of a stable interlocutor who could deal with the local communities on their own terms, without surrendering unity of purpose and operation. This function is what the French describe with the adjective 'fédérateur' (which does not mean 'federal'). One of the central gestures of kingship is giving or granting; it formed the core of many local roles, examined above. Its importance extends beyond its pervasiveness in all contexts, Greek and non-Greek (giving is the corollary of taking, and one of the factors for legitimacy in an 'early state' such as the Hellenistic kingdom; royal gifts also express power precisely by avoiding talking about power, in a collaborative conversation between all parties involved). To this trope, the kings assimilated the act of granting privileges or statuses: the particular shapes of local existence in communities, whatever their differences, admitted the existence of a ruling power who could make such grants; diversity itself amounted to a paradoxical affirmation of the existence of a larger, stable authority which posited itself as the ultimate horizon of the local communities. Alexander made grants of local rights to Lydians and Greek cities alike. Antiochos III dealt with Greek *poleis* such as Teos, non-Greek communities such as Iranian peasants and the spice city of Gerrha, eastern kings such as Xerxes of Armenia or Euthydemos of Baktria; to all, his interaction took the form of negotiation (against the background of violence, actual or potential), culminating in a royal grant. Other phenomena played a similar function of subsuming the local. Ruler cult in the Ptolemaic realm took on a variety of forms, but centred on the same few persons; the cult of Arsinoe II, fostered by Ptolemy II, was celebrated by Greek households in Egypt, Egyptians, households in cities of the Ptolemaic overseas empire and cities named Arsinoe founded across the Eastern Mediterranean, from Asia Minor to Keos (Robert 1968b: 192–210; Jones and Habicht 1989): across cultural borders and a vast geographical space, this cult created a concert of celebration centring on the same figure, and manifesting unity of purpose and authority, even in diversity. A similar analysis might be given for the variegated armies fielded by the Seleukids, and which were manifestations of 'imagined empire' (Sherwin-White and Kuhrt 1993: 53–6, 212–14).

Earlier, I presented the Hellenistic kings as deeply involved in local role-playing before different constituencies with powerfully entrenched and self-confident traditions. But in this section, I have insisted on the kings as the centre of a state, with concrete operations of administration and a strong ideology. What is the relation between these two analyses? One answer would be to view the relation as one of equilibrium. The kings must obtain local consent to their power before they can proceed to the vital operations of extraction; the roles they play represent a cover for their power, but, conversely, they are also the imposition of terms and conditions by the local communities. The end result is nonetheless to establish the existence of a unitary royal state, underlying the plethora of local commitments and made acceptable by these commitments, the price to pay for local accommodation. This leads to the second possible interpretation, centred on the ideological angle developed in this section. The diversity of roles played by the kings only reinforces the unitary ideology: it shows the existence of the boundary-crossing kings, whose multiplicity in interaction expresses identity of purpose and authority. Conversely, the existence of a central authority creates the value of local privilege, granted by the ruling power, and in contrast with an unprivileged and directly ruled elsewhere: the tacit contrast with the latter state is constantly assumed in the negotiation of privilege. Here also, the final effect is to assume the king's single authority. Antiochos III ended up paying the traditional oil-grant to Herakleia under Latmos; but the Herakleians ended up paying taxes, direct and indirect, to the Seleukid state; more importantly, they accepted the integration within a supra-local empire, whose legitimacy they accepted and whose vastness they bore in mind as they gratefully enjoyed local privileges. Resistance is possible, and the whole thing can be rejected as a self-fulfilling con-game, if the local communities have the material strength to do so. Smyrna and Lampsakos refused an offer from Antiochos III to 'grant their liberty', and thus convert their political existence into statuses created by royal speech-act (Livy 33.38); Ptolemaic Egypt saw serious revolt, in the second century, and the priestly elites may have been far less co-operative than the synod decrees wish us to believe (Huss 1994; McGing 1997). Even so, the ideological coherence and totalizing power of royal ideology remain striking.

4   Dominant Ethno-class and Ethno-power Games

The scheme of analysis developed above focused on the relation between local role-playing and unitary ideology, a *jeu d'emboîtement* in which diversity takes on particular meanings within a system of power. A particular case is the ethnicity of the Hellenistic king, since many of the examples of local traditions are non-Greek (Babylonian, Egyptian): how did the Greco-Macedonian king fit? How did the local role playing affect his ethnic identity? This case should be examined separately, because it concerns the Greekness of the Hellenistic king, in view of the recent insistence on the adoption of pharaonic behaviour by the Ptolemies, and on the Seleukids' conduct as Babylonian 'king of lands'.

Just as there existed a unitary royal state, aiming at control and extraction, the various Hellenistic kingdoms were characterized by a single dominant ethnic group, the Macedonians and Greeks who monopolized the ruling positions, starting with that of the kings and ending with the landlord colonists installed in foundations on royal land, often living off the labour of native peasants (Briant 1982). The Macedonians were mostly the descendants of the conquest group which, under Alexander, had taken over the Achaimenid dominion; identity was defined by a Macedonian father, and hence could survive marriage with non-Macedonian women (Antiochos I, the son of Seleukos I and the Iranian Apame, was nonetheless a Macedonian). The king was Macedonian, identified as such in public documents both Greek and non-Greek (e.g. Paus. 6.3.1, 10.7.8; *OGIS* 239; Briant 1994a; 1999). Admission to the group was possible, by various channels (royal grant, habit, belonging to certain military units); but generally, the Macedonians constituted a self-conscious colonial elite. As Macedonians, the kings and their states showed continuities with institutions developed in the Argead kingdom, mostly by Philip II (Hatzopoulos 1996): court, Friends, royal pages, land grants, military recruitment and institutions to interact and integrate Macedonian cities within the royal state. As for the other element of the dominant group, the Greeks were the citizens of the communities in the Greek world, mostly Old Greece and Asia Minor; they served the kings as mercenaries, officers, administrators and Friends in the court system (Savalli-Lestrade 1998). Macedonians and Greeks seem to have constituted politically dominant groups, defined by ethnic identity, perceived and proclaimed. They can usefully be described with a concept developed by P. Briant, the 'dominant ethno-class' (Briant 1988; 1996). The concept was developed to study the Iranian elites of the Achaimenid empire; in the Hellenistic period, this group lost its dominant position, after Alexander's attempt at integrating them into the various spheres of Macedonian dominance (army, court, elite families). The Iranian diaspora left strong traces of its implantation (notably in Asia Minor), and individual members found local niches for themselves, but the Iranians' position, as responsible members of an imperial system, from which they profited, was taken by the Macedonian colonists scattered in their own diaspora across the Hellenistic world.

Concretely, Macedonians and Greeks occupy the high positions of authority within the royal states: the King, his court of Friends, his administrators and military officers, even to a large extent the striking forces in his army, were drawn from the dominant ethno-class (just as the Achaimenid ruling and fighting group was almost entirely Persian). This conclusion, notably argued by Chr. Habicht, seems confirmed by recent research (Habicht 1958; *contra* Sherwin-White and Kuhrt 1993; but see now Savalli-Lestrade 1998). The cultural manifestations of kingship, produced by the central institutions, were expressed in Greek. Military power and legitimacy was expressed by the concept of spear-won land and the emblem of the small, round, bronze-covered shield embossed with central sunburst and concentric crescents and stars, the Macedonian phalangite's shield. These cultural phenomena represented Greek military superiority and right to rule (Billows 1995: chapter 2). Major features of kingly practice, from the centre of power, were Greek: the Hippodamian plan, Greek population and Greek-style festivals of the royal foundations (Sherwin-White and Kuhrt 1993: 141–87); the coinage, with its naturalistic portraits, its visual vocabulary and the language of its inscriptions; the paraphernalia of kingship, the diadem, sceptre and purple chlamys (Smith 1988: chapter 4; *OGIS* 248 with Robert *OMS* 4.251). Peer interaction between Hellenistic kings took place largely in the Aegean, in the form of strategic competition, or simply war. This peer interaction was a collaborative venture to define the exercise of kingship (explicitly stated at Diod. 20.53): the language was Greek, and the space the ancient Greek lands, in spite of the diversity of the individual kingdoms.

A clear sign of the perceived centrality of Greekness in Hellenistic kingship can be seen in their imitation by smaller kingdoms ruled by non-Greeks, for instance Bithynia, Cappadocia, Pontos and the Hasmonaean state. Correspondence occurred in Greek even between kings further East, as shown by a royal letter found carved on a cliff in Armenia (Sherwin-White and Kuhrt 1993: 194–7; the site is Armavir, the writer and recipient are local dynasts). Closer to the Aegean, the arena for interaction between the major kingdoms, the Bithynian king Prusias I offered benefactions to Byzantion, and was offended when the Byzantines were slow to acknowledge a festival he had created, and to erect statues they had decreed for him (Polyb. 4.49.3; generally Hannestad 1996). Cappadocia is another example of a kingdom which adopted Greek as the language of administration, and whose kings energetically sponsored cultural Hellenism (high literary culture, *gymnasion* culture; euergetism abroad), to gain acceptance in the international scene (Robert 1963: 490–7). The non-Greek kings imitated the cultural traits of the dominant group in the great Hellenistic kingdoms: Hellenization of dynasts took over from the earlier phenomenon of Iranization of elites under the Achaimenids (names, visual style, use of Aramaic for public and private inscription, culture). The shift corresponded exactly to the emergence of the Greco-Macedonian 'dominant ethno-class' to replace the earlier Achaimenid imperial groups.

But how does Greco-Macedonian kingship interact with the diversity of local roles, in non-Greek idioms? The variety of forms taken by Hellenistic kings corresponded to the need for communication with different constituencies, to each in its own language; a crucial aim was to locate power within traditions of legitimacy, and hence obtain the agreement of the ruled, and their willingness to rationalize the king's presence. But P. Briant has made clear that ethnic diversity reinforced the message of dominance by a specific ethnic group, in Ptolemaic Egypt and the Seleukid empire. Ethnic diversity enabled the kings to play what we might call 'ethno-power games', by manipulating the economy of ethnic relations: continuities co-existed with rupture. The background to interaction remained the awareness of the king's foreignness, and Greekness, shared by ruler and ruled and sometimes explicitly stated. The phenomenon is worth illustrating, since the details show the deftness, and the symbolical violence, which the kings could deploy to make domination visible. The process starts with Alexander. At Sardis, the first Achaimenid centre he took over, and an important settlement in its own right, he maintained continuity both as concerns administrative structures (tribute, officers), and local privileges (the 'ancestral laws' of the Lydians, the *asylia* of a major sanctuary). But he also took the step of building a shrine to Zeus Olympios, the Macedonian god, in the Lydian palace on the acropolis: a symbolical manifestation of rule, but also the visible proclamation of his ethnic identity as Macedonian king come to this particular place, characterized by its traditions and history, associated with Lydian and Persian rule over Asia. Arrian's account locates the initiative for the gesture in a storm sent by Zeus. This is perhaps an echo of contemporary explanations for the rupture represented by Alexander's decision, or an indication of how this gesture could be read: conspicuous because of its ethnic content, and expressing divinely sanctioned power (Arr. *Anab.* 1.17.3–8, with Briant 1993).

Another case is that of Seleukid Babylonia. A Babylonian chronicle describes Seleukos I marching to Macedonia, 'his land'; the Borsippa cylinder, even as it purports to show Antiochos I performing temple-building rites in the role of Babylonian 'king of lands', breaks the surface by introducing a new, very un-traditional title: 'the Macedonian'. Even as they interacted in locally defined spaces and gestures, both foreign king and local priest knew that the former belonged to a *Herrenvolk* of external conquerors (Briant 1994a). I would interpret in similar fashion the naked 'royal hero' on Seleukid official sealings found in Uruk. The image associated official authority with images which were highly Greek (muscular, divine nudity) in a community whose culture remained Babylonian; the foreign nature of the rulers was made clear in practical transactions, since the sealings represented state validation of business contracts or tax payments (Smith 1988: 14; Sherwin-White and Kuhrt 1993: 149–50).

In Ptolemaic Egypt, images can be seen performing similar functions. The priestly decree passed for Ptolemy IV after his victory at Raphia orders the production both of Egyptian style images (as 'Horus who has vindicated his Father', etc.) and of a hybrid image, as seen on the best preserved stele: surrounded by the hieroglyphic inscription, framed by Egyptian gods, smiting a kneeling Asiatic king, wearing the pharaonic crown (pschent), Ptolemy IV nonetheless is shown as a dashing horseman, complete with prancing horse, Greek breastplate, and long lance – a Macedonian image of prowess, seen for instance in the 'Alexander Mosaic' (figure 11.2; Gauthier and Sottas 1925; Stewart 1993a: chapter 5; Briant 1999: 114–15. Admittedly, the lance is held overarm rather than in the Macedonian underarm style, but I don't think this detail is very significant). Here, as in the Borsippa cylinder, continuity is deliberately broken, by inserting an alien representation of kingly identity within traditional discourses: Egyptian viewers saw the foreign origin and ways of the king; Greek viewers, if any bothered to look at this Egyptian document, might have recognized the familiar representation of the charging king on horseback, and seen a reminder, transpiring even in an Egyptian representation, of the dominance of a Greek king over an ancient, non-Greek land. Some 'hybrid' Ptolemaic portraits, play similar games (Smith 1988: 92–3; 1996; S. Ashton 2001). They mingle traditional pharaonic representations and Greek features (the carefully disarrayed locks – a distant allusion to Alexander's hairstyle – poking out, as from a diadem, under the Egyptian headgear: nemes and uraeus; the cornucopia so noticeably, perhaps even incongruously, carried by Egyptian-style representations, in traditional basalt or granite, of Ptolemaic queens). To Egyptian viewers, such images might have acted as a reminder of the foreign origins and traditions of the king. Simultaneously, they present a message to Greek audiences

Figure 11.2 Spot the Macedonian king. The Raphia stele (the best surviving example of a particular trilingual document commemorating the victory of Ptolemy IV over Antiochos III at Raphia in 217) shows, amidst an Egyptian scene, the king as 'Macedonian cavalryman': riding a prancing warhorse, wearing a Greek-style corslet with *pteruges* as well as an Egyptian crown, and wielding, one-handed, the long cavalry lance. To what effect this rupture of ethnically determined visual discourse? (From Gauthier and Sottas 1925)

of the Greekness of the king ruling over Egypt; at least, these images try to make rule over Egypt clear in Greek visual terms (see Dunand 1981 and Erskine 1995, for the various audiences of the grand procession of Ptolemy II, held in Alexandria).

To grasp the exact patterns of intent, decision-making, unconscious gesture, perception, communication, interference, would need close reading of documents like the Raphia decree; even in the case of such detailed texts, the exact actors involved in producing these overlapping discourses (king, local elites, local communications experts, bilingual members of the system) largely escape our knowledge. But the ethnic strategies, the fields of power created, their link with royal domination, are clear enough. Both in Babylon and in Egypt, words and images reminded the non-Greeks of the domination by the Greco-Macedonian king, with his own traditions and his own men. In itself, such manipulation of local discourse was a means of domination and even violence upon the subject population: it expressed power, and the ethnic origins of power. A further function was to provide a context for those cases of interaction where the kings did adopt the roles ascribed by local, non-Greek tradition. The ruler escaped any claim by the local tradition to exclusive representation of kingship: the Hellenistic king, in performing local gestures of kingship, co-opted local images of authority and legitimacy, so that diversity, in the realm of ethnic relations as in that of negotiation with the traditions of Greek *poleis*, was meant to underline the unity of the kings' power. Furthermore, the openly asserted Greekness of the kings meant that participation in non-Greek rituals could be construed as a special case of piety and goodwill. The extension of the kingdom beyond the local, in matters of ethnicity as well as simple territorial power, gave particular value to local interaction, and, again, constituted it as a privilege, and hence a reflection of power.

5   Towards a (Cultural) History of Hellenistic Kingship

The analyses offered above for the economy of diversity and unity in creating ideological force for the Hellenistic kingdom, and the strategic coexistence of expression in local, ethnically diverse idioms and dominant ethnic group, were developed by P. Briant, for the Hellenistic period, in the prolongation of his analysis for the same phenomena under the Achaimenids (Briant 1988; 1996; 1999). 'To each in his own language' is the expression used by the Book of Esther to describe the operation of the extensive, multi-ethnic empire of Ahasuerus/Artaxerxes. One local tradition was that of the Greek cities in Asia Minor. These had their local gods, to be interacted with: Darius I protected a shrine of Apollo near Magnesia on Maeander (*ML* 12); Xerxes sacrificed a thousand oxen to Athena Ilias (Hdt. 7.43). But they also had their local political traditions to be accommodated: after the Ionian revolt, the Achaimenid state, which had earlier fostered local tyrants, supported the local tradition of *polis* democracy, responding to developments in *polis* culture, from archaic aristocrats and tyrants to middling citizen regimes (Hdt. 6.92). In Egypt, Darius could be represented as pharaoh, but also in deliberately Persian style, as in a statue carved by Egyptian workmen: the king wears Persian garb and paraphernalia (akinakes, lotus flower), and while the hieroglyphic inscriptions on the base and the robe call Darius 'king of Upper and Lower Egypt', the inscription in Old Persian proclaims the power of the dominant ethno-class: 'A great god is Ahura Mazda . . . who made Darius king. This is the statue which Darius the king has ordered be made in Egypt, so that the viewer might know in future that the Persian man holds Egypt . . . ' (Briant 1999, esp. 105–9; the Old Persian text from the French translation by F. Vallat). As Briant points out in his analysis of the Raphia relief, the continuities are direct (Alexander took over the Achaimenid state and its operations), but also structural: strategies for subsuming local diversity and converting it to signs of central power were the only way to constitute empire.

The findings of the 'New Achaimenid History' are indispensable to understanding Hellenistic kingship, its problems and its ideological manoeuvres when faced with local communities, Greek and non-Greek. The Achaimenid paradigm is a determinant factor in the genealogy of Hellenistic kingship; *mutatis mutandis*, Achaimenid solutions became those of the Ptolemies, Seleukids, Antigonids and Attalids, extended to the greater part of the Greek world as well as the ancient near east. All the same, this factor of origins and continuity should not obscure the major difference: the disappearance of Achaimenid stability, in favour of competing super-powers. Actual control of any local community could be surprisingly precarious, in the absence of any 'balance of power' (Austin 1986). The cities' margin of manoeuvre, between competing kingdoms and their desire for freedom, never quite disappeared, and gave the transactions between rulers and ruled an underlying tension that prevented the relation from being one of pure domination (Ma 1999). The analysis offered above tried to show the ideal workings of royal ideology, as an Achaimenid-style manifestation of its own stability and dominance. It assumes an ideal type, dominant in the Hellenistic world, as the outcome of the history of the Greek world in the fourth century. But this analysis is abstract, and, in assuming the existence of a stable type, neglects the great diversity of situations the Hellenistic kings confronted in the history of the period and the institution. Stability could be wishful thinking, not always self-fulfilling. If the economy of concrete power relations between subject and ruler changed, the ideological operations of subsuming diversity could reveal their hollowness: they ended up covering the king's weakness rather than expressing, more or less directly, the king's dominance. This is perhaps the case of the later Ptolemies faced with native rebellion, or of the later Seleukids' relations with the Jews: because of dynastic strife in the centre of power, the kingly gestures of granting privileges within local traditions became a matter of pretending to offer what the kings could not refuse (Ma 2000c).

Generally, the history of Hellenistic kingship is much more diverse than the ideological strategy studied in this essay. One aspect that will modify the standard picture is the recent work on Macedonian kingship, the institutions of the Argead kingdom, perpetuated by the Antigonids, but also, to some extent, by the other dynasties (Hatzopoulos 1996, as mentioned briefly section 4 above). In the ethnically diverse Seleukid empire, there existed a class of cities, all royal colonies, which kept institutions which originated in the Macedonia of Philip II: a council bearing the Macedonian name of *peliganes*; the single official called *epistates*, chosen among the civic elite, governing the city for the king but answerable to the civic community, in conjunction with which he elaborated decrees (Hatzopoulos 1996; Hatzopoulos, *BE* 00, 453). Seleukeia on the Tigris in Babylonia, and Seleukeia in Pieria, in Northern Syria, are the two known examples; I would also draw attention to the 'Greek' citizenry of Seleukid Babylon, with their *epistates* (known in cuneiform texts, where the word is transcribed): this might be another instance of a Seleukid foundation with an ancestral Macedonian constitution (van der Spek 2001). But the existence of such communities raises more questions than it answers. In Macedonia, the 'federal' or 'national' institutions functioned to integrate the cities, as municipal units, within the national kingdom which they provided with manpower and whose constituent parts they were. Hatzopoulos' picture is closer to that of an ancient 'constitutional mon-archy' or *état de droit* than to the structures of domination which I have studied above. The Macedonian ethno-elite in the time of the Successors to Alexander and in the early Hellenistic period thus came from a vital political culture of their own, just as the Iranian elite of the Achaimenid empire came from a specific culture with its defining traits. The Antigonid realm ran itself along the traditional institutions until its end, proving their suitability for the exceptionally large, rich and populous state in northern Greece. But such institutions were not extended out of Macedonia, for instance into southern Greece. To what extent did these Macedonian insti-tutions contribute to the central structures of kingship in the Hellenistic world? The picture is still unclear. To start with, we do not know whether Alexander's cities were founded along the lines of 'Macedonian' institutions: how would the latter have suited the much vaster scale of his empire? It seems clear that neither Ptolemies nor Attalids founded cities of Macedonian settlers organized along the traditional constitution. The Seleukids kept the system, at least in part, to organize the Macedonian diaspora that formed the core of their army (but not for all of their foundations): was this remnant of Macedonian organization a fossilized marker of ethnic difference *qua* reminders of practice in a faraway land of origin? Why in the Seleukid empire only?

Finally, a topic that cannot be approached in these pages is the Hellenistic king as object for cultural history (mostly in the Greek material), rather than ideological analysis: the impact of kingship on political culture and hopes – why did the revolted slave Eunous, in second-century Sicily, call himself King Antiochos (Robert *OMS* 4.210–1)? Why did the Maccabees, creating their post-Seleukid state, turn into a Hellenistic kingdom of their own? A cultural history would also have to take into account many other features: the connection between kingship and the important phenomenon of Hellenistic 'colonization'; the impact of royal lifestyle and morality on conceptions of the self; the dynastic, familial and sexual life of the royal houses (Ogden 1999); the court as place of artistic and philosophical patronage; the imagined and emotional king of art, philosophical writing and literature (for instance Plutarch's brilliant, moralizing, reworking of Demetrios Poliorketes along explicitly theatrical models; or even the spot-on application of Cavafy's neo-Hellenistic sensibility to E. Bevan's history of the Hellenistic dynasties).

One such element that can be examined here is the creation of a royal timespace (for the concept, I. Morris 2000), combining vivid involvement in the present and the local with broader scales and perspectives. This combination was not simply an ideology of domination (as argued in this chapter): it also was the very exercise of kingship, and its deepest, most essential pleasure. It mobilized huge resources to come into existence, richly rewarding those involved in the enterprise.

An obvious instance is the kings' practice of Big War: fought on a strategic scale where the immediacy and danger of physical engagement alternated with a geography of vast movements, royal warfare converted place into space. A patchily preserved poem, in elegiacs, shows a king's anger, upon receiving some piece of news (attack by the Galatians?): 'Those men of violence and foolishness (*hubristai te kai aphrones*)...the salary of this piece of madness...they will know after learning their lesson...strong enslavement...to the deep-wealthy Medes...the furious Galatian man...not in purple clothes nor with perfumes...anointing his soft skin...but sleeping on the ground and under the open sky...' (*Supp. Hell.* no. 958). The latest editors see this poem as a Ptolemaic document, but I consider it a piece of Seleukid court poetry (even though it was found in Egypt: perhaps a piece of booty?). Sweeping movement across space, from the hereness of the scene to the thereness of the next enemy, is driven by the king's temper and vision; geographical distance, but also cultural boundaries (hard people/soft people), are transcended by royal energy. Less bombastically but just as strikingly, a Babylonian astronomical diary records a strike force of twenty elephants, passing through on its way from Baktria to fight in the First Syrian War: the local community watches on as the king's will makes things happen, in this case to make war elephants walk from one end of the empire to the other (Briant 1994a: 458–9, on Sachs and Hunger 1988, year 273; also Sherwin-White and Kuhrt 1993: 46). A whole segment of historiography recognized and perhaps helped constitute royal time space: Hieronymos' narrative of the contest between Eumenes and Antigonos Monophthalmos focused on the leaders' mastery of geography, their strategic sense as well as their tactical skill (Syme 1995: chapter 18); narratives of sieges showed the moments when the extension of a king's power came to bear on a single point, but also when a local obstacle threatened to disrupt the fluidity of strategic movement across the space of royal war.

Other features of Hellenistic life could be related to the royal timespace of local involvement and boundary crossing. Alexandrian poetry collected elements from local religion and culture (these, it is worth insisting, enjoyed great vitality and continued relevance), and converted them into avant-garde court poetry: the operation is related to games of identity and power within royal timespace. The regimen of the king's body, alternating between the strenuous and the luxurious; the liking for gigantic or exorbitantly expensive objects; the infliction of torture and violence, and hence the breaking down of social boundaries concerning the body (van Proosdij 1934; Fontenrose 1960) – these too belonged to the pleasures of kingship, to be found in the managing of interaction, of boundaries and of scale. All these issues appear clearly in the story of Antiochos III, who provided the opening vignettes of this essay: the diversity of these images offered a way into the central trope of kingship, the subsuming of the local into the unitary, by concrete and ideological operations. Diversity and unity have proved as important, to understand the Hellenistic kings, as change and continuity: diversity determined the experiences, as well as the ideologies, of kingship.

ACKNOWLEDGEMENT

I would like to thank A. Erskine and A. Bertrand for their invitation to write this chapter, and their patience on editorial matters. J.-M. Bertrand illuminated the issues in conversation, indeed sketched the chapter out in a few sentences; P. Brown very early on asked me questions which I could not answer; M. Hatzopoulos asked me the questions to which I had hoped he had the answers. To all many thanks.

FURTHER READING

The collection of articles edited by P. Bilde et al. (1996) gives a sense of recent evolution in research on kingship, and especially the way in which the topic has grown much more complex, in integrating smaller kingdoms and non-Greek evidence (NB Gruen, this volume).

Two conceptual advances really affect the way we talk about Hellenistic kingship. The first is J.-M. Bertrand's rethinking of royal power as discourse (1990): speech-act theory helps us understand how kingdom was created as royal pronouncement. The second is the 'new Achaimenid history', which has culminated in P. Briant's massive *Histoire de l'empire perse* (1996); see also Briant 1990, 1994a, 1999, on imperial strategies and continuities. Both Bertrand's and Briant's work inform the present essay (as they did my book on Antiochos III: Ma 1999).

On ethnicity and kingship, D. J. Thompson's book on Ptolemaic Memphis (1988), and L. Koenen's essay on the old theme of the Ptolemies' religious and ethnic identity (1993) are illuminating; the Seleukid side is dominated by Sherwin-White and Kuhrt 1993, arguing for the Near-Eastern nature and base of the Seleukid kingdom. Kuhrt and Sherwin-White 1991, on the Borsippa cylinder, is a *tour de force* and an eye-opener.

On the structure of the kingdoms, Austin's essay on warfare and Hellenistic kingship (1986) is essential; Bikerman 1938 is important on the legal concepts that shaped Seleukid rule. Billows 1995 is a recent survey of issues in administrative history. M. Hatzopoulos (1996, 2001) has studied a particular case, the 'national kingship' of the Macedonians. On the important institution of royal benefaction, and civic honours, Gauthier 1985 is *incontournable*.

But more important than the various currents of interpretation are the documents, visual and textual. R. R. R. Smith's essay on Hellenistic royal portraits (1988) is also a study on Hellenistic kingship, as well as a lesson in how to read sculpture as documents; see also A. Stewart's book on Alexander's 'faces of power' (1993a). The catalogue to the 1998 exhibition in Paris, *La gloire d'Alexandrie*, gives a lavish image of the culture of one, very special, royal city. The other place to look is at the epigraphical material, gripping in its directness and vividness: the inscriptions record, but also embody, the transactions between king and local community. Louis Robert has treated documents in ways that illuminate aspects of Hellenistic kingship (e.g. Robert 1968b; Robert and Robert 1954; 1983). Among recent (or not so recent) finds, I would single out the Teian decrees for Antiochos III (Herrmann 1965a, *SEG* 41.1003), the interaction between Sardis and Antiochos III (Gauthier 1989, *SEG* 39.1283–5), and the negotiations between Antiochos III and Herakleia under Latmos (Wörrle 1988, *SEG* 37.859); the latter case is fundamental to understanding the creation of legitimacy between the ruled and the ruling parties. Equally exciting is a recently found set of royal letters (*SEG* 47.1745, from publication by L. Jonnes and M. Ricl, 1997; BD 43): Eumenes II grants the status of *polis* to a community in Phrygia, Tyriaion, after receiving an embassy (which included one Brennos, probably a Celtic mercenary or military colonist, or the descendant of such a man). One can read a letter by an Attalid king lecturing a community in Phrygia, including the bearers of Celtic names, on the importance of being a *polis*, just as one can read a Babylonian account of a Seleukid king kneading mud-brick and boasting about it: the Hellenistic period, and the study of Hellenistic kings, abound in such effects.

CHAPTER TWELVE

Cities

Richard Billows

Scholars who have written histories of the Greek city-states have most often tended to draw their histories to a close with the advent of the Hellenistic Era, on the assumption that the creation of the Hellenistic empires brought the great age of the Greek cities to an end. This is exactly the opposite of reality; for in reality, the Hellenistic era was in many respects the most important period in the history of the Greek cities, a period of dramatic growth and development. Geographically, the reach of the Greek city was enormously expanded by the foundation of several hundred new cities throughout western Asia from the Mediterranean coast all the way to modern Afghanistan and Pakistan. Not only was there a far greater number of Greek cities in the Hellenistic era, covering a much greater geographical range, but the size of Greek cities had increased. The largest Greek cities of Classical times, Athens and Syracuse, had populations on the order of a hundred to a hundred and twenty five thousand persons, or perhaps as much as a quarter of a million if one includes their surrounding territories. A number of Hellenistic cities were much larger than this – Antioch-on-the-Orontes and Seleukeia-on-the-Tigris may have reached half of a million, Alexandria in Egypt may even have reached a million – and there were quite a few cities that were as large as classical Athens and Syracuse.

Besides sheer numbers and size, one must also consider the sophistication of urban development, both physical and cultural, and the nature of inter-city contacts and relations – far more elaborate during the Hellenistic than during previous eras. In terms of city-state culture, what is clearly observable is the extension of certain uniform institutions and norms throughout the Hellenistic world. Most obvious is the triumph of the Hellenistic *koine* dialect over local (Doric, Aeolic, Ionic, etc.) dialect forms in all Greek cities. It is worth emphasizing that the *koine* (or 'common') dialect was a slightly modified form of the Attic dialect of classical Athens. For it is clear that, as in language, so in virtually all cultural matters, the Hellenistic Greek cities modelled themselves on classical Athens. Attic drama was everywhere admired and watched; city after city prided itself on being a democracy; Athenian higher education, in the form of Iso-kratean rhetoric, became the standard Greek higher education; and so on. This same cultural uniformity, based in great part on the Athenian model, is found in physical infrastructure and accompanying administrative institutions. Several authors – Dio Chrysostom (*Or.* 48.9) and Pausanias (10.4.1) most notably – present what is virtually a checklist of the physical infrastructure a city must have to be considered worthy of the term *polis*: surrounding walls, a monumentally defined *agora*, a theatre, at least one *gymnasion*, stoas, fountain houses, a council house and/or *prytaneion* (town hall). And with this infrastructure went administrative offices – the *agoranomos* (market warden), the *gymnasiarchos* (head of gymnasium), *amphodarchai* (street governors), *astynomoi* (city wardens) – each of which should be properly defined and regulated by administrative laws.

In all of this one can see that in the Hellenistic period a broad consensus had emerged on what it meant to be a Greek city, and on the basic cultural components of Greek civic life. This consensus was created and fostered by a host of inter-city contacts and relations of every sort, both at the individual, private level and at the official, public level. It is, for instance, common to find in Greek cities decrees honouring both individual citizens of other cities, and whole cities, for benefactions conferred; these honorific decrees look remarkably similar throughout the Hellenistic world; and a very common element found in the explanatory segment of such decrees is a statement to the effect that the individual or city honoured has done his/its best to be of service both privately to individual citizens of the honouring city, and to the city as a whole. The widespread proliferation of such decrees gives a clear impression of a community of Greek cities in constant friendly contact with each other. Hellenistic Greeks were aware of this, and spoke of the *oikoumene* – the inhabited, civilized world – meaning the world of the Greek cities. Greek cities arbitrated disputes among fellow Greek cities, asked for and sent panels of respected citizens to expeditiously settle backlogs of court cases in each others' communities, made agreements to respect each other's sanctuaries as 'holy and inviolate', and in general interacted and co-operated in a host of other ways besides. There were, of course, outbreaks of warfare from time to time between neighbouring or rival cities, but even such hostilities – so common in the archaic and classical eras – were mitigated in the Hellenistic era by the quickness of other cities to intervene with offers of arbitration. In general, one may say that the world of the Hellenistic Greek cities was one of considerable, peaceful interconnectedness.

1 The Geographic Extension and Size of the Greek Cities

The idea of extending the reach of Greek urban civilization by founding new Greek cities in new territories was hardly a new one at the beginning of the Hellenistic Era: the Greeks had already gone through a great age of overseas colonization between about 750 and 550 BC, during which the shores of the Mediterranean, north Aegean and Black Seas were settled with perhaps as many as 150 or more new Greek cities. Available sites for such colonization had, however, been largely used up by the middle of the sixth century; yet the Greek population growth that had fuelled the colonization continued, as can be seen from the growth in size of Greek towns and cities during the late sixth and fifth centuries. During the fourth century there was in the Greek world a substantial 'surplus' population of political exiles, adventure seekers, rootless and impoverished people, and the like, according to conservative political writers like the Athenian Isokrates (Seibert 1979; McKechnie 1989). Isokrates proposed in various speeches and pamphlets (most notably in the *Panegyrikos* and the *Philippos*) a solution to this problem: a unified Greek attack on the Persian Empire that would open up western Asia to a new wave of Greek settlement, and create a new life for the rootless and disfranchised in new Greek cities to be founded in Asia.

This is precisely what happened during the half-century or so between Alexander the Great's crossing to Asia in 334 and the settling down of the lands he conquered into the three major Hellenistic Empires in the 270s: the second great age of Greek colonization. This new phase of colonization had its beginning with Alexander's orders to found Alexandria in Egypt in 333/2: Alexandria was the first of the new cities in the lands of the former Persian Empire, and was destined to become the largest and most famous. Alexander followed up on this by founding a dozen or more colonies – mostly likewise named Alexandria after himself – in inner Asia to garrison and hold down the eastern provinces of his empire. He achieved thereby a great, indeed somewhat exaggerated, reputation as a city-founder, for in fact the chief credit for founding new cities in the conquered lands of western Asia must go to Alexander's successors Antigonos the One-eyed and Seleukos Nikator (Billows 1990; G. Cohen 1978; Grainger 1990b), and to a more limited degree to their rival Lysimachos and to Seleukos' successor Antiochos I.

The end result of this colonizing work was the emergence of scores of new Greek cities throughout Asia Minor, Syria, Palestine and Mesopotamia, and to a more limited extent also further east in the trans-Tigris regions of Media, Baktria and the other so-called 'upper satrapies'. Many of these 'new' cities were in fact continuations of old native cities or settlements with the imposition of a Greek population element, Greek civic institutions and a Greek (often dynastic) name: thus Susa became Seleukeia-on-the-Eulaios, Sumerian Uruk became, it seems, Antioch-on-the-Ishtar-Canal, Gaza became another Seleukeia, and even Jerusalem famously almost became an Antioch, sparking the Maccabaean revolt (van der Spek 1987: 73; Sherwin-White and Kuhrt 1993: 161–87). It was certainly normal for new Greek cities to have a substantial native population included in them, particularly the larger new cities (Billows 1995: 154), and this inevitably led over the course of a generation or two to the Hellenization of the natives thus included. Some ancient native cities were permitted to remain as they were – Babylon and Jerusalem for example – but inevitably they tended to decline due to the rivalry of new Greek cities, as Babylon did to Seleukeia-on-the-Tigris, or succumb to the lure of Hellenization, as Jerusalem threatened to do (van der Spek 1987). In the end, there were well over a hundred new Greek cities by even the most conservative computation (G. Cohen 1995; Tscherikower 1926), and each of them had in its way received the extensive physical, legal, social, cultural and religious elaboration that was required in order to be a Greek city in a meaningful sense. That is to say that the structures and social, political, religious and cultural norms and institutions of Greek urban civilization were now to be found throughout western Asia as well as in Greece and the older colonial regions; and in fact in some respects these older regions of Greek culture were outshone by the 'new Greece' of the Hellenistic colonial world. Many of the new cities, and by and large the most important of them, bore dynastic names, that is names based on those of the kings who founded them and of their relatives. Thus in addition to a number of Alexandrias, cities named Seleukeia (after Seleukos Nikator) and Antioch (Antiocheia, after Seleukos' father and son, both named Antiochos) abounded, and there were quite a few named after female members of the Seleukid dynasty: Laodikeia (Lao-dike), Apameia (Apame), Stratonikeia (Stratonike), etc. Usually the many homonym-ous cities that resulted from this practice are distinguished from each other by some geographic designation: for example Antioch-on-the-Orontes, Antioch-in-Pisidia, Antioch-in-Persis; or Seleukeia-in-Pieria (on the Syrian coast), Seleukeia-on-the-Tigris, Seleukeia-on-the-Kalykadnos (in Cilicia), etc. Other cities, usually smaller and less important ones, were named after cities in Macedonia and the rest of Greece: Europos (Dura), Pella, Larisa, and so on.

Although we have no reliable ancient population statistics, and although the physical extent of Hellenistic cities is often hard to figure due to incomplete excav-ation, the existence of modern cities on the sites of ancient ones, and/or the presence of a Roman overlay not always easy to distinguish from Hellenistic layers, it remains clear nevertheless that many Hellenistic cities reached a substantial size in both population and extent compared to classical Greek cities. The largest Hellenistic cities were very much larger than the largest classical cities: not only the famous Alexandria in Egypt, Antioch-on-the-Orontes, and Seleukeia-on-the-Tigris, but quite a few other Hellenistic cities were of a very respectable size by any standards. This is hardly the place to give a list, but one may mention such cities as Alexandria Troas, Nikaia, Ephesos, Smyrna, Pergamon, Stratonikeia-in-Karia, Laodikeia-by-the-Sea, Apameia-on-the-Orontes, to name just a few. Population estimates for these cities are problem-atic and controversial, but few would doubt that cities such as the great Alexandria, Antioch and Seleukeia counted many hundreds of thousands of inhabitants: Pliny *HN* 6.122 mentions 600,000 for Seleukeia; Diod. 17.52.6 claims, purportedly based on Ptolemaic census records, that Alexandria had over 300,000 free inhabitants *c*. 58 BC, and by this he presumably means the citizen community, excluding Egyptian and servile inhabitants who will certainly have outnumbered the citizen class (and see Downey 1963 on Antioch). That cities with a hundred thousand or more inhabitants were no longer the great rarities they had been in the fifth and fourth centuries is also not controversial: such cities of old Greece as Athens, Corinth, Argos and Syracuse continued to be major metropolitan centres during the third and early second centur-ies at least, and newer cities like Pergamon, the refounded Ephesos and Smyrna, Stratonikeia-in-Karia, Seleukeia-in-Pieria and Apameia-on-the-Orontes were certainly of this order of size. Of course most cities were smaller, but it is clear that most Greeks in western Asia at least did not live very far away from a substantial city, and that there was a scattering of truly large cities; and in view of the greater ease and security of travel, it was possible for quite a few Greeks to at least visit a large city, even if they did not live in one, so that the experience of truly urban life, as opposed to small town life, was much more widespread in Hellenistic than in earlier times.

2 Town Planning and Physical Infrastructure

During the classical period, the so-called Hippodamian town plan – streets laid out on a rectangular grid around central public spaces – had become common, and during the Hellenistic era it was essentially universal for all newly founded cities as well as for re-founded or modernized older cities (Owens 1991: 74–93 for a good overview). The basis for the success of this pattern of town planning lay, of course, in its simplicity: it was easy to lay out a city on this pattern, and when built the city was easy for its inhabitants and visitors to get around in. It is of course for these same reasons that this grid pattern has been adopted in many modern cities, as very famously in New York for example. There is no doubt that this generalized grid plan created a certain sameness in Hellenistic cities: Wycherley (1962: 35) speaks of 'the mass-production of new Hellenistic cities in Asia which took place under Alexander and his successors', and Green (1990: 160), quoting this, adds that 'their axial-grid plans [were] as monotonously repetitive as those of the American Midwest'. One should not exaggerate this sameness: these cities were founded in widely different locales, and the Greeks were very alive to the need to adapt their town planning to the specific geography of the site. As a result, there is in fact a great deal of variation in shape and arrangement of Hellenistic cities within the basic axial-grid form. But without doubt, the sameness of the axial plan was an attraction: settlers in the new cities and visitors between cities could feel at once comfortable and at home in an urban environment that was basically similar wherever they went.

How this axial-grid town planning was fitted to the topographical realities of actual settlement sites to produce this basic sameness and familiarity, while at the same time responding to the features of the landscape so as to make the best of each site and introduce a suitable variety, can best be illustrated by looking in detail at some well known examples. I will examine Priene, Ephesos and Pergamon: three well excavated and studied sites that show the variety introduced by differing landscapes, and also illustrate a different kind of variety – Priene being a town of rather moderate size, Ephesos a large and important city and Pergamon a royal city, capital of the second rank but still wealthy and important Attalid kingdom.

Priene was an ancient Ionian city which was moved to a new site some time in, most probably, the third quarter of the fourth century: the very end of what we call the 'Classical' era and beginning of the Hellenistic. It is therefore one of the very earliest Hellenistic cities, and is also one of the best preserved: since the city dwindled in importance in the early Roman period, it has little Roman overlay on the Hellenistic remains, and the site was abandoned at the end of antiquity and never resettled. We have therefore an almost perfectly undisturbed Hellenistic city, thoroughly excavated under the German archaeologists Humann and Wiegand in the late nineteenth century (see e.g. Akurgal 1990: 185–206). The city was founded on the southern slope of the Cape Mykale peninsula, overlooking the Gulf of Latmos to the south – though today, due to the continued silting action of the River Maeander, it overlooks a wide flat agricultural plain. It represents an almost perfect example of the axial-grid plan: it is basically circular in shape, though with irregularities to take advantage of the terrain, with public spaces and buildings at the centre; its axial grid is formed of wide (*c.* 14–15 ft.) avenues running east–west, and narrower (*c.* 8 ft.) cross streets running north–south (figure 12.1). The defensive advantages of the site are obvious – to its immediate south lay the Gulf of Latmos, and to the north a steep cliff on the top of which a fortified outpost formed a kind of acropolis – and it was surrounded from the start by a strong city wall. The complex of public buildings at the centre of the city comprised, north to south, a theatre, a gymnasium, a *bouleuterion* (council house) and *prytaneion* (city hall) side by side, a grand stoa, and finally – again side by side – a two part *agora* and a *temenos* of Zeus Olympios. All basic civic requirements – political, social, commercial, religious and cultural – were therefore met in this large central agglomeration. The two part *agora* is noteworthy: a large main *agora* covering two whole city blocks was flanked to the west by a smaller area – roughly half a block – that seems to have been a commercial market place (Akurgal 1990: 193). This separation of the political/social and commercial functions of the *agora* into two distinct spaces was quite a normal feature of Hellenistic town planning, as we shall see. A little to the west of the main group of public buildings/spaces lay a subsidiary group comprising the temple of Athena, patron goddess of the city, and a probably commercial stoa to its immediate south. Another important temple, to the goddess Demeter, lay in the north-west quadrant of the city; but the most important additional public space was at the southern edge of the town: a large second gymnasium and a stadium, undoubtedly built there to take advantage of the flatter terrain in this area.

In its basic orientation, the city is dominated by the north–south slope of the flank of Mt. Mykale it sits upon. The main avenues run east–west because they thus are flat; and it is the narrower north–south cross streets that negotiate the slope, which is in places quite steep, reducing the streets to stairs. The city blocks in effect sit on a series of terraces, and most buildings, public and private, face to the south to take advantage of the open vista over the Gulf and the winter sunlight this terracing afforded. Many of the housing blocks are divided into four dwellings, each fairly commodious by Greek standards, though there are of course larger and smaller dwellings. In addition to defence and public buildings and spaces, careful thought in establishing the city was given to a public water supply. The water was brought into Priene from the mountains by aqueduct and collected in settling tanks, from which earthenware pipes distributed it to stone fountains set in the walls of buildings throughout the city (Akurgal 1990: 187; Owens 1991: 65–6). Over all, we clearly see a very well organized, well set up small city (figure 12.2). It had all the basic physical features and amenities to be expected of a Hellenistic Greek city, often in an unusually fine form. Accessible by highways from east and west, it enjoyed a beautiful view over the Gulf of Latmos to the headland on which sat Miletos to the south; and a small port town, Naulochos, lay not far away. Based on the number of housing blocks provided by the axial-grid street system, one can estimate the number of private dwellings as somewhere around 260 (about 65 or so housing blocks with on average four dwellings per block); if one guesses at around 10–12 inhabitants per dwelling (family, dependents, slaves) that would give a very approximate population for the city of Priene of 2600 to 3000. Definitely a small town, therefore, though for the state of Priene one should of course add the population of the territory of the city-state, including subsidiary towns like the aforementioned Naulochos.

Ephesos was, like Priene, an ancient Ionian city re-founded at the beginning of the Hellenistic era, but a very much larger and more important one. The initiative in re-founding Ephesos came, according to our sources, from the Diadoch Lysimachos, who ruled Asia Minor from 301 until his death in battle in 281. The city was apparently in decline at its original site, probably as a result of silting by the river Kaystros on which it lay, and the site chosen by Lysimachos was by universal acclaim far superior: certainly Ephesos flourished in its new location and became one of the largest and most prosperous cities of the Hellenistic and Roman world. The topography of Ephesos is very different than that of Priene, and likewise therefore the town planning. Ephesos was built on the coast in a valley between two hills: Mt. Pion (modern Panayirdag) to the north and east and Mt. Koressos (modern Bulbuldag) to

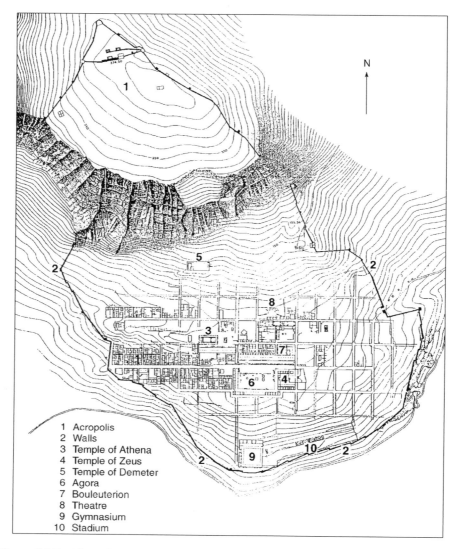

1 Acropolis
2 Walls
3 Temple of Athena
4 Temple of Zeus
5 Temple of Demeter
6 Agora
7 Bouleuterion
8 Theatre
9 Gymnasium
10 Stadium

Figure 12.1 Plan of Priene, founded in the second half of fourth century BC. After G. Kummer and W. Wilberg

the south. The city has two parts: an upper city on the west slope of Mt. Pion and in the valley between Pion and Koressos, and a lower city along the coast in front of and around the harbour (figure 12.3). One of the best preserved and most thoroughly excavated ancient cities, as a result of successive Austrian archaeological expeditions between 1895 and the present day (Akurgal 1990: 142–71, 354–60), it is neverthe-less the case that the very extensive Roman overlay – the vast majority of the buildings

Figure 12.2 Reconstruction of Priene as seen from the south, by A. Zippelius, courtesy of DAI Istanbul

visible today are of Roman date – prevents us from knowing as much as we would like about Hellenistic Ephesos. However, as far as town planning goes, there can be no doubt that the basic arrangement of the city was set in the Hellenistic period, the Romans merely expanding or adding to what was already there.

The layout of Ephesos was affected not only by the topography of the two hills between which it lay and the harbour in front, but also by the hugely important suburban temple of Artemis, one of the seven wonders of the ancient world. The main avenue of Ephesos, around which the street plan was established, was oriented with both the temple of Artemis and the local topography in mind. A processional way, beginning at the temple, ran more or less directly south until it reached the eastern 'Magnesian Gate' of the city, between the slopes of Pion and Koressos; there it turned west, entering the city and proceeding at an angle slightly north of due west along the valley between the hills until it reached the open harbour plain in front of Mt. Pion; there it turned north along the west front of Pion to the north gate of the city, from where it turned east and regained the temple of Artemis. It was from this non-axial avenue that the street grid of Ephesos radiated out, in two basic patterns. In

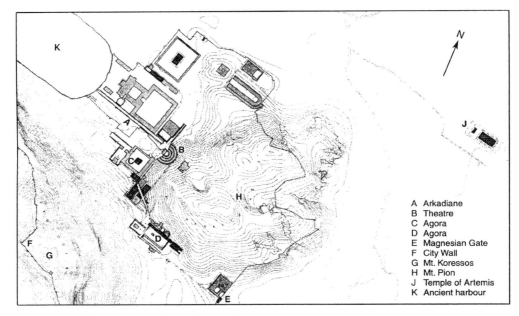

A Arkadiane
B Theatre
C Agora
D Agora
E Magnesian Gate
F City Wall
G Mt. Koressos
H Mt. Pion
J Temple of Artemis
K Ancient harbour

Figure 12.3   Plan of Roman Ephesos, following the arrangement of the Hellenistic city; after W. Oberleitner

the upper city, between the hills, streets branched off and climbed the slopes on either side in a basically axial way, though not meeting the avenue at the normal right angle; in the lower city the axiality was more complete, as streets branched off from the avenue at right angles to the west, and were in turn intersected by subsidiary north–south streets. Most important was the great colonnaded street later called the 'Arkadiane' (after it was rebuilt and decorated by the emperor Arcadius) that led straight down to the harbour, bisecting the lower city. This urban layout, of course, meant that the public buildings and spaces of Ephesos could not, as in Priene, be concentrated in a central location; instead they were divided between the upper and lower cities, but always sited in relation to the main avenue and its subsidiary, the 'Arkadiane'.

In the upper city, as one walked into the town along the avenue from the Magnesian Gate, one came to the political centre of the city: the main *agora*, with stoas along its sides and, on the north, a *bouleuterion* in the form of a small auditorium and beside it the *prytaneion*: though the surviving edifices are all of Roman imperial date, Hellenistic remains have been found under the *agora* and its north stoa, and it is most likely that Hellenistic predecessors underlie all of these buildings. In the lower city were placed an array of commercial and cultural spaces and buildings. At the point where the main avenue turns north lies, to its west, a second *agora* intended for commercial use and linked to the harbour by the 'Arkadiane'. Originally built in Hellenistic times, its surviving architecture dates to the time of Augustus. Diagonally across from the commercial market square, built into the west slope of Mt. Pion, lies

Figure 12.4 The theatre at Ephesos with the Arkadiane in the foreground. Photo: R. Billows

the magnificent theatre, one of the most beautiful and best preserved of its kind. Its plan and the first two of its three tiers of seating are Hellenistic, though in Roman times it was expanded with a built-up *skene* and a third tier of seats. At its largest, it could seat 24,000, giving an indication of the large population of late Hellenistic and Roman Ephesos, presumably well over 100,000 (Figure 12.4). The stadium of Ephesos, near the north gate, is Roman, but very likely on the site of a Hellenistic predecessor; the four gymnasia – near the Magnesian gate, near the harbour, near the theatre and just inside the north gate next to the stadium – are likewise all Roman, but obviously several of them continue Hellenistic gymnasia. Though, again, the surviving waterworks of the city are mostly Roman, Hellenistic fountain houses do survive near the theatre at the junction of the main avenue and the 'Arkadiane', and just before the avenue enters the *agora* in the upper city, making it clear that the city's water supply was well attended to in the Hellenistic period. Besides the theatre, the most impressive visible remnant of Hellenistic Ephesos is without doubt the long stretch of fortification wall on the ridge of Mt. Koressos (another small angle of Lysimachos' wall survives at the north-east corner of Mt. Pion).

The harbour was one of the most important features of ancient Ephesos, determining its location and giving it its importance and prosperity. Though it is today completely silted up, its outline is still clearly visible on the ground, especially from the upper seats of the theatre which overlooks it. A long narrow channel from the sea opened up into a large, almost circular basin providing one of the finest sheltered harbours on the west coast of Asia Minor. Besides the great colonnaded avenue and the magnificent commercial *agora* to which it led, it is clear that some of the bathing and exercise complexes near the harbour served the commercial visitors who thronged Ephesos in Roman times, as did a variety of less public establishments such as brothels and the souvenir shops selling religious paraphernalia connected with Artemis/Diana attested in the *Acts of the Apostles* (19.23–7). We can reasonably guess again, that these will have had Hellenistic predecessors. The private housing was located, in the upper city, on the slopes of Pion and Koressos leading up from the main avenue and, in the lower city, mostly to the north of the harbour. All in all, Ephesos was clearly a large, successful and magnificently planned and appointed city, one of the jewels of Hellenistic city planning.

Unlike Priene and Ephesos, Pergamon was not an ancient city re-founded in the Hellenistic period. Though it had clearly existed for centuries before the Hellenistic era, it was essentially a fortified outpost on a prominent hill overlooking the lower Kaikos valley until it came under the control of the Attalid dynasty who, in the course of the third and second centuries, built it up into the capital city of a small but wealthy kingdom in the north-west corner of Asia Minor which, at its height under Roman patronage between 189 and 133, controlled all of western Asia Minor. In terms of layout, it is virtually the opposite of Ephesos: as we have seen, Ephesos lay in a coastal plain and valley in front of and between two hills, and spread up their slopes; Pergamon lay on the top of a substantial hill and spread down its slopes. This imposed a very different town plan, and as a result Pergamon is the least axial of the three cities here examined in detail (figure 12.5). The natural topography divides Pergamon into an upper, a middle and a lower city. As at Ephesos, there is substantial Roman overlay masking the Hellenistic city, but the German excavations of the late nineteenth and twentieth centuries under, successively, Humann, Dörpfeld, Wiegand and (now) Radt enable us to grasp the city plan quite well. The lower city is essentially of Roman date, though there was likely some suburban habitation in the area in Hellenistic times, and the great suburban sanctuary of Asklepios, which attained widespread renown in the Roman period, certainly dates back to the third century at least. The Hellenistic city proper was restricted to the upper and middle regions, on the crest and slopes of the hill of Pergamon (Akurgal 1990: 69–111, 360–1). The division between upper and middle cities is not just topographical: it also corresponded to social and political realities of Pergamon: the upper city had at its core the royal palace and military complexes, and was rounded out by various public buildings and spaces; the middle city held the main residential quarters, but also a number of important public complexes.

Noteworthy is that we find at Pergamon the same division into two distinct *agorai* of political (upper city) and commercial (middle city) functions that we saw at Ephesos and, in rather embryonic form, at Priene. The crest of the hill, or acropolis, forms a long slightly curving terrace roughly north–south in orientation. The northern two-thirds or so are taken up by the royal compound. At the extreme north end lay a set of arsenals; to the south of them, along the eastern side of the hill, lay barracks and officers' housing; and to the south of them again lay royal palaces built by various kings of the dynasty. On the north-west side of the acropolis, across from the barracks and officers' quarters, stands the temple of Trajan built in the reign of Hadrian. Whatever Hellenistic building originally lay here was thoroughly destroyed by the levelling of the site for the Trajaneum. To the south of this temple, across from

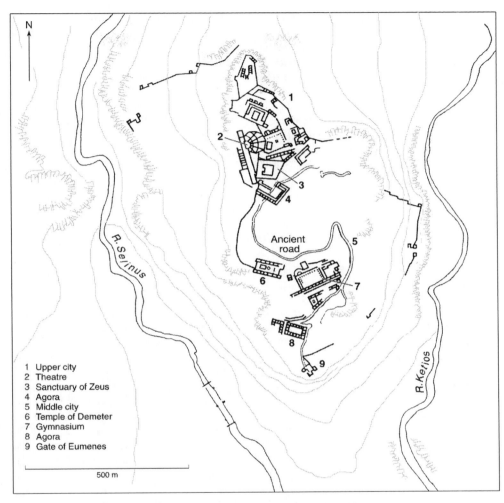

1 Upper city
2 Theatre
3 Sanctuary of Zeus
4 Agora
5 Middle city
6 Temple of Demeter
7 Gymnasium
8 Agora
9 Gate of Eumenes

500 m

Figure 12.5 Plan of Pergamon, built by the Attalids in the third century; after E. Akurgal

the royal palaces, lay one of the most interesting buildings in Pergamon, the great library; modelled on the famous library of Alexandria, it is said to have contained upwards of 200,000 books at its peak, before many volumes were removed to Alexandria on the orders of Mark Anthony, to replace losses to the great library of the Ptolemies. The library begins the sequence of public buildings and spaces filling the southern end of the acropolis, for access to it was from the second floor of a stoa built along the northern side of the sanctuary of Athena, patron goddess of the city. This sanctuary consisted of a large open square with stoas on its north, east and south sides, and on the west, set at a slight angle, the Doric temple of Athena of early third century date. To the south of this sanctuary again lay yet another stoa, two-aisled, of late Hellenistic date. South-west from this stoa was a row of shops facing south and overlooking a Heroon in honour of kings Attalos I and Eumenes II. To the south-east lay a sanctuary of Zeus with the famous great altar at its centre, whose remains now adorn the Berlin Museum; and below it the extensive political *agora*, colonnaded and with a small temple at its north-east end.

The upper city is thus seen to be largely a display piece of royal and public buildings, fulfilling security, religious, cultural and political functions and making a proud crown to this great city. On the west slope of the hill, this public area was rounded off by a magnificent theatre and temple complex. Built into the slope of the hill was perhaps the most unusual Greek theatre known to us: to fit the topography, it was built with an almost vertiginous steepness, and it curved much less than 180 degrees, rather than the normal 190–200. It consisted of 80 rows of seats, and held some 10,000 spectators. The upper city, which like the theatre faced west, was in effect curved around the theatre which thus formed its centrepiece, and afforded the spectators a magnificent view west across the coastal plain to the sea. At the base of the theatre was a terrace running north–south and providing an access road, with stoas on either side, from the *agora* in the south to the theatre, and then beyond it to a small temple of Dionysos, patron god of Greek drama, at the north end of the terrace. The *skene* of the theatre was set up, on a temporary basis whenever dramas were staged, on this terrace.

Some little way down the hill from the acropolis, in the midst of the basically residential middle city, there is a second large group of public buildings which included – as one descends the city – a temple of Demeter, the *prytaneion*, a magnificent three part gymnasium complex and a second *agora* surrounded by stoas and undoubtedly intended for commercial purposes. There were also two monumental fountains, and the upper gymnasium included an auditorium that may, given its size and location next to the *prytaneion*, have served when needed as a *bouleuterion*, though it should be noted that like much of the surviving architecture of the upper gymnasium, it is of Roman date. Magnificent Hellenistic fortification walls, of which substantial sections still remain, surrounded the middle city. The three-part gymnasium is one of the most remarkable structures of Pergamon. The upper gymnasium, the largest and most elaborate of the three, was for general use by the 'young men' of Pergamon, while separate gymnasia were provided for youths (the middle gymnasium), and boys (the lower gymnasium), which probably doubled as schools for the youngsters of the citizen class. For athletic competitions, the upper gymnasium had an indoor running track; but a suburban stadium of Roman date may perhaps mark the site of a Hellenistic open-air stadium. All in all, it is clear that all the necessary amenities of a Greek city were magnificently provided for.

What is, I think, remarkable about these cities is the degree of sameness within such a wide variation. It is clear, in the first place, that to Greek city planners the axial-grid system was an amenity, not a straitjacket: they readily adapted it or to a greater or lesser degree abandoned it if the topography of the city location called for it. It is noteworthy, in fact, how carefully Hellenistic city planning took topography into account and made the best of the physical features of the locale, blending with them, exploiting them, but never forcing them into the Hippodamian system where it did not fit. Where a city was built – on a slope, in a valley, on a hill-top – determined its shape and layout and therefore its particular character. Within this physical variety, and the additional variety of size, we find a basic sameness. In each city, whether royal metropolis (Pergamon), large commercial city (Ephesos), or small provincial town (Priene), the citizens' basic needs with respect to politics, religion, social/cultural life, commerce and basic security found essentially the same provision in the form of monumental public buildings and spaces: an *agora* with nearby *prytaneion, bouleuterion* and stoas to provide offices for magistrates and the like (politics); temples and sanctuaries (religion); a gymnasium or gymnasia, a theatre, a stadium and sometimes another auditorium or a library (social/cultural life); a commercial *agora* with stoas to provide rooms for shops (commerce); city walls and an ample and well set-up water supply (basic security). These buildings and spaces might differ in number and size according to the size of the city and its population, but they clearly conformed to the same overall conception of what a city should be. It was a conception that found expression, as I noted above, in literary works; and it was also worked out in a whole variety of other ways in the life of the community.

3   Civic Life and Urban Culture

Associated with the various forms of physical infrastructure that made up the city were an array of political and cultural institutions and norms that framed and shaped the life of the citizens in their communities. During the Hellenistic period the notion that democracy was the only appropriate form of constitution for an autonomous Greek city became part of Greek urban culture (Musti 1966; Quass 1979; Gruen 1993b; O'Neil 1995: chapter 5). Along with the political form of democracy, borrowed essentially from classical Athens, went another borrowing from fifth- and fourth-century Athens: the so-called 'epigraphic habit'. Democratic government required public record keeping in order for laws, institutions, policies and the like to be out in the open and retained in the public memory. The way the Greeks kept and published civic records was to inscribe them in stone, either on the walls of temples and other public buildings, or on stelae set up in cult sanctuaries, on the acropolis, or in the *agora*. As a result, we possess enormous numbers of inscriptions from the Hellenistic era documenting, among other things, how the Greek cities functioned and were governed. From them we can see that Hellenistic cities prized their local autonomy and democratic institutions greatly, that government by duly elected or appointed magistrates, state council and assembly of citizens was virtually universal, and that the magistrates, councils and assemblies of the Hellenistic cities were kept very busy. We can see that, limited as the autonomy of Greek cities was due to the realities of imperial power, the local self-governance was real. It was concerned primarily with six main issues: religious matters and festivals, relations with kings and dynasts, relations with other cities, honouring benefactors, the food supply and the upkeep of public buildings and amenities. Although the public business of Hellenistic cities is sometimes dismissed as unimportant trifling compared to the issues of real significance dealt with by classical city-states like Athens and Sparta (e.g. by Green 1990: 155–70), it should be clear from the above list that matters of real import to the citizens were routinely dealt with; and in any case that attitude overstates the freedom of most classical city-states – for Athens and Sparta were exceptions, and most cities never had much more real autonomy than they had in the Hellenistic era.

What we can see from the epigraphic evidence is that, though Greek cities never at any time developed proper administrative bureaucracies, there was in the Hellenistic era a considerable elaboration of the civic magistracies charged with overseeing the various aspects of public life and business, and that the amenities and services cities provided their citizens likewise became more elaborate. One of the best (and most frequently cited and quoted) pieces of evidence in this regard is a long inscription from Pergamon recording substantial portions of the administrative code of that city (*OGIS* 483; Klaffenbach 1954; Austin 216 trans.). There are detailed instructions for upkeep of the road network in and around the city, specifying the minimum width of main roads (*c.* 30 ft.) and side roads (*c.* 12 ft.). The *astynomoi* (city wardens) are charged with chief responsibility for this, with under them street governors (*amphodarchai*) who have actual oversight of ensuring that the city streets are clean and in good repair. Those owning property along the streets are required to pay for the actual work of cleaning and repairing them when necessary, with the *amphodarchai* overseeing them, and if necessary the *astynomoi* stepping in to contract the work out and exact the money to cover the resulting expense from the property owners. Over the *astynomoi*, to ensure that they do their job, are the *strategoi* (lit. generals, the city's chief magistrates) and the *nomophylakes* (guardians of the law). Precise fines and punishments are laid down for those at each level who fail to fulfil their responsibilities properly. It is strictly forbidden to damage the streets, and any such damage is to be made good at the wrongdoers' expense. The *astynomoi* are further charged with inspecting party walls and seeing to it that the owners keep them in good repair, with detailed provisions for how the cost is to be allocated. The *astynomoi* are likewise charged with ensuring that the public fountains are kept clean and that the flow of water is not obstructed, and to fine heavily those who misuse them. They are also charged with keeping a record of the water cisterns in the city and ensuring that they are properly maintained, fining heavily owners who do not do so, and reporting on this to the *strategoi*. Similarly, the city's public toilets and sewers are under their care, with the charge to ensure that the toilets are clean and the sewers covered.

The *astynomoi* emerge from this document as important officials charged with crucial responsibilities for seeing to it that the physical fabric of the city was properly maintained. They reported on this to two of the top magistracies of the city – the *strategoi* and the *nomophylakes* – and had lesser magistrates serving under them for specific tasks, like the aforementioned *amphodarchai*. Such *astynomoi* are met with in inscriptions from quite an array of other cities (see e.g. the evidence cited by A. Jones 1940: 349 n. 5), and we know that they formed part of an array of magistracies charged with the maintenance of public amenities. The best known is no doubt the *gymnasiarchos*, charged with upkeep and oversight of the gymnasium and its proper use. Other important and quite well known magistracies are: the *agoranomoi*, who oversaw the marketplace and made sure that merchants and traders used proper weights and measures, the right coinage and in general that the market place was used fairly and peacefully; the *sitophylakes* or *sitonai*, charged with overseeing the city's grain-storage facilities and, so far as possible, ensuring the import of an adequate supply of grain to feed the population at an affordable price; *nuktostrategoi* or *nuktophylakes* (night generals or guards), or sometimes *eirenarchai* (peace wardens), charged with the police function of maintaining public order, especially (as the title of 'night' general or guard indicates) at night – ancient cities were not well lit after dark (A. Jones 1940: 211–50, 348–9). One might also mention *paidonomoi* (child wardens) in charge of overseeing the education of citizen boys – and sometimes also girls – in some cities, and various sorts of treasurers (*tamiai*) in charge of the receipt and disbursement of public funds.

In general, it is plain that Hellenistic cities were rather well and carefully governed and maintained by a whole network and hierarchy of magistracies which collectively saw to it that the city looked good and functioned smoothly, and that the needs of the citizens were taken care of. All of these magistrates were appointed by the citizen body, and were ultimately responsible to the citizen assembly for the proper fulfilment of their duties. Again it is clear from this that the self-governance of Hellenistic cities was not an empty honour (as for instance Green 1990: 155), but that the citizen assemblies had matters of real importance to them upon which to deliberate and decide at their meetings. It comes as no surprise, therefore, to find that evidence exists to show that assemblies were well attended. Records of voters present at assemblies, or of citizens voting in favour of a measure, are known from various cities – Halikarnassos, Magnesia-on-the-Maeander and Kolophon for instance – and the numbers given are large enough to indicate that a substantial percentage of citizens frequently attended (Gauthier 1984: 96–7; Gruen 1993b; 354). However, discussion of magistracies and citizen assemblies, important as they were to the functioning of the cities, gives only part of the picture of how the cities were run.

One of the characteristic features of Greek cities, in the Hellenistic no less than in the Classical period and earlier, was that they tended to have rather diminutive public revenues, too small to meet all of the communities' public expenses. Just as Greeks resisted the holding of salaried jobs, considering working regularly for another to be demeaning (banausic) and slavish, so they also resisted the imposition of taxes on their incomes – irregular as they often were – considering such taxes to be harsh and a sign of submission on the part of the taxpayer. Public finances therefore rested on more irregular and unpredictable sources: market and harbour taxes, import and export duties, sometimes property taxes (usually only imposed in emergencies) and fines and confiscations of various sorts. Shortfalls in the revenues needed to cover expenses were hence chronic. The cities met this situation by appealing to the generosity of wealthy benefactors (*euergetai*), fellow citizens in the first place who had a self-interested motive to contribute to the well-being of the community, but during the Hellenistic period also increasingly benevolent foreigners, including dynasts and kings. A huge number of inscriptions from all around the Hellenistic world recording the thanks and honours accorded such benefactors attests to the practice and its importance (see esp. Gauthier 1984; also Veyne 1976). Almost every conceivable form of public activity – upkeep of city walls, public buildings, fountains; provision of massage oil for the gymnasia; funding of public education; and above all, underwriting of the grain supply – received crucial financial support from wealthy *euergetai*; and the rendering of proper thanks and honours to them was evidently one of the major preoccupations of the public assemblies.

This process of benefaction and honouring should not be dismissed as an empty or purely formulaic activity: it goes to the very heart of the functioning of the cities, of the maintenance of harmonious relations between rich and poorer citizens, of the continuance of public spirit within the cities (Gauthier 1984; Gruen 1993b; Billows 1995: 70–80). The cities needed this active involvement by their wealthy elites, not only to make up for their shortfalls in public finances, but also because, in the absence of substantial civic administrative bureaucracies, they relied on the personal business staffs and business contacts of the wealthy to get things actually done. By being willing to give of their wealth for the public good, the rich of the Hellenistic cities won a public goodwill and gratitude that allayed nascent resentments about the disparity between rich and poor citizens. And the interaction between citizen assemblies, civic magistracies and the wealthy elites in taking care of the cities' infrastructures and needs showed that civic morale and public spirit remained high despite the reduced independence of the Greek cities in the new world of Hellenistic Empires. It is worth quoting a few examples of the honorific decrees of this period, not just to illustrate how the citizens thanked and honoured their benefactors, but also to show the kinds of services such benefactors performed for their fellow citizens.

From Halikarnassos, for instance, a decree honoured those who had provided the city with interest free loans towards the construction of a new stoa, reading in part: '. . . so that those who have advanced money for the stoa which the *demos* (people) is dedicating to Apollo and to King Ptolemy should be known to all, the controllers (*exetastai*) in whose period of office the stoa is completed shall inscribe on the side wall of the stoa the names and patronymics of all those who have advanced without interest sums of not less than 500 drachmas, prefacing the list with the words "The following men gave to the *demos* money without interest for the construction of the stoa". They shall inscribe first the person who gave most' (*OGIS* 46, trans. as Austin 100). The raising of funds by public subscription, either as here in the form of an interest free loan or as an outright gift, was a common way for Hellenistic cities to meet special needs of all kinds and is widely attested (Migeotte 1992). Another form of benefaction was the donation of large capital sums to be invested on behalf of the city, the proceeds to finance special civic services. This form of benefaction was used in several cities that we know of to create public schools, for example, at which the sons – and in at least one case the daughters too – of the citizens could receive a free education (Miletos: *SIG*³ 577, trans. Austin 119; Teos: *SIG*³ 578, trans. Austin 120).

One of the most important benefactions reflected in the surviving honorific decrees was the provision of help with the cities' grain supply. A decree from Delos, for example, honours one Aristoboulos of Thessalonike, a *sitones* of the Macedonian king Demetrios II for help given to the Delians while he resided there in his capacity of grain purchaser for the king (Durrbach 1921: no. 48, trans. Austin 114); but a decree from the city of Histiaia on Euboia honouring a Rhodian for helping with the grain supply is particularly revealing:

> The *archontes* proposed that the *boule* (council) submit to the *demos* (people) this resolution: whereas Athenodoros son of Peisagoras the Rhodian continues to provide services, both privately to any citizen in need, and publicly to the city; and whereas he provided ready aid in every way to the *sitonai* sent by the city to Delos, lending them money without interest and enabling them to carry out their duties as quickly as possible, placing the good of the city above his own private gain; therefore, so that all may know that the *demos* of the Histiaians knows how to honour its benefactors, and more people may compete to provide benefits to the city when they see worthy men being honoured; with good fortune, be it decided by the *demos* to honour Athenodoros son of Peisagoras the Rhodian for his goodwill towards the city and to crown him with an olive wreath for his excellence and his goodwill towards the *demos* of the Histiaians, to proclaim the crown at the festival of the Antigoneia, and that the *agonothetes* (official in charge of the festival) shall see to the proclamation; to grant to him and to his descendants citizenship

according to the law and priority access to the *boule* and the *demos*, first after sacred matters; to inscribe this decree on a stone stele and set it up here (Histiaia) in the sanctuary of Dionysos and at Delos in the sanctuary of Apollo after requesting a place from the koinon of the Delians; the expense for the inscription shall be covered by the presiding treasurer. (*SIG*³ 493)

Particularly noteworthy here is the clause in which the Histiaians expressed the hope that others would compete to benefit their city when they saw that the Histiaians knew how to render proper thanks and honours: Greek culture was always highly competitive, and like everything else public benefactions were seen as a competition, a competition for honour – indeed this competition to benefit the city and so win honour was likened by the Athenian orator Aischines (3.180) to the competition among athletes at the Olympic games. The Greek cities manipulated this competition for honour in order to extract benefactions from the wealthy; and this system of euergetism and associated honours was extended to relations between cities and kings. The Greek philosophy of kingship required the king to be a *euergetes*, and seeing that the kings had adopted this public pose the cities called their bluff and manipulated them into granting a wide array of privileges and benefactions, making them live up to the benefactor image they wished to sustain (Billows 1995: 70–80). In this way, relations between kings and cities remained mostly cordial and respectful throughout the Hellenistic era, despite the often rather severe restrictions the kings placed on civic freedom. Cities also helped each other, pursuing this same philosophy of euergetism in a different sphere. One of the hallmarks of the Hellenistic Era is the high degree of interconnectedness the community of Greek cities displayed (see especially Giovannini 1993 for this). They passed decrees declaring each other's cults and temples to be 'holy and inviolate' (Rigsby 1996); they made so-called *isopoliteia* agreements, creating a limited form of shared citizenship among the contracting cities (Gawantka 1975); they arbitrated disputes for each other, helping to decrease greatly the instances of warfare between rival cities (Ager 1996); they sent panels of citizens to act as judges in nearby cities, clearing up backlogs of court cases that many cities found it hard to cope with themselves (Crowther 1995; 1998; 1999). There was, in other words, a genuine sense of a community of cities with shared language, culture, religion, institutions, ideals, values; a community of cities that ought to get along and interact in a friendly and peaceful way, that ought to help each other and respect each other. Of course there was still a great deal of inter-city hostility and rivalry, and wars were still fought; but the expectation, the norm even, clearly was for peaceful and friendly interaction unless strong reasons existed to go against that.

In conclusion, I want to emphasize that by the Hellenistic Era there had emerged in Greek culture an idea of what a city ought to be, of a set of physical, social, political, cultural and religious structures, amenities, institutions, norms and practices to which all cities ought to adhere. This was not just an idea: it is very clear that the Hellenistic cities strove mightily to make it a reality. I will bring forward one final piece of evidence to illustrate this fact, and provide a fitting close to this chapter. It has long been pointed out that in the Hellenistic period the gymnasium became the most characteristic institution of social and cultural life in the cities, that frequenting the gymnasium was the hallmark – the *sine qua non* almost – of the Greek citizen (so e.g.

Davies 1984: 308; Giovannini 1993; also Green 1990: 319, with a characteristically negative cast). We happen to have preserved for us an inscription of the early second century BC from the town of Beroia in Macedonia, recording the citizens' decision to establish a law regulating in detail the running of the gymnasium (Hatzopoulos and Gauthier 1993; Austin 118, trans.). The preamble to this law makes interesting reading: 'When Hippokrates son of Nikokrates was *strategos*, on the 19th of Apellaios, at a meeting of the assembly, Zopyros son of Amyntas the gymnasiarch, Asklepiades son of Heras, and Kallipos son of Hippostratos proposed: since all the other magistracies are exercised in accordance with the law, and in the cities in which there are gymnasia and anointing is practised the laws on gymnasiarchs are deposited in the public archives, it is therefore appropriate that the same should be done among us and that the law which we handed over to the auditors (*exetastai*) should be inscribed on a stele and placed in the gymnasium and also deposited in the public office...' The people of Beroia, that is to say, had become aware of an anomaly: in other Greek cities how the gymnasium was run, who had access and when, the precise duties of the gymnasiarch, and so on, were set out in a written law displayed for all to see; Beroia lacked such a law. This anomaly needed to be addressed: in order for Beroia to take its place as a full-fledged *polis* in the community of Greek *poleis* it too should have such a law. The law was duly passed and inscribed, and happens to have survived through the centuries down to our own time as an eloquent witness to the fact that Hellenistic Greek cities strove to conform to an ideal of what a city ought to be, and made that ideal a reality so far as they could achieve it.

FURTHER READING

The fullest and best treatment of the Greek cities during the Hellenistic Era is still A. H. M. Jones 1940. A great deal of new evidence – epigraphic, archaeological and, to a more limited extent, papyrological – has come to light since then, but Jones' work has yet to be superseded. More recent works that in various ways do update it have been cited in the text above: Davies 1984: 304–20; Green 1990: chapter 10; Gruen 1993b; Giovannini 1993. Akurgal 1990 is still an excellent overview of the archaeological remains of cities in Asia Minor, for which L. Robert 1962 has much that is valuable also; for cities further east see e.g. the papers in Kuhrt and Sherwin-White 1987. The successive volumes, city by city, of the *Inschriften Kleinasiens* edited by Merkelbach, Engelmann, and others and published out of Bonn have made the bulk of the best epigraphic material easily accessible (= *IK*); for the rest the *SIG*3, *OGIS* and *ISE* collections are excellent; Austin 1981 provides translations of many of the more important inscriptions; and see Ma 2000a for recent epigraphic studies. On Alexander's foundations, Fraser 1996. The Greek settlements in Asia are treated in Tscherikower 1926 and, for Asia Minor, G. Cohen 1995; we await Cohen's second volume treating the further east. For the process of settlement G. Cohen 1978 is invaluable, and see also Grainger 1990b and Billows 1995: chapter 6. For town planning Owens 1991: ch. 5 provides a good recent treatment, and Wycherley 1962 is still valuable. For the governance of the cities: Gauthier 1984 and Migeotte 1992; for the crucial role of benefactors, Gauthier 1985 and Veyne 1976; for relations between kings and cities, Orth 1977, Billows 1995: chapter 3, Bringmann 1993, and Herz 1996; for relations between cities see the studies of individual varieties of interaction by Gawantka 1975, Marek 1984, Rigsby 1996, Ager 1996 and Crowther 1995, 1998, 1999 (to be developed more fully in his forthcoming book). Gregory 1997 treats relations between city and countryside in an excellent but regrettably still unpublished dissertation. Finally, there are numerous studies of individual cities or groups of cities, for example Downey 1963, Fraser 1972, Bernand 1998, Cartledge and Spawforth 1989, Habicht 1994 and 1997, Berthold 1984, and Ma 1999, to name a few.

CHAPTER THIRTEEN

The Past in a Hellenistic Present: Myth and Local Tradition

Tanja S. Scheer

1   Myth as History According to the Greeks

The inhabitants of the city of Tarsos in Cilicia, according to the geographer Strabo, originally came from Argos: 'They say that Triptolemos was sent by the Argives in search of Io, who first disappeared in Tyre, and that he travelled through Cilicia; there several of his Argive companions left him and founded Tarsos' (16.2.5). The strange foundation myth of the Tarsians is a typical example of how people in the Hellenistic period dealt with past and present. We hear for the first time that a search party was sent out to find the Argive princess and priestess Io. It must have seemed very curious to experts in Greek mythology – and every citizen of a *polis* counted himself as such – that Triptolemos should have taken on such a task, that ended finally in the founding of cities in distant, barbaric places.

The relationship of Hellenistic Greeks to their past is shaped by much older traditions. In particular two important points characterize the relationship to the past: its genealogical structuring and its re-shaping by epic poetry. It is already clear from the Homeric epics that the Greeks thought in familial structures: 'Who are you? Where do you come from? What is the name of your home city and your parents?' These questions are posed in epic when strangers meet (e.g. Hom. *Od.* 1.170). Self-definition as well as assessment by others are marked by genealogical connections. The past of his own family, of his home city, of his tribe defines the identity and status of the individual in the present: Glaukos and Diomedes find out on the battlefield that their families are bound together by ancestral ties of guest-friendship (Hom. *Il.* 6.234–6). Even much later individuals in Greece set great store by ancestry. But whole cities also prided themselves on their ancestors and founders. Xenophon makes Sokrates praise the outstanding descent of the Athenians (Xen. *Mem.* 3.5.3) and the whole city allegedly talks about the supposed divine origin of the young Athenian Lysis (Plato *Lysis* 205c). Herodotos reports that other nations occasionally outdo the Greeks in genealogical ambition, namely when an Egyptian priest responds merely with a smile to the ancestral line of Hekataios of Miletos, which reaches back sixteen generations (Hdt. 2.143). The past in the form of genealogy had an effect right up to the present in Greece through the emphasizing of family structures: it gave rise to expectations and claims. These might for instance have consisted of territorial claims, but might also have applied to 'familial behaviour': allied cities and families were expected to stand by each other in war or in economic crises.

This pronounced Greek interest in ancestry and kinship was, however, not properly historical. The past was only of importance when it was marked by famous personalities or by deeds of mythical heroes. A family tree that ended with an anonymous smallholder was of little use. Even as proof of the great age of a family it could not offer much help: for great age only really began when the genealogy could be traced back to heroic times and thereby into the society of heroes or even gods (Strubbe 1984; Weiß 1984; Scheer 1993: 6ff.; Gehrke 1994).

Even if there had been a general interest in the authentic past, if the Greeks had looked for objective answers, the problems with the sources would have quickly driven them to the limits of possibility (Forsdyke 1956: 13; Patzek 1992: 2ff.) The knowledge of Linear B script had been lost. People were at a loss when confronted with written or archaeological discoveries from their own past, which chance had brought to light. The Greeks reconstructed the past not so much through concrete evidence from early times but rather with the help of their traditional stories, of myth. In cases of doubt an oracle was readily consulted, for instance when they sought an explanation for the discovery of colossal bones. The answers were bound by the framework of established tradition. It might then emerge for instance that they were dealing with the kneecap of Ajax, son of Telamon, from the Homeric epic or the skeleton of the giant Orontes, which at the same time would provide a plausible explanation for the colossal size of the finds (Pfister 1909–12: 507ff.; Scheer 1996: 354ff.). Similar explanations probably presented themselves in the case of visible remains of buildings from the Mycenean Age (Hampl 1975: 75; Tausend 1990: 152). Questions about the past led to heroic, not historically correct, answers (see also Dowden 1992: 60ff.; Sourvinou-Inwood 1987: 215–16). The possibility is not absolutely excluded that historical memory has here and there preserved the reality of early Greece. Already long before Hellenistic times, however, Greek logographers and historians had made the fictional events of epic the focal point of their history and accepted them as containing at least a core of truth. Even Thucydides speaks of the autochthony of the Athenians, of the naval supremacy of King Minos, and of the Trojan War as historical facts from which one only needs to expunge the improbable additions (Thuc. 1.2.5; 1.4.1; 1.9.1). The swift spread of the Homeric epics throughout Greece had clearly extinguished or at least 'reshaped' real memory. The memory of a more or less exiguous real past was hardly a match for the epic alternative of heroic martial renown (Strasburger 1972: 15–16; Scheer 1993: 62).

The connection between epic and self-definition through heredity is established without difficulty if one stresses the role of the ancestors of cities and of individuals in specific mythological incidents. Mythical tradition becomes mythical construct. Already in the ancient world the Athenians saw themselves confronted with the accusation that they had inserted supposedly appropriate lines into the *Iliad* (Hereas of Megara *FGrH* 486 F1; Plut. *Sol.* 10). Or else individual families traced their ancestry in a direct line back to epic heroes: the family of the Philaides, to which the historian Thucydides belonged, claimed to be descended from Ajax, son of Telamon (Hdt. 6.35; Pherekydes *FGrH* 3 F2), the orator Andokides even claimed descent from Odysseus and Hermes (Plut. *Alc.* 21; [Plut.] *Mor.* 834b). The habit of evaluating the qualities of individuals and even of cities on the basis of their ancestry understandably encouraged the desire to number the gods themselves – or at least the heroes of epic – among one's own ancestors.

2   Past and Present in the Hellenistic Period

The interconnection of past and present reached hitherto unprecedented levels in the Hellenistic period. The basic constants remained the same: the interest in genealogy continued unabated, and the past as re-fashioned by epic, in which the products of the poetic imagination have taken the place of reality, is established and recognized as a valid representation of the Greek past. What changed and developed, however, was the role that the past played in the present. The immediate cause of this was the upheaval brought about by the campaigns of Alexander the Great.

In his treatment of the past Alexander connected seamlessly with the traditional perception. Already for generations the Argeads had attached great value to a prestigious ancestral line that went right back to Herakles as its progenitor. The Macedonian royal house, at first not recognized as truly Greek, found it particularly necessary to claim mythological-cum-historical proof of their noble descent. It was the propagation of a family tree which went back to Argos and Herakles that made possible their admission to the Olympic Games (Hdt. 5.22; 8.137–9; Thuc. 2.99.3). At the time of Philip II this ancestry was largely recognized (though for dissent, see Dem. 9.31) and significantly in his case it also had an influence on the present; the history of the family imposed an obligation. Thus the political writer Isokrates could present Herakles as a model for his descendant Philip (*Panath.* 76–7). The deeds of Herakles in the first conquest of Troy were used to legitimate, and also to oblige, Philip to carry out successful military action in the present – that is the campaign against the Persians (Isoc. *Phil.* 111–15). The young Alexander through his mother, the Epeirote princess Olympias, also counted Achilles, Homer's most courageous hero at Troy, among his ancestors (Paus. 1.11.1; Funke 2000: 167). Through Herakles and Achilles, therefore, Alexander was of divine descent both on his father's and on his mother's side: he had the sea-goddess Thetis, the mother of Achilles, and Zeus, king of the gods, the father of Herakles, in his family tree. Alexander as king emphasized his connection to a divine, or at least glorious heroic, past not only through his own ancestry but also through his conduct. His campaign against the Persians could already be regarded – completely in the tradition of Philip – as a war of vengeance designed to punish the outrage previously committed by the Persians in Greece (Polyb. 5.10.8; Diod. 17.4.9; Just. 11.2.5; Bellen 1974). Furthermore, the action was permeated with repeated allusions to the mythical past. He presented himself as a new fighter against Troy: when he landed on Asiatic soil, he leapt from his ship, like Protesilaos before him, and hurled his spear as a gesture of ownership into enemy ground. In addition he pointedly visited the sites of ancient Ilion and sacrificed in the temple of Athena. He had Trojan weapons from this temple carried ahead of him as a standard from then on, a consequence of his well-documented personal interest in the epic that praised his ancestor Achilles (Arr. *Anab.* 1.11.6–12.2; Plut. *Alex.* 5.8). The continued influence of the mythological past on the present is clear: it is the motivating yardstick for the new Achilles (Stewart 1993a: 78–86; Erskine 2001: 226–31).

3   The Greeks Abroad

In the course of Alexander's campaigns the interaction of past and present gained a new dimension. The advance of the Macedonian army changed the Greek view of the world (cf. Geus, this volume). The way they dealt with this expanded, apparently endless, world is significant: they evidently abstained from extravagant advertisement of the claim to be the first to have ever advanced so far. Instead the stress was placed over and over again on familiar elements in these foreign lands: the geographical opening up of the world took place in the footsteps of great forerunners, of gods and heroes from the mythical past.

Throughout his campaign Alexander recognized Greek gods and heroes in foreign lands; he called on them pointedly and paid honour to them. He recognized his ancestor Herakles in the Phoenician Melqart of Tyre. In remote Cilicia he sacrificed to the Asklepios of Soloi and hailed the hero Amphilochos of Mallos as a direct relation (Arr. *Anab.* 2.16.7; 2.5.5; 2.5.9). The whole campaign of Alexander can be interpreted as a venture following the trail of the mythical past: like Herakles, who had travelled the world and fought against the barbarians, Alexander too took up the fight with the barbarian foe. In the footsteps of Dionysos he travelled to India, beyond the boundaries of the known world (Arr. *Ind.* 1.4–5; 5.12).

In the case of Alexander's campaigns this emphasis on the mythical past of the Macedonians and Greeks tended to integrate rather than exclude. The aim was by no means a one-sided ennobling of the Macedonians at the expense of the indigenous peoples whom they encountered. Family relationships based on myth did not have the function of an exclusive patent of nobility. Alexander and his generals endeavoured on the contrary to establish a connection between Greeks and Persians. Strabo records the creation of a family relationship between the Thessalians and the inhabitants of Armenia and Media which was promoted by followers of Alexander (11.14.12). This idea of kinship between the inhabitants of Asia and the Greeks was not completely new. Already in the Homeric epic Greek gods had sons in both camps: one thinks of Aeneas, Sarpedon and Memnon. Herodotos had already reported that the kings of Lydia were descended from Herakles (1.7). And in the run up to the Persian Wars Persian envoys are supposed to have come to Argos in an attempt to win the Argives over to their side – by appealing to their mutual mythical ancestor Perseus (Hdt. 7.150; Braun 1982: 31; Speyer 1989).

This integrating use of the mythical past was not simply an unselfish mark of respect or recognition for non-Greek civilizations on the part of the Greeks. At stake surely was the need to prevent the Greek claim to power from appearing to the conquered as foreign rule. At least as important, however, was the opportunity for the Greeks to take mental possession of these new lands. In this aim the structure of the traditional stories of the Greeks was of considerable assistance. A common method of intellectual subjugation of unfamiliar lands consisted in making them accessible through eponymous heroes: every river, every tree, every region, according to the Greek view, was inhabited by local supernatural powers. Once the areas which they reached were mythically personalized, then the local family trees could easily be connected to well-known Greek heroes. Indeed if it was possible to recognize a prominent Greek hero as progenitor, then the new members could be regarded as having been successfully fitted into the system. But in addition the propagation of parallels between

Alexander and successful models from the past must have had positive consequences. The example of mythical wandering heroes and gods like Herakles and Dionysos, in whose footsteps they could imagine themselves to be following, helped the Macedonians cope with the pressures of an alien environment. The foreign land was not really unknown: their own ancestors had after all once passed through it victoriously (Arr. *Anab.* 5.26.5). The cultivation of a mythical past was valuable for the Hellenistic present; even in the most far-flung foreign land traces of old familiar patterns could be discovered. Thus, the new world could be integrated into the old as something already familiar.

The person of Alexander himself became in the end a new fixed point of the more recent past, which in its turn had an influence on the present. Alexander's deeds allowed him to grow in the eyes of contemporaries and descendants to a truly superhuman stature. Just as rulers and cities had tried to obtain a share in the Homeric epic, so they now strove to establish a link to this latterday hero, who had proved himself to be a true successor to the gods and heroes. Alexander became the focus of competition among kings and cities; not only were genealogical claims made but relics of the dead king were highly-prized. The desire to have a share in Alexander led Ptolemy I, for example, to stylize himself as a descendant of Herakles and an Argead (Theocr. *Id.* 17.26; Paus. 1.6.25; Curt. 9.8.22). What is more, Ptolemy was able to secure Alexander's corpse for his own capital city, Alexandria, where Alexander later acquired the status of a founding hero and of a local guardian hero, who kept watch from his tomb over the future of his foundation (Payne 1991: 170; Erskine 2002a). In the kingdom of Macedon itself the genealogical connection to Alexander remained a central ideological element. Polybios describes the ambition of Philip V who throughout his life had emphasized his family connection with Alexander (5.10.10). The hard-pressed Macedonian king Perseus is supposed to have made his ill-fated journey to the city of Pydna in 168, because he wanted to make a sacrifice there to Herakles, the ancestor he shared with Alexander (Plut. *Aem.* 19).

4   The Past for Kings: Hellenistic Pergamon

Alexander had already, in the course of his campaign, founded a number of cities. His successors carried this policy further: the establishment of new Greek cities in areas hitherto unexploited by the Greeks is probably rightly regarded as a particularly typical element of the Hellenistic period. The kings quickly recognized the significance of cities in the territorial exploitation of defeated regions (Brodersen 2001). Many of these new foundations were not, however, actually new. Probably only a very few were really planned on the drawing-board. The places of settlement had, on the contrary, frequently already been settled and were now simply restructured by a Greek component in the population. Several cities acquired a completely new significance as a result. Their new political importance called for ideological underpinning. The past also played an important role for a Hellenistic 'new foundation'. 'Newness' was not a positive factor for the Greeks – just the opposite. This was true for most spheres – beginning with the inauguration of customs or laws, which were attributed to the earliest possible ancestor, and whose obligatory nature derived from their allegedly great age; and applying also to cities and tribes who liked to claim the greatest possible antiquity for themselves. In the course of the following discussion the significance of myth for past and present in the Hellenistic period will be shown through two examples: firstly a royal capital; secondly the relationships between long-established Greek cities and others, hitherto only superficially Hellenized, situated at the edge of the Greek world.

Greek myth and local tradition played an important role in the history of the city of Pergamon from the beginning of the Hellenistic period. Pergamon was not a new foundation of its first Hellenistic ruler, Philetairos. Traces of settlement go back to second millennium BC. Already in the fifth century a place called Pergamon is recorded in this region. The Persian king presented it to a follower from Eretria called Gongylos (Xen. *Hell.* 3.1.6). But before the Hellenistic Age this settlement was probably not a Greek city; it could not be compared with the nearby Ionic foundations on the west coast of Asia Minor, rich in tradition. It never became a city with a purely Greek population; funerary inscriptions show that, even in its Hellenistic heyday when a replica of the Athena Parthenos was set up in the Pergamene library, a large part of the population still bore non-Greek personal names (Scheer 1993: 101–2). For the Hellenistic rulers, who chose the city of Pergamon as their seat, the decisive factor was probably not some kind of ideological prestige possessed by the place but rather the impregnability of its acropolis. The previous insignificance of the place, its existence as a settlement in Asia Minor in the backwaters of history, was appropriate to the humble origins of its new ruler. Philetairos, son of Attalos and Boa, came from Tieion, a small city in Paphlagonia. His mother Boa did not even bear a Greek name. It shows the value which the Greeks attached to personal descent when the ancestry of the Attalid ruling family from a Paphlagonian forebear could still lead to denigration hundreds of years later: Boa was abused by poets as a barbarian flute-girl – after all what good could come out of Paphlagonia (Strabo 14.1.39; Athen. 13.577b)?

The rise of Pergamon to be the capital of a new, prosperous and liberal dynasty directed an attention never before known on settlement and ruler – and also on the history of both (for the city, Billows, this volume, section 2; for the dynasty, Kosme-tatou, this volume). The rivals with whom it was essential to be of equal birth were the other Hellenistic ruling families with their claims to divine or at least Argead descent and the neighbouring Greek cities with an ancient cultural tradition. By the reign of Attalos I, who was the first Pergamene to take the title of king, the real ancestry of the ruling family and the real history of the settlement had long ceased to matter in dynastic and civic self-representation. Philetairos had sent donations on a grand scale to the most important sanctuaries of the Greek world, to Delphi, Delos and Olympia among others. His successors were a match for him in this respect. At the end of the third century in the sanctuary at Delos a votive offering was donated which was of particular significance for the self-conception and self-representation of the Attalids: the so-called Teuthrania offering (Schalles 1985: 127; Hintzen-Bohlen 1992: 146; Scheer 1993: 127). The inscriptions on the bases of five or six statues give the name and parents of the person represented. That the Pergamene rulers Eumenes I and Attalos I appear here is not surprising. It is interesting, however, that the rulers of Pergamon are seen in company with eponymous local heroes from the area around their royal capital. One of these is Midios, son of Halisarne and Gyrnos. Midios can be identified as hero of a place called Midapedion, Halisarna was already named by

Xenophon as a place near Pergamon. In later sources Gyrnos, the father of Midios, was explicitly described as founding hero of the sanctuary of Apollo at Gryneion. The remaining inscriptions of the Teuthrania offering also give information about the mythological systematization to which the area around Pergamon was clearly subjected: one of them refers to personifications of local stretches of water. A final statue is a representation of 'Teutras'. Called 'Teuthras' by the literary sources, he was a well-known mythical hero of the region. According to the Attic tragedians he is king of a city called Teuthrania – and stepfather of the famous hero Telephos.

The inscriptions of the Teuthrania offering briefly mentioned here show how the system of mythological genealogy can be used for the mental appropriation, incorporation and ennobling of a city previously of little importance, and how it allows the creation of new focus points. Features of the landscape are personalized in the form of eponymous heroes of the past and given a genealogical connection. On the basis of the preserved inscriptions of the Teuthrania offering no direct personal genealogical connection of the royal family of Pergamon with the local heroes can be proved. Nevertheless the family trees gather together local traditions from the surrounding area and bring them closer to the new royal capital and its rulers. Visually at least the rulers of Pergamon in the Hellenistic present and the local heroes are to be seen on the same level. The comparatively new rulers demonstrate their attachment to the region, as if they had been settled there since the times of Teuthras' government. The Teuthrania offering is located not in the Mysian hinterland nor in Pergamon itself but in the famous ancient sanctuary of Apollo of Delos: the whole Greek world is addressed there in the language of myth.

The Attalid representation of the past was to go further than this. In another major Greek sanctuary, Delphi, the ruling family's connection to an eponymous hero of Pergamon must have played a role (Scheer 1993: 123–4). It is not clear whether Philetairos, the founder of the dynasty, had this in mind when he made his donations to Delphi, but Attalos I surely drew on this when endowing the sanctuary at Delphi with a stoa. This building, the stoa of Attalos, occupies a special position in the sanctuary: it is the only building allowed to interrupt the Temenos wall (Schalles 1985: 110; Jacquemin and Laroche 1992: 248–9; Hintzen-Bohlen 1992: 127), and consequently it is situated in direct proximity to the *heroon*, or hero-shrine, of Pyrrhos-Neoptolemos (Paus. 10.24.6; on the current discussion about the location of the temenos of Neoptolemos, see Funke 2000: 88–9). Pyrrhos-Neoptolemos played an important part in Delphi but also quite fundamentally in Homeric epic and classical tragedy. At first he had not played a particularly creditable role in Delphi. He is said to have burnt down a temple of Apollo because he blamed Apollo for his father Achilles' death. The punishment was not long in coming: Pyrrhos-Neoptolemos died suddenly at the hands of a murderer in the sanctuary at Delphi (e.g. Eur. *Andr.* 1073–4). For the Attalids this hero was special because of his mythological family tree. Through his father Achilles, the greatest Greek hero at Troy, he belonged to the first rank of mythical heroes. Even more interesting, however, were his descendants. From the Trojan booty he was awarded Andromache, the widow of Hektor; he went with her to Epeiros and fathered three children there: Pielos, Molossos and a son called Pergamos (Paus. 1.11.1). That the Attalids had knowledge of this genealogy of heroes is as good as certain, considering their well-known cultural ambitions and their huge library. In addition Pausanias records a double shrine for Andromache and Pergamos in the city of Pergamon itself (1.11.1–2). The proximity of the stoa of Attalos and the shrine of Pyrrhos is unlikely to be due to chance. Pergamos of Epeiros might at first sight appear to be a rather colourless hero, but the Attalids could see in him the eponymous hero of their city, or at least a relative, and such a connection was open to a particularly honourable interpretation according to Greek standards: the family tree of Pergamos made it possible to link the Attalids with the most courageous heroes of both sides at Troy: to Achilles and, through Andromache, also to the Trojan prince Hektor. Andromache also belonged to a royal family of Asia Minor (Hom. *Il.* 6.395ff.). Relationship to the ancestors of the royal family of Epeiros also brought with it a relationship that reached right up to the Hellenistic present: with Olympias, the mother of Alexander. And just as Alexander had justified his claim to divine and heroic ancestry through appropriately heroic deeds against the barbarians, so Attalos of Pergamon legitimized himself too as a 'new Pyrrhos': during the Galatian invasion of Greece in 279, according to the Delphians, Pyrrhos-Neoptolemos had joined the battle through an epiphany and repulsed the enemy. Attalos I, conqueror of the Gauls at the Kaikos springs, built his stoa not without reason in the neighbourhood of the father of the eponymous hero of Pergamon.

The local heroes of Mysia, as well as the eponymous hero Pergamos, in comparison to the founding legends and founding heroes of the famous old Greek cities, were rather pale figures. However the emphasis placed on the Mysian heroes by the Attalid kings, which took the mythological names of a whole area as the basis of civic identity, made possible the revaluation of the Pergamene past with the help of a really prominent hero-figure of Greek myth: Telephos. He had already entered the scene in the epic cycle – as a successful protector of his homeland from Greek intruders, even the equal of Achilles as a warrior. Attic tragedy, and above all the drama *Telephos* of Euripides, had conclusively moved the fate of this hero into the best-known group of mythological material. At least since Sophocles' play *The Aleades* it was also clear that the Mysian king Telephos was actually a Greek by birth: a son of Herakles, the greatest Greek hero, and Auge, a princess of Tegea (Scheer 1993: 71ff.).

The first definite evidence for the appropriation of Telephos by the Attalids and simultaneously the acceptance of this mythological ancestry by the Hellenistic present comes from the year 209: the inhabitants of Aigina donated a statue of Telephos to Attalos I for a joint temple with the island's hero Aiakos (Allen 1971; Scheer 1993: 127–8). The reason given for this on the inscription was: Attalos was related to Aiakos through his descent from Herakles (i.e. through Telephos). That the city of Pergamon had played no role in the whole previous tradition of the legend of Telephos clearly did not disturb anyone: the city (or sometimes also the surrounding area), in which Telephos is traditionally said to have been king, was always called Teuthrania in the sources. A small place of this name still existed in the Hellenistic period – but it was not identical with the Hellenistic metropolis Pergamon. But if Pergamon had, in the meantime, proclaimed the heroes of Mysia to be its own in the most important sanctuaries of the Greek world, so Telephos, king of Teuthrania, could also in this way become an ancestor of the Pergamenes and of their royal family. That the ancestry of Telephos did not, indeed, just relate to the royal family of Pergamon is shown by the existence of a civic tribal group called Telephis in the late Attalid period. With Telephos as their ancestor the rulers of Pergamon had completed the historical connection to a past worthy of the new importance of their city. Appropriately the hero's adventures found their place on the Telephos frieze of the Pergamon altar (Bauchhenß Thüriedl 1971; Schalles 1986; Dreyfus and Schraudolph 1996). The comparison between this pictorial representation of the myth and the written records shows a careful selection or adaptation of the mythological versions in circulation. Already on the larger frieze of the altar Telephos' father Herakles appears in a central position. The smaller Telephos frieze highlights and gives especial importance to specific elements in the story of Telephos: for instance when the infant hero was exposed he was not, as he was still in Sophocles, suckled by a hind but by a much more royal beast – by a lioness. In addition the Pergamenes placed particular emphasis on their hero's Greek origin. Other versions of the Telephos myth told that the child Telephos, along with his mother Auge, was put out to sea in a chest and came to the Mysian coast from Arkadia via Nauplia. The native king Teuthras married Auge and brought Telephos up as his son (Strabo 13.1.69). The Telephos frieze tells a different story: after Telephos had been brought up in Greece, he came as an adult at the head of a troop of Greek soldiers – potential founders of cities – to Mysia. An adult son in search of his mother Auge, the Tegean priestess of Athena, obviously corresponded more closely to the ideal of the Pergamene clients than the infant thrown on the mercy of non-Greeks.

Telephos as ancestral hero guaranteed the city of Pergamon, especially through his father Herakles, a connection with the Greek cities of the Hellenistic present – and, once more, with Alexander the Great. Even the origin of Telephos in the Arkadian city of Tegea – a rather insignificant place in Hellenistic times – could be useful in the matter of prestigious family connections: the Arkadians were regarded as one of the most ancient peoples in Greece – as ancient as the moon (Dem. 19.261). The antiquity of Pergamene cults could also be reinforced through the Tegean connection: Telephos' mother Auge was supposed to have brought the statue of the Tegean Athena Alea with her to Pergamon (*I.Perg.* 156). And the myth of Telephos was also highly suitable for a Hellenistic dynasty: the founding hero was numbered among the Homeric kings and could trace his ancestry back to Zeus, the king of the gods. Telephos, son of Herakles and grandson of Zeus, had successfully defended his homeland Mysia against enemies from outside: his descendants, the kings of Pergamon, produced the proof that his blood still flowed in their veins not least by similar heroic deeds, such as their victory over the Galatians, barbarians who scorned the gods. Interesting in their treatment of their supposed civic history is the way the kings of Pergamon linked up to 'local' traditions. It is superfluous to give as the reason for the choice of the Telephos legend the need to turn to authentic local figures of the remote past (e.g. Sayce 1925; Barnett 1956; against such interpretative approaches, Ünal 1991). Whether the Pergamenes knew of the existence of a Hittite mythical figure called Telipinus is more than doubtful. They linked onto a local tradition rather through the form set in advance by the Homeric epics: for Greek-speaking people Mysia was above all the scene of epic events connected with the Trojan War. Every authentic memory was hopelessly inferior to this tradition. Even if the recent past of Pergamon in the Hellenistic period was fabricated, nevertheless it must be accepted that structurally any number of well-known mythical narratives of the Greeks could have been considered suitable and appropriated accordingly. The Pergamenes did not, however, make arbitrary use of anything from the pool of stories available.

A certain plausibility was required in the founding legend: it ought to permit an inherently logical integration of one's own city into the mythical-historical system of coordinates that helped make up the Greek world picture. This was best achieved by recourse to pseudo-local tradition: by linking in to the picture of the landscape of Mysia drawn by epic. At this point the question of the reception of the Pergamene 'past' and its success is posed: did Telephos, as progenitor of the Pergamenes, get only an ironic smile in Greek cities and Hellenistic empires? Clear signs indicate acceptance of the newly arranged Pergamene past. The people of Aigina were hardly pleased about the new Pergamene rule in the year 209. Nevertheless, they erected a statue to Attalos with explicit reference to his relationship with them. This made it possible for them to save face at least outwardly. One could also understand the reference to their mutual forebear as an appeal to the new rulers to behave towards Aigina according to the rules of family dealings.

That the ancestry claim of the Pergamenes also found sympathetic listeners on the Greek mainland is shown by the reaction of the city of Tegea, the mythical birthplace of Auge and Telephos. Instead of jealously claiming the hero for their own history and rejecting the claim of the Pergamenes as that of a usurper, Tegean envoys set off straightaway for Pergamon with acclamations of approval. Tegea offered the Pergamenes mutual citizen rights (*I.Perg.* 156). The mutual conferring of civic rights on account of the family connection with Telephos lent Pergamon's model of its past official recognition and confirmation. That the Pergamenes clearly gave the embassy from Tegea a friendly reception is not surprising. The motives of the Tegeans are surely to be sought both in the ideal and in the concrete sphere. Concrete was the hope that the Attalids would prove themselves as generous in the Arkadian town as they had been in numerous other cities on the Greek mainland. In the ideal sphere a specifically Hellenistic development revealed itself: Tegea was indeed a famous old city, but, as a medium-sized member of the Achaian League, it was a political lightweight. As in Pergamon, there was a certain imbalance between the current importance of the city and the past, to which they referred – but in the opposite direction. Here a possibility began to emerge of balancing this out. If the Athena of Pergamon was a daughter cult of Tegea, this dependence raised the prestige of the Tegean cult to a considerable degree. What applied to the sphere of the cult also applied to the prestige of Tegea as a whole. To be the mother city of a Hellenistic royal capital and to possess a rich, famous and influential daughter city certainly gave the Tegeans a considerable increase in self-confidence in relation to their neighbouring cities and allies in the Achaian League.

The emphasis on ancient family relationships was, however, not just the result of ephemeral political constellations and short-term opportunistic hopes. As the political relationships between the members of the Achaian League, to which Tegea belonged, and Pergamon grew worse after 175, the Arkadian Telephos still continued to be highly thought of in Pergamon. The reasons for this are indeed obvious (in spite of the occasional astonishment of modern scholars, Kertész 1982: 210; Bastini 1987: 129; Schindler 1988: 154): Telephos was important for the Pergamenes not because they wanted to curry favour with the Achaian League, nor even because they wanted to take advantage of the civic rights of Tegea. Rather the mythical forefather Telephos gave the Pergamene dynasty, in competition with the other Hellenistic dynasties and empires, the chance to mark out its own place. The Pergamenes did not seek to preserve the balance between past and present through short-lived political involvements but through participation in the complex network of myth that spread across the Greek world.

5   The Greek Past for Cilician Cities: the Race for Argos

Not only Hellenistic royal families, who wanted to claim a distinguished past as their own, sought a connection to prominent heroes. In the Hellenistic period a large number of cities suddenly began to emphasize their hitherto unknown Greek past with the presentation of mythical founders. The settlements on the Cilician plain in southern Asia Minor offer an example of this. The case of Tarsos has already been mentioned at the beginning of this chapter; it claimed, among other things, to have been founded by the Argives as they wandered around together with Triptolemos in search of Io.

Up to this time Cilicia was far from being a centre of Greek civilization. In contrast to Pergamon its cities were not situated in the neighbourhood of ancient Greek cities rich in tradition. The Cilicians were hardly touched by the Greek colonization of the eighth century and until the fourth century they were under Persian control. From the perspective of a Greek from the motherland the region was absolutely marginal. It was inhabited by people who could not even speak proper Greek: the expression '*soloikizein*' for someone with a strange and uncultivated accent was connected with the Cilician city of Soloi (Strabo 14.2.28).

In the Hellenistic period a past was in great demand not only in Cilicia itself but also along the whole south coast of Asia Minor: from Pamphylia to Syria they all now suddenly remembered their own civic history (Strubbe 1984; Weiß 1984). The focal points of this memory are sometimes suspiciously similar. From Aspendos in Pamphylia, Soloi, Mallos, Tarsos and Aigeai in Cilicia as far as the new Hellenistic capital of Antioch in Syria, a common claim united them: they (along with a whole number of further candidates) were related to the Greek city of Argos.

Practically everything speaks against the legitimacy of such claims. According to our standards they are not historically correct (Scheer 1993: 337ff.). The city of Argos did not feature prominently during the great Greek colonization. At best Rhodian sailors and merchants had established occasional trading posts in prehellenistic times. Soloi, for instance, could have been such a trading post. The Cilician cities' claim to a past did not, however, refer to the times of archaic colonization, as the Tarsian foundation legend already makes clear. It reached further back, into mythical prehistory, when gods and heroes were acting in person as city founders. While no records of any kind referring to figures from Greek mythology are preserved for Cilician cities from archaic and classical times, that changed during the Hellenistic period. Tarsos did not, indeed, claim to have been founded by anonymous Rhodian sailors but by the hero Triptolemos himself.

New Argives

But what made the Tarsians, and along with them numerous other cities in the region, think of Argos of all places as their mother city? This fact is an important indicator of the shaping of historical thought by mythological categories in the

Hellenistic period. Argos possessed in the ancient world a considerable and very special mythological prestige. Throughout the whole of ancient history it was regarded as the homeland of famous mythological kings and in Attic tragedy it became the homeland of Agamemnon. Since Homer the Argives were also famous as descendants of Herakles. Other important states in Greece, such as Rhodes and Kos, had for a long time proudly traced their ancestry back to the Argos of Herakles (Hom. *Il.* 2.662; Strabo 14.2.6). The genealogical connection of Argos with Alexander, who for his own part had stressed his descent from gods and heroes, was not only of interest to the new rulers of Hellenistic empires but also to individual cities. The high standing of Argos lasted until Roman imperial times. The Emperor Claudius was still describing the citizens of Kos as Argives (Tac. *Ann.* 12.61). If a hierarchy of the most distinguished cities were to be drawn up, educated people like Dion of Prusa were of the opinion that Sparta, Athens and Argos were the first cities of Greece (Dio Chrys. 44.6).

The reference to Argives offered even further opportunities: the Homeric epics had created an ambiguity in the term 'Argive'. Argives and Achaians were used there to mean the same: when someone spoke of Argives they might mean the residents of the city of Argos or the entire gathering of Greek heroes at Troy. Understood in such a way, 'to be an Argive' signified a connection with the Homeric epics and brought those so designated universal respect in the Greek world as genuine Greeks. The cities of the south coast of Asia Minor referred in this context especially to the many versions of the narratives about the homecoming of the Greeks after the fall of Troy. Amongst these were, for instance, the tradition of the Greek seer Kalchas, who foresaw the shipwreck of the fleet and therefore refused to go on board ship. He went along the coast of Asia Minor towards the south with other heroes (Scheer 1993: 153ff.). According to some versions he died in Klaros, in a competition with another seer, Mopsos (Strabo 14.1.27 = Hesiod fr. 278MW). Other sources make Kalchas travel further with his fellow seers Mopsos and Amphilochos, along with other heroes, to Pamphylia, Cilicia and Syria (Hagias in Proklos, Davies *EGF*: 67; Hdt. 7.91). According to popular mythological genealogy none of those involved, with the exception of Amphilochos, actually came from Argos. The vagueness of the term 'Argive' allowed them all, however, to become kings of the Argives, 'reges Argivorum' (cf. Cic. *Div.* 1.88; Scheer 1993: 210–11).

Alexander and the Greek founding heroes of Cilicia

Why did the cities of Cilicia suddenly discover their mythical past in the Hellenistic period? Here again the campaigns of Alexander seem to represent the deciding factor. As the Macedonian army reached Cilicia the cities of the area experienced different treatment. The city of Soloi unambiguously supported the Persians. She was punished for this: she received a garrison and had to pay an indemnity of 200 talents. On the other hand Alexander behaved much more generously towards neighbouring Mallos: he sacrificed there to Amphilochos (Arr. *Anab.* 2.5). Whether there was a sanctuary to Amphilochos before that time is unknown: the oldest records mention Amphilochos rather in connection with the neighbouring city of Soloi. But for Alexander it was obviously possible without difficulty to offer the hero a public sacrifice in Mallos. Possibly *Interpretatio Graeca*, the habit of recognizing Greek mythical figures in foreign mythology, played a role here once more. Whomsoever Alexander had identified as Amphilochos, the residents of Mallos had every reason from then on to commemorate Amphilochos and did this in the form of a complicated foundation legend (Strabo 14.5.16). The discovery of the hero Amphilochos by Alexander gained for the Mallians exemption from the taxes they had previously had to pay to the Persians. According to Arrian, Alexander had expressly given as the reason for his kindness to Mallos the argument that the Mallians were colonists from Argos. Amphilochos, as the son of Amphiaraos, originally came from there according to mythical genealogy. And the same passage states that Alexander had counted himself among the Heraklids from Argos (Arr. *Anab.* 2.5.9). Even though Alexander, after battles in the surrounding territory, in the end also sacrificed to Asklepios of Soloi and held magnificent games there, still the emphasis on the old family connection and the prestige attached to it remained limited to Mallos. The historical circumstances of the founding of Mallos must have been just as unfamiliar to the Macedonians as those of Soloi. According to archaeological evidence Soloi, which possibly had at one time been an *emporion* of Rhodian sailors, perhaps actually had a greater right to boast of its Greek ancestry. However it clearly did not depend on the real past: in comparison the mythical-heroic version of the past carried much more weight than the reality. The preferential treatment of Mallos by Alexander clearly brought local consequences with it. Mythological ambition was now awoken also in Soloi, which sought proof of its own mythological relationships: apparently embassies went directly to Argos and claimed the Argive seer Amphilochos for Soloi. They were successful, since privileges for the Solians in the Argive people's assembly are attested by inscriptions from the end of the fourth century onwards (Stroud 1984). And Argos was not the only place that the Solians approached. The far-reaching echo of the Solian claim to ancient Greekness in the Hellenistic period is also reflected in Polybios (21.24.4): in the disputes with Rome the Rhodians gave support to Soloi – with the argument that they were both related and both came originally from Argos. The Solians had emphasized the connection with Rhodes through inscribed votive offerings to the temple of Athena Lindia (*FGrH* 532.33).

The sudden proliferation of foundation myths that followed the Macedonian conquest indicates how places, which had previously been peripheral, were now trying to shape their conception of the world according to Greek categories. In this attempt however they did not proceed in a purely arbitrary manner. For one thing the link to Homeric epic again came into play. Over and above that, the presence of heroic seers in Cilicia cannot have been a coincidence. For centuries the ancient Kizzuwatna of the Hittites had been a region of particularly sacral character, in which purification and atonement rituals played an important role (Burkert 1983; Scheer 1993: 266ff.).

If settlements like Mallos and Soloi had gained prestige through stressing their alleged Greekness, which was rooted in the heroic past, clearly the important city of Tarsos could not be left behind in this matter. When Xenophon went through Cilicia in the early fourth century on the occasion of the Anabasis, he had – contrary to his usual practice – nothing to say about Greeks resident there. Before the campaigns of Alexander, Tarsos was apparently not recognized as a veiled Greek city. Nothing is known about Alexander's reaction to the cults of Tarsos. In contrast to neighbouring Soloi, there is no direct epigraphic evidence that Tarsos sent embassies to the Greek motherland to seek confirmation of a prestigious foundation legend. Nevertheless it is clear, not just from Strabo, but also from later sources, that the Tarsians wanted to be Argives (Dio Chrys. 33.41). While Soloi and Mallos put the main emphasis regarding their past on Greek seers who came from Troy, the Tarsians accentuated their past in a different way: among other things they claimed to be descendants of Triptolemos and the Argives who accompanied him in search of Io. If the city possessed Argive founders, then it was also connected to Herakles and Alexander.

And at this point we come back to the questions posed at the beginning of this chapter: what had Triptolemos to do with Argos in the mythological tradition of the Greeks? What connected him to Io? Why do we hear now of an organized search for the Argive woman who, according to earlier sources, was driven across the world in the shape of a cow by a gadfly? In the classical versions of the Triptolemos myth Argos was not even mentioned. Strabo is the earliest evidence for this. The hero Triptolemos, who had brought the world the Eleusinian Mysteries and the art of agriculture, was from earliest times an Attic national hero. The Argive claim to Triptolemos appears first in Pausanias: even before he went to Athens, he is said to have established mysteries in Argos (Paus. 1.14.2). The search for Io is also first verified in the Hellenistic period. Here it seems to involve a 'further thinking out of the myth' by Hellenistic scholars: the similarity in this case with another better known story is only too clear – with the search for another of Zeus' loves, Europa (Hdt. 4.147; Davison 1991: 54; Scheer 1993: 276ff.). Just as Europa's father had sent out her brothers at the head of a band of men with instructions to bring their sister home again and with the condition that they were not to return home without her, so now a group of Argives with a well-known leader went in search of the missing princess of Argos. Whether a relationship between Triptolemos and Io was postulated does not emerge from the sources but would not be surprising. It was also said of the unsuccessful pursuers of Europa that they had founded cities in faraway places, since a return home without the missing princess was denied them.

Where this version of the myth of Triptolemos and Io originated can only be conjectured: the forced linking of Triptolemos with Argos in another context, too, would point to the involvement of Argos itself. There are probably several reasons why the city of Tarsos thought up such an uncanonical foundation legend: like the neighbouring cities it sought a connection with the Argives and therefore a kinship with Alexander. For the realization of this claim the best contenders in Greek mythology were the migrant hero Triptolemos and Io who is said to have gone to Egypt through Asia Minor driven by the anger of Hera: in this way the Tarsian claim could be fitted to some extent logically into the Greek traditions.

In addition, however, the local traditions of the Cilician hinterland may have inspired this Tarsian foundation legend: from the fifth century onward coins of Tarsos already bore an ear of corn (*BMC* Cilicia 1900: 164 no. 11; table 28, 12). The Cilician plain was already famous for its fertility and for its abundance of corn under the Assyrians and Persians. The native god Baal Tarz was, after all, represented with ears of corn and bunches of grapes in his hands (Chuvin 1981: 314). To recognize the Greek bringer of corn in him was natural.

But it was not only the link to Argive traditions, conferring equal status with other Cilician cities, that Triptolemos made possible. The corn-bringer was also very popular in the Seleukid heartland of the Syrian Tetrapolis, which bordered on Cilicia to the north east. Seleukos Nikator settled descendants of Triptolemos in Antioch (Strabo 16.2.5). Much later Libanios took up the tradition: Triptolemos is supposed to have finally settled in Antioch (Lib. 11.51–2). The city of Antioch even pointed to the grave of Io, while Tarsos had to be satisfied with being founded by anonymous Argive companions of Triptolemos. Even in later times they apparently did not possess a *heroon* of a prominent founder. To be connected to an important royal capital like Antioch could not do the Tarsians any harm.

Barbarian relations? The Argives on the Panhellenic stage

The ambition of Cilician cities to find a familial connection with the most famous cities and the most ancient traditions of Greek myth, therefore, need not cause surprise. But how was this noble ancestry, the frequently attested aristocratic lineage (*eugeneia*) of the proud city of Argos, compatible with cities of highly questionable Greekness, which were suddenly knocking on the gates and wishing to be recognized as relatives of long standing?

That the Argives wanted to make their glorious past productive in the Hellenistic present is demonstrated by the cultivation of their relationship to the Macedonian kings long after Alexander (Livy 32.22.11). The delegations from the fringes of the ancient Greek world also benefited from this attitude. They were clearly by no means turned away with disdain nor fobbed off as discreetly as possible – quite the contrary. The Argives bragged about their 'ancient' connections in the Eastern Mediterranean. This is shown for instance by an Argive decree from the end of the fourth century (Stroud 1984). The Argives not only granted citizen rights to the people of Aspendos, a Pamphylian city with a not too well-established Greek past (Scheer 1993: 203ff.), but they expressly pointed out that the Rhodians and the Cilician Solians already enjoyed the same privileges as kin. Three copies of the inscription were set up in prominent places: in the civic sanctuary of Apollo Lykeios, in the Argive Heraion and finally in the panhellenic temple precinct of Zeus of Nemea, a sign of the value that was placed on the publicizing of these familial connections.

Kinship with cities of questionable Greekness in Pamphylia and Cilicia was, therefore, no longer something to conceal with shame. The behaviour of Argos is particularly instructive here, as Pausanias certified that the Argives were filled with particular pride on account of their glorious past and in this respect were in constant competition with the Athenians: 'among the Greeks the ones who compete most of all with the Athenians with regard to their antiquity and the gifts which they claim to have received from the gods are the Argives' (1.14.2).

So the changes in the Greek world picture reveal themselves not only in the dealings of the famous old Greek cities with Hellenistic kings. The city-states of the Greek motherland had lost political influence compared with the new territorial states of Alexander and his Hellenistic successors. Power and wealth were no longer concentrated in Greece itself, the centres had shifted eastwards. Pamphylia, Cilicia and Syria along with the new Seleukid capital of Antioch were no longer peripheral areas, inhabited by semi-barbarians, whose strange dialects were a cause of merriment. Instead they were prosperous areas in the immediate shadow of royal power, and it was worthwhile even for venerable cities like Argos to be bound to them by family ties.

The expansion of the world in the Hellenistic present resulted in a re-ordering of the past. The tendency of the Hellenistic period towards the systematizing of a world whose current upheavals no doubt seemed ominous to many revealed itself also in the systematizing of the past. The traditional tales of the Greeks proved themselves once more to offer constructive possibilities. Myth had never been a canonical text in the sacred sense. It was open to new combinations and new emphases: it could be logically 'thought out further'. And so the inclusion of the new structures of the present was successful, since their roots could be discovered in the past. And the hitherto marginal regions, addressed in the language of myth, responded swiftly. As participants in myth numerous cities – from Tarsos to Pergamon – achieved integration in the new political systems, which were dominated by Greeks. Their integration occurred on the basis of familial connections with the retention of local features. The broadening of the mythic system of co-ordinates helped the inhabitants of cities with an ancient Greek tradition, from Argos to Tegea, to come to terms with the Hellenistic present – by looking back to the mythical past.

FURTHER READING

The diverse approaches of research and interpretation on the theme of Greek Mythology are outlined, for instance, in Bremmer 1987, Edmunds 1990, Dowden 1992. Gehrke 1994 analyses the relationship of myth and history, cf. also the collection of essays, Pozzi and Wickersham 1991. To be recommended on the disputed question about the possibility of a historical core in Greek mythology is Patzek 1992 with its focus on Homer and Mycenae. Scheer 1993 offers a detailed examination of the role of mythical founders in Greek cities. Musti 1963, Curty 1995, C. Jones 1999b and Erskine 2001 discuss the use of myth in inter-state kinship. For the imposition of Greek mythology on non-Greeks, Bickerman 1952. For further reading on Pergamon, Kosmetatou, this volume; on Telephos, Stewart 1996b; on the hero Pergamos, Kosmetatou 1995. Isager 1998 and Lloyd-Jones 1999 publish an important recent inscription from Halikarnassos which gives a sense of the place of local tradition within a community.

CHAPTER FOURTEEN

Space and Geography

Klaus Geus

Alexander the Great in his youth had Aristotle as his tutor, a circumstance that has led to excited speculation among scholars. What knowledge and insight might Aristotle have imparted to his pupil? The ancient sources do not supply us with unequivocal information, they even cast doubt on the assumption that both were on good terms. Nevertheless it is not unreasonable to suppose that in the course of the three years during which Aristotle tutored Alexander the subject of geography came up for discussion. In some cases it is even possible to demonstrate that Alexander proceeded with his campaigns on the basis of geographical conceptions which are mentioned in the works of Aristotle (Schachermeyr 1973: 87–9). I will also try to argue that some of the methods and arguments used by Alexander to assess and explain new discoveries can be traced back to his teacher.

1 The World Before Alexander

In the generation of Aristotle a new scientific conviction became increasingly popular among Greek scholars: that the earth was not a flat disc but a sphere. This theory had implications for the way in which people thought about the earth's surface. Longstanding questions about the distribution of water and land mass as well as the geographical position of the continents were being asked afresh, especially by scholars belonging to the school of Aristotle, such as Dikaiarchos and Straton (Geus 2000a: 84–6).

Aristotle believed that in comparison with other stars the earth was not large. He noted that 'the mathematicians' who tried to determine its circumference put it at 400,000 stades (*Cael.* 2.14, 298a); although he does not say who they were, it is possible that Eudoxos of Knidos was one of those he had in mind. How these 'mathematicians' reached this conclusion is not known, but their method need not have been mathematical or astronomical. It would be more than a century before Eratosthenes came up with such a technique for calculating the circumference. Presumably, they worked with information gathered from descriptions of journeys by sea (*periploi*) and by land (*itineraria*) and then estimated any distances that were still unknown (cf. Arist. *Mete.* 2.5, 362b).

Aristotle also produced a model to map the surface of the earth. Possibly following Parmenides, he divided the earth into zones which extended round the globe in broad strips. The earth consisted of five zones, two habitable and three uninhabitable. The Greeks lived in the zone 'towards the upper pole', which was bounded by the Arctic Circle in the north and the Tropic of the Cancer in the south. Another habitable zone existed towards the south pole. This latter hypothesis was revolutionary, as it led inevitably to the conclusion that unknown peoples may live either in the southern hemisphere ('antipodes') or at the rear of the northern zone ('perioikoi'). The old conviction that the Greeks were at the centre of the world had started to break down.

After discovering that the region in which we live is only a part of the earth's surface, the Greeks needed a new term to distinguish the known parts of the world from the unknown parts of the world: *oikoumene*, i.e. the 'inhabited (earth)'. The earlier maps based on the out-dated flat-earth theory had to be changed. Around 500 Hekataios of Miletos had still drawn a circular map. Now the *oikoumene* was superimposed on these circular maps in the form of a rectangle.

In the decades that followed, geographers argued about the extent of the *oikoumene* and its appearance. Demokritos proposed a ratio of 3:2 for the relationship between the *oikoumene*'s length (from west to east) and its breadth (from north to south); Eudoxos preferred 2:1; Dikaiarchos chose 3:2, and according to Eratosthenes, who called the *oikoumene* '*chlamys*-shaped' (Zimmermann 2002), it was 'more than 2:1'. Aristotle estimated by means of *periploi* and *itineraria* that the ratio was 'more than 5:3' (*Mete.* 2.5, 362b). The edges of the *oikoumene* were terminated by distant countries or geographical cornerstones: Lake Maeotis and Scythia were in the north, India in the east, Ethiopia in the south and the Pillars of Herakles in the west. According to the hellenocentric view the – geographically speaking – central position of Greece had endowed the Greeks with the good qualities of the northern and southern peoples. From this circumstance Aristotle could derive a legitimate claim to Greek supremacy (*Pol.* 7.7, 1327b20–33).

Further arguments were put forward. Several scholars imagined the region around the Pillars of Herakles as joined to India and in support of their contention they offered the fact that elephants were to be found at the extremities of both lands, a suggestion that Aristotle considered to be 'not utterly incredible' (*Cael.* 2.14, 298a). It is interesting to see here how a (rather vague) zoological observation could lend credibility to a geographical hypothesis – or rather had to, since the Greeks of that time lacked more advanced means for determining the latitude and especially the longitude of an observer. As a result, it was the standard procedure of the philosophers of that time, who thought all things to be interconnected, to draw upon information from different scientific disciplines and to arrive at far-reaching conclusions.

This new model of the world, developed by philosophers and geographers, was also adopted by laymen, albeit in a more primitive form. Strabo, our main source for hellenistic geography, and the Christian monk Kosmas Indikopleustes both report how the fourth-century historian Ephoros made use of a rectangular map (Strabo 1.2.28; Cosm. *Christian Topography* 2: 148). In the fourth book of his *Histories* Ephoros sketched out the *oikoumene* in the form of a parallelogram (where the south is on the upper side).

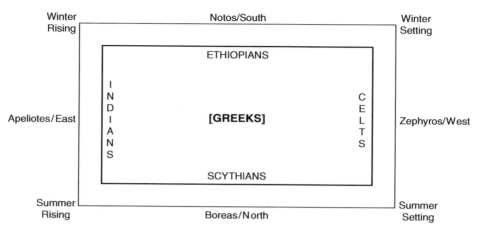

Figure 14.1   The Parallelogram of Ephoros

Ephoros equated each side and angle of the parallelogram with 'compass points' expressed in terms of winds and with astronomical points, i.e. where the sun rises and sets on the day of the summer and winter solstice. Each side is also bounded by one of the outlying peoples. While the Scythians are in the north and the Celts in the west, the Ethiopians are situated along the south and the Indians along the east (figure 14.1). The northern and southern lines are said to be longer than the eastern and western which underlines the fact that the relative horizon, marked by certain fixed points, is terminated by a Greek observer (Heidel 1937: 16–18).

Thus, the model of Ephoros was based on the old conception that Greece, or rather the Greeks, were located at the centre of the *oikoumene*. It is still influenced by the tradition of the old Ionian circular maps. Like his predecessor Hippokrates, Ephoros followed the principle of dividing up the edges of the *oikoumene* among the main peoples according to the horizon of a Greek observer. Furthermore, the influence of the ethnological tradition on geography is clearly visible. At the centre of this ethnological view of the earth, that is to say in Greece, there is normalcy (order and civilization), whereas as one moves towards the outer rim conditions grow increasingly archaic and primeval. The Greek ethnographer had no second thoughts about populating the periphery of the *oikoumene* with fantastic peoples and creatures. Blissful barbarians, such as the Hyperboreans, Scythians and Ethiopians, lived in the north and south. Fantastic lands stretched out to the west and east: the garden of the Hesperides and Erytheia lay in the west, India over to the east and Amazonia to the north-east (Romm 1992). The further the distance from the centre, the less accurate the information Greeks had at their disposal. Later, the Hellenistic authors of utopian literature were to fall back on just such a model. Unlike Aristotle, whose more abstract and more scientifically advanced theory uses distant yet known countries and geographical cornerstones as boundaries, Ephoros seems to owe much to this ethnological model when he states that the *oikoumene* is bounded by certain peculiar peoples. This way of thinking was not without influence on the first Greeks to visit these lands. For example, when Alexander's Macedonians heard about armed female

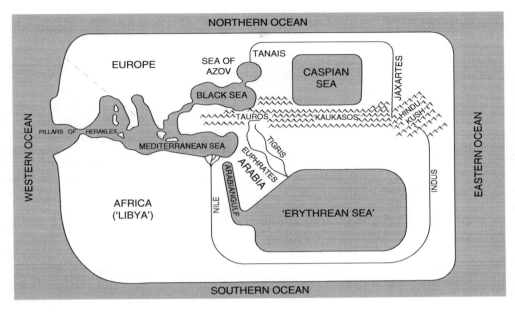

Figure 14.2 The world before Alexander

warriors living in the vicinity of Chorasmia, they were quick to identify them with the Amazons of legend (Arr. *Anab.* 4.15.4).

It is safe to say, therefore, that in the time of Aristotle common knowledge about the *oikoumene* was by no means uniform (figure 14.2). The coasts of the Mediterranean Sea had been explored extensively, but until the late fourth century when Pytheas of Massalia ventured out into the Atlantic Ocean the Greeks would have been unable to form an accurate picture of northwestern Europe. As for the northeast, Aristotle was better, if not always correctly, informed. He held that the border between Europe and Asia was formed by the Black Sea, the Caucasian Isthmus and the Caspian Sea. Unlike Hekataios of Miletos he did not consider the Caspian Sea to be a gulf of the northern Ocean and instead favoured Herodotos' idea that it was an inland sea, but he mistakenly assumed that a distinction needed to be made between the Caspian Sea and the Hyrkanian Sea (Arist. *Mete.* 2.1, 354a; cf. Plut. *Alex.* 44, 2; for a different view, Tarn 1948: II.5–6).

Knowledge about Eastern Asia had not improved since the era of the Achaimenid Great Kings Darius I (522–486) and Xerxes (486–465). The whole Iranian plateau region from Armenia to the Hindu Kush went by the name of 'Kaukasos'. According to Greek tradition the Indians inhabited the eastern part of the *oikoumene*. Aristotle believed the eastern Ocean to be very close, 'within view when one has crossed the Hindu Kush' (*Mete.* 1.13, 350a). His geographical and biological information about India was derived from the notoriously unreliable account of Ktesias, the Greek doctor who had served at the court of Artaxerxes II (Bosworth 1993's preference for 'standard gazetteers', *periodoi*, such as written by Eudoxos of Knidos, fails to convince).

The Greeks knew even less about the south-east of the *oikoumene*. The fifth-century geographer, Damastes of Sigeion, for example, had described the Arabian Gulf as an inland lake (*FGrH* 5 F8 = Strabo 1.3.1). Some Greeks, therefore, gathered vaguely that the Arabian Gulf and the Persian Gulf were joined in the south and called these two seas by a single name, the 'Erythrean Sea'. It was, however, subject to debate whether this southern 'Okeanos' was an inland sea bounded by a land bridge that connected Africa with India or was actually part of the 'Okeanos' which surrounded the western, southern, eastern and maybe even the northern (disputed by Herodotos) outskirts of the *oikoumene*. Aristotle tried to reconcile both assumptions and maintained 'that the Erythrean Sea communicates with the Ocean outside the straits by only a narrow channel' (*Mete.* 2.1, 354a; for an alternative view, Scylax 112 = *GGM* I.95; cf. H. Berger 1903: 316–17, n. 3). In consequence Aristotle pictured the Erythrean Sea as a relatively small inland sea.

Information about Libya (Africa) had been lost since Pharaonic and Persian times. During the reign of Pharaoh Necho II (610–594) Phoenician seamen had already sailed around Africa (Hdt. 4.42.2–4), but their account was doubted in Hellenistic times (Poseidonios in Strabo 2.2.4; cf. Polyb. 3.38.1–3) despite the fact that there had been other enterprises of that kind, such as those by Hanno, Sataspes and Magos. The narrative of Skylax of Karyanda, who sailed from the Upper Indus to Suez in the time of Darius I, was also met with disbelief (Högemann 1985: 65, n. 19). Ephoros' discussion of the location of Kerne, an island off the Atlantic coast of Africa, may serve as an example to illustrate how knowledge about southern Africa had declined in the period shortly before Alexander: 'Ephoros states that vessels approaching Kerne from the Red Sea (Erythrean Sea) are unable to advance beyond the Columns – that being the name of certain islands – because of the heat' (Pliny *HN* 6.199). Thus, Ephoros argued that the hot zone above the equator prevented mariners from sailing to the southern parts of Africa and around to its Atlantic coast. Obviously he had in mind the Aristotelian model of the five zones in which the zone between the tropics was considered uninhabitable owing to the heat. In this way theory dominated and ousted first-hand knowledge.

This, then, was the kind of information Alexander would have had at his disposal when he hurled his spear onto Asian soil at the Hellespont in May of 334. Insights into the outlying regions of the *oikoumene* had been lost, and Alexander's knowledge of Asia would have been especially deficient. As ruling Asia appears to have been Alexander's goal from the very start, he must have imagined Asia to be substantially smaller than it actually was. We must ask, therefore, to what extent the Greek image of the world was changed by Alexander's campaigns.

2 Alexander's Campaigns

The first stage of Alexander's campaign up until the capture of the Persian capitals of Babylon, Susa and Persepolis did not pose any major geographical problems. The Greeks had long been familiar with the expanse of land that lay between the west coast of Asia Minor and Mesopotamia. Alexander could even fall back on an account in Xenophon's *Anabasis*, when in the spring of 333 he marched his troops from the ancient Phrygian capital city of Gordion in Cilicia across the Tauros, a vast mountain range between the Mediterranean Sea and the Anatolian mainland. The route to

Egypt along the coast of the Mediterranean Sea was also well-known. Once Alexander had reached Egypt, the mystery of the Nile is said to have prompted him to send out a scientific expedition in search of its source (Lucan 10.272–5; cf. Phot. *Bibl.* cod. 2489: 441b).

However, after Alexander had captured the Persian capitals and had begun his pursuit of the Great King Darius and later Bessos into the east, he was moving into unfamiliar territory. Although he had been declared 'king of Asia' on the battlefield of Gaugamela in 331, his knowledge of the eastern part of his realm, the so-called 'Upper Satrapies', was vague at best. Starting with Ekbatana, the ancient capital of Media, the east was *terra incognita* to the Greeks. This marked a turning-point. The campaign of retaliation had now reached its conclusion and what followed was in part at least a voyage of exploration. The change in the character of the campaign is evident in Alexander's treatment of his Greek allies; officially dismissed, they are allowed to continue as mercenaries. Alexander thus not only conquered the eastern regions, he also explored them. For that purpose he had at his disposal a group of specialists called 'bematists', whose duty it was to measure and calculate distances covered by the main body of the army as well as by special detachments. In addition to this they also recorded their observations on the native population, flora, fauna and other matters of interest in the territory through which they passed (Bretzl 1903: 3; Berve 1926: I.51). Alexander himself scrutinized 'the description of the whole country prepared for him by those best acquainted with it' (Strabo 2.1.6).

Giving chase to Darius, Alexander crossed the Elburz Range and reached the south coast of the Caspian Sea in 330. Whether this was an inland sea or rather a bay or a gulf belonging to the northern Ocean was a problem that had for a long time perplexed geographers, but for Alexander it was no mere academic question. If the Caspian Sea gave easy access to the Ocean, then possession of this coast would prove invaluable for future military campaigns. For the first time Alexander had to face the possibility that he had finally reached the Ocean, the end of the world. After some investigation, however, he concluded that the Caspian Sea was an inland sea which was 'not smaller than the Euxine' and stretched almost all the way to Lake Maeotis (Sea of Azov), or was a stagnant overflow from Lake Maeotis (Plut. *Alex.* 44.1–2; Curt. 6.4.18–19; Alexander also corrected the error of Aristotle, who had assumed that the Caspian Sea consisted of two distinct bodies of water). The Macedonian king based his conclusions on two observations: firstly, the water of the Caspian Sea was less salty than that of other seas, and, secondly, that it produced large serpents (Polykleitos in Strabo 11.7.4; cf. Diod. 17.75.3; Curt. 6.4.18). The fact that geographical conclusions were based on this sort of observation is reminiscent of a way of thinking found also in the works of Aristotle, who stated that the distance between Eastern India and the Pillars of Herakles was relatively small because there were elephants at the extremities of both lands.

The political situation forced Alexander to postpone his plans to explore the Caspian Sea (Arr. *Anab.* 7.16.1–2). To pursue the murderers of Darius Alexander had to invade the lands east of the Caspian Sea. Approaching from the south, he marched his army across the Hindu Kush into Baktria in the spring of 329. Aristotle had thought that the Hindu Kush (called by himself Parnassos, by others Paropamisos) was the extension of the Tauros mountains in Asia Minor and that it reached as far as the Ocean, thus forming the eastern end of the *oikoumene* (*Mete.* 1.13, 350a). Alexander's latest military expedition effectively disproved this, at the same time reviving but not resolving the question of the eastern Ocean. All, however, need have not been strictly scientific. Something of the character of this newly-acquired geographical knowledge is suggested by the Macedonian belief that here in this legendary mountain range they had found the cave of Prometheus (Arr. *Anab.* 5.3.2; *Ind.* 5.11).

While he was still pursuing Bessos, Alexander happened upon the Amu-Darya river; Ktesias and Aristotle had called this the Araxes river, but Alexander found out that it was actually named the Oxus. A rather confused Aristotle had also believed that the river Tanais, which flowed into the Sea of Azov and is today known as the Don, was a tributary of this Araxes river. It is safe to assume that it was this that led Alexander to believe the Tanais river was in the immediate vicinity. So, when he arrived at a second river, called Jaxartes by the natives, he was convinced that he had reached the upper course of the Tanais. In truth, Alexander had discovered the Syr-Darya river. Again, this misinterpretation was nurtured by botanical observation; for the country on the far side of the river was said to produce fir-trees, and since the Tanais was the traditional boundary between Europe and Asia and since such trees were believed to grow only in Europe and not in Asia, it was not difficult to imagine that this must indeed be the Tanais (Strabo 11.7.4; cf. Bretzl 1903: 220–6, 345–7). Accordingly, the far side of the river Jaxartes must be Europe again. Alexander, therefore, named the city which he founded on the Asian bank of the river Alexandria Eschate, the 'furthest Alexandria'. By the same reasoning, he named the nomads living across the Jaxartes 'European Scythians', and the nomads roaming the lands on his side of the river he called 'Asian Scythians'. The earlier idea that the Caspian Sea was an inland sea was now considered to be an established fact, as the Tanais could only circle it to the north. Clearly, Alexander had not received information concerning the Aral Sea, into which these two rivers, the Amu-Darya and the Syr-Darya, flowed (for a different view, Tarn 1948: II.5–13). As a result of these geographical errors Alexander would have for the first time been persuaded that he had reached the boundary of his Asian realm.

Ambassadors and prisoners confirmed the assumption of both Herodotos and Aristotle that there were extensive steppes north of the Caspian Sea. Earlier, Ionian geographers had believed this region of the *oikoumene* to be surrounded by the Ocean. However, since these tracts of land were regarded as parts of Europe proper, they did not figure significantly in Alexander's plans at the time. When Pharasmenes, the ruler of Chorasmia, invited Alexander to assist him in a campaign against the neighbouring Kolchians and Amazons, Alexander refused, a stance indicative of his more ambitious plans to conquer 'all of Asia'. As far as Alexander was concerned, 'all of Asia' meant especially India. Although he was to be embroiled in severe fighting in Baktria and Sogdiana for the next two years, he was already preparing an invasion of India along the valley of the Kabul river. One of his aims was to find the Indus, which was then considered to be the largest river in Asia, the Ganges not yet having been discovered.

The rather fabulous ideas about India entertained by Greeks at that time were mainly based on the writings of Skylax, Hekataios, Herodotos and Ktesias. Above all, it was Ktesias who had moulded the Greek sense of far eastern geography. He believed the sea near India to be no larger than the Aegean and it was probably he who was responsible for Aristotle's claim that on crossing the Hindu Kush one could see the Ocean (*Mete.* 1.13, 350a).

The general direction of the expedition shows that Alexander corrected the long-standing error made by Hekataios and Herodotos, both of whom thought that the Indus flowed eastwards and into the Ocean. They had confused the Indus with the Kabul river, and even Aristotle still placed the origin of the Indus in the Hindu Kush. Alexander, however, recognized the difference between the Kabul river and the Indus, calling the former Kophen. It remains uncertain whether this distinction was based on what he learned from the native population or rather on an earlier source of geographical information, such as Skylax.

After encountering fierce opposition, Alexander finally reached the Indus. When the Macedonians spotted crocodiles living in the region, they were immediately reminded of the Nile, which was also infested with crocodiles (Arr. *Anab.* 6.1.1). This gave renewed credibility to the old theory that the Nile and the Indus were connected (Arist. frag. 248 Rose; cf. Aesch. *Supp.* 284–6; [Aesch.] *PV* 807–15). In the course of the following weeks, this idea was supported by the repeated discovery of crocodiles in the Hydaspes (modern Jhelum), the next river that he came across. Furthermore, along the third river, the Akesines (modern Chenab), they discovered sacred lotus growing, a plant known to the Greeks as the 'Egyptian bean'. The thinking is well expressed by Arrian:

> Alexander had already seen crocodiles on the Indus, as on no other river except the Nile, and beans growing on the banks of the Akesines of the same sort as the land of Egypt produces and, having heard that the Akesines runs into the Indus, he thought he had found the origin of the Nile; his idea was the Nile rose somewhere thereabouts in India, flowed through a great expanse of desert, and there lost the name of Indus, and then, where it began to flow through inhabited country, got the name of Nile from the Ethiopians in those parts and the Egyptians... (*Anab.* 6.1.2–3; cf. Strabo 15.1.25; Arr. *Ind.* 6.8, adapted from E. Iliffe Robson)

Arrian and Strabo both say that it was Alexander himself who had made this discovery. Obviously, they, or rather their common source Nearchos, thought that Alexander personally drew the conclusion, and they may be right in that respect. For the third time we are told that a key problem in geography was solved by means of biological observation.

At this time Alexander believed that he was near the source of the river Nile. One might note that this particular view was also held by the Persians. Twenty years before Alexander's campaign Artaxerxes III had been planning to hold at bay the rebellious Egyptians by diverting the upper course of the Nile, here equated with the Indus ([Arist.] *De inundatione Nili*, F248 Rose: 193). Alexander may well have picked up the idea from the Persians in his entourage. Implicit in this odd geographical notion is a way of thinking about the world which sees the south as the mirror image of the north: just as the River Tanais, which was said to originate from a sizeable lake in the 'Kaukasos' mountains, circles the Caspian Sea to the north and finally flows into the Sea of Azov, that is to say the northern extension of the Mediterranean, so the Indus, likewise originating from the 'Kaukasos', circles the Erythrean Sea to the south and eventually empties its lower course, i.e. the Nile, into the Mediterranean (cf. figure 14.2). As a result of this geographical hypothesis, which was heavily influenced by the old Ionian mindset of symmetry already criticized by Herodotos a century earlier (4.36), Alexander pictured the Erythrean Sea as a (relatively) small inland sea and so was bound to seriously underestimate the dimensions of the southeastern (as well as the northern) *oikoumene*. For the people living at the time the world, rather strangely, appeared to be shrinking.

Without a doubt these ideas exerted a significant influence on Alexander's subsequent plans. We have credible evidence that after the victory over Poros near the Hydaspes river Alexander instructed his admiral Nearchos to construct a great fleet in order to sail back to Alexandria via the Nile, from its source to its estuary (Strabo 15.1.25; cf. Diod. 17.89.4–5; Curt. 9.1.3–4). Assenting to the views of Aristotle and thus believing himself to be near the eastern end of the *oikoumene*, he crossed the Hydraotes and proceeded to the Hyphasis river (modern Beas) before the construction of the fleet was complete. During his advance east, however, Alexander learnt from the Indian rulers Phegeus and Poros that the far bank of the Hyphasis was in fact not the eastern end of the *oikoumene*. On the contrary, he would find a vast expanse of desert which would take twelve days to cross and then he would be faced with another large river; according to later geographers and historians this was the Ganges but this claim must remain unproved (Bosworth 1996: 186–200). When Alexander was furthermore informed by the natives that the Hydaspes and Akesines rivers were tributaries of the Indus, whose twin estuaries emptied into the 'Great Sea', he was forced to modify his conception of world geography accordingly, as the Indus could no longer feasibly be held to be the upper course of the Nile. He, therefore, cancelled the part of his letter to his mother Olympias where he contended that he had discovered the source of the Nile (Arr. *Anab.* 6.1.4; cf. Strabo 15.1.25). The eastern end of the *oikoumene* seemed more remote than ever before. It is hardly surprising that this news caused distress among Alexander's soldiers; with no end in sight to the current campaign, they simply refused to go any further east.

Thus, Alexander was compelled to re-think his goals. If the eastern end of the *oikoumene* was unattainable, then maybe he could at least reach the southern limits? He marched his army back to the Hydaspes, where in the meantime the construction of the fleet had been completed. They travelled downstream beyond the Hydaspes and Akesines rivers and arrived at the delta of the Indus in July 326. Reaching the estuary of the Indus provided confirmation of the belief that the Indus and the Nile were actually two distinct rivers. In consequence, there could be no land bridge connecting India and eastern Africa. In addition to the previously unknown phenomenon of a tidal sea, the sighting of whales lent further support to the belief that Alexander had indeed reached the southern Ocean (Arr. *Ind.* 30.1). In this respect the ancient Ionian view of the world was corroborated, as was the symmetrical mindset inherent in it, which conceived of geographical conditions as mirrored across the *oikoumene*: for whales were also regarded as typical of the western Ocean beyond the Pillars of Herakles (cf. Plut. *Mor.* 22e; [Scymn.] 161–2 (*GGM* I.201); Avien. *Or.* 102, 127, 410). It is to be noted that for the fourth time during Alexander's campaigns zoological information is used to resolve geographical issues, which is hardly surprising at a time when the individual sciences had not yet separated from philosophy but were still considered to be parts of the latter.

But if, as the Ionian philosophers had believed, all of the *oikoumene* was surrounded by the Ocean, it was entirely possible to reach every point along the fringes of the *oikoumene* by sea. It does not seem at all far-fetched to imagine that this insight made a strong impression on Alexander, whose plans for future campaigns suggest that his earlier land-based approach came to be superseded by a more maritime way of thinking (Högemann 1985: 61–72). Subsequent expeditions, as well as the so-called 'last plans', were mainly maritime by nature. Since Alexander thought that the Erythrean Sea and Persian Gulf were identical, his next task was to explore the coastline between the delta of the Indus and the estuary of the Euphrates and Tigris, something that had already be done by the Karian Skylax in the time of Darius. Alexander instructed Nearchos to sail along the Indian coast as far as the Persian Gulf, while he himself marched his army back across the Gedrosian Desert. Nearchos' expedition was a success. The information gathered on his voyage from the delta of the Indus river to the mouth of the Tigris provided conclusive evidence that it was possible to travel from Babylon to India by ship.

The success of Nearchos inspired Alexander to devise further projects based on the assumption that the *oikoumene* was surrounded by a continuous Ocean. As geographical knowledge changed and developed, so long-standing and more recent theories were called into question: Was the Caspian Sea really an inland sea, as Alexander had surmised in 330? Was it true that the Jaxartes river was identical to the Tanais/Don? To answer these questions Alexander sent a man called Herakleides, son of Argaios, to Hyrkania with orders to build a fleet and explore the Caspian Sea (Arr. *Anab.* 7.16.1; cf. Pfister 1961: 43–4).

The next scheme was to trace the sea route to the south-west. Alexander, believing the Red Sea to be a gulf of the southern Ocean, was now planning to circumnavigate the Arabian Peninsula with a view to opening up a direct sea route from Babylon to Alexandria. For this project Alexander ordered the construction of an enormous fleet, which required timber to be transported overland to Babylon from as far away as Phoenicia. The venture, however, was brought to a halt by Alexander's premature death in June 323. The royal archives contained outlines of projects far more ambitious than this Arabian expedition. Although the authenticity of these plans has been the subject of much controversy, there is no valid reason to reject them outright. Their sheer audacity is consistent with Alexander's character, as is their far-reaching geographical scope. Above all, the change to a more maritime outlook is clearly evident, as the coasts of the *oikoumene* defined these plans.

In addition to the Arabian fleet that was being constructed in Babylon, a second fleet was to be built on the coast of Phoenicia and Syria, which was intended to travel westwards along the African coast of the Mediterranean until it reached the Pillars of Herakles. Similarly, the plan to circumnavigate Africa, conceived by Alexander in 324 should be taken seriously (Plut. *Alex.* 68, 1; Arr. *Anab.* 5.26.2; 7.1.2–3; Bosworth 1988: 185–97); less probable, however, are the reports that he planned to search for the source of the Nile and to visit Ethiopia (Curt. 4.8.3; Lyd. *Mens.* 4.197; cf. Desanges 1978: 246–7). When one looks at modern maps, scepticism about Alexander's plans for exploration is so much easier, but Alexander himself would have had no clear notion of the southward extension of Africa, and in all probability grossly underestimated the size of Arabia and Libya. His conception of Asia in one sense demanded a survey of the north African coast; he believed that 'only after the

conquest of Libya and Carthage could he rightfully be called king over all of Asia'
(Arr. *Anab.* 7.1.2). This statement is firmly rooted in ancient Ionian tradition, which
held Libya to be part of Asia; only later did it rise to the rank of an independent
continent (Zimmermann 1999: 36–54).

Alexander's geographical outlook was fully in keeping with his times. His approach
reveals the influence not only of Aristotle but also of the Ionian tradition; the latter,
with its emphasis on symmetry, applied the conditions of a known region of the
oikoumene to an unknown region as though it were its mirror image. Similarly the way
Alexander dealt with scientific information was also typical of the period.

As it became increasingly difficult to obtain reliable geographical information
during the second half of his campaign, Alexander began to draw geographical
conclusions from observations of a biological nature. We have seen how interpretations were based on the presence or absence of such things as serpents, fir-trees,
crocodiles, beans and whales. The questionable nature of such thinking did not
escape notice in antiquity; Arrian criticized Alexander for 'drawing conclusions
about important things from very slender indications' (Arr. *Anab.* 6.1.4). Such a
method can be called inductive or phenomenological: a set or system of rules is
derived from or even proved by a single observation. In the case of Alexander, it is
especially striking that the information submitted to him was discussed on the spot
and apparently assessed by himself (and not by competent specialists and scientists –
there were none at that time). It is tempting to see here the influence of Aristotle who
had been conducting research in the field of biology shortly before and during his
time as Alexander's tutor (Düring 1966: 510, 523). Indeed a much-quoted passage
of the Elder Pliny tells how Alexander had assisted Aristotle in the collection of
zoological data (*HN* 8.16.44). Alexander, of course, was doing something very
different from Aristotle; there was no concern with biological theory, but in his
treatment of empirical data and in the often far-reaching conclusions he drew from
it an Aristotelian influence can be detected.

3   The World after Alexander

Alexander's campaigns brought with them a wealth of new, albeit unconfirmed –
geographical, ethnological, anthropological, zoological, botanical, sociological, political, historical and economic – information about the inhabited world, causing a
surge of interest in geography. Numerous travel accounts, written in early Hellenistic
times, such as those of Nearchos, Pytheas and Megasthenes, bear witness to this
growing interest. Furthermore the regions untouched by Alexander's campaigns
attracted attention. If information could not be obtained, it was often invented.
Both Strabo and Arrian claim that the Macedonians deliberately falsified geographical
data in order to promote the glory of Alexander (Strabo 11.7.4, Arr. *Anab.* 5.3.2–3;
Ind. 5, 10). Above all, there grew up a sizeable body of utopian literature: the
writings of such as Hekataios of Abdera, Euhemeros and Iamboulos, and the legends
about the fantastic voyages of Alexander. The fictitious travelogues and ethnographic
accounts about peoples living at the edges of the world so characteristic of this
literature encouraged people to disbelieve even trustworthy narratives like that of
Pytheas on Thule. These fanciful tales, sometimes treated as reliable sources by the
later writers such as Strabo and Diodoros, shattered traditional geographical and

ethnographic conceptions no less than authentic accounts of expeditions and for a long time would exert considerable influence over Greek ideas about the fringes of the world (cf. Geus 2000b). The centrifugal forces released by the enlargement of the *oikoumene* catapulted Greece off its central position. The ancient Ionian circular maps had become obsolete by the era of Alexander. But the time was not yet ripe for a new model of the world, not even as succeeding generations of the Greeks acquired new information about Taprobane (modern Sri Lanka), the Ganges, north-eastern Europe, the Caspian Sea and Arabia.

Since the individual sciences were considered parts of philosophy, all this new information about the world was classified according to the leading philosophical systems. Four great schools of thought had emerged at the beginning of the third century BC: the Academy, the Peripatos, the Stoa and Epicureanism. By the middle of the century the founders and the first generation of pupils were dead, and their successors were wearing themselves out in petty quarrels and polemics. The masters' theories became dogmatic. New information was not supposed to question old convictions or to arrive at new conclusions, but to corroborate existing dogmas. Despite assiduously gathering information, the Aristotelians integrated it into the system founded by Aristotle without analysing it for some greater goal. They were content with the idle collection of data. The Academy, the Stoa, and the Epicureans were also conservative in terms of scientific thought; there were even setbacks, such as Epicurus' theory of motion which caused him to discard the idea of a spherical earth. It is hardly surprising that when scientific progress was made, it was done by individuals who did not belong to any particular philosophical school or at least by philosophers who had managed to break free from constraints imposed by their school. The individual sciences received fresh impetus in the time after Alexander. Geography was pressed forward in particular by Eratosthenes, Hipparchos and Ptolemaios.

Eratosthenes of Cyrene (276–194) secured his place in the history of scientific thought with his calculation of the circumference of the earth, based not on conjecture but on mathematics and astronomy (Geus 2002: 223–38). He also drew a new map of the *oikoumene*, one which was a major improvement on the older maps with their characteristic features of analogy, symmetry and speculation. Eratosthenes seems to have renounced this old method, which had been used by Alexander; turning against those who tried to base geographical boundaries on botanical observation, he, rather sarcastically, pointed out that the fir-tree also grew in India (Strabo 11.7.4). He was also the first geographer to draw parallel circles and meridians and develop them into a proper system. By means of known distances and the localization of central points within his system of co-ordinates it was now possible for him to construct a new map of the *oikoumene*. Despite certain conceptual imperfections his theories put the study of geography on a new scientific basis. The cornerstones of his map consisted no longer of peoples ('the Indians', 'the Celts' etc.), but of cities (Meroe, Thule, Tamaros etc.) and significant geographical points (Cape Notu Keras etc.). Eratosthenes' geographical construct was not only more accurate than that of his predecessors, but was also devoid of ethnological implications and connotations. It was, however, only the first step towards a more scientific approach. Eratosthenes was unable to determine more than a handful of parallel circles (and even less meridians) running through some of the most important cities of early Hellenistic times (Alexandria, Rhodes, Byzantion, Carthage, Massalia, Cadiz). Thus, since these cities were chosen in part because of their political status, they formed no completely abstract and geometrical set of co-ordinates (Prontera 1997). So, the *modus operandi* of Eratosthenes must not be judged as a complete break with geographical tradition. The Cyrenean geographer trod both old and new paths. On the one hand, he appreciated the need to determine the relevant locations on the basis of astronomical observations, on the other hand there was not enough data available to allow him to ignore all the empirical information he had at hand. His *Geographika* were dictated by insight and restraint. From that point of view Eratosthenes' geographical achievements may be considered to be an expedient compromise between the claims of theory and practical feasibility (Geus 2000a: 92; 2002: 288).

Later astronomers and geographers criticized Eratosthenes for his extensive use of itineraries and *periploi* to determine the positions of the meridians and parallel circles. Hipparchos of Nikaia, working in the latter half of the second century BC, is said to have demanded that the relative positions of places be determined solely by astronomical observations (Strabo 1.1.12). Nonetheless, he was too far ahead of his time in stating the principle to be able to follow it in practice, since his access to astronomical data was limited to only a small number of places. He did not think the system of Erastosthenes could be modified. In consequence, Hipparchos preferred to use the old Ionian maps, even though they were less accurate (Strabo 2.1.38; cf. H. Berger 1903: 109; Prontera 1997). Hellenistic geography, therefore, reached an impasse at the point where Eratosthenes left it and may even have slipped back again.

Eventually, it was Klaudios Ptolemaios (AD 100–180) who renewed the scientific foundation of geography by separating it into a theoretical and a descriptive subdiscipline. By eliminating all political, historical and sociological aspects and by concentrating purely on cartographic data, he elevated cartography to new heights. The major part of his *Geography* consists of a catalogue of no less than 6700 co-ordinates, based on latitude and longitude. The geographical work of Ptolemaios is an impressive demonstration of applied mathematics, i.e. on the one side, it is very accurate, but it also lacks vividness and colour (at least to the layman).

If we compare the ways the Greeks saw the *oikoumene* before and after Alexander, we can discern a tendency towards a more objective and scientific and less ethnological and hellenocentric view. Just as geography became fully emancipated as an individual science with its own methods (and not borrowing them from other sciences or deriving them from philosophical precepts) in the time after Alexander, so the way was paved for a new view of the world.

FURTHER READING

The fragmented character of the sources on Hellenistic geography (a useful source book is Kish 1978) is mirrored by the modern scholarly literature. A comprehensive English account is still a *desideratum*. The (partly outdated) standard works by Bunbury 1879, H. Berger 1903, Warmington 1934, Thomson 1948, Tozer 1964, Pédech 1976, and Jacob 1991 dedicate but a few pages to the Hellenistic period. Fraser's excellent chapter on 'Geographical Writing' in his *Ptolemaic Alexandria* (1972: I.520–53, II.750–90) covers most aspects and remains a good starting point. Dilke 1985 is a modern classic, but concentrates exclusively on cartography. The question whether and to what extent maps were actually used in antiquity has caused great controversy: Janni 1984 and Brodersen 1995 deny that maps were common outside the scientific community; for some particular aspects see Heidel 1937 and Aujac 1987.

The Hellenistic period brought about the distinction between descriptive, theoretical and didactic geography, thus making it difficult to illuminate more general aspects and developments. In consequence, more recent publications have focused on single geographers, especially on our most important source, Strabo of Amaseia: K. Clarke 1999 (who also covers Polybios and Poseidonios), J. Engels 1999, Dueck 2000; on Eratosthenes: Aujac 2001 and Geus 2002, but H. Berger 1880 remains indispensable; on Ephoros: Forderer 1913 and Barber 1935; on Pytheas: Bianchetti 1998; on Polybios: Walbank 1948; on Hipparchos: Dicks 1960; on Poseidonios: Edelstein and Kidd 1989–99; on Pseudo-Skymnos: Bianchetti 1990. Recent studies try to show how utopian voyages, a very popular genre in hellenistic times, exerted great influence on contemporary geography: See Romm 1992 and Geus 2000b. On ethnological conceptions see K. Müller 1972–80 and Jacob 1991. On Alexander's geographical notions and the influence of Aristotle, note the contrasting views of Hamilton 1969 and Schachermeyr 1973; a good overview is Burr 1947; for particular aspects: Tarn 1948 and Bosworth 1993.

PART IV

Greeks and Others

CHAPTER FIFTEEN

Town and Country in Ptolemaic Egypt

Jane Rowlandson

1 Introduction

Even to Thebes
in Egypt, where vast treasures lie piled in the houses
And there are a hundred gates, through each of which two hundred men
Surge forth with their horses and chariots. (Homer, *Iliad* 9.381–4)

If western scholars have often tended to treat the Greek *polis* as the consummate urban form, superior to the cities which developed very much earlier elsewhere in the Near East, the Greeks themselves were sufficiently impressed by the urban glories of Egypt, already over two thousand years old when Alexander the Great founded his city of Alexandria on the Egyptian coast in spring 331 BC.

The annual inundation of the Nile valley and Delta created the fertile conditions to support a relatively high population, while discouraging dispersed settlement. Communities clung to the sides of the valley above flood level or perched on mounds which rose ever higher with the accumulation of waste, at flood time resembling islands in the sea (Hdt. 2.97.1). Even if a centralized state was not exactly a prerequisite for the successful exploitation of the Nile's hydrology, and agriculture could be organized at a local level using 'natural' irrigation basins (Butzer 1976: 106–11), the desire to improve upon nature by the control of water, and the construction of canals to distribute it most effectively, undoubtedly encouraged the growth of a strong state and homogeneous administrative system based on the division of the whole country into 36 districts (*nomes* in Greek; the number later rose to over 40) each with a principal town as well as numerous villages. Despite the ease of communication by water (boats travelling south benefited from the prevailing wind; the current assisted those going north), tension between central control and local particularism was a constant feature of Egyptian history, and the union of 'The Two Lands' remained precarious as the centre of royal power shifted between Upper (south) and Lower Egypt (for map of Egypt, figure 7.1).

In the course of over two millennia, different pharaohs bestowed their patronage on many different cities, including Heliopolis (near modern Cairo), and Tanis and Sais in the Delta. But the two cities to develop the most enduring importance were Thebes and Memphis, with their vast and hugely wealthy temple complexes. Although there were, of course, significant differences between the structure and layout of Egyptian cities and Greek *poleis* (cf. Alston 1997), we must beware of ethnocentric prejudice when interpreting the significance of the grid plan design of the new Ptolemaic foundations in Egypt (section 3 below). Egyptian town planners were also capable of adopting a rectilinear design, particularly during the Middle Kingdom (Kemp 1989: 149–66); and the main contrast is between planned communities, often constructed under royal patronage, and those which developed more organically over the long term. It is true, however, that in the New Kingdom, Egyptian planners made little attempt to extend the rectilinear pattern into areas of private housing (most conspicuous at Akhenaten's short-lived foundation at Amarna; Kemp 1989: 294).

On the edge of the desert just beyond the limit of cultivation were sited the burial places for the valley towns. These necropoleis themselves developed resident populations of embalmers and priests to serve the mortuary cults; at Memphis these virtually constituted an alternative city on the desert escarpment overlooking the valley city (D. J. Thompson 1988: 10). On the west bank of the Nile at Thebes were several communities which grew from the need for workers to build and service royal tombs and mortuary temples; the town of Djeme in the shadow of the temple of Rameses III at Medinet Habu has yielded documentation of everyday life right through until after the Arab conquest. In the New Kingdom, workers on the royal tombs in the Valley of the Kings were segregated in a specially constructed village at Deir el Medina, where thorough excavation has revealed detailed archaeological evidence of domestic housing as well as documents relating to the business dealings and private lives of the workers which affords comparison with the Ptolemaic evidence discussed in this chapter (McDowell 1999; Meskell 2002: 38–44).

Thus, when Alexander the Great arrived to liberate Egypt from Persian rule in autumn 332 BC, Egypt already possessed a long urban tradition, embracing the two major cities of Memphis and Thebes, some forty further nome capitals, and thousands of smaller towns and villages. Diodoros' claim of 'more than thrice ten thousand' at the time of Ptolemy I is far too high and sounds suspiciously conventional, though the manuscript may anyway be corrupt (1.31.7, cf. Theocr. *Id.* 17.82–4; Rathbone 1990: 104). Later there were about 120 villages in the Oxyrhynchite nome, which is probably not untypical.

Also by the time of Alexander's conquest, Egypt included several resident communities of Greeks. Herodotos tells how the seventh-century pharaoh Psammetichos provided his Ionian and Karian mercenaries with two settlements called the 'Camps' in the Nile Delta near Bubastis; in the next century, pharaoh Amasis moved them to cosmopolitan Memphis (2.154; D. J. Thompson 1988: 84). Psammetichos, too, was responsible for the Milesian *emporion* of Naukratis in the western Delta, which Amasis made the base for all Greeks who traded with Egypt, both permanent and temporary residents (Strabo 17.1.18; Hdt. 2.178). Thus local Greeks, as well as ambassadors and Alexander's own troops, will have appreciated the games he held at Memphis during the winter; and on his departure in spring 331, the notorious Kleomenes of Naukratis was able to seize sole control of the country, ruining

Alexander's attempt to leave a government which balanced the power of different interest groups (Arr. *Anab*. 3.1.5).

Alexander's most famous city foundation, Alexandria on the Egyptian coast, must have anticipated from the start a significant further influx of Greeks into Egypt; but it was left to his general Ptolemy, who obtained control of Egypt after Alexander's death (Thompson, this volume, section 1), to carry out the policy of attracting large numbers of immigrants. Although we cannot document the process by which the citizen body of Alexandria was first constituted, and the rapid growth of its population to include non-citizen Greeks, Egyptians, Jews and other Semitic peoples, as well as other groups, within a generation or so it had clearly overtaken Athens as the largest, and wealthiest, city of the Greek world (Fraser 1972: vol. I chapter 2).

But Greek immigration was by no means confined to Alexandria. Ptolemy decided to found only one further Greek *polis* in Egypt, Ptolemais, clearly intended to provide a focus for the new regime in the south, as Alexandria was in the north. Instead he chose to cement the loyalty of his mercenaries by granting them allotments (*kleroi*) throughout the countryside, mostly in existing communities where Egyptians lived side by side with the new settlers. This had profound implications for the future course of Egypt's social and cultural development (Diod. 19.85.4, 20.47.4; Uebel 1968; Bagnall 1984). The fortuitous survival of tens of thousands of papyrus documents, in Greek and Egyptian, enables us to look in detail at some of these communities, and the process by which the immigrants settled on the land and were progressively assimilated with the existing population. The dry conditions suited to the preservation of papyrus, however, are found only in certain parts of Egypt, particularly the cemeteries along the fringes of the Nile valley and around the periphery of the Fayum, the 'semi-oasis' to the south-west of Memphis which was subject to much development and settlement under the early Ptolemies (Thompson, this volume, section 2). Thus our information is very patchy; and ironically we know much more about some obscure villages (such as Kerkeosiris; section 4 below) than about the Greek cities of Naukratis and Ptolemais, which are both very scantily documented in the papyri. Even Alexandria has produced no papyri directly – because of the high water table throughout the Delta – although it is attested in various ways by numerous papyri from other parts of Egypt, as well as in much other literary, documentary and archaeological evidence.

This review of town and country in Ptolemaic Egypt will start with a look at these three 'true' Greek *poleis* of Egypt, before proceeding to the communities of the *chora* (countryside). Despite considerable variation in size, pretensions and the extent to which they were hellenized, the *chora* communities shared a lack of autonomous political institutions, and were all subject to the administration of royal officials. In contrast to chapter 7, which traces the main outlines of Ptolemaic history, this chapter aims to concentrate on trying to convey, from the wealth of evidence available, something of what life was like for the ordinary inhabitants of Ptolemaic Egypt.

2   Alexandria and the Other Greek *Poleis* of Egypt

The city of Alexandria was built on a low limestone ridge facing the island of Pharos, already familiar to educated Greeks as the abode of Proteus (Hom. *Od*. 4.355) and to become synonymous with the lighthouse built *c*. 280 BC by Sostratos of Knidos, one of the seven wonders of the world. Constricted by lake Mareotis to the south, the city was described by ancient writers as shaped like a *chlamys* (cloak), some 6 km east to west but less than 2 km north to south. Its grid plan design was attributed to the famous architect Deinokrates of Rhodes, and the unusually broad principal streets, bisecting each other, were a source of marvel for visitors to the city throughout antiquity (Strabo 17.1.8; cf. Ach. Tat. 6.1). Changes in the coastline due to seismic activity and the silting up of the *heptastadion* (the causeway built to link Pharos to the mainland, thereby creating two excellent harbours), combined with the continuous inhabitation of the site, have until recent decades seriously hampered archaeological investigation of the ancient city. And even now, despite the spectacular results of rescue excavations on land and underwater exploration of the ancient harbour and palace areas (Empereur 1998; Goddio et al. 1998), our understanding of its basic topography must start from ancient descriptions, particularly the detailed eyewitness account of Strabo (17.1.6–10) written only a few years after the downfall of Kleopatra and the Ptolemaic regime.

Between a quarter and a third of the city's total area was occupied by the royal palaces, which embraced Cape Lochias and dominated the eastern side of the Great harbour. In the palace area were situated the famous Museum and Library, and the monumental tomb of Alexander and the Ptolemies; and there were open spaces and gardens to which the general public were admitted, at least during festivals (Theocr. *Id.* 15; see below). Nearby was the theatre and the temple of Poseidon. Further temples were spread throughout the city, including one to the deified Arsinoe II; but the most important sacred site was the great temple of Sarapis on a hill in the southwestern district called Rhakotis. This, according to ancient tradition, had been an Egyptian village before Alexander arrived (Strabo 17.1.6; cf. Ps.-Callisthenes I.31.4) – although it has recently been claimed that the name simply means 'building site' in Egyptian – and arose from the natives' rather derogatory way of referring to the new Greek city (Chauveau 2000: 57). But a predominantly Egyptian population in the adjacent suburb of Necropolis is certainly implied by Strabo's reference to embalming there. Excavation at the Sarapeum (the site of 'Pompey's Pillar'; actually a monument of Diocletian) has unearthed foundation plaques which clearly date the main temple to the reign of Ptolemy III, although evidence of earlier finds is suggestive of religious activity on the site back to the start of the Ptolemaic period, if not earlier (Stambaugh 1972: 6). The temple was Hellenic in style, and the cult statue anthropomorphic (although its attribution to Bryaxis poses a chronological difficulty; Clem. Al. *Protr.* 4.48); it is commonly held that Ptolemy I inaugurated the cult to provide the immigrants with a religious focus that they could identify with their new home but was not alien to them like the Egyptian zoomorphic deities. This may underestimate the significance of Egyptian elements right from the start (includ-ing the bilingual foundation deposits and pair of sphinxes which may have formed a *dromos*); indeed, the number of pharaonic-style statues recovered in the recent underwater excavations suggests that the whole city may have had a more Egyptian visual aspect than has usually been assumed (Rowe 1946: 14; Goddio et al. 1998).

In the middle of the city, between the palace area to the north-east and the perhaps more Egyptianized religious focal point to the south-west, were the main civic buildings. It is significant that Strabo singles out for particular mention the gymna-sium and law court (*dikasterion*), rather than more strictly political institutions, like a *prytaneion* or *bouleuterion*; political activity was always seriously attenuated by the overpowering royal presence, and at some point (maybe as one of Ptolemy VIII's repressive measures in 145; Athen. 4.83, trans. Burstein 105) Alexandria lost its *boule* altogether. Nor do we hear of an active assembly. Yet membership of the citizen body was strictly regulated, and organized into tribes and demes on the normal Greek model, and the city enjoyed its own legal system (*P.Hal.* I; excerpted in *Sel.Pap.* II 201–2). Until very recently, Alexandrian evidence for domestic housing of Ptolemaic date was entirely lacking, and inferences had to be drawn from tomb architecture; but now rescue excavation has started to reveal houses back to the early third century with mosaic flooring (Empereur 1998: 60–1), to be set alongside evidence from other Delta sites, such as Athribis (Alston 2002: 236).

According to Diodoros, Alexandria in his day (*c.* 59 BC) had 300,000 'free' inhabitants, implying a total population of around half a million; a plausible enough figure, even if we remain sceptical about Diodoros' testimony (17.52.6; cf. Rathbone 1990: 119–20). A sense of the unusually dense and cosmopolitan character of life in the city is best conveyed by Theocritus' *Idyll* 15 of the 270s BC, a conversation between two ladies attending an Adonis festival, in which the danger of the crowded streets is repeatedly stressed:

> O ye gods, what a big crowd! However are we to get through this crush, and how long will it take? Ants, numberless and immeasurable! You've conferred a great many benefits on us, Ptolemy, since your father (Ptolemy I) went off to join the gods. Nowadays no criminal harms the passer by, sneaking along in Egyptian fashion.

Later, the two women boast to one of the other onlookers of their Doric dialect, reflecting their Syracusan (and ultimately Corinthian) ancestry. A recent study has confirmed that an identity and accent associated with one of old Greek cities, or with Macedonia, was a mark of high status in the early Ptolemaic period, and that it was not until the second century that the elite became more regularly identified with Alexandria itself (Clarysse 1998).

For such a large and cosmopolitan population lacking opportunities for political expression, the spectacle offered by frequent and magnificent festivals provided the cement which united the disparate elements to one another, and all to the ruling dynasty. While royal patronage could extend to the festival of any god (again illustrated by Theocr. *Id.* 15), the greatest scope for the projection of Ptolemaic bounty and power, both to the Alexandrian population and visitors to the city, lay in the festivals for the cult of the ruling house itself. If this reached its apogee in the 'Grand Procession of Ptolemy Philadelphos' whose description is preserved by Athenaeus (5.197–203; Erskine 1995: 43–5; D. J. Thompson 2000), almost certainly one of the earliest celebrations of the four-yearly Ptolemaieia, or festival of the deified Ptolemy I and his queen Berenike I founded in 279, there were other royal festivals, notably the Basileia (Austin 234), and the Arsinoeia in honour of Arsinoe II, deified on her death in 270. The distinctive blue faience *oinochoai*, or 'Queen Vases', presumably emanate from the popular celebration of the cult of Arsinoe and later queens (D. B. Thompson 1973). A papyrus fragment of Satyrus' *On the Demes of Alexandria* also preserves the regulations for sacrificing to Arsinoe on altars of sand as the priestess made her way through the streets (*P.Oxy.* XXVII 2465).

From Arsinoe II onwards, the Ptolemaic queens seem to have attracted a deep and genuine affection among the people of both Alexandria and Egypt as a whole. Thus the murder of Arsinoe III in the power struggle at court following her husband's death (Ptolemy IV, 204 BC) provoked the Alexandrian population, including upper-class women and even children, to exact from the perpetrators and their families a horrific revenge by which a controlled, charivari-like public humiliation (the women were led naked, on horseback, to the stadium) culminated in their being literally torn limb from limb (Polyb. 15.25–35, excerpted in Rowlandson 1998: no. 7; Barry 1993). This riot set a trend, and the Alexandrians made several more interventions in dynastic squabbles, ending with their insurgence in disapproval at Caesar's support of the young Kleopatra VII, during which part of the Library allegedly went up in flames (Fraser 1972: I.334–5, II.493–4). Lacking any legitimate means of political expression, the Alexandrians found a way to make their voice heard.

With the foundation of Alexandria, Naukratis lost its *raison d'être* as the main port for Greek trade with Egypt; in 380 BC, Nectanebo I had devoted a tithe of the customs revenue from this trade to the nearby temple of Neith at Sais (Lichtheim 1980: 86–9. The pair of this 'Naukratis stele' has recently been discovered by underwater excavations at the coastal port of Thonis/Herakleion; Yoyotte 2002). In fact Naukratis may have continued to have some role as a port (Coulson 1996: 14), and it certainly retained its status as a self-governing *polis*, although a resident royal official, *oikonomos*, supervised royal property and interests in the city (*OGIS* 89; cf. Sherk 1992: 268–9). But it seems gradually to have slipped into relative obscurity.

By contrast, Ptolemais (called Psoi in Egyptian) retained its importance to the end of the Ptolemaic period. Strabo declared it the largest city of the Thebaid (Thebes had been reduced to a series of villages by the rebellions of 88–85 and 26 BC), comparable to Memphis in size and possessing a Greek constitution (17.1.42, 46). We can only guess at an actual population figure – a conservative estimate would be around 50,000 (cf. D. J. Thompson 1988: 35) – at any rate, it must have been perceptibly larger than the ordinary nome *metropoleis*. Surviving city decrees provide testimony to its Greek cultural, as well as political, life, with reference to a theatre, and including a decree of the Dionysiac artists based in the city (*OGIS* 49, 50; cf. *OGIS* 48, trans. Austin 233). Some of the settlers may have been drawn from Argos and Thessaly (*SEG* 20.665). From 215/4 BC, an eponymous dynastic cult was instituted at Ptolemais parallel to that at Alexandria, which is reflected in the date clauses of many private documents from Upper Egypt (Sherk 1992: 263–4). But the intended role of Ptolemais as a bulwark of hellenism and loyalty to the dynasty in the south did not prove sufficient to prevent the series of rebellions which afflicted that region in particular from the end of the third century onwards.

3   The Impact of Greek Settlement in the Egyptian *Chora*

The popular Athenocentric view of Greeks as valuing political autonomy above all is contradicted by the enthusiasm with which many immigrants to Egypt settled in mixed rural communities with no vestige of self-government. Their aspirations for wealth and social prestige were fulfilled in their new homes; and it is clear that, particularly in the areas of most intensive settlement, the Fayum and northern part of the Nile valley, considerable effort was put into creating the distinctive infrastructures and ambience necessary for a 'civilized' Greek lifestyle.

This is seen most clearly, and may indeed have been most thoroughly put into practice, at the 'model town' of Philadelphia, whose very name (referring to Ptolemy II's sister-wife Arsinoe Philadelphos) is testimony to its links with the ruling dynasty. The 10,000 aroura (2,750 ha.) estate nearby which the king granted to his favoured minister, Apollonios the *dioiketes*, was developed using the latest agricultural ideas (not always approved of by the Egyptian workforce: Austin 240) under the supervision of his assistant Zenon of Kaunos (in Karia), whose papers of some 2000 surviving letters and accounts provide a level of detailed knowledge unparalleled in the Hellenistic world (Rostovtzeff 1922a; Orrieux 1983, 1985). Newly dug canals and irrigation ditches divided the whole area into regular rectangular portions; the two Greek staple crops, vines and olives, were planted on a massive scale, and experiments made with novel cash crops such as poppies or the planting of two crops of wheat annually (Orrieux 1983: 79–92; D. J. Thompson 1984; 1999b). The town of Philadelphia itself was also laid out on an orderly grid plan, aligned parallel to the main ancient canal, as an air photograph of 1925 shows clearly (Edgar 1931: plate 1). Although strictly speaking it remained a *kome* (village) without any self-government, its size and level of urbanism attracted ready settlers, who found it natural to describe it as a *polis*:

> Apollophanes and Demetrios, brothers, craftsmen in all the skills of weaving women's clothing, to Zenon, greeting. If you please and you happen to have the need, we are ready to provide what you need. For hearing of the reputation of the *polis* in that you, its leading man, are a good and just person, we have decided to come to Philadelphia to you, we ourselves, and our mother and wife. (*PSI* IV 341, trans. Rowlandson 1998: no. 201)

Although lacking political institutions, Philadelphia possessed the two key Greek cultural institutions, a gymnasium and theatre; there was also a stoa, a distinctively Greek arcaded street. A wide range of temples served Greek deities (Zeus, Demeter, the Dioskouroi), Egyptian (Souchos, Thoeris, Poremanres), and Greco-Egyptian (Isis and Sarapis), as well as the ruling dynasty (Arsinoe, the Brother-Sister gods; the gods of Samothrace who were also particularly associated with Arsinoe) (Pestman 1981: II.512). Some private houses were built on an impressively grand scale, designed and decorated according to Greek taste, as this decorator's estimate addressed to Zenon reveals:

> About the work in the house of Diotimos: for the portico, [I undertake] to have the cornice painted with a purple border, the upper part of the wall variegated, the lower course like vetch-seed, and the pediments with circular veining; providing myself with all materials, for 30 drachmas. For the dining room with seven couches, I will do the vault according to the pattern which you saw, and give the lower course an agreeable tint and paint the Lesbian cornice, for 20 drachmas. And for the dining room with five couches, I will paint the cornices, providing myself with all materials, for 3 drachmas. The sum total is 53 drachmas. But if you provide everything, it will come to 30 drachmas. (*Sel.Pap.* I 171; cf. *P.Mich.Zenon* 38)

If Philadelphia marked an extreme of development under royal patronage, all around the Fayum similar developments were being undertaken on a more modest scale. Survey work at Kom Talit (ancient Taleithis) again shows regularly planned streets aligned with a canal newly dug in the mid-third century (Kirkby and Rathbone 1996), and even at remote Soknopaiou Nesos on the barren northern shore of the lake, the earliest settlement phase, also of the mid-third century, shows large, stone-built houses on a rectilinear plan (Boak 1935: 17–20). Connection with the ruling dynasty was reflected in many Fayum village names, such as Theadelphia, Ptolemais, Philotera (after a sister of Ptolemy II), Dionysias or Bacchias, as well as in the designation of the whole region from *c.* 257 BC as the Arsinoite nome in honour of Philadelphos' deified sister-wife Arsinoe.

Census records suggest that by the second half of the third century, sixteen per cent of the population of the Fayum were classed as Greek, some military settlers (kleruchs) and their families, others civilians; in some villages they formed over half the population (Clarysse 1994: 75; D. J. Thompson 2001: 309). The introduction of a privileged 'colonial' population on this scale undoubtedly led to jealousies and tensions with the local inhabitants (such as over billeting: see Thompson, this volume, section 2), but for several reasons the social and ethnic composition of these rural communities was very much more complex than a simple dichotomy between immigrant Greek colonists and native Egyptians. For one thing, the expansion of agricultural land meant that some of the Egyptians had relocated from other parts of the country, such as Heliopolis (Austin 240) or Oxyrhynchos (Pintaudi 1990). For another, immigration was not confined to Greeks and other hellenized groups such as Thracians or Karians, but included Syrians, Jews, Samarians and other Semitic immigrants from the Ptolemaic overseas empire. Even more significantly, the census records make clear that some of those described as 'Hellenes' and privileged by exemption from the obol tax were in fact partly or wholly of Egyptian ancestry; it was possible to acquire the status, for instance through service in the civil administration (D. J. Thompson 2001). The records also show Greeks and Egyptians living in close proximity to one another, in adjacent households, and although even with the help of these detailed lists it is difficult to estimate confidently the extent of intermarriage, this undoubtedly occurred. The Greeks resident in the Egyptian *chora* were not affected by the legal restrictions on marriage with non-citizens which applied to citizens of Greek poleis (including presumably Alexandria – although we do apparently find one marriage of an Alexandrian citizen resident in the Fayum with an Egyptian woman; Clarysse 1992: 51–2).

The settlement of kleruchs and civilians also occurred on a wide scale in the northern part of the Nile valley adjacent to the Fayum (and no doubt also in the Delta, although evidence from that important area of Egypt is very thin). Our best evidence concerns the Herakleopolite and Oxyrhynchite nomes, mainly from the cemetery of El Hibeh, supplemented by later evidence from the same area. Here the village names remained almost entirely Egyptian, with no suggestion of links with the ruling dynasty; but the settlement of kleruchs at almost every village is demonstrated by the fact that plots of land continued to be known for many centuries afterwards by the name of the original recipient, for example 'the *kleros* of Nikanor' (Pruneti 1975; 1981; Falivene 1998). How actively these kleruchs were involved in the actual cultivation of their land is a moot point; it was often leased out, partly, it has been argued, because the kleruchs themselves lacked the necessary capital to make it productive, and might prefer to hand it over to civilian middlemen who would provide finance and hire Egyptians to work it (Bingen 1973; 1978b).

Apart from private contracts like leases and loans, most of our documents relate to routine local administration, such as collection of taxes in kind or money, or the arrest of delinquents. For instance, a small group of letters addressed to a village official called Ptolemaios circa 245 BC includes the following:

> Zenodoros to Ptolemaios, greeting. When you receive this letter, send to us under guard the woman who was handed over to you in possession of contraband oil, and send also the person who handed her over to you. And if you do not stop your evil-doing in the village, you will repent of it. Farewell. Year [.], Epeiph 10th. (*P.Hib.* I 59)

> Demophon to Ptolemaios, greeting. Do all you can to send me the flute-player Petoüs with both the Phrygian flutes and the others; and if any expense is necessary, pay it, and you will get it back from me. Send me also Zenobios the feeble with a drum and cymbals and castanets, for he is wanted by the women in connection with the sacrifice; and let his dress be as elegant as possible. Also get the kid from Aristion and send it to me. And if you have apprehended the slave, hand him over to Semphtheus to bring to me. Send me as many cheeses as you can, new earthenware, all kinds of vegetables, and some relish if you have any. Farewell. Put them on board with the guards who will assist in bringing the boat. (*P.Hib.* I 54)

Interpreted within the context of literally thousands of other documents of similar types, these texts illustrate many aspects of rural society in this period, from the working of the monopoly on the processing and disposal of oil crops (cf. *P.Rev.*, trans. BD 95) to the use of boats for much local, as well as long-distance, transport, the reliance on personal contacts to provide both necessities and luxury goods, or the interpenetration of official duties with the private interests of the colonial entrepreneurs (cf. Orrieux 1983). The obscure reference to Ptolemaios' misdeeds reflects the fact that even low level officials like Ptolemaios held power over the village community which, if misused, threatened to undermine the ideology whereby royal officials were the instruments which disseminated pharaoh's role as guarantor of *Ma'at* (justice, or balance) to the people at large (D. Crawford 1978). Hence the need for a multiplicity and apparent duplication of officials, all keeping check on one another in the attempt to minimize abuse. The preparations, clearly for a local festival, further illustrate how closely newcomers and the native population could co-operate if they wanted to; after all, both Greeks and Egyptians could enjoy a good festival, in the villages of the *chora* no less than in the more opulent setting of Alexandria during the 'Grand Procession of Ptolemy Philadelphos'. Our information is ambiguous as to whether the celebration under Demophon's patronage was basically Greek or Egyptian in form; Phrygian flutes are familiar from the Greek world, but their player's name is Egyptian, whereas castanet dancing was distinctively Egyptian, although apparently provided by a Greek. This degree of integration is instructive at a date when many Greeks would still be first- or second generation immigrants to Egypt.

The scale of Greek settlement in Middle Egypt south of Oxyrhynchos is difficult to establish because of lack of evidence, although later documents suggest that there must have been widespread kleruchic settlements there at some point in the

Ptolemaic period. Some Greeks were also settled under the first two Ptolemies in the Thebaid, notably at the strategic point of Elephantine island opposite modern Aswan (the location of a Jewish garrison in the fifth century), from which comes the earliest surviving marriage contract in Greek (*P.Eleph.* 1, dated 311 BC; cf. Porten et al. 1996), and at Edfu (*Sel.Pap.* II 207; Lukaszewicz 1999). Kleruchic settlement in the Apollonopolite nome (of which Edfu was the metropolis) was never on a large scale, however; in 119/8 the nome had only some 657 arouras of kleruchic land compared with over 20,000 arouras of 'privately owned' land (*P.Haun.* inv. 407; contrast Kerkeosiris, section 4 below). And generally, evidence from this region suggests the persistence of earlier patterns of land tenure and social structure to which the relatively few immigrants brought only slow change, particularly in the third century, before rebellion provoked more active royal intervention through garrisons and 'dynastic' urban foundations (Manning 1999; 2003; Thompson, this volume, section 5, cf. also section 4 below).

Thebes itself, despite a number of attestations of Greeks from the 290s BC onwards, all in demotic Egyptian texts (Clarysse 1995; Depauw 2000: 52), remained overwhelmingly Egyptian in ambience, under the influence of the hugely wealthy and ancient temples and their priestly families. Even the non-Egyptologist can gain some sense of the milieu in which these families lived – and not only the wealthiest – from the collections of family papers which they carefully preserved in their houses (Depauw 1997: 156–7; 2000). Because the texts are predominantly in demotic, these 'family archives' from Thebes are perhaps less well-known to non-specialists than similar archives from elsewhere in Egypt (section 4 below; cf. Lewis 1986: chapters 6 and 8), but they deserve attention not least because several date back to the very early Ptolemaic period, when documentation in Greek is scarce. One of the most interesting relates not to a single family, but traces the history of a house through a series of transactions over fifty years from 324, when the first-attested owner, Djufachi, assigned it jointly to two of his sons, Petechons and Phib (other adjacent property went to another son) who only many years later divided it physically into two separate dwellings. In 315, it was included (still undivided) in Petechons' marriage agreement; and twenty years after that Petechons' widow used her now divided share as security for a loan, selling it two years later to the mortgagee, Pleehe. In 290, Pleehe entered into a detailed contract with his neighbour Tahib allowing her to extend her house up to his west wall, provided that she inserted no new timbers into his wall, and left an adequate light well opposite his two windows. Subsequently, Pleehe made the property over to his wife, Teihor, who after his death sold the house in 279 to its last known owner, another woman, Teianteus, from whose period of occupancy we have a series of tax receipts and a lease of the house to her sister (Glanville 1939; Pestman 1989).

This example provides insight into both the physical conditions in which the residents of Thebes (and of smaller communities throughout the Nile valley) lived, with dark mud-brick houses crammed closely against each other overshadowing the narrow streets, and into the social and legal relationships of the families who lived in such close proximity to one another, and who mostly came from the lower echelons of the priesthood (for instance, Pleehe is entitled 'lector of the Ape'). Modest though these mud-brick constructions were, they represented a source of wealth that could be used as security against a loan or a dowry, as well as the space in which wife and husband hoped to raise children who would inherit. We can see the sophistication of the Egyptian legal system before it had interacted to any extent with that of the immigrant Greeks (cf. also the existence of demotic Egyptian legal 'handbooks': Depauw 1997: 113–14). Records of each transaction were carefully preserved, to be produced in court in the event of any dispute arising with neighbours or other family members, such as the so-called 'Hermias case' (*P.Tor.Choach.*), or the family dispute from Siut (P. BM 10591 published by H. Thompson 1934). Anyone familiar with the treatment of women in Greek law will also note that here women appear as parties to contracts without the need for any male guardian, and their favourable treatment with regard to marital property (see further Pestman 1961; Smith 1995).

The Ptolemies were responsible for relatively little building work in the temple complexes at Thebes, and it is difficult to escape the conclusion that they viewed its powerful and conservative priestly establishment with suspicion (in contrast to their close relationship with the priests of Ptah at Memphis; Thompson, this volume, section 3). They preferred to counterbalance Theban power by patronizing major rebuilding projects at other religious sites in the south, most notably the temple of Isis at Philai (begun under Ptolemy II), and that of Horus at Edfu, begun in 237 under Ptolemy III (Arnold 1999). This unfortunately left too little vested support at Thebes for the Ptolemaic state to prevent its secession for two decades from 207/6 BC under two rebel pharaohs who, whatever the original cause of the rebellion, played the 'nationalist' propaganda card (Thompson, this volume, section 5).

4 Ethnicity and Society in the Late Ptolemaic *Chora*

By 186 BC, when the royal power of Ptolemy V was finally restored throughout the country, Greeks and Egyptians had been living side by side in the *chora* for several generations. The combination of social mobility and intermarriage had produced a more ethnically and culturally mixed population than the documents superficially suggest (Clarysse 1985 and further below). However, we continue to find isolated instances of racial tension (always surprisingly rare in our sources), perhaps inflamed by the 'nationalistic' colour of the rebellions against the state (examples in Goudriaan 1988, especially 42–57, on Ptolemaios the 'Recluse' at the Memphite Sarapeion, widely discussed elsewhere).

The consequences for a small town community, both of the continued unrest through the second and early first centuries, and of government measures to restore order, can be traced in detail in the unusually well-documented case of Pathyris (modern Gebelein), some 30 km south of Thebes. It was a garrison town (one of four strategically located to the north and south of Thebes), and when the garrison was reinforced in the mid-second century, it became the home of a cavalry officer called Dryton, a citizen of Ptolemais perhaps of Cretan descent. He already had an eight-year-old son, Esthladas, by a former wife Sarapias (who was also a citizen – *aste* – of Ptolemais), but in 150 married Apollonia alias Senmouthis of a local Greco-Egyptian family, whose father and other male ascendants were infantrymen from the *politeuma* of the Cyreneans (a form of military association, membership of which may, but does not necessarily, point to some real Cyrenaean ancestry).

On any account, Dryton's family illustrates the ethnic and cultural complexities of Ptolemaic society at this period, but the precise interpretations put upon the evidence have varied considerably (not least because new documents come to light). Whereas Lewis (1986: 88–103) saw Dryton's marriage to Apollonia as leading to his 'Egyptianization' after the relatively 'pure' Greek milieu of Ptolemais, more recently Vandorpe has argued that Dryton was already used to dealing with Egyptian legal contracts before he met Apollonia, and that on the contrary, it was she who, with his assistance, gradually began to conduct her business activities in Greek (Vandorpe 2002a; 2002b). In this, she was following a more general pattern (see below), but it is interesting that after Dryton's death in 126, we hear no more of Apollonia's business activities, and the couple's five daughters do not seem to have continued the hellenizing trend. In his last will (superseding two earlier ones) of 29 June 126, Dryton made an approximately equal division of his property between Esthladas on the one hand (who also received his father's armour and horse, having followed him in a military career), and the five daughters on the other. This reflects less a characteristically Greek preference for males over females in succession than an attempt to achieve a balance between the offspring of his two marriages; after all, if he had not remarried, Esthladas would have inherited the whole estate. More obvious Greek influence is seen in Dryton's possession of four household slaves attested by the will (probably all female, and with impeccably Greek names). But four of the five known witnesses to the will signed in Egyptian demotic, 'because in these places there is not a sufficient number of Greeks' (*P.Grenf.* I 21 with *Pap. Lugd.-Bat.* XIX 4 ii 1–25, widely reproduced and translated).

This interesting archive also directly documents how the entire population of Egypt was potentially affected by the political unrest of the later second century. In 130 Esthladas, who was serving with the forces of Ptolemy VIII in the civil war against his sister Kleopatra II, wrote home to reassure his family:

> Esthladas to his father and his mother (sc. stepmother), greeting and good health. As I write to you frequently to keep up your courage and take care of yourself until things settle down, once again please reassure yourself and our household. For news has come that Paos (the king's general) is sailing up in the month of Tybi (= the following month) with sufficient forces to subdue the mobs in Hermonthis and deal with them as rebels. (*Sel.Pap.* I 101; Burstein 44)

We can sense here the nervousness of a family, whose entire livelihood and social identity was constituted through loyal service to the king, in face of a violent threat to his rule. The conflict was by no means a simple opposition between 'Greeks' and 'Egyptians'; but the dissension within the Ptolemaic ruling house provided an occasion for the pursuit and magnification of more local enmities. The priests of Hermonthis and Pathyris were embroiled in a decades-long land dispute (*P.Lond.* VII 2188; cf. Van't Dack et al. 1989: 39–48); hardly surprising, then, that the two neighbouring towns found themselves on opposite sides in the civil war. Some years later political unrest again impinged on the family, when Dryton's five daughters complained to the regional governor that one Ariston son of Athenodotos of Thebes 'in times of unrest' had violently occupied the vineyard they inherited from their father and claimed it for his own (*P.Lond.* II 401: 13, trans. Rowlandson 1998: no. 87).

Other texts to survive from later Ptolemaic Pathyris include a register of landholdings (P. Berlin 13608), and a plan using coloured ink and annotated in Greek and demotic (P. Cairo 31163), as well as several further bilingual family archives (Depauw 1997: 130, 152, 155–6). One such archive, consisting of 21 documents in Greek and 49 in demotic, may have been discovered intact in the original pot (*P.Adler*, cf. the contemporary archive of Totoes, found in two pots at Deir el Medina: Depauw 1997: 156–7). The use of Greek for legal documents progressively expanded at the expense of Egyptian, partly because after 146 BC demotic contracts required registration in Greek to be fully effective (Depauw 1997: 24); and paradoxically, the protection offered to Egyptian law in the 'Amnesty Decree' of 118 BC only accelerated this trend (Austin 231, lines 207–20; Pestman 1985). But Greek texts start to reflect Egyptian legal practices; for instance, the woman Nahomsesis regularly employed Greek contracts without using a guardian, despite apparently not being literate in Greek herself (Rowlandson 1998: no. 184). The texts from Pathyris end abruptly in 88 BC, when the Thebaid experienced yet another rebellion.

Land allotments to soldiers continued to be made right through the second century and beyond, though now the recipients were not immigrants, but locally born, and the apparent ethnic distinction between *machimoi* (Egyptian foot-soldiers) and the higher status 'Macedonians of the katoicic cavalry' who received larger plots is not all it seems. This, among other aspects of late Ptolemaic rural society, is best illustrated from the papers of Menches, village secretary (*komogrammateus*) of Kerkeosiris in the penultimate decade of the second century. A recent study has done much to elucidate the precise nature of this 'archive' (the surviving texts were discarded from the village secretary's archive, reused for various private jottings, and later formed the wrappings of 26 mummified crocodiles at nearby Tebtunis!), and the activities of Menches himself (Verhoogt 1998). Kerkeosiris was a remote and not very prosperous agricultural village, with thin soil overlying the limestone bedrock, and afflicted by sand sweeping in from the desert; the texts reveal a constant struggle against derelict land. It is surprising, therefore, to find Menches in regular contact not only with other local and regional officials, but also with the *dioiketes* in Alexandria. Whether this was typical of Ptolemaic village secretaries it is difficult to say; Menches enjoyed the patronage of an influential courtier named Dorion (who apparently paid the fee to renew Menches' term of office; *P.Tebt.* I 9–11, trans. Austin 260), and he held office at a time when there was an attempt to restore good administration after the chaotic conditions of civil war between Ptolemy VIII and his former wife Kleopatra II (see Menches' copy of the famous 'Amnesty Decree' of 118; *P.Tebt.* I 5, trans. Austin 131).

Much of Menches' duties concerned the administration and reclamation of land, and surviving texts include not only a summary of the entire village lands for 118 BC (*P.Tebt.* I 60), but also registers detailing the precise use of individual plots (of which D. Crawford 1971 remains the fundamental study, although further texts have since been published in *P.Tebt.* IV). Of a total area of 4700 arouras, Crown land comprised almost half (2427 ar.), and kleruchic land almost another third (1565 ar.). The village itself occupied some 70 ar. There was surprisingly little sacred land (292 ar.), orchards were very scarce (21 ar.), and no privately owned land is listed at all (contrast the figures for Edfu, above). All known landholders were male, another significant contrast with our evidence from Upper Egypt (and indeed with the neighbouring Herakleopolite nome; see *BGU* XIV: 226)

Women do appear incidentally in some texts, however, including as victims of a curious raid on the homes of several farmers of Crown land one summer day in 113 BC, during which household furniture, possessions and items of women's and children's clothing were stolen (*P.Tebt.* I 45–7, IV 1095–6). The Greek names of the ringleaders, Pyrrhichos son of Dionysios, *katoicic* cavalryman, and Herakleios son of Posidippos, might make one suspect ethnic tension as the cause of trouble (cf. Lewis 1986: 121), but this is never stated explicitly; and by well before this period, names had come to reflect a person's social position rather than ethnicity (Clarysse 1985, 1992). Thus 'Maron alias Nektsaphthis son of Petosiris' gradually mutated over a number of years (apparently on promotion from the lower ranks into the *katoicia*) into 'Maron son of Dionysios, Macedonian of the katoicic cavalry' (*P.Tebt.* I p. 547; cf. D. Crawford 1971: 134–5). Maron may have wanted to leave his Egyptian identity behind; but it was common to keep both a Greek and an Egyptian name on a permanent basis, using each in the appropriate context. So Menches was also known as Asklepiades, and his whole family had double names. This practice went far up the social scale: at Edfu, Ptolemaios/Pamenches who held the court rank of 'kinsman' under Ptolemy VIII, is commemorated with his wife and son in two quite separate series of grave monuments, in Egyptian hieroglyphs and Greek verse respectively (Yoyotte 1969; cf. D. J. Thompson 2001: 315–16).

Thus by the late Ptolemaic period, although Greek and Egyptian culture remained largely distinct, many individuals were effectively 'bicultural'. This included many, perhaps most, of the *katoicic kleruchs*. Their *kleroi*, originally revocable by the King, had now become hereditary, and even alienable to others of similar status, creating a stable, comfortably off, landowning class throughout the *chora* (Bingen 1983). The Egyptian background of this class (despite their apparently wholly Greek persona when viewed through Greek texts) is well illustrated by a unique demotic will of Heti, a *katoicic* cavalryman from Panopolis in 69 BC. Heti was evidently so much more at home with Egyptian as not merely to buck the general trend towards the use of Greek for private contracts, but even to import into Egyptian from Greek law the concept of a will, which was alien to the Egyptian legal tradition (Malinine 1967; cf. with caution Oates 2001).

Heti's house was situated in the north-west quarter of Panopolis, a nome metropolis. We also find *katoicic* cavalrymen residing in the metropolis (all in the street of Kleopatra Aphrodite) in the few documents to survive from Oxyrhynchos over the last half-century of Ptolemaic rule (earlier texts from this site, one of our main sources for the Roman period, have presumably succumbed to damp). But whether these cases are representative of a more general trend among *kleruchs* (or other landholders) to move from villages into the metropolis, we are unfortunately unable to assess through lack of evidence. While we may share Bingen's (1975) scepticism of the traditional view that Ptolemaic *metropoleis* were mere agglomerations of population, no better than villages in the facilities they offered, the fact is that neither written nor archaeological evidence has yet allowed detailed study of any Ptolemaic metropolis (other than the exceptional Memphis and Thebes of course).

Roman rule undoubtedly encouraged the *metropoleis* to flourish at the expense of the surrounding villages, developing the appearance and infrastructure of Greek cities. The Roman administration classed the entire population of the *chora* (other than Roman citizens; and citizens of Alexandria, Naukratis and Ptolemais) as 'Egyptians', while privileging within this group some metropolitan residents (given reduced poll tax, and membership of a more hellenized 'gymnasial' class). In both respects this marked, not a fundamental change of direction for the relationship of town and country, but an acute recognition of the complex ethnic and cultural legacy of the Ptolemaic period.

FURTHER READING

On papyri, see Erskine, this volume, section 5 with further reading there. *P.Haun.* inv. 407 (unpublished) is to be published by Thorolf Christiansen. On Alexandria, Fraser 1972 is the standard work; for a briefer introduction, see Jacob and de Polignac 2000. True and Hamma 1996 focuses particularly on art, but also covers Alexandrian society. On the recent excavations, Empereur 1998 and Goddio et al. 1998. The World Wide Web is a good source for latest discoveries; see especially: http://www.franckgoddio.org/english/projects. Recent publications on Naukratis deal only incidentally with the Ptolemaic period (e.g. Coulson 1996), and Plaumann 1910 remains the only study of Ptolemais; in contrast, both Memphis and Thebes have received recent attention (D. J. Thompson 1988; Vleeming 1995). On specific villages and archives, note especially Crawford 1971 and Verhoogt 1998 on Kerkeosiris, and Vandorpe 2002a and 2002b on Dryton at Pathyris (Vandorpe is also engaged on a more general study of the Pathyris archives).

On Ptolemaic society, Chauveau 2000 ranges more widely than its title suggests, offering a lively introduction to the later part of the period from an Egyptologist's perspective, a useful balance to the predominantly Hellenic perspective of most earlier work (e.g. Lewis 1986). Over recent decades, important work by Demotists (particularly Clarysse) has revolutionized our perception of how Greeks and Egyptians interacted under Ptolemaic rule, perhaps best characterized as marking a shift from 'colonial' to 'post-colonial' perspectives (for the earlier view, see Rostovtzeff 1941). Johnson 1992 provides a valuable, if inevitably fragmented, attempt to debate the 'multi-cultural' character of late Egyptian society on the basis of artistic as well as written evidence (but note that there is significant cultural change from the Ptolemaic to the Roman period; Johnson covers both, and the Persian period also). Manning 2003 (again informed by a background in Egyptology) offers a major new synthetic analysis of Ptolemaic land tenure and society.

In general, this is a rapidly developing field, partly through the publication of new texts, but more significantly because the dialogue between Hellenists and Egyptologists encourages new questions and perspectives on the material.

CHAPTER SIXTEEN

Jews and Greeks

Erich S. Gruen

Alexander the Great burst like a thunderbolt upon the history of the Near East. Within a dozen years in the late fourth century BC, he humbled the mighty Persian empire, marching its length and breadth, defeating its armies, toppling its satraps, terminating its monarchy and installing a Greek hegemony from the Hellespont to the Indus. No direct confrontation occurred between the great Macedonian conqueror and the Jews of Palestine. Fanciful tales sprang up later, in which Alexander paid homage to the High Priest in Jerusalem and Yahweh sanctioned his subjugation of Persia (Jos. *AJ* 11.304–5). None of them has a basis in fact. Palestine was of small interest to the king who captured the great fortress of Tyre, then marched straight to Egypt and subsequently to Mesopotamia, on the way to the heartland of the Persian empire. Judaea was spared – and largely ignored.

The long-term impact on Jewish history and culture, however, was enormous. The encounter of Jews with the language, literature and learning of the Hellenic world created a cultural revolution. The Greeks may not have noticed it much. But ancient Judaism was never quite the same again. The adjustments entailed by that encounter played a profound role in the reshaping of Jewish self-conception.

The interplay of Hellenism and Judaism is an endlessly fascinating subject. Did it constitute a confrontation? The coming of the Greeks to the world of the Jews has generally been viewed as a threat to tradition and faith. Increasing Hellenization would entail erosion of ancestral Jewish practice and belief. The Jews, on this interpretation, faced a choice: either assimilation or resistance to encroaching pagan culture. Indeed the terms 'Hellenism' and 'Judaism' (or 'Hellenism' and 'Hebraism') have served as metaphors for a tension between reason and religion, between rationality and spirituality, throughout the ages.

The matter is not so simple. This was no zero-sum game in which every win for Hellenism was a loss for Judaism – or vice versa. Nor did adaptation to the Greek world necessarily require compromise of Jewish principle or practice. To take only the most striking illustration, when a Greek gymnasium, a central exemplar of Hellenic society, was introduced into Jerusalem in the early second century BC, the Jewish High Priest himself installed it on his own initiative. And other Jewish priests soon found themselves in the palaestra, engaging in physical exercise and exploiting the institution to their advantage (II *Macc.* 4.9). They evidently did not regard this activity as undermining their priestly duties for the Temple. The notion of an irreconcilable cultural conflict needs to be abandoned.

Jews had previously lived under a Persian yoke, a light one and a relatively benign one. The centres of royal power lay at a great distance, in Susa and Persepolis, with little direct effect upon the society of the Jews. A major change occurred with the coming of the Greeks. Alexander's vast holdings splintered after his death, as his powerful marshals divided and fought fiercely over the territories he had claimed. In the new configurations of the Hellenistic kingdoms, Greco-Macedonian dynasts held sway and Hellenism became the culture of the ruling class in the major cities and states, both old and new, of the Near East, in places like Sardis and Ephesos, in Alexandria and Antioch, in Babylon, in Tyre and Sidon and in the coastal communities of Palestine.

1   The Homeland

The political constellation affected Jews everywhere – most directly and immediately in the homeland. The Ptolemies ruled Palestine for about a century, from the time of Ptolemy I's occupation of the land at the end of the fourth century to its acquisition by the Seleukids at the beginning of the second century. How firm or loose that rule was is difficult to say. Military governors exercised authority, and revenues were earmarked for Alexandria. But the Ptolemies leased out tax collection to contractors, often, if not regularly, local or regional figures, like the Jewish family of the Tobiads (Tcherikover 1959: 59–73). In Judaea itself, the High Priest retained a position of eminence, with extensive religious and political authority. He governed in collaboration with respected Jewish leaders in Jerusalem. The Ptolemies would have little need for or purpose in repressing local governance, so long as the area remained stable – and continued to produce revenues (Hengel 1974: 18–47).

Nor did Ptolemaic overlordship require the imposition of Hellenic culture upon the inhabitants of Palestine. But the infiltration of Hellenism seeped inevitably into the land. Cities with a hybrid population of Greeks and indigenous peoples emerged along the Mediterranean coast from Acco-Ptolemais to Raphia, in Transjordan from Gadara to Philadelphia-Ammon, and around Lake Tiberias. The existence of Greek-speaking communities (even if the ethnic mix was diverse) which adopted names like Apollonia, Pella, Dion, Ptolemais, Philadelphia and Skythopolis was bound to penetrate the consciousness of the Jews (Schürer 1979: 85–183). Commercial contacts increased the interconnections and made use of the Greek language a convenience. Service by Jews as mercenaries or as functionaries in the Ptolemaic administration accelerated the process. And intermarriages blurred older boundaries. Palestine became part of a larger Hellenistic world. The political and religious institutions of Judaea retained their integrity. Jewish traditions, laws and allegiance to the teachings of the Torah remained undiminished. But Judaea was no island fortress. Greek practices, language and learning would gradually show their impact.

International rivalries supervened to shake up the political structure. The energetic young Seleukid ruler Antiochos III revived the fortunes of his house in the late third century. His aggressive campaigns of 219 and 218 wrested much of Phoenicia and

Palestine from the grasp of the Ptolemies (Gera 1998: 9–20). The gains proved to be temporary as Antiochos suffered a celebrated defeat at Ptolemaic hands in the battle of Raphia in 217. But when Ptolemy IV Philopator died *c.* 204, leaving a young boy on the throne of Egypt, surrounded by ambitious advisors unpopular among their own people, Antiochos seized the occasion for a renewed invasion. This time success was enduring. In the 'Fifth Syrian War' Antiochos captured Jerusalem, drove Ptolemaic garrisons out of Palestine, and took full control of the country (Gera 1998: 23–35).

The Jews were beneficiaries rather than victims. They (or at least some of them) had assisted the Seleukid cause in expelling Ptolemaic forces from the citadel in Jerusalem in 198. In return, Antiochos promised to rebuild those parts of the city ravaged by war, authorized completion of work on the Temple, supplied animals for the sacrifice, food and other needs, abolished taxes for three years, relieved the people of one third of their tribute so as to restore losses, granted special exemptions to the Jewish, priests, and other Temple functionaries and pronounced his guarantee that Jews could live under their own laws (Jos. *AJ* 12.138–44). The documents that carried these declarations were, to be sure, delivered to the Jews by a Seleukid official acting on the king's orders. Royal authority in the region was unquestioned. But the arrangements between Antiochos and the Jews were negotiated by a Jewish representative (II *Macc.* 4.11). And the favours bestowed indicate a willingness on the part of the Syrian regime to promote internal autonomy in Judaea, backed by the resources of the Seleukids. The policy did not stem from altruism. It would add stability to the situation and earn the Seleukids wider support against any reintroduction of Ptolemaic influence.

The collaboration bore fruit. Appointment of the High Priest was subject to ratification by the king. But that office remained in the hands of the Oniads, who had long enjoyed its prerogatives. A smooth relationship held between Antiochos III and the High Priest Simon the Just. And that cordiality endured into the next generation between Antiochos' successor, Seleukos IV and Simon's successor Onias III. Seleukos indeed pursued his predecessor's favours toward Jerusalem, paying conspicuous honour to the Temple, and subsidizing the sacrifices out of his own pocket (II *Macc.* 3.1–3).

Tensions mounted, however, in the last years of Seleukos IV and the beginning of the reign of his successor, Antiochos IV Epiphanes. Internal quarrels within the Jewish establishment sparked the troubles, a clash between the High Priest Onias III and the overseer of the Temple, Simon, each appealing to the Seleukid court for intervention. Seleukos IV was tempted by the prospect of utilizing money from the Temple treasury, but did not press the matter over Jewish objections. Divisions within the Jewish leadership widened when a new ruler took the Seleukid throne in 175. Onias' brother Jason seized the opportunity to ingratiate himself with Antiochos IV, offering increased revenues to the Seleukids in return for support for his claims on the High Priesthood. Backing from Antioch put Jason in control and allowed him to institute a gymnasium, an ephebate and a community of 'Antiochenes' in Jerusalem (II *Macc.* 3–4). The events, striking and memorable, have generally been taken as the forcible imposition of 'Hellenism' upon the Jews by a 'Hellenizing party' implementing the wishes of Antiochos IV (e.g. Hengel 1974: 277–309).

Matters were not so simple. The initiative came from Jason, not from Antiochos. And nothing in the evidence indicates resistance to the Greek institutions that Jason introduced. The construction of a gymnasium implies that Greek schooling had already earned a place in Judaea. The priests themselves welcomed the gymnasium and supported games in the palaestra. The adoption of Greek names like Jason, Menelaos and Antigonos by some in the Jewish elite suggests that Hellenic culture had already become part of the social scene in Jerusalem. Jason had taken advantage of a new man on the Seleukid throne to press his own agenda. The episode represents competition for power within Judaea, not a clash between Hellenism and Judaism. The fact was underscored three years later when Menelaos, another member of the priestly establishment but not of Oniad lineage, outbid Jason in turn for the favour of Antiochos and was awarded the High Priesthood (II *Macc.* 4.23–9). The king, it appears, took little interest in the fraternal squabbles of the Judaean aristocracy. His eyes were trained on a prospective invasion of Egypt, the eve of the Sixth Syrian War. For that purpose additional cash from Jerusalem would come in handy. Co-operation with Menelaos would serve his ends. Antiochos conducted no campaign of coercive Hellenization. Egypt was the objective.

The king, in fact, led two expeditions into Egypt, in 170/169 and in 168. With Menelaos' assistance he entered the Temple in Jerusalem and carted off some of its treasures to finance his military ventures (I *Macc.* 1.20–8; II *Macc.* 5.15–21). The second invasion ended badly. The Roman legate Popillius Laenas, his arm strengthened by Rome's victory in the Third Macedonian War, arrived in Egypt in 168 and brusquely demanded Antiochos' withdrawal from that land. The Seleukid monarch had no recourse but to comply. The consequences proved to be grave for the Jews. There had been further internal upheaval in Judaea, as Jason's faction had re-emerged to oust Menelaos from power, but then engaged in a reign of terror that backfired and drove Jason once again to Transjordan. Antiochos Epiphanes returned to Jerusalem and ordered widespread massacre and enslavement in 168. And that was only the beginning. In the following year, the king sent forces to occupy the citadel, terrorize the populace, and install a military colony. Dissident Jews fled to the desert and the mountains. Antiochos then imposed his most extreme measures in late 167. He forbade sacrifices in the Temple, ordered erection of pagan altars, banned circumcision, burned copies of the Torah and engaged in wholesale violations of Jewish practices. The Temple itself was re-dedicated to Zeus Olympios, and pigs were slaughtered on the altar. Jews who refused to conform were ruthlessly punished (Tcherikover 1959: 175–203).

The cataclysmic events mark a critical moment in Jewish history. Resistance to Antiochos' persecutions began as a guerrilla movement, then swelled into an army under Judas Maccabaeus. When the king turned his attention to other adventures in the east, Judas and his followers inflicted a series of defeats upon the royal forces sent to quell the rebellion. The Jewish successes culminated in the recovery of Jerusalem, then the cleansing and re-dedication of the Temple in December of 164, a moment celebrated through the ages and to this very day with the festival of Hanukkah (Bar-Kochva 1989: 151–290).

It is easy and tempting to interpret these dramatic developments as a confrontation of Jew and Greek, a clash of Judaism and Hellenism, the reassertion of the nation's traditions against the coercive application of an alien culture (e.g. Bickermann 1937: 117–36; Tcherikover 1959: 152–74, 193–203). But the dichotomy is deceptive and misleading. Hellenism had long since entered into the life of Palestinian Jews (Hengel

1974: 58–106). The turmoil of these years arose from internal tensions and competitive rivalries. And Antiochos Epiphanes had shown no inclination before or after to conduct a crusade of forcing Hellenic culture down the throats of the peoples in his empire. His violent reactions in the wake of his compelled withdrawal from Egypt may reflect an effort to reassert his power and to halt any perceived decline in his authority in the Near East, or to punish recalcitrant Jews who had raised tumult during his absence in Egypt. But there is little to indicate that he sought to convert subject peoples to Hellenism (Gruen 1993a).

Nor, for that matter, did Judas Maccabaeus represent himself as a relentless foe of Greeks and the Seleukid empire, let alone of 'Hellenizers' among his own countrymen. He directed his military campaigns in large part against enemies who had dwelled in the lands surrounding Judaea long before the advent of the Greeks. Insofar as Judas rallied his forces against the foe, he hoisted a biblical standard aimed at the indigenous dwellers of the region, not primarily against the Greeks themselves. Clashes between Jewish forces and Seleukid armies occupy a prime place in the historiography of the Maccabaean era. But they should not obscure the interaction of Jew and Greek at the leadership level. Repeated negotiations took place between the Seleukid officialdom and the Jews during the lifetime of Judas Maccabaeus. The pacts and agreements proved to be short-lived, mere temporary cessations of hostility. But a more fundamental understanding endured. The Seleukids backed off from requiring abandonment of Jewish faith or conformity with Hellenic practices. Antiochos IV had been an aberration. And his successors did not revive such policies. Intermittent hostilities continued. But a pattern of reciprocal relations and mutual dependency took shape in subsequent decades, no irremediable antagonism (Gruen 1998: 3–12).

Hasmonaean (Maccabaean family) pre-eminence in Judaea survived Judas' death in 160. His brother Jonathan took the reins of leadership and maintained a *modus vivendi* with the Seleukids. Indeed, rivalries within the Seleukid house played into Jonathan's hands. Contenders for the Syrian throne sought his support for their ambitions, rewarded his assistance with appointment to the High Priesthood, and designated him as 'friend of the king' (I *Macc.* 10.15–21). The arrangement basically restored the situation that held prior to Antiochos IV: the Jewish High Priest exercised authority in Jerusalem under the patronage of the Seleukid ruler. Relations were often rocky, and shifting fortunes might bring setbacks. But parallel advantages undergirded the relationship. The kings needed Jewish support to shore up their positions against rivals and pretenders, and the crown's imprimatur gave vital backing to Hasmonaean leadership within Judaea. Distinctions conferred upon the High Priest also declared the king's right to bestow them.

The accession of Simon, yet another brother, to power after the death of Jonathan in 143 marked no break in the pattern. Despite claims in the sources (I *Macc.* 13.33–42; Jos. *AJ* 13.213–4) that his years brought a shaking off of the Seleukid yoke and real autonomy for the Jews, the evidence suggests a more nuanced picture. Demetrios II provided a peace treaty, authority over the fortresses that Jews had built, a remission of taxes and enrolment of the Jews into Seleukid forces. But Simon had initiated the negotiations, and his request, in effect, conceded the station of the overlord. It was Demetrios who forgave all the 'errors and offences' committed by the Jews (I *Macc.* 13.36–40). The Seleukid vantage-point takes precedence. And the

Jews' own inscription, affixed to a monument on Mt. Zion in 140, records that the Syrian monarch himself secured for Simon the office of High Priest, made him one of the king's Friends, and accorded him great honour (I *Macc.* 14.25–49).

Enhancement of Hasmonaean authority came not through successes against the Seleukids, but through weakness and divisions within the Syrian realm. Simon's re-occupancy of the citadel in Jerusalem constituted a gain of high symbolic significance. But the pattern of Seleukid contenders seeking Hasmonaean support and Hasmonaeans backing first one, then another of the Seleukid rivals persisted into the High Priesthood of Simon's son John Hyrkanos. Hasmonaeans still controlled Judaea as surrogates for Seleukid power. Interminable civil strife within the house of Seleukos allowed Jewish ambitions to burst former confines. Hyrkanos' expansionism included Hasmonaean advances into Transjordan, Idumaea and Samaria – but no assaults on Seleukid centres (Tcherikover 1959: 238–51). Hyrkanos' successor Aristoboulos became the first of his line to take the title of king and don the diadem (Jos. *AJ* 13.301; *BJ* 1.70). The move proclaimed a station equal to that of Hellenistic rulers. And the long reign of Alexander Jannaeus from 103 to 76 underscored the rise in international stature. Jannaeus conducted major military campaigns in Transjordan and the Galilee, issuing in the reduction of numerous Hellenistic cities by his forces (Schürer 1973: 219–28). The Hasmonaeans had now broken decisively with Antioch. There was nothing more to be gained from the disintegrating dynasty whose internal splits forecast impending doom. But Jannaeus' operations brought him within the shadow of the Ptolemaic realm, stirred the forces of Egypt against him, and compelled him to engage in devious negotiations with the rulers of that nation (Jos. *AJ* 13.324–355). Even in the reign of Jannaeus, most conspicuous for independence of Seleukid influence and spread of Jewish nationalist power, the Hasmonaeans still operated within a Hellenistic world to which they had adapted rather than one which they had rejected.

No confrontation of Hellenism and Hebraism disturbed the age of the Maccabees. Jason as High Priest had introduced the gymnasium and the ephebate. And, so far as our evidence goes, Judas Maccabaeus, his brothers and their successors kept them in place. Hasmonaeans and their prominent supporters adopted Greek names (a practice hardly confined to a 'Hellenizing party'). The purple vestments of the High Priest represented Seleukid court practice. Simon, traditionally claimed as champion of Jewish autonomy, constructed a massive family tomb that imitated Hellenic archetypes and received honours through a formal decree inscribed on bronze tablets that echoed Greek expressions of gratitude to benefactors. John Hyrkanos inaugurated the practice of minting coinage in Judaea, with Hellenistic symbols. Alexander Jannaeus took matters a step further by sporting Greek inscriptions on the obverse of his coins – while adding Hebrew lettering on the reverse and refraining (as did all Hasmonaeans) from placing any human portraits on them (Gruen 1998: 35–7). Hyrkanos was the first of the Jewish rulers to hire foreign mercenaries, a practice common to Hellenistic princes everywhere, but he and his successors maintained a majority of nationals in their forces (Jos. *AJ* 13.249, 13.374–8). And Aristoboulos, who adopted the diadem and royal title to place him on a footing with Hellenistic monarchs and styled himself 'philhellene', also engaged in nationalist expansionism and even insisted upon the circumcision of gentiles who had come under his authority (Jos. *AJ* 13.318). The Hasmonaeans advertised their regime as one that absorbed the ways of the Greeks and worked within the traditions of the Jews. Their coinage serves as an appropriate emblem: it spoke in both Greek and Hebrew, but to the same constituency – the Jews for whom Hellenism expanded and reinforced their identity.

Internal problems, rather than contests with Greeks, plagued the Jews under the later Hasmonaeans. Alexander Jannaeus' aggressive campaigns against Arabs and against coastal cities of Palestine put a heavy strain on Jewish resources, stirring dissension and rebellion among his own people – and prompting some brutal retaliation as a consequence. The degree to which this represents religious resistance by more traditional elements in society exemplified by the Pharisees remains uncertain. Jannaeus' harsh reactions, in any case, seriously exacerbated rifts among the Jews themselves. They spilled over into the reign of his widow Salome Alexandra and burst into violent dynastic conflict between her sons Hyrkanos II and Aristoboulos II in the 60s BC (Schürer 1973: 219–36). The fierce hostilities led directly to the most ominous development for the Jews: the coming of Rome.

A treaty of alliance had held between Rome and the Jews ever since the time of Judas Maccabaeus. It was twice renewed under Jonathan and Simon, and appealed to more than once in the High Priesthood of John Hyrkanos I (I *Macc.* 8.20–31, 12.1–4, 14.16–18; Jos. *AJ* 13.259–64). But it existed largely as a diplomatic formality, perhaps a source of pride for the Hasmonaeans, never a reason for Roman action or intervention. All this changed in the 60s when Pompey led Roman forces in the East, eliminated the rickety monarchy of the Seleukids, and reduced Syria to the status of a Roman province. Delegates from the factions of both Hyrkanos II and Aristoboulos reached Pompey in Syria, with mutual recriminations, and they were joined by a third set of envoys who denounced both and advocated theocracy without a king – the fruit of continuing internal discontent with the Hasmonaeans. Roman power decided the issue. Pompey, evidently eager to round off his successes and declare a stable situation in the East before his return to Rome, turned against Aristoboulos, overcame fierce resistance in Jerusalem, captured the citadel, and even entered the Holy of Holies in the Temple (Schürer 1973: 236–42). The events constituted a fateful turning point for Jewish history in the homeland.

Splits among the Jews reflected more than just partisan rivalries between dynastic contenders. They involved contests between supporters and opponents of the Hasmonaeans, between a rural and an urban populace, and between those willing to accept foreign rule and those determined to resist. Pompey's settlement could hardly resolve all disputes. The general refrained from annexing Judaea as a Roman province. Indeed, he showed respect for the Temple cult, leaving sacred objects untouched, ordering the Temple to be cleansed, and even offering sacrifice to Yahweh – useful insurance for his own success in the region. Pompey installed Hyrkanos II as High Priest, while prohibiting the title of King, and sent Aristoboulos as a captive off to Rome. Tribute was imposed upon Jerusalem and the countryside, perhaps to contribute to the costs of maintaining a Roman administration in Syria, and as a reminder of Roman presence and influence. And Pompey liberated many cities, including those on the Mediterranean coast, from the Hasmonaeans (Jos. *AJ* 14.72–6; *BJ* 1.153–7). But Rome exercised no direct rule in Judaea itself. The Jewish religious and political leadership remained intact. So also did the internal friction and discontent.

Hyrkanos had Roman backing, and retained it for the final thirty years and more of his life. He benefited from the Roman civil war in the 40s when first Caesar, then

Caesar's assassins elevated his stature in return for loyalty during their conflicts. But none of this discouraged tumult and upheaval within Hyrkanos' own domain. At least four times in that period risings occurred against the regime by the family and supporters of Aristoboulos, and each of them gathered considerable numbers before being suppressed (Schürer 1973: 267–80). The episodes disclose sharp discontent with Hasmonaean rule, perhaps resentment with Roman overseership, and genuine nationalist sentiments among the Jews.

In the course of these events, a new leader of remarkable energy, shrewdness and unscrupulous conduct rose to prominence. The notorious Herod emerged from Idumaean, rather than Judaean, origins to attain power in Jerusalem and hold it successfully for nearly four decades. Herod attained influence, first through his father, chief deputy to Hyrkanos, then through ingratiating himself with Roman leaders in the last turbulent years of the Roman Republic. He gained the patronage in turn of Sex. Caesar, governor of Syria, Cassius, the assassin of Caesar, Mark Antony, Octavian and Agrippa, managing to land on his feet with each shift in fortunes in Rome. He succeeded even in obtaining the title of king of Judaea, endorsed in 40 BC by both Antony and Octavian before their falling out. And he retained it throughout his life (Richardson 1996: 95–130, 153–73, 262–94). Secular power was now severed from priestly rule. More than deft diplomacy operated here. Rome evidently preferred to have Judaea as an independent client kingdom than as an appendage to the province of Syria, thus perhaps as greater counterweight to Egypt. Herod, in any case, took full advantage. Roman backing allowed him to expand his territorial holdings from Judaea to Galilee and Peraea, to add Idumaea, Samaria and parts of Transjordan, and to acquire key cities on the Mediterranean coast. The execution of Hyrkanos II in 31 BC ended the Hasmonaean line, giving Herod free rein to appoint his own High Priests – which he did with frequency, a sharp diminution of that office's authority and prestige, and further indication that Herod held the whip hand. Not that the years were trouble-free. Discontent expressed itself more than once in Herod's realm, and murderous quarrels within his own household marred his rule almost throughout (Richardson 1996: 216–39). But he held control, exercised extraordinary power, and made Judaea a major player in the Near East until his death in 4 BC.

Herod's links to the classical world were intimate, indeed ostentatiously paraded. His lavish building program in Palestine and elsewhere announced his passion for Hellenic cultural traditions. And homage paid to the Roman imperial house through conspicuous structures that rose in his own realm declared Herod's promotion of Augustan interests. Little wonder that Herod has a tawdry image in Jewish memory. Did the king, in fact, compromise the integrity of Judaism by his commitment to the world of Greeks and Romans?

It might seem so. Herod authorized the building of a theatre, an amphitheatre and a hippodrome in Jerusalem itself, striking emblems of classical culture in the very heart of the nation. Elsewhere he subsidized the construction of similar emblems, including pagan temples and gymnasia, with abandon: in Caesarea, Ptolemais, Jericho, Damascus, Tyre, Sidon and Tripolis. Even more notable, he sponsored the building of temples to Roma and Augustus, in Caesarea, Sebaste (Samaria) and Panion, direct homage to the imperial cult (Richardson 1996: 174–215; Roller 1998: 85–213). The king spread his bounty well outside the homeland. He bestowed benefactions upon a whole array of Greek cities in Asia Minor, the Aegean and Greece

Proper. Among other things, he endowed the Olympic Games at Elis and dedicated a structure in the holy isle of Delos (Roller 1998: 214–38). All of this exhibited the wealth and generosity of Herod, setting himself in the mould of Hellenistic monarchs, spreading his patronage and his name, and declaring himself an international figure at home in the Hellenistic world.

But none of this required diminution of piety toward the ancestral faith. Herod's most dazzling legacy, in fact, was his rebuilding of the Temple in Jerusalem in elaborate and splendid style (Richardson 1996: 245–9). And he had priests themselves trained as masons and carpenters, so that construction could take place in proper hands, a clear acknowledgement of sensitivity to traditional feelings (Jos. *AJ* 15.390, 15.421). Herod indeed made a point of exhibiting his adherence to tradition, as in his abstention from pork. Augustus once quipped that he would feel safer as Herod's pig than as his son (Macrob. *Sat.* 2.4.11). Shrines to Roma and Augustus arose only outside Jerusalem, a gesture towards Jewish feelings but also towards pagans who could conduct their rites with Herod's support. Theatres and hippodromes now became established institutions, raising no furor or resistance, Hellenistic features that Jews found entirely agreeable without sacrifice of principle. Herod may have been ruthless toward family and foes and obsessed with shameless self-advertisement, but his embrace of classical culture was perfectly consistent with the maintenance of a Jewish heritage.

2 Beyond the Homeland

The encounter of Judaism and Hellenism did not confine itself to Palestine. Jews spread themselves far and wide in the Mediterranean during the Hellenistic period. On the information of I *Maccabees*, composed in the late second century BC, they found their way not only to Egypt, Syria, Mesopotamia and the Iranian plateau, but to the cities and principalities of Asia Minor, to the islands of the Aegean, to Greece itself, to Crete, Cyprus and Cyrene (I *Macc.* 15.22–23). Reliable figures elude us. But there can be little doubt that Jews in the diaspora far outnumbered those in the homeland.

What induced so massive a migration? Some of it, to be sure, was forced and unwelcome, like the prisoners of war who followed Ptolemy I to Egypt after his victories in Palestine in the late fourth century or the political refugees victimized by civil strife in the land. But compulsory dislocation cannot have accounted for more than a fraction of the diaspora. The vast bulk of Jews who dwelled abroad did so voluntarily. Even where initial deportation came under duress, the relocated families remained in their new residences for generations – long after the issue of forced dislocation had become obsolete. Multiple motives operated. Large numbers of Jews found employment as mercenaries, military colonists or enlisted men in the regular forces. Others seized opportunities in business, commerce or agriculture. The new and expanded communities that sprang up in the wake of Alexander's conquests served as magnets for migration.

Communal life sustained the Jews of the diaspora. The institutions they created and the activities they conducted supplied the means to preserve traditions and advance the interests of the clan. But they did not promote private enclaves or segregated seclusion. Jews strove to engender circumstances that would enable them to maintain their ancient heritage while engaging comfortably and productively in the classical lands wherein they dwelled. Even in the diaspora they faced no stark choice between assimilation or adherence to the faith.

The synagogue was ubiquitous in the Hellenistic era. Testimony is fragmentary but decisive – from archaeological, epigraphic, papyrological and literary sources. Jewish houses of worship stood in Antioch and Damascus, in Alexandria and Leontopolis, as well as numerous other sites in Lower and Middle Egypt, in Cyrenaica, in Cyprus, in a wide range of cities in Asia Minor, on the shores of the Black Sea, in the islands of Delos, Samos, Kos and Rhodes, at various places in mainland Greece, and as far away as Italy, where Ostia and even Rome itself housed a substantial Jewish community (Binder 1999: 227–341; Levine 2000: 74–123; Gruen 2002). It is unlikely that many Jews in such far-flung locations resorted either to isolationist purity or to outright apostasy. In Alexandria, for instance, Jews could and did live anywhere in the city. But the majority chose to make residence in two particular districts that became known as the Jewish quarters (Philo *In Flacc.* 55). They mingled freely and (in some cases) lived among the gentiles, but most preferred the company of their co-religionists. Jews were not ghettoized. But, at the same time, their identity was undisguised and their peculiar customs conspicuous. Greek and Latin authors frequently comment on Jewish embrace of monotheism, observance of the Sabbath, dietary restrictions and the practice of circumcision (M. Stern 1976; 1980). Attachment to distinctive traditions continued to mark diaspora existence. And Jews did not have to hide them away in subterranean regions.

The synagogue provided a setting for a range of services. Jews engaged in a number of civic and sacral activities that marked their distinctiveness and expressed their communal identity. A common term for the institution, *proseuche*, indicates its central character: a house of prayer. Some of those in Egypt at least even obtained the grant of *asylia*, the right of asylum, from the Ptolemies, an acknowledgement of their sacral nature (*CIJ* 1449). Manumissions could take place in their precincts, with dedications to the divinity (Gibson 1999: 127–52). But religious activities constituted only a part of their role. Study and instruction held a prominent place in the functions of the synagogue. In the view of Philo, the learned Alexandrian Jew, it qualified as a Jewish replica of a philosophical academy, the *didaskaleion* (Philo *Mos.* 2.216). It supplied a venue for examination and interpretation of holy writ. Synagogues afforded the setting for communal dining, particularly for the celebration of festivals, the commemoration of key events in Jewish tradition that helped to define the community. They could also serve as places to adjudicate internal disputes among Jews, to conduct the formal process of manumission, or to assemble for the passage of decrees or for the meetings of a burial society. Synagogues acted as repositories for sacred monies, a means for display of votive offerings and dedicatory inscriptions, and archives for public records (Binder 1999: 389–450; Levine 2000: 124–59; Gruen 2002). Not that all these functions were performed in all synagogues. Local circumstances doubtless dictated numerous divergences. But the range of activities is impressive and telling. They were not carried out in secret enclaves. Synagogues stood in public view, sabbath observances were well known to gentiles, inscriptions announced decisions of the congregation, and the collection of moneys and their shipment to Jerusalem were conspicuous. The testimony underscores thriving and vigorous Jewish communities, self-assured in the exhibit of their traditions and the fostering of their special character.

The mechanisms for internal stability seem clear. But to what degree did Jews move outside their own circles and participate (or were permitted to participate) actively in the wider affairs of the Greek world in which they dwelled? Evidence here is scantier but not insignificant.

The best testimony comes from Egypt. It suggests that Jews in the Ptolemaic era fared surprisingly well. The author of the *Letter of Aristeas*, an Alexandrian Jew writing in Greek, reports that Ptolemy I removed up to 100,000 Jews from Palestine to Egypt, and then installed 30,000 of them in garrisons and fortresses throughout his realm (12–13, 35–6). The numbers are inflated and incredible. But the fact of Jewish soldiers serving in the Ptolemaic armies need not be doubted. Ample evidence, literary, epigraphic and papyrological, attests to it. Jews enrolled in regular units of the army, could obtain officer rank, and received land grants like any others in the lists of the royal forces (*CPJ* 18–32). Inscriptions in Aramaic and Greek from Alexandrian cemeteries in the early Ptolemaic period disclose Jews, evidently mercenary soldiers, buried alongside Greeks from all parts of the Hellenic world (*CIJ* 1424–31). One need not credit Josephos when he claims that Ptolemy VI appointed two Jewish officers as generals over the entire army, particularly when he makes the identical claim for Kleopatra III a generation later (Jos. *Ap.* 2.49; *AJ* 13.285–7, 13.349). Nevertheless, a substantial Jewish element plainly existed in the armed forces of the Ptolemaic domain. Jews, in fact, can be found at various levels of the Hellenistic administration in Egypt, as tax-farmers and tax-collectors, as bankers and granary officials (Kasher 1985: 58–63). No barriers, it appears, existed to prevent their engagement in the social and economic world of Ptolemaic Egypt. By the time of the early Roman principate (and doubtless earlier) the Jews in that land were shop-owners, farmers, merchants, shippers, traders and artisans. They even turn up as policemen (Kasher 1985: 55–8).

The gymnasium marked the capstone of higher education in Greek cities all around the Mediterranean and beyond. That institution, with its attendant corps of ephebes, the select youth of upper echelon families, signalled the cultural and intellectual elite of the Hellenistic world. Blanket statements about Jewish participation are impossible in view of the slim testimony. But there is enough to show that they did take part at least in some cities. Lists of ephebes, for instance, from Cyrene and from the Karian city of Iasos include unmistakable Jewish names (*SEG* 20.740–1; Robert 1946: 90–108). The effect of gymnasium education upon Jews cannot be gainsaid. Jewish authors adapted the Greek language and Greek literary genres to rewrite biblical stories, to produce historical narratives and to create fictional fantasies. They include the translators of the Pentateuch into Greek, the historian Demetrios, the authors of historical fiction like *The Letter of Aristeas* and III Maccabees, the tragedian Ezekiel, Aristoboulos the philosophic writer and supposed teacher of Ptolemy VI, and the wildly inventive Artapanos who recast tales from Genesis and Exodus to his own peculiar mold (Gruen 1998: 110–60; Collins 2000: 29–46, 186–95, 224–30). The anticipated readership of these authors must have been largely Jewish. Diaspora communities, scattered in the eastern Mediterranean, were predominantly Greek speaking, their knowledge of the Bible dependent upon the Septuagint, with most of their numbers no longer conversant with Hebrew. But the composers of these works plainly had access to higher education and to Hellenic cultural traditions.

Those who mastered Hellenic literary genres and wrote in elegant Greek must have had gymnasium education or its equivalent.

Diaspora Jews were no strangers to the athletic activities associated with Greek gymnasia. The evidence of the Alexandrian Philo makes this clear. He discourses knowledgeably about both the subtle tactics and the brutality of boxers, the fierce and draining battles of the pancratiasts, the tremendous powers of endurance exhibited by wrestlers, the pitfalls encountered by sprinters and jumpers, and the rabid spectators at chariot races, some of whom rushed out onto the race-course and were crushed by the vehicles. In addition, his works frequently made use of the imagery of athletic contests and physical training for purposes of analogy and simile (H. Harris 1976: 55–70). Philo clearly took for granted that his readers, primarily Jews, had a close acquaintance with them. Nor did Jewish fascination with and participation in gymnasia confine itself to the diaspora. Herod built three gymnasia (at least) in Palestine (Jos. *AJ* 15.268–271, 15.341, 17.194).

Jews, it appears, could even share in the governing process of gentile cities. Whether or not they held citizenship in individual communities (or indeed desired it) remains unclear. But the Jews of Alexandria certainly partook of political privileges and freely termed themselves 'Alexandrians' (Philo *In Flacc.* 53; Jos. *AJ* 14.188). They possessed similar status in Antioch, and in several cities of Asia Minor (Jos. *AJ* 12.119, 14.235; *BJ* 7.44). And they were able to attain high office in Cyrene (Applebaum 1979: 186–9). If more evidence were available, we might indeed find them elsewhere as well. Certainly the Jewish communities in Rome contained a substantial number who had even acquired Roman citizenship (Philo *Leg.* 157–8) – and others who held that franchise in Hellenistic cities abroad (like Paul of Tarsos). No barriers excluded Jews from becoming full-fledged beneficiaries of Roman imperial power. Of course, this does not translate into untroubled existence everywhere and all the time. But diaspora existence, insofar as we can make it out, managed to combine access to the classical world with affirmation of a traditional identity.

It remains to ask what relations held between Jews in the diaspora and those in the homeland and what role Jerusalem played in the self-perception of Jews abroad. The Temple still stood, a reminder of the hallowed past, and a Jewish regime existed in Palestine. Yet those in the diaspora, from Italy to Iran, constituted the vast bulk of Hellenistic Jewry. Few of them had ever seen Jerusalem, and few were likely to. Had Jerusalem then lost its significance for Jews long since settled in the communities of the Hellenistic world?

Far from it. The sanctity of Jerusalem retained a central place in the consciousness of Hellenistic Jews, wherever they happened to reside. References to Palestine as 'the holy land' and Jerusalem as the 'holy city' occur frequently in diaspora writings (e.g. II *Macc.* 1.12; Philo *Leg.* 225). And even the pagan geographer Strabo takes note of Jewish devotion to their sacred 'acropolis' (16.2.37). Loyalty to one's native land was a deep commitment in the rhetoric of the Hellenistic world. Jews naturally adopted a similar stance. Philo more than once endorsed the idea that adherence to one's *patris* has compelling power. For that philosopher, neglect of the *patris* stands on a level with failure to worship God (Philo *Mos.* 2.198). Other Jewish writers produced comparable formulations. Jerusalem as concept and reality remained a powerful emblem of Jewish identity, in no way disavowed by those who dwelled afar.

Do such pronouncements suggest discontent in the diaspora, a desire to pull up stakes and return to the fatherland (see van Unnik 1993)? That inference would be erroneous. Assertions about love of one's country accord with general Hellenistic attitudes and expressions (e.g. Polyb. 1.14.4). They do not require that residence abroad be abandoned and native environs reinhabited lest life remain unfulfilled. It is noteworthy that the texts which speak of reverence for the *patris* make no mention of the 'Return' as a goal. Jewish settlements abroad were often characterized as *apoikiai*, 'colonies' (e.g. III *Macc.* 6.10; Philo *Mos.* 1.71, 2.232). That designation presented them as offshoots from the metropolis. But the term, in customary Greek usage, lacked negative overtones. And, as employed by Jewish writers, its implications were, in fact, decidedly positive. Philo proudly details the 'colonies' that had been sent out from Judaea over the years to places all over the Mediterranean and the Near East (*Leg.* 281–2). Josephos echoes that sentiment in asserting that Jewish participation in colonies dispatched by other nations gave them an honoured presence in those settlements from the start (*Ap.* 2.38). Philo indeed affirms that for those sent to a colony, the *apoikia*, rather than the *metropolis*, becomes the *patris* (*Conf.Ling.* 78). Jerusalem, in short, remained the mother city. But, as is clear, the expression 'colony' had a ring of pride and accomplishment, signalling the spread of the faith and its adherents, not a fall from grace. Philo elsewhere offers a striking depiction of Jewish attitudes both towards Jerusalem and towards the lands where they now (and for generations) had made their home. As he puts it, they considered the holy city as their *metropolis*, but the states in which they were born and raised and which they acquired from their fathers, grandfathers and distant forefathers they adjudged their *patrides* (*In Flacc.* 46). That fervent expression eradicates any 'doctrine of the Return'. Diaspora Jews, in Philo's formulation, held a fierce attachment to the adopted lands of their ancestors.

Jews around the Mediterranean appear unapologetic and unembarrassed by their situation. They did not describe themselves as part of a diaspora. They did not suggest that they were cut off from the centre, leading a separate, fragmented and limited existence. People from communities and nations everywhere settled outside their places of origin in the fluid and mobile Hellenistic world without abandoning their identities as Athenians, Macedonians, Phoenicians, Antiochenes or Egyptians. The Jews equally eschewed justification, rationalization, or tortured explanation for their choice of residence. They felt no need to construct a theory of diaspora.

Commitment to the local community and devotion to Jerusalem were entirely compatible. That devotion had a public and conspicuous demonstration every year: the payment of a tithe to the Temple from Jews all over the Mediterranean. The ritualistic offering carried deep significance as a bonding device. The fact impressed itself notably upon the Romans. When the Roman senate in the 60s BC passed a series of decrees forbidding the export of gold, they had not reckoned with this Jewish institution. A howl of protest arose. The episode, as disclosed in a speech of Cicero, no fan of the Jews, demonstrates the earnest obligation of Jews everywhere to provide funds annually to the Temple from Italy and from all provinces of the Roman empire. Cicero remarks both on the pressure and the size of the Jewish assemblage in Rome that had gathered to support their compatriots elsewhere (Cic. *Flac.* 66–8). The event exhibits the solidarity of sentiments among diaspora Jews from Italy to the Near East in the matter of expressing their allegiance to Jerusalem. Philo reinforces the testimony of Cicero. His comment on the large Jewish community in Rome at the time of Augustus also associates it with zeal, for gathering the sacred tithes to be delivered by envoys to Jerusalem – a fact well known to the *princeps* (*Leg.* 155–6). The stark symbolism of the tithe had a potent hold upon Jewish sentiment. The repeated, ritualistic contributions emblematized the unbroken attachment of the diaspora to the centre.

Did the outpouring of cash for the Temple by Jews from Italy to Iran imply that the diaspora was reckoned as fleeting and temporary, an interim exile or refuge, an affliction to be endured until restoration to the Holy Land? In fact, the reverse conclusion holds. The continuing pledge of allegiance proclaimed that the diaspora could endure indefinitely and quite satisfactorily. The communities abroad were entrenched and successful, even mainstays of the centre. Their fierce commitment to the tithe did not signify a desire for the Return. To the contrary. It signalled that the Return was unnecessary.

A comparable phenomenon confirms the conclusion: the pilgrimage of diaspora Jews to Jerusalem (Safrai and Stern 1974: 191–204). Major festivals could attract them with some frequency, and in quantity. Huge crowds from abroad at Passover were evidently common. The women's court at the Temple was large enough to accommodate those who resided in the land and those who came from abroad – a clear sign that female pilgrims in some numbers were expected visitors (Jos. *BJ* 5.199). The delivery of the annual tithe itself brought diaspora Jews to Jerusalem on a regular basis, a ritual performance analogous to, even identical with a pilgrimage. The visits to the homeland and gifts to the Temple followed the appropriate mode of expressing homage. But the demonstration of devotion did not entail a desire for migration. Pilgrimage, in fact, by its very nature, signified a *temporary* payment of respect. The holy city had an irresistible and undiminished claim on the emotions of diaspora Jews. It was indeed a critical piece of their identity. But home was elsewhere.

The self-perception of Hellenistic Jews projected a tight solidarity between centre and diaspora. The connection emerges with impressive frequency in both fictitious representations and historical events. The author of II *Maccabees*, for example, provides a letter from the Jews of Jerusalem to their brethren in Egypt, urging them to celebrate the new festival that honoured the recovery and purification of the temple after the desecration by Antiochos IV (II *Macc.* 1.9, 1.18, 2.16–17). The *Letter of Aristeas*, celebrating the translation of the Hebrew Bible into Greek, has King Ptolemy II write to the High Priest in Judaea, asserting that the purpose of the translation was to benefit not only the Jews of Egypt but all Jews throughout the world – even those not yet born (38).

The community of interests could have direct effect on the events of Jewish history. In the late second century BC, Kleopatra III, Queen of Egypt, contemplated an invasion of Judaea, but was dissuaded by the advice of a Jewish general in her army. He claimed that any attack on the High Priest and his land would make enemies of all the Jews in Egypt. Kleopatra prudently dropped the idea (Jos. *AJ* 14.127–37). A half century later, when Julius Caesar was besieged in Alexandria, a troop of three thousand Jewish soldiers marched to his rescue from Palestine. A hostile group of Egyptian Jews dwelling in Leontopolis temporarily blocked their path until their general brandished a letter from the High Priest in Jerusalem. No further persuasion was necessary. The Jews of both Lentopolis and of Memphis declared themselves for

Caesar and helped to turn the tide of war (Jos. *AJ* 17.300–1). The sense of Jewish solidarity and the respect for the High Priest's authority had an impressive impact. Other episodes offer similar illustrations. Fifty envoys came from Judaea to Rome in 4 BC after the death of Herod the Great, pressing Augustus for an end to Herodian rule. Eight thousand Jews in Rome immediately materialized to support their lobbying efforts. And when a pretender to the throne emerged, claiming to be a reincarnation of one of Herod's sons, he found widespread backing from Jews in Crete, in Melos and in Rome itself (Jos. *AJ* 17.321–8). These events provide a revealing window upon the lively interest and occasionally energetic engagement of diaspora Jews in the affairs of Palestine.

A moving passage in Philo's corpus neatly encapsulates the theme. Philo who thrived in the diaspora, enjoyed its advantages, and broadcast its virtues, nevertheless found even deeper meaning in the land of Israel. In his discussion of Jewish festivals, he interprets Pentecost as a celebration of the Jews' possession of their own land, a heritage now of long standing, and a means whereby they could ease their wandering over continents and islands and their existence as foreigners and vagabonds dwelling in the countries of others (*Spec.Leg.* 2.168). Philo saw no inconsistency or contradiction. Diaspora Jews might find fulfilment and reward in their communities abroad, as he himself did. But they honoured Judaea as refuge for the formerly displaced and unsettled, and the prime legacy of all.

Josephos makes the point in a quite different context but with equal force. In his rewriting of the biblical Book of Numbers, he places a sweeping prognostication in the mouth of the Midianite priest Balaam. To the consternation of the king of Moab who had expected a dark oracle for the Israelites, Balaam predicted a glorious future. They will not only occupy and hold forever the land of Canaan, a chief signal of God's favour, but their multitudes will fill all the world, islands and continents, outnumbering even the stars in the heavens (*AJ* 4.115–6). That is a notable declaration. Palestine, as ever, merits a special place. But the diaspora, far from being a source of shame to be overcome, represents a resplendent achievement.

The respect and awe paid to the Holy Land stood in full harmony with commitment to local community and allegiance to gentile governance. Diaspora Jews did not bewail their fate and pine away for the homeland. Palestine mattered, and it mattered in a territorial sense. But not as a required residence. Gifts to the Temple and pilgrimages to Jerusalem announced simultaneously a devotion to the symbolic heart of Judaism and a singular pride in the accomplishments of the diaspora. Jewish Hellenistic writers took the concurrence for granted. They were not driven to apologia. Nor did they feel obliged to reconcile the contradiction. There was none.

FURTHER READING

The most valuable general narratives of Jewish experience in the Hellenistic world are Tcherikover 1959 and Schürer 1973. More specific studies on the pre-Maccabaean and Maccabaean periods appear in Gera 1998. A fuller treatment of the reign of Herod can now be found in Richardson 1996.

The pivotal work on the relationship between Judaism and Hellenistic culture in this era is that of Hengel 1974 which made a powerful case for the early and extensive infiltration of Hellenism into Palestine. The subject of Jewish-Hellenistic literature as emblematic of that cultural interchange has received recent discussion in Gruen 1998 and Collins 2000.

The topic of Jewish life outside Palestine, in the diaspora, is explored in a broad-gauged, extensive and judicious work by Barclay 1996. A different approach can be found now in Gruen 2002. More detailed studies pursue this topic in particular regions of the Mediterranean: On Cyrene, Applebaum 1979; on Egypt, Kasher 1985, Mélèze-Modrzejewski 1995; on Asia Minor, Trebilco 1991. Two major surveys of the role of the synagogue in the promotion of Jewish identity in both Palestine and the diaspora have appeared very recently: Binder 1999 and Levine 2000. On the attitudes of Greeks toward the Jews in their midst, the invaluable collection by M. Stern, *Greek and Latin Authors on Jews and Judaism* (1976–80) is essential reading.

CHAPTER SEVENTEEN

The Galatians:
Representation and Reality

Stephen Mitchell

During the later months of 280 BC well organized bands of Celtic warriors gathered in the southern Balkans, poised to invade first Greece, in 279, and then Asia Minor in the following year (Mitchell 1993: I.13–15; Strobel 1996; figure 17.1). These incursions and the subsequent settlement of Celtic peoples in central Asia Minor, in the region which was known thereafter as Galatia, were episodes of far reaching importance in the formation of the Hellenistic world. Greek writers used the name Galatai to refer both to the Celtic peoples of Gaul and to the Celts of Asia Minor, and the latter were also known as Gallograeci to Latin authors. In modern terminology the term Galatians is applied exclusively to denote the Celtic peoples of the eastern Balkans and especially of Asia Minor.

1 The Attack on Greece in 279

The fullest surviving account of the Galatian invasion of Greece, and the key text for our understanding of the impact of the newcomers, was written by Pausanias in the third quarter of the second century AD. He was in no doubt as to the significance of these events:

> My description of the council chamber at Athens contains some observations on the Galatian expedition into Greece. I wanted to provide a clearer record of them in my account of Delphi, because these were the greatest of all the deeds which the Greeks accomplished against the barbarians. (10.12.5; referring back to 1.4.1–6)

The narrative which follows this introduction is derived from an excellent early Hellenistic source, perhaps the historian Hieronymos of Kardia, and is one of the longest of Pausanias' invaluable excursuses on Hellenistic history (Habicht 1985: 95–117; Ameling 1994). He saw the Galatian war as a prime illustration of how the Greeks could act collectively in defence of their most prized possession, their freedom. After the Persian War of 480/79, he set the repulse of the Galatians alongside Greek resistance to the Macedonian power of Philip at Chaironeia in 338 and of

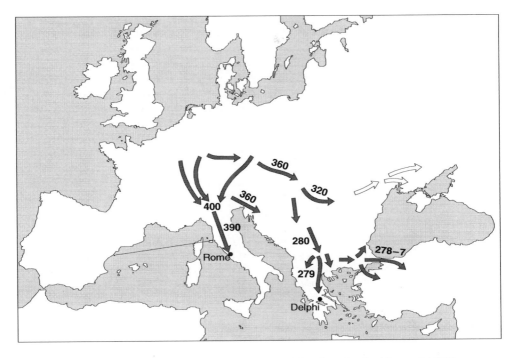

Figure 17.1   Map showing migrations of Celtic peoples; from Darbyshire et al. 2000

Antipater during the Lamian war of 322, as true tests of this patriotic panhellenic spirit (Habicht 1985: 106–7).

The invasion of Greece during the winter of 279/8 focused on the heroic but unsuccessful defence of Thermopylai, and a decisive battle at Delphi. The Greeks recalled that Apollo's divine intervention had combined with the forces of nature, a violent winter storm, to aid the defenders, and contributed to the total extirpation of the Galatian forces (Bearzot 1989). In practice, the key military contribution to the defence of Delphi came from the Aitolians, who thereafter took control of the Amphiktyonic League which ran the sanctuary (Nachtergael 1977). Pausanias explicitly highlighted the parallels between the defence of Greece in 279 and Herodotos' account of the Persian invasion two centuries earlier (Ameling 1994: 145–58). He matched the catalogues of Greek allies on each occasion with one another (10.20.1–5) and compared the Galatian battle unit known as the *trimarkisia*, in which the unmounted attendants of each cavalryman replaced their master if he fell, with the Persian 'immortals' of Xerxes' army (10.19.10–11). In the same spirit he recalled the deeds of the fallen Athenian warrior Kydias, by quoting his inscribed memorial dedicated to Zeus Eleutherios (10.21.5). The Athenians, under the command of Kallippos, who led the Greek forces at Thermopylai in 279, were fully the equal of their Spartan counterparts in the struggle with the Persians (1.4; cf. 7.15.3), and indeed the Greek achievement as a whole even exceeded the earlier one, as the struggle was not merely for their freedom, but for their very existence against the merciless barbarian foe (10.19.12).

The comparison of the two invasions was no invention of Pausanias but had been a commonplace of Hellenistic historiography. Polybios' account of Roman campaigns against the Celts in northern Italy compared those events with Greek resistance to the Persian and Galatian invasions. He claimed that such written accounts of heroic resistance to the barbarians made no mean contribution to the defence of the common good of the Greeks and to the struggles which continued against the Galatians in Asia Minor until Polybios' own times (Polyb. 2.35.7–9). Propaganda and historical myth-making were as important to the Greek cause as arms, leadership and manpower.

Most of the contemporary descriptions of these struggles, like so much Hellenistic historical writing, are now lost, but inscriptions, sculptures and other monuments from the third and second centuries indicate that the myth of the defence of Delphi and Greece, and the comparison with the Persian invasion, were created in the immediate aftermath of the conflict. In the spring or early summer of 278 the people of Kos passed a resolution to send a delegation to attend the new festival, which had been founded to celebrate the saving of Delphi, and to sacrifice in their own city to Pythian Apollo, to Zeus the saviour, and to Victory. The preamble runs:

> Diokles son of Philinos proposed: since, when the barbarians had made an expedition against the Greeks and against the sanctuary at Delphi, it has been reported that those who attacked the sanctuary had encountered vengeance from the god and from the men who had come to the aid of the sanctuary on the occasion of the barbarian invasion, and the temple had been protected and adorned with the shields of the attackers, and that most of the remaining fighting men had perished in the battles with the Greeks; – so that the people (of Kos) may demonstrate its joy at the victory and give thanks to the god both for his appearance at the moment of the sanctuary's peril and for the safety of the Greeks: – it was resolved . . . (*SIG*³ 398; trans BD 17)

Three themes were emphasized in the Delphic propaganda, which was immediately adopted across the Greek world: the gods' divine protection, Greek unity in defence of the sanctuary and the overriding theme of salvation, identified in the name of the new festival, the *Sotéria*. The Aitolians, who made immediate political capital from their decisive contribution, at once set their own deeds on a level with those of the Athenians during the Persian invasion. Pausanias, who had seen them, tells us that the shields mentioned in the Koan decree had been placed by the Aitolians in the metopes of the west and south sides of the temple of Apollo to complement the gilded shields set up on the east and north by the Athenians after the battle of Marathon (Paus. 1019.3; Schalles 1985: 107).

Later writers, as well as contemporary inscriptions, laid enormous stress on the cruelty and savagery of these new barbarians. Plunder, rape and wanton murder were claimed to be their stock in trade, and horrific stories were told about how they treated their enemies:

> They butchered every human male of that entire race, the old men and the children at the breast; and the Gauls drank the blood and ate the flesh of the slaughtered babies . . . Any woman and mature virgins with a spark of pride committed suicide as soon as the city fell;

those who lived were subjected with wanton violence to every form of outrage by men as remote from mercy as they were remote from love.... Others were to die by famishing hunger and sleeplessness, outraged in an endless succession by pitiless and barbarous men: they mated with the dying; they mated with the already dead. (Paus. 10.22.2)

This description of the atrocities inflicted on the Kallieans in Thessaly, with its hysterical crescendo rising from butchery, cannibalism and gang rape to necrophilia, is the most extreme example of the demonization of the Galatians, but the grotesque exaggeration carries little historical conviction. No doubt conflicts were brutal and violent, but the evidence of contemporary Asia Minor inscriptions from Thyateira (*TAM* 5.2.881), Erythrai (*SIG*³ 410) and two villages of the Lykos valley (*I.Laodikeia* I.1, trans. Burstein 19) indicates that the Galatians, rather than slaughter their victims, preferred to take captives with the aim of obtaining ransom payments, or held hostages to secure the compliance of Greek communities that opposed them.

2   The Crossing to Asia in 278

The military threat of the Galatians passed from Greece to Asia Minor, as the tribes of the Tolistobogii (or Tolistoagii), Trocmi and Tectosages crossed the Hellespont and the Bosporus in the winter months of 278/7 (Just. 25.2.7). The terror which they instilled in the cities of western Asia Minor is documented in a series of inscriptions from the 270s, before they were effectively confined to their permanent settlements in central Anatolia (Mitchell 1993: I.15–18). The responsibility and the credit for crushing the threat now passed from the Aitolians and the cities of Greece to the Hellenistic kings. Within a decade the dynasties of the Antigonids, the Seleukids and the Ptolemies each stridently claimed that it had rescued the Greeks from the new barbarian enemy and made this feat the basis of its own claims to legitimate rulership.

In 277 Antigonos Gonatas defeated an army of 15,000 Celts at Lysimacheia on the European shore of the Hellespont and assumed the title *Sôtêr* (saviour) for the first time. He thus sealed his claim to the kingship of Macedonia. Sometime between 275 and 268 Antiochos I rendered a similar service to the communities of western Asia Minor by defeating a Galatian army at the so-called 'Battle of the Elephants'. The echoes of this victory resonated widely. The terracotta workshops of Myrina near Pergamon produced figurines depicting elephants trampling Galatian warriors. These were doubtless modelled on the trophy, depicting only an elephant, which Antiochos had erected after the battle (Bienkowski 1928: 141–50). The literary traditions surrounding the event lie behind a brief, but epic description of the battle in Lucian's short essay *Zeuxis*. Appian tells us that Antiochos was first called *Sôtêr* after the battle (*Syr.* 65) and the title first appears on inscriptions of the 260s. Even in Egypt Ptolemy II was able to exploit a triumph over the Gauls to enhance his own monarchic prestige. Callimachus, in his *Hymn to Delos*, and other poets compared the crushing of a mutiny of 4000 Celtic mercenaries on an island in the river Nile with the victory of the gods over the giants and with Apollo's recent triumph at Delphi (Strobel 1994: 78–9). Galatian shields were depicted in the decoration of the temple of the Ptolemaic ruler cult at Limyra in Asia Minor.

A generation later Attalos I of Pergamon constructed his own monarchy on exactly the same foundations. Polybios tells us that Attalos only received the title of king after his victory over the Galatians, forty-four years before his death in 197 BC (Polyb. 18.41.7). He will have claimed the title *Sōtēr* at the same time. This takes us back to around 240, the context of his victories first over the Galatian tribe of the Tolistobogii in a battle fought in Mysia at the sources of the river Kaikos and then over the Galatians fighting in alliance with the Seleukid Antiochos Hierax (Mitchell 1993: I.21–2; for translations of the inscriptions of the victory monument, Burstein 85).

The claim that victory over barbarian, and especially Galatian forces, elevated the Hellenistic kings to be the saviours of the Greeks continued to be a crucial theme of royal propaganda in the second century, as is clear from an inscription of Telmessos in Lykia, set up in honour of Eumenes II in 184 to celebrate his victories over the Bithynian king Prusias and his Galatian allies.

> King Eumenes, our saviour and benefactor, took up the war not only on behalf of his own subjects but also on behalf of the other inhabitants of Asia, and surmounted the danger; having summoned the gods to his assistance and struggled against Prusias and Ortiagon and the Galatians and their allies, he triumphed brilliantly and splendidly and so as to make us give thanks to the gods. (Robert 1934: 284–6)

3   The Saviours of Civilization

The ideology of salvation was a vital feature in the legitimization of the Hellenistic monarchies. During the forty-five years which separated the death of Alexander the Great in 323 from the Galatian attack on Delphi in 279/8 Alexander's Macedonian successors had fought with one another to control his empire but had established no claims to be legitimate rulers of the Greeks. As Pausanias shows better than any other ancient writer, their authority was bitterly resented by the independent cities of Greece and Asia Minor. Alexander asserted that he had fought to free the Greeks of Asia from the Persians, but his mission had been betrayed by his successors. The appearance of the Galatians was thus providential for the next generation of rulers. The Celtic intruders had been identified by the Greeks themselves as an external threat comparable to the Persians. Without exception the major Hellenistic monarchies used their own Galatian victories to argue that they had saved the Greeks from the new barbarian peril and thus to justify their own right to rule.

Architecture and sculpture were exploited in spectacular fashion to promote the myth of the kings as saviours of the Greeks. The victories over the Galatians in particular became the cornerstone of the programme of the Attalids to promote themselves as the dominant power in Asia Minor and the Aegean world through paintings, sculptures and building programmes. Their impact can be seen in the major centres of the Greek world: Delphi, Athens, Delos, and naturally at their own capital Pergamon.

The aspirations of the Attalid kings are visibly embodied in the buildings of the sanctuary of Athena on the acropolis of Pergamon (Schalles 1985: 51–104; Radt 1999). The temple itself was a relatively modest Doric building, probably founded by Barsine, a Persian mistress of Alexander the Great, between 330 and 325 BC. At an early date the cult was identified as that of Athena Polias, reflecting the close link between Pergamon and Athens, whose cultural and political leadership would be

Figure 17.2   The Dying Gaul, Capitoline Museum, Rome. Photo: S. Mitchell

emulated by the Attalids. However, the appearance and scale of the sanctuary were definitively transformed after the victories over the Galatians. The earliest monument to be added was a colossal statue placed on a circular base which was dedicated to Athena by Attalos I as a thank-offering for his victory over the Tolistobogii at the sources of the river Kaikos (*OGIS* 269). It is likely that this base carried a statue of Athena Promachos, as did its fifth-century counterpart on the Athenian acropolis. Another base, which carried statues carved by the sculptor Epigonos, was dedicated to Zeus and Athena as a votive after victories over the Galatians and Antiochos Hierax, and probably displayed the mounted figure of Attalos in battle with his enemies (*OGIS* 280). The *pièce de résistance* of this sculptural programme was a nineteen-metre-long base set in front of the south wall of the sanctuary which was dedicated to Athena by Attalos himself. Seven further inscriptions identified the major battles which Attalos fought against the Galatians and the Seleukids to establish his authority in Asia Minor between 240 and 223 BC, the date at which the monument was set up (*OGIS* 273–9; translated Burstein 85). After much controversy, there is now a growing scholarly consensus that the most famous sculptural representations of the Galatians, the figure of the Dying Gaul (figure 17.2) and the group depicting a Galatian chieftain in the act of plunging his sword into his own breast while supporting the slumped body of his slain wife, both known in fine marble copies of the Roman imperial period, were displayed on this base, as part of a programme depicting the king's defeated foes (for an alternative reconstruction of the base, Marszal 2000: figure 10.1). It is clear that the choice of sculptural subjects, which included oriental as well as northern barbarians, was designed to represent Attalos not as the victor over his Seleukid rivals in Asia Minor, but as the conqueror of barbarian forces that threatened Greek civilization.

The symbolic importance of victory over the Galatians was emphatically reinforced when the sanctuary was enlarged and remodelled by Eumenes II (193–159). The area around the temple was enclosed by two-storey stoas erected to the north, east and south. The balustrades in the upper storey of the north and east stoas and those of the new propylon carried friezes depicting Galatian weapons, most distinctively their large oval shields with spindle-shaped bosses. Architectural sculpture was certainly also complemented by paintings, which have not survived. Pausanias mentions that he had seen a painting depicting a battle against Galatians on the Pergamene acropolis (1.4.6). Eumenes himself fought major campaigns against the Galatians in 184/3 and 168–6. His final victory, at a battle in Phrygia, was hailed with jubilation by the cities of western Asia Minor, and celebrated with new festivals founded in his honour (*OGIS* 305, 763, trans. Burstein 88). Fragments of a frieze found at Ephesos depict a battle with Galatians, which is probably to be associated with one of these wars. At Pergamon itself Eumenes now undertook the last great building operation of the dynasty on the Pergamene acropolis, the construction of the Great Altar, a work which defined the cultural and political claims of Pergamon as surely as the Parthenon had done for Athens. The main frieze took a mythological subject, the wars of the gods and the giants, the cosmic counterparts of the Greeks' earthly enemies, but the latter were represented iconographically in the guise of northern barbarians, with their thick manes of unkempt hair and full beards, an unmistakable allusion to the Galatians (Strobel 1991: 110–11). Thus the victories over barbarian foes were harnessed to the key aims of Pergamene propaganda, to present the Attalid regime as proponents of civilization and culture against the forces of barbarian disorder and as saviours and protectors of the Greeks from the Galatian threat.

The message was spread by vigorous cultural imperialism, focusing on the most important sanctuaries and cities of Greece. The earliest Attalid monuments outside Pergamon appear to have been built at the sanctuary of Apollo on the island of Delos. At either end of the south portico, which stood on the east side of the processional way to the temple, stood two large statue bases, very similar in dimensions to those set up in honour of Attalos I at Pergamon, whose subjects were, respectively, Attalos in battle with the Galatians, and his general Epigenes, depicted on horseback (*IG* 11.4.1109–10). They should be dated to the period 228–23 (Schalles 1985: 60–8). Sculptures depicting Galatians have also been found on Delos, although none can be demonstrably linked to the south portico. It is likely, but not proven, that the victories over the Galatians were commemorated in similar fashion at Delphi. Attalos I was certainly responsible for building a stoa above a new terrace in the north-west part of the sanctuary, in front of which stood one or more statue bases carrying his dedications. Unfortunately there is no direct evidence for the choice of subjects for the sculptures, and the building is better dated around 210/9, when Attalos received the honorary post of general in the Aitolian League, than to the immediate aftermath of his victories in the late 220s (Ameling in Bringmann and von Steuben 1995: 143–50). However, the design of the terrace and its stoa was closely modelled on a similar structure which the Aitolians had built on the opposite side of the sanctuary and adorned with spoils and other reminiscences of their defeat of the Gauls in 279, and it is unlikely that the Attalid building failed to highlight the same theme. Both structures with their decorative programmes also deliberately recalled predecessors built in the fifth century to commemorate Greek victories over the Persians (Schalles 1985: 104–23).

Pausanias is once again our only written source for a monument erected by a Pergamene king on the acropolis of Athens:

> Next to the south wall Attalos set up a monument depicting the legendary war of the giants, who once lived around Thrace and on the isthmus of Pallene, the battle of the Athenians against the Amazons, the struggle at Marathon against the Persians and the defeat of the Galatians in Mysia. Every figure was two cubits high. (1.25.2)

Marble sculptures from Rome, known as the small Galatian monuments to distinguish them from those of Attalos I at Pergamon itself, depicting giants, amazons, Persians and Galatians, have been identified as copies derived from this dedication, and their style suggests that the originals probably date to the period of Attalos II (159–53) rather than Attalos I. The composition vividly illustrates the whole thrust of Pergamene cultural propaganda, which deliberately assimilated their victories over the Galatians with the mythological defeat of the giants by the gods, of the Amazons by the Athenians, and with Athens' historical triumph over the Persians in 490 (see also Kosmetatou, this volume, section 3; Stewart, this volume, section 2).

The Galatians thus provided the Hellenistic world with a new barbarian model to replace that of the Persians of the fifth and fourth centuries. Just as the identity of Classical Greece in important ways had been shaped in self-conscious reaction to the image of the oriental barbarian, so the hellenized world after Alexander, which stretched far across former Persian territory, found its own identity in the contrast with the new type of the northern barbarian, embodied by the Galatian invaders. The Macedonian dynasties, whose arbitrary authority was deeply offensive to most Greek cities, now justified their claims to rule by offering protection to their subjects from the new enemies.

4   Historical Realities

The historical reality of Galatian history and culture as it entered into contact with the hellenized world bore little resemblance to the way they were represented by their enemies. A perspective that comes much closer to this reality than those of the propagandist sources reviewed so far is provided by the local historian, Memnon of Herakleia, who describes how the newcomers were brought across to Asia after they had been exerting pressure on the last city of Europe, Byzantion:

> (Nikomedes, king of Bithynia) arranged to bring them across on friendly terms. The terms were: the barbarians would always maintain a friendly attitude toward Nikomedes and his descendants, and without the approval of Nikomedes they would ally with none of those who sent embassies to them, but they would be friends with his friends and enemies to those who were not his friends; and also they would ally with the Byzantines, if by chance there were need, and with the Tians and the Herakleotes and the Chalkedonians and the citizens of Kieros and with some other rulers of peoples. On these terms Nikomedes brought the Galatian hordes into Asia. There were seventeen prominent leaders, and of these the most eminent and chief were Leonnorios and Luturios. At

first the crossing of the Galatians to Asia was believed to have led to harm for the
inhabitants, but the result proved it to have been to their advantage. For, while the
(Seleukid) kings were eager to deprive the cities of democracy, the Galatians especially
secured it by opposing those attacking it. (Memnon *FGrH* 434 F11; trans. Burstein 16,
modified)

The first implication of this passage is that the Galatians, far from being a tumultuous
horde, were disciplined warrior bands with responsible and effective leaders. This
impression, which is also implicit in Pausanias' account of the invasion of Greece, is
fully borne out by detailed analysis of the social organization of the successful and
aggressive La Tène cultures of Europe. As these Celtic populations grew and
expanded in search of new lands, they formed smaller, specialized bands of warriors,
to exert military and diplomatic pressure on target areas, thus forming the advance
guard of an aggressive colonial enterprise. The process has many parallels with the
formation of new and aggressive Gothic and Germanic groupings on the north
frontier of the Roman Empire in the third and fourth centuries AD, and their creation
of 'barbarian' kingdoms in the former Roman provinces (Strobel 1996). The actual
name Galatai, which seems to derive from a Celtic root which denoted military
capacity, was adopted by the Celts themselves to describe these warrior groups
(Schmidt 1994). They also provided a formidable resource of fighting men for
anyone in search of military reinforcement. Celtic mercenaries had been employed
in the Classical world since the early fourth century. Thus in reality their presence was
an opportunity, rather than a threat, for the Hellenistic monarchies.

As Memnon reveals, Nikomedes struck a treaty of alliance with the Galatians. The
advantages for the king were those which the passage expounds: a fighting force
capable of protecting the Greek cities of northern Asia Minor and his own kingdom
from the major power in Asia Minor, the Seleukids. The Galatian side of the bargain,
which was doubtless spelled out in the original treaty, becomes clear in the narrative
which follows: they took a major share of the war booty, but above all they obtained
their primary objective, land for settlement in the central areas of Asia Minor which
lay south-east of Bithynia and also formed a buffer against Seleukid territories, namely
the new Galatia. The northern parts of central Anatolia in the early third century, after
the decline of the Phrygians, had no natural overlords, and contained land of
excellent agricultural potential, whose inhabitants could easily be subjected to new
masters (Strobel 1996). As its subsequent history showed, the region offered an ideal
environment for the creation of a new Celtic state. The Galatians maintained their
distinctive cultural and political groupings in central Anatolia for 250 years, before
they were incorporated into a Roman province, which even then retained many
distinctive marks of Galatian cultural identity. A form of the Celtic language was
spoken in the region until the sixth century AD (Mitchell 1993: I.42–58).

Despite the attempt by Nikomedes to reserve Galatian military assistance for
himself, in practice they at once played a significant role in the military calculations
of all the Hellenistic monarchies. Galatians served as mercenaries in virtually every
major campaign from the 270s until the battle of Actium in 31 (Launey 1949–50).
According to Livy, Nikomedes of Bithynia had initially introduced 10,000 Galatian
warriors to Asia Minor. The rulers who had made the greatest capital from having
defeated them were the first to enlist Galatian contingents to their forces. Antigonos

Gonatas, after his victory at Lysimacheia, hired 9000 Galatians to help suppress his Macedonian rival Antipater Etesias. The Seleukid Antiochos Hierax formed an alliance with the Galatians in his rebellious war against his brother Seleukos II, whom he defeated at a battle near Ankyra. The location of the battle is clear evidence for the significance of the Galatian role in this war. Ptolemy II hired a contingent of 4000 Gauls to reinforce his control of Alexandria and the Delta, and grave monuments of Galatian warriors are a feature of the epigraphic record of Egypt. The eastern Anatolian dynasties of Ariobarzanes I in Cappadocia and Mithradates II in the Pontic region used the help of Galatian contingents to repel a Ptolemaic naval incursion into the Black Sea. In 218 BC, five years after the end of the long struggle with the Galatians and Seleukids for control of Lydia and Mysia, Attalos I settled a new Galatian tribe, the Aigosages, in the neighbourhood of Abydos on the Hellespont, doubtless to strengthen his hand in the contest for control of north-west Asia Minor with the Bithynian king Prusias I. Prusias reacted with a pre-emptive strike by destroying the Galatian force a year later (Polyb. 5.77–8, 5.111).

Thus the military activities of the Galatians should only exceptionally be explained as wars or raids undertaken at their own initiative. In the majority of these actions they were serving as major, but subordinate, players in the contests of Hellenistic kings for control of Anatolia (Strobel 1991). The victories of Antigonos Gonatas, Antiochos I, Attalos I and Prusias I demonstrated clearly that they could be decisively defeated by large, well-organized Hellenistic armies, and it would probably have been within the capacity of any of the kings to drive the Galatians definitively from their new settlements and bring an end to the Celtic occupation in Asia Minor, had they chosen to do so. However, they were too useful and important as a source of military manpower for this step to be contemplated, and periodic victories over the Galatians were too important a source of prestige to be neglected.

The Roman defeat of Antiochos III at the battle of Magnesia in 190, and the subsequent treaty of Apameia, which excluded the Seleukids from Anatolia north of the Tauros, and reinforced the authority of the Attalids as the main force in the region, fundamentally redefined power relationships in Asia Minor. Rome was now potentially or actually the strongest player in regional politics, and its capacity for action was underlined immediately after Magnesia by the expedition of Manlius Vulso in 189, who made his way through former Seleukid territory in Karia, Pisidia and Phrygia and ended his campaign with two successful battles against the Galatians in their own territory. The historical tradition about this war, principally derived from a long account in Livy, represents the Galatians as the main target of Manlius' expedition. The two battles were described as major Roman victories over a deadly foe, although the details suggest that Galatian forces were no match for the legions opposed to them, and the outcome can never have been in any doubt. This tradition doubtless began with Manlius himself, who sought to gain maximum prestige and recognition for having destroyed another source of 'Gallic terror'. However, this Roman triumph over the Galatians was in fact exploited for propaganda reasons just as surely as the earlier victories of Hellenistic kings had been. Moreover, a close look at the details of the campaign has shown that its real aim was not to extirpate the Galatians, but to harry and put pressure on remaining Seleukid forces in Asia Minor, as Roman negotiators thrashed out the uncompromising terms of the treaty of Apameia (Grainger 1995b).

In fact at least until the middle of the second century the Galatians remained what they had been before, a significant but subordinate player in the power struggles of the region. Although they clearly fell within the Pergamene sphere of influence and authority, they remained an independent force. They formed alliances with the kings of Bithynia and of the Pontic region, in their continuing wars with the Attalids. There are hints that this was not to the dislike of the Romans who preferred not to intervene in these regional wars and were happy that the competing forces balanced one another. Equilibrium was preserved until the next major alignment of political forces was initiated by the creation of the Roman province of Asia out of the former Pergamene kingdom after 133, and the steady growth of the power in the Pontic region under Mithradates V and Rome's great enemy, Mithradates VI Eupator.

5   Galatian Settlement and Society

The Galatians survived these political changes and thrived in their Anatolian homelands. Our knowledge of Galatian society and political organization in this period derives from two sources. The first is the account of their constitution, provided by Strabo in the time of Augustus but evidently relating back to the period before 86 BC, when Mithradates VI massacred the Galatian leaders in a devastating *putsch*, which virtually annihilated their political leadership:

> The three tribes used the same language and differed from one another in no other respect; they were divided each into four sections, and called them tetrarchies, each having its own tetrarch, one judge, one military commander, subordinate to the tetrarch, and two junior commanders. The council of the twelve tetrarchs consisted of three hundred men, And they assembled at the so-called *Drynemetos*. The council decided major cases, the tetrarchs and the judges all the others. (12.5.1)

There is no reason to doubt that this description, derived from an unknown source, is substantially accurate, and details of Galatian political organization and the functions of its tribal leaders can be paralleled from Celtic societies in western Europe. In the east, the Galatians were gradually affected by the process of hellenization. Some of their leaders and surely most of those who served for long periods as mercenaries learned to speak Greek. In the first century BC, especially after the massacre of the leading Galatians by Mithradates, a pattern of hereditary dynastic rule replaced the old tribal organization. Galatians were assimilated into local religious structures, which themselves became recognizably hellenized. Thus the leaders of the Anatolian sanctuary of the Great Mother at Pessinous in western Galatia, known by the Phrygian cult names as Attis and Battakes, included Galatians, and an imperial inscription suggests that the hierarchy comprised a college of ten priests, five each of local and of Galatian origin (Mitchell 1993: I.48). The temple itself, however, had been rebuilt from white marble in Greek form as an Attalid benefaction around the mid second century BC.

Inscriptions of the Roman imperial period show that the Galatians preserved their own ethnic identity, not only through the survival of the Celtic language but through their nomenclature, religious cults and forms of social organization (Mitchell 1982). Important archaeological discoveries also show that they created a characteristic

Figure 17.3 The site of Tabanlıoğlu Kale in north-west Galatia, probably to be identified with Peion, the treasury of the Galatian ruler Deiotaros in the mid first century BC. It occupies a fortified promontory above the winding course of the Girmir Çay. Sophisticated ashlar masonry and the design of the towers and gate indicate Hellenistic influence

pattern of regional settlement on the Anatolian landscape. Strabo and other sources indicate that the most important type of settlement were fortresses, occupied by local chieftains. Thanks to recent field work over twenty-five such forts have now been located, mostly in the region west of Ankyra occupied by the tribes of the Tolistobogii and the Tectosages. Typically they are located on strategic hilltops, which control the system of local communications, but which also dominate extensive stretches of agricultural territory. They have well built dry-stone walls, with carefully protected gateways, projecting towers and other sophisticated defensive features (Darbyshire et al. 2000). Only the latest and most elaborate of these forts, which have been identified as the strongholds of Deiotaros, the most powerful Galatian king of the first century BC, show the influence of Hellenistic military architecture (figure 17.3; Mitchell 1974). The others all represent local traditions of building and design. It is also clear that these forts did not function simply as strongholds or refuges, but as the kernel of important agricultural settlements. Surface observations indicate that they were invariably surrounded by buildings and field systems. The pattern is unmistakable evidence for the settlements of a large local population, living in organized village communities and dependent on agriculture for their livelihood. These settlements give an insight into the stable base on which Galatian society was built. They are clear testimony to the success of the Galatian colonization of Asia Minor and explain how these Celtic peoples retained their identity through the Hellenistic and Roman periods.

Their influence was not confined to the core region west and east of modern Ankara. Burials which can be associated with the Galatians have been found in fertile agricultural plains in eastern Bithynia, near Bolu and in the middle Sangarios valley. Hilltop fortresses with close affinities to those in Galatia have been identified by a recent survey of Paphlagonia. They are evidence for the expansion of Galatian settlement substantially beyond the original area of settlement. Object finds are reported from an even wider geographical range. Belt-buckles, decorative torques, fibulae and weapons of distinctive La Tène types have now been recovered from widely dispersed locations in Asia Minor, including Cappadocia in the south-east, Lykia and Pisidia in the south-west, Paphlagonia in the north as well as findspots along the western Asia Minor coast. In some cases these may have been associated with Galatian settlements, but others may reflect the diaspora of Galatian mercenaries, whose families often settled in the Greek cities of Asia Minor (Mitchell 1993: I.57).

The Galatians have hitherto occupied a marginal place in modern reappraisals of the Hellenistic world. This perception rests on a major historical misjudgement. The presence of these new barbarians in Greece and Asia Minor, and the terror which their presence inspired, proved less of a threat than an opportunity for the Hellenistic kings to redefine their role in relation to their Greek subjects. Galatian victories enabled the kings to claim to be the protectors of civilization from chaos and barbarous annihilation. Their very legitimacy as monarchs was reinforced by such claims and by the ruler cults which the Greeks initiated for their new saviours (Habicht 1970). The northerners replaced the Persians as an archetypal symbol of non-Greek barbarians, and thus contributed to the new definition of what it was to be Greek in a hellenized world which now encompassed much of Asia.

The Celts meanwhile established themselves as the most successful and long-lasting external migrants into the Hellenistic world, and took second place only to the Jews in forming the most successful and enduring non-Greek cultural group within the western parts of Alexander's former empire. Literary and documentary evidence has long been available to show how extensive and persistent their settlements in Anatolia were. It is reasonable to hope that future archaeological discoveries, in addition to those which have already dramatically changed our understanding of Galatia, will finally set the record straight and restore the region and its people to proper prominence.

FURTHER READING

Modern scholarship has placed increasing emphasis on the disparity between the image of the Galatians as barbaric enemies of civilization, which derives from propagandistic documentary and literary sources, and the dispassionate evidence from archaeology, which is the source of our information about their way of life in their new Anatolian homeland. For the image of the Galatians see in particular Schalles 1985, Hannestad 1994, Strobel 1994; for a sceptical re-thinking of the image in Pergamene art, Marszal 2000. The Delphic evidence is discussed in detail by Nachtergael 1977. Launey 1949–50 is an authoritative and detailed account of their role as mercenaries in the Hellenistic world. Mitchell 1993 and Darbyshire et al. 2000 provide extensive information about the archaeological evidence for Galatian settlements in Asia Minor, and Schmidt 1994 is the most recent discussion of the evidence of their language. Strobel 1996 is the first part of a promised two-volume study of the Galatians, and offers a highly detailed and authoritative analysis of the historical development of Galatian society, which draws extensive parallels with processes of tribal formation among north European barbarian groups in late antiquity.

CHAPTER EIGHTEEN

Beyond Greeks and Barbarians: Italy and Sicily in the Hellenistic Age

Emma Dench

1 Introduction

In 214 BC Philip V of Macedon wrote to the people and magistrates of Larisa in Thessaly as follows, urging them to be less exclusive in granting their citizenship to outsiders, and using Rome as an example to which they might aspire:

> For that it is the fairest thing of all for the city to grow strong, with as many as possible having a part in the state, and for the land to be worked not badly, as is now the case, I believe that not one of you would disagree, and it is also possible to look at the others who make use of similar enrolments of citizens. Among these are the Romans, who receive into their state even slaves, when they have freed them, giving them a share in the magistracies, and in such a way not only have they augmented their own fatherland, but they have also sent out colonies to almost seventy places. (*SIG*³ 543; trans. as BD 32; also Austin 60)

This extract from the letter hints at complex issues of heritage and identity in the Hellenistic world: not least the need for new models in a changing political and social environment. Importantly, Roman behaviour regarding the citizenship, which would have seemed extraordinary from the perspective of a Greek *polis*, is portrayed in terms that recall respectably Greek precedents, but these are carefully selected and amalgamated elements. Rome is the exemplar of inclusiveness, a virtue that was attributed by Thucydides to early Athens (1.2.6; cf. 2.39.1), but that has a new urgency in the changed conditions of the Hellenistic Mediterranean. Philip V is of course silent about the sometimes more exclusive thought and behaviour of classical Athens regarding the citizenship (e.g. Parker 1987; Rosivach 1987; Loraux 1993; Ogden 1996: chapter 5). Rome's alleged ability to send out nearly seventy colonies casts her in the mould of Alexander the Great. The figure of seventy, which bears no relation to the number of Roman and Latin colonies actually sent out by Rome by 214, is not plucked out of the air, but recalls traditions on the number of Alexander's own foundations (cf. Plut. *Mor.* 328E). It is within such old and new models that Rome's potentially shocking and distinctively non-Greek habit of enfranchising considerable numbers of ex-slaves is framed. Philip V's letter is a prime example of the increasing recognition of Rome on the part of mainland Greece, as well as Rome's own increasing interest in the image of Alexander and the Hellenistic kingdoms. But it is important to contextualize this mutual recognition within the broader environment of peninsular Italy and Sicily, over which Rome was beginning to gain supremacy in the decades immediately following the death of Alexander the Great. It is only within this broader context that we can begin to distinguish the more peculiar aspects of Roman expansion and rule.

This chapter explores the ideological and cultural dynamics of massive political changes in Italy and Sicily in the Hellenistic age: in short, it asks in what sense and in what form Italy became Roman and Rome became Italian, at a time when Rome was becoming mistress of the Mediterranean world. There are obvious dangers in writing an overly teleological account of ancient Italy, one that constantly projects the future greatness of Rome and devalues the historical significance of other peoples, cultures and communities in Italy and Sicily. It is important to understand the history of the emergence of Rome within the context of the peculiar dynamics of Italy and Sicily, partly precisely in order to avoid believing that Roman hegemony was inevitable, and partly in order to avoid exaggerating the uniqueness of Roman behaviour. Nevertheless, Roman hegemony in Italy and Sicily, or indeed in the Mediterranean world, did not entail the loss of individual local identities, of distinctive histories, or of divergent cultural models, and questions about the nature of ethnic and cultural plurality in the Roman west correspond to the interesting questions scholars are currently asking about the Hellenistic East (cf. Cartledge 1997: 4–6; for map of the west, figure 4.1 this volume).

2 Historiography

The political fragmentation of the Hellenistic Mediterranean world, the lack of a central point, whether this is perceived as a handicap to the study of this period or, alternatively, one of the aspects that makes it so exciting, has had an obvious effect on the traditional historiography of Hellenistic Italy and Sicily. 'Greek' and 'Roman' history, as it has been traditionally studied in schools and universities, has been driven by major extant 'great' ancient textual narratives, from Herodotos and Thucydides to Polybios, Livy and Tacitus. From such a perspective Italy and Sicily are important arenas for major political and military events, such as the Athenians' Sicilian expedition in 415 BC, the Roman conquest of Italy in the fourth and third centuries, or the outbreak of the First Punic War. In contrast, the histories of Syracuse, of Tarentum, of Neapolis (modern Naples), or of the Samnites, Etruscans, Umbrians or Lucanians, based on a combination of lesser or fragmented texts, and above all on material evidence, are traditionally perceived as 'local' histories of, at best, tangential relevance to the mainstream histories of Greece and Rome.

This problem of a place in history is well illustrated by the arrangement of material into chapters and volumes in the new edition of the *Cambridge Ancient History*: any sense of continuity is disrupted by apportioning some aspects of the history of Italy and Sicily to essentially Greek or Roman political narratives, and relegating others to area studies (Millar 1995). The concentration on the major political narratives of Greece and Rome reflects a series of nineteenth- and early twentieth-century intellectual traditions in the western world. Strands in the tradition that are particularly relevant to the ancient history of Italy and Sicily include the impact of the modern ideology of unification in later nineteenth- and twentieth-century Italy, with ancient Rome perceived as the first bringer of unity to Italy. More broadly, nineteenth- and early twentieth-century theories of the naturalness and inevitability of nations have had a major impact on modern readings of the making of Roman Italy, while the appropriation of Rome as a model for a number of European empires, including the British Empire, has influenced perceptions of the place of Rome and Roman culture within Italy (e.g. Mouritsen 1998; Ceserani 2000; Hingley 2000). In the English-language academic tradition within which the *Cambridge Ancient History* needs to be contextualized, the problem is compounded by the comparatively late recognition of the value of archaeology for the understanding, rather than the illustration, of the ancient world (e.g. M. Clarke 1959: 120; Stray 1998: 207, 310–11). The subsequent development of an essentially separate discipline of archaeology that maintains a somewhat strained relationship with ancient history has to some extent hindered the integration of properly analysed text with properly analysed material evidence (Halsall 1997).

If we look now at the problem from the opposite direction, a traditional emphasis on grand Hellenocentric or Romanocentric narratives has historically encouraged the development of proudly or romantically 'small' histories of the peoples or *poleis* of Italy and Sicily. Such accounts gained momentum in the particular ideological conditions of Italy of the late eighteenth and early nineteenth centuries, when there was a tendency amongst, in particular, the bourgeoisie of central and southern Italy to identify with the pre-Roman peoples of Italy, emphasizing traditions of a proud, independent past (Torelli 1999: 2). It is, however, worth noting that this was part of a much broader humanistic interest that had in the seventeenth and earlier eighteenth centuries focused particularly on the Etruscans. Some of the impetus for eighteenth century Italian enthusiasm for the Etruscans and other non-Roman peoples came from an unpublished manuscript, *De Etruria Regali*, written by Thomas Dempster, a Scot by birth, who had died in 1625 a professor at Bologna (Momigliano 1966: 18–20). For rather different reasons, there remains today, especially in Italian publications aimed at a broad audience, a strong focus on the origins and Iron Age, pre-Roman cultures of Italy: fostering a sense of distinctive, individual and sometimes independent local identities has a strong popular appeal. The importance of regional identities in modern Italian culture is also sometimes part of the impetus for extremely reputable scholarly enterprises, well presented museums and well-catalogued exhibitions (e.g. Dench 1995: 8 for Molise, ancient Samnium). These kinds of interests in pre-Roman history are based on the assumption (tacit or otherwise) that individual local identities were compromised or destroyed by the Roman conquest.

There are also other, more regionally specific 'ways of seeing' with longer or shorter histories that have shaped the modern historiography of Hellenistic Italy. These include the 'problem' of South Italy, that is, modern perceptions of the permanent and intransigent nature of a range of aspects associated with the south, particularly at the end of the nineteenth and during the first half of the twentieth century, including economic decline, depopulation and organized crime (Gribaudi 1996; J. Dickie 1997). Such perceptions are reflected in the motif of the timelessness of life in non-urban southern Italy that is to be found in some modern accounts of the area in ancient times (e.g. Barker 1995). There has, more specifically, sometimes been a tendency in modern writing to elide the very different historical circumstances of the late nineteenth and earlier twentieth century with the perceived decline of, especially, the Greek *poleis* around the time of the Roman conquest (e.g. Toynbee 1965: I.162–3; II.35). *Ancient* historiographical traditions 'explaining' why the *poleis* of Magna Graecia succumbed to Roman conquest have sometimes been brought in to enhance the picture of timeless decline, ignoring the culturally peculiar emphasis on luxury and excess (Purcell 1994: 389 with bibliography).

More recently, questions have been raised about the origins and cultural identity of what today is northern Italy. While the bourgeoisie of central and southern Italy were dreaming of their pre-Roman past, their counterparts in the north dreamed rather of their proud status during the Renaissance (Torelli 1999: 2). Most recently, questions of the cultural roots of the north have again become profoundly politicized in some quarters: here, an insistence on the essentially 'Mediterranean' nature of Hellenistic culture, unobjectionable from the perspective of an ancient cultural historian, may be extremely provocative to those who would prefer to insist on distinct, 'northern' roots (Denti 1991: 7–10).

I have already begun to hint at ways in which scholarship has been moving beyond an over-emphasis on Rome in the Hellenistic age, whether this is manifested in accounts that end with the Roman conquest and the implied death of local identity and culture, or in accounts that constantly look forward to the coming of the nation-state with the coming of Rome. These are obviously two sides of the same coin. Since the mid-1970s, the emphasis of (especially French- and Italian-speaking) sophisticated individual and collected studies of, especially, material evidence has been on modes of interaction rather than on romantically fragmented individual histories (P. Zanker 1976; *Modes de contacts* 1983; *Italici in Magna Grecia* 1990; Mertens and Lambrechts 1991). These have contributed to a more sensitive understanding of the processes of what are traditionally described as 'Hellenization' and 'Romanization'. These processes include the appropriation and adaptation of different cultural 'languages', including 'Greek' motifs, to articulate in unique ways individual cultural concerns. They also include the understanding of patterns of local settlement and the expression of local identities before, during, and after the Roman conquest of Italy.

These studies have serious general consequences for our perceptions of the growth and articulation of Roman power and Roman identity, which is revealed as both more and less extraordinary within the context of Hellenistic Italy and Sicily. One of the remaining problems of modern scholarship is that these sophisticated studies of Sicily and Italy have had little impact on major narratives and collected works on the Hellenistic world as a whole: there is still a tendency to privilege the Hellenistic kingdoms of the East on the one side, and the coming of Rome, somewhat decontextualized from Italy, on the other side. This may in part explain a tendency to begin to be interested in Roman history only at the beginning of the First Punic War. It may also begin to explain scholarly preoccupation with the Roman reception of Greek culture during and immediately after Roman intervention in the Greek mainland and the Hellenistic kingdoms of the east, neglecting, to some extent, Roman reception of other cultures in Italy, and, indeed, earlier reception of Greek culture through contact with south Italy and Sicily.

3   Characterizing Relationships: Old Ways of Seeing in a New World

We need to understand the relationship between peoples and cultures in Hellenistic Italy and Sicily within the context of current scholarly debates about relationships during the archaic and classical periods. For example, the commonly used phrase 'Greek colonization' has recently been problematized in scholarly accounts. Questions have been asked about how far there was anything 'Greek' about the 'colonization' of Italy and Sicily in either the sense of collective activity or in the sense of self-conscious or recognized shared culture. While recent scholarly accounts suggest the possibility of an emerging, aggregative sense of Greek identity in the archaic period, what seems most important in the 'colonies' of Italy and Sicily is the relationship with individual mother-cities, as well as the establishment of distinctive identities for the new settlements. The term 'colonization' is reminiscent of the activity of modern, European empires, and might carry overtones inappropriate to the archaic Mediterranean, such as those of a deliberate process, of a cultural, technological and/or religious polarity between 'natives' and 'colonists'. We should instead imagine a whole range of relationships formed between the newly arrived and local peoples: the emergent *poleis,* with their restricted territories, of necessity grew up to a greater or lesser extent dependent on local resources and peoples, while the ever-expanding world was mapped by mythological genealogies of wandering heroes – Odysseus, Herakles or Aeneas – that tended to write in rather than exclude new peoples (e.g. Bickermann 1952; Graham 1964; Malkin 1987; 1998; C. Morgan 1991; 1993; Dougherty 1993; Dench 1995: 47–50; J. Hall 1997; Erskine 2001).

It is in the fifth century, in the aftermath of the Persian Wars, that the notion of 'Greekness' defined in opposition to the barbarian first appears as an important means of thinking about identity, although this notion always exists in competition with other ways of figuring identity, such as those based on the individual *polis* (E. Hall 1989; cf. Walbank 1951). The notion of a common, even 'global' barbarian enemy is illustrated by explicit references to western contexts in contemporary Greek literature. As early as 470, Pindar celebrated in an ode the victory in the chariot-race at Delphi of Hieron I, tyrant of Syracuse. In the course of this, he linked Syracuse's rout of 'Tyrrhenians' (Etruscans) and Carthaginians at Cumae on the Bay of Naples with the victory of the Athenians over the Persians at Salamis, and that of the Spartans at Plataia. This tradition suggested an equation of Carthaginians and 'Tyrrhenians' with Persians, and the western battles with the battles of Salamis and Plataia, which had rapidly acquired a quasi-mythological status (*Pyth.* I.72 ff.; cf. Hdt. 7.166; E. Hall 1989).

The most convenient aspect of the rhetorical proclamation of Greek superiority to 'the barbarian' was, of course, the multitude of experience amongst the various Greek states that could be encompassed within it. The Athenians' claims for hegemony in and beyond the Aegean through their role in fending off 'the barbarian' were only the start of it. In southern Italy, a world in which ethnic relations were more complex, the Tarentines, who periodically both enjoyed and found comfortable ways of talking about their close relationship with their Oscan-speaking neighbours, the Samnites, were especially eager to advertise in certain contexts their own part in the struggle against the now generic barbarian. Pausanias describes two *ex votos* offered by the Tarentines at the panhellenic sanctuary at Delphi during the fifth century, both apparently emphasizing Tarentine supremacy over various south Italian *barbaroi*, the Messapians in the first and the Peucetii and their Iapygian ally, Opis, in the second. Pausanias' juxtaposition of the second to the Greek dedication after Plataia is no accident (10.10.6; 10.13.9–10).

At first, we might want to think of the examples discussed above as, essentially, participation in a new, pan-Mediterranean discussion of what it was to be Greek. But we should also emphasize the particularity of local circumstances. For the *poleis* of Sicily and southern Italy, the period from the late fifth century until well into the third was one of real change. Above all, the political independence of the *poleis* was challenged and compromised by competing powers, not least when the Samnites and Romans competed for supremacy in peninsular Italy from the last decades of the fourth century. The most striking individual examples include the political takeover of the Greek *polis* Poseidonia by Oscan-speaking people by the end of the fifth century, and the takeover of Messana in the 280s by the Oscan-speaking mercenaries of Agathokles, after his death (Costabile 1984; Dench 1995: 55–6). The expression of Greek superiority over the barbarian, essentially in cultural terms, was an important way of conceptualizing these changes: Greekness is imagined to be threatened by the arrival of the 'barbarian', and needs actively to be preserved. The perceived threat to the Greek language is not infrequently repeated (e.g. [Plato] *Ep.* 8.353e on Sicily; Athen. 14.632a on Poseidonia/Paestum).

It is essential that we realize the aspirational nature of this cultural dichotomy between Greek and barbarian: it does not describe at all literally the closely interactive nature of both cultures and relationships between peoples in central and southern Italy before, during or after the fourth century, or the kind of cultural continuities that we can observe here. One might think, for example, of the spatial geography of Paestum, the most clear-cut example of political change, where the political spaces of the former Greek *polis*, Poseidonia, were apparently retained unchanged (Greco and Theodorescu 1983: 81ff.; Curti et al. 1996: 183). Lessons in the subtlety of cultural identity and cultural change can also be learned from the remarkable corpus of Poseidonian/Paestan tomb-painting which spans from the fifth century to the third, that is from the period of the 'Greek' city through the political takeover by Oscan-speakers to the aftermath of the Roman conquest. The careful creation of typologies and of close iconographical readings of individual tombs, the painted walls of which create a narrative, make this a particularly suggestive body of evidence. Taking the famous example of the Tomb of the Diver from the first half of the fifth century, that is, the 'Greek' period, the immediate question to ask is how 'Greek' is painting of this kind, when the closest and most obvious points of comparison are to be found within the Etrusco-Campanian environment. Nor can the 'arrival of the barbarians' be tracked through any abrupt cultural caesura or through the 'deterioration' of cultural expression, although such interpretations are suggested in older art historical works (e.g. Trendall 1967: 150–5, 185–8). What one notices above all in fourth-century Paestan tomb-painting, and, indeed, grave-goods in Paestum, is a certain kind of cultural continuity. The culturally-specific preoccupations of a non-Greek elite are emphasized by the use of motifs common to various peoples of south

Italy: it is, above all, the formula and the emphases that are distinct. For example, vases suggesting an enduring taste for 'Greek' mythological scenes are placed with the dead, but, in contrast with the burials of the 'Greek' phase of the town, with their sparse grave-goods, there is clearly now a concern to mark and differentiate both the social status and the gender of the dead. Evidence of this kind acts as a powerful reminder of the fact that the categories of 'Greek' and 'barbarian' do not exist as culturally hermetically sealed entities (Greco Pontrandolfo 1979; Pontrandolfo and Rouveret 1992).

While the theme of Greek superiority to the Barbarian was clearly a powerful one for the Greek *poleis* of south Italy, the paradox was that it was not necessary for a community to identify itself, or to be identified, as Greek in order to appropriate this particular way of expressing superiority. It is again in Paestan tomb-painting that we can begin to glimpse the 'transferability' of this idea. For example, a tomb with a particularly suggestive sequence was discovered during the nineteenth century, and then unfortunately destroyed, the paintings known only from drawings made at the time. Paintings on the walls of the tomb, to which a date between the late fourth and early third centuries BC has been ascribed, show scenes of the life of the dead man, with emphasis on his status as a horseman and warrior, in a manner familiar to Paestan and Campanian tomb-painting. On the two long walls, the horseman is shown in full Paestan panoply, with characteristic plumed helmet and cuirass, fighting an Amazon in one scene, and a man in a Phrygian-style helmet in the other. That we are meant to draw parallels between the two scenes seems clear, and the motif of the Amazon indicates both a real comprehension of Greek symbolism, which regularly casts Amazons and Phrygians in the losing role of the barbarian, pitted against the victorious Greek. But more striking still are indications of the way in which such imagery is being re-deployed. The identity of the Phrygian-helmeted man whose losing position answers to that of the Amazon in the other scene is not entirely clear, but the possibility remains open that this is a Greek. If this is the case, assertions of Greek superiority over the barbarian would not just be elegantly re-interpreted, but also turned upside-down (Rouveret and Greco Pontrandolfo 1983; 1985; Curti et al. 1996: 183–4).

Finally, we can observe Rome enter this particular dimension by studying a late fourth-century series of polychrome vases from Arpi, a Daunian community which, under pressure from its hostile Samnite neighbours, appealed for Roman support and was received into a treaty of alliance (Livy 9.13.7). This series of vases represents winners and losers in battle, and follows a clearly identifiable set of iconographical rules: the winners are made to occupy the role of 'Greeks', while the losers are attributed the representational space and posture of 'barbarians'. In the clearest example, the winner in the role of the 'Greek' is to be identified by his unmistakable Roman armour, the loser in the role of the 'barbarian' by his characteristically Samnite armour (Mazzei 1987; Curti et al. 1996: 184).

The impact of Alexander the Great on ideologies of 'imperial' expansion, power and indeed monarchy itself is most familiar to us in late Republican and Augustan Rome. We might think, for example, of Pompey's acquired epithet, Magnus, or portraits of Pompey, or well-publicized anecdotes of Octavian paying his respects to Alexander's corpse, all examples of a complex relationship, emphasizing simultaneously Rome's closeness to and distance from Hellenistic models (Treves 1953;

Weippert 1972; P. Zanker 1988: 8–11; Smith 1988: 135–9; Carlsen 1993). Roman 'reception' of Alexander may in fact be traced much further back in time, as we have already begun to see from the example of Philip V's letter. We need also to understand Roman 'reception' of imagery and ideas associated with Alexander and the Macedonian kingdoms within the broader context of the 'reception' of such motifs in Hellenistic Italy and Sicily. Along with motifs that have their origins in the classical Greek world, such as Greeks and barbarians, the imagery associated with Alexander and the Macedonian kingdoms is part of the shared conceptual range of the post-classical world in which Rome gradually emerges as a serious contender.

In a digression from his narrative of the Samnite Wars, Livy poses the question of what would have happened if Alexander the Great had come to Italy and tried his luck against Rome. His long rhetorical 'proof' of how Alexander would have been beaten soundly by these manliest of men is no more and no less than a marvellous example of much-maligned counter-factual history (9.17–19). We might, however, want to pose a more serious set of questions about the contemporary and near-contemporary impact of Alexander and, above all, early Hellenistic kingship in Italy and Sicily, and specifically about the models of power that this came to represent. The most precise examples are those of the tyrants of Syracuse at the end of the fourth century and beginning of the third. In a manner that seems altogether typical of the self-consciously post-classical world that was Hellenistic Italy and Sicily, tales that self-consciously linked them to an older tradition of tyranny in the Greek world were an important aspect of their image (Lewis 2000). Such story-telling was, however, combined with flirtation with newer models of monarchy. For example, Agathokles of Syracuse became closely involved with Ptolemy I of Egypt, approaching the threat of Carthage from a new angle, and subsequently assumed the royal title of *basileus* in the last years of the fourth century BC, in apparent self-conscious emulation of the Diadochoi (Diod. 20.54.1; Meister 1984). Rome's future ally, Hieron II, was also proclaimed *basileus* in 270, and, in Hellenistic fashion, conferred upon himself the regal diadem associated with Dionysian victory (Smith 1988: 34–40).

More generally, in the last decades of the fourth century, south Italian ideological languages of opposition and conquest were much inspired by Macedonian regal images of victory: the advertised acquisition of 'spear-won territory' was a crucial aspect of Macedonian kingship (Walbank 1984c: 66). The representation of Nike, the goddess of victory, driving her chariot towards the heavens, ultimately dedicated in the late Republic on the Capitol by Lucius Munatius Plancus is attributed by the Elder Pliny to Nikomachos of Thebes, who worked for the Macedonian court, while the broader identification of the Roman mid-Republican cult of Victoria with Hellenistic Nike is a real possibility (*HN* 35.108; Hölscher 1967). This interest may prefigure the Roman fascination with these models of monarchy and regal behaviour that are clearly an important cultural reference-point from at least the second century BC (Rawson 1975; Walbank 1984c: 99). Nike was popular in Tarentine iconography of the late fourth century, being represented in the form of statues, on the coinage of the Tarentine leader Archytas, and on coin issues commemorating the feats of the various generals who arrived from mainland Greece to join forces against the local 'barbarians'. The poses in which Nike is represented recur: she drives her chariot – in south Italy, the two-horsed chariot is favoured – crowns conquering horsemen, or bears a trophy (Weinstock 1957).

Meanwhile, confusing nicely the dichotomies of which Greek thought was fond, the conquests of Alexander reawakened interest in the orientalized taste of 'the barbarian', an image that has its origins in fifth-century Athenian representations of Persians. Depictions of Persians were in vogue in South Italy, in and beyond the Greek *poleis*, as can be seen most famously in the case of the so-called Darius Vase, a large volute-crater found at Canosa, depicting the protection of Hellas by Athena, Asia lured to her doom by a Fury, Darius himself in full costume directly under Zeus, and an assortment of grovelling Oriental vassals bringing tribute to the coffers as the bottom scene (Metzger 1967; Trendall and Cambitoglou 1982: 495 with plate 176.1; Francis 1990: 36–9; Dench 1997: 130–1).

The Darius Vase offers clues to a revival of interest in themes of luxury, success and failure, and the rise and fall of empires, through Alexander's conquest of the Persian Empire. Such themes are apparent in Hellenistic historiography on the decadence and decline of the *poleis* of Magna Graecia as Rome begins to be dominant in the early third century BC: decadence every bit as shocking as that ascribed to Persia can usefully explain the subordination of the Greeks to a more austere enemy. We can also trace late fourth-century Tarentine traditions about the Pythagorean leader Archytas, who allegedly discoursed in the presence of Plato and the wise Samnite leader, Pontius Herennius, on vice and virtue in the form, respectively, of the denial of pleasures and the promotion of austerity. Thus, one implication is Archytas' Tarentum might be distanced from other, decadent *poleis* of Magna Graecia, escaping defeat and decline (Cic. *Sen.* 39–41; cf. Athen. 12.545a). The idea of 'barbarian' involvement in such discussions can be traced elsewhere in the late fourth century. Archytas' Tarentum, not coincidentally in need of manpower, was apparently engaged in a dialogue with the Samnites, creating for them an ancestry in common with their own Spartan roots, as well as a range of suitably austere ethnographical traditions (Strabo 5.4.12). Early third-century Lucanian tomb-paintings, like the grave-goods of Paestum, suggest an emphasis on austerity and controlled behaviour. It is within such contexts that traditions about the legendary austere behaviour of mid-Republican Roman generals, such as M'. Curius Dentatus, who supposedly refused Samnite bribes of gold while dining on turnips from coarseware, begin to look like more than just later Republican back-projection. What we can see here is the reinterpretation within new contexts and with new meaning of essentially classical and pre-classical modes of thought about success and failure, as various peoples of south Italy competed to claim for themselves the success that surely attended austere behaviour (Dench 1995: 101–2; 1997: 138).

We can see, then, that the ideology of victory and conquest inspired by Macedon, Pythagorean traditions on success and failure, and even that most 'Greek' of all themes, the definition of 'Greek' in opposition to the 'barbarian', were very far from being exclusive to the Greek *poleis*, emphasizing once again the high degree of communication between the various peoples of central and southern Italy. The intensely competitive environment of late fourth- and early third-century Italy may be illustrated by the alacrity with which different peoples seized on these vocabularies, casting themselves, or their friends, in the 'winning' roles. When Rome and the Samnites fought for hegemony over peninsular Italy, and particularly for the friendship of the more powerful of the Greek *poleis*, such as Neapolis in 327 BC, the ultimate card was philhellenism, the rules of which both societies knew very well (D.H. *Ant.*

Rom. 15.5ff.; Frederiksen 1984: 201 ff.; Dench 1995: 54). As always, it is the winning side that we, as historians, hear most clearly, and, in this case, we know most about the continued preoccupation of Rome in the later Republic and well beyond with the kind of themes that we have explored in this section and the previous one: the precariousness of imperial success and the constant need to regulate the behaviour of the elite; Rome as the civilized, 'Greek' centre of urbanity, rightly dominant over a barbarian, rustic Italy; the delineation of increasingly prominent individuals by reference to Hellenistic monarchs.

In these ways, the peoples of central and southern Italy used common ideological motifs to create culturally specific 'languages' of their own. We are inclined to place a disproportionate amount of emphasis on aspects of these 'languages' that we identify as 'Greek'. This is partly because of the prestige of Greekness, recognized and asserted in so much of the Mediterranean in different ways in the classical, Hellenistic and imperial periods, and partly because of the aesthetic judgements and preoccupations peculiar to our own, modern societies with their own complex histories of 'receiving' classical culture. It is for these reasons that we look for, and worry about, the 'Hellenization' of Rome and Italy, rather than 'Italicization' or 'Lucanization' (cf. Curti et al. 1996: 188).

That said, however, the discussion of the 'Hellenization' of Rome and Italy, or, slightly less provocatively, 'Hellenism' in Italy, has by and large taken place on a sophisticated level. Pioneering studies looked for models and parallels in the modern world, and it is perhaps Clara Gallini's article of 1973, 'Che cosa intendere per ellenizzazione' ('What is the meaning of Hellenization?'), that still offers greatest insight into what 'Hellenization' is, and, above all, the sorts of questions that we need to ask before making any assumptions. Gallini's models for the 'Hellenization' of Rome were modern African states such as Tanzania that had appropriated European political and cultural motifs in their struggle for independence, and the Japanese appropriation of American modes of production and culture that were instrumental in the emergence of Japan as an economic world-leader, challenging the status of the USA. In both cases, 'foreign' cultural motifs were used in the assertion of forcefully independent identities in a manner that is suggestive for later Republican Rome.

Besides emphasizing the active processes of creativity on the part of the 'Hellenized' Romans, as well as the fact that 'Hellenization' had different significance at different historical moments, the real value of Gallini's article was that, for example, the Japanese appropriation of American culture is not envisaged to require the assumption of an identity that is not Japanese (Curti et al. 1996: 182). In this context, it is worth spelling out the fact that, in ancient Italy, the 'Hellenization' of non-Greek peoples that we may catalogue is extremely rarely accompanied by the acceptance of a change in character to a Greek *polis*. Rome's supporters, ranging from Herakleides of Pontos to Dionysios of Halikarnassos, might have mused on the Greekness of her identity, while, amongst the Romans themselves, 'foreignness' might periodically be perceived to compromise 'real' Romanness, whatever that was imagined to be (Cornell 1995: 398; Beard et al. 1998: 87–98). But the case of Rome was in no ways parallel to that of the once-Bruttian town of Petelia, which, despite the Oscan nomenclature of her magistrates in the third to second centuries, sent a *theorodokos* to Delphi, and proudly recorded the names of gymnasiarchs (Manganaro 1964; Costabile 1984: 67).

In the decades since Gallini's article was published, scholarly awareness of the dangers suggested by the term 'Hellenization' has grown: awareness of the danger of implying agency, a process that is always the same, the existence of an active and a passive player in the process, is to be generally noted. Linguistic metaphors for the expression of individual cultural identities, and the creation of new identities, have been usefully explored, and get close to the subtlety required of this field of study (e.g. Gruzinski and Rouveret 1976; Wallace-Hadrill 1998).

However, one interesting, and potentially dangerous phenomenon to be observed in recent studies – or rather critiques – of both 'Hellenization' and 'Romanization' is a tendency to play down, almost to the point of eliminating, any sense of power relations between different peoples or even amongst one people, of cultural prestige, or of expressions of anxiety about identities perceived to be compromised by 'foreign' culture, which are to be plainly seen in the very different contexts of Rome and Judaea. There are hints here of a modern western sensitivity about relationships of power, a sensitivity fostered by studies of gender, race and class in both the modern west and the post-colonial world. Some of the very different perspectives on the processes of cultural change may be seen in a selection of recent scholarly work written by individuals from a number of different cultural, intellectual and disciplinary backgrounds (e.g. Bénabou 1976; Hengel 1980; Gruen 1992; 1998; Webster and Cooper 1996; Mattingly 1997; Woolf 1998; Curti 2001).

4 Plural Societies

'Traditional' Roman openness to foreigners and 'generosity' with her citizenship was, Rome's friends liked to claim, nothing new (Gauthier 1974). For a number of different reasons, Athens is the model most frequently cited or hinted at by authors with stances as different as those of Livy and Dionysios of Halikarnassos in the Augustan age, and Aelius Aristides of the so-called Second Sophistic (Livy 1.8.6; D. H. *Ant. Rom.* 2.15.3–4, cf. Thuc. 1.2.5–6; Aristid. *Rom. Or.* 60–1; *Panath.* 332). Such references speak volumes about the periodic importance of Athens as a cultural reference-point for Rome in the early imperial period, but should not lead *us* to ignore the more immediate context of Hellenistic Italy and Sicily that will show up more clearly the peculiarity of Rome.

Athens is not, from a modern perspective, the most obvious exemplar of inclusiveness. While recent studies have, interestingly, emphasized the role of the Piraeus as a booming multi-ethnic and multi-cultural community on which the success of the *polis* depended, the Periklean citizenship-law of 452/1 represents an attempt to restrict the citizenship on an unusually tight definition of descent (von Reden 1995; 1998; Cartledge 1998). In the broad context of Mediterranean history, it is Athens that seems the anomaly, but it is through Athenian eyes that we most immediately judge the rather different environment of the west. Most famous of all are Thucydidean images of late fifth-century Sicily, of ethnic and historical fragmentation, of the disparate hugeness that might recall a Herodotean Persian Empire, of the fault-lines hoped for by Athenian fortune-hunters doomed to tragic failure (Harrison 2000).

From a western perspective, early attempts to conceptualize in geographical terms new collectivities – Italia or Magna Graecia – suggest on an ideological plane the physical necessity of looking outwards. Not that this was without difficulty: conflicting traditions on the limits of Italia, beginning with fragments of the fifth-century western Greek writer, Antiochos of Syracuse, suggest the fraught dynamics of power between the *poleis* of the far south, and there is no sense of linear growth. There are interesting hints, however, of attempts to write in the ethnic diversity of the south. In spatial terms, this might be seen in conceptualizations of Italia as an isthmus (the boundaries of which differ according to context), combining coast-line and interior, thus writing in the relevant local peoples of the interior (Prontera 1986; cf. Lepore 1963). In mythographical terms, this can be seen in Dionysios of Halikarnassos' representation of antiquarian tradition on the successive kings of southern Italy, including Italus, Morges and Siculus, as if someone somewhere had tried to make sense of a composite ethnic reality by putting it into a pseudo-historical order (*Ant. Rom.* 1.11). It is Dionysios too who credits Hellanikos of Lesbos, the fifth-century mythographer and geographer, with a version of the naming of Italia that involves dialogue between Herakles and the local people of south Italy, as he looks for his lost calf. This version seems clearly to mythologize some of the realities both of the foundation and the survival of the Greek colonies of southern Italy (*FGrH* 4 F111 = *Ant. Rom.* 1.35; Lepore 1985; Dench 1995: 11).

Investigation of the term Magna Graecia, or, in Greek, Megale Hellas, ascribed usually to varying areas of southern Italy, again suggests a sense of competing versions, leading to intense debates amongst both ancient authors and modern scholars. One of the more suggestive interpretations of the term is its association with fourth-century post-Pythagorean thought of the kind that we have seen above, centred on the figure of Archytas of Tarentum. Megale Hellas was, according to this interpretation, an expandable ideal that could (in some versions) bring in non-Greek leaders, and even whole peoples, accommodating them through ideologies of good government and moral behaviour (Calderone 1976; Musti 1988; Dench 1995: 60). While we should never underestimate competition and tensions within traditions, the idea that we might see here some attempt to talk about what was literally common ground is highly suggestive.

The challenge of manpower in the relatively small, sometimes beleaguered *poleis* of southern Italy and Sicily gave impetus to more inclusive ideologies and behaviour. The most obvious solution to the problem of manpower was to recruit forces from neighbouring non-Greek peoples, and different *poleis* understood and formalized this relationship in different ways at different times. The Deinomenids, tyrants of Syracuse provided a fifth-century precedent for the ever-more pressurized *poleis* of the late fourth and early third centuries when they appealed to the 'mainstream' ideology of citizen soldiers by enfranchising the non-Greek forces they employed as manpower, reversing but retaining the ideological connection between citizenship and fighting for the *polis* (Frederiksen 1984: 193; cf. 203, n. 120; Purcell 1994: 385). The extension of the citizenship both rewarded these forces by allowing access to privileges and formalized the obligation to fight for the *polis* (Tagliamonte 1994: 114–23). For the Tarentines in the latter part of the fourth century BC, the Samnite forces they had recruited were conceptualized as the long-lost Pitanate cousins of the originally Spartan Tarentines: the unfavourable image of using mercenary forces was avoided by appeal to the common 'language' of shared origins (Strabo 5.4.12; Dench 1995: 53–61).

These are the general contexts within which we need to understand early instances of Roman concessions of citizenship and other statuses, which is in itself intimately bound up with the development of a specifically Roman sense of Italia. Some instances seem very close to western Greek examples, such as the status of *cives sine suffragio* ('citizens without the vote'), possibly a Roman version of honorific, non-participatory citizenship, held in conjunction with one's original citizenship, and acceptance *in fidem* (under the 'protection' of Rome) (Frederiksen 1984: 193–8). While being careful to think of early Roman concessions of the citizenship in appropriately comparative terms, after 338 BC, when the Romans secured the submission of all the neighbouring Latin peoples and some others, we can begin to see signs of peculiar developments. Significant leaps of imagination and experiments were required, and these were to provide the models upon which future developments in the Roman Empire were based. As we move into the third century BC, the Roman settlement of peninsular Italy after her wars of conquest begins to set Rome apart from her western Greek neighbours, partly in terms of scale, although we will continue to observe practice that recalls theirs. The treaties drawn up between Rome and individual Italian communities were based on manpower, and vast numbers were mobilized. Roman territory itself was also extended on a massive scale: M'. Curius Dentatus carved a swathe of Roman territory all the way to the Adriatic at the beginning of the third century, incorporating the inhabitants originally as *cives sine suffragio*, perhaps reinterpreted now as a punitive measure. In his boast of victory over so many men and their land, we may want to see echoes of the ideology of Hellenistic kingship, with its emphasis on victory and 'spear-won territory' (A. Sherwin-White 1973: 38–53; Purcell 1990a).

There were few juridically Roman colonies: in the third and early second centuries, colonies were largely Latin in status. This reinterpretation of an ethno-geographical term as a term used to delineate a particular juridical status in relation to dealings with Roman citizens is extremely significant. In part, we might see here an attempt to manage the vastness of the new Roman world: the colonists, many of whom would originally have been Roman, are envisaged to have a privileged relationship with Rome, but the communities in which they live are imagined as independent. This is the sort of conceptual leap upon which changing ideas of the Roman citizenship, and Roman identity itself, will be based.

While it may be that the idea of sacred space bounded by water is very ancient, it may be no accident that the earliest Roman notices suggesting the application of this idea to peninsular Italy refer to the third century. Huge boundaries are thereby set for the potential efficacy of Roman ritual practice (Diod. 27.2; Livy 28.38.12; cf. 28.44.11; Dio fr. 57.52; Catalano 1978; M. Crawford 1990). This highly proprietorial expression of what Italy means is only strengthened by the apparently new practice of reporting prodigies, signs of disturbance to be expiated by Roman ritual practice, from Latin areas in the late third century and from allied territories by the end of the second (Bradley 2000: 194). Such indications should really be thought about in connection with modern discussions about the distinctive nature of Roman rule. Nicolet has proposed that we should begin only in the Augustan age to think about empire as 'a territorial state', suggesting that emphasis on the control of physical space on a vast scale is a new phenomenon (1991: 1–2; cf. the slightly earlier chronology of Richardson 1991). And yet the Roman conquest of Italy in general was emphatically directed not only towards the subjugation of peoples but towards the transformation of land on ultimately a very large scale. In other words, it fits

Nicolet's definition of the 'territorial state' of the Roman Empire, while predating the Augustan age by several centuries (Purcell 1990a; 1990b).

If early hints of an interest specifically in the refiguration of the land of conquered peoples can already be observed in M.' Curius Dentatus' conquest of the Sabines, two major examples taken from the next decades begin to suggest the beginnings of an idea of Italy as a whole, a whole which can be redrawn according to a pattern determined by the Romans. One is the building of a network of huge, permanent roads, all leading outwards from the city, in the course of the third and into the second century. The building of roads is apparently closely connected to the foundation of colonies: a consideration of the dates of Latin colonies suggests a sense of symmetry and balance which seems to imply an overall vision of Italy, and a will to refigure the landscape, both in terms of large-scale geography, and in terms of the redistribution of land in the territory of the colony itself, through confiscation, centuriation and redistribution. The roads themselves alter forever the sense of ways in which individual areas interconnect, while defying what would seem to be topographical constraints, such as rivers and even mountains (Chevallier 1976; Pasquinucci 1985; Coarelli 1988; Laurence 1999; Curti et al. 1996). There are some limited comparisons to be drawn here with the 'Royal Road' of the Achaimenid Empire, at least in terms of the impression and impressiveness of drawing a vast line that refigures the connections between ethnically diverse peoples and symbolizes in a very visible way the power of the rulers (Briant 1996: 67–82; Purcell 1990a; 1990b). A second major example is that of the resettlement of populations in the third and second centuries: for example, in 269, Picentes were moved to the territory just outside Paestum. It is hard to overestimate both the impact of the rearrangement of huge numbers of people and the will behind the impulse to do this (Curti et al. 1996: 187).

While Italy is not traditionally considered within the context of discussions of the 'provincialization' of space in the Roman empire, in some ways transformations of Italian land from the third century are in fact a paradigm for what will become a distinctively Roman emphasis on the reorganization of space in the Roman empire. It is the intimacy of the relationship of Italy to Rome that both determines the intensity of Roman intervention at this early date, and which has often deterred us from discussing these events within the context of the distinctive character of Roman rule.

I have so far emphasized, even at the risk of over-emphasizing, the deliberate nature of the Roman conquest and the profound consequences it had on the reconfiguration of peoples and lands in Italy. In doing so, I take a line rather different from that of much recent scholarship on 'Romanization' and the creation of empire which, as we saw above, tends to emphasize local initiative in change at all levels, minimizing the effects of power-relations and institutional structures which need to be taken into account, even if the especially permeable nature of the Roman citizenship meant that, for some, crossing line was a much greater possibility than it was in any other ancient Mediterranean society after the archaic period.

To conclude this chapter, I will consider briefly what happens to local identities in Italy and Sicily as a result first of the processes of conquest and alliance and ultimately through being offered and accepting grants of the citizenship. On the more traditional view, distinctive local cultural identities, and, by implication, a sense of individual local identity, begins to 'disappear' from the Roman conquest, and this process escalates rapidly after the enfranchisement of Italy in the 80s BC. In its starkest versions, this 'disappearance' is interpreted as a by-product of 'becoming Roman', the process of beginning to look to Rome and aspire to the citizenship (Brunt 1965; Toynbee 1965: I.93; cf. Mouritsen 1998 for a systematic critique). We should perhaps start by observing some distinctions between the third and second century on the one hand and the first century on the other, rather than imagining a continuous process of cultural 'Romanization'. It is in the second century that scholars begin to trace especially in central and south-central Italy the flourishing of what appears to be common architectural aspirations, especially temple and theatre complexes that seem to hint at shared urban ideals. Despite a degree of homogeneity, such ideals are interpreted very differently within different local cultures, and even methods of building can vary a great deal (La Regina 1976; Morel 1976). While in the course of the second century, we can observe some adoption by non-Roman, non-Latin peoples of distinctively Roman culture, such as Latin loan-words (Campanile 1979), it is the great Hellenistic cities of the Eastern Mediterranean that seem to be the most obvious cultural reference-points. None of this is to deny the profound effects of the Roman conquest on local dynamics and identities. One striking example is to be found in the foundation of the Latin colony of Luceria founded on the borders of Samnium and Apulia in the late fourth century. The celebration there of the 'Trojan' cult of Athena Ilias renewed and reinterpreted an older assertion in Daunian culture of descent from the Greek hero Diomedes, associated with the 'Palladian' cult of Athena, and emphasized strong 'family' links with the Romans, friends to the Daunians against their common Samnite enemies (Torelli 1999: 172). Specifically local 'roots' asserted in mythological terms, perhaps the most profound way of expressing identity in the ancient world, are subtly reconfigured by the Roman conquest, but remain peculiarly local.

The cultural, but more particularly the political orientation of first-century Italy is rather different. The profound effects of enfranchisement and political incorporation on local communities are to be found manifested in numerous areas towards the middle of the century. While Italians must go to Rome to vote for laws and magistrates, to exercise magistracies, or to benefit from food-doles, incorporation within the Roman state has a marked effect on the physical appearance of individual communities, and above all in the configuration of local identities: perhaps the greatest irony of what is often described as the 'unification' of Italy is the effect that it has on distinctive local identities, dynamics and rivalries. One example is the sense of competitive pride taken in statuses granted by Rome, most notably those of *municipium* and *colonia*; this seems to be particularly marked in the towns of the north, the most newly Roman communities of the late Republic (Rudd 1959; Wiseman 1985; Cenerini 1989; Criniti 1994). Another is the creation of space within urban communities such as Alba Fucens, Herdonia and Pompeii, in the *campus*, the Latin equivalent to the *gymnasium*, for honours granted to individual Roman patrons (Torelli 1991). In areas such as the remoter parts of the Central Apennines, where urban ideals had hitherto had least impact, there are clear signs of real changes simultaneously in elite behaviour and in the very fabric of communities, at the same time as some individuals begin to aspire to a political life at Rome, in the increasing use of wealth in more 'private' contexts, and in the building of baths and aqueducts (J. Patterson 1991; Dench 1995: 140–53). It was perfectly possible to look simultaneously to Rome and to the local environment, as is illustrated by the inscription dedicated by the people of

Superaequum to their patron Q. Varius Geminus, 'the first of all the Paelignians to become a senator' (*ILS* 932).

It is surely not a coincidence that the end of the Republic and the first century of the Empire is the period when an interest in Italian local origins and histories is most noticeable. One does not necessarily have to imagine that what we see is the 'invention of tradition' from scratch in order to recognize significant contemporary impulses, above all that of reasserting distinctive local identities in a newly Roman world as well as that of renegotiating Roman identity in a newly Italian world. Earlier experiments in thinking about Roman identity as a plural entity, via the myth of the rape of the Sabine women, the formulation of *Graecus ritus*, or the expandable blood relationship of Latins (Thomas 1990; Scheid 1996; Arieti 1997), were much further developed in antiquarian and historical treatments of Rome's Italian roots, from Varro's *de Lingua Latina* to Virgil's *Aeneid* (Zetzel 1997; Horsfall 1997; 2001). The stylized variegation of the literary topos of *laudes Italiae* is a rhetorical counterpart to the Augustan creation of the Italian *regiones* with sometimes evocative ethnic names, such as 'Sabinum et Samnium' or Etruria (Thomsen 1947; Nicolet 1991). At a local level, two very different examples of the proud assertion of local roots include Livy's twinning of the foundation by Antenor of his native Padua with that by Aeneas of Rome at the beginning of his history, and the so-called Elogia of Etruscan Tarquinii, relating episodes of a pre-Roman independent past, that seem studiously not to mention Rome (Torelli 1975; Laurence 1998a: 104–6). Perhaps the most obvious case of a distinctive local identity that seems to have been deliberately fostered by Rome is that of Neapolis, proudly Greek, but Greek in ways only imaginable in the context of being part of the Roman state, well into the imperial period (M. Crawford 1978; Lomas 1997). These treatments coexist with flatter treatments of the making of Roman identity, such as Cicero's formulation of dual identity in his *de Legibus* (2.2.5), and Velleius Paterculus' narrative of 'Roman Italy' as a long and continuous process of incorporation, interrupted only by the Social War (Gabba 1973: 347ff.).

A traditional narrative of ancient Italy would end with Augustus' emphasis on the support of *tota Italia* ('the whole of Italy') for his leadership against an increasingly 'orientalized' Antony (*RG* 25). While the Battle of Actium and the Egyptian war formally mark the end of the Hellenistic period, the individual local histories of Italy are, as I have tried to show, by no means over, while the history of Roman Italy is inextricably linked to the history of the Roman Empire. As we have seen, the past, an increasingly complex amalgam of archaic, classical, Hellenistic and more recent motifs, continued to be understood as a remarkably rich repository of *exempla*, its cultural and geographical emphases shifting in different contexts. Almost as soon as distinctively Roman ideas about Italy began to be formulated in the third, second and first centuries BC, these in turn were used as precedents for the understanding and organization of territories and peoples overseas (Giardina 1994, cf. Gabba 1978). While the Emperor Claudius' insistence that extending the Roman citizenship on the other side of the Alps was nothing more than the continuation of a process as old as the city of Rome itself was, to put it kindly, a selective view of history, but there is no doubt that Roman experience in Italy encouraged the development of the distinctively plural shape of the Roman Empire, with its ultimately vast, multi-ethnic citizenship (*CIL* 13.1988; cf. Tac. *Ann* 11.23–5).

FURTHER READING

There is a rapidly expanding English-language bibliography on Hellenistic Italy and Sicily that fortunately includes some translated work, but few general overviews. Pallottino 1991 exemplifies some of the methodological problems in attempting to write an 'Italic' history, while J.-M. David 1996 is rather Romanocentric. Mouritsen 1998 is a useful antidote to the latter work. Despite the organizational problems mentioned in this chapter, the new edition of the *Cambridge Ancient History* has some excellent individual essays (NB Purcell 1994, Cornell 1989, M. Crawford 1996). Torelli 1991, concentrating on the period of the Roman conquest, begins to show those who do not read Italian something of what they might be missing: the historical readings of material culture are particularly striking.

Monographs in English on individual peoples, varying in chronological focus, perspective and the kinds of evidence privileged, include: Salmon 1967; W. Harris 1971, Frederiksen 1984; Spivey and Stoddart 1990; Ross Holloway 1991; Lomas 1993; Dench 1995; Bradley 2000.

For those who want to go further, Italian and French are indispensable, and bibliography of the major players can be chased via essays in the *Cambridge Ancient History*, the more recent monographs listed above, or Curti et al. 1996. Classic, paradigm-shifting collections of generally excellent essays include: P. Zanker 1976, *Modes de contact* 1983, Mertens and Lambrechts 1991. The Longanesi series of archaeological monographs on individual Italian peoples gives an idea of the distinctive emphases of Italian scholars: excellent volumes include those of Tagliamonte on the Samnites (1996), Guzzo on the Bruttians (1989), and Greco Pontrandolfo on the Lucanians (1982). For those who have the opportunity to visit sites and museums in Italy, the *Guide Archeologiche Laterza* series, divided into volumes by modern regions, is indispensable, and includes some classics that are of themselves scholarly works, e.g. Coarelli and La Regina (1984) on Abruzzo and Molise (the area that includes ancient Samnium).

PART V

Society and Economy

CHAPTER NINETEEN

Family Structures

Riet van Bremen

The interest of the family group overruling that of the individual is a historical constant until recent times. (Vérilhac and Vial 1998: 375)

There are different ways of approaching the concept of family structures. The major role played by kinship in the organization of Hellenistic cities, and the pervasiveness of what may be called 'family-thinking' in civic self-representation and in the collective mentality of those who lived in cities, are structural to society in a different sense from the 'structural' that is concerned with demography, with the size of households and the shape of kinship groups, or with marriage and inheritance patterns. It is with the former, and with the connection between what is conventionally called the 'private' and the 'public' that this chapter will be largely concerned, although one of its themes will be that of the impact of changes in the wider, political, world, upon the nature of the family group and its individual members. It will take as its focus the world of the cities, because it is here, in the cities of Greece, the Aegean islands, and western Asia Minor, that a reasonably coherent body of evidence exists and some level of generalization about developments is possible. It is also here that some of the more interesting tensions emerged between the Hellenistic world's two main organizational and representational systems: that of dynastically-orientated monarchies and equality-orientated civic communities.

I

1 Civic Endogamy: the Case of Latmos and Pidasa

Sometime in the years between 323 and 313 BC, the two cities of Latmos and Pidasa in Karia, in western Asia Minor, entered into a *sympoliteia*: a union of their communities. The treaty, ratified by an oath and inscribed in stone, survives virtually intact (Blümel 1997; C. Jones 1999a, cf. figure 19.1). Of the two cities, Latmos was the larger, situated at the foot of the mountain of the same name. The centre of Pidasa,

Figure 19.1 Inscription recording a treaty between Latmos and Pidasa, photo courtesy of W. Blümel. **Translation**: (line 3) The officials should also immediately lay on a sacrifice so that the city may live in harmony. (4)A new *phyle* should be added to the existing ones and it should be named Asandris. Men from all the *phylai* and *phratoria* in Latmos and in (8)Pidasa should be allocated to it by lot. And the remaining Pidaseans should be allocated to the remaining (three) *phylai* as evenly as possible. The Pidaseans who have been so distributed should be allowed to partake in all cultic activities: as members of the *phratoriai* in the cultic activities of the *phratoriai*, (12)and as members of the *phylai* in the cultic activities of the *phylai*, to whichever one they have been allocated. And the revenue which accrues to the Pidaseans and Latmians, from sacred or other sources, they are to have in common, (16)and there is not to be any separate income for either of the cities. And the debts which exist in either city until the month of Dios are to be settled separately by each of the (cities). And the Latmians should provide for the (20)Pidaseans sufficient living and stabling accommodation for a period of one year. And so that they will also intermarry with one another it will not be permitted to a Latmian to give a daughter to a Latmian nor to take (from him), and for a Pidasean (to give) to a Pidasean [or take from him], (24)but a Latmian must give to and take from a Pidasean and a Pidasean to and

whose territory adjoined that of Latmos to the south, was located in Mt. Grion, above the road that runs south-east from Miletos, towards Euromos and Mylasa. We do not know the name of the newly formed community, but it is clear from the treaty that Latmos was the dominant partner. Soon after, towards the very end of the fourth century, Latmos was refounded as Herakleia (by Latmos) on a site half a kilometre further east, probably by the Macedonian king Antigonos Monophthalmos. At this time the new city may still have consisted of Latmo-Pidaseans but we know that in the longer term the arrangement was not successful: the Pidaseans left the union sometime in the early third century. Pidasa continued to exist under its own name for more than a century, until it was integrated into neighbouring Miletos in the early second century BC in another – well-documented – *sympoliteia* (*Milet* I.3, no 149; translation and bibliography in *Milet* VI.1, 184–5; Gauthier 2001).

The union of Latmos and Pidasa was imposed by a higher authority, the satrap of Karia, Asandros whose allegiance at this time was to Antigonos Monophthalmos. His name is attached to the new *phyle*, Asandris, which the Latmians added to their existing three *phylai*. The treaty contains arrangements for the redistribution of citizens of both cities into the four *phylai*. It deals with the entitlements of the newly constituted citizen body, with the sharing of income, the setting up of joint boards of magistrates, and with arrangements for the Latmians to provide housing and stables for Pidaseans for the duration of a year. It is also concerned with the mixing of the two citizen bodies into one, for the purpose of which two extraordinary measures are taken: a rigorous, six-year prohibition of civic endogamy and a concomitant obligation to marry exclusively someone from the other city. (In describing eight separate permutations of daughter-giving-and-taking the Greek text manages to use the word *thugater*, 'daughter', only once, thus leaving no doubt about the male focus of the transaction):

> and so that they will also intermarry with one another (*epigamias poieisthai*) it will not be permitted to a Latmian to give a daughter to a Latmian nor to take (from him), and for a Pidasean (to give) to a Pidasean [or take from him], but a Latmian must give to and take from a Pidasean and a Pidasean to and from a Latmian for a period of six years. (ll. 22–5)

This rather striking example of ancient social engineering, for which so far no parallels exist, has been described as 'breaking with the old particularisms' (Gauthier, *BE* 1999, no. 462), implying that what we see here, at the very beginning of the Hellenistic period, is a new development, which runs counter to established structures and mentalities. But does it?

---

from a Latmian for a period of six years. And the magistracies must be filled from both Latmians and Pidaseans. It will be permitted to the Pidaseans to build houses (28)in the city on the common land wherever they wish. And one hundred Pidasean men, as designated by the Latmians, and two hundred Latmians as designated by the Pidaseans, are to swear an oath over a bull and a boar in the marketplace (32)to abide by this decree and this constitution. And the decree will be inscribed on stone *stelai* of which one is to be set up in the sanctuary of Zeus at Labraunda, and one in Latmos in the sanctuary of Athena. (36)The officials who are allocated to Aropus must take care of the arrangements. The oath which the Latmians are to swear: 'I swear by Zeus, Ge, Helios, Poseidon, Athena Areia and (Artemis) Tauropolos and the other gods. I will share citizenship with the Pidaseans. . . . '

Both civic endogamy and *epigamia* emerged from the structural, underlying, connection that existed in Greek cities between private kinship networks and political organization. If, fundamentally, marriage was an arrangement concerning two households, and a contract concluded between two individual men (a woman's father and his prospective son-in-law), it was also communal and political in the sense that it was through marriage that legitimate citizenship was continued and guaranteed and through affiliation in the male line that membership of a city's constituent bodies was perpetuated. This structural continuum between the individual/private (*idion*) and the communal/civic (*politikon*) developed in the course of the archaic and Classical periods and became one of the most fundamental characteristics of the Classical city. The Pidasa/Latmos treaty shows clearly the various networks that linked individuals with one another and with their city. *Phylai* (usually translated as 'tribes') and *phratoriai* ('brotherhoods') were organizational subdivisions of male citizens through which political activity was channelled and political status secured. The legitimacy of citizen status, and all the rights and obligations that adhered to it were closely linked to membership of a *phyle* and to further social subdivisions which formed the link between the private and the public: in this case *phratoriai*; elsewhere we hear of *syngeneiai, patrai*, etc. Units like these, taking their name from kinship terminology – though not necessarily based on real kinship groups – coexisted with other, numerically constituted ones (e.g. *chiliastyes*: 'thousands') and with geographical units like demes (N. Jones 1987).

The ancient Greek citizen body was a closed community, with strict rules as to who was 'in' and who was 'out'. The connection between marriage and citizenship was carefully guarded and exclusive: only from a marriage between two citizens could legitimate children be born. In most cities, citizen descent going back one generation on both father's and mother's side had been a requirement of full citizenship at least from the early fourth century onwards (in some, a three-generation rule existed for certain magistracies and priesthoods). In practice, therefore, a system of civic endogamy ('in-marrying') prevailed, and although marrying outside one's community was never prohibited, doing so drastically altered one's status. Under normal circumstances, the son of a Latmian man and a Pidasean woman would have been without full citizen rights: in Latmos his status would have been that of *nothos* (bastard). In the same city, the son of a Latmian mother and a Pidasean father would have had the status of foreigner (*xenos*) or resident foreigner (*metoikos, paroikos*), for the son's status was derived primarily from that of the father. The prohibition of civic endogamy in the Latmos–Pidasa treaty, therefore, appears, at first sight, to be an inversion of the normal situation.

Epigamia, too, is a device familiar from across the Greek world; it enabled cities to arrange the necessary or desirable incorporation of outsiders into the civic community but without losing control of the principles that governed its basic structures. Along with other rights adhering to citizenship it might be granted *en bloc* to citizens who had entered into a shared, new, *politeuma*, as we saw above, or in a mutual gesture of exchange, to cities that were members of the same larger federation (such as the Aitolian League) or, as an integral right, to individuals to whom citizenship of a city other than their own had been awarded as a particular favour or as part of a special arrangement between two communities. In all these cases, *epigamia* was granted as a right; never, as far as we know, was it used as a mechanism of enforcement as in the case of Latmos and Pidasa. It could therefore be claimed that, in this respect too, we see a departure from the normal situation.

We cannot generalize from this unique case, nor even be certain that the forced mixing of these two communities was typical of new-style autocratic interference rather than the brainchild of the two communities themselves. If the former, as is certainly possible, then it is only in this, the autocratic enforcing, that the novelty of the situation lies, not in the mechanisms used. Both the prohibition on civic *endogamia* and the encouraging of *epigamia* can be seen as variations on an existing mode of thinking about the interrelation between family and city, as temporary 'adjustments' in an extraordinary situation, but using existing devices rather than departing from established principles. There is every reason to think that after the six-year period, the situation was meant to revert back to normal and the usual, exclusive, rules of civic endogamy would once more apply, though now within a newly-mixed and redefined citizen-body of Latmo-Pidaseans (Herakleians?). Therefore, in the end, no fundamental principles or particularisms were violated and no different structures invented.

2 Changes?

Even so, given the date of the treaty, it must be asked whether the particularist principles underlying the union of Pidasa and Latmos belonged squarely in the 'old' world of the Classical *polis*, even perhaps at the tail-end of the latter's evolution, or whether they continued to be characteristic of cities in the 'new' Hellenistic world. The question is relevant in the context of this chapter: it has often been argued that in the Hellenistic period the old structures and certainties of the Classical *polis* weakened, and that this process profoundly affected the status of individuals as members of families and, by extension, the dynamics of the family itself. Several recent studies of Hellenistic families start from this position, and it can be found also in studies of Hellenistic women. At its core is the idea that Hellenistic society underwent fundamental changes as a result of large-scale migration whose effects are commonly referred to as 'deracination': in the wake of Alexander's campaigns and the wars fought by the Successors, hundreds of thousands of men, ex-soldiers and others, settled in newly conquered territories and in newly founded cities. 'Older' cities were depleted of men and needed to recruit new citizens. Emigration and settlement in foreign territory had the effect of 'severing people both from their forebears and their descendants', as one historian has put it. Emigrants were thus 'not only separated from (their) blood relations but could scarcely pretend to be a member of long-established artificial kinship groups' (Pomeroy 1997b: 108–9). The result was a weakening of the 'old' family-ties and 'old' *polis*-structures, 'major changes in the relationship between *oikos* and *polis*', and the invention of new, more flexible, family structures (in particular, the loosening of the principle of transmitting status and wealth through the male line, giving more weight to cognatic links and more scope to women for wielding influence and using their own wealth: Pomeroy 1997b: 109–12; 1997a: 205).

Parallel to this, and partly for the same reasons, that well-known ancient condition, 'Hellenistic individualism' is said to have developed. 'This was a world in which it was often more important to be an *anthropos* than a *polites*' is how one recent study of the Greek family sums up the idea that the bringing of cities under monarchic rule and the wider perspective of the new monarchies served to loosen the individual's ties with his *polis*, changing his citizen-perspective to a more cosmopolitan one while at the same time focusing his immediate attention on the domestic sphere and on personal relationships (C. Patterson 1998: 191; cf. also e.g. Shipley 2000: 105–6). The new societal structures that are said to have developed as a result of these forces are supposed also to have caused a weakening of authority within families, and allowed women to be treated as individuals and as capable of owning and disposing of property in their own right, often dispensing with the control of a male *kyrios* or tutor: by almost general consensus, the position and status of women 'improved' in this period, while that of their male tutors declined.

While some of these developments are undeniably characteristic of the Hellenistic period, it is extremely difficult to use them to underpin broad generalizations, linking what may in fact be quite separate phenomena into one apparently – and satisfyingly – logical sequence, into which isolated observations can then be inserted and 'explained' as part of the same causal chain. One of the most obviously characteristic features of the Hellenistic period is certainly the large-scale movement, during the first half of the third century, of Macedonians and Greeks from the 'old' cities across the newly conquered territories, as soldiers or as settlers, or both. So, indeed, is the foundation of large numbers of new cities on the model of the old, across Asia Minor and the Near East. But while some scholars have emphasized the estranging effects which this dispersion had on individuals, others have instead seen a increasing structural and cultural homogeneity and a surge in 'connectivity' between Greek cities old and new, as a main feature of the Hellenistic world (e.g. Billows, this volume).

How to assess the effects on the fundamental connection between individual, family and city of developments seemingly pulling in different directions? One could put it flippantly, though not entirely unseriously: how many deracinated Greeks did it take to change the basic structures of a *polis*, or to change the collective memories and mentalities that determined communal and individual actions, and how many new *poleis* did it take to counter the trend? Were all cities affected equally or some more than others? Was the sense of being uprooted equally strong if one settled as a Cretan in Miletos, a Macedonian in Egypt, or a Thessalian in furthest Baktria? The answer to the last question has to be no. Acculturation was more problematic, and adaptation and change more necessary – or more likely to be resisted, or more likely to fail: the possible permutations are many – the greater the cultural distance between settlers and natives and the greater the structural difference between the kind of communities in which each group had been used to organizing itself.

A recently published inscription documenting a new city foundation in a remote part of Phrygia shows that new-*polis*-packages came with all the familiar ingredients including the traditional subdivisions of the citizen body, and with laws that conformed to Greek norms:

> Submit (your laws) to us, so that we may inspect them for anything contrary to your interests; if (you are not satisfied with them) let us know and we shall send you the laws capable of setting up both the council and the magistrates, of distributing the people and assigning them to *phylai*, and of building a gymnasium and providing oil for the *neoi*.

(The Attalid king Eumenes II to the new city of Tyriaion in Phrygia, 180s BC; Jonnes and Riçl 1997; *SEG* 47.1745; BD 43)

Familiar, or deceptively familiar? Were recognizable Greek institutions, laws and terminologies merely a veneer, overlying different indigenous structures and customs? Did they hide fundamental changes within the families that made up these new citizen bodies? More often than not, we cannot tell. The insurmountable problem in the case of most new cities is that we simply do not have the evidence to investigate – on either the public or the private level – the dynamics of the civic communities that were created or the implications of acculturation of settlers and natives during the first few centuries of their existence.

Those postulating changes in the dynamics of family relationships in this period are therefore in practice limited to taking their evidence from two better documented contexts: Ptolemaic Egypt, and the cities of Greece, western Asia Minor and the Aegean islands. The implications of this limitation need to be clearly spelled out. In Egypt, many tens of thousands of Macedonians and Greeks settled in small groups dispersed over the countryside (the *chora*), mostly in villages and alongside native Egyptians. Differences between Egyptians and settlers were considerable in many aspects of life, and there is evidence both of conflict and of selective adaptation and adoption of Egyptian customs by Greek settlers and *vice versa*. Intermarriage between Greeks and Egyptians was more frequent in the second century than in the third, more common in the *chora* than in the *metropoleis*, and among the lower social classes than among the elites: within the latter, Greek tended to marry Greek. Not surprisingly, when thus thrown together, Greeks from different backgrounds attempted to settle through personal contracts what the laws of their respective cities had once regulated and supervised. Thus, marriage contracts (of which no more than a handful survive in any detail), and other documents on papyrus illustrating the private and communal arrangements between Greeks, and between Greeks and Egyptians, show both adherence to common Greek practice and deviations from the old and the accustomed. Here, obviously, 'major changes in the relationship between *oikos* and *polis*' occurred, because the framework of the *polis* itself was largely absent (so already Wolff 1939: 82). It is much less easy than is sometimes suggested, however, to detect subsequent developments, such as, e.g. the postulated weakening of male authority within families or changes in inheritance patterns. Significant though this evidence is in showing the circumstances that prevailed in the Egyptian *chora* (and occasionally in the new *metropoleis*), we cannot easily generalize from it beyond the specific Egyptian context, (Vatin 1970: chapter 4; Ogden 1996: chapters 13 and 14; Vérilhac and Vial 1998: chapters 1 and 5; Rowlandson 1998: chapters 3 and 4).

It is in the cities of the 'old' Greek world: those in Greece, the islands, and western Asia Minor, that questions about changes to the basic structures of civic and familial organization acquire some meaning. But even here much of the evidence is indirect, dispersed and fragmentary, and often hard to fit into a sequence of cause and effect. It is salutary to realize, for instance, that in the case of Cretans in Miletos, briefly alluded to above, we have one of the very few documented examples of *groups* of emigrants making their home in another Greek city. At the end of the third century BC (in 234/3 and 229/8) large groups of Cretan soldiers were persuaded by the Milesians to come to their city in order to provide military assistance. There were possibly about

1000 men in total, though only about 400 names survive; 78 men are accompanied by 'families' of some description. Upon the Cretans' request, and after the Milesians had consulted the oracle at Didyma, they were naturalized as Milesian citizens, given land in Milesian territory (or rather in the territory of a small neighbouring *polis*, Myous, which had been absorbed by Miletos in a *sympoliteia*) and integrated into the existing structures of Miletos, in many cases together with their families. Lists of their names survive, inscribed together with the decrees, on one of the walls of the sanctuary of Apollo Delphinios (*Milet* I.3, 33–8; discussion pp. 166–203).

Here one might legitimately ask what, if any, effects 'deracination' would have had on a structural level. There is nothing to suggest that these men and their families, once naturalized, would have had any option other than to conform to the laws and customs of the Milesians (which might not in any case have struck them as very different from their own). Would they have felt the need to create more 'flexible' family structures or even been able to do so, while fully subject to the laws of the Milesians? Unusually, we have some information about our Cretans some thirty years after their naturalization. When in 201 BC, the Macedonian king Philip V forced the Milesians to give up Myous, granting the latter with its territory to the neighbouring city of Magnesia, the 'Cretans' suddenly found themselves without the land on which they had been settled, or rather with a citizen-status that no longer fitted that of their land. The Magnesians attempted to repatriate the naturalized soldiers to Crete. A decree of one of their home cities, Gortyn, refusing repatriation, survives (*IC* 4.176, ll. 34–8 with W. Günther 1988: 393–6). What we can tentatively conclude from this is that, one generation on, the Cretans still apparently formed a separate community within the larger Milesian state, and had not intermarried with 'real' Milesians to any significant extent: the Milesian citizen body was still predominantly a family of citizens into which groups of outsiders, even when naturalized, were integrated but slowly if at all. If this conclusion has any validity, might a further hypothesis be that during their first few decades in Miletos the Cretans resorted to practising close-kin endogamy within their own community either from choice or from necessity? Or to marrying *metoikoi* resident in Miletos, thus producing offspring that would not have had full citizen status? These are possible strategies that might, in the longer term, have affected the character of the Milesian citizen body. But answers are not forthcoming. Given such a level of ignorance even here, in one of the better documented cities of the Hellenistic world, it would be rash to want to put forward any further hypotheses about weakening of family ties or other changes in family behaviour as a result of migratory movements.

There is much evidence to show that, within the cities themselves, rather than a weakening of the continuum between 'old' family-ties and 'old' *polis*-structures, there was a continuation or even a reinforcing of the essential relationship between the two spheres throughout much of the Hellenistic period. Several recent studies all emphasize the persistence, continuity and vitality of the 'old' structures rather than their instant demise (Gauthier 1972a and 1988; Savalli 1985; N. Jones 1987; Vérilhac and Vial 1998: chapter 2). When, more than a hundred years after their failed *sympoliteia* with the Latmians, in the early 180s BC, the Pidaseans were integrated into the Milesian citizen body, the decree ratifying the *sympoliteia* stipulated that 'the Pidaseans will be citizens of the Milesians, together with their children and their wives, insofar as the latter are Pidasean by birth, or citizens of a Greek city' (*Milet* I.3, no.

149, ll. 10–12, translated in *Milet* VI.1, 184–5). The concession concerning the wives' citizen status *appears* to imply Pidasean disregard for the 'two-parent' rule. One could imagine it fitting perfectly in an argument about the loosening of *polis* structures. But that the concession, and the practices underlying it, were exceptional, is emphasized in a recent study (Vérilhac and Vial 1998) in which Pidasa is discussed as one of only two known Hellenistic cities which 'practised exogamy'. The unusual stipulation is sometimes explained as a blanket exclusion of Karian spouses (Miletos was on the edge of Karia, Pidasa in origin a Karian community), but this does not ring true at a time when civic identity had long superseded ethnic identity, and the fact that the earlier *sympoliteia* does not appear to be similarly concerned with 'barbaric' elements within the Pidasean citizen body further undermines this explanation. Given its very small size, and its evident history of negotiations with several larger neighbouring cities, it is more likely than not that the Pidaseans had over the years entered into *epigamia* arrangements with neighbours which had resulted in non-Pidasean wives being married and domiciled in Pidasa. Even if the children of these unions were legitimate under the specific arrangements of one *epigamia* arrangement, their privileges were not valid in Miletos, and a special case had to be made.

What this example shows first of all is the very great care the Milesians took to define precisely the different kinship relationships that were acceptable and those that were not. The principle of civic membership through male filiation was not abandoned. Secondly, small, landlocked Pidasa's status as an 'exogamous' city (the other known case is the equally small and landlocked city of Euaimon in Arkadia) can only be explained if we realize that the kind of circumstances that led to this 'habit' of civic exogamy were specific and local. In support of this, we need only to look at large commercial cities like Miletos itself, or Rhodes, or Alexandria, or to the commercial centre that was the small island of Delos, all of which had substantial populations of foreigners ('immigrants' of a different kind), both resident and temporary, but at the same time, and very likely because of the size of the non-citizen population, took some care to preserve the principle of civic endogamy throughout the Hellenistic period.

The overall increase in numbers of resident foreigners in places like these (among whom resident Romans became an important group from the second century onwards) and the juxtaposition of a closed (even if not impermeable), privileged citizen body with a large group of non-citizen residents is an interesting phenomenon in its own right – to which no justice can be done in a brief chapter – and one which, within the large and interconnected economies of the Hellenistic kingdoms certainly became more common than it had been in the Classical period. The elaborate organizational structures (called *koina*) that were developed, for instance, by the metic population on Rhodes, were *sui generis*, and are the more interesting for being modelled on the *polis* in many of their aspects (Gabrielsen 1997: chapter 5). Even more interesting are the connections (economic, social, religious) that developed between these associations and members of the Rhodian elite. But it was only here, in large commercial centres like Rhodes, that intermarriage between Greeks from different cities became a major factor and anything like a non-citizen population sufficiently large to start creating its own social organizations developed, thus, if not directly undermining, at least contributing to changes in the structure of the Rhodian state. In most other cities, the size of the metic and foreign population was substantially smaller and it is doubtful whether it was ever substantial enough to change the fundamental principles that shaped Hellenistic cities. Unlike the mixed marriages of the Egyptian *chora*, those that occurred, among *metoikoi* on the periphery of citizen bodies, remained part of the overall framework of a city and were subject to its laws as well as integrated into its rituals, as the following example shows.

When, around the mid-second century BC, on the island of Tenos, Medeios 'having given away (*egdidomenos*) his daughter Philippe', and his son-in-law Souniadas 'having accepted her (*lambanón*)' jointly decided to celebrate their happy transaction, they invited all (male) citizens and (male) foreigners to banquets and distributions of wheat (*IG* 12.5.863–6). This kind of ritual reinforcement of what was in essence a shared Greek practice closely tied to the perpetuation of civic structures, meant that migrating to cities other than one's own did not necessarily result in estrangement from one's roots, customs, or even laws. In the next section I attempt to show just how important a role was played by collective ritual in the shaping and reinforcing of that civic reality and how collective (and thus individual) mentality were shaped more by notions of common descent, kinship and inclusiveness than by notions of cosmopolitanism, rootlessness and detachment.

II

3 The Civic Family

In Hellenistic cities divisions within the family extended into the public sphere. The ideology of equality and solidarity, which dominated male civic behaviour and which emerged from a political tradition that gave a central decision-making role to the assembly of male citizens, strongly affected the public *personae* of women and the young. In the public sphere households re-grouped themselves along lines of gender and age, forming in a certain sense a collective family of citizens. For civic purposes, families dissolved into collectives of men (*neoi*: young men, formed a separate and important group), women (referred to as *gynaikes* or *politides*), boys of different ages (*paides*: young boys, *epheboi*: boys in their upper teens) and unmarried girls (*parthenoi*). This functional separation affected office-holding, including religious office-holding, and gave structure to civic and religious ritual and to the acculturation and education of (future) citizens. The principle of it is well shown in the following passage from an inscription of Halikarnassos (*SIG*³ 1015, *LSAM* 73) but it could be illustrated from many other public documents:

> He who buys the priesthood of Artemis Pergaia has to provide a priestess who is a citizen woman of citizen descent (*aste ex astón*) over three generations and on both father's and mother's side. She who buys it is to be priestess for life and is to perform both public and private sacrifices.... (14) The treasurers are to give to the prytaneis 30 drachmas for the public sacrifice to Artemis. The sacrifice is to be prepared by the wives of the prytaneis, having taken what has been given from the polis. She (the priestess) is to perform the sacrifice in the month of Herakleios on the twelfth. And she is to receive the same portion of the sacrificial victims as the wives of the prytaneis in the case of the victims sacrificed publicly. (*SIG*³ 1015, *LSAM* 73, ll.4–8 and 14–23; 3rd c. BC)

Here, the wives of the *prytaneis* form a small, female collective, whose position as wives of the city's main body of magistrates gave them a specific part to play alongside the priestess: essential is that they carry out their role in the ritual as part of the collective of women; in no way are they linked in their activities to their husbands, even if their status and privileges are derived from the latter's position; for public purposes they are autonomous, just as the collective of citizen wives had a separate identity from that of their citizen husbands. In understanding public–private relations within Classical and Hellenistic Greek cities nothing could be more wrong than to say, as is commonly done, that women belonged to the domestic, or private, sphere, and men to the public. It was inherent in Greek society from early on that there existed a public role for women and for the young. It is particularly in the period after Alexander that the development of institutions concerned with these specific sub-groups took off (and at the same time becomes more visible to us): civic gymnasia for *paides*, ephebes and *neoi* became central to the acculturation and training of the young, while magistracies like the *gymnasiarchia, paidonomia* and *gynaikonomia* developed more widely.

It is unfortunate – though an inevitable result of the focus on women's history over the past decades – that the public regulation of women is often treated separately from that of other civic groups. The occurrence of *gynaikonomoi*, (male) supervisors of female public conduct, has thus been variously described as retrogressive, an expression of nostalgia, and typically aristocratic (Pomeroy 1997a: 214; 1997b: 63). The title of *gynaikonomos* is often translated, following Cicero's attempt at explaining the magistracy in Roman terms (*Rep.* 4.6), as 'censor of women', some-times more broadly as a 'police des moeurs' (Pouilloux 1954: 407–10; Wehrli 1962) and his role explained as concerned with the reining in of unruly women, the curbing of 'excessive display of wealth' 'lavish parties' or 'overindulgence in disorderly expres-sions of grief' (Shipley 2000: 105; Pomeroy, as above). These are interpretations that are too narrowly conceived and too negative and stereotypical in their emphasis on controlling female excess. The evidence, from a range of cities, and with dates ranging from the fourth to the first century BC, shows the *gynaikonomoi*'s role variously as that of supervising female participation and dress during religious ceremonies, pro-cessions, civic festivals and funerals, and, at times, supervising young girls. So for instance in Magnesia on the Maeander, in the early second century BC, in a list of prescriptions concerning the cult of Zeus Sosipolis, by decision of the people the *gynaikonomoi* were to delegate nine girls and the *paidonomoi* nine boys to participate in the sacrificing of a bull. In another example, from Alexandria, the *gynaikonomos* can be seen testifying to a young man's citizen credentials on his mother's side (Wehrli 1962; Vatin 1970: 254–61; Ogden 1996: 364–75).

Aristotle, in the *Politics*, does indeed describe the *gynaikonomos*, together with the *paidonomos* and 'other magistracies exercising similar supervisory functions', as aris-tocratic, not democratic, elements in constitutions ('because the poor have to make their wives and children work'); he also lists the *gynaikonomia* with the *paidonomia, nomophylakia* and *gymnasiarchia* under the heading of magistracies that 'are con-cerned with *eukosmia* (good order, decorum) and specific to cities that have a certain amount of leisure and wealth' (*Pol.* 1300a4; 1322b39; 1323a4). But neither the *paidonomia* nor the *gymnasiarchia* are ever described by modern scholars with such value-laden terms as 'retrogressive' or 'nostalgic'; nor is the title of *paidonomos* (identically constituted to *gynaikonomos*) usually translated as 'censor of boys' or his concern with boys' potential unruliness or excesses singled out. The *paidonomos* supervised *paides* (sometimes also *parthenoi*), and was responsible for their public appearances such as participating in processions or singing hymns. The *gymnasiarchos* supervised *paides*, ephebes and *neoi* in the context of the gymnasium, guarding *eukosmia* by preventing any contact between the young boys and older age groups during exercising and generally keeping undesirable individuals from entering the premises (Austin 118; Hatzopoulos and Gauthier 1993). In our period, these magistracies had developed from being specific only to certain types of cities to being virtually ubiquitous and characteristic of cities' concern with acculturating the young and with guarding the public decorum and moral integrity of those groups that were deemed to be in need of supervision precisely because they were essential to the integrity of the citizen body as a whole. The main point is to try to understand the *gynaikonomia* not in isolation, but in context, as part of a general mentality and a general regulatory and organizational system.

More than thirty years ago, Cl. Vatin pointed out the distinction made by Cicero between the Roman *censor* and the Greek *gynaikonomos* (and, implicitly, between the two societies): the former's function was to 'teach husbands how to rein in their wives' while the second was truly a *praefectus* – a magistrate – of women, implicitly criticizing Greek men for abdicating what, in Roman eyes, was the role of the *paterfamilias*. But in the Greek city, in our period even more visibly and explicitly than before, the 'community of women' was a collective as was that of men, with collective roles and duties. Vatin's observation that 'the Ciceronian ideal was that of a patriarchal society, composed of family units into which political power (the State) did not intervene directly' (1970: 260) is acute, but it needs some slight modification: seeing the Greek system as one in which the 'State' interfered directly does not do justice to the fact that there *was* no 'State' other than that same collective of citizen men, who jointly delegated some of their own number to be gymnasiarchs, *gynaikonomoi, paidonomoi* etc., thus collectively entrusting these magistrates with supervising the totality of their sons, daughters and wives.

4   Family Thinking and Collective Ritual

A public ordinance of Kos (dated to shortly after 198 BC) is concerned with the sale of the priesthood of Aphrodite Pandamos (of the entire People) and with regulations for her cult:

> So that the honours of the goddess are increased, all those of the female citizens, *nothai* and resident foreigners (*paroikoi*) who are getting married must be seen to honour the goddess to the best of their ability, all who are to marry, having sworn an oath (?); and all are to sacrifice a victim to the goddess within one year after their marriage. . . . Those who do not sacrifice as is prescribed, are to be fined, and they owe the priestess a fine of ten drachmas . . . (*Iscr.Cos*. ED 178, ll. 15–20; 24–6; cf. Dillon 1999)

This text raises issues about civic 'family thinking' that are not easily discussed in a few paragraphs. The stated aim of this section of the ordinance is that 'the goddess' honours be increased'. We might conclude from what follows in the text that this was partly achieved by increasing income from sacrificial animals and from fines ('she was made richer') and in part by enhancing her civic profile through frequently repeated acts of sacrifice ('she got more attention'). But was that really what the Koans understood by 'increasing her honours'?

We must ask what wider considerations generated these measures. Can we, in particular, conclude from this ordinance that the proper sanctioning of marriages and propitiating the right deity was a matter of collective, civic concern and thus in need of prescriptive regulation? It has been pointed out (Parker and Obbink 2000) that marriage rituals such as these, though commonly found in Greek cities of both the Classical and Hellenistic periods, were not normally prescribed by law, and were customary only, and that we must not try to conclude too much from the two known instances where civic regulation has been specifically attested (the one other case, a late-fourth-century sacred law from Cyrene, concerned with purification, contains prescriptions for brides to sacrifice to Artemis or risk pollution, exclusion and a fine: Parker 1983: 345; Dillon 1999: 67).

But if Aphrodite, like Artemis and Hera, to name but the most obvious female deities, was customarily associated with marriage in her own right, then why in this case *Pandamos*, 'of the entire people'? This was not Aphrodite in a guise suited to an essentially private even if socially expected act. This Aphrodite's primary role was not, as one might at first think, that of patron of love, and therefore of marriage. As *Pandamos* her role was primarily linked with the collective well-being of the civic community. Aphrodite's role as protectress of mutual affection and harmony within marriage, of good relations between husbands and wives, certainly explains, associatively, her more general role as protectress of harmony and understanding within collectives of people, hence her epithet *Pandamos*: 'of the entire people' (at Athens, with the same epithet, she was associated with the *synoikismos* of the people of Attika into one *polis*). It also explains why, more particularly, all over the Greek world, she was the goddess who guarded good relations within bodies of magistrates. In many cities, magistrates made dedications to Aphrodite at the end of their term of office and in these cases she frequently took her epithet from the specific body she protected: thus we find Aphrodite *Strategis* ('of the *strategoi*' – not, in this period a military function), *Nomophylakis, Timouchos* ('of the *timouchoi*'), or even *Synarchis* ('of joint office-holding'). *Peithó* (Persuasion), *Homonoia* (Concord) and the *Charites* (Graces) all feature in similar contexts and were often associated with Aphrodite in magistrates' dedications, just as they were associated also, on a private level, with marriage and concord between spouses (L. Robert, *BE* 1959, no 325 and 1961, no 487; Sokolowski 1964; Croissant and Salviat 1966; Dillon 1999).

The underlying connection in the case of Kos, as in many other places (for we should not unduly emphasize the difference between custom and regulation) was, however, not simply one of *associating* good relations within marriage with good relations within the citizen body. It has recently been written that 'the Greeks liked to think associatively about familial concord and civic concord, comparing living *en famille* to living as a citizen body, or comparing a good statesman to a good father' (Thériault 1996: chapter 4). But explaining this kind of thinking in terms of association only is to see as two-dimensional something that was multi-faceted, and as detached something that was intricately entangled. The collective mentality and identity of the citizens of Kos, or any other ancient citizen body, were characterized not just by associative *thinking* (which might, anyway, be better described as connective thinking with a strong historical dimension) but also, and especially, by connective *acting*, both collectively and individually. On Kos, as elsewhere, whether by obligation or 'only' by custom, the private served to reinforce the public and the complex of associations evoked by 'Aphrodite' was reflected in a tangle of civic acting, both public and private. Women who had recently married had to sacrifice to Aphrodite *Pandamos* so that, through guaranteeing the well-being of their marriage they guaranteed the well-being of the city; domestic concord was intrinsically connected to public concord in the same way as concord within bodies of magistrates was. It was thus that they actively 'increased the honours' of the goddess, and we should read it as meaning that Aphrodite *Pandamos* and everything she stood for needed to be properly anchored in all areas of civic life. Through repeated sacrificing the community's order and harmony were guaranteed. The continuum between *idion* and *koinon* underlies the rituals and gives them meaning, and it is in no way unusual that *nothai* and female *paroikoi* also had to share in the sacrificing: the harmony of *their* marriages was as essential to the entire city's well-being as was that of the inner circle of *politides*.

5   Civic and Royal Families

Something similar to the Koan prescriptions is being aimed at in the following set of regulations recorded in a decree of the city of Iasos (and can we really tell whether the 'older' rituals onto which the new are being grafted, had been 'customary' rather than prescribed by law?):

> Let [the people] elect [each year] a maiden (*parthenos*) [as priestess] of queen Aphro[dite La]odike; in the formal processions let her wear a headband of mingled white; let it not be possible for the same to be priestess twice . . . this honour on the [. . . day of] Aphrodision, on which day queen Laodike was born, and let all the . . . be present and let the men who are about to wed and the women who are about to wed [after the completion of their wedding] sacrifice to Queen [Laodike . . . according to] their means, each one . . . of the queen; let . . . all the priestesses and the [maidens about to wed] all take part in the procession . . . first fruit offering. (Decree of Iasos for queen Laodike, wife of Antiochos III, *c.* 196 BC. *I.Iasos* 4, B 14–28; trans. as Ma 1999: no. 26)

The major innovation, here, of course, is the accommodation of an aspect of the new reality of monarchic power into the ritual complex of a city. By remodelling existing ritual practices new meaning was added without losing the meaning of the old. In Iasos an existing ritual connected with marriage was turned into a joint celebration of royal power and the power of Aphrodite, and the symbolic importance of Laodike's role as royal wife was expanded into that of protectress of marriage through her association with Aphrodite. Elsewhere, in Teos, a fountain in the *agora* was dedicated to Laodike from which water for the ritual baths of brides was to be drawn. In both cities, rituals focused on the person of the queen complemented others which elevated and incorporated Antiochos' power (Ma 1999: chapter 4; Savalli-Lestrade 1994).

Despite the evident ability of civic ritual systems to incorporate new political realities, the interaction of royal and civic ideology created areas of tension in Hellenistic cities and in some ways profoundly altered civic structures. In a recent book John Ma (1999) has shown the fundamental disjunctions that existed between the language and ideology of Hellenistic kingship and that of the civic community. In their negotiations both kings and cities had to find a common language of representing what was fundamentally unequal interaction, and express, in terms of reciprocity and dialogue, a relationship which was in real terms one of ruler and subject. This disjunction of the royal and the civic was felt also on the level of family thinking.

The overlap between the public/political and the private within a monarchy is, of course, total. Power and authority are vested in the person of the king, indirectly in his wife and children. Monarchical succession is based on the successful producing of offspring, and alliances are forged and reforged through marriages. The Hellenistic court was a community of *intimi*, around whom circles of *philoi*, friends (who were at the same time officials) replicated and reinforced royal behaviour and ideology (the 'court' of the Ptolemaic *strategos* on Cyprus is an interesting case in point). And just as the private thoughts of the king became public – and became command – through the device of the royal letter, so, through the same medium of communication, did the intimate language of the court find its way into the public sphere. Queen Laodike, in a letter thanking the citizens of Sardis for instituting a cult and festival, refers to her 'brother and husband', the king, and her *paidia*, her 'little ones', using a term of endearment belonging to the intimacy of a household (Gauthier 1989: chapter 2; Ma 1999: no. 2). A letter of Antiochos III giving instructions to set up a cult for queen Laodike his 'sister and wife' refers to her *philostorgia* towards himself and mentions his own *philostorgia* for her as a motivation. (*RC* 36–7; Ma 1999: no. 37). *Philostorgia* is *the* word for familial affection: like *paidia*, it is used in private between parents and children, or spouses. With precisely those private connotations it occurs on hundreds of tombstones; but although it was part of a common Greek language, it was not part of the public and political discourse of Greek cities.

Cities needed to respond to this emphasis on the dynastic, the familial and the private, and incorporate it into their own very different language of equality and civic solidarity. In doing so, they could not help giving at least some of it a civic twist. When, for instance, the royal Seleukid couple Antiochos III and Laodike were incorporated into the ritual and representational world of Teos, they were separated, just as the Halikarnassian *prytaneis* and their wives had been, into a male and a female half, each with its own domain. At Teos the focus of Antiochos' ritual and cultic presence in the city was in the *bouleuterion*, while Laodike's fountain in the market-place was at the centre of entirely separate rituals (though cult images of both as common saviours were also erected in the temple of Dionysos alongside that of the god). And when, at Iasos, Laodike complemented her husband's benefactions to the city by promising an annual gift of wheat from the sale of which dowries were to be funded for poor citizen girls, the Iasians instituted, in return, a priestess for her from among the city's girls. Everywhere, queens were served by their own priestesses, often by unmarried girls. Hellenistic royal couples were not, at any time, served by couples of priests. The contrast with the provincial and civic Roman imperial cult is striking: imperial priests were husband and wife teams, and even if the priestess was separately responsible for the female members of the imperial household the joint 'front' presented was that of a married couple (van Bremen 1996: 12–13).

Some of the aspects that characterized the public *personae* of queens were remarkably absent from the way citizen women acted and were represented in public. Their capacity to intercede with their royal husbands was frequently appealed to and is well-documented (see below for an example). Characteristically, queens would supplement the benefactions of their husbands, often specializing in more humanistic or philanthropic gifts (Laodike's concern with poor girls' dowries has a precedent in that of Phila, daughter of Antipater and wife of Demetrios Poliorketes, who married off, at her own expense, daughters and sisters of poor soldiers; Diod. 19.59.4). The language in which their own benefactions were phrased never failed to refer explicitly to those of their royal husbands, as in Laodike's letter to the Iasians quoted below. It is interesting to note, incidentally, that Laodike's gift was specifically aimed at assisting Antiochos' effort to 'increase the citizen body', underlining the advantage to the entire people of poor citizen girls being able to marry so that the citizen body might replenish itself 'from within':

> He gave back to you your liberty and your laws, and in other matters he strives to increase the citizen body (*politeuma*) and to bring it in a better condition, and making it my own intention to act in accordance with his zeal and eagerness, and, because of this, to confer some benefaction on the poor among the citizens, and a general advantage among the whole people.... If you remain as is right in your behaviour towards my brother and generally towards our house, and if you gratefully remember the benefactions which you have met with, I shall try to procure for you other favours that I can think up, since I make it my intention in all matters to concur with the will of my brother... (Letter of Laodike to the Iasians ll. 8–14; 25–30; trans. as Ma 1999: no. 26)

Royal couples presented themselves consistently as a couple or *en famille* and civic well-wishing formulas therefore often included wives and children. Even those who were royal only by association, or had dynastic pretensions, like Olympichos, Seleukos II's *strategos* in Karia, received this treatment: in a letter to the citizens of Mylasa, Olympichos refers to the city's envoys who had promised 'to honour me, my wife Nikaia, and my children with due honours' (Crampa 1969: no. 6). In nearby Panamara, the local *koinon* honoured the Macedonian king Philip V, decreeing that the priest of Panamaran Zeus was to 'pray on behalf of the safety of the king and the queen and their children' (*I.Stratonikeia* 3).

On the civic level, the inclusion of a man's wife and children in any honours or public commemoration was unheard of. The ideology of civic politics was determined by notions of 'good citizenship'. In both its male and female versions the 'ideal' citizen was, as M. Wörrle has memorably described him, a 'Polisfanatiker' whose every effort, including his wealth, was at the service of his fellow citizens (Wörrle 1995; cf. van Bremen 1996: chapter 6). Even though this period sees the emergence of the civic benefactor, or *euergetes*, within civic politics, and the concomitant emergence of female euergetism, the wives of major Hellenistic *euergetai* were never associated with their husbands in public nor were they even referred to by name, and vice versa. Since women, in their own name, and as members of the body of *polites*, regularly took on priesthoods or – religious – liturgies in a female pendant to the male system of civic duties, it was predominantly in this context that female euergetism developed. It is therefore too simplistic (and actually wrong) to say that it was royal example (i.e. the inclusion of royal wives and the emphasis on a different familial model in which there was a place for women) that was responsible for the emergence of women as civic benefactresses in their own right. The reality was different and a great deal more complex.

The increasing visibility of women in the public sphere (more visible also to us, in honorific or in dedicatory inscriptions) and the evident wealth some women were able to employ for the good of their fellow citizens, should be understood as an intrinsic part of the more general development of euergetism as a political factor within Hellenistic cities and the gradual oligarchization of civic politics. The roots and causes of this development are themselves complicated and cannot be discussed in detail here, but are well analysed in Veyne 1976 and Gauthier 1985. Too often this feature of Hellenistic civic life is explained as a direct result of the loosening of family restrictions on women and their consequent ability to control their 'own' wealth. It is placed within an evolutionary scheme and held up as a sign of women's advancement relative to 'their' position in the Classical period. The explanatory value of such schemes in a more general sense is doubtful (on this see now C. Patterson 1998: chapter 1) and more often than not, they distort and misunderstand actual historical contexts.

In a seminal discussion of the development of euergetism as a political factor in the Hellenistic period, Ph. Gauthier rightly argued that the – inevitable – disjunction between institutional developments and conventional period boundaries meant that in terms of developments within Greek civic institutions, a meaningful 'break' occurred (or becomes visible) only in the course of the second century BC, not at the beginning of the Hellenistic period. The fourth, third and early second centuries BC were very much part of a continuum (Gauthier 1985: introduction). This observation is equally valid for the aspects of civic, and private, life that this chapter has been concerned with. The centuries after Alexander constitute the period during which civic 'family thinking' reached its culmination, as did the particular civic model whose features were already in place in the fourth century (and even before, in the fifth). In the course of the second century BC changes began to appear which, though not entirely undermining the model, nevertheless shifted its internal emphasis away from the egalitarian 'family of citizens' towards an ideology that placed the families of those who governed at the centre of civic ideology, language and imagery. For a considerable time, the gradual verticalization of the relationship between the wealthy and politically active 'few' and their less active (or less wealthy) fellow citizens was contained by the traditions and assumptions of the Classical Greek city; by notions of equality and solidarity and the political–communal aspects of civic life. The royal family model took some time to filter down to the level of civic politics but it is easy to see how its language and ideology fitted that of an emerging civic elite. It is here, in the abandoning of the 'old' continuum between the private and the public and the 'old' solidarity between those that made up the collective family of citizens, that the greatest shifts in terms of family dynamics took place.

But whether it was this, rather than the increased mobility of individuals and the new patterns of settlement that emerged, which affected the fundamental principles that shaped Greek collective existence, is not easy to say, nor is it possible to gauge the precise extent of the changes. To look for linear patterns of cause and effect in a world as complex as the Hellenistic is simplistic and, ultimately, unsatisfactory. The two broad aspects of the relationship between political community and private family group that I have discussed in this chapter never moved at the same pace and it is not easy to show that, or how, changes in one generated changes in the other, or vice versa. The functional connection between the private and the public (civic endogamy and everything that follows from it) and the transcendent, representational connection which affected mentality, behaviour, language and individual psychologies, stood in a complex relationship to one another, never exactly expressing the same reality. Collective memories and mentalities feed on a multitude of realities past and present, internal and external, and are capable, in their turn, of shaping reality. For the historian it is the ever-shifting disjunction between these two areas of ancient life which it is as challenging to try to understand as that between the rapid movements of high politics and the slower pace of institutional changes.

FURTHER READING

Some of the best books and articles on this subject are written in languages other than English. By far the best recent discussion of Greek marriage practice in the widest sense of the word is Vérilhac and Vial 1998. Vatin 1970 is ambitious in scope and stimulating, but should be read with the review of Gauthier 1972b. Davies 1977–78, though discussing Classical Athens, is excellent for underlying concepts and therefore relevant for our period; Ogden 1996 discussed bastardy in the Classical and Hellenistic periods. On civic organization see N. Jones 1987; on *sympoliteia*, Reger 2004, C. Jones 1999a and Gauthier 2001; on foreigners in Greek cities the two collective volumes edited by Lonis 1988 and 1992; on naturalization in Hellenistic cities, Savalli 1985 and on the sale of citizenship Robert 1940: chapter 6. On Rhodes, Gabrielsen 1997 is thought-provoking.

Brulé 1990 and Pomeroy 1997(a and b) both try to draw wide-ranging demographic and general historical conclusions from the Cretan (and other) naturalization inscriptions from Miletos, and from the one other surviving inscription (from Ilion) documenting naturalization of a large group of individuals, but their conclusions are unreliable. Pomeroy's interpretation of the Ilion document is shown to be unsound in L.-M. Günther 1992.

For Ptolemaic Egypt best is Vérilhac and Vial 1998; cf. also Ogden 1996. There is now a good collection of sources with introduction and commentaries discussing issues of family structure, acculturation etc.: Rowlandson 1998.

The best general article on Hellenistic queens is by Savalli-Lestrade 1994; Macurdy 1932 is still useful for the comprehensiveness of its evidence.

Dillon 1999 is inspiring on Aphrodite Pandamos, as is L. Robert in *BE* 1959, no. 325 however brief, on Aphrodite and magistrates. Van Bremen 1996 focuses on the public roles of women and discusses civic ritual. For women's religious roles, Krohn 1996; for *gynaikonomoi* best is Ogden 1996. Ma 1999 is excellent on the differing ideologies of kings and cities, and translates a large range of relevant and illuminating documents.

CHAPTER TWENTY

The Economy

Gary Reger

1 Introduction

A long inscription from Kos lays obligations on sailors: 'When they shall complete their journey by sea let those who serve in the big ships sacrifice to Aphrodite Pontia on her aforementioned altar an adult victim worth 30 drachmas for each tent, or let them pay the priestess instead of her traditional gifts 10 drachmas for each tent and one drachma in the offering-box' (Parker and Obbink 2000: 416–17, lines 5–9). The fundamental purpose here is religious – to give thanksgiving for coming back safely from the sea. But the obligations drew the sailors into the local economy: someone raised the sheep to be sacrificed; someone brought that sheep to market (the *agora*), where he haggled with the sailors' representatives over the price; the priestess received either part of the animal (which she could sell or keep) or cash. And the sailors had to have 30 or more drachmas in cash to pay for their purchase – money obtained as pay from the state or from their own resources. Economic transactions saturated the act of piety, and so it was in virtually every aspect of Hellenistic life. The economy was everywhere.

Analysis over the last century of the Hellenistic economy has operated along two main dimensions. One is the 'primitivist–modernist' dichotomy. The 'modernizing' view (associated, not always fairly, with Michael Rostovtzeff, but going back to Eduard Meyer) saw the Hellenistic economy as dominated by price-setting markets that embraced the whole Hellenistic world. 'Capitalist' enterprises, operating on a considerable scale, produced, transported and sold goods over long distances in completely monetarized markets. The competing 'primitivist' view (associated with M. I. Finley, but going back to Karl Bücher) argued instead for an ancient economy composed of an enormous number of tiny, 'autarchic' (self-sufficient) units – sometimes, but not always, equivalent to a *polis* – that operated almost without interaction. The other dimension was the 'formalist–substantivist'. Formalists saw the economy as a separate sphere, like the economy today, if less sophisticated. Substantivists (Finley again, following especially Karl Polanyi) saw the economy instead as 'socially embedded and politically overdetermined and so ... conspicuously conventional, irrational, and status-ridden' (Cartledge 2002: 15; cf. Loomis 1998: 251–4; Morris in Finley 1999: ix–xxxvi).

More recent work has tended to reject such stark dichotomies. It is becoming clearer that the Hellenistic economy was not a monolith that can be described within a single, complete analytical framework. On the one hand, the majority of people living in the three centuries of the Hellenistic period were certainly small-scale, largely subsistence farmers who never travelled much beyond where they were born. At the same time, these people were connected to a wider world through their local polity and through the markets which they patronized, whether to buy goods they could not produce on their own (pottery, worked metal goods) or to sell their own surpluses to get cash. Cash formed part of their reserve against bad times, which they might use to buy imported staples like grain, olive oil, or wheat when their own crops failed; or to buy up neighbour's land (as Hesiod advised many years before); or to pay the taxes imposed by the *polis* or the sovereign. At a wider level, there were regional units of exchange (Horden and Purcell 2000) within which goods and people flowed, sometimes centred around a famous sanctuary like Delphi or Delos, sometimes created by the realities of geography, sometimes the result of exercise of political and military power, whether present or a residue of the past. Finally, the new big kingdoms – the Antigonids in Macedon and Greece, the Ptolemies in Egypt, and the Seleukids almost everywhere else – created *loci* of economic activity, of production, exchange and consumption. In the context of these more complex levels there were people and goods that travelled far and wide; these are often the most visible to us. There were also extraordinary differences in wealth – nothing as extreme perhaps as came later with the Romans, but still the distance was extraordinary between Diogenes, who only wanted Alexander the Great to stop blocking the sun and recommended begging for one's meals at temples (D.L. 6. 38; Plut. *Alex.* 14), and the owner of the 'Maison des comediens', one of the most magnificent houses on Delos – to say nothing of the resources commanded by a Ptolemy II Philadelphos or a Seleukos Nikator. The scene is then one of enormous complexity and diversity, operating on many different levels and many different scales at the same time, in changing relations to each other across time and space. Some work has now begun to appear attempting to model such economic interrelationships. As these models are articulated, critiqued and revised, new ways of looking at the Hellenistic economy and new questions to ask about it will undoubtedly emerge (see especially Davies 1998).

The fundamental feature of the economy – as in all pre-modern economies – was the production of food (Isager and Skydsgaard 1992). Such production took place largely in the countryside (though many *poleis* had considerable empty space within the town that might be turned over to gardens or even larger agricultural production). In Greece and much of western Asia Minor the countryside was subject to *poleis* and the owners of the land were citizens. The agricultural commodities produced on this land – grain, olives and their oil, wine, vegetables and fruits like figs, cheese from sheep and goats, meat – were consumed largely by the producers themselves or were sold in the local market, the *agora*, to fellow-citizens. This economic activity remains largely invisible to us, though its character and in some cases something of its quantity occasionally peeps through the veil. The operation of this agricultural enterprise depended fundamentally on the conditions of production that prevailed in the ancient eastern Mediterranean.

2   Physical Preconditions

Greece and the eastern Aegean basin lie within a Mediterranean climate zone. The region experiences basically two seasons, summer and winter. Summers typically are hot and dry, winters cool to cold and rainy. Most of the rain that falls comes between October or November and April or May. This general climatic regime imposes a particular approach to the growing of food. Generally speaking, farmers planted (and still plant) cereal crops (largely wheat and barley) in the fall with the onset of the rains. Harvest came in spring or early summer, after the rains ended. The amount of rainfall can vary drastically from year to year ('high interannual variability'). In a dry farming regime – that is, with reliance on rainfall alone and no or little irrigation – wheat demands at least 300 mm of precipitation during the growing season, barley rather less (200–250 mm). Generally speaking, Greece and the Aegean basin generally get fewer than 300 mm every other year, fewer than 200 mm every fourth or fifth year. Crop failures were therefore a built-in element of the agricultural regime of the Hellenistic world. Further, highly variable transient local conditions could make life miserable for a farmer while sparing a neighbour (some examples in Reger 1994b: 102–4). Alkiphron, an artful writer of the second century AD, has left us a collection of fictional letters by ordinary people. In one a farmer writes to his neighbour:

> A severe hailstorm has cut down our crops, and there's no remedy for hunger. We can't buy imported wheat because we have no money. I hear you still have stores left from last year's good yield. Lend me twenty *medimnoi*, so I can survive, me and my wife and kids. When harvest comes, we'll pay you back 'measure for measure, and better', if there's any abundance. Don't ignore good neighbours being destroyed in a tight season. (2.3)

At typical levels of consumption, twenty *medimnoi* would keep a family of four for about a year (Reger 1994b: 86–9). It was in part to temper the effects of such variations that Greek farmers typically practised highly scattered farming, with small plots in different micro-environments (Halstead and Jones 1989; Gallant 1991: 41–5).

But the Hellenistic world embraced much more than the old Aegean basin, and conditions in the new kingdoms of Egypt and Asia could be very different. The high Anatolian plateau, for example, presents in parts desert-like conditions; summers are fiercely hot and winters bitterly cold, with snow; the agricultural regime there demands cereal cultivation in the summer. Mesopotamia, a heartland of the Seleukid empire, was home to one of the world's oldest irrigation regimes. Because the bed of the Euphrates lies higher than the Tigris 'many canals have been cut from it, some of which are always running and supply water to the inhabitants on either bank, while others are constructed as occasion requires, whenever they are short of water to irrigate the land; for in general this country gets no rain'. Alexander the Great found the weirs built on the Tigris an obstruction to navigation and removed them; but rather than intended, as Arrian has him say, to foil attack by naval forces, they were likely part of the irrigation system (Arr. *Anab.* 7.7.3–7, trans. Brunt).

3 Human Resources

Two basic questions are the total size and the distribution of the population of the Hellenistic world. A recent rough estimate puts the population of Alexander's empire – thus essentially the whole Hellenistic world – at 30–35 million (Aperghis 2001: 72–7, but the matter requires thorough re-examination; for a penetrating analysis of Roman Egypt, Scheidel 2001; brief general overview in Corvisier and Suder 2000: 44–9). This figure can be used to estimate total taxation, demand for food and other economic variables *en gros*. The total resources available to the Seleukid kings, for instance, have been estimated at about one talent per thousand population per year (based largely on data from Mesopotamia; Aperghis 2001). Such a population would demand roughly 120–175 million *medimnoi* of grain per year (one *medimnos* Attic held roughly 52 kg). Such estimates help us grasp the total size of economic activity in the Hellenistic world, but elide important details. Distribution of the population is an equally important variable. The majority of the population certainly lived on the land – whether in nucleated villages or isolated farmsteads, for both patterns can be found (Saprykin 1994; 1997: 179–208; Spencer 1995; Kolesnikov and Jacenko 1999). These people farmed for a living and supplied most of their own needs for food. In some cases people preferred to live aggregated in a single settlement within the territory of a polity, but as long as the territory was small, like the island of Melos, people could still commute to their farms and live off the production (Renfrew and Wagstaff 1982: 251–6). It was in bigger places like Attica where a considerable portion of the population did not farm that questions of food supply became a matter of continual concern (Garnsey 1988).

But the Hellenistic world saw the creation of truly large cities, such as Alexandria in Egypt, Seleukeia on the Tigris, Antiocheia on the Orontes and many others of lesser size (Billows, this volume). Such foundations in the newly conquered territories had the effect of creating new centres of high urban density and of drawing at least their ruling and military elite from the population of Greece. That is to say, there was undoubtedly also a marked transfer of population eastward and southward (to Egypt). Whether the population as a whole grew, declined, or remained stable over time is difficult to say. Recent archaeological research (surveys) has suggested that, in some parts at least of old Greece, the number of rural habitations declined over the Hellenistic period (Alcock 1993: 33–92, but see Corvisier and Suder 2000: 112–17 for a different view and see the important critique of conclusions about rural habitation for the Athenian deme of Atene based on survey work: Osborne 1996: 55–6). This discovery can be conjoined with a famous complaint of Polybios: 'In our time the whole of Greece has been subject to a low birth rate and a general decrease of the population, owing to which cities have become deserted and the land has ceased to yield fruit, although there have neither been continuous wars or epidemics.' Polybios attributes this decline to greed: people refused to marry, or refused to have children, or were unwilling to raise more than one or two children, so as to leave them the whole of their patrimony; when one or more died prematurely, 'houses must have been left unoccupied, and as in the case of swarms of bees, so by small degrees cities became resourceless and feeble' (Polyb. 36.17.5–6, trans. Paton). Two letters of Philip V of Macedon to the city of Larisa in Thessaly show his concern to repopulate the city and restore its agricultural base. Larisan ambassadors came to him and 'revealed to me that your city needs more inhabitants on account of the wars'; he instructed Larisa to enrol resident Greeks as citizens. These actions were intended to ensure that 'the land will be cultivated to a greater extent' (SIG^3 543; Austin 60; Dench, this volume, section 1). But the issue here, as in Sparta too (E. David 1981: 142–70), was not depopulation in general, but a decline in the number of citizens. Philip was quite confident that enough people lived at Larisa to keep the land farmed; the problem was their exclusion from the land because they lacked citizen rights. And Polybios' complaint is framed in moral, not economic, terms.

What all this suggests is that patterns of settlement changed in the Hellenistic period. In the short term cities might by devastated by war or other disasters (like the famous Rhodian earthquake); in these cases intervention by higher authorities might ameliorate or even solve the problem. In other cases the actions of kings themselves rearranged settlement patterns, as when they moved populations to form new cities (G. Cohen 1995; Reger 2004). But there were longer-term and larger-scale trans-formations as well, like the transfer of population to Egypt and the Middle East, that followed from structural changes in the Hellenistic world. These changes could not help but reorganize aspects of the economy, though we must be cautious in suppos-ing that such changes were always fundamental and complete. For example, despite the planting of many new Greek cities in the Middle East, the basic structure of economic life there seems to have been relatively little affected. These changes – if changes they were – were neither exclusively Hellenistic phenomena nor uniformly distributed over the Hellenistic world. Even if the regions of Asia and Africa that came under the suzerainty of Hellenistic kings saw a net import of people (Davies 1984: 266–7), people moved in the reverse direction as well. A garrison of at least 120 men established by the Ptolemies on the Aegean island of Thera consisted largely of soldiers from Pisidia and Pamphylia in Asia Minor, under the command of an Aspendian (*IG* 12.3.325 with p. 230 and 3 Suppl. p. 283; L. Robert 1963: 388, 411–18); 39 of 42 soldiers stationed at Delphi by King Attalos in 208 hailed from Pergamon (*ISE* 2.81). Traders from the Levant settled on Delos, like a family from Tyre (Le Dinahet-Couilloud 1997). And some parts of the old Greek world must have continued to be able to export population, at least for part of the Hellenistic period. Macedon, for one, continued to supply soldiers and settlers in the third century, and Crete remained a very fertile source for mercenaries throughout the Hellenistic centuries (Corvisier and Suder 2000: 44–8).

For the most part, productive labour was exercised by individuals and their families on their own farms, as the Grouch in Menander's play, who eschewed even the help of his neighbours (lines 328–31). But even in the sphere of self-sufficient agriculture, the rhythms of labour demand were such that farmers must have depended at harvest time on the assistance of others, whether mutual help of neighbours or the services of paid seasonal labourers (Gallant 1991: 60–112, 143–69). These forms of labour exchange have left almost no traces in our sources. For wealthier farmers – whether owner-operators or absentee landlords – another labour option existed: slavery (Gabrielsen, this volume). Typically our sources for agricultural slavery (as opposed to other forms) are poor, but they suffice, especially given how scattered and casual they are, to guarantee that slave labour was a standard feature of the rural landscape. For example, in the early second century a citizen of Mylasa in Karia 'came to the *boule* and the assembly and declared that a slave (*soma*) of his had run away and come to Myndos'; the Mylaseans appointed an ambassador to go to Myndos and seek relief (*I.Mylasa* 102.23–6; see generally Burford 1993: 208–22).

Manumission, the freeing of slaves, was a relatively common feature of Hellenistic slavery, but manumission was often tempered by conditions that secured continued use of part of the slaves' economic value for the former owner. When sometime in the third century one female slave and three males bought their freedom and that of their wives and children from their owner Attinas (for a total of 325 gold staters), they were obligated to 'remain with Attinas while Attinas lives and do whatever Attinas orders' (*ISE* 109; trans. Burstein 54) – a highly conditional freedom indeed. A great many such conditional manumissions are known from Macedon, Thessaly, Delphi, Kalymna and other places, sufficient to prove that the practice was widespread and typical.

Many *poleis* could avail themselves of another type of labour, provided by the services of subordinated populations. The helots of Sparta are the most famous example (Alcock 2001; Ducat 2002), but there are plenty of other examples from the Hellenistic world. At Priene in Asia Minor a subordinated group called the Pedieis ('plain-dwellers') rebelled against their Greek masters in the 280s with the help of a neighbouring *polis*. The terror the insurrection provoked and the heavy punishments meted out to the rebels appear in inscriptions that refer to the events (*I.Priene* 14.5–7, 14, 3.14–15; Burford 1993: 206–7).

4   Forms of Movement

Sokrates famously remarked that the sights outside Athens had no attraction for him, and although he was perhaps extreme in his love of the town, certainly most people in the Hellenistic world never travelled far from where they were born. Short-distance movement, of course, was nevertheless a mainstay of the very local economy. Agricultural commodities and rural products – grain, olive oil, wines, vegetables, meat, wood for fire and construction, stone – all had to be transported from their points of origin to points of sale and consumption. Mules loaded with faggots of wood or sacks of grain, like those evoked in a fourth-century speech of Demosthenes (42.5–7), must have been common sights. A landowner of Mylasa in Karia had to move the grapes grown on his estates to the press in his house in town (*en tei polei*; *I.Mylasa* 205–6 and unpublished material). Heavier commodities, like building stone, were moved in wagons pulled by yokes of oxen. An inscription from Athens dated to 330/29 honours Eudemos of Plataia, who 'has now given 1000 pairs of oxen for the making of the Panathenaic stadium and theatre' (*IG*2² 351.15–18; cf. Loomis 1998: 110–11), no doubt for the transport of building stone (though whether over longer distance, say from the quarries, or on-site, is unclear).

For long distances, recent work in Roman Italy has suggested that the network of roads built there had a trade component, or at least served incidentally to enhance trade. Handbooks like Cato the Elder's *De agricultura* seem to presuppose the existence of a land transportation network and its usability for transport of farm products (Laurence 1998b). For western Asia Minor Strabo describes a Common Road running from Ephesos to Magnesia on the Maeander and then along the river into Phrygia (14.2.29). This road may have existed already in the Achaimenid period (French 1998). As a conduit for military and civilian traffic, it helped to assure the prosperity of a brace of small communities strung out along it (Marchese 1986: 139–

41). Strabo describes Karoura, a town along the road, as 'a village having inns (*pandocheia*) and springs of hot water' (Strabo 12.8.17, trans. French 1998: 32). The economics of land transport will have varied from place to place and time to time. Clearly, the emergence in Italy of Rome in the third and second centuries as a massive urban conglomeration, heavy with demand for food and the ability to pay for it, will have seeded the development of a regional, or supra-regional, network of trade to satisfy those demands. The role of roads like that between Athens and Thebes, of which a picturesque description survives (Austin 83), will have been more modest. But in any case, we can be confident that land transport played an important role in the movement of goods and people; the quandary remains, as so often, our inability to quantify (see still Burford 1960).

Transportation by sea was always more important because of the vastly reduced expense, especially for the movement of bulk goods. The bustling intersection between sea and land is evoked nicely in a story from a fourth-century handbook on surviving sieges. The agora of the besieged town was filled with boxes packed with clothes or other goods, crates, mats, partially woven sails, jars of chaff and wool, baskets of raisins and figs, amphorae full of wheat and dried figs, gourds and a load of firewood (Aen. Tact. 29.1–10). Some of these items may have come from close by and others brought in from long distances – it is impossible to be sure, though one may guess (see Reger 2003). Even if harvested locally, as is not unlikely, firewood was probably transported (like other bulky goods) by water if possible; this situation is reflected both in the Delian regulations on the sale of wood and wood products (*ID* 504; Descat 2001) and a fourth-century inscription from Torone, in which a merchant begs a colleague to 'send to me straight away if you have a ship, buying seven talents (of wood) if it is possible' (Henry 1991; cf. Davies 2001).

Our knowledge of the typical size and fittings of Hellenistic ships derives mostly from wrecks. Literary accounts like Moschion's of a great ship built by Hieron of Syracuse (301–215) tend to focus on the exceptional (Athen. 5.206d–9b with Casson 1986: 191–9). Ships mentioned in documents seem to have ranged typically from 95 to 165 tons. These figures may not represent the full capacity since they come from reports of cargoes, usually grain; the ships may have carried other goods as well, as both Moschion's report and wrecks suggest. According to a recent comprehensive study, many Hellenistic wrecks were small ships, of 50 tons burden or less, with mixed cargoes suggesting that '[t]he predominant activity represented by these wrecks may have been tramping – the speculative and small-scale contractual transport of goods along coastal routes, often within an established economic region' (Gibbins 2001: 294). This picture however does not preclude some highly-organized, 'destination-conscious' shipping, particularly of either luxury goods or staples like grain intended for large and predictable markets like Athens. But shipwrecks, horrible as they no doubt were for those who experienced them, tell a good deal about the nature of trade.

The trade about which we are best informed is that in staples like grains, wine and olive oil. The reasons are simple, but make analysis difficult. Grain appears again and again as a consequence of the efforts of *poleis* to secure satisfactory supplies at satisfactory prices (Migeotte 1984; 1991; 1998). In many cases this means grain grown locally, as for example in the Samian law regulating the sale of grain grown in the Samian Peraia (*IG* 12.6.172; Bresson 2000: 253–7).

In other cases, grain was imported from long distances. As in the Classical period before, Athens remained the chief example of a city dependent on long-distance imported grain. According to the *Constitution of the Athenians* attributed to Aristotle and certainly composed in the 320s (48.4; Rhodes 1981), the Athenian assembly was required to deliberate about the grain supply at its chief monthly meeting; in his *Rhetoric* Aristotle himself recommends that the aspiring politician familiarize himself with the supply of grain as one of five crucial areas of knowledge (1359b–60a). The role of grain merchants becomes especially clear in times of stress.

Another body of evidence that contributes to our understanding of trade is amphorae. Large pottery containers with tapered bottoms to make for easy packing in ships, amphorae were produced in massive quantity in many parts of the Hellenistic world. They were used for the shipment of a wide variety of goods – chiefly wine and olive oil – but in fact almost any commodity that could be put in a jar. Sometimes the origin of amphorae can be determined from an analysis of the fabric of the pots themselves (Whitbread 1995), but for many centres of production the preliminary work has only begun. In other cases the jars were marked with official stamps, typically on one or both of the handles, indicating the magistrate under whom the jar was thrown and, sometimes, the origin. The stamps were probably used for local fiscal purposes (and surely not as trade names, guarantors of quality, or for other purposes aimed at end-consumers: see Garlan 1999: 75–83), though this has not been absolutely established. At first blush a veritable quarry of economic information, these stamps are in fact devilishly difficult to analyse (Lawall 1998; Garlan 1999; Finkielsztejn 2001b).

A good case study is fourth-century Thasos. There is little doubt that the chief product shipped in Thasian amphorae was wine. Thasian amphorae have been found in greatest abundance in the Black Sea region, and there is evidence for return shipment of goods from that region to Thasos, notably grain ([Dem.] 50.14–21; for Black Sea products in the third century, Polyb. 4.38). The apogee of finds of Thasian amphorae dates roughly to the 350s–340s, with a marked drop-off thereafter. But what this pattern means for the economy of Thasos or trade patterns is less clear. A later fourth-century Athenian speech ([Dem.] 35.35) reveals a cargo of wine headed for the Black Sea composed of products from Attica, Peparethos, Kos, Thasos, Mende and other cities – here clearly the trade in Thasian wine was not in Thasian hands, although there is also evidence for Thasian ships carrying their own product. Complicating our understanding of the structure of this trade is the rarity of Thasian coins in the Black Sea (Garlan 1999: 83–92).

Finally, we may consider briefly the classic example, the amphorae of Rhodes. The Rhodian material provides in many ways the greatest interpretative temptations, because the Rhodians came to stamp their amphorae most consistently of all the Hellenistic ateliers. But the practice entails problems. Because the Rhodians stamped both handles of each amphora (albeit with different information), the numbers of stamped Rhodian handles found at any site always overwhelm those of other centres of production. Apparent Rhodian predominance must therefore always be tested (for an example of the result of this exercise, Gibbins 2001: 290–3). Moreover, we cannot know with certainty the numbers for other centres found at the same site, since many of competitors' amphorae may have remained unstamped (Lawall forthcoming). Finally, the Rhodians' own practices were not consistent over time. They stamped relatively few handles early in the Hellenistic period; by the later third and second centuries, in contrast, the majority of amphorae produced were probably stamped (Finkielsztejn 2001a: 181–5). With these cautions in mind, we may note a trend. There is some evidence to suggest that a predominance enjoyed by Rhodian amphorae in the third and first half of the second centuries fell off after 170 or so. Knidian amphorae seem to replace Rhodian in the second half of the second century, although never achieving the same level of predominance. This change has been attributed to a new preference for Knidian wine especially among the Romans. Attractive as this explanation may seem at first, it has holes; not least, that there is essentially no archaeological confirmation for Knidian wine imports into Italy (Gibbins 2001: 291; generally now on the chronology of Rhodian amphorae, Finkielsztejn 2001b).

5   Institutions of the Economy

The study of institutions is a fruitful way to think about economies which lack data to permit more quantitative analysis (North 1990). For the Hellenistic economy, it may be useful to examine six out of many possibilities: mechanisms for setting prices; banking, finance and credit; the *polis*; forms of inter-state economic co-operation; the role of the Hellenistic kingdoms; and money.

Price setting

In the retail trade there can be little doubt that prices were typically set in the *agora*, the market, as a result of face-to-face negotiations between sellers and buyers. Anthropological studies of recent 'bazaar economies' have emphasized the sophistication of such interactions today (Geertz et al. 1979: 123–313: a classic study). Much depends on the information each side controls, the time of day, expectations – or guesses – about the future. A series of barley prices from Delos shows intense competition between sellers to supply the sanctuary with feed for the sacred geese under circumstances of apparently declining price (Reger 1994b: 10–11). A poet at Iasos found himself abandoned when the bell pealed announcing the opening of the fish market; in fish, freshness is all (Strabo 14.2.21). An inscription from Magnesia on the Maeander gives a sense of the hustle and bustle of the agora, with people selling linen, wool, dried fish, onions, and cheeses (*I.Magn.* 121); likewise an Athenian inscription mentioning Persian dried fruit, nuts from Herakleia, pine-cones, chest-nuts, Egyptian beans, dates, dried fruits, lupines, olives, almonds and other goods sold by weight (*IG*2^2 1013 with Meritt 1938: 127–46, no. 27). But the state had interests in overseeing prices. An inscription from Kyparissa in Messenia of the late fourth or early third century sets out regulations related to the collection of the *pentekoste*, the two per cent tax imposed by many *poleis* on imports and exports. People who imported goods (*emporia*) into the *chora* of the *polis* had to register with the *pentekostologoi* (the officials charged with collecting the tax) before they could display or sell their goods. Exporters were also required to pay the tax. And anyone who underpriced his goods – for the purpose, obviously, of evading part of the tax – was to be compelled by the *pentekostologoi* to 'do business according to the contract' (*SIG*^{3} 952; Vélissaropoulos 1980: 208–9). Market disequilibrium might also provoke state intervention. An *agoranomos* from Paros was honoured for tamping down bread prices and assuring availability (*IG* 12. 5.129). On a larger scale, the *polis* might seek to soften grain prices by buying stocks for sale at a price below market, whether as a one-time action or from a fund specifically created for these purposes (Migeotte 1991; 1998; Reger 1993). Festivals offered opportunities for profiteering, particularly when many strangers gathered together; states sought to regulate such affairs. For example, for a festival at Andania in the Peloponnese the regulations for the *agora* say:

> Let the priests designate a place in which all items are to be sold. Let the *agoranomos* for the city be in charge, so that the sellers sell genuine and ritually acceptable goods and use the same weights and measures as the public ones, and let him not determine the price for which something must be sold nor the time nor let him exact a fee from the sellers for the place. As for those who do not sell as prescribed, let him whip the slaves but fine free men twenty drachmae, and let the fine be sacred. (*SIG*³ 736)

Here the *agoranomos* is forbidden from fixing prices, but clearly he could have been granted that authority (Bresson 2000: 173–4). Fish were especially a subject of price regulation, as a recently published Athenian inscription has re-emphasized (Bresson 2000: 151–82). The retail trade was carried out in part through shops; a Samian regulation of 245/4 relating to four shops owned by Hera and rented out gives some sense of the conditions of such arrangements (*IG* 12.6.169). Archaeological finds of shops, or potential shops, include a considerable number of buildings off the agora in Athens (Young 1951) and houses at Olynthos of late fourth century date that included equipment for processing olives or grapes (Robinson and Graham 1938: 337–43, and now Cahill 2002). On Delos another facility with presses, beds, storage jars and other equipment associated with olive oil processing has been identified as a perfumery (Brun 1999). Evidence then for retail trade of various types and for local manufacturing establishments is abundant.

It has recently been argued that Athenian officials in the fourth and third century were able to set desirable (but not obligatory) wholesale prices for grain and to encourage large-scale importers to abide by them through the award of public honours (Bresson 2000: 183–210). Whether such price-setting was possible, or attempted, for other goods (except fish and some meats) is unclear. Athens may in any case have been exceptional because of the scale of its imports – by the fourth century, if not long before, the Athenians were certainly far from feeding themselves from the harvest of their own territory – and the regulations imposed to guarantee imported grain. Smaller *poleis* may well have been more at the mercy of merchants and highly variable supply and demand.

Finally, we may consider briefly whether there was a price-setting market that embraced the whole, or much of, the Hellenistic world. This view was certainly held by some earlier scholars, and has recently been revived in a modified form for grain prices in the context of the Aegean (Bresson 2000: 263–307). It is however certainly not the case that grain prices (those for which we are best informed) were linked throughout the Hellenistic world, as a glance at prices from Babylon as compared to Delos and Egypt will show (Drexhage 1991; Slotsky 1997; van der Spek 2000; Aperghis 2001: 83–5). The degree to which prices may have moved in tandem on a regional basis is less clear. Certainly, people in nearby cities may sometimes have entertained similar notions about the appropriate level of price for basic goods like grain, and may even, when their city had the economic might, striven to obtain such prices from importers. It is also true that travelling merchants must have had plenty of opportunity to compare prices in different towns on their routes. But we are still very far from being able to say with assurance enough about the structure of individual markets – amount of local production, level of local demand and so forth (with some, but still too few exceptions; see Reger 1994b) – to mark with any confidence the degree to which prices were linked at different times and places. My own view is that such linkage, when it existed, was likely to be exceptional and transient rather than permanent and structural.

Banks, financing, credit

Sources for credit and financing in the Hellenistic world included kings and their courtiers, whose wealth sometimes financed building projects or helped cities in natural or man-made disasters; sanctuaries, which often controlled massive reserves of wealth built up over centuries; public banks run by the *poleis*; private banks; and private groups and individuals who might lend money without interest. Interest-bearing loans were typically secured by 'hypothecation' of real property – land, buildings, ships and/or their cargo, slaves. Hypothecation differed from modern mortgages in that default led to the forfeiture of the entire value of the hypothecated good(s) to the creditor, even if their value exceeded the amount owed. But that did not necessarily mean that property-owners could not borrow repeatedly and simultaneously on the security of a single piece of property, as an Athenian inscription of 367/6 makes perfectly clear (*Agora* 19.P5.1–39).

Public banks appear in many documents. At Miletos, a gift of money by three brothers in 206/5 was administered through a public bank to generate interest (*Milet* I.3.145; *SIG*[3] 577). When fifty years later King Eumenes II gave a large financial gift to Miletos, this too was administered through the public bank, which made 'commercial loans' (*emporika daneia*) with the capital (*I.Didyma* 488; Bogaert 1968: 259–61). A Rhodian public bank is also well attested (Gabrielsen 1997: 82). Another source of capital was loans made by the state. Many *poleis* had funds from which money was lent to private persons; the income from these loans might then be used to finance a festival or dedications to the god(s). The stoa given to Miletos by Antiochos falls into this category; so too, on a much smaller scale, do the loans on Delos which financed the dedication of vases to Apollo (Reger 1992).

Private banks also existed (for the lively debate about banking and the economy in fourth-century Athens, Millett 1991 and E. Cohen 1992). On Delos much of the business of keeping money was entrusted to a series of private bankers in the early second century (*ID* 442A1–55). A loan made by a banker on Lemnos is attested by a '*horos* of the land and house and the things belonging to the land and the house hypothecated to the banker Agathokles son of Philippos and to Polyphilos son of Archedemos (of the Athenian deme of) Halai, for 200 drachmas, silver, for the tomb of Hedea, to have and control according to the contract kept by Drakontides son of Archagathos of Phearrio' (Beschi 1992–3: 263). The purpose of the loan may have been to finance the tomb or funeral rites, though this is not made explicit. Loans by private individuals and private groups are also attested. Many of the loans recorded on

the Athenian security *horoi* (brief texts inscribed on stones and placed by hypothecated property to show that the property secured a loan; Lalonde in *Agora* 19: 18–21;
Finley 1985) were granted by private individuals. Interest-free loans could be provided by *eranoi*: *ad hoc* groups who lent to an individual for a specific need. A number
of such loans are attested in Athens in the 330s for the manumission of slaves (e.g.,
IG2².1553.20–3, etc.) and in *horoi* (e.g., IG2².2721).

Maritime loans formed a special category. Two documents preserve terms in whole
or in part of such loans. The most complete is embedded in a speech delivered in
Athens in the 340s ([Dem.] 35.10–13). In it an Athenian and a citizen of Karystos, a
town on Euboia, lent 3000 drachmas to two men from Phaselis on the south coast of
Asia Minor for a trip from Athens into the Black Sea and back. The loan, secured on
the cargo of the ship, which was to be wine bought at Mende, carried an interest rate
of 25 per cent, or 30 per cent if they left after Arktouros rose in mid-September
(Morton 2001: 259). The loan was to be repaid within twenty days of return to
Athens, except on cargo jettisoned by common decision of the crew or goods taken
by enemies. The lenders had full power to extract from the borrowers' property to
recover any monies owed under the contract but not paid. Another, similar loan,
though couched in somewhat enigmatic language (Bogaert 1965: 146–54), dates to
the second century and was struck at Alexandria (Wilcken 1925; Vélissaropoulos
1980: 308–10). These texts differ from more ordinary, land-based loans in many
particulars, but most notably because the lenders could not control the property that
secured the loans and because the loans did not need to be repaid unless the trip was
successful; in this respect they shaded into a kind of insurance, their function also as a
source of capital cannot be forgotten (Bresson 2003: 158–61).

It has long been argued whether private non-maritime loans were made for
'productive' or 'consumptive' ends. Finley believed that most were destined for
consumption, many as dowries for the property owners' daughters. In an inscription
from Mykonos we can see explicitly how property was used for this purpose: 'Kallixenos has given his daughter Timekrate to Rhodokles and as dowry 700 drachmas, of
this 300 as clothing; Rhodokles agrees that he has the clothing and 100 drachmas,
but for 300 drachmas Kallixenos has hypothecated the house in the city to which the
house of Ktesidemos son of Chairelas is neighbour' (*SIG*³ 1215.15–20). But there
can be no doubt that loans were also put to 'productive' ends. Several Athenian *horoi*
attest to the hypothecation of productive assets, as for example an Athenian *horos*
taken on a workshop (*ergasterion*) and the slaves who worked in it (*SEG* 32.236,
c. 350). The *emporika daneia* granted by the Milesian public bank have already been
mentioned; whether these were maritime loans, as some have thought, or land-based,
their name makes their purpose clear.

The polis

The *polis* remained a vibrant and fundamental institution in Greece and western Asia
Minor throughout the Hellenistic period (Billows, this volume). The *polis* was
marked by certain fundamental features: in particular, from an economic point of
view, tight linkage between the urban centre (the *asty*) and its associated agricultural
hinterland (the *chora*), and a clear distinction between citizens (*politai*), who enjoyed
full access (if male and adult) to the protection of the state, and non-citizen residents
(*metoikoi*, 'metics', *paroikoi*, and other terms: Papazoglou 1997) and visitors (some-

times called *xenoi*). These characteristics helped to mark out each *polis* as a distinct economic unit, which nevertheless interacted with outsiders in the form of trade and exchange. But these features of the *polis* were not uniform over time and space, and some changes can be seen in the course of the Hellenistic period. Here I would like to focus on three issues: the relationship between the *polis* and its rural hinterland; taxation and other forms of income and spending; and the growing role of non-citizens in economic life in at least some *poleis*.

The economic life and health of all *poleis* was closely linked to agricultural production in the territory. Not only did most citizens of the *polis* farm, but the city itself, whether directly or through public sanctuaries, owned agricultural estates that were leased out (e.g., Delos: Reger 1994b: 189–238; Charre and Le Dinahet-Couilloud 1999; Thespiai: Sosin 2000; Athens: Behrend 1970; Mylasa: *I.Mylasa* 201–32, 801–54; Dignas 2000; 2002: 95–106). A *polis* might express its control over such properties, which could be important sources of income, through the terms of leases; a late fourth-century lease from Arkesine on Amorgos stipulated that the renter of a sacred estate 'shall apply each year 150 measures of manure, in a wicker basket holding one *medimnos* 4 *hemiekta*. If he does not apply, he shall pay 3 obols per basket. He shall make a pledge before the *neopoiai*, that he has indeed applied the manure according to the lease' (*IG* 12.7.62.20–5).

Control of the hinterland meant defining as precisely as possible its boundaries, especially with regard to neighbouring states. The Thessalian towns Ambrakia and Charadros appointed three (?) commissioners each to set the boundaries between the cities:

> Let them proceed to the land starting at the corner of the wall, just as prescribed in the written agreement, and let them set boundary-markers just as the agreement orders wherever seems good to both sides, and let them measure the distances from the walls of the polis of the Ambrakians so as to proceed toward the marker at the hilltop, measuring anything else they need to measure by distance from this marker.... (Charneux and Tréheux 1988)

The economic interests that coloured boundary disputes appear for example in the long-standing dispute between Priene and Samos over the control of territory from which the Samians derived part of their public grain supply (*I.Priene* 37; *IG* 12.6.172.23–7). Boundaries might be studded with fortifications and patrolled by troops (Ober 1985; Habicht 1997: 137; Rousset 1999; Ma 2000b; Baker 2000), even along borders that technically ceased to exist after the political unification of two neighbouring towns (Schmitt 1994; Rousset 1999).

The basic tax, known already from the Classical period, was the 'contribution', the *eisphora*, an impost on personal fortunes, typically imposed at times of special need (Migeotte 2000: 164–5; 2002: 41–2). Indirect taxes of various kinds were perhaps more common and formed the chief basis of *polis* income. The *pentekoste* has already been mentioned. An inscription from Teos in Ionia gives a sense of the range of such taxes, from which certain new citizens were exempted for four years: the *choregia*, the *boegia*, the *lampadarchia*, all taxes connected with civic festivals; the taxes on plough oxen and on pack animals and slaves involved in the wood trade; taxes on sheep or pigs; the tax that supported the public doctor; the taxes on the production of clothing made from Milesian wool and on purple-dyeing; and the taxes on gardens and beehives (J. and L. Robert 1976; Austin 99). Taxes were often collected not directly but through tax-farming: private individuals bought the right to collect a certain tax, earning a profit from the difference between the purchase price and the amount actually collected. An inscription from Kos (which is not complete) lists sale of taxes on grain, wine, bread, gardens, wood, prostitutes, rental houses, women slaves (probably again used for prostitution), vineyards and many other goods and services (*SIG*³ 1000; Pleket 1964: no. 23).

Fines for violation of all kinds of laws were imposed by all cities. Towards the end of the second century the Amphyktiony that controlled the sanctuary of Apollo at Delphi legislated a fine of 200 drachmas for persons violating a currency law, half going to the individual who denounced the offender, the balance to the *polis* (*SIG*³ 729). *Poleis* also obtained income through rental property, whether on real estate owned directly by the *polis* or by a sanctuary. *Poleis* had recourse also to loans from various sources. In the early third century the sanctuary of Zeus Olympios at Lokroi Epizephyrioi lent money to the city on several occasions and issued regulations to guarantee that it would recover money owed by defaulting debtors if third parties bought property belonging to them (Bogaert 1976: no. 33–4). The Argives, in desperate need, borrowed 100 talents from the Rhodians to repair their fortification walls and fill the ranks of their cavalry (*ISE* 1.40; Migeotte 1984: no. 19). Loans from private persons are attested at Olbia in the Black Sea, Halikarnassos and Arkesine on Amorgos (Migeotte 1984: nos. 43, 103, 49; *IG* 12.7.67B). Subunits of the *polis* lent money too. The Koan deme of Antimacheia honoured two sacred treasurers (*hierotamiai*) who 'provided the deme with many great benefits, and, when the money which the *polis* owed was repaid during their term of office, had care that it be lent out with suitable hypothecations and added monies of their own so that the deme's incomes should grow...' (Paton and Hicks 1891: no. 383).

Finally, *poleis* received gifts, whether from their own citizens and residents in the form of voluntary contributions or from kings or other high officials (Migeotte 1992; Bringmann and von Steuben 1995). In the aftermath of the earthquake that devastated southwestern Asia Minor in 199/8, King Antiochos III and his wife Laodike contributed money and grain to the town of Iasos. In addition and on her own Laodike ordered the conveyance to Iasos for ten years of 1000 *medimnoi* of grain, the sale of which would provide dowries for girls of poor families (*I.Iasos* 4; Ma 1999: 180–2, 329–35 no. 26). Perhaps the most famous of such gifts came from a host of kings to Rhodes after the earthquake of 227/6 that toppled the famous Colossus (Polyb. 5.88.90–4). But some gifts created civic income. Around 299

> Antiochos, the eldest son of King Seleukos... seeing his own father exerting every effort on behalf of the sanctuary at Didyma (near Miletos)... promises to construct a stoa one stadion (approximately 200 m) in length for the god (Apollo) in the city from which there shall be derived every year income, which he thinks ought to be spent for works undertaken in the sanctuary at Didyma, and the structures built with these revenues shall be his own dedications. (*OGIS* 213; Bringmann and von Steuben 1995: 338–41 no. 281; trans. Burstein 2)

Even more impressive, perhaps, was the gift to Miletos in the second century of 160,000 *medimnoi* of grain and the necessary wood to build a gymnasium (Herrmann 1965b: 71–90 no. 1; Bringmann and von Steuben 1995: 346–8 no. 284 trans. Burstein 40). At a rough estimate of 5–10 drachmas per *medimnos* for wheat (Reger 1993: 305 Table 1, 312–14), this gift represented 800,000–1,600,000 drachmas, or 133–266 talents.

Civic income became civic budget. Cities had many expenses – salaries for public officials, pay for attendance of public functions like the assembly (*I.Iasos* 20.5–7; Gauthier 1990), public building projects, especially in sanctuaries (see Burford 1969 for Epidauros), purchase and upkeep of public slaves, financing of military operations, to name only a few. How annual – or longer term – budgets were drawn up is a difficult topic. An inscription from Ilion of 77 BC shows the city planning to make adjustments in expenditures authorized currently against future income when the actual amount of that income becomes known (*SEG* 4.664; Pleket 1964: no. 36). In late fourth or early third century Oropos diverted 'all funds' of the city 'for the repayment of money borrowed for the (fortification) walls, except money for sacred matters, for salaries of the financial officers (*hyperetai*), and for any other civic expenditure set by law or decree' (Petrakos 1997: 210–1, no. 302 [*SEG* 16.295]).

Greek *poleis* had always had inhabitants who were not citizens and whose ability to participate in the economic life of the city was correspondingly limited. In the fourth century the Athenian Xenophon in his *Poroi* offered suggestions for expanding the access of such foreigners to Athenian economic life, and the establishment of *dikai emporikai* to which foreign merchants had access was a concrete step in that direction (Vélissaropoulos 1980: 235–67; Todd 1993: 334–7). The Hellenistic period shows many examples of non-citizens' increased access to the political, social and economic life of the *poleis*. Groups formed at Lindos on Rhodes for economic and social purposes included non-citizens (e.g. *Lindos* 300a4–6, 384b15–16; Gabrielsen 2001a: 223). Delians owned land within the territory of the neighbouring *polis* of Rheneia (*ID* 442A23–4), and for a time on Delos non-citizen merchants exerted considerable influence within the Athenian-controlled government (see Reger 2003 with further references).

Forms of inter-state co-operation

The Hellenistic period saw the development or elaboration of a number of mechanisms to tighten links between *poleis* and to facilitate interactions between them. Most of these institutions existed in earlier times, but became increasingly common in this period. Their sole purpose was not economic – typically political and social goals predominated – but in many cases they had important economic consequences.

Proxenia was the granting of honours by one state to a citizen or citizens of another. Such awards were often bestowed as a consequence of political actions (serving as a foreign judge or ambassador; obtaining favours from a sovereign) but the honours granted often included economic benefits, such as the right to import or export goods without paying taxes (*ateleia*). Individuals who enjoyed these benefits may only occasionally have availed themselves, but they created at least opportunities for economic activities (Marek 1984; Gauthier 1985).

Other institutions created ties between states. Grants of *asylia*, for example, secured freedom for sanctuaries from seizures and reprisals; this was a genuinely Hellenistic institution, as study of the documentary evidence has shown, though it had roots in earlier practice. A declaration of *asylia* kept the sanctuary safe and contributed to its role as a locus for economic activity, especially during festivals (Rigsby 1996). Grants of *isopoliteia*, which allowed citizens of one *polis* to become citizens of another, and declarations of *sympoliteia*, which created new political units where there had before been separate polities, facilitated economic interchange between *poleis* (Gawantka 1975; Reger 2004). A good recent example of the benefits and the care with which cities entered into such agreements appears in an *isopoliteia* agreement between Xanthos and Myra in Lykia (Bousquet and Gauthier 1994: 319–47).

Hellenistic kingdoms

The economic activities of the great territorial kingdoms of the Hellenistic period related for the most part to their chief preoccupation: war (Austin 1986). Recent study of the taxation and coinage practices of the Seleukid kingdom, the largest by far of the successor states, has shown that almost all of taxes collected and money coined can be accounted for by reference to military costs (Aperghis 2001; cf. Papagopoulou 2000, 2001 on Antigonos Gonatas with analogous conclusions). The coinages of Mithradates VI can be very tightly correlated to the rhythms of his military activity against the Romans (de Callataÿ 2000: 355–9). The costs of war were considerable. Hellenistic armies were largely mercenary. Pay rates attested in inscriptions suggest that mercenaries might be paid roughly 6–8 obols/day (Attic standard; see still the useful discussion in Griffith 1935: 294–307). The costs associated with a major conflict, like the battle of Raphia in 217 when 75,000 Ptolemaic troops faced 68,000 Seleukid (according to Polyb. 5.79), were an exceptional strain, but the troops in garrisons on Thera or in Delphi needed their pay too; troops surrendering at Theangela in Karia insisted on their four months' back pay (L. Robert 1936: 69–86 no. 52). Aside from soldiers' salaries, Hellenistic kings built and maintained fleets; secured corps of elephants and their handlers; supported weapons workshops; built, repaired and staffed fortifications; and founded cities peopled with ex-soldiers intended to provide local security and forces that could be called upon in case of need (Migeotte 2000; Baker 2000; Aperghis 2001).

It is no wonder, with the fiscal demands on their treasuries, that kings imposed broad tax burdens on their subjects. In an inscription from Herakleia in Karia, the king exempts citizens from taxes on bringing things in and out, on produce of the land, on pasturage dues for bees and herds (time and number of animals to be determined), taxes on grain imported into the city and taxes on goods brought into the city from royal land, whether for personal use or resale (Wörrle 1988; Ma 1999: 340–5 no. 31). This considerable range of taxes over which royal authority extended finds its echo in a phrase that recurs in many honorary decrees from *poleis* under royal authority. When recipients were awarded tax exemption, *ateleia*, the *polis* was often careful to add, 'from taxes over which the *polis* has authority' (*I.Iasos* 37.8–9 and many other texts; Gauthier 1991).

Money

The reasons for the origin of coined money (invented in Asia Minor in the Archaic period) and its functions throughout antiquity have long been debated (the current discussion starts from Howgego 1990; see now de Callataÿ 2000: 341–4; for the technology, Rihll 2001). A recent view argues that states started to coin because they saw ways to profit from coining; soon thereafter came the exploitation of coins – with their distinctive emblems denoting the issuing authority, the 'type' – for purposes of self-assertion and propaganda (Le Rider 2001; *contra* T. Martin 1985). From an economic point of view, two great interests of the state (whether Hellenistic kingdom or *polis*) in coins lay in their use for payment, particularly of expenses associated with war and bureaucracy, and income, in taxes and other receipts (booty, indemnities, etc.). The second great question for the historian is the degree to which coins monetarized the economy, that is to say, the degree to which exchanges came to be conducted exclusively, or almost exclusively, in coined money. Related to this question is whether coining entities – the *poleis* or the Hellenistic kingdoms – recognized this role for the coins they struck and coined explicitly to facilitate exchange.

In the Classical period, Athenian coins with the owl as the obverse type set the standard for coins throughout the Aegean world; they were, in Plato's phrase, the 'common Greek coinage' (*Laws* 742a). Struck from highly pure silver, they adhered to a weight standard of 4.2–4.3 g. for a drachma, or 16.8–17.3 for a tetradrachma. Other weight standards and other coinages of course existed, but when Alexander the Great decided to issue coinage, he chose the Attic standard. These coins – Alexander struck issues in gold as well – and similar ones issued by his successors (the Lysimachoi, for example), became extraordinarily popular. Many entities issued copies and they were often explicitly demanded for payment (M. Price 1989; Knoepfler 1997). These coinages circulated widely alongside the issues of smaller states, which were often more confined in their circulation, and seem to have served the bulk of the need of the economy for money for about a century (see de Callataÿ in de Callataÿ, Depeyrot and Villaronga 1993: 13–46). In the second century – the date remains unclear – the Athenians began to strike a new coinage, the so-called New Style Coinage (M. Thompson 1961). By 145 the Athenians were striking this coinage annually, and it was accepted widely, like Athens' coinages of earlier times. At the same time, many *poleis* continued to strike their own coins, in silver or bronze or both, and some larger entities, notably the Ptolemaic and the Pergamene kingdoms, rejected the standard Attic coinage and created their own 'closed' economic zones based on a coinage at a reduced weight standard (Kleiner and Noe 1977; Mørkholm 1982; but see on 'closed economy' the caveat of Davies 1984: 279).

6 How Monetarized Was the Economy?

For certain large-scale payments, there is no doubt that the economy was entirely monetarized in, or by, the Hellenistic period. Payments to troops were made exclusively or essentially in coined money. As early as 347 at Delphi a general of Phokis struck coins from precious metal dedications at the sanctuary of Apollo to pay his troops, who clearly wanted coined money, not even bullion (Diod. 16.56.5–8). The treaty between Rhodes and Hierapytna on Crete regulating the supplying of soldiers stipulates payment of salary in money (*IC* 3.3.3A26–9). War indemnities were often paid in coin as well. It has recently been suggested that the New Style Athenian coinage may have been introduced as currency for the payment of the Aitolian indemnity to Rome after the end of their war in 189; at least, the terms of the treaty preserved in Polybios state explicitly that the Aitolians are to pay in 'coinage not worse than Attic' (21.32.8, cf. 21.43.19–22 for the indemnity imposed on Antiochos III in 188; Dreyer 2000). Be that as it may, a series of countermarks – stamps added to existing coins by some third party – on coins issued in various cities of Pamphylia and eastern Lykia in the 180s have been argued to represent the payment of a war indemnity by Antiochos III to Eumenes II, king of Pergamon, imposed by the treaty of 188 that ended the war between Antiochos and Rome and its allies, including Eumenes (Bauslaugh 1990). Sulla ordered Lucullus to collect the 20,000 talent indemnity imposed on the cities of Asia Minor – and to coin it (Plut. *Luc.* 4.1).

Private transactions frequently called for coined money as well. We have seen many examples in the course of this chapter. A series of inscriptions from Amorgos recording loans by private persons to the Amorgian *poleis* reveals something of the expectations of the nature of the coins that private persons might want: a clause in one contract stipulates repayment in 'Attic or Alexandreian coinage which the city uses besides the Attic, of full weight, legal, not subject to seizure, unencumbered, free of all taxes' (Migeotte 1984: 168–77 no. 49.20–1; Picard 1996). The reference to 'Attic' and 'Alexandreian' money (the latter coinage on the Attic standard issued by Alexander himself or, more commonly, by his successors or other authorities in his name and sometimes bearing his image) reflects the emergence of Attic-standard coinage as the 'common currency' of the Hellenistic world often preferred for payments to foreigners. But *poleis* continued to strike their own coins for local use, often of different or lighter weight standards. Such coins may have dominated local exchange for locally produced and sold goods and services (Marcellesi 2000 with Picard 1996).

The role of money in small-scale exchanges is illustrated by coinage in 'bronze' (actually copper alloys). First struck in the late fifth and early fourth century, bronze coinage became widespread in the Hellenistic period (Picard 1998: 9); at Athens, for example, an entire mint building was devoted to the production of bronze coins (Camp and Kroll 2001). There is plenty of evidence for cash payments in small sums. On Delos the sanctuary sold eggs laid by the sacred geese for as little as 3 obols (we are not told how many eggs this sum bought) or two geese for 4.5 obols (*IG* 11.2.287A17). A *phiale* apparently used for small cash offerings brought in amounts as small as a quarter of an obol (*IG* 11.2.287A17–25). Some of these payments may have been made in small silver, which was no doubt more common than finds suggest (Behrend 1984). But at Thasos, we know of payments made in small change in bronze (Picard 1994). In the fourth century, we are told, Timotheos struck bronze to replace silver so that he could pay troops, but he guaranteed this coinage for the suspicious merchants (*emporoi* and *agoraioi*) with silver ([Arist.] *Oec.* 1351a1). The Sestos decree of a little before 120 BC makes plain this city's motivations for coining in bronze: 'so that the city's coin type should be used as a current type and the people (*demos*) should receive the profit resulting from this source of revenue' (*I.Sestos* 1; *OGIS* 339.44–5, trans. Austin 215; Le Rider 2001: 242–7).

But it would be a mistake to suppose that all exchange was conducted exclusively in coins. Barter and other non-monetarized exchanges persisted (Le Rider 1993–94: 815–19), and many people must have exchanged with their neighbours on such bases, like the farmer in Alkiphron who pleads for a loan of grain. We cannot quantify these sectors of economic activity. We can only say that the activity most visible to us – large-scale public and private exchanges, trade over long distances, and the like – seems pretty thoroughly monetarized, and that the spread of bronze coinage from the fourth century clearly enabled the monetarization of all kinds of small-scale exchanges which would have been harder to conduct before. The popularity of bronze issues and the measures *poleis* took to protect confidence in them makes it clear that ordinary people enjoyed the convenience of carrying out even the smallest market exchanges with money (on the Archaic and Classical periods, cf. Kim 2001).

7   Did States Have 'Economic Policies'?

A famous inscription from Teos in Ionia records the terms under which King Antigonos Monophthalmos sought to unite Teos and its neighbour Lebedos into a single entity. In the negotiating back and forth between the king and his subjects, the Lebedeans asked for the right to import grain. Antigonos expressed his reluctance:

> Previously we were unwilling that any city should undertake the importation of corn or maintain a (subsidised) grain supply, for we were not willing to have the cities spend for this purpose large sums of money unnecessarily; we did not wish even now to give this permission, for the crown land is near and if a need of grain arose, we think there could easily be brought from there whatever one wishes. (*RC* 3–4, trans. Welles; Austin 40)

Antigonos claims that his sole interest here is to avoid unnecessary expense and to enable the cities to 'become free of debt', for, he says, 'there is no private profit for us in the business'. That Greek cities under the Seleukid kings had to obtain permission to import grain, however, is well attested in many documents. The practice has recently been explained as a continuity from the policies of the Achaimenid kings who ruled Asia Minor before Alexander. The matter in fact is treated in the *Oeconomica* attributed to Aristotle (2.1.3 with Briant 1994b). There, the kings clearly are eager to be able to sell off excess goods such as grain which have been produced on their behalf but which are surplus to the needs of army and court. This clarifies the source of the grain and other goods, particularly agricultural goods but also wood products originating from the kings' great forest holdings (Gauthier 1989: 22–33), that the kings had at their disposal to give to places like Iasos and Rhodes. Otherwise, conversion into money provided all the more cash needed to hire mercenaries and keep up a court. In this respect the Seleukids clearly did have a kind of economic policy, and Antigonos' avowal of complete disinterest may be taken with a certain irony. But we must remember at the same time that the fundamental policy interest of the great Hellenistic kings was to stoke their armies. The need to provide booty for redistribution to maintain loyalty led to a self-reinforcing cycle of warfare that helps to explain many of the large-scale features of the period (Billows 1995; but see Billows 1990: 286–91 for a different reading of Antigonos' economic policy).

Antigonos' reluctance to let go of a mechanism for generating cash takes on a new meaning in this context.

The Ptolemies of Egypt provide a rather different example. As is well known, elephants became an important feature of warfare in the Hellenistic period. To compete with their Seleukid rivals, the Ptolemies developed an infrastructure to capture elephants in Africa for shipment back to the Nile valley. Early on this activity was routed through the north end of the Red Sea and a canal of Achaimenid date re-opened by the kings. But the northern Red Sea was difficult to navigate, and by the middle of the third century Ptolemy II had established a network of settlements on the mid- and southern Red Sea shore. These connected to the Nile via desert caravan routes leading from Berenike and Myos Hormos (Alcock et al., this volume). As early as 255 a papyrus mentions an official charged with 'the conveyance of elephants into the Thebaid' (Mitteis and Wilcken 1912 1(2).513–15 col. II.78–80). In the later Ptolemaic period and especially under Roman rule, trade in luxury goods – spices, frankincense, ivory, tortoise shells, pearls, etc. – flourished in this region, funnelled into Alexandria for redistribution to the Mediterranean world. Some of the trade goods are mentioned in a famous inscription of 'Soterichos…who has been dispatched by Paos, relative [of the king: a title] and general of the Thebaid, for the collection of precious stones and in charge of the ships and to provide security for those who convey from the harbour at Koptos cargoes of frankincense and other foreign goods' (Bernand 1977: 253–61 no. 86). The linkage between the elephant trade of the third century and this text (along with other evidence) has led to the view that the Ptolemies pursued an articulated mercantile policy on the Red Sea and Indian Ocean. The ports on the Red Sea and the caravan routes to the Nile offered an entrée to a wider region. The result, according to some, followed from a plan of the Ptolemies to create a mercantile policy based on the trade in luxuries and a royal monopoly on their sale. But, as has recently been stressed, this picture leaves out the fundamental royal interest in the third century (elephant hunting), the discontinuities in the political life of the kingdom (especially the great Thebaid revolt; Thompson, this volume, section 5), and, perhaps most important, the role of indigenous Red Sea and Indian Ocean merchants in running the trade (de Romanis 1996: 121–46). Here, rather than a royal mercantile policy, it is better to see the trade in luxury items as an adventitious growth on an infrastructure put in place for the elephant trade.

So much for the 'big kingdoms'. What about ordinary *poleis*? A congeries of evidence can be cited to suggest a kind of mercantile policy for the island *polis* of Thasos. Thasos was famous in antiquity for the production of wine. A series of laws, whose interpretation is not always easy, regulated the wine trade (Salviat 1986). Wine was exported in transport amphorae which have been recovered in enormous quantities all over the eastern Mediterranean, but with particular concentration in the Black Sea region (Garlan 1999). Exploration of the Thasian countryside has revealed many farms, often with distinctive towers attached to the farm complex (Osborne 1986) and *ateliers* where the amphorae were made (Garlan 1999: 2–4). Put together, this evidence suggests that the Thasians concentrated on the production of wine for export to the non-Greek kingdoms of the Black Sea, and that the Thasian state sought to regulate and promote this trade (Picard 1994). This is no surprise as the people who owned the wine orchards were certainly also the wealthy elite who controlled political life on Thasos. For example, there is good evidence to suppose that the family that used the names Pylades and Demes, who produced amphorae, included members who served as priest of Demeter Eleusinia and as *theoros*, a high Thasian official (Garlan 1999: 46–7). But in all this there is one curious feature. After about 310 and until the 180s the Thasians stopped coining in silver. All their issues in those decades were bronzes intended for local, internal use. How did they manage foreign trade and accumulation of wealth without silver coinage? Like many others in the Hellenistic world, they relied on the abundant 'common Greek coinage' (Plato *Laws* 742a) issued as Alexanders, Lysimachoi and a few other types on the Attic weight standard (M. Price 1989; Mørkholm 1991; Marcellesi 2000).

I leave aside other, well-known examples of possible policies, such as that of Kleomenes of Naukratis in Egypt (Le Rider 1997).

8 The Impact of Rome

From about 200, the Romans were a constant presence in the Hellenistic world. Roman armies and navies contested control of small *poleis* and great territorial kingdoms; they defeated the Aitolians, the Antigonids and the Seleukids; they inherited the kingdom of the Ptolemies; they created new structures for imperial control, and ultimately brought the entire Hellenistic world more or less up to the Euphrates under their authority (chapters 4–6 above). With the military came traders, tax collectors, loan sharks, settlers (military colonists at Corinth), students (Cicero's son at Athens), and a host of others, whether Romans or Italians. Eventually, after a horrible period of civil wars that devastated much of the Greek world, came peace – marked symbolically and in fact by, among other things, the emperor Augustus' leisurely tour of the East and the commissions of his trusted subordinate Agrippa to try to clean things up.

This subject is far too big to cover here in any kind of systematic or complete way; that would take a book. Rather, we shall look at a few topics with the question in mind, to what degree did the coming of Rome affect the structures and character of the Hellenistic economy?

Keith Hopkins has offered a model for describing one way in which Roman intervention may have affected the Hellenistic east. Hopkins argued that the wealth brought into the Italian peninsula by successful military operations in the Greek east was reinvested largely in land in Italy. Since the investors were large landowners, not proprietary farmers, they worked the land with slave labour. A major source of slaves was war captives. Positive feedback loops generated increased pressure for warfare as the source of new wealth and new slaves, and the reinvestment of this wealth transformed the economic and social landscape of Italy, forming an important component of the Social War and the collapse of the Roman Republic in the first century (Hopkins 1978: 1–98). Whatever subsequent research has made of this view, it deserves consideration if only as an attempt to model and explain economic change. Hopkins' interests focused largely on the impact in Italy, but it is not hard to see how constant Roman military exercises in the Greek east might have transformed the economy.

Indeed, texts of the first century especially are full of evidence of the dislocations, disruptions and impoverishment that warfare, particularly the civil wars, but also wars of 'resistance' to Roman rule, had on the Greek world. An inscription from Mylasa in Karia recounts the suffering of that city attacked in 40 BC by Labienus, a Roman rebel: the city was captured, many citizens were taken prisoner and others had been killed, fires burnt in the city, and 'the enemies' brutality did not keep away from the holiest temples or sanctuaries' (*I.Mylasa* 602; Canali De Rossi 2000: 172–8). Examples could easily be multiplied, and lead to the inference that the Greek east suffered terribly in the last century, not least from having typically picked, or been forced to pick, the wrong side in conflicts from the First Mithradatic War to the war between Octavian and Mark Antony and Kleopatra.

Another realm in which the impact of Roman rule may appear is civic finances. The Romans imposed war indemnities and other payments on the Greeks. These were collected by Roman tax farmers, who often profited from their contracts by lending money at high interest rates to impecunious cities. Public inscriptions attest to the kindness of some of these figures. In the first century L. Aufidius Bassus wrote off part of a large civic debt owed by the island of Tenos to his father and then to him and reduced interest on others debts (*IG* 12.5.860); the brothers Cloatii were honored in 71 for lending large sums to the city of Gytheion (*SIG*[3] 748). Literary texts are blunter. Most famous is the incident in which Cicero became involved with Roman financiers trying to collect a huge debt from Salamis on Cyprus (Cic. *Att.* 5.21.10–13 = Migeotte 1984: no. 75). But examples are widespread. Paintings were removed from Sikyon to Rome to pay off a public debt (Pliny *HN* 35.127 = Migeotte 1984: no. 18). Apollonia tried to avoid paying civic debts with a bribe (Cic. *Pis.* 86 = Migeotte 1984: no. 35). A series of towns in Karia owed Clodius money and failed in their obligations (Cic. *Fam.* 13.56.1–3 = Migeotte 1984: no. 106). The list could easily be expanded.

Clearly Roman entry into the Greek east had important economic effects, including many not treated here; perhaps most notably the massive infusion of Italian and Roman traders, tax farmers and others whose presence helped spark the First Mithradatic War. Surely, however, one large and important consequence of Roman hegemony was an increased linkage of the eastern Mediterranean with the west. The flow of goods and people in both directions, but especially toward Italy, played out in the first few centuries of the common era, when a truly Mediterranean-wide economic sphere can be said to have emerged. But that is another story.

FURTHER READING

This is an exciting time to study the Hellenistic economy. A decade or two ago the student interested in learning more would first have been directed to M. I. Finley's *The Ancient Economy*, the prevailing theoretical study of the economy of the Greco-Roman world, where she would have found disappointingly little about the Hellenistic period (a few words at p. 183; see Davies 2001: 11–14). Then would have come Rostotzveff's massive three volumes of text, notes, and plates – dense, full of marvellous detail, gravid with sources. Beyond these two classics lay an intimidating morass of specialized technical studies. Today research in the topic has enjoyed a wonderful reinvigoration, not least thanks first to J. K. Davies, who has worked now for two decades to outline ideas toward new approaches (starting in Davies 1984); in particular, he has offered ways of making and testing new models (Davies 1998; forthcoming). Work which owes its impetus in one way or another to Davies's efforts can now be accessed easily through the essays in Archibald et al 2001. Nor can one ignore Hopkins 1978, whose model of the impact of slavery in the economy of Italy in the third through first centuries retains extraordinary interest for economic historians despite criticism. Another recent collection of stimulating essays appears in Cartledge et al 2001. On the finances of Greek *poleis* and the trade in grain, Léopold Migeotte's work continues to deepen our understanding; he has now summarized his views in an elegant little book worth a translation into English (2002). Alain Bresson's challenge to the standard view of the *polis* as unconcerned with commerce is now required reading, with the articles of his colleague Raymond Descat. The contribution of archaeology to economic history has been changed forever by the emergence of the survey, Alcock et al, this volume. Despite new publications, there is still no better place to begin to see how survey archaeology can be interpreted than Alcock 1993, although her interests range far beyond the economy *per se*. The discoveries of the archaeologists have yet to be fully integrated into our picture of the economy, but a sense of what such work might look like can be found, in part, in Rousset 1999. And as comprehensive studies of amphora like Garlan's magnificent corpus-in-progress for Thasos (1999) appear, we may finally be able to begin to integrate this important but difficult category of evidence into our understanding of the economic (and indeed political and social) life of the Hellenistic world (for an example of what might be done, Finkielsztejn 2001a). The economic life of Babylonia and the east has been largely beyond the scope of this chapter, but is now becoming better known as cuneiform texts are published or reinterpreted: Slotsky 1997; van der Spek 1998, 2000; Vargyas 1997.

CHAPTER TWENTY-ONE

Reading the Landscape: Survey Archaeology and the Hellenistic *Oikoumene*

Susan E. Alcock, Jennifer E. Gates and Jane E. Rempel

A fascinating, if somewhat humbling, exercise is the honest assessment of how far the nature of our sources dictate the questions we ask, and the framework we use, to analyse a historical period. For the Hellenistic age, a heavy reliance on textual evidence, and principally Greek textual evidence at that, long tilted scholarly perspectives on the Hellenistic *oikoumene*, or 'inhabited world'. We once perceived that world as fundamentally transformed by the arrival of Hellenic culture, as deeply divided from whatever had come before, as a newly created and somehow homogeneous entity (Droysen 1887–88; Rostovtzeff 1941: 1040; Tarn and Griffith 1952: 3).

It is not news to announce that such perspectives are, to a great extent, misguided, that (to present-day eyes) they appear the somewhat absurd product of a particular and limited reading of a particular and limited body of evidence (see the criticisms of, among others, Préaux 1978: 5–9; Briant 1982: 7–12; Kuhrt and Sherwin White 1987). Such attitudes have been assailed from many directions: in particular, through a theoretical sea-change in our conception of the relationships possible between Greek and non-Greek peoples, through the addition of native voices in languages other than Greek, and through the more wide-ranging use and sensitive analysis of archaeological data. This chapter speaks to one distinctive and increasingly attractive approach to the Hellenistic world – the contribution of survey (or landscape) archaeology – through the presentation of three diverse regional case studies.

1 Landscape, Survey and the Hellenistic World

Landscape is a difficult concept to define but an extremely useful one to employ. In current archaeological analysis, 'landscape' revolves around human experience, perception and modification of the world. All aspects of human activity – settlement patterns, boundaries, ritual sites, roads, monuments, burial places – together with their intersection with the natural world, are bound up in the concept, which also highlights emotional ties to particular places and the memories invested within them (Bender 1993; Hirsch and O'Hanlon 1995; Basso and Feld 1996; Shipley and Salmon 1996; Ashmore and Knapp 1999). Landscape offers a means by which to assess changing local conditions over time; through it we can observe, for example, the impact of newly constituted political or economic regimes, such as the formation of the Hellenistic kingdoms.

One principal means to assemble archaeological data at the broader scale required by the study of landscape (as opposed to individual site-based analysis) is through the practice of regional survey. Archaeological survey has taken many forms since its introduction to the Mediterranean and Near East in the 1950s and 1960s, but increasingly it involves the intensive examination of the earth's surface, by field teams engaged in counting, collecting and analysing all traces of cultural debris. Today many other disciplines contribute to this type of regional study, such as geologists (to warn about significant geomorphological or riverine changes), botanists (to advise about climatic alterations), anthropologists (to observe how present-day populations interact with their world), or remote sensing experts (for example, to detect ancient patterns of irrigation or road networks in satellite imagery) (for a wide ranging recent review of survey and ancillary techniques, see Barker and Mattingly 1999–2000).

While specific survey methodologies can vary dramatically, regionally-based projects share certain common goals: they aim to gather, in systematic fashion, evidence for human activity in a defined geographical area over long spans of time (Cherry 1995; Francovich and Patterson 2000). Categories of evidence (and the inferences those data make possible) have expanded to include not only the distribution of human settlement, but land use and land tenure patterns, ritual, ceremonial and mortuary landscapes, and networks of communication and exchange. That expansion is visible in this chapter's three case studies. One investigates what a consideration of road networks can reveal; another observes the changing interactions of rural communities and burials; the third notes the respect paid to prehistoric monuments. Survey is also deliberately diachronic in its coverage; for many of the surveys conducted in the modern countries which once comprised the Hellenistic world, the time span of interest stretches from Palaeolithic to Early Modern times. From such a perspective, the Hellenistic period thus appears as only part of a richly detailed, long-term history in a particular region.

We would argue that this landscape approach offers considerable advantages to the study of the Hellenistic world, especially as a corrective to the past biases noted at the outset of this chapter. One benefit, for example, is that it forces us to consider just how far the Hellenistic age was indeed 'newly transformed': just how different was life in that period compared to what came before and what would follow? In what senses was it different, and to what extent could this be attributed to the workings of Hellenic culture – as opposed, for example, to the introduction of new political and exploitative regimes? Moreover, adopting this perspective willy-nilly embraces all dwellers in a particular landscape: rich and poor, urban and rural, Greek and indigenous. Obviously, it is often easier to 'see' some of these people than others through their remaining material traces. Nonetheless, for anyone armed with evidence for settlement or ritual patterning across an entire region, a single-minded search for 'the Greeks' or 'Greek influence' will no longer seem desirable, or even possible.

Finally, numerous locally-based regional studies can test the notion of Hellenistic uniformity, the impression that this entire (very far-flung and diverse) *oikoumene* followed similar developmental trajectories. One previous analysis has already contested that model; through the comparison of fifty different regional survey projects (admittedly of varying quality and intensity), divergent patterns were seen to emerge across the expanse of the Hellenistic world and beyond (Alcock 1994). The remainder of this chapter will develop this theme of local distinctiveness. As the existence of a single, unitary Hellenistic landscape comes to appear increasingly improbable, we can instead acknowledge – and analyse more closely – the possibility of regional differentiation. Shared characteristics across the Hellenistic world may yet emerge: but only as they manifest themselves from the 'ground up', and not be assumed from the 'top down'.

What follows are three short case studies, drawn from different parts of the Hellenistic world: a peninsular kingdom, an economically strategic desert, a politically divided island. These regions differ in environmental and ecological terms; they interacted in various fashions with the major Hellenistic kingdoms; they have been explored to different degrees, with different methodologies. Disparate as they will appear, what has to be remembered is that they represent only a small fraction of the diversity covered by what we bravely summarize as 'the Hellenistic world'.

2   Social Change and Rural Settlement in the Bosporan Kingdom[1]

' . . . here, at the far edge of the ancient world, for the most part in peculiar conditions, Greek traditions existed in very different realms of rural life and practice, demonstrating amazing viability, over a long period of time'. With these words A. A. Maslennikov (1998: 271) concludes his recent volume on the rural territory of the Bosporan kingdom. The author's choice to end on this note is telling: one of the most fundamental, and problematic, aspects of this Black Sea state was its heterogeneous population, including the descendants of Greek colonists, Scythians and various Maeotian groups, as well as the interactions between them. This quasi-Greek kingdom, composed primarily of urban Hellenes and largely rural local populations, experienced none of the political or territorial upsets we associate with the beginning of the Hellenistic period, but at first glance it easily agrees with our ideas about Hellenistic kingdoms. In fact, this 'Hellenistic aspect' was the result of a long process of change that began well before 323 BC; indeed Minns, in his 1913 opus on Scythians and Greeks, considered it to be a forerunner of the other Hellenistic kingdoms (1913: 563).

Located on the north coast of the Black Sea at the mouth of the Sea of Azov (figure 21.1), the Bosporan kingdom, which originated as a loose confederation of Greek colonial *poleis* in the early fifth century BC, was ruled by the Thracian-tinged dynasty of the Spartokids from 438/7 until 108/7 BC (when Mithradates VI took over the kingdom). A key supplier of grain to Greece, and to Athens in particular, the kingdom also prospered from trade with the neighbouring Scythians and Maeotians. The fourth century BC, in particular, was a period of great wealth, and it is during this period that the Bosporan kingdom begins to look particularly 'Hellenistic'. At

---

1   This section of the paper is primarily the work of Jane E. Rempel.

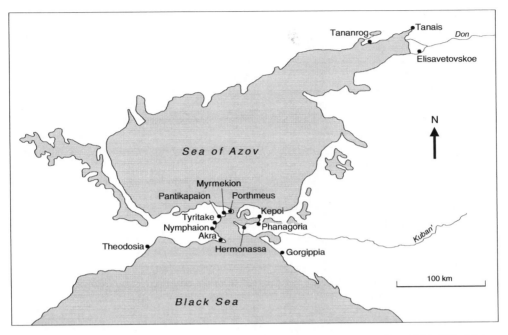

Figure 21.1 Map of the Bosporan kingdom. After Triester and Vinogradov 1993: 522. 20.1

this time, the kingdom expanded to include not only the territory of the Greek colonies, but also that of the neighbouring populations, and the Spartokid rulers began to call themselves 'kings' in addition to the title of 'archon' they had previously employed. By the third century BC, the rulers used king as their sole title, and even began to mint coinage that bore their own portraits, much like other Hellenistic leaders (Hind 1994b: 490, 496–501). Although the settlements of the Bosporan kingdom had probably always had mixed populations (Tsetskhladze 1998: 45), it is in the fourth century that evidence for the incorporation of non-Greek representations of status and power by the Bosporan elite begins to become especially striking. For example, large and lavish burial mounds were erected close to the main cities of the kingdom, clearly recalling the Scythian mounds that already dotted the landscape, but also allying themselves, through their location, with the Bosporan cultural sphere (Rempel forthcoming; throughout this section, the term 'Bosporan' is used not as a geographical descriptor, but in reference to all aspects of the kingdom itself). At the non-elite level, otherwise Greek-seeming burials contained Scythian-style weapons, and local burials incorporated markers of Greek inspiration (Hind 1994b: 506–8). Greek, Scythian, Maeotian: all elements interacted in this environment, in which expressions of identity and representations of power could, and did, transcend strict cultural boundaries. Signals from Greek culture, and from those of the steppe, were read together, and informed each other, in a decidedly Hellenistic, but uniquely 'Bosporan', frame of reference.

This complex cultural mix was echoed in the complex and disjointed landscape of the kingdom. From Theodosia in the west to Gorgippia in the east, the territory was bounded, defined and dissected by water: relatively flat plains were punctuated by a myriad of bays, lakes and inlets, or alternately swept down to dramatic cliffs at the shore, or petered out to marshy land. The disunity of this geography lies in stark contrast to the large vistas it afforded, creating a sense of visual connection and an awareness of the physical evidence of its occupation history. By the fourth century BC, ancient fortification ditches, Scythian burial mounds and long-established trade routes were juxtaposed with Greek-style agricultural settlements and land-divisions, charging the landscape with implications of power and control, and structuring individual experiences within it.

How the territory of the Bosporan kingdom functioned has always been a question of importance for archaeologists working in this region. Beginning with the 1953 publication of Blavatskii's *Agriculture in the Ancient States of the Northern Black Sea Littoral*, the rural territories of the kingdom have received considerable attention, and additional comprehensive studies of settlement patterns, and how they change through time, have been published more recently (Kruglikova 1975; Paromov 1986, 1989, 1990; Abramov and Paromov 1993; Maslennikov 1998; Scholl and Zin'ko 1999). The survey methodology traditionally employed in the investigation of Greek colonies on the north coast of the Black Sea (including the Bosporan kingdom) is very intensive; although systematic fieldwalking is not always employed, the region has been explored for years through the use of a variety of techniques (including general topographic reconnaissance, systematic and non-systematic fieldwalking, aerial photography, and geophysical survey, as well as on-site collection of surface finds) (e.g. Shcheglov 1983: 18–24; Paromov 1986: 71; 1989: 73; 1990: 161–2; Maslennikov 1998: 32). These investigations have been primarily concerned with the ancient Greek and Roman occupation of the territory, and as a result they have focused on specific questions: the physical organization of the Greek *poleis* and the location of their *choras*, and – for the Bosporan kingdom – its economic and administrative organization, and the distribution of settlements throughout the territory under its control.

Although this research has produced a wealth of information and opened up numerous avenues of research, it remains more of a two-dimensional map of the archaeological residue of human activity than a consideration of human interaction in and with the landscape. As Tilley (1994: 9) has warned, when space is viewed as an abstract stage for human activity, it is 'divorced from any consideration of structures of power and domination...divorced from humanity and society'; accordingly, a conception of landscape as a socially dynamic force must be added to more traditional economic and political explanations of change. The rural landscape of the Bosporan kingdom, contested and controlled in various ways, is an ideal forum for investigating the complex social and cultural dynamics of interaction that informed Bosporan society. It is ideal, precisely because this same landscape was an *active participant* in structuring those interactions, a force in informing social behaviour and in contesting and negotiating relations of power and dominance.

During the fourth and continuing into the third century BC, there was a dramatic increase in the number of settlements constructed in the rural territory of the Bosporan kingdom (figure 21.2). Although this territory had been settled to a certain

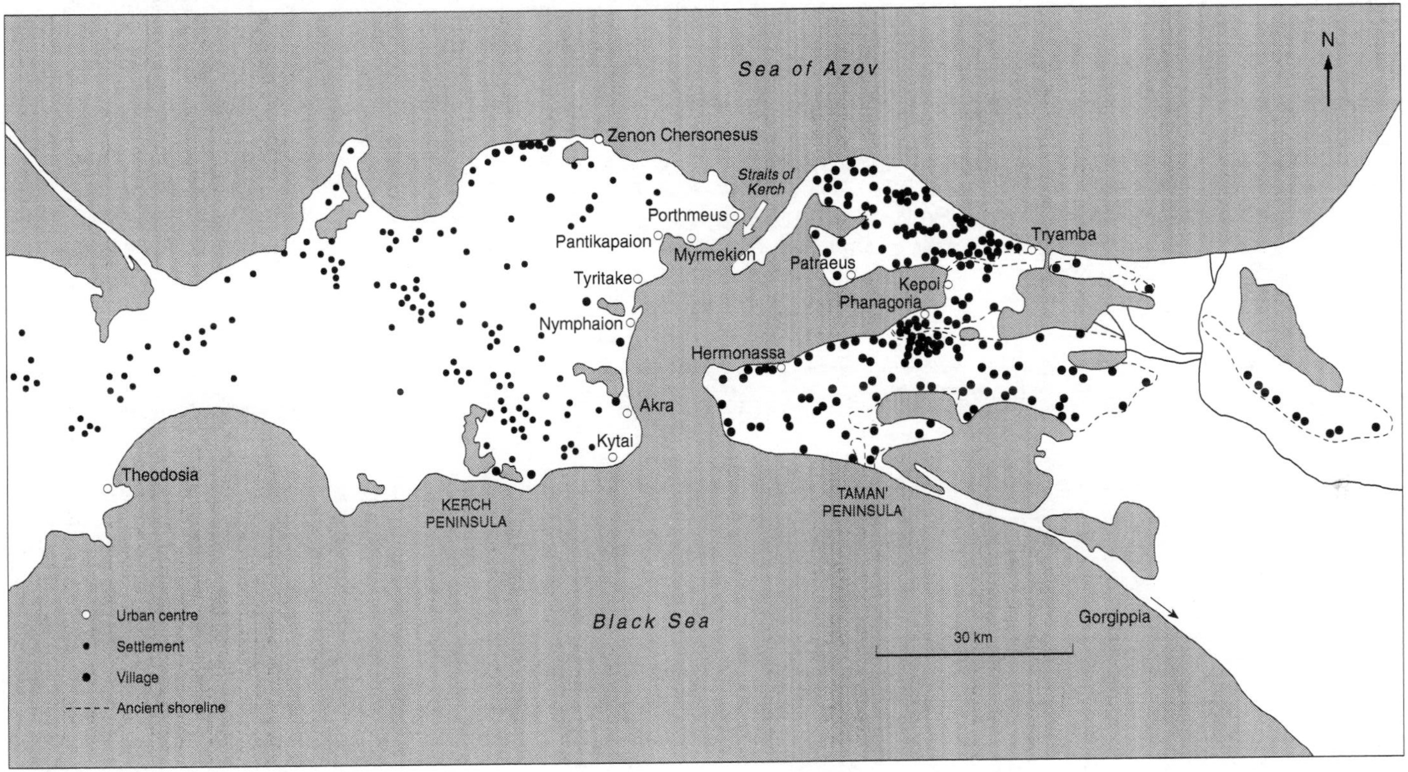

Figure 21.2 Settlement distribution in the Bosporan kingdom, fourth–third centuries BC. After Maslennikov 1998: **43**, 77 (Kerch peninsula); Paromov 1986, 1989 (Taman' peninsula)

extent in the sixth century BC, when the area was first colonized by the Greeks, this new 'flowering' of settlement marks an important change in the landscape of the Bosporan kingdom (Kruglikova 1975: 53–101). Farmsteads, similar to those found in Attica, and small local villages sprang up beside each other; all were caught up in networks of fortifications and roads. Historically, this development coincides with the Bosporan annexation of the neighbouring Sindoi and other Maeotian populations, which first occurred during the reign of Leukon (393/2–354/3 BC); certainly this reconfiguration of power dynamics in the region had a fundamental impact on patterns of settlement and land use. It has also been demonstrated that these settlements were intimately linked with the administrative and economic system of the Bosporan kingdom (Maslennikov 1989). This fourth century 'flowering', however, is also indicative of, and was a participant in, the ever-changing social dynamics of the kingdom, and serves to illuminate the nature of cultural interactions in the region from a new perspective.

Both sides of the strait witnessed an increase in rural settlement, but an increase manifested in different ways (figure 21.2). The eastern Taman peninsula was, during the classical period, a series of islands, separated by bays and branches of the Kuban River delta, and the difficulty of identifying the ancient coastlines with precision has, of course, affected the study of its territory (Paromov 1986: 71). Nonetheless, much investigation has been undertaken since the end of the eighteenth century, and the settlement organization is well understood (despite the unpublished state of much of Paromov's work; see Paromov 1986; 1989; 1990; Abramov and Paromov 1993; cf. Scholl and Zin'ko 1999: 8). From the earliest periods of colonization, rural settlements were constructed throughout the Taman peninsula; in the fourth to third centuries, however, the number of such settlements nearly doubled, and they were united by a more sophisticated network of roads and land plots. It has been postulated that almost all of the available land was under cultivation during this period, and that therefore the local Sindic and Maeotian populations must have been actively involved in this process, even living in the cities and towns along with the Bosporan Greeks (Paromov 1989: 78; 1990: 163).

The coastlines of the western Kerch peninsula have also changed (Maslennikov 1998: 16; Scholl and Zin'ko 1999: 11), but not as drastically as those of the Taman peninsula. For various reasons, exploration of the rural territory of this part of the Bosporan kingdom only began in earnest about 50 years ago, but since then it has been studied in detail. In contrast to the Taman peninsula, here there was relatively little rural settlement in the sixth and fifth centuries BC, and it was only in the second quarter of the fourth century that the occupation of the hinterland steeply increased (figure 21.2). This occupation included Greek-style farmsteads and villas, the introduction of land plots in the *choras* of the *poleis*, as well as the formation of the 'Bosporan *chora*' (settlements outside the colonial *choras*, on 'crown land' as it were). In addition, many small villages were constructed in this period that, judging by their architecture, finds and frequent grouping near burial mounds, were inhabited by a local segment of the population (Kruglikova 1975: 54–8, 75; Maslennikov 1998: 42, 46, 72–89, 292–3).

Of course, the Bosporan landscape is not well represented by the black and white of settlement distribution maps. Fortification systems, trade routes, road networks, burial mounds and land divisions all complicate the archaeological map produced by recent investigations. In addition, subtleties of settlement type and construction, and of topographic location, are constituent parts of any landscape. But for the purposes of this brief case study, the changing settlement patterns of the fourth and third century BC serve as a metonym through which to illustrate the intimate links between the landscape, the people that inhabited it, and the society in which they functioned.

Presumably, an influx of population into the countryside accompanied the foundation of the settlements themselves. This rural territory thus became a more active and crowded stage for interaction, contact and exchange, and the level of interaction increased at the same time as it was being *actively structured* by the physical manifestations of Bosporan control. In this sense, these new rural settlements served to formalize interactions in the landscape within a frame of reference that was explicitly linked with the hegemony of the cosmopolitan Bosporan state, and helped actively to define that state as a distinct and separate entity. Pre-existing settlements, boundaries, roads and burial mounds were also absorbed into this new Bosporan framework, and their original meanings and resonances would have been altered, even subverted, by this new context. For example, the earlier burial mounds, often set on hilltops and along trade routes (Maslennikov 1998: 28; Paromov 1986: 72), and quite possibly speaking of non-Greek control of the landscape, would, in the fourth and third centuries, have been 'read' in conjunction with the proliferation of newly constructed burial mounds commemorating the Bosporan elite. In other words, these former statements of 'steppe' presence and authority were overlaid with 'Bosporan' implications. In a similar way, the isolated hilltop farmsteads constructed in the *polis choras* in the sixth and fifth centuries – potent statements of a Greek colonial presence in the landscape – would have now participated in the larger statement of Bosporan control in the context of other fourth and third century settlements. The rural landscape of the Bosporan kingdom in this period made a palpable statement about Bosporan *exclusion* from the rest of the steppe.

This exclusion, however, should not be interpreted as that of Bosporan Greeks versus the Barbarians of the steppe. Rather it was the consolidation of the Bosporan kingdom, as both a physical and conceptual entity, that defined the exclusion. The relatively fluid engagement with varying cultural traditions that was visible in elite self-presentation during this period meant that not only were cultural identifiers polyvalent, but that this polyvalency was legitimated within Bosporan power structures. The Bosporan kingdom had a culturally heterogeneous population, and while people may have possessed Greek, Sindic, Maeotian or Scythian identities, separately or in combination, they constructed those identities in a dialogue that acknowledged, even incorporated, a mixed bag of cultural traditions. The vocabulary of this uniquely Bosporan dialogue was at least conceptually accessible to everyone who engaged in it, and this accessibility made distinct statements about inclusion. These overtones of inclusion must be read into the rural landscape as well. However much the network of settlements, roads and fortifications represented, in a physical way, the Bosporan state's control of the region, these constructions were also active participants in the dialogue, constantly being interpreted and affecting interpretations in the process. Settlements, roads, burials and boundaries all structured interactions with the landscape, but were also constantly claimed through that interaction. In this way, the obvious cultural specificities of a Greek-style farmstead or a Scythian burial mound were transcended by an overarching awareness of their individual roles and fluid meanings in Bosporan society. Through this awareness, the rural landscape of the Bosporan kingdom also spoke of *inclusion* for the people who inhabited it during this period.

In the Bosporan kingdom, as in most parts of the Hellenistic world, moving beyond the Hellenocentric nature of our sources, discipline, training and proclivities, in order to understand the complexities of multicultural interactions and transformations, is difficult – to say the least. And yet such interactions flesh out our historical and economic narratives by providing a social framework for human action. The relative anonymity of landscape, and its ability to speak of change through time and space, provide both a fresh perspective and a powerful investigative tool.

3   Landscape and Commerce in the Egyptian Eastern Desert[2]

In their recent edited volume, Ashmore and Knapp assert that no landscape study can be objective, with the exception of 'measurable economic impacts on a landscape' (1999: 8). To be sure, Ashmore and Knapp are thinking here of questions such as 'how much agricultural land was irrigated by state-controlled canals?' or 'what is the average size of the production plot for a household practising subsistence farming?' These 'economic' questions are concerned with quantifying and understanding the way in which a landscape was utilized, divided or perhaps marked in the process of eking out a living in a physically brutal world. Yet in what way is this an 'objective' economic landscape? What do numbers and patterns mean without some sort of interpretive framework?

The ancient economy and, by default, the economic aspects of landscape, have been under-studied because of the very nature of historical economic studies. The contrast between the messy cultural aspects of society and the logical, rational features of economy is a powerful paradigm. Although anthropologists have long pointed out that economic actions are culturally determined, economy is still too often kept largely separate from religious, social and political spheres of inquiry (Plattner 1989: 4). The assumption is that although the cultural aspects of ancient economies may have in fact been different from our own, rational choice behaviours are still quantifiable and analysis need not move beyond them. As a result, many researchers interested in historical economic behaviours spend their time looking for scientific ways to discuss the ancient economy. The raw data of economic discussions are produced this way, but the next step is equally important: the economy, like so many other facets of ancient culture, is embedded in society and must be studied as an aspect of social life, rather than as a separate and distinct entity (Gudeman 1986). We must ask ourselves why certain economic choices 'worked' for the persons making them.

How do these questions intersect with the study of ancient landscapes? Other aspects of society – religious, political and social behaviours – are routinely 'read' in the landscape. The manifestation of symbolic and cognitive systems, and their physical correlates, are accepted as part of the constructed and natural landscape. Economic action can also be seen in the landscape as part of, and just as important as,

---

2   This section of the paper is primarily the work of Jennifer E. Gates.

other co-existing modes of behaviour which make up the warp and weft of social fabric in antiquity. The study of a wholly 'economic' landscape, therefore, is as unrealistic as the study of a purely 'sacred' landscape. These aspects exist simultaneously.

The challenge becomes how to observe, in the landscape, the subtle interplay between social and economic aspects of society. One possibility is to turn to new research in material culture and economic studies. Consumption studies, for example, offer a fresh look at the relationship between economic behaviours and abstract cultural discourses (Glennie 1996). The substance of such research is that economic behaviours, specifically the complex act of consuming a commodity, are not subordinate to other social factors, but worked with and through them.

Like the consumption of a single object, the creation of landscape presents features of all these social dynamics; it is shaped by actions and decisions which take into account multiple reasons and complicated priorities. Thus the 'economic' landscape is a landscape shaped by demonstrably 'economic' activities, but with implications for much much more. In the Hellenistic period, this is a particularly important point. The Hellenistic economy is frequently described as if it were a single, unified system with uniform practices and goals spread out across the whole of a Hellenized eastern Mediterranean. Yet, as we have already noted, the sheer diversity of the physical world covered under the umbrella of 'the Hellenistic' demands that we look more critically at regional economic practices.

As an example, we can turn to the Ptolemaic period trade system that connected Berenike and the Nile cities of Edfu and Koptos (figure 21.3). This system was but a single vein in the larger organism of the Ptolemaic economy, yet it provides us with an opportunity to examine one particular 'space' where economy and culture met. As is well known, the geography of Egypt is extremely diverse. From the brilliant green of the Nile Valley to the vast expanse of the Western Desert and the rugged mountains of the Eastern Desert, its topographical features are as varied as the experiences they suggest. It is not surprising that the sacred world of Egypt was closely identified with the landscape and certain physical aspects of the land's form embodied ideas that were at the centre of Egyptian religious thought (Richards 1999: 83–100).

The 'sacred', however, is but a single layer of a more complex landscape (Alcock 1993: 6–7). Many concepts of place – civic, political and economic – are at work in the geography of Egypt. At no time is this more true than in the later periods of Egyptian history when foreign regimes dominated the country and the landscape was affected by large, regional powers: first the Hellenizing culture of the Ptolemies, and later, the Mediterranean empire of Rome. Landscape, as an analytical tool, highlights the ways in which these elements interact and how the experience of the physical world, and of geography itself, were part of Egypt's larger cultural environment.

The Eastern Desert is a particularly fascinating example of just such a lived and dynamic archaeological landscape. East of the Nile, between that river valley and the Red Sea, it is bordered to the North by the Delta and Sinai, and to the south by the deserts of Nubia in modern Sudan. This is an arid, desert region, very mountainous and dry (figure 21.4). The mountain ranges are traversed by sandy wadis (dry stream beds), which direct the occasional seasonal flash flood. The wadis provided (and still provide) a natural means of navigating through the mountains; ancient roads often, if not always, used them as tracks. These ancient roads are an important source of

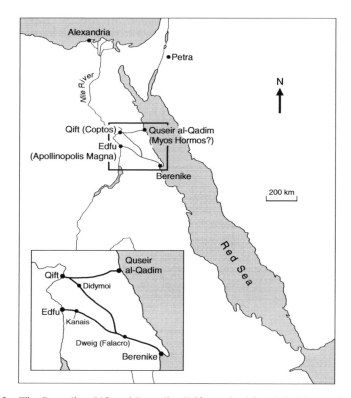

Figure 21.3   The Berenike–Qift and Berenike–Edfu roads. After Gabolde and Galliano 2000

information for the kinds of activity taking place in the region, and for relationships between its population and the rugged world in which they lived.

The unique topography of the Eastern Desert makes field walking or other standard methods of archaeological survey quite difficult! Rather than imposing any very regular system of exploration upon the landscape, reconnaissance strategies must be modified to accommodate the rocky and mountainous terrain. The wadis themselves are navigable, but moving through the region is more complicated than it might first appear. The sand is loose and vehicles often become stuck, so light transport, driven by guides who are experienced 'sand drivers', is a necessity (figure 21.4). Survey usually takes place in the wadis, where ancient remains and ceramic scatters stand out obviously on the surface of the sand. The remarkable preservation of the archaeological remains in this dry region also means that standing architecture is often visible, allowing sites to be located on that basis as well.

Once a site is located, a GPS (ground positioning system) reading is normally taken, any standing architectural features are recorded and a pottery sample drawn and analysed. This information is used to create maps of artefact and site distributions, which in turn help to identify the course of the ancient roadways. In some cases, built-up areas and markers, as well as the occasional inscription, can be observed along the line of the ancient route.

Figure 21.4   Survey in progress at Samut. Note the vehicles and the Ptolemaic and Roman period fort. Courtesy of Brandon Foster

In short, the Eastern Desert roads were part of a system that moved goods from sub-Saharan Africa and the Red Sea to the Nile, on which they were transported to Alexandria, to be consumed there or in more distant parts of the Mediterranean (figure 21.3). Gold, exotic animals, spices, beads, slaves and other commodities were exchanged along these routes by merchants and traders. One of the primary Ptolemaic port cities in the Eastern Desert region was Berenike on the Red Sea. Around 275 BC, Ptolemy II Philadelphos founded this city, together with others along that coastline, to facilitate trade with groups in the south and with Red Sea merchants. The major routes through the desert connected Berenike to trans-shipment centres on the Nile. These river cities in turn acted as distribution centres that oversaw the shipping of goods up the Nile towards the Mediterranean and the major cities in the Delta. The two important Nile cities were Apollinopolis Magna (modern Edfu) to the south and Koptos (modern Qift) to the north (figure 21.3; on this network, see Maxfield 2001; Zitterkopf and Sidebotham 1989: 155–89; 1991: 571–622; Sidebotham et al. 1995; 1996; 1998; 1999; 2000; Sidebotham 1996: 181–92; Sidebotham and Zitterkopf 1997: 221–37; Maxfield 2001).

What can these roads tell us about the cultural and economic situation of Hellenistic Egypt? They hint at a complex and significant set of issues. For example, cultural identity was very much a debated topic in Ptolemaic and Roman Egypt. The language you spoke, your name, your occupation, the objects with which you surrounded yourself: all were immensely important in articulating a kind of fluid personal identity

Figure 21.5 View of ruins at Umm Garahish on the Berenike–Edfu road. Courtesy of
Brandon Foster

which came into play as part of daily life (Bowman 1986). Trade, of course, introduced new elements into this mix. New objects, representative of foreign places and
exotic experiences, broadened the immediate material surroundings of the merchants, traders, townsfolk and transporters who moved these goods through the
port cities and along the Eastern Desert roads.

Archaeological reconnaissance has made clear that these exotic commodities
(which are sometimes found at the port city of Berenike) simply do not appear
at the desert sites along the roads. Yet it is certain that such goods passed slowly
along the desert routes before their arrival in Alexandria and in other Mediterranean
cities where they were destined for the homes of the wealthy or the storehouses of the
Ptolemaic monarchs (Bagnall et al. 2000). How would this task of transit, and the
objects at its centre, have been 'understood' by the individuals who moved them
through the desert? And how was it part of a conception of their own social, cultural
and economic place – as the movers and not the takers – in the emergent new, multi-
ethnic order of Ptolemaic Egypt?

The relationship between the landscape and the archaeological remains of the road
networks may suggest one way in which this problem was negotiated. Since we lack
any evidence that these desirable elite imports were ever diverted to the desert way-
stations along the roads (figure 21.5), the participation of Egyptian traders cannot be
explained by simply assuming that they had hoped to acquire these goods and yet

were unable to do so. If they had such hopes, some hint of emulation of what they saw passing by, or some trace of their use of such goods, would surely appear in the archaeological record. Their attitudes to these objects were likely much more complex, as was their conception of their own social and cultural situation. The non-elite Egyptian groups involved in this trade were not just moving materials for a 'foreign' elite; they were interacting with the desert in a way that was essential to their understanding of their own role and identity in Ptolemaic society.

The degree of autonomy exercised by the traders and desert dwellers – the choice of station and fort placement, the routes chosen through the desert – all these aspects of the network were, in a sense, statements of their relationship with the landscape and their assertion of the literal 'way' that this trade should take place. The harsh desert that they knew and navigated was a zone that *demanded* familiarity. Water and resources, even in seasons of more abundance, would not have been common. The ability to move through, and survive in, the convoluted wadis would itself have been a precious commodity.

Thus, their familiarity with, and understanding of, the landscape was part of the cultural capital which these individuals brought to the Eastern Desert trade. Control of the landscape may have been an assertion of their own authority in the face of, and – ironically – in the service of, a Hellenizing upper class that desired the commodities they carried. In a sense, the landscape of the Eastern desert and its particular characteristics became a source of power; the archaeological remains stand as testimony to the close relationship between the Ptolemaic traders and the landscape they travelled. Although the activities they pursued on these roads were in one sense primarily 'economic', an intrinsic part of those actions was also eminently 'cultural'. Issues of power, identity and knowledge of a distinctly Egyptian landscape may have been 'cultural commodities' that were just as important to the Eastern Desert trade as any measurable 'economic impact' on the Hellenistic landscape.

4   The Divided Landscape of Crete[3]

'A very uncomfortable place': such was the dry verdict passed on Hellenistic Crete by a twentieth-century student of the island (Bosanquet 1939–40: 72), and the reasons for discomfort are not far to seek. During the Hellenistic period, the island remained divided among numerous independent cities; although Hellenistic monarchs periodically sought alliances with one or more of these *poleis*, royal policy encouraged internal insular dissent (Davies 1984: 309). And dissent there was, for probably the most salient feature of Hellenistic Crete (especially in the third and second centuries BC) was ongoing, often violent inter-city conflict and competition. Frequently this took the form of one city expanding at the expense of other, usually smaller polities. Successful communities included Gortyn, Hierapytna, Kydonia, Lyttos and Knossos; the vanquished included Tylissos (by Knossos), Phaistos (by Gortyn), Rhaukos (by Gortyn and Knossos), and Praisos and Istron (by Hierapytna) (figure 21.6). The political organization of the island was thus radically altered, with a significant reduction in the number of independent civic units. Some of these communities

---

3   This section of the paper is primarily the work of Susan E. Alcock.

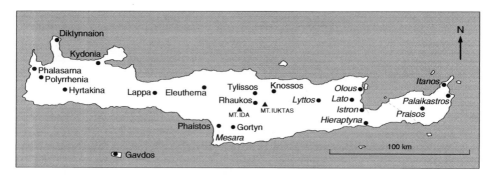

Figure 21.6   Map of Crete, with principal communities mentioned in the text. After Sanders 1982

may have survived their loss of independence, but others were clearly terminated (Sanders 1982: 11–12).

Explaining this endemic strife has engaged commentators since Polybios in the second century BC – although to Polybios, such Cretan viciousness was no more than he expected (see, for example, Polyb. 24.2.3). Scholars today instead point to the trouble-making of external powers, and also propose more internal factors, such as a likely rise in population and increasing inequality in land holding patterns (Chaniotis 1995). Whatever the causes behind the internecine friction, Crete emerges as a restless, 'uncomfortable' part of the Hellenistic world.

How far can this restlessness be perceived in the island's landscape? And, more important perhaps, what can that landscape add to our understanding of the island at this difficult time? The ability even to ask, let alone answer, such questions for historic Crete is quite new. From the early work of Arthur Evans around the turn of the twentieth century, archaeological work on Crete focused almost exclusively on the prehistoric period, the epoch of the Minoan palaces (S. Morris 1992: 173; MacGillivray 2000). Today, however, a growing interest is manifest in 'post-Minoan' Crete, and that includes the work of numerous regional surveys. In one recent count, some twenty projects, from all parts of Crete, could be named, although some remain at an early stage of publication (Moody et al. 1998: 88). Two parts of the island – east Crete and the Mesara plain – are, however, sufficiently well-explored to build up a picture of Hellenistic developments in the countryside. These are also areas especially affected by the expansionist activities of, respectively, Hierapytna and Gortyn.

In the east, we can concentrate on ancient Praisos, the ancestral home of the Eteocretans (or 'true' Cretans, reputedly the autochthonous inhabitants of the island) until its destruction by Hierapytna around 145 BC. Archaeological prospection at this site extended over both the urban centre and its immediate rural hinterland. Results of this work both reveal a thriving city in Classical and earlier Hellenistic times and testify to its violent mid-second century BC end. Surface survey here traces a sharp disruption in local patterns of life, disruptions paralleled in other parts of east Crete thanks to the interventions of Hierapytna (for Praisos, Whitley et al. 1995; Whitley 1998; other projects: Hayden et al. 1992; Haggis 1996). Another regional survey, conducted in the high tablelands south-west of Praisos, may possibly suggest what happened to at least some of that community's inhabitants. The Ziros Project noted its first signs of permanent settlement in the Hellenistic period, a development possibly reflecting the displacement and resettlement of the Praisos population (Branigan 1998: 90).

The very real, and deep-running, impact of civic dissension can also be traced in the fertile Mesara plain, in the south-central part of the island, and to the rise of Gortyn (later the Roman capital of the province of Crete and Cyrenaica). In the later Hellenistic period, Gortyn annexed the territories of several cities, of which Phaistos, situated on the site of a Minoan palace, is most famous. Survey work, both extensive and intensive, has emphasized marked rural change in the Mesara and beyond in response to that development (Sanders 1976: 136–7; Watrous et al. 1993: 232–3; Alcock 1994: 180). For example, settlement expanded dramatically in the vicinity of one of Gortyn's ports (Matala), while in a remote valley to the south of the Mesara, habitation seemed to 'drift' north, towards Gortyn and its surrounding plain (Blackman and Branigan 1977: 75; Hope Simpson et al. 1995: 397–9). All in all, regional survey effectively demonstrates that Hellenistic warfare, and the rewriting of the island's political geography, resulted in significant – if variable – transformations in the pattern of people's lives.

The study of landscape, as the preceding two case studies have made clear, can reach beyond questions of settlement or economics; it can say much about human response to changed conditions of life. Looking at other elements in the Cretan landscape offers one opportunity to gauge how people reacted to these disruptions, or coped with anxiety about their uncertain situation. One very clear reaction, for example, is an investment in the past, in monuments and places perceived to be ancient.

This phenomenon takes many forms. One manifestation is the appearance of numerous small rural cults in Hellenistic times, many of which were located in recognizably 'old' settings (Sanders 1982: 39). The Mesara plain offers several good examples, particularly the area around Phaistos. Close to that community lay the famous Minoan villa site of Ayia Triada. Excavation here recovered not only important prehistoric occupation, but signs of later cultic use (votives, fine pottery), dating to the Iron Age and also to the Hellenistic period (D'Agata 1998). Nestled close to a prehistoric tholos tomb in the Mesara – Kamilari Tomb I – lay a small shrine to Demeter, of late Classical and Hellenistic date. Excavation and survey alike reveal this juxtaposition of activity; the later finds included terracotta plaques, female figurines and miniature horns of consecration (Alcock 1991: 459, n. 53; Cucuzza 1997: 72–4). An intensive survey of the western Mesara plain adds additional cases; for example the discovery of Hellenistic pottery in close proximity to Late Minoan tombs. Summing up the situation, that project's directors came to the conclusion: 'Minoan sites in the Mesara became the focus of cult during the Hellenistic period' (Watrous et al. 1993: 231–2, quote at 231).

The well-explored Mesara plain may offer the most instances of this 'return to old places', but they are to be found scattered elsewhere across the island. A Hellenistic shrine was placed atop a Minoan country house at Pyrgos, on the south coast of the island not far from Hierapytna (figure 21.7; Cadogan 1981: 169–71); Hellenistic ceramics adorned the relieving triangle of a Late Minoan tholos tomb at Stylos

Figure 21.7   View across the Minoan country house at Pyrgos, in which was later inserted a Hellenistic shrine. Courtesy of J. F. Cherry

Sternaki to the west (Alcock 1991: 563, no. 12). Nor was this merely a matter of cult activity at ancient monuments. Hellenistic settlements too overlay visible prehistoric remains, for example at the palace site of Phaistos (Levi 1964: 11–12). Historic episodes of ritual practices in Cretan caves – often the site of prehistoric activity – were not new in Hellenistic times, but they definitely increased in number, leading one student of the phenomenon to comment on an apparent 'desire to visit "old" cult places . . .' (Tyree 1974: 150; see also Rutkowski and Nowicki 1996; Watrous 1996). Finally, one could note cases where Hellenistic graves are placed within older cemeteries or in association with older tombs: most remarkably at the well-excavated North Cemetery at Knossos, where Hellenistic graves were inserted – carefully and deliberately – within the Iron Age cemetery (Coldstream and Catling 1996).

What can be gained from this evidence for the ritual and commemorative land-scapes of Hellenistic Crete? Strong interest and investment in ancient places suggests a deep concern with preserving memories of the local past. In some cases, this seems to have been overtly political and territorial in intent. It could be argued, for example, that cult at Ayia Triada offered one means for the community at Phaistos to maintain control of that area (as has been said for its Iron Age practices: D'Agata 1998: 24). Such an interpretation is supported by the fact that the Ayia Triada cult ends around the same time that Phaistos was swallowed up by Gortyn, and thus lost any right to claim its own territory. Similar explanations may well account for other examples reviewed here; in the uncertain conditions of the Hellenistic age, the desire to make such claims, and buttress them in many ways, would seem an understandable development. As at Ayia Triada, some of these manifestations of interest in the local past appear to end with the loss of civic autonomy; certainly almost all are abandoned with the Roman conquest, when arguments over boundaries and independence became – to a great extent – moot.

What we see in the Hellenistic landscape of Crete should not, however, be reduced merely to matters of territory and political authority. Claims to land were also claims to identity and to a sense of belonging; the veneration of an old monument or hallowed landmark was one way to combat the vulnerability felt by many Cretan communities. If Cretans of the Hellenistic age faced the very real danger of displacement and dispossession (as the regional survey evidence suggests), they did not accept this passively. We knew they waged war vigorously. What the evidence of landscape reveals is that they resisted change and loss in other ways as well, by turning to the past as a source of power, or of comfort.

5   Conclusion

This triad of brief case studies demonstrates the degree of regional variation at work across the Hellenistic *oikoumene*. Yet each of the three treatments, in their different ways, touches on common themes – not least considering the impact of that world's changing configuration, with its larger political units and greater velocity of contact; they all share a sense of how conditions in one locale could well be influenced, even dictated, by circumstances and events far away. Adopting a landscape perspective is one positive way to explore this ongoing dialectic between the local and the global. Another common element, of course, is a concern for evolving notions of identity and ethnicity at this time, and how these concepts could be materially negotiated and expressed. Such topics form, of course, the subject of much current scholarship on the Hellenistic world.

What landscape archaeology can *uniquely* offer is a new dimension to the study of Hellenistic society. If certain elements – the illiterate, the rural, the poor, the inhabitants of regions beyond the scope of our textual accounts – had before been almost automatically neglected, studies such as those offered here can now retrieve something of their lives, their decisions, their attitudes. We return to where we began: our understanding of the Hellenistic *oikoumene* is very much the product of the sources we employ. The infusion of evidence from innumerable regional landscapes – which is only now beginning to be assimilated – will leave that understanding both radically altered, and much improved.

FURTHER READING

For regional archaeology in the Mediterranean world, the five volume set – *The Archaeology of Mediterranean Landscapes* – generated by the POPULUS Project provides an excellent and comprehensive recent review (Barker and Mattingly 1999–2000). There is no real equivalent for other parts of the Hellenistic world, but for regional studies in the Near East, see Adams 1981, Hole 1987, and Wilkinson 2000. For an early comparison of regional data in a Hellenistic context, with bibliography, Alcock 1994. For an overview of the topography of the Bosporan kingdom and its investigation, Braund 2000; for a historical overview, Hind 1994b; for an archaeological survey, Triester and Vinogradov 1993. Methodologies of archaeological survey in the area are discussed by Scholl and Zin'ko 1999. Minns 1913 and Rostovtzeff 1922b remain the only extensive treatments of this region in English. For general treatments of the Hellenistic economy at large, Archibald et al. 2001, Davies 1984, Mattingly and Salmon 2001, Reger, this volume. Hölbl 2001 is a recent study of the Ptolemaic empire. Other recent publications on the Eastern Desert, apart from those cited in the chapter, include Redde and Golvin 1987 and Peacock 1997. On 'post-Minoan Crete', Cavanagh and Curtis 1998, Chaniotis 1999, and Myers, Myers and Cadogan 1992. For an excellent ecological review of the island over time, see Rackham and Moody 1996. For more on the Hellenistic and Roman 'commemorative landscapes' of Crete, Alcock 2002.

CHAPTER TWENTY-TWO

Warfare

Patrick Baker

In the middle of the fourth century, with the establishment of the Macedonian state under Philip II and the reforms he made to the army, the Macedonian military become the principal force to be reckoned with on the battlefields of the Greek world. And when Alexander succeeded his father in 336, he lost no time in readying his troops for war and launching his Asian conquests. Thus began a new era whose political foundations were largely shaped by military phenomena. When I was asked to write a chapter on warfare during the Hellenistic period, the editor of this volume was especially interested in whether fundamental changes occurred with the advent of the kings as dominant powers. Framed in this manner, this question points to a more fundamental one, dealing with the Hellenistic period as a whole: Did it constitute a break with – or a continuation of – the classical Greek world? The military history of the Hellenistic period is primarily that of kingdoms and their armies. Over the centuries, countless pages have been written on how these armies were commanded and on the troops which filled their ranks. Much attention has also been paid to the movement of armies; to how they were introduced to and supplied in different parts of the Greek world; to the tactics and strategies used in great battles, as described by ancient historians; to the ethnic makeup of the troops; and so forth. As a result, certain subjects have become tired and clichéd.

Regardless of the specific theme which interests them, historians of the Hellenistic period must always acknowledge the Greek heritage which stubbornly persists on the Hellenistic landscape. Yet they must also recognize all of the new elements which, taken together, serve to distinguish the period from previous ones, elements which sometimes suggest a clean break with the archaic and classical worlds. The Hellenistic period – break with or continuation of the Greek world? Any attempt to provide a definitive answer to this question would be mistaken. Things certainly changed, sometimes substantially, but rarely is it possible to speak in terms of a clean break with the classical period. Nevertheless, the changes were substantial enough to make it difficult to simply speak in terms of continuity. Thus, the question remains: Did warfare change during the Hellenistic period? The discussion which follows focuses on one aspect of this question. Studying warfare naturally involves an interest in those who actually participated in war, and this is probably the area where changes were most striking. But studying warfare during the Hellenistic period also requires that a distinction be made between the war and those who took part in it. This distinction has a direct influence on the overall portrait of Hellenistic warfare painted below.

Hellenistic warfare can be approached from several different perspectives. The most popular of these is innovation (or difference). Thus, Hellenistic military history involves great armies supported by equally impressive supply networks and increasingly sophisticated military machinery. The troops of the period were more diverse than the traditional hoplite phalanx, which had constituted the bulk of those military forces drawn from the city-states of the old Greek world. From this perspective, war was henceforth a matter of military resources. The battlefield no longer seemed home to citizen-soldiers, both because they were now far outnumbered by other troops and because what was at stake in the conflicts went far beyond the local or regional interests of city-states or federations of city-states. Likewise, ancient authors' accounts of battles usually stress the multitude of soldiers present on the battlefield; the size of the battlefield itself, which sometimes covered entire mountains and valleys; and the thunderous clamour of troops fired up by their generals. (e.g. I *Macc.* 6.39–41; Plut. *Sull.* 16).

For part of my discussion, I will adopt a perspective which is less well represented in the historiography. It focuses on city-states at war during the Hellenistic period. I will show how, at this level, warfare had changed very little and how it is possible to speak in terms of continuity with the archaic and classical worlds. In the process, I will offer some general reflections related to my recent research. These take the form of questions regarding what needs to be understood about the place and the role of Hellenistic city-states in a world where it seemed (and this idea is unfortunately still frequently promoted in modern historiography) that city-states no longer had a place, drowned as they were in a sea of vast kingdoms which took responsibility for the most important aspects of international politics and whose vicissitudes, by themselves, provided sufficient inspiration to the historians and authors of antiquity. Thus, these kingdoms have remained at the centre of the historical narrative. Of course, not all works discussing the political history of the Hellenistic world neglect to mention individual city-states when these played a role in an important event. However, with the exception of great cities like Rhodes, such passages tend to be rare and anecdotal, while the larger narrative remains focused on the Hellenistic kings, on their military campaigns and on their dynastic struggles with their kin. This begs another set of questions which better orient the discussion which takes shape below. What is the place (or the role) of Greek city-states in this world which could, *a priori*, be described as new in comparison to the archaic and classical periods? Is it even possible to speak in terms of city-states at war during the Hellenistic period?

1 War and Hellenistic Political History

A quick glance at Hellenistic society reveals a world of permanent warfare, with conflicts occurring at various levels, and with the different levels often proving to be linked together in practice. First of all, there were the wars between the Greco-Macedonian kingdoms created from the division of Alexander's empire. Large-scale rivalries, these conflicts even took place between kingdoms which did not share borders. Sometimes, individual kingdoms were torn apart when, in ensuring their succession to the throne, brothers and sisters were quick to take up arms. These conflicts overshadow local rivalries between city-states, which had by no means been pacified. Indeed, conflicts involving city-states continued as they had in previous periods. Many of them would have been drawn into royal wars, and it is impossible to know in detail the experiences of every individual city-state in the Aegean Basin. Nevertheless, epigraphic documents – which, thankfully, are abundant for this period – leave no doubt as to the fact that previous antagonisms were still very strongly felt and that recourse was being made to familiar tactics, be they war or diplomacy, to resolve tensions.

Not only was warfare a permanent fixture on the Hellenistic landscape, but it can also be seen as the founder of Hellenistic states, both through foreign conquests and within the borders of existing kingdoms. The process began with Alexander's conquest, a military expedition in which every inch of conquered territory was won at the point of a spear. It continued when the wars between Alexander's successors brought about the fragmentation of his universal empire. Thus, the Hellenistic kingdoms were, from the very beginning, military rivals. War was the primary means of resolving differences, and the monarchs all followed a more or less imperialist strategy (especially in third-century Egypt) by fighting amongst themselves for territories like Koile-Syria or the islands in the Aegean Sea, by making alliances against one another and even by taking their penchant for conquest abroad. For example, in Italy, Pyrrhos organized an alliance of Greek city-states against Rome and Carthage between 280 and 275 (Bengtson 1975: 98–100). Similarly, in India, the Seleukid kingdom never fully succeeded in securing the allegiance of the Baktrian satraps. As for the creation of new states within existing kingdoms, the Seleukid kingdom in Asia constitutes a particularly striking example. Fed by the mutual animosities of the numerous tribes united under royal authority, war raged uninterrupted. By the third century, the territory originally ceded to Seleukos I had fragmented into numerous smaller states, and Antiochos III, the dynasty's fifth monarch, had to re-conquer the territory of his forefathers. The example of the Seleukids clearly shows how the Hellenistic kings, as sovereigns of lands conquered by force of arms, were never at peace, not even at home. The Ptolemies paid dearly for giving the Egyptians the opportunity to liberate themselves when the latter were integrated into Ptolemaic contingents for the battle of Raphia in 217 (Will 1982: 40–4). Thus, Hellenistic warfare both established and erased frontiers (Austin 1986: 454–7).

During the Hellenistic period, war also laid the foundations of royal power and authority. Such power was not completely new; Greek city-states had been confronted with this type of government since the Macedonian expansion of the fourth century. Now, however, it represented the primary form of state authority in all territories touched by Hellenistic civilization, and this was the case for the entire length of the Hellenistic period. Alexander and his successors became kings by virtue of the 'law of the sword'. Kings were above all generals, generalissimos. Their dress was that of the Macedonian soldier, including the sandals, the *chlamys*, and the hat. They led their troops to combat (ten of the fourteen Seleukid monarchs died in battle) and their victories were celebrated in hymn, in honorific epithets (Great, Poliorketes, Saviour, Kallinikos), and in the numerous sources recording their military accomplishments (including stone inscriptions, papyri, Nike-type coins specially issued following a victory, statues and trophies). Battlefield victories were a key element of royal cults. A kind of royal mystique, coupled with a theology of victory, was developed during the Hellenistic period, when the king came to be associated with the goddess Nike, Victory personified. For example, the reaction of the inhabitants of Koile-Syria to Ptolemy's victory at Raphia (Polyb. 5.86) can be summed up by quoting an inscription describing Ptolemy in the days following the battle: King Ptolemy Great God Saviour, Philopator and Nikephoros (*OGIS* 89). The monarchs themselves were conscious of the importance accorded to military victory in legitimizing their power over the people, and the art of war rapidly became a science studied by numerous kings and military leaders. It was believed that a good king, like a good general, had to combine within his person audacity, clear-sightedness, and self-control (Plut. *Pyrrh.* 8; *Phil.* 4; Lévêque 1968: 276–9; Austin 1986: 457–9).

Finally, is it really necessary to point out that war was a source of profit? Even if the objectives in expanding a kingdom's borders were primarily political or strategic, the spoils of victory served both to satisfy the troops in the field and to fill the royal treasury, insofar as newly-conquered peoples were added to the tax rolls and, in certain cases, to the lists of those required to pay tribute. More specifically, the conquest of ports in the Aegean Islands or along the coasts of Greece and Asia Minor meant that a Hellenistic king could open up his kingdom to the resources of Arabia, Upper Egypt and the Red Sea, not to mention the forests of Koile-Syria (a very precious commodity when it came to naval construction). Thus, war offered the means for achieving greatness while it stimulated the economy by increasing the demand for and the circulation of goods and currency (Austin 1986: 459–61). For example, the widespread use of mercenaries, which was also an important source of cultural exchange during the Hellenistic period, constituted one of the important vectors of economic and commercial vitality whose effects can be seen today in archaeological digs which document the widespread circulation of goods and currency.

During the Hellenistic period, the fourth-century hegemonic ideal of certain great classical cities like Athens, Thebes and Sparta was inherited by the Greco-Macedonian kingdoms whose reach was infinitely more vast. In this new context, city-states would have naturally held a smaller, more limited place. And it is tempting to assume that since city-states no longer carried the same weight, they did not have a significant role to play in the history of the period, one which began with all of the city-states being subjugated to larger kingdoms, a form of power they had been aware of but which had supposedly been absent from the Greek political landscape up to that point. Yet it can easily be shown that this state of subjugation was by no means new. Any disruption caused by the conquest of Greece by Philip II, and later by Alexander's campaign, had relatively little effect on the Greek city-states beyond the multiplication of their numbers (Gauthier 1984; Ma 2000a: 107). Thus, the traditional model of democratic government – which gave the people control over political life, over justice and over community administration – persisted in a new, though not necessarily inferior, form. This phenomenon was most striking in the Greek city-states of Western Asia Minor which had endured centuries of Persian domination. Their political framework, by contrast with that of the city-states of Greece itself, did not result from a long evolution, nor did it rely on a well-established tradition. After being declared free by Alexander the Great, many of them entered a significant phase of political, economic and cultural development. As for the city-states within Greece itself, on the Aegean islands and in the Peloponnese, both the Athenian imperialism and the political context of the fourth century had, long before the Hellenistic period, made them familiar with a state of international politics where ideological, political and military stakes regularly went far beyond their local interests.

For city-states of all kinds, written documents from the period attest to an important increase in the number of diplomatic contacts, to the founding of important religious festivals, and to the diversity and prosperity of commercial activity, notwithstanding occasional periods of uncertainty related to the vicissitudes of international politics. Meanwhile, archaeological finds show how their prosperity was reflected in the construction of great panhellenic sanctuaries, or of monumental fortified walls still visible to this day. Thus, contrary to a once widespread opinion whose adherents are becoming progressively fewer in number, the Hellenistic period was not one of decline for Greek city-states. Rather, it represented the height of their development. Granted, despite successive declarations by Alexander and the Diadochoi making them independent, some of them lost no time in falling back into a state of subjugation. Ephesos provides a good example. With the exception of a few brief periods of independence, it remained a royal capital ruled by a governor with a permanent garrison at his disposal from 334 BC until the Roman Conquest. Samos did not obtain independence from the Ptolemaic kingdom until about 192 BC. The beginning of the second century is also the period when epigraphic documents related to that city's affairs first appeared and proliferated. But Ephesos and Samos are two exceptions which should not distract from the experience of hundreds of other cities which, in many cases, have left an extensive written record.

2 Means of War

Diversified troops

The military resources of the great kingdoms have proved a subject of utmost interest to both the authors of antiquity and modern scholars. Like Alexander's army, the troops of the Greco-Macedonian armies were both numerous and cosmopolitan. When he began his conquest, Alexander had an army of between 40,000 and 50,000 men, the core of which was made up of Macedonians, both infantrymen and horsemen, who fought alongside a number of specialist contingents, manned by Greek allies or mercenaries: Greek infantry and cavalry, Cretan archers and slingers, Thracian or Balkan light infantry and cavalry, etc. Over time, Alexander's army became increasingly diversified, although it maintained a hierarchy largely based on ethnic criteria: Macedonian and Greek heavy infantry; Persian or Cretan archers and spearmen; horsemen of diverse origins; Greek engineers charged with building or maintaining siege machines and artillery and with digging mines; and so on. The famous divisions of Asian elephants were soon added to the mix, and later became particularly common in the Seleukid armies. Finally, to round out the forces, a number of interpreters and tradesmen were required (D. Engels 1978: 11–26; Rochette 1997). When the army reached India, it included some 120,000 men, although this number was reduced to 80,000 by the time of Alexander's death. And while the army's ranks were continually replenished by the very tribes it subjugated along its route, Greeks were established in the military colonies to serve as occupying armies. It was the members of this latter group which quickly began organizing themselves into genuine Greek city-states.

Like Alexander's 'founding' army, those of his successors were composed of troops which were both cosmopolitan and great in numbers. After all, Ptolemy II Philadelphos could rely on a force of 240,000 men (App. *Preface* 10), though the figure was greatly reduced under the reign of Philopator, whose forces numbered only 75,000 men (Polyb. 5.65). While statistical data gleaned from the authors of antiquity must always be viewed with a critical eye, they nevertheless provide rough estimates which can be used for the purposes of parallel and comparison. Thus, in 217, Antiochos III mobilized almost 62,000 infantrymen and 6000 horsemen against his Ptolemaic enemies. These numbers are similar to those he is reported to have commanded at the battle of Magnesia in 189: 60,000 infantrymen and 12,000 horsemen (Polyb. 5.79; Livy 37.18).

Most soldiers were mercenaries, and demand for their services was great. During the third century, Macedonians and Greeks answered the call in great numbers by visiting recruitment centres established across the eastern Mediterranean. Material conditions (pay, etc.) were relatively good, since the new kingdoms created following the division of Alexander's empire were at the height of their power. Texts nevertheless describe problems with recruitment and pay which constantly faced monarchs and military leaders. Take, for example, the contract made between Eumenes of Pergamon and his soldiers on the subject of pay (*OGIS* 266, trans. Austin 196; Launey 1950: 742–3; Virgilio 1982), the one entered into by the Karian dynast Eupolemos with the defenders of Theangela, whom he had just conquered (Robert 1936: 78–9), or the difficulties the Ionian city-state of Erythrai had in providing for the pay of its mercenaries (*I.Erythrai* 24). In the second and first centuries, material conditions deteriorated and recruiters increasingly sought out barbarians: Semites, Jews, Asians. Indigenous contingents were also recruited in Egypt and Asia, while the Macedonian army conserved a more national character (Griffith 1935: 308–16).

Over the course of three centuries, Ptolemies, Seleukids and Attalids succeeded in standardizing the recruitment of troops. They did so in such a way as to ensure both a regular supply and an equal presence across the entire territory occupied by their respective kingdoms. In Egypt, a system of kleruchia (*klérouchia*) was established: in exchange for a parcel of land to be developed (whose size varied according to the recipient's rank), the kleruch (*klérouchos*) could be mobilized (with payment) and taxed. Though originally based on a form of individual tenure where the occupant's rights were limited to usufruct, the kleruchia was gradually transformed into hereditary and alienable property. Thus, the kleruch could cede his property to his sons by gift or inheritance, or sell it to a third party, just as well as he could lose it for having badly managed it (e.g. Sijpesteijn 1979: 151–8). This was an individual and essentially rural system, where the sons of kleruchs became kleruchs in turn, giving the Ptolemaic forces the appearance of a permanently garrisoned army across the territory. The Seleukids and the Attalids preferred to establish permanent rural or urban settlements responsible for their own defence and, eventually, for regular military service in the royal army. These settlements sometimes took the form of city-states, more often of military colonies (G. Cohen 1991: 41–50). By contrast to the Ptolemaic kleruchic system, this collective system attracted immigrants to settlements which were in keeping with their traditions, sometimes forcing the neighboring Greek city-states to trade with their new neighbours (e.g. *OGIS* 229, Austin 182).

Given their large numbers, mercenaries were conspicuous figures in Hellenistic society. Leading no real civic life, they could nevertheless vote decrees and exercise political influence on their employers. Their influence was mainly a cultural one, with the spread of their gymnasia, cults and Greek lifestyles continuing at least until the third century. Subsequently, their influence was felt to a lesser extent. Although writers seldom portrayed them in a favourable light, and they were often an object of derision in the literature of the period (Polyb. 6.52; 15.25; or the mercenaries in the comedies of Menander: Thrasonides in *Misoumenos*, Polemon in *Perikeiromene* and Stratophanes in *Sykionios*), their superiority to the citizen-soldier was nevertheless widely recognized (Diod. 29.6).

Diversified tactics

The distinctiveness of the great kingdoms' military resources is usually most striking from a technical perspective. First of all, the diversity of troops constituted a clean break with what had been known in the classical Greek city-states, despite the fact that mercenaries had been increasingly used since the fourth century. The phalanx remained the heart of the army, the Macedonian version proving even heavier and more monolithic than its Greek counterpart, making it a wonder of the Hellenistic world. The technical specifications of the phalangite's equipment changed very little. He wore a coat of mail (which protected him better than the simple breastplates worn by Greek heavy hoplite infantry) and a helmet, while he carried a shield and a straight sword. Nevertheless, the Macedonian *sarissa* replaced the Greek pike which had been shorter (2.5 m) and, as a result, less effective. Measuring between 5 and 6 metres, the *sarissa* had to be held with two hands, thereby hindering the movement of the phalanx. Not that increased mobility was necessary, as the phalanx could simply lie in wait for an enemy charge. In fact, the *sarissa* had a sharp point at both ends, allowing it to be stuck in the ground, thereby creating an almost impenetrable wall of spikes (Markle 1977; 1978; 1982).

From a tactical perspective, land combat appears to have evolved very little, in spite of the introduction of many new categories of troops and specialized contingents. Although Alexander and Pyrrhos proved themselves to be brilliant tacticians, most battles were still decided by the clash of two phalanxes, accompanied by smaller skirmishes, with the elite troops being concentrated in the right wing. Yet Alexander's conquest included only four engagements – the battles of Granikos (334), Issos (333), Gaugamela (331), and the River Hydaspes (326) – fought in the same manner as those which had occurred in previous centuries. Across the entire period, while battles were fought with the idea of two compact masses in mind, they also took forms which reflected the armies' increasingly diverse troops. In the middle of the period, the clash of the Macedonian phalanx and the Roman legion was the source of great surprise and bitter defeat. The ultimate tool of war in the Greek world for almost six centuries had found a superior enemy. By far the best account of the struggle (notwithstanding the author's obvious bias) comes from Polybios, who tells the tragic story of the crushing of Philip V by Flamininus at Kynoskephalai (18.29–32; also Livy 31.34).

Hellenistic armies' light troops were numerous and diverse, thanks to the recruitment of barbarians and semi-barbarians (the latter category refers to barbarians from the border regions of the Greek world who used a combination of armament and tactics). As technicians of warfare, capable of managing both technical and cultural diversity, the Greeks were often sought after to prepare and even command troops. As I mentioned before, so-called 'light' troops varied significantly from one army to the next – both internally in terms of ethnicity and across time – making it impossible to provide a detailed description here. I will merely underscore the fact that although the cavalry was frequently used by Alexander – he made it his primary assault force, going so far as to charge enemy infantry on the flanks and from the back – it proved to be a less popular weapon in subsequent periods, when it was used mainly as a light contingent for skirmishes, harassing enemy troops during their movements (Brunt 1963; Hammond 1978). But although the connection between phalanx and cavalry became much less important after Alexander, it should be noted that this coincided with the emergence of squadrons with well established reputations, such as the Tarentine mounted spearmen (Griffith 1935: 246–50; Launey 1949: 601–4).

Despite their lack of efficiency, one of the most commonly evoked elements of Hellenistic armies was their dreadful scythed chariots, copied from the Persians (war chariots had not been used by the Greeks since the so-called Dark Ages). They were first described by Xenophon, who wrote of their invention by Cyrus (*Cyr.* 6.1). They subsequently appeared in the armies of Antiochos III, in 189; of Mithradates, in 86; and of Pharnakes II, son of Mithradates, in 47 (Glover 1950). Another interesting (and substantial) component of Hellenistic royal armies were Indian elephants, soon followed by their African counterparts; the latter variety proved less docile and consequently less useful. Occasionally, these animals were a decisive element for the success of an army in the field. Seleukos I apparently gathered almost 480 of them at the battle of Ipsos in 301. They were a gift of Seleukos' new ally, the Mauryan king of India, Chandragupta (Sherwin-White and Kuhrt 1993: 12). Antiochos III fielded 102 at Raphia, where his opponent, Ptolemy IV, had 73 (Polyb. 5.79). However, despite the novel and spectacular nature of these living weapons, they were far from ideal, since they could easily turn against those who used them and consequently required special precautions (Polyaen. 4.6.3). Elephants virtually disappeared from Greek battlefields after the defeat of Antiochos III at Magnesia in 189 (Scullard 1974: 180–5).

In the distinctively Greek tradition of naval warfare, exemplified by Athens and the Delian League, maritime forces came to play a critical role in the wars between Hellenistic kingdoms. After all, if the Eastern World had traditionally seen the Mediterranean as little more than another in a long list of natural boundaries, it remained the centre of the world for the Hellenistic dynasties. Consequently, it was the site of innumerable naval battles and focus of a veritable 'arms race', both in terms of the number of vessels built (150 to 200 units for Ptolemy I; 500 for Demetrios Poliorketes; 200 for Pyrrhos in Sicily) and in terms of their size (twenty, thirty and even forty-bank ships!). Triremes nevertheless remained the vessel of choice, with *pentereis* and even *heptereis* also proving particularly common. Although the Macedonians were never great mariners, Ptolemies and Seleukids fought over the forests of Koile-Syria, which were essential for naval construction. And throughout the third century, the Ptolemies controlled the Aegean Basin and Straits, a powerful maritime position which subsequently passed for a time to the great city of Rhodes, which acted as a veritable maritime policeman (Ormerod 1924: 128–50; Berthold 1984: 98–101; Gabrielsen 1997: 42–4). In any case, the size and the weight of the fleets meant that there could be nothing subtle about maritime battles, which most often took the form of clashes between two lines of ships. That much is known from the descriptions of battles given in the sources. Naturally, there might also have been smaller skirmishes at sea, notably with pirates, which would have more closely resembled the naval battles of the classical era (e.g. *SIG*[3] 567; Baker 1991: 24–30).

The *poliorketika* – literally the science of siege warfare – reached its height by the end of the fourth and into the third century, by which time virtually all cities had been fortified. The remnants of these fortifications bear witness to elaborate plans and to the application of a continually improved know-how. These coveted assets integrated such elements as trenches, forward-walls, towers, *crémaillères* and sawtooth layouts, and postern-gates (McNicoll 1997). Throughout the period, siege machines, together with the mobility of light troops, were comparable to those developed during the fourth century, especially by one of the Diadochoi, famous for his ability to win over besieged cities, Demetrios son of Antigonos justly named Poliorketes, the Besieger: these included rolling towers, battering rams, artillery, etc. (Garlan 1974; 1984).

3 Warfare and City-States

Civic armies and means of war

There are several sources available to the modern historian for appreciating the military resources of Hellenistic city-states. The most obvious of these are the still-visible fortifications that surrounded virtually every city, which naturally have great archaeological significance and provide important technical and tactical insights. However, these fortifications also bear witness to the complex work of military organization and planning overseen by civic bodies, the details of which can be found in various texts. For example, the construction and maintenance of walls are documented in agreements reached between city-states and their contractors, as well as in administrative documents honouring the citizens responsible for this work: for example the epistates of the ramparts, *epistates teichon* were usually organized into a college, as they were at Erythrai (*I.Erythrai* 23). Meanwhile, short texts from Smyrna and Stratonikeia clearly show how the layout of that part of the city lying within the walls was also the object of planning by civic bodies, with an eye to essentially military concerns (*I.Smyrna* II.1.613a–c; *I.Stratonikeia* II.1.1003–4; Varinlioglu 1994: 189–91). Furthermore, information on the financing of fortification projects can be found in subscriptions raised for that purpose, notably those voted by the people of Kolophon at the very end of the fourth century (Migeotte 1992: 214–23). Finally, fortifications were also built to protect a city's outlying territory, and the more modest ruins of various small forts and fortresses are still visible to those who choose to stray from the beaten path (on the costs of fortifications and their manning, Baker 2000).

But while the mere existence of these fortifications is noteworthy, the individuals who manned them are even more significant. Texts describe the quartering of citizen-soldiers in the small forts around the city's territory or in the citadel. Clearly, these men did not hesitate to take up arms in defence of the interests of their community. Furthermore, numerous military offices were filled by citizens, following democratic elections. And in the vast majority of Hellenistic city-states, efforts were made to educate future citizens in the arts of war. I use the plural deliberately, for to a great extent the city-states kept up with the technical advances of their time. Thus, while youth still studied the traditional tactics of hoplite warfare, they also received instruction in archery, firing catapults and combat in light arms. These examples are taken from the numerous inscriptions found in gymnasia, principally lists of champions (Gauthier 1997).

Clearly, evidence of Hellenistic city-states' military resources is not lacking. And yet this evidence has long remained largely ignored, perhaps because of the diverse nature of the sources. No single text provides a clear understanding of the actual situation in a given city. But by assembling all of the available evidence, it is nevertheless possible to sketch an overall view by drawing on the experiences of certain cities as recorded in inscriptions (for example, see the study of military expenses in the cities by Migeotte 2000). Thus, the impossibility of knowing the details surrounding each individual city-state's civic militia is no longer an excuse for raising doubts regarding the very existence of those institutions.

City-states at war

Determining the military means at the disposal of Hellenistic city-states only partially addresses the question of their defence. From a more pragmatic perspective, it remains to be seen exactly whom they had to defend themselves against and what concrete dangers they actually faced. The first element which set the Hellenistic period apart was a new form of political power, essentially founded on the might of astonishingly large armies. As a result, city-states also had to come to terms with a new form of war, or rather new reasons for making war. Integrated into great kingdoms which were being made and remade all around them – sometimes to their advantage, sometimes at their expense – city-states were required to operate a two-fold foreign policy. On the one hand, they actively fought to maintain their political autonomy, although autonomy and liberty were occasionally marred by compromises which brought alternating periods of democracy and oligarchy or, in earlier periods (i.e. under Alexander's successors), occasional subjugation to the authority of a tyrant. On the other hand, city-states pursued a 'traditional', smaller-scale, foreign policy based on shifting alliances and conflicts with neighbouring city-states. These territorial squabbles, settled by arms or by negotiation, may have been essentially local in nature, but they were no less important for the city-states involved. The attitude of Hellenistic city-states to this complex political landscape bears witness to their desire to maintain their independence from any and all foreign powers.

This political landscape represented various kinds of threats to city-states, and naturally elicited various kinds of military and political reactions. In the case of hostile royal armies, responses could range from simply accepting the subjection of the city-state to obstinacy and a desire to make a stand. The latter option brought about armed conflicts whose outcomes were rarely favourable to the city-states (there are numerous examples, e.g. Phokaia and Teos in 190 BC: Polyb. 21.6.1–6; Livy

37.11.15; 27.9; 28.1–2; 32.1–8). In these conflicts with Hellenistic kingdoms, city-states were primarily concerned with preserving their liberty and autonomy. Meanwhile, the royal attacker was normally interested in a city for the strategic importance of such features as its urban centre or its port, which could serve as strategic posts within a much larger territory. This helps explain why such conflicts usually took the form of a siege of a city rather than an open war on its territory. From another perspective, several factors might have led a royal army to linger on a city's territory. Perhaps it had been unable to subjugate the city's besieged population and was seeking vengeance on the hinterland. Or perhaps the attacker was trying to draw the defending troops out of the city. A final explanation would apply to cases where the king had no real interest in the city itself. Rather, he was simply taking advantage of its territory's resources to supply his troops. From yet another perspective, city-states did not hesitate to attack their counterparts. And when the enemy was another city-state, conflicts rarely centred on the siege of a city. Instead, they focused on extracting the hinterland's economic and material resources. However, it is difficult to know whether these conflicts mirrored the agonistic battles of earlier times or whether they reflected the evolution begun in the fourth century by becoming more drawn out affairs involving wars of attrition and raids.

In any case, the defence of city and hinterland alike was tirelessly maintained. Diplomatic contacts with neighbouring cities were increased and military alliances or assistance agreements were increasingly common in the course of relations between city-states. Kings or their representatives were also the object of diplomatic overtures on the part of plenipotentiary representatives sent by city-states concerned with the security of their national territories and of their inhabitants. For most city-states, the armies they maintained were primarily charged with defending the civic space (significant examples can be found in epigraphic documents: Miletos and Herakleia under Latmos made an alliance, *SIG*³ 633; Priene organized against the Gauls, *OGIS* 765; other measures taken against the Gauls at Erythrai, *I.Erythrai* 28; etc.). This fact brings to mind the famous document describing the emergency measures taken by the Ephesians during one of the Mithradatic wars, in December 87 and January 86 BC: 'as great dangers threaten the sanctuary of Artemis, the city and all of its citizens, along with all of the inhabitants of the city and its territory, it is necessary that all show solidarity in facing this period; may it please the people, the affair pertaining to the defence, security and safety of the sanctuary of Artemis, of the city and its territory...' (*OGIS* 742.23–8).

This naturally leads to new questions regarding the nature of these localized conflicts. What were these minor clashes which were part of the ordinary course of life for Greek city-states and which are frequently mentioned in the epigraphic sources? Are we to see here warfare as a means of settling border disputes, as the prelude to peace treaties, as the result of shifting military alliances? Though relatively less intense and requiring fewer resources, these conflicts remained very serious from the perspective of the city-states themselves, since they dealt directly with the integrity of the civic space.

A series of documents traces the relations between the city-states in the lower Maeander valley for a period of about 75 years, covering the latter part of the third century and first half of the second century. Although it often deals with isolated and seemingly unrelated incidents, this rich epigraphic dossier describes numerous border disputes, wars and alliances which attest to both the military conflicts and the political relationships which developed between city-states sharing a common territory (Baker 2001).

During the years 184–180 BC a peace treaty was negotiated between the cities of Miletos and Magnesia-on-the-Maeander and the respective allies, Herakleia under Latmos and Priene. The treaty brought an end to a war about which little is known, except what can be deduced from the clauses of the treaty itself, the majority of which relate to the ownership of a territory disputed by the two city-states (SIG^3 588, trans. Burstein 37; Ager 1996: 292–6). The territory, known as Peraia, probably constituted all or part of what the city-states of the lower Maeander had been fighting over for several decades. Indeed, a common thread is woven through both the documents related to those conflicts and the treaty signed between Miletos and Magnesia. The war between these two city-states was caused by conflicting claims to arable lands situated in the valley at the edges of their respective territories. Fighting had previously erupted over the ownership of these lands between Priene and Magnesia (SIG^3 679; Ager 1996: 321–7), Priene and Miletos (*I.Priene* 26, 27, 28; Ager 1996: 271–3), and later Miletos and Herakleia under Latmos (SIG^3 633; Ager 1996: 290–2). As early as the last third of the third century, the introduction of Cretan soldier-colonists to the valley by Miletos created problems for both the Milesians and the Cretan settlers when the territory passed into the hands of the Magnesians, following the intervention of Philip V in 201 (Athen. 3.78c). Later, at the beginning of the second century, Asia Minor's history was affected by Antiochos III's campaign against Rome, a well known event whose repercussions were felt by the coastal city-states, including those in Ionia, which were among the main strategic points sought by the Seleukid king. Unfortunately, details are often lacking, except for sporadic comments in the works of Polybios and Livy. The Ionian city-states found themselves closely caught up in events opposing the Senate to the ambitions of Antiochos III. Forced to allow foreign armies on their territory and to provide lodging, supplies, or military support (depending on changing contexts and on what the great powers involved imposed on them), these city-states were obviously facing a difficult period. But the larger war was not the only thing which held their attention, and Maeander Valley inscriptions clearly show that civic and political activity continued regardless of the circumstances, that the city-states involved were just as (perhaps more) interested in other conflicts, and that they did not hesitate to declare war against an overly ambitious neighbour.

In the complex game of relations between city-states, former enemies frequently became allies until such time as a new disagreement separated them again. Thus, behind the dominant narrative of Hellenistic history, well documented by the authors of the period, there lies a parallel history dealing primarily with the affairs of the city-states. And yet, in previous centuries, it was this second layer which had single-handedly held the attention of historians for essentially the same reasons that they subsequently shifted their attention to the activities of great kingdoms. Thus, the theme of warfare during the Hellenistic period can actually be given a variety of definitions and explanations. For the city-states, the context of international politics had changed and, inevitably, the ways and means of making war had changed as well. In terms of their financial and human resources, as well as in terms of pragmatic imperatives, they were able to adapt themselves to the changes while keeping up with technological progress (e.g. the range of weapons taught in the gymnasia, Launey

1950: 815–35). On this subject, I will limit myself to a single example. Several epigraphic documents allow for a relatively detailed analysis of how the islands of Kos and Kalymna organized the defence of their territory between 205 and 200. Their efforts consisted of public subscriptions calling for a general effort on the part of the population, as well as decrees in honour of particularly devoted citizens (*SIG*[3] 567, 569; Habicht and Hallof 1998: 116–21). Yet the two successive conflicts which these islands participated in had implications which went beyond merely local concerns. The first, called the 'Cretan War' because of the participation of several Cretan city-states, was instigated by the Macedonian king, Philip V. The second involved the Macedonian fleet itself. The course of events is well known, thanks especially to Polybios, and the sources leave no doubt as to the fact that Kos and Kalymna, then allies of the mighty city of Rhodes, were cast as actors, extras and victims in a drama whose plot extended far beyond their own borders. Nevertheless, the civic spirit, still very much alive, allowed them to efficiently organize the defence of the national territory of the two islands (Baker 1991).

4 Peace

In a world of incessant wars, the idea of peace retained the positive connotations it had begun to take on during the fourth century. In principle, the treaties negotiated during the period were permanent, although their clauses sometimes included provisions for changes or renewals. These treaties presented peace 'as a state which must be restored, conserved, renewed, confirmed' (Préaux 1961: 234). That being said, the kings played a paradoxical role in the concert of international relations. Not simply warriors, they were also responsible for restoring and conserving order, especially from the perspective of their subjects and that of the city-states under their authority, by whom they were often heralded as saviours, protectors and benefactors. Even Alexander presented himself as the world's conciliator and peacemaker, despite the fact that his mission was essentially one of military conquest. Thus, the king embodied the 'peace of the magnanimous victory' (Préaux 1961: 233). And while the exploits of princes were the subject of official praise, many decrees also praised the work of peacemakers, diplomats and ambassadors. As the kings rarely undertook the work of negotiation themselves, these individuals were normally extremely important, recognized for their great abilities and eloquence.

This situation inexorably points to a more brutal reality: clearly, when they sought peace, kings usually had military considerations in mind. Often finding themselves in a state of temporary weakness following a less-than-successful military campaign, they saw peace as an opportunity to buy time or to seek out a weaker adversary. In other words, war was ever-present in the kings' minds while peace was merely a means of freeing up resources and 'regrouping'. Thus, the political balance was always precarious and continually put into question. The kings' preferred way of making peace was by following traditional procedures, thereby limiting the degree of innovation and retaining the idea of peace as a contract. However, negotiations often proved difficult and the terms imposed were not always fully accepted by one party or the other, resulting in ongoing tensions and leading to new conflicts (e.g. Koile-Syria, that eternal bone of contention between the Ptolemies and the Seleukids). Furthermore, there was no organization standing above the kingdoms, in a position to act as referee or as guarantor of the treaties. With few exceptions, from the middle of the second century until the end of the period, even the Roman Senate only intervened as a party to the conflicts, and not as a superior power. Thus, while Roman military power gradually overcame that of the Hellenistic kingdoms, Rome's dominance was felt as a military adversary, and not as a referee.

Meanwhile, relations between city-states proved both constant and intense, even if they were often carried on under the shadow of the great powers. The latter were sometimes called on for help, which explains why local quarrels of limited scope are sometimes mentioned in general treaties which put an end to vast wars between great powers. On top of all this there was piracy as well as the social conflicts taking place within individual city-states. Thus, relations between Greeks had changed very little. In many cases, evidence of conflicts comes from attempts to resolve differences. Arbitration, an ancient form of conflict resolution, continued to be practised during the Hellenistic period, as numerous epigraphic documents attest. However, this abundance of documentation does not necessarily mean that it had become an increasingly popular or effective tool for securing peace. The initiative for negotiations often came from outside: a king (at least at the beginning of the period), a confederation, a neutral city-state, or the Senate after 200 BC. But warring city-states could also take the initiative and request that an external neutral power intervene as arbitrator, be it a city-state (or city-states), a king, a confederation, or the Senate. The procedures remained the same as in earlier times, although the agreements reached were fragile and often put into question, for want of institutions capable of imposing punishment for breaches. Only Alexander, the Diadochoi, and the Senate (after 146 BC) seem to have had enough authority to impose settlements. The city of Rhodes might also have played such a role for a certain time, especially during the third and at the beginning of the second centuries.

City-states were reconciled by way of alliance treaties, which settled their past differences and determined their future relations (e.g. *symmachia*), as well as by various judicial procedures which multiplied and intensified with time: mutual agreements of inter-marriage law (*epigamia*), of property law (*egktesis*) and even reciprocity of civic rights (*isopoliteia*: Gawantka 1975); purely judicial agreements (*symbola*) opened the courts of other cities to the citizens of participating city-states; proxeny decrees multiplied (Marek 1984), as did decrees of *asylia* (Rigsby 1996), notably on the part of the Aitolians who, by exempting certain cities from the risk of pillage, created a web of relationships in the Aegean Sea. 'The details naturally varied greatly from one case to the next, but there was a strong continuity in the spirit and operation of negotiations from the classical period to its Hellenistic successor. The world of the city-states persisted from one era to the next' (Préaux 1961: 259).

5 Conclusion

According to Lévêque (1968: 279), there were really only four short periods of peace in the Hellenistic world between 323 and 150: 299–297, 249–248, 205–204 and 159–149. Subsequently, war essentially raged without interruption. And although wars did not erupt everywhere at the same time, their impact on the international political landscape was nevertheless widespread. Sometimes harsh and cruel, they also bore witness to acts of chivalry (Poliorketes, Gonatas, Pyrrhos) and clemency (treatment of prisoners, recognition of the territorial immunity of certain city-states or sanctuaries) (Shipley 2000: 80–3). Fighting no longer took place as it did in archaic and early classical times, and instead saw the further development of practices introduced during the fourth century, at least insofar as the great kingdoms were concerned. Furthermore, on a smaller scale, the study of the armies in Hellenistic Greek city-states clearly shows an unconditional and enduring attachment of civic bodies to their territory and their city. On this subject, it is safe to say that for the city-states, especially those in the Aegean Basin, there never was a break with the past as fundamental as that which scholars still too often describe when discussing such key historical events as the creation of the Hellenic League by Philip II, Alexander's conquest, or the subsequent division of the Empire by Alexander's successors.

The defence of the city-state and its territory remained a national, and purely civic, preoccupation. It lay at the heart of all the relations maintained with the outside world by Hellenistic city-states, regardless of whom they dealt with. Thus, whether it was a matter of negotiating with a king or his representative for the withdrawal of a royal garrison (e.g. at Erythrai, SIG^3 285), or with regards to a treaty creating a military alliance between two cities (e.g. Miletos with Herakleia under Latmos SIG^3 633), the desire to preserve territorial integrity and civic independence was always a central motivation for city-states. Likewise, the multiplication of agreements leading to the amalgamation of the territory of a small city or township into that of its larger neighbour also underscores this attachment to the land and the desire to enlarge its area, or at least to maintain its limits. Just as the citizen-soldier is closely linked to the origins of democracy and to the history of democracy during the classical period, he remains relevant to the history of the city-state and to the persistence of democracy during the Hellenistic period.

As I bring this chapter to a close, it seems appropriate that I return to the question posed at the outset and which has served as an organizing thread: Did warfare during the Hellenistic period change with the advent of the kings as dominant powers in Greek political history, which henceforth encompassed the whole of the known world? However important this question might be, it remains difficult to offer a definitive or straight answer. Although the kingdoms left a profound mark on the destiny of the Greek world and the face of international politics, the more traditional world of the city-state, the same one which had begun to slowly take shape during the eighth century BC, had not changed very much. In good times and bad, the defensive needs of the city-state remained the same, even with the addition of other, less immediate, considerations which went far beyond the local context. While the city-states could not ignore this additional level of political consideration, they did not necessarily have a firm grasp on its significance. Warfare during the Hellenistic period took various forms and benefited, in terms of its technical and tactical development, from financial means which, up to that point in Greek history, were unparalleled. From this perspective, it can be said that the appearance of the kings on the political landscape constituted a factor of change in the practice of war. Likewise, the necessity of preserving the integrity of states originally conquered by force, and the inevitable temptation to subsequently expand their borders, made the resort to armed conflict a common feature of international politics. But was this really a new state of affairs for the Greeks? It is true that, except for the unique case of the conquest of Messenia by the Spartans, the Greek city-states were not tempted by wars of conquest;

nonetheless, their attachment to the lands they defended sunk roots so deep in history that only mythology could explain it. But to resolve territorial conflicts – that is to say those which touched the states at the very deepest level – the military solution had long presented itself as the only one imaginable. 'In the politics of ancient city-states . . . , if there was a conflict, usually a territorial conflict, between two city-states, normally bordering each other, and if it was impossible to settle the differences peaceably, violence and war were the solution, and Greek history is covered by such battles fought over a piece of territory taken, lost, retaken, depending on the circumstances' (Robert *OMS* 5.141). For the Greeks, violence was an ordinary political tool (Garlan 1972: 197–203).

FURTHER READING

For a general account of military developments, Shipley 2000: 334–41; Tarn 1930 remains a classic, and the short book by Adcock (1957) can also serve as a starting point. Two general works dealing which the whole of Antiquity provide a particularly good overview for the uninitiated: Hackett 1989 and Hanson 1999. See Hammond 1981, D. Engels 1978 and Milns 1976 for information on Alexander and his army; Bar-Kochva 1976 on the Seleukid army, and Lesquier 1911 on the Ptolemaic army. For Roman warfare the detailed study of Cannae, Daly 2002. The subjects of fortification and siege warfare are amply covered by Garlan 1984 and 1974, and McNicoll 1997, 1986 and 1978 (Lawrence 1979 and Winter 1971 discuss fortifications from an essentially archaeological perspective). On mercenaries, a vast subject if all its facets are taken into consideration (social, economic, etc.), Griffith 1935 and Launey 1949–50 provide contextualized presentations which are rich in references. With regard to naval warfare and naval forces in general, the literature is rather sparse. Some information can be gleaned from the works already cited. Gabrielsen 1997 looks specifically at the case of Rhodes, and Hauben 1970 deals with the Ptolemaic example. More general works include Starr 1989, who dedicates a chapter of his short book to the Hellenistic period, as well as Casson 1991 and Rougé 1981. Ma 2000b offers an interesting account of the situation as it was experienced by city-states (in a book in preparation I cover the question of military institutions and armies in the Greek city-states of the Western coast of Asia Minor). Finally, two very stimulating studies on violence by the Greeks: de Romilly 2000 and Bernand 1999.

CHAPTER TWENTY-THREE

Piracy and the Slave-Trade

Vincent Gabrielsen

1 Introduction

We cannot fully appreciate the special quality which the concept of 'freedom' had for the inhabitants of the ancient world without taking into account a grim fact of life: that a person was also viewed as a commodity, to be appropriated, sold, or resold to a new owner. The pervasiveness of chattel slavery as an institution ensured that every free individual, high or low, had to live with the fear of losing his or her personal liberty and thus become another person's property. When it occurred, such a horrendous change in a person's legal status was almost unexceptionally accompanied by the no less ruinous act of physical dislocation to a far-off place. As a result, individuals were deprived of one of their most cherished privileges, families were deprived of their members, and cities of their very life-blood, that is, their citizens. No wonder, therefore, that freedom was regarded as both a precious and a highly precarious possession. Hence its intimate, even though intricate, relationship to another highly-valued notion: 'protection'.

The sources of peril were actually few, but immensely grave. To fall into captivity in connection with warfare was one of them. To be suddenly seized by someone exercising the customary right of reprisal (*syle, rhysia*) was another. A third one was to be snatched by a band of brigands or pirates. All three of these involved the use of violence, made no fine distinctions between humans and other valuables, put the captives wholly at the mercy of their captors and, as we shall see, shared between them some fundamental structural features. Still, whatever its specific mode, the act of appropriation itself was but the prelude to a further operation, whereby the 'catch' entered for good the domain of profit-generating transactions. For like any other commodity that of human captives was part and parcel (and a very large one at that) of the wider economic life, with an established supply/demand system, points of distribution and sale, a host of purveyors, shippers, dealers and buyers and price-setting routines – all in all, a *market in humans*; and, of course, the same system also expedited the movement, or rather the recycling, of captives already possessing the status of slaves. All three 'sources of peril', jointly exercising absolute control over at least the supply side of the market, carried prime responsibility for the intermarriage between organized violence and economic activity.

The whole gamut, from the capture of the 'commodity' to the final transaction deciding its fate, was operating in the classical period and continued doing so in the Hellenistic world, without anyone (state or individual) ever feeling any compunction about it. Already in the fourth century, Aristotle had thrown a good measure of his intellectual weight into demonstrating the primacy of this business as a perfectly rational and justified component of economic life: man-hunters, he explained, are those who live from 'booty-seizure' (*leisteia*), a profession as natural as animal-hunting and fishing; man-hunting, moreover, is a sub-category of warfare, which itself is by nature an art of acquisition (*ktetike techne*) practised against 'such people who, even though naturally created for subjection, do not submit to it voluntarily' (*Pol.* 1256a36–b27). Should anyone have had moral scruples about engaging in 'freedom stealing' and slave trafficking, that might indeed have been the proper antidote. But in fact no one did. In the period after Alexander, all went on happily observing the old convention – indeed 'a universal law' (Xen. *Cyr.* 7.5.73) – that persons and their property appropriated in war belong to those who had seized them. Serious trouble began whenever this very convention was observed (and it was so frequently) by people who, allegedly or factually, disregarded all other conventions about the use of organized violence. Enter the infamous pair: the pirate and the brigand.

2   Hellenistic Piracy

'The pirate', Tarn remarked, 'had a most useful place in the economy of the old world; he was the general slave merchant' (1913: 88). Concurring with this, Ros-tovtzeff adds: 'Scores of inscriptions refer to piratical raids and to the tragic experiences of men, women and children kidnapped by the pirates and sold into slavery.... This ancient practice had now [in the Hellenistic period] become very common and was carried on with cynical ruthlessness' (1941: I.202). Subsequent scholarship agrees that the difference from previous periods was above all a quantitative one: its intensity having increased (at times dramatically) in Hellenistic times, predatory activity came to play a markedly greater role in the slave-trade than it had before (Pöhl 1993: 33–6, but see de Souza 1999: 59–64). Any attempt to quantify that role more precisely is, of course, defeated by our lack of the necessary data; for instance, our current knowledge about such a basic requisite for any further analysis as the size of 'slave populations' remains deplorable (cf. W. Harris 1980). But even if we had the figures themselves, the task of estimating, diachronically, the relative volume and value of the pirate's share in the slave-trade would hardly become any the more easier. To appreciate this we shall have to look more closely at predatory activity, especially the economic processes of which it was part (sections 2–4) and the historical structures defining its character (section 5).

As historical phenomena, piracy and brigandage are by far the most complex of the 'sources of peril' mentioned above. What needs to be noted at the outset is that in the Hellenistic period, as earlier, one and the same label (*leistes*, or the less common *peirates*) was used indiscriminately for the practitioners of both activities. Thus we are really faced with a single phenomenon, not two. To concentrate on the seaward *operateur* only (as is done in this chapter), is simply to acknowledge that in volume his activity surpassed that of the brigand: His chosen element enabled him to prey over an area that was both much larger and far richer in catch, that is, the high seas as well as the Mediterranean and Black Sea littorals; in addition, his unequally greater ease of movement, besides minimizing the risk of capture, afforded him the advantage of hitting, within a given time, many more targets than his landward counterpart could hope for; moreover, even though he plied the seas by ship, his operations were often amphibious. It seems therefore defensible to regard the maritime *leistes* as historically and economically the more significant of the two, a fact also accentuated by the substantial investment of precisely that agent in the technological improvement of his 'hunting equipment', the light, fast-sailing galley; an investment that put him in 'the vanguard of military progress' (Davies 1984: 286).

Modern scholarship, too, recognizes this to be the archetypal predator, who, the violent part of his work being done, brought his human merchandise to the points of distribution and sale. Indeed, a slave market was to be found in practically every port. Some of them, notably Side, Phaselis, Alexandria, Rhodes and Delos, as well as the ports of Crete and the Black Sea, at various periods, dwarfed the rest in scale. Fine-grained evidence detailing the economic performance of these seaward markets and their inland counterparts, such as, for instance, Karian Mylasa (Men. *Sik.* 3–7), is sparse in the extreme; that applies especially to the numbers of piracy-related captives which these markets expedited monthly or annually. Delos, of course, is a well-known exception. And yet, it is only by chance that we are informed of the island's function as a market in the late third century (*SEG* 3.666) – and as a pirate base in the early second century (*SIG*[3] 582). More importantly, Strabo offers a vivid description of the momentous boost experienced by Delos after 145 (Maroti 1969–70; Rauh 1993: 41–68), an expansion of the island's in- and outgoing traffic in slaves that might have prompted the construction of facilities related to that trade (Coarelli 1982: the Delian 'Agora of the Italians' was essentially a slave market). Yet even that description is not an independent comment on economic trends but simply part of an explanation of political events, i.e. violent upheaval in the Southeastern Mediterranean and Roman disinterest in it. Strabo says:

> The export of slaves was an especially strong inducement to this wrongdoing, as it was extremely profitable. They were easily caught and not too far away there was the market of Delos; large and wealthy, it could have a turnover of ten thousand slaves a day. From where comes the proverb, 'Merchant, sail in, unload, everything has been sold'. The cause of all this was that the Romans became wealthy after the destruction of Carthage and Corinth and used many slaves. The pirates, seeing what easy profit there was, bloomed forth in large numbers, operating as both pirates and slave-traders. (14.5.2)

That all these slave markets, small and great, were also fed by the pirates themselves, often directly – note Strabo's switch from 'pirate' to 'merchant', when the captor enters the harbour – is thus incontestable. What seems less so is the notion that the 'open market' constituted the pirate's sole, or even main, field of economic activity. There is much to indicate that, when it came to selling his human merchandise, the pirate's first choice was another and equally important branch of the market.

3   Ransom: the 'Domestic' Branch of the Market

In about 470 the citizens of Teos, no doubt as an act of despair, pronounced a collective curse against those of their citizens and others who practised piracy (*ML* 23). But as time passed their imprecation apparently lost much of its force; around 200 Teos suffered a devastating assault by pirates, who, holding a large number of its inhabitants as hostages, demanded a seemingly astronomical sum of money in ransom. A grand-scale fund-raising operation was immediately launched for buying back the captives (*SEG* 44.949). A similar mishap hit the city of Aigiale on Amorgos in the third century. Arriving by sea suddenly one night, a gang led by one Sokleidas raided and plundered the countryside, a reminder of the amphibious nature of piratical operations; then, after having prudently scuttled the ships in the harbour to prevent a chase, they made a quick escape with, among other valuables, thirty girls, women and other persons, free and slave. Shortly afterwards two among the citizen captives persuaded the gang-leader, in return for ransom, to release the free persons and some of the freedmen and slaves, while they themselves volunteered to stay as hostages until the agreed sum of money had been paid. Thus, even though some loss was suffered (i.e. a number of freedmen and slaves were excluded from the bargain), the worst was avoided, thanks to the courageous initiative of the two citizens, who were recompensed accordingly by the city with rewards of honour (*SIG*[3] 521).

These instances are not unique. Timesa, a woman citizen of the Amorgan city of Arkesine, ransomed from her own means all the citizens who had been taken by pirates (*SEG* 29.762). During the Chremonidean war Epichares, the military commander of the Attic deme Rhamnous, made a deal with the pirates who had captured a number of the deme's inhabitants; the sum of 120 drachmas was paid for each captive (*SEG* 24.154). In roughly the same period, a foreign resident of Ephesos ransomed both free and slaves from pirates (Robert 1960: 132–5). Later in the century Eumaridas, a citizen of Cretan Kydonia living in Athens, contributed from his own pocket towards the 120 talent ransom agreed for the release of 'a large number of citizens and others', who had been captured by the Aitolian Boukris and carried off to Crete; Eumaridas even lent the captives money for their travel expenses (*SIG*[3] 535, trans. Austin 88). Around the same time ambassadors from Aulon on Naxos successfully negotiated the ransoming of 280 of their citizens from Aitolian raiders (*SIG*[3] 520). While sailing to the Crimea to announce the Pythian Festival of 194, Delphian *theoroi*, an especially exposed group of travellers, fell into the hands of pirates and were then ransomed by the citizens of Chersonesos (*SIG*[3] 604). And so forth.

What all these instances attest is the 'domestic' branch of the market, a branch also used by rulers and city-states for converting their war captives into cash; this is one of the elements making piracy and warfare parts of a single historical structure. If the captive was a free person, relatives were those immediately expected to put up the money required in ransom (e.g. Livy 34.50.5; App. *Hann.* 28). The same goes for entire cities. In 210 the inhabitants of Aigina asked their captor, the Roman proconsul P. Sulpicius, to allow them to appeal to kindred states for payment of ransom money. Being ultimately assured that this was the custom (*ethos*) of the Greeks, the proconsul reversed his initial denial to a positive answer, but the Aiginetans were largely failed by their 'kindred states' with the result that they were all sold into slavery (Polyb. 9.42.5–8). If, on the other hand, the captive was a slave, the obligation to pay ransom fell on the owner, provided he found it worthwhile. Mass capture, demographically vexing for any city, could instance the canvassing of community-wide financial support, either in the form of loans to be repaid with interest (cf. the case of Teos above), or as free gifts (cf. the case of Eumaridas above). Thus an old means of gaining distinction via private benefaction gained new impetus, at least in texts published on stone: the public-spirited man who had helped ransom captives, a topos in fourth-century Attic oratory (Pritchett 1991b: 269–71), surfaces all the more frequently in Hellenistic inscriptions.

Underneath all this, however, lay three hard facts: Firstly, that sometimes the captive was failed by his own relatives, a situation which, if the city did not step in to recover its 'life-blood', forced him to put his fate in the hands of profiteering money lenders. Secondly, that, mostly as a consequence of the latter, often the bill for his release had to be footed by the captive himself, failing which he became the property of his ransomer; the legal complexities of these matters, it should be noted, exercised thinkers from Aristotle to Cicero (*Eth. Nic.* 1165a; *Off.* 2.16.56). Thirdly, and more to the point, that what the man-hunter exploited here was not the old vocation of slave-trafficking but the perhaps older habit of extortion. In economic terms, 'freedom-selling' was far more lucrative for the simple reason that humans could fetch a much higher price if sold back to their own – or to themselves – than as slaves in the open market.

The ransom of 120 talents paid for the victims shipped by Boukris to Crete is definitely a very large sum. By comparison in 415 the Athenian general Nikias sold the entire population of Hykkara in South Italy as slaves, about 7500 people, for exactly the same amount (Thuc. 6.62). Even if the price per head in the Boukris incident is reckoned as low as 500 drachmas, the resulting total number of captives taken to Crete would still be too high to render that (presumed) price credible. Half a talent (3,000 dr.) seems more like it. Equally high sums were demanded by states, which often ransomed their war captives out of the same economic rationale as the pirates (Ducrey 1968: 246–54; Volkmann 1990: 110–18, 165–7; Pritchett 1991b: 247–55). In 189, for instance, the Epeirotes initially demanded five talents for each of the four Aitolian envoys they had captured; after further negotiations the sum came down to three talents per head (Polyb. 21.26). Roman captives in Achaia went for 500 drachmas and in Delphi for 300 to 600 drachmas each (Livy 34.50; Hatzfeld 1913). Earlier, in 254, the Romans themselves released the 14,000 inhabitants of Sicilian Panormos who could afford the 2000 drachma ransom; the remaining 13,000 were sold as slaves (Diod. 23.18). Noticeably lower than these sums is the 120 drachmas per head demanded by the kidnappers of the people from Rhamnous in Athens (see above). But price variation is what would be expected, anyway, since the pirate most likely set the price tag on his catch individually, according to status and wealth; Hannibal is reported to have done just that with his captives from the battle of Cannae in 216 (Livy 22.58). The same logic underlies the story about Julius Caesar's capture by pirates, perhaps on his way to Rhodes, in around 74 BC. Realizing what a 'big fish' that they had caught, the pirates demanded 20 talents in ransom. Piqued by this, Caesar raised the amount to 50 talents; after 38 days of captivity, the sum arrived from Miletos (Plut. *Caes.* 2). Even when due allowance is made, as indeed it must be, for an upward bias in some of these amounts, they are well in excess of ordinary 'slave prices' in the open market (Ducrey 1968: 248–9). So the pirate Sokleidas whose raid on Aigiale was observed above did not really have to be 'persuaded' to release those of his captives who could pay ransom; if he, just as any other in that profession, abstained from exploiting the 'domestic' branch of the market, a middleman stood ready to profit from freshly-caught persons.

   This latter agent is a shadowy figure, whose role can only be disclosed by lifting the shroud of philanthropy usually enveloping his action. Our clearest evidence for the way he operated stems from shortly after 368. The Athenian Nikostratos was captured by a trireme and sold to a man in Aigina. Heart-breaking letters were immediately dispatched to Nikostratos' family at home describing the captive's 'dreadful condition' and informing them that he would be released for a ransom of 2600 drachmas. Eventually, Nikostratos, receiving no help from his family, had to borrow this amount as well as 300 drachmas for travel expenses from others who demanded payment of both principal and interest within thirty days or else they would claim him as their property ([Dem.] 53.6–10). It was not the original captor/vendor who profited most from this transaction but rather the retailer in Aigina. The same situation is indicated by Hellenistic evidence. In the early second century, Epikles, a Cretan based on Cyprus, was seized by pirates and then 'sold [as slave] in Amphissa'; but soon afterwards Epikles gained his freedom by somehow raising the money with which to pay 'the ransom', *ta lytra*, to the man who had bought him (SIG^3 622). When the Karian city of Theangela commends a Delian for having 'purchased' a number of Theangelan women who were 'among the booty that resulted from the raid of the pirates', the suspicion arises that his action was not pure altruism but that he let them return home on receipt of ransom (*SEG* 3.666). The elusive middleman, using the open market as an intermediate point, was sometimes the pirate's close collaborator, sometimes his competitor.

   Judged by the *number* of documents that refer to it, the ransoming of captives, especially by pirates, seems indeed to have occupied a marginal place in this market in humans (so Pritchett 1991b: 283). Not necessarily so, however, if the emphasis is shifted to the *character* of these documents. For what we do have a record of are precisely those cases which, by their very nature, were habitually deemed meritorious to be publicized on inscriptions: that is, the intervention of benefactors, collective or individual. What we totally lack (and shall probably never get) is epigraphic evidence for the presumably far superior number of cases of captives being bought back by their own families, something usually not publicized through inscriptions. The more probable view is therefore that the 'domestic' branch of the market was both substantial and the pirates' favourite. One class of captives, of course, more often remained outside than inside that branch: persons already possessing the status of slaves. The redistribution of these to new owners constituted a relatively larger part in the overall contribution of piracy to the slave-trade (Finley 1962: 57–8; de Souza 1999: 64–5). If, for some reason, the pirate proved unable to ransom his hostages, he turned them over to the professional dealers who also helped armies move their captives.

   Nevertheless, auctioning captives in the slave market and obtaining ransom for their release were transactions situated very closely within one and the same spectrum of economic activity, often so closely that they became tangled. No one would therefore have been able to quantify even approximately the pirate's share in the slave-trade. Strabo's '10,000 slaves a day' for post-145 Delos is no more than a shorthand for 'exceptionally many'; nor does it offer a clue about how many of these were bought back by their own and how many went on to join the existing hordes of forced labour.

4 The Naval Protector

Alongside piracy, another time-honoured tradition was inherited by the Hellenistic world: the obligation (purportedly a moral one) of the hegemonic power currently enjoying maritime supremacy (*thalassocracy*) to fight, and preferably to suppress, that perennial evil. Whoever wielded power was expected to offer protection. A long succession of these eminent 'policemen of the seas' is paraded in our record. King Minos, archaic Corinth and classical Athens number among the early representatives; the task was taken over by Alexander, then by successors such as Antigonos and Demetrios and the Ptolemies; in the mid third century it was the turn of the Rhodians, and from 102 it was taken up in earnest by the Romans, who effectively finished the job off when Pompey in 67 annihilated the claimed plague of those times, the so-called Cilician pirates, right at their very base in Korakesion.

The relevance of this vast topic to our own derives from the propensity of modern scholarship to use this 'succession list' as an index of the fluctuations in the volume of piratical activity. Briefly, the assumption is that periods distinguished by the absence or presence of a strong maritime *hegemon* are also periods of flourishing or declining piracy: for instance, Plutarch records the plundering of thirteen sanctuaries and the capture of 400 cities by pirates in the early first century owing to the absence of a power to check their activities (*Pomp.* 24). By the same token, it becomes possible to isolate periods during which the volume of piracy-related slave-trade increased or decreased (Ormerod 1924: chapters. 4, 6; Rostovtzeff 1941: I.195–204, II.607–10 with notes). However, for four main reasons, which can only be touched upon here, all this is too simplistic.

Firstly, piratical contingents were very often incorporated into the fleets of major states, including that of the naval *hegemon*. The archpirate who put his flotilla and brilliant tactical skills at the service of the kings is a common figure in Hellenistic naval operations (Launey 1949: 34–35, 180–95; Ducrey 1968: 178). Ample historiographic coverage is received by a few celebrities: the Phokian Ameinias (hired by Antigonos Gonatas), the Illyrians Agron and Demetrios of Pharos (employed by Demetrios II and Antigonos Doson respectively), their compatriot Skerdilaidas (in the service of Philip V), and the Aitolian Dikaiarchos, who having served Philip V shifted his allegiance to Egypt, where Ptolemaic favour materialized in the grant of a lucrative concession placing him in a key-post within the Egyptian slave market (Westermann 1929: 1–3, 22–5; cf. Launey 1949: 192). But these should not get all of our attention at the expense of their far more numerous, though less well-known, colleagues: for instance, the archpirate Nikandros, who in 190 operated in Antiochos III's fleet, or one Timokles, who served under Demetrios Poliorketes during the siege of Rhodes (Livy 37.11.16; App. *Syr.* 24; Diod. 20.97). The latter's flotilla of three ships was deemed to be the best one among the host of pirates who had joined Demetrios – the sort of profiteers who customarily 'rush together where there are wars and plundering' (Diod. 20.110); interestingly, in addition to these there were some 1000 ships belonging to 'merchants and marketeers', who during the siege operated in exactly the same way as the pirates (Diod. 20.82.4–5, 84.5–6, 97.5). What was in it for both the pirates and the 'merchants', besides the rich loot to be had if Rhodes fell, is indicated by the deal made by Demetrios and the Rhodians: that those of their captives who could pay ransom should be exchanged, a free man going for a thousand, a slave for five hundred drachmas (Diod. 20.84.6); implicit in this agreement is the circumstance that all those who proved unable to pay these amounts were to be sold as slaves. So, frequently, the pirate and the 'policeman of the seas' stood not in opposition to each other but co-operated. That was recognized long ago (Rostovtzeff 1941: I.196, 607–8; Garlan 1978). What has not been sufficiently stressed is that as a consequence the proceeds from piracy, humans and other valuables, went piggyback on, and therefore were indistinguishable from, those of warfare (Heinen 1976–77).

Secondly, the suppression of piracy was generally used by the maritime *hegemon* as a mere pretext for pursuing his own political objectives, that is, first and foremost to legitimize his right to rule and to increase his own power (de Souza 1999: 241–2). To this should be added that when politically or economically opportune he might choose to look the other way. Strabo, for instance, charges the Ptolemies with assisting the Cilician pirates out of hostility to the Seleukids and then, judging carefully what he considers politically correct (or safe), he comes close to saying that the Romans did nothing effective to curb the Cilicians mainly out of economic opportunism: the westward movement, via Delos, of eastern captives coincided with Roman interest in satisfying the increased demand for forced labour, a demand which according to modern scholarship was created by the expanding Italian agriculture (Strabo 15.5.2; Hopkins 1978: chapter 2). A corresponding demand, this time arising east of the Adriatic and satisfied by regular warfare, is evidenced by the counter-flow of huge numbers of Italian captives who had been sold by Hannibal all over Greece after 216; the fate of these captives became a strong Roman concern in 194 and again in 189 (Diod. 28.13; Livy 34.50, 37.60; cf. Hatzfeld 1913). The economic and demographic consequences of warfare are also reflected in numerous other massive movements of human resource both within the territory of Old Greece and Macedonia and between the new Hellenistic monarchies: for example, after his victory over Demetrios at Gaza in 312 Ptolemy brought 8000 captives to Egypt, while his successors maintained a fairly steady supply mainly from Syria and Phoenicia (Diod. 19.85.3; Ducrey 1968: 83–7; Volkmann 1990; Pritchett 1991b: 226–34).

Economic opportunism is in evidence also with minor rulers, not least those of the Black Sea areas. Indeed, their stand is often described in positive terms. Around 240 the Bithynian king Ziaelas reassured the people of Kos that he would guarantee the safety of their seafarers (*RC* 25); Eumelos, king of the Kimmerian Bosporos, is said to have 'cleared the sea of pirates', waging war against the Heniochoi, Tauroi and Achaei, barbarian tribes which regularly plundered those sailing in the region (Diod. 20.25). Yet, the rich flow of high-quality slaves from the Black Sea to the Mediterranean reported by Polybios (4.38) only makes sense in the light of Strabo's later remarks about the piratical activities of the Heniochoi, Zygoi and Achaei: that 'they are sometimes assisted by those who hold power in the Bosporos, the latter supplying them with landings and a market and the means of disposing their loot' (11.2.12). In short, naval powers were prepared to exploit piracy in order to cultivate their own interests. The 'policeman of the seas' was not really interested in the elimination of piracy.

Thirdly, that lack of interest became further assisted by a strong economic incentive inherent in the performance of the naval *hegemon* as a genuine protector, *prostates*. Protection was a marketable commodity in very high demand, which could be purchased by consumers through payments in cash or in kind; tribute is one form of such payments. Politically and psychologically, the terms *phylake* or *asphaleia* which designated that product had come to rank almost as high in value as the word 'freedom'. In the fourth century Athenian naval commanders would sell protection to traders and their cities, sometimes for huge sums of money which were euphemistically known as 'benevolences' and routed through the treasury (Gabrielsen 2001b: 235–6). This practice was later adopted by Athens' Hellenistic successors, in particular by the Rhodians. In 298 Delos paid, probably to Rhodes, at least 5000 drachmas for its 'protection against Tyrrhenian pirates' (*IG* 11.2.148.73). In 220 the imposition by Byzantion of tolls on shipping to and from the Black Sea compelled all the traders to complain to the Rhodians, 'as they regarded them to be the protectors of those using the sea' (Polyb. 4.47). Political issues aside, the traders were surely discontented with having a new item of expenditure (i.e. the tolls) added to an existing one (i.e. protection charges), while the Rhodians, taking prompt action, were keen to show their ability to deliver what they were highly esteemed for. In this line of business a good reputation was essential: by calling a special class of choice-craft in their fleet 'protection ships' the Rhodians advertised both their resolution to perform the role of protector seriously and the high quality of their own product (Gabrielsen 1997: 108–9).

Where the 'policeman of the seas' failed (or demanded exorbitantly high protection prices), the raider himself moved in to grab a part of this market. In the mid third century, for example, the Aitolians made a bid for the Aegean market (e.g. *SIG*[3] 442.5: protection to Chios; cf. Benecke 1934; Scholten 2000). In these and other instances, though, the profit took the form of political advantages rather than of hard currency: renowned raider-states, such as the Aitolians or Cretans, frequently granted potential victim-cities immunity (*asylia*) from violent seizure (Ducrey 1968: 289–311; documents in Rigsby 1996). Others, however, insisted on receiving cash. Early in the third century the Istrians had been paying the Thracian ruler Zoltes and his 'pirates' for abstaining from raiding their city and its territory, first five talents, then 7500 drachmas (*SEG* 24.1095, trans. Austin 98). Towards the end of our period, the Lipari islands were buying exemption from raids by paying the pirates a fixed amount of money every year (Cic. II *Verr.* 3.85). Thus the perennial fear of a violent assault fuelled a thriving field of economic activity, which for most of the time was under the control of the naval protector. Eliminating those producing that fear would inevitably result in his having to shut down his operations in the business of protection, something not only economically undesirable but politically catastrophic.

Fourthly, and finally, the naval protector's systematic and organized pirate chasing, for which the word 'war' (*polemos*) was most often used, was itself a more direct source of profit. In their treaty with the Cretan city of Hierapytna, the Rhodians spell out the obligation of their allies: to participate with all their strength and at their own expense 'when the Rhodians wage war at sea against the pirates or those who provide them with shelter or assistance'. The text goes on to specify that in the division of any profits that might accrue from such campaigns the Rhodians are to receive the largest share (*SIG*[3] 581, trans. Austin 95). Indeed, just as in all other operations of this kind, a 'war' it was and so the terminology of war was appropriately used for the entire haul of the naval 'protector', whether captives (*aichmalotoi*) or generally booty (*laphyron*). Accordingly, the only law applying to the catch, persons as well as valuables, was the old 'universal law', that persons and their property appropriated in war belong to the captor (cf. section 1 above), which in most instances meant that the fate of the pirates themselves *and* of their own captives was decided neither by a court of law nor by humanitarian principles, but simply by the price they could fetch in ransom (e.g. Polyb. 27.14) or in the slave market (Diod. 20.93; Gabrielsen 2001b: 236; *contra*: Ducrey 1968: 191–3). Like the proceeds of any war, these ones too went to the coffers of the 'protector', after of course he had offered part of them as a tithe to a principal deity (e.g. *I.Lindos* 88).

Another interesting case concerns the resolute and solicitous action of the Astypalaians, known from an inscription of the late second or early first century. After they had successfully chased the raiders who had been harassing Ephesos, they brought the captured pirates and their Ephesian victims back to Astypalaia. The pirates they 'punished immediately in a manner worthy of their wickedness'. The rescued Ephesians themselves (citizens only) they treated 'like their own children', providing for their daily needs, while, most commendably, they took care of the upbringing (*agoge*) and education (*paideia*) of all the free children who had been seized. To interpret 'punishment' as capital punishment is to load the word with more legalistic content than it can possibly bear here; and being sold as slaves is a punishment equally worthy of the pirates' 'wickedness'. Again, we should not let the rhetoric of philanthropy – plentiful in this fragmentary document – blur our vision: after one appearance the slaves among the pirates' captives vanish completely; more importantly, one wants to know why the Astypalaians had kept the distressed Ephesians and their children away from their home city for so long. The reality behind all this apparent care may well be that all the slaves were sold, while the Ephesians were allowed to return home only after ransom had been forwarded from Ephesos; that they meanwhile had a pleasant stay in Astypalaia is not refuted by this view (*IG* 12.3. Suppl. 1286).

War against the pirates meant raids on the raiders themselves, which if successful resulted in the seizure of 'booty from booty'. Between the pirate and the slave market stood the biggest fish of all, one representing the pirate's greatest occupational hazard: that is, the fleet of the naval protector. Hence an additional reason for the pirate to prefer a quick ransom deal. From an economic point of view, both the pirate and the 'policeman of the seas' were enmeshed in the same business. Taking a count of the captives shipped to Delos or to any other slave market was not really a difficult task; telling who among these captives had fallen into that plight because of piracy was a different matter.

The upshot of this all is that the yardstick conventionally used to gauge the intensity of piratical activity and, by extension, the fluctuations in the volume of piracy-related slave-trade is deceptive.

5   Who Were the Pirates?

In the preceding sections, 'pirate' and 'piracy' have been used as if they were uncomplicated terms. They are not. Two major advances made in this area by recent scholarship should be noted. One is an increasing acknowledgement of the fact that 'pirate' and 'piracy', or rather their principal Greek equivalents, *leistes* and *leisteia*, were subjective terms, consistently applied, especially from the fourth century onwards, as pejorative labels on enemies and their acts. Endowed with an admirable stereotyping effect, one that quintessentially flagged out 'inhuman' as well as 'illegitimate' behaviour, they offered themselves as convenient tools by means of which a dominant power, often assisted by history writers, sought to construct a specific image of its political opponents – whether rival states, recalcitrant allies, or headstrong insurrectionists. In that sense, 'the difference between warfare and piracy is in the eye of the beholder' (Pritchett 1991b: 317). Inevitably, the same holds true also about the difference between war captives and the pirates' captives.

The other advance is a radical shift in the basic explanatory tenet, that is the answer to the question: what made people resort to acts which our sources describe as piratical? Earlier scholarship's inclination to point at 'personal, destructive disposition' has been abandoned in favour of explanations that stress 'social and political pressures'. Thus, whereas Ormerod spoke of the 'ruffians', Garlan, Brulé and others prefer now to speak of the 'underprivileged classes' and 'politically oppressed people', who were forced by circumstances to resort to unlawful acts with devastating effects. In combination, these new insights portray piracy as an historical phenomenon oscillating between two extremes: the realm of political constructs and that of reality. They therefore render it most urgent to meet two challenges: (a) to establish, at least approximately, the boundary between construct and factual; and, perhaps more importantly, (b) to try to determine what, *in the eye of any beholder*, was the most essential factor which gave the 'booty-seizer' (*leistes*) his unfortunate baggage of 'inhumanity' and 'illegitimacy'.

First, the limits of the construct. Cases of egregious and deliberate terminological abuse can be dealt with very briefly here, even though the record of smear campaigns launched against prominent adversaries is a long one. For Cicero, for example, Mark Antony was a mere bandit (*Fam.* 10.5; 10.6; 12.12). The Lykian ruler Kleon, an associate of Antony and later of Octavian, was branded by Strabo as a pirate leader (12.8.8–9). Caesar, too, sweepingly called all his adversaries during the Civil Wars pirates (*BC.* 3.110). These and numerous other attacks on an enemy's reputation can be comfortably traced back to the fourth century, when the main protagonists in a mutual mud-casting contest were the Athenians and the Macedonian king Philip II (Dem. 10.34; [Dem.] 12.2, 5; 7.14–15). Their malicious character notwithstanding, such charges were part of the time-honoured ritual of political denigration, and indeed the specific terms in which they were made really instanced no ambiguity either for their authors themselves nor for anybody else.

Some measure of ambiguity, however, enters the picture with a different set of instances. Obvious candidates for membership into this class include, firstly, the Spartan king Nabis, whose power-political project is cast by our tradition in terms of his excessive acquisitive drive: he not only filled the Peloponnese with temple robbers, highwaymen and assassins, the profits of whose misdeeds he shared, but he also co-operated with the Cretans 'in acts of piracy' (Polyb. 13.6–8; Livy 34.32.17–20; contrast Cartledge and Spawforth 1989: chapter 5). Secondly, there were army leaders such as the Aitolians Dorimachos and Skopas, whose land- and seaward operations in the Peloponnese during the latter part of the third century are said to have been motivated by their insatiable appetite for booty; Polybios held Dorimachos to be the embodiment of the 'violent and greedy disposition of the Aitolians' (4.3.5). A third candidate would be the coalition of Cretan cities which fought against Rhodes and its allies in the so-called First Cretan War, a conflict purportedly caused by acts of Cretan piracy (Diod. 27.3; for inscriptions referring to seaborne raids during the war: Brulé 1978: 29–56; Baker 1991).

   This ambiguity is at its most pronounced in the long and predatory career of the Cilicians. Even in the rather sensationalist reports of Appian, Dio and Plutarch, it is inextricably linked to specific power-political conflicts. The emergence of Cilician piracy is traditionally associated with the unsuccessful revolt of the Seleukid military officer Diodotos Tryphon from his power-base in western Rough Cilicia in the mid second century (Strabo 14.5.2). Then, after Tryphon's death various local pretenders, variably called tyrants, generals, archpirates or kings, attempted to carve out for themselves small principalities in Syria and Cilicia (App. *Mith.* 92, 117; cf. Strabo 14.5.7; Memnon *FGrH* 434 F1.53; Cic. II *Verr.* 5.77); it is especially during these upheavals that the Cilician slave-trade at Side and Delos is said to have flourished. A different kind of conflict, one commonly seen as signalling the peak of Cilician piracy as a menace in the eastern Mediterranean, broke out in 88. That year marked the beginning of the Pontic king Mithradates VI's fierce and protracted wars against Roman rule, during which the king allegedly received massive assistance from entire pirate navies (App. *Mith.* 62–3, 92, 119; but cf. de Souza 1999: 125–8). Another major conflict was the very last and most effective of a series of Roman attempts to suppress political unrest in Southern Anatolia – Pompey's campaign of 67 – which resulted in the elimination of Cilician piracy.

   Where construct ends and reality begins is problematic. Ambiguity is not least manifest in the prevailing modern opinion that, although all these and several other 'pirates' were the creation of their political enemies, they did indeed deserve their reputation (cf. de Souza 1999: 75 on the Aitolians). Or in the recent, and still unorthodox, view that the 'Cilician pirates' were actually not pirates at all (Avidov 1997; *contra* Rauh 1998). What creates that ambiguity, however, is simply the circumstance that these examples concern states or their leading representatives, who pursued political objectives which strongly challenged the existing hegemonial order, through large-scale use of unconventional (i.e. predatory) tactics, and/or with war-chests so poorly fed by conventional fiscal devices as to make 'booty-seizure' (*leisteia*) a principal mode of financing their operations. It is particularly the latter that blurred even more the thin line separating the application of violence as a means of enrichment ('booty-seizure') from its application as a means of securing or promoting 'national'-political interests (warfare proper). Thus the pinning of 'piracy' and related labels onto this kind of performance was not entirely subjective, though claims that such a performance exclusively distinguished *some* belligerents certainly were subjective. From this point on, however, all else is unequivocally outside the realm of construct. Essential in an appraisal of the prime factors that produced the 'genuine' predator is recognition of two diametrically opposed views held by states on what constituted legitimate organized violence.

   One of these views surfaces in the evidence for the activities of Eumaridas, a Cretan resident in Athens. Besides having mediated the ransoming of captives taken to Crete by Boukris (section 3 above), Eumaridas also proved useful to his host country in another way. As a member of an Athenian embassy to Crete, he used his persuasive skills and personal connections there to obtain a positive response to an Athenian request. The Cretans' cities customarily granted to those sailing into their harbours and to their own citizens 'the right of violent seizure'. Eumaridas, therefore, asked these cities to revoke that grant (*SIG*[3] 535; on the meaning of *hoi katapleousi*, Bravo 1980: 824–7, against Brulé 1978: 16–23). A positive answer to a similar petition by Athens, one dating from the early second century, is preserved in a fragmentary inscription, which announces the decision of an unknown Cretan city to exempt the Attic territory from its grant of 'the right of violent seizure' (*IG*2[2] 1130). Likewise, Cretan Lattos favoured Teos with a similar exemption (*I.Cret.* 1: 111, no. 2.24–31). So Eumaridas and his co-ambassadors did not ask the Cretan cities to remove entirely that custom but only to ban its use against Athenian targets.

Another people wholeheartedly subscribing to that custom were the Aitolians. Indeed, they are said to have held so firmly onto it that in 198/7 a general petition to remove it was sternly met with the reply that they 'would rather remove Aitolia from Aitolia than that custom'. Polybios presents the Aitolians' custom in the garb of a quasi-technical expression, 'to take booty from booty' (*agein laphyron apo laphyrou*). Then he has one of their most fierce enemies, the Macedonian king Philip V, explain its precise meaning to the Roman commander Flamininus by giving what to all intents and purposes is an unabashedly distorted interpretation of a practice well-known to all: namely, the issuing by certain states of a general permission to their citizens and others to plunder practically everyone, including the plunderer himself (18.4–5; Gabrielsen 2001b: 227 n. 37). Here it is crucial to differentiate between three types of publicly issued permits for violent seizure: (a) those not limited to a particular occasion or target, of which the 'custom' of the Cretans and the Aitolians mentioned above are examples; (b) those issued by warring states against their enemy during a particular armed conflict (Polyb. 4.36.6: 'The Spartans declared the right of seizure against the Achaians'); and (c) the proclamations of reprisals (*syle, rhysia*), carried out, at any time, by a community or individuals against another community or some of its citizens with a view to exacting retribution for wrongs allegedly perpetrated by the target (Polyb. 4.53.2: 'The Knossians proclaimed reprisals against the Rhodians'; *pace* Ducrey 1968: 181–2, 'unspecified seizure' and 'reprisals' are clearly distinguished in e.g. *IG* 9.1[2] 1, 179.20–1).

What put the first of these into a class of its own were its unlimited field of application in both space and time and, most significantly, its being regarded as strictly illegitimate by a number of states. Matters were greatly complicated, however, by the fact that almost all states recognized the legitimacy of the other two types, even though they abhorred the effects. As in practice all three types were largely indistinguishable, it was therefore fairly easy for the practitioners of type (a) to claim that they were actually effectuating type (c). Booty-seizure of the 'non-licit' kind could thus become embellished with a legitimate cause. Symptomatic of this was the tendency of states authorizing 'unlimited' illegitimate seizure to make grants of 'immunity from reprisals' to potential victims and so imply that they were abstaining from something that was perfectly licit. On the issue of what constituted legitimate violence political communities had entrenched themselves into either one of two opposing camps; and this, in turn, created plenty of scope for a Manichean world-view (Brulé 1978: 46; Davies 1984: 286).

It is true that definite steps towards a tolerable mode of coexistence were taken. The Aitolians issued *ad hoc* exemptions from their custom by declaring 'the right of violent seizure' to be inapplicable to the citizens of a certain city, for instance to Athenians or Mytilenians (*SV* III.470.10; *IG* IX 1² 1, 189.1–6), or to a particular group of professionals, such as the artists of Dionysos (*SIG*³ 399, 507), or, finally, on a specific occasion such as the Pythian Festival (*SIG*³ 483.15–16). Such exemptions were also made by other states and all did so for exactly the same reason: to win political advantages. Akin to these are two other kinds of *ad hoc* convention, both of which add to the evidence showing that the danger of losing one's freedom was real and immense. One consisted of bilateral agreements by which the signatories bound themselves to abstain from *seizing* each other's citizens, as was agreed, for instance, between Delphi and Achaian Pellana and between Miletos and Phaistos (Haussoullier 1917; *Milet* I.3, no. 140c.55–9). The other consisted of pledges exchanged by cities to the effect that they would not knowingly *purchase* each other's citizens (and sometimes slaves too), when these were offered for sale (e.g. *SV* III.482, trans. Austin 89). All such steps did help to establish inter-communal relations through their propensity to create, or at least demonstrate, political goodwill. Nonetheless, the richer they grew in number and variety the more they underscored the insistence of some states on regarding as an exceptional concession precisely what others held to be a universally valid convention. In the Hellenistic period the gap separating these two kinds of states had become unbridgeable.

Just how unbridgeable is illustrated by an incident involving still another people who recognized the legitimacy of private plunder: the Illyrians. In 230 the Illyrian Queen Teuta received a formal Roman complaint about the persistent seaborne raids of her subjects against Italian shipping. Her reply is reported by Polybios as follows: 'so far as concerned private activities it was not customary for Illyrian rulers to preclude their subjects from augmenting their fortunes at sea', a response so outrageously unacceptable (and insulting) to the Romans that they reacted immediately with a declaration of war, the First Illyrian War (2.8.8; Derow, this volume, section 1). Obviously, the vast cultural distance between the two communities on this point made mutual forbearance impossible. But Teuta's response brings also to the fore another important feature distinguishing the official authorizations of privately-conducted plunder: their predominantly economic rationale. Hence they signalled the continuing adherence, by both grantor and grantee, to the very old notion that organized violence was a perfectly acceptable mode of acquisition (Hom. *Od.* 14.222–34, 17.424–33, section 1 above); and, as a corollary of this, that private enrichment constituted just as legitimate a cause for the use of violence as did the furtherance of community-wide interests. Maurice Holleaux characterized Illyrian piracy as 'a public institution, a state industry' (in Ducrey 1968: 180). Actually, the reverse was the case. For what clashed with Roman – and for that matter also with dominant Greek – perceptions was Queen Teuta's total lack of interest in claiming the 'industry of plunder' as the exclusive prerogative of the state, one restricted to the public arena and rigorously guarded through governmental controls. Plunder as such was not objected to by anyone. Therefore it cannot have been the existence of disparate moral notions about its practice that situated states into diametrically opposed camps – and fuelled the Manichean world-view. Vehement condemnations of the 'inhumanity' of the predator are indeed abundant in our record. Yet besides often turning out to be blatantly hypocritical, these too availed themselves of distinctions – moral or otherwise – whose validity depended on 'the eye of the beholder'.

So too did the three major components of a long-term trend observable from Thucydides (1.5) to Plutarch (*Ant.* 29). The trend itself is quite simply that predatory activity increasingly attains ethnic specificity, and to such a degree as to create a widely-used classificatory system that proved as resilient to change as it was overly simplistic. The first and most conspicuous of its components is reflected in the fact that the 'succession list' of maritime protectors mentioned in section 4 above is matched by a similar list of 'rogue states' or 'rogue peoples', all of which had won renown for their addiction to predatory activity: most notably (and in crude chronological order), the Karians, Ozolian Lokrians, Akarnanians, Tyrrhenians, Illyrians, Aitolians, Cretans, Pamphylians and Cilicians. The second component consists of the virtual correspondence which our sources claim existed between these 'rogue states' and the inhabitants of areas commonly branded with the stigma of cultural and political backwardness. The third one is that the very primitiveness of these peoples is said to have a direct cause–effect relationship with their 'addiction' (cf. Thuc. 1.5, on Asia Minor and western Greece; for Polybios on the Aitolians and Cretans, Davies 1984: 290).

The classification is, therefore, expressed in terms of ethnicity or civilization, but underlying this there is a much more fundamental difference which, *in the eye of any beholder*, situated political communities in two diametrically opposed camps. That difference lay in their respective socio-political structures and comes to the surface in the way each of them chose to answer the crucial question: who has a legitimate right to exercise violence? In certain states, organized violence had become the absolute monopoly of the central political authority, which accordingly had taken all such activity under its purview, legally restricted its usage to the pursuit of 'national' objectives and claimed for itself the exclusive right to any material proceeds (*laphyron*, *leia*) that might accrue therefrom: for these there was only one legitimate 'booty-seizurer' – the state – and one field furnishing a justifiable cause for performing that role – that of the political. Within such a system no room was allowed for either the private entrepreneur or his main motive, economic gain. Both were therefore expelled from the area of the legitimate chiefly because their very existence was irreconcilable with the monopolistic claim to power by the central political authority. Heading the list of states adhering to this organization are of course the entire group of naval protectors and particularly the major Hellenistic monarchies: total personal command over vast and highly effective military machines ceaselessly kept busy in warfare was the life-line of the Hellenistic kings, constitutionally as well as economically (Austin 1986).

By contrast, the central political authority of the Illyrians, the Aitolians, the Cretan city-states and other communities was willing to share the right to exercise violence with the private entrepreneur, whether a native citizen or a foreigner in need of an operational base in which his trade remained legally undisputed. Ultimately, therefore, it was neither political oppression nor poverty that created the predator. Indeed, historically he had been there all along and continued to enjoy a thriving existence. What did mark a significant turning point, however, was the emergence of the non-legitimate variant ('pirate', 'brigand') right after the adoption of monopolistic violence systems by states which eventually proved successful (because powerful enough) at usurping the concept of 'legitimacy'. Moral castigation and political marginalization of their competitor was only a natural sequel. Still, from the perspective of all those unfortunate enough to have forfeited their freedom, such distinctions might have seemed largely immaterial: it would have brought little comfort to captives waiting to be ransomed or sold as slaves to know that the 'man-hunter' in to whose hands they had fallen was of the licit rather than of the illicit variety.

FURTHER READING

An updated, chronologically organized and lucid account of ancient piracy that challenges previous views on several points is de Souza 1999. Its predecessor, Ormerod 1924, often employs comparative material to present some interesting views and can still be consulted with profit. A good many of the sources for Hellenistic piracy are cited in the notes of Rostovtzeff 1941 III (cf. index s.v.), which assesses the general impact of piracy on the Hellenistic world. Much fuller is the catalogue of sources on piracy and raids, including raids in reprisal, in Pritchett 1991b: 312–63. Several works cover particular areas: Dell 1967 (Illyria), Benecke 1934 (Aitolia), Avidov 1997 and Rauh 1998 (diverging views on the Cilicians); Brulé 1978 (Crete) stands out as a well-documented study demonstrating attentiveness to the need to see piracy within a broader historical perspective. Fruitful and insightful analyses of the social and economic ramifications of the phenomenon at large are offered by Garlan 1978, 1989, esp. chapter 8, and Davies 1984. Bravo 1980, even though less easily accessible, contains interesting interpretations, of which those relating to the Greek vocabulary for the violent seizure of persons and goods have been contested, cf. Pritchett 1991b: 68–152. On the Black Sea slave trade: Finley 1962, with M. Crawford 1977 for post-163 trends; also Braund and Tsetskhladze 1989. On the important subject of brigandage, not treated in this chapter, cf. Robert 1937: 90–110 and Briant 1976. On Hellenistic warfare Launey 1949–50 is fundamental. Rich in material on captives (from war and piracy), slavery and ransom are Volkmann 1990 (updated edn of 1961 original) and Pritchett 1991b: 203–312. But good treatments of these topics within their historical setting are offered by Ducrey 1968 (still the best starting point for future studies), Heinen 1976–77 and Hopkins 1978.

PART VI

Gods and Men

CHAPTER TWENTY-FOUR

Hellenistic Religion

David Potter

1   Religion

In thinking about the subject of 'Hellenistic' religion two problems are immediately obvious, the first being the parameters allowed to the concept of religion, the second being whether or not the adjective makes any sense in conjunction with the noun. In the first case, I will argue that the subject must be permitted to encompass a very broad range of human behaviours conditioned by the belief that powerful divinities controlled every feature of human existence from the moment of conception to the moment of death and beyond. These behaviours include, but are not restricted to, the actions associated with the formal worship of the gods. In recent years important work on other religious systems has called into question the distinction that has often been employed since the Reformation to distinguish between 'true' and 'false' worship, or between 'religion' and 'magic'. The thrust of this work has been to show that forms of behaviour that have been relegated to the category of 'magic' are better seen as alternative forms of religious behaviour. I think that this view is the correct one, and I have argued elsewhere that a distinction may usefully be drawn between 'active' and 'passive' forms of religious behaviour (Potter 1994). By 'active' I mean behaviours that seek new knowledge of the divine world, or to control divine action. By 'passive' I mean behaviours sanctioned by tradition that seek to describe the relationship between the mortals and divinities. These actions are 'passive' because they imply an acceptance of existing guidelines. The two modes of religious behaviour are complementary as discoveries made through 'active' investigation serve to reform, reshape and update traditional behaviours, enabling a religious system to progress as the culture that supports it progresses. So crucial is the interaction between 'active' and 'passive' behaviours that ways of seeking new information were an integral part of sacrifice, the central act of Greek cult. The gods were thought to have decreed the form of sacrifice, were invited to participate in the sacrificial meal, and to indicate their approval or disapproval of the person offering the sacrifice.

The question whether or not the adjective 'Hellenistic' can properly be transferred from the context of political history to that of religion has recently become problematic. Important work on the cult system of Athens in particular has drawn attention to large areas of continuity, making it hard to isolate elements of religious behaviour that are genuinely new in this period (Mikalson 1998: 315–23; Parker 1996: 256). This is quite correct, but, as I will suggest, concentration on civic cult in the traditional Greek homeland tells only one part of the story. The central questions facing the study of Hellenistic religion must then be linked with the broader evolution of societies between the death of Alexander and the rise of both the Roman and Parthian states. One of these must be whether or not the changed horizons of the Greek world altered the way that people saw their relationship with the divine, or whether what appears perhaps most strikingly new (the use of cultic formulae to honour living people) can be linked primarily or solely to behaviours that were already current within the pre-existing *polis* structure. A second question is whether the emergence of supra-regional Greek states effected the practice of cult in the individual cities of the Aegean homeland in other ways, and, if so, to what degree? Finally, there is the question of the relationship between the *polis* religion of the Greek Aegean and the religious systems of the Near East. Should the redefinition of the relationship between the Mesopotamian world and Mediterranean world that is characteristic of the political history of this period be reasonably allowed some role in conditioning attitudes towards the divine? Perhaps the most significant feature of this period is the interaction between points of continuity and areas where new forms of conduct evolved, or, to return to my earlier point, the interaction between 'active' and 'passive' aspects of religion that resulted from the transformation of the power structure of the vastly expanded Greek world.

2   Continuity

The main form of political organization among the Greeks at the end of the period under consideration was, as it had been for the previous four hundred years, the *polis*. Within the *polis* the basic structures of religious organization and theory remained largely unchanged: prices at which priesthoods were sold might vary, but priesthoods were still sold to the highest bidder in the majority of Greek cities. Priests still served male divinities, and priestesses were usually charged with the oversight of female divinities. Where this division by gender was not observed it was usually a sign that the cult in question was of non-Greek origin. With regard to the cults celebrated in each *polis*, the issue of ritual purity was of the foremost importance. Only a person who was *hagnos* (pure) could approach the gods.

The requirement that a person be ritually pure in order to address the divinities is significant in a number of ways (Parker 1983: 144–50). On a very basic level, it helps explain the emphasis on physical action in laws governing cult activity, including the terms under which a person who was not *hagnos* could become so. Thus in a law concerning who might make a sacrifice from the city of Metropolis in Ionia it is stated that: 'He will be *hagnos* twelve days after the death of a kinsman, two days after having had sex with his wife, three days after having had sex with a prostitute' (*LSAM 29*). In a law from Maionia, datable to 147–6 BC, it is stated that: 'he will be *hagnos* on the fifth day after the death of a kinsman of his own blood, of another on the third day, after sex with his wife he may enter on the same day having been cleansed in the designated place in the Metroon; after sex with a prostitute he may be cleansed in the same way on the third day' (*LSAM* 18, cf. 12 from Pergamon). The terms of these laws, which are ubiquitous from the end of the sixth century BC well into the years of Roman domination, reflect a fundamental division between the human and divine spheres. The ease with which everyday acts of purification can be performed reflects a sense that fundamental aspects of the human life cycle result in pollution (*miasma*). This in turn reflects a view that the world is an essential source of corruption, while the realm of the gods is seen as being pure. If one wished to contact the gods in their *hieron*, the earthly sanctuary that was devoted to their use and thus infused with the awe that one should feel when approaching the divine, one had to attempt to remove impurity from oneself. To do otherwise would be to injure the gods. If the gods were injured, they would take vengeance upon the mortal who offended them (Parker 1983: 145–6). That person would become 'accursed' – *enages*. The negative defin-ition of persons who were not *hagnos* reflects a sense of the human propensity to fall away from the condition in which they might rightfully contact the gods. It may also be connected with the Greek sense of the gods as anthropomorphic being – as the bodies of the gods were pure, the bodies of humans were not, a reflection of the 'necessary tension between the darkness in which the visible human body is steeped and the radiant light with which the god's body shines' (Vernant 1991: 49).

While the Greeks often used myth to explain why a god was worshipped, the governing body of each cult made the rules for their own cult. Myths might be invented, remembered or adapted to explain why a cult worked in a certain way but there was no direct link between the universalizing texts of the archaic period such as Hesiod's *Theogony* and *Works and Days*, or the Homeric cycle, and individual Greek cults. Indeed, the practice may be seen as being akin to the terms of the laws quoted above: while they all agree that sex or contact with death brings pollution they all differ somewhat in describing the way that the pollution needed to be removed. These differences did not occur on a simple *polis*-to-*polis* basis, but within a *polis* on a cult-by-cult basis. Thus a law from Pergamon (albeit of the third century AD, but using language that is fundamentally the same as the texts just quoted) states that a man who wished to sleep in the temple of the god Asklepios had to abstain from sex with his wife for ten days (*LSAM* 14.1–2). It may be that as sleeping in the temple involved closer contact with the god, so the level of purification had to be greater.

Pollution was not ordinarily, in and of itself, seen as a moral fault. The closest that Greek thought came to a sense that moral turpitude should keep a person from approaching the god appears in some texts that state that a person must approach with a pure mind as well as a pure body, but this too leaves it up to the individual to ensure that he or she is doing the right thing (Chaniotis 1997b). It is only a crime if one does not, and the category of crime is separate from that of simple pollution. The same law from Pergamon includes a second category of persons 'who wish to be freed from a crime (*ponos*)' (*LSAM* 14.3–4; cf. *SEG* 9.347). *Miasma* that arose from physical acts of violence was entirely a different matter, though again it is linked with the notion of touching something that was impure. In the case of murder, the blood of the victim was thought to cling to the hand of the murderer, who had to be excluded from all contact with society. The presence of such a person in a city threatened all who lived there as it was thought that the spirit of the victim or of avenging deities could affect all who came into contact with the killer (Parker 1983:

104–6; 126–30). In the end, of course, the gods would exact their revenge, but it was best if humans could speed the process up. The notion that divine revenge could affect a large number of people was deeply imbued in the Greek consciousness, for no person could be innocent if that person did not take a proactive role in stamping out pollution. So too did the notion that the gods were ultimately involved in avenging crimes. A human could evade civic justice systems if he or she sought protection from a god, the situation envisioned in clauses of sacred laws such as that from Pergamon. A criminal could approach the God as a suppliant, *hiketes*, and obtain purification for his or her crime. The temples of the gods were places where the agents of human justice could not penetrate, all of them having some area surrounding the altar that had *asylia*, or sanctuary. The *hiketes* remained within the temple until he or she received the desired purification.

The connection between city and divinity was demonstrated by civic efforts to eliminate sources of pollution, and, in a more positive way, by annual festivals to the gods, and the dedication of things that were precious to a divinity, making the temple a reserve treasury for the city, as befitted the house of a wealthy resident. Most crucially, the link between the god and the civic order was represented by the fact that a priest or priestess of a divinity was a civic official. Priesthoods served to link secular society to the shrines of the gods within the city. As we have seen, the land that was attached to a shrine belonged to the god. The priest or priestess did not; they were holders of positions that, in the case of civic cults, belonged to the city. As a city's representative to a shrine, a priest or priestess was obviously an important person, but they were not 'religious leaders' in anything like the modern sense of the word: they did not propound doctrines about the gods as a result of their holding office, they did not 'preach the gospel' of their god, and they did not set the rules of engagement between the community and the divinity. They were there to make sure that the rules were enforced and to manage the bureaucratic aspects of the cult: somebody had to organize annual festivals, make sure the shrine was in good order and so forth. The rewards for this service could include civic benefits such as front seats at the theatre, the right to wear special clothes, free lunch, and a fee for each sacrifice that could be paid in money, meat or other animal parts (*LSAM* 12.14; 24). A text from around the end of the fourth century from Miletos offers a good idea of just what was involved:

> He will take the skins and the other prerequisites; if one animal is sacrificed he will take the tongue, the loin with meat on it and the *óré*; if more than one animal is sacrificed, he will take a loin with meat on it from each animal, the tongue and one thigh bone with flesh on it from the lot, and the priest who serves all of the other gods in the *temenos* will take the same prerequisites and the thigh with meat on it in place of the *óré* if the *basileus* should not take it; if the *polis* should sacrifice a victim whose skin is singed, he will take the tongue, the loin with meat on it, and the *óré*. If some foreigner should wish to make a sacrifice to Apollo, whichever citizen the foreigner should choose will give all of the prerequisites which the city would give except for the skin; if any foreigner should wish to make a sacrifice at the Apollonia . . . (*LSAM* 46)

Aside from the fact that no one is quite sure now what is meant by the *óré*, the organization here is reasonably straightforward. First and foremost it is clear that the animals sacrificed in this cult are large, and that the god shared space in his precinct (the *temenos*) with other gods who had a single priest to look after their affairs. This priest had a claim to meat if multiple offerings were made to the principal divinity, perhaps a recognition that he could expect less business and thus needed to share in that of the chief god to make his priesthood worthwhile. It appears that another priest, the *basileus*, also had some claim to the animals (the reason why is obscure). Direct approach to the god here seems to have been limited to citizens, a feature that is not without parallel in the case of important cults elsewhere (*SIG*³ 548.10). The multiple claims to parts of a sacrificial animal suggest that this was indeed seen as a significant benefit of office. In other texts it appears that the priest was not expected to be present every time that a sacrifice was made and that the sacrificer was supposed to leave the appropriate portion of the animal on a table where the priest could collect it. Another text from Miletos suggests that people were not always as scrupulous in the observance of this rule as they might be: a person who had failed to leave the portion of the offering due to the priestess of Artemis would be enrolled amongst the civic debtors and banned from participation in public life until appropriate recompense was made (*LSAM* 45).

Perhaps the most significant feature of the Miletos text is the fact that the penalties are civil. The city debt collector is the person who will collect from the defaulter; it is the civic authority that bans the defaulting sacrificer from public affairs. The sacrificer incurred no stain of *miasma* for the failure to pay the priest. This is the clearest possible indication that an offence against the person or income of a priest was not a *de facto* religious offence. The god had nothing to do with the choice of the priest/priestess. Increasingly, priesthoods were sold to the highest bidder, and the sums realized by the *polis* for the sale of multiple priesthoods could be substantial, leading, in some cases, to a secondary market in priesthoods as a person who had purchased a priesthood for life might transfer it to another (for a fee). A fascinating text from Erythrai, dating to the first part of the third century BC, gives a list of priests (always listed with an *egguétēs* or guarantor), annual prices for priesthoods, and sales on the secondary market, which included a transfer tax to the city (*LSAM* 25). If a human could not be found to hold a priesthood, it was possible through a legal fiction to transfer the priesthood to the god or goddess herself. Under these circumstances it appears that the money spent by the god to hold the priesthood was treated as a loan from the god's treasury to the city, which would have to be repaid.

A vast conceptual space separated the practices connected with ritual impurity, which assumed an extraordinarily activist posture by the divinity, and the priesthood that served to manage the civic affairs of a divinity. The mundane affairs of priests should not obscure the fact that the temple was still sacred, *hieros*, and the belief that the divinity could be physically present in the shrine. A shrine was both a civic monument, celebrating the *polis*' association with the divinity, and a direct link with the divine plane. The negotiation of the space between the human and divine was not something that could be left to priests. This space was filled instead by a wide range of professionals whose speciality was either sacred law or direct communication with the divinity.

As agents of passive religion, Greek priests were not empowered to decide either what gods were to be worshipped in a *polis* context, or how they were to be worshipped. Their positions depended on decisions taken elsewhere. It was a god or goddess who decided to reside in a *hieron*, and it was a divinity who told humans how the cult should work. The perceived role of the gods in this way is so central to Greek religion that, while it is possible to rationalize all of this into a series of human decisions, it would be wrong to do so. As we have seen, the fundamental world-view that informed the structure of *polis* cult assumed that the gods were different from mortals. While humans might question the validity of individual cult practices within a *polis*, there were very few, if any, genuine agnostics in the Greek world. People knew that the gods were in contact with them because the gods spoke to them, and told them how they were to be worshipped. A text that has recently come to light from Kallatis contains a list of gods who are worshipped in the city and a collection of Delphic oracles listing gods who ought to be celebrated (*SEG* 45.911–13). It was also typical for an oracle establishing a new cult to decree who should participate, what should be sacrificed and how. In the light of the content of these oracles, it is likely, though this cannot be proved on the basis of the texts themselves, that the portions of sacred laws that are connected with ritual purity and participation go back to an oracle that had approved their content. If an oracle was not involved in the establishment of a cult, it was typical for there to be some other form of direct divine action. Thus the *Sotereia* that was instituted at Delphi after the repulse of the Gauls in 278 is explicitly connected with the epiphany of the god during the battle, and the new festival of Artemis Leukophryene at Magnesia on the Maeander is said to have been the result of an epiphany of the goddess (*I.Magn.* 16; Nachtergael 1977: 25, 163–4). So too the cult of Sarapis was reshaped into a 'national' cult under the Ptolemies as the result of a vision of Ptolemy I, and the shrine of Sarapis at Delphi includes a text describing the vision of Sarapis to the founder of that shrine (Nock 1930: 50–4; Fraser 1972: I.267–8; Dunand 1973: 45–66). At Epidauros and other shrines, the miraculous cures of Asklepios proved to all who went to the temple and read the record of the god's mercy what he could do (Edelstein 1945). The sudden upsurge in the inscription of these stories in the third century is perhaps a response to the public stress on the manifestation of divine action in other quarters.

In the course of celebrating the gods, the moment of sacrifice was a critical point where the active and passive intersected. The mode of sacrifice, the date upon which it was offered, if offered by the city, and, indeed, the decision by an individual to offer the sacrifice are all elements of passive religion in that they depend upon the existing expectation that contact with the god will be made in a certain way at a certain time. Participation in the sacrifice also varied depending upon who offered it – a civic sacrifice could very well involve the participation of the whole community, which might then share in a banquet. A private sacrifice would plainly involve only those persons whom the sacrificer deemed necessary. The presence of priests was always necessary at a public sacrifice, but not at a private one – a further sign of the priest's role as a representative of the community to the god rather than of the god to the community.

The moment of sacrifice, however, injected an element of the active; for the god was, in theory, invited to participate in the sacrifice, and the sacrificer attached great importance to signs that the god had accepted the sacrifice. The course of the sacrificial ceremony was centred on the decisive moment when the god's presence would be manifest. Thus it began with a procession in which the sacrificial animal was led to the altar, and when it arrived, the participants stood in a circle, washing their hands with lustral water and taking a handful of grain (Burkert 1985: 55–7; Vernant

1991: 290–302). Once the humans were prepared, water was sprinkled on the head of the animal so that it would nod in agreement to its fate. In the case of an animal with hair (we do not know what happened in the case of birds or fish) a lock was then cut from its forehead to be thrown onto the fire that was burning on the altar. The chief sacrificer then uttered a prayer to the god, and those who were also participants threw their handfuls of barley onto the fire. The sacrificer then cut the animal's throat (larger animals were stunned first) and women who accompanied the procession let out a cry (the *ololygē*). The animal was then butchered, with the god's portion being placed on the altar, and the priest's prerequisites left on a table nearby (or placed on the image of the god). Every stage of the operation was watched closely for signs of divine approval: if there was trouble with the sacrificial animal, it was a bad sign; if the fire did not flare up when the god's portion consisting of fat and bones was placed upon it, that was also a bad sign. If some fault appeared within the animal after it was sacrificed, that too was a bad sign. On the other hand, if all went well, the sacrificer could then turn to the further butchery of the animal and the preparation of the feast for those who had participated. The symbolic ordering of events makes the meaning of the ceremony very clear: the god comes first, if the human has succeeded in making positive contact with the god, then the human may participate in a meal that the divinity has agreed to join. If not, it was up to the human to figure out what went wrong, and, quite possibly to do so by asking a god what the problem was with the aid of a professional consultant.

Professional consultants came, broadly speaking, in two varieties: those who specialized in deductive prognostication on the basis of signs, and those who were divinely inspired. In general terms, words for inspired prophets involved compounds of words for speech – *prophetes, thespiodos, chresmologos* – while those for other specialists involved compounds derived from their method of divination: an *oinopolos* sought meaning from the flight of birds, an *astrologos* from the movement of the stars and so forth. The significant exception to this general tendency is the word *mantis*, connected with *mainomai*, to rant or rage. Even in the classical period, the word was used loosely to designate any expert, despite what would appear to be an original derivation from the practice of inspired prophecy: the *mantis* raged because he could not control the god who spoke through him (Burkert 1985: 112–13). In some cases their function appears to have been to suggest sacrifices that would yield accurate results, giving the *mantis* a reasonable claim to have offered material assistance in winning a battle. Others seem to have been less skilled and functioned simply to interpret omens for which they could take no particular credit. Certainly when a city needed advice, standard practice appears to have been to approach an oracle rather than a local specialist. The prophets at oracles were evidently felt to be in closer touch with the divine than others.

The range of professionals was vast, ranging from people who had their own predictive methods, such as interpreting cheeses, to those who were specialists in the wisdom that appeared in books of prophecy that were the professed work of prophets who had lived in the distant past (Potter 1994: 10–11). The practice of these people, ordinarily referred to as *chresmologoi*, was widespread as early as the sixth century, and their impact will be felt later in this chapter when we turn to the question of discourse between Greek and non-Greek modes of religious thought (section 5).

3 *Polis* Cult and *Polis* Dignity

The connection between cult and civic life made it inevitable that a city should attempt to promote its own cults as a form of civic aggrandizement. This was anything but new in the centuries after Alexander, as the history of Delphi or Olympia, Dodona or Delos in the classical period (or before) make abundantly clear. The Athenian use of the cult of Athena in the period of its fifth century empire was more aggressive than anything attempted by the supra-regional kingdoms after Alexander, and for obvious reasons. While the Seleukids could make much of their devotion to Apollo, or the Ptolemies of their links to Herakles and Zeus, they were perforce referring to the generalized Olympian divinity rather than any individual city cult. The one exception to this rule (which may prove the point) is the close association between the Attalids and the cult of Zeus at Pergamon, for, unlike the other Hellenistic monarchies they started from a *polis* base rather than a base provided by the Macedonian people in arms, and they never asserted a desire for control of 'the whole'. The fact that monarchs might patronize *polis* cults as a way of demonstrating their good qualities might have had the collateral effect of encouraging new forms of expression through which cities could assert their own importance through the promotion of their own cults.

The development of the right of asylum is one of these significant changes in civic practice during the Hellenistic period, and while it was by no means universal, it was widespread enough to be seen as a characteristic of the period (Rigsby 1996: 4–6). This change did not involve the abandonment of earlier practices, but rather the addition of a new practice.

It appears that the request for such rights did not emerge directly from temples (whose gods could look after their own interests). Rather it stemmed from a complex of factors, not the least of them being the repulse of the Gauls from Delphi, and the recollection of a tradition of panhellenic success against barbarian foes (Rigsby 1996: 26–7). Prior to the middle of the third century, the only place in the Greek world that had been recognized in historical time as permanently 'sacred and inviolable' was Plataia. The repulse of the Gauls was presented to the world as an event of similar magnitude to the defeat of the Persians, the language with which it was described evoked the events of 480/79 and a suitable miracle was reported (Nachtergael 1977: 1, 21–5; Mitchell, this volume). What is more, and this point while not made directly by anyone would perhaps have been clear to everyone, it was a victory won by Greek *poleis* without the aid of a king.

The temple of Athena Itonia at Koroneia in Boiotia, the federal shrine of the Boiotian league, is the first temple that we know to have been the object of a decree of inviolability. Like Delphi, the shrine had historic significance, but in this case the decree may have been motivated by an actual desire to protect a place that might be threatened in the course of the Chremonidean war that was raging between the Antigonids of Macedon and an alliance of Greek states led by Athens and Sparta (Rigsby 1996: no. 1; Scholten 2000: 70, 75–7). Although this move may be associated with an effort by states in mainland Greece to assert their independence, the sudden reassertion of royal power after the Antigonid victory may have suggested that efforts at civic assertion move into a different context. Assertion of a glorious past, or of miracles on another plain could offer avenues without challenging the power of the kings, now shown to be a fruitless activity. At the same time there seems to have been an increase in the number of cities that were seeking panhellenic status for themselves through the foundation of new games. Requests for the status of 'sacred and inviolable' are often found in the context of these new games – as are requests for other forms of civic embellishment. Thus on an inscription from Lebadeia we find that:

> Kalliklidas the Lokrian from Opous, having gone down to the oracle of Trophonios announced that Lebadeia is to be dedicated to Zeus Basileus and Trophonios, and Akraiphia to Apollo Ptoios, and no one is to wrong these (peoples). They are both to collect sacred funds, for the common good, in every land, and proclaim the holy contest. Whoever repairs the temple of Zeus Basileus will wear the crown. (Rigsby 1996: no. 2, trans. slightly altered)

It would, perhaps, be easy to read this text as a sign that divine cult had become a ritualized farce in the struggle for civic improvement. So too might it be possible to read the decree of the people of Magnesia on the Maeander proclaiming their festival of Artemis Leukophryene as a blatant attempt to gain status on the basis of claims about a divine apparition (Rigsby 1996: no. 66). Likewise, in reading replies such as those of Ptolemy to the people of Kos as a publicity stunt motivated by the desire to be seen to be as reasonable as others; for he states that the fact that others have recognized their festival in honour of Asklepios is a factor in motivating his acceptance (Rigsby 1996: no. 8). But in all these cases there is a consistent pattern. What is needed, first and foremost, is a sign of divine will either in the form of a specific intervention, or, in other cases, because success can be attributed to the longstanding favour of the divinity who is to be celebrated. The crucial point is that a convincing case needed to be presented that the divinity had taken the initiative. Instead of seeing these actions as a sign that local cults had lost their meaning, it is perhaps better to see them as reinforcing the importance of local cults in civic life.

A phenomenon that runs parallel to the search for asylum is the use of 'history' (usually mythological) to negotiate with other states. In this case, of course, there was a long tradition of mythological diplomacy and the creation of fictive kinship in Greek history (Curty 1995; C. Jones 1999b; Erskine 2001; 2002b). But that does not make the phenomenon, which increased dramatically in the centuries after Alexander, any less significant. The stories of gods and heroes provided the ideological glue that held the Greek world together. While not, strictly speaking, religious, neither is this form of discourse, strictly speaking, secular. It represents the close linkage of local cult and local identity. The use of stories about gods and heroes as 'ice-breakers' between two states is very similar to the use of miracle stories to justify claims for 'sacred and inviolable' status. Although in the modern world these accounts may be viewed as 'constructed history', there is no proof that they were conceived of this way in the ancient (C. Jones 1999b: 132–3). In a sense the discourse of miracle and myth contextualized current concerns within a greater world history.

4 Cult for Humans

One aspect of the discourse of myth and miracle was the fact that mortals had become gods in the Greek tradition long before the time of Alexander. So too temples were repositories of items that were of importance to a city. The two traditions are of equal importance in explaining how it was that there was a rapid increase in the number of people who received divine honours after the death of Alexander. This is a phenomenon that, strictly speaking should not be referred to as ruler cult (hence the title for this section). As we shall see, people who were never in a position to claim the title of *basileus* received such honours, and the practice of granting such honours to kings emerges from a context in which individuals of all sorts were acquiring honours in a divine context. The dividing line between the placement of an image of a human being in a temple and celebrating a festival in honour of a person whose image has been erected in a temple is not nearly as vast as the gulf between human and divine. What it reflects is a melding of civic interest and divine location in a new way rather than an altogether new phenomenon.

The crucial point for understanding the development of divine cult for humans is that by the second half of the fourth century it was not unusual for honours that a city had voted to an individual to be inscribed on a stele that was placed within a temple precinct. Thus at some point between 334 and 332 the people of Delphi ordered that a decree for the historian Kallisthenes and the philosopher Aristotle be placed in the temple of Apollo at Delphi (*SIG*³ 275). In 333 the people of Priene ordered that a statue of Mexyboxos the Ephesian be placed in their temple of Athena (*SIG*³ 282). In 334 the people of Erythrai ordered that stele commemorating the actions of their citizen Phanes, who had played a role in expelling the Persians from the city, be placed in the temples of Athena and Herakles, and in 332/1 the Athenians ordered that a stone stele honouring the historian Phanodemos for his service to Amphiareus be placed in the temple itself (*SIG*³ 285, 287). In 328/7 they ordered similar honours for Androkles, the priest of Asklepios, in the temple of the god he had served (*IG* 2² 352). At Samos the citizens of the restored *polis* honoured a certain Gorgo, who had played some role in negotiating the removal of the Athenian colony with Alexander, and inscribed the decree on a stele that was erected in the temple of Hera (*SIG*³ 312). The Athenians had not left peacefully after Alexander's decree, and had arrested a group of Samians that had attempted to return, transporting them to Athens where they were sentenced to death. A man named Antileon, from Chalkis on Euboia, intervened to save them from their fate. In his case the Samians voted that Antileon should receive 'a statue] of bronze in the temple [of Hera' as well as a variety of other honours (Habicht, *MDAI(A)* (1957) no. 1).

The practice of dedicating statues or other images in temples for individuals who had merely spent a great deal of money or time on some temple or other civic matter raised the question of what to do for someone whose ability to act went far beyond that of the ordinary civic benefactor (Nock 1930: 61; Habicht 1970: 163–4)? The fusion of honours in the civic context brings out 'the ease with which an ancient could put what we call human honours and what we should call divine honours on a level without any inevitable mental confusion between the objects of each or the categories to which those objects belonged' (Nock 1930: 51). As we have seen, it was the city that determined what gods should be worshipped and how – the honours were the city's to bestow.

It was on Samos, in the wake of Lysandros' defeat of Athens, that cult honours were first offered to a living man – Lysandros' restoration of Samos went far beyond what any ordinary benefactor could offer, so it may have made sense to honour him in a way that no other man was honoured. So too at Syracuse in 357, there is evidence that an altar was erected in honour of Dion after he had ended the tyranny. There is no need to think that this decision was taken because of what the Samians had done earlier – Lysandros had, after all, come to a bad end – rather it is likely that the Syracusans were independently motivated by the same logic. He had done something extraordinary, and so deserved an extraordinary honour. In Macedonia a cult appears to have been established for Amyntas, possibly in his own lifetime, at Pydna, and the same was almost certainly done for Philip at Amphipolis. Somewhat later, as his armies marched through western Asia Minor, taking advantage of under-prepared Persian defences, Philip received divine honours at Eresos and Ephesos. Philip himself appears to have taken all this one step further when he appeared as the thirteenth god in a procession at Pella on the last day of his life. He was, after all, a benefactor to the Greek world (at least in his eyes, and those of his supporters) unlike any other man, and so he integrated himself into a local form of celebration in his capital. Given the honours for Philip, it is scarcely surprising that Alexander first received cult from the cities of Asia Minor, and then, it appears, promoted suggestions of his own divinity after his visit to Siwa (Habicht 1970: 3–36; Chaniotis, this volume).

Despite the special claims that they may both have had and sought to promote, Philip and Alexander did not remove divine honours from a civic context. Two decrees are of great significance for understanding the spread of divine honours for mortals after the death of Alexander. The first of these decrees concerns a man named Thersippos in the small island *polis* of Nesos, who obtained significant influence with various Macedonian generals after Alexander's death. Here the statement with regard to divine honours is explicit, for the people 'will crown him on three successive days and offer a *euaggelia* and a *sôtéria* and a *panagyris* at public expense' (*OGIS* 4.41–3). The second, known only through a much later honorific decree from Kolophon, refers to a temple called the Prepelaion. The Prepelaion honoured a general of Lysimachos who had arranged for the city to be preserved when the king had desired to transfer its population in its entirety to Ephesos (J. and L. Robert 1989: 77–85).

Cult to benefactors, either as individuals or as a group continued for the next several centuries (Robert 1926: 499–500; S. Price 1984: 47–9). Thus in 117 a decree of the Macedonian city of Letai in honour of a Roman quaestor named Marcus Annius states that the citizens will establish 'a contest involving horse races in his honour each year in the month of Daisios when they celebrate the contests in honour of the other benefactors' (*SIG*[3] 700.38–40). At Athens the ephebes were charged in the late second century with offering 'the established sacrifices to the gods and the benefactors' and the gymnasiarch at Pergamon was ordered to 'make the proper sacrifices to the gods in the gymnasium and to the benefactors' (*IG* 2[2] 1006.15–16; *MDAI*(A) (1910) no. 410.10). The language used in these and other cases reveals that the cult of the benefactors was closely linked with other celebrations of the past. Thus in addition to participating in festivals such as the Dionysia and the Eleusinian mysteries, the Athenian ephebes would appear at sacrifices at the Aianteia on Salamis, make an offering to Zeus Tropaios, offer sacrifice at the public tomb at Marathon, and appear in the procession of Artemis Agrotera, all festivals connected with the Persian wars of the fifth century. Likewise they would go and 'enquire about the proprietary rights of Athens at the Amphiaraion', acquired in 287, as a way of asserting Athenian ownership (Mikalson 1998: 248–9). Benefactors and old battles were part and parcel of the civic tradition.

Similar to the cult of benefactors who were alive was the establishment of hero cults to those who had died. The category of hero or 'demi-god', a category that occupied an area between the mortal and divine realms, was a peculiarly Greek institution. In outward form it involved the creation of a special grave, a *heroon*, that was separated from other graves, the offering of regular sacrifice and votive gifts and, sometimes, a spectacular monument. The rites with which heroes were celebrated were, to some degree, a 'chthonic counterpart' to the rites with which the gods were celebrated – involving blood sacrifice, offerings of food and libations (Burkert 1985: 203–6). Some sites appear to have made provision for bathing and lamentation for the dead hero appears to have been routine. The sacrifice was always accompanied by a banquet at which the hero was thought to be present, and, in some cases, by a festival that was equal to that offered to a god. In other cases the celebration was less spectacular, and the accomplishment that qualified a person for heroic status was allegedly no more than having died – 'why don't you hang yourself and become a hero in Thebes' appears in an Attic comedy and might be best rendered in English as 'drop dead' (Fraser 1977: 78).

One of the crucial aspects of the hero or heroine was that he/she only lived once and thus could only have one true resting place. This led to a significant connection between hero cult and community identity. If all places might have a Zeus, only one place could be the resting-place of Achilles' son, Pyrrhos, whose tomb was at Delphi. The connection between community history and hero cult would appear to go back to the formative period of the practice (probably the eighth century) and it may be no accident that it was connected with the epic cycle as a feature of the archaic reification of tradition. In some cases actual sites were connected with the Mycenean past – the graves of the Hyperborean maidens on Delos are the remains of Mycenean tombs – and it may be that the epic tradition itself helped shape this form of commemoration. As the epic cycle gave shape to Greek notions of their past, hero cult enabled Greeks of later generations to lay claim to a piece of that tradition. Hero cult plainly had a strong political aspect from the sixth century onwards when Athenians laid claim to Salamis on the basis of Homer, and Sparta to a dominant position within the Peloponnese on the basis of the Achaian tradition invented around the bones of Orestes. The strength of these traditions as part of a national myth during the Hellenistic period may be seen, for instance, in the actions of the Athenian ephebes described above, and their visit to a pair of hero shrines – those of Ajax and Amphiareus – in the course of their annual peregrinations and their participation in the Theseia, the festival celebrating the role of Theseus in the foundation of the Attic state. As historical figures, heroes were no more figures of the distant past than were other benefactors, and the tradition of celebrating benefactors as heroes is important as a later development in the cult of benefactors. It was a basic premise of benefactor cult that the benefactor who received the honours was still alive, while it was a basic premise of hero cult that the honorand was deceased.

Benefactor cult, and the extension of benefactor cult to hero cult, may be seen as logical developments of existing *polis* institutions, and extensions that might have taken place even if Philip or Alexander had never lived – cult had, after all, been offered to Lysandros in the wake of his destruction of Athenian power in 404. In a sense it is important to keep benefactor cult within the civic context separate from ruler cult, an extension of benefactor cult that moved in a wholly new direction, and the subject of next chapter of this book. For present purposes, however, it will be sufficient to note that one of the truly interesting features of this phenomenon was the way that it facilitated the redefinition of Greek traditions within native contexts in the realm of the Ptolemies, where it developed. What evolved in Egypt was a combination of elements derived from benefactor cult with indigenous traditions to create a new form of discourse that proved remarkably powerful as a political institution, providing the structures upon which the later Roman imperial cult would evolve. It also offers a paradigm for the differential integration of new religious elements in the Greek world. Contact between Greek and non-Greek resulted in forms of discourse that had multiple meanings depending upon the perspective of the participant in the discourse, and it is to this broader context that we must now turn.

5 Interactions

The interchange between Greek and non-Greek traditions of religious thought is by far the most important feature of the Hellenistic period from the perspective of the broader history of religious thought. As we shall see, there was no one model that fits all forms of contact, and one word will be avoided in the description of any of them. This word is 'syncretism', a word in that, in religious studies, describes the influence of one religion upon another (Colpe 1987: 218–27; L. Martin 1987: 10–11). But the forms of this interaction are so varied as to make the term virtually meaningless – instead of saying that some behaviour is the result of 'syncretistic synthesis' (which should be a tautology) or 'syncretistic evolution' it is perhaps better to be content with terms like synthesis, symbiosis, acculturation, transformation, distortion, absorption. It is perhaps more useful to examine parallelism, interaction and identification, all of which have been identified as different forms of 'syncretism', in their own right rather than as features of something else. In speaking of the evolution of ideas about the gods, it might be better to think of confrontation or theocrasy (a rather useful term to describe the way that cults of very different sorts came to resemble each other). All of these phenomena are amply attested in the record of religious interaction between Greek and non-Greek in the centuries after Alexander.

It is from the very limit of Greek rule in central Asia that some of the most intriguing evidence for synthesis comes. The excavations at Ai Khanoum on the Oxus in modern Afghanistan did not reveal the foundations of a Greek temple before the political crises of recent years forced their termination. But they did reveal the foundations of a Mesopotamian-style temple, 'the temple of the niches' on the main street of the town, containing what appears to be a colossal statue of a seated Zeus along with a variety of other dedications (Liger and de Valence 1984: 125). An inscription that dates to the middle of the second century BC reveals that the gods of the gymnasium were still being worshipped at that point. Inscriptions from the treasury show officials with both Greek and Persian names working side by side in the administration. The coins of the Baktrian kings were replete with images of the gods of the Aegean, and it appears that they claimed a particular affinity to Zeus (Holt 1999: 120–1).

Plutarch claimed that the people of Baktria learned to honour the Greek gods after Alexander, and the evidence cited above may be taken as proving his point, but only on a most superficial level (*Mor.* 328d). Thus the Artemis who was also worshipped at Ai Khanoum, giving her name to the current site, seems to have been 'Lady Moon' in the local dialect. Her cult was assimilated to that of the Mesopotamian Goddess Anahita, and, as the modern tradition suggests, both divinities may have resonated with the worship of a goddess prior to the arrival of the Achaimenids. So too, while 'the temple of the niches' contains the aforementioned statue of Zeus it also contains an image of Kybele, and numerous objects that look back beyond the Achaimenid era to older kingdoms such as Urartu and Assyria. The best explanation of the miscellany that has emerged from the study of objects found in niches (which have no parallel in Mesopotamian architecture) is that they are connected with the worship of a divinity or divinities by the indigenous people (Liger and de Valence 1984: 122–5). The collocation of objects in the temple of the niches, assembled between 280 and 150, is of particular interest as the temple appears to have ceased to function as a temple in the 'late period' of the habitation of the site, the period after the end of direct Greek control. The temple's fate would seem to suggest that it was seen as a building connected in some significant way to the previous regime, which was evidently loathed by the nomadic Yue-tche who sacked the city in 145 (Liger and le Cuyot 1992: 2–3, 289–94). If that is the case, then the temple may well represent not so much the coexistence between Greek and indigenous cults as it did the gradual ascent of an indigenous cult so that it became a cult of the ruling power. This in turn may help confirm what would otherwise seem the obvious conclusion to draw from an altar dedicated, in Greek, at Takht-i Sangin by a man named Atrosokes to Oxus. In this case, of course, we have a man with a Persian name making a dedication to a central Asian god in the language that he had assimilated from the ruling class (Litvinsky and Pichikyan 1981–2: 195–206). The temple in which he made his dedication was, like the temple of the niches at Ai Khanoum, in the Mesopotamian style (Hannestad and Potts 1990: 95). The system was thus neither Greek nor truly that of the original system of the indigenous peoples, but rather a blending of three different systems: Greek, Persian and central Asian.

If, in the later period of the Baktrian kingdom, local cults were becoming significant for the ruling class, it should also be noted that in the earlier period of the kingdom, the flow of influence was set in the opposite direction. The front of the *heroon* of Kineas (probably the city founder) at Ai Khanoum was originally marked by three columns containing the one hundred and fifty or so 'Sayings of the Seven Sages', carefully copied by the peripatetic philosopher Klearchos from Delphi and inscribed at what was the farthest point in the Greek world (Robert 1968a: 416–57; Yailenko 1990: 239–56). About twenty years later, on the borders of the Mauryan kingdom of Asoka, a number of pillars were erected, in a variety of languages, to inform the king's subjects of his personal moral code (Thapar 1997: 271–82). One of these, erected in the tenth year of his reign, was placed in the city of Kandahar, known to the Greek world as Alexandria in Arachosia, inscribed in both Greek and Aramaic. The Greek version reads as follows:

Ten years having passed, king Piodasses (= Asoka) revealed piety to men. Thenceforth he made men more pious and made all things prosper throughout the entire land. The king abstained from [eating] living creatures, and [following his example] other men did likewise, and all who were hunters or fishermen have ceased their work. Those lacking self-control, have, as far as possible, overcome their weakness, and, unlike before, have become obedient to their father, mother, and elders. By doing these things they will live more profitably in the future. (trans. Thapar 1997: 260–1)

The Greek phrasing of this text reveals many close points of contact with the Delphic maxims, and there is direct evidence for Greek philosophers who had visited the court of the Mauryan kings. The Deimachos who negotiated the treaty between Seleukos I and Asoka's father, Bindousara, appears to have been the author of a work *On Piety*, *Peri Eusebeias*, in Greek, but in the text presented here, the word *eusebeia* translates precisely the word *Dhamma* (Strabo 1.10; 2.10; Yailenko 1990: 253). Whether or not Deimachos' work was composed before, during or after his stay in the court of Bindousara does not really matter, for it is clear from other evidence (the request that Bindousara made of Antiochos I for another philosopher) that the ideas that he espoused were, in general terms, of interest (Athen. 14.652–3). Ptolemy II was sufficiently aware of this to make sure that he included a philosopher in the embassy that he sent to the same court. Asoka himself sought to continue the dialogue, on his own account, by sending Brahmins to discuss matters with the Greeks. This may reasonably be taken as an example of constructive discourse between two different modes of thought. But does it mean that Asoka's thought was conditioned or altered in some significant way by the encounter with Greek philosophy? The evidence can be read in two very different ways. According to one reading, the verbal parallels between Asoka's Greek text and the language of the Delphi maxims suggest that there was a very real influence (Yailenko 1990). Another reading, when Asoka's Greek text is read in the context of his other edicts, might suggest something very different – that Asoka had a scribe who was familiar with the seven sages and used the language of that text as a guide to translating Asoka's thought into Greek (Thapar 1997: 279).

   If the second view is accepted (and I think it the more likely) then there is a very interesting parallelism between the Indian and Greek behaviours towards each other. Asoka's interest in Greek philosophy may be seen as a vehicle for communication with his subjects rather than as a profound intellectual engagement. He is using Greek to express Indian thought. At the same time, Greeks may be seen transforming Indian culture into something that was comprehensible to themselves. To the very Klearchos who brought *Delphic Maxims* to Ai Khanoum are attributed two remarks of staggeringly blinkered religious ethnography. According to Diogenes Laertius he declared that the 'Naked sophists' were the descendants of the magi. He also appears to have maintained that all opinions concerning nature could be found to originate 'among philosophers outside of Greece, some amongst the Brahmins of India, others in Syria amongst those who are called the Jews' (D.L. 1.9; Jos. *Ap.* 1.179; Robert 1968a: 447). Indeed, he appears to have argued that the Jews were actually descendants of the Brahmins. Whatever he was actually told, Klearchos plainly only heard it according to his own preconceived notions of the way that knowledge was transmitted from one culture to another. The case of Klearchos' encounter with the wise men of the east may reasonably be compared with the fate of one man who did try to explain an eastern religion, in its own terms, and in Greek.

The man in question is Berossos, who was connected in some way with the cult of Marduk at Babylon, and who composed a history, probably entitled the *Babyloniaka*, to demonstrate the importance of Babylon in the history of the Near East. In this history he plainly drew upon texts in his native language, and he seems to have tried to present this material in a way that conformed to the tastes of his rulers (Kuhrt 1987: 32–56). He failed, quite possibly because his version of Babylonian history and religion (including a talking Fish Man), was so completely at odds with the version of Near Eastern history and religion that the people he was trying to educate already knew. There was no room in the Greek version of the Near East for a Babylon that was distinct from Assyria and Persia. Nor, it seems, was there room for a religious system that did not involve the magi. Berossos' history seems to have attracted relatively little notice until the first century BC when the historian Alexander Polyhistor produced a condensed version of it. After that it seems to have been ignored save by the authors of other specialized tracts on Babylonian history and commentators in Greek on Hebrew scripture (Sterling 1992: 116–17).

As if to complete the act of cultural appropriation, Berossos himself was transformed within the Greek tradition from a real human being to an object of fiction. Vitruvius wrote that Berossos was the first of the Chaldeans who were versed in astrology to come west, and that he settled on Kos (*FGrH* 680 T5). A number of other western authors cite his alleged doctrines with approval and the Elder Pliny even records that there was a statue of him in the gymnasium at Athens with a golden tongue, erected 'because of his divine predictions' (*FGrH* 680 T6). The astrological doctrines associated with his name, however, are all Greek (Kuhrt 1987: 36–48). In another tradition he becomes the father of a sibyl who was said to have lived in the very earliest period of human history.

Appropriation may also result in parallelism, or, at best, a one directional flow of intellectual influence. The Seleukids (like all Greeks) regarded indigenous temples as sacred places. But, with the exception of Seleukos I's patronage of the temple of Marduk at Babylon, they also paid them little heed, preferring to found temples to Greek gods in their new cities and allowing traditional cults to continue without interruption. Two sites in particular reveal possible models of interaction, quite different from each other, albeit contemporaneous. These are Masjid-i Solaiman and Bard-è Néchandeh, both in the southeastern part of Iran that had once comprised the ancient kingdom of Elam and the homeland of the Achaimenids, and would, before the end of the Hellenistic period, house the kingdom of Elymais. Bard-è Néchandeh was constructed in the second century BC by the Elamite king Kamniskires I in the form of a traditional Zoroastrian shrine with three basic elements; a terrace that supported a podium upon which sat an *atestgah*, the high tower that housed, in a chamber at the top, a sacred fire. As the excavator notes, the shrine was constructed as if the Greeks had never been (Ghirshman 1976: 282). Masjid-i Solaiman, by way of contrast, shows some signs of contact with the Greek world. The original shrine, with its terrace–podium–*atestgah* structure dates to the early Achaimenid period, and in this context two votive objects of extreme antiquity have been discovered, one being an Assyrian cylinder containing a treaty between Esarhaddon and the Medes, the other being a casket of Tutmoses III (Ghirshman 1976: 67). In the course of the late third or early second century BC (probably) the terrace was expanded to the north and west to hold two new temples, which have been identified as being to Athena Hippia, the other to Herakles, probably dating to the reign of Antiochos III (Ghirshman 1976: 187–91 but see caveats on the date in Hannestad and Potts 1990: 115; Potts 1999: 371). In neither case did the temple resemble a temple of the Aegean world, in both cases the style of construction resembles that of the Seleukid temple at Uruk, modelled on Mesopotamian structures (Heinrich 1982; Hannestad and Potts 1990: 107). In other words, if these are Greek cults, they are Greek cults in thoroughly non-Greek buildings. The three temples appear to have coexisted throughout the Seleukid period as independent entities – a true parallelism. The lack of local respect for the Greek tradition amongst the indigenous population may be reflected by the fact that the temple of Athena was sacked in the course of the Parthian conquest, and both temples were re-dedicated to Parthian divinities: Anahita and Verethragna (Ghirshman 1976: 282–3).

Aside from the shape of the building in which they were worshipped there is no evidence to suggest that Persian attitudes affected the way that the Greek colonists viewed their gods. On the other hand, when the shrine of Herakles became unquestionably one of Verethragna, his worshippers recognized him in an anthropomorphic form. This was a very real departure from earlier traditions, a sign that temple architecture can only take us so far in determining what people thought about the gods who were worshipped within their walls. It is quite reasonable to think that architecture was more conservative than theology. In the realm of theology, the anthropomorphization of Persian gods may be paralleled by at least one significant development in Zoroastrian thought. This development is the view that history can be described as a succession of kingdoms (initially four) followed by an eschatological catastrophe. This scheme is attested in a thirteenth-century AD Persian manuscript, but in such a way as to make it clear that it had entered Zoroastrian thinking in the early Hellenistic period (Eddy 1961: 10; Boyce 1984: 68). From there it appears to have entered Jewish thought where it is adumbrated most famously in the *Book of Daniel*. In Greek thought the scheme, which has its origins in the Hesiodic myth of ages, became so well established that uses of the pattern were not always eschatological. Dionysios of Halikarnassos exploited the notion as a way of praising Rome in the preface to his *Roman Antiquities*, pointing out that Rome was superior to the four previous kingdoms, and another Augustan historian, Pompeius Trogus, adopted it to give structure to his universal history (J. W. Swain 1940: 16–17; Gabba 1991: 193). In the second century Appian used it in the preface to his collected histories of Rome and of Rome's wars and civil wars in a way that was very similar to Dionysios.

The contact between Greek and Iranian, Indian and central Asian systems of thought thus allowed for a wide range of different results, though, in the main, Greek ideas were adapted to indigenous systems of thought in ways that were largely consistent with their own traditions. And, as far as the Greeks went, it would appear that their habits may have assimilated more in the direction of eastern thought than eastern traditions assimilated themselves to the Greek. Perhaps the most striking example of this was the ultimate conversion of the Greek kings who established themselves in the Indus valley at the end of the second century to Buddhism (Woodcock 1966: 112–4; Sharma 1980). A rather different set of results obtained father west, where *polis* traditions were much stronger, in the case of various divinities that were native to Anatolia, though, even here, earlier ideas about the relationship between mortal and immortal are detectable.

Perhaps as a result of the vast distances involved, and the relatively small number of Greeks, the interactions between peoples in Central Asia and Iran had no significant impact upon the Mediterranean World – it is Asoka who tells us of the missionaries he sent to the kingdoms of the west, no Greek source reports them (Thapar 1997: 255–6; Holt 1999: 53). Indeed, after Seleukos I's vigorous interventions in Central Asia, it would appear that the Seleukid kings lost interest in the area, which may account for the relatively rapid rise of independent states there in the course of the third century BC which may help explain the increasing openness of Greeks to indigenous ideas (Bernard 1994: 509–11). The same cannot be said of developments further to the west.

There were two basic models of interaction between Greek thought and those of Anatolia and Syria: one resulted in the alteration of a local god into a form of a Greek divinity, usually retaining the original identity in the form of a specific cult title, for example Zeus Ampelites; the other was the adaptation of the divinity under its own name into a Greek context (Robert 1983: 523–48). Three cults, those of Kybele, Atartagis and the Jewish god Yahweh, may offer useful insight into the later process. They are, in certain institutional ways, quite similar (if one will allow that there was no parallel to the extensive literature generated by the followers of Yahweh, and that auto-castration was never a part of his cult). All three had a single primary cult centre: Pessinous in Galatia for Kybele, Hierapolis in Syria for Atartagis and Jerusalem for Yahweh. In the cases of Yahweh and Atartagis we know that the temple cults were governed by elaborate rules of procedure before the time of Alexander. Likewise, again in the cases of Yahweh and Atartagis, there was also a pronounced henotheistic element, meaning that the divinity in question was thought to be the 'greatest' by his or her followers. We know somewhat less about the cult of Kybele, but it is clear that, like Atartagis, she was originally a divinity connected with fertility, while Yahweh had affinities with the widespread Aramaic cult of Hadad. What is, however, most significant about all three (although Atartagis was often assimilated to Kybele) is that they resisted ready assimilation to any Olympian divinity. Their followers created communities in Greek cities, made offerings in Greek (in the case of Yahweh's followers they translated their sacred literature into Greek and created a further Greek literature) but they appear to have retained the essential integrity of their practice. As we saw with Asoka, the use of Greek as a vehicle for expression does not mean that the cult was 'hellenized' in the sense that it was transformed by Greek ideas, rather the use of Greek made it possible to communicate with people beyond the homeland more freely.

The cult centres of Atartagis at Hierapolis, of Kybele at Pessinous and of Yahweh at Jerusalem were essentially 'temple-states' in that primary temporal and religious authority resided with a high priest (Debord 1982; Boffo 1985: 18–23). The essential elements of such states are spelled out in a quite detailed fashion by Strabo in his description of another temple-state, that of the goddess Ma:

> In this Anti-Tauros are deep and narrow valleys, in which are situated Komana and the temple of Enyo, whom people there call Ma. It is a considerable city; its inhabitants, however, consist mostly of 'divinely inspired' people and the sacred slaves who live in it.

Its inhabitants are Kataonians, who, though in a general way classified as subjects of the king, are in most respects subject to the priest. The priest is master of the temple, and also of the sacred slaves, who, on my sojourn there, were more than six thousand in number, both men and women together. Also, considerable territory belongs to the temple, and the revenue is enjoyed by the priest. He is second in rank in Cappadocia after the king. (12.2.3)

While the study of temple states may belong more properly to an account of Hellenistic land tenure rather than one of religion, the very existence of such states raises significant issues for the history of religion. Chief among these is the relationship between the priest in the governing temple and votaries outside the immediate territory of the temple state. There appear to have been no hard and fast rules here. We know, for instance, that when a cult image of Kybele was brought to Rome from its original home at Pessinous in 203, an official cult was established that bore no resemblance to practices in Asia Minor. Indeed, the Roman State accommodated two quite different styles of worship for the goddess – the second form being modelled on procedures in Asia Minor. What we do not know is what impact the removal of the goddess had on the celebration of her cult at home. So too it is clear that the many Jewish communities around the Mediterranean and throughout the Near East retained a formal connection with the temple of Yahweh at Jerusalem, as signified, above all else by the annual tax that was paid each year to the High Priest (Schürer 1979: 272–4; Gruen, this volume). Similarly, the priests who proclaimed the glories of Atargatis around the Mediterranean World were, in theory at least, to bring the money they collected for the goddess back to her shrine at Hierapolis.

The tale of eastern divinities could be vastly expanded, and, to be sure, the cults of Isis and Sarapis offer significant parallels to those of Yahweh and Atartagis, especially the cult of Isis where a basic text, the so-called *Aretology of Isis*, was transmitted from the central temple in Egypt (Dunand 1973: 1–4). Like the later translations of Jewish scripture into Greek, the *Aretology of Isis* appears to have retained the sense of the original text, although it appears to have been more open to the influence of Greek thought than were Jewish texts. Indeed, the cult of Isis remained as recognizably an Egyptian cult as the cult of Yahweh remained a recognizably Palestinian one, just as the cult of Hadad, even if celebrated at Delos, remained recognizably Syrian (Mikalson 1998: 233). The fact that each cult adapted differently in the Greek environment is a sign that the degree of adaptation was conditioned by the indigenous worshippers.

The lack of significant evidence for these cults in the Aegean world prior to Alexander's conquests, especially given the significant increase in evidence for these cults in the next century, should not be seen as representing some profound shift in religiosity. Rather it is evidence for a profound shift in political culture resulting from the demise of the Persian Empire. The devotees of Phoenician, Egyptian and Syrian cults were coming into the Aegean if not in greater numbers (this we cannot tell) then at least with greater confidence in the advertisement of their faith. Perhaps too, with the removal of Persian domination, the Greek cities of the Aegean world were not only more interesting, but also more welcoming to outsiders who might no longer be seen as representatives of a power that threatened the life-style of the *polis*. Furthermore, the great stress that Ptolemaic or Seleukid kings laid upon their relationship with Greek cities may have drawn the attention of other peoples, who might previously have been less interested, to those places.

Greek *poleis* had always, of course, had the capacity to welcome new gods. In the years after Alexander they welcomed more than they had before, but it would be wrong to assume that this represented any significant new spirituality. Cults from Syria and Egypt did attract worshippers from traditional *poleis*, but this should be taken as a sign of the vitality of traditional *polis* religion: Athens or Delos could provide space for an Isis, Sarapis or Hadad.

6 Oracles

This chapter has so far stressed institutional aspects of religion as being most readily traceable across the vast spectrum of the Hellenistic world. There is, however, an equally significant area of religious activity that has only been touched upon in passing, but where the exchange of ideas between systems of religious thought may have been even more powerful than on the institutional level. This area is the realm of the individual professional, of the magician, the astrologer, the prophet and the *chresmologos*. These practitioners are fundamentally the agents of active religious activity in that they sought direct divine information for those who consulted them, or provided information about the gods that was simply not available through the mechanisms of public cult (Potter 1994: 12–13). Their qualifications were determined by the results that they obtained rather than through any hard and fast rules as to what constitute licit and illicit activity.

Magicians performed valuable services for the individual in need, be it in finding a missing slave, a lover, or a change in the weather. They were threatening figures in that they might be able to channel the power of a god to do some actual harm to one person while helping another. A person who wished to ensure that he (or a friend) would win an athletic contest might seek a spell that would weaken an opponent, a man who had been rejected by a lover (our evidence for this sort of activity is overwhelmingly from the male perspective) might seek a spell to compel the object of his affections to accept him. If one person hated another, he might seek a spell that would incapacitate his enemy, or ruin his crops. So too a person who was uncertain about the future might consult a prophet or an astrologer about some business activity, the advisability of a journey, or a question of personal health in the same way that a city would seek the advice of the gods about these same matters. On the other hand, this same person might be seeking information that would work to the disadvantage of another – if you knew that your neighbour was going to die, why not break your agreement with him. From a very early period states legislated against efforts to channel divine energy to the hurt of another, while allowing practitioners to function freely if they did not do such things.

The search for ways to compel divine power to work for private individuals led to an interest in what was perceived as 'eastern wisdom'. It appears to have been generally agreed in the classical period that various eastern peoples, especially the Persians and the Egyptians had special knowledge of the divine (Potter 1994: 183–212). After the ruin of the Persian Empire the search for eastern wisdom picked up pace, sometimes actually involving the integration of genuine eastern traditions into existing practice. There is some evidence for Babylonian calculations being used by Greek astrologers, and other evidence for people seeking to meet the religious professionals of eastern cultures (Neugebauer 1975: 1–4; 1988: 301–4). In time this would impact on local traditions, especially in Egypt where temple officials would know what Greeks were looking for and provide 'improved' versions of local wisdom that conformed with Greek expectations (Frankfurter 1998: 217–48). It might also lead to the translation of actual books of native lore into Greek. Perhaps the best example of this, in the Egyptian context, is offered by a book known as *The Oracle of the Potter.*

It appears that *The Oracle of the Potter* was originally composed in the first part of the third century BC in Demotic, as a piece of local propaganda directed against the Ptolemies (Koenen 1968; 1984). Two of our extant versions (on papyri of the Roman period) seem to have been rewritten at the end of the second century after the failure of a rebellion led by a man named Harsiesis. In this version, the redactor tried to associate the text with an oracle of Ammon that made reference to a king of two years in an effort to reconcile the situation predicted by the Potter with events occurring in his own time. Another redactor seems to have quoted the passage in *The Lamb of Boccharis* (a text of the late Persian period) that reads 'the one of two, who is not our (king), the one of fifty-five is our king', in order to correct the first interpretation (Zauzich 1983: 165–74). Since Harsiesis' rebellion had lasted only two years, the second author may be commenting on Harsiesis' failure by pointing out that he cannot have been the saviour of Egypt predicted in the oracles, and commenting also on the possibility that king Ptolemy Euergetes II, who may have been looked upon as that saviour by some when he reached the fifty-fourth year of his reign in 116 BC, was not the right one either.

The Oracle of the Potter thus shows how wisdom could pass from an Egyptian context to a Greek context outside the avenues of cult. It also shows how people would use these texts as guides to the world around them, and how religious language substituted for 'plain speaking'. As we saw in the case of mythological diplomacy, one value of appealing through the ancestors, heroes, gods and other myths was that it provided an authority to a case that present circumstances might not otherwise justify. Oracular language was by definition the language of the gods themselves – it carried with it an authority derived from its divine origin that ordinary readings of events lacked. By removing contemporary events from their temporal context and placing them in a deeper, world-historical scheme, oracles validated the desires of their readers, and enabled their authors to achieve some distance from the partisan realities of present circumstance. It is thus often to oracular literature that we must turn to gain a perspective removed from the rhetoric of current circumstance. *The Book of Daniel*, for instance, elevated the struggle of the Maccabaean rebels against the Seleukids from a struggle over control of the temple and an internal dispute over the way that Yahweh ought to be venerated, by placing it within a universal scheme of world history (albeit one borrowed in places from Greek thought). The struggle of the Jewish people for their distinctive ethnic identity lay in the construction of history that allowed Daniel to overcome persecution and win due regard from the great powers of the earth through Yahweh's revelations. As we now know, thanks to the discoveries at Qumran, there were earlier versions of parts of the book of Daniel that were reused and updated in the composition of the new text (Kratz 1991). As the Qumran texts also show, prophetic texts and their interpretation could help validate the claims of groups within Judaism to the propriety of their version of history (Vanderkam 1994).

One power that recognized the authority of the Maccabaean dynasty at an early date was Rome. Rome's place in the Hellenistic world was likewise the subject of oracular prediction, in both supportive and hostile ways. The oracle that welcomed Scipio's armies to the Hellespont in the campaign against Antiochos III was most likely composed somewhere in the Troad as a way of contextualizing the rise of the new power, just as the Trojan myth had been used to establish links between the cities of the Aegean world and the great power to the west. So too would oracles be used to establish the credentials of Rome's foes. Poseidonios notes the oracles that were recited throughout the east in support of Mithradates' first invasion of the province of Asia, and it is no doubt to this context that an extraordinary account of anti-Roman oracles preserved in the second century AD as an antiquarian curiosity by Phlegon of Tralles, a freedman of the emperor Hadrian, also belongs. The story opens after Antiochos' defeat at Thermopylai when Buplagos, an officer of Antiochos who had been killed, rose from the dead on the day following the battle and walked into the Roman camp where he delivered a prophecy 'in a soft voice' to the effect that Zeus would send a mighty race against Italy and put an end to the rule of the Romans; he then dropped dead again. The Romans, who were understandably upset by this turn of events, sent ambassadors to Delphi, where the Pythia told them to cease their invasion on the spot and return home, for Athena was preparing a powerful army that would destroy their kind. After receiving the Delphic oracle, the Romans were withdrawing towards Naupaktos when an officer named Publius fell into a prophetic fit and predicted that the Romans would suffer disaster on their way home from the conquest of Asia. When asked to explain what this meant, Publius described, in reasonable detail, what would occur during the rest of the war with Antiochos. He also observed that the returning army would be attacked by Thracians and lose some of its booty. He then fell into another prophetic fit, foreseeing, among other things, the destruction of Rome at the hands of an invading army and his own consumption by a wolf to prove that he had spoken the truth. The wolf duly arrived and ate Publius, leaving only the head, which, once again, burst into prophetic song, telling the Romans that Athena hated them, and that she would send a powerful army from Asia which would destroy Italy and drag its people off into slavery. The account ends with the statement that, 'hearing these words, they (the Romans) were deeply upset and established a temple and altar of Apollo Lykios where the head had lain and got onto their ships and each one went to his own land. All the things that Publius predicted have come true' (*FGrH* 257 F36 III; Gauger 1980; W. Hansen 1996 for a translation).

Not only does this story allow for multiple interpretations – it could be read as a tale of Sulla as easily as of Mithradates – it also validates the importance of Delphi as a source of true wisdom in the new world of Rome. It is precisely this sort of flexibility that enabled oracular literature to mediate between traditions in a way that was not possible for traditional *polis* cult. *Polis* cult might represent tradition, and as such it was invaluable, but in an ever-changing world, it was to oracles that people might turn in order to understand how their past would survive.

7 Conclusions

There are, of necessity, multiple avenues of approach to Hellenistic religion. Religion in antiquity was in many ways a metaphor for power, both that of nature, which could not be controlled, and that of mortals for which it offered a vehicle of expression. The study of religious institutions will often tell a quite different story than the study of individual behaviours, and this is as it should be. As the foundation for the passive aspect of religion, that aspect that served as a stabilizing force within society institutions remained static. If seven Athenians had gone to sleep in a cave on Hymettos in 336 to awaken in 100 BC they would not have been greatly confused by the religious structures that they confronted. Athena Polias was still in charge, the Eleusinian Mysteries were still revered, great festivals of the past still would run their course through the city. They might well wonder where some strange new gods had come from, but they would know that the *polis* had a way of incorporating new cults that was long sanctioned by tradition. They might be a bit taken aback by festivals for kings who had received divine honours, but they might also recall that the city had come close enough to creating such honours before they had gone to their long nap. What would astonish them, however, would be a trip through the lands of the collapsing Seleukid or Ptolemaic kingdoms. It is outside the structure of traditional *polis* cult that religious life was changing, and had changed.

The interaction between Greek and non-Greek cults was, of course, not new. What was different was the vitality of the discourse, and this is what should be meant by terms such as hellenization and syncretism. Neither is much use in describing an end result (a moving target in any case). But as terms that may describe discourse between different groups they have genuine value, for they presume a process through which ideas were exchanged, new habits formed, and old certainties questioned. It is the tension between the stability of institutions like *polis* cult and the creation of new institutions, the dialogue between groups, that reflects the intimate connection between temporal and divine power in the ancient world.

ACKNOWLEDGEMENT

Many years ago, my friend George Forrest asked me to write something on the Hellenistic world rather than the Roman. When the editor invited me to write this essay, I took it as an opportunity to acknowledge George's request, and if it has some merit, that will be owed to George's insistence that Greek religion can best be understood through the record of behaviours in the documentary record.

FURTHER READING

For nearly a century work on the documents of the Hellenistic world has offered a dynamic picture of developments in the realm of religion. The bibliography here does not come close to representing the contribution of Louis Robert to the subject, and any person interested in the serious study of Hellenistic religion must begin with a perusal of the seven volumes of his *Opera Minora Selecta*. The insights offered in Nock 1930 are of critical importance for understanding the relationship between Greek and non-Greek systems of religious thought. Likewise the individual studies collected in Nock 1972 are in many cases still fundamental.

For the structures of *polis* cult, Burkert 1985 and Vernant 1991, as well as Parker 1983, which is crucial on ideas relating to ritual purity. The most important recent development in the subject has stemmed from the study of the cult system at Athens. Parker 1996 and Mikalson 1998 offer excellent treatments, calling attention to continuity with the classical past and raising questions about what is genuinely significant about religious developments in the period. Parker 2000 offers a valuable insight into the part played by religon in personal names. Rigsby 1996, Curty 1995, C. Jones 1999b and Erskine 2001 are of critical importance for looking at the role of religion in shaping diplomatic language. This in turn supports the views of Habicht 1970, Nock 1972: 202–51 and Ma 1999: 219–26 about the place of cult for mortals in a civic context. Ma offers a particularly detailed reading of cult for Antiochos III in the formation of civic history.

For the study of the relationship between Greek and non-Greek, the work of Koenen 1993 and Dunand 1973 on Ptolemaic ruler cult and the cult of Isis is of great importance for viewing the interaction between Greek and Egyptian traditions. Their conclusions are expanded upon in an exciting way by Frankfurter 1998, and taken in new directions in Dillery 1999, a careful study of narrative types in Manetho. They show that the view of Momigliano 1975 that Greeks tended to read all eastern traditions through Greek lenses is in some need of emendation (though it remains true in many cases). Perhaps the most significant challenge to Momigliano's view has emerged in recent years as a result of the superb French excavations at Ai Khanoum, and the collaborative work now being done by French and Russian scholars in the territory of the former Soviet Union. In some cases early conclusions such as those in Ghirshman 1976 are open to challenge, as shown in Potts 1999, but the evidence is now coming to light that enables a new understanding of the eastern reaches of the Seleukid empire, see especially Bernard 1994 and the evidence collected in Holt 1999. For the Asoka texts Thapar 1997 remains critical. Study of indigenous cults in Asia Minor has been undertaken with genuine perception by Debord 1982 and Boffo 1985.

For the study of oracles and questions about the paradigm with which to view classical religion, see Potter 1994. The problem of the relationship between religion and magic (for which Graf 1997 is an excellent traditional introduction) has been moved in new directions by the work of anthropologists who have concentrated on the performative nature of ritual, see esp. Gardner 1983.

CHAPTER TWENTY-FIVE

The Divinity of Hellenistic Rulers

Angelos Chaniotis

1   Introduction: the Paradox of Mortal Divinity

When King Demetrios Poliorketes returned to Athens from Kerkyra in 291, the Athenians welcomed him with a processional song, the text of which has long been recognized as one of the most interesting sources for Hellenistic ruler cult:

> How the greatest and dearest of the gods have come to the city! For the hour has brought together Demeter and Demetrios; she comes to celebrate the solemn mysteries of the Kore, while he is here full of joy, as befits the god, fair and laughing. His appearance is majestic, his friends all around him and he in their midst, as though they were stars and he the sun. Hail son of the most powerful god Poseidon and Aphrodite. (Douris *FGrH* 76 F13, cf. Demochares *FGrH* 75 F2, both at Athen. 6.253b-f; trans. as Austin 35)

Had only the first lines of this ritual song survived, the modern reader would notice the assimilation of the *adventus* of a mortal king with that of a divinity, the etymological association of his name with that of Demeter, the parentage of mighty gods, and the external features of a divine ruler (joy, beauty, majesty). Very often scholars reach their conclusions about aspects of ancient mentality on the basis of a fragment; and very often – unavoidably – they conceive only a fragment of reality. Fortunately, in this case the rest of the hymn is preserved:

> For the other gods are either far away, or they do not have ears, or they do not exist, or do not take any notice of us, but you we can see present here; you are not made of wood or stone, you are real.

It is not surprising that this section of the hymn underlines the close and visible presence of Demetrios the God. The visibility of divine power (*epiphaneia*) is an essential feature of Greek religious beliefs. Surprising is rather the obvious inconsistency of these lines, in which doubt is cast upon the existence of other gods, and the hymn's first lines, which welcome Demeter, praise Poseidon as a most powerful god, and regard him and Aphrodite as Demetrios' divine parents. Inconsistencies in Greek texts with a religious content should not surprise us – not after the series of studies which Henk Versnel has devoted to this phenomenon (1990; 1994). An inscription from Perinthos presents a nice example (*I.Perinthos* 146). It quotes a funerary epigram that denies life after death: 'What is the point of saying "hail, passers-by"? Life is what you see here; a singing cicada stops soon; a rose blossoms, but it soon withers; a skin had been bound, now unfastened it has given up its air; when alive the mortal speaks, when he dies he is cold; the soul is carried away, and I have been dissolved'. And yet this poem is part of the funerary inscription of a member of a cult association of worshippers of Dionysos (the *speire* of the *Sparganiotai*) who must have been initiated in this cult exactly because of its eschatological content. Instead of looking for arguments to clear up the inconsistency in Demetrios' hymn, it is more fruitful to ask what the composer of this text aimed at by diminishing the importance of other gods and underlining the presence, visibility and reality of Demetrios. This becomes clear in the last lines:

> And so we pray to you: first bring us peace, dearest; for you have the power. And then, the Sphinx that rules not only over Thebes but over the whole of Greece, the Aitolian sphinx sitting on a rock like the ancient one, who seizes and carries away all our people, and I have no defence against her (for it is an Aitolian habit to seize the property of neighbours and now even what is far afield). Most of all punish her yourself; if not find an Oedipus who will either hurl down that sphinx from the rocks or reduce her to ashes.

What makes Demetrios divine is his power to offer protection to the Athenians and vengeance against those who had attacked them. In this sense the poem fully corresponds to the Greek idea of divinity, an essential feature of which is not immortality, but the willingness to hear the prayers of men and offer them help in need. Greek religion knows of several gods – notably Asklepios, Dionysos and Herakles – who had ascended Olympos after their death as mortals, and a legion of privileged (and restless) dead who had the ability to provide assistance, especially in war, and received the worship of grateful (or terrified) humans. Extraordinary achievements, such as athletic victory or the successful foundation of a colony, placed some mortals above the common dead and gave them the capacity to be at work even after death. In this sense they overcame their mortality. In the early Hellenistic period, Euhemeros of Messene, a philosopher at the court of Kassandros, gave this idea a theoretical foundation. In his *Hiera anagraphe*, or 'Sacred Narrative', he describes a journey to an island in the Indian Ocean which was the Olympians' land of origin; the Olympians were mortal kings who were worshipped after their death as gods because of their virtues (Euhemeros *FGrH* 63). Of course, there is a difference between the heroized or deified dead and living, divine kings. The protective power of the former manifests itself after their death, whereas the latter were expected to care for their subordinates during their lifetime. Although the cult of kings continued – and sometimes was established for the first time – after their death, there is no reference to the miraculous appearance of a deceased ruler, analogous to the reports of the epiphany of heroes; with the exception of Arsinoe II Philadelphos, protector of seamen, people do not seem to have appealed to the protection of a deceased ruler. If kings had a claim to divine honours it was because of their achievements and benefactions. This is what the epithets attributed to monarchs indicate: 'the Saviour' (*Soter*, attested, e.g., for Antigonos Monophthalmos and Demetrios Poliorketes, Ptolemy I, Antiochos I, Antigonos Gonatas, Attalos I, Achaios, Philip V, Eumenes I, Seleukos III, Ptolemy IX and Kleopatra), 'the one with the manifest power' (*Epiphanes*, attested for Antiochos IV); or 'the winner of fair victories' (*Kallinikos*, attested for Seleukos II and Mithradates I). Of these epithets, *Soter* and *Epiphanes* (or *Epiphanestatos*) are attested for a large number of deities, while *Kallinikos* is a common epithet of Herakles. What places the kings on the same level with the gods is the protection they offer. This idea is expressed in an epigram from Pergamon (*c.* 250–220; [*SEG* 37.1020]; H. Müller 1989) written on the base of the statue of the satyr Skirtos. The statue was dedicated by an admiral of the Attalid fleet, Diony-sodoros, to both Dionysos *and* King Attalos I; such joint dedications to a god and a king are not uncommon (e.g. *OGIS* 17; *SEG* 37.612; 39.1232). In the last line the dedicator expresses his expectations: 'may both of you take care of the dedicator'. The expectation that a mortal take care of another person does not necessarily make him divine; but in this case the king and the god are associated not only in their function as protectors of Dionysodoros but also as joint recipients of his dedication. With both 'gods' Dionysodoros had a close personal relationship; he was in the service of Attalos, but he was also the 'gift' of Dionysos (Dionyso-doros), the patron god of the Attalids.

The power to offer protection is an essential feature of the king's mortal divinity; this explains why in the earliest phases of Hellenistic royal cult it was not the ruler himself who declared his divinity, but usually the real or potential recipient of his benefactions (cf. section 4 below). Since Hellenistic kings, or at least most of them, resembled the immortal gods in the care they took for humans, they deserved to receive similar expressions of gratitude as the gods. The Greek phrase which is often used to describe the establishment of divine honours expresses no more and no less than this: the king is to receive *isotheoi timai* (e.g. *IG* 12.7, 506; *SEG* 41.75), i.e. honours equal to those bestowed upon the gods. Rather than equating the king to the gods, with this phrase the grateful community asserts in a subtle way that the king *is not* a god, even though he receives the same honours from the thankful community. The attribute *theos* ('god') was usually given to a king or a queen only posthumously (e.g. *OGIS* 246). The sharp distinction between the immortal gods and the mortal recipients of divine honours is clear in a letter of Zeuxis, Antiochos III's governor in Asia Minor, in which he quotes a decree of Herakleia upon the Latmos (*SEG* 37.859, *c.* 196). Zeuxis refers to the establishment of a monthly sacrifice for 'the gods (*theoi*), the king and queen, and their children'. The word *theoi* does not comprise the royal family, albeit the latter shares in the same monthly sacrifice. The godlike royals receive godlike honours, but are not gods; their mortality makes all the difference. Even the most divine of rulers, Alexander, is said to have made a bitter joke exactly on his own mortality; when wounded, he assured his companions that what they saw was blood, not '*ichor*, that which runs in the veins of the blessed divinities' (Plut. *Alex.* 28). As the 'royal journals' report, until the very end of his life Alexander behaved as a mortal, never neglecting to sacrifice to the gods (*FGrH* 117 F3).

2   Historical Development and Local Variants

Long before the beginning of the Hellenistic period the Greeks had been bestowing divine honours upon extraordinary individuals (city-founders, athletes, etc.) after their death, but the first mortal known to have received godlike honours during his own lifetime was the Spartan general Lysandros (Douris *FGrH* 76 F71 and 26): the Samians erected an altar, offered him sacrifices, sang cultic songs and renamed the festival of Hera the Lysandreia (*c.* 404). These honours foreshadow later developments: in response to the extraordinary achievements of an individual (victory over the Athenians) and as an expression of gratitude for a service (the return of the Samian oligarchs) a mortal received honours that were commonly reserved for the gods. But still substantial differences between the worship of the gods and the honours for the mortal can be observed: there is, for instance, no reference to a cult statue or to a shrine, and there can be little doubt that these rituals were ephemeral. The immediate predecessor of Hellenistic ruler cult is the cult of two Macedonian kings, Amyntas III, to whom a shrine (Amynteion) is said to have been dedicated at Pydna, and his son Philip II. Leaving aside several controversial testimonies concerning a divine cult introduced by Greek cities (Amphipolis, Ephesos and Eresos) and a report that Philip himself insinuated his divinity shortly before he was murdered, by having his (cult?) image carried in a procession together with the images of the twelve Olympians (Diod. 16.92.5), we now have unequivocal evidence for his cult at Philippi, possibly already in existence in his lifetime. An inscription from there concerning the sale of sacred land (*temene*) lists among the possessors not only gods (Ares and Poseidon) and the Heroes but also Philip (*SEG* 38.658; *c.* 350–300). Of course, Philippi is a particular case, as it was a city founded by Philip II, who was worshipped there as the *ktistes* ('founder') according to a widespread custom which was followed also by the Hellenistic kings in the cities that they founded.

The worship of Alexander is a complex phenomenon, heavily obscured by unreliable anecdotes. Although it was based on an existing tradition, it still differs from both its immediate predecessors and later developments. The very fact that his military achievements had surpassed anything the Greeks had hitherto known made a big difference; in his attack against Aornos the Macedonian conqueror competed with Herakles, who had allegedly failed to take this citadel, and his conquest of India was comparable in the eyes of contemporaries with its mythological precedent, India's conquest by the god Dionysos (Edmunds 1971; Hahn 2000: 16–19, 68–9, 82–6). New too was the influence of non-Greek practices, such as the display of obeisance in the Persian court or the divine worship of the pharaoh. But other facets of the divine worship of Alexander during his lifetime can be paralleled with earlier phenomena and with later Hellenistic developments. That he counted among his ancestors heroes, the sons of gods themselves (Achilles and Herakles), was not uncommon in his world; in Athens the Kynnidai claimed descent from Apollo and the Asklepiadai of Kos were regarded as the descendants of Asklepios; this tradition of consanguinity with heroes and gods was continued by most Hellenistic dynasties, for example with the Ptolemies claiming descent from both Herakles and Dionysos and the Seleukids from Apollo. The divine ancestry of the ruling king also had a long tradition in Egypt, where Alexander as the ruling pharaoh was the son of Ammon-Re; naturally, this belief was adopted by the Ptolemies in their very careful amalgamation of indigenous Egyptian religious elements and their own distinctive royal ideology. Alexander introduced, however, an additional element in his divinity with the claim that he was the son of Zeus. The date and the circumstances in which this claim was made (after his visit to the oracle at Siwa?) are a matter of controversy, but it should be noted that such a claim was not unknown in Greek history. As late as the fifth century the famous Thasian athlete Theagenes was believed to be the son of Herakles and his colleague Euthymos of Lokroi was regarded as the son of the river-god Kaikinos (Paus. 6.9.2, 6.6.4). Alexander's claim to a direct descent from a god found at least one follower among his successors; a hymn discovered in Erythrai regards Seleukos I as the son of Apollo (*I.Erythrai* 205 = *LSAM* 24B). In most respects the cult of Alexander continued and strengthened the existing traditions. It was established in many cities in Asia Minor, probably already during his campaign, in response to his achievements and his benefactions (Habicht 1970: 17–25) and in content and form it did not differ from earlier cases (erection of an altar and sometimes a shrine, offering of sacrifices, contests (*agones*), dedication of a statue in the temple of another god, establishment of a priesthood, naming civic tribes after him). These separate honours have an entirely different quality from the joint celebration of Alexander's divinity that occurred shortly before his death, when, as a result of a proclamation he had issued demanding divine honours for himself, the cities of the Greek mainland sent sacred envoys to Babylon to honour the king as a god (Arr. *Anab.* 7.23.2).

An important difference from the cult of both earlier mortals and that of later kings is the wide diffusion, popularity and persistence of Alexander's worship (Habicht 1970: 25, 185). In Egypt, the cult of Alexander was supported by Ptolemy I as part of his efforts to legitimize his rule, and this worship was continued under the later Ptolemies. But the cult remained popular also in areas in which it was not part of the monarchical ideology. An interesting piece of evidence came to light recently: the ancient visitors to a Macedonian grave of the fourth century in Pella incised on its walls dedicatory texts addressed to Herakles, *Heros Alexandros* and Kassandros; the mention of Herakles in this context rules out the possibility that Alexandros and Kassandros were some ordinary dead; we are dealing with a private worship of Alexander the Great and King Kassandros (*SEG* 47.933). In Priene in the second century private persons repaired his shrine, the Alexandreion (*I.Priene* 108, 75); Erythrai's budget in the early second century included funds for sacrifices to his honour (*LSAM* 26, 90); in the second century AD Bargylia replaced (or repaired) a statue of 'Alexander the God' (*OGIS* 3), and priests of King Alexander are still attested in Ephesos in the second century AD (*I.Ephesos* 719) and in Erythrai as late as the third century AD (*IGRR* 1543 = *I.Erythrai* 64). A statue of Alexander dedicated by Thessalonike in the Severan period designates him as 'the great king Alexander, the son of Zeus' (*SEG* 47.960, *c.* AD 200–250). We can associate with Alexander's worship also a series of contests by the name of 'Alexandreia' or 'Alexandreios agon' that existed centuries after Alexander's death (e.g. in Alexandria, Beroia, Rhodes and Smyrna).

The honouring of achievement, benefaction, military success and protection with divine honours had already a long tradition when Alexander's successors received the title of 'king'. Even 'ordinary' companions were honoured with festivals, as, for instance, Aristonikos for whom the *agon* Aristonikeia was established in Karystos (Athen. 1.19a, *IG* 12.9.207, 41); Philetairos, the Pergamene dynast who never received the title of 'king', was honoured with festivals in Kyme and Kyzikos (Manganaro 2000). All the Successors were honoured with cults in cities supported or subordinated by their troops, and of course they received the traditional worship as founders in the cities they (re-)founded (e.g. Kassandros in Kassandreia, Demetrios Poliorketes in Demetrias, Lysimachos in Ephesos, the first Seleukids in Antioch on the Maeander and in Mygdonia, Apollonia in Karia and Pisidia, Laodikeia on the Lykos, Nysa, etc.). In the study of royal cult one should make a distinction between the (more widely attested) introduction of the worship of a living king or queen by a *polis* and the establishment of a royal cult by the royal administration. This latter procedure entails two different aspects, the establishment by a king of the worship of a deceased family member (father, parents, wife), a phenomenon attested from the beginning of the Hellenistic period, and, at a much later date, the introduction by the ruler of a cult of himself.

The first procedure, the creation of a cult of the ruler by a *polis*, is best demonstrated by the cult of Antigonos the One-Eyed and Demetrios Poliorketes in Athens, set up after the expulsion of Kassandros' garrison (Plut. *Demetr.* 8–13; Diod. 20.45.2; Polyaen. 4.7.6; Habicht 1970: 44–8). Antigonos and Demetrios were regarded as saviours (*Soteres*) and liberators of the city. A decree introduced the office of the 'priest of the Saviours' (cf. Dreyer 1998), an altar was erected, the names of the benefactors were given to two new tribes (Antigonis and Demetrias), and an annual festival, with procession, sacrifice and *agon*, was founded. A similar procedure was repeated countless times in many cities and for almost every known monarch; the many new inscriptions that come to light usually confirm the same stereotypical practice. One of the most recent finds is a letter of queen Laodike (213 BC), with which she accepts the honours bestowed to her by Sardis. The Sardians decreed the foundation of a sacred enclosure or *temenos* (Laodikeion), an altar, a yearly festival or *panegyris* (Laodikeia) on her birthday, the 15th of Hyperberetaios, a procession, and a sacrifice to Zeus Genethlios, protector of the royal family; for three days during the Laodikeia Antiochos III granted an exemption from taxes (*SEG* 39.1284–5; Gauthier 1989, nos. 2–3; Ma 1999: 285–8). An instructive example is also provided by the decree of Pergamon concerning the establishment of the cult of Attalos III in the Asklepieion after a victorious campaign: the demos was to dedicate a statue representing the victorious king standing on war booty in the temple of Asklepios Soter, 'so that he may be sharing the temple with the god' (*synnaos toi theoi*); another statue representing the king on a horse was to be erected next to the altar of Zeus Soter; on this altar the eponymous magistrate, the king's priest, and the official responsible for competitions were to burn every day incense 'for the king'; an annual procession and sacrifice celebrated the anniversary of the king's return to Pergamon (*I.Perg.* 246; Virgilio 1993: 23–7). Sometimes the establishment of the cult was sanctioned with the help of an oracle, as in the case of the cult of Arsinoe Philadelphos in Kos (*Iscr. Cos.* ED 61).

The second procedure, the deification of a deceased king or queen by the royal administration, is best attested in the Ptolemaic kingdom. When Ptolemy I died in 283, his son and successor Ptolemy II declared him a god; the same honour was bestowed upon Ptolemy's widow Berenike in 279. The deceased royal couple was worshipped under the name *theoi soteres* (the saviour gods). When Arsinoe, Ptolemy II's wife and sister died (July 270), her cult was introduced in the temples of all the native gods; her death may have also prompted Ptolemy II to attach his cult and that of Arsinoe to the cult of Alexander, adding the name of the 'Brother-Sister Gods' (*theoi Philadelphoi*) to the title of Alexander's priest; his successor did the same, and the other kings followed this example. Thus this cult in Alexandria was transformed into an eponymous state cult; the reference to its eponymous priest in the dating formula of documents fulfilled an important symbolic function, underlining both dynastic continuity and the monarchy's divine nature. Thus the text of the Rosetta stone under Ptolemy V reads: 'during the priesthood of Aetos, son of Aetos, priest of Alexander and Saviour Gods and the Brother-Sister Gods and the Benefactor Gods and the Father-loving Gods and the Manifest and Beneficent God' (*OGIS* 90). In addition to this cult, the Ptolemies were also worshipped as 'temple-sharing deities' (*synnaoi theoi*) in the Egyptian temples and received daily libations and incense offerings (Lanciers 1993: 214–15; cf. Huss 1994). Their Greek cult-names (Soter, Euergetes, Philadelphos, Philopator, Philometor, Epiphanes, Eucharistos) sounded Greek to the Greeks, but at the same time captured many of the tenets of Egyptian titulary and allowed the native population to recognize in them their pharaoh (Koenen 1993); in general, the native population accepted the ruler cult.

The third procedure, the establishment of cult of the living monarch in the entire kingdom by the ruler himself, is best documented in the kingdom of Seleukids. In the early Hellenistic period the cult of the Seleukids did not differ substantially from that of other monarchs: cults of the living kings and queens were established at the initiative of individual cities, and the deification of the deceased monarch was a standard procedure from the time of Antiochos I. The first Seleukid king who established his own cult during his lifetime was Antiochos III the Great. A series of letters to the provincial governors that request the nomination of a high priest in the provinces for his wife Laodike mention an already existing high priest for the cult of Antiochos himself and for that of his ancestors (*RC* 36; *SEG* 37.1010); this office (*archiereus*) was introduced in 209 (Lanciers 1993: 218–19; Ma 1999: 288–92; H. Müller 2000). When the Attalids took over the largest part of Asia Minor (188/187) they retained the institution of the high priest for their own dynastic cult (*SEG* 47.1519). In the Seleukid kingdom the ruler cult seems to have been limited only to the Greek population (Lanciers 1993).

Things were different in the realm of the Antigonids, where the Greek traditions were strong. The cult of the monarch was widespread, but only as a *polis* institution; even Antigonos Gonatas, who for a long time was believed to have rejected the establishment of his cult in cities under his control, is now known to have received godlike honours in Athens (Habicht 1996).

At the periphery of the Hellenistic world, where the non-Greek element was predominant, ruler cult was sometimes based on an elaborate theological background, as is the case with Kommagene, where Antiochos I introduced cult reforms that combined Iranian cultic elements with his royal ideology. But these forms of divine worship of the king are different in nature from the cult as it was established by and practised within the Greek cities. The organization and content (section 3 below) as well as the role of ruler cult in the Hellenistic world (section 4 below) are essentially Greek phenomena, both in the sense that they continue Greek traditions and in the sense that they are related to the interaction between Hellenistic rulers and Greek cities.

3 Organization and Content

The organization of ruler cult was from its very beginning modelled after the worship of the gods. It was centred around the ritual of the sacrifice (*thysia*) which is one of the indispensable elements of a Greek festival (*panegyris*, rarely *heorte*); additional elements were the procession (*pompe*) and an athletic or musical competition (*agon*). The festivals in honour of kings and queens were named after the person they intended to honour (Attaleia, Eumeneia, Alexandria, Ptolemaia, etc.). When the cult was established during the lifetime of a ruler or a member of the royal family, the rituals usually took place on his or her birthday – similarly, the birthday of a deity is the day of its major festival. Exactly as in the worship of the gods, a sacrifice was offered not only annually, but every month on the same day. When the cult was introduced after a person's death, it was celebrated either on the anniversary of the death (Habicht 1970: 17 n. 5) or on the birthday (Habicht 1998 on *I.Didyma* 488). Other important occasions were the anniversary of the accession to the throne, the anniversary of a victory, or the day the new magistrates assumed office; for example, during the reign of Ptolemy III the 25th day of every month was 'the day of the king', a festival which commemorated the king's accession to the throne on 25th Dios 246 (*I.Louvre* 5); in *c.* 246/244 Ilion established a 'good-tidings-sacrifice' (*euangelia*) for Seleukos II (*I.Ilion* 35). Occasionally the celebration of the ruler was appended to an already existing festival. In addition to the monthly and annual sacrifices, a particular achievement or benefaction could be the occasion for the offering of an extraordinary sacrifice.

The festival began with a procession to which all the citizens were invited, wearing wreaths and their best clothes (e.g. *OGIS* 11; *SIG*[3] 372). The city processions could not compete in glamour with those organized by the royal administration but they were influenced by them. The most impressive procession was the one organized by Ptolemy II in honour of his deceased father; its description by Kallixeinos of Rhodes is the fullest description of an ancient celebration (in Athen. 5.194a–203b, Rice 1983). Highlighting the royal family's affinity to the gods, this Ptolemaic procession demonstrated the king's political and military supremacy as it progressed through the streets of Alexandria; the population was here the audience for a lavishly-staged spectacle, in contrast to the city processions which enlisted the inhabitants as active performers. Religious songs too would be sung at festivals; an inscription from Erythrai, for instance, preserves part of a hymn which calls Seleukos a son of Apollo (*I.Erythrai* 205 = *LSAM* 24B). The city festivals for kings offered an additional opportunity for the organization of athletic and musical contests which very often survived long after a king's death. At Laodikeia on the Lykos the annual athletic *agon* Antiocheia, named after the founder of the city, Antiochos II, continued to be celebrated into the second century (*I.Laodikeia* 5); and in Pergamon the cult of the deceased ruler was still practised long after his death, even after the end of the dynasty (Virgilio 1993). Our most detailed evidence for the organization of a festival comes from the decree of the Euboian cities about the Demetria in honour of Demetrios Poliorketes (*IG* 12.9.207).

The offering of the sacrifice required an altar, which was usually erected in a sacred precinct (*temenos*) which bore the king's name (e.g. Philetaireion in Iasos). An important difference between ruler cult and the cult of the gods is that temples (*naoi*) were rarely dedicated to rulers, either living or dead; only literary sources refer to temples of kings (of Alexander in Athens, of Seleukos I in Lemnos, of Ptolemy II in Byzantion) and only in the context of the *polis* cult. Little is known about the architectural form and decoration of the *temene* and temples, and only a few excavated buildings have been tentatively identified as places of ruler worship (Radt 1989: Pergamon; Borchhardt 1991: Limyra). The erection of a statue was an intrinsic part of the honours, but it is often difficult to distinguish between honorific and cult statues. When the documents designate the king's image as an *agalma* (not an *eikon* or an *andrias*) they usually refer to a cult statue. One of the earliest epigraphic testimonies for ruler cult, a decree of Skepsis in honour of Antigonos Monophthalmos (*OGIS* 6, trans. in Austin 32), expresses the establishment of divine honours with the phrase 'let the city mark off a sacred precinct for him, erect an altar and set up a (cult) statue as beautiful as possible'. The Hellenistic kings were often worshipped as 'temple-sharing gods' (*synnaoi*) through the erection of their statue in the temple of other deities (e.g. Attalos I in Aigina and Sikyon, Antiochos III and Apollonis in Teos, Attalos III in Pergamon, Ariarathes V in Athens and Mithradates VI on Delos: Schmidt-Dounas 1993–4). In Hellenistic Egypt not the living kings, but only the deceased ones seem to have received a cult as *synnaoi* in the temples of other deities (Fishwick 1989). In general, Hellenistic cities preferred to honour a king by establishing a separate shrine for him, naturally in the city's most prominent place. Sometimes the sanctuaries of rulers were the places where public documents are inscribed; it seems quite natural that in Arsinoe in Cilicia public documents were inscribed in the sanctuary of the queen to whom the city owed its name, Arsinoe II (*SEG* 39.1426). Sacrifices and shrines in most cases required the existence of a special priest; the priesthood of Eumenes II, for example, was one of the many priesthoods offered by Kos for sale (*Iscr.Cos.* ED 182). In the long list of the city's priesthoods at Seleukeia in Pieria two priests of the rulers feature (*OGIS* 245, *c.* 187–175): one for the deceased kings (Seleukos Zeus Nikator, Antiochos Apollon Soter, Seleukos Kallinikos, Seleukos Soter, Antiochos, Antiochos Megas) and another for the living monarch (Seleukos IV). Sometimes the priest was the eponymous official of the city (e.g. the priest of Lysimachos in Kassandreia, the priest of Seleukos I in Dura-Europos, the priest of Antiochos III and his homonymous son in Xanthos).

4 Historical Significance

In order to understand the historical significance of Hellenistic royal cult one should rather exclude the cult of Alexander from the discussion; his exceptional achievements and his personal idiosyncrasies probably confuse the general picture. It would be tempting to claim that the royal cult was introduced in the beginning of the Hellenistic period in order to provide Alexander's successors with the legitimacy they lacked. Indeed, there can be little doubt that the Hellenistic kings exploited their cult in order to underscore the charismatic nature of their rule. But do the results of the royal cult necessarily explain the intentions behind its introduction? How can we explain the fact that to best of our knowledge in the early Hellenistic period the cult of living monarchs was always established at the initiative of *poleis* and not at the initiative of monarchs? Unlike the cult of Alexander which was imposed on the *poleis* towards the end of his life – Hypereides uses the verb *anankazo* ('force, compel') twice with regard to Alexander's cult in Athens (6.21) – there is no such reference with regard to the successors; on the contrary, Demochares (*FGrH* 75 F1) reports that Demetrios Poliorketes was deeply annoyed at the flattery of the Athenians. Do we solve this problem by simply suspecting that the *poleis* introduced ruler cult as a response to the monarch's expectations or to the discreet requests of his friends? Were the Hellenistic cities and their political leaders the passive recipients of royal commands or suggestions? It is mainly the epigraphic evidence that compels us to look for an explanation for civic ruler cult not in the intentions of the monarchs but in the interests of the *poleis*. The relevant inscriptions suggest that royal cult was an instrument used by the *poleis* in order to establish a close relationship with a monarch and directly express both their gratitude for past and their expectation of future benefactions. The *narratio* of the relevant decrees explains the cult not as recognition of superhuman, godlike achievements, but as recognition of past services. This idea is clearly expressed in a decree of the League of Islanders: 'the Islanders were the first to have honoured Ptolemy Soter with godlike honours because of his services to individuals' (*IG* 12.7.506, trans. in Austin 218; cf. *IG* 12.5.1008; *I.Cret.* 3.4.4). Similarly, the kings and queens responded to these honours by promising to consider the interests of the cities. Eumenes II, for example, writes to the Ionian League: 'the honours I accept kindly and having never failed, as far as it lay in my power, to confer always something of glory and honour jointly upon you all and individually upon your cities, I shall now try not to diverge from such a precedent' (*RC* 52; cf. *RC* 22; *SEG* 39.1284B).

A common feature of Hellenistic decrees is the so-called hortatory formula, which usually states that a city honours a benefactor in public in order to demonstrate its gratitude and thus encourage others to behave in a beneficial way (e.g. *SEG* 1.366, trans. Austin 113: 'so that we may be seen to be honouring good men and encouraging many citizens to follow the same course of action'). The same strategy of delicate negotiations between *polis* and benefactor explains to a great extent why it is the *polis* which takes the initiative in introducing the cult of the living king. In order to encourage royal liberality, the cities accepted for themselves the image of the inferior, weak and needy, constructing in exchange for the monarch an image of supremacy and unlimited power. This theatrical behaviour underlies many aspects of the fragile balance of power between the monarchic aspirations and the pretensions of urban populations (Chaniotis 1997a: 252–3; cf. Ma 1999: 179–242). By compelling the king to live up to his godlike image, the *poleis* secured for themselves his protection. This is, of course, not to say that the monarchs did not recognize the potential inherent in these honours and did not actively promote their cult. Eumenes II again provides a characteristic example when accepting honours from the Ionian League in 167/166: 'In order that for the future, by celebrating a day in my honour in the Panionian Festival, you may make the whole occasion more illustrious, I shall present you with an adequate income from which you will be able to remember us suitably' (*OGIS* 763, *RC* 52, trans. Welles). As a religious phenomenon the ruler cult corresponds to the mentality of *do ut des* that characterizes the relations of the Greeks to their gods, in general (cf. Grotanelli 1991).

Within their kingdoms the royal cult gave the monarchs, especially the Ptolemies and the Attalids, an additional ideological support for their power. It also allowed the native population to participate in a worship in which it would have been able to recognize familiar elements both in the cult practice and in the religious vocabulary. The interdependence of Greek and native elements has been observed in Ptolemaic ruler cult: in 263 the quota of produce (*apomoira*) from vineyards and orchards not attached to the temples, which had previously been paid to the native Egyptian temples, was diverted to the cult of Arsinoe II (Clarysse and Vandorpe 1998) and the dates of dynastic festivals often followed Egyptian traditions (Koenen 1993).

In cities under the direct or indirect control of a monarch, the existence of a priest of the living king or his ancestors underlined this position of dependence. In Xanthos, for instance, the priest of Ptolemy IV Philopator, Berenike and Ptolemy V was one of the eponymous priests of the city (*SEG* 38.1476, 206/205), and in both Nagidos and Arsinoe the cults of Ptolemy II and Arsinoe II were of central importance (*SEG* 39.1426, *c.* 238). In such dependent cities an important instrument of monarchical power was the garrison; the commander and his soldiers became bearers of the dynastic ideology, primarily through their dedications addressed to, for the welfare of, or in honour of the king and members of the royal house. In Thera all dedications addressed to the deified Ptolemaic kings, in which the names of the dedicators are known to us, were initiated by members of the garrison. The role of garrisons in the promulgation of the royal cult can be seen best in Itanos on Crete, precisely because the dynastic cult is a peripheral phenomenon on this island. A Ptolemaic garrison was established there during the reign of Ptolemy III at the latest. During his reign the Itanians dedicated a *temenos* to the king and to Queen Berenike and established annual sacrifices; in the relevant document Ptolemy is praised for protecting the city and its laws (*I.Cret.* 3.4.4, *c.* 246?). Once established, the dynastic cult could be continued, obviously under the care of the garrison commanders, the *phrourarchoi*. It is the commander of the garrison, a Roman, who made a dedication to Ptolemy IV Philopator and Queen Arsinoe (*I.Cret.* 3.4.17, *c.* 217–209). It is less certain that the dynastic cult of the Ptolemies in Cyprus was established by the garrisons (Bagnall 1976: 68–73), but it was certainly promoted by them. In Ephesos, a commander of troops and the soldiers made a dedication to Ptolemaios II, Arsinoe II and the Theoi Soteres (i.e. Ptolemy I and Berenike) after having offered a sacrifice to them (*SEG* 39.1234). With such actions – whether guided by the royal administration or not – the garrisons reminded the local population that there was a divine element inherent in kingship and made the presence of the king felt in the city (Chaniotis 2002).

Although royal cult was primarily promoted by cities and kings, it did not possess only an official character. The private worship of the dead or living monarch was explicitly requested in some decrees. In Teos, for example, the inhabitants of noncitizen status were asked to celebrate the festival for Antiochos III and Laodike and offer sacrifices in their houses (*SEG* 41.1003 II 25–6) and to bring first-fruit offerings to the king's cult statue (II 53–5); the water of a fountain dedicated to Laodike was to be used in sacrifices, purifications and wedding rituals (II 70–83). At Iasos, the newlyweds were obliged to offer a sacrifice to Laodike (*I.Iasos* 4.85–8; Ma 1999: 329–35). In a few cases we know of dedications made to Hellenistic kings and queens by individuals (e.g. *OGIS* 17). Usually these individuals were soldiers or officials in the royal administration who expressed in this way loyalty, solidarity with the monarch, gratitude or hopes for patronage (e.g. *SEG* 37.1020; *I.Cret.* 3.4.17). The expression of loyalty and gratitude also explains the worship of sovereigns by the

Dionysiac associations, for instance in Pergamon (Radt 1989) and in Athens (*IG* 2²
1330). Things are different in the case of Arsinoe II who was posthumously assimilated with Isis and Aphrodite and became one of the most popular goddesses in Egypt
and on Cyprus. Two of the earliest attestations of Arsinoe's cult are private dedications: the Ptolemaic admiral Kallikrates dedicated a temple of Arsinoe/Aphrodite at
Cape Zephyrion, near Kanopos, and in Halikarnassos Chairemon established a sanctuary of Sarapis, Isis and Arsinoe Philadelphos; Kallikrates' dedication underscores
the worship of Arsinoe as a patron of sailors, an aspect which may be explained either
in the light of her assimilation with Aphrodite Euploia or in the light of Arsinoe's
maritime policy (Malaise 1994). From Cyprus we know of more than twenty altars for
the household cult of Arsinoe in various cities; her cult was continued for a century
after her death (Nicolaou 1993; Anastassiades 1998). Altars for the cult of Arsinoe
Philadelphos have been found in private houses as far away as Eretria and Miletos
(*SEG* 40.763; *Milet* I.7, nos. 288–9); their owners may have had trade contacts with
Egypt. Occasionally, we get insights into the practice of ruler cult; for instance, in a
village in the Delta an association of farmers honoured the benefactor Paris by
crowning his statues on the festive days (*eponymoi hemerai*) on which sacrifices to
the kings were offered (Bernand 1992: no. 40; 67 and 64 BC). At the border between
public and private cult we find the cult of the ruler in the gymnasium, often in
gymnasia that had received royal benefactions. Here where the young men, especially
those of the elite, were educated and imbued with the values of their community,
ruler cult played a crucial part.

Ruler cult established a close relationship between the subject and the object of a
benefaction; it was quite natural that it influenced a similar relationship between *poleis*
and benefactors who did not possess royal status. Already at the beginning of the
Hellenistic period friends of Demetrios Poliorketes received heroic honours in Athens
(Habicht 1970: 55–8). A new interesting document from Laodikeia on the Lykos
(*I.Laodikeia* 1, *c.* 267) attests divine honours for Achaios, a member of the Seleukid
family, and his officials Banabelos and Lachares; they were honoured by the inhabitants of Neon Teichos and Kiddiou Kome with the establishment of their cult for their
services during a war against the Gauls. A yearly sacrifice of an ox was to be offered to
Achaios Soter in the sanctuary of Zeus in Baba Kome, a sacrifice of three rams to
Lachares and Banabelos Euergetai in the sanctuary of Apollo in Kiddiou Kome. Long
after the abolishment of the Attalid monarchy, the Pergamenes modelled the divine
honours bestowed upon their benefactor Diodoros Pasparos after the honours they
had decreed for king Attalos III (*OGIS* 332, *c.* 139–133). The honours included the
erection of cult statues, the establishment of a *temenos* and a temple, the celebration
of a festival, the appointment of a priest, the creation of an eponymous tribe and his
praise as a founder or *ktistes* (Radt 1986; Virgilio 1995).

The success of ruler cult both as a medium for the communication between ruler
and subordinate civic community and for the legitimation of monarchical power can
be best seen in the fact that it continued long after the end of the Hellenistic period as
part of the ideology of the Principate. The Greek cities used this familiar instrument
from the very beginning of their relations with Roman generals: T. Quinctius Flamininus was the first Roman to have received godlike honours (in Chalkis), and others
followed. Provincial governors, in particular, were honoured in the same way Greek
cities used to honour monarchs (Halfmann 1987). Late Ptolemaic Egypt played a

very important part in the transmission of the ruler cult to Rome. It is probable that Caesar received divine honours in Alexandria (Fishwick 1987), and it is certain that Mark Antony was assimilated with Dionysos and Herakles (Heinen 1995). The Kaisareion in Alexandria, whether first dedicated to Divus Julius, Mark Antony or Octavian, presents an early example of a shrine for a Roman general. It is not surprising that in the Greek East, the cult of Octavian/Augustus was modelled after Hellenistic traditions. Exactly as Hellenistic sovereigns were assimilated to Greek divinities (e.g. Seleukos I-Zeus, Antiochos I-Apollo, Arsinoe II-Isis, Demeter and Aphrodite, etc.) so too was Augustus, especially to Zeus (*SEG* 46.754; 47.218; Reynolds 1996) and Apollo (Mavrojannis 1995); the story that Octavian's father was Apollo himself was probably created sometime after the sea battle at Actium (Kienast 1982: 376) and recalls similar traditions about Alexander and Seleukos. His reluctance to accept the erection of temples to his honour can be explained by the fear of opposition in Rome, but is also paralleled by a similar reluctance on the part of Hellenistic monarchs. Octavian accepted instead the construction of a temple of Dea Roma in Pergamon (29 BC), where he was worshipped as a *synnaos theos* by the representatives of the province of Asia; the provincial emperor cult was established later in other provinces as well and became one of the most important social and cultural institutions of the Imperial period in the Roman East. The model of a joint cult of Roma and Augustus was also followed in Athens (19 BC?). In other cities cult statues of Augustus were set up in the temples of other divinities, for instance in the temple of Zeus in Kalindoia (*SEG* 35.744) and of Apollo in Delos (Mavrojannis 1995). Other honours (e.g. tribes and months named after him, *agons*, the epithet *Soter* in Athens) followed Hellenistic models. His iconography can also be seen against the background of the iconography of Hellenistic sovereigns (La Rocca 1994), and the ceremonial context of the *agons* which were organized in honour of Augustus and the later emperors can be traced back to the cult of mortals in the Hellenistic period (Herz 1997).

At some time between 27 BC and AD 14, still during Augustus' lifetime, the citizens of Ioulis on Keos dedicated a building, probably a Sebasteion located near the sanctuary of Apollo. The dedicatory inscription states that the building was dedicated for the well-being of Theos Kaisar Sebastos (Divus Caesar Augustus); as if it were not strange enough that a dedication was made for the well-being of a 'god' (Theos), the dedication is addressed not only to the Olympian Gods but also to the Theoi Sebastoi, i.e. to Divus Augustus himself and to Livia (who bears here the unofficial title of an Augusta). Augustus' cult is Hellenistic in this respect too: it was no less paradoxical than the mortal divinity of Hellenistic kings.

FURTHER READING

Sources.   The evidence for ruler cult is being continually increased through new epigraphic finds that supplement and modify our understanding of the worship of Hellenistic kings or certain of its aspects. It had long been believed, e.g., that Antigonos Gonatas did not accept divine worship, but a new find from Rhamnous (*SEG* 41.75) not only demonstrated that this was the case in Athens, but also urges us to reconsider other evidence as well, e.g. from Ios (*IG* 12 Suppl. 168; Habicht 1996). The new epigraphic evidence published from 1987 onwards is presented in the *Epigraphic Bulletin for Greek Religion* in *Kernos* (6, 1991 and subsequent years).

Historical background: This has received much attention in recent years, especially hero cult and heroization (Kearns 1989, 1992, Antonaccio 1994, Larson 1995, Lyons 1997, Johnston 1999), the predecessors of ruler cult, e.g. for Lysandros, Amyntas III and Philip II (Habicht 1970: 3–16), the ideological/philosophical background (Piérart 2001). The cult of Philip II now seems certain (Habicht 1970, Fredricksmeyer 1981), despite the sceptical remarks of Badian 1981. In the case of several dedications to a king Philip it is disputed whether they refer to Philip II or Philip V (*SEG* 47.917, Hatzopoulos 1996: no. 78). The divinity and cult of Alexander the Great, the exact date of its introduction (*c.* 332, 327 or later), the role of the oracle of Ammon in Siwa, the initiative of cities, Alexander's own understanding of his divinity and the consanguinity with Zeus, are still matters of dispute, and the controversial statements of the sources add to the confusion (e.g. Strabo 14.1.22, Ephippos *FGrH* 126 F5). To give but one example, the reciting of a Homeric verse (*Iliad* 340: '*ichor*, that which runs in the veins of the blessed divinities') in connection with the blood running from Alexander's wounds, is sometimes attributed to the king himself, sometimes to a companion, sometimes as an (self-)ironical remark, sometimes as flattery (F. Jacoby, *FGrH* IID Kommentar: 519). New finds rarely add something new. The cult of Hephaistion as a hero, not as a god, seems now to be confirmed by a relief stele from Pella; it is dedicated to Hephaistion soon after his death (late fourth century), and the text designates him an *heros* (Voutiras 1990, Despinis et al. 1997: no. 23). It is also possible that the divine honours decreed by the Greek cities originated in Alexander's wish to introduce the posthumous cult of Hephaistion, a wish to which the Greek cities may have responded with the joint introduction of both Hephaistion's cult as a hero and that of Alexander as a god (Habicht 1970: 28–36). On Alexander's divinity: Balsdon 1950, Habicht 1970, Edmunds 1971, Fredricksmeyer 1979, Badian 1981, 1996, Cawkwell 1994. The cult of the sovereign has, naturally, received more attention in Egypt (e.g. Lanciers 1988, Koenen 1993, Huss 1994, Bingen 1997, Melaerts 1998, Quaegebeur 1998) and in the Seleukid kingdom (e.g. H. Müller 2000). For the cult of Antiochos I of Kommagene, at the periphery of the Hellenistic World: Şahin 1991, Waldmann 1973, 1991, Schwertheim 1991, Allgöwer 1993, Dörner 1996. For Pergamon see Schwarzer 1999.

Organization and content: The best presentation of the development and content of the Hellenistic ruler cult is still that offered by Habicht 1970, cf. Price 1984: 23–53, Walbank 1987. Specific aspects, such as the festivals established by or for kings (Hintzen-Bohlen 1992), sacrificial practices (Lanciers 1993), cult officials (Minas 1998 on the Kanephoros of Arsinoe II) or the archaeological evidence (Bergmann 1998, Kotsidou 2000), have been discussed in a plethora of studies. A very instructive example of a decree establishing the royal cult is that of Teos for Antiochos III and Laodike (*SEG* 41.1003; Herrmann 1965a; *c.* 204/3). One of the most important pieces of evidence is Kallixeinos on Ptolemy II's procession (in Athen. 5.194a-203b): Dunand 1981, Rice 1983, Köhler 1996, Walbank 1996, D. J. Thompson 2000. Its date is still a matter of controversy: Foertmeyer 1988, Habicht 1992, Hazzard 2000: 59–79.

Historical significance: The important part played by the *poleis* in the establishment of the ruler cult has been underlined by Habicht 1970: 160–71. The integration of the ruler cult in a system of exchange (cf. Ma 1999: 178–242, esp. 219–26) is paralleled by the similar role of the imperial cult in the Roman East (Price 1984: 65–77). Stevenson 1996 has argued more recently that the figure of the ideal benefactor underlies the cult of mortals in the Greco-Roman world. The early stages of the emperor cult in Roman Egypt, especially its forerunners – the Ptolemaic ruler cult, the cult of Caesar, the establishment of a Kaisareion in Alexandria for Julius Caesar – are discussed by Grenier 1995, Fishwick 1987, Heinen 1995, Huzar 1995, and Ruggendorfer 1996. Useful overviews of the cult of Augustus are presented by Kienast 1982: 202–14 and Clauss 1999; cf. Fishwick 1987–92, Bosworth 1999. For a detailed bibliography on this subject, Krause et al. 1998: 399–412. Clauss 1996 argues that Julius Caesar and Augustus were regarded as gods during their lifetime not only in the eastern provinces, but also in the western part of the Empire, even in Rome. The origins of the emperor cult in Asia Minor have been recently illuminated by a series of studies by Campanile (1993, 1994a, 1994b); cf. S. Price 1984, Friesen 1993, Herrmann 1994. Among other areas, the cult of Augustus in Athens has received much attention, because of the abundance of sources: Clinton 1997, Mavrojannis 1995, Hoff 1996, Spawforth 1997. A very interesting aspect of Hellenistic and Imperial ruler cult is the *adventus* of the monarch: Lehnen 1997; it is possible that the ceremonial *adventus* has influenced early Christian liturgy (K. Berger 1991).

PART VII

Arts and Sciences

CHAPTER TWENTY-SIX

Empires of Knowledge: Medicine and Health in the Hellenistic World

Rebecca Flemming

It has become commonplace in a range of disciplines – in (at least parts of) history and literary studies, for instance, as well as anthropology and sociology – to approach empire as a type of knowledge project. 'Colonial knowledge both enabled conquest and was produced by it', states historical anthropologist Nicholas Dirks, 'in certain ways knowledge was what colonialism was all about' (1996: ix). The point is, in a sense, an obvious one. Successful conquerors need not just military strength and organization, together with some political skills, but also intelligence. Conquest itself is a learning process, both for the victors and the vanquished, and this feeds into the system of domination which is then established and consolidated. The management of knowledge – its continued but controlled generation, its rightful ordering, differential possession, and ongoing productivity – counts amongst the most vital technologies of colonial rule. It may also become a site of resistance.

The principle is generally illustrated with examples from the 'Grand Era' of European imperialism in the eighteenth and nineteenth centuries. Here, as Canadian historian Ruth Roach Pierson points out:

> Hand-in-hand with European conquerors, explorers, slave traders, merchants, missionaries, and imperial and colonial administrators, European cartographers, botanists, biologists, and budding anthropologists fanned out over the globe, returning home with the booty that fueled the mania for classification and categorization. These were at the heart of the great urge to control, the will to power, through the creation of a 'new global order of cultural knowledge' ... (Pierson 1998: 3; citing McClintock 1995: 3)

Thus the histories of these scientific, or more broadly scholarly, disciplines (and others such as geology and geography) in this period, their institutions and heroes, are increasingly written as a part of European imperial history (e.g. Brockway 1979; Stafford 1989; Gascoigne 1998). It is, moreover, precisely in these centuries that these subjects really took off: expanding with the empires that needed and sustained them, and establishing themselves in something like their modern forms. Western medicine also has a deeply imperialist past. It too participated in the extension and consolidation of systems of European international domination, and a host of studies have tracked, described and analysed the multifarious forms of this participation (e.g. Arnold 1988; MacLeod and Lewis 1988).

There are also obvious resonances with the Hellenistic world, though scholars have been reluctant to use words like 'colonial', and even 'imperial', in this context. Alexander the Great was accompanied on his campaigns by surveyors, physicians, historians and philosophers; indeed it might be argued that the desire *to know*, intertwined as it was with the will to power, formed a key part of his *pothos*. Even discarding the Roman encyclopaedist Pliny the Elder's much later story of his systematic collection of animal specimens for Aristotle's study (*HN* 8.17), it is clear that Alexander's conquests greatly increased the range and repertory of Greek natural history. Many descriptions of exotic lands and peoples are also traced back to the companions of Alexander, such as Nearchos (Arr. *Anab.* 7; Pliny *HN* 6.21). More-over, this is just the beginning of the explosion in, and systematization of, knowledge that marks the Hellenistic period. This is, after all, the age of mathematicians such as Euklid and Archimedes of Syracuse (whose mechanical interests also overlapped with those of men such as Ktesibos of Alexandria), and of Aristarchos of Samos with his heliocentric model of the cosmos. It is the era of the formation of significant new philosophical schools, and of the creation of various literary corpora and canons; not to mention the medical developments that are the focus of this paper.

The explanations offered for this efflorescence of learning certainly make reference to the geo-political situation created by Alexander's acquisition of empire, followed by its break-up into the Successor Kingdoms, but in a somewhat muted, even euphemistic, manner. The eminent student of Greek scientific enterprise, G. E. R. Lloyd, for example, speaks of 'a certain widening of the mental horizons', as 'closer intellectual and cultural contacts between Greeks and Barbarians became possible' (Lloyd 1973: 2). He also emphasizes the importance of kingly patronage to Hellen-istic science (Lloyd 1973: 3–5), a theme which others have also picked up on and elaborated. It is, however, not just monarchy that is at issue here, but empire. Horizons have been widened by conquest – by territorial expansion and the subjuga-tion of other peoples – and the contact between 'Greeks and Barbarians' was, at a basic level, contact between victor and vanquished, ruler and ruled; not a neutral, even-handed affair. The particular shape the Hellenistic world settled into after the death of Alexander, and the subsequent division of spoils, diverges in a number of important respects from the world of eighteenth- and nineteenth century imperial-ism; but it also shares certain features of no less significance.

The point is not just a moral one, but also one of understanding. If we place the considerable developments in medical knowledge during the Hellenistic era in a more explicitly *imperialist* framework than hitherto, and make use of the various insights about the intimate relations between knowledge and empire gained from other periods in history, might it not help us to understand the phenomena rather better? That is what I propose to find out in this account of Hellenistic medicine. Caution will, of course, be needed in implementing such a comparative approach. The intention is certainly not simply to adopt models from the extensive scholarship on 'colonial' or 'imperial' medicine, focused as it is on the particularities of the modern era; but rather to benefit from the ways in which these discussions have recently been both broadened out to deal with issues of power and culture, domination and discourse, in more inclusive ways, and have become more sensitive to various specificities and complexities of context.

1 Bodies of Medical Knowledge/Imperial Knowledge

The medical development which dominates most discussions of scientific endeavours in the Hellenistic period is, of course, the introduction (and conclusion) of the practice of systematic human dissection (and vivisection) in early third-century Alexandria. This anatomical moment – which is coterminous with the careers of just two men, Herophilos of Chalkedon and Erasistratos of Ioulis on Keos – has perhaps gained more importance in the history of medicine from the defining role that the dissection of human cadavers has played (and rather surprisingly still plays) in the self-identity of modern medicine and its practitioners, than from any consideration of its more immediate effects. None the less, it certainly counts as a moment in which classical medical knowledge (if not practice) was transformed. The rather loosely conceived, and imaginative, approach to the human interior which characterizes the writings of the Hippocratic Corpus, had up till now been supplemented and steadied only by the comparative anatomy of Aristotle, and others who dissected animals. In early Ptolemaic Alexandria, this figuration was decisively overlaid with a detailed description of each human part, 'its position, colour, shape, size, arrangement, hardness, softness, smoothness, interrelationships, processes and depressions, and whether any part is inserted into or receives another part' (Celsus *Med*. pr.24). Names were given to each feature discovered, and, though the actual works of the Alexandrian anatomists have been lost, their terminology – particularly that of Herophilos – proved much more resilient. Even today, various bodily items still bear their Herophilean monikers, albeit in a Latinized form, such as the terms 'cornea' ('horn-like', from *keratoeides*, Rufus *Onom*. 12–13) and 'retina' ('net-like', from *amphiblestroeides*: Rufus *Onom*. 153), for two of the four tunics of the eye which Herophilos was the first to identify.

The amount of knowledge about the human body was thus vastly increased, as befits the imperial setting; but the effects this had on the understanding of how the body worked, fell ill and was cured were rather less dramatic, and serve (along with various other complications) to give this imperialist theme a particular shape and stress. Some aspects of somatic formation and functioning did come more clearly into focus. One of Herophilos' major achievements, for example, was identifying the nerves as distinct entities, separate from the arteries and veins, if not always from various sinews and tendons. Both he and Erasistratos further distinguished between sensory and motor nerves, though they diverged on which parts of the brain and spine constitute the origin, or centre, of these systems. This allowed a clear differentiation to be made between involuntary motions based on the arteries – primarily the pulse, a subject on which Herophilos was also very influential – and voluntary motion involving the nerves and muscles; a differentiation which could then take a pathological form. As Galen, the great physician of the Roman imperial era whose copious (but far from disinterested) writings provide much of the evidence for earlier medical theories and practices, explains it, Herophilos held that the disease cluster of tremor, palpitation and spasm were all diseases of the operation of voluntary movement, and so affections of the nerves, not the arteries, as his teacher, Praxagoras of Kos, had argued (Gal. *Trem. Palp.* 5: 7.605–6 K). However, the practical ramifications of this pathological reassignment are hard to detect. There seems, for example, to be little therapeutic response to the new conceptualization.

Moreover there is still the underlying question of what causes these problems: what so badly affects the nerves so as to result in this dysfunction of voluntary motion, these tremors, palpitations and spasms? Here teacher and pupil seem to have been in agreement, not only with each other but with established Hippocratic doctrine too. As a later medical handbook ascribed to Galen explains:

> Some people attributed both the constitution of things that are in accordance with nature and the causes of things which are contrary to nature to the humours alone, as did Praxagoras and Herophilos. ([Gal.] *Intro.* 9: 14.698–9 K)

And Galen himself describes this as 'emulating' Hippokrates (Gal. *PHP* 8.5.24: *CMG* 5.4.1.2 510.1–5). Despite all his anatomical discoveries, the accuracy and detail of his innovative topographical descriptions of the human interior, therefore, Herophilos remained committed to a very traditional understanding of health (which is always in accordance with nature) and disease (which is the contrary condition); one that was based on age-old notions of balance and imbalance, manifested in the humoural mixture of the body. This is, furthermore, a conception which operates at a very general level of somatic organization, not a more anatomically specific one. It is about the fluids – the humours – that pervade the whole body rather than being tied to any specific location or organ.

Erasistratos, on the other hand, did break with Hippocratic tradition, and in a manner that was clearly related to the new anatomy. He took the separation of the three somatic networks – arteries, veins and nerves – a step further than Herophilos by separating out also the substances they transported around the body. Most controversially, Erasistratos confined blood (considered in ancient medical thought to perform a nourishing role) to the veins, asserting that the arteries contained only vital *pneuma*, that is *pneuma* (warm air that became integral to bodily functioning) which simply sustains life, whereas the *pneuma* in the nerves was implicated in perception and action. For him then, all disease was caused by the 'transference of blood into the arteries' ([Gal.] *Intro.* 13: 14.728–9 K); that is by the break down of this systemic and substantial division. There was also a very clear therapeutic consequence of all this. Erasistratos was opposed to blood-letting, that most fundamental feature of the ancient curative armoury from the Hellenistic era onwards.

Even Erasistratos, however, left many of the key assumptions and basic understandings of the medical tradition he inherited entirely intact. He, and indeed Herophilos, may have provided some new answers to old questions, but they rarely thought to change the questions, or challenge the set of presumptions from which they arose. Indeed, to some extent the newness of their answers was a matter of detail and precision, of the kind of extended account which could now be given with their recently acquired anatomical knowledge; rather than any more dramatic innovation. This, and the general failure of these developments to deliver any obvious therapeutic results, has all been a considerable disappointment to many modern commentators, particularly those most committed to the inherently, and intensely, revelatory powers of human dissection. But, as well as offering a salutary lesson in the general limitations of empirical knowledge of this type, there is a more specific surprise in this conceptual conservatism. For the undertaking of systematic human dissection for the first time *was* a radical one, and did entail breaking with traditions of a rather stronger, more socially and religiously entrenched, variety than those which shaped the medical community as such. The inhibitions against opening up the human body were bound up with a number of deep cultural commitments and long-standing practices relating to life and death, the proper treatment of the corpse and its polluting properties, and the integrity and aesthetic qualities of the body. They were, moreover, only briefly overcome. Why then did the boldness that took these men through these barriers not carry right through their research? What, indeed, made them want to anatomize at all, if it had so few tangible results, and seems so incidental to the wider medical enterprise?

This apparent paradox would be resolved if it were the ideological rather than the practical results of the new human anatomy that were of primary concern here; if it were the simple desire to bring knowledge of the human body decisively within the estate of the medical art – a move hinted at by Hippocratic speculations and Aristotelian animal dissections – which was crucial in this case, without any particular consideration of the precise therapeutic rewards that might be reaped from this conquest, or even of the exact way the newly won territory would relate to the existing heartlands. The somatic interior invited capture: to be able to claim mastery over it was a goal in itself, the achievement of which would both bring glory to those responsible and give strength to the medical art more generally.

This is, obviously, to implicate Herophilos and Erasistratos more directly in the imperialism of their age than most scholars have been inclined to do hitherto; and it is all highly speculative, as any discussion of their motivations, and indeed many of their activities, must be in the absence of their own works, or any contemporary reports. However, it is an interpretation which fits in well with the other factors that are invoked to explain this ancient anatomical moment. For the most important of these all relate to the political realities of the world shaped by Alexander's conquests. First there is the moral and practical support offered by the early Ptolemies – in the shape of 'condemned men, provided alive by the kings from prison' (Celsus *Med.* pr.23–4) to cut open and inspect while still breathing – as part of their attempt to establish Alexandria as a centre of cultural achievement. The culture in question was, of course, Greek, the culture of the conquerors, and its promotion was about legitimizing the new ruling dynasty, providing the Ptolemies with more than just a military basis for their regime. Second there is their success in attracting an intelligentsia, drawn from all over the Greek world, and committed to innovation and enterprise in both sciences and letters. The first two Ptolemies invested substantial amounts of the wealth they acquired with their empire in cultural projects, establishing the Library and the Museum to this end; and though there is nothing to link Herophilos or Erasistratos directly with either, the fact that the boundaries of knowledge and literature were being extended all around them surely had some indirect effects. Third there are the ways in which the newness of the city itself, its 'frontier' qualities, added to the adventurous brew (von Staden 1992: 232). Alexandria was the first of Alexander's city foundations, and, in many ways, the foremost herald of his new order.

The explanatory emphasis in all this is clearly, if not explicitly, on the *colonial* situation in Hellenistic Egypt (particularly in its early phases) as intellectually and imaginatively enabling for the colonizers. Cultural life, including scientific enquiry, was part of the consolidation of empire. It was the continuation of territorial expansion by other means, the expression of the superiority of the rulers over both their subject peoples and rival Macedonian regimes. This expression was, moreover, invigorated as well as necessitated, by the colonial encounter with difference and novelty, by the challenge and freedom of living 'on the frontier', among non-Greeks. And, even if the suggestion that human dissection might have taken either techniques or permission from native Egyptian practices or beliefs, particularly from mummification, is currently out of favour, there is another direct contribution the Egyptian population could have made to these researches. Rather surprisingly, no one has yet speculated about the ethnic identity of those criminals who were provided by the Ptolemies from their prisons to be vivisected. Instead the debate has focused on the impossibility of 'civilized' Greeks behaving in such a barbaric manner, despite the unequivocal reports to the contrary of a number of reasonably reliable, though certainly not contemporary, witnesses, such as the early imperial Latin writer Celsus. This 'argument from inconceivability' has now fallen into disrepute, as the cruelties practised by the Greeks in a range of areas, including their judicial and penal systems, have come more to prominence in the scholarship (a relevant example here is Bosworth 1996). But would it not have made the Ptolemies' task easier if the condemned men they were handing over to this terrible fate were Egyptians not Greeks or Macedonians?

It should be added immediately that, whether or not this was the case, the anatomy of Herophilos and Erasistratos was not an anatomy of difference. There is no indication that they dissected, as some of their nineteenth-century successors did (e.g. Stepan 1982), in order to distinguish between varieties of human being, to provide interior confirmation and meanings for a racial hierarchy. Indeed, their approach to the one difference they were clearly concerned with – that between women and men – appears to be one which brings the two closer together rather than pushing them further apart. One of the more substantial surviving quotes from Herophilos' *Anatomy*, contained in a work of Galen, opens: 'On the uterus, growing out sideways, one from each part, are the *didymoi* (literally "twins" but here "testicles"), and they differ only a little from those of males' (Gal. *Sem.* 2.1.15: *CMG* 5.3.1 146.22–4). Nor does the similarity between male and female end with them both possessing testicles (though not, it should be said, contributing equally to the formation of offspring); both Herophilos and Erasistratos held, in their own distinct ways, that female bodies were composed from the same stuff as male ones, worked and failed in the same way, and so that there were no diseases peculiar to women, nor cures (Sor. *Gyn.* 3.1; Flemming 2000).

The final area that benefits from this more imperialist reading of Hellenistic anatomy is, appropriately, its end. For, despite various suggestions to the contrary (e.g. Edelstein 1967), there is no evidence that either human vivisection or dissection continued after the lifetimes of Herophilos and Erasistratos (most cogently argued in von Staden 1989 and 1992). This is, in large part, seen as a reversion to normality, as traditional values and behaviours dominate once more after the initial dynamism, the early pioneering period, of Ptolemaic rule fades away. These traditional values being, it is further stressed, now not just Greek or Macedonian, but Egyptian too, as native culture has reasserted itself, becoming, along with various sections of the Egyptian elite, of more concern to successive Ptolemies as the new order beds down. There is much to recommend this basic understanding, but thinking about anatomizing as conquest helps the process of reversion. For conquest is not something that needs to be repeated. It is, by definition, a one-off occurrence, though often the platform for further developments. Once the knowledge of the body has been won – the territory mapped and named – then that is the end of it, though it may be the beginning of something else. In these terms, human vivisection and dissection thus came to its natural conclusion as Herophilos and Erasistratos completed their project. The terms had changed, however, by the time that men like Galen and Rufus of Ephesos (explicitly or implicitly) regret their inability to open up the human body (Gal. *AA* 1.2: 2.218–27 K; Rufus *Onom.* 10), several centuries, and many shifts in the medical (not to mention political and cultural) situation, later.

One such medical shift is also to be located in Hellenistic Alexandria, and both emerges out of and helps terminate its anatomical moment. It is, furthermore, a development that has received considerable scholarly attention in its own right (e.g. von Staden 1982, and Hankinson 1995, for two different kinds of scholarly treatment). That is the inauguration of medical sects, based on epistemological divisions of the medical art. The link with anatomy is twofold. First, and most personally, it is when a pupil of Herophilos – Philinos of Kos – left his teacher's circle to initiate the foundation of a rival school or sect (*hairesis*) which developed a different conception of the medical art, that the Hellenistic phase of the debate about what constituted medical knowledge – about where the boundaries of relevance, utility and necessity lie, and about what qualifies as knowledge – took a sharper, definitional and organizational turn. The new grouping launched by Philinos became known as the *empirikoi* or 'empiricists', and those they had broken with, such as those around Herophilos and Erasistratos, were characterized, almost by default, as the *logikoi* or 'rationalists'. The epistemological dichotomy which thus crystallized has been summarized by philosopher Michael Frede:

> Very roughly speaking, the empiricists were called 'empiricists' since they took the view that knowledge is just a matter of a certain kind of complex experience (in Greek *empeira*), whereas the rationalists were so called since they assumed that mere experience, however complex, does not amount to knowledge, that knowledge crucially involves the use of reason (*logos* in Greek, *ratio* in Latin), for example to provide the appropriate kind of justification for our belief. (Frede 1990: 225)

Second, while complex experience encompassed incidental examination of the bodily interior, when confronted, for example, by someone who needed treatment for having been cut open by a sword, systematic dissection and vivisection fell outside this category. According to Celsus, the empiricists held that these activities were not only useless and unnecessary, but also, at least in the case of vivisection, cruel (*Med.* pr. 40–4). For nothing is more foolish than assuming that the human body remains the same during this kind of intervention, through dying and death, when it is, after all, living bodies and their repair which are of real interest to doctors. What they need to know, therefore, is what treatment has been beneficial for which pathological condition in the past, based primarily on their own observation, and on the critical assimilation of the reports of others.

It is possible, therefore, to see empiricism as a complex response to the new anatomy, based in part on ethical considerations, but also on the extrinsic qualities of the knowledge which had been produced. All that was resting on this detailed topographical understanding of the somatic interior was a broad claim to medical authority, nothing more specific than that; and that was a claim which could be anchored elsewhere, in experience and history. Both factors, as well as the continuing drive to innovate, to differentiate oneself from other physicians and their ideas in the continuing competition for patients and pupils that characterized classical medicine, suggested that this kind of anatomy be rejected, and contributed to the demise of human dissection (see esp. von Staden 1992 for this latter point). It is harder to see any more directly imperialist motivation in this move, in this epistemological division of the medical landscape, prefigured as it was by differences in the Hippocratic Corpus. Though it might perhaps be speculated that the totalizing aspect of the empiricist vision, the sense in which their definition of the knowledge requisite to the medical endeavour coincided with their definition of knowledge *per se* owed something to the totalizing vision of empire, to the scale and ambition of the Greek world of Alexander. Division and competition were also, of course, facts of political life thereafter.

At least one empiricist was also associated with the later Ptolemaic court. The commentary on the Hippocratic treatise *On Joints* by Apollonios of Kition is the only Hellenistic medical treatise to survive intact, and each of its three books opens with an address to King Ptolemy, on whose orders the work was undertaken. The Ptolemy in question is generally held to be Auletes, who reigned from 80 to 51 BC, thus demonstrating the long-term success of Philinos' sectarian foundation. More important to the theoretical development of empiricism, however, are figures like Serapion of Alexandria, Philinos' successor and the man generally credited with establishing the sect's main tenets, and Herakleides of Tarentum, who repeated Philinos' original apostasy, leaving the school of Herophilos for the ranks of the *empirikoi* in the early first century BC. This shows, in addition, the continuing vitality of the Herophilean lineage itself, though, unable to continue opening up human bodies, they largely 'turned their backs on anatomy' (von Staden 1989: 446), and diversified into other areas, several of which – such as pharmacology, surgery and Hippocratic philology and exegesis – were also of much interest to the empiricists, and tied in with some broader cultural movements too. The followers of Erasistratos were an identifiable group throughout the Hellenistic age also, though they too seem to have neglected anatomy while remaining committed to the basic tenets of Erasistratos' physiology, pathology and therapeutics, as Galen's polemics against the Erasistrateans active in the Rome of his day emphasize (Gal. *Ven. Sect. Er. Rom.* 11: 187–244 K; and see Brain 1986).

When exactly the first Erasistrateans reached Rome is unknown – it may have been not till after Actium. If so, they were beaten to the capital of this new Mediterranean power, this new empire, by a physician who appears to have taken some of Erasistratos' ideas a good deal further than any of his followers. Asklepiades of Prusias in Bithynia, arrived in Rome in the later part of the second century BC, and seems to have been remarkably successful there in his promulgation both of innovative theories about the human being in sickness and health, and an original (though less dramatic-ally so) therapeutic package to accompany them. He argued that the human body (like the rest of the cosmos) was constructed out of fundamental (but frangible) particles which percolated through the body in various passages or pores. Their balanced, free-flowing movement constituted health, and their impaction in the passages, with resultant blockage, was the sole cause of disease. His curative prescrip-tions were notoriously gentle, based on 'passive exercise' (such as being rocked in a hammock), baths, massage, drinking wine and water, or occasionally abstaining from the same, or even food. All of these are elements of traditional dietetics, albeit sometimes rather minor ones, but re-formulated, and given different emphases and explanations in a more selective package.

The pleasant qualities of Asklepiades' cures have been suggested as the key to his spectacular success (see e.g. Pliny *HN* 7.124, and also 26.12–17). There may well be something to the allegation, but Asklepiades also won many adherents to his theor-etical positions. Dioscorides, writing his highly influential work on medical materials in the late first century AD, includes a list of recent pharmacological authors in his preface, and they are Asclepiadeans to a man (*Materia medica* pr. 2). Like Herophilos before him, however, Asklepiades suffered an early, and significant, defection from the ranks of his followers. His pupil Themison of Laodikeia gradually separated himself from his teacher, and formulated an alternative 'method' of medicine, centred on the observation of certain common characteristics of disease ('stricture', 'flux', and 'mixture'), which a physician needs to be able to recognize in any sick individual and take as, in themselves, indicative of their treatment (so that, for example, 'stricture' requires relaxing, and so forth). These notions formed the core commit-ments of the 'methodist sect', which flourished in the Roman imperial era.

2   Medicines for an Empire

The Asclepiadean interest in medical materials followed on from a general increase in the attention devoted to this area of healing practice, not only by the medical community as a whole, but the wider literate population too. Pharmacology entered the Hellenistic era consisting mainly of simples – that is of drugs derived from a single active ingredient, whether animal, vegetable or mineral – and left it dominated by compound drugs, often involving lengthy lists of ingredients. Herophilos himself called medicaments the 'hands of the gods' (Scribon. *Comp. Ep.* 1), and many of his followers zealously pursued his lead. One – Mantias – is indeed credited with founding the compound drug tradition, and it is his errant pupil, Herakleides of Tarentum, who heads the roll-call of respected Empiricist writers on pharmacology. Other notable contributors to Hellenistic drug-lore, such as Iollas of Bithynia and Krateuas the Root-cutter (or Rhizotomist, that is a medical practitioner located in a strongly plant-based tradition of healing), operated outside any particular medical lineage or sectarian grouping. But it was not just the number of items that might go into a remedy which increased at this time, the number of items that might be therapeutically called on in any way dramatically expanded, and in some particular directions, bringing the imperialist theme to the fore again. Prior to Alexander's conquests, cultural and economic contacts around the Eastern Mediterranean had already infiltrated a number of 'Egyptian', 'Indian', and other exotic ingredients into

Greek drug-lore; and this process of assimilation massively increased in the Hellenistic period.

This assimilation was about more than simply expanding the pharmaceutical repertoire of Greek medicine; it also helped to bring order to the contents of the newly conquered territories, to generate and manage knowledge about their flora, fauna and minerals, in acceptable and familiar ways. The plants, animals and stones of the Hellenistic world could be pharmacologically mapped and organized, and so brought into a beneficial relationship with humanity, and its Greek portion in particular, as this organization occurred around an established Greek centre, taking Greek literary forms. The dietetic aspects of these things could also be treated in the same way, thus incorporating new foodstuffs within existing, and distinctively Greek, patterns of understanding and evaluation; a task which seems to have begun in the age of the Diadochoi themselves, as Diphilos of Siphnos' work *On Foodstuffs* dates, according to Athenaeus who cites it extensively, 'to the age of Lysimachos' (2.51a). Another contribution to the same enterprise, one that found particular favour outside the strictly medical arena, was writing on poisonous (or at least dangerous) animals, plants and some minerals, together with remedial responses to them. New threats were thus placed alongside the old, and, as far as possible, matched with antidotes. The only surviving examples of this rich Hellenistic genre are the twin didactic poems on the subject – the *Theriaka* and *Alexipharmaka* – composed by Nikander of Kolophon, probably in second-century BC Pergamon. His main inspiration is thought to have come from one Apollodoros, who wrote similar works in early third-century BC Alexandria; but the Herophilean Andreas also wrote a treatise *On Poisonous Animals* later in the same century, and a series of more medical as well as poetic successors are known.

Poisons and their antidotes were, of course, a particular preoccupation within ruling circles, and royal patronage undoubtedly played a role in the rise, and shape, of Hellenistic pharmacology. Andreas is, for example, one of the few Herophileans who can be directly linked to the Ptolemaic court, indeed he even managed to get himself killed in place of his king – Ptolemy IV Philopator – on the eve of the battle of Raphia in 217 BC (Polyb. 5.81.6). Krateuas the Root-cutter is generally associated with the king of antidotes, Mithradates VI of Pontos himself. Not, it should be said, with the monarch's testing of possibly poison nullifying substances on criminals condemned to death (presumably by poison), a practice which had apparently been pioneered by Attalos III of Pergamon before him (Justin also has Attalos experimenting likewise on his 'friends': 36.4.3), but perhaps with Mithradates' wider medical investigations. Pliny the Elder explicitly aligns these with the king's position as conqueror and colonial ruler, and has him collecting medical information from 'all his subjects, who comprised a great part of the world' (*HN* 25.5–7). Pliny also mentions an antidote favoured by Antiochos the Great against all poisonous creatures except the asp (*HN* 20.264), and one of that monarch's physicians – Apollophanes of Seleukeia – may have been famous for his plasters (a kind of externally applied medicament) as well as his political activity (see e.g. Gal. *Comp. Med. Loc.* 8.9 and *Comp. Med. Gen.* 7.7: 13.220 and 979 K; as well as Polyb. 5.56 and 5.58–61, though the name alone is not enough to prove identity). Doctors from the Antigonid court seem to have had the least impact on the historical and medical record, but Celsus (7.21.3) describes one such (whose name is unfortunately lost to us) as 'a not undistinguished physician, a pupil of Chrysippos' (perhaps Chrysippos of Knidos, the teacher of Erasistratos, or, if chronology requires it, the Chrysippos whom Erasistratos himself taught: D.L. 7.186). Following Alexander's precedent, not to mention various more practical impulses, therefore, every Hellenistic dynasty included physicians within their courtly circles, and drew them from all over the Greek world.

Returning, however, to the particular environs of the Pontic court, the figure of Krateuas illuminates other features of the Hellenistic medical landscape. Though the reputation of his work is better attested than its contents, the indications are that he distanced himself from some of the murkier aspects of classical Greek *rhizotomia*, from the kind of root-cutting associated, for example, with the sorceress Medea (Macrob. *Sat.* 5.19.10). Rather than paying attention to rituals of cutting – performing the task by the new or full moon, for instance, with (or without) special implements, having purified or otherwise prepared oneself – Krateuas seems to have concentrated on the plants themselves; on how to identify them (for which purpose illustrations were provided), and their properties. Some of these properties might be classified as 'wonderful', such as the ability of the plant *onothuris* to calm all fierce animals when sprinkled with wine (Pliny *HN* 22.167), but most are more mundane, such as Krateuas' prescription of lettuce juice for dropsy (*HN* 20.63). Similarly marvellous powers of things can also be found in Nikander, in the Hellenistic paradoxographers, and in a related literary genre which took this kind of folklore in a different direction. This is the development of a literature of learned magic, a literature full of this kind of information – about plants such as the *ophiusa* from Elephantine and the *thalassaegle* of the Indus which both cause visions and derangement, or the Persian plant *hestiateris* that produces conviviality and promotion at court (*HN* 24.163–5) – but which frames it in a very particular fashion. The data is presented as wisdom derived, not from local root-cutters, but from more exotic and prestigious sources, most especially the *magi* of Persia, but also, for example, Egyptian priests and kings. Its transmission from these foreign quarters into Greek forms is then ascribed either to a hellenized sage of some kind, or to a Greek philosopher – usually Demokritos or Pythagoras – who trafficked with the purveyors of Eastern learning. It was these specific names that two of the chief architects of this new magical literature – Bolos of Mendes (probably active in the early second century BC) and Kleemporos the physician (of uncertain date) – chose, respectively, to write under.

The overlap of content, and also form, between these organized catalogues of the magical properties of various natural substances – plants, animals and minerals – and medical writings is obvious, even without Kleemporos' professional designation. None the less, the birth and growth of this literary genre, this expansion in occult knowledge about nature, is often seen as standing in contrast with, if not opposition to, the more rationalistic medical developments outlined so far. It is, however, put down to the same causes: the broadening of horizons and monarchic structures of the Hellenistic world. There was, it is argued, a critical loss of confidence, of the 'special sort of confidence that only self-determination can produce' (Green 1990: 53), as a result of the rise of Macedonian monarchy, allied with a general dislocation and disorientation as old institutions and patterns of organization gave way to the new. To allay these anxieties Greeks either turned inwards, following the teachings of new Hellenistic philosophies to a fulfilment based on individual conduct rather than community participation, or turned further outwards, beyond the boundaries of civic religion or established reason, to mystery cults, magic and astrology.

Now it may be that Hellenistic monarchy is big enough to hold both elaborate discourses of rationality and irrationality in its embrace, to contain both supreme confidence and a loss of nerve. Indeed it is possible that an overwhelming rationalism will inevitably produce its opposite, or that the sectarian disputes of the third century BC fuelled a search for alternative approaches. Overall, however, these contrasts seem too sharply drawn, the picture constructed seems too simple given the many factors involved, and the considerable continuities evident between the Classical and Hellenistic eras. Certainly the development of bodies of occult knowledge about nature can be seen as the *extension* of methods of organization, of systematization, established in more 'rational' areas of natural knowledge, rather than their contradiction. Both Bolos and Krateuas, for example, participate in the discourse of *dynameis*, of determining and describing the powers or properties naturally inherent in things, a concept that has Aristotelian connections amongst others. They simply place the emphasis differently, both from each other and from others who use the same explanatory mechanism. Bolos is most interested in the more marvellous powers of things, Krateuas in their healing properties; others, like Herophilos, in the *dynameis* of various bodily organs, or indeed of the human body itself. Just as widely shared was the notion of sympathy and antipathy which provides the other explicatory thread in the world of natural magic. Indeed, one of Bolos' pseudo-Demokritean creations was called alternatively, *Natural Properties* or *On Sympathies and Antipathies* (*Suda* B482); and the two concepts are clearly intertwined as it is, for example, in the nature of menstruating women to be lethally antipathetic to caterpillars (Columella 11.3.64). Again, however, there is a shift of emphasis from the sympathy evoked in Stoicism and medical writings (where there are sympathetic connections between parts of the body which may find pathological expressions of various kinds), to the antipathy that appears to dominate the more magical works. Still, it is a commitment to the interconnectedness, the ordering, of all things which underlies both.

By invoking these explanatory mechanisms, men such as Bolos and Kleemporos are, as the classical scholar Richard Gordon has suggested (1997), attempting to rationalize pre-existing Greek practices, embedded in a set of almost entirely tacit assumptions and understandings. They are, effectively, taking established folk traditions, expanding them, placing them in an explicatory framework formed out of strands of current thinking about how things work, interrelate and interact, and dressing them up in exotic clothes – the clothes of ancient Eastern and Egyptian learning. For, though Greek borrowing from Babylonian and Egyptian astronomy and astrology is reasonably clear, even if the precise path to, and date of, this merging of traditions remains a matter of debate, the suggestions of a comparable process in the more earthly realms of knowledge are much weaker and less convincing (M. Dickie 1999: 183–9 has to work much too hard to make the connections he wants in this respect; see also M. Dickie 2001: 120–4 for astrological comparisons). So it is the clothes alone that are borrowed here, and even these are more like theatrical costumes than authentic attire.

The benefits of such an authorial strategy are obvious. In laying claim not only to the names of Demokritos and Pythagoras, but also to the wisdom of Zoroaster and the *magi*, of Egyptian priests, kings and gods, these texts laid claim to both an authority and a novelty they otherwise lacked. That authority was at once philosophical and religious, rational and mystical, rooted inside and outside established tradition. Nor did the benefits accrue solely to the authors themselves: the works thus framed gave the recently conquered but venerable cultures of the Achaimenid Empire a place in the new world order, just as they gave the recently arrived Greeks a place in the old. The subordinate position of this ancient wisdom was clear – it lay underneath, behind, an invigorated extension of Greek learning – and, by translating difference into an exotic colouring for the familiar, it also provided justificatory 'roots' for Greek settlement in the new territories, a legitimating lineage for the consolidation of conquest. To conclude from this growth of orientalist pseudepigraphica, as ancient historian Arnaldo Momigliano did in his fundamental study of 'alien wisdom', that Hellenistic civilization 'had all the marks of a conquering and ruling upper class – except faith in its own wisdom' (1975: 149) is, therefore, seriously to misconstrue the meaning of this discourse (as well as seriously overrating its importance). It was very much a part of, not at odds with, a discourse of domination, as self-serving as any other imperialist interpretation of the cultural traditions of colonized (or otherwise dominated) peoples, regardless of their enviable antiquity or spiritual strengths.

Bolos, Krateuas, Nikander, Andreas and Herakleides can all be seen, along with Herophilos, Erasistratos, and many others, as contributing to the 'new global order of cultural knowledge' that was an integral part of the formation and maintenance of the Hellenistic world. That is not all they did, and their contributions were not identical; but each had something to offer, and each took from, and was supported by, his political, social, economic and ideological context in his work. One final, but undoubtedly significant, medical development of the Hellenistic period is of a rather different character, however. This is the rise of the cult of Asklepios, the most specialized healing deity in the Greek pantheon, and the associated increase in the emphasis on, and attention paid to, the Asklepios-like curative and more generally protective powers of various other divinities, both old and new. This phenomenon is not primarily an expansion of knowledge, distinguishing it from the other developments discussed so far; but there are epistemic elements to the improvement in the fortunes of divine healing, along with the obvious elements of expansion, which connect with events in other areas of Hellenistic medicine none the less.

3   Medicine and Divinity

Temples, altars, sanctuaries, priestly personnel, festivals and other rituals associated with Asklepios (and, increasingly, his whole family) spread and accumulated across the Greek world in the Hellenistic period. In the wake of the foundation of the new *polis* of Kos in the mid fourth century BC, for example, architectural developments began at a nearby cult site which was to become home of one of the most notable Asklepieia of antiquity. Major building work commenced around 300 BC, and the first temple complex was completed by 242 BC, with a new and larger temple, together with various other structures, being added in the second century. At Lebena in Crete too it is the early third century BC that sees the creation of the Asklepieon proper, and there are similar developments in Pergamon, also made grander and more monumental in the following century, under Attalid patronage. The god is represented on

Pergamene coinage in the reign of Eumenes II, as he is on the obverse of Koan coins from the mid second century BC, further attesting to the official commitment to, and identification with, the cult. Older sanctuaries, like those at Athens and, most famously, Epidauros, also experienced expansion at around the same time. The former gained a new temple around 300 BC, and the latter, having benefited from a lavish building programme in the early fourth century, went on to acquire more structures, such as a hostel, baths and stoa in the third. Many other examples of such growth and investment could be offered, and there is additional evidence for the greater use and popularity of these sites in the Hellenistic era that seems to have gone hand in hand with their aggrandizement. The number of anatomical votives, generally thought to be offered either in connection with a request, or in thanks, for cure of the particular part of the anatomy in question, found in sanctuaries of Asklepios increases very substantially, 'from the fourth century onwards' (van Straten 1981: 149).

These more numerous votives are, moreover, not the exclusive property of Asklepios. In Hellenistic Athens, for example, anatomical *ex votos* were deposited in the sanctuaries of Amynos and the Hero Doctor, as well as in that of Asklepios himself. Both heroes were traditionally associated with healing, but votives to the more recently arrived Ptolemaic deities, Isis and Sarapis, have also been found in the Asklepieion on the Acropolis. Sarapis' healing powers were certainly acquired early on in his divine career. Demetrios of Phaleron, the Peripatetic philosopher and statesman, not only wrote hymns in honour of Sarapis after being miraculously cured of blindness by him in Alexandria during the reign of Ptolemy I (D.L. 5.76), but also focused on cures carried out by him in his sanctuaries in his five books *On Dreams* (Artem. 2.44). Isis too acquires medical associations, though perhaps somewhat later in her development. Diodoros, writing his histories in the first century BC, even gives her a foundational role for medicine in Egypt – as the discoverer of drugs and guardian of medical knowledge – a role similar to that played by Asklepios elsewhere (1.25.2).

This final point needs stressing, for Asklepios was the divine patron of, the divine legitimation for, the medical art and its mortal practitioners; not just an alternative route to health. Physicians were, therefore, intimately connected with, not antagonistic to, the cult of Asklepios, and did not draw sharp distinctions between seeking medical help from amongst their own number and from their patron deity. In a world in which the ability to make well was assumed to be among the powers of the gods, was indeed an intrinsic element of their identity, turning to a deity when ill was an obvious, and rational, response. Turning to Asklepios in particular only served to bring that response closer to going to a mortal doctor. That Greeks and Macedonians seem to have visited the sanctuaries of healing gods with greater frequency in the Hellenistic age than before cannot, therefore, be taken as a rejection of other avenues to cure, or as a manifestation of irrationalism. Nor can it be interpreted as an indication of a widening social malaise, of greater anxiety and illness, since it could just as easily be explained as resulting from increased wealth, mobility, expectations and access, combined with the added allure of these now truly magnificent sites. However, there are aspects of the cult of Asklepios and his healing colleagues which do chime in with other aspects of the age and which might indicate some of the more conceptual reasons why healing gods and their sites were both promoted and aggrandized by kings and cities and increasingly frequented by their populations. For divinity was, as ancient historian Simon Price has argued (1984: esp. 23–52), a key resource for the negotiation of power in the ancient world, a resource that was more explicitly drawn on by Macedonians and Greeks, as both rulers and subjects, in the Hellenistic period than before. Asklepios offered a model of power that was particularly protective and curative, that engendered a more acceptable form of dependence, and which, therefore, was peculiarly apt and productive for many of those involved in the ongoing representations of, and responses to, Hellenistic patterns of power.

Thus we return to the imperialist dimension, to the imperialist theme of this paper, adding another layer to its complexity, but also its suitability as an analytical tool for understanding the range of medical developments in the Hellenistic world – from dissection to incubation. Not that this is the only useful approach to adopt towards these phenomena, and each requires a much fuller examination than has been possible here; but thinking about the intimate intrinsic connections between knowledge and empires is certainly as beneficial in this context as it has been in many others.

FURTHER READING

For an insight into the broader historical relations between medicine and empire see the collections of Arnold 1988, and MacLeod and Lewis 1988. As for the fragmentary remains of Hellenistic medicine itself: Herophilos is the best served, by the magisterial work of von Staden 1989. Ivan Garofalo's collection of Erasistratos' fragments (1988) is a much less ambitious publication, and we await von Staden's forthcoming Erasistratean volume to do this innovative physician justice. The remains of the *empirikoi* are mostly contained in Deichgräber 1930/1965; and more general discussions of the Hellenistic sects include von Staden 1982, Hankinson 1995 and G. Lloyd 1995. On Asklepiades, Vallance 1990. The most recent discussion of Hellenistic magic can be found in M. Dickie 2001: 96–123; which should be read alongside Gordon 1997. The starting place for any study of the cult of Asklepios is E. and L. Edelstein 1945 (repr. 1998 with a new introduction containing much intervening bibliography). Further reading dealing with many aspects of Hellenistic medicine and its context includes Fraser 1972, G. Lloyd 1973, and Nutton 2004.

CHAPTER TWENTY-SEVEN

The Institutions of Hellenistic Philosophy

Phillip Mitsis

1 Philosophical Institutions: Ancient and Modern

One feature of philosophy in the Hellenistic period often remarked upon is the way that philosophical argument and study become increasingly the domain of trained professionals. Whereas Sokrates, who ironically was to serve as the intellectual inspiration for so much of Hellenistic philosophy, approached his interlocutors with philosophical arguments that were both immediate and non-technical, Hellenistic philosophers often produced enormous amounts of specialized technical work clearly accessible only to fellow professionals. However much they may claim to be interested in alleviating the psychic distress of humanity at large, it is equally the case that they often write to score points with fellow professionals against other professionals and with a style and vocabulary that could only befuddle the uninitiated. The establishment and standardization of philosophical topics, the routine rehearsal of common objections and responses, the intensity of focus on argumentative niceties, the creation of a specialized vocabulary to be wielded and understood only by trained technicians – all indicate a discipline progressively leaving any amateur behind.

Of course, the notion of philosophers as professionals writing for other professionals is something to which we have grown accustomed and a layperson picking up a piece of professional philosophy today often might just as well be approaching an advanced medical textbook or the latest issue of a physics journal. We may lament this feature of contemporary philosophical argument or we may think it just as essential to developments in philosophy as special technical equipment is to the progress of other specialized disciplines. Regardless of our views here, however, one thing seems undeniable. What underwrites the contemporary practice of professional philosophy is an extended system of institutional support and reward. Without stable university positions, salaries, fellowships, professional journals and presses, endowments and all the other kinds of familiar institutional support that underwrite the practice of contemporary philosophy, professional philosophy, as we know it, would cease to exist.

It is tempting to assume initially, perhaps, that as it took on an increasing professional aspect, philosophy in the Hellenistic period similarly was supported by institutions of increasing complexity, scope and power. How else to account for the unparalleled persistence of the four storied schools of Hellenistic philosophy – the Epicurean, Stoic, Academic and Peripatetic – and the enduring intellectual influence of their great centres in Athens – the Garden, Stoa, Academy and Lyceum respectively? Such an assumption becomes even more tempting, no doubt, when we dip into standard accounts of Hellenistic philosophy. Although few now would subscribe to the easy analogies drawn by nineteenth century European philologists between the ancient philosophical schools and modern universities, it is not uncommon to find contemporary scholars making use of language and metaphors that suggest fairly straightforward correspondences between ancient and modern institutions of philosophy.

A moment's reflection serves to make clear some fundamental differences, however. First, and most obvious, perhaps, is the fact that philosophical schools do not exist today as independent, freestanding institutions dedicated to the study and teaching of philosophy. The contemporary study of philosophy is supported within a larger institutional framework provided by colleges and universities and is thus subject to a wide variety of constraints from without, as are its teachers and students. Although scholars have sometimes described the ancient philosophical schools as 'the universities of antiquity' or have tried to trace the origins of the idea of the university to practices in the ancient philosophical schools, nothing could be more misleading at the level of institutional description. Whatever continuities or parallels might exist between the methods and aims of teaching in these respective ancient and modern pedagogical contexts, any attempt to draw parallels between actual ancient and modern institutions quickly runs into a series of obstacles. This is because no ancient philosophical school had anything remotely resembling philosophy's place or support in the wider institutional structures of the modern (or even medieval) university. Indeed, in many ways the flourishing of philosophy in the Hellenistic period presents a rather stark challenge to the notion that there is any strict correlation between the power and resources of established institutions and the complexity, influence and professional quality of the philosophical thinking and writing that they underwrite. The Stoics, for instance, adherents of arguably both the most technically dextrous and most enduringly influential of the Hellenistic schools, probably never managed to acquire a single piece of property or the slightest bit of any other form of common endowment. So too, although one sometimes hears talk of a long, uninterrupted line of Stoic scholarchs throughout the Hellenistic period holding forth to generations of students in the Stoa, we have good evidence that Chrysippos, surely one of the most accomplished and professionally visible of Stoic scholarchs, gave up teaching in the Stoa to teach in the Lyceum, Academy and the entrance of the Odeon – the very haunts of those old adversaries of Sokrates, the sophists. And he may have done so quite consciously, since he claimed that the philosopher should make money by charging for his teaching and 'being a sophist' (Plut. *Mor.* [*Stoic Contradictions*] 1034b). Any talk of a Stoic 'school', therefore, is likely to be misleading if it implies a particular ongoing institution with a recognizable identity, structure, or even location over and above the individuals or groups who happened to gather together and identify themselves as Stoics at particular times and places.

By way of contrast, modern institutions of higher learning support and lend continuity to the study and teaching of philosophy independently, in a real sense, of any particular individuals. In the Hellenistic period, only the Garden of the Epicureans provided anything remotely like this kind of institutional continuity. But it was a striking exception. The fortunes of the other schools often very much depended on the abilities, intellectual influence, and in some cases, the means of particular individuals. Nor should we forget that, for the most part, what we actually have any real evidence for are very short flurries of creative philosophical activity followed by periods of silence that periodically are interrupted by what might best be described as attempts to reformulate doctrines either in the face of new scientific developments or of new philosophical challenges. It might be the case, as many have assumed, that this evidence can best be accounted for by postulating coherent underlying institutions that provided for the continuity, survival and development of the chief philosophies of the Hellenistic period. But institutional continuity is certainly not the only possible explanation, especially since any hard evidence, even for briefly surviving institutions, is remarkably scarce. Moreover, in several important cases we have much better reasons for concluding that, to the contrary, philosophical activity was occurring either without any institutional support or under the banner of an institution that in reality was long since defunct.

2   Institutions: Doctrines and Practice

In turning to the evidence, we face several methodological questions. Chief among them initially, perhaps, is how to understand the relations between the stated doctrines of a school and its institutional practices. Given the extreme paucity of evidence for institutions of any kind or for any of the practices carried on within them, it has often been tempting to try to reconstruct features of the schools from the varieties of evidence that we do have – philosophical doctrines in the main, sometimes augmented by anecdotal evidence about philosophers' personalities or about incidents occurring at lectures, reactions to their teaching, etc. After all, one might suppose, it hardly seems implausible to assume a certain continuity between a school's overt doctrines and its educational practices and one certainly might expect a school's arrangements to reflect or at least attempt to reflect in some measure the very doctrines that gave rise to it in the first place. On closer inspection, however, one soon discovers how difficult it is to make even the most simple inferences of this kind and how spectacularly such inferences can go awry.

We might find gaps between doctrines and actual school practices less surprising, perhaps, if we pause to reflect for a moment on institutions for which we are much better informed. Armed only with the New Testament, for instance, one might go on to make some badly mistaken inferences about the likely forms of association that have occurred among various groups of Christians in particular historical periods. This is not only because the Gospels are open to a bewildering range of interpretations, but also because a host of other considerations can condition the dynamics within groups. Conversely, if one were in possession of evidence only for the behaviour and institutional practices of certain groups of avowed Christians, one might be extremely hard pressed to recover the revealed doctrines they are meant to reflect. Moreover, even in those cases where we both are well informed about the practices of a particular group and have direct access to its guiding texts, we still may be at a loss to understand the exact nature of the connections its members saw between their doctrines and their institutions. How much more precarious, then, to make inferences from doctrines to institutional practices in the case of the philosophical schools. Typically we have next to nothing in the way of evidence for internal practices, and often, to complicate matters further, fairly strong evidence of doctrinal disagreements.

Although few scholars today would move with any confidence between, say, the educational ideals expressed in Plato's *Republic* and the little we know about what may have gone on in the Academy, it is not uncommon for scholars to claim, based on perceived contrasts in philosophical doctrines, that, at the very least, a different ethos pervaded and gave shape to the respective institutional arrangements of the various schools. Martha Nussbaum (1994), for instance, who argues that sharply contrasting forms of association, pedagogical methods and intellectual goals were to be found in the Peripatos and the Garden of Epicurus, has offered a particularly strong statement of this kind of view and one that well illustrates our methodological problem. The Garden of the Epicureans, she claims, was a place where members were proselytized by a series of careful techniques that speak to our deepest psychological anxieties. Once these anxieties were laid bare, would-be Epicureans were subjected to a whole battery of coercive techniques whose object was inculcating Epicurean doctrine and integrating individuals into a homogeneous community of true believers. Among other things, new members would undertake to memorize authoritative doctrines and to put themselves under the spiritual control of superiors who had mastered Epicurean techniques and who would keep them on the right path by administering strong verbal admonitions. Community life in the Epicurean school was structured by a shared concern for constant vigilance and strict adherence to Epicurean doctrines. Thus members were urged to report the backsliding of others and to confess their own lapses in belief or in behaviour.

The key contrast with the Peripatos and its centre, the Lyceum, revolves around questions of rationality and respect for individual autonomy. For Nussbaum, the Garden was a place where the practical goals of therapy were placed above concerns for the autonomy of individuals and for their rational understanding of the doctrines they were absorbing. The Peripatos, on the other hand, embodied in a certain sense the liberal ideals of the modern research university. It fostered free and unencumbered inquiry with no constraints other than making one's views or results stand up to the rigorous rational scrutiny of one's fellows. Students came to the Lyceum in search of knowledge and to engage in dialectical examination with fellow researchers; they did not come because they were driven to address some deep inner psychological turmoil or because they were seeking personal salvation. Presumably, in keeping with Aristotle's own views about the importance of early habituation for future moral and intellectual inquiry, the Lyceum attracted students with very different backgrounds from those of the Garden and with different psychological experiences, intellectual attainments, and an upbringing more conducive to free dialectical inquiry. As for the nature of communal interaction in the Peripatos, one should imagine (an idealized) Harvard or Oxford versus the alternative Moonie communities run by the Epicureans.

Although many might disagree either with details of Nussbaum's characterization or with the sharpness of her contrast, it is safe to say that her views capture a general consensus that something very different was going on in the Garden and in the Peripatos with respect to teaching, research goals and methods, social interactions and experiences, etc. And certainly at a general level it would be hard to deny that this may very well have been the case. But the question we face is whether we are in any position to recover actual differences in school practice and whether we are warranted in making inferences from the doctrines we find in philosophical texts toward this end.

Did, as Nussbaum's account suggests, generations of peripatetic teachers engage in the dialectical examination of philosophical topics with their students, show concern to foster their independent research skills, display a healthy respect for their intellectual autonomy and avoid unappealing displays of paternalism when disagreeing with them? And were they encouraged to do this on the basis of abiding institutional structures that reflected Aristotelian commitments to such pedagogical methods and goals? From the perspective of what we actually know about pedagogical practices in the Lyceum, such questions, frankly, are likely to look a little absurd. We are only very rudimentarily informed about the fortunes of the Peripatos, and then not even for its first hundred years. At that point the Peripatos itself, perhaps, but certainly any surviving evidence of its activities as an institution, disappears precipitously. What remains, in addition to Aristotle's own works, is a substantial body of work by his immediate successor as head of the school, Theophrastos, but thereafter only some fragments and reports for Straton and Lykon, the next two heads of the school. What are we in a position to conclude, therefore, about the ongoing pedagogical practices in the Peripatos? Were Straton's lectures on microvoids and his classroom manner less authoritarian and more openly dialectical, say, than the mathematical lectures of the Epicurean Philonides? Straton apparently defended a unitary view of the soul. Should we conclude that he affirmed or denied Aristotle's views of habituation, with their corresponding implications for student admission? Was Straton's reported talent for refutation aimed at students in ways that fostered or hindered the development of their rational autonomy? When we turn from Straton to his successor, is there any way of deciding whether the apparently well-dressed and affable Lykon dealt with students in a more or less authoritarian manner than his highly-strung and anorexic predecessor? Lykon was said to be a vastly popular lecturer. But given his reported predilections for pleasures and erotic pursuits, can we be sure that he avoided demeaning entanglements with his students based, not on respect for their autonomy and a concern for their intellectual growth, but purely as an expression of his own desire and superior power?

We obviously are in no position to form judgements about any of these matters responsibly, and indeed the only glimmers of evidence we have about actual pedagogical practice suggest that as time went on the Lyceum engaged more in instruction than in discussion and dialectic (Lynch 1972: 84ff.). Whether this was a decision made at a broader institutional level or whether some prominent individuals preferred to teach this way in the face of earlier practices is anybody's guess. If we remember as well Wilamowitz's complaint that Aristotle's choice of Theophrastos as the next head of the Peripatos over Eudemos (Aulus Gellius 13.5) was autocratic and smacked of paternalism (when compared to the elections of scholarchs in the Academy), conclusions about a general liberal ethos pervading the actual institutional arrangements of the Peripatos seem, at best, merely fanciful. We therefore should be strongly suspicious, I think, about any attributions of a particular ethos to the Lyceum as an institution generally. It may be that the dialectical nature of the works that survive under Aristotle's name gives theoretical witness to a respect for individual autonomy and reflects Aristotelian views of the importance of our own rationality in assessing and understanding beliefs about ourselves and the world. But such textual features, on their own, provide an insufficient warrant for inferring that the ongoing pedagogical methods of peripatetics displayed any special concern for autonomy or rationality, especially given that the few bits of evidence that we do have about institutional life in the Peripatos actually tend to tell against such a view.

Nussbaum's reconstruction of institutional life in the Garden raises a connected methodological worry, that of the relation between doctrines and particular practices in those few cases where we actually have some evidence for the latter. In making her argument that life in the Garden was rigidly hierarchical, coercive and ever vigilant against heterodoxy, she relies heavily on Philodemos' *On Frankness* along with texts of Epicurus that treat philosophy as analogous to therapy. Philodemos offers our most complex and richly detailed discussion of pedagogical and social practices associated with any ancient school. At the same time, however, *On Frankness* is a text two hundred years removed from the days of Epicurus and one whose discussion clearly may be influenced by later developments in groups far removed from the original Garden in time, place, cultural and political milieu, etc. Thus, although Philodemos alludes, for instance, to what looks like a developed hierarchical system of Epicurean trainers and trainees, we have no independent evidence for such a hierarchy within the institutions of early Epicureanism. Nor, indeed, do we have any evidence for the type of close-knit community seemingly envisaged by Philodemos' text. Indeed, one persistent misconception about the Garden is that a kind of alternative community lived within its grounds committed to Epicurus' injunction to 'Live hidden'. Epicurus' will leaves to his followers a garden and a small house separate from it, the latter for the use of his innermost circle and their children (D.L. 10.19). But there is no serious evidence to suggest that Epicurus himself ever envisaged groups coming together to live in the Garden in obedience to his principles; nor do we have any evidence of any permanent residences in the Garden at any period. At one time, it was fashionable to postulate camps of humble little huts, *à la* Lucretius book 5 no doubt, thronging the Garden. But in retrospect, this vision of a kind of perpetual tent city in Athens abutting the walls of the Academy hardly can fail to strain our credulity. It is much more likely that Epicureans went back and forth from their residences to the Garden just as members of other schools went from their homes to their meeting places. How they got there, of course, is a different matter. Our most influential recent collection of Hellenistic philosophical texts, by A. A. Long and David Sedley, includes an illustration of the ancient philosophical schools in which the Academy is chock-a-block with serious-looking men and youths reading and striking thoughtful poses. Next door, at the Epicurean Garden are two huts, what appears to be a series of vegetable plots, and one solitary fellow walking away from what is either a very long-eared horse or a donkey. Old stereotypes die hard, it seems. It is difficult to know what to say about the vegetable plots, except that they seem more English than Greek. The donkey, as the saying goes, is hard to dispute with, especially if we are meant to view him, not as the companion of a permanent resident, but as having just dropped off a visitor (Long and Sedley 1987: 4 for illustration).

It is unlikely that Nussbaum's picture of a closed, alternative community of Epicureans corresponds, therefore, to any historically-occurring group associated with the original Garden in Athens. Other Epicurean groups in such places as Rhodes or Kos may have practised differently, but that remains a matter of speculation. On the other hand, we do have good evidence that memorizing authoritative doctrines of the master was a practice encouraged from the very beginnings of the school. Does this count as evidence that prevailing in the Garden was a general ethos of disregard for rationality and individual autonomy? Certainly not on its own, I think, since this practice can be open to a variety of interpretations. When taken out of Nussbaum's more claustrophobic account of Epicurean group dynamics, memorizing doctrine begins to look far less sinister and threatening to individual autonomy. Nussbaum aligns memorization with Epicurean sayings that stress the therapeutic aspect of philosophy, e.g. 'Empty are the words of that philosopher who offers therapy for no human suffering . . . there is no use in philosophy if it does not expel the suffering of the soul' (Long and Sedley 1987: no. 25C = Porphyry, *To Marcella* 31). But we also have Epicurean statements (and ones more likely to have been memorized by adherents) that suggest a strong commitment to truth and individual understanding: 'One should not pretend to philosophise, but actually philosophise. For what we need is not the semblance of health, but real health' (Long and Sedley 1987: no. 25D = *Vatican Sayings* 54). In this different light, it is possible to see how memorizing might function as an initial aid to one's further rational understanding of doctrine, not merely as a replacement for it. Thus, Elizabeth Asmis (2001), for example, takes the Epicurean practice of memorizing authoritative sayings as part of the initial stages of Epicurean education, a basic first step by which one comes to eventually understand the thought of the Master rationally. She also finds nothing objectionably coercive in the sort of hierarchies described by Philodemos, but rather views them as an institution grounded in friendly guidance – guidance of the sort that is respectful of students' autonomy and slowly leads them to rationally understand the truths of Epicureanism for themselves.

How then are we to choose between these two diametrically opposed visions of life in the Garden? Both try to link the Epicurean practice of memorizing authoritative sayings to textual doctrines. However, texts can be found that put this behaviour in a different light. Moreover, it is clear that different groups can engage in the same practice for different purposes, regardless of any textual warrant. Our problem is that we have insufficient historical evidence to decide how the practice of memorization was actually carried on within the Garden and what internal institutional functions it was meant to serve. We do not know, that is, the kinds of connections groups of Epicureans themselves might have seen between their authoritative texts and this practice, or between their doctrines and their institutions more generally. Presumably some of their members never achieved the requisite rational understanding of Epicurus' thought, regardless of the time they spent in memorizing, while others perhaps did. But our evidence does not allow us to discriminate finely enough to determine the exact nature of this practice and its function in the Garden. Any conclusions about a general ethos in the Garden seem, therefore, to be on much the same footing as those made about the Peripatos, even though we initially may seem better informed about some features of the Epicureans' institutional life. This is because, given the limitations of our evidence, we are not in a position to decide how particular practices were actually carried on nor can we be sure of their point. Making this claim, I hope, is not to give in to some lamentable form of historical scepticism; rather, it is meant as a gentle reminder of the kinds of evidence we would need to defend claims about the general ethos of institutions. The Epicureans were doctrinally philosophical dogmatists in the way that members of the Peripatos presumably were not. But how this difference in philosophical attitude translated into the institutions and actual pedagogical practices of their two respective schools is not something that we can hope to recover on the basis of inferences from perceived contrasts in philosophical doctrine, even at a general level.

3   Institutions and Their Scope

It is unfortunate that although we have some intriguing and suggestive titles in booklists (e.g. *Peri Askeseos, Peri Agoges, Didaskalos*, etc.), there are no surviving treatises from any of the founders of the four schools that take up in a theoretical way such questions as a philosophical school's proper arrangements, its institutions, the best and most productive forms of institutional life, etc. Moreover, although it seems plausible to assume that the founders themselves took at least some pains over the ongoing internal arrangements of their schools, our evidence is largely silent on this point. Indeed, it is surprising how little provision they seem to have made for the survival of their schools at all, if they had any hopes that it would be through such institutions that their thought would endure and continue to be propagated. Plato taught both at the Academy and later in an adjoining garden at Kolonos when he returned from Sicily for the first time (D.L. 3.5, 3.20). His will, however, makes no mention of the garden and makes no provision for the continuation of his school (D.L. 3.41–3). We therefore have no evidence to suggest that Plato believed that his school would continue its activities after his death, nor do we know if he cared. We do know, however, that he took no special steps to ensure its future institutional life, even by making the minimal gesture of naming a successor. Aristotle, too, made no provisions for any particular institution to survive him, though he seems to have picked a successor. Being a resident foreigner, he could not legally own property in Athens. Moreover, given his flight from Athens for political reasons, it is unlikely that he could have ever imagined such an institution coming into being in a city that had become so hostile. The Stoic Zeno, likewise, was a resident foreigner at Athens, as was his successor Kleanthes. Although feted by the Athenians for his services to virtue with a gold crown and a tomb upon his death (D.L. 7.10–12), in his lifetime Zeno could have harboured no hopes for the kind of private grounds and facilities enjoyed by the Epicureans. Among the four so-called founders, then, it is really only Epicurus, who made any material provisions for an institution to outlast him. Whether or not we accept Diskin Clay's thesis that Epicurus further tried to ensure the survival of his thought by depositing central works in the archives of Athens (Clay 1998: 40–54), he is the only one of the four who consciously provided physical resources for the survival of his school. In this he was preceded by Aristotle's successor, Theophrastos, who acquired and bequeathed a garden for the Peripatos that provided a private space for the next few generations of that school. We know that Plato's garden as well, presumably inherited by his nephew Speusippos, came to serve as a meeting place for his immediate successors, though after the death of its third head, Polemon, no more mention of it is made in our sources. It is worth noting these simple points, perhaps, since when we speak of the Academy, Lyceum, Garden and Stoa it is often easy to think of something much more grand and to forget on just how fragile a foundation, in the sense of private material support, the ancient schools survived. Of course, some prominent members of schools, such as Theophrastos, were exceedingly well off. But ongoing resources for the support of philosophy at any kind of institutional level were decidedly minimalist. Apart from some small bits of property which usually were alienated among philosophically interested family members for their own use, but then often lost for the future use of the school, some pieces of furniture, and small collections of books, which also tended quickly to go out of groups' possession, the material resources available for most practising philosophers as members of schools were practically nil. Schools in the material sense typically consisted of little more than a private place where members could meet and make use of the library belonging to the school's head. Moreover, except for the Epicureans, it is not clear that any of the schools enjoyed even such modest amenities for more than their first few generations. The Stoics managed on less. Illustrative of their institutional resources is the story that Kleanthes, after becoming the second head of the Stoa, augmented the money gained from his teaching by engaging in the lowly profession of water-carrier (D.L. 5.168).

   When we speak of the ancient schools, then, we are speaking of institutions that primarily relied on traditions of teaching and on the ongoing relations of individuals for their continuity and survival. This is one reason why analogies to our contemporary institutions can be so misleading. In fact, one of the greatest impediments to our understanding of the ancient schools as institutions is perhaps simply our habit of calling them 'schools', since so many of the associations that this word holds for us do not apply in the ancient context. Take, for instance, a representative claim by the great French historian of education, Henri-Irenee Marrou. In the course of what is often taken to be the standard account of education in the philosophical schools, he claims that a small number of elite students went on to study philosophy after completing the regular Hellenistic *enkyklios paideia* (roughly 'general education') and that they would begin their studies with lectures in the history of philosophy (Marrou 1956: 309). This should all sound rather familiar, since it corresponds to our own experience of a few elite students going directly on to study philosophy in schools after finishing their preliminary studies. Nor is this familiarity unplanned. This is because, for Marrou, the Hellenistic schools are in many ways not only paradigmatic of Greek educational principles generally, but also the source for our own educational institutions. Moreover, he subscribes to a *longue durée* conception of institutions (cf. Too 2001: 2–10) in which one explains historical phenomena by means of resemblance, analogies and parallels to subsequent contexts. There is an obvious danger of anachronism in such a procedure, one might think, but the claim is that this vision of the historical connections among institutions holds out the promise of discovering deep underlying correspondences between practices that we might otherwise miss.

   Such an account, however, whatever its use in helping to isolate paradigmatic and static trans-historical structures – and ones that serve as models for later historical periods – blurs what, if anything, is to my mind most characteristic of the teaching of philosophy in the Hellenistic period. And that is the ever-shifting plurality of forms of association, many of them evanescent, which arose among particular philosophical groups, groups whose composition and intellectual focus rarely remained stable. Did some elite students go on to study philosophy after finishing their preliminary studies? There can be little doubt. But it is hard to believe that the Epicureans and Stoics, regardless of their increasing concern with philosophical polemics, started their students off with lectures in the history of philosophy. Indeed, we have evidence that they did not, since in their view there would be little value in getting things out of focus immediately by exposing students to a regrettable history of philosophical error. More important, however, Marrou's account treats philosophical education as being the next potential step in a larger, more systematic process of Greek *paideia* and one that depends on one's prior education. But this claim, apart from admitting of many exceptions, more worryingly assimilates philosophical study into a wider institutional structure that it never enjoyed. Philosophical education was typically viewed as something separate and unconnected, and certainly never a part of *enkyklios paideia*. The story of Epicurus turning to philosophy because his schoolmaster could not explain to him the meaning of 'chaos' in Hesiod (D.L. 10.2) is just one of many illustrations of the fact that philosophical questions were viewed as something apart from standard education. Indeed, Epicurus exhorted those interested in philosophical questions and the good life to shun the standard education entirely: 'Hoist all sail, my dear boy, and steer clear of all education' he urges his follower Pythokles (D.L. 10.6). Philosophical study was viewed by the Epicureans as a replacement for standard education, not as a next step following upon it. Similarly for Stoicism, it is hardly likely that a student like Kleanthes, for instance, had much prior education, since he was a boxer from an impoverished background. The jibes of his fellow students, moreover, by no means suggest that he could be characterized as the elite product of a system of general education. But my point is not to line up exceptions to Marrou's claim, since there are many. It is to dispute his general picture of philosophical study as duly taking up its assigned place, much as in our own day, in the wider institutional structures of cultural and political life. Such an account implies the kind of stable ongoing system of institutional support that the study of philosophy in the 'schools' of the Hellenistic period just did not have.

4   Schools and Their Adherents

In antiquity, a variety of terms were used to refer to the activities of philosophers (see Glucker 1978: 159ff.). Some, such as *exedra* (a form of hall), *peripatos* (a walkway) and *kepos* (garden), referred to the places where they met and strolled. *Schole* and *diatribe* came to be used to describe courses of study and lectures. *Hairesis* and *agoge*, in the sense of choices of a particular type of philosophical life and view of one's *telos* (end or philosophical goal), become more prominent later in the period. Indeed, it became a matter of controversy whether some philosophers, e.g. cynics, could be said to belong to a *hairesis*. Hippobotos, in his *On the Sects*, denied a place to cynics among the 'schools' precisely because they produced no body of coherent doctrine and they seemed to be unable to specify a *telos* for their style of life (Bracht Branham and Goulet-Cazé 1996: 21–3). Whether we agree with Hippobotos' definitional strictures here, it is perhaps salutary to reflect on the way he formulates the problem. He believes that a philosophical school is primarily a group of adherents who share the same view of the *telos*. Obviously, such a criterion raises problems of its own. It is too general to capture readily such phenomena as the strong shifts in doctrines that occurred among Academics; nor can it pretend to account sufficiently for any of the fine-grained relationships that doubtlessly structured membership in the schools. Clearly, life in philosophical groups was shaped by a myriad of personal relationships, rivalries and personal research agendas, for which we have only the most inadequate, scattershot testimony. But it is perhaps worth following out some of the implications of this claim, however general, if only as a corrective to the kinds of misconceptions we are likely to fall prey to if we follow Marrou's lead in thinking of philosophical activity as taking place in schools in the familiar sense.

Obviously such generalizations can be crude, but in looking at the overall history of philosophy in the period, we can see in each *hairesis*, as it were, some roughly similar patterns consisting of brief flurries of philosophical activity followed by intervals of silence and, in some cases, short-lived revivals. Obviously, we need to be on our guard not to substitute one form of anachronism for another, but in some ways it may be helpful to think of ancient philosophical 'schools', in the first instance, as emerging and initially functioning in a way that corresponds to how we might today view the 'school' of Wittgenstein and his followers, or the 'schools' of Leo Strauss or Ayn Rand. The analogy is by no means perfect, of course, since followers of these modern scholarchs typically are supported individually within universities and thus lead intellectual lives that, while more secure, are both more dispersed and isolated than their ancient counterparts. But the point of the analogy is to try to pick out some common features shared by groups of adherents to schools of thought – schools of thought that wax and wane in popularity and prestige, perhaps, but that manage to continue attracting individuals who subscribe to their particular doctrines. To be sure, one could not describe these contemporary groups as comprising schools in the familiar sense of a group of individuals gathered together under the aegis of a common, stable institution with fixed curricula, degrees, legal status, formal admission requirements, dedicated positions, etc. But we can recognize them as adherents to particular schools of thought, nonetheless, by the rough, if changing, similarity of their views and their shared intellectual commitments.

Although there are several significant differences that must be taken into account, it may be worth pursuing this analogy further since it captures some additional features of schools of thought and the behaviour of their adherents that may be relevant to our discussion. Like the followers of Wittgenstein, Strauss or Rand, the first followers of Plato, Aristotle, Zeno and Epicurus were attracted by their masters' compelling combination of philosophical talent and personal charisma. There is no need to retail the ancient lore in support of this point, especially since too much ancient evidence for modern tastes typically is directed precisely at demonstrating this often problematic feature of the psychology of philosophical groups. No doubt connected to this characteristic of philosophical groups is the way that, at least among the generation of students who have had direct contact with the master, there arises a deep concern to understand and propagate the master's thought. At the same time, although personal study and conversation with the great master can serve as a special mark of distinction, it is also something that can colour doctrinal disputes with charges of loyalty and betrayal and it certainly can foster personal jockeying based on claims to the master's favour, etc. Not surprisingly, therefore, internal disputes often arise among the first generation of adherents about the exact import of particular doctrines or actions of the master, occasionally leading to bitter disputes, charges of apostasy, excommunications, etc. One further important consideration here is that within ancient philosophical groups, family relationships were similarly involved and added their own special dynamic to the mix.

But a clear difference that one typically sees between this first generation of students and those generations with no personal experience of the master is that the personal force and character of such worries begins to wane in later generations. In the same way, say, that Wittgenstein's immediate students took on some of his personal mannerisms along with his doctrinal ones, so some of Plato's immediate students began to mimic his stoop (Plut. *Mor.* 26b, 53c) as well as his manner of argument. But the stooping Platonist and the impossibly arrogant, abrupt and laconic Wittgensteinian rarely makes an appearance in the generation which has had no direct personal experience of the master. Such affectations are not likely to carry weight with members of these later generations, in any case. So too, among those adherents of subsequent generations, it is harder to find those with the same kind of commitment to the master's particular projects or to find those who wish to take on the mantle of his thought with the same doctrinal reverence as those who experienced that thought firsthand. To style oneself a Wittgensteinian today, for example, is a very different proposition from what it meant, say, forty years ago in the days of Norman Malcolm, and it involves an altogether different level of commitment to a cult of personality.

Even the most cursory look at the early history of Peripatetic, Academic, or Stoic thought shows how quickly corresponding shifts of focus and doctrine appear with each new generation. The history of Academic philosophy in the Hellenistic period, for example, presents such profound shifts in doctrine that scholars are at a loss to find even the thinnest of common threads uniting its first few generations. For the most part, its 'institutional' history and continuity consists of little more than a list of scholarchs. The early and short-lived Peripatos undergoes deep shifts in focus, if not doctrine, and the later renewal of Aristotelianism under Kritolaos seems to be much more an exploration of Aristotelian possibilities and positions in the face of new philosophical challenges than attempts to examine and revive actual doctrines of the master. Stoicism, too, along with some strong early doses of infighting, undergoes measurable shifts in focus, although these shifts are typically presented as capturing the true spirit of the founder's thought. But they are shifts, nonetheless, and again it is only the Epicureans who maintain an easily recognizable doctrinal continuity along with their institutional continuity and thus provide an exception to this pattern. But even here the overall rigidity in Epicureanism can be overdone. Later Epicureans such as Zeno of Sidon and Diogenes of Tarsos seemed perfectly willing to recast works of the master in different forms. And although it has been claimed that Epicureans were deeply concerned to establish canonical texts, we do not find among them, as we might expect if this were the case, a parallel tradition of commenting on texts such as we find in later Aristotelianism (Snyder 2000: 54).

One further feature of philosophy in the Hellenistic period that bears on this analogy is the manner in which talented philosophers took up the mantle of one of the great masters' thought and attempted to breathe life into neglected doctrines e.g. Kritolaos' 'revival' of Peripatetic thought or Arkesilaos' reinvigoration of Academic philosophy. Correspondingly, in a few generations, perhaps, some powerful thinker might again take up the mantle of Wittgenstein and revive aspects of his thinking that have fallen out of fashion. When Kritolaos did this for Aristotelianism, and identified himself as a Peripatetic, the Lyceum had been defunct as an institution for over one hundred years. His adherence to the 'Peripatos' was thus not a pledge to any ongoing institution, but to a school of thought.

Of course, it would be misleading to suppose that this notion of a school of thought can capture all the varieties of philosophical association that occurred in our period. But it can perhaps help us to see something whose importance for the survival and success of Hellenistic philosophy cannot be underestimated, although it is sometimes overlooked in accounts of institutions. Contemporary adherents to schools of thought are typically supported by established institutions, but nonetheless the long-term power and influence of their philosophies depend less on institutional mandates, in many ways, than on their own talent and teaching. In this they provide a clear and important parallel to Hellenistic philosophers. This is because it is primarily to these more intimate personal rhythms of philosophical life – and not to any institutional backing provided by something called 'the Stoa' or 'the Lyceum' – that we owe the survival, power and professional complexity of Hellenistic philosophy.

FURTHER READING

Complete texts of Hellenistic philosophy have survived very poorly, in striking contrast to the work of predecessors such as Plato and Aristotle. The best point of access to this fragmented material is the source collection by Long and Sedley (1987), Vol. 1 giving texts in translation, Vol. 2 in the original language. The recent *Cambridge History of Hellenistic Philosophy* (1999), edited by K. Algra et al., offers a comprehensive treatment and full bibliography; otherwise overviews can be found in Long 1974 (clear, though now rather old), Cambiano 1983, Erler 1983, the brief Sharples 1996. In the past couple of decades Hellenistic philosophy has become the subject of lively debate; some sense of the directions this has taken can been seen in the essays gathered in Barnes et al. 1980 (on epistemology), Schofield and Striker 1986 (on ethics), Laks and Schofield 1995 (on political thought). There are numerous studies of different aspects of the philosophical schools. For the Peripatos: Wehrli 1967–78, 1983, Gottschalk 1972 (on the wills of the scholarchs), Lynch 1972 (on the Lyceum as an institution), Moraux 1973–84, Natali 1991; for the Academy (and scepticism): Cherniss 1945, Dal Pra 1975, Glucker 1978, L. Tarán 1981, Tarrant 1985; for the Stoa: Ioppolo 1986 (on the debate with the Academy), Erskine 1990, Schofield 1991 (the latter two concerned especially with political thought); for the Epicureans: Clay 1998, Sedley 1998a, Asmis 2001, Warren 2002; for Cynicism: Goulet-Cazé and Goulet 1993 in French, some of the essays of which are translated in Bracht Branham and Goulet-Cazé 1996. Sedley 1998b considers the relation between philosophical schools and the city. On education, in addition to Marrou 1956, note Snyder 2000, Cribiore 2001 and the essays in Too 2001.

CHAPTER TWENTY-EIGHT

Literature and its Contexts

Richard Hunter

1   Survival and Loss

Our view of Hellenistic literature is fragmented and skewed by the chances of survival. The high poetry of the third century, particularly that associated with the court of the Ptolemies at Alexandria, holds centre-stage, but (for example) Hellenistic oratory and tragedy are all but completely lost, and we must reconstruct most of the literary scholarship of the period from scattered fragments and the scholia to the texts of earlier ages, which were now properly 'edited' for the first time. The natural concentration upon Alexandria can obscure the flowering of a brilliant Doric literary culture in the West: Theocritus allows us a glimpse of this, but one would give much to have one of Rhinthon's tragic parodies from the same period and area (cf. Taplin 1993: 48–52). The literature of the second and first centuries has, in particular, fared badly: epigrams (including those of Meleager of Gadara, whose 'Garland', an anthology of poems by himself and others, may still be glimpsed within the surviving *Palatine Anthology*), the *Europa* of Moschos, some bucolic poems which probably survived because of their association with Theocritus, Bion's *Epitaph for Adonis* (Reed 1997), and the anonymous *Epitaph for Bion* are practically all the poetry which survives intact from this crucial transitional period. Nevertheless, it is also important to remember that a very important part of 'literary experience' in this period was constructed through the great texts of the past, most notably perhaps Homer and Euripides, and it is through the constant re-interpretation and appropriation of these texts, an appropriation that took place in thousands of elementary schoolrooms as well as in theatres and in the books of learned men, that they may be considered as much 'Hellenistic' as 'archaic' or 'classical'. The Hellenistic age is indeed one of the more remarkable and important periods of Homeric reception, and in the world after Alexander, the *alter Achilles* himself, a world of powerful 'kings' (*basileis*) of many different shades of legitimacy, the *Iliad* became again a strongly didactic text about (*inter alia*) power and conflict, as the *Odyssey* became an obvious pre-echo of the apparently ever-expanding geographical horizons of Greek culture.

If readings of Homer represent large-scale reactions to a shifting social geography, the new possibilities of movement, dislocation and loss are perhaps reflected at a micro-level in the hundreds of 'literary' funeral epigrams of the Hellenistic period. The epigram offers the ever-moving 'passer-by' a brief moment of stillness, while the deceased's often bitterly brief moment of *kleos* asserts the value of life in the face of the hopelessness of human mortality. Thus the following poem of Callimachus unites his own community of Cyrene in grief,

> At dawn we buried Melanippos, and while the sun
>   Was setting the maiden Basilo died
> By her own hand, unable to live once she had placed
>   Her brother on the pyre. The house of their father
> Aristippos looked upon evil doubled, and all Cyrene plunged
>   In grief, seeing that home of noble children orphaned.
>   (Epigram 20 Pf., trans. Nisetich)

whereas in another poem the separation and loss of death is cruelly actualized in geographical distance:

> If you come to Kyzikos, it's small trouble (*ponos*) to find Hippakos
>   and Didyme, for in no way obscure (*aphanes*) is the family.
> And you must say to them a painful word (*epos*), but say it
>   All the same: I hold their son, Kritias, here.
>   (Epigram 12 Pf., trans. Nisetich)

The poem quite literally 'fills out' the narrative of grief which lies behind the factual details – ' "Who lies here?" "X from Y" ' – of the standard epitaphic epigram, which here frame the poem (Kyzikos . . . Kritias). There is an obvious contrast, pointed by the semantic range of *ponos*, 'trouble, effort' as well as 'grief', between the 'small trouble' which the passer-by needs to endure to pass on the message, once he reaches Kyzikos, and the grief which that message will cause (Walsh 1991). No one wishes to be the bearer of bad tidings, and the epigram exploits the unease which the passer-by/reader will feel; there is no pressure, no 'command' to tell the news to the parents, but rather a conditional, 'If you travel to Kyzikos . . .'. Only by adopting such a low key can the grief be controlled. The very distance, however, between Kyzikos on the Propontis and wherever the 'epitaph' now stands (is it being read in North Africa?) both complicates the assertion of 'little trouble' and pathetically underscores the irretrievable distance between Kritias and his parents; though his family may be 'in no way obscure' (*aphanes*), Kritias has disappeared (i.e. is *aphanes*) for ever, and the confident assertion of v.2 has more than a touch of desperate whistling in the dark.

If, however, these poems reflect some of the mobility of the Hellenistic world, we nevertheless know far too little about Greek literature reflecting the cultural inter-change of the high Hellenistic period, though various texts, such as the 'Letter of Aristeas', which describes the translation of the Septuagint by Jewish sages at Alexandria, and the *Exagoge* of Ezekiel, a tragic dramatization of the Septuagint story of the flight of Moses and the Jews from Egypt, allow us a glimpse of Jewish culture in second-century Alexandria. Papyri and inscriptions reveal that Greek literature was read and performed all over the world opened up by Alexander, but of the new compositions which that new world brought forth, only traces remain. We know, for example, almost nothing of the influential works of the Cynic Menippos of Gadara, in whom Semitic and Arabic traditions of 'prosimetrum' (i.e. compositions which use both prose and verse) have reasonably been thought to have left their mark.

2   Display and Self-Representation

If 'Greek' and 'other' is one opposition which both structures and is constantly interrogated in Hellenistic literature, another is that of 'high/elite' vs. 'low/popular' culture. It is frequently argued that in the post-classical world the gulf between elite and non-elite culture became a yawning chasm, one propped ever wider by the circulation of written texts to be enjoyed by a relatively tiny, though socially powerful, minority; on the other side of the gap, so the argument goes, will have been a kaleidoscopic performance culture, most of which has perished for ever, but for occasional notices in compilers such as Athenaeus and a fitful epigraphic record which preserves the names of poets and performers of all kinds and all levels of formality. Like many sharply drawn distinctions, there is some truth in this. There certainly are clear differences in, particularly, metrical and verbal style between 'high literature' and what we can reconstruct of this almost wholly lost world of perform- ance and popular entertainment (Hunter 1996a: 7–13). On the other hand, the opposition itself is, in part at least, the creation of the elite texts themselves: thus, Theocritus' hexameter mimes and Herodas' *Mimiamboi*, in an old-fashioned metre and a literary reconstruction of an archaic dialect, call attention to (and hence reify)'the mime' as a separate area of cultural experience, precisely by 'translating' it to a different mode. A famous epigram of Callimachus (cf. below) is precisely built upon the fragility of such elite constructions, though the elite prose literature of subsequent centuries, which never tires of unfavourable comparisons between the 'morally beneficial' reading and recitation practices of the educated classes and the 'vulgar' entertainments of the common people, does not seem to have listened. Such distinctions trace their intellectual heritage to Plato's remarks (*Laws* 3.700c–d) on the increasing effacement of distinctions between generic types, which results from a pandering to vulgar taste, and Aristotle's discussion of the different modes of humour practised by the educated and the vulgar (*Eth. Nic.* 4.1128a). Ultimately, of course, this self-consciousness about language use goes back, as also does the intellectual framework of many of the scholarly practices of the Alexandrian Museum, to the central concerns of the sophistic era. The literature of 'display', which has at its heart the assertion or confirmation of group or individual identity, is always concerned to mark difference between itself and 'other'.

'Display', *epideixis*, is indeed a crucial element in some Hellenistic poetry: Lyko- phron's *Alexandra*, with its extraordinary riddling catalogue of Greek myth, the dark curses of Euphorion's *Thrax* and the didactic poems of Nikander on poisons and snake-bites are among the prominent examples usually cited. Metrical experimen- tation now comes to the fore. Sotades of Maroneia transposed the *Iliad* into 'sexy' sotadeans (an ionic metre), and Philikos, a member of the group of writers of tragedy known (at least later) as the 'Pleiad' and an important priest of Dionysos at Alexan- dria, composed a poem on the rape of Persephone and the grief of Demeter in choriambic hexameters and offered this novelty as a gift to the *grammatikoi* (*Supp.*

Hell. 676–80). Scholarship and learning are indeed not spared from the pervasive irony which colours the best poetry of the period. Thus, for example, the poetry of Simichidas, the pompous young poet of Theocritus' *Seventh Idyll*, is characterized by a 'display' of his knowledge of obscure Arcadian cult, and the pedantic poetic voice of Callimachus' *Aitia* (cf. below) is constantly the subject of gentle humour; at fr. 75.8 ('Acontius and Cydippe') the poet's 'much knowledge' nearly lands him in a serious blasphemy. One of Callimachus' most famous epigrams deals explicitly with the folly of elitist self-delusion:

> I hate recycled poetry (*poiema kuklikon*), and get no pleasure
>   From a road crowded with travellers this way and that.
> I can't stand a boy who sleeps around, don't drink
>   at public fountains, and loathe everything vulgar (*demosion*).
> Now you, Lysanies, sure are handsome ... But before I've repeated
>   'handsome', 'and some ... one else's' cuts me off.
>   (Epigram 28 Pf., trans. Nisetich)

The poet proclaims his disdain for all things common or banal which must be widely shared: 'cyclic' poetry, the broad highway, a promiscuous lover, a fountain available to all. The variety of the verbs in the first four verses marks the poet's fastidiousness and care, whereas the very prosaic expression for the things which are rejected enacts at the verbal level the banality which is being imputed to them. What is rejected also involves or implies movement: the poem 'which circles around', the path with its bustling crowd, the boy who roams from one admirer to the next, the fountain to which one must travel; against this chaos is set the stillness of the poet, fixed in his opinions and the privacy of his superiority. The final couplet modifies this picture. The play with echo suggests the emergence of a truth which previously was (consciously or unconsciously) suppressed (Walsh 1990: 11–12); the poet's brave words turn out to be a protective barrier which conceal as much as they reveal, and only the operation of echo, which is beyond human control, can unmask the truth. The 'vulgar', embodied in a popular, 'non-elitist' pronunciation which makes the echo possible, triumphs. The poem thus explores the fissure inherent in the whole business of seeking to write 'elitist' epigrams about *eros*, an emotion to which we are all vulnerable (it is always *demosion*) and one which is no respecter of aesthetic principles; it is not merely that the store of epigrammatic literary *topoi* is finite, but so is that of experience – hierarchies of literature are, in the end, as vain as hierarchies of kinds of lover.

If it is literary taste to which Callimachus gives pride of place in his (as it will turn out, crumbling) sense of himself, then this too is representative of an important feature of Hellenistic literary culture. When scholars and poets dispute over the quality of Antimachos' poetry (Krevans 1993; Cameron 1995: 303–38) or over the relative merits of Homer and Hesiod, it is of course the present which is as much at issue as the past; in one sense this is merely an intensification of the attitudes parodically described already in, for example, Aristophanes' *Clouds*: 'modernity' (or, as it now is and was already with the sophists of the late fifth century, different manifestations of 'modernity') is expressed through adhesion to particular intellectual and poetic modes. This intensification, however, depends upon an equally intensified sense of the monumentality of the past, a phenomenon most easily recognizable perhaps in the rise of scholarship. Although the clear sense of a 'break' in literary culture after Alexander is explicit only in the critics of the Augustan age, various indications point in the same direction for the earlier period of the Hellenistic age: Eratosthenes did not carry his chronographical work on the Olympian victors beyond the death of Alexander, and Aristarchos and Aristophanes of Byzantion did not receive anyone 'of their own time' into the lists of approved authors (Quintilian *Inst. Or.* 10.1.54).

The past was quite literally monumentalized and made available in physical form in the unparalleled collection of texts in the Library of Alexandria, which could, if need be, themselves assume human form. Thus Callimachus (*Iambus* 1) brings the archaic Ionian poet Hipponax, himself an object of serious scholarly endeavour, back from the dead to introduce a 'modern' version of Hipponactean poetry and to contrast the wisdom of the legendary Seven Sages with the petty squabbles of their Alexandrian descendants; the modernity matters, for in a matching poem (*Iambus* 13) Callimachus also makes the point that mindless copying of archaic and classical poetic modes is not what 'poetry' should be about. The past is something to be engaged with, creatively exploited, sometimes indeed surpassed, not merely reproduced. The same message is delivered by Apollo himself to Callimachus in perhaps the most famous and influential passage of Hellenistic poetry:

> The very first time I sat down and put
> A writing tablet on my lap, my own
> Lykian Apollo said to me: 'Make your sacrifice
> as fat as you can, but keep
> your Muse on slender rations. And see that you go
> where no hackneys plod: avoid the ruts
> carved in the boulevard, even if it means
> driving along a narrower path.
>   (*Aitia* fr.1.21–8, trans. Nisetich)

Avoiding the 'broad highway' is a matter of using the past intelligently, not of a fruitless search for 'originality'. So it is that Hellenistic elite poetry is intensely intertextual in its constant allusive reference to archaic and classical texts, particularly of course Homer. This is not a matter of setting puzzles for the reader, but of using creatively the most important shared aspect of experience between poet and reader, namely the experience of previous literature. This past heritage can no more be wished away than can the future; the young Cyclops of Theocritus' *Eleventh Idyll*, trapped in a language and a future which Homer has created for him, offers a particularly amusing vision of this paradoxical modernity.

3   Hellenistic Comedy

The most important Hellenistic literary form, in terms of the breadth and longevity of its cultural impact, was New Comedy. We have enough Menander to feel reasonably confident about the nature of this dramatic form, though his rivals and successors survive only in fragments and through the Latin adaptations of Plautus and Terence.

New Comedy was performed all over the Greek world and its role, enacted both through performance in the theatre and through private reading and recitation, in spreading a particular set of 'civilizing' values and even indeed forms of social behaviour, ought not to be underestimated. Set in a contemporary world and reflecting the concerns and assumptions of well-to-do *oikoi*, no texts offer as rich an opportunity for the exploration of certain Hellenistic moral and social patterns. It has often been thought that the repeated narrative motif of family separation and ultimate, wish-fulfilling recognition and reunion, together with the prominent role of Tyche, 'Fortune', reflects the great upheavals and dislocations and the almost continuous warfare of the age; what is clear, however, is that, although the political and social life of Athens can be readily mapped as background into many of the plays, the plots no longer depend upon a detailed knowledge of any one city and the focus is on the lives of individuals and individual families, whose fate is not symbolic of the life of the *polis* in the complex manner which is familiar from Aristophanes. Even the best preserved play of Menander, the *Dyskolos*, whose setting at a shrine of Pan and the Nymphs in the mountainous Attic deme of Phyle might have been expected to exploit and demand local knowledge of its audience, proves almost entirely devoid of regional specificity. Rather, under the sign of Pan who grants fertility to the flocks, the play opposes a universal ideal of communality and social cohesion, expressed through the idea of marriage and cultic practice, to the misanthrope Knemon's rejection of society and impossible dream of autarky, based on his experience of dog-eat-dog reality:

> One mistake, perhaps, I *did* make – I believed that I was the
> One man in the world who could be self-contained (*autarkes*), and wouldn't require
> Help from any man. However, I've seen now that death can strike
> Suddenly and with no warning, and I've realised that my
> Past belief was wrong. You always need someone who'll lend a hand,
> Someone on the doorstep. By Hephaestus, I thought nobody
> On this earth could show real friendship to another – that's how far
> Off the rails I'd gone through studying all the different ways of life,
> How men in their calculations angle for gain.
>
> (*Dyskolos* 713–21, trans. Arnott)

So too, Daos' account in *Aspis* of the battle in which he believes his young master to have been killed is geographically specific ('There is a river in Lykia called the Xanthos . . .'), but nothing hangs on that specificity.

The foregrounded values of New Comedy are generosity in the broadest sense (*philanthropia*), gentleness and self-knowledge. The opening of the *Misoumenos* ('The Hated Man'), one of the most famous scenes of Menander in antiquity, foreshadows the emergence of those virtues in the play to come through the opening presentation of the soldier Thrasonides, whose sexual restraint in the matter of his captive Krateia marks him as worthy eventually to become a full member of the citizen body:

> O Night – for you've the largest share in sex
> Of all the gods, and in your shades are spoken
> Most words of love and thoughts charged with desire –

Have you seen any other man more racked
With misery? A lover more ill-starred?
Now either at my own front door I stand,
Here in the alley, or I saunter up
And down, when I could lie asleep
Till now, when you, O night, have nearly run
Half course, and clasp my love. She's in there – in
My house, I've got the chance, I want it just
As much as the most ardent lover – yet
I don't . . . I'd rather stand here shivering
Beneath a wintry sky – chatting to you!
(Misoumenos 1–14, trans. Arnott)

Old Comedy's concern with 'real' persons was, however, taken over in the Hellenistic age by the literature of anecdote. Some 470 verses survive (preserved in Athenaeus' *Deipnosophistai*) of the *Chreiai* ('Anecdotes') of the comic poet Machon of Corinth or Sikyon. These verse anecdotes tell of the doings and witty sayings of courtesans, parasites and poets; great men are not absent (one or more Ptolemies, Demetrios Poliorketes), but they are only rarely very important to the anecdotes and are there rather to make the anecdotes interesting by lending a flavour of 'naughtiness in high places'. Machon was probably active at Alexandria in the middle of the third century, but the anecdotes of the *Chreiai* cover the period from the late fifth to the early third centuries, and it is likely that Machon drew on the genre of prose *Chreiai*, *Apophtheg-mata* and *Apomnemoneumata* which flourished from the later fourth century on (perhaps in particular the work of Lynkeus of Samos, the brother of the historian Douris).

4 Alexandria and the Ptolemies

Much of what survives of elite third-century poetry was written at Alexandria during the reigns of the first three Ptolemies. The twin institutions of the 'Museum' (lit. 'shrine of the Muses') and the Library (Pfeiffer 1968: 96–104; Fraser 1972: 312–35; Erskine 1995), together with the fabulous wealth of the Ptolemies, served as a magnet to intellectuals, poets and scientists from all over the Greek world and simultaneously marked the Ptolemies as the true heirs and preservers of Greek cultural traditions. There are, of course, many interwoven strands of tradition. The Ptolemies were, on one hand, celebrated by poets as the true successors of Alexander and through him of Herakles, the great civilizer (cf. Theocr. *Id.* 17.13–33); in another way, Alexandria was the new Athens, i.e. the cultural and mercantile capital of the world. In the first 'mimiamb' of Herodas the bawd Gyllis seeks to persuade a younger friend that her man has forgotten all about her in the midst of the delights of Alexandria:

> The home of the goddess is there. For everything in the world that exists and is produced is in Egypt: wealth, wrestling schools, power, tranquillity, fame, spectacles, philosophers, gold, youths, the sanctuary of the sibling gods, the King is an excellent chap, the Museum, wine, every good thing he could desire, women, as many as by Hades' Maid as the stars that heaven boasts of bearing . . . (Herodas 1.26–33, trans. Cunningham, adapted)

So too, in Theocritus' *Fifteenth Idyll* the description of a Ptolemaic 'spectacle' (Arsinoe's festival in honour of Adonis) is combined with the representation of Alexandria as a *cosmopolis* to which all the people and goods of the world flow (Rowlandson, this volume, section 2).

The Ptolemaic dimension of some 'Ptolemaic' poetry is completely explicit. The royal house figures in many contemporary epigrams, and both Theocritus and Callimachus draw an analogy between Apollo's birth on Delos, as narrated in the *Homeric Hymn to Delos*, and Philadelphos' birth on Kos (Theocr. *Id.* 17.58–76, Callimachus *Hymn to Delos* 160–95); in Callimachus, in fact, Philadelphos' birth is foretold by Apollo while still unborn in Leto's womb. In other texts, a more oblique link with the royal house and with Ptolemaic ideology is a plausible hypothesis. Thus, for example, the story of Heracles' strangling of the snakes and his early education in Theocritus 24 has been attractively read as a way of imaging a Ptolemaic prince, perhaps the young Philadelphos (Koenen 1977: 79–86; Griffiths 1979: 91–8). The only surviving Hellenistic epic, the *Argonautica* of Apollonios of Rhodes, who served as Librarian of the Royal Library in the middle years of the century, takes the Argonauts on an increasingly fantastic journey to the eastern edges of the Black Sea and then back to Greece via central Europe, Italy and North Africa; there are obvious resonances of Alexander's eastern travels, but, more specifically, the Argonauts come into contact with areas of considerable political interest to the Ptolemies – the Aegean islands, the Black Sea, Cyrenaica – and the epic as a whole suggests the important themes of inter-cultural contact, Hellenization, and the widening intellectual and physical horizons of the Hellenistic world (Hunter 1991; 1993: 152–69; 1995). The present and recent past is everywhere in the religious and social practices of the poem, and the foreshadowing of the present in the past is a technique which Apollonios perhaps inherited from Pindar and Attic tragedy and which he bequeathed to Virgil.

More problematic has proved the attempt to find within Ptolemaic poetry ideas and narrative motifs which exploit Egyptian and pharaonic themes; the apparent lack of interest of third-century Alexandrian scholarship in things Egyptian may seem to discourage even searching for such material. Nevertheless, powerful arguments have been advanced for seeing Egyptian patterns within particular poems which directly concern the royal house, such as Callimachus' 'Lock of Berenice' in which Berenice's dedication of a lock of hair for the safe return of her 'brother'-husband Euergetes seems to exploit the mourning of Isis for Osiris (Koenen 1993; Selden 1998); in such poems both Greek and Egyptian themes may resonate, thus inscribing the duality of Ptolemaic kingship within the poem.

5   Writing the Past

The *Eighteenth Idyll* of Theocritus records an epithalamian which a choir of Spartan maidens sang outside the wedding-chamber of Menelaos and Helen:

> Now, in Sparta once, in the palace of golden-haired Menelaus,
> There were girls who wound fresh hyacinths into their hair, and
> Stepped into the dance outside his freshly painted bridal room –
> Twelve girls, from the city's foremost families, the great glory of
> Sparta's youthful womanhood, at the time when Atreus' younger son,

> Successful in his wooing, had locked the doors on them with his
> Adored Helen, daughter of Tyndareus. So the girls sang in unison,
> And moved their feet to the dance's complex measures,
> While all the palace echoed to the sound of their wedding hymn.
>
> (Theocr. *Id.* 18.1–8, trans. Verity)

The sense of a distant pastness ('once upon a time') which pervades the poem extends to both subject-matter and form. As early as Homer, Menelaos and his comrades belong to an earlier, stronger, and more 'heroic' generation than 'men of the present day', and Hesiod (*Works and Days* 156–73) had assigned the heroes of the Trojan war to the 'divine race of hero men, who are called "demigods" ' and had expressed regret that he lived in a degenerate present; for the poets of the third century BC, however, Homer and Hesiod were themselves paradigmatic icons of a now distant past. In another poem, *Idyll* 16 in honour of Hieron of Syracuse, the poet pictures potential patrons who conceal their miserliness behind the existence of Homer: 'Who would listen to another poet? Homer is enough for all.' The irony of the presentation should not conceal the urgency of the question: the undying fame which Homer conferred upon the characters of his poems (Theocr. *Id.* 16.48–57, 17.116–20) both offered the prime example of the power of poetry, but was also an ever-present reminder of the seeming impossibility of measuring up to the past.

The *Eighteenth Idyll* also recreates an apparently past world of Spartan maiden-songs, that world most familiar to us from the lyric poetry of Alkman. The sacred geography of Spartan legend shapes the rite which the choir foretells that it will perform in Helen's honour:

> As for us, early tomorrow we'll go to the flowering
> Meadows where we race, to pick scented garlands, full of
> Memories of you, as suckling lambs long for their mothers' teats.
> We shall be the first to plait for you a wreath of ground-loving
> Clover to hang on a shady plane-tree, and we shall be the first
> To make an offering of gleaming oil, dripped from our silver flasks,
> Under that plane tree's shade. In its bark we shall cut these words, that
> Passers-by may read its Dorian message: 'Respect me; I am Helen's tree'.
>
> (Theocr. *Id.* 18.39–48, trans. Verity)

This appeal to a reader's power to imagine the (real or believed) cult of remote places or times, combined with an interest in the origins, the 'aetiology', of that cult is one of the most powerful currents which run through Hellenistic literature. The urge to catalogue and record does not, of course, of itself imply recognition of impending loss – not all archaeology and anthropology is of the 'rescue' variety – but, like the collection of rare and dialect words ('glosses') which flourished in third-century scholarship, such practices can themselves define an area of 'otherness', which reinforces a sense of difference from the world of the reader.

This sense of 'otherness', of the conjuring of a world which is no longer ours, ought in fact to be connected to the very nature of literature in the Hellenistic world. The spread of higher-level literacy, a flourishing book trade and the growth of libraries and scholarly activity meant that works were now composed with an 'international' audience in mind, an audience bound together by a sense of a common cultural and intellectual heritage which expressed itself, in part, through a displayed interest – which today might be termed, somewhat misleadingly, 'antiquarian' – in the local traditions and stories of the whole Greek world. Callimachus' most influential and famous poem, the *Aitia*, a treatment in four books and perhaps some 6000 elegiac verses of the origins of customs and cults from all over the Greek world, is the most powerful and important witness to these developments. The great centres of cultural and (sometimes) political power – Alexandria, Pergamon, Athens, Pella, Antioch – became the market-places in which such knowledge was exchanged and membership of this intellectual elite confirmed.

Although such exchange now regularly took place through the medium of exchanged writing, there was a real continuity, which is not to be underestimated, however much it was also exaggerated and to some extent constructed by the elite themselves, between these practices and the sympotic world of intellectual and cultural exchange depicted by archaic poets and the narratives of Herodotos. Perhaps the best illustration of this is the episode (fr. 178 Pf.) in the *Aitia* in which the poet meets Theogenes, a visitor to Alexandria from the Aegean island of Ikos (modern Alonnisos); he meets him at a symposium at the house of Pollis, an Athenian who keeps all the celebrations of the Athenian sacred calendar, though living in Alexandria. Theogenes and the poet are 'two of a kind', interested in intellectual conversation which wears the elite badge of allusion to famous texts of Homer and Hesiod (Hunter 1996b; Fantuzzi and Hunter 2002: 97–104). Unlike Theogenes, however, Callimachus stays in Alexandria and gathers the tales of those who pass through or (what amounts to the same thing) whose books reach the Library – an Odysseus who 'saw the cities of many men and came to know their minds' (or, with Zenodotos, 'customs'), but whose journeys are those of the mind. So too, the festivals which Pollis nostalgically re-creates in a 'foreign' city doubtless remained for him and some of his guests markers of Athenian identity, as they were in their true home, but participation in them now marks as well a broader, more 'international' form of identity.

6   The Real and the Written

As early as the latter part of the fifth century there is evidence for the gradual dissolution of the Greek 'song culture' and its replacement in part by a 'book culture' and in part by a new kind of specialist music culture in the hands of experts and *virtuosi* whose performances were no longer necessarily tied to specific performance occasions, whether public festivals or private celebrations. Certainly, by the end of the fifth century the great age of choral poetry was over, and most poetry of the high Alexandrian period is in unaccompanied dactylic hexameters or elegiac couplets. The two crucial performative contexts for high poetry were now recitation, whether to one's fellow poets or at the court of a patron or at a public poetry festival, and reading. The 'internationalization' of literature, together with this dual loss of the original nexus between words, music and metre and of the specific, often local performance context of (particularly lyric) poetry led not only to the standardization of poetic form, but also to a radical liberation of poets from the, partly self-imposed, tyranny of convention determined by geography and occasion. No set of texts illustrates these phenomena as brilliantly as Callimachus' *Hymns*.

Callimachus inherited a broad and permeable distinction between hexameter poems of the kind which have survived for us as the 'Homeric hymns', which were probably performed in much the same context as epic narrative, and the lyric, choral hymns which formed part of cultic performance. In the changed circumstances of the third century, in which grand lyric poetry of the old style was no longer possible, Callimachus recuperated the experience of the cultic performance of poetry by writing three of his hymns (to Apollo, Athena and Demeter) as 'scripts' being performed during a religious ceremony; in *Apollo* and *Athena* the celebrants, respectively at an unspecified rite (though perhaps the Karneia at Callimachus' native city of Cyrene) and at an Argive ceremony in which the image of Athena was bathed in the river, are waiting for the epiphany of the god (or his or her image), and in the *Demeter* the female celebrants are taking part in a sacred procession on a day of fasting, such as is familiar from the Athenian 'Thesmophoria'. These 'scripts' elaborate the self-reference of the early hymns to the choir and the festival in a way that was unnecessary when the hymns actually were part of a performance (Depew 2000; Fuhrer and Hunter 2002). Here are the openings of the hymns to Apollo and Athena:

> How Apollo's laurel sapling shook, how the whole
> Temple shook with it! Back, *back*, all who have sinned!
> The doors are rattling: it must be
> Apollo striking them with his gleaming foot.
> Can't you see? All of a sudden
> The Delian palm nodded with joy, and now
> The swan is singing, high in the air, his lovely song.
> Up now, bars, swing free of the gates!
> Let them go, bolts: the god is no longer distant.
> And you, young men, begin the singing and dancing.
> > (*Hymn to Apollo* 1–8, trans. Nisetich)

> All who pour water for the bath of Pallas,
> Come out, come out! Just now I heard
> The mares of the goddess whinny: she too
> Is anxious to go! Hurry, then,
> Blond daughters of Pelasgia, hurry.
> > (*Hymn to Athena* 1–4, trans. Nisetich)

The scripted excitement is, on one hand, a recognition that listening to a recitation or reading a text are modes of engagement which are clearly different from actually taking part in a ceremony, but it also celebrates the extraordinary power of 'the mind's eye' to envision the absent.

A similar celebration is an important part of the prominent place in Hellenistic poetry held by descriptions of (real or imaginary) works of art: a marvellously sculpted wooden bowl in Theocritus' *First Idyll*, the richly decorated cloak which Jason wears to meet Hypsipyle in the first book of Apollonios' *Argonautica*, the basket with scenes from the Io story which Europa takes with her to the beach for the fateful meeting with the 'Zeus-bull' in Moschos' *Europa*, the tapestries and images in honour of Aphrodite and Adonis in Theocritus' *Fifteenth Idyll* (cf. below). Both literary tradition (the 'Shield of Achilles' in *Iliad* 18) and developments in 'realistic' representational art itself (Pollitt 1986: 141–7) have contributed to these passages, which are, however, also to be connected with the new importance of reading and the demands upon the imagination that this brings with it. This 'ecphrastic' style may also occur in narrative which does not explicitly purport to describe a work of art. In Theocritus 22 the Dioskouroi come upon Amykos, king of the Bebrykians, as they are wandering away from the other Argonauts to admire the beauties of nature:

> There,
> At the foot of a smooth cliff, they found an ever-flowing spring,
> Brimming with pure water; in its depths pebbles gleamed, as if
> Made of crystal or silver. Around it grew tall pines, poplars,
> And plane trees, and leaf-crowned cypresses, and fragrant flowers,
> Such as carpet meadows at the end of spring and summon hairy bees
> To cheerful husbandry. There sat a giant of a man, taking his ease
> In the sun. He was an awesome spectacle: his ears were thickened
> By blows from leather mitts, and his huge chest and broad back swelled
> Like the iron flesh of a hammered statue. Where his shoulders and hard arms
> Met, the muscles jutted out like rounded boulders, polished smooth
> By the whirling onrush of a winter torrent. A lion's skin, tied by its paws,
> Hung from his neck and over his back.
>
> (Theocr. *Id*. 22.37–52, trans. Verity)

We see both the pool and Amykos with the eyes of the Dioskouroi, here depicted as 'outsiders', tourists with refined and modern aesthetic sensibilities (v.36). What they (and thus we) 'see' is a pool which conforms to the most verdant beauties of the *locus amoenus* (Hunter 1999: 12–17), i.e. a description shaped by prior texts and one which foregrounds the mediating role of the poet, and a man who resembles the figures of 'realistic' Hellenistic statuary, such as the famous 'Terme boxer' (Pollitt 1986: 145–7; Hunter 1996a: 62–3; figure 28.1). More broadly, the juxtaposition of the narratives of Polydeukes and Kastor in *Idyll* 22 displays two apparently opposed modes of representation, one which emphasizes *techne* and *kosmos*, 'art' and 'artificiality' – the passage just considered, the unparalleled stichomythia in hexameters which follows – and one (the Kastor narrative) which seems to be an experiment in almost 'unmediated' narrative. In this juxtaposition lies a further exploration of the new possibilities of book literature.

The fluctuation in Hellenistic texts between the description of 'real', often famous, works of art and the creation of imaginary artefacts within the text is one manifestation of a persistent concern with the closeness or distance of 'literary' experience from 'lived' experience; this concern is in part a result of the new contexts of reception and of the growth of the idea of literature as a discrete area of activity and one whose enjoyment is a mark of inclusion in a particular cultural group. Inclusion, however, also involves the exclusion of 'others', and the frequency with which elite Hellenistic literature depicts the lives of 'ordinary people', i.e. the excluded, may be taken as a further manifestation of the changed functioning of written texts. There was, of course, ample archaic and classical precedent in, for example, Homer's Eumaios and the low life of Ionian iambus, but the new prominence of such characters seems clear, even after every allowance for the chanciness of survival (G. Zanker 1987). The lives of 'ordinary' people are described in very 'unordinary'

Figure 28.1 Bronze statue of a boxer, late Hellenistic. Rome, National Museum of the Terme. Reproduced by permission of the Soprintendenza Archeologica, Roma

language in the epigrams of Leonidas of Tarentum, and Callimachus' *Hekale*, a hexameter poem of uncertain length (?? *c.* 1200 verses), which told the story of how Theseus, on his way to fight the bull of Marathon, was entertained in the Attic countryside by a peasant woman called Hekale, when he took shelter in her hut from a storm; on returning after his triumph over the bull, the hero found that Hekale had died, and so he gave her name to the local deme and founded a shrine of Zeus Hekaleios (Hollis 1990). Hekale, rather than Theseus, clearly held centre-stage in this poem, and the description of her rustic life and the traditional peasant fare she set before Theseus was for later antiquity the most famous part of Callimachus' poem (cf. Ovid's tale of Baucis and Philemon, *Met.* 8.626 ff.). Very similar is the depiction of the peasant Molorkos in the so-called 'Victoria Berenices' (*Supp. Hell.* 254–269), which opened the third book of Callimachus' *Aitia*; this poem is an epinician-style (though elegiac) celebration of victory at the Nemean Games by a chariot team entered by Queen Berenice, the Cyrenean wife of Ptolemy Euergetes. At the centre of the poem stood the story of how Heracles, on his way to fight the Nemean lion, was humbly entertained at Kleonai by Molorkos; on returning to Molorkos after killing the lion, Heracles related a prophecy of Athena regarding the crowning of future victors in the Nemean and Isthmian Games. In this poem, too, Heracles' heroic feat is displaced from the centre of interest by the description of Molorkos' rustic life. Even the battle with the Nemean lion took second place to Molorkos' constant and 'epic' struggle with mice (*Supp. Hell.* 259.5–33 = fr. 177 Pf.).

In the *Hekale* and the 'Victoria Berenices' the effect of such material depends upon the fact that it appears within a conventionally 'high' poetic context. Other texts, however, claim a representational purchase upon 'real life', such as the mime texts of Theocritus (*Id.* 2, 14, 15) and Herodas, in which a clash between subject-matter ('ordinary', often rather 'sordid' lives) and form (Theocritus' hexameters and the choliambs and archaizing literary Ionic of Herodas) problematizes the kind of realism on show, as also does the ironic distance created by the fact that the characters are female, but the audience of the poetry almost certainly largely male. Moreover, it is not simply through a common debt to the mime tradition that both Theocritus 15 and Herodas 4 confront their characters with the 'realism' of representational art (Goldhill 1994: 216–23). In *Idyll* 15 Gorgo and Praxinoa admire the tapestries in the royal palace at Alexandria:

> Lady Athena, to think of the weaving that went into them!
> Such artists, to make their designs appear so true to life.
> How naturally the figures stand, how naturally they move!
> They seem alive, not woven. Ah, what a clever creature man is!
> And how wonderfully *he* reclines on his silver couch,
> With the first downy growth spreading from his temples:
> Thrice-adored Adonis, adored even beside Acheron.
>   (Theocr. *Id.* 15.80–86, trans. Verity)

In Herodas 4 two women admire famous works of art in a temple of Asklepios:

> Don't you see, dear Kynno, what works are here! You would say that Athene carved these lovely things – greetings, Lady. This naked boy, if I scratch him, won't he have a wound, Kynno? For the flesh is laid on him in the painting, pulsing like warm springs. And the silver fire-tongs, if Myellos or Pataikiskos son of Lamprion sees them, won't they lose their eyes thinking they are really made of silver? And the ox, and the man leading it, and the woman following, and this hook-nosed man and the one with his hair sticking up, don't they all have the look of life and day? If I didn't think I was acting too boldly for a woman, I should have cried out, in case the ox might do me some harm: he glances sideways so, Kynno, with the one eye. (Herodas 4. 56–71, trans. Cunningham)

The temptation to see in these passages a kind of self-reflexive parody of the simple platitudes of both literary and art criticism is strengthened by a further ecphrasis in the sixth mimiamb. In this poem two women discuss a maker of marvellous leather dildoes; in vv. 65–73 his products are described:

> His work, what work it is! You would think you were seeing the handiwork of Athene, not Kerdon; when I saw them – for he came with two, Metro – my eyes swelled out at first sight; men do not make stands – we are alone – so straight; and not only that, but their smoothness is sleep, and the little straps are wool, not straps; if you look for another cobbler better disposed to a woman, you will not find one. (Herodas 6.65–73, trans. Cunningham)

The possibility that the virgin goddess Athena might have been interested in dildoes is certainly not recorded elsewhere, but the claim that these artificial aids are 'better than the real thing' exploits the rhetoric of ecphrasis in brilliant new directions. Can art do 'nature's work' better than nature herself?

The Hellenistic appeal to 'realism' is thus a function of the place of 'literature' in elite society. It is also, of course, always subject to the constraints of genre, and the third century saw the creation of at least one new genre in which the construction of nature by art was central. Theocritus' hexameter *Bucolics* present themselves as elaborate literary versions of a song-culture alive in the traditions of illiterate shepherds and goatherds in the countryside of the Greek west and the islands. Implicit, then, in this new genre is a literary-historical construction analogous to Aristotle's tracing of the origin of tragedy and comedy to less formalized song traditions (*Poetics* 1449a9–14), and it is very difficult to accept any simplistic explanation for the emergence of bucolic in a desire to find relief from the pressures of life in the large conurbations of the Hellenistic world. On the other hand, these poems can, with hindsight, be seen as very significant texts in the history of the imagination of the countryside as a separate space of emotional, particularly erotic, experience. One of the most haunting of all Greek poems, Theocritus' 'Thalysia' (*Id.* 7), describes a walk 'away from the town' into a song-filled landscape where the narrator meets an extraordinary goatherd who has many of the attributes of the divine. The pattern is familiar enough – we may think of Philippides' meeting with Pan in the wilds of the Peloponnese (Hdt. 6.105) – but the emphasis upon the beauty of the countryside and the search for respite from the ache of longing were to have permanent influence upon the western pastoral tradition (Hunter 1999: 12–17).

7   All for Love

The apparent prominence of *eros*, including the emotional torments of women, in Hellenistic poetry has often been remarked. Here again, of course, we are at the mercy of the chances of survival. The erotic epigrams of Asklepiades, Callimachus, Disocorides and others are the knowing heirs of the sympotic lyric (Anakreon etc.) and elegy (Theognis etc.) of the archaic period, and *eros* is never far from the symposium. The emotions are, like everything, the object of second-order reflection in this self-conscious poetry: thus a poem (*AP* 12.17 = *HE* 988–91), which may be by Asklepiades or Poseidippos, contrasts the pleasures and pains of homo- and heterosexual desire and love-making, a theme familiar from Plato and Xenophon. There is some evidence that, in particular contexts, poets could treat paederastic desire as a phenomenon of the inherited past (cf. Theocr. *Id.* 12, 13, 28, 29, Hunter 1996a: 167–95), though this does not (of course) necessarily make heterosexual desire itself a marker of 'modernity'. What is perhaps new is the elaboration with which male poets are prepared to lay bare their helplessness, dramatized in the recurrent motif of the *komos* to the beloved's door (S. Tarán 1979), before the onslaught of desire (of all kinds); whether conclusions can be drawn from this poetic motif about changes in notions of masculinity is at least doubtful, but it is certain that it is within Hellenistic poetry that the origins of an important element of the ambiguous *personae* of the Roman elegists is to be sought.

Female characters (whether in love or not) play central roles in what survives of Hellenistic poetry: Apollonios' depiction of Medea's infatuation with Jason and her terrifying anxiety on the journey back, Moschos' wittily naive Europa, the chattering 'housewives' of Herodas and Theocritus, Simaitha's confused emotions and magical practices, set off by her knowing self-presentation as the wronged innocent, in Theocritus' *Second Idyll*, and Callimachus' exploration of maternal grief and discomfort in the *Hymns* to Athena and Demeter are memorable creations. This female prominence has often been associated with an increasing legal and social freedom of, at least, elite women in the Hellenistic period and the political influence wielded (so it is claimed) by the leading women of the royal houses. Over-interpretation is a constant danger here. Thus, for example, it would be difficult to draw sociological conclusions from Apollonios' brilliantly funny depiction of the all-female assembly at Lemnos, where physical desire and 'rational' argument happily flow together (as they often do in politics), and it is far from clear that Simaitha's 'forwardness' in 'making the first move' towards Delphis is a manifestation of a new-found female freedom rather than a marker of her dependent social position; the literary strategy by which the gender roles in a standard erotic narrative are partly reversed (itself perhaps to be associated with the poem's affiliations to the mime) ought not, by itself, to be taken as evidence of large-scale social change. A principal conceit of Theocritus' poem, the fact that the male 'seduction speech' (cf., e.g., Archilochos' 'Cologne Epode') is given in direct speech but as recollected and reported by the female (Andrews 1996), perhaps tells us more about the interest of Hellenistic poetry in experimentation with voice than it does about female consciousness. Nevertheless, the profusion of female voices in Hellenistic poetry and the exploration of female emotion and desire in a depth which is foreshadowed only sporadically in earlier poetry (Sappho, Euripides' *Hippolytus* etc.) perhaps reflects and certainly implies a heightened sense of female identity (in a broad sense). We never really know what Nausikaa *feels*, but Apollonios leaves us in no doubt about the long night of Medea's soul:

> But on Medea sweet sleep could get no hold, kept
> Wakeful as she was by worrying over Jason
> In her longing for him, and dreading the great might of the bulls
> That would bring him an ill fate there on Ares' ploughland.
> Close and quick now beat the heart in her bosom,
> As a shaft of sunlight will dance along the house wall

When flung up from water new-poured into pail or cauldron:
Hither and thither the swiftly circling ripples
Send it darting, a *frisson* of brightness; in just such a way
Her virgin heart now beat a tattoo on her ribs,
Her eyes shed tears of pity, constant anguish
Ran smouldering through her flesh, hot-wired her finespun
Nerve ends, needled into the skull's base, the deep spinal
Cord where pain pierces sharpest when the unresting
Passions inject their agony into the senses.

(*Argonautica* 3.751–65, trans. Green)

FURTHER READING

There are several recent and accessible introductions to the central literary issues of the period, particularly as concerns poetry: Bulloch 1985; the essays by Gelzer, Parsons, and Henrichs in Bulloch et al. 1993; Hunter 1996a: chapter 1; Hunter 1997 with bibliography; Fantuzzi in Fantuzzi and Hunter 2002: chapter 1. The first part of Bing 1988 is a fundamental study of the 'writtenness' of Hellenistic poetry. Hutchinson 1988 surveys the whole period, with chapters (or parts of chapters) devoted to each of the major figures in turn, except Menander. Fantuzzi and Hunter 2002 is not a survey, but offers advanced discussion of several key texts and genres (Callimachus' *Aitia*, the *Argonautica* of Apollonios, Theocritus' *Bucolics*, epyllion etc.). Cameron 1995 ranges widely and provocatively over much more than merely the structure of the *Aitia*. On scholarship and its reflection in and effects upon literature: Pfeiffer 1968; Fraser 1972: Part II; Weber 1993; Rengakos 1993.

On the principal surviving genres and authors

Menander and New Comedy: Handley 1965; Goldberg 1980; Gomme and Sandbach 1973; Hunter 1985; Vogt-Spira 1992; Zagagi 1994; Hunter in Fantuzzi and Hunter 2002. Herodas: Cunningham 1971; Mastromarco 1984; Simon 1991. Theocritus and bucolic poetry: Gow 1952; Segal 1981; Halperin 1983; Hunter 1996a, 1999; Gutzwiller 1991; Harder et al. 1996; Stanzel 1995; Fantuzzi in Fantuzzi and Hunter 2002. Apollonios, *Argonautica*: Beye 1982; Fusillo 1985; Hunter 1993; Knight 1995; DeForest 1994. Rengakos and Papanghelis 2001 offers an up-to-date bibliographical guide. Callimachus: in addition to the works listed above, much recent bibliography can be traced through the essays in Harder et al. 1993 and Montanari 2002. Epigram: S. Tarán 1979; Gutzwiller 1998; Fantuzzi in Fantuzzi and Hunter 2002.

CHAPTER TWENTY-NINE

Hellenistic Art, AD 1500–2000

Andrew Stewart

1   Whose Laokoon?

When I think of Hellenistic art (which is often) I think of the Laokoon (figures 29.1 and 29.3). The study of Hellenistic art in the second millennium begins and ends with it. No single work of ancient art has been more fertile or more controversial (cf. Bieber 1942/1967; Brilliant 2000). So I want to use it as a springboard for a millennial *Ringkomposition*. After sketching its history, I want to outline the development and present state of the field as a whole, ending with three examples of the ways in which it is currently moving – the Laokoon being number 3.

Writing in AD 77, Pliny the Elder locates the Laokoon 'in the house of the *imperator* Titus' and judges it 'superior to all other works of painting and sculpture' (*HN* 36.37). He attributes it to the virtuoso Rhodian sculptors Hagesandros, Athanodoros and Polydoros, who had allegedly carved it all from a single mighty block of stone. Yet frustratingly, he omits to date it.

Discovered in Rome on 14 January 1506, at once identified as Pliny's and Titus' very statue, and swiftly installed in the Cortile del Belvedere of the Vatican, the Laokoon immediately captivated the Renaissance imagination. For the first time an ancient masterpiece had appeared that was apparently well documented and even complemented a 'classic' poetic text: Virgil's description of the Sack of Troy in *Aeneid* Book 2. Recognized as the supreme *exemplum doloris* and soon enthroned at the centre of the *paragone* debate (the contest over the relative merits of painting and sculpture), in 1533 the group was restored in proto-'baroque' fashion by Giovanni Montorsoli with Laokoon's right arm extended towards the sky (figure 29.1). When in 1550 Vasari selected it and the Belvedere Torso as the two seminal works of his *terza maniera* (Vasari 1550: Vol. 4.1: 7, ed. Barocchi) – the High Renaissance style of which Michelangelo was the supreme exponent – its canonization was complete.

Two centuries later, the pioneering art historian J. J. Winckelmann (1717–68) followed Pliny in making the group the culmination of ancient art in his *Geschichte der Kunst des Alterthums* (Winckelmann 1764). Arguing that Laokoon sighs rather than screams, Winckelmann categorized him (oddly to our eyes) as the epitome of 'noble

Figure 29.1   Laokoon, Vatican. As restored by Giovanni Montorsoli in 1532–3. Photo: Vat. neg. IX.27.27

simplicity and quiet grandeur' and dated him to the 'beautiful' or late classic period of the fourth century BC. Almost immediately, however, the critic G. E. Lessing (1729–81) published a brilliant essay entitled *Laokoon: Oder, Über die Grenzen der Mahlerey und Poesie* (1766) that challenged this chronology. Arguing that the group was based on Virgil and Roman in date, he used their two narratives to revisit the ancient rivalry between text and image. To him, Laokoon's restraint was not merely classical but a matter of artistic decorum. Art history and art criticism had begun to part company.

Figure 29.2 Athena panel from the Gigantomachy of the Great Altar of Pergamon, Berlin. From *Altertümer von Pergamon*

In the nineteenth century this debate over chronology sharpened, as archaeologists excavated the Great Altar of Pergamon and its baroque-style Gigantomachy frieze (figure 29.2), discovered inscriptions recording other works by the Hagesandros family, began to sort out the sequence of Hellenistic sculptural styles, and quietly jettisoned Winckelmann's chronology.

In the great project of classification that now engrossed the field, the Laokoon's correct placement was of critical importance. Should it belong with the Great Altar around 170 BC, as its 'baroque' style implied? (The Altar's excavator, Alexander Conze, had even exclaimed when it was found, 'Now we've got our own Laokoon!') Or should one trust its flat, 'one-sided' composition and its sculptors' reconstructed family tree and date it much later? Is it truly a baroque original or a sheep in wolf's clothing – a reproduction announcing an extended baroque revival? Is it a product of the Hellenistic world's zenith, of its long twilight, or even of Imperial Rome?

In 1960 fresh evidence re-energized the debate. A new restoration by Filippo Magi (Magi 1960; figure 29.3) confirmed that *pace* Pliny the three sculptors had used no fewer than seven blocks of marble. One, at the back of the altar upon which Laokoon sits, came from an Italian quarry at Carrara which was not opened until Augustan times – but could be a repair. Magi also replaced Montorsoli's upraised arm with a

Figure 29.3 Laokoon, Vatican. As restored by Filippo Magi in 1960. Photo: Vat. neg.
XXXIV.22.9

flexed one discovered in a Roman stonemason's shop in 1906, and moved the right-
hand son further away from his father. So is this boy escaping? If so, the Rhodians'
source cannot have been the *Aeneid*, where all three die.

   Almost simultaneously, a seaside cave at a villa at Sperlonga (midway between
Rome and Naples) yielded a huge cache of sculptures in the same style as the
Laokoon. One of the groups was even signed by the same three Rhodians, but with
different patronymics than previously conjectured (Conticello and Andreae 1974;
figure 29.4). At first identified as fragments of another Laokoon, these new-found
marbles were soon attributed to no fewer than four groups featuring Odysseus
(rescuing Achilles' body at Troy, trying to steal the Trojan Palladion from Diomedes,
escaping from Skylla, and blinding Polyphemos).

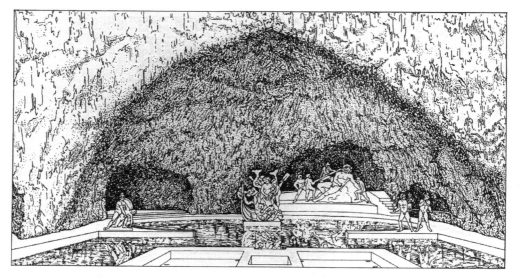

Figure 29.4 Reconstruction of mythological groups (Skylla, Polyphemos and others) at Sperlonga, signed by Athanodoros, Hagesandros, and Polydoros of Rhodes. Drawing by Candace Smith

But were they imported or made for the Sperlonga cave? Had they been looted from the east or commissioned by one of the villa's owners – perhaps even by the Emperor Tiberius' whose narrow escape when its roof collapsed in AD 26 is vividly narrated by Suetonius and Tacitus (*Tib.* 39; *Ann.* 4.59)? Were they inspired by Virgil, by Tiberius' favourite Hellenistic poet, Euphorion (275–*c.* 210 BC; cf. Stewart 1977), by Homer and the Cyclic epics; or by some other source? Were they and the Laokoon merely superb replicas of lost, High Hellenistic bronzes? When did their sculptors live? And so on.

At the end of the millennium the pattern has repeated itself. A sumptuous conference volume has treated the Laokoon in its Vatican context (Winner 1998). Two scholars have independently proposed a new interpretation of it, one text-based and the other from autopsy (Lahusen 1999; Queyrel 1997 [published 2001]). A third has produced a string of monographs on it, Sperlonga and Rome (Andreae 1987; 1988; 1991b; 1994; 1999). A fourth, following Winckelmann and Lessing, examines its contribution to 'the aesthetics of pain' (Richter 1992). A fifth offers a postmodern treatment of the discourses that have shaped it across the centuries (Brilliant 2000). A reviewer of his (Mary Beard, *TLS*, 2 February 2001: 3–4) doubts whether the 'new' arm belongs; and two other sceptics argue that it is not Pliny's Laokoon anyway (Albertson 1993; Koortbojian 2000).

Of course, investigation of the scholarly tradition is nothing new, though Brilliant's veritable snake pit of no fewer than six Laokoons is unprecedented. His Laokoon A is Pliny's statue; Laokoon B is its hypothetical mid-Hellenistic prototype; Laokoon I is the group discovered in 1506 and subsequently restored by Montorsoli; Laokoon II is Winckelmann's and Lessing's; Laokoon III is Magi's; and Laokoon IV is Brilliant's own.

Scholars have long questioned the group's findspot as well. For the Renaissance accounts only place it 'near' the holding tanks of Trajan's Baths (the so-called Sette Sale) on the Esquiline, in a richly embellished room six *bracchia* (3.5 m) below ground. This area was part of the gardens of Augustus' favorite *savant* and Virgil's patron, Maecenas. Over the centuries, scholars have placed its findspot almost everywhere on the hill, even (quite wrongly) in Nero's Golden House. Indeed, since the Flavian emperors lived on the Quirinal, more than a kilometre away, some have argued that our Laokoon is not Pliny's and Titus' at all (Albertson 1993; Koortbojian 2000; cf. S.H.A. *Tyr. Trig.* 33; cf. Suet. *Dom.* 1). Finally, Pliny's Laokoon was 'made from one stone', but ours is made from several, and by 1600 at least four more alleged Laokoons (all now lost) had appeared in Rome.

Yet in AD 77, when Pliny published his *Natural History*, dedicated it to the *imperator* Titus and placed the Laokoon in his house (*HN* 36.37), Titus was indeed merely *imperator* ('crown prince') and not yet emperor, so he could have been living anywhere (Haeuber 1991; Haeuber, forthcoming). Suggestively, when Tiberius had returned from exile in AD 2 as Augustus' designated successor, he lived in the Gardens of Maecenas (Suet. *Tib.* 15.1). Yet even so, we still do not know exactly where our Laokoon was found, whether it belonged to a larger sculptural program, when to date it, and whether Maecenas himself or someone else commissioned it.

Yet as so often in archaeology a stalemate on one front has been countered by a major advance on another. Examination of Laokoon's eyes in raking light has shown that they still retain traces of paint but that their irises apparently have no pupils (Queyrel 1997; 2002). Laokoon is neither 'seeking help from a higher power' as Winckelmann thought nor callously turning away from his stricken sons as others later argued. He is probably blind. As one scholar has argued independently of this startling discovery (Lahusen 1999), his pose and agonized demeanour best fit the only extant text that describes him thus: Quintus of Smyrna's third century AD epic the *Posthomerica*. In a long passage (12.389–497) that must be based on some earlier but still unidentified source, Quintus attributes the injury to a vengeful Athena:

> Then even as from destruction shrank the lads,
> Those deadly fangs had seized and ravined up
> Them both, outstretching to their father dear
> Their pleading hands: no power to help had he.
> (12. 474–77; trans. Loeb Classical Library)

Yet Quintus cannot be describing the Vatican statue itself, for while his Laokoon escapes with his life, the marble one just as clearly will not.

This new twist in the plot suggests that our Laokoon is pre-Virgilian, since after his *Aeneid* was published in 19 BC his version of the tale immediately became canonical at Rome. It places its manufacture within the lifetime of Maecenas (*c.* 70–8 BC), Virgil's patron, it catapults Laokoon's status as the supreme *exemplum doloris* to an entirely different level, and it opens up exciting new avenues of interpretation. A seer who cannot see; a prophet of doom whose prophecy dooms him; a truth-teller whose tale

Figure 29.5   Dead Giant, Amazon, and Persian, and Dying Gaul, Roman copies after the Lesser Attalid dedication on the Athenian Akropolis. Photo: Brogi

is a classic misstep (*hamartia/error*) that brings on his own destruction – this is the stuff of Greek tragedy at its most classic. I will return to it at the end of this chapter.

The Laokoon's story in the second millennium AD, then, is the story of Hellenistic art in microcosm. For both are:

- Protean (the Laokoon is simultaneously both 'baroque' and 'classic', Hellenistic and Roman);
- Geographically fuzzy (this acknowledged masterpiece of Hellenistic art was found in Rome and was perhaps made for Romans);
- Chronologically precarious;
- Open-ended;
- Intertextual;
- Slippery; and
- Unpredictable.

Now for attempts to bring this art to order.

2   'Bricks in the Edifice of Knowledge'

In 1865 the German art historian Heinrich Brunn (1822–94) gave a lecture to the German Archaeological Institute in Rome. In one brief hour he rescued a key monument of Hellenistic sculpture – the so-called Lesser Attalid Dedication on the Athenian Acropolis – from 1500 years of oblivion. Using plaster casts, Brunn put together nine small marble statues of defeated, wounded and dead barbarians: a Gaul in Paris; a Giant, Amazon, Persian, and Gaul in Naples; a Persian in the Vatican; and three Gauls in Venice (figure 29.5, cf. Stewart forthcoming a; Otto Benndorf added a tenth statue, a Persian in Aix, in 1876). Brunn saw that in scale and subject these figures match a remark by the traveller Pausanias (1.25.2), penned around AD 170:

> By the [Acropolis's] south wall Attalos dedicated the legendary battle of the Giants; the Athenians' battle against the Amazons; the Persian affair at Marathon; and the Gauls' destruction in Mysia. Each figure is about two cubits high.

Assigning the monument to the first King Attalos of Pergamon (regn., 241–197 BC), Brunn dated it to the year 200, when the Macedonians were ravaging Attica like barbarians and threatening the city's very existence. In his ensuing publication (Brunn 1870) he added some new ancient testimonia, discussed alternative reconstructions of the monument and evaluated other possible attributions to it. Finally, he sketched a history of the 'Pergamene School' of sculpture. He examined what Pliny and others had said about its practitioners, especially the bronzecasters Isigonus (a textual corruption for the Epigonus of *HN* 34.88?), P[h]yromachus, Stratonicus and Antigonus who 'did the battles of Attalus and Eumenes against the Gauls' (*HN* 34.84), and brought key works such as the Suicidal (Ludovisi) and Capitoline Gauls, Barberini Faun and Marsyas/Uffizi Scyth into its orbit.

All this represented a real breakthrough, especially because it concerned not Classical art, which Brunn had already done much to map, but the *terra incognita* of Hellenistic art. Pliny had stigmatized most of the period as artistically barren (*HN* 34.52), alleging that bronze sculpture 'stopped' in 292 BC and resumed only in 156 in the hands of 'inferior' artists. The word 'Hellenistic' had been coined only thirty years before; works attributed to the period were few and virtually unresearched; and Pergamon's treasure-trove of architecture and sculpture was still undiscovered. Yet at one stroke Brunn had found a major Pergamene monument, attributed it, pinpointed it to the year and contextualized it: a milestone in a chaotic and jumbled landscape.

Brunn was a positivist. Since positivism in some form has dominated the study of Hellenistic art ever since, but now is often used as a term of abuse, it is good to be clear about what it meant in mid nineteenth-century Germany. As Richard Popkin (1999: 668) has remarked:

> The term 'positivism' is semantically slippery since its original referent, the philosophy of Auguste Comte and his disciples which promulgated a systematic religion of humanity, was quickly replaced, especially in Germany, by any view that restricted knowledge to what could be attained using the methods of observation, induction, and mathematical analysis found, paradigmatically, in the empirical science of nature.

Brunn's lecture of 1865 was a classic exposition of these principles. As Donald Preziosi (1989: 82) explains:

> The modern discipline of art history might be viewed in one sense as a reaction, within the frameworks of the nineteenth-century dreams of scientificity, to the Romanticist entanglements with the double binds of the intentional-affective fallacies, resulting in a displacement of the problematics of production and reception beyond the purview of the new formalist, historicist science … [It] endeavored to demonstrate that its practice was as disciplined and rigorous as any other academically instituted science … by mounting a discourse that was tough-minded, logical, detached, objective, and grounded in expertise.

So in Foucauldian terms this new discourse was a technology of power. It programmatically replaced opinion with fact, fancy with evidence, speculation with induction, dilettantism with expertise and romanticism with science.

Any reader of Brunn's essay (Brunn 1870) is instantly impressed by his careful autopsy of the originals and by his painstaking accumulation of plaster casts, ancient texts and Renaissance documents to build his thesis. But his formidable research skills should not overshadow his unrivalled command of positivist methodology. Witness his forthright and sober statements of principle; his discriminating, rigorous and objective application of material, formal and historical analysis; and his end result – a tightly reasoned and historically plausible construct complete with its own criteria for inclusion and exclusion. To use a favourite positivist metaphor, he had indeed contributed a brick – indeed, a whole course of bricks – to the edifice of knowledge.

Yet the method had definite limitations.

Under the influence of nineteenth-century scientism and the great tradition of mimetic art criticism from Xenokrates (*c.* 300 BC), Pliny the Elder (AD 23–79), and Vasari (1511–74) through Winckelmann, it attributed an equally empiricist and evolutionist character to the artworks it studied. It assumed that Greek art sought naturalism or realism (rarely distinguishing them) above all else and gradually evolved towards this goal. But although everybody agreed that this process climaxed in the Hellenistic period, their idealist bias led them to privilege Pheidian classicism above all else. The summit of perfection in the visual arts, the Pheidian style was enthroned as the Aristotelian mean between the two extremes of the 'primitive' Archaic and the 'degenerate' Hellenistic.

Strict positivism also entailed other distressing consequences, often collectively termed the 'positivist fallacy'. Its 'scientific' focus upon the objects – upon what survives – immediately turned the historian into a Doubting Thomas: truly the Ur-positivist! For strict positivists must either assume that artefacts are both archaeologically *and* historically significant in proportion to their rate of survival or stop extrapolating from them altogether. Yet most ancient material culture is irretrievably lost, including whole classes of artefacts like Hellenistic panel-paintings, clothing and tragedies. Survival rates for the rest are utterly lopsided and often inversely related to their value in antiquity. (For example, we have vast quantities of pottery and barely a scrap of any gold and ivory statue.) Though some important survivals were pre-selected by the ancients themselves, this was not because they were typical but because they were considered special or collectible – like seven tragedies each of Aeschylus, Sophocles and Euripides, and the dozen Hellenistic erotic groups reproduced in Roman copy. The thousands of Hellenistic private portraits in bronze known from inscribed bases and decrees, on the other hand, generated no copies and are utterly lost, all having been melted down; likewise the victors from Brunn's Attalid dedication (figure 29.5).

So strictly positivist interpretations (which Brunn's was not) are necessarily minimalist and timid. By refusing to 'go beyond the evidence' they prejudge their own conclusions, are self-limiting and impoverish the world they study. And no amount of such evidence – of bricks new or old – tells us anything about the *meaning* of the edifice itself. Despite positivism's power as a heuristic device – as a method of recovering facts about the past – it offers no guide to interpretation. And in careless hands it can easily create monstrosities.

For Brunn's very success immediately tempted lesser folk to add bricks of their own – to multiply attributions, and thus inevitably to turn his tightly-constructed edifice into a ramshackle slum. Indeed, he even essays some of the more dubious tricks practised by his followers: arguing from silence or in circles; special pleading; resurrecting famous names; making serial attributions (A > B > C > D, but by now D has little to do with A); using dated material to date unrelated 'floating' work; and basing historical judgements on personal views of artistic quality – all are products of positivism's hunger to create facts at any price, of its thirst for 'positive' results, and Brunn was by no means innocent of them.

Brunn's work was soon enriched in ways he could never have imagined. Rome and its environs had been continuously excavated since the fifteenth century, and Pompeii and Herculaneum since the eighteenth. Yet systematic digging in the Hellenistic east began only in the mid nineteenth, inaugurating a process that still continues. Some of the earliest excavations – at Alexandria (1863), Delos (1873) and Pergamon (1878), for example – are still in progress. Others soon followed: in the Aegean area, at Pella, Priene, Miletos, Magnesia, Rhodes, Lindos and Kos; to the west, at Taranto, Syracuse and Morgantina; and to the east, at Antioch, Nemrud Dag, Seleukeia-on-the-Tigris and Taxila. Most have yielded much Hellenistic architecture and pottery, and some (especially Rome, Pompeii, Herculaneum, Pella, Pergamon, Delos and Alexandria) have produced much Hellenistic sculpture, painting and/or mosaic. Supplementing these finds, shipwrecks at Antikythera (1900), Mahdia (1907) and Cape Artemision (1926) produced precious 'time-capsules' of Hellenistic bronzes and marbles. And from the 1970s, new finds at Vergina in Macedonia (Andronikos 1984), at Ai Khanoum in Afghanistan (Bernard 1973–) and in the sea off Alexandria (Empereur 1998) have transformed our knowledge of the Hellenistic world.

Yet how was all this material – already abundant by 1900 – to be organized? As Winckelmann had discovered, classical Greek art of the fifth and fourth centuries was intractable enough. For Hellenistic art the problem is far worse, chiefly because of Pliny's notorious 'black hole' between 292 BC and 156 (*HN* 34.52). He does include the above-mentioned four bronzecasters who 'did the battles of Attalus and Eumenes against the Gauls' (*HN* 34.84) and seven more 'inferior' ones assigned to the year 156 (*HN* 34.52) but notes only a handful of others. Two diligent German scholars (Overbeck 1868; Löwy 1885) had gathered all the available literary and epigraphical testimonia for Hellenistic art, but against the wealth of evidence for the classical period it was modest indeed.

Moreover, the compilation of *corpora* of objects or types – a favourite nineteenth-century activity – was a partial solution only. For among the dozens of 'Neo-Attic' reliefs, the hundreds of grotesques from all over the East and the several thousand gravestones from Asia Minor, only a handful could be dated externally and many of these looked disturbingly late – i.e., Roman.

Like nature, scholarship abhors a vacuum. Fortunately, two powerful new analytical and documentary tools – formalism and photography – together seemed to offer a remedy.

The formalists' agenda was simple. They wanted to bring order to the chaos of Hellenistic art by discovering evolutionary stylistic changes that had escaped earlier, less sophisticated critics, and by creating chronologies out of them. Their databases were the photographic arsenals now available in the published *corpora* and at the

German Archaeological Institute at Rome, and their mentors were master formalists like Adolf Hildebrand (1847–1921), Alois Riegl (1858–1905) and Heinrich Wölfflin (1864–1945). Late in life Wölfflin even promoted an 'art history without artists', arguing that all significant stylistic change was supra-personal. For scholars of Hellenistic art, badly off for personalities, dates and contexts, these ideas had immediate appeal.

By 1910 one German scholar had already convinced many that on stylistic grounds Brunn's Attalid monument should belong after the Great Altar rather than before it, in the reign of Attalos II (159–138), and more *ad hoc* adjustments to the canon soon followed. Others began with concepts imported from the more recent past, gathering works that looked 'Baroque', 'Rococo' or 'Neoclassic' in style and writing monographs about them (e.g. Klein 1921). Some of these styles seemed at home in a single centre, like the baroque in Pergamon and the 'rococo' in Rhodes, others not. Conversely, a city like Alexandria with a rich literary and cultural tradition but a spotty archaeological record attracted all sorts of speculative attributions. These ranged from new styles like pictorial and sculptural 'Impressionism' to new genres like landscape reliefs and grotesques (Schreiber 1885; 1889–94; etc.).

In Hellenistic sculpture, formalism's high priest was Gerhard Krahmer (1890–1931), a brilliant connoisseur. His dissertation, grandly entitled 'Stilphasen der hellenistischen Plastik' ('Style-Phases of Hellenistic Sculpture') was published in 1924. It traced the art's supposed advance from the 'closed' form of the first two Hellenistic phases (the 'simple' of *c*. 330–230 BC and the 'pompous' or 'pathetic' of *c*. 230–150) to the 'open' form of the late Hellenistic period (*c*. 150–100). Three years later, his magisterial study of what he called 'one-sided' groups argued that the Laokoon and its ilk were designed to be seen solely from the front, like a relief. In a classicizing retreat from the late, 'open' phase (Krahmer 1927), they sought a Hildebrandian ideal of well-bounded clarity and purity of form where despite an often 'baroque' content, contour again reigned supreme and all internal relations were completely intelligible from the frontal plane.

Yet awkwardly this development apparently had begun as early as *c*. 150. For several of Brunn's Attalid figures (figure 29.5) were suspiciously flat, but since Pausanias had specified their dedicator as 'Attalos' they could not post-date the reign of the last Pergamene king, Attalos III, who died in 133 (Krahmer 1927: 71). So there they had to stay.

Krahmer's disciples extended his ideas to other genres and even to architecture. Mosaic and painting, rarer and more heterogeneous, remained on the sidelines, and many areas of the field could take no real account of them at all. Architectural historians continued to publish buildings and to research the development of building types and their key elements. Numismatists continued to classify the extensive coinages of the kings and cities. Ceramicists continued to sort out the various relief wares like 'Megarian' bowls and plain fabrics like Athenian black ware and eastern *terra sigillata*; and so on.

Even in the field of sculpture non-Germans were quite resistant to Krahmer's theories, with one notable exception. This was the American scholar Rhys Carpenter (1889–1980), a brilliant teacher and powerful writer who in 1960 produced a late and highly influential reworking of them in his book *Greek Sculpture: A Critical Review*.

Like Wölfflin, Carpenter also wanted an 'art without artists' but went further, characterizing Greek sculpture as the 'anonymous product of an impersonal craft . . . strictly conditioned by evolutionary laws which are in turn dependent upon the unchangeable dictates of the mechanism of human vision' (1960: v–viii). Accordingly, he put his Laokoon in the mid second century by rejecting Magi's flat, 'one-sided' restoration (figure 29.2) for a more three-dimensional one that turned the elder son at right angles to his father. Next he posited a 'renascence of classic form' after 150 that became a haven for many masterpieces expelled from the fourth century; and finally a wholesale 'intrusion of plastic form' after 100, as stonecarvers began to imitate the fluid, shifting epidermis of bronzes made from freely modelled wax. Carpenter's follower Christine Havelock soon canonized these ideas in a well-illustrated college textbook on Hellenistic art (1970) which is still often read as gospel by the unwary.

Yet as Richard Wollheim (1980: 145) has explained in another context:

> [The formalists] had far too narrow a conception of the range of devices operative in art . . . Secondly, they had no theoretical means of fitting together stylistic changes on the general or social level with changes of style on an individual or expressive level: Wölfflin's famous program of 'art history without names' is in effect the denial that there is any need to make the fit since all change occurs primarily or operatively on the more general level. Thirdly, all these writers were confused about the status of their investigation. From the fact that it is in the nature of art that it changes or has a history, they tried to move to the conclusion that the particular history it has, the particular changes that it undergoes, are grounded in the nature of art.

Krahmer and Carpenter themselves slide from a quasi-positivist reliance on induction from close observation to an idealist imposition of an *a priori* system of organic formal development (ultimately derived from Winckelmann) upon their material. So although they use dated monuments wherever possible their reasoning is basically circular and often relies on concepts alien to antiquity and problematic even on their home turf of the Renaissance and Baroque. The pattern is familiar. An originally flexible heuristic device becomes a rigidly predictive one – a way of creating ironclad typologies – and an all-too-recognizable spectre lurks behind the scenes. For the entire scheme implicitly assumes some kind of universal *Zeitgeist* at work. But why did these alleged trends begin, develop and end as they did? Having ditched the artist as both independent artificer and social being, they failed to produce a plausible group psychology to take his place.

Worse, they overlooked a mass of evidence that Hellenistic styles are cumulative not successive, often genre-specific and sometimes remarkably stable. They homogenized works from different genres and even different continents into a single, monolithic development. They relied excessively upon a few precariously dated sculptures (like the Magnesia frieze, then dated *c.* 140 but now often to *c.* 200; or even the Laokoon). They argued away or simply ignored anomalies like the Lesser Attalid Dedication (figure 29.5). And they failed to see that their systems could never determine the particular case. Why, for example, should an observation about a particular characteristic of *some* Hellenistic groups be generalized into a teleological account of the development of *all* Hellenistic groups, let alone into a prediction about the dates of other, *as yet undiscovered* Hellenistic groups?

So what Krahmer, Carpenter and their followers produced was a series of elegantly argued theories of internal stylistic evolution. Yet unlike Pliny, Vasari and Winckelmann they offered no account of causes, motivations or goals, and were arbitrarily restrictive in their selection of 'significant' devices or traits for analysis. For example, since sculptural groups necessarily involve interpersonal relations, why not select increases (or decreases) in melodrama, pathos, violence, humour or eroticism, or at least crosscheck these with one's supposed changes in style? If this suggestion seems absurdly subjective, it is no more so than privileging a selection of traits based on Hildebrand's transcultural theories about relief and plane, or Wölfflin's pendulum of 'closed' to 'open' form and back again.

After the Second World War the field turned to less grandiose concerns but only rarely explicitly questioned either Krahmer's results or the formalist agenda *per se*. (French structuralism and post-structuralism, so influential in the study of Attic vase painting, for example, have barely touched it.) Yet some had already sidestepped the formalist preoccupation with evolutionary development. In 1940, for example, Giovanni Becatti produced a lengthy study of Athenian Hellenistic sculpture, arguing that the vast prestige of Pheidias and Praxiteles, reinforced by Athens' nostalgia for its classical golden age, essentially conditioned the city's Hellenistic sculptors to produce endless variations upon the classical style (Becatti 1940; cf. Stewart 1979). Their speciality was naturally the prestigious cult statue, until second to first century Pergamenes and Romans began to demand reproductions of all sorts. At Athens, in other words, conservative patronage and group psychology apparently coincided to widespread profit and stylistic stagnation.

Today, most commentators would agree that Hellenistic styles in all media are cumulative, not successive, and conditioned by a complex mixture of region, site, patron, period, genre and function – not necessarily in that order. Predictably, then, site- and genre-based studies (and with them the atomization of the field) are multiplying fast. At the turn of the millennium, in addition to ongoing publication of excavations and individual objects in museums, one detects the following trends – many of which of course overlap:

- Regional and site studies. Buildings or artefacts from a specific kingdom, region or site (e.g., Mesopotamian or Egyptian temples; the rock tombs of Petra; Macedonian paintings, mosaics and reliefware; Athenian fine and coarse pottery; Delian sculpture and mosaics; Seleukid coins; etc.) are published for the first time or studied afresh with a view to determining local preferences, developments and responsiveness to external trends.
- Genre and typological studies. Also essentially nineteenth-century *corpora* in updated form (e.g., of texts; architectural sculpture; ruler-and philosopher-portraits; fishermen and peasants; erotic groups; decorative busts; engraved gems; metal vessels; etc.), these seek to define styles and iconographies specific to the genre or type in question, and often to investigate its social roots and sociopolitical significance. In extreme cases, they become essays in the social history of art.
- Thematic studies. These include investigations of monuments that address a specific agenda, whether artistic (e.g., realism; the grotesque; erotica; the nude), political (royal patronage; theomorphic ruler portraits; portraits of careworn local politicians; political allegories), cultic (cult statues; medical votives), social ('bour-

geois' gravestones; luxury and *tryphe*), or literary/rhetorical (theatricality; narration; etc.).

- Studies of individual buildings, artefacts, artists, etc. Reconsidering key and often problematic monuments and personalities (e.g., the Temple of Apollo at Didyma; the Great Altar of Pergamon; the Alexander and Nile Mosaics; the Getty Bronze; the Drunken Old Woman; the Farnese Bull; the Laokoon; Damophon of Messene; the Tazza Farnese; Ptolemy II's Great Procession; etc.), these often propose a radical re-dating or reinterpretation of their subjects.
- Exhibition catalogues. Exhibitions arranged around a historical personality, a monument, a deposit, or a collection (e.g., Alexander or Kleopatra; the Telephos frieze; the Mahdia wreck; the Walters collection of Hellenistic art) are increasingly popular and promote republication and in-depth reconsideration of specific objects and of the field in general.
- Symposia and anthologies. Assembling scholars of different backgrounds, disciplines and/or nationalities, these usually attempt to shed light on a specific theme (e.g., images, ideologies and self-definition; state and citizen; etc.), specific monuments (Pergamon/Sperlonga; palaces; sculptural groups; small bronzes; pottery), regions and localities (western versus eastern Hellenism; Alexandria and Alexandrianism; sculptural schools), or more rarely personalities (the architect Hermogenes; the sculptor Phyromachos).
- Syntheses. These range from college-type textbooks covering all the major arts (architecture, sculpture, painting, mosaic), through concept-based studies (e.g., on *ekphrasis* and *enargeia*; the Hellenistic culture of viewing; the Hellenistic body; etc.) and more traditional, parallel accounts of art and literature or art and thought, to surveys of individual media. Of the media, sculpture is easily the most popular. Approaches range from far-reaching correlations with political events and social trends to an almost total scepticism about dates, attributions and stylistic continuity.

3   Directions

To express a preference for one approach or body of work over another is a good way to make enemies and in the present climate of research doomed to rapid obsolescence. So the remainder of this chapter is intended to be illustrative, not prescriptive. It summarizes three directions in my own work that in some ways typify current scholarly trends: redating, reattribution and reinterpretation.

Hellenistic finds at Tel Dor, Israel: losses and gains

Dor is a crossroads (E. Stern 2000). Situated beside the coast road from Egypt to Syria, blessed with splendid harbours to north and south, and offering easy access to the interior, the city was first settled in the Middle Bronze Age. In Hellenistic times it withstood sieges by Antiochos III of Syria in 218–17 and by Antiochos VII Sidetes and Simon Maccabee in 139–38. Around 100 it fell to the brutal Hasmonaean (Maccabean) King Alexander Jannaeus. In 63 Pompey the Great restored its autonomy, and soon it became the southernmost port of Provincia Syria. It continued to flourish despite the foundation of Caesarea Maritima by Herod the Great (regn.,

37–4 BC), shunned the Jewish revolt of AD 66–70, and prospered thereafter until for some unknown reason it was abandoned around AD 235.

In the late nineteenth century the Turks stripped Dor of much of its stone, so that when the British archaeologist John Garstang began excavations there in 1923 little remained above ground (Garstang 1924). Yet the impressive ruins of a huge Ionic building were still visible along the western, seaward side of the mound, and another big foundation to the south of it. Both were built of massive blocks of the local sandstone (figure 29.6). Garstang identified the northern building as an early Hellenistic temple, 'poised on a high platform in the Syrian style, surrounded by a great stone temenos wall which fronted to the sea' (1924: 97). Connecting it with Poseidon or his supposed son Doros (the city's eponymous hero), he linked it with a hexastyle temple with central arch and robed, sceptred figure inside, pictured on the Roman coins of Dor. He said nothing about the southern foundation.

Malaria drove him off in 1924, leaving Dor undisturbed for two generations. The Hebrew University of Jerusalem reopened it in 1980; drawn by the prospect of an incompletely excavated Hellenistic temple and by several anomalies in Garstang's brief report, I was persuaded to join them with a U.C. Berkeley team in 1986.

Twelve excavation seasons later, we know that the huge northern building looked nothing like Garstang's 'temple . . . in the Syrian style'. Measuring around 70×35 m, it was probably a huge pi-shaped stoa facing east, built over an underground corridor or *cryptoporticus* – a Roman invention. The southern building is even more suspicious. 31 m (105 Roman feet) square, it looks like an Italic *peripterus sine postico*: a cella surrounded by a colonnade on three sides, with a massive cross-wall substituting for a Greek-style rear (western) porch or *posticum* (Vitr. *De arch.* 3. 2. 5 and 4. 7. 2, reading *alae* instead of *aliae*). Concomitantly, these buildings' stratigraphy, the artefacts from their foundation trenches, floors and approaches, and the occasional remains of concrete show that they cannot predate AD 150. They may even be Severan (suggestively, Garstang's coins date to AD 205/6 and 210/11). So was this huge project the town's last gasp before its final demise in the 230s?

Yet once more losses on the swings are countered by significant gains on the roundabouts. On the eastern and western sides of the mound the town plan looks both characteristically Phoenician/Hellenistic and is essentially stable from *c.* 500 BC through to early Roman times. The rooms have yielded masses of stratified pottery and other artefacts, including the best collection of Hellenistic relief ware ('Megarian Bowls') in the Levant. Furthermore, fragments of a limestone and sandstone Doric building from its south side are stratigraphically pre-Roman and were found with late second-century BC pottery and lamps. The columns' 1 : 7 lower diameter : height ratio is distinctively Hellenistic, and a Nike akroterion was found with them (Stewart 2001; Stewart and Martin, forthcoming).

These finds, made in 2000, open up exciting new horizons. Was this perhaps a temple built to celebrate Antiochos' defeat in 217 but destroyed by Alexander Jannaeus around 100 – his way of punishing pagan cities for resisting the resurgent Jewish state? Yet the vandals apparently spared a superb mosaic in *opus vermiculatum vermiculatum* later thrown into a nearby Roman pit (figure 29.7). Showing a theatre-mask of a young dandy wearing a fantastic basketlike hat, placed amidst exuberant bouquets of fruits and flowers, it finds its closest parallels in second-century Pompeii,

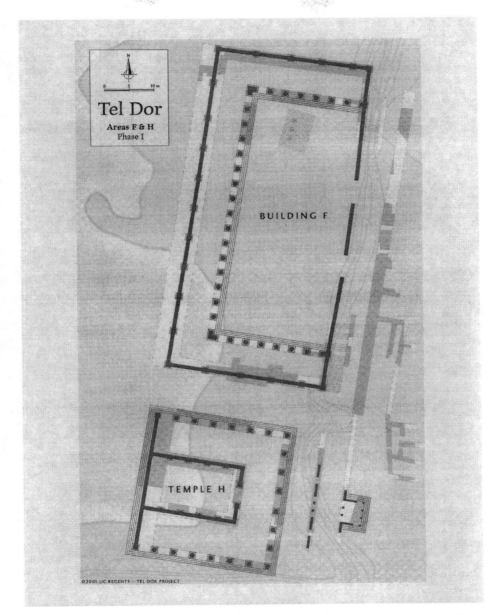

Figure 29.6 Restored plan of the temple and other buildings on the west side of Tel Dor, Israel. Reconstruction by Erin Dintino

Pergamon, Delos and Alexandria (Stewart and Martin, 2003; cf. Westgate 2000). A Greek tyrant, Zoilos, ruled Dor in 100. Perhaps the mosaic embellished his banquet room or *andron*, in a palace yet to be found.

Figure 29.7 Mosaic of a mask of a young dandy (detail) from Tel Dor, Israel. Photo: Gabi Laron

All these discoveries are presently unique in Israel. The Doric 'temple' and *akroterion* are the only certainly pre-Herodian examples of their kind, and the mosaic has no equal there until the third century AD.

The Farnese Bull: Eumenes II of Pergamon or Mark Antony?

Among the monuments of antiquity, few remind us more forcibly than the Farnese Bull (figure 29.8) that the past truly is a foreign country. Yet as its critical stock has fallen – from a 'marvellous mountain of marble' (Federico Zuccaro 1607) to a 'dreary mountain' of the same (Martin Robertson 1975) – scholarly investment in it has risen proportionately. For discoveries of other versions of it have prompted no fewer than one exhibition catalogue, two monographs, a long encyclopaedia entry and half a dozen articles in the last ten years alone.

Found at Rome in the Baths of Caracalla in 1545, restored in 1579 and taken to Naples in 1789, the group was soon connected with Pliny's report of a great Hellenistic marble group in the collection (*Monumenta*) of Asinius Pollio (76 BC–AD 4): 'Zethus and Amphion along with Dirce, the Bull, and the rope – all carved from the same piece of stone – a work by Apollonius and Tauriscus brought from Rhodes. These men caused a controversy about their parents, professing that, although Menecrates appeared to be their father, their actual father was Artemidorus' (*HN* 36.33–4). The Naples version is now usually seen as a Severan copy, and its lost

Figure 29.8 'Toro Farnese' (Dirke, Amphion, Zethos, and the Bull), Naples. Photo: author

original is often placed at the beginning of the late Hellenistic period, around 160 BC. Current opinion is that King Eumenes II of Pergamon (regn., 197–158) perhaps dedicated this original at Rhodes; Cassius plundered it in 42; Pollio acquired it by 39; and its many replicas begin with an isolated set of Etruscan ash-urns around 150 and resume when it reached Rome (Kunze 1998). Since I disagree with most of this, here is my own reading of the evidence:

1   Pliny does not say that the group was plundered, merely that it was 'brought' from Rhodes. Moreover, other accounts of Cassius' extortions in 42 suggest that he chiefly wanted cash and valuables. Pliny himself attests that thousands of statues

remained on the island a century later, and Dio Chrysostom (*Or.* 31. 147–9) denies that any were plundered. But none of this matters if the group *post-dates* 42 . . .

2   Pliny's adoption tale, the signature of an [. . .]ates son of Menekrates (ethnic unknown) on the Great Altar of Pergamon, and a late Roman schoolbook's garbled mention of a 'Menecrates' as one of the world's seven great architects cannot be safely or even plausibly combined to yield a High Hellenistic date for the two sculptors. Instead, a statue-base at Magnesia on the Maeander signed by an Apollonios son of Tauriskos of Tralleis in a late Hellenistic or early imperial script suggests a triumviral or Augustan date.

3   The simplest inference from Pliny's note is that Pollio himself brought the group from Rhodes. Although he apparently built his museum in 39, he could have acquired the Bull at any time. So the only safe *terminus* is his death in AD 4. Indeed, if a late Hellenistic statue of a Roman general from Naxos carrying a maenad in its outstretched hand and bearing (*inter alia*) the Dirke scene on its breastplate is correctly identified as Mark Antony, and if this relief indeed echoes Apollonios' and Tauriskos' group (perhaps more accurately than the Farnese version), then this group presumably was still on display at Rhodes in the 30s.

4   The Bull fits no Pergamene mytho-propagandistic scenario with precision, but does fit both Mark Antony's devotion to Dionysos and his liberation of Rhodes from Cassius and his allies in 42. In this case the avenging brothers would stand for Antony himself and Octavian; Dirke would represent their defeated opponents, the 'enslavers' of Rhodes and the rest of Greece.

So did the Rhodians themselves commission both Bull and Naxian statue as dedications to Dionysos, to thank the triumvir for their freedom and for restoring Naxos and their other territories confiscated by Cassius? And after Actium, did Antony's erstwhile supporter, Pollio (who had reconciled him and Octavian in 40) then tactfully 'depoliticize' the Bull by rescuing it for his own collection?

This scenario is supported by the following circumstantial evidence:

A   The Farnese group's style is irrelevant. The original could have been made at any time after *c.* 230; the Severan copyist clearly modernized the drapery, and every head except the bull's is restored.

B   The Hellenistic Etruscan urns that supposedly reproduce the group differ from it both compositionally and iconographically. And after these urns and the Naxian statue, the next echoes are from Augustan Rome.

C   Rhodian Hellenistic marbles are generally small-scale votives or decorative pieces. The closest Rhodian counterparts to Apollonios and Tauriskos are the carvers of the Laokoon – Hagesandros and family – who on present evidence freelanced for the late republican/early imperial elite. Perhaps they were Apollonios' and Tauriskos' rivals. For they too carved massive, complex marble groups, favoured dramatic, 'baroque' subjects, and produced an eclectic mixture of 'original' works and amplified versions of earlier ones.

D   According to Pliny, Pollio's collection was heavily biased towards contemporary sculptors. Apollonios and Tauriskos fit comfortably into this ambience, which complements Pollio's enthusiasm for and occasional patronage of contemporary Latin *novi poetae* such as Catullus, Gallus, the young Virgil and Horace.

There is a saying in American jurisprudence that circumstantial evidence is as good as fact if there is enough of it. This speculative combination of the two, along with all its artistic and political implications, may serve to indicate what is still possible in the field.

Laokoon: some final musings

If the discovery that Laokoon is blind holds water, it would prove that the group cannot be based on Virgil. Yet the three Rhodians worked in Italy for Romans and Virgil's account dominated the Roman imagination from the moment of its publication in 19 BC. So the group should either pre-date Virgil or (less likely) post-date him and 'improve' upon his account.

Whatever the truth, this discovery reinforces Laokoon's status as the ultimate *exemplum doloris*. But it also prompts another question. Many of the great 'baroque' groups (the Pasquino – now persuasively identified as Ajax heroically rescuing Achilles' body after his ambush by Paris and Deiphobos; Achilles and Penthesileia; Marsyas; Dirke; etc.) are based on epic/tragic themes. So what is there about the baroque that lends itself to this particular heroic mode?

Of course, Hellenistic art's theatricality is a cliché of the handbooks, and the baroque is certainly the most theatrical of its styles. But the connection goes deeper. Hellenistic culture was above all a rhetorical one where 'the categories of eloquence were imposed on every form of mental activity' (Marrou 1956: 195). So when a grandiloquent, theatrical rhetoric devoted to *psychagogia* or the swaying of the soul emerged in third-century BC Asia Minor, it soon dominated not only public speaking but also the production of literature, especially of epic, tragedy and historiography, throughout the region and even elsewhere.

Wilamowitz first connected this flamboyant 'Asian' rhetoric with the Pergamene baroque in the year 1900. These 'baroque' groups display many of the same characteristic traits as the example he chose, the Gigantomachy of the Great Altar (Stewart 1993b: 133–7; figure 29.2). They share its love of *auxesis* (amplification), *megaloprepeia* (grandeur), *deinosis* (intensity), *ekplexis* (shock), *enargeia* (vividness), *antithesis* and *pathos*. But they do more. Whereas the Gigantomachy creates melodrama by overliteralizing, they both move us to pity and fear, and explore the disastrous outcome of a tragic error (*hamartia*). All of this strongly recalls Aristotle's definition of tragedy (Stewart, forthcoming). So, paradoxically, could the Hellenistic baroque represent the 'classic' realization in stone of Greek culture's central literary achievement: Greek tragedy itself?

Envoi

On the Dor excavation we have a saying, facetiously called the Third Law of Archaeology: 'Only the future is immutable; the past is always changing'. Hellenistic art remains our strongest witness.

FURTHER READING

The sites are described and referenced in Stillwell 1976. Useful introductory mono-graphs on two major ones (Alexandria and Pergamon) are Grimm 1998 and Radt 1999, with Ginouvès 1994 on Macedonia.

The best survey of Hellenistic art is Pollitt 1986, with Boardman 1994 on its diffusion. Webster 1964, Onians 1979 and Fowler 1989 offer wide-ranging, impres-sionistic correlations with literature and philosophy. Beard and Henderson 2001 is resolutely iconoclastic. There is no good architecture survey in English: see Lauter 1986 (in German), with Lawrence 1996 for an introduction; Steele 1992 is unreliable and includes much that is Roman. Sculpture surveys abound: see Bieber 1961; Stewart 1990; R. Smith 1991; Moreno 1994; Ridgway 1990, 2000a and 2002; and Andreae 2001. Painting and mosaic are almost as badly served as architecture, largely because a continuous history is impossible: see Pollitt 1986 for comments, with introductions to Ling 1991, 1998 and Dunbabin 1999; also, e.g., Andronikos 1984 and especially Rouveret 1989 (in French). For numismatics see Mørkholm 1991; and for engraved gems, Plantzos 1999. Hellenistic minor arts are covered only in general surveys of these media, in site reports and in specialist articles; for synopses and selected bibliographies see *The Dictionary of Art* (London, Macmillan, 1996) under 'Greece, Ancient: Pottery: Metalwork; Terracotta; Other Arts'.

For an accessible sample of current trends, see Reeder (ed.) 1988 for an up-to-date exhibition catalogue of a single museum's holdings; Bulloch et al. (eds.) 1993 on images and ideologies; Stewart 1993a on Alexander portraits; Meyboom 1995 on the Nile Mosaic; P. Zanker 1995 on philosopher portraits; True and Hamma 1996 on Alexandria; Dreyfus and Schraudolph 1996 on the Telephos exhibition; Stewart 1996a on the Hellenistic body; A. Cohen 1997 and Pfrommer 1998 on the Alexan-der Mosaic; Mattusch 1997 on the Getty bronze athlete; de Grummond and Ridgway 2000 on Pergamon and Sperlonga; Hellenkemper-Salies 1994 on the Mahdia wreck; and Walker and Higgs 2001 on Kleopatra. The most thought-pro-voking foreign-language work in the field is represented by P. Zanker 1989, 1998 and Wörrle and Zanker 1995.

Bibliography

Abramov, A. P. and Paromov, Y. M. 1993. Ranneantichnie poseleniya Tamanskogo poluostrova. *Bosporskii Sbornik* 2: 25–98.

Adams, R. McC. 1981. *Heartland of Cities*. Chicago.

Adams, W. and Borza, E. (eds). 1982. *Philip II, Alexander the Great, and the Macedonian Heritage*. Washington.

Adcock, F. E. 1957. *The Greek and Macedonian Art of War*. Berkeley.

Africa, T. 1961. *Phylarchus and the Spartan Revolution*. Berkeley.

Ager, S. 1989. Judicial imperialism: the case of Meliteia. *AHB* 3.5: 107–14.

Ager, S. 1996. *Interstate Arbitrations in the Greek World, 337–90* BC. Berkeley.

Akurgal, E. 1990. *Ancient Civilizations and Ruins of Turkey.* 7th edn. Istanbul.

Albertson, F. 1993. Pliny and the Vatican Laokoon. *MDAI* (R) 100: 133–40.

Alcock, S. E. 1991. Tomb Cult and the post-classical polis. *AJA* 95: 447–67.

Alcock, S. E. 1993. *Graecia Capta: The Landscapes of Roman Greece*. Cambridge.

Alcock, S. E. 1994. Breaking up the Hellenistic world: survey and society. In Morris 1994: 171–90.

Alcock, S. E. 2001. A simple case of exploitation? The Helots of Messenia. In Cartledge et al. 2001: 185–99.

Alcock, S. E. 2002. *Archaeologies of the Greek Past: Landscape, Monuments and Memory.* Cambridge.

Alcock, S. E., Cherry, J. F. and Elsner, J. (eds). 2001. *Pausanias: Travel and Memory in Roman Greece*. Oxford.

Alexander, P. 2001. Essay with commentary on post-biblical Jewish literature. In J. Barton and J. Muddiman (eds), *The Oxford Bible Commentary*. Oxford. 792–829.

Algra, K. 1999. *The Cambridge History of Hellenistic Philosophy.* Cambridge.

Allen, R. E. 1971. Attalos and Aegina. *BSA* 66: 1–12.

Allen, R. E. 1983. *The Attalid Kingdom: a Constitutional History.* Oxford.

Allgöwer, D. 1993. Antiochos Ier de Commagène entre sceptre et Diadème. *AION* (arch.) 15: 257–87.

Alston, R. 1997. Ritual and power in the Romano-Egyptian city. In H. M. Parkins (ed.), *Roman Urbanism: Beyond the Consumer City.* London. 147–72.

Alston, R. 2002. *The City in Roman and Byzantine Egypt.* London.

Ameling, W. 1994. Pausanias und die hellenistiche Geschichte. In J. Bingen (ed.), *Pausanias Historien*. Entretiens Hardt 41. Geneva. 117–60.

Ameling, W. and Jonnes, L. 1994. *The inscriptions of Heracleia Pontica*. Bonn.

Anastassiades, A. 1998. Ἀρσινόης Φιλαδέλφου: aspects of a specific cult in Cyprus. *RDAC*: 129–40.

Andreae, B. 1987. *Plinius und der Laokoon*. Mainz.

Andreae, B. 1988. *Laokoon und die Gründung Roms*. Mainz.

Andreae, B. 1990. Der Asklepios des Phyromachos: ein Kolossalkopf pergamenischen Stils. In B. Andreae (ed.), *Phyromachos-Probleme: mit einem Anhang zur Datierung des grossen Altares von Pergamon*. Mainz. 45–100.

Andreae, B. 1991a. The image of the Celts in Etruscan, Greek, and Roman art. In S. Moscati, E. Arslan, O. Frey, V. Kruta, and M. Szabo (eds), *The Celts*. New York. 61–77.

Andreae, B. 1991b. *Laokoon und die Kunst von Pergamon: Die Hybris der Giganten*. Frankfurt.

Andreae, B. 1994. *Praetorium Speluncae: Tiberius und Ovid in Sperlonga*. Stuttgart.

Andreae, B. 1999. *Odysseus: Mythos und Erinnerung*. Mainz.

Andreae, B. 2001. *Skulptur des Hellenismus*. Munich.

Andreau, J., Briant, P. and Descat, R. (eds). 2000. *Économie antique 5. La guerre dans les économies antiques*. Saint-Bertrand-de-Comminges.

Andrews, N. E. 1996. Narrative and allusion in Theocritus, Idyll 2. In Harder et al. 1996: 21–53.

Andronikos, M. 1984. *Vergina: The Royal Tombs and the Ancient City*. Athens.

Antonaccio, C. 1994. *An Archaeology of Ancestors: Tomb Cult and Hero Cult in Early Greece*. Lanham.

Antonetti, C. 1987. *Agraioi* et *Agrioi*. Montagnards et bergers: un prototype diachronique de sauvagerie. *DHA* 13: 199–236.

Antonetti, C. 1990a. Il santuario apollineo di Termo in Etolia. In M.-M. Mactoux and E. Geny (eds), *Mélanges P. Lévéque* 4. Paris. 1–28.

Antonetti, C. 1990b. *Les Étoliens: Image et religion*. Paris.

Aperghis, M. 2001. Population – production – taxation – coinage: a model for the Seleukid economy. In Archibald et al. 2001: 69–102.

Applebaum, S. 1979. *Jews and Greeks in Ancient Cyrene*. Leiden.

Arafat, K. 1996. *Pausanias' Greece: Ancient Artists and Roman Rulers*. Cambridge.

Archibald, Z. 1998. *The Odrysian Kingdom of Thrace. Orpheus Unmasked*. Oxford.

Archibald, Z., Davies, J. K., Gabrielsen, V. and Oliver, G. J. (eds). 2001. *Hellenistic Economies*. London.

Arieti, J. 1997. Rape and Livy's view of Roman history. In S. Deacy and K. Pierce (eds), *Rape in Antiquity*. London. 209–29.

Arnold, D. 1999. *The Last Temples of Ancient Egypt*. Oxford.

Arnold, D. (ed.). 1988. *Imperial Medicine and Indigenous Societies: Disease, Medicine and Empire in the Nineteenth and Twentieth Centuries*. Manchester.

Arnott, W. G. (trans.) 1979–2000. *Menander*, 3 vols (Loeb Classical Library). Cambridge, Mass.

Arnusch, M. 2000. Argead and Aetolian relations with the Delphic polis in the late fourth century BC. In R. Brock and S. Hodkinson (eds), *Alternatives to Athens: Varieties of Political Organization and Community in Ancient Greece*. Oxford. 293–307.

Ashmore, W. and Knapp, A. B. (eds). 1999. *Archaeologies of Landscape: Contemporary Perspectives*. Oxford.

Ashton, R. 1994. The Attalid poll-tax. *ZPE* 104: 57–60.

Ashton, S. 2001. *Ptolemaic Royal Sculpture from Egypt: the Interaction Between Greek and Egyptian Traditions*. Oxford.

Asmis, E. 2001. Basic education in Epicureanism. In Too 2001: 209–39.

Aujac, G. 1987. The growth of an empirical cartography in Hellenistic Greece. In J. Harley and D. Woodward (eds), *The History of Cartography.* Vol. I: *Cartography in Prehistoric, Ancient, and Medieval Europe and the Mediterranean.* Chicago. 148–60.

Aujac, G. 2001. *Ératosthène de Cyrène, le pionnier de la géographie: sa mesure de la circonférence terrestre.* Paris.

Auliard, C. 1995. La spécificité des premiers contacts diplomatiques de Rome avec les monarchies hellénistiques avant la fin du IIIe siècle av. J.C. In E. Frézouls and A. Jacquemin (eds), *Les relations internationales.* Paris. 433–52.

Austin, M. M. 1981. *The Hellenistic World from Alexander to the Roman Conquest. A Selection of Ancient Sources in Translation.* Cambridge.

Austin, M. M. 1986. Hellenistic kings, war and the economy. *CQ* 36: 450–66.

Austin, M. M. 2001. War and culture in the Seleucid empire. In T. Bekker-Nielsen and L. Hannestad (eds), *War as a Cultural and Social Force. Essays on Warfare in Antiquity.* Copenhagen. 90–109.

Avidov, A. 1997. Were the Cilicians a nation of pirates? *Mediterranean Historical Review* 10: 5–55.

Aymard, A. 1967. Sur quelques vers d'Euripide qui poussèrent Alexandre au meurtre. *Études d'histoire ancienne.* Paris. 51–72.

Badian, E. 1958a. *Foreign Clientelae.* Oxford.

Badian, E. 1958b. The Eunuch Bagoas: a study in method. *CQ* 8: 144–57.

Badian, E. 1959. Rome and Antiochus the Great: a study in cold war. *CP* 54: 81–99 (reprinted in his *Studies in Greek and Roman History.* Oxford. 1964. 112–39).

Badian, E. 1962. Review of M. J. Fontana, *Le lotte per la succesione di Alessandro Magno dal 323 al 315* (Palermo, 1960). *Gnomon* 34: 381–7.

Badian, E. 1967. The testament of Ptolemy Alexander. *Rh.Mus.* 110: 178–92.

Badian, E. 1971. The family and early career of T. Quinctius Flamininus. *JRS* 61: 102–11.

Badian, E. 1981. The deification of Alexander the Great. In H. Dell (ed.), *Ancient Macedonian Studies in Honor of Charles F. Edson.* Thessaloniki. 27–71.

Badian, E. 1996. Alexander the Great between two thrones and heaven: variations on an old theme. In Small 1996: 11–26.

Bagnall, R. 1976. *The Administration of the Ptolemaic Possessions outside Egypt.* Leiden.

Bagnall, R. 1984. The origins of Ptolemaic cleruchs. *Bulletin of the American Society of Papyrologists* 31: 7–20.

Bagnall, R. 1995. *Reading Papyri, Writing Ancient History.* London.

Bagnall, R. 2001. Archaeological work in Hellenistic and Roman Egypt 1995–2000. *AJA* 105: 225–43.

Bagnall, R. and Derow, P. 2004. *The Hellenistic Period: Historical Sources in Translation.* Oxford

Bagnall, R. and Frier, B. 1994. *The Demography of Roman Egypt.* Cambridge.

Bagnall, R., Helms, C. and Verhoogt, A. 2000. *Documents from Berenike.* (Papyrologica Bruxellensia 31). Brussels.

Baines, J. and Málek, J. 1980. *Atlas of Ancient Egypt.* Oxford.

Baker, P. 1991. *Cos et Calymna, 205–200 a. C.: esprit civique et défense nationale.* Québec.

Baker, P. 2000. Coûts des garnisons et fortifications dans les cités à l'époque hellénistique. In Andreau et al. 2000: 177–96.

Baker, P. 2001. La vallée du Méandre au IIe s. a. C.: relations entre les cités et institutions militaires. In Bresson and Descat 2001: 61–73.

Bakhuizen, S. C. 1987. De Vikingen van Hellas – Strooptochten van de Aetoliërs, een Grieks bergvolk. *Utrechtse Historische Cahiers* 3: 21–39.

Bakhuizen, S. C. 1992. The town wall of Aitolian Kallipolis. In S. Van de Maele and J. M. Fossey (eds), *Fortificationes Antiquae.* Amsterdam. 171–84.

Bakhuizen, S. C. 1993–4. Veloukhovo. *Archaeological Reports.* 33–5.

Balsdon, J. P. V. D. 1950. The 'divinity' of Alexander. *Historia* 1: 363–88.

Bar-Kochva, B. 1976. *The Seleucid Army. Organisation and Tactics in the Great Campaigns.* Cambridge.

Bar-Kochva, B. 1989. *Judas Maccabaeus. The Jewish Struggle Against the Seleucids.* Cambridge.

Barbantani, S. 2001. *Phatis Nikephoros. Frammenti di elegia encomiastica nell'età delle Guerre Galatiche: Supplementum Hellenisticum 958 e 969.* Milan.

Barber, G. L. 1935. *The Historian Ephorus.* Oxford.

Barclay, J. M. G. 1996. *Jews in the Mediterranean Diaspora.* Edinburgh.

Barker, G. (ed.). 1995. *A Mediterranean Valley: Landscape Archaeology and* Annales *History in the Biferno Valley.* London.

Barker, G. and Mattingly, D. 1999–2000. *The Archaeology of Mediterranean Landscapes.* 5 vols. Oxford.

Barnes, J., Burnyeat, M. and Schofield, M. 1980. *Doubt and Dogmatism: Studies in Hellenistic Epistemology.* Oxford.

Barnett, R. D. 1956. Ancient Oriental influence on Archaic Greece. In S. Weinberg (ed.), *The Aegean and the Near East. Studies Presented to Hetty Goldman.* New York. 212–38.

Baronowski, D. 1991. The status of the Greek cities of Asia Minor after 190 B.C. *Hermes* 119: 450–63.

Barry, W. D. 1993. The Ptolemaic crowd and the riot of 203 B.C. *Echos du monde Classique/ Classical Views* 12: 415–31.

Basso, K. and Feld, S. (eds). 1996. *Senses of Place.* Santa Fe.

Bastini, A. 1987. *Der achäische Bund als hellenistische Mittelmacht.* Frankfurt.

Bauchhenß-Thüriedl, C. 1971. *Der Mythos von Telephos in der antiken Bildkunst.* Würzburg.

Bauslaugh, R. 1990. Cistophoric countermarks and the monetary system of Eumenes II. *Numismatic Chronicle* 150: 39–65.

Baynham, E. 1998. *Alexander the Great: the Unique History of Quintus Curtius.* Ann Arbor.

Beard, M. and Henderson, J. 2001. *Classical Art: from Greece to Rome.* Oxford.

Beard, M., North, J., Price, S. 1998. *Religions of Rome.* Vol. 1. Cambridge.

Bearzot, C. 1989. Fenomeni naturali e prodigi nell'attacco celtico a Delfi (279 a. C.). In M. Sordi (ed.), *Fenomeni naturali e avvenimenti storici nell'antichità.* Milan. 71–86.

Becatti, G. 1940. Attikà – Saggio sulla scultura attica nell' ellenismo. *Rivista dell' Istituto d'Archeologia e di Storia dell'Arte* 7: 7–116.

Beck, H. 1997. *Polis und Koinon: Untersuchungen zur Geschichte und Struktur der griechischen Bundesstaaten im 4. Jahrhundert v. Chr.* Stuttgart.

Behrend, D. 1970. *Attische Pachturkunden.* Munich.

Behrend, D. 1984. Réflexions sur les fractions du monnayage grec. In A. Houghton (ed.), *Festschrift für Leo Minderberg.* Wettern. 7–30.

Bellen, H. 1974. Der Rachegedanke in der griechisch-persischen Auseinandersetzung. *Chiron* 4: 43–67.

Bénabou, M. 1976. *La résistance africaine à la romanisation.* Paris.

Bender, B. (ed.). 1993. *Landscape: Politics and Perspectives.* Oxford.

Benecke, H. 1934. *Die Seepolitik der Aitoler.* Hamburg.

Bengtson, H. 1975. *Herrschergestalten des Hellenismus.* Munich.

Béquignon, Y. 1937. *La vallée du Spercheios.* Paris.

Berger, H. 1880. *Die geographischen Fragmente des Eratosthenes.* Leipzig.

Berger, H. 1903. *Geschichte der wissenschaftlichen Erdkunde der Griechen.* 2nd edn. Leipzig.

Berger, K. 1991. Die Bedeutung von Elementen des antiken Herrscherkultes für Liturgie und Eschatologie des Christentums im 1. Jahrhundert. In J. Assmann (ed.), *Das Fest und das Heilige. Religiöse Kontrapunkte zur Alltagswelt.* Gütersloh. 146–54.

Bergman, J. 1968. *Ich bin Isis – Studien zum memphischen Hintergrund der griechischen Isis-Aretologien.* Uppsala.

Bergmann, M. 1998. *Die Strahlen der Herrscher. Theomorphes Herrscherbild und politische Symbolik im Hellenismus und in der römischen Kaiserzeit.* Mainz.

Bernand, A. 1977. *Pan du désert.* Leiden.

Bernand, A. 1992. *La prose sur pierre dans l'Égypte hellénistique et romaine.* I: *Textes et traductions.* II: *Commentaires.* Paris.

Bernand, A. 1998. *Alexandrie la Grande.* 2nd edn. Paris.

Bernand, A. 1999. *Guerre et violence dans la Grèce antique.* Paris.

Bernard, P. 1973–present. *Fouilles d'Ai Khanoum.* Paris.

Bernard, P. 1994. L'Asie centrale et l'empire séleucide. *Topoi* 4: 473–511.

Berthold, R. 1984. *Rhodes in the Hellenistic Age.* London.

Bertrand, J. M. 1990. Formes de discours politiques: décrets des cités grecques et correspondance des rois hellénistique. In C. Nicolet (ed.). *Du pouvoir dans l'antiquité: mots et réalités.* Paris. 101–15.

Berve, H. 1926. *Das Alexanderreich auf prosopographischer Grundlage.* 2 vols. Munich.

Beschi, L. 1992–3. Nuove iscrizioni da Efestia. *Annuario* 54/55: 259–74.

Bevan, E. R. 1902. *The House of Seleucus.* 2 vols. London.

Beye, C. R. 1982. *Epic and Romance in the Argonautica of Apollonius.* Carbondale, Southern Illinois.

Beyer, K. 1984. *Die aramäischen Texte vom Toten Meer.* Gottingen.

Beyer-Rotthoff, B. 1993. *Untersuchungen zur Außenpolitik Ptolemaios' III.* Bonn.

Bianchetti, S. 1990. *Sulle tracce di una periegesi anonima.* Florence.

Bianchetti, S. 1998. *Pitea di Massalia: L'Oceano.* Pisa.

Bianchi, R. et al. (ed.). 1988. *Cleopatra's Egypt: Age of the Ptolemies.* Brooklyn Museum Catalogue.

Bickerman, E. 1952. Origines Gentium. *CP* 47: 65–81.

Bickerman, E. 1966. The Seleucids and the Achaemenids. In *Convegno sul tema: la Persia e il mondo greco.* Rome. 87–117.

Bickermann, E. 1937. *Der Gott der Makkabäer.* Berlin.

Bieber, M. 1942, 1967. *Laocoon, The Influence of the Group since its Rediscovery.* New York (rev. edn Detroit 1967).

Bieber, M. 1961. *The Sculpture of the Hellenistic Age.* New York (rev. edn).

Bienkowski, P. 1928. *Les Celtes dans les arts mineurs gréco-romains.* Kraków.

Bikerman, E. 1938. *Institutions des Séleucides.* Paris. (= E. Bickerman)

Bilde, P., Engberg-Pedersen, T., Hannestad, L. and Zahle, J. (eds). 1990. *Religion and Religious Practice in the Seleucid Kingdom.* Aarhus.

Bilde, P., Engberg-Pedersen, T., Hannestadt, L. and Zahle, J. (eds). 1992. *Ethnicity in Hellenistic Egypt.* Aarhus.

Bilde, P., Engberg-Pedersen, T., Hannestad, L. and Zahle, J. (eds). 1996. *Aspects of Hellenistic Kingship.* Aarhus.

Bilde, P., Engberg-Pedersen, T., Hannestadt, L. and Zahle, J. (eds). 1997. *Conventional Values of the Hellenistic Greeks.* Aarhus.

Bilde, P., Engberg-Pedersen, T., Hannestad, L., Randsborg, K. and Zahle, J. (eds). 1994. *Centre and Periphery in the Hellenistic World.* Aarhus.

Billows, R. 1990. *Antigonos the One-Eyed and the Creation of the Hellenistic State.* Berkeley.

Billows, R. 1993. IG XII 9, 212: a Macedonian officer at Eretria. *ZPE* 96: 249–57.

Billows, R. 1995. *Kings and Colonists. Aspects of Macedonian Imperialism.* Leiden.

Binder, D. D. 1999. *Into the Temple Courts: The Place of the Synagogues in the Second Temple Period.* Atlanta.

Bing, P. 1988. *The Well-Read Muse. Present and Past in Callimachus and the Hellenistic Poet.* Göttingen.

Bingen, J. 1973. Présence grecque et milieu rural ptolémaique. In M. I. Finley (ed.), *Problèmes de la terre en Grèce ancienne.* Paris. 215–22.

Bingen, J. 1975. Le milieu urbain dans la chôra égyptienne à l'époque ptolémaïque. In *Proceedings of the XIV International Congress of Papyrologists.* London. 367–73.

Bingen, J. 1978a. *Le Papyrus Revenue Laws: tradition grecque et adaptation hellénistique.* Opladen. Translated into English in Bingen, forthcoming, ch. 12.

Bingen, J. 1978b. The third-century BC land-leases from Tholthis. *Illinois Classical Studies* 3: 74–80.

Bingen, J. 1983. In Van't Dack et al. 1983: 1–11.

Bingen, J. 1997. I. Philai I 4, un moment d'un régne, d'un temple et d'un culte. In B. Kramer et al. (eds), *Akten des 21. Internationalen Papyrologenkongresses, Berlin, 13.-19.8.1995.* Stuttgart. I. 88–97.

Bingen, J. Forthcoming. *Hellenistic Egypt: Monarchy, Society, Economy, Culture.* Edited with introduction by R. S. Bagnall. Edinburgh.

Blackman, D. and Branigan, K. 1977. An archaeological survey of the lower catchment of the Ayiofarango valley. *BSA* 72: 13–84.

Blavatskii, V. D. 1953. *Zemledelie v antichnikh gosudarstvakh Severnogo Prichernomor'ya.* Moscow.

Blümel, W. 1997. Vertrag zwischen Latmos und Pidasa. *EA* 29: 135–42.

Boak, A. E. R. 1935. *Soknopaiou Nesos. The University of Michigan Excavations at Dimé in 1931–2.* Ann Arbor.

Boardman, J. 1994. *The Diffusion of Classical Art in Antiquity.* Princeton.

Bodson, L. 1991. Alexander the Great and the scientific exploration of the Oriental part of his empire: an overview of the background, trends and results. In *Ancient Society* 22: 127–38.

Boffo, L. 1985. *I re ellenistici e i centri religiosi dell'Asia Minore.* Florence.

Bogaert, R. 1965. Banquiers, courtiers et prêts maritimes à Athénes et à Alexandrie. *Chronique d'Egypte* 40: 140–56.

Bogaert, R. 1968. *Banques et banquiers dans les cités grecques.* Leiden.

Bogaert, R. 1976. *Epigraphica III. Texts on Bankers, Banking, and Credit in the Greek World.* Leiden.

Bommeljé, L. 1988. Aeolis in Aetolia: Thuc. 3.102.5 and the origins of the Aetolian *Ethnos. Historia* 37: 297–316.

Bommeljé, L. and Doorn, P. 1991. Transhumance in Aetolia, Central Greece: a mountain economy caught between storage and mobility. *Rivista di Studi Liguri* 56: 81–97.

Bommeljé, L., Doorn, P., Deylius, M., Vroom, J., Bommeljé, Y., Fagel, R. and van Wijngaarden, H. 1987. *Aetolia and the Aetolians.* Utrecht.

Bommeljé, L. S., Doorn, P. K., Deylius, M.,Vroom, J., Bommeljé, Y., Fagel, R. and van Wijngaarden, H. Forthcoming. *An Inland Polity: The Spatial Organization of Eastern Aetolia in Antiquity.* Amsterdam.

Borchhardt, J. 1991. Ein Ptolemaion in Limyra. *RA*: 309–22.

Borza, E. N. 1990. *In the Shadow of Olympus. The Emergence of Macedon.* Princeton.

Bosanquet, R. C. 1939–40. Dicte and the temples of Dictaean Zeus. *BSA* 40: 60–77.

Bosworth, A. B. 1971. The death of Alexander the Great: rumour and propaganda. *CQ* 21: 112–36.

Bosworth, A. B. 1988. *From Arrian to Alexander: Studies in Historical Interpretation.* Oxford.

Bosworth, A. B. 1993. Aristotle, India and the Alexander Historians. *Topoi* 3. 407–24.

Bosworth, A. B. 1996. *Alexander and the East: the Tragedy of Triumph.* Oxford.

Bosworth, A. B. 1999. Augustus, the *Res Gestae* and Hellenistic Theories of Apotheosis. *JRS* 89: 1–18.

Bosworth, A. B. and Wheatley, P. 1998. The origins of the Pontic house. *JHS* 118: 155–64.

Bouché-Leclercq, A. 1913–14. *Histoire des Séleucides*. 2 vols. Paris.

Bousquet, J. 1985. L'Hoplothèque de Delphes. *BCH* 109: 718–26.

Bousquet, J. 1988. La stèle des kyténiens au Letôon de Xanthos. *REG* 101: 12–53.

Bousquet, J. 1989. *Les comptes du quatrième et du troisième siècle*. Paris.

Bousquet, J. and Gauthier, P. 1994. Inscriptions du Létôon de Xanthos. *REG* 107: 319–61.

Bowersock, G. 1965. *Augustus and the Greek World*. Oxford.

Bowersock, G. 1983. *Roman Arabia*. Cambridge, Mass.

Bowersock, G. 1984. Augustus and the east: the problem of the succession. In F. Millar and E. Segal (eds), *Caesar Augustus: Seven Aspects*. Oxford. 169–88

Bowman, A. 1986. *Egypt after the Pharaohs: 332 BC–AD 642: From Alexander to the Arab Conquest*. London (corr. edn. 1990, Oxford).

Bowman, A. 1994. *Life and Letters on the Roman Frontier: Vindolanda and its People*. London.

Bowman, A. and Rogan, E. (eds). 1999. *Agriculture in Egypt: from Pharaonic to Modern Times*. Proceedings of the British Academy 96. Oxford.

Bowman, A. and Woolf, G. (eds). 1994. *Literacy and Power in the Ancient World*. Cambridge.

Boyce, M. 1984. On the Antiquity of Zoroastrian Apocalyptic. *Bulletin of the Society of Oriental and African Studies* 47: 56–78.

Bracht Branham, R. and Goulet-Cazé, M.-O. (eds). 1996. *The Cynics: the Cynic Movement in Antiquity and its Legacy*. Berkeley.

Bradley, G. 2000. *Ancient Umbria: State, Culture, and Identity in Central Italy from the Iron Age to the Augustan Era*. Oxford.

Brain, P. 1986. *Galen on Bloodletting: A Study of the Origins, Development and Validity of his Opinions, with a Translation of the Three Works*. Cambridge.

Branigan, K. 1998. Prehistoric and Early Historic Settlement in the Ziros Region, Eastern Crete. *BSA* 93: 23–90.

Braun, T. 1982. The Greeks in the Near East. *CAH*² 3.3: 1–31.

Braund, D. 1984. *Rome and the Friendly King: the Character of Client Kingship*. London.

Braund, D. 1985. *Augustus to Nero: a Sourcebook on Roman History, 31 BC–AD 68*. London.

Braund, D. 1994. *Georgia in Antiquity: a History of Colchis and Transcaucasian Iberia 550 BC–AD 562*. Oxford.

Braund, D. 2000. Map 87 inset: Cimmerius Bosphorus. In R. J. A. Talbert (ed.), *Barrington Atlas of the Greek and Roman World*. Princeton.

Braund, D. and Tsetskhladze, G. 1989. The export of slaves from Colchis. *CQ* 39: 114–25.

Bravo, B. 1980. *Sulan*. Représailles et justice privée contre des étrangers dans les cités grecques. Étude du vocabulaire et des institutions. *ASNP* Ser. III, Vol. 10.3: 675–987.

Bremmer, J. (ed.). 1987. *Interpretations of Greek Mythology*. London.

Bresciani, E. 1978. La spedizione di Tolomeo II in Siria in un ostrakon demotico inedito da Karnak. In Maehler and Strocka 1978: 31–7.

Bresson, A. 2000. *La cité marchande*. Bordeaux.

Bresson, A. 2003. Merchants and politics in Ancient Greece: social and economic aspects. In A. Giardina and C. Zaccagnini (eds), *Mercate e politica nel mondo antico*. Rome. 143–67.

Bresson, A. and Descat, R. (eds). 2001. *Les cités d'Asie Mineure occidentale au IIᵉ siècle a.C.* Bordeaux.

Bretzl, H. 1903. *Botanische Forschungen des Alexanderzuges*. Leipzig.

Briant, P. 1976. Brigandage, dissidence et conquête en Asie achéménide et hellénistique. *DHA* 2: 163–80.

Briant, P. 1982. *Rois, tributs, et paysans. Études sur les formations tributaires du Moyen-Orient ancien*. Paris.

Briant, P. 1985. Iraniens d'Asie Mineure après la chute de l'empire achéménide. *DHA* 11: 167–95.

Briant, P. 1988. Ethno-classe dominante et populations soumises: le cas de l'Egypte. In A. Kuhrt and H. Sancisi-Weerdenburg (eds), *Achaemenid History* III. Leiden. 137–73.

Briant, P. 1990 The Seleucid kingdom, the Achaemenid empire and the history of the Near East in the first millennium BC. In Bilde et al. 1990: 40–65.

Briant, P. 1993. Alexandre à Sardes. In Carlsen 1993: 13–27.

Briant, P. 1994a. De Samarkande à Sardes et de Suse au pays des Hanéens. *Topoi* 4: 455–67.

Briant, P. 1994b. Prélevements tributaires et échanges en Asie Mineure achéménide et hellénistique. In *Economie antique. Les échanges dans l'Antiquité: le rôle de l'état.* Saint-Bertrand-de-Comminges. 69–81.

Briant, P. 1996. *Histoire de l'empire Perse de Cyrus à Alexandre.* Paris.

Briant, P. 1999. Inscriptions multilingues d'époque achéménide: le texte et l'image. In Valbelle and Leclant 1999: 91–115.

Brilliant, R. 2000. *My Laocoon: Alternative Claims in the Interpretation of Artworks.* Berkeley.

Bringmann, K. 1993. The king as benefactor: some remarks on ideal kingship in the age of Hellenism. In Bulloch et al. 1993: 7–24.

Bringmann, K. and von Steuben, H. 1995. *Schenkungen hellenistischer Herrscher an griechische Städte und Heiligtümer.* I. *Zeugnisse und Kommentare.* Berlin.

Briscoe, J. 1973. *Commentary on Livy, Books XXXI–XXXIII.* Oxford.

Briscoe, J. 1981. *Commentary on Livy, Books XXXIV–XXXVII.* Oxford.

Brockway, L. 1979. *Science and Colonial Expansion: The Role of the British Royal Botanic Gardens.* New York.

Brodersen, K. 1989. *Appians Abriss der Seleukidengeschichte (Syriake 45, 232–70, 369).* Munich.

Brodersen, K. 1995. *Terra Cognita: Studien zur römischen Raumerfassung.* Hildesheim.

Brodersen, K. 2001. In den städtischen Gründungen ist die rechte Basis des Hellenisierens. Zur Funktion seleukidischer Städtegründungen. In S. Schraut and B. Stier (eds), *Stadt und Land, Bilder, Inszenierungen und Visionen in Geschichte und Gegenwart.* Stuttgart. 355–71.

Brodersen, K. (ed.). 1999. *Zwischen Ost und West. Studien zur Geschichte des Seleukidenreichs.* Hamburg.

Brulé, P. 1978. *La piraterie crétoise hellénistique.* Paris.

Brulé, P. 1990. Enquête démographique sur la famille grecque antique. *REA* 42: 233–58.

Brun, J.-P. 1999. *Laudatissimum fuit antiquitus in Delos insula.* La maison IB du Quartier du stade et la production des parfums à Délos. *BCH* 123: 87–155.

Brunet, M. (ed.). 1999. *Territoires des cités grecques. Actes de la table ronde internationale organisée par l'Ecole Francaise d'Athenes, 31 octobre–3 novembre 1991.* Athens.

Brunn, H. 1870. I Doni di Attalo. *Annali del Instituto di correspondenza archeologica.* 292–323 (= Brunn, *Kleine Schriften* Vol. 2 [Leipzig 1905], 411–30).

Brunt, P. 1963. Alexander's Macedonian cavalry. *JHS* 83: 27–47.

Brunt, P. 1965. Italian aims at the time of the Social War. *JRS* 55: 90–109.

Brunt, P. 1980. On historical fragments and epitomes. *CQ* 30: 477–94.

Buck, R. 1993. The Hellenistic Boiotian League. *AHB* 7. 3: 100–6.

Buckler, J. 1980. *The Theban Hegemony.* Cambridge, Mass.

Buckler, J. 1989. *Philip II and the Sacred War.* Leiden.

Budé 2001. *Appien. Histoire romaine. Tome VII, Livre XII. La Guerre de Mithridate.* Texte établi et traduit par Paul Goukowsky. Paris.

Bulloch, A. 1985. Hellenistic Poetry. In P. Easterling and B. Knox (eds), *The Cambridge History of Classical Literature,* I: *Greek Literature.* Cambridge. 541–621.

Bulloch, A., Gruen, E., Long, A. and Stewart, A. (eds). 1993. *Images and Ideologies: Self-Definition in the Hellenistic World.* Berkeley.

Bülow-Jacobsen, A. 1979. *P. Haun.* 6. An inspection of the original. *ZPE* 36: 91–100.

Bunbury, E. H. 1879. *A History of Ancient Geography among the Greeks.* London (repr., Amsterdam 1979).

Buraselis, K. 1982. *Das hellenistische Makedonien und die Ägäis*. Munich.

Burford, A. 1960. Land transport in Classical Antiquity. *Economic History Review* 13: 1–18.

Burford, A. 1969. *The Greek Temple Builders at Epidaurus*. Liverpool.

Burford, A. 1993. *Land and Labor in the Greek World*. Baltimore.

Burkert, W. 1983. Itinerant diviners and magicians: a neglected element in cultural contacts. In R. Hägg (ed.), *The Greek Renaissance of the Eighth Century* BC: *Tradition and Innovation*. Lund.

Burkert, W. 1985. *Greek Religion*. Oxford (orig. in German, Stuttgart 1977).

Burr, V. 1947. Das geographische Weltbild Alexanders des Großen. *Würzburger Jahrbücher für die Altertumswissenschaft* 2: 91–9.

Burstein, S. 1978. *The Babyloniaca of Berossus*. Malibu, Ca.

Burstein, S. 1982. Arsinoë II Philadelphos: a revisionist view. In Adams and Borza 1982: 197–212.

Burstein, S. 1985. *The Hellenistic Age from the Battle of Ipsos to the Death of Kleopatra VII*. Cambridge.

Burstein, S. 1989. *Agatharchides of Cnidus: On the Erythraean Sea*. London.

Burstein, S. 1996a. *The Hellenistic Period in World History*. Essays on global and comparative history. American Historical Association, Washington DC.

Burstein, S. 1996b. Ivory and Ptolemaic exploration of the Red Sea: the missing factor. *Topoi* 6: 799–807.

Burton, P. 1996. The summoning of the Magna Mater to Rome (205 BC). *Historia* 45: 36–63.

Butzer, K. W. 1976. *Early Hydraulic Civilization in Egypt*. Chicago.

Cabanes, P. 1976. *L'Épire de la mort de Pyrrhos à la conquête romaine*. Paris.

Cabanes, P. 1980. Société et institutions dans les monarchies de Grèce septentrionale au IVe siècle. *REG* 113: 324–51.

Cabanes, P. 1985. Le pouvoir local au sein des états fédéraux: Épire, Acarnanie, Étolie. In *Actes du colloque international 'La Béotie antique'*. Paris. 343–57.

Cabanes, P. 1988. *Les Illyriens de Bardylis à Genthios: IVe–IIe siècles avant J.-C*. Paris.

Cabanes, P. 1989. Cité et *ethnos* dans la Grèce ancienne. In M-M. Mactoux and E. Geny (eds), *Mélanges P. Lévêque* 2. Paris. 63–82.

Cabanes, P. 1993a. Histoire comparée de la Macédoine, de l'Épire et de l'Illyrie méridionale (IVᵉ–IIᵉ s. a.C.). *MDAI* (A) 5: 293–311.

Cabanes, P. (ed.). 1987. *L'Illyrie méridionale et l'Épire dans l'antiquité*. Vol. 1. Clermont-Ferrand.

Cabanes, P. (ed.). 1993b, 1999. *L'Illyrie méridionale et l'Épire dans l'antiquité*. Vols 2 and 3. Paris.

Cadell, H. 1998. À quelle date Arsinoé II Philadelphe est-elle décédée? In Melaerts 1998: 1–3.

Cadogan, G. 1981. A probable shrine in the country house at Pyrgos. In R. Hägg and N. Marinatos (eds), *Sanctuaries and Cults in the Aegean Bronze Age*. Lund. 169–71.

Cahill, N. 2002. *Household and City Organization at Olynthus*. New Haven.

Calderone, S. 1976. La conquista romana della Magna Grecia. In *La Magna Grecia nell'età romana*. Naples. 33 ff.

Callieri, P. 1995. Note d'information. Une borne routière grecque de la région de Persépolis. *CRAI*: 65–7.

Cambiano, G. 1983. *La filosofia in Grecia e a Roma*. Rome.

Cameron, A. 1995. *Callimachus and his Critics*. Princeton.

Camp, J. M. and Kroll, J. 2001. The Agora Mint and Athenian Bronze Coinage. *Hesperia* 70: 127–62.

Campanile, E. 1979. Le strutture magistratuali degli stati osci. In E. Campanile and C. Letta, *Studi sulle magistrature indigene e municipali in area italica*. Pisa. 15 ff.

Campanile, M. 1993. Osservazioni sul culto provinciale di Augusto in Asia Minore. *Epigraphica* 55: 207–11.

Campanile, M. 1994a. *I sacerdoti del Koinon d'Asia (I sec. a.C.-III sec. d.C.)*. Pisa.

Campanile, M. 1994b. I sommi sacerdoti del Koinón d'Asia: Numero, rango e criteri di elezione. *ZPE* 100: 422–6.

Canali de Rossi, F. 2000. Tre epistoli di magistrati romani a città d'Asia. *EA* 32: 163–81.

Carlsen, J. (ed.). 1993. *Alexander the Great: Reality and Myth*. Rome.

Carney, E. 1987. The reappearance of royal sibling marriage in Ptolemaic Egypt. *Parola del Passato* 237: 420–39.

Carney, E. 1994. Arsinoë before she was Philadelphus. *AHB* 8: 123–31.

Carney, E. 2000. *Women and the Macedonian Monarchy*. Norman, Oklahoma.

Carpenter, R. 1960. *Greek Sculpture: A Critical Review*. Chicago.

Cartledge, P. 1997. Introduction. In Cartledge et al. 1997: 1–19.

Cartledge, P. 1998. Introduction: defining a *kosmos*. In Cartledge et al. 1998: 1–12.

Cartledge, P. 2002. The economy (economies) of Ancient Greece. In W. Scheidel and S. von Reden (eds), *The Ancient Economy*. Edinburgh. 11–32.

Cartledge, P. and Spawforth, A. 1989. *Hellenistic and Roman Sparta: a Tale of Two Cities*. London.

Cartledge, P., Cohen, E. and Foxhall, L. (eds). 2001. *Money, Labour and Land in Ancient Greece: Approaches to the Economics of Ancient Greece*. London.

Cartledge, P., Garnsey, P. and Gruen, E. (eds). 1997. *Hellenistic Constructs: Essays in Culture, History and Historiography*. Berkeley.

Cartledge, P., Millett, P. and von Reden, S. 1998. *Kosmos: Essays in Order, Conflict, and Community in Classical Athens*. Cambridge.

Caskey, J. 1982. Koroni and Keos. In *Studies in Attic Epigraphy, History, and Topography Presented to Eugene Vanderpool*. Princeton. 14–16.

Casson, L. 1986. *Ships and Seamanship in the Ancient World*. 2nd edn. Princeton.

Casson, L. 1991. *The Ancient Mariners. Sea Farers and Sea Fighters of Ancient Times*. 2nd edn. Princeton.

Catalano, P. 1978. Aspetti spaziali del sistema giuridico-religioso romano. Mundus, templum, urbs, ager, Latium, Italia. *ANRW* 16.1: 440–53.

Cavanagh, W. and Curtis, M. (eds). 1998. *Post-Minoan Crete*. London.

Cawkwell, G. L. 1994. The deification of Alexander the Great: a note. In I. Worthington (ed.), *Ventures into Greek History*. Oxford. 293–306.

Cenerini, F. 1989. O colonia quae cupis ponte ludere longo (Cat. 17): cultura e politica. *Athenaeum* 67: 41 ff.

Ceserani, G. 2000. The charm of the Siren: the place of Classical Sicily in historiography. In Serrati and Smith 2000: 174–93.

Champion, C. 1995. The Soteria at Delphi: Aetolian propaganda in the epigraphical record. *AJP* 116: 213–20.

Champion, C. 1996. Polybius, Aetolia and the Gallic attack on Delphi (279 BC). *Historia* 45: 315–28.

Chaniotis, A. 1995. Problems of 'Pastoralism' and 'Transhumance' in Classical and Hellenistic Crete. *Orbis Terrarum* 1: 39–89.

Chaniotis, A. 1996. *Die Verträge zwischen kretischen Poleis in der hellenistischen Zeit*. Stuttgart.

Chaniotis, A. 1997a. Theatricality beyond the theater. Staging public life in the Hellenistic world. *Pallas* 47: 219–59.

Chaniotis, A. 1997b. Reinheit des Körpers – Reinheit der Seele in den griechischen Kultgesetzen. In J. Assmann and T. Sundermeyer (eds), *Schuld, Gewissen und Person*. Gütersloh. 142–79.

Chaniotis, A. 2002. Foreign soldiers – native girls? Constructing and crossing boundaries in Hellenistic cities with foreign garrisons. In A. Chaniotis and P. Ducrey (eds), *Army and Power in the Ancient World*. Stuttgart.

Chaniotis, A. (ed.). 1999. *From Minoan Farmers to Roman Traders: Sidelights on the Economy of Ancient Crete*. Stuttgart.

Charneux, P. and Tréheux, J. 1988. Sur le règlement frontalier entre les cités d'Ambracie et de Caradros. *BCH* 112: 359–73.

Charre, R. and Le Dinahet, M.-Th. 1999. Sites de fermes à Rhénée. In Brunet 1999: 135–57.

Chauveau, M. 2000. *Egypt in the Age of Cleopatra*. Ithaca.

Cherniss, H. 1945. *The Riddle of the Early Academy*. New York.

Cherry, J. F. 1995. Regional survey in the Aegean: the 'New Wave' (and after). In P. N. Kardulias (ed.), *Beyond the Site: Regional Studies in the Aegean Area*. Lanham, MD. 91–112.

Chevallier, R. 1976. *Roman Roads*. Berkeley.

Chuvin, P. 1981. Apollon au trident et les dieux de Tarse. *JSav.* 305–26.

Clarke, K. 1999. *Between Geography and History: Hellenistic Constructions of the Roman World*. Oxford.

Clarke, M. L. 1959. *Classical Education in Britain 1500–1900*. Cambridge.

Clarysse, W. 1980. A royal visit to Memphis and the end of the Second Syrian War. In Crawford, Quaegebeur and Clarysse (eds) 1980: 83–9.

Clarysse, W. 1983. Literary papyri in documentary 'archives'. In Van't Dack et al. 1983: 43–61.

Clarysse, W. 1985. Greeks and Egyptians in the Ptolemaic army and administration. *Aegyptus* 65: 57–66.

Clarysse, W. 1992. Some Greeks in Egypt. In Johnson 1992: 51–6.

Clarysse, W. 1993. Egyptian scribes writing Greek. *Chronique d'Egypte* 68: 186–201.

Clarysse, W. 1994. Greeks and Persians in a bilingual census list. *Acta Demotica: Acts of the Fifth International Congress for Demotists; Pisa, 4th–8th September 1993*. Pisa. 69–77.

Clarysse, W. 1995. Greeks in Ptolemaic Thebes. In Vleeming 1995: 1–19.

Clarysse, W. 1998. Ethnic diversity and dialect among the Greeks of Hellenistic Egypt. In A. Verhoogt and S. Vleeming (eds), *The Two Faces of Graeco-Roman Egypt*. Pap. Lugd.-Bat. 30. Leiden. 1–13.

Clarysse, W. 2000a. Ptolémées et temples. In Valbelle and Leclant 2000: 41–65.

Clarysse, W. 2000b. The Ptolemies visiting the Egyptian chora. In Mooren 2000: 29–53.

Clarysse, W. 2000c. Les décrets égyptiens et leur affichage dans les temples. In Valbelle and Leclant 2000: 41–65.

Clarysse, W. and Thompson, D. J. 1995. The salt-tax rate once again. *Chronique d'Egypte* 70: 223–9.

Clarysse, W. and van der Veken, G. 1983. *The Eponymous Priests of Ptolemaic Egypt*. Pap. Lugd.-Bat. 24. Leiden.

Clarysse, W. and Vandorpe, K. 1995. *Zénon: un homme d'affaires grec a l'ombre des pyramides*. Leuven.

Clarysse, W. and Vandorpe, K. 1998. The Ptolemaic apomoira. In Melaerts 1998: 5–42.

Clarysse, W. and Willems, H. 2000. *Les empereurs du Nil*. Leuven.

Clauss, M. 1996. Deus praesens. Der römische Kaiser als Gott. *Klio* 78: 400–33.

Clauss, M. 1999. *Kaiser und Gott. Herrscherkult im römischen Reich*. Stuttgart.

Clay, D. 1998. *Paradosis and Survival: Three Chapters in the History of Epicurean Philosophy*. Ann Arbor.

Clinton, K. 1997. Eleusis and the Romans: Late Republic to Marcus Aurelius. In Hoff and Rotroff 1997: 161–81.

Coarelli, F. 1982. L'agora des Italiens a Delo: il mercato degli schiavi? In F. Coarelli, D. Musti and H. Solin (eds), *Delo e l'Italia*. Rome. 119–39.

Coarelli, F. 1988. Colonizzazione romana e viabilità. *DdA* 6: 35–48.

Coarelli, F. and La Regina, A. 1984. *Abruzzo, Molise*. Rome.

Cohen, A. 1997. *The Alexander Mosaic: Stories of Victory and Defeat*. Cambridge.

Cohen, E. 1992. *Athenian Economy and Society. A Banking Perspective.* Princeton.

Cohen, G. M. 1978. *The Seleucid Colonies. Studies in Founding, Administration and Organization.* Stuttgart.

Cohen, G. M. 1991. Katoikiai, Katoikoi and Macedonians in Asia Minor. *AncSoc* 22: 41–50.

Cohen, G. M. 1995. *The Hellenistic Settlements in Europe, the Islands, and Asia Minor.* Berkeley.

Coldstream, J. N. and Catling, H. W. (eds). 1996. *Knossos North Cemetery: Early Greek Tombs.* London.

Collins, F. 1980. The Macedonians and the revolt of Aristonicus. *Ancient World* 3: 83–7.

Collins, J. J. 2000. *Between Athens and Jerusalem: Jewish Identity in the Hellenistic Diaspora.* 2nd edn. Grand Rapids.

Colpe, C. 1987. Syncretism. In M. Eliade (ed.), *The Encyclopedia of Religion* 14. New York. 218–27

Conticello, B. and Andreae, B. 1974. Die Skulpturen von Sperlonga. *Antike Plastik* 14.

Cornell, T. J. 1989. The conquest of Italy. *CAH*^{2} 7.2: 351–419.

Cornell, T. J. 1995. *The Beginnings of Rome: Italy and Rome from the Bronze Age to the Punic Wars (c. 1000–264 BC).* London.

Corsten, T. 1999. *Vom Stamm zum Bund – Gründung und territoriale Organisation griechischer Bundesstaaten.* Würzburg.

Corvisier, J. N., and Wieslaw, S. 2000. *La population d'antiquité classique.*

Costabile, F. 1984. *Istituzioni e forme costituzionali nelle città del Bruzio in età romana.* Naples.

Coulson, W. 1996. *Ancient Naukratis II: the Survey of Naukratis and Environs: Part I: the Survey at Naukratis.* Oxford.

Coulton, J. J. 1976. *The Architectural Development of the Greek Stoa.* Oxford.

Cowey, J. M. S. and Maresch, K. 2001. *Urkunden des Politeuma der Juden von Herakleopolis (144/3–133/2 v. Chr.). (P. Polit. Iud.).* Wiesbaden.

Crampa, J. 1969. *Labraunda III.1: the Greek Inscriptions, Part I: 1–12 (Period of Olympichus).* Lund.

Crawford, D. J. 1971. *Kerkeosiris: an Egyptian Village in the Ptolemaic Period.* Cambridge.

Crawford, D. J. 1978. The good official in Ptolemaic Egypt. In Maehler and Strocka 1978: 195–202.

Crawford, D. J. 1980. Ptolemy, Ptah and Apis in Hellenistic Memphis. In Crawford et al. 1980: 1–42.

Crawford, D. J., Quaegebeur, J. and Clarysse, W. 1980. *Studies on Ptolemaic Memphis.* Leuven.

Crawford, M. H. 1977. Republican denarii in Romania: the suppression of piracy and the slave trade. *JRS* 67: 117–24.

Crawford, M. H. 1978. Greek intellectuals and the Roman aristocracy. In P. Garnsey and C. Whittaker (eds), *Imperialism in the Ancient World.* Cambridge. 193–207.

Crawford, M. H. 1990. Origini e sviluppi del sistema provinciale romano. In *Storia di Roma ii: L'impero mediterraneo; 1. La repubblica imperiale.* Turin.

Crawford, M. H. 1996. Italy and Rome from Sulla to Augustus. *CAH*^{2} 10: 414–33.

Cribiore, R. 1996. *Writing, Teachers, and Students in Graeco-Roman Egypt.* American Studies in Papyrology 36. Atlanta, Ga.

Cribiore, R. 2001. *Gymnastics of the Mind. Greek Education in Hellenistic and Roman Egypt.* Princeton.

Criniti, N. (ed.). 1994. *Catullo e Sirmione: società e cultura della Cisalpina alle soglie dell'impero.* Brescia.

Criscuolo, L. and Geraci, G. (eds). 1989. *Egitto e storia antica dall'ellenismo all'età araba: bilancio di un confronto.* Bologna.

Croissant, F. and Salviat, F. 1966. Aphrodite gardienne des magistrats: gynéconomes de Thasos et polémarques de Thèbes. *BCH* 90: 460–71.

Cross, G. N. 1932. *Epirus*. Cambridge.

Crowther, C. 1995. Iasos in the second century BC. 3, Foreign Judges from Priene. *BICS* 40: 91–138.

Crowther, C. 1998. Aus der Arbeit der Inscriptiones Graecae. 1, Drei Dekrete aus Kos für Dikastagogoi. *Chiron* 28: 87–100.

Crowther, C. 1999. Aus der Arbeit der Inscriptiones Graecae. 4, Koan Decrees for Foreign Judges. *Chiron* 29: 251–319.

Cucuzza, N. 1997. Considerazioni su alcuni culti nella Messarà di epoca storica e sui rapporti territoriali fra Festòs e Gortina. *Atti dell'Accademia nazionale dei Lincei. Rendiconti* 9.8: 63–93.

Cunningham, I. C. 1971. *Herodas, Mimiambi*. Oxford.

Curti, E. 2001. Toynbee's legacy: aspects of the Romanization of Italy. In S. Keay and N. Terrenato (eds), *Italy and the West: Comparative Issues in Romanization*. Oxford.

Curti, E., Dench, E. and Patterson, J. 1996. The archaeology of central and southern Roman Italy: recent trends and approaches. *JRS* 86: 170–89.

Curty, O. 1995. *Les parentés légendaires entre cités grecques*. Geneva.

D'Agata, A.-L. 1998. Changing patterns in a Minoan and post-Minoan sanctuary: the case of Agia Triada. In Cavanagh and Curtis 1998: 19–26.

Dal Pra, M. 1975. *Lo scetticismo Greco*. Rome.

Daly, G. 2002. *Cannae: the Experience of Battle in the Second Punic War*. London.

Dany, O. 1999. *Akarnanien im Hellenismus: Geschichte und Volkerrecht in Nordwestgriechenland*. Munich.

Dao, J. 2002. One nation plays the great game alone. *The New York Times*, Sunday 7 July 2002 (*from* Week in Review Desk; repr. in *Le Monde*, 14–15 July, 2002).

Darbyshire, G., Mitchell S. and Vardar, L. 2000. The Galatian settlement in Asia Minor. *Anatolian Studies* 50: 75–97.

Daux, G. 1955. L'expansion étolienne vers le nord à la fin du IIIe siècle avant J.-C. In *Studia Antiqua Antonio Salac Septuagenario Oblata*. Prague. 35–9.

David, E. 1981. *Sparta between Empire and Revolution (404–243 BC)*. *Internal Problems and their Impact on Contemporary Greek Consciousness*. Salem, Mass.

David, J.-M. 1996. *The Roman Conquest of Italy*. Oxford.

Davies, J. K. 1977–8. The Descent group and its alternatives. *CJ* 73: 105–21.

Davies, J. K. 1984. Cultural, social and economic features of the Hellenistic world. *CAH²* 7.1: 257–320.

Davies, J. K. 1998. Ancient economies: models and muddles. In Parkins and Smith 1998: 225–56.

Davies, J. K. 2001. Hellenistic economies in the post-Finley era. In Archibald et al. 2001: 11–62.

Davies, J. K. Forthcoming. Flow models for ancient economies. In I. Morris and J. Manning (eds), *Ancient Economies. Evidence and Models*. Stanford.

Davison, J. 1991. Myth and the Periphery. In Pozzi and Wickersham 1991: 49–63.

de Callataÿ, F. 1997. *L'Histoire des guerres mithridatiques vue par les monnaies*. Louvain.

de Callataÿ, F. 2000. Guerres et monnayages à l'époque hellénistique. Essai de mise en perspective suivi d'une annexe sur le monnayage de Mithridate VI Eupator. In Andreau et al. 2000: 337–64.

de Callataÿ, F., Depeyrot, G. and Villaronga, L. 1993. *L'argent monnayé d'Alexandre le Grand à Auguste*. Brussels.

de Grummond, N. and Ridgway, B. (eds). 2000. *From Pergamon to Sperlonga*. Berkeley.

de Meulenaere, H. 1995. La prosopographie thébaine de l'époque ptolémaïque à la lumière des sources hiéroglyphiques. In Vleeming 1995: 83–90.

de Romanis, F. 1996. *Cassia, cinnamomo, ossidiana. Uomini e merci tra Oceano Indiano e Mediterraneo.* Rome.

de Romilly, J. 2000. *La Grèce antique contre la violence.* Paris.

de Souza, P. 1999. *Piracy in the Graeco-Roman World.* Cambridge.

de Ste Croix, G. E. M. 1981. *The Class Struggle in the Ancient Greek World.* London.

Debevoise, N. D. 1938. *Political History of Parthia.* Chicago.

Debord, P. 1982. *Aspects sociaux et économiques de la vie religieuse dans l'Anatolie gréco-romaine.* Leiden.

Decourt, J.-Cl. 1990. *La vallée de l'Énipeus en Thessalie.* Paris.

Decourt, J.-Cl., Helly, B. and Gallis, K. 1995. *La Thessalie: Colloque internationale d'archeologie: Quinze années de recherches (1975–1990), bilans et perspectives.* Athens.

DeForest, M. M. 1994. *Apollonius' Argonautica: a Callimachean Epic.* Leiden.

Deichgräber, K. 1930/1965. *Die greichische Empirikerschule: Sammlung der Fragmente und Darstellung der Lehre.* Berlin (repr. with additional material 1965).

DeLacy, P. 1952. Biography and tragedy in Plutarch. *AJP* 73: 159–71.

Delev, P. 2000. Lysimachus, the Getae and archaeology. *CQ* 50: 384–401.

Dell, H. J. 1967. The origin and nature of Illyrian piracy. *Historia* 16: 344–58.

Dell, H. J. 1970. Demetrius of Pharus and the Istrian war. *Historia* 19: 30–8.

Dench, E. 1995. *From Barbarians to New Men: Greek, Roman, and Modern Perceptions of Peoples from the Central Apennines.* Oxford.

Dench, E. 1997. Austerity, Excess, Success, and Failure in Hellenistic and Early Imperial Italy. In M. Wyke (ed.). *Parchments of Gender: Deciphering the Bodies of Antiquity.* Oxford. 121–46.

Denti, M. 1991. *I Romani a nord del Po: archeologia e cultura in età repubblicana e augustea.* Milan.

Depauw, M. 1997. *A Companion to Demotic Studies.* Brussels.

Depauw, M. 2000. *The archive of Teos and Thabis from Early Ptolemaic Thebes.* Monographies Reine Élisabeth 8. Turnhout.

Depew, M. 2000. Enacted and represented dedications: genre and Greek hymn. In M. Depew and D. Obbink (eds), *Matrices of Genre. Authors, Canons, and Society.* Cambridge. 59–79.

Derow, P. S. 1970. Polybios and the embassy of Kallikrates. In *Essays Presented to C. M. Bowra.* Oxford.

Derow, P. S. 1973a. Kleemporos. *Phoenix* 27: 118–34.

Derow, P. S. 1973b. The Roman calendar, 190–168 BC. *Phoenix* 27: 345–56.

Derow, P. S. 1976. The Roman calendar, 218–191 BC. *Phoenix* 30: 265–81.

Derow, P. S. 1979. Polybius, Rome and the east. *JRS* 69: 1–15.

Derow, P. S. 1984. Review of Walbank 1979. *JRS* 74: 231–5.

Derow, P. S. 1989. Rome, the fall of Macedon, and the sack of Corinth. *CAH*² 8: 290–323.

Derow, P. S. 1990. Review of Ferrary 1988. *JRS* 80: 197–200.

Derow, P. S. 1991. Pharos and Rome. *ZPE* 88: 261–70.

Derow, P. S. and Forrest, W. G. 1982. An inscription of Chios. *BSA* 77: 79–92.

Desanges, J. 1978. *Recherches sur l'activité des Méditerranées aux confins de l'Afrique (VIᵉ siècle avant J.-C. – IVᵉ siècle après J.-C.).* Paris.

Descat, R. 1994. La cité grecque et les échanges. Un retour à Hasebroek. In *Économie antique. Les échanges dans l'antiquité: le rôle de l'état.* Saint-Bertrand-de-Comminges. 11–30.

Descat, R. 2001. La loi délienne sur les bois et charbons et le rôle de Délos comme marché. *REA* 103: 125–30.

Despinis, G., Stefanidou Tiveriou, T. and Voutiras, E. 1997. *Catalogue of Sculpture in the Archaeological Museum of Thessaloniki.* Vol. 1. Thessaloniki.

Dickie, J. 1997. Stereotypes of the Italian south 1860–1908. In R. Lumley and J. Morris (eds), *The New History of the Italian South: the Mezzogiorno Revisited.* Exeter. 114–47.

Dickie, M. 1999. The learned magician and the collection and transmission of magical lore. In D. R. Jordan, H. Montgomery and E. Thomassen (eds), *The World of Ancient Magic.* Bergen. 162–93.

Dickie, M. 2001. *Magic and Magicians in the Greco-Roman World.* London.

Dicks, D. R. 1960. *The Geographical Fragments of Hipparchus.* London.

Dietz, S., Kolonas, L. et al. 1998. Surveys and excavations in Chalkis, Aetolias, 1995–1996. First preliminary report. *Proceedings of the Danish Archaeological Institute* 2: 233–315.

Dignas, B. 2000. The leases of sacred property at Mylasa. An alimentary scheme for the Gods. *Kernos* 13: 117–26.

Dignas, B. 2002. *Economy of the Sacred in Hellenistic and Roman Asia Minor.* Oxford.

Dilke, O. A. W. 1985. *Greek and Roman Maps.* London.

Dillery, J. D. 1999. The first Egyptian narrative history: Manetho and Greek historiography. *ZPE* 127: 93–116.

Dillon, M. 1999. Post-nuptial sacrifices on Kos (Segre, *ED* 178) and ancient Greek Marriage Rites. *ZPE* 124: 63–80.

Dirks, N. 1996. Foreword. In B. S. Cohen, *Colonialism and its Forms of Knowledge: The British in India.* Princeton. ix–xvii.

Dixon, M. 2000. Disputed territories: international arbitration in the northeast Peloponnesos, *ca.* 250–150 BC. (Dissertation, Ohio State University). Columbus.

Donally, W. 1989. The pre-state community in Greece. *Symbolae Osloenses* 64: 5–29.

Dörner, F. K. 1996. Sculpture and Inscription Catalogue. In D. H. Sanders (ed.), *Nemrud Daği. The Hierothesion of Antiochus I of Commagene 1.* Winona Lake. 175–377.

Dougherty, C. 1993. *The Poetics of Colonization: from City to Text in Archaic Greece.* Oxford.

Dowden, K. 1992. *The Uses of Greek Mythology.* London.

Downey, G. 1961. *A History of Antioch in Syria from Seleucus to the Arab Conquest.* Princeton.

Downey, G. 1963. *Ancient Antioch.* Princeton.

Drexhage, H.-J. 1991. *Preise, Mieten/Pachten, Kosten und Löhne im römischen Ägypten bis zum Regierungsantritt Diokletians.* St Katharinen.

Dreyer, B. 1998. The *Hiereus* of the *Soteres:* Plut. *Dem.* 10.4, 46.2. *GRBS* 39: 23–38.

Dreyer, B. 1999a. *Untersuchungen zur Geschichte des spätklassischen Athen (322–c.230 v. Chr.).* Stuttgart.

Dreyer, B. 1999b. Zum ersten Diadochenkrieg: der Göteborger Arrian-Palimpsest (ms Graec I). *ZPE* 125: 39–60.

Dreyer, B. 2000. Roms Ostpolitik, Athen und der Beginn der Neustil-Silberprägung. *ZPE* 129: 77–83.

Dreyfus, R. and Schraudolph, E. (eds). 1996. *Pergamon: the Telephos Frieze from the Great Altar.* San Francisco.

Droysen, J. G. 1877–8. *Geschichte des Hellenismus.* Gotha (repr. Basel 1952).

Ducat, J. 1994. *Les Pénestes de Thessalie.* Paris.

Ducat, J. 2002. The Obligations of Helots. In M. Whitby (ed.), *Sparta.* London. 196–211.

Ducrey, P. 1968. *Le traitement des prisonnieres de guerre dans la Grèce antique: des origines à la conquéte romain.* Paris.

Dueck, D. 2000. *Strabo of Amaseia.* London.

Dunand, F. 1973. *Le culte d'Isis dans le bassin orientale de la méditerranée.* Leiden.

Dunand, F. 1981. Fête et propagande à Alexandrie sous les Lagides. In *La fête, pratiques et discours. D'Alexandrie hellénistique à la mission de Besançon (Annales Littéraires de l'Université de Besançon, 262).* Paris. 13–40.

Dunbabin, K. 1999. *Mosaics of the Greek and Roman World.* Cambridge.

Düring, I. 1966. *Aristotle: Darstellung und Interpretation seines Denkens.* Heidelberg.

Durrbach, F. 1921. *Choix d'inscriptions de Delos.* Paris.

Eckstein, A. 1995. *Moral Vision in the Histories of Polybius.* Berkeley.

Eckstein, A. 1999. Pharos and the question of Roman treaties of alliance in the Greek east in the third century BCE. *CP* 94: 395–418.

Eddy, S. K. 1961. *The King is Dead.* Lincoln.

Edelman, M. 1988. *Constructing the Political Spectacle.* Chicago.

Edelstein, E. and L. 1945. *Asclepius: Collection and Interpretation of the Testimonies.* Baltimore (repr. 1998 with new introduction).

Edelstein, L. 1967. The history of anatomy in antiquity. In O. and C. Temkin (eds), *Ancient Medicine: the Selected Papers of Ludwig Edelstein.* Baltimore. 247–301.

Edelstein, L. and Kidd, I. G. 1989. *Posidonius.* Vol. 1: *The Fragments.* 2nd edn. Cambridge.

Edgar, C. C. (ed.). 1931. *Zenon Papyri (P. Michigan I).* (University of Michigan Studies, Humanistic Series 24). Ann Arbor.

Edmunds, L. (ed.). 1990. *Approaches to Greek Myth.* Baltimore.

Edmunds, L. 1971. The religiosity of Alexander. *GRBS* 12: 363–91.

Edson, C. F. 1958. Imperium Macedonicum: the Seleucid empire and the literary evidence. *CP* 53: 153–70.

Ehrenberg, V. and Jones, A. H. M. 1976. *Documents Illustrating the Reign of Augustus.* 2nd edn. Oxford.

Ehrhardt, C. 1975. Studies in the reigns of Demetrios II and Antigonos Doson. (Dissertation, State University of New York). Buffalo.

Ehrhardt, C. 1978. Demetrios ὁ, Αἰτωλικός and Antigonid Nicknames. *Hermes* 106: 251–3.

Eilers, C. 2002. *Roman Patrons of Greek Cities.* Oxford.

Elwyn, S. 1990. The reorganization decree for the Delphian Soteria and the date of Smyrna's inviolability. *JHS* 110: 177–80.

Empereur, J.-Y. 1998. *Alexandria Rediscovered.* London.

Engelmann, H. 1975. *The Delian Aretology of Sarapis.* Leiden.

Engelmann, H. and Merkelbach, R. 1972–3. *Die Inschriften von Erythrai und Klazomenai* I-II. Bonn.

Engels, D. 1978. *Alexander the Great and the Logistics of the Macedonian Army.* Berkeley.

Engels, J. 1999. *Augusteische Oikumenegeographie und Universalhistorie im Werk Strabons von Amaseia.* Stuttgart.

Erler, M. 1983. *Die Hellenistische Philosophie,* Vol. 4.1 of H. Flashar (ed.), *Die Philosophie der Antik.* Basel.

Errington, R. M. 1970. From Babylon to Triparadeisos, 323–320 BC. *JHS* 90: 49–77.

Errington, R. M. 1978. The nature of the Macedonian state under the monarchy. *Chiron* 8: 77–133.

Errington, R. M. 1989a. Rome and Greece to 205 BC. *CAH*² 8: 81–106.

Errington, R. M. 1989b. Rome against Philip and Antiochus. *CAH*² 8: 244–89.

Errington, R. M. 1990. *A History of Macedonia.* Berkeley.

Erskine, A. 1990. *The Hellenistic Stoa: Political Thought and Action.* London

Erskine, A. 1994. The Romans as common benefactors. *Historia* 43: 70–87.

Erskine, A. 1995. Culture and power in Ptolemaic Egypt. The museum and Library of Alexandria. *Greece and Rome* 42: 38–48.

Erskine, A. 2000. Polybios and Barbarian Rome. *Mediterraneo Antico* 3: 165–82.

Erskine, A. 2001. *Troy between Greece and Rome: Local Tradition and Imperial Power.* Oxford.

Erskine, A. 2002a. Life after death: Alexandria and the body of Alexander. *Greece and Rome* 49: 163–79.

Erskine, A. 2002b. O Brother, where art thou? Tales of kinship and diplomacy. In Ogden 2002, ch. 6.

Étienne, R. and Knoepfler, D. 1976. *Hyettos de Béotie et la chronologie des archontes fédéraux entre 250 et 171 avant J.-C.* Paris.

Étienne, R. and Piérart, M. 1975. Un décret du *koinon* des hellènes à Platées, en l'honneur de Glaucon, fils d'Étéoclès, d'Athènes. *BCH* 99: 51–75.

Falivene, M. 1998. *The Herakleopolite Nome*. Atlanta, Ga.

Fantuzzi, M. and Hunter, R. 2002. *Muse e Modelli. La poesia ellenistica da Alessandro Magno ad Augusto.* Rome.

Fellman, W. 1930. *Antigonos Gonatas, König der Makedonier und die griechischen Staaten.* Würzburg.

Ferguson, W. S. 1906. The premature deification of Eumenes II. *CP* 1: 231–4.

Ferrary, J.-L. 1988. *Philhellénisme et impérialisme: aspects idéologiques de la conquête romaine du monde hellénistique.* Rome.

Feyel, M. 1942. *Polybe et l'histoire de Béotie au IIIe siècle avant notre ère.* Paris.

Finkielsztejn, G. 2001a. Politique et commerce a Rhodes au IIe s. a.C.: Le témoignage des exportations d'amphores. In Bresson and Descat 2001: 181–96.

Finkielsztejn, G. 2001b. *Chronologie détaillée et révisée des éponymes amphoriques rhodiens, de 270 à 108 av. J.-C. environ.* Oxford.

Finley, M. I. 1962. The Black Sea and Danubian regions and the slave trade in antiquity. *Klio* 40: 51–9.

Finley, M. I. 1985. *Studies in Land and Credit in Ancient Athens. The* Horoi *Inscriptions. With an Introduction by Paul Millett.* New Brunswick.

Finley, M. I. 1999. *The Ancient Economy. Updated with a new foreword by Ian Morris.* 3rd edn. Berkeley.

Fishwick, D. 1987–92. *The Imperial Cult in the Latin West. Studies in the Ruler Cult of the Western Provinces of the Roman Empire.* Leiden.

Fishwick, D. 1987. The Caesareum of Alexandria Again. *AJAH* 12: 62–72 [1995].

Fishwick, D. 1989. Statue taxes in Roman Egypt. *Historia* 38: 335–47.

Flacelière, R. 1937. *Les Aitoliens à Delphes. Contribution à l'histoire de la Grèce centrale au IIIe siècle av. J.-C.* Paris.

Flemming, R. 2000. *Medicine and the Making of Roman Women: Gender, Nature, and Authority from Celsus to Galen.* Oxford.

Foertmeyer, V. 1988. The Dating of the Pompe of Ptolemy II Philadelphus. *Historia* 37: 90–104.

Fontenrose, J. 1960. The crucified Daphidas. *TAPA* 91: 83–99.

Forderer, J. 1913. *Ephoros und Strabon.* Tübingen.

Forsdyke, J. 1956. *Greece before Homer. Ancient Chronology and Mythology.* London.

Fossey, J. M. 1986. *The Ancient Topography of Eastern Phokis.* Amsterdam.

Fossey, J. M. 1990. *The Ancient Topography of Opountian Lokris.* Amsterdam.

Fowler, B. H. 1989. *The Hellenistic Aesthetic.* Madison.

Francis, E. D. 1990. *Image and Idea in Fifth-Century Greece: Art and Literature after the Persian Wars.* London.

Francovich, R. and Patterson, H. (eds). 2000. *Extracting Meaning from Ploughsoil Assemblages.* Oxford.

Frankfurter, D. 1998. *Religion in Roman Egypt: Assimilation and Resistance.* Princeton.

Fraser, P. M. 1972. *Ptolemaic Alexandria.* 3 vols. Oxford.

Fraser, P. M. 1977. *Rhodian Funerary Monuments.* Oxford.

Fraser, P. M. 1996. *Cities of Alexander the Great.* Oxford.

Frede, M. 1990. An empiricist view of knowledge: memorism. In S. Everson (ed.), *Epistemology.* Cambridge. 225–50.

Frederiksen, M. 1984. *Campania.* London.

Fredricksmeyer, E. A. 1979. Three notes on Alexander's deification. *AJAH* 4: 1–9.

Fredricksmeyer, E. A. 1981. On the background of the ruler cult. In *Ancient Macedonian Studies in Honor of Charles F. Edson*. Thessaloniki. 145–56.

Freeman, E. A. 1893. *A History of Federal Government in Greece and Italy.* 2nd edn by J. B. Bury. London.

Freitag, K. 2000. *Der Golf von Korinth. Historisch-topographische Untersuchungen von der Archaik bis in das 1. Jh. v. Chr.* Munich.

French, D. H. 1998. The Persian royal road. *Iran* 36: 15–43.

Friesen, S. J. 1993. *Twice Neokoros. Ephesus, Asia, and the Cult of the Flavian Imperial Family.* Köln.

Frösén, J. (ed.). 1997. *Early Hellenistic Athens. Symptoms of a Change.* Helsinki.

Fuhrer, T. and Hunter, R. 2002. Imaginary gods? Poetic theology in the *Hymns* of Callimachus. In Montanari 2002: 143–87.

Fuks, A. 1970. The Bellum Achaicum and its social aspect. *JHS* 90: 78–89.

Funke, P. 1985. Untersuchungen zur Geschichte und Struktur des aitolischen Bundes. Habilitations dissertation. Cologne.

Funke, P. 1987. Zur Datierung befestigter Stadtanlagen in Aitolien. *Boreas* 10: 87–96.

Funke, P. 1991a. Zur Ausbildung städtischer Siedlungszentren in Aitolien. In E. Olshausen and H. Sonnabend (eds), *Raum und Bevölkerung in der antiken Stadtkultur.* Bonn. 313–32.

Funke, P. 1991b. Strabone, la geografia storica e la struttura etnica della Grecia nord-occidentale. In F. Prontera (ed.), *Geografia storica della Graecia antica: tradizioni e problemi.* Rome. 174–93.

Funke, P. 1997. *Polis*genese und Urbanisierung in Aitolien im 5. and 4. Jh. v. Chr. *CPCActs* 4: 145–88.

Funke, S. 2000. *Aiakidenmythos und epirotisches Königtum. Der Weg einer hellenistischen Monarchie.* Stuttgart.

Fusillo, M. 1985. *Il tempo delle Argonautiche.* Rome.

Gabba, E. 1973. *Esercito e Società nella tarda repubblica romana.* Florence.

Gabba, E. 1978. Il problema dell' 'unità' dell'Italia romana. In E. Campanile (ed.), *La cultura Italica.* Pisa. 11–27.

Gabba, E. 1991. *Dionysius and the History of Archaic Rome.* Berkeley.

Gabbert, J. J. 1987. The anarchic dating of the Chremonidean war. *CJ* 82: 230–5.

Gabbert, J. J. 1997. *Antigonus II Gonatas: a Political Biography.* London.

Gabolde, M. and Galliano, G. 2000. *Coptos: l'Egypte antique aux portes du désert.* Lyon.

Gabrielsen, V. 1997. *The Naval Aristocracy of Hellenistic Rhodes.* Aarhus.

Gabrielsen, V. 2001a. The Rhodian associations and economic activity. In Archibald et al. 2001: 215–44.

Gabrielsen, V. 2001b. Economic activity, maritime trade and piracy in the Hellenistic Aegean. *REA* 103: 219–40.

Gallant, T. 1991. *Risk and Survival in Ancient Greece.* Stanford.

Gallini, C. 1973. Che cosa intendere per ellenizzazione. Problemi di metodo. *DdA* 7: 175–91.

Garaöanin, M. 1982. The Stone Age in the central Balkan Area. *CAH*[2] 3.1: 75–135.

Gardner, D. S. 1983. Performativity in ritual: the Mianmin case. *Man* 18: 346–60.

Garlan, Y. 1972. *La guerre dans l'Antiquité.* Paris.

Garlan, Y. 1974. *Recherches de poliorcétique grecque.* Athens.

Garlan, Y. 1978. Signification historique de la piraterie grecque. *DHA* 4: 1–16.

Garlan, Y. 1984. War and Siegecraft. *CAH*[2] 7.1: 353–62.

Garlan, Y. 1989. *Guerre et économie en Grèce ancienne.* Paris.

Garlan, Y. 1999. *Les timbres amphoriques de Thasos, I. Timbres protothasiens et thasiens anciens.* Paris.

Garnsey, P. 1983. Grain for Rome. In P. Garnsey, K. Hopkins and C. Whittaker (eds), *Trade in the Ancient Economy.* London. 118–30.

Garnsey, P. 1988. *Famine and Food Supply in the Greco-Roman World. Responses to Risk and Crisis*. Cambridge.

Garofalo, I. (ed.) 1988. *Erasistrati Fragmenta*. Pisa.

Garstang, J. 1924. Tanturah (Dora). *Bulletin of the British School at Jerusalem* 4: 35–47; 6: 65–75.

Gascoigne, J. 1998. *Science in the Service of Empire: Joseph Banks, the British State, and the Uses of Science in the Age of Revolution*. Cambridge.

Gauger, J.-D. 1980. Phlegon von Tralles Mirab. III: zu einem dokument geistigen Widerstandes gegen Rom. *Chiron* 10: 223–61.

Gauthier, H. and Sottas, H. 1925. *Un décret trilingue en l'honneur de Ptolémée IV*. Paris.

Gauthier, P. 1972a. *Symbola: les étrangers et la justice dans les cités grecques*. Nancy.

Gauthier, P. 1972b. Review of Vatin 1970. *REG* 1972: 208–13.

Gauthier, P. 1974. Generosité romaine et avarice grecque: sur l'octroi du droit du cité. In *Mélanges W. Seston*. Paris. 207–15.

Gauthier, P. 1984. Les cités hellénistiques: épigraphie et histoire des institutions et des régimes politiques. In *Acts of the Eighth International Conference on Greek and Latin Epigraphy Athens, 3–9 October, 1982*. Athens. 82–107.

Gauthier, P. 1985. *Les cités grecques et leurs bienfaiteurs (IVe-Ier siècle avant J.-C.). Contribution à l'histoire des institutions*. Paris.

Gauthier, P. 1988. Métèques, périèques et *paroikoi*: bilan et points d'interrogation. In Lonis 1988: 23–46.

Gauthier, P. 1989. *Nouvelles inscriptions de Sardes II*. Geneva.

Gauthier, P. 1990. L'inscription de Iasos relative à l'*ekklesiastikon* (*I. Iasos* 20). *BCH* 114: 417–43.

Gauthier, P. 1991. Ατελεια του σώματος. *Chiron* 21: 49–68.

Gauthier, P. 1993. Epigraphica II.4. *Prostagmata* attalides à Egine (*OGI* 329). *Revue de Philologie* 67: 41–8.

Gauthier, P. 1996. Bienfaiteurs du gymnase au Létôon de Xanthos. *REG* 109: 1–34.

Gauthier, P. 1997. Notes sur le rôle du gymnase dans les cités hellénistiques. In Wörrle and Zanker 1997: 1–11.

Gauthier, P. 2001. Les Pidaséens entrent en sympolitie avec les Milésiens: la procédure et les modalités institutionelles. In Bresson and Descat 2001: 117–27.

Gawantka, W. 1975. *Isopoliteia: ein Beitrag zur Geschichte der zwischenstaatlichen Beziehungen in der griechischen Antike*. Munich.

Geertz, C., Geertz, H. and Rosen, L. 1979. *Meaning and Order in Moroccan Society*. Cambridge.

Gehrke, H.-J. 1994. Mythos, Geschichte, Politik – antik und modern. *Saeculum* 45: 239–64.

Gelzer, T. (ed.) 1979. *Le Classicisme à Rome aux Iers siècles avant et après J.-C*. Entretiens Hardt 25. Geneva.

Gera, D. 1998. *Judaea and Mediterranean Politics, 219 to 161 BCE*. Leiden.

Geus, K. 2000a. Eratosthenes. In W. Hübner (ed.), *Geographie und verwandte Wissenschaften*. Stuttgart. 75–92.

Geus, K. 2000b. Utopie und Geographie: Zum Weltbild der Griechen in Frühhellenistischer Zeit. *Orbis Terrarum* 6: 55–90.

Geus, K. 2002. *Eratosthenes von Kyrene: Studien zur hellenistischen Kultur- und Wissenschaftsgeschichte*. Munich.

Ghirshman, R. 1976. *Terrasses sacrées de Bard-è Néchandeh et Masjid-i Solaiman*. Mémoires de la Délégation archéologique en Iran 45. Paris.

Giardina, A. 1994. L'identità incompiuta dell'Italia romana. In *L'Italie d'Auguste à Dioclétien*. Rome. 1–89.

Gibbins, D. 2001. Shipwrecks and Hellenistic Trade. In Archibald et al 2001: 273–312.

Gibson, E. L. 1999. *The Jewish Manumission Inscriptions of the Bosporus Kingdom*. Tübingen.

Ginouvès, R. 1994. *Macedonia: from Philip II to the Roman Conquest*. Princeton.

Giovannini, A. 1971. *Untersuchungen über die Natur und die Anfänge der bundesstaatlichen Sympolitie in Griechenland*. Göttingen.

Giovannini, A. 1993. Greek cities and Greek commonwealth. In Bulloch et al. 1993: 265–86.

Glanville, S. 1939. *Catalogue of Demotic Papyri in the British Museum I: a Theban Archive of the Reign of Ptolemy I Soter*. London.

Glennie, P. 1996. Consumption within Historical Studies. In D. Miller (ed.), *Acknowledging Consumption*. New York. 164–203.

Glew, D. G. 1981. Between the wars: Mithridates Eupator and Rome, 85–73 BC. *Chiron* 11: 109–30.

Glover, R. F. 1950. Some curiosities of ancient warfare. *Greece and Rome* 16: 5–8.

Glucker, J. 1978. *Antiochus and the Late Academy*. Gottingen.

Goddio, F. et al. 1998. *Alexandria: the Submerged Royal Quarters*. London.

Goldberg, S. 1980. *The Making of Menander's Comedy*. London.

Goldhill, S. 1994. The naive and knowing eye: ecphrasis and the culture of viewing in the Hellenistic world. In S. Goldhill and R. Osborne (eds), *Art and Text in Ancient Greek Culture*. Cambridge. 197–223.

Gómez Espelosín, F.-J. 1991. Plutarch and Justin on Aristotimus of Elis. *AJP* 112: 103–9.

Gomme, A. W. and Sandbach, F. H. 1973. *Menander: a Commentary*. Oxford.

Gordon, R. 1997. *Quaedam veritatis umbrae:* Hellenistic magic and astrology. In Bilde et al. 1997: 128–58.

Gottschalk, H. 1972. Notes on the wills of peripatetic scholarchs. *Hermes* 100: 314–42.

Goudriaan, K. 1988. *Ethnicity in Ptolemaic Egypt*. Amsterdam.

Goulet-Cazé, M.-O. and Goulet, R. (eds). 1993. *Le Cynisme ancien et ses prolongements*. Actes du colloque international du CNRS (Paris, 22–25 July 1991). Paris.

Gow, A. S. F. 1952. *Theocritus*. 2nd edn. Cambridge.

Graf, F. 1997. *Magic in the Ancient World*. Cambridge, Mass.

Graham, A. J. 1964. *Colony and Mother City in Ancient Greece*. Manchester.

Grainger, J. D. 1990a. *Seleukos Nikator: Constructing a Hellenistic Kingdom*. London.

Grainger, J. D. 1990b. *The Cities of Seleukid Syria*. Oxford.

Grainger, J. D. 1991. *Hellenistic Phoenicia*. Oxford.

Grainger, J. D. 1995a. The expansion of the Aetolian League, 280–260 BC. *Mnemosyne* 48: 312–43.

Grainger, J. D. 1995b. The campaign of Cn. Manlius Vulso in Asia Minor. *Anatolian Studies* 45: 23–42.

Grainger, J. D. 1997. *A Seleukid Prosopography and Gazetteer*. Leiden.

Grainger, J. D. 1999. *The League of the Aitolians*. Leiden.

Grainger, J. D. 2000. *Aitolian Prosopographical Studies*. Leiden.

Granberg, D. 1993. Political perception. In S. Iyengar and W. McGuire (eds), *Explorations in Political Psychology*. Durham. 70–112.

Grandjean, Y. 1975. *Une nouvelle arétologie d'Isis à Maronée*. Leiden.

Grayson, A. K. 1975a. *Assyrian and Babylonian Chronicles*. Locust Valley, NY.

Grayson, A. K. 1975b. *Babylonian Historical-Literary Texts*. Toronto.

Greco Pontrandolfo, A. 1979. Segni di transformazioni sociali a Poseidonia tra la fine del V e gli inizi del III sec. a.C.. *DdA* 1: 27 ff.

Greco Pontrandolfo, A. 1982. *I Lucani: etnografia e archeologia di una regione antica*. Milan.

Greco, E. and Theodorescu, D. 1983. *Poseidonia-Paestum* 2: *L'Agora*. Rome.

Green, P. 1990. *Alexander to Actium: the Hellenistic Age*. Berkeley (corr. edn 1993).

Green, P. 2000. Pergamon and Sperlonga: a historian's reactions. In de Grummond and Ridgway 2000: 166–90.

Green, P. (ed.). 1993. *Hellenistic History and Culture*. Berkeley.

Green, P. (trans.) 1997. *The Argonautika by Apollonios Rhodios.* Berkeley.

Gregory, A. 1997. *Village Society in Hellenistic and Roman Asia Minor.* (Dissertation, Columbia University) New York.

Grenier, J.-C. 1995. L'Empereur et le Pharaon. *ANRW* II.18.5: 3181–94.

Gribaudi, G. 1996. Images of the south. In D. Forgacs and R. Lumley (eds), *Italian Cultural Studies: an Introduction.* Oxford. 72–87.

Griffith, G. T. 1935. *The Mercenaries of the Hellenistic World.* Cambridge (repr. Chicago, 1984).

Griffiths, F. T. 1979. *Theocritus at Court.* Leiden.

Grimm, G. 1998. *Alexandria: Der erste Königstadt der hellenistischen Welt.* Mainz.

Grotanelli, C. 1991. Do ut des? In G. Bartoloni, G. Colonna and C. Grotanelli (eds), *Atti del convegno internazionale 'Anathema. Regime delle offerte e vita dei santuari nel mediterraneo antico', Roma 15–18 Giugno 1989 (Scienze dell'antichità* 3–4, 1989/90). Rome. 45–55.

Gruen, E. S. 1972. Aratus and the Achaean alliance with Macedon. *Historia* 21: 609–25.

Gruen, E. S. 1976. The origins of the Achaean War. *JHS* 96: 46–69.

Gruen, E. S. 1984. *The Hellenistic World and the Coming of Rome.* Berkeley.

Gruen, E. S. 1985. The coronation of the Diadochoi. In J. Eadie and J. Ober (eds), *The Craft of the Ancient Historian: Essays in Honor of C. G. Starr.* Lanham. 253–71.

Gruen, E. S. 1990. *Studies in Greek Culture and Roman Policy.* Leiden (repr. Berkeley 1996).

Gruen, E. S. 1992. *Culture and National Identity in Republican Rome.* Ithaca.

Gruen, E. S. 1993a. Hellenism and persecution: Antiochus IV and the Jews. In Green 1993: 238–64.

Gruen, E. S. 1993b. The polis in the Hellenistic world. In R. Rosen and J. Farrell (eds), *Nomodeiktes. Greek Studies in Honor of Martin Ostwald.* Ann Arbor. 339–54.

Gruen, E. S. 1996. Puzzles, problems and possibilities. In Bilde et al. 1996: 116–25.

Gruen, E. S. 1998. *Heritage and Hellenism: the Reinvention of Jewish Tradition.* Berkeley.

Gruen, E. S. 2000. Culture as policy: the Attalids of Pergamon. In de Grummond and Ridgway 2000: 17–31.

Gruen, E. S. 2002. *Diaspora: Jews amidst Greeks and Romans.* Cambridge, Mass.

Gruzinski, S. and Rouveret, A. 1976. 'Ellos son como niños'. Histoire et acculturation dans la Mexique colonial et l'Italie méridionale avant la romanisation. *Mélanges de l'École Francaise de Rome (Antiquité)* 88: 159 ff.

Gschnitzer, F. 1955. Stammes- und Ortsgemeinden im alten Griechenland. *Wiener Studien* 68: 120–44.

Gudeman, S. 1986. *Economics as Culture: Models and Metaphors of Livelihood.* New York.

Günther, L.-M. 1992. Zur Familien- und Haushaltsstruktur im hellenistischen Kleinasien (am Beispiel zweier Inschriften aus Milet und Ilion). In F. Schwertheim (ed.), *Studien zum antiken Kleinasien* 2 (Asia Minor Studien 8).

Günther, W. 1988. Milesische Bürgerrechts- und Proxenieverleihungen der hellenistischen Zeit. *Chiron* 18: 383–419.

Gutzwiller, K. 1991. *Theocritus' Pastoral Analogies. The Formation of a Genre.* Madison.

Gutzwiller, K. 1998. *Poetic Garlands: Hellenistic Epigrams in Context.* Berkeley.

Guzzo, P. 1989. *I Brettii: storia e archeologia della Calabria preromana.* Milan.

Gygax, M. D. 2000. Ptolemaios, Bruder des Konigs Ptolemaios III. Euergetes, und Mylasa: Bemerkungen zu. I. Labraunda Nr. 3. *Chiron* 30: 353–66.

Habicht, C. 1956. Über die Kriege zwischen Pergamon und Bithynia. *Hermes* 84: 90–110.

Habicht, C. 1957. Eine Urkunde des akarnanischen Bundes. *Hermes* 85: 86–122.

Habicht, C. 1958. Die herrschende Gesellschaft in den hellenistischen Monarchien. *Vierteljahrschrift für Soziologie und Wirtschaftsgeschichte* 45: 1–16.

Habicht, C. 1970. *Gottmenschentum und Griechische Städte.* 2nd edn. Munich.

Habicht, C. 1979. *Untersuchungen zur politischen Geschichte Athens im 3. Jahrhundert v. Chr.* Munich.

Habicht, C. 1982. *Studien zur Geschichte Athens in hellenistischer Zeit*. Göttingen.

Habicht, C. 1985. *Pausanias' Guide to Ancient Greece*. Berkeley.

Habicht, C. 1989. The Seleucids and their rivals. *CAH*² 8: 324–87.

Habicht, C. 1992. Athens and the Ptolemies. *Classical Antiquity* 11: 68–90.

Habicht, C. 1994. *Athen in hellenistischer Zeit: gesammelte Aufsatze*. Munich.

Habicht, C. 1996. Divine honours for King Antigonus Gonatas in Athens. *SCI* 15: 131–4.

Habicht, C. 1997. *Athens from Alexander to Antony*. Cambridge, Mass.

Habicht, C. 1998. 'Zur ewig währenden Erinnerung'. Ein auf das Nachleben zielender Topos. *Chiron* 28: 35–41.

Habicht, C., Hallof, L. and K. 1998. Aus der Arbeit der *Inscriptiones Graecae* II. Ehrendekrete aus dem Asklepieion von Kos. *Chiron* 28: 101–42.

Hackett, J. (ed.). 1989. *Warfare in the Ancient World*. New York.

Haegemans, K. and Kosmetatou, E. 2002. Aratus and Polybius's Achaean background. In G. Schepens and J. Bollansée (eds), *The Shadow of Polybius. Intertextuality as a Research Tool in Greek Historiography, International Colloquium Organized by the Ancient History Section, September 21–22 2001*. Katholieke Universiteit Leuven. Leuven.

Haeuber, C. 1991. *Horti Romani. Die Horti Maecenatis und die Horti Lamiani auf dem Esquilin: Geschichte, Topographie, Statuenfunde*. Dissertation. Köln.

Haeuber, C. Forthcoming. Zum Fundort der Laokoongruppe. *Jahrbuch des deutschen archäologischen Instituts*.

Haggis, D. C. 1996. Archaeological survey at Kavousi, East Crete: preliminary report. *Hesperia* 65: 373–432.

Hahn, J. (ed.). 2000. *Alexander in Indien, 327–325 v. Chr.* Stuttgart.

Halfmann, H. 1987. Ein neuer Statthalterkult in der Provinz Asia. *EA* 10: 83–90.

Hall, E. 1989. *Inventing the Barbarian: Greek Self-definition Through Tragedy*. Oxford.

Hall, J. 1997. *Ethnic Identity in Greek Antiquity*. Cambridge.

Halperin, D. M. 1983. *Before Pastoral: Theocritus and the Ancient Tradition of Bucolic Poetry*. Yale.

Halsall, G. 1997. Archaeology and history. In M. Bentley (ed.), *Companion to Historiography*. London. 805–27.

Halstead, P. 1987. Traditional and ancient rural economy in Mediterranean Europe: Plus ça change? *JHS* 107: 77–87.

Halstead, P. and Jones, G. 1989. Agrarian ecology in the Greek islands: time stress, risk, and scale. *JHS* 109: 41–55.

Hamilton, J. R. 1969. *Plutarch: Alexander*. Oxford.

Hammond, N. G. L. 1966. The kingdoms in Illyria *circa* 400–167 BC. *BSA* 61: 239–53.

Hammond, N. G. L. 1967. *Epirus*. Oxford.

Hammond, N. G. L. 1978. A note on 'pursuit' in Arrian. *CQ* 28: 136–40.

Hammond, N. G. L. 1981. *Alexander the Great, King, Commander and Statesman*. London.

Hammond, N. G. L. 1982. Illyris, Epirus and Macedonia in the early Iron Age. *CAH*² 3.1: 619–56.

Hammond, N. G. L. 1989. *The Macedonian State: the Origins, Institutions, and History*. Oxford.

Hammond, N. G. L. and Griffith, G. T. 1979. *A History of Macedonia*. Vol. 2. Oxford.

Hammond, N. G. L. and Walbank, F. W. 1988. *A History of Macedonia*. Vol. 3. Oxford.

Hampl, F. 1975. Die Ilias ist kein Geschichtsbuch. In I. Weiler (ed.), *Geschichte als kritische Wissenschaft*. Vol. 2. Darmstadt 51–99.

Handley, E. W. 1965. *The Dyskolos of Menander*. London.

Hankinson, R. J. 1995. The growth of medical empiricism. In D. Bates (ed.), *Knowledge and the Scholarly Medical Traditions*. Cambridge. 60–83.

Hannestad, L. 1994. Greeks and Celts. In Bilde et al. 1994: 15–37.

Hannestad, L. 1996. 'This contributes in no small way to one's reputation': the Bithynian kings and Greek culture. In Bilde et al. 1996: 67–98.

Hannestad, L. and Potts, D. T. 1990. Temple architecture in the Seleucid kingdom. In Bilde et al. 1990: 91–124.

Hansen, E. V. 1971. *The Attalids of Pergamon*. 2nd edn. Ithaca.

Hansen, M. H. 1993. Introduction. The *Polis* as a citizen-state. *CPCActs* 1: 7–29.

Hansen, M. H. (ed.). 1993–8. *Acts of the Copenhagen Polis Center*. Vols. 1–5. Copenhagen.

Hansen, W. 1996. *Phlegon of Tralles, Book of Marvels*. Translated with introduction and commentary. Exeter.

Hanson, V. D. 1999. *The Wars of the Ancient Greeks*. London.

Harder, M. A., Regtuit, R. F. and Wakker, G. C. (eds). 1993. *Callimachus*. Groningen.

Harder, M. A., Regtuit, R. F. and Wakker, G. C. (eds). 1996. *Theocritus*. Groningen.

Hardie, P. 1986. *Virgil's Aeneid: Cosmos and Imperium*. Oxford.

Harris, H. A. 1976. *Greek Athletics and the Jews*. Cardiff.

Harris, W. V. 1971. *Rome in Etruria and Umbria*. Oxford.

Harris, W. V. 1979. *War and Imperialism in Republican Rome, 327–70* BC. Oxford.

Harris, W. V. 1980. Towards a study of the Roman slave trade. In J. H. D'Arms and E. C. Kopff (eds), *The Seaborne Commerce of Ancient Rome*. Rome. 117–40.

Harrison, T. 2000. Sicily in the Athenian imagination: Thucydides and the Persian Wars. In Serrati and Smith 2000: 84–96.

Harter-Uibopuu, K. 1998. *Das zwischenstaatliche Schiedsverfahren im achaeischen Koinon: zur friedlichen Streitbeilegung nach den epigraphischen Quellen*. Cologne.

Hassal, M., Crawford, M. and Reynolds, J. M. 1974. Rome and the Eastern provinces at the end of the second century BC. *JRS* 64: 195–220.

Hatzfeld, J. 1913. Esclaves italiens en Grèce. In *Mellanges Holleaux*. Paris. 93–101.

Hatzopoulos, M. 1996. *Macedonian Institutions under the Kings*. 2 vols. Athens.

Hatzopoulos, M. 2001. *L'organisation de l'armée macédonienne sous les Antigonides. Problèmes anciens et documents nouveaux*. Paris.

Hatzopoulos, M. and Gauthier, P. 1993. *La Loi gymnasiarchique de Beroia*. Athens.

Hauben, H. 1970. *Callicrates of Samos, a Contribution to the Study of the Ptolemaic Admiralty.* Leuven.

Hauben, H. 1983. Arsinoé II et la politique extérieure de l'Égypte. In Van't Dack et al. 1983: 99–127.

Hauben, H. 1990. L'expédition de Ptolémée III en Orient et la sédition domestique de 245 av. J.-C. *APF* 36: 29–37.

Haussoullier, B. 1917. *Traité entre Delphes et Pellana: étude de droit grec*. Paris.

Havelock, C. 1970. *Hellenistic Art: the Art of the Classical World from the Death of Alexander the Great to the Battle of Actium*. Greenwich, Conn.

Hayden, B., Moody, J. and Rackham, O. 1992. The Vrokastro survey project, 1986–89: research design and preliminary results. *Hesperia* 61: 293–353.

Hazzard, R. A. 2000. *Imagination of a Monarchy: Studies in Ptolemaic Propaganda*. Toronto.

Heckel, W. 1992. *The Marshals of Alexander's Empire*. London.

Heidel, W. 1937. *The Frame of the Ancient Greek Maps: with a Discussion of the Discovery of the Sphericity of the Earth*. New York.

Heinen, H. 1972. *Untersuchungen zur hellenistischen Geschichte des 3. Jahrhunderts v. Chr.: zur Geschichte der Zeit des Ptolemaios Keraunos und zum Chremonideischen Krieg*. Wiesbaden.

Heinen, H. 1976–7. Zur Sklaverei in der hellenistischen Welt: I and II. *AncSoc* 7: 127–49 and 8: 121–54.

Heinen, H. 1984. The Syrian-Egyptian Wars and the new kingdoms of Asia Minor. *CAH*² 7.1: 412–45.

Heinen, H. 1995. Vorstufen und Anfänge des Herrscherkultes im römischen Ägypten. *ANRW* II.18.5: 3144–80.

Heinen, H. 1997. Der κτίστης Boethos und die Einrichtung einer neuen Stadt, Teil II. *APF* 43: 340–63.

Heinrich, E. 1982. *Die Tempel und Heiligtümer in alten Mesopotamien*. Berlin.

Hellenkemper-Salies, G. 1994. *Das Wrack: Die antike Schiffsfund von Mahdia*. Köln.

Helly, B. 1995. *L'État thessalien. Aleuas le Roux, les tétrades et les tagoi*. Paris.

Hengel, M. 1974. *Judaism and Hellenism*. London.

Hengel, M. 1980. *Jews, Greeks, and Barbarians: Aspects of the Hellenization of Judaism in the Pre-Christian Period*. Philadelphia.

Henry, A. S. 1991. A lead letter from Torone. *L'Année Épigraphique*: 65–70.

Herman, G. 1997. The court society of the Hellenistic age. In Cartledge et al. 1997: 199–224.

Herrmann, P. 1965a. Antiochos der Große und Teos. *Anadolu* 9: 29–159.

Herrmann, P. 1965b. Neue Urkunden zur Geschichte von Milet im 2. Jahrhundert v. Chr. *MDAI* (I) 15: 71–117.

Herrmann, P. 1994. Milet unter Augustus. C. Iulius Epikrates und die Anfänge des Kaiserkults. *MDAI* (I) 44: 203–36.

Herz, P. 1996. Hellenistische Könige: zwischen griechischen Vorstellungen von Königtum und Vorstellungen ihrer einheimischen Untertanen. In Small 1996: 27–40.

Herz, P. 1997. Herrscherverehrung und lokale Festkultur im Osten des römischen Reiches (Kaiser/Agone). In H. Cancik and J. Rüpke (eds), *Römische Reichsreligion und Provinzial-religion*. Tübingen. 239–64.

Hind, J. 1994a. Mithridates. *CAH*² 9: 129–64.

Hind, J. 1994b. The Bosporan kingdom. *CAH*² 6: 476–511.

Hingley, R. 2000. *Roman Officers and English Gentlemen: the Imperial Origins of Roman Archaeology*. London.

Hintzen-Bohlen, B. 1992. *Herrscherrepräsentation im Hellenismus. Untersuchungen zu Weih-geschenken, Stiftungen und Ehrenmonumenten in den mutterländischen Heiligtümern Delphi, Olympia, Delos und Dodona*. Cologne.

Hirsch, E. and O'Hanlon, M. (eds). 1995. *The Anthropology of Landscape: Perspectives on Place and Space*. Oxford.

Hoddinott, R. F. 1981. *The Thracians*. London.

Hoepfner, W. 1996. Der vollendete Pergamonaltar. *Archäologischer Anzeiger*. 115–34.

Hoepfner, W. 1997. Model of the Pergamon Altar (1:20). In Dreyfus and Schraudolph 1997: 23–58.

Hoff, M. 1996. The politics and architecture of the Athenian imperial cult. In Small 1996: 185–200.

Hoff, M. and Rotroff, S. (eds). 1997. *The Romanization of Athens*. Oxford.

Högemann, P. 1985. *Alexander der Große und Arabien*. Munich.

Hölbl, G. 2001. *A History of the Ptolemaic Empire*. London.

Hole, F. 1987. *The Archaeology of Western Iran: Settlement and Society from Prehistory to the Islamic Conquest*. Washington, DC.

Holleaux, M. 1921. *Rome, la Grèce et les monarchies hellénistiques au IIIème siècle avant J.-C.* Paris.

Holleaux, M. 1928. The Romans in Illyria. *CAH* 7: 822–57.

Holleaux, M. 1930a. Rome and Macedon: Philip against the Romans. In *CAH* 8: 116–37.

Holleaux, M. 1930b. Rome and Macedon: the Romans against Philip. In *CAH* 8: 138–98.

Holleaux, M. 1930c. Rome and Antiochus. In *CAH* 8: 199–240.

Holleaux, M. 1952. *Etudes d'épigraphie et d'histoire grecques. Tome IV*. Paris.

Holleaux, M. 1957. *Etudes d'épigraphie et d'histoire grecques. Tome V*. Paris.

Hollis, A. S. 1990. *Callimachus, Hecale*. Oxford.

Hölscher, T. 1967. *Victoria Romana: archäologische Untersuchungen zur Geschichte und Wesenart der römische Siegesgöttin*. Mainz.

Holt, F. 1999. *Thundering Zeus: the Making of Hellenistic Bactria*. Berkeley.

Hope Simpson, R. et al. 1995. The archaeological survey of the Kommos area. In J. and M. Shaw (eds), *Kommos I: the Kommos Region and Houses of the Minoan Town. Part I*. Princeton. 325–402.

Hopkins, K. 1978. *Conquerors and Slaves*. Cambridge.

Hopp, J. 1977. *Untersuchungen zur Geschichte der letzten Attaliden*. Munich.

Horden, P. and Purcell, N. 2000. *The Corrupting Sea: a Study of Mediterranean History*. Oxford.

Hornblower, J. 1981. *Hieronymus of Cardia*. Oxford.

Horsfall, N. 1997. The unity of Italy: some anomalies. *SCI* 16: 71–6.

Horsfall, N. 2001. The unity of Italy: anomalies in context. *SCI* 20: 39–50.

Howgego, C. 1990. Why did ancient states strike coins? *Numismatic Chronicle* 150: 1–25.

Hunter, R. L. 1985. *The New Comedy of Greece and Rome*. Cambridge.

Hunter, R. L. 1991. Greek and non-Greek in the *Argonautica* of Apollonius. In S. Said (ed.), *ΕΛΛΗΝΙΣΜΟΣ. Quelques jalons pour une histoire de l'identité grecque*. Leiden. 81–99.

Hunter, R. L. 1993. *The Argonautica of Apollonius. Literary Studies*. Cambridge.

Hunter, R. 1995. The divine and human map of the Argonautica. *Syllecta Classica* 6: 13–27.

Hunter, R. L. 1996a. *Theocritus and the Archaeology of Greek Poetry*. Cambridge.

Hunter, R. L. 1996b. Callimachus swings (frr. 178 and 43 Pf.). *Ramus* 25: 17–26.

Hunter, R. L. 1997. Hellenismus. In H.-G. Nesselrath (ed.), *Einleitung in die griechische Philologie*. Stuttgart. 246–68.

Hunter, R. L. 1999. *Theocritus. A Selection*. Cambridge.

Hunter, R. L. 2003. *Theocritus. Encomium of Ptolemy Philadelphus*. Berkeley.

Huss, W. 1976. *Untersuchungen zur Außenpolitik Ptolemaios' IV*. Munich.

Huss, W. 1977. Eine ptolemäische Expedition nach Kleinasien. *AncSoc* 8: 187–93.

Huss, W. 1978. Eine Revolte der Ägypter in der Zeit des 3. Syrischen Kriegs. *Aegyptus* 58: 151–6.

Huss, W. 1994. *Der makedonische König und die ägyptischen Priester. Studien zur Geschichte des ptolemäischen Ägypten*. Stuttgart.

Huss, W. 1998. Ptolemaios der Sohn. *ZPE* 121: 229–50.

Huss, W. 2001. *Ägypten in hellenistischer Zeit 332–30* BC. Munich.

Hutchinson, G. 1988. *Hellenistic Poetry*. Oxford.

Huzar, E. G. 1995. Emperor worship in Julio-Claudian Egypt. *ANRW* II.18.5: 3092–143.

Invernizzi, A. 1994. Seleucia on the Tigris: centre and periphery in Seleucid Asia. In Bilde et al. 1994: 230–50.

Ioppolo, A. M. 1986. *Opinione e scienza: il dibattito tra Stoici e Accademici nel III e nel II secolo a C*. Naples.

Isager, S. 1990. Kings and gods in the Seleucid empire: a question of landed property in Asia Minor. In Bilde et al. 1990: 79–90.

Isager, S. 1998. The Pride of Halikarnassos: editio princeps of an inscription from Salmakis. *ZPE* 123: 1–23.

Isager, S. and Skydsgaard, J. 1992. *Ancient Greek Agriculture: an Introduction*. London.

Italici in Magna Grecia. Lingua, insediamenti e strutture, Atti Convegno (Acquasparta 1986). 1990. Venosa.

Jacob, C. 1991. *Géographie et ethnographie en Grèce ancienne*. Paris.

Jacob, C. and de Polignac, F. 2000. *Alexandria, Third Century* BC: *the Knowledge of the World in a Single City*. Alexandria.

Jacoby, F. 1949. *Atthis: The Local Chronicles of Ancient Athens*. Oxford.

Jacquemin A. and Laroche D. 1992. La Terasse d'Attale Ier revisitée. *BCH* 116: 229–58.

Jacquemin, A. 1985. Aitolia et Aristaineta: Offrandes monumentales étolienne à Delphes au IIIe s. av. J.-C. *Ktèma* 10: 27–35.

Jähne, A. 1974. Die 'Syrische Frage'. Seleukeia in Pierien und die Ptolemäer. *Klio* 56: 501–19.

Janni, P. 1984. *La mappa e il periplo: Cartografia antica e spazio odologico*. Rome.

Johnson, J. H. (ed.). 1992. *Life in a Multi-Cultural Society. Egypt from Cambyses to Constantine and Beyond*. Chicago.

Johnston, S. I. 1999. *Restless Dead: Encounters Between the Living and the Dead in Ancient Greece*. Berkeley.

Jones, A. H. M. 1940. *The Greek City from Alexander to Justinian*. Oxford.

Jones, C. P. 1971. *Plutarch and Rome*. Oxford.

Jones, C. P. 1974. Diodoros Pasparos and the Nikephoria of Pergamon. *Chiron* 4: 183–205.

Jones, C. P. 1993. The decree of Ilion in honor of a King Antiochus. *GRBS* 34: 73–92.

Jones, C. P. 1995. Graia Pandetur ab Urbe. *HSCP* 97: 233–41.

Jones, C. P. 1999a. The union of Latmos and Pidasa. *EA* 31: 1–7.

Jones, C. P. 1999b. *Kinship Diplomacy in the Ancient World*. Cambridge, Mass.

Jones, C. P. 2000. Diodoros Pasparos revisited. *Chiron* 30: 1–14.

Jones, C. P. and Habicht, C. 1989. A Hellenistic inscription from Arsinoe in Cilicia. *Phoenix* 43: 317–46.

Jones, N. F. 1987. *Public Organization in Ancient Greece: a Documentary Study*. Philadelphia.

Jonnes, L. and Ricl, M. 1997. A new royal inscription from Phrygia Paroreios: Eumenes II grants Tyriaion the status of a polis. *EA* 29: 1–30.

Jost, M. 1985. *Sanctuaires et cultes d'Arcadie*. Paris.

Kallet-Marx, R. 1995. *Hegemony to Empire. The Development of the Roman Imperium in the East from 148 to 62 BC*. Berkeley.

Kase, E., Szemler, G., Wilkie, N. and Wallace, P. 1991. *The Great Isthmus Corridor Route*. Vol. 1 of *Explorations of the Phokis-Doris Expedition*. Dubuque.

Kasher, A. 1985. *The Jews in Hellenistic and Roman Egypt*. Tübingen.

Kästner, V. and Heilmeyer, W. 1997. New arrangement and interpretation of the Telephos frieze from the Pergamon Altar. In Dreyfus and Schraudolph 1996: 68–82.

Kearns, E. 1989. *The Heroes of Attica*. London.

Kearns, E. 1992. Between God and man: status and function of heroes and their sanctuaries. In A. Schachter (ed.), *Le sanctuaire grec*. Entretiens Hardt 37. Geneva. 65–99.

Kemp, B. J. 1989. *Ancient Egypt: Anatomy of a Civilization*. London.

Kertész, I. 1982. Der Telephosmythos und der Telephosfries. *Oikumene* 3: 203–15.

Kidd, I. G. 1988. *Posidonius*. Vol. 2: *The Commentary*. Cambridge.

Kidd, I. G. 1999. *Posidonius*. Vol. 3: *The Translation of the Fragments*. Cambridge.

Kienast, D. 1982. *Augustus, Prinzeps und Monarch*. Darmstadt.

Kim, H. S. 2001. Small change and the moneyed economy. In Cartledge et al. 2001: 44–51.

Kind, E. 1922. Krateuas (2). *RE* 11.2: 1644–6. Stuttgart.

King, H. 1998. Asklepios and women's healing. In H. King (ed.), *Hippocrates' Woman: Reading the Female Body in Ancient Greece*. London. 99–113.

Kinns, P. 1999. Attic weight Drachms of Ephesus. *Numismatic Chronicle*: 47–98.

Kirkby, C. and Rathbone, D. W. 1996. Kom Talit: the rise and fall of a Greek town in the Faiyum. *Egyptian Archaeology* 8: 29–31.

Kish, G. 1978. *A Source Book in Geography*. Cambridge.

Klaffenbach, G. 1954. *Die Astynomeninschrift von Pergamon*. Berlin.

Klein, W. 1921. *Vom antiken Rokoko*. Vienna.

Kleiner, F. 1980. Further reflections on the early Cistophoric coinage. *ANSMN* 25: 45–52.

Kleiner, F. and Noe, S. 1977. *The Early Cistophoric Coinage*. New York.

Knauss, F. 2001. Persian rule in the north. Achaemenid palaces on the periphery of the empire. In I. Nielsen (ed.), *The Royal Palace Institution in the First Millennium BC*. 125–43.

Knight, V. 1995. *The Renewal of Epic: Responses to Homer in the Argonautica of Apollonius.* Leiden.

Knoepfler, D. 1993. Les *Kryptoi* du stratège Épicharès à Rhamnonte et le début de la guerre de Chrémonidès. *BCH* 117: 327–41.

Knoepfler, D. 1995. Les relations des cités eubéennes avec Antigone Gonatas et la chronologie delphique au début de l'époque étolienne. *BCH* 119: 137–59.

Knoepfler, D. 1997. Alexandreion nomisma. L'apparition et la disparition de l'argent d'Alexandre dans les inscriptions grecques. Quelques refléxions complementaires. *Topoi* 7: 33–50.

Koenen, L. 1968. Die Prophezeiungen des 'Töpfers'. *ZPE* 2: 178–209.

Koenen, L. 1977. *Eine agonistische Inschrift aus Ägypten und frühptolemäische Königsfeste.* Meisenheim.

Koenen, L. 1984. A supplementary note on the Oracle of the Potter. *ZPE* 54: 9–13.

Koenen, L. 1993. The Ptolemaic king as a religious figure. In Bulloch et al. 1993: 25–115, with response by Walbank, 116–29.

Koester, H. (ed.). 1998. *Pergamon. Citadel of the Gods. Archaeological Record, Literary Description, and Religious Development.* Harrisburg.

Köhler, J. 1996. *Pompai. Untersuchungen zur hellenistischen Festkultur.* Frankfurt.

Kolesnikov, A. and Jacenko, I. 1999. Le territoire agricole de Chersonesos taurique dans la région de Kerkinitis. In Brunet 1999: 289–321.

Koortbojian, M. 2000. Pliny's Laocoön? In A. Payne et al. (eds), *Antiquity and its Interpreters.* Cambridge. 199–216.

Korres, M. 1983. Vorfertigung und Ferntransport eines athenischen Grossbaus und zur Proportionierung von Säulen in der hellenistischen Architektur. In *Bauplannung und Theorie der Antike* (Diskussionen zur archäologischen Bauforschung 4). Berlin. 201–7.

Kosmetatou, E. 1995. The legend of the hero Pergamos. *AncSoc* 26: 133–44.

Kosmetatou, E. 1997. Pisidia and the Hellenistic kings from 323 to 133 BC. *AncSoc* 28: 5–37.

Kosmetatou, E. 1998. Cistophori and Cista Mystica. A new interpretation of the iconography of the early Cistophoric types. *Révue belge de Numismatique* 144: 11–19.

Kosmetatou, E. 1999. The Mint of Ephesos under the Attalids of Pergamon. In H. Friesinger and F. Krinziger (eds), *100 Jahre Österreichische Forschungen in Ephesos. Akten des Symposions Wien 1995.* Vienna. 185–93.

Kosmetatou, E. 2000. Lycophron's 'Alexandra' Reconsidered. The Attalid Connection. *Hermes* 128: 32–53.

Kosmetatou, E. 2001. Ilion, the Troad, and the Attalids. *AncSoc* 31: 107–32.

Kotsidou, H. 2000. Τιμὴ καὶ δόξα. *Ehrungen hellenistischer Herrscher im griechischen Mutterland und in Kleinasien unter besonderer Berücksichtigung der archäologischen Denkmäler.* Berlin.

Krahmer, G. 1923–4. Stilphasen der hellenistischen Plastik. *MDAI* (R) 38–9: 138–84.

Krahmer, G. 1927. Die einansichtige Gruppe und der späthellenistischen Kunst. *Nachrichten von der Gesellschaft der Wissenschaften in Göttingen. Philologisch-Historische Klasse* 1: 53–91.

Kramer, B. 1997. Der κτίστης Boethos und die Einrichtung einer neuen Stadt, Teil I. *APF* 43: 315–39.

Krasilnikoff, J. A. 1992. Aegean mercenaries in the fourth to second centuries BC. A study in payment, plunder and logistics of Ancient Greek armies. *Classica et Mediaevalia* 43: 23–36.

Kratz, R. G. 1991. *Translatio Imperii. Untersuchungen zu den aramäischen Danielzählungen und ihrem theologiegeschichtlichen Umfeld.* Düsseldorf.

Krause, J.-U., Mylonopoulos, J. and Cengia, R. 1998. *Bibliographie zur römischen Sozialgeschichte 2. Schichten, Konflikte, religiöse Gruppen, materielle Kulturr.* Stuttgart.

Kreissig, H. 1978. *Wirtschaft und Gesellschaft im Seleukidenreich.* Berlin.

Krevans, N. 1993. Fighting against Antimachus: the *Lyde* and the *Aetia* reconsidered. In Harder et al. 1993: 149–60.

Krohn, U. 1996. Priesthoods, dedications, and euergetism. What part did religion play in the political and social status of Greek women? In P. Hellström and B. Alroth (eds), *Religion and Power in the Ancient Greek World*. Uppsala. 139–82.

Kruglikova, I. 1975. *Sel'skoe khozyaistvo Bospora*. Moscow.

Kuhrt, A. 1987. Berossus' *Babyloniaka* and Seleucid rule in Babylonia. In Kuhrt and Sherwin-White 1987: 32–56.

Kuhrt, A. 1996. The Seleucid kings and Babylonia: new perspectives on the Seleucid realm in the east. In Bilde et al. 1996: 41–54.

Kuhrt, A. and Sherwin-White, S. (eds). 1987. *Hellenism in the East. The Interaction of Greek and Non-Greek Civilizations from Syria to Central Asia after Alexander*. London.

Kuhrt, A. and Sherwin-White, S. 1991. Aspects of Seleucid royal ideology: the cylinder of Antiochus I from Borsippa. *JHS* 111: 71–86.

Kunze, C. 1998. *Der farnesische Stier und die Dirkegruppe des Apollonios und Tauriskos*. Berlin.

Kuttner, A. 1995. Republican Rome takes a look at Pergamon. *HSCP* 97: 157–78.

La gloire d'Alexandrie: 7 mai-26 juillet 1998. Une exposition des musées de la ville de Paris. Paris.

La Regina, A. 1976. Il Sannio. In Zanker 1976: 219–44.

La Rocca, E. 1994. Theoi epiphaneis. Linguaggio figurativo e culto dinastico da Antioco IV ad Augusto. In K. Rosen (ed.), *Macht und Kultur im Rom der Kaiserzeit*. Bonn. 9–63.

Lahusen, G. 1999. Bemerkungen zur Laokoon-Gruppe. In *Hellenistische Gruppen: Gedenkschrift für Andreas Linfert*. Mainz. 295–305.

Laks, A. and Schofield, M. 1995. *Justice and Generosity: Studies in Hellenistic Social and Political Philosophy*. Cambridge.

Lampela, A. 1998. *Rome and the Ptolemies of Egypt*. Helsinki.

Lanciers, E. 1988. Die Vergöttlichung und die Ehe des Ptolemaios IV. und der Arsinoe III. *APF* 34: 27–32.

Lanciers, E. 1993. Die Opfer im hellenistischen Herrscherkult und ihre Rezeption bei der einheimischen Bevölkerung der hellenistischen Reiche. In J. Quaegebeur (ed.), *Ritual and Sacrifice in the Ancient Near East. Proceedings of the International Conference Organized by the Katholieke Universiteit Leuven from the 17th to the 29th of April 1991*. Leuven. 203–23.

Lang, F. 1994. Veranderungen des Siedlungsbildes in Akarnanien von der klassisch-hellenistischen zur romischen Zeit. *Klio* 76: 239–54.

Larsen, J. A. O. 1968. *Greek Federal States*. Oxford.

Larson, J. 1995. *Greek Heroine Cults*. Madison.

Launey, M. 1949–50. *Recherches sur les armées hellénistiques*. 2 vols. Paris (repr. of original edition with additional comments by Y. Garlan, P. Gauthier, C. Orrieux, 1987).

Laurence, R. 1998a. Territory, ethnonyms and geography: the construction of identity in Roman Italy. In R. Laurence and J. Berry (eds), *Cultural Identity in the Roman Empire*. London. 95–110.

Laurence, R. 1998b. Land transport in Roman Italy: costs, practice and the economy. In Parkins and Smith 1998: 129–48.

Laurence, R. 1999. *The Roads of Roman Italy: Mobility and Cultural Change*. London.

Lauter, H. 1986. *Die Architektur des Hellenismus*. Darmstadt.

Lawall, M. 1998. Ceramics and positivism revisited: Greek transport amphoras and history. In Parkins and Smith 1998: 75–101.

Lawall, M. Forthcoming. Stamp collecting and Hellenistic economies: interpreting amphoras from Athens, Ilion and Koptos. In Z. H. Archibald, J. K. Davies, and V. Gabrielsen (eds), *What's New about Ancient Economies – Making, Moving, and Managing, c.330–31 BCE*.

Lawrence, A. W. 1979. *Greek Aims in Fortifications*. Oxford.

Lawrence, A. W. 1996. *Greek Architecture*. 5th edn. New Haven.

Le Bohec, S. 1993. *Antigone Dósón, roi de Macédoine*. Nancy.

Le Dinahet-Couilloud, M.-T. 1997. Une famille de notables tyriens à Délos. *BCH* 121: 617–66.

Le Rider, G. 1973. Un tétradrachme d'Athéna Niképhoros. *Révue Numismatique* 15: 66–79.

Le Rider, G. 1986. Les Alexandres d'argent en Asie Mineure et dans l'Orient Séleucide au II siècle av. J.-C. (*c.* 275–*c.* 225). Remarques sur le système monétaire des Séleucides et des Ptolemées. *JSav.*: 3–51.

Le Rider, G. 1989. La politique monétaire du royaume de Pergame après 188. *JSav.*: 163–90.

Le Rider, G. 1990. Un groupe de cistophores de l'époque attalide. *BCH* 114: 683–701.

Le Rider, G. 1991. Ephèse et Arados au IIe siècle avant notre ère. *Quaderni ticinesi di numismatica e antiquità classiche* 20: 193–212.

Le Rider, G. 1992. Les clauses financières des traités de 189 et de 188. *BCH* 116: 267–77.

Le Rider, G. 1993–4. Histoire économique et monétaires de l'Orient hellénistique. *Annuaire de la Collège de France* 94: 815–21.

Le Rider, G. 1997. Cléomene de Naucratis. *BCH* 121: 71–93.

Le Rider, G. 2001. *La naissance de la monnaie. Pratiques monetaires de l'Orient ancien.* Paris.

Le Rider, G. and Drew-Bear, T. 1991. Monnayage cistophorique des Apaméens, des Praipénisseis et des Corpeni sous les Attalides. Questions de géographie historique. *BCH* 115: 361–76.

Lefèvre, F. 1995. La chronologie du IIIe siècle à Delphes, d'après les actes amphictioniques (280–200). *BCH* 119: 161–206.

Lefèvre, F. 1998a. *L'Amphictionie pyléo-delphique – histoire et institutions.* Paris.

Lefèvre, F. 1998b. Traité de paix entre Démétrios Poliorcète et la confédération étolienne (fin 289?). *BCH* 122: 109–41.

Lefèvre, F. 2002. *Documents amphictioniques.* Corpus des Inscriptions de Delphes 4. Paris.

Lehmann, G. 1988. Der 'lamische Krieg' und die 'Freiheit der Hellenen': Überlegungen zur hieronymianischen Tradition. *ZPE* 73: 121–49.

Lehnen, J. 1997. *Adventus Principis. Untersuchungen zu Sinngehalt und Zeremoniell der Kaiserankunft in den Städten des Imperium Romanum.* Frankfurt.

Lepore, E. 1963. L'Italia nella formazione della communità romano-italico. *Klearchos* 5: 89ff.

Lepore, E. 1985. La tradizione antica sul mondo osco e la formazione storica delle entità regionali in Italia meridionale. In E. Campanile (ed.), *Lingua e cultura degli Osci, Testi linguistici* 9. Pisa. 55–67.

Lerat, L. 1952. *Les locriens de l'ouest.* Paris.

Lerner, J. D. 1999. *The Impact of Seleucid Decline on the Eastern Iranian Plateau.* Stuttgart.

Lesquier, J. 1911. *Les institutions militaires de l'Égypte sous les Lagides.* Paris (repr. Milan, 1973).

Lessing, G. E. 1766. *Laokoon: Oder, Über die Grenzen der Mahlerey und Poesie.* Berlin.

Lévêque, P. 1957. *Pyrrhos.* Paris.

Lévêque, P. 1968. La guerre à l'époque hellénistique. In J.-P. Vernant (ed.), *Problèmes de la guerre en Grèce ancienne.* Paris. 261–87.

Levi, D. 1964. *The Recent Excavations at Phaistos.* Lund.

Levick, B. M. 1967. *Roman Colonies in Southern Asia Minor.* Oxford.

Levick, B. M. 1971. The beginning of Tiberius' career. *CQ* 65: 478–88.

Levick, B. M. 1976. *Tiberius the Politician.* London.

Levick, B. M. 1996. Greece (including Crete and Cyprus) and Asia Minor from 43 BC to AD 69. *CAH*[2] 10: 641–75.

Levine, L. I. 2000. *The Ancient Synagogue.* New Haven.

Lewis, N. 1986. *Greeks in Ptolemaic Egypt. Case Studies in the Social History of the Hellenistic World.* Oxford.

Lewis, S. 2000. The tyrant's myth. In Serrati and Smith 2000: 97–108.

Lichtheim, M. 1980. *Ancient Egyptian Literature III: the Late Period.* Berkeley.

Liger, J.-Cl. and de Valence, R. 1984. In H.-P. Francfort, *Fouilles d'Aï Khanoum* III. *Le sanctuaire du temple à niches indentées. 2. Les trouvailles.* Paris.

Liger, J.-Cl. and le Cuyot, G. 1992. In Rapin 1992.

Ling, R. 1991. *Roman Painting.* Cambridge.

Ling, R. 1998. *Ancient Mosaics.* Princeton.

Lintott, A. 1993. *Imperium Romanum: Politics and Administration.* London.

Litvinsky, B. A. and Pichikyan, I. 1981–2. Découvertes dans un sanctuaire du dieu Oxus de la Bactriane septentrionale. *RA*: 195–206.

Lloyd, A. B. 1982. Nationalist propaganda in Ptolemaic Egypt. *Historia* 31: 33–55.

Lloyd, A. B. 2000. The Ptolemaic period (323–30 BC). In I. Shaw (ed.), *The Oxford History of Ancient Egypt.* Oxford. 395–421.

Lloyd, G. E. R. 1973. *Greek Science after Aristotle.* London.

Lloyd, G. E. R. 1995. Epistemological arguments in early Greek medicine in comparativist perspective. In D. Bates (ed.), *Knowledge and the Scholarly Medical Traditions.* Cambridge. 25–40.

Lloyd-Jones, H. 1999. The Pride of Halicarnassus. *ZPE* 124: 1–14.

Lomas, K. 1993. *Rome and the Western Greeks, 350 BC–AD 200: Conquest and Acculturation in Southern Italy.* London.

Lomas, K. 1997. Constructing 'the Greek': ethnic identity in Magna Graecia. In T. Cornell and K. Lomas (eds), *Gender and Ethnicity in Ancient Italy.* London. 31–42.

Long, A. A. 1974. *Hellenistic Philosophy: Stoics, Epicureans, Sceptics.* London (2nd edn 1986).

Long, A. A. and Sedley, D. 1987. *The Hellenistic Philosophers.* 2 vols. Cambridge.

Lonis, R. (ed.). 1988, 1992. *L'Étranger dans le monde grec.* Vols 1 and 2. Nancy.

Loomis, W. T. 1998. *Wages, Welfare Costs and Inflation in Classical Athens.* Ann Arbor.

Loraux, N. 1993. *The Children of Athena: Athenian Ideas about Citizenship and the Division between the Sexes.* Princeton.

Lorton, D. 1971. The supposed expedition of Ptolemy II to Persia. *EA* 57: 160–4.

Löwy, E. 1885. *Inschriften griechischer Bildhauer.* Leipzig (repr. Osnabruck 1965 and Chicago 1976).

Luce, T. J. 1977. *Livy, the Composition of his History.* Princeton.

Lukaszewicz, A. 1999. Le papyrus Edfou 8 soixante ans après. In *Tell-Edfou soixante ans après. Actes du colloque franco-polonais. Le Caire – 15 Octobre 1996.* Cairo. 29–35.

Lund, H. S. 1992. *Lysimachus: a Study in Hellenistic Kingship.* London.

Lynch, J. P. 1972. *Aristotle's School: a Study of a Greek Educational Institution.* Berkeley.

Lyons, D. 1997. *Gender and Immortality: Heroines in Ancient Greek Myth and Cult.* Princeton.

Ma, J. 1999. *Antiochos III and the Cities of Western Asia Minor.* Oxford. Paperback edn, 2002, contains an extra chapter with afterthoughts.

Ma, J. 2000a. The epigraphy of Hellenistic Asia Minor: a survey of recent research (1992–1999). *AJA* 104: 95–121.

Ma, J. 2000b. Fighting Poleis of the Hellenistic world. In H. van Wees (ed.), *War and Violence in Ancient Greece.* London. 337–76.

Ma, J. 2000c. Seleukids and speech-acts: performative utterances, legitimacy and negotiation in the world of the Maccabees. *SCI* 19: 71–112.

MacDowell, D. W. and Taddei, M. 1978. The early historic period: Achaemenids and Greeks. In F. R. Allchin and N. Hammond (eds), *The Archaeology of Afghanistan from Earliest Times to the Timurid Period.* London.

MacGillivray, J. A. 2000. *Minotaur: Sir Arthur Evans and the Archaeology of the Minoan Myth.* New York.

MacLeod, R. and Lewis, M. (eds). 1988. *Disease, Medicine and Empire: Perspectives on Western Medicine and the Experience of European Expansion.* London.

Macurdy, G. 1932. *Hellenistic Queens. A Study of Woman-power in Macedonia, Seleucid Syria and Ptolemaic Egypt*. Baltimore.

Maehler, H. and Strocka, V. M. (eds). 1978. *Das ptolemäische Ägypten*. Mainz.

Magi, F. 1960. Il Ripristino del Laocoonte. *Atti della Pontificia Accademia Romana di Archeologia*, ser. 3: Memorie 9. 1. Rome.

Magie, D. 1950. *Roman Rule in Asia Minor to the End of the Third Century after Christ*. 2 vols. Princeton.

Malaise, M. 1994. Le culte d'Isis à Canope au IIIe siècle avant notre ère. In M.-O. Jentel and G. Deschênes-Wagner (eds), *Mélanges en l'honneur de Tran tam Tinh*. Québec. 353–70.

Malay, H. 1996. New evidence concerning the administrative system of the Attalids. *Arkeoloji Dergisi* 4: 83–6.

Malay, H. 1999. *Researches in Lydia, Mysia amd Aiolis*. Vienna.

Malinine, M. 1967. Partage testamentaire d'une propriété familiale (Pap. Moscou no. 123). *Révue d'Egyptologie* 19: 67–85.

Malkin, I. 1987. *Religion and Colonization in Ancient Greece*. Leiden.

Malkin, I. 1998. *The Returns of Odysseus: Colonization and Ethnicity*. Berkeley.

Manganaro, G. 1964. Città di Sicilia e santuari panellenici nel III e II sec. a.C. *Historia* 13: 414ff.

Manganaro, G. 2000. Kyme e il dinasta Philetairos. *Chiron* 30: 403–14.

Manning, J. 1999. The land-tenure regime in Ptolemaic Upper Egypt. In Bowman and Rogan 1999: 83–105.

Manning, J. 2003. *Land and Power in Ptolemaic Egypt: the Structure of Land Tenure, 332–30 BCE*. Cambridge.

Marasco, G. 1980. *Sparta agli inizi dell'Età ellenistica: Il regno di Areo I (309/8–265/4 a. C.)*. Florence.

Marcellesi, M.-C. 2000. Commerces, monnaies locales et monnaies communes dans les états hellénistiques. *REG* 113: 326–58.

Marchese, R. T. 1986. *The Lower Maeander Flood Plain: a Regional Settlement Study*. Oxford.

Marek, C. 1984. *Die Proxenie*. Frankfurt.

Markle, M. M. 1977. The Macedonian Sarissa, spear and related armor. *AJA* 81: 323–39.

Markle, M. M. 1978. Usage of the Sarissa by Philip and Alexander of Macedon. *AJA* 82: 483–97.

Markle, M. M. 1982. Macedonian arms and tactics under Alexander the Great. In *Macedonia and Greece in Late Classical and Early Hellenistic Times. Studies in the History of Art*. Vol. 10: 82–111.

Maroti, E. 1969–70. Der Sklavenmarkt auf Delos und die Piraterie. *Helikon* 9–10: 24–42.

Marrou, H.-I. 1956. *A History of Education in Antiquity*. New York.

Marsden, E. W. 1971. *Greek and Roman Artillery. I. Historical Development; II. Technical Treatises*. Oxford.

Marszal, J. R. 1991. *The Representation of the Gauls in the Hellenistic and Roman Imperial Periods*. (Dissertation Bryn Mawr College). Ann Arbor.

Marszal, J. R. 1998. Tradition and innovation in early Pergamene sculpture. In O. Palagia and W. Coulson (eds), *Regional Schools in Hellenistic Sculpture*. Oxford. 117–27.

Marszal, J. R. 2000. Ubiquitous barbarians: representations of the Gauls at Pergamon and elsewhere. In de Grummond and Ridgway 2000: 191–234.

Martin, L. 1987. *Hellenistic Religions: an Introduction*. Oxford.

Martin, T. 1985. *Sovereignty and Coinage in Classical Greece*. Princeton.

Maslennikov, A. 1989. O tipologii sel'skikh poselenii Bospora. *Sovetskaya Arkheologiya* 2: 66–78.

Maslennikov, A. 1998. *Ellinskaya khora na krayu Oikumeni. Sel'skaya territoriya evropeiskogo Bospora v antichnuyu epoku*. Moscow.

Masson, O. 1962. *Les fragments du poète Hipponax. Édition critique et commentée.* Paris.

Mastrocinque, A. 1979. *La Caria e la Ionia meridionale in epoca ellenistica (323–188).* Rome.

Mastrocinque, A. 1987–8. La guerra di successione siriaca. Realtà storica o invenzione moderna? *Annali dell'istituto italiano per gli studi storici* 10: 65–92.

Mastrocinque, A. 1995. Les médecins des Séleucides. In P. van der Eijk, H. Horstmanshoff and P. Schrijvers (eds), *Ancient Medicine in its Socio-Cultural Context.* Vol. 1. Amsterdam. 143–51.

Mastromarco, G. 1984. *The Public of Herondas.* Amsterdam.

Mattingly, D. J. (ed.). 1997. *Dialogues in Roman Imperialism: Power, Discourse, and Discrepant Experience in the Roman Empire.* JRA Supp. 23. Portsmouth, R.I.

Mattingly, D. J. and Salmon, J. (eds). 2001. *Economies Beyond Agriculture in the Classical World.* London.

Mattusch, C. C. 1997. *The Victorious Youth.* Malibu.

Mavrojannis, T. 1995. Apollo Delio, Atene e Augusto. *Ostraka* 4: 85–102.

Maxfield, V. A. 2001. Stone quarrying in the Eastern Desert with particular reference to Mons Claudianus and Mons Porphyrites. In Mattingly and Salmon 2001: 115–42.

Mazzei, M. 1987. Nota su un gruppo di vasi policromi con scene di combattimento, da Arpi (FG). *AION* 9: 167ff.

McClellan, M. C. 1997. The economy of Hellenistic Egypt and Syria. In B. B. Price (ed.), *Ancient Economic Thought.* Vol. I. London. 172–87.

McClintock, A. 1995. *Imperial Leather: Race, Gender and Sexuality in the Colonial Contest.* New York.

McCredie, J. R. 1966. *Fortified Military Camps in Attica.* Princeton.

McDowell, A. G. 1999. *Village Life in Ancient Egypt: Laundry Lists and Love Songs.* Oxford.

McGing, B. C. 1986. *The Foreign Policy of Mithridates VI Eupator King of Pontus.* Leiden.

McGing, B. C. 1997. Revolt Egyptian style. Internal opposition to Ptolemaic rule. *APF* 43: 273–314.

McInerney, J. 2000. *The Folds of Parnassos: Land and Ethnicity in Ancient Phokis.* Austin.

McKechnie, P. 1989. *Outsiders in the Greek City in the Fourth Century.* London.

McNicoll, A. W. 1972. The development of urban defenses in Hellenistic Asia Minor. In P. Ucko, R. Tringham and G. Dimbleby (eds), *Man, Settlement and Urbanism.* London. 787–91.

McNicoll, A. W. 1978. Some developments in Hellenistic siege warfare with special reference to Asia Minor. In E. Akurgal (ed.), *Proceedings of the Xth International Congress of Classical Archaeology, Vol. I, Ankara–Izmir 20–23 Sept. 1973.* Ankara. 405–20.

McNicoll, A. W. 1986. Developments in techniques of siegecraft and fortification in the Greek World *ca.* 400–100 BC. In P. Leriche and H. Tréziny (eds), *La fortification dans l'histoire du monde grec. Actes du colloque international de Valbonne, 1982.* Paris. 305–13.

McNicoll, A. W. 1997. *Hellenistic Fortifications from the Aegean to the Euphrates* (with revision and an additional chapter by N. P. Milner). Oxford.

Mehl, A. 1980–1. ΔΟΡΙΚΤΗΤΟΣ ΧΩΡΑ. Kritische Bemerkungen zum 'Speerwerb' in Politik und Völkerrecht der hellenistischen Epoche. *AncSoc* 11/12: 173–212.

Mehl, A. 1986. *Seleukos Nikator und sein Reich. 1. Seleukos' Leben und die Entwicklung seiner Machtposition.* Leuven.

Meister, K. 1984. Agathocles. *CAH*² 7.1: 384–411.

Melaerts, H. (ed.). 1998. *Le culte du souverain dans l'Égypte ptolémaïque au IIIe siècle avant notre ère.* Leuven.

Mélèze-Modrzejewski, J. 1995. *The Jews of Egypt.* Philadelphia.

Mellor, R. 1975. ΘΕΑ ΡΩΜΗ. *The Worship of the Goddess Roma in the Greek World.* Göttingen.

Meritt, B. D. 1938. Greek Inscriptions. *Hesperia* 7: 77–146.

Merker, I. C. 1970. The Ptolemaic officials and the League of the Islanders. *Historia* 19: 141–60.

Merker, I. L. 1989. The Achaians in Naupaktos and Kalydon in the fourth century. *Hesperia* 58: 303–11.

Mertens, J. and Lambrechts, R. 1991. *Comunità indigene e problemi della romanizzazione nell'Italia centro-meridionale (IV–III sec. av. C.).* Brussels.

Meskell, L. 2002. *Private Life in New Kingdom Egypt.* Princeton.

Metzger, H. 1967. A propos des images apuliennes de la bataille d'Alexandre et du conseil de Darius. *REG* 80: 308–13.

Meyboom, P. 1995. *The Nile Mosaic of Palestrina: Early Evidence of Egyptian Religion in Italy.* Leiden.

Meyer, E. 1925. *Blüte und Niedergang des Hellenismus in Asien.* Berlin.

Meyers, E. (ed.). 1997. *The Oxford Encyclopedia of Archaeology in the Near East.* 5 vols. Oxford.

Migeotte, L. 1984. *L'emprunt public dans les cités grecques. Recueil des documents et analyse critique.* Quebec.

Migeotte, L. 1991. Le pain quotidien dans les cités hellénistiques. A propos des fonds permanents pour l'approvisionnement en grain. *Cahiers du Centre G. Glotz* 2: 19–41.

Migeotte, L. 1992. *Les souscriptions publiques dans les cités grecques.* Geneva.

Migeotte, L. 1998. Les ventes de grain public dans les cités grecques aux périodes classique et hellénistique. In *La memoire perdue. Recherches sur l'administration romaine.* Rome. 229–46.

Migeotte, L. 2000. Les dépenses militaires des cités grecques: essai de typologie. In Andreau et al. 2000: 145–76.

Migeotte, L. 2002. *L'économie des cités grecques.* Paris.

Mikalson, J. 1998. *Religion in Hellenistic Athens.* Berkeley.

Mileta, C. 1998. Eumenes III. und die Sklaven. Neue Überlegungen zum Charakter des Aristonikos Aufstandes. *Klio* 80: 47–65.

Millar, F. 1983. Epigraphy. In M. Crawford (ed.), *Sources for Ancient History.* Cambridge. 80–136.

Millar, F. 1984a. State and subject: the impact of the monarchy. In F. Millar and E. Segal, *Caesar Augustus: Seven Aspects.* Oxford. 37–60.

Millar, F. 1984b. The Mediterranean and the Roman revolution: politics, war and the economy. *Past and Present* 102: 3–24.

Millar, F. 1993. *The Roman Near East: 31 BC–AD 337.* Cambridge, Mass.

Millar, F. 1995. The last century of the republic: whose history? *JRS* 85: 236–43.

Millett, P. 1991. *Lending and Borrowing in Ancient Athens.* Cambridge.

Milns, R. 1976. The army of Alexander the Great. In A. B. Bosworth (ed.), *Alexandre le Grand. Image et réalité.* Entretiens Hardt 22. Geneva. 87–130.

Minas, M. 1998. Die κανηφόρος. Aspekte des ptolemäischen Dynastiekults. In Melaerts 1998: 43–60.

Minns, E. H. 1913. *Scythians and Greeks: a Survey of Ancient History and Archaeology on the North Coast of the Euxine from the Danube to the Caucasus.* Cambridge.

Mitchell, S. 1974. Blucium and Peium: the Galatian forts of King Deiotarus. *Anatolian Studies* 24: 61–75.

Mitchell, S. 1976. Legio VII and the garrison of Augustan Galatia. *CQ* 26: 298–308.

Mitchell, S. 1982. *Regional Epigraphic Catalogues of Asia Minor II. The Inscriptions of North Galatia.* British Institute of Archaeology at Ankara Monograph 4. Oxford.

Mitchell, S. 1993. *Anatolia. Land Men and Gods in Asia Minor.* 2 vols. Oxford.

Mitteis, L. and Wilcken. U. 1912. *Grundzüge und Chrestomathie der Papyruskunde. Erster Band: Historischer Teil. Zweiter Hälfte: Chrestomathie.* Berlin.

Modes de contacts et processus de transformation dans les sociétés anciennes. 1983.

Momigliano, A. 1966. *Studies in Historiography.* London.

Momigliano, A. 1975. *Alien Wisdom: the Limits of Hellenization*. Cambridge.

Momigliano, A. 1977. *Essays in Ancient and Modern Historiography.* Oxford.

Montanari, F. (ed.). 2002. *Callimaque*. Entretiens Hardt. Geneva.

Moody, J., Nixon, L., Price, S. and Rackham, O. 1998. Surveying poleis and larger sites in Sphakia. In Cavanagh and Curtis 1998: 87–95.

Mooren, L. 1977. *La hiérarchie de cour ptolémaïque. Contribution à l'étude des institutions et des classes dirigeantes à l'époque hellénistique.* Leuven.

Mooren, L. (ed.). 2000. *Politics, Administration and Society in the Hellenistic and Roman World.* Leuven.

Moraux, P. 1973–84. *Der Aristotelismus bei den Griechen.* 2 vols. Berlin.

Morel, J.-P. 1976. Le Sanctuaire de Vastogirardi et les influences hellénistiques en Italie centrale. In Zanker 1976: 255–9.

Moreno, P. 1994. *Scultura Ellenistica.* Rome.

Morgan, C. 1991. Ethnicity and early Greek states: historical and material perspectives. *PCPS* 37: 131–63.

Morgan, C. 1993. The origins of panhellenism. In N. Marinatos and R. Hägg (eds), *Greek Sanctuaries: New Approaches.* London. 18–44.

Morgan, T. 1998. *Literate Education in the Hellenistic and Roman Worlds.* Cambridge.

Mørkholm, O. 1966. *Antiochus IV of Syria.* Copenhagen.

Mørkholm, O. 1979. Some reflections on the early Cistophoric coinage. *ANSMN* 24: 47–61.

Mørkholm, O. 1982. Some reflections on the production and use of coinage in Ancient Greece. *Historia* 31: 290–305.

Mørkholm, O. 1991. *Early Hellenistic Coinage from the Accession of Alexander to the Peace of Apamea (336–188 BC).* Cambridge.

Morris, I. (ed.). 1994. *Classical Greece: Ancient Histories and Modern Archaeologies.* Cambridge.

Morris, I. 2000. *Archaeology as Cultural History: Words and Things in Iron Age Greece.* Oxford.

Morris, S. P. 1992. *Daidalos and the Origins of Greek Art.* Princeton.

Morton, J. 2001. *The Role of the Physical Environment in Ancient Greek Seafaring.* Leiden.

Mouritsen, H. 1998. *Italian Unification: a Study in Ancient and Modern Historiography.* London.

Müller, H. 1989. Ein neues hellenistisches Weihepigramm aus Pergamon. *Chiron* 19: 499–553.

Müller, H. 2000. Der hellenistische Archiereus. *Chiron* 30: 519–42.

Müller, K. 1972–80. *Geschichte der antiken Ethnographie und ethnologischen Theoriebildung.* 2 vols. Wiesbaden.

Musti, D. 1963. Sull'idea di συγγένεια in inscrizioni greche. *ASNP*[2] 32: 225–39.

Musti, D. 1966. Lo stato dei Seleucidi: dinastia, popoli, città da Seleuco I ad Antioco III. *Studi Classici e Orientali* 15: 61–197.

Musti, D. 1984. Syria and the East. *CAH*[2] 7.1: 175–220.

Musti, D. 1988. I Greci e l'Italia. In *Storia di Roma, I: Roma in Italia.* Turin. 39ff.

Myers, J., Myers, E. and Cadogan, G. (eds). 1992. *The Aerial Atlas of Ancient Crete.* London.

Nachtergael, G. 1977. *Les Galates en Grèce et les Sôtéria de Delphes.* Brussels.

Nafissi, M. 1995. Zeus Basileus di Lebadea. La politica religiosa del koinon beotico durante le guerra cleomenica. *Klio* 77: 149–69.

Nafissi, M. 2001. L'iscrizione di Laodice (IvIasos 4): revisione del testo e nuove osservazioni. *Parola del Passato* 56: 101–46.

Nagy, G. 1998. The Library of Pergamon as a classical model. In Koester 1998: 185–232.

Natali, C. 1991. *Bios Theoretikos: La Vita di Aristotele e l'orginizzazione della sua scuola.* Bologna.

Neugebauer, O. 1975. *A History of Ancient Mathematical Astronomy.* Heidelberg.

Neugebauer, O. 1988. A Babylonian lunar ephemeris from Roman Egypt. In E. Leichty, M. Ellis and P. Gerardi, *A Scientific Humanist. Studies in Memory of Abraham Sachs*. Philadelphia. 301–4.

Newell, E. T. 1936. *The Pergamene Mint under Philetaerus*. New York.

Nicolaou, I. 1993. Inscriptiones Cypriae Alphabeticae XXXII, 1992. *RDAC*: 223–32.

Nicolet, C. 1991. *Space, Geography and Politics in the Early Roman Empire*. Ann Arbor.

Nicols, J. 1990. Patrons of Greek cities in the early principate. *ZPE* 80: 81–100.

Nielsen, I. 1994. *Hellenistic Palaces*. Aarhus.

Nielsen, T. 1996. Arkadia. City ethnics and tribalism. *CPCActs* 3: 117–63.

Nielsen, T. and Roy, J. (eds). 1999. *Defining Ancient Arkadia. CPCActs* 6. Copenhagen.

Nisetich, F. (trans.). 2001. *The Poems of Callimachus*. Oxford.

Nock, A. D. 1930. *Conversion: the Old and the New in Religion from Alexander the Great to Augustine of Hippo*. Oxford.

Nock, A. D. 1972. *Essays in Religion and the Ancient World*. Oxford.

North, D. C. 1990. *Institutions, Institutional Change and Economic Performance*. Cambridge.

Nussbaum, M. C. 1994. *The Therapy of Desire: Theory and Practice in Hellenistic Ethics*. Princeton.

Nutton, V. 1992. Healers in the medical market place: towards a social history in Graeco-Roman medicine. In A. Wear (ed.), *Medicine in Society: Historical Essays*. Cambridge. 15–58.

Nutton, V. 2004. *Ancient Medicine*. London.

O'Neil, J. L. 1995. *The Origins and Development of Ancient Greek Democracy*. Lanham.

Oates, J. F. 2001. Observations on a demotic will (69 BC) of a Katoikos Hippeus. In *Alexandrian Studies II in Honour of Mostafa el-Abbadi (BSAA 46 [2000]; Cairo)*. 29–38.

Oates, J. F. et al. 2001. *Checklist of Editions of Greek, Latin, Demotic and Coptic Papyri, Ostraca and Tablets*. 5th edn. Bulletin of the American Society of Papyrologists, Supp. 9, Oakville, Conn. (also available and regularly updated at http://odyssey.lib.duke.edu/papyrus/texts/clist.html).

Ober, J. 1985. *Fortress Attica. Defense of the Athenian Land Frontier, 404–322 BC*. Leiden.

Ober, J. 1989. *Mass and Elite in Democratic Athens. Rhetoric, Ideology, and the Power of the People*. Princeton.

Oberhummer, E. 1887. *Akarnanien, Ambrakia, Amphilochen, Leukas im Altertum*. Munich.

Ochs, P. 1966. Cops of the world, from *Phil Ochs in Concert*.

Oelsner, J. 1986. *Materialien zur babylonischen Gesellschaft und Kultur in hellenistischer Zeit*. Budapest.

Ogden, D. (ed.). 2002. *The Hellenistic World: New Perspectives*. London.

Ogden, D. 1996. *Greek Bastardy in the Classical and Hellenistic Periods*. Oxford.

Ogden, D. 1999. *Polygamy, Prostitutes and Death: the Hellenistic Dynasties*. London.

Oliva, P. 1971. *Sparta and Her Social Problems*. Amsterdam.

Oliver, G. 2001. Regions and microregions: grain for Rhamnous. In Archibald et al. 2001: 137–55.

Onians, J. 1979. *Art and Thought in the Hellenistic Age: the Greek World View, 350–50 BC*. London.

Ormerod, H. A. 1924. *Piracy in the Ancient World*. Liverpool (repr. New York, 1987).

Orrieux, C. 1983. *Les papyrus de Zénon. L'horizon d'un grec en Égypte au IIIe siècle avant J.C.* Paris.

Orrieux, C. 1985. *Zénon de Caunos, parepidemos, et le destin grec*. Paris.

Orsi, D. P. 1987. La rivolta di Alessandro, governatore di Corinto. *Sileno* 13: 103–22.

Orth, W. 1977. *Königlicher Machtanspruch und städtische Freiheit. Untersuchungen zu den politischen Beziehungen zwischen den ersten Seleukidenherrschern (Seleukos I. Antiochos I. Antiochos II.) und den Städten des westlichen Kleinasien*. Munich.

Osborne, R. 1986. Island towers: the case of Thasos. *BSA* 81: 67–178.

Osborne, R. 1996. *Classical Landscape* revisited. *TOPOI* 6: 49–64.

Ossana, M. 1999. *Santuari e Culti dell'Acaia antica.* Naples.

Overbeck, J. A. 1868. *Die antiken Schriftquellen zur Geschichte der bildenden Kunste bei den Griechen.* Leipzig (repr. Hildesheim 1959).

Owens, E. J. 1991. *The City in the Greek and Roman World.* London.

Pakkanen, P. 1996. *Interpreting Early Hellenistic Religion: a Study Based on the Mystery Cult of Demeter and the Cult of Isis.* Helsinki.

Pallottino, M. 1991. *A History of Earliest Italy.* London.

Pantos, P. A. 1985. Τὰ Σφραγίσματα τῆς αἰτωλικῆς Καλλιπόλεως. (Dissertation). Athens.

Papagopoulou, E. 2000. *Antigonos Gonatas: Coinage, Money and the Economy.* (Dissertation University College London). London.

Papagopoulou, K. 2001. The Antigonids: patterns in a royal economy. In Archibald et al. 2001: 313–64.

Papapostolou, I. A. 1983–98. Θέρμος. *Ergon.*

Papapostolou, I. A. 1987–1990. Ἀνασκαφὴ Θέρμοῦ. *Praktika.* Vols. 142–5.

Papazoglou, F. 1978. *The Central Balkan Tribes in Pre-Roman Times.* Amsterdam.

Papazoglou, F. 1997. Λαοί et πάροικοι. *Recherches sur la structure de la société hellénistique.* Belgrade.

Parke, H. W. 1933. *Greek Mercenary Soldiers from the Earliest Times to the Battle of Ipsos.* Oxford (repr. 1970).

Parker, R. 1983. *Miasma: Pollution and Purification in Early Greek Religion.* Oxford.

Parker, R. 1987. Myths of early Athens. In Bremmer 1987: 187–214.

Parker, R. 1996. *Athenian Religion: a History.* Oxford.

Parker, R. 2000. Theophoric names and the history of Greek religion. In S. Hornblower and E. Matthews (eds), *Greek Personal Names and their Value as Evidence.* Oxford. 53–79.

Parker, R. and Obbink, D. 2000. Aus der Arbeit der *Inscriptiones Graecae* VI. Sales of priesthoods on Cos. *Chiron* 30: 415–49.

Parkins, H. and Smith, C. (eds). 1998. *Trade, Traders, and the Ancient City.* London.

Parkinson, R. 1999. *Cracking Codes. The Rosetta Stone and Decipherment.* London.

Paromov, Y. M. 1986. Obsledovanie arkheologicheskikh pamyatnikov Tamanskogo poluostrova v 1981–1983 gg. *Kratkie Soobshcheniya Instituta Arkheologii* 188: 69–76.

Paromov, Y. M. 1989. Obsledovanie arkheologicheskikh pamyatnikov Tamanskogo poluostrova v 1984–1985 gg. *Kratkie Soobshcheniya Instituta Arkheologii* 196: 72–8.

Paromov, Y. M. 1990. Intervention sur la péninsule de Taman. In O. Lordkipanidze and P. Lévêque (eds), *Le Pont-Euxine vu par les grecs: sources écrites et archéologie.* Paris. 161–4.

Pasquinucci, M. 1985. Centuriazione e catastazione: la politica di Roma verso l'Italia settentrionale. In *Misurare la terra: centuriazione e coloni nel mondo romano: città, agricoltura, commercio: materiali da Roma e dal suburbio.* Modena. 20–3.

Paton, W. R. and Hicks, E. 1891. *The Inscriptions of Cos.* Oxford.

Patterson, C. 1998. *The Family in Greek History.* Cambridge, Mass.

Patterson, J. 1991. Settlement, city and elite in Samnium and Lycia. In J. Rich and A. Wallace-Hadrill (eds), *City and Country in the Ancient World.* London. 147–68.

Patzek, B. 1992. *Homer und Mykene. Mündliche Dichtung und Geschichtsschreibung.* Munich.

Payne, M. 1991. Alexander the Great: myth, the polis and afterward. In Pozzi and Wickersham 1991: 164–81.

Peacock, D. P. S. 1997. *Mons Claudianus: 1987–1993: Survey and Excavation.* Cairo.

Pearson, L. 1960. *The Lost Histories of Alexander the Great.* New York.

Pédech, P. 1976. *La géographie des Grecs.* Paris.

Pédech, P. 1989. *Trois historiens méconnus: Théopompe, Duris, Phylarque.* Paris.

Pelling, C. B. R. 1987. *Plutarch, Life of Antony.* Cambridge.

Pelling, C. B. R. 1996. The triumviral period. *CAH²* 10: 1–69.

Peremans, W. 1978. Les révolutions égyptiennes sous les Lagides. In Maehler and Strocka 1978: 39–50.

Peremans, W. 1981. Sur la *domestica seditio* de Justin (XXVII, 1, 9). *L'Antiquité Classique* 50: 628–36.

Peremans, W. 1987. Les Lagides, les élites indigènes et la monarchie bicéphale. In E. Lévy (ed.), *Le système palatial en Orient, en Grèce et à Rome*. Strasbourg. 327–43.

Pestman, P. W. 1961. *Marriage and Matrimonial Property in Ancient Egypt: a Contribution to Establishing the Legal Position of the Woman*. Leiden.

Pestman, P. W. 1981. *A Guide to the Zenon Archive*. 2 vols. Leiden.

Pestman, P. W. 1985. Agoranomoi et actes agoranomiques: Krokodilopolis et Pathyris, 145–88 BC. In P. W. Pestman (ed.), *Textes et études de papyrologie grecque, démotique et copte*. Pap. Lugd.-Bat. 23. Leiden. 9–44.

Pestman, P. W. 1989. Het huis van Teianteus. In *Familiearchieven uit het land van Pharao*. Zutphen. 14–23.

Pestman, P. W. 1995. Haronnophris and Chaonnophris: two indigenous pharaohs in Ptolemaic Egypt (205–186 BC). In Vleeming 1995: 101–37.

Petrakos, B. C. 1997. *Oi epigraphes tou Oropou*. Athens.

Pfeiffer, R. 1968. *History of Classical Scholarship from the Beginnings to the End of the Hellenistic Age*. Oxford.

Pfister, F. 1909–12. *Der Reliquienkult im Altertum*. Gießen.

Pfister, F. 1961. Das Alexander-Archiv und die hellenistisch-römische Wissenschaft. *Historia* 10: 30–67.

Pfrommer, M. 1998. *Untersuchungen zur Chronologie und Komposition des Alexandermosaiks auf antiquarischer Grundlage*. Mainz.

Picard, O. 1979. *Chalcis et la confédération eubéene: Étude du numismatique et d'histoire (IVᵉ–Iᵉʳ siècle)*. Paris.

Picard, O. 1994. Monnaies et commerce a Thasos. In *Economie antique. Les échanges dans l'Antiquité: le role de l'Etat*. Saint-Bertrand-de-Comminges. 31–45.

Picard, O. 1996. Monnaie oloscheres, monnaie de poids reduit, *apousia* en Eubée, à Délos et ailleurs. In *Character. Aphieroma ste Manto Oikonomidou*. Athens. 243–50.

Picard, O. 1998. La valeur des monnaies grecques en bronze. *Revue numismatique* 1998: 7–18.

Piejko, F. 1990. Episodes from the Third Syrian War in a Gurob papyrus, 246 BC. *APF* 36: 13–27.

Piejko, F. 1991. Antiochus III and Ilium. *APF* 37: 9–50.

Piérart, M. 2001. Le blanc, le pourpre et le noir. Les funérailles des εὔθυνοι dans les 'Lois' de Platon et le culte des grands hommes. In E. Delruelle and V. Pirenne-Delforge (eds), *Κῆποι. De la religion à la philosophie*. Kernos Supp. 11. Liège. 153–66.

Pierson, R. 1998. Introduction. In R. Pierson and N. Chauduri (eds), *Nation, Colony, Empire: Historicizing Gender and Race*. Bloomington. 1–20.

Pintaudi, R. 1990. Oxyrhyncha e Oxyrhynchites: P. Vat. Gr. 65: Lettera di Dionysodoros ad Asclepiades. *Tyche* 5: 101–4.

Plantzos, D. 1999. *Hellenistic Engraved Gems*. Oxford.

Plattner, S. 1989. *Economic Anthropology*. Stanford.

Plaumann, G. 1910. *Ptolemais in Oberägypten*. Leipzig.

Pleket, H. 1964. *Epigraphica I. Texts on the Economic History of the Greek World*. Leiden.

Pleket, H. 1996. Epigraphy, Greek. *OCD³*: 539–43.

Pöhl, H. 1993. *Die römische Politik und die Piraterie im östlichen Mittelmeer vom 3. bis zum 1. Jh. v. Chr.* Berlin.

Pollitt, J. J. 1986. *Art in the Hellenistic Age*. Cambridge.

Pollitt, J. J. 2000. The phantom of a Rhodian school of sculpture. In de Grummond and Ridgway 2000: 92–110.

Pomeroy, S. B. 1984. *Women in Hellenistic Egypt, from Alexander to Cleopatra*. New York.

Pomeroy, S. B. 1997a. Family values: the uses of the past. In Bilde et al. 1997: 204–19.

Pomeroy, S. B. 1997b. *Families in Classical and Hellenistic Greece. Representation and Realities*. Oxford.

Pontrandolfo, A. and Rouveret, A. 1992. *Le tombe dipinte di Paestum*. Modena.

Popkin, R. H. 1999. *The Columbia History of Western Philosophy*. New York.

Porten, B. et al. 1996. *The Elephantine Papyri in English*. Leiden.

Porter, W. H. 1937. *Plutarch's Life of Aratus*. Cork.

Potter, D. S. 1994. *Prophets and Emperors: Human and Divine Authority from Augustus to Theodosius*. Cambridge, Mass.

Potter, D. S. 1999. Roman religion: ideas and actions. In D. Potter and D. Mattingly, *Life, Death and Entertainment in the Roman Empire*. Ann Arbor. 113–67.

Potts, D. T. 1999. *The Archaeology of Elam: Formation and Transformation of an Ancient Iranian State*. Cambridge.

Pouilloux, J. 1954–8. *Recherches sur les l'histoire et les cultes de Thasos*. 2 vols. Paris.

Pouilloux, J. 1975. Glaucon fils d'Éteoclès d'Athènes. In J. Bingen, G. Cambier and G. Nachtergael (eds), *Le monde grec – Pensée, littérature, histoire, documents: Hommages à Claire Preaux*. Brussels. 376–82.

Pozzi, D. and Wickersham, J. (eds). 1991. *Myth and the Polis*. Ithaca.

Préaux, C. 1939. *L'économie royale des Lagides*. Brussels.

Préaux, C. 1961. La paix à l'époque hellénistique. In *Recueils de la Société Jean Bodin*, XIV: *La Paix*. Brussels. 227–301.

Préaux, C. 1978. *Le monde hellénistique*. 2 vols. Paris.

Preziosi, D. 1989. *Rethinking Art History*. New Haven.

Price, M. J. 1989. *The Coinage in the Name of Alexander the Great and Philip Arrhidaeus*. London.

Price, S. R. F. 1984. *Rituals and Power: the Roman Imperial Cult in Asia Minor*. Cambridge.

Pritchett, W. K. 1965, 1985, 1989. *Studies in Ancient Greek Topography*. Parts 1, 5, and 6. Berkeley.

Pritchett, W. K. 1974. *The Greek State at War*. Part 1. Berkeley.

Pritchett, W. K. 1991a, 1992. *Studies in Ancient Greek Topography*. Parts 7 and 8. Amsterdam.

Pritchett, W. K. 1991b. *The Greek State at War*. Part 5. Berkeley.

Pritchett, W. K. 1996. *Greek Archives, Cults, and Topography*. Amsterdam.

Prontera, F. 1986. *Imagines Italiae*: sulle più antiche visualizzazioni e rappresentazioni geografiche dell'Italia. *Athenaeum* 64: 295ff.

Prontera, F. 1997. Sulle basi empiriche della cartografia greca. *Sileno* 23: 49–63.

Pruneti, P. 1975. I *kleroi* del nomo Ossirinchite: ricerche topografica. *Aegyptus* 55: 159–244.

Pruneti, P. 1981. *I centri abitati dell'Ossirinchite: repertorio toponomastico*. Florence.

Purcell, N. 1990a. The creation of provincial landscape: the Roman impact on Cisalpine Gaul. In T. Blagg and M. Millett, *The Early Roman Empire in the West*. Oxford. 7–29.

Purcell, N. 1990b. Maps, Lists, Money, Order and Power. *JRS* 80: 178–82.

Purcell, N. 1994. South Italy in the Fourth Century BC. *CAH*[2] 6: 381–403.

Quaegebeur, J. 1988. Cleopatra VII and the cults of the Ptolemaic queens. In Bianchi et al. 1988: 41–54.

Quaegebeur, J. 1989. The Egyptian clergy and the cult of the Ptolemaic dynasty. *AncSoc* 20: 93–116.

Quaegebeur, J. 1998. Documents égyptiens anciens et nouveaux relatifs à Arsinoé Philadelphe. In Melaerts 1998: 73–108.

Quass, F. 1979. Zur Verfassung der griechischen Stadte im Hellenismus. *Chiron* 9: 37–52.

Queyrel, F. 1989. Art pergaménien, histoire, collections: Le Perse du Musée d'Aix et le petit ex-voto attalide. *Revue archéologique*: 583–96.

Queyrel, F. 1997. La cécité du Laocoon. *Bulletin de la Société des Antiquaries de France*. 88–96.

Queyrel, F. 2002. Lo Sguardo del Laocoonte. *Archeo* 18.7: 38–43.

Rackham, O. and Moody, J. 1996. *The Making of the Cretan Landscape*. Manchester.

Radt, W. 1986. In M. Wörrle (ed.), *Die Altertümer von Pergamon XV.1. Die Stadtgrabung. Teil I. Das Heroon*. Berlin. 121–6.

Radt, W. 1989. Zwei augusteische Dionysos-Altärchen aus Pergamon. In N. Basgelen and M. Lugal (eds), *Festschrift für Jale Inan*. Istanbul. 199–209.

Radt, W. 1998. Recent research in and about Pergamon: a survey (*ca*. 1987–1997). In Koester 1998: 1–40.

Radt, W. 1999. *Pergamon. Geschichte und Bauten, Funde und Erforschung einer kleinasiatische Metropole*. Cologne (rev. edn).

Rajak, T. 1994. The Jews under Hasmonean rule. *CAH*² 9: 274–309.

Rapin, C. 1992. *Fouilles d'Aï Khanoum. 8, La trésorerie du palais hellénistique d'Aï Khanoum. L'apogée et la chute du royaume de Bactriane*. Paris.

Rathbone, D. W. 1990. Villages, land and population in Graeco-Roman Egypt. *PCPS* 36: 103–42.

Raubitschek, A. E. 1954. Epigraphical notes on Julius Caesar. *JRS* 44: 65–82.

Rauh, N. 1993. *The Sacred Bonds of Commerce: Religion, Economy, Trade and Society at Hellenistic and Roman Delos*. Amsterdam.

Rauh, N. 1998. Who were the Cilician pirates? In S. Swiny et al. (eds), *Res Maritimae: Cyprus and the Eastern Mediterranean from Prehistory to Late Antiquity. Proceedings of the Second International Symposium 'Cities on the Sea', Nicosia, October 18–22, 1994*. Atlanta. 263–83.

Rawson, E. 1975. Caesar's Heritage: Hellenistic Kings and their Roman Equals. *JRS* 65: 148–59.

Ray, J. D. 1976. *The Archive of Hor*. Egypt Exploration Society. Texts from excavations 2. London.

Ray, J. D. 1994. Literacy and language in Egypt in the Late and Persian Periods. In Bowman and Woolf 1994: 51–66.

Redde, M. and Golvin, J.-C. 1987. Du Nil à la Mer Rouge: documents anciens et nouveaux sur les routes du désert oriental d'Égypte. *Karthago* 21: 5–64.

Reed, J. D. 1997. *Bion of Smyrna: the Fragments and the Adonis*. Cambridge.

Reeder, E. D. (ed.). 1988. *Hellenistic Art in the Walters Art Gallery*. Baltimore.

Reger, G. 1985. The date of the Battle of Kos. *AJAH* 10: 155–77.

Reger, G. 1992. Private property and private loans on independent Delos (314–167 BC). *Phoenix* 46: 322–41.

Reger, G. 1993. The public purchase of grain on independent Delos. *Classical Antiquity* 12: 300–34.

Reger, G. 1994a. The date and historical significance of *IG* XII 5.714 of Andros. *Hesperia* 63: 309–21.

Reger, G. 1994b. *Regionalism and Change in the Economy of Independent Delos*. Berkeley.

Reger, G. 1994c. The political history of the Kyklades, 260–200 BC. *Historia* 43: 32–69.

Reger, G. 2001. The Mykonian *Synoikismos*. *REA* 103: 157–81.

Reger, G. 2003. Aspects of the role of merchants in the political life of the Hellenistic world. In C. Zaccagnini (ed), *Mercanti e politica nel mondo antico*. Rome. 165–97.

Reger, G. 2004. *Sympoliteiai* in Hellenistic Asia Minor. In S. Colvin (ed), *The Greco-Roman East (Yale Classical Studies 31)*. Cambridge. 144–80.

Reinach, A. J. 1911. Un monument delphien: L'Étolie sur les Trophées Gaulois de Kallion. *Journal international d'archéologie numismatique* 13: 177–240.

Rempel, J. Forthcoming. Where are the Greeks? Understanding cultural categories in the Bosporan kingdom. In G. R. Tsetskhladze (ed.), *Proceedings of the Second International Congress on Black Sea Antiquities*. Oxford.

Renfrew, C. 1986. Introduction. In C. Renfrew and J. Cherry (eds), *Peer Polity Interaction and Socio-political Change*. Cambridge. 1–18.

Renfrew, C. and Wagstaff, J. (eds). 1982. *An Island Polity: the Archaeology of Exploitation on Melos*. Cambridge.

Rengakos, A. 1993. *Der Homertext und die hellenistischen Dichter*. Stuttgart.

Rengakos, A. and Papanghelis, T. (eds). 2001. *A Companion to Apollonius Rhodius*. Leiden.

Reynolds, J. 1996. Ruler cult at Aphrodisias in the Late Republic and under the Julio-Claudian emperors. In Small 1996: 41–50.

Rhodes, P. J. 1981. *A Commentary on the Aristotelian* Athenaion Politeia. Oxford.

Rice, E. E. 1983. *The Grand Procession of Ptolemy Philadelphus*. Oxford.

Richards, J. 1999. Conceptual landscapes in the Egyptian Nile valley. In W. Ashmore and A. Knapp (eds), *Archaeologies of Landscape: Contemporary Perspectives*. Oxford. 83–100.

Richardson, J. 1991. *Imperium Romanum*: Empire and the Language of Power. *JRS* 81: 1–9.

Richardson, P. 1996. *Herod: King of the Jews and Friend of the Romans*. Columbia.

Richter, S. 1992. *Laocoon's Body and the Aesthetics of Pain: Winckelmann, Lessing, Herder, Moritz, Goethe*. Detroit.

Ridgway, B. S. 1989. Laokoon and the Foundation of Rome. *JRA* 2: 171–81.

Ridgway, B. S. 1990. *Hellenistic Sculpture I: the Styles of ca. 331–200* BC. Madison.

Ridgway, B. S. 2000a. *Hellenistic Sculpture II: the Styles of ca. 200–100* BC. Madison.

Ridgway, B. S. 2000b. The Sperlonga sculptures: the current state of research. In de Grummond and Ridgway 2000: 78–91.

Ridgway, B. S. 2002. *Hellenistic Sculpture III: the Styles of ca. 100–31* BC. Madison.

Rigsby, K. 1996. *Asylia. Territorial Inviolability in the Hellenistic World*. Berkeley.

Rihll, T. 2001. Making money in classical Athens. In Mattingly and Salmon 2001: 115–42.

Rizakis, A. D. 1991. *Archaia Achaia kai Elia: anakoinoseis kata to proto Diethnes Symposio, Athena, 19–21 Maiou 1989*. Athens.

Rizakis, A. D. 1995. *Achaie I: sources textuelles et histoire regionale*. Athens.

Rizakis, A. D. 1998. *Achaie II: la cité de Patras: epigraphie et histoire*. Athens.

Robert, J. and L. 1954. *La Carie. Histoire et géographie historique, avec le recueil des inscriptions antiques. 2: Le plateau de Tabai et ses environs*. Paris.

Robert, J. and L. 1976. Une inscription grecque de Téos en Ionie. L'union de Téos et de Kyrbissos. *JSav*: 154–235.

Robert, J. and L. 1983. *Fouilles d'Amyzon en Carie. 1: Exploration, histoire, monnaies et inscriptions*. Paris.

Robert, J. and L. 1989. *Claros 1: décrets hellénistiques*. Paris.

Robert, L. 1926. Notes d'épigraphie hellénistique XIII-XXIII. *BCH* 50: 469–522 (= Robert *OMS* 1: 33–86).

Robert, L. 1934. Documents d'histoire hellénistique. *Revue de Philologie* 60: 284–6 (= Robert *OMS* 2: 1183–5).

Robert, L. 1936. *Collection Frœhner I: les inscriptions grecques*. Paris.

Robert, L. 1937. *Études anatoliennes. Recherches sur les inscriptions grecques de l'Asie Mineure*. Paris.

Robert, L. 1940. *Hellenica*. Vol. 1. Limoges.

Robert, L. 1946. *Hellenica*. Vol. 3. Paris.

Robert, L. 1960. *Hellenica*. Vols 11–12. Paris.

Robert, L. 1961. Épigraphie. *Encyclopédie de la Pléaide*. Paris. 453–97.

Robert, L. 1962. *Villes d'Asie Mineure. Études de geographie ancienne.* 2nd edn. Paris.

Robert, L. 1963. *Noms indigènes dans l'Asie Mineure gréco-romaine.* Paris.

Robert, L. 1968a. De Delphes à l'Oxus: inscriptions nouvelles de la Bactriane. *CRAI*.: 416–57.

Robert, L. 1968b. Sur un décret d'Ilion et sur un papyrus concernant des cultes royaux. In *Essays in honor of C. Bradford Welles.* New Haven. 175–211 (= Robert *OMS* 7: 599–635).

Robert, L. 1973. Statues des héros mysiens à Délos. *BCH* Supp. 1: 478–85.

Robert, L. 1983. Documents de l'Asie Mineure. *BCH* 107: 523–48 (= Robert 1987: 367–92).

Robert, L. 1987. *Documents d'Asie Mineure.* Paris.

Robinson, D. M., and Graham, J. W. 1938. *Excavations at Olynthus. Part VIII. The Hellenic House.* Baltimore.

Robinson, E. S. G. 1954. Cistophors in the name of King Eumenes. *Numismatic Chronicle* 14: 1–8.

Rochette, B. 1997. Les armées d'Alexandre le Grand et les langues étrangères. *Antiquite Classique* 66: 311–18.

Roesch, P. 1982. *Études béotiennes.* Paris.

Roller, D. W. 1998. *The Building Program of Herod the Great.* Berkeley.

Romer, F. 1979. Gaius Caesar's military diplomacy in the East. *TAPA* 109: 199–214.

Romm, J. S. 1992. *The Edges of the Earth in Ancient Thought: Geography, Explorations, and Fiction.* Princeton.

Rosivach, V. 1987. Autochthony and the Athenians. *CQ* 37: 294–306.

Ross Holloway, R. 1991. *The Archaeology of Ancient Sicily.* London.

Rostovtzeff, M. 1922a. *A Large Estate in Egypt in the Third Century* B.C.: *a Study in Economic History.* Madison.

Rostovtzeff, M. 1922b. *Iranians and Greeks in South Russia.* Oxford.

Rostovtzeff, M. 1941. *The Social and Economic History of the Hellenistic World.* 3 vols. Oxford.

Rougé, J. 1981. *Ships and Fleets of the Ancient Mediterranean.* Middletown.

Rousset, D. 1989. Les doriens de la Métropole: Étude de topographie et de géographie historique. *BCH* 113: 199–239.

Rousset, D. 1990. Les doriens de la Métropole: Nouveaux documents épigraphiques et prosopographie. *BCH* 114: 445–72.

Rousset, D. 1999. Centre urbain, frontière et éspace rural dans les cités de Grèce centrale. In Brunet 1999: 35–77.

Rouveret, A. 1989. *Histoire et imaginaire de la peinture ancienne: Ve siècle av. J.-C.–Ier siècle ap. J.-C.* Rome.

Rouveret, A. and Greco Pontrandolfo, A. 1983. La rappresentazione del Barbaro nell'ambiente magno-greco. In *Modes de contacts et processus de transformation dans les sociétés anciennes.* 1051ff.

Rouveret, A. and Greco Pontrandolfo, A. 1985. Pittura funeraria in Lucania e Campania: puntualizzazioni cronologiche e proposte di lettura. In *Richerche di pittura ellenistica: lettura e interpretazione della produzione pittorica dal IV secolo a. C. all'ellenismo.* Quaderni dei Dialoghi di Archeologia 1: 91ff., 120–1.

Rowe, A. 1946. *Discovery of the Famous Temple Enclosure of Serapis at Alexandria.* Cairo.

Rowlandson, J. 1998. *Women and Society in Greek and Roman Egypt: a Sourcebook.* Cambridge.

Rudd, N. 1959. Colonia and her bridge: a note on the structure of Catullus 17. *TAPA* 90: 238–42.

Ruggendorfer, P. 1996. Zum Kaisareion von Alexandria. In F. Blakolmer et al. (eds), *Fremde Zeiten. Festschrift für Jürgern Borchhardt zum sechzigsten Geburtstag am 25. Februar 1996 dargebracht von Kollegen, Schülern und Freunden*, Vienna. II. 213–23.

Russell, D. 1972. *Plutarch.* London.

Rutkowski, B. and Nowicki, K. 1996. *The Psychro Cave and Other Sacred Grottoes in Crete.* Warsaw.

Sachs, A. J. and Hunger, H. 1988. *Astronomical Diaries and Related Texts from Babylonia* I: *Diaries from 652* BC *to 262* BC. Vienna.

Sachs, A. J. and Hunger, H. 1989. *Astronomical Diaries and Related Texts from Babylonia* II: *Diaries from 261* BC *to 165* BC. Vienna.

Sacks, K. S. 1990. *Diodorus Siculus and the First Century.* Princeton.

Safrai, S. and Stern, M. 1974. *The Jewish People in the First Century.* Vol. 1. Philadelphia.

Şahin, S. 1991. Forschungen in Kommagene II: Topographie. *EA* 18: 114–31.

Said, E. W. 1978. *Orientalism: Western Conceptions of the Orient.* London (repr. with new afterword 1995).

Said, E. W. 1993. *Culture and Imperialism.* London.

Salmon, E. T. 1967. *Samnium and the Samnites.* Cambridge.

Salviat, F. 1986. Le vin de Thasos. In *Recherches sur les amphores grecques.* Paris. 145–96.

Samuel, A. E. 1989. *The Shifting Sands of History: Interpretations of Ptolemaic Egypt.* Lanham.

Sánchez, P. 2001. *L'Amphictionie des Pyles et de Delphes. Recherches sur son rôle historique des origines au 11e siècle de notre ère.* Stuttgart.

Sanders, I. F. 1976. Settlement in the Hellenistic and Roman periods on the Plain of the Mesara, Crete. *BSA* 71: 131–7.

Sanders, I. F. 1982. *Roman Crete: an Archaeological Survey and Gazetteer of Late Hellenistic, Roman and Early Byzantine Crete.* Warminster.

Saprykin, S. 1994. *Ancient Farms and Land-Plots on the Khora of Khersonesos Taurike: Research in the Herakleian Peninsula, 1974–1990.* Amsterdam.

Saprykin, S. 1997. *Heracleia Pontica and the Tauric Chersonesus before Roman Domination, 6th to 1st Centuries* BC. Amsterdam.

Savalli, I. 1985. I neocittadini nelle città ellenistiche. *Historia* 34: 387–431.

Savalli-Lestrade, I. 1994. Il ruolo pubblico delle regine ellenistiche. In S. Alessandri (ed.), *Historie. Studi offerti degli allievi a Giuseppe Nenci in occasione del suo settantesimo compleanno.* 415–32.

Savalli-Lestrade, I. 1998. *Les philoi royaux dans l'Asie hellénistique.* Geneva.

Savalli-Lestrade, I. 2001. *Les Attalides et les cités grecques au IIe Siècle.* In A. Bresson and R. Descat 2001.

Sayce A. H. 1925. Perseus and the Achaeans in the Hittite Tablets. *JHS* 45: 161–3.

Schachermeyr, F. 1973. *Alexander der Große: Das Problem seiner Persönlichkeit und seines Wirkens.* Vienna.

Schachter, A. 1981–6. *Cults of Boiotia.* Parts 1 and 2. London.

Schalles, H.-J. 1985. *Untersuchungen zur Kulturpolitik der pergamenischen Herrscher im 3. Jh. v. Chr.* Tübingen.

Schalles, H.-J. 1986. *Der Pergamonaltar. Zwischen Bewertung und Verwertbarkeit.* Frankfurt.

Schaps, D. M. 1979. *Economic Rights of Women in Ancient Greece.* Edinburgh.

Scharrer, U. 1999. Seleukos I und das babylonische Königtum. In Brodersen 1999: 95–128.

Scheer, T. S. 1993. *Mythische Vorväter. Zur Bedeutung griechischer Heroenmythen im Selbstverständnis kleinasiatischer Städte.* Munich.

Scheer, T. S. 1996. Ein Museum griechischer 'Frühgeschichte' im Apollontempel von Sikyon. *Klio* 78: 353–73.

Scheid, J. 1996. *Graeco ritu.* A typically Roman way of honouring the gods. *HSCP* 98: 15–31.

Scheidel, W. 2001. *Death on the Nile.* Leiden.

Scherberich, K. 2001. *Koine Symmachia. Untersuchungen zem Hellenenbund Antigonos Dosons und Philipps V.* Aachen.

Schiffman, L. and Vanderkam, J. 2000. *Encyclopedia of the Dead Sea Scrolls.* New York.

Schindler W. 1988. *Mythos und Wirklichkeit in der Antike.* Berlin.

Schmidt, K.-H. 1994. Galatische Sprachreste. In Schwertheim 1994: 15–28.

Schmidt-Dounas, B. 1993–4. Statuen hellenistischer Könige als Synnaoi Theoi. *Egnatia* 4: 71–141.

Schmitt, H. H. 1964. *Untersuchungen zur Geschichte Antiochos' des Grossen und seiner Zeit.* Stuttgart.

Schmitt, H. H. 1969. *Die Staatsverträge des Altertums III: Die Verträge der griechisch-römischen Welt von 338 bis 200 v. Chr.* Munich.

Schmitt, H. H. 1994. Uberlegungen zur Sympolitie. In G. Thur (ed.), *Symposium 1993. Vortrage zur griechischen und hellenistischen Rechtsgeschichte.* Cologne. 35–44.

Schober, L. 1984. *Untersuchungen zur Geschichte Babyloniens und der Oberen Satrapien, 323–303 v. Chr.* Frankfurt.

Schoch, M. 1997. *Beiträge zur Topographie Akarnaniens in klassischer und hellenistischer Zeit.* Würzburg.

Schofield, M. 1991. *The Stoic Idea of the City.* Cambridge.

Schofield, M. and Striker, G. 1986. *The Norms of Nature: Studies in Hellenistic Ethics.* Cambridge.

Scholl, R. 1987. Alexander der Große und die Sklaverei am Hofe. *Klio* 69: 108–21.

Scholl, T. and Zin'ko, V. 1999. *Archaeological Map of Nymphaion (Crimea).* Warsaw.

Scholten, J. B. 1990. The date of the Delphic Archon Eudocus II. *ZPE* 83: 289–91.

Scholten, J. B. 2000. *The Politics of Plunder: Aitolians and their Koinon in the Early Hellenistic Era, 279–217* BC. Berkeley.

Schreiber, T. 1885. Alexandrinischen Skulpturen in Athen. *MDAI* (A) 10: 380–400.

Schreiber, T. 1889–94. *Die hellenistische Reliefbilder.* Leipzig.

Schürer, E. 1973. *The History of the Jewish People in the Age of Jesus Christ.* Vol. 1, rev. and ed. by G. Vermes, F. Millar and M. Black. Edinburgh.

Schürer, E. 1979. *The History of the Jewish People in the Age of Jesus Christ.* Vol. 2, rev. and ed. by G. Vermes, F. Millar and M. Black. Edinburgh.

Schwartz, J. 1978. Athènes et l'Étolie dans la politique lagide (à la lumière du Pap. Haun. 6). *ZPE* 30: 95–100.

Schwarzer, H. 1999. Untersuchungen zum hellenistischen Herrscherkult in Pergamon. *MDAI* (I) 49: 249–300.

Schwertheim, E. (ed.). 1994. *Forschungen in Galatien.* Asia Minor Studien 12. Bonn.

Schwertheim, E. 1991. Iupiter Dolichenus, der Zeus von Doliche und der kommagenische Königskult. *Asia Minor Studien* 3: 29–40.

Scullard, H. H. 1974. *The Elephant in the Greek and Roman World.* London.

Sedley, D. 1998a. *Lucretius and the Transformation of Greek Wisdom.* Cambridge.

Sedley, D. 1998b. Le scuole filosofiche e le città. In S. Settis (ed.) *I Greci*, vol. 2.3. Turin. 467–82.

Segal, C. 1981. *Poetry and Myth in Ancient Pastoral.* Princeton.

Seibert, J. 1967. *Historische Beiträge zu den dynastischen Verbindungen in hellenistischer Zeit.* Wiesbaden.

Seibert, J. 1976. Die Schlacht bei Ephesos. *Historia* 25: 45–61.

Seibert, J. 1979. *Die politischen Fluchtlinge und Verbannten in der griechischen Geschichte.* Darmstadt.

Selden, D. 1998. Alibis. *Classical Antiquity* 17: 289–412.

Serrati, J. and Smith, C. (eds). 2000. *Sicily from Aeneas to Augustus: New Approaches in Archaeology and History.* Edinburgh.

Sharma, G. R. 1980. *The Inscription of Menander and the Indo-Greek Invasion of the Ganga Valley.* Allahabad.

Sharples, R. 1996. *Stoics, Epicureans and Sceptics: an Introduction to Hellenistic Philosophy.* London.

Shcheglov, A. 1983. Razvedki i raskopki antichnikh sel'skikh poselenii i agrarnikh sistem: Instruktsiya. In D. Shelov (ed.), *Metodika polevikh arkheologicheskikh issledovanii*. Moscow. 12–30.

Shear, T. L. 1978. *Kallias of Sphettos and the Revolt of Athens in 286* BC. Princeton.

Sherk, R. K. 1984. *Rome and the Greek East to the Death of Augustus*. Cambridge.

Sherk, R. K. 1992. The eponymous officials of Greek cities IV. *ZPE* 93: 223–72.

Sherwin-White, A. N. 1973. *The Roman Citizenship*. 2nd edn. Oxford.

Sherwin-White, A. N. 1984. *Roman Foreign Policy in the East: 168* BC *to* AD *1*. London.

Sherwin-White, A. N. 1994. Lucullus, Pompey and the east. *CAH*² 9: 229–73.

Sherwin-White, S. 1978. *Ancient Cos: an Historical Study from the Dorian Settlement to the Imperial Period*. Göttingen.

Sherwin-White, S. 1987. Seleucid Babylonia: a case study for the installation and development of Greek rule. In Kuhrt and Sherwin-White 1987: 1–31.

Sherwin-White, S. and Kuhrt, A. 1993. *From Samarkhand to Sardis: a New Approach to the Seleucid Empire*. London.

Shipley, G. 2000. *The Greek World after Alexander 323–30* BC. London.

Shipley, G. and Salmon, J. (eds). 1996. *Human Landscapes in Classical Antiquity*. London.

Sidebotham, S. 1996. Newly discovered sites in the eastern desert between Abu Sha'ar-Nile and Quseir-Nile roads. *JEA* 82: 181–92.

Sidebotham, S. and Zitterkopf, R. 1997. Survey of the Via Hadriana by the University of Delaware: the 1996 season. *Bulletin de l'Institut français d'archéologie orientale de Caire* 97: 221–37.

Sidebotham, S., Wendrich, W. and Aldsworth, F. 1995. *Berenike 1994: Preliminary Report of the 1994 Excavations at Berenike (Egyptian Red Sea Coast) and the Survey of the Eastern Desert*. Leiden.

Sidebotham, S., Wendrich, W. and Aldsworth, F. 1996. *Berenike 1995: Preliminary Report of the 1995 Excavations at Berenike (Egyptian Red Sea Coast) and the Survey of the Eastern Desert*. Leiden.

Sidebotham, S., Wendrich, W. and Aldsworth, F. 1998. *Berenike 1996: Report of the 1996 Excavations at Berenike (Egyptian Red Sea Coast) and the Survey of the Eastern Desert*. Leiden.

Sidebotham, S., Wendrich, W. and Aldsworth, F. 1999. *Berenike 1997: Report of the 1997 Excavations at Berenike (Egyptian Red Sea Coast) and the Survey of the Eastern Desert*. Leiden.

Sidebotham, S., Wendrich, W. and Bagnall, R. 2000. *Berenike 1998: Report of the 1998 Excavations at Berenike and the Survey of the Egyptian Eastern Desert, Including Excavations in Wadi Kalalat*. Leiden.

Sijpesteijn, P. 1979. Report concerning Kleroi. *AncSoc* 10: 151–8.

Simon, F -J. 1991. τὰ κύλλ'ἀείδειν. *Interpretationen zu den Mimiamben des Herodas*. Frankfurt.

Simpson, R. H. 1954. The historical circumstances of the peace of 311. *JHS* 74: 25–31.

Slotsky, A. 1997. *The Bourse of Babylon Market Quotations in the Astronomical Diaries of Babylonia*. Bethesda.

Small, A. (ed.). 1996. *Subject and Ruler: the Cult of the Ruling Power in Classical Antiquity*. *JRA* Supp. 17. Ann Arbor.

Smith, H. S. 1995. Marriage and the family in ancient Egypt I: marriage and family law. In M. J. Geller and H. Maehler (eds), *Legal Documents of the Hellenistic World*. London. 46–57.

Smith, R. R. R. 1988. *Hellenistic Royal Portraits*. Oxford.

Smith, R. R. R. 1991. *Hellenistic Sculpture: a Handbook*. New York.

Smith, R. R. R. 1996. Ptolemaic portraits: Alexandrian types, Egyptian versions. In True and Hamma 1996: 203–15.

Snodgrass, A. M. 1980. *Archaic Greece. The Age of Experiment*. London.

Snodgrass, A. M. 1993. The rise of the *polis*. The archaeological evidence. *CPCActs* 1: 30–40.

Snyder, H. G. 2000. *Teachers and Texts in the Ancient World*. London.

Sokolowski, F. 1964. Aphrodite as guardian of Greek magistrates. *HTR* 57: 1–8.

Solmsen, F. 1961. Greek philosophy and the discovery of the nerves. *Museum Helveticum* 18: 150–97.

Sordi, M. 1953. Le origini del koinon etolico. *Acme* 6: 419–45.

Sordi, M. 1958. *La lega tessala fino ad Alessandro magno*. Rome.

Sosin, J. D. 2000. A missing woman: the Hellenistic leases from Thespiae revisited. *GRBS* 41: 47–58.

Sourvinou-Inwood, C. 1987. Myth as history: the previous owners of the Delphic Oracle. In Bremmer 1987: 215–41.

Spawforth, A. J. S. 1997. The early reception of the imperial cult in Athens: problems and ambiguities. In Hoff and Rotroff 1997: 183–201.

Spencer, N. 1995. *A Gazetteer of Archaeological Sites in Lesbos*. BAR International Series 623. Oxford.

Speyer, W. 1989. Die Griechen und die Fremdvölker. Kulturbegegnungen und Wege zur gegenseitigen Verständigung. *Eos* 77: 17–29.

Spivey, N. and Stoddart, S. 1990. *Etruscan Italy*. London.

Staden, H. von. 1982. Hairesis and heresy: the case of the *haireseis iatrikai*. In B. Meyer and E. Sanders (eds), *Jewish and Christian Self-Definition*. Vol. 3. London. 76–100.

Staden, H. von. 1989. *Herophilus: the Art of Medicine in Early Alexandria*. Cambridge.

Staden, H. von. 1992. The discovery of the body: human dissection and its cultural contexts in ancient Greece. *The Yale Journal of Biology and Medicine* 63: 223–41.

Stafford, R. A. 1989. *Scientist of Empire: Sir Roderick Murchison, Scientific Exploration and Victorian Imperialism*. Cambridge.

Stambaugh, J. 1972. *Sarapis under the Early Ptolemies*. Leiden.

Stanzel, K.-H. 1995. *Liebende Hirten: Theokrits Bukolik und die alexandrinische Poesie*. Stuttgart.

Starr, C. G. 1989. *The Influence of Sea Power on Ancient History*. Oxford.

Steele, J. 1992. *Hellenistic Architecture in Asia Minor*. London.

Stepan, N. 1982. *The Idea of Race in Science: Great Britain, 1800–1960*. London.

Sterling, G. E. 1992. *Historiography and Self Definition. Josephus, Luke-Acts and Apologetic Historiography*. Leiden.

Stern, E. 2000. *Dor – Ruler of the Seas*. Jerusalem.

Stern, M. 1976, 1980. *Greek and Latin Authors on Jews and Judaism*. Jerusalem.

Stevenson, T. R. 1996. Social and psychological interpretations of Graeco-Roman religion: some thoughts on the ideal benefactor. *Antichthon* 30: 1–18.

Stewart, A. 1977. To entertain an emperor: Laokoon, Sperlonga, and Tiberius at the dinner-table. *JRS* 67: 76–90.

Stewart, A. 1979. *Attika: Studies in Athenian Sculpture of the Hellenistic Age*. London.

Stewart, A. 1990. *Greek Sculpture: An Exploration*. New Haven.

Stewart, A. 1993a. *Faces of Power: Alexander's Image and Hellenistic Politics*. Berkeley.

Stewart, A. 1993b. Narration and allusion in the Hellenistic baroque. In P. Holliday (ed.), *Narrative and Event in Ancient Art*. Cambridge. 130–74.

Stewart, A. 1996a. *Art, Desire, and the Body in Ancient Greece*. Cambridge.

Stewart, A. 1996b. Telephos/Telepinu and Dionysos: a distant light on an ancient myth. In Dreyfus and Schraudolph 1996: 109–20.

Stewart, A. 2000. *Pergamo ara marmorea magna*: On the date, reconstruction, and functions of the Great Altar of Pergamon. In de Grummond and Ridgway 2000: 32–57.

Stewart, A. 2001. Victory on the harbor: Greek remains found at Dor. *Biblical Archaeology Review* 27.4: 17.

Stewart, A. 2004. *Attalos, Athens, and the Akropolis. The Pergamene 'Little Barbarians' and their Roman and Renaissance Legacy.* Cambridge.

Stewart, A. Forthcoming. Baroque classics: the tragic muse and the *Exemplum*. In J. Porter (ed.), *Classical Pasts: the Classical Traditions of Greco-Roman Antiquity.*

Stewart, A. and Martin, S. R. 2003. Hellenistic discoveries at Tel Dor (Israel). *Hesperia* 72: 121–46.

Stillwell, R. et al. (eds). 1976. *The Princeton Encyclopedia of Classical Sites.* Princeton.

Strasburger, H. 1972. Homer und die Geschichtsschreibung. In *Sitzungsberichte der Heidelberger Akademie der Wissenschaften.* Winter. 1.

Straten, F. T. van. 1981. Gifts for the gods. In H. Versnel (ed.), *Faith, Hope, and Worship: Aspects of Religious Mentality in the Ancient World.* Leiden. 65–151.

Stray, C. 1998. *Classics Transformed: Schools, Universities, and Society in England 1830–1960.* Oxford.

Strobel, K. 1991. Die Galater im hellenistischen Kleinasien: Historische Aspekte einer keltischen Staatenbildung. In J. Seibert (ed.), *Hellenistiche Studien. Gedenkschrift für H. Bengtson.* Munich. 101–34.

Strobel, K. 1994. Keltensieg und Galatersieger. Die Funktionalisierung eines historischen Phänomens als politischer Mythos der hellenistischen Welt. In Schwertheim 1994: 67–96.

Strobel, K. 1996. *Die Galater. Geschichte und Eigenart der keltischen Staatenbildung auf dem Boden des hellenistischen Kleinasiens. I. Untersuchungen zur Geschichte und historischen Geographie des hellenistischen und römischen Kleinasiens.* Berlin.

Stroud, R. S. 1984. An Argive decree from Nemea concerning Aspendos. *Hesperia* 53: 193–216.

Strubbe, J. H. M. 1984. Gründer kleinasiatischer Städte, Fiktion und Realität. *AncSoc* 15/17: 253–304.

Sullivan, R. D. 1990. *Near Eastern Royalty and Rome, 100–30* B.C. Toronto.

Swain, J. 1940. The theory of the four empires. *CP* 35: 1–21.

Swain, S. 1996. *Hellenism and Empire: Language, Classicism and Power in the Greek World,* AD 50–250. Oxford.

Syme, R. 1995. *Anatolica. Studies in Strabo.* A. Birley (ed.). Oxford.

Tagliamonte, G. 1994. *I figli di Marte: mobilità, mercenari e mercenariato italici in Magna Grecia e Sicilia.* Rome.

Tagliamonte, G. 1996. *I sanniti: caudini, irpini, pentri, carricini, frentani.* Milan.

Tait, W. J. 1988. Rush and reed: the pens of Egyptian and Greek scribes. In *Proceedings of the XVIII International Congress of Papyrology, Athens 25–31 May 1986.* Athens. II.477–81.

Tait, W. J. 1994. Egyptian fiction in Demotic and Greek. In J. R. Morgan and R. Stoneman (eds), *Greek Fiction: the Greek Novel in Context.* London. 203–22.

Taplin, O. 1993. *Comic Angels.* Oxford.

Tarán, L. 1981. *Speusippus of Athens.* Leiden.

Tarán, S. L. 1979. *The Art of Variation in the Hellenistic Epigram.* Leiden.

Tarn, W. W. 1913. *Antigonos Gonatas.* Oxford.

Tarn, W. W. 1930. *Hellenistic Military and Naval Developments.* Cambridge (repr. New York 1966).

Tarn, W. W. 1940. Phthia-Chryseis. *HSCP* Supp. 1: 483–501.

Tarn, W. W. 1948. *Alexander the Great.* 2 vols. Cambridge.

Tarn, W. W. and Griffith, G. T. 1952. *Hellenistic Civilisation.* 3rd edn. London.

Tarrant, H. 1985. *Scepticism or Platonism? The Philosophy of the Fourth Academy.* Cambridge.

Tausend, K. 1990. Sagenbildung und Heroenkult. *Gymnasium* 97: 145–53.

Tausend, K. 1992. *Amphiktyonie und Symmachie: Formen zwischenstaatlicher Beziehungen im archaischen Griechenland*. Stuttgart.

Tcherikover, V. 1959. *Hellenistic Civilization and the Jews*. Philadelphia.

Thapar, R. 1997. *Asoka and the Decline of the Mauryas*. Oxford.

Themelis, P. 1979. Ausgrabungen in Kallipolis (Ost-Aetolien) 1977–1978. Άρχαιολογικὰ Άνάλεκτα 12: 249–75.

Thériault, G. 1996. *Le culte d'Homonoia dans les cités grecques*. Lyon.

Thomas, Y. 1990. L'Institution de l'origine. Sacra principiorum populi Romani. In M. Detienne (ed.), *Tracés de fondation*. Paris. 143–70.

Thompson, D. B. 1973. *Ptolemaic Oinochoai and Portraits in Faience: Aspects of the Ruler Cult*. Oxford.

Thompson, D. J. 1984. Agriculture. In *CAH*² 7.1: 363–70.

Thompson, D. J. 1988. *Memphis under the Ptolemies*. Princeton.

Thompson, D. J. 1990. The high priests of Memphis under Ptolemaic rule. In M. Beard and J. North (eds), *Pagan Priests*. London. 95–116.

Thompson, D. J. 1992. Language and literacy in early Hellenistic Egypt. In Bilde et al. 1992: 39–52.

Thompson, D. J. 1994a. Egypt, 146–31 BC. *CAH*² 9: 310–26.

Thompson, D. J. 1994b. Literacy and power in Ptolemaic Egypt. In Bowman and Woolf 1994: 67–83.

Thompson, D. J. 1997. The infrastructure of splendour: census and taxes in Ptolemaic Egypt. In Cartledge et al. 1997: 242–57.

Thompson, D. J. 1999a. Irrigation and drainage in the early Ptolemaic Fayyum. In Bowman and Rogan 1999: 107–22.

Thompson, D. J. 1999b. New and old in the Ptolemaic Fayyum. In Bowman and Rogan 1999: 123–38.

Thompson, D. J. 2000. Philadelphus' procession: dynastic power in a Mediterranean context. In Mooren 2000: 365–88.

Thompson, D. J. 2001. Hellenistic Hellenes: the case of Ptolemaic Egypt. In I. Malkin (ed.), *Ancient Perceptions of Greek Ethnicity*. Cambridge, Mass. 301–22.

Thompson, D. J. 2002. Families in early Ptolemaic Egypt. In Ogden 2002: ch. 8.

Thompson, H. 1934. *A Family Archive from Siut from Papyri in the British Museum*. Oxford.

Thompson, M. 1961. *The New Style Silver Coinage of Athens*. New York.

Thomsen, R. 1947. *The Italic Regions from Augustus to the Lombard Invasion*. Copenhagen.

Thomson, J. O. 1948. *History of Ancient Geography*. Cambridge.

Thornton, J. 2001. *Lo storico, il grammatico, il bandito: momenti della resistenza greca all'imperium romanum*. Catania.

Tilley, C. 1994. *A Phenomenology of Landscape: Places, Paths and Monuments*. Oxford.

Todd, S. C. 1993. *The Shape of Athenian Law*. Oxford.

Too, Y. L. 2001. *Education in Greek and Roman Antiquity*. Leiden.

Torelli, M. 1975. *Elogia tarquiniensia*. Florence.

Torelli, M. 1991. Il 'diribitorium' di Alba Fucens e il 'campus' eroico di Herdonia. In Mertens and Lambrechts 1991: 39ff.

Torelli, M. 1999. *Tota Italia. Essays in the Cultural Formation of Roman Italy*. Oxford.

Toynbee, A. 1965. *Hannibal's Legacy: the Hannibalic War's Effects on Roman Life*. 2 vols. London.

Tozer, H. F. 1964. *A History of Ancient Geography*. New York (Rev. edn by M. Cary).

Trampedach, K. 1994. *Platon, die Akademie und die Zeitgenössische Politik*. Stuttgart.

Trebilco, P. 1991. *Jewish Communities in Asia Minor*. Cambridge.

Treggiari, S. 1978. *Cicero's Cilician Letters*. LACTOR no. 10. London.

Tréheux, J. and Charneux, P. 1998. Décret des Athéniens de Délos en l'honneur d'un épimélète de l'île. *BCH* 122: 239–76.

Trendall, A. D. 1967. *The Red-Figured Vases of Lucania, Campania and Sicily.* Oxford.

Trendall, A. D. and Cambitoglou, A. 1982. *The Red-Figured Vases of Apulia.* 2. *Late Apulian.* Oxford.

Treves, P. 1953. *Il mito di Alessandro e la Roma d'Augusto.* Milan.

Triester, M. and Vinogradov, Y. 1993. Archaeology on the north coast of the Black Sea. *AJA* 97: 521–63.

Troxell, H. 1971. The Peloponnesian Alexanders. *ANSMN* 17: 41–81.

True, M. and Hamma, K. (eds). 1996. *Alexandria and Alexandrianism; Papers Delivered at a Symposium Organized by the J. Paul Getty Museum and the Getty Center for the History of Art and the Humanities and held at the Museum, April 22–25, 1993.* Malibu, Ca.

Tsangari, D. 2002. Corpus des monnaies d'or, d'argent et de bronze du Koinon étolien. (Dissertation.) Paris.

Tscherikower, V. 1926. *Die hellenistische Stadtegrundungen von Alexander dem Grossen bis auf die Romerzeit.* Leipzig.

Tsetskhladze, G. 1998. Greek colonisation of the Black Sea area: stages, models, and native population. In G. Tsetskhladze (ed.), *The Greek Colonisation of the Black Sea Area: Historical Interpretation of Archaeology.* Stuttgart. 9–68.

Tunny, J. A. 2000. Ptolemy 'the Son' reconsidered: are there too many Ptolemies? *ZPE* 131: 83–92.

Turner, E. G. 1980. *Greek Papyri: an Introduction.* 2nd edn. Oxford.

Turner, E. G. 1984. Ptolemaic Egypt. *CAH²* 7.1: 118–74.

Tyree, L. 1974. Cretan sacred caves: archaeological evidence. (Unpublished Ph.D. thesis.) University of Missouri-Columbia.

Uebel, F. 1968. *Die Kleruchen Ägyptens unter den ersten sechs Ptolemäern.* Berlin.

Ünal, A. 1991. Two peoples on both sides of the Aegean Sea: did the Achaeans and the Hittites know each other? In *Essays on Ancient Anatolian and Syrian Studies in the 2nd and 1st Millennium* B C. *Bulletin of the Middle Eastern Culture Center in Japan* 4. 16–44.

Urban, R. 1979. *Wachstum und Krise des achäischen Bundes.* Wiesbaden.

Valbelle, D. and Leclant, J. (eds). 1999. *Le décret de Memphis.* Paris.

Vallance, J. T. 1990. *The Lost Theory of Asclepiades of Bithynia.* Oxford.

van Bremen, R. 1996. *The Limits of Participation. Women and Civic Life in the Greek East in the Hellenistic and Roman Periods.* Amsterdam.

van der Spek, R. 1987. The Babylonian city. In Kuhrt and Sherwin-White 1987: 57–74.

van der Spek, R. 1998. Cuneiform documents on Parthian history: the Rahimesu archive. Materials for the study of the standard of living. In J. Wiesehoefer (ed.), *Das Partherreich und seine Zeugnisse.* Stuttgart. 205–58.

van der Spek, R. 2000. The Seleucid state and the economy. In E. Lo Cascio and D. Rathbone (eds), *Production and Public Powers in Classical Antiquity.* Cambridge. 27–36.

van der Spek, R. 2001. The theatre of Babylon in cuneiform. In W. Soldt et al. (eds), *Veenhof Anniversary Volume. Studies presented to Klas R. Veenhof on the occasion of his sixty-fifth birthday.* Leiden.

van Minnen, P. 2000. An official act of Cleopatra (with a subscription in her own hand). *AncSoc* 30: 29–34.

van Proosdij, B. A. 1934. De morte Achaei. *Hermes* 69: 347–50.

van Straten, F. 1993. Images of gods and men in a changing society: self identity in Hellenistic religion. In Bulloch et al. 1993: 245–64.

van Unnik, W. C. 1993. *Das Selbstverständnis der jüdischen Diaspora in der hellenistisch-römischen Zeit.* Leiden.

Van't Dack, E. 1977. Sur l'évolution des institutions militaires lagides. In *Armées et fiscalité dans le monde antique, Paris 14–16 Oct. 1976*. Paris. 77–106.

Van't Dack, E. et al. 1989. *The Judaeo–Syrian–Egyptian Conflict of 103–101* BC. Collectanea Hellenistica 1. Brussels.

Van't Dack, E., van Dessel, P. and van Gucht, W. (eds). 1983. *Egypt and the Hellenistic World*. Leuven.

Vanderkam, J. 1994. *The Dead Sea Scrolls Today*. Grand Rapids.

Vandorpe, K. 2000a. Paying taxes to the thesauroi of the Pathyrites. In Mooren 2000: 405–36.

Vandorpe, K. 2000b. The Ptolemaic epigraphe or harvest tax (*shemu*). *APF* 46: 169–232.

Vandorpe, K. 2002a. *The Bilingual Family Archive of Dryton, his Wife Apollonia and their Daughter Senmouthis*. Collectanea Hellenistica 4. Brussels.

Vandorpe, K. 2002b. Apollonia, a businesswoman in a multicultural society (Pathyris, 2nd–1st centuries BC). In H. Melaerts and L. Mooren (eds), *Le rôle et le statut de la femme en Egypte hellénistique, romaine et byzantine* (Studia Hellenistica 37). Lourain.

Vargyas, P. 1997. Les prix des denrées alimentaires de première necessité en Babylonie a l'époque achéménide et hellénistique. In J. Andreau, P. Briant and R. Descat (eds), *Economie antique. Prix et formation des prix dans les économies antiques*. St Bertrand-de-Comminges. 335–54.

Varinlioglu, E. 1994. La fortification hellénistique de Stratonicée, archéologie et épigraphie. *REA* 96: 189–91.

Vasari, G. 1550. *Vite de' piu eccellenti architetti, pittori et scultori italiani*. Florence.

Vatin, C. 1970. *Recherches sur le mariage et la condition de la femme mariée à l'époque hellénistique*. Paris.

Vegetti, M. 1998. Between knowledge and practice: Hellenistic medicine. In M. Grmek (ed.), *Western Medical Thought from Antiquity to the Middle Ages*. Cambridge, Mass. (orig. Italian, Rome 1993). 72–103.

Vélissaropoulos, J. 1980. *Les naucleres grecs. Recherches sur les institutions maritimes en Grèce et dans l'Orient*. Geneva.

Verhoogt, A. 1998. *Menches, komogrammateus of Kerkeosiris. The Doings and Dealings of a Village Scribe in the Late Ptolemaic Period (120–110* BC). Pap. Lugd.-Bat. 19. Leiden.

Vérilhac, A. M. and Vial, C. 1998. *Le Mariage grec, du VIᵉ siècle av. J.–C. à l'époque d'Auguste*. *BCH* Supp. 32. Paris.

Vernant, J. P. 1991. *Mortals and Immortals: Selected Essays*. Princeton.

Versnel, H. 1990. *Inconsistencies in Greek and Roman Religion. 1. Ter unus. Isis, Dionysos, Hermes. Three Studies in Henotheism*. Leiden.

Versnel, H. 1994. *Inconsistencies in Greek and Roman Religion. 2. Transition and Reversal in Myth and Ritual*. Leiden.

Veyne, P. 1976. *Le pain et le cirque*. Paris.

Virgilio, B. 1982. Eumene I e i mercenari di Filetereia e di Attaleia. *Studi Classici e Orientali* 32: 97–140.

Virgilio, B. 1993. *Gli Attalidi di Pergamo. Fama, eredità, memoria*. Pisa.

Virgilio, B. 1995. La città ellenistica e i suoi 'benefattori': Pergamo e Diodoro Pasparo. *Athenaeum* 82: 299–314.

Vittmann, G. 1997. Das demotische Graffito vom Satistempel auf Elephantine. *MDAI* (C) 53: 263–81.

Vleeming, S. P. (ed.). 1995. *Hundred-gated Thebes. Acts of a Colloquium on Thebes and the Theban Area in the Graeco-Roman Period*. Pap. Lugd.-Bat. 27. Leiden.

Vogt-Spira, G. 1992. *Dramaturgie des Zufalls: Tyche und Handeln in der Komödie Menanders*. Munich.

Volkmann, H. 1990. *Die Massenversklavungen der Einwohner eroberter Städte in der hellenis-tisch-römischen Zeit*. 2nd edn. Stuttgart.

von Reden, S. 1995. The Piraeus – a world apart. *Greece and Rome*. 42: 24–37.

von Reden, S. 1998. The well-ordered polis: topographies of civic space. In Cartledge et al. 1998: 170–90.

von Reden, S. 2001. The politics of monetization in third century BC Egypt. In A. Meadows and K. Shipton (eds), *Money and its Uses in the Ancient World*. Oxford. 65–76.

Voutiras, E. 1990. ῾Ηφαιστίων ἥρως. *Egnatia* 2: 123–73.

Walbank, F. W. 1933. *Aratos of Sicyon*. Cambridge.

Walbank, F. W. 1944. The causes of Greek decline. *JHS* 64: 10–20.

Walbank, F. W. 1948. The geography of Polybius. In *Classica et Mediaevalia* 9: 155–82.

Walbank, F. W. 1951. The problem of Greek nationality. *Phoenix* 5: 41–60 (= Walbank 1985: 1–19).

Walbank, F. W. 1957 (Vol. 1), 1967 (Vol. 2), 1979a (Vol. 3). *A Historical Commentary on Polybius*. Oxford.

Walbank, F. W. 1965. *Speeches in Greek Historians*. Third Myres Memorial Lecture. Oxford (= Walbank 1985: 242–61).

Walbank, F. W. 1972. *Polybius*. Berkeley.

Walbank, F. W. 1975. *Symploke*: its role in Polybius' histories. In D. Kagan (ed.), *Studies in the Greek Historians in memory of Adam Parry* (*Yale Classical Studies* 24). 197–212 (= Walbank 1985: 313–24).

Walbank, F. W. 1976–7. Were there Greek federal states? *SCI* 3: 27–51 (= Walbank 1985: 20–37).

Walbank, F. W. 1979b. Egypt in Polybius. In J. Ruffle, G. Gaballa and K. Kitchen (eds), *Orbis Aegyptiorum speculum: Glimpses of Ancient Egypt; Studies in Honour of H. W. Fairman*. Warminster. 180–9.

Walbank, F. W. 1982. Sea-power and the Antigonids. In Adams and Borza 1982: 213–36.

Walbank, F. W. 1984a. Macedonia and Greece. *CAH²* 7.1: 221–56.

Walbank, F. W. 1984b. Macedonia and the Greek Leagues. *CAH²* 7.1: 446–81.

Walbank, F. W. 1984c. Monarchies and monarchic ideas. *CAH²* 7.1: 62–100.

Walbank, F. W. 1985. *Selected Papers. Studies in Greek and Roman History and Historiography.* Cambridge.

Walbank, F. W. 1987. Könige als Götter. Überlegungen zum Herrscherkult von Alexander bis Augustus. *Chiron* 17: 365–82.

Walbank, F. W. 1988. Review of Kuhrt and Sherwin-White 1987. *Liverpool Classical Monthly* 13: 108–12.

Walbank, F. W. 1989. Antigonus Doson's attack on Cytinium (*REG* 101 [1988], 12–53). *ZPE* 76: 184–92.

Walbank, F. W. 1992. *The Hellenistic World*. London (rev. edn; orig. 1981).

Walbank, F. W. 1994. Supernatural paraphernalia in Polybios' Histories. In I. Worthington (ed.), *Ventures into Greek History.* Oxford. 28–42.

Walbank, F. W. 1996. Two Hellenistic processions: a matter of self-definition. *SCI* 15: 119–30.

Waldmann, H. 1973. *Die kommagenischen Kultreformen unter König Mithradates I. Kallinikos und seinem Sohne Antiochos I.* Leiden.

Waldmann, H. 1991. *Der kommagenische Mazdaismus*. Tübingen.

Walker, S. and Higgs, P. 2001. *Cleopatra of Egypt from History to Myth*. London.

Wallace, J. 1998. A (hi)story of Illyria. *Greece and Rome*. 45: 213–25.

Wallace-Hadrill, A. 1998. To be Roman, go Greek: thoughts on Hellenization at Rome. In M. Austin, J. Harries and C. Smith (eds), *Modus Operandi: Essays in Honour of Geoffrey Rickman*. London. 79–92.

Walsh, G. B. 1990. Surprised by self: audible thought in Hellenistic poetry. *CP* 85: 1–21.

Walsh, G. B. 1991. Callimachean passages: the rhetoric of epitaph in epigram. *Arethusa* 24: 77–105.

Warmington, E. H. 1934. *Greek Geography.* London.

Warren, J. 2002. *Epicurus and Democritean Ethics: an Archaeology of Ataraxia.* Cambridge.

Watrous, L. V. 1996. *The Cave Sanctuary of Zeus at Psychro: a Study of Extra-Urban Sanctuaries in Minoan and Early Iron Age Crete.* Liège.

Watrous, L. V. et al. 1993. A survey of the western Mesara plain in Crete: preliminary report of the 1984, 1986 and 1987 field seasons. *Hesperia* 62: 191–248.

Weber, G. 1993. *Dichtung und höfische Gesellschaft.* Stuttgart.

Webster, J. and Cooper, N. 1996. *Roman Imperialism: Post-Colonial Perspectives.* Leicester.

Webster, T. B. L. 1964. *Hellenistic Poetry and Art.* London.

Wehrli, C. 1962. Les Gynéconomes. *Museum Helveticum* 19: 33–8.

Wehrli, C. 1968. *Antigone et Démétrios.* Geneva.

Wehrli, F. 1967–78. *Die Schule des Aristoteles.* 10 vols with 2 vols supp. Basel.

Wehrli, F. 1983. Der Peripatos bis zum Beginn den romischen Kaiserzeit. In H. Flashar (ed.), *Grundriss der Geschichte der Philosophie: Die Philosophie der Antik.* Vol. 3. Basel. 461–599.

Weinstock, S. 1957. Victor and Invictus. *HTR* 50: 211–47.

Weippert, O. 1972. *Alexander-Imitatio und römischer Politik in republikanischer Zeit.* Augsburg.

Weiss, P. 1984. Lebendiger Mythos: Gründerheroen und städtische Gründstraditionen im griechisch-römische Osten. *Würzburger Jahrbücher* 10: 179–207.

Welwei, K. 1967. Das makedonische Herrschaftssystem in Griechenland und die Politik des Antigonus Dosons. *Rh.Mus.* 110: 306–14.

Wenke, R. J. 1990. *Patterns in Prehistory.* 3rd edn. Oxford.

Wenning, R. 1978. *Die Galateranatheme Attalos I.: Eine Untersuchung zum Bestand und zur Nachwirkung pergamenischer Skulptur* (PergForsch 4). Berlin.

Westermann, W. L. 1929. *P. Col. Inv. 480, Upon Slavery in Ptolemaic Egypt.* New York.

Westermark, U. 1961. *Das Bildnis von Philetairos von Pergamon.* Stockholm.

Westgate, R. 2000. *Pavimenta atque emblemata vermiculata*: regional styles in Hellenistic mosaic and the first mosaics at Pompeii. *AJA* 104: 255–76.

Westlake, H. D. 1935. *Thessaly in the Fourth Century* BC. London.

Whitbread, I. K. 1995. *Greek Transport Amphorae: a Petrological and Archaeological Study.* Athens.

Whitehorne, J. 1993. *Cleopatras.* London.

Whitley, J. 1998. From Minoans to Eteocretans: the Praisos region, 1200–500 BC. In Cavanagh and Curtis 1998: 27–39.

Whitley, J., O'Conor, K. and Mason, H. 1995. Praisos III: a report on the architectural survey undertaken in 1992. *BSA* 90: 405–28.

Wilamowitz-Moellendorf, U. von. 1900. Asianismus und Attizismus. *Hermes* 35: 1–52.

Wilcken, U. 1925. Punt-Fahren in der Ptolemaerzeit. *Zeitschrift für ägyptische Sprache und Altertumskunde* 60: 86–102.

Wilkinson, T. J. 2000. Regional approaches to Mesopotamian archaeology: the contribution of archaeological surveys. *Journal of Archaeological Research* 8: 219–67.

Will, E. 1979–82. *Histoire politique du monde hellénistique.* 2nd edn. 2 vols. Nancy.

Will, E. 1984. The succession to Alexander and the formation of the hellenistic kingdoms. *CAH*² 7.1: 23–61, 101–17.

Winckelmann, J. J. 1764. *Geschichte der Kunst des Alterthums.* Dresden.

Winner, M. (ed.). 1998. *Il Cortile delle Statue/Der Statuenhof des Belvedere im Vatikan.* Mainz.

Winter, F. E. 1971. *Greek Fortifications.* Toronto.

Winter, F. E. 1984. Building and townplanning. *CAH*² 7.1: 371–83.

Wiseman, T. P. 1985. *Catullus and his World: a Reappraisal.* Cambridge.

Wolff, H. J. 1939. *Written and Unwritten Marriages in Hellenistic and Postclassical Roman Law.* Oxford.

Wollheim, R. 1980. *Art and Its Objects, An Introduction to Aesthetics.* 2nd edn. Cambridge.

Woodcock, G. 1966. *The Greeks in India.* London.

Woolf, G. 1998. *Becoming Roman: the Origins of Provincial Civilization in Gaul.* Cambridge.

Wörrle, M. 1975. Antiochos I. Achaios der Ältere und die Galater. Eine neue Inschrift in Denizli. *Chiron* 5: 59–87.

Wörrle, M. 1988. Inschriften von Herakleia am Latmos I: Antiochos III., Zeuxis und Herakleia. *Chiron* 18: 421–76.

Wörrle, M. 1995. Von tugendsamen Jüngling zum gestressten Euergeten. Überlegungen zum Bürgerbild hellenistischer Ehrendekrete. In Wörrle and Zanker 1995: 241–50.

Wörrle, M. and Zanker, P. (eds). 1995. *Stadtbild und Burgerbild im Hellenismus.* Munich.

Wright, H. and Johnson, G. 1975. Population, exchange, and early state formation in south-western Iran. *American Anthropologist* 77: 267–89.

Wycherley, R. E. 1962. *How the Greeks Built Cities.* 2nd edn. London.

Yailenko, V.-P. 1990. Les maximes delphiques d'Aï Khanoum et la formation de la doctrine du *dhamma* d'Asoka. *DHA* 16: 239–56.

Yardley, J. C. (trans.), and Develin, R. (ed.). 1994. *Justin: Epitome of the Philippic History of Pompeius Trogus.* Atlanta.

Young, R. S. 1951. An industrial district of ancient Athens. *Hesperia* 20: 135–288.

Yoyotte, J. 1969. Bakhthis: Religion égyptienne et culture grecque à Edfou. In *Religions en Égypte hellénistique et romaine: Colloque de Strasbourg 16–18 mai 1967.* Paris. 127–41.

Yoyotte, J. 2002. Guardian of the Nile: Thonis rediscovered. *Minerva* 13.3: 32–4.

Zagagi, N. 1994. *Comedy of Menander: Convention, Variation, and Originality.* London.

Zahle, J. 1990. Religious motifs on Seleucid coins. In Bilde et al. 1990: 125–39.

Zanker, G. 1987. *Realism in Alexandrian Poetry.* London.

Zanker, P. 1988. *The Power of Images in the Age of Augustus.* Ann Arbor.

Zanker, P. 1989. *Die trunkene Alte: Das Lachen der Verhohnten.* Frankfurt.

Zanker, P. 1995. *The Mask of Socrates: the Image of the Intellectual in Antiquity.* Berkeley.

Zanker, P. 1998. *Eine Kunst für die Sinne: Zur hellenistischen Bilderwelt des Dionysos und der Aphrodite.* Berlin.

Zanker, P. (ed.). 1976. *Hellenismus in Mittelitalien.* Göttingen.

Zauzich, K.-T. 1983. Das Lamm des Bokchoris. In *Papyrus Erzherzog Rainer (P. Rainier Cent.)* 1. Vienna. 165–74.

Zauzich, K.-T. 1984. Von Elephantine bis Sambehdet. *Enchoria* 12: 193–4.

Zetzel, J. 1997. Rome and its traditions. In C. Martindale (ed.), *Cambridge Companion to Virgil.* Cambridge. 188–203.

Zgusta, L. 1955. *Die Personennamen griechischer Städte der nördlichen Schwarzmeerküste.* Prague.

Zgusta, L. 1964. *Anatolische Personennamensippen.* Prague.

Zimmermann, K. 1999. *Libyen: Das Land südlich des Mittelmeers im Weltbild der Griechen.* Munich.

Zimmermann, K. 2002. Eratosthenes' chlamys-shaped world: a misunderstood metaphor. In Ogden 2002: ch. 2.

Zitterkopf, R. and Sidebotham, S. 1989. Stations and towers on the Quseir-Nile road. *JEA* 75: 155–89.

Zitterkopf, R. and Sidebotham, S. 1991. Survey of the Abu-Sha'ar–Nile road. *AJA* 95: 571–622.

Zoumbaki, S. and Mendoni, L. 1998. Θεοὶ Σεβαστοί. In L. Mendoni and A. Mazarakis Ainian, *Kea-Kythnos. History and Archaeology. Proceedings of an International Symposium, Kea-Kythnos, 22–25 June, 1994.* Athens. 669–78.

Chronological Guide

The following chronology is intended as a guide. Many dates in the Hellenistic period, especially those in the third century, are uncertain and disputed. For chronology of 323–311, see p. 34 above.

Fourth Century BC

359	Accession of Philip II
356	Birth of Alexander
338	Battle of Chaironeia
337	Establishment of League of Corinth
336	Philip assassinated; accession of Alexander
335	Destruction of Thebes
334	Battle of Granikos
333	Battle of Issos
331	Foundation of Alexandria
	Battle of Gaugemela
330	Death of Darius
326	Alexander reaches Indus
323	Death of Alexander at Babylon (June)
	Allotment of satrapies: Ptolemy gets Egypt, Lysimachos Thrace and Antigonos Greater Phrygia
	Outbreak of Lamian War
	Birth of Alexander IV
322	Battle of Krannon
	Deaths of Aristotle and Demosthenes
321	Ptolemy seizes Alexander's body
320	Perdikkas invades Egypt; killed by his officers
	Conference at Triparadeisos; Antipater made regent
319	Death of Antipater; Polyperchon becomes regent
	Outbreak of war between Polyperchon and Kassandros
317	Demetrios of Phaleron takes power in Athens
	Execution of Philip III Arrhidaios
316	Eumenes' successes in Asia
	Agathokles takes power in Syracuse
315	Kassandros executes Olympias; founds Kassandreia and Thessalonike
	Antigonos executes Eumenes; forces Seleukos out of Babylon
314	Proclamation of Tyre: Antigonos proclaims freedom of the Greeks

312/11	Battle of Gaza; Seleukos recovers Babylon; Seleukid era begins
c. 312	Zeno of Kition arrives in Athens
311	Peace between Ptolemy, Lysimachos, Kassandros and Antigonos
310	Murder of Alexander IV and Roxane; end of Argead dynasty
309	Execution of Herakles, son of Barsine
308	Seleukos makes pact with Antigonos
c. 308–303	Seleukos campaigns in East, including war against Chandragupta
307	Demetrios captures Athens from Kassandros
307/6	Epicurus begins teaching in Athens
306	Demetrios defeats Ptolemy off Salamis and captures Cyprus
	Antigonos I and Demetrios I take title of 'king'
305–4	Demetrios' failed siege of Athens; earns name Poliorketes (Besieger)
304	Ptolemy, Seleukos and probably Lysimachos become kings
302	Kassandros becomes king (most likely date)
	Antigonos and Demetrios establish new League of Corinth
301	Defeat and death of Antigonos I at battle of Ipsos

Third Century BC

300/299	Seleukeia in Peiria and Antioch on the Orontes founded
298/7	Death of Kassandros
295	Ptolemy recaptures Cyprus
294	Demetrios I Poliorketes becomes king of Macedon
	Antiochos I co-ruler with Seleukos I
293	Foundation of Demetrias
c. 292	Death of Menander the dramatist
288	Macedon divided between Pyrrhos and Lysimachos
c. 287	Death of Theophrastos, head of Lyceum; succeeded by Straton
286	Demetrios I captured by Seleukos I
285	Ptolemy II Philadelphos co-ruler with Ptolemy I
283	Deaths of Ptolemy I Soter (naturally) and Demetrios I (in captivity)
281	Defeat and death of Lysimachos at Koroupedion against Seleukos I
	Ptolemy Keraunos assassinates Seleukos I; becomes king of Macedon
	Re-establishment of the Achaian League
280–275	Pyrrhos in Italy and Sicily
280–279	Celts invade Macedon and Greece; death of Ptolemy Keraunos
277	Antigonos II Gonatas defeats Celts at Lysimacheia; becomes king of Macedon
278	Celts cross to Asia
c. 275	Ptolemy II marries sister Arsinoe II
274	Pyrrhos invades Macedonia
274–271	First Syrian War: Ptolemy II v. Antiochos I
273	Ptolemaic embassy to Rome
272	Death of Pyrrhos in fighting at Argos
c. 270	Antiochos I defeats Galatians (Celts) in the 'elephant battle'
	Death of Arsinoe II (or 268)
270	Death of Epicurus the philosopher

268/7	Chremonidean War begins (or 265/4)
263	Death of Philetairos of Pergamon; succeeded by Eumenes I
c. 262	Antigonos Gonatas captures Athens
	Death of Zeno; Kleanthes of Assos becomes head of Stoa
261	Death of Antiochos I Soter, succeeded by Antiochos II Theos
c. 260–253	Second Syrian War: Ptolemy II v. Antiochos II
252	Antiochos II marries Berenike II, daughter of Ptolemy II
251	Aratos ousts tyrant at Sikyon, which then joins Achaian League; around this time Alexander, Macedonian governor in Corinth, rebels
246	Death of Ptolemy II Philadelphos, succeeded by Ptolemy III Euergetes
	Death of Antiochos II Theos, succeeded by Seleukos II Kallinikos
246–241	Third Syrian War: Ptolemy III v. Seleukos II
245	Aratos becomes *strategos* of Achaian League for the first time
	Antigonos re-takes Corinth
244	Romans found Brundisium
c. 244	Agis IV becomes king in Sparta
243	Aratos captures Acrocorinth; Corinth joins Achaian League
241	Execution of Agis in Sparta
	Death of Eumenes I; accession of Attalos I
240/39	Death of Antigonos Gonatas; Demetrios II becomes king of Macedon
	Outbreak of war for Asia Minor between Seleukos II and his brother Antiochos Hierax
235	Megalopolis joins Achaian League
	Accession of Kleomenes III at Sparta
c. 232	Chrysippos succeeds Kleanthes as head of Stoa
230	Roman embassy to Illyrians
229	Athens gains independence from Macedon
	Antigonos III Doson succeeds Demetrios
	First Illyrian War: Rome v. Teuta
228	Attalos I forces Hierax out of Asia Minor to Alexandria
	Romans admitted to the Isthmian Games
227	Death of Hierax in Thrace
	Kleomenes III's revolution at Sparta
	Antigonos Doson in Karia
227/6	Earthquake at Rhodes
226/5	Seleukos III Keraunos succeeds Seleukos II
224	Achaians make agreement with Antigonos Doson
223	Accession of Antiochos III after assassination of Seleukos III
222	Battle of Sellasia: Kleomenes defeated by Macedonians
222–220	Revolt of Molon against Antiochos III
221	Ptolemy IV Philopator succeeds Ptolemy III Euergetes in Egypt
	Philip V succeeds Antigonos Doson in Macedon
220	Achaios proclaims himself king in Asia Minor
220–217	Social War: Philip V and Achaians v. Aitolians
220/19	Death of Spartan king Kleomenes III in Egypt
219–217	Fourth Syrian War: Ptolemy IV Philopator v. Antiochos III
218–202	Second Punic War: Rome v. Carthage

217	Battle of Raphia: Antiochos III defeated by Ptolemy IV
	Battle of Lake Trasimene: Hannibal defeats Rome
	Peace of Naupaktos
216	Battle of Cannae: Hannibal defeats Rome
216–213	Antiochos overcomes Achaios
215	Treaty between Philip V and Hannibal
214–205	First Macedonian War
211	Treaty between Aitolia and Rome
212–205/4	Antiochos III campaigns in East
208/7	Magnesia-on-the-Maeander launches successful campaign for panhellenic festival in honour of Artemis Leukophryene (after failed attempt of 221/20)
207	Nabis becomes Spartan king
207–186	Rebellion in Upper Egypt
206	Aitolians make peace with Philip V
	Aitolian diplomatic campaign in support of re-building of Kytinion
205	Peace of Phoinike
205/4	Cult of Magna Mater imported from Asia Minor to Rome
204	Ptolemy V Epiphanes succeeds Ptolemy IV
	Battle of Zama: Rome defeats Carthage in North Africa
202–200	Fifth Syrian War: Antiochos III v. Ptolemy V Epiphanes
200	Battle of Panion: Antiochos defeats Ptolemy and seizes Koile Syria

Second Century BC

200–197	Second Macedonian War: Rome v. Philip V
197	Battle of Kynoskephalai: Rome defeats Philip V
	Eumenes II succeeds Attalos I
197/6	Lampsakene embassy to Rome
	Antiochos re-founds Lysimacheia in Thrace
196	Romans announce the freedom of the Greeks at the Isthmian Games
	Meeting between Antiochos and Romans at Lysimacheia
	Rosetta decree, Egypt
195	Roman war against Nabis
	Smyrna establishes cult of Roma
194	Romans withdraw army from Greece
194/3	Embassy of Antiochos to Rome
192	Assassination of Nabis; Sparta brought into Achaian League
192–188	War between Rome and Antiochos III
189	Aitiolians submit to Rome
	Battle of Magnesia: Romans defeat Antiochos
188	Peace of Apameia
187	Seleukos IV Philopator succeeds Antiochos III
187–183	War between Eumenes II and Prusias of Bithynia
183	Revolt of Messene from Achaian League
183–179	War between Eumenes II and Pharnakes of Pontos
181	Eumenes II re-founds Nikephoria festival as panhellenic

180	Ptolemy VI Philometor succeeds Ptolemy V
	Philip V executes Demetrios his son
179	Perseus succeeds Philip V in Macedon
175	Assassination of Seleukos IV; succeeded by Antiochos IV Epiphanes
	Jason becomes High Priest in Jerusalem
172	Eumenes II denounces Perseus in Rome
171–168	Third Macedonian War: Rome v. Perseus
169–168	Sixth Syrian War: Antiochos IV v. Ptolemy VI
169–164	Joint rule of Ptolemy VI, Ptolemy VIII Euergetes II and Kleopatra II
168	Battle of Pydna: Romans defeat Perseus
	C. Popillius Laenas demands Antiochos IV leave Egypt
167	End of Macedonian kingdom; replaced by four republics
	Delos made a free port and given to Athens
	Polybios among Achaian hostages taken to Italy
166	Antiochos IV's parade at Daphne
c. 166–164	Maccabaean revolt against Antiochos IV in Judaea
164	Antiochos IV dies campaigning in East
	Re-dedication of the Temple in Jerusalem
	Ptolemy VI visits Rome to reclaim throne
164/3	Rhodian treaty with Rome
163	Ptolemy VI ruler of Egypt and Cyprus, Ptolemy VIII ruler of Cyrene
162	Demetrios escapes from Rome and seizes Seleukid throne from Antiochos V
161	Treaty between Rome and Judas Maccabaeus
160	Demetrios defeats and kills Judas Maccabaeus
158	Attalos II succeeds Eumenes II
156–154	War between Prusias II of Bithynia and Pergamon
155	Ptolemy VIII Euergetes announces decision to bequeath kingdom to Rome
155–153	War between Rhodes and Crete
150	Demetrios defeated and killed by Alexander Balas
149–148	Rising of Andriskos in Macedon
146	War between Rome and Achaian League; destruction of Corinth
	Roman destruction of Carthage ends Third Punic War
	Macedon assigned to a Roman commander as a *provincia* from here on
145	Ptolemy VI dies after defeating Alexander Balas; Ptolemy VIII succeeds in Egypt, Demetrios II in Syria
c. 145–139/8	Diodotos Tryphon attempts to usurp power in Syria
140–139	Scipio Aemilianus' embassy to Eastern Mediterranean
139	Demetrios II captured by Parthians
135/34	Antiochos VII Sidetes besieges Jerusalem
133	Attalos III dies, bequeathing his kingdom to Rome
132–129	Aristonikos defeated by Rome as attempts to claim Attalid throne
129	Antiochos VII killed campaigning against Parthia
129–126	M. Aquillius reorganizes Asia; the beginning of the Roman province
120	Mithradates VI Eupator succeeds to Pontic throne
116	Death of Ptolemy VIII Euergetes II
c. 115	Mithradates VI begins Black Sea expansion

107	Ptolemy X Alexander I rules in Egypt, Ptolemy IX Soter II in Cyprus, Ptolemy Apion in Cyrene
c. 103/2	Mithridates VI and Nikomedes III of Bithynia dispute over Cappadocia
102	M. Antonius' piracy command in Cilicia

First Century BC

99/8	Embassy of C. Marius to Eastern Mediterranean
96	Mithradates obeys Roman order to leave Cappadocia
91–87	Social War in Italy (largely over by 89)
89–85	First Mithradatic War
88	Massacre of Romans and Italians in Asia
	Athens supports Mithradates
	Ptolemy X ousted from Egypt; sack of Thebes by Ptolemy IX
86	Fall of Athens to Sulla
85	Mithridrates makes peace settlement at Dardanos with Sulla
83–81	Second Mithradatic War: L. Licinius Murena raids Pontos
74	Nikomedes IV of Bithynia dies, bequeathing his kingdom to Rome
73	Mithradates seizes Bithynia
73–63	Third Mithradatic War: Rome v. Mithradates
67	Pompey's successful campaign against piracy
66	Pompey appointed to command against Mithradates
64–62	Pompey reorganizes the East; remains of Seleukid kingdom becomes the Roman province of Syria
63	Suicide of Mithradates
58	Rome annexes Cyprus
53	Roman invasion of Parthia ends in defeat at battle of Carrhae
52 and 51	Parthians invade Syria
51	Death of Ptolemy XII Auletes; joint rule of Kleopatra VII and Ptolemy XIII
49	Roman civil war between Caesar and Pompey begins
48	Caesar victorious at Battle of Pharsalos; Pompey assassinated in Egypt
	Caesar in Egypt; relationship with Kleopatra VII
47	Birth of Ptolemy XV (Caesarion); death of Ptolemy XIII
	Battle of Zela: Caesar defeats Pharnakes II of Pontos (*veni vedi vici*)
44	Assassination of Caesar in Rome
43	Conspirators Brutus and Cassius forcibly raise money from East
42	Battle of Philippi: Antony and Octavian defeat Brutus and Cassius
41	Antony begins relationship with Kleopatra VII
41–39	Parthians invade Syria in alliance with Q. Labienus
40	Birth of twins to Kleopatra
37/6	Antony acknowledges paternity of twins
36	Antony's Parthian expedition ends in defeat
34	Antony invades Armenia
31	Battle of Actium: victory of Octavian over Antony and Kleopatra
30	Octavian captures Alexandria; deaths of Antony and Kleopatra VII
	End of kingdom of Ptolemies

30–29	Octavian re-organizes the East78
27	Octavian takes name Augustus; provincial system re-structured
25	Galatia annexed as province
23–21	Agrippa in authority in East
21–19	Augustus visits East
18–13	Agrippa returns to supervise East
4	Herod of Judaea dies; Archelaos succeeds
6BC–AD2	Tiberius lives in retirement on Rhodes

First Century AD

4	Augustus' grandson Gaius dies after Armenian campaign
6	Archelaos deposed; creation of province of Judaea
14	Death of Augustus; accession of Tiberius

Index

41768191R00356

Made in the USA
Lexington, KY
27 May 2015